D1514686

Cities and Society

Cities and Society

THE REVISED READER IN URBAN SOCIOLOGY

EDITED BY

PAUL K. HATT

LATE OF NORTHWESTERN UNIVERSITY

AND

ALBERT J. REISS, JR.

VANDERBILT UNIVERSITY

THE FREE PRESS, GLENCOE, ILLINOIS

The personal and professional association which this writer shared with the late Paul Hatt led to the joint editorship of the first edition of this *Reader in Urban Sociology*. Professor Hatt's untimely death in January of 1953 took from professional sociology one of its most productive scholars, and a warm colleague. The loss of his association raised some question as to the wisdom of revising this Reader when it went out of print two years ago. For a variety of reasons, the writer decided to assume the responsibility for a revision.

Substantial changes were made for this revision. Twenty-two of the 57 selections in the first edition are omitted and 27 selections added, for a total of 62 selections in the second edition. The four criteria applied for the selection of papers in the first edition also were used for the selection of new papers for this one. It was considered desirable to select the new papers primarily from the literature published since this Reader first appeared in 1951. A few papers again were written especially for this Reader, including a number by the editor. They were written either to summarize the research findings from a number of sources in a single paper, or to bring research findings to bear upon a particular point of view in urban studies. It was difficult to reach decisions to exclude and retain papers for this revised edition. A list of the reasons for excluding papers appearing in the first edition from appearance in the second one almost requires a separate statement of reasons for each of the papers deleted. The reorganization of sections and the overlap of a new selection with one from the first edition perhaps account for most of the exclusions.

Special attention again was given to the second criterion in the selection of new papers—to include only those papers which clearly refer to urban phenomena. The city so often is regarded simply as a community context within which other phenomena are investigated; these investigations add little to our knowledge of urban phenomena and how they behave. The selections in the revised edition deal largely with generic urban community variables, even though in many cases it is not possible to separate them empirically from closely related ones, such as the independent influence of technology and industrialization.

The general statements which introduce the selections in each section are expanded and rewritten. Again, no attempt was made to cover all the problems of a particular area of urban studies. The general statements, however, try to lay out the major problems in each area in somewhat greater detail, and to indicate more clearly the contribution of each paper to the problems of the section. It is intended that the selections in this edition should comprise a balanced introduction to the sociology of cities. The bibliography also has been reorganized somewhat and publications from the recent literature are included.

The value of the volume again depends in large measure on the contributions of the authors and their publishers who generously gave their permission to reprint them. Gratitude to them is great. The critical contributions of Otis Dudley Duncan, sometime collaborator and colleague of the writer, as always, are gratefully acknowledged. G. Franklin Edwards, Wayland J. Hayes and R. Heberle also made helpful suggestions. To Jeremiah Kaplan, editor and publisher of The Free Press, a special debt of gratitude is owed for his warm friendship and encouragement. Special thanks go to Mrs. Dorothy P. Griffin for secretarial aid in the preparation of materials for this edition.

ALBERT J. REISS, JR.

Vanderbilt University
September, 1956

The enormous significance of the city in determining patterns of life throughout modern society is obvious. The very term "modern society" connotes a way of life characterized by a rationalized industrial structure, complex markets, rapid transportation and efficient communication. More than this, modern society connotes a way of life so related to the requirements of the city that it is almost the equivalent of "urban society."

The importance of the city has by no means been overlooked by the social sciences. An abundant and penetrating literature testifies to this. Characteristically, however, this literature is widely scattered both with reference to the disciplines which have produced it and with reference to the publications in which it appears. Attempts at integration are singularly rare and generally unsatisfactory. The sociology of the city, in fact, frequently has been treated as if it were the study of all social behavior which takes place in a city. This assumes that somehow the city as such is automatically relevant to all behavior which occurs within its limits. The editors do not agree with this point of view and have attempted to select writing in which the relevance of the problem to the city, as a mode of life, not merely as a locus of the problem, is explicit.

The criteria applied were essentially four. The two most important were the excellence of the selection on its own merits and its significance for an analysis of the city as a phenomenon *sui generis,* which is the aim of the volume. The third criterion was, in those cases where more than one piece met these criteria equally well, to choose that one least accessible to the student. There remained certain lacunae in the literature which were covered by hitherto unpublished research. A number of scholars therefore were asked to contribute selections.

The several sections are introduced by short general statements which are intended to lay out the major problems in that particular area, thus giving each piece a relationship to broader principles. Since it would be impossible to cover all problems, no attempt was made to do so. While there will doubtless be disagreement both as to the emphasis given various subjects and as to some of the selections, the volume represents what, at least in the opinion of the editors, should be a balanced introduction to the sociology of the city. A bibliography, covering a much larger literature than that actually covered in the Reader, has been included.

The careful critical contributions of the advisory board are gratefully acknowledged. Their work has contributed greatly to the volume. Of course, they bear no responsibility for the finished volume.

In the final analysis, any value which the volume may have depends upon the authors and publishers who have given permission to reprint their works. Our gratitude to them is great. A further debt of gratitude is owed to Jeremiah Kaplan, editor of The Free Press, for his interest and co-operation in undertaking the publication of a series of Readers in the social sciences.

PAUL K. HATT
ALBERT J. REISS, JR.

Northwestern University
University of Chicago
September, 1951

Contents

Introduction

THE SOCIOLOGY OF URBAN LIFE: 1946-1956

The field of urban sociology was recognized early within the formal discipline of sociology in the United States. Rural sociology perhaps developed somewhat earlier as a specialized field than did urban sociology. The 1916 meetings of the American Sociological Society were devoted to the field of "Rural Sociology," but it was not until 1925 that the Society similarly devoted an annual meeting to "Urban Sociology." The papers from the 1925 annual meeting were published under the editorship of E. W. Burgess under the general title of *The Urban Community* (13). Prior to this, in 1925, Park, Burgess, and McKenzie published a volume, *The City* (63), a collection of essays they had separately published in the previous decade. These essays attest to the establishment of a field of urban sociology during this period (19). The major outlines of the field from 1915 to 1935 probably were laid down by students of Park and Burgess at the University of Chicago (35). Their general approach to urban study perhaps is best summarized either in Park's early 1915 essay on "The City as a Social Laboratory" (63), or in the later essay by Louis Wirth, "Urbanism as a Way of Life" (86).

The studies in urban sociology at the University of Chicago were not, however, the only source of a sociological interest in the study of urban life during this period. There were the community studies such as those by the Lynds of *Middletown* in 1929, the systematic treatment of rural and urban sociology by Sorokin and Zimmerman in 1929, and the Columbia University dissertation of Adna Weber on *The Growth of Cities in the Nineteenth Century* as early as 1899—to mention only a few of the other main currents leading to the sure establishment of urban sociology as a field in sociology by 1930. No attempt is made here to trace its origin systematically. The Bedford *Readings in Urban Sociology* in 1927 and the Anderson and Lineman text, *Urban Sociology,* in 1928 appear to be the earliest attempts at full classroom treatment by sociologists in the United States. The number of urban sociology texts currently available for classroom use numbers some twenty.

The influence which European inquiry into cities had upon the development of urban sociology in the United States also is not traced here. The

Revised version of a paper originally published in *Sociology in the United States of America,* edited by Hans L. Zetterberg, UNESCO, 1956.

intellectual origins of the American students of sociology, of course, included familiarity with men like Tönnies, Simmel, Durkheim, and Weber. It seems reasonable to postulate, however, that the major impetus to urban study in sociology was the rapid industrialization of Europe and the United States in the late nineteenth and early twentieth centuries. To the nascent American sociology, the problems generated by the "new technology," the "Americanization" of immigrants in cities, the slum, corruption in municipal government, and a host of "problematic aspects of urban living" provided the major impetus to an urban sociology for the American sociologist who was rapidly turning his efforts to the empirical observation of social reality. These problems at the same time were dramatized by the muckrakers like Lincoln Steffens and other news writers. To the American newspaperman and sociologist, Robert Park, the city was a "social laboratory" for the study of *all* human behavior, and in this sense, urban sociology was a basis for a generalizing science of human society.

The brief presentation which follows describes the development of the field of "urban sociology" or "the sociology of city life" in the 1946 to 1956 period. A few comments about development to this point may be in order. Park, and later Wirth, saw three broad areas of sociological inquiry into urban life: the study of the ecology of the city, of its social organization, and of the psychology of its inhabitants. Empirical studies in urban sociology up to 1946 were not spread equally among these three divisions. The early studies by Park and his students usually included all three aspects in the investigation of phenomena such as vice, juvenile delinquency, the Jewish ghetto, land values, or the taxi-dance hall. Individual studies often ignored the treatment of the social psychological study of city life, however. Studies in urban sociology during this period were more likely to focus on the demography and ecology of the city, on the one hand, or on special aspects of the social organization of the city on the other. The 1915 essay by Park (63) raised a large number of questions which appear to have guided research during this period. A few of these questions around which the research of the period centered are: What makes a city grow, and is it reproducing itself? Do cities follow a regular pattern of urban growth? What is the nature of urban neighborhoods? Is the slum a disorganized area? What are the effects of the division of labor in cities? What happens to local institutions and populations when cities grow? To what extent is the city selective of social types and to what degree does it create them?

The study of individual communities as functioning entities became a major type of investigation during this period. The earliest investigations in American sociology included community study, but beginning with the nineteen-thirties, community studies were more likely to seek a description of the "total community" in the tradition of ethnography. These investigations were not "total" in the sense that all aspects of human life in the community were studied, however. Many aspects of community life were ignored. Few, for example, ever detailed the patterns of food and

alcohol consumption in a community—facts of social life which no anthropologist would ignore in studying a primitive community. The political
structure of these communities often was not investigated as well, to mention a second example. The interest in community study continues among
sociologists, although they now are more likely to treat the urban community as a context for, rather than as an object of, investigation.

URBAN ECOLOGY AND DEMOGRAPHY. Human ecology in the United
States is developed both as a specialized field of study and as an aspect of
rural and urban sociologies. Park and McKenzie were largely responsible
for the development of a theoretical frame of reference for the study of
human ecology. No formal treatise on human ecology was available until
the writings of Hawley (38) and Quinn (66) were published in 1950, although texts in urban sociology always include a section on urban ecology.
The contributions of both Hawley and Quinn are based on several decades
of research findings in urban ecology. The work of Quinn is primarily a
codification of research findings, while that of Hawley makes a formal
contribution to urban ecology in presenting human ecology as a theory
of "community structure."

Generally speaking, more of the sociological research in urban ecology
during the past ten years was concentrated on the study of ecological
organization than on the study of ecological aggregates. This does not
mean that only a small amount of attention was given to investigation of
the composition of the population, its growth, and population balance, but
simply that relatively more sociologists devoted their effort to research on
ecological organization. The study of ecological aggregates in the United
States usually is based on data from the decennial censuses of population
and housing, while the studies of ecological organization usually depend
either upon field work by the investigator or the analysis of data collected by
organizations as a part of their regular operation. A series of monographs by
individual scholars, under the joint sponsorship of the U.S. Bureau of the
Census and the Committee on Census Monographs of the Social Science
Research Council, were published first in 1955. These studies are based on
data from the 1950 Census of Population. Their publication redresses somewhat the balance between the two types of investigation (28, 45, 61).

The spatial dimension of urban agglomerations was an early interest of
ecologists exploring the ecological organization of the city. The interest
continues to be a major one. Less attention perhaps now is given to investigation of the spatial patterns of urban growth in the manner of the
earlier studies on the zonal, sector, and multiple-nuclei hypotheses. One
of the more important recent investigations of spatial pattern has been
the study of the effect of bombing on the spatial pattern of cities in the
postwar period. The studies provide information on the relative influence
of socio-psychological as compared with ecological correlates in determining pattern (46). The pattern of internal differentiation within the
metropolitan complex has been given much attention in recent studies.

The work of Shevky and his associates (6, 79) and of Kish (51) are examples of this type of investigation. The tracing of a large number of American cities with 50,000 or more inhabitants has done much to facilitate this comparative analysis. There continues to be controversy over the relative influence of "cultural variables" vis-à-vis "symbiotic variables" in intra-urban area differentiation, generated most recently by the empirical work of Firey (31). There also is an increasing awareness that studies of "suburbanization" are but an aspect of the process of internal differentiation of metropolitan areas attested to by investigators of the "decentralization" of the urban population and its institutions. There now are fewer studies of the "suburb" and more of the "rural-urban fringe" and the "rural non-farm" population. The most comprehensive of these perhaps is a study by Hawley on metropolitan area growth since 1900 (37). The nature of the institutional organization and attitudes of fringe populations have been studied as well as the aggregation process itself (8, 59). A closely related research problem is that of determining the "relative influence" or dominance of metropolitan centers. Attention has largely centered on an empirical delineation of the area of metropolitan influence. The most original works in this area have been those of John Q. Steward on "social physics" (80), the "input-output" models for metropolitan regional analysis by Isard (47), and the study of metropolitan gradients by Bogue (9). The effect of technology on the spatial pattern of cities has been given some consideration in recent years. Ogburn's research on the effect of inventions of local transportation on patterns of urban settlement is of special interest (62). Little attention has been given to the study of industrial location or the functional specialization of urban places, since in the United States these problems are more generally considered by urban geographers or land economists, rather than by sociologists. The Kitagawa and Bogue (52) and Reeder (67, 68) studies are noteworthy exceptions. The work of the economist Loesch is a major contribution to ecological location theory (56).

The growth of cities and the process of urbanization is an object of continued investigation. This includes a continued interest in the problem of differentials induced by city size as well as by metropolitan organization. The investigation of two aspects of urban growth merit particular mention. (a) The interest of urban planners in "optimum city size" has led to research on that problem. The work of Duncan is of particular interest in this regard, since he concluded that the "optimum size of cities" will vary according to what criterion one selects as an "optimum condition," but that there appears to be no obvious way in which the various optima may be objectively equilibrated (26). (b) One of the earliest American works on cities is a study of world urbanization by Adna Weber published in 1899. This aspect of urbanization was generally ignored by American sociologists until quite recently, however. The work of Kingsley Davis and his associates reopened this area to investigation (20, 21). The interest of American social scientists in the "economic development" of underdeveloped areas also has stimulated research on urban agglomerations and the process of urbanization in the less economically advanced countries of the world (87, 75).

The temporal dimension of urban life usually was ignored in early studies in ecology. During the past decade there was an increased awareness of this dimension, manifesting itself primarily in two types of studies —those of the daily movement of urban inhabitants between workplace and residence (11, 17, 25, 77) and the residential mobility of urban populations (14, 76). There is documentation in some of these studies not only of the pattern and incidence of movement, but of the attitudes of persons toward such movement (76), and the effect of residential turnover on characteristics of the inhabitants (81).

Park and McKenzie focused observation on the process of ecological organization in an attempt to understand how cities assume the kind of structure they have and how particular functional aspects of cities might be explained. The interest in process has declined somewhat during the past decade, while students have worked somewhat more on describing structure. This does not deny a strong research interest in ecological process. Most of the research on process, however, focuses either on the process of expansion of the urban organization into a hinterland or on the processes of segregation, invasion and succession in urban areas. The interest in ameliorating the position of minority groups seems to be the major source of interest in the study of these latter ecological processes.

SOCIAL ORGANIZATION. Investigations of urban life, until recently, were studied within a theoretical framework of social disorganization. This no longer remains a central theoretical and empirical focus of investigation, as the study of urban social structure and its corollary functions seems to have replaced it. The largest number of investigations of urban social structure during the past decade are on social stratification in small urban communities. The studies have been severely criticized largely on the ground that what is measured refers to non-communal rather than communal systems of stratification (36, 64). There now appears to be a wholesome shift away from the simple descriptive study of class structure in small communities to a study of their power structures and the process of decision-making in communities. The investigation of the power structure in Atlanta, Georgia, by Floyd Hunter reported in *Community Power Structure* merits particular notice (44) as the most comprehensive effort in this area of investigation.

Some twenty years ago Thorndike published a treatise on the "goodness of cities" as places to live. This general interest has been reformulated in the study of the social and moral integration of cities as, for example, in the work of Angell (2), Gillen (34), and Anderson (1). There is considerable difficulty in defining and measuring social integration, and the empirical indexes in these studies therefore are very crude.

The effect of the rapid growth of cities on urban organization, and the effect of industrialization on small communities, agricultural areas or less economically advanced countries have become matters for investigation. The studies of Willow Run (16) and of the Hampton Roads communities (58), are examples of studies investigating the effect of wartime industrialization on communities in the United States. The urbanization and industrialization of the southern region of the United States (42, 83) and of underdeveloped areas outside the United States (18, 43, 55, 87), have achieved considerable attention, particularly in the reports of a recent conference on the effects of cities and urbanization on economic development (75). Many of these published papers lack data on the social structure of communities outside the United States, a fact which makes a truly comparative approach to the study of urban social structure very difficult. There are, however, a growing number of case studies of cities in areas undergoing rapid industrialization and urbanization which shortly may facilitate a comparative approach.

. There is some evidence that a concern with describing specific urban social institutions is diminishing. The earlier urban studies devoted considerable attention to these institutions and their organization—real estate boards, ethnic institutions, vice, and so on. Urban sociologists now seldom foster investigations of this type. A few of the formerly "neglected," but pervasive urban institutions, such as the industrial corporation and the leisure institutions, recently have been given increased attention. A separate field within sociology on work or industry, in fact, has arisen around the former interest. Similarly, the effect of urban living on specific social groups no longer holds the attention of students of urban life, except for a continued interest in the family (49, 53), the neighborhood (15, 29, 33), and participation in voluntary associations (4, 7, 24, 70, 88). What is generally called collective behavior has with few exceptions become a neglected problem area; the exceptions are the study of the mass phenomena of communication and opinion formation. There is, finally, less concern with an investigation of the problems associated with organizing and maintaining life in cities, except for that of application of sociological findings in urban planning (23, 30, 39, 48).

Early studies of cities focused on the personal and social problems which arise in, and contribute to, the "disorganized atmosphere" of cities. This interest perhaps was generated by a spirit to reform cities, and later by an economic depression. A decade or so of full employment may have influenced some professionals to shift away from this concern. A more important influence perhaps is a professional attitude that these personal and social problems are not the proper theoretical problems of sociology. They are rather thought of by a growing proportion of intellectuals in sociology as the province of "action sociologists." Despite this attitude, three of the major problems of American society during the past decade were studied intensively in an urban context—those of aging, race relations, and juvenile and adult crime. The demand by applied sociologists and anthropologists for research related to action programs has, however, led to a body of research on *how* groups and organizations in cities can more effectively implement their programs. The problem of the racial desegregation of American schools affords a case in point (85). This research has led to an emphasis on the "organization of communities" to meet their problems, rather than on a particularistic approach to the "solution" of particular problems. The work of Bradley Buell and his associates (12) and of Hayes (41) are good examples of this approach.

SOCIAL PSYCHOLOGY OF URBANITES. There has been, on the whole, very little investgiation of the effect of urban living on the personality structure of urban dwellers. There are, nonetheless, more investigations in this area during the past decade than in previous ones. Several studies merit particular attention. The writings of Riesman and his associates (71, 72, 73), while not strictly oriented toward an urban context have nevertheless dealt with personality development and character analysis in the "mass urban American society." Mangus and his associates (57) and Sewell (78) perhaps have undertaken the best comparative studies of differences in personality between rural and urban children, but their conclusions on personality differences among rural and urban dwellers are not in agreement. No social scientist appears to have attempted a study of intra-urban variation in personality development suggested by the earlier writings of James Plant (65).

The continued development and application of poll techniques and attitude measurement has, however, led to rather large bodies of data on differences in the opinions and attitudes of rural and urban inhabitants, and of inhabitants of different-sized urban agglomerations (5). The exploration of the source of this variation among various groups or aggregates within the city seldom is undertaken. The Detroit, Michigan, area inhabitants have been studied rather intensively through the Detroit Area Study at the University of Michigan (22) and a study at Wayne University (54). There nonetheless are few studies of the extent to which urban living conditions these attitudes and opinions, as most of the correlates are demographic or stratification variables.

A major shift in research emphasis has been a return to the study of social interaction in urban settings. The concern with studying interaction represents a growing awareness that this, after all, is the theoretical starting point of sociology. The study of differential social participation in communal settings (4, 88) and of reference groups (60, 70, 82) reflects this awareness. It formerly was taken for granted that neighborhood life is at a "minimum" in cities except in ethnic areas and among children. Recent studies of interaction in urban areas have questioned this general assumption about interaction in cities, pointing to data on close interpersonal relations in many urban neighborhoods (4, 24, 33). Studies of factories and other business institutions in cities have emphasized the primary interaction in these contexts, while a recent study of the urban local community press (50) emphasizes the primary relations orientation of these local media of communication. These studies appear to build upon the earlier studies of primary relations in ward politics and ethnic groups in American cities.

THEORY AND METHOD. There have been several major attempts to re-formulate the theories of urban demography and ecology during the past decade, the most comprehensive being the work of Amos Hawley (38). Little attempt has been made to reformulate theories about the social organization of cities, although there is evidence of a growing dissatis-faction with the formulations by Wirth and others (1, 32, 33, 50). This dissatisfaction is based on a number of criticisms: (a) the theories do not rest on a comparative urban approach, (b) the ideal-typical formulations are not too helpful in empirical research, and (c) the conception of com-munity in social organization theory is not properly related to this con-ception in human ecology.

There have been rather substantial advances in technique in demo-graphic and ecological research. These include, in particular, a literature on segregation indexes culminating in the recent work of the Duncans (27), the application of multiple regression and covariance analysis to urban data by Bogue (10), and the development of special techniques for area analysis (40). There have been, also, two major foci of critique —a critique of the use and interpretation of the ecological correlation (74) and of the logic and methodology of community rseearch (3, 69). No apparent technical developments have arisen in other kinds of urban studies, although "the current" study generally is characterized by greater methodologcial and technical sophistication (largely that of survey tech-niques and statistical methodology). Research reports are perhaps less "literary" than the reports of previous decades, with nonstatistical language usually employed only to describe the statistical findings. The studies may, therefore, be less attractive to the nontechnically oriented scholar.

CONCLUSION. There seems to be a decline of interest in research on cities and city life, if the research in urban demography and human ecology is excluded from consideration. This is in part due to the fact that much of the research simply considers the urban community to be a *context* within which a particular kind of theoretical problem is studied, but the context itself is not often made the object of investigation. This also means that a comparative sociology of urbanism is lacking, although seriously needed for future development of urban and/or community theory. This lack is not to be traced solely to a failure of American sociologists to take account of data from other cultures, since often these data are not available except in the demographic and ecological spheres of investigation. A second reason for the decline in urban research activity is the fact that there has been a shift in the problem-area division of sociological knowledge so that certain of the problems formerly conceptualized as "urban sociology" now are viewed within another frame of reference or theory. This is true, for example, of what now are called the problem fields of industrial sociology, social stratification and mass communication. There is some reason to believe that the sociology of city life will limit itself largely to a consideration of urban structure (in the sense of community) during the next decade and that the fragmentation of the field will continue. A more genuine comparative urban sociology should make its appearance, however .

REFERENCES

1. Anderson, C. Arnold. "Community Chest Campaigns as an Index of Community Integration," *Social Forces,* 33 (October, 1954), 76-81.
2. Angell, Robert C. *The Moral Integration of American Cities.* Chicago: University of Chicago Press, 1951.
3. Arensberg, Conrad M. "The Community-Study Method," *American Journal of Sociology,* 60 (September, 1954), 109-124.
4. Axelrod, Morris. "Urban Structure and Social Participation," *American Sociological Review,* 21 (February, 1956), 13-18.
5. Beers, Howard W. "Rural-Urban Differences: Some Evidence From Public Opinion Polls," *Rural Sociology,* 18 (1953), 1-11.
6. Bell, Wendell. "The Social Areas of the San Francisco Bay Region," *American Sociological Review,* 18 (February, 1953), 39-47.
7. Bell, Wendell, and Force, Maryanne T. "Urban Neighborhood Types and Participation in Formal Associations," *American Sociological Review,* 21 (February, 1956), 25-34.
8. Blizzard, Samuel W. "Research on the Rural-Urban Fringe," *Sociology and Social Research,* 38 (January-February, 1954), 143-149.
9. Bogue, Donald J. *The Structure of the Metropolitan Community: A Study of Dominance and Subdominance.* Ann Arbor: University of Michigan Press, 1949.
10. Bogue, Donald J. and Harris, Dorothy L. *Comparative Population and Urban Research Via Multiple Regression and Covariance Analysis.* Oxford, Ohio: Scripps Foundation, Miami University, 1954.
11. Breese, Gerald. *The Daytime Population of the Central Business District of Chicago.* Chicago: University of Chicago Press, 1949.
12. Buell, Bradley, and associates. *Community Planning for Human Services.* New York: Columbia University Press, 1952.
13. Burgess, E. W., (ed.). *The Urban Community.* Chicago: University of Chicago Press, 1926.
14. Caplow, Theodore. "Incidence and Direction of Residential Mobility in a Minneapolis Sample," *Social Forces,* 27 (May, 1949), 413-17.
15. Caplow, Theodore, and Forman, Robert. "Neighborhood Interaction in a Homogeneous Community," *American Sociological Review,* 15, (June, 1950), 357-66.
16. Carr, Lowell J. and Sterner, James E. *Willow Run: A Study of Industrialization and Cultural Inadequacy.* New York: Harper and Brothers, 1952.
17. *The Chicago Urban Analysis Project.* University of Chicago: Chicago Community Inventory, Reports 5, 13, 17 and 20.
18. Comhaire, J. "Some Aspects of Urbanization in the Belgian Congo," *American Journal of Sociology,* 61 (July, 1956), 8-13.
19. Davie, Maurice R. "The Field and Problems of Urban Sociology," in L. L. Bernard, editor, *The Fields and Methods of Sociology.* New York: Ray Long and Richard Smith, Inc., 1934.
20. Davis, Kingsley. "The Origin and Growth of Urbanization in the World," *American Journal of Sociology,* 60 (March, 1955), 429-37.
21. Davis, Kingsley and Hertz, Hilda. "The World Distribution of Urbanization," *Bulletin of the International Statistical Institute,* 33, Part IV.

22. Detroit Area Study. *Social Profile of Detroit.* University of Michigan, 1952, 1953, and 1954.

23. Dewey, Richard. "Peripheral Expansion in Milwaukee County," *American Journal of Sociology,* 53 (May, 1948), 417-22.

24. Dotson, Floyd. "Voluntary Associations Among Urban Working Class Families," *American Sociological Review,* 16 (October, 1951), 687-93.

25. Duncan, Beverly. "Factors in Work-Residence Separation: Wage and Salary Workers, Chicago, 1951," *American Sociological Review,* 21 (February, 1956), 48-56.

26. Duncan, Otis Dudley. "Optimum Size of Cities," in Paul K. Hatt and Albert J. Reiss, Jr., (editors), *Reader in Urban Sociology.* Glencoe: The Free Press, 1951.

27. Duncan, Otis Dudley, and Duncan, Beverly Davis. "A Methodological Analysis of Segregation Indexes," *American Sociological Review,* 20 (April, 1955), 210-17.

28. Duncan, Otis Dudley, and Reiss, Jr., Albert J. *Social Characteristics of Rural and Urban Communities: 1950.* New York: John Wiley & Sons, Inc., 1956.

29. Festinger, Leon, Schachter, Stanley, and Back, Kurt. *Social Pressures in Informal Groups.* New York: Harper and Brothers, 1950.

30. Firey, Walter. "Ecological Considerations in Planning for Rurban Fringes," *American Sociological Review,* 11 (August, 1946), 411-23.

31. Firey, Walter. *Land Use in Central Boston.* Cambridge: Harvard University Press, 1947.

32. Fisher, Robert Moore, (ed.). *The Metropolis in Modern Life.* New York: Doubleday & Company, 1955.

33. Foley, Donald L. *Neighbors or Urbanites? The Study of a Rochester Residential District.* New York: University of Rochester, 1952.

34. Gillen, John Bates. *The Distribution of Occupations as a City Yardstick.* New York: The Kings Crown Press, 1951.

35. Gillen, John Lewis. "The Development of Sociology in the United States," *Publications of the American Sociological Society,* Volume XXI, 1927, pp. 1-25.

36. Hatt, Paul K. "Stratification in the Mass Society," *American Sociological Review,* 15 (April, 1950) 216-222.

37. Hawley, Amos. *The Changing Shape of Metropolitan America: Deconcentration Since 1920.* Glencoe, Illinois: The Free Press, 1956.

38. Hawley, Amos. *Human Ecology: A Theory of Community Structure.* New York: The Ronald Press, 1950.

39. Hawley, Amos. "Municipal Government Expenditures in Central Cities," *Journal of Social Issues,* VII, Nos. 1 and 2, 1951, pp. 180-188.

40. Hauser, Phillip M., Duncan, Otis Dudley, and Duncan, Beverly Davis. *Methods of Urban Analysis: A Summary Report.* Air Force Personnel & Training Research Center, TN-56-1.

41. Hayes, Wayland J. *The Small Community Looks Ahead.* New York: Harcourt, Brace and Company, 1947.

42. Heberle, Rudolf and Bertrand, Alvin. "Social Consequences of the Industrialization of Southern Cities," *Social Forces,* 27 (October, 1948), 29-37.

43. Hoselitz, Bert F. "The City, The Factory, and Economic Growth," *American Economic Review,* XLV (May, 1955), 166-184.

44. Hunter, Floyd. *Community Power Structure.* Chapel Hill: University of North Carolina Press, 1953.

45. Hutchinson, E. P. *Immigrants and Their Children.* New York: John Wiley & Sons, Inc., 1956.

46. Ikle, Fred C. "The Effect of War Destruction Upon the Ecology of Cities," *Social Forces,* 29 (May, 1951), 383-91.

47. Isard, Walter and Kavesh, Robert. "Economic Structural Interrelations of Metropolitan Regions," *American Journal of Sociology,* 60 (September, 1954), 152-162.

48. Isaacs, Reginald R. "The 'Neighborhood Unit' as an Instrument for Segregation," *Journal of Housing,* 5 (August, 1948), 215-18.

49. Jaco, E. Gartly, and Belknap, Ivan. "Is A New Family Form Emerging in the Urban Fringe?," *American Sociological Review,* 18 (October, 1953), 551-57.

50. Janowitz, Morris. *The Community Press in an Urban Setting.* Glencoe: The Free Press, 1952.

51. Kish, Leslie. "Differentiation in Metropolitan Areas," *American Sociological Review,* 19 (August, 1954), 388-98.

52. Kitagawa, Evelyn R. and Bogue, Donald J. *Suburbanization of Manufacturing Activity Within Standard Metropolitan Areas.* Oxford, Ohio: Scripps Foundation for Research in Population Problems, 1955.

53. Koos, Earl. *Families in Trouble.* New York: The Kings Crown Press, 1946.

54. Kornhauser, Arthur. *Detroit as the People See It: A Survey of Attitudes in an Industrial City.* Detroit: Wayne University Press, 1952.

55. Le Tourneau, Richard. "Social Change in the Muslim Cities of North Africa," *American Journal of Sociology,* 60 (May, 1955), 527-35.

56. Loesch, August. *The Economics of Location.* Translated from the Second Revised Edition by William W. Woglom with the assistance of Wolfgang F. Stolper. New Haven: Yale University Press, 1954.

57. Mangus, A. R. "Personality Adjustment of Rural and Urban Children," *American Sociological Review,* 13 (October, 1948), 566-75.

58. Marsh, Charles F., (ed.). *The Hampton Roads Communities in World War II.* Chapel Hill: University of North Carolina Press, 1952.

59. Martin, Walter T. *The Rural-Urban Fringe: A Study of Adjustment to Residence Location.* Eugene: The University of Oregon Press, 1953.

60. Merton, Robert K., and Kendall, Patricia. "Patterns of Influence," in *Communications Research, 1948-1949.* Edited by Paul F. Lazarsfeld and Frank Stanton. New York: Harper and Bros., 1949.

61. Miller, Herman P. *Income of the American People.* New York: John Wiley & Sons, Inc., 1955.

62. Ogburn, William F. "Inventions of Local Transportation and the Patterns of Cities," *Social Forces,* 24 (May, 1946), 373-79.

63. Park, Robert E., *et al. The City.* Chicago: University of Chicago Press, 1925.

64. Pfautz, Harold and Duncan, Otis Dudley. "A Critical Evaluation of Warner's Work in Community Stratification," *American Sociological Review,* 15 (April, 1950), 205-215.

65. Plant, James. *Personality and the Culture Pattern.* New York: The Commonwealth Fund, 1937.

66. Quinn, James A. *Human Ecology.* New York: Prentice Hall, Inc., 1950.

67. Reeder, Leo G. "Industrial Deconcentration as a Factor in Rural-Urban Fringe Development," *Land Economics,* 31 (August, 1955), 275-80.

68. Reeder, Leo G. "Industrial Location in the Chicago Metropolitan Area with Special Reference to Population," Unpublished Ph.D. dissertation, University of Chicago Libraries, 1952.

69. Reiss, Albert J., Jr. "Some Logical and Methodological Problems in Community Research," *Social Forces,* 33 (October, 1954), 51-57.

70. Reissman, Leonard. "Class, Leisure and Social Participation," *American Sociological Review,* 19 (February. 1954), 76-84.

REFERENCES

71. Riesman, David. *Individualism Reconsidered.* Glencoe: The Free Press, 1954.
72. Riesman, David. *The Lonely Crowd: A Study of the Changing American Character.* New Haven: Yale University Press, 1950.
73. Riesman, David. *Faces in the Crowd: Individual Studies in Character and Politics.* New Haven: Yale University Press, 1952.
74. Robinson, W. S. "Ecological Correlations and the Behavior of Individuals," *American Sociological Review,* 15 (June, 1950), 351-56.
75. *The Role of Cities in Economic Development and Cultural Change: Proceedings of a Conference Held at the University of Chicago, May 24-26, 1954. Economic Development and Cultural Change,* Vol. III, Nos. 1 and 2.
76. Rossi, Peter. *Why Families Move: A Study in the Social Psychology of Urban Residential Mobility.* Glencoe, Illinois: The Free Press, 1955.
77. Schnore, Leo. "The Separation of Home and Work: A Problem for Human Ecology," *Social Forces,* 32 (May, 1954), 336-43.
78. Sewell, William H., and Amend, Eleanor H. "The Influence of Size of Home Community on Attitudes and Personality Traits," *American Socioloical Review,* 8 (April, 1943), 180-84.
79. Shevky, Eshref and Williams, Marilyn. *The Social Areas of Los Angeles.* Los Angeles: The University of California Press, 1949.
80. Stewart, John Q. "Suggested Principles of 'Social Physics'," *Science,* CVI (August, 1947).
81. Suellenger, T. Earl. "The Social Significance of Mobility: An Omaha Study," *American Journal of Sociology,* 55 (May, 1950), 559-64.
82. Sykes, Gresham M. "The Differential Distribution of Community Knowledge," *Social Forces,* 29 (May, 1951), 376-82.
83. Vance, Rupert B. and Demerath, N. *The Urban South.* Chapel Hill: University of North Carolina Press, 1955.
84. Watson, Jeanne, Breed, Warren, and Posman, Harry. "A Study in Urban Conversation: Sample of 1,001 Remarks Overheard in Manhattan," *Journal of Social Psychology,* 28 (1948), 121-33.
85. Williams, Robin M., Jr. and Ryan, Margaret W. *Schools in Transition: Community Experiences in Desegregation.* Chapel Hill: University of North Carolina Press, 1954.
86. Wirth, Louis. "Urbanism as a Way of Life," *American Journal of Sociology,* 44 (July, 1938).
87. "World Urbanism." *American Journal of Sociology,* 60 (March, 1955), 427-92.
88. Zimmer, Basil. "Farm Background and Urban Participation," *American Journal of Sociology,* 61 (March, 1956), 470-75.

1

THE NATURE OF THE CITY

A central fact of modern human existence is that the world increasingly comprises urban inhabitants, although it still is made up predominantly of rural ones. In the course of human history, an ever larger proportion of men have come to spend at least a portion of their lives within the confines of the city. Those who have not dwelt within cities have nonetheless been influenced to a growing extent by city life as the influence of the city spreads to the hinterland. The mode of life, the goals and problems of the peoples of the world have undergone many changes in the span of human history. The city and its civilization is the locus of many of these changes, for the city serves not only as a focal point for the integration of human activity, but also as a source for the initiation and control of social life.

Cities are social facts of many dimensions. Men have described and analyzed them from a variety of perspectives: as moral entities, as products of human history, as a relationship between man and his habitat, as a set of economic interrelationships, as centers of political control and as a distinct mode of human existence. Not all of these perspectives are of central interest in the sociological analysis of the city. Rather, the sociologist generally views the city as a mode or form of human community—a kind of community where there are particular symbiotic and commensalistic forces of integration, where human beings acquire certain traits by association, and where institutions and forms of organization arise giving to human life a characteristic aspect which we call "urban."

Sociologists, then, consider the city a *distinct form of human community*. The development of a consistent frame of reference and theory for the study of urban communities among other forms of community does not exist in the present state of development of the sociological discipline. There are, rather, three major approaches to the analysis of urban phenomena which are used in sociological description and analysis of urban phenomena: they are the ideal-type community approach, the trait-complex approach, and the rural-urban continuum approach. Often these approaches are combined in the work of a particular sociologist, and it is difficult to maintain any clear differentiation among them. They are treated separately here primarily because they represent recognizable emphases in methods of analyzing the phenomena of city life and urbanization.

Ideal-type analysis often is thought of as a method *sui generis*. The ideal type is a construct of the theorist or investigator which is obtained by abstracting the characteristics of an object in which one is interested to their logical extreme and perfection. They are in this sense pure logical abstractions; no empirical instance can ever be found to correspond exactly with the type. Ideal-type constructs of an urban community always include several ideal characteristics, and the more characteristics there are in the type, the less closely do empirical cases of communities approximate the ideal-type construct. Some ideal types are polar conceptions, but the definition of an ideal type does not require that they be polar; rural and urban societies frequently are thought of as polar ideal types, while the feudal society is not considered a polar type.

The technique of ideal-type analysis is a form of comparative method. Actual empirical instances are compared with the ideal type to see how closely they approximate the ideal type. The polar ideal-type analysis compares empirical cases with the two logical extremes. It generally assumes there is a continuum between the two polar types along which empirical cases order themselves.

There are a rather large number of examples in sociology of ideal-type definitions of communities. Among the earlier definitions are those of Maine and Toennies. The polar distinction involved in these definitions is between an intimate and traditional form of association in a village community and the formal and deliberately contractual association of an urban society. Durkheim's distinction between the society based on the sharing of sentiments with the society based on complementary functions resembles these distinctions but emphasizes a somewhat different contrast. Redfield's writings on the polar types of folk and urban societies have drawn considerable attention since he has become one of the principal supporters of ideal-type community analysis among contemporary American social scientists. He defines the folk society as a small, isolated, nonliterate and homogeneous society where the members have a strong sense of group solidarity. The logically opposite characteristics define the urban society.[1]

The trait-complex is closely related to the ideal-type approach. The difference between the two approaches is that the trait-complex approach employs *empirical* attributes or variables in the definition which are presumed to be causally connected. Some trait-complex definitions postulate a causal generating variable from which the others presumably follow. For Sorokin and Zimmerman, this variable is occupation,[2] while for others it is size or/and density of settlement. Trait differences may be either qualitative or quantitative. Sorokin and Zimmerman consider the occupational difference between rural and urban communities an example of a qualitative difference,[3] while size and density of settlement are purely quantitative ones. The traits employed in trait-complex definitions of communities usually are purely quantitative differences between communities since there appear to be few demonstrably qualitative ones.

A majority of urban sociologists in the United States appear to disregard the approach of a rural-urban dichotomy, of nonpolar ideal types of communities, *sui generis,* and of empirical trait definitions of rural and urban. One reason for the rejection of these definitions perhaps is that the correlation among the traits, attributes or ideal characteristics is far from perfect, so that it is difficult to work empirically with them. The most commonly accepted approach is the idea of a rural-urban continuum where there is *a continuous gradation from rural to urban* such that all human communities can be empirically placed at some point on the continuum. When rural and urban are defined in terms of a quantitative difference in traits, a continuum of difference is postulated automatically. The definitions of folk and urban *polar* ideal-types of communities similarly imply a continuum of community where all empirical instances of communities can be placed somewhere on the continuum.

The conception of a rural-urban continuum entails a number of empirical

1. See, Robert Redfield, "The Folk Society," *American Journal of Sociology,* 52 (January, 1947), 293-308.

2. See P. A. Sorokin and C. C. Zimmerman, *Principles of Rural-Urban Sociology* (New York: Henry Holt and Co., 1929).

3. *Ibid.,* p. 56.

difficulties. Are the characteristics which define the continuum themselves variables? If so, do the measures of the defining characteristics vary considerably for each community so that they fail to define consistently a continuum position for the community? And, if the values of the measures vary considerably for a community, can one weight the measures in such a way that each community can be assigned a specific place on a continuum which validly measures whether one community is more or less urban (or rural) than another? These questions do not receive a clear answer in the sociological literature. The paper by Miner in this section raises additional questions about the validity of the ideal-type method and the folk-urban continuum in a critical attempt to evaluate its usefulness as a frame of reference for community study. Duncan's paper is a careful empirical investigation of the hypothesis that there is consistent variation in patterns of behavior with gradations on the rural-urban continuum. Assuming that gradations in community size are a measure of the rural-urban continuum, Duncan shows that only some of the criteria of urbanism vary consistently, as postulated in the continuum idea.

The attributes or variables which define urban communities sociologically are chosen from four major sets of community characteristics. There are the characteristics which define it as (a) an ecological community, (b) a unique demographic structure, (c) a characteristic form of social action or organization and, (d) a set of values or subjective perceptions. The variables which delineate the area of functional interdependence of a population with reference to its daily requirements are the characteristics of the ecological community. The specific operational measures chosen are measures of the distribution of the population which regularly turns to a common center to satisfy its daily requirements. Some of the operational ways in which the urban ecological community has been

defined include the delineation of service areas of organizations such as newspapers and department stores, and the delineation of commutation areas, particularly of commutation to the city center. The two most commonly chosen demographic variables are absolute size and density of a settled area. The attributes of social organization employed in definitions of the urban community include its legal status as an urban corporation, the complexity of the division of labor, the quality of the industrial and occupational structures (primary, secondary, tertiary, and quaternary industries, for example), the opportunities for territorial and social mobility, the kind and degree of social cohesion among the members of a population, and the nature of the system of social interaction. Attributes such as the quality of institutions, of attitudes and sentiments, and the subjective awareness of, or identification with, a common community are characteristics which are presumed to define the community as a set of values or subjective perceptions.

There is good reason to assume that the attributes and variables sociologists use to define urban communities are not all of equal value in generating a valid and theoretically useful definition of "urban." There are considerable differences among the criteria in the ease with which they can be used in research, the degree to which they provide meaningful theoretical and empirical differentiation, their constancy in time and space, their cultural relativity, and their causal connection or interrelationship. A variable such as community size, for instance, has greater ease of operationalization and more freedom from cultural bias, and it is less subject to change in time and space, than is one such as the opportunity for social mobility. The problem of definition, of course, is relatively easy to state in a formal logical sense—the several analytical elements in the definition should be in the nature of the intersection, or logical product, of several sets which are not null sets, and its complements should be few so that it has the power of discrimination required of a definition in science. It is quite another matter to satisfy these logical criteria in a theoretical frame of reference for community study.

A growing number of sociologists appear to share the point of view that the formal criteria of a scientific definition of urban phenomena is satisfactorily met by defining communities solely in terms of their demographic uniqueness—the variables of population and area. "Urban" usually is defined, then, as a function of absolute population size and density of settlement. Most so-called urban variables then are considered causal consequences of variation in size and density of settlement.

Sociologically speaking, the city is a special mode of existence or a way of life. The paper by Wirth in this section accepts this orientation and defines the city in terms of three major variables which generate or cause these differences in way of life. They are absolute numbers of population in a permanently settled area, density of the settlement, and heterogeneity of the population. The central problem for the sociologist of the city, then, is to discover the forms of social action and organization which are generic to settlements of this kind. Actually, in the continuum form of the relationship, it is expected that the larger, the more densely populated and the more heterogeneous a permanent settlement, the more extreme the value of the measure associated with urbanism should be. The writings of Sorokin and Zimmerman, Robert Park, Nicholas J. Spykman, Georg Simmel and Louis Wirth, among others, focus on a number of characteristics presumed to be the causal consequences of urbanness. As urbanness increases, it is postulated that the following also increase: (1) qualitative differences in the occupational structure and increasing complexity of the division of labor and system of social stratification; (2) territorial and social mobility; (3) partici-

pation in voluntary interest groups or associations; (4) spatial segregation; (5) functional interdependence; (6) personal anonymity in interpersonal contacts, segmentalization of social roles and of role interactions, and the ratio of secondary to primary social contacts; (7) the toleration of social differences; (8) the degree to which behavior is controlled by indirect means; (9) normative deviance.

These are only some of the postulated structural and behavioral consequences of size. Rigorous scientific tests of these relationships are difficult to find; this is so for a number of reasons. First, it is difficult to develop valid and reliable operational measures of these characteristics. Second, data from various cultures and historical periods are not available to test the generality of the differences observed in a particular culture or historical period. It is known, for example, that only about one-half of the almost 900 large cities in the world are located in countries where the degree of literary, of industrialization, of per capita income, and of urbanization is high enough to approximate the conditions taken for granted by most writers on urbanism. Whether the hypotheses hold for the less industrialized and urbanized cultures of the world is questioned. Third, the effect of urbanness cannot easily be measured by comparing rural-urban or even size-of-place differences within a common culture, since there is contact and communication among these places, particularly among places in highly urbanized and industrialized societies. The effect of this contact and communication is not known, although all writers on urbanism assume that the effect is to reduce the difference between rural and urban ways of life. The possibility that under certain conditions contact and communication between the two ways of life may actually cause a greater divergence usually is not entertained. Inasmuch as most empirical studies concern places in highly urbanized countries, results of these comparisons may be least valid, at least as to the magnitude of differences, providing the assumption that contact decreases differences is correct. Closely related to the second and third points is a fourth one, viz., that it is too frequently assumed that the correlation between a variable and urbanness represents a causal connection between the two; often, however, the presumed consequence is a function of some other variables which may themselves have generated urbanness. The complexity of technology, for example, varies with size of place, but technology is not, for this reason, an urban variable. And the ethnic heterogeneity of large American cities probably is more a function of its settlement history and immigration policies than it is of size of place. Fifth, the consequences of urbanness may appear in other community contexts as well. The frontier community, for example, appears to generate temporarily many of the presumed effects of urbanness. The kind of confusion to be avoided is this: a factor such as anonymity may vary with city size, but this does not mean that anonymity occurs only in cities. The question of whether cities cause anonymity to increase is a problem of first knowing what the conditions are which cause anonymity and then learning whether these conditions are more common to cities as their size increases.

Many of the papers in this volume are selected to show the empirical relationship between variables presumed to measure urbanness and variables presumed to measure its consequences.

Not all the empirical data support the hypotheses set forth in the paper by Wirth. Duncan's paper, for example, raises doubts about the adequacy of the rural-urban continuum idea. Sjoberg's paper questions the postulate that a small, unstable, kinship group is a necessary correlate of city life by showing that kinship solidarity is an integral aspect of the pre-industrial city, while Axelrod's paper suggests that urbanites are more likely to maintain contacts with kinship and other informal groups than is sometimes assumed. Such findings do not negate the hypothesized relationships between size of place and other variables. They do affect, however, the degree to which they are related, and they may call into question causal connections.

Anyone who approaches the study of urban sociology for the first time may be surprised to learn that the ratio of accepted theory and established knowledge to speculation and conjecture in this discipline is low. If so, it should be kept in mind that any science seeks to ascertain the degree of reliability in such knowledge as it has, and not to attain the impossible goal of absolutely reliable knowledge. This Reader attempts to present the best examples that social science has to offer in urban sociology. The student is invited to identify for himself the many unsolved problems confronting investigators trying to develop a scientific knowledge of city life and the determinants and consequences of urbanization.

THE FOLK-URBAN CONTINUUM

Horace Miner

An evaluation of the utility of the *folk* ideal type and its contrast with the urban societal type seems appropriate at this time. Developments in the past two years ambiguously indicate both a decline and a resurgence in the use of the continuum.

The conceptual scheme is now over twenty years old. Some aspects of it seem still to be misunderstood and some of the limitations which have become apparent have not yet been adequately stated. It is our purpose to examine the basic propositions of the folk-urban continuum in the light of experience and criticism, in an effort to determine its inherent advantages and limitations for research and theory building.

Briefly stated, Redfield's scheme defines an ideal type, the *folk society*, which is the polar opposite of urban society. The ideal type is a mental construct and "No known society precisely corresponds to it. . . ."[1] It is "created only because through it we may hope to understand reality. Its function is to suggest aspects of real societies which deserve study, and especially to suggest hypotheses as to what, under certain defined conditions, may be generally true about society."[2]

The folk type of society is characterized as follows:

> Such a society is small, isolated, nonliterate, and homogeneous, with a strong sense of group solidarity. The ways of living are conventionalized into that coherent system which we call "a culture." Behavior is traditional, spontaneous, uncritical, and personal; there is no legislation or habit of experiment and reflection for intellectual ends. Kinship, its relationships and institutions, are the type categories of experience and the familial group is the unit of action. The sacred prevails over the secular; the economy is one of status rather than of the market.[3]

Redfield concerns himself largely with the folk pole of the continuum. It is the characteristics of the folk society which receive his descriptive attention. These are derived by discovering the common traits of those societies which are least like our own.[4] The definitive qualities of the urban

---

Reprinted from the *American Sociological Review*, Vol. 17 (October, 1952), pp. 529-37, by permission of the author and the *American Sociological Review*. (Copyright, 1952 by the American Sociological Society.)

1. Robert Redfield, "The Folk Society," *The American Journal of Sociology*, 52 (January, 1947), p. 294.
2. *Ibid.*, p. 295.
3. *Ibid.*, p. 293.
4. *Loc. cit.*

type are then left as the logically opposite ones to those which characterize
the folk. Urban society is never actually discussed here as an ideal type
and is not explicitly named. Redfield usually refers to it as "modern urbanized society" or some variant of the phrase. Implicit in the use of this pole
as an ideal type, however, is the idea that it stands for urbanized society
in general and that modern Western society represents the specific case
most closely approximating the polar category. The term "urban society"
would appear to represent the content of the ideal type more adequately.

   The folk-urban continuum developed, of course, from earlier conceptual schemes. Maine, Tönnies, and Durkheim contributed important dichot-
omies of societal characteristics. Redfield's formulation took elements of
these characteristics and others which he saw to be related and put them
together as the definitive traits of the polar types. A factor influencing the
research work of Redfield was that of concern with empirical method. To
this interest must be attributed the fact that he executed, in Yucatan, one
of the rare field projects in which a series of communities was selected
and studied to test a specific hypothesis. Consistent with the express purpose of the formulation of the ideal type, its characteristics suggested the
hypothesis. Concerning the Yucatan study, Redfield writes:

   The problem is seen as one of the relation among variables. No one of these
is the sole cause of the others, but it is assumed, subject to proof, that, as certain
of these vary, so do others. *For the purposes of this investigation* the isolation
and homogeneity of the community are taken together as an independent variable. Organization or disorganization of culture, secularization, and individualization are regarded as dependent variables. The choice of isolation and
homogeneity as independent variables implies the hypothesis that loss of isolation and increasing heterogeneity are causes of disorganization, secularization,
and individualization. Even if this should be established, it would not follow
that these are the only causes of these effects or that these are the only covariant
or causal relationships to be discovered in the same data.[5]

   Consideration of the data from Yucatan leads Redfield to the conclusion that ". . . increase of contacts, bringing about heterogeneity and
disorganization of culture, constitutes one sufficient cause of secularization
and individualization."[6] No formal generalization is attempted with regard
to the nature of the processes through which the variables affect one another,
although the analysis of the data is full of demonstration of their specific
interdependence in Yucatan. Comparison of the Yucatan material with
that from Guatemala leads Redfield to the final conclusion that ". . . there
is no single necessary cause for secularization and individualization."[7]
   The pertinent research in Guatemala is that of Sol Tax. It is essentially
exploratory in nature—an attempt to discern if, in another cultural milieu
than Yucatan, the variables of the ideal type are related in the same way.

---

* Italics mine.
5. *The Folk Culture of Yucatan,* Chicago: University of Chicago Press, 1941, p. 344.
6. *Ibid.,* p. 369.
7. *Loc. cit.*

Tax says Guatemalan societies are "small . . . homogeneous in beliefs and practices . . . with relationships impersonal . . . and with familial organization weak, with life secularized, and with individuals acting more from economic or other personal advantage than from any deep conviction or thought of social good."[8] As trade and commerce were important in Guatemala even in pre-Spanish times, Redfield regards Tax's observations as suggesting that the development of important commerce and a money economy may be another sufficient cause of secularization and individualization.[9] Tax points out that there seem to be two aspects of culture which cut across the dichotomy of the continuum. He finds the Guatemalan Indian "world view" or "mental apprehension of reality" to be folk in character but their kind of social relations to be those of the civilized (urban) type.[10]

Turning to other relevant research, Redfield's introduction to the writer's study of a comparatively isolated, French-Canadian community points out that this culture is intermediate on the continuum.[11] (He originally used the term "folk" to indicate this sort of society rather than the polar type, as Oscar Lewis has pointed out.) The Quebec study was not oriented toward any proposition explicitly related to the folk-urban continuum, but the writer agrees with Redfield's further observations that as the folklike community lost its isolation, through contact with the city, it became more heterogeneous, a market economy developed, and indications of disorganization appeared.

In a subsequent study of Timbuctoo, French West Africa, the writer did try to determine whether or not this densely populated, heterogeneous, non-isolated community showed social disorganization and was characterized by secular behavior and impersonal relationships, even in the absence of influences from Western civilization. As the report of this work is not yet available,[12] the following comments must, for the moment, be taken at their face value as evidence of the author's experience with and involvement in the folk-urban conceptual scheme.

The previous lack of interest, among anthropologists, in the urban pole of the continuum has already been alluded to. This polar type is logically also an ideal type, yet its characteristics have frankly been derived from a consideration of our own society. Further, in the series of Yucatan communities, decreasing isolation was in fact due to increased contact with Western urban civilization. This was explicitly recognized by Redfield.[13] But

8. "Culture and Civilization in Guatemalan Societies," *The Scientific Monthly,* 48 (May, 1939), p. 467.

9. *The Folk Culture of Yucatan,* p. 369.

10. "World View and Social Relations in Guatemala," *American Anthropologist,* 43 (January-March, 1941), p. 37.

11. *St. Denis, A French-Canadian Parish,* Chicago: University of Chicago Press, 1939.

12. *The Primitive City of Timbuctoo,* Princeton: Princeton University Press, 1953.

13. *The Folk Culture of Yucatan,* p. 360.

inherent in the continuum, as a hypothesis-provoking construct, is the idea that increased contact with any dissimilar society, not just with Western urban society, results in change in other variables of the ideal type. The Timbuctoo study was an attempt to avoid the limitations of the Yucatan research and of relevant rural-urban studies which have also been made in situations of rural contact with cities of Western civilization.

Briefly, the theoretical implications of the Timbuctoo data are that lack of isolation, marked population density and heterogeneity seem to be accompanied by disorganization, secularization and impersonalization, even in the absence of Western influences. The market economy appears as the system which makes possible the basic ecological conditions, holds the diverse cultural elements together, and mediates most relationships among them. Having said this, certain qualifications are immediately required. Evidence of disorganization and of secular and impersonal behavior, is most evident in relationships between members of different ethnic elements of the community. Familial relationships within each group seem to be strong, sacred and personal. Other intra-ethnic relationships are only somewhat less folk-like in character. Any attempt to characterize the whole society, and to compare it with others, highlights the fact that the folk-urban continuum deals with problems of the relative degree of presence or absence of polar characteristics, which vary not only between cultures but within them, and that no adequate methodological techniques exist for operationalizing and quantifying the characteristics themselves. To this point we shall want to return.

Certainly the most adverse comment on the utility of the folk-urban continuum is Oscar Lewis' critique which concludes his restudy of Tepoztlán. Both because this is a restudy of a community analyzed earlier by Redfield and because of the limited amount of research conducted with the continuum explicitly in mind, Lewis' comments deserve careful consideration.

Lewis points out that the folk concept is an ideal type and hence a matter of definition. It is upon its heuristic value that the type and its related continuum must be judged. He makes the following six criticisms of the conceptual framework, with regard to its utility for the study of culture change and for cultural analysis:[14]

(1) The folk-urban conceptualization of social change focuses attention primarily on the city as a source of change, to the exclusion or neglect of other factors of an internal or external nature. . . .

We would agree that Redfield's writing and research does neglect other sources of change than urban contact. We can not agree that the folk-urban continuum excludes other conceptualization. Most social scientists believe that the evolution of cities and civilizations has resulted from increased cultural interaction and interdependence. The operation of this

---

14. Quotations extracted from *Life in a Mexican Village*, pp. 432-440.

process is evident in Tax's Guatemalan data and in the Timbuctoo material. However, it would be erroneous to say that even loss of isolation need always be considered the independent variable in change. Any other variable might do, so far as the continuum is concerned. The very consideration of what other characteristics might be so employed leads immediately to the fruitful observation that some of the type traits seem to presuppose others. For example, great heterogeneity in the division of labor requires a large population, while a large population may exist with a relatively unelaborate division of labor.

(2) . . . culture change may not be a matter of folk-urban progression, but rather an increasing or decreasing heterogeneity of culture elements. For example . . . the incorporation of Spanish rural elements, such as the plow . . . did not make Tepoztlán more urban, but rather gave it a more varied rural culture. . . .

The fact that Lewis says "may not be a matter of folk-urban progression" can be taken to mean that homogeneity and the other variables of the ideal type are interrelated only in certain circumstances. His phraseology also suggests an identification of the concepts "folk" and "rural."

While it is possible that homogeneity may vary independently from the other variables, the following excerpts from Lewis' monograph demonstrate that this was not the case with regard to the increase of heterogeneity resulting from the addition of plow cultivation to hoe agriculture in Tepoztlán.

The differences between hoe culture (*tlacolol*) and plow culture are not limited merely to the use of different tools; each system has far-reaching social and economic implications.[15]

Tlacolol is practiced on communally owned land and necessitates a great deal of time and labor but very little capital. Plow culture is practiced on privately owned land and requires relatively little time and labor but considerable capital. In the former, there is dependence almost exclusively upon family labor; in the latter, there is a great dependence upon hired labor.[16]

Tlacolol is essentially geared to production for subsistence, while plow culture is better geared to production for the market. It is significant that most families who work *tlacolol* are landless and that *tlacolol* has traditionally been viewed as the last resort of the poor.[17]

[An informant says of Tepoztlán during the Diaz régime,] ". . . The presidents of the municipio, in agreement with the *caciques*, forbade the sowing of *tlacolol* and so the poor had no way of helping themselves. This prohibition was due to the fact that if the poor planted *tlacolol*, the rich or *caciques* would not have the peones during the rainy season to seed their lands. . . ."[18]

. . . in the years immediately following the Revolution, that is between 1920 and 1927, relatively few individuals became *tlacoloteros*. The population of the village was still small (the Revolution having reduced the population to about half its previous figure) and there was a relative abundance of rentable land. . . .

15. *Ibid.*, p. 129.
16. *Ibid.*, p. 130.
17. *Ibid.*, p. 131.
18. *Ibid.*, p. 93.

In 1927 the municipio lost control of the *tlacolol* lands, which passed to the jurisdiction of the forestry department. . . . With the rapid increase of population in the thirties, the shortage of land became acute and the need for the *tlacolol* land urgent. Many individuals began to open *tlacolol* plots and were fined.

In 1938 a group of Tepoztecans . . . stated that they would open *tlacolol* even if it meant violence and arrest. Following this demonstration the *tlacololeros* were allowed to work without government interference, and the number of *tlacololeros* increased.[19] . . . one of the crucial problems in Tepoztlán . . . (now is) the rapid increase of population with no accompanying increase in resources or improvement in production techniques. On the contrary, the increase in the number of *tlacololeros* represents a return to a more primitive type of production in an effort to escape the devastating effects of a money economy during a period of inflation. . . . Although it is helping to resolve the immediate problem, it by no means offers a satisfactory solution. In fact, it increases the problems to be faced.[20]

The writer knows of no better demonstration than that above of the manner in which two tools and their associated techniques form the core of social subdivision within a society. While it would certainly be unjustifiable to attribute the land-use system and its attendant problems in Tepoztlán solely to the co-occurrence of plow culture and *tlacolol,* it is equally unjustifiable to say that they are unrelated. Lewis' material indicates specifically that the introduction of plow agriculture and its coexistence with hoe agriculture is directly related to phenomena of population density, family cooperation, market economy, group solidarity, and conflicts indicative of social disorganization. What is more, this heterogeneity of technique seems to be related to shifts in the other variables away from the folk and, hence, toward the urban type. Tepoztlán is rural, in that it is an agricultural community, but it has a rural culture which shows definite urban influences and characteristics.

(3) Some of the criteria used in the definition of the folk society are treated by Redfield as linked or interdependent variables, but might better be treated as independent variables. . . .

The argument supporting this statement cites Tax's work and Lewis' own material showing that commercialism is accompanied by little evidence of family disorganization in Tepoztlán. This point is obviously a more generalized statement of that immediately preceding it. The only comment required is to note that the continuum, as defined, does not require that the type traits change at the same rate or that they are all interdependent in the same way in all circumstances. This is implicit in Redfield's statement, ". . . the societies of the world do not range themselves in the same order with regard to the degree to which they realize all of the characteristics of the ideal folk society."[21] It is explicit in his comparison of the Yucatan and Guatemala evidence.[22]

19. *Ibid.,* pp. 148-49.
20. *Ibid.,* p. 157.
21. "The Folk Society," p. 306.
22. *The Folk Culture of Yucatan,* pp. 364-369.

(4) The typology involved in the folk-urban classification of societies tends to obscure . . . the wide range in the ways of life and in the value systems among so-called primitive peoples. . . . the criteria used . . . are concerned with the purely formal aspects of society. . . . Focusing only on the formal aspects of urban society reduces all urban societies to a common denominator and treats them as if they all had the same culture. . . . It should be clear that the concept "urban" is too much of a catchall to be useful for cultural analysis. Moreover, it is suggested here that the question posed by Redfield, namely, what happens to an isolated, homogeneous society when it comes into contact with an urbanized society, cannot possibly be answered in a scientific way because the question is too general and the terms used do not give us the necessary data. What we need to know is what kind of an urban society, under what conditions of contact, and a host of other specific historical data.

We should amend two of these statements slightly to bring them in line with the facts before discussing them. Obviously the reduction of "all urban societies to a common denominator" treats them as though they had *something in common,* but not "as if they all had the same culture." Secondly, we see again a confusion between the conceptualization of the continuum and Redfield's research concern with a particular kind of loss of isolation, namely urban contact.

Granted that it is desirable to study the total configuration of a society and the specific historical factors which gave rise to that pattern, limiting our interests to such inquiry produces a methodological and descriptive science, such as linguistics. If we want to develop a social science with general principles applicable to all societies, despite their cultural differences, we are forced to abstract categories of phenomena which are applicable to all cultures.

Differences in ethos are important in understanding culture, as Lewis says in his discussion, citing the individualism and competitiveness of the Plains Indians. But because the urbanite and the Indian hunter share these features, does this mean we should cease to consider individualism and competition as specifically related to other aspects of urban life? It may also argue that we need to know how and in what circumstances individualism is systematically related to other systems than the urban.

As for the polar types being "catchalls," too generally defined for scientific investigation, Lewis seems to be restating Redfield's remarks:

> The problems suggested in that earlier paper defining the types are too comprehensive in scope and too vague in definition to be suitable guides for research. Nine or ten characters, each simply denoted by a phrase or two, are thrown together and called a "type." It is not clear how we are to determine how any particular society partakes more or less of any of these characters. It is not made clear how we are to determine which of these characters is naturally associated with any other. It is necessary to ask many more special questions, and to relate them to particular fact, to define more precise lines of inquiry.[23]

The continuum is an oversimplifiation, but at least it is a simplification

---

23. *Ibid.,* p. 344.

of a mass of data on cultural variation and change. As a rudimentary conceptual device, the continuum requires elaboration—elaboration which will produce a different conceptual scheme. Science does advance by asking the general questions. The crude answers to the general questions are the basis of increasingly more specific inquiry. The real query is, do we have a better initial answer than the folk-urban continuum to the general question of how to account for the similarities and differences observable among societies?[24]

(5) The folk-urban classification has serious limitations in guiding field research because of the highly selective implications of the categories themselves and the rather narrow focus of problem. The emphasis upon essentially formal aspects of culture leads to neglect of psychological data and, as a rule, does not give insight into the character of the people. . . .

The new element of critique here is that the continuum is not specifically concerned with psychological variables. This is perfectly true. The continuum does, however, invite the use of any body of theory which can explain the nature of the interrelationships among the variables.

(6) Finally, underlying the folk-urban dichotomy as used by Redfield, is a system of value judgments which contains the old Rousseauan notion of primitive people as noble savages, and the corollary that with civilization has come the fall of man. . . . It is assumed that all folk societies are integrated while urban societies are the great disorganizing force. . . .

To the extent that this is a criticism of Redfield rather than the continuum, we are not here concerned with the argument. This is, in part, the case, for there are no explicit value judgments placed on the polar types in their definition. The organization-disorganization variable, however, does lead to questions of value orientation. The concepts of "function" and what Merton calls "dysfunction," along with the idea of "degree of integration," are all closely allied in this problem. Social scientists do sometimes treat organization, function, and integration as though they were better than disorganizaion, dysfunction, and lack of integration. Much of our theory about culture change relies upon the belief that people experience conflict as punishing and that they restructure their behavior so as to eliminate the conflict. The fact that culture change often introduces new conflicts gives us pause to consider, but we still use this motivation of conflict-reduction as an essential element in explaining culture change. The basis for such motivation in the non-cultural reactions of organisms is quite clear. The value connotation of "organization" and "integration" seems to be a quality of data, not of the investigator, and as such is not bias.

Quite a different consideration concerning disorganization as a feature

---

24. Ralph Beals, in his review of Lewis' work, comments, "Even if we cannot define the significant variables satisfactorily, it seems hard to avoid recognition of important differences between urban and non-urban culture and behavior." *American Sociological Review,* 16 (December, 1951), p. 896.

of urban society is that this characteristic may not be dependent upon the other variables of the polar type but may be a function of the rate of social change. Such an explanation is consistent with change theory and might explain why ancient urban civilizations seem to have been less disorganized.

The foregoing discussion has introduced many of the sorts of inadequacies which some social scientists have seen in the folk-urban concept. Rather than to continue here piecemeal treatment, further questions will be introduced into any attempted systematic formulation of all of the arguments, with a view to making some judgment as to what the status of the continuum might profitably be in our theoretical thinking.

Criticisms of the folk-urban concept might be classed under three general headings: (1) the problem of lack of fit between the empirical evidence on particular societies and the nature of these societies which one might expect from the ideal-type construct, (2) the problem of definition of the characteristics of the ideal types, (3) the limited theoretical insight provided by the continuum.

(1) *The problem of fit.* Redfield deals with the ideal type as a mental construct which will be productive of testable hypotheses concerning society. This construct itself is commonly referred to as a hypothesis. It is the testing of this hypothesis which we here refer to as "the problem of fit." The fundamental hypothesis inherent in the formulation of the ideal type and the related continuum is that "There is some natural or interdependent relation among some or all of these characters (of the ideal type) in that change with regard to certain of them tends to bring about or carry with it change with respect to others of them."[25] Implied also is a general tendency for the characters to change in the same direction.

A. L. Kroeber raises two questions which essentially involve problems of fit.[26] One, which he does not develop, concerns the nature of the characteristics of the neglected, urban polar type. He asks if we can project the urban characteristics "forward into the future to a vanishing point." In other words, how can we conceive of a completely nonisolated, secular, heterogeneous, individualistic society? Kroeber's question is also applicable to the folk pole, although somewhat less so. While we might conceive of a completely isolated, sacred, personal, and kin-oriented society, what is a completely small or homogeneous society? These questions do not destroy the rationale of the continuum. They point up the fact that the empirically possible polarities must be located short of the logical extremes. Answers to the problem of what the minimal and maximal societal requisites are in this regard involve important knowledge about the basic nature of society.

Kroeber's other concern is the fact that if culture change is considered as movement along the continuum, it is an irregular progression, sometimes reversing its trend and moving at varying rates. These facts about culture

---

25. *The Folk Culture of Yucatan*, p. 343.
26. *Anthropology*, New York: Harcourt, Brace and Co., 1948, pp. 280-86.

change would only vitiate the continuum if it contended that change is always at the same rate or in the same direction. This it does not do. The fact that the direction of most change along the continuum corresponds with the ethnocentric idea of "progress" also suggests to Kroeber the possibility of bias. The conflict between this point and Lewis' view that Redfield has a value bias in favor of the folk pole makes it apparent that this sort of value judgment is not really inherent in the continuum.

The diffuseness of the hypothesis implied by the continuum is such that many specific cases of lack of fit do not in themselves invalidate the concept. If, considering all known societies, there is shown to be no general tendency for the elements of the type to co-occur, then obviously the ideal type is not valid. So far as the writer knows, no one has claimed that the general tendency does not exist.

There is another problem of fit which became apparent in the studies of Guatemala and Timbuctoo and in the restudy of Tepoztlán. This concerns the fact that the continuum requires that the investigator characterize a whole society as to the degree to which it partakes of each trait of the ideal type. The continuum states that some cultures are more folk-like than others; it admits that some characteristics of a single society may be more folk-like than other characteristics of the same society. What the continuum does not take into account is the fact that a single characteristic varies in its degree of folkness in different aspects of life in a single society. To ignore this fact in a summary characterization of the whole society blurs differences which are relevant and probably important. This observation seems to imply a need for the addition of some new dimension to the continuum.

(2) *Definition of characteristics.* Attempts to find the degree of fit between actual societies and the ideal type presupposes a precise definition of the characteristics of the type. The definition must be operationalized so that all observers of societies can categorize the cultural characteristics in the same way. Inasmuch as the traits of the ideal type are variables, there must be some way not only to identify them but also to quantify them, or at least to rank the variations of each trait in some consistent fashion.

Widely different societies conceivably might be ranked by judicious rule-of-thumb methods. There is definite evidence, however, that even this procedure is unsatisfactory. The difference between Redfield and Lewis in their conclusions concerning Tepoztlán is in large part attributable to the use of different standards by the two workers. It is even questionable if Redfield and Tax share a common standard, although they worked in close cooperation. Redfield seems to have had some reservations as to Tax's characterization of Guatemalan culture as secular and individualistic with weak familial institutions.[27]

Tax points out that the Indian *municipios* are highly specialized among

27. *The Folk Culture of Yucatan,* p. 364; "The Folk Society," p. 308.

themselves and in continuous intercommunication.[28] He characterizes each *municipio*, however, as being internally homogeneous.[29] This homogeneity is then used as characterizing Guatemalan societies. The designation of the community pattern as the social pattern would appear to be legitimate only in instances in which the communities are isolated or in which they are undifferentiated and intercommunity structure is undeveloped. The writer would be inclined to regard Guatemalan society as heterogeneous.

The study of Timbuctoo may also be open to different interpretation from that which the writer has made. The attention given to cases of conflict may be seen by others as observer bias. Actually instances of conflict were specifically sought, as they were regarded as indicative of disorganization. There is nothing novel about this approach but it suggests that some scale of conflict indexes should be applied to the whole range of the organization-disorganization variable, instead of using it solely at one pole. Past practice has often been to categorize organization by a "see how well it all fits together" description. This led, for example, to the anomaly of Lewis discovering that there were over a hundred cases of crime in Tepoztlán during the time that Redfield was observing the integrated nature of folk culture there. In his later work Redfield came to recognize four different categories of organization.[30] Disorganization, in the sense of lack of internal consistency, stands as the polar opposite to only one of these. All four need some uniformly applicable and scalable treatment.

Others of the characteristics of the ideal type lend themselves to more explicit handling than has been accorded them. Population size and density are easily metricized. Indices of amount of isolation could be developed on the basis of amount of movement of persons and goods in and out of the community, as well as the amount of mail and mechanical communication. The degree of functional importance of these contacts to the society is less readily dealt with, but this factor is probably more significant than the gross quantity of contact.

The presence of three distinct culture groups in Timbuctoo, and their organization in a ramifying division of labor and class structure, was used as indicative of marked heterogeneity. An itemization of distinctive roles based on kinship, economy, politics, religion, etc., might fruitfully be derived from such data for single numerical comparison with similar material from other societies. Taking population size into account, one would have an index of heterogeneity of roles. It is not suggested that this is the only important kind of heterogeneity, but its relevance to degree of individualization and impersonalization is clear.

It should be said in passing that the Yucatan study suffers less from

28. "World View and Social Relations in Guatemala," pp. 29-30.
29. "Culture and Civilization in Guatemalan Societies," *The Scientific Monthly,* (May, 1939), p. 467.
30. *The Folk Culture of Yucatan,* p. 346.

scaling difficulties than the other studies. In the first place, Redfield was familiar with most of the communities studied and his personal definition of the variables could be applied in each case. More important, the communities all presented varieties of traits with a common historical basis. It is relatively easy to judge the significance of traits which have been added to or dropped out of a particular ceremony. It is much more difficult to compare cross-culturally the significance of differences between utterly unrelated *rites de passage*.

The weight of evidence seems to be that, irrespective of the merits of the folk-urban continuum for theory building, the characteristics of the ideal type must be operationalized before relevant theory can be reliably tested cross-culturally.

(3) *The limited theoretical insight.* G. P. Murdock has criticized the folk-urban concept because it does not make use of historical, functional or psychological theory and method.[31] Melville Herskovits antedates Lewis in dissatisfaction with the type categories because they emphasize form rather than process.[32] These criticisms point up accurately the basic nature of the continuum. It does deal with the form rather than with the content of culture traits. As a predictive device it is a weak hypothesis. This doubtless accounts for the fact that Redfield does not refer to it as a hypothesis at all.

It will place the continuum in its proper perspective if we ask what utility remains for it, if it provides little exact fit or predictive value and if no theory concerning function or process is involved. To answer simply, we can only rephrase Redfield's original exposition. The ideal type is a conceptual recognition of a general tendency for certain formal characteristics of cultures to vary together. The continuum stands as an insistence that social science has something to explain here. Any body of theoretical knowledge in the social sciences can be related to the continuum if it can contribute to our understanding of the processes through which the characteristic traits are interrelated.

We note the Spencerian principle that as population density increases, so does differentiation, i.e., heterogeneity. This principle must be refined by the addition of Durkheim's idea of "social density," or frequency of contact and interchange within a population. This essential intervening variable lends itself not only to ecological treatment[33] but also to sociopsychological considerations of communication. In other words, there are bodies of theory which, when applied to the heterogeneity of population, and size and density characteristics, can go a long way toward explaining the processes through which they tend to vary together.

---

31. Review of *The Folk Culture of Yucatan, American Anthropologist,* 45 (January-March, 1943), pp. 133-136.

32. *Man and His Works,* New York: Alfred A. Knopf, 1948, pp. 604-07.

33. See, for example, Amos Hawley, *Human Ecology,* New York: The Ronald Press Co., 1950, Chapter 11.

Probably the most valuable feature of the continuum is the fact that it provides a framework within which various theoretical fields may be integrated to provide greater understanding of the nature and course of culture change. It is clear that such theoretical progress will involve the clarification, refinement, and addition of important variables in such change. Whether or not these developments take place with the continuum specifically in mind, they will, of necessity, have to take into account the cultural facts upon which the continuum rests. It is hardly prophetic to predict that the linear continuum will evolve into a more complex and more insightful construct. The ideal types are useful as a basis for such development.

COMMUNITY SIZE AND
THE RURAL-URBAN CONTINUUM

Otis Dudley Duncan

Despite the ubiquity and convenience of the dichotomous classification, urban *vs.* rural, most students of urbanism have long agreed that it is but a crude device at best. Thus, alongside well-known efforts to typify "the city" or "the rural world," one finds such cautions as the following: "In reality the transition from a purely rural community to an urban one . . . is not abrupt but gradual. . . . There is no absolute boundary line which would show a clearly cut cleavage between the rural and the urban community."[1] Or the following: "The city and the country may be regarded as two poles in reference to one or the other of which all human settlements tend to arrange themselves."[2]

Actually, no competent sociologist, for at least a generation, has maintained that the distinction between urban and rural is a sharp one. Even the standard Census Bureau classification, employed in much sociological research, involves three categories—urban, rural nonfarm, and rural farm—and is supplemented by such concepts as that of the "metropolitan district." Yet, in recent years writers on rural-urban sociology seem to have found it necessary to rediscover the inadequacy of the "rural-urban dichotomy,"[3] and a new label for an old idea has crept into the literature: the "rural-urban continuum."

This paper suggests that students take a careful look at the new terminology before admitting it permanently to the professional argot. Nothing is gained by replacing an objectionable concept with one having equally misleading, if somewhat different, connotations. The approach of the paper is empirical, as well as critical; and an incidental objective is to set forth some recent data on one type of intercommunity differentiation. These data have descriptive value independent of the paper's argument.

It is convenient to take as a point of departure a succinct formulation of the "hypothesis of the rural-urban continuum." A current text asserts

---

Published for the first time in this volume.

1. Pitirim Sorokin and Carle C. Zimmerman, *Principles of Rural-Urban Sociology* (New York: Henry Holt and Co., 1929), p. 14.

2. Louis Wirth, "Urbanism as a Way of Life," *American Journal of Sociology*, XLIV (July, 1938), p. 3.

3. For example, Neal Gross, "Sociological Variation in Contemporary Rural Life," *Rural Sociology*, 13 (September, 1948), 256-269; Irving A. Spaulding, "Serendipity and the Rural-Urban Continuum," *Rural Sociology*, 16 (March, 1951), 29-36.

that "there is a continuous gradation in the United States from rural to urban rather than a simple rural-urban dichotomy and . . . as human communities are arrayed along this rural-urban continuum, consistent variations occur in patterns of behavior."[4] Insofar as this statement is a substantive proposition, and not a mere definition or terminological convention, it is subject to acceptance or rejection on adequate empirical grounds. To accept the hypothesis, one would require essentially unequivocal confirmation by a large body of evidence, even if the proposition is left in the form of a statement in the present tense about a single country, and not extended to cover other places or time periods. On the other hand, even a small number of significant negative instances—cases where the proposition is incorrect or intolerably imprecise—would require its outright rejection or substantial modification. Thus, although this paper perhaps exhibits more "pro" than "con" instances, the latter are the more important as a test of the proposition's cogency.

Before turning to the data it is necessary to consider briefly two key terms in the foregoing statement of the "continuum" hypothesis: "continuous gradations" and "consistent variations." Even if a "continuum" exists, it can be analyzed only by using discrete categories. The range of the variable must, perforce, be broken down into intervals. In this paper eleven such intervals are used. This is a much larger number than is ordinarily employed in rural-urban comparisons, and should afford ample basis for a practical judgment as to whether "continuous gradation" is in evidence. The meaning of "consistent variations" in the present context is not entirely clear. But the term seems to imply that as one moves from the rural to the urban pole of the "continuum" any variable related to urbanism should increase (or decrease) in magnitude monotonically, or any attribute related to urbanism should increase (or decrease) in relative frequency monotonically. Minor irregularities aside, then, one would count as evidence against the hypothesis a case in which a dependent variable has a low value at the rural pole, a high value at some intermediate point, and a low value again at the urban pole. From the standpoint of "continuous gradation," another negative case for the hypothesis would be one in which a dependent variable is practically constant over a considerable part of the range of the "rural-urban continuum" and then increases abruptly with the next interval. Inasmuch as the paper sets forth the data on which its conclusions rest, the reader may form an independent judgment of the acceptability of those conclusions.

DATA AND PROCEDURE. A key assumption of this paper is that the most natural way to approach the construction of a "rural-urban continuum"

---

4. Stuart A. Queen and David B. Carpenter, *The American City* (New York: McGraw-Hill Book Co., 1953), p. 38. There is no intention here to single out these authors for criticism. Their statement, rather than some other one, is cited only because it states the "continuum" hypothesis concisely. For a similar point of view, see, for example, James A. Quinn, *Urban Sociology* (New York: American Book Co., 1955), pp. 24-27.

is to classify communities by size. Almost all writers on rural-urban differences stress the significance of community size. And while most of
them agree that "characterization of a community as urban on the basis
of size alone is obviously arbitrary,"[5] no one has suggested a practical
basis for including other variables among the criteria of urbanism to be
applied to all communities in standard fashion. The acceptability of this
assumption is discussed further below.

The community size classification, then, stands for the "rural-urban
continuum" as an independent variable. Several dependent variables are
related to the independent variable, and their regressions on community
size are examined for evidence of "continuous gradation" and "consistent
variation." Both the community size classification and the population characteristics studied as dependent variables are drawn from a 1950 Census
Report, *Characteristics by Size of Place.*[6]

Table 1 presents the community size classification, together with the
distribution of the population by community size groups. The first four
size categories include the 157 urbanized areas recognized in 1950. The
concept of "urbanized area" was first introduced in the 1950 Census, and

Table 1—Distribution of Population by Size of Community, for the United States: 1950

Size of Community	Number of Places	Per cent of Total Population
Total	17,217*	100.0
Urbanized areas		
3,000,000 or more	3	14.0
1,000,000 to 3,000,000	9	11.1
250,000 to 1,000,000	37	11.6
50,000 to 250,000	108	9.3
Places outside urbanized areas		
25,000 or more	193	4.7
10,000 to 25,000	547	5.5
2,500 to 10,000	2,513	7.9
1,000 to 2,500	4,158	4.3
Under 1,000 (incorporated)	9,649*	2.7
Nonvillage rural†		
Nonfarm	..	13.9
Farm	..	15.0

* Does not include unincorporated places of under 1,000 population.
† Includes population of unincorporated places of under 1,000 population.

it has some important advantages for a study of the present type. In
general, an urbanized area consists of a "central city" of at least 50,000
population plus its adjacent or nearby incorporated "suburbs," and, in

5. Wirth, *op. cit.,* p. 4.
6. Special Report, P-E No. 5 A (Washington: Government Printing Office, 1953).
The data in this report are based on a 3-1/3 per cent sample of the returns of the
1950 Census enumeration. Summary figures based on these data are, therefore, subject
to sampling variability. It is doubtful, however, that the amount of sampling variability
is large enough to affect this paper's conclusions materially.

addition, such unincorporated territory as is contiguous, or nearly so, to any other part of the area and has a closely spaced street pattern with at least 500 dwelling units per square mile, or which is the site of commercial or industrial activities functioning in close relation to the central city. Several urbanized areas contain more than one central city; for example, Minneapolis-St. Paul and San Francisco-Oakland. The important point is that the entire agglomeration is treated as a single unit, and its size classification is determined by the aggregate population. Hence, in the community size classification, a suburban municipality of, say, 10,000 population is regarded simply as part of a large "city," and not as comparable with an independent town of 10,000 population.

The next five size classes include progressively smaller places outside urbanized areas. Not only incorporated places, but also some 1,430 unincorporated places of 1,000 population or more, are included in these categories.

The two final categories include that part of the "rural" population (population outside places of 2,500 inhabitants or more) not included in places of 1,000 to 2,500 or in incorporated places of less than 1,000. The distinction between the nonfarm and farm parts of this rural residual is not, strictly speaking, based on community size. Nonetheless, on an *a priori* basis it seems reasonable to regard the farm category as "more rural" on the whole than the nonfarm. It should be noted that in most Census tabulations all population in the last four categories is classified as "rural," with the bulk of the population in villages of 1,000 to 2,500 and under 1,000 inhabitants falling into the "rural nonfarm" category. The separation of villages from the other rural categories is one of the virtues of the community size classification.

Some difficulties with the community size classification must be recognized. The delineation of urbanized areas was not carried out for central cities of less than 50,000 population. But smaller cities, as well, have "suburbs" and "fringe" populations. A more thoroughgoing classification would doubtlessly result in shifting some of the present "rural" and small town population into higher size groups.[7] Another source of error is the heterogeneity of the rural nonfarm (RNF) category. Perhaps one-sixth, or more, of the population in this category resides in unincorporated villages of less than 1,000 and properly belongs with the incorporated places of this size. Another substantial segment, no doubt, consists of residents of the "fringe" around small cities and towns and of the "satellite" territory of larger places. The RNF category also includes disproportionate numbers of persons in the Armed Forces, living on military posts outside cities and

7. Moreover, because the Census Bureau had to delineate the urbanized areas in advance of the 1950 enumeration, there are 21 places of 50,000 or more which attained that size for the first time in 1950 and were not included in urbanized areas, but in places outside urbanized areas of 25,000 or more. This overlap between the size class 50,000 to 250,000 and the size class 25,000 or more is probably a minor source of error for the purposes of this paper, however.

towns, and persons living in institutions (prisons, sanatoria, and the like). In addition to these disparate population elements, persons residing in the open country but not on farms are classified as rural nonfarm residents. Evidently, any summary of the characteristics of the RNF category must be interpreted with caution.

In relating dependent variables to community size, one must realize that there is considerable variability in the characteristics of communities in the same size group. With communities aggregated into size classes the most that can be done is to determine *average relationships* of dependent variables to community size. It is beyond the scope of this paper to consider the relative importance of other factors in intercommunity differentiation in comparison to community size.

DEFINITION OF URBANISM. In accepting the community size classification as an operational counterpart to the hypothetical "rural-urban continuum," one violates the premise of many authorities that urbanism must be defined in terms of several characteristics. One should inquire, therefore, how community size is related to other criteria of urbanism. Wirth's definition of a "city" specified as minimal elements size, density, and "social heterogeneity."[8] Sorokin and Zimmerman, in their "compound definition," included these elements, and several others, among which they emphasized the importance of agricultural occupations as a criterion of rurality.[9]

Table 2 shows the relation to community size of population density, the frequency of farm occupations, and as the only available indicator of "heterogeneity," the proportions of the population classified as nonwhite and foreign-born white.

Density figures are not available for villages, and it is perhaps doubtful whether a meaningful density could be computed for the RNF category. But over the first seven size categories density declines regularly with decreasing community size. The density of the entire rural population (village and nonvillage rural) is undoubtedly well below that of any of the urban categories. On the average, then, classifying communities by size yields an ordering in terms of density as well.

As community size increases, there is a decline in the proportion of the working force engaged in farm occupations (farmers and farm managers, and farm laborers and foremen). The "consistent variation" of farm pursuits with community size is disturbed only by the somewhat lower figure for the RNF category than for the smaller villages. It is noteworthy that even the "most rural" category has scarcely more than three-fourths of its employed males engaged in farm occupations, and even in moderately large towns and small cities there is a significant number of farm workers. The criterion of farm occupation, like density, is generally consistent with that of community size.

It is not so easy to measure "social heterogeneity," a characteristic

---

8. Wirth, *op. cit.*, p. 8.
9. Sorokin and Zimmerman, *op. cit.*, Chapter II.

which is usually discussed somewhat diffusely.[10] But one frequently mentioned aspect of heterogeneity is ethnic diversity. There is a theoretical basis for expecting ethnic diversity to vary with other criteria of urbanism. Large communities are supposed to recruit their populations through immigration from a more extended territory than that on which smaller places draw. The data in Table 2 do reveal a tendency for the proportions of nonwhites and foreign-born whites to vary directly with community

Table 2—Characteristics Defining "Urbanism"

Size of Community	Population per Square Mile	Per cent of Employed Males in Farm Occupations	PER CENT NONWHITE		PER CENT FOREIGN-BORN WHITE	
			North and West	South	North and West	South
Urbanized areas						
3,000,000 or more	7,679	0.5	8.9	..§	16.4	..§
1,000,000 to 3,000,000	6,776	0.3	10.7	22.4	11.7	4.8
250,000 to 1,000,000	4,468	0.5	5.7	21.5	8.2	2.7
50,000 to 250,000	3,869	0.8	3.7	22.7	8.6	2.5
Places outside urbanized areas						
25,000 or more	3,339*	1.3	3.0	21.7	6.6	2.0
10,000 to 25,000	2,721*	2.3	2.6	21.0	5.9	1.6
2,500 to 10,000	1,992*	3.9	1.6	19.8	5.6	1.3
1,000 to 2,500	..†	6.3	1.3	18.1	5.4	1.0
Under 1,000 (incorporated)	..†	12.6	0.7	16.5	4.0	0.6
Nonvillage rural						
Nonfarm	..†	11.2	3.0	18.9	5.5	1.0
Farm	13‡	76.8	1.6	26.6	4.2	0.6

* Based on incorporated places only. Land areas are for 1940 or are roughly estimated for 12 per cent of the incorporated places of 10,000 to 25,000 and 9 per cent of the incorporated places of 2,500 to 10,000. The corresponding density figures are probably slightly too high.
† Not available.
‡ Total farm population divided by total land in farms.
§ No community of this size in the South.

size. But there are several exceptions to this relationship at the rural end of the community size scale. In fact the highest proportion of nonwhites occurs in the rural-farm (RF) category for communities in the South. Even with the South removed, the nonwhite proportion is higher in the RF category than in villages in the remainder of the country. The RNF category has higher proportions of both nonwhites and foreign-born whites than would be expected from its position on the community-size scale. In fact, the least ethnic heterogeneity is observed in the case of the small villages (under 1,000). To explain the deviations from a regular relationship one has only to refer to the historical concentration of Negroes on southern farms and the segregation of American Indians in rural parts of the West. However, unless one takes the position that these historical facts "explain away" the deviations, the data on ethnic diversity raise a doubt as to the unidimensionality of a "rural-urban continuum" compounded of variables of size, density, farm occupations, and heterogeneity.

DEMOGRAPHIC CHARACTERISTICS. One of the most familiar rural-urban

10. See Sorokin and Zimmerman, *op. cit.*, pp. 23-28, and Wirth, *op. cit.*, pp. 16-18.

differences is the high proportion of males in rural areas as compared to cities. On the hypothesis of the "rural-urban continuum," then, one would expect the proportion of males in the population to increase with decreasing community size. Instead, as is shown in Table 3, the masculinity of the population is virtually constant over the first nine community size categories, then increases abruptly for the RNF and RF categories. The contrast is all the more striking in that females outnumber males in each of the urban and village categories, whereas the reverse is true of the nonvillage rural population. If one drew a line between "rural" and "urban" between the RNF category and the small villages, instead of between places of 2,500 or more and places under 2,500 (the Census classification), he would certainly note an "abrupt transition" from rural to urban rather than a "continuous gradation."

Table 3—Demographic and Socio-Economic Characteristics

Size of Community	Per Cent Male	Per Cent 65 Years Old and Over	Intra-county Mobility Rate*	Per Cent High-School Graduates†	White-Collar Workers as Per Cent of All Nonfarm Workers‡	Median Income§ (dollars)
Urbanized areas						
3,000,000 or more	48.5	7.8	9.5	39.4	43.8	2,492
1,000,000 to 3,000,000	48.5	7.6	10.5	39.9	39.8	2,443
250,000 to 1,000,000	48.4	7.8	14.3	39.9	39.9	2,160
50,000 to 250,000	48.3	8.0	13.7	38.3	37.9	2,057
Places outside urbanized areas						
25,000 or more	48.4	8.4	14.4	38.9	38.3	1,899
10,000 to 25,000	48.2	8.8	14.2	37.9	37.0	1,822
2,500 to 10,000	48.2	9.3	13.5	35.4	35.6	1,700
1,000 to 2,500	48.5	10.3	12.0	33.0	33.7	1,634
Under 1,000 (incorporated)	48.4	13.5	11.0	30.3	35.9	1,368
Nonvillage rural						
Nonfarm	51.4	7.3	14.3	27.3	26.0	1,605
Farm	52.3	7.5	9.6	19.0	21.7	1,111

* Per cent of all persons one year old and over living in the same county in 1950 as in 1949 who lived in a different house in 1949.
† Persons 25 years old and over.
‡ Employed males 14 years old and over.
§ For persons 14 years old and over with income in 1949.

Table 3 shows a rather "continuous gradation" in one aspect of age distribution, the percentage of the population 65 years old and over. However, the gradient extends only over the urban and village size groups and is abruptly broken when the RNF and RF categories are reached. The latter are actually more similar to the largest cities in their proportions of old persons than to any of the intervening size groups.

A third demographic variable exhibits still a different type of departure from expectations based on the "continuum" hypothesis. An approximation to the amount of local residential mobility is given by expressing the number of persons living in a different house within the same county as a percentage of all those living in the same county in 1950 as in 1949. This calculation disregards persons who moved from one county to another over the one-year period. The figures in Table 3 show that the intracounty mobility rate is lowest for the largest urbanized areas and for the non-village rural-farm population, and rises to a peak toward the middle of the community size scale. The high RNF value is an exception to this relationship. In this case, then, the extremes of the "continuum" resemble each other more closely than either resembles the median points.

SOCIO-ECONOMIC CHARACTERISTICS. On the whole, measures of socio-economic status fall into the regular gradient pattern expected on the "continuum hypothesis." As Table 3 shows, educational attainment, the percentage of white-collar workers in the nonfarm labor force, and the median cash income of persons with income are highest at the upper end of the community size scale and lowest at the rural pole. There are some minor fluctuations from one size category to the next, but perhaps the only serious disturbance of the pattern is the comparatively high median income for the RNF category.

One remark should be made, however. In the case of each of the three socio-economic series, the index value for the largest urbanized areas is about twice as large as that for the RF category. In the case of median income the middle size category (places of 10,000 to 25,000) is about half-way between the two extreme categories. But for the percentages of high-school graduates and white-collar workers, places of 10,000 to 25,000 are much closer to the largest cities than to the RF category. This finding means that one must expect to discover different types of community size gradients, even within the class of those relationships which are generally consistent with the "continuum hypothesis."

FAMILY CHARACTERISTICS. Many authorities believe that one of the most basic differences between rural and urban communities lies in the greater strength of familistic values in the former. On the "continuum hypothesis" one would expect various measures of family organization and functioning to exhibit a regular gradient pattern by size of community. The data in Table 4 provide general support for this expectation, but reveal some significant exceptions.

If allowance is made for variations in age distribution, the percentage of married females increases regularly from a low point in the largest communities to a maximum in RF areas. The extreme difference of 12 percentage points in the age-standardized proportion married and the step-wise progression of the proportions yield a pattern as closely in line with the "continuum hypothesis" as one might hope to find. The finding for males is not quite so neat: The differences are smaller and less regular; and after reaching a maximum for the two groups of villages, the proportions drop rather sharply for the RNF and RF categories. A major part of the explanation for this drop undoubtedly lies in the excess of males over females in RNF and RF areas; i.e., males in these areas have less opportunity for marriage.

Labor force participation of females belongs in a discussion of family characteristics, because gainful employment of women outside the home represents a departure from traditional familistic patterns. As Table 4 shows, there is a marked rural-urban contrast in the proportion of women in the labor force. However, a community size gradient is observed only for places under 25,000, and the labor force participation rate is practically constant among the five categories of places larger than 25,000. This finding is a bit surprising in view of the variation in proportion married and in marital fertility among the larger community size groups. Since employment competes with marriage and childbearing, one would expect labor force participation to be highest where the proportion married and the index of fertility are lowest. Perhaps if the labor force participation rates were standardized for marital status and number of children, one would actually find lower rates in the largest communities than in those of intermediate size.

Table 4 reveals a regular gradient pattern in the fertility ratio, here defined as the number of children under the age of five per 100 married women aged 14 to 44. The RF fertility ratio is nearly 50 per cent larger than that of the largest communities.

In view of the finding on fertility, one might expect a gradient in size of family. The statistics in Table 4 are for primary families, which means families comprised of a household head and all of his or her relatives by blood or marriage living in the same household (household heads living alone, or with nonrelatives only, are not included). There is, indeed, a pronounced rural-urban contrast, i.e., a substantial difference between the RNF and RF categories and all other community size categories, in

Table 4—Family Characteristics

Size of Community	Per Cent Married (Standardized for Age)* Male	Per Cent Married (Standardized for Age)* Female	Per Cent of Females in the Labor Force†	Fertility Ratio‡	Average Size of Primary Families
Urbanized areas					
3,000,000 or more	65.2	61.4	34.0	56	3.41
1,000,000 to 3,000,000	65.2	61.5	33.0	61	3.53
250,000 to 1,000,000	68.0	62.9	33.9	62	3.44
50,000 to 250,000	68.4	63.5	34.1	63	3.47
Places outside urbanized areas					
25,000 or more	68.2	63.6	33.9	64	3.44
10,000 to 25,000	69.3	64.6	32.6	63	3.45
2,500 to 10,000	70.0	66.4	30.4	66	3.53
1,000 to 2,500	70.4	68.5	27.2	69	3.59
Under 1,000 (incorporated)	70.2	70.4	23.4	70	3.53
Nonvillage rural					
Nonfarm	67.7	71.2	21.1	78	3.91
Farm	67.8	73.7	16.0	83	4.14

* Persons 14 years old and over. Standardized by the indirect method, on the basis of age-specific percentages married for the entire population of the United States.
† Females 14 years old and over.
‡ Children under five years old per 100 married women 14 to 44 years old.

the mean number of persons per family. But over the nine categories of urban and village communities there is relatively little variation in family size. The finding on average family size provides a negative case for the "continuum hypothesis" similar to that on the proportion of males.

CONCLUSIONS. The empirical materials of this paper reveal several "negative instances" for the "hypothesis of the rural-urban continuum," i.e., relationships between community size and dependent variables which do not fall into the pattern one would expect if the hypothesis had high descriptive validity. It appears that there are two important ways in which the hypothesis may prove misleading. (1) Suppose that an investigator working with a simple rural-urban dichotomy has observed a substantial difference between rural and urban areas on some important characteristic. He might then reason from the "continuum hypothesis" that if he established a scale of several intervals along a rural-urban dimension, an index of the characteristic in question would change gradually from one step on the scale to the next. Such an expectation would be in error for characteristics like the masculinity of the population or the size of families. The point is not wholly academic, for it is a common misconception that large cities have higher proportions of females, on the average, than do small cities and towns. (2) Suppose that an investigator has observed a consistent relationship between some dependent variable and community size over part of the range of community sizes. He might then reason from the premise of the "rural-urban continuum" that the relationship would hold over the entire range. Such an extrapolation, as has been shown, would lead to erroneous results for variables like the proportion of persons 65 years old and over, the intracounty mobility rate, the proportion of non-whites in the population, or the female labor force participation rate.

The results of the study certainly support what might be called the "weak form" of the "continuum hypothesis," i.e., the merely negative assertion that there is no unique, sharp breaking point between rural and urban. In particular, the Census Bureau's practice of designating as "urban" communities of 2,500 population or more is justified solely on grounds of convenience. In dealing with characteristics like those studied here one finds as often as not that villages resemble small towns (in the "urban" category) more closely than they do the nonvillage rural areas. Clearly, the data presented above demonstrate the value of working with a classification of communities more detailed than the rural-urban dichotomy or the trichotomy of rural farm, rural nonfarm, and urban residence.

On the other hand, the "strong form" of the "continuum hypothesis" does not withstand careful examination, for even the few series of statistics examined here contain several instances where either "continuous gradation" or "consistent variation" is not to be found. To accord this conclusion the emphasis it deserves, these supporting points are offered: (1) While this study is limited to an analysis of census data, it touches on a number of characteristics usually thought to be fundamental in a consideration of rural-urban differences or regarded as basic correlates of urbanization.[11] It is doubtful that equally clear-cut results, for or against the hypothesis, could be obtained for characteristics inferred from a smaller quantity of data or less precise data than those of the census. (2) The results of the study depend, but only in part, on the use of a community size classification as the operational counterpart to the hypothetical "rural-urban continuum." It is doubtful that the outcome would be different in net effect, if communities were scaled according to population density or the proportion engaged in agriculture, rather than according to size. In view of the conceded significance of community size as an indicator of urbanism, it would be difficult to accept as valid an empirical scaling of the "continuum" which disregarded community size. In any case, the results of the study place on the proponent of the "continuum hypothesis" the burden of *exhibiting* a measuring instrument which performs in the hypothesized manner. One may note that it is rather easier to posit a hypothetical "continuum" than to demonstrate the empirical relationships which it suggests. (3) There are defects in the community size classification, especially the ambiguity of the RNF category. But although the characteristics of this category are perhaps more frequently out of line with the "continuum hypothesis" than those of any other single category, none of the paper's conclusions rests on this fact alone. Even if one disregards the data on RNF category, there remain several cases in which the hypothesis does not withstand scrutiny.

The writer's general position is that careful inductive classifications of communities are of greater scientific value than hypothetical constructs like the "rural-urban continuum." The latter perhaps has some heuristic value in suggesting one kind of intercommunity variation. But it is highly doubtful that the unidimensional continuum, in any rigorous, mathematical sense, is a sufficiently realistic model for research on intercommunity variation. Realistic classifications will almost necessarily be multidimensional ones. Moreover, the precision of measurement along the various dimensions will doubtlessly be much less than is suggested by the idea of a continuum in mathematics. If this is true, then does not the social scientist reveal more pretentiousness than insight in insisting on a term like "continuum"? Finally, although it does not provide a "rural-urban continuum" in a definitive sense, the community size classification employed here—or, better, a refinement thereof—will no doubt prove to be a useful tool in research.

---

11. For an analysis of a number of other census characteristics and a fuller treatment of those discussed in this paper, see the monograph by the writer and Albert J. Reiss, Jr., *Social Characteristics of Urban and Rural Communities, 1950* (New York: John Wiley and Sons, 1956), Part I.

URBANISM AS A WAY OF LIFE

Louis Wirth

I. The City and Contemporary Civilization. Just as the beginning of Western civilization is marked by the permanent settlement of formerly nomadic peoples in the Mediterranean basin, so the beginning of what is distinctively modern in our civilization is best signalized by the growth of great cities. Nowhere has mankind been farther removed from organic nature than under the conditions of life characteristic of great cities. The contemporary world no longer presents a picture of small isolated groups of human beings scattered over a vast territory, as Sumner described primitive society.[1] The distinctive feature of the mode of living of man in the modern age is his concentration into gigantic aggregations around which cluster lesser centers and from which radiate the ideas and practices that we call civilization.

The degree to which the contemporary world may be said to be "urban" is not fully or accurately measured by the proportion of the total population living in cities. The influences which cities exert upon the social life of man are greater than the ratio of the urban population would indicate, for the city is not only in ever larger degrees the dwelling-place and the workshop of modern man, but it is the initiating and controlling center of economic, political, and cultural life that has drawn the most remote parts of the world into its orbit and woven diverse areas, peoples, and activities into a cosmos.

The growth of cities and the urbanization of the world is one of the most impressive facts of modern times. Although it is impossible to state precisely what proportion of the estimated total world-population of approximately 1,800,000,000 is urban, 69.2 per cent of the total population of those countries that do distinguish between urban and rural areas is urban.[2] Considering the fact, moreover, that the world's population is very unevenly distributed and that the growth of cities is not very far advanced in some of the countries that have only recently been touched by industrialism, this average understates the extent to which urban concentration has proceeded in those countries where the impact of the industrial revolution has been more forceful and of less recent date. This shift from a rural to a predomi-

Reprinted from *The American Journal of Sociology*, Vol. 44 (July 1938), by permission of the author and the publisher. (Copyright 1938 by *The American Journal of Sociology*.)

1. William Graham Sumner, *Folkways* (Boston, 1906), p. 12.
2. S. V. Pearson, *The Growth and Distribution of Population* (New York, 1935), p. 211.

nantly urban society, which has taken place within the span of a single generation in such industrialized areas as the United States and Japan, has been accompanied by profound changes in virtually every phase of social life. It is these changes and their ramifications that invite the attention of the sociologist to the study of the differences between the rural and the urban mode of living. The pursuit of this interest is an indispensable prerequisite for the comprehension and possible mastery of some of the most crucial contemporary problems of social life since it is likely to furnish one of the most revealing perspectives for the understanding of the ongoing changes in human nature and the social order.[3]

Since the city is the product of growth rather than of instantaneous creation, it is to be expected that the influences which it exerts upon the modes of life should not be able to wipe out completely the previously dominant modes of human association. To a greater or lesser degree, therefore, our social life bears the imprint of an earlier folk society, the characteristic modes of settlement of which were the farm, the manor, and the village. This historic influence is reinforced by the circumstance that the population of the city itself is in large measure recruited from the countryside, where a mode of life reminiscent of this earlier form of existence persists. Hence we should not expect to find abrupt and discontinuous variation between urban and rural types of personality. The city and the country may be regarded as two poles in reference to one or the other of which all human settlements tend to arrange themselves. In viewing urban-industrial and rural-folk society as ideal types of communities, we may obtain a perspective for the analysis of the basic models of human association as they appear in contemporary civilization.

II. A SOCIOLOGICAL DEFINITION OF THE CITY. Despite the preponderant significance of the city in our civilization, however, our knowledge of the nature of urbanism and the process of urbanization is meager. Many attempts have indeed been made to isolate the distinguishing characteristics of urban life. Geographers, historians, economists, and political scientists have incorporated the points of view of their respective disciplines into diverse definitions of the city. While in no sense intended to supersede these, the formulation of a sociological approach to the city may incidentally serve to call attention to the interrelations between them by emphasizing the peculiar characteristics of the city as a particular form of human association. A sociologically significant definition of the city seeks to select those elements of urbanism which mark it as a distinctive mode of human group life.

3. Whereas rural life in the United States has for a long time been a subject of considerable interest on the part of governmental bureaus, the most notable case of a comprehensive report being that submitted by the Country Life Commission to President Theodore Roosevelt in 1909, it is worthy of note that no equally comprehensive official inquiry into urban life was undertaken until the establishment of a Research Committee on Urbanism of the National Resources Committee. (Cf. *Our Cities: Their Role in the National Economy* [Washington: Government Printing Office, 1937].)

The characterization of a community as urban on the basis of size alone is obviously arbitrary. It is difficult to defend the present census definition which designates a community of 2,500 and above as urban and all others as rural. The situation would be the same if the criterion were 4,000, 8,000, 10,000, 25,000, or 100,000 population, for although in the latter case we might feel that we were more nearly dealing with an urban aggregate than would be the case in communities of lesser size, no definition of urbanism can hope to be completely satisfying as long as numbers are regarded as the sole criterion. Moreover, it is not difficult to demonstrate that communities of less than the arbitrarily set number of inhabitants lying with the range of influence of metropolitan centers have greater claim to recognition as urban communities than do larger ones leading a more isolated existence in a predominantly rural area. Finally, it should be recognized that census definitions are unduly influenced by the fact that the city, statistically speaking, is always an administrative concept in that the corporate limits play a decisive role in delineating the urban area. Nowhere is this more clearly apparent than in the concentrations of population on the peripheries of great metropolitan centers which cross arbitrary administrative boundaries of city, county, state, and nation.

As long as we identify urbanism with the physical entity of the city, viewing it merely as rigidly delimited in space, and proceed as if urban attributes abruptly ceased to be manifested beyond an arbitrary boundary line, we are not likely to arrive at any adequate conception of urbanism as a mode of life. The technological developments in transportation and communication which virtually mark a new epoch in human history have accentuated the role of cities as dominant elements in our civilization and have enormously extended the urban mode of living beyond the confines of the city itself. The dominance of the city, especially of the great city, may be regarded as a consequence of the concentration in cities of industrial and commercial, financial and administrative facilities and activities, transportation and communication lines, and cultural and recreational equipment such as the press, radio stations, theaters, libraries, museums, concert halls, operas, hospitals, higher educational institutions, research and publishing centers, professional organizations, and religious and welfare institutions. Were it not for the attraction and suggestions that the city exerts through these instrumentalities upon the rural population, the differences between the rural and the urban modes of life would be even greater than they are. Urbanization no longer denotes merely the process by which persons are attracted to a place called the city and incorporated into its system of life. It refers also to that cumulative accentuation of the characteristics distinctive of the mode of life which is associated with the growth of cities, and finally to the changes in the direction of modes of life recognized as urban which are apparent among people, wherever they may be, who have come under the spell of the influences which the city exerts by virtue of the power of its institutions and personalities operating through the means of communication and transportation.

The shortcomings which attach to number of inhabitants as a criterion of urbanism apply for the most part to density of population as well. Whether we accept the density of 10,000 persons per square mile as Mark Jefferson[4] proposed, or 1,000, which Wilcox[5] preferred to regard as the criterion of urban settlements, it is clear that unless density is correlated with significant social characteristics it can furnish only an arbitrary basis for differentiating urban from rural communities. Since our census enumerates the night rather than the day population of an area, the locale of the most intensive urban life—the city center—generally has low population density, and the industrial and commercial areas of the city, which contain the most characteristic economic activities underlying urban society, would scarcely anywhere be truly urban if density were literally interpreted as a mark of urbanism. Nevertheless, the fact that the urban community is distinguished by a large aggregation and relatively dense concentration of population can scarcely be left out of account in a definition of the city. But these criteria must be seen as relative to the general cultural context in which cities arise and exist and are sociologically relevant only in so far as they operate as conditioning factors in social life.

The same criticisms apply to such criteria as the occupation of the inhabitants, the existence of certain physical facilities, institutions, and forms of political organization. The question is not whether cities in our civilization or in others do exhibit these distinctive traits, but how potent they are in molding the character of social life into its specifically urban form. Nor in formulating a fertile definition can we afford to overlook the great variations between cities. By means of a typology of cities based upon size, location, age, and function, such as we have undertaken to establish in our recent report to the National Resources Committee,[6] we have found it feasible to array and classify urban communities ranging from struggling small towns to thriving world-metropolitan centers; from isolated trading centers in the midst of agricultural regions to thriving world ports and commercial and industrial conurbations. Such differences as these appear crucial because the social characteristics and influences of these different "cities" vary widely.

A serviceable definition of urbanism should not only denote the essential characteristics which all cities—at least those in our culture—have in common, but should lend itself to the discovery of their variations. An industrial city will differ significantly in social respects from a commercial, mining, fishing, resort, university, and capital city. A one-industry city will present different sets of social characteristics from a multi-industry city, as will an industrially balanced from an imbalanced city, a suburb from a satellite, a residential suburb from an industrial suburb, a city within a metropolitan

4. "The Anthropogeography of Some Great Cities," *Bull. American Geographical Society*, XLI (1909), 537-66.

5. Walter F. Willcox, "A Definition of 'City' in Terms of Density," in E. W. Burgess, *The Urban Community* (Chicago, 1926), p. 119.

6. *Op. cit.*, p. 8.

region from one lying outside, an old city from a new one, a southern city from a New England, a middle-western from a Pacific Coast city, a growing from a stable and from a dying city.

A sociological definition must obviously be inclusive enough to comprise whatever essential characteristics these different types of cities have in common as social entities, but it obviously cannot be so detailed as to take account of all the variations implicit in the manifold classes sketched above. Presumably some of the characteristics of cities are more significant in conditioning the nature of urban life than others, and we may expect the outstanding features of the urban-social scene to vary in accordance with size, density, and differences in the functional type of cities. Moreover, we may infer that rural life will bear the imprint of urbanism in the measure that through contact and communication it comes under the influence of cities. It may contribute to the clarity of the statements that follow to repeat that while the locus of urbanism as a mode of life is of course, to be found characteristically in places which fulfil the requirements we shall set up as a definition of the city, urbanism is not confined to such localities but is manifest in varying degrees wherever the influences of the city reach.

While urbanism, or that complex of traits which makes up the characteristic mode of life in cities, and urbanization, which denotes the development and extensions of these factors, are thus not exclusively found in settlements which are cities in the physical and demographic sense, they do, nevertheless, find their most pronounced expression in such areas, especially in metropolitan cities. In formulating a definition of the city it is necessary to exercise caution in order to avoid identifying urbanism as a way of life with any specific locally or historically conditioned cultural influences which, while they may significantly affect the specific character of the community, are not the essential determinants of its character as a city.

It is particularly important to call attention to the danger of confusing urbanism with industrialism and modern capitalism. The rise of cities in the modern world is undoubtedly not independent of the emergence of modern power-driven machine technology, mass production, and capitalistic enterprise. But different as the cities of earlier epochs may have been by virtue of their development in a preindustrial and precapitalistic order from the great cities of today, they were, nevertheless, cities.

For sociological purposes a city may be defined as a relatively large, dense, and permanent settlement of socially heterogeneous individuals. On the basis of the postulates which this minimal definition suggests, a theory of urbanism may be formulated in the light of existing knowledge concerning social groups.

III. A THEORY OF URBANISM. In the rich literature on the city we look in vain for a theory of urbanism presenting in a systematic fashion the available knowledge concerning the city as a social entity. We do indeed have excellent formulations of theories on such special problems as the growth of the city viewed as a historical trend and as a recurrent process,[7] and we have a wealth of literature presenting insights of sociological relevance and empirical studies offering detailed information on a variety of particular aspects of urban life. But despite the multiplication of research and textbooks on the city, we do not as yet have a comprehensive body of compendent hypotheses which may be derived from a set of postulates implicitly contained in a sociological definition of the city, and from our general sociological knowledge which may be substantiated through empirical research. The closest approximations to a systematic theory of urbanism that we have are to be found in a penetrating essay, "Die Stadt," by Max Weber,[8] and a memorable paper by Robert E. Park on "The City: Suggestions for the Investigations of Human Behavior in the Urban Environment." [9] But even these excellent contributions are far from constituting an ordered and coherent framework of theory upon which research might profitably proceed.

In the pages that follow we shall seek to set forth a limited number of identifying characteristics of the city. Given these characteristics we shall then indicate what consequences or further characteristics follow from them in the light of general sociological theory and empirical research. We hope in this manner to arrive at the essential propositions comprising a theory of urbanism. Some of these propositions can be supported by a considerable body of already available research materials; others may be accepted as hypotheses for which a certain amount of presumptive evidence exists, but for which more ample and exact verification would be required. At least such a procedure will, it is hoped, show what in the way of systematic knowledge of the city we now have and what are the crucial and fruitful hypotheses for future research.

The central problem of the sociologist of the city is to discover the forms of social action and organization that typically emerge in relatively permanent, compact settlements of large numbers of heterogeneous individuals. We must also infer that urbanism will assume its most characteristic and extreme form in the measure in which the conditions with which it is congruent are present. Thus the larger, the more densely populated, and the more heterogeneous a community, the more accentuated the characteristics associated with urbanism will be. It should be recognized, however, that in the social world institutions and practices may be accepted and continued for reasons other than those that originally brought them into existence, and that accordingly the urban mode of life may be perpetuated under conditions quite foreign to those necessary for its origin.

---

7. See Robert E. Park, Ernest W. Burgess, *et al.*, *The City* (Chicago, 1925), esp. chaps. ii and iii; Werner Sombart, "Städtische Siedlung, Stadt," *Handwörterbuch der Soziologie,* ed. Alfred Vierkandt (Stuttgart, 1931); see also bibliography.

8. *Wirtschaft und Gesellschaft* (Tübingen, 1925), Part I, chap. viii, pp. 514-601.

9. Park, Burgess, *et al., op. cit.,* chap. i.

Some justification may be in order for the choice of the principal terms comprising our definition of the city. The attempt has been made to make it as inclusive and at the same time as denotative as possible without loading it with unnecessary assumptions. To say that large numbers are necessary to constitute a city means, of course, large numbers in relation to a restricted area or high density of settlement. There are, nevertheless, good reasons for treating large numbers and density as separate factors, since each may be connected with significantly different social consequences. Similarly the need for adding heterogeneity to numbers of population as a necessary and distinct criterion of urbanism might be questioned, since we should expect the range of differences to increase with numbers. In defense, it may be said that the city shows a kind and degree of heterogeneity of population which cannot be wholly accounted for by the law of large numbers or adequately represented by means of a normal distribution curve. Since the population of the city does not reproduce itself, it must recruit its migrants from other cities, the countryside, and—in this country until recently—from other countries. The city has thus historically been the melting-pot of races, peoples, and cultures, and a most favorable breeding-ground of new biological and cultural hybrids. It has not only tolerated but rewarded individual differences. It has brought together people from the ends of the earth *because* they are different and thus useful to one another, rather than because they are homogeneous and like-minded.[10]

There are a number of sociological propositions concerning the relationship between (a) numbers of population, (b) density of settlement, (c) heterogeneity of inhabitants and group life, which can be formulated on the basis of observation and research.

Size of the Population Aggregate. Ever since Aristotle's *Politics*,[11] it has been recognized that increasing the number of inhabitants in a settlement beyond a certain limit will affect the relationships between them and the

---

10. The justification for including the term "permanent" in the definition may appear necessary. Our failure to give an extensive justification for this qualifying mark of the urban rests on the obvious fact that unless human settlements take a fairly permanent root in a locality the characteristics of urban life cannot arise, and conversely the living together of large numbers of heterogeneous individuals under dense conditions is not possible without the development of a more or less technological structure.

11. See esp. vii. 4. 4-14. Translated by B. Jowett, from which the following may be quoted:

"To the size of states there is a limit, as there is to other things, plants, animals, implements; for none of these retain their natural power when they are too large or too small, but they either wholly lose their nature, or are spoiled. . . . [A] state when composed of too few is not as a state ought to be, self-sufficing; when of too many, though self-sufficing in all mere necessaries, it is a nation and not a state, being almost incapable of constitutional government. For who can be the general of such a vast multitude, or who the herald, unless he have the voice of a Stentor?

"A state then only begins to exist when it has attained a population sufficient for a good life in the political community; it may indeed somewhat exceed this number. But, as I was saying, there must be a limit. What should be the limit will be easily ascertained by experience. For both governors and governed have duties to perform; the special functions of a governor are to command and to judge. But if the citizens of a

character of the city. Large numbers involve, as has been pointed out, a greater range of individual variation. Furthermore, the greater the number of individuals participating in a process of interaction, the greater is the *potential* differentiation between them. The personal traits, the occupations, the cultural life, and the ideas of the members of an urban community may, therefore, be expected to range between more widely separated poles than those of rural inhabitants.

That such variations should give rise to the spatial segregation of individuals according to color, ethnic heritage, economic and social status, tastes and preferences, may readily be inferred. The bonds of kinship, of neighborliness, and the sentiments arising out of living together for generations under a common folk tradition are likely to be absent or, at best, relatively weak in an aggregate the members of which have such diverse origins and backgrounds. Under such circumstances competition and formal control mechanisms furnish the substitutes for the bonds of solidarity that are relied upon to hold a folk society together.

Increase in the number of inhabitants of a community beyond a few hundred is bound to limit the possibility of each member of the community knowing all the others personally. Max Weber, in recognizing the social significance of this fact, pointed out that from a sociological point of view large numbers of inhabitants and density of settlement mean that the personal mutual acquaintanceship between the inhabitants which ordinarily inheres in a neighborhood is lacking.[12] The increase in numbers thus involves a changed character of the social relationships. As Simmel points out:

[If] the unceasing external contact of numbers of persons in the city should be met by the same number of inner reactions as in the small town, in which one knows almost every person he meets and to each of whom he has a positive relationship, one would be completely atomized internally and would fall into an unthinkable mental condition.[13]

The multiplication of persons in a state of interaction under conditions which make their contact as full personalities impossible produces that segmentalization of human relationships which has sometimes been seized upon by students of the mental life of the cities as an explanation for the "schizoid" character of urban personality. This is not to say that the urban inhabitants have fewer acquaintances than rural inhabitants, for the reverse

state are to judge and to distribute offices according to merit, then they must know each other's characters; where they do not possess this knowledge, both the election to offices and the decision of law suits will go wrong. When the population is very large they are manifestly settled at haphazard, which clearly ought not to be. Besides, in an overpopulous state foreigners and metics will readily acquire the rights of citizens, for who will find them out? Clearly, then, the best limit of the population of a state is the largest number which suffices for the purposes of life, and can be taken in at a single view. Enough concerning the size of a city."

12. *Op. cit.*, p. 514.

13. Georg Simmel, "Die Grosstädte und des Geistesleben," *Die Grosstadt,* ed. Theodor Petermann (Dresden, 1903), pp. 187-206.

may actually be true; it means rather that in relation to the number of people whom they see and with whom they rub elbows in the course of daily life, they know a smaller proportion, and of these they have less intensive knowledge.

Characteristically, urbanites meet one another in highly segmental roles. They are, to be sure, dependent upon more people for the satisfactions of their life-needs than are rural people and thus are associated with a greater number of organized groups, but they are less dependent upon particular persons, and their dependence upon others is confined to a highly fractionalized aspect of the other's round of activity. This is essentially what is meant by saying that the city is characterized by secondary rather than primary contacts. The contacts of the city may indeed be face to face, but they are nevertheless impersonal, superficial, transitory, and segmental. The reserve, the indifference, and the blasé outlook which urbanites manifest in their relationships may thus be regarded as devices for immunizing themselves against the personal claims and expectations of others.

The superficiality, the anonymity, and the transitory character of urban-social relations make intelligible, also, the sophistication and the rationality generally ascribed to city-dwellers. Our acquaintances tend to stand in a relationship of utility to us in the sense that the role which each one plays in our life is overwhelmingly regarded as a means for the achievement of our own ends. Whereas, therefore, the individual gains, on the one hand, a certain degree of emancipation or freedom from the personal and emotional controls of intimate groups, he loses, on the other hand, the spontaneous self-expression, the morale, and the sense of participation that comes with living in an integrated society. This constitutes essentially the state of *anomie* or the social void to which Durkheim alludes in attempting to account for the various forms of social disorganization in technological society.

The segmental character and utilitarian accent of interpersonal relations in the city find their institutional expression in the proliferation of specialized tasks which we see in their most developed form in the professions. The operations of the pecuniary nexus lead to predatory relationships, which tend to obstruct the efficient functioning of the social order unless checked by professional codes and occupational etiquette. The premium put upon utility and efficiency suggests the adaptability of the corporate device for the organization of enterprises in which individuals can engage only in groups. The advantage that the corporation has over the individual entrepreneur and the partnership in the urban-industrial world derives not only from the possibility it affords of centralizing the resources of thousands of individuals or from the legal privilege of limited liability and perpetual succession, but from the fact that the corporation has no soul.

The specialization of individuals, particularly in their occupations, can proceed only, as Adam Smith pointed out, upon the basis of an enlarged market, which in turn accentuates the division of labor. This enlarged market is only in part supplied by the city's hinterland; in large measure it is found among the large numbers that the city itself contains. The dominance of the city over the surrounding hinterland becomes explicable in terms of the division of labor which urban life occasions and promotes. The extreme degree of interdependence and the unstable equilibrium of urban life are closely associated with the division of labor and the specialization of occupations. This interdependence and instability is increased by the tendency of each city to specialize in those functions in which it has the greatest advantage.

In a community composed of a larger number of individuals than can know one another intimately and can be assembled in one spot, it becomes necessary to communicate through indirect media and to articulate individual interests by a process of delegation. Typically in the city, interests are made effective through representation. The individual counts for little, but the voice of the representative is heard with a deference roughly proportional to the numbers for whom he speaks.

While this characterization of urbanism, in so far as it derives from large numbers, does not by any means exhaust the sociological inferences that might be drawn from our knowledge of the relationship of the size of a group to the characteristic behavior of the members, for the sake of brevity the assertions made may serve to exemplify the sort of propositions that might be developed.

Density. As in the case of numbers, so in the case of concentration in limited space, certain consequences of relevance in sociological analysis of the city emerge. Of these only a few can be indicated.

As Darwin pointed out for flora and fauna and as Durkheim [14] noted in the case of human societies, an increase in numbers when area is held constant (i.e., an increase in density) tends to produce differentiation and specialization, since only in this way can the area support increased numbers. Density thus reinforces the effect of numbers in diversifying men and their activities and in increasing the complexity of the social structure.

On the subjective side, as Simmel has suggested, the close physical contact of numerous individuals necessarily produces a shift in the mediums through which we orient ourselves to the urban milieu, especially to our fellow-men. Typically, our physical contacts are close but our social contacts are distant. The urban world puts a premium on visual recognition. We see the uniform which denotes the role of the functionaries and are oblivious to the personal eccentricities that are hidden behind the uniform. We tend to acquire and develop a sensitivity to a world of artifacts and become progressively farther removed from the world of nature.

We are exposed to glaring contrasts between splendor and squalor, between riches and poverty, intelligence and ignorance, order and chaos. The competition for space is great, so that each area generally tends to be put to the use which yields the greatest economic return. Place of work tends to become dissociated from place of residence, for the proximity of indus-

14. E. Durkheim, *De la division du travail social* (Paris, 1932), p. 248.

trial and commercial establishments makes an area both economically and socially undesirable for residential purposes.

Density, land values, rentals, accessibility, healthfulness, prestige, aesthetic consideration, absence of nuisances such as noise, smoke, and dirt determine the desirability of various areas of the city as places of settlement for different sections of the population. Place and nature of work, income, racial and ethnic characteristics, social status, custom, habit, taste, preference, and prejudice are among the significant factors in accordance with which the urban population is selected and distributed into more or less distinct settlements. Diverse population elements inhabiting a compact settlement thus tend to become segregated from one another in the degree in which their requirements and modes of life are incompatible with one another and in the measure in which they are antagonistic to one another. Similarly, persons of homogeneous status and needs unwittingly drift into, consciously select, or are forced by circumstances into, the same area. The different parts of the city thus acquire specialized functions. The city consequently tends to resemble a mosaic of social worlds in which the transition from one to the other is abrupt. The juxtaposition of divergent personalities and modes of life tends to produce a relativistic perspective and a sense of toleration of difference which may be regarded as prerequisites for rationality and which lead toward the secularization of life.[15]

The close living together and working together of individuals who have no sentimental and emotional ties foster a spirit of competition, aggrandizement, and mutual exploitation. To counteract irresponsibility and potential disorder, formal controls tend to be resorted to. Without rigid adherence to predictable routines a large compact society would scarcely be able to maintain itself. The clock and the traffic signal are symbolic of the basis of our social order in the urban world. Frequent close physical contact, coupled with great social distance, accentuates the reserve of unattached individuals toward one another and, unless compensated for by other opportunities for response, gives rise to loneliness. The necessary frequent movement of great numbers of individuals in a congested habitat gives occasion to friction and irritation. Nervous tensions which derive from such personal frustrations are accentuated by the rapid tempo and the complicated technology under which life in dense areas must be lived.

Heterogeneity. The social interaction among such a variety of personality types in the urban milieu tends to break down the rigidity of caste lines and to complicate the class structure, and thus induces a more ramified and differentiated framework of social stratification than is found in more integrated societies. The heightened mobility of the individual, which brings him within the range of stimulation by a great number of diverse

15. The extent to which the segregation of the population into distinct ecological and cultural areas and the resulting social attitude of tolerance, rationality, and secular mentality are functions of density as distinguished from heterogeneity is difficult to determine. Most likely we are dealing here with phenomena which are consequences of the simultaneous operation of both factors.

individuals and subjects him to fluctuating status in the differentiated social groups that compose the social structure of the city, tends toward the acceptance of instability and insecurity in the world at large as a norm. This fact helps to account, too, for the sophistication and cosmopolitanism of the urbanite. No single group has the undivided allegiance of the individual. The groups with which he is affiliated do not lend themselves readily to a simple hierarchical arrangement. By virtue of his different interests arising out of different aspects of social life, the individual acquires membership in widely divergent groups, each of which functions only with reference to a single segment of his personality. Nor do these groups easily permit of a concentric arrangement so that the narrower ones fall within the circumference of the more inclusive ones, as is more likely to be the case in the rural community or in primitive societies. Rather the groups with which the person typically is affiliated are tangential to each other or intersect in highly variable fashion.

Partly as a result of the physical footlooseness of the population and partly as a result of their social mobility, the turnover in group membership generally is rapid. Place of residence, place and character of employment, income and interests fluctuate, and the task of holding organizations together and maintaining and promoting intimate and lasting acquaintanceship between the members is difficult. This applies strikingly to the local areas within the city into which persons become segregated more by virtue of differences in race, language, income, and social status, than through choice or positive attraction to people like themselves. Overwhelmingly the city-dweller is not a home-owner, and since a transitory habitat does not generate binding traditions and sentiments, only rarely is he truly a neighbor. There is little opportunity for the individual to obtain a conception of the city as a whole or to survey his place in the total scheme. Consequently he finds it difficult to determine what is to his own "best interests" and to decide between the issues and leaders presented to him by the agencies of mass suggestion. Individuals who are thus detached from the organized bodies which integrate society comprise the fluid masses that make collective behavior in the urban community so unpredictable and hence so problematical.

Although the city, through the recruitment of variant types to perform its diverse tasks and the accentuation of their uniqueness through competition and the premium upon eccentricity, novelty, efficient performance, and inventiveness, produces a highly differentiated population, it also exercises a leveling influence. Wherever large numbers of differently constituted individuals congregate, the process of depersonalization also enters. This leveling tendency inheres in part in the economic basis of the city. The development of large cities, at least in the modern age, was largely dependent upon the concentrative force of steam. The rise of the factory made possible mass production for an impersonal market. The fullest exploitation of the possibilities of the division of labor and mass production, however, is possible only with standardization of processes and products. A money economy goes hand in hand with such a system of production. Progressively as cities have developed upon a background of this system of production, the pecuniary nexus which implies the purchasability of services and things has displaced personal relations as the basis of association. Individuality under these circumstances must be replaced by categories. When large numbers have to make common use of facilities and institutions, an arrangement must 'be made to adjust the facilities and institutions to the needs of the average person rather than to those of particular individuals. The services of the public utilities, of the recreational, educational, and cultural institutions must be adjusted to mass requirements. Similarly, the cultural institutions, such as the schools, the movies, the radio, and the newspapers, by virtue of their mass clientele, must necessarily operate as leveling influences. The political process as it appears in urban life could not be understood without taking account of the mass appeals made through modern propaganda techniques. If the individual would participate at all in the social, political, and economic life of the city, he must subordinate some of his individuality to the demands of the larger community and in that measure immerse himself in mass movements.

IV. The Relation between a Theory of Urbanism and Sociological Research. By means of a body of theory such as that illustratively sketched above, the complicated and many-sided phenomena of urbanism may be analyzed in terms of a limited number of basic categories. The sociological approach to the city thus acquires an essential unity and coherence enabling the empirical investigator not merely to focus more distinctly upon the problems and processes that properly fall in his province but also to treat his subject matter in a more integrated and systematic fashion. A few typical findings of empirical research in the field of urbanism, with special reference to the United States, may be indicated to substantiate the theoretical propositions set forth in the preceding pages, and some of the crucial problems for further study may be outlined.

On the basis of the three variables, number, density of settlement, and degree of heterogeneity, of the urban population, it appears possible to explain the characteristics of urban life and to account for the differences between cities of various sizes and types.

Urbanism as a characteristic mode of life may be approached empirically from three interrelated perspectives: (1) as a physical structure comprising a population base, a technology, and an ecological order; (2) as a system of social organization involving a characteristic social structure, a series of social institutions, and a typical pattern of social relationships; and (3) as a set of attitudes and ideas, and a constellation of personalities engaging in typical forms of collective behavior and subject to characteristic mechanisms of social control.

Urbanism in Ecological Perspective. Since in the case of physical structure and ecological processes we are able to operate with fairly objective indices, it becomes possible to arrive at quite precise and generally quantitative results. The dominance of the city over its hinterland becomes explicable through the functional characteristics of the city which derive in large measure from the effect of numbers and density. Many of the technical facilities and the skills and organizations to which urban life gives rise can grow and prosper only in cities where the demand is sufficiently great. The nature and scope of the services rendered by these organizations and institutions and the advantage which they enjoy over the less developed facilities of smaller towns enhances the dominance of the city and the dependence of ever wider regions upon the central metropolis.

The urban-population composition shows the operation of selective and differentiating factors. Cities contain a larger proportion of persons in the prime of life than rural areas which contain more old and very young people. In this, as in so many other respects, the larger the city the more this specific characteristic of urbanism is apparent. With the exception of the largest cities, which have attracted the bulk of the foreign-born males, and a few other special types of cities, women predominate numerically over men. The heterogeneity of the urban population is further indicated along racial and ethnic lines. The foreign born and their children constitute nearly two-thirds of all the inhabitants of cities of one million and over. Their proportion in the urban population declines as the size of the city decreases, until in the rural areas they comprise only about one-sixth of the total population. The larger cities similarly have attracted more Negroes and other racial groups than have the smaller communities. Considering that age, sex, race, and ethnic origin are associated with other factors such as occupation and interest, it becomes clear that one major characteristic of the urban-dweller is his dissimilarity from his fellows. Never before have such large masses of people of diverse traits as we find in our cities been thrown together into such close physical contact as in the great cities of America. Cities generally, and American cities in particular, comprise a motley of peoples and cultures, of highly differentiated modes of life between which there often is only the faintest communication, the greatest indifference and the broadest tolerance, occasionally bitter strife, but always the sharpest contrast.

The failure of the urban population to reproduce itself appears to be a biological consequence of a combination of factors in the complex of urban life, and the decline in the birth-rate generally may be regarded as one of the most significant signs of the urbanization of the Western world. While the proportion of deaths in cities is slightly greater than in the country, the outstanding difference between the failure of present-day cities to maintain their population and that of cities of the past is that in former times it was due to the exceedingly high death-rates in cities, whereas today, since cities have become more livable from a health standpoint, it is due to low birth-rates. These biological characteristics of the urban population are significant sociologically, not merely because they reflect the urban mode of

existence but also because they condition the growth and future dominance
of cities and their basic social organization. Since cities are the consumers
rather than the producers of men, the value of human life and the social
estimation of the personality will not be unaffected by the balance between
births and deaths. The pattern of land use, of land values, rentals, and
ownership, the nature and functioning of the physical structures, of housing, of transportation and communication facilities, of public utilities—these
and many other phases of the physical mechanism of the city are not isolated phenomena unrelated to the city as a social entity, but are affected
by and affect the urban mode of life.

Urbanism as a Form of Social Organization. The distinctive features of
the urban mode of life have often been described sociologically as consisting of the substitution of secondary for primary contacts, the weakening of
bonds of kinship, and the declining social significance of the family, the
disappearance of the neighborhood, and the undermining of the traditional
basis of social solidarity. All these phenomena can be substantially verified
through objective indices. Thus, for instance, the low and declining urban-
reproduction rates suggest that the city is not conducive to the traditional
type of family life, including the rearing of children and the maintenance of
the home as the locus of a whole round of vital activities. The transfer of
industrial, educational, and recreational activities to specialized institutions
outside the home has deprived the family of some of its most characteristic
historical functions. In cities mothers are more likely to be employed, lodgers are more frequently part of the household, marriage tends to be post-
poned, and the proportion of single and unattached people is greater.
Families are smaller and more frequently without children than in the
country. The family as a unit of social life is emancipated from the larger
kinship group characteristic of the country, and the individual members
pursue their own diverging interests in their vocational, educational, religious, recreational, and political life.

Such functions as the maintenance of health, the methods of alleviating
the hardships associated with personal and social insecurity, the provisions
for education, recreation, and cultural advancement have given rise to highly
specialized institutions on a community-wide, state-wide, or even national
basis. The same factors which have brought about greater personal insecurity also underlie the wider contrasts between individuals to be found in
the urban world. While the city has broken down the rigid caste lines of
pre-industrial society, it has sharpened and differentiated income and status
groups. Generally, a larger proportion of the adult-urban population is
gainfully employed than is the case with the adult-rural population. The
white-collar class comprising those employed in trade, in clerical, and in
professional work, are proportionately more numerous in large cities and
in metropolitan centers and in smaller towns than in the country.

On the whole, the city discourages an economic life in which the individual in time of crisis has a basis of subsistence to fall back upon, and

it discourages self-employment. While incomes of city people are on the average higher than those of country people, the cost of living seems to be higher in the larger cities. Home ownership involves greater burdens and is rarer. Rents are higher and absorb a larger proportion of the income. Although the urban-dweller has the benefit of many communal services, he spends a large proportion of his income for such items as recreation and advancement and a smaller proportion for food. What the communal services do not furnish the urbanite must purchase, and there is virtually no human need which has remained unexploited by commercialism. Catering to thrills and furnishing means of escape from drudgery, monotony, and routine thus become one of the major functions of urban recreation, which at its best furnishes means for creative self-expression and spontaneous group association, but which more typically in the urban world results in passive spectatorism on the one hand, or sensational record-smashing feats on the other.

Being reduced to a stage of virtual impotence as an individual, the urbanite is bound to exert himself by joining with others of similar interest into organized groups to obtain his ends. This results in the enormous multiplication of voluntary organizations directed toward as great a variety of objectives as there are human needs and interests. While on the one hand the traditional ties of human association are weakened, urban existence involves a much greater degree of interdependence between man and man and a more complicated, fragile, and volatile form of mutual interrelations over many phases of which the individual as such can exert scarcely any control. Frequently there is only the most tenuous relationship between the economic position of other basic factors that determine the individual's existence in the urban world and the voluntary groups with which he is affiliated. While in a primitive and in a rural society it is generally possible to predict on the basis of a few known factors who will belong to what and who will associate with whom in almost every relationship of life, in the city we can only project the general pattern of group formation and affiliation, and this pattern will display many incongruities and contradictions.

Urban Personality and Collective Behavior. It is largely through the activities of the voluntary groups, be their objectives economic, political, educational, religious, recreational, or cultural, that the urbanite expresses and develops his personality, acquires status, and is able to carry on the round of activities that constitute his life-career. It may easily be inferred, however, that the organizational framework which these highly differentiated functions call into being does not of itself insure the consistency and integrity of the personalities whose interests it enlists. Personal disorganization, mental breakdown, suicide, delinquency, crime, corruption, and disorder might be expected under these circumstances to be more prevalent in the urban than in the rural community. This has been confirmed in so far as comparable indices are available; but the mechanisms underlying these phenomena require further analysis.

Since for most group purposes it is impossible in the city to appeal individually to the large number of discrete and differentiated individuals, and since it is only through the organizations to which men belong that their interests and resources can be enlisted for a collective cause, it may be inferred that social control in the city should typically proceed through formally organized groups. It follows, too, that the masses of men in the city are subject to manipulation by symbols and stereotypes managed by individuals working from afar or operating invisibly behind the scenes through their control of the instruments of communication. Self-government either in the economic, the political, or the cultural realm is under these circumstances reduced to a mere figure of speech, or, at best, is subject to the unstable equilibrium of pressure groups. In view of the ineffectiveness of actual kinship ties we create fictional kinship groups. In the face of the disappearance of the territorial unit as a basis of social solidarity we create interest units. Meanwhile the city as a community resolves itself into a series of tenuous segmental relationships superimposed upon a territorial base with a definite center but without a definite periphery and upon a division of labor which far transcends the immediate locality and is worldwide in scope. The larger the number of persons in a state of interaction with one another the lower is the level of communication and the greater is the tendency for communication to proceed on an elementary level, i.e., on the basis of those things which are assumed to be common or to be of interest to all.

It is obviously, therefore, to the emerging trends in the communication system and to the production and distribution technology that has come into existence with modern civilization that we must look for the symptoms which will indicate the probable future development of urbanism as a mode of social life. The direction of the ongoing changes in urbanism will for good or ill transform not only the city but the world. Some of the more basic of these factors and processes and the possibilities of their direction and control invite further detailed study.

It is only in so far as the sociologist has a clear conception of the city as a social entity and a workable theory of urbanism that he can hope to develop a unified body of reliable knowledge, which what passes as "urban sociology" is certainly not at the present time. By taking this point of departure from a theory of urbanism such as that sketched in the foregoing pages to be elaborated, tested, and revised in the light of further analysis and empirical research, it is to be hoped that the criteria of relevance and validity of factual data can be determined. The miscellaneous assortment of disconnected information which has hitherto found its way into sociological treatises on the city may thus be sifted and incorporated into a coherent body of knowledge. Incidentally, only by means of some such theory will the sociologist escape the futile practice of voicing in the name of sociological science a variety of often unsupportable judgments concerning such problems as poverty, housing, city-planning, sanitation, municipal administration, policing, marketing, transportation, and other technical issues. While the sociologist cannot solve any of these practical problems—at least not by himself—he may, if he discovers his proper function, have an important contribution to make to their comprehension and solution. The prospects for doing this are brightest through a general, theoretical, rather than through an *ad hoc* approach.

THE PROCESS OF URBANIZATION:
UNDERLYING FORCES AND EMERGING TRENDS

National Resources Committee

Preconditions of Urbanization

There remain to be considered the underlying forces that have brought about the decisive differences between country and city and among different types of cities and that are even now at work in transforming our cities and our national life. If the cities are as significant a phase of civilized existence as they appear to have been throughout history, then we must regard the determining factors in urbanization as more or less identical with those that have shaped civilization itself.

AGRICULTURAL SURPLUS. A precondition for the emergence and growth of cities is a level of agricultural production sufficiently high to release a substantial part of the population from agricultural labor, and to permit the concentration in cities of people engaged in nonagricultural enterprises formerly performed on the farm and in the village. But since in all but the industrialized parts of the world it still requires approximately three agricultural workers to support each person engaged in nonagricultural pursuits, urbanization has proceeded slowly in most regions outside the Western World. Except for a few large port and capital cities, these regions have developed only a low degree of urbanization when contrasted with Western Europe and the United States.

The general conclusion that urbanization rests upon a surplus of agricultural products beyond the bare subsistence requirements of the rural population itself does not, however, justify the inference that only those countries can evolve an urban type of civilization which produce an agricultural surplus within their own national boundaries. This may well have been true in more primitive cultures when the technology of transportation and storage was technologically crude; but it is no longer in a country that has access to the products of the whole world and has mastered the mechanical problems of transportation and preservation of the necessities of life. This is well illustrated in the case of highly urbanized and industrialized England, which supports a relatively enormous population on a disproportionately small territory by exchanging its industrial products and

Reprinted from *Our Cities: Their Role in the National Economy,* published by the National Resources Committee, Washington, D.C., United States Government Printing Office, 1937, pp. 29-41.

services for the agricultural produce of its overseas colonies and the other countries of the world.

It would be even more misleading to assume that cities are dependent upon the agricultural surpluses of the immediate hinterlands which they dominate. Under conditions made possible by modern technology and the intricate web of commercial interrelations, the basis of subsistence of the urban center is often far-flung, indirect, and world-wide rather than local. It is not so much the state of agriculture in its immediate vicinity as the degree of agricultural efficiency reached by the larger world with which it is interconnected that conditions the existence and growth of the city. In the United States, which until recently was virtually a virgin territory, even an extensive agriculture was able to provide a vast surplus. This great disproportion between men and resources is a significant factor in the unprecedented rapidity of the urbanization of the nation. Through the application of the technology produced in the city, agricultural productivity has been enhanced and rural conditions of living have been lifted to a higher level.

CENTRIPETAL INFLUENCE OF STEAM. The growth of cities since about the beginning of the 19th century in Western Europe and the United States in particular is attributable, secondly, to the scientific discoveries and mechanical inventions which facilitated the development of power-driven machinery. Of these revolutionizing innovations none was probably more fundamental than the application of steam as a source of power for industry and transportation to supplement and replace the previously available sources of power, especially water. Prior to the steam era, few cities exceeded 100,000 and it is doubtful whether any city, even such renowned centers as Rome, Peking, or Nanking, ever exceeded 1 million in population. Not until the great economic and social changes that we identify as the Industrial Revolution had been set in motion did the modern great city become possible. The emergence of the great city, however, itself in turn became a major force in revolutionizing man's existence.

Steam not only made possible a vast increase in man's potential means of subsistence and, consequently, in his numbers but indirectly by releasing a rapidly increasing proportion of the population from the actual tilling of the soil, it became an overwhelming force in the cityward migration and played a major role in determining the internal structure of the city and of the economic organization of which it became the nucleus. In the pre-steam era, because of the crude, inefficient, and expensive means of transportation which man had at his disposal, the provisioning of large cities was difficult, as was the supplying of raw materials and the distribution of finished products over a wide area. Consequently most manufacturing was local.

Apart from the military necessity of concentrating the largest number of inhabitants and structures within the smallest possible walled area, the city before the age of steam had no need for marked concentration into a "down town" or central-business district which is a distinguishing mark of the modern city. Steam has operated as a concentrative force through its direct use as power. Since steam is most cheaply produced in large quantities and must be used close to where it is produced, from which point the power it generates can be extended only over limited distances by means of shafting, belts, and pulleys, it fostered the concentration of manufacturing processes and large units of production. But since it could not be used economically for local transportation, its use as power in manufacturing tended also to concentrate managerial and wholesale distributing activities and above all, population, near the factory. Moreover, the great economies in long-distance transportation, which steam made possible, further accentuated the concentration of industry and population into large urban centers which, because of their favorable situation from the standpoint of production and markets, continued to attract ever more industries, commerce, and population. The large, densely built up and rapidly growing city with a single center where transportation lines and hence traffic converge, derives its principal structural features in large measure from the centripetal influence of steam.

ELECTRICITY AND THE AUTOMOBILE. In recent years, and while steam was molding the pattern of urbanization, a new force has come upon the scene. Whereas steam has had a concentrative effect, electricity and the internal-combustion engine, which became available after the pattern of American cities had already become fixed, have tended to have precisely the opposite effect. The dispersive influence of electricity is due to the fact that it can be transmitted economically even now over distances up to about 300 miles and that it can be used as power with almost equal efficiency in large or small units. It also has decided advantages over steam for rapid local transportation. It has at least the potentiality of exercising a centrifugal influence upon cities as contrasted with the centripetal force exerted by steam. Up to the present, however, electricity, through its use as power for the fast electric elevator and for urban and suburban transit, has mainly accentuated concentration as in the skyscraper and in the overdeveloped, congested, central business district.

In addition to its use as power, electricity, as distinguished from steam, has a quality which has to be reckoned with as a reconstructive element in urban life, the urban structure and our entire social order, namely its use in communication. This use in the form of the telegraph, the telephone, and the radio has only recently been felt and appreciated. It gives promise of having at least as great an influence in reshaping our cities and our civilization during the twentieth century as steam did during the nineteenth.

If to the influences of electricity we add the flexibility, the speed and the individualization of transportation effected by the internal-combustion engine as embodied in the automobile and the airplane, we may say that these new technological devices are likely to alter the structure of the urban community and national life profoundly whether or not we consciously use them as instruments to improve our mode of living.

THE TECHNOLOGICAL REVOLUTION. One of the most striking consequences of modern transportation, commerce, and communication is the fact that despite physical distances, national boundaries, and sectional differences, the world, at least from a technological standpoint, has become more uniform and interdependent. Hence the advances made in one part of the world are readily and rapidly diffused to all the rest. With reference to cities this means that their size, rate of growth, structure, and function depend less upon local circumstances than upon the general level of knowledge and civilization achieved anywhere at a given point in time.

Indeed so far has mechanization progressed that nowadays a good share of what may properly be called agricultural production and the work of the farmer is actually carried on in urban communities. The farmer no longer, generally speaking, produces his own agricultural tools and implements, but procures them from urban factories and through urban mail-order houses. Our grain is transformed into flour and other food products for man and animals in huge urban factories and shipped back, in large part, to the farmer as a finished product. The same is true of meat and fibers. There is ample evidence that whatever its traditional repute may be, the city is no longer a predatory parasite content with consuming the products that the country has produced and giving nothing in return. A new division of labor between country and city has emerged which neither can afford to undermine without sinking to a lower level of security and well-being.

SANITATION. The development of modern sanitation is another significant precondition to the existence of the modern city. Life for large masses of people spatially removed from and yet closely dependent upon a constant supply of water, food, fuel, and raw materials is in itself conditioned by a high degree of technological development and the perfection of administrative organization. But the task of conquering the hazards of life among a vast congested population, such as inhabits a great city, in the face of disease, can be appreciated better if we consider that before the advent of modern sanitation the deaths in cities of the Western World regularly exceeded the births by a considerable margin. If in addition we recall that the population of the western countries was frequently afflicted by epidemics that swept away a large portion of their inhabitants and that this is still in a measure true of backward countries, we can realize the significance of modern sanitation for urban existence. The ample provision of pure water, the perfection of centralized sewerage and waste disposal systems, the insurance of a safe food supply, and the prevention and control of contagious diseases are the chief measures that for more than a century have made it possible for most western cities to maintain population by lowering the death rate. This was accomplished in spite of the adverse effects of heavy migration upon the health of the urban population.

Specific Urbanizing Forces and Emerging Urban Trends

Having considered the principal preconditions for urbanization, we may now turn to examine some of the factors that are shaping this process today, and paying particular attention to recent urban trends, note the future prospects of urban America.

The basic factors that operate to produce the city, determine its character and growth and generate its problems and indirectly those of our Nation, have two major aspects: (1) National or interurban, (2) internal or intraurban. Cities come into existence as products of and as focal points in the social and economic life of a people that has reached a certain stage of development. The resulting division of labor presupposes and furthers urbanization. When a civilization arrives at such a stage of maturity that its life is no longer local and self-sufficient but is intertwined in a nexus of national and world commerce, technology, population movement, social, and intellectual intercourse and cultural and political contact, cities emerge because they discharge certain vital functions. The very existence and the growth of cities in turn sets into operation forces that create problems both within the city and in the Nation at large.

REPRODUCTION OF POPULATION. In view of the fact that the city is apparently not conducive to family life and the rearing of children, it is significant to present the factors that underlie the growth of urban population. The proof for the failure of the cities to maintain themselves is found in their reproductive indexes, or the ratios of children under 5 to women of 20 to 44 years of age. In 1930 only three cities of over 100,000 had a reproduction index above 1.0. The still existing surplus of births over deaths in other cities is due only to the fact that for the time being their age composition is favorable to a low death rate and a high birth rate, which will be of less significance in the coming years. The postponement of marriage because of the prolongation of the period of educational preparation and economic handicaps, the greater probability of broken families, the emancipation of women and their entry into the vocations and professions, the spread of birth control, the diminution of child labor and the consequent depreciation of children as economic assets, the premium put upon small families by virtue of economic insecurity coupled with the craving for status and a high standard of living, and the rapidly declining proportion of immigrant families—are among the forces reducing the urban birthrate, especially in the largest cities, to a point insufficient to reproduce the population.

This fact is of greater national significance today than formerly, since it applies now to the majority of the American population. It follows, therefore, that if the larger cities are to grow or even to maintain themselves, their population must be recruited in the future to an increasing extent from other communities. With foreign immigration practically cut off, the domestic rural areas are the only possible sources of recruitment. But since the rural population constitutes considerably less than half of the total and since the rural birth rate is also declining rapidly, a marked slowing down of city growth is impending. Our urban growth in the present decade will probably not exceed half that of the previous one. Furthermore, our urban population probably will be recruited increasingly from the economically and culturally least favorable rural areas where the reproduction rates for the time being remain high. This may affect the quality of the urban stock adversely, may put added burdens upon urban institutions and may involve personal and social costs of readjustment.

The prospects of a marked slowing down of population growth, especially that of cities, presages a number of important changes in the economic and social life of cities and of the Nation as a whole. Those enterprises, both public and private, the growth of which depends upon and responds to increase in population, should become more stable. Thus we may look forward to a lessened need for the expansion and to an increased need and opportunity for improving the quality of public utilities, of welfare and educational institutions, and to much more gradual changes in land values. With slower growth and lessened migration the urban population will tend to be older, and consequently the power and interests of older people will probably bulk larger in the future. It will be easier to provide education for the young, a fact already evident in many cities through the lessened enrollment in the elementary schools; and there will be increasing need for adult education. Industry and business will have to adjust themselves to using older workers or the community will have to assume greater responsibility for the support of its aged. The scarcity of children and youths will correspondingly call for greater concern about the conservation of these potential human resources.

If our present immigration policy is continued, our white urban population will tend toward greater cultural homogeneity. At the same time we may expect our cities to contain a greater proportion of Negroes recruited from the rural South. If the low-reproduction rate should turn out to be inherent in city life, we must ultimately face the prospect of declining population not only in the city but in the Nation as well, or we must attempt to reverse the trend toward urbanization. If, on the other hand, the lowered urban reproduction rate is due either to conditions merely incidental to city life, a social policy seeking to create conditions more favorable to reproduction is to be envisaged. The declining rural-reproduction rate, which is coming to characterize modern industrial countries generally, suggests the possibility, however, that the rural-urban differential in reproduction is a result of the impact of industrial civilization upon the manner of life and the attitudes of modern man generally. Naturally, this impact would manifest itself first in cities but not confine itself to them. It should not be assumed that a stationary or even a declining population is undesirable either from a personal or from a social standpoint. Nor need we assume that a trend toward lowered reproduction rates is irreversible once it has begun. The quantity and the quality of population of the country at large and of the cities is, however, of utmost concern to the cities of the future and must be considered in shaping national policies.

METROPOLITAN AREAS. There is a significant trend in urbanization which in recent decades has become quite marked. It is revealed by the extraordinarily rapid growth of small satellite towns and rural communities within the orbit of metropolitan centers as compared with the central cities themselves.[1] This is in a sense an expression of the coming into more general use of the automobile, electric service, the telephone, and the extension of urban utilities into the surrounding territory. As a result, a new type of urban community has come upon the scene—the metropolitan region.

The metropolis subsists not merely upon its own hinterland but it has become the most vital link in world affairs so that the lines of communication and transportation that link the great metropolitan centers with one another may be thought of as the Main Streets of the world. Since the trend toward a greater concentration of the Nation's population and industry into great metropolitan centers is almost wholly the unplanned product of interacting forces of which we are as yet scarcely conscious, we may infer that these metropolitan aggregations perform essential functions in the national and world economy and owe their genesis and growth to the vital role they play in modern civilization.

The growth of the 96 metropolitan districts recognized by the United States Census in 1930 will serve to illustrate the nature of this regional development of the urban community in the United States. Since 1900 the rate of population increase has been greater in the satellite areas surrounding those large cities than that within their limits. While the central cities in the decade 1920–30 increased 22.3 percent, those portions of the metropolitan districts lying outside the central cities increased at about twice this rate, or nearly six times as much as the nonmetropolitan part of the United States. The central cities contain a declining proportion of the total population of the metropolitan districts, indicating that metropolitan growth is in even larger degree than formerly a suburban trend. But what might at first glance appear to be a decentralization of population, therefore, is revealed upon closer inspection to be merely a redistribution of the urban population within metropolitan regions or a dispersion from the central city into the adjacent suburban periphery. It is not a general devolution of cities or a flight from the city. What is actually happening is, rather, that the urbanite is steadily being transformed into the suburbanite. While the movement of the last 100 years toward the centralization of population apparently continues, actually satellite cities and satellite rural areas are increasing so rapidly as to evidence a powerful dispersive force within urban

1. "It is a familiar fact, however, that the population of the corporate city frequently gives a very inadequate idea of the population massed in and around the city, constituting the "greater" city, as it is sometimes called, and that as regards large cities, in few cases do the boundaries of the city limit the urban population which that city represents or of which it is the center. The suburbs are from many standpoints as much a part of the city as the area which is under the municipal government. The suburban residents share in the economic and social activities of the city; many of them have their business or employment in the city; and to a less extent persons residing in the city are employed in the suburbs." Fifteenth Census, 1930; Metropolitan Districts (Washington: Government Printing Office, 1932), p. 5.

regions. This dispersion has not yet become a definite centrifugal movement, but might well develop into one.

Far from being on the decline, the city thus gives evidence mainly of a new phase of its growth by emptying at the center and spilling over its own corporate boundaries. The basis of this centrifugal tendency is to be sought in the urge on the part of those who have the means to escape the congestion, the disadvantageous family life, the undesirable and expensive housing and living conditions, and the high taxation which urban life so frequently involves. The hegira from the city is motivated by the ease of commutation and communication giving ready access to urban technical and cultural facilities combined with the lower taxes and land values, the better housing, more desirable family and community life, and more healthful conditions of existence prevailing in the suburbs. The intraregional dispersion of industry follows in the main from the same factors. Sometimes it precedes and stimulates and at the other times it follows and eccentuates the centrifugal movement of population.

The redistribution of the urban population into the peripheries of metropolitan regions involves the close and constant dependence of the suburban communities upon the economic and technical functions and cultural opportunities which the metropolis provides. The model suburb, whether it is industrial or residential, however superior, aloof, and detached it may believe itself to be, has its basis of existence and draws much of its sustenance from the noisy, grimy city of which economically and culturally it is an integral part, but from which it has managed to remain independent politically.

It has been said that the suburbanite shuttles back and forth from a place where he would rather not live to a place where he would rather not work. In his daily or periodical pendular movement, of which the clock and the time schedule are symbolic, the suburban commuter exhibits the peculiar segmentalization between working and living so characteristic of modern urban society. The bedrooms of American cities are increasingly to be found in the dormitory colonies of the suburbs. The suburbanite, who in his daily routine oscillates between his vocation involving the humdrum, high-speed, technical work of business, industry, and the professions in the heart of the metropolis, and his avocation, which may range from amateur gardening and similar pastoral activities to suburban politics, is not an exception to the urban type of personality but is merely a variety of it. The motives leading to this type of existence are to be sought in the urge to escape the obnoxious aspects of urban life without at the same time losing access to its economic and cultural advantages. In the process, the form and the functions of the city are being revolutionized.

THE CITY AS A CONSUMER OF HUMAN RESOURCES. In the 140 years of our national history depicted by the United States Census, our rural population grew from 3.7 millions to 53.8 millions, while the urban population grew from less than a quarter of a million to 68.9 millions. Apparently the city is the principal consumer of man. Its role in the national economy in the broadest sense, therefore, centers around the utilization of human resources.

While cities had their origin as fortresses, as military and administrative centers, as religious shrines, or in the fairs symptomatic of industry, commerce, and transportation in the industrialized portions of the world, their growth was conditioned by agrarian reform, a surplus of rural births, and world-market politics. The extraordinarily rapid urbanization of the United States, however, has been significantly influenced by the tremendous disproportion between natural resources and manpower, which has attracted immigration to a vast unexploited frontier and, by putting a premium upon labor-saving devices, has stimulated industry. The virtual cutting off of foreign immigration may be regarded as indicative of the fact that the frontier has vanished and that the reflux to the cities has begun.

Internal migration will, therefore, be more important than foreign immigration for the future of our cities. During the decade 1920–30 about two-thirds of the States suffered losses in farm population. The Southern and the Middle Western farm areas, especially, sent such large numbers of youth to the cities that they could not maintain their own numbers. Without this migration, amounting to a net movement of 6 million people away from the farms in the decade 1920–30, the American cities could not have grown as they did in the past and without it they cannot even maintain their numbers in the future.

Cities as Commercial and Service Centers. The national trend in urbanization is merely a phase of the development of the Nation as a whole. In the past it has been conditioned basically by national trends in industry. Of late, however, the rapid growth of the larger cities has reflected their increasing importance as commercial and service centers rather than as industrial centers. The shift in emphasis from industry to commercial and service enterprises is indicated by the increasing proportion of the workers in large cities who are classified as white-collar workers. The mechanization of industry in the United States has proceeded at a pace faster than the increase in the Nation's wage earners. From 1900 to 1929 the horse-power per wage earner in manufacturing industries more than doubled, but the number of wage earners increased by only about one-third. While the increase in the index of production during this period was almost 100 percent, the population increase was only 29 percent. As industry and population in a city increase, and as larger areas outside of the city are brought within the orbit of its influence, the demand for service functions increases. As industry and business enter the mass production and mass distribution stage, the clerical and managerial functions require a relatively larger personnel. The range of occupations, of incomes and, consequently, of standards of living tends to increase with the size of the city, producing great diversity and contrasts between various sections of the urban population. The city is thus both a product and a cause of the division of labor and of specialization.

Types of Cities. Similarly, individual cities themselves acquire a specialized role in the national economy. They become differentiated partly as a result of differences in access to suitable resources, transportation facilities, and labor supply. In addition to these natural and technological factors, cities in the course of time become distinguishable from one another also because of the initiative of entrepreneurs and of the advantages derived from an auspicious start, which are cumulatively enchanced by tradition and reputation so that certain cities acquire a prestige and renown for the production of certain goods. Such factors will in the course of time shape the industrial contour of the community. Furthermore, certain industries can exist advantageously only where others upon which they depend are already established. Some cities, therefore, develop a highly specialized economic base, while others, offering more general locational advantages, attract a variety of industries and thus become more balanced economic entities.

The functional differentiation of cities, moreover, proceeds not merely on the basis of industrial specialization but is conditioned also by the commercial, governmental and social roles which cities assume. Thus we have developed in the United States some cities whose economic base rests primarily upon the extraction of natural resources from the immediate or nearby sites. Mining cities, oil cities, fishing cities, and lumber cities are familiar examples of specialized urban communities. Others derive their specialized industrial character from the presence of less localized advantages. The selection of Gary, Ind., as a site for a steel producing center proved eminently successful despite the absence of either coal or iron ore in the immediate territory, because of the economical accessibility of the raw materials for steel manufacture derived from its position intermediate between coal fields and ore fields, combined with proximity to a great market and a source of labor. Again, such a city as Chicago has risen on an economic base as a transportation focus and transshipment center, just as others have centered around a port. Still other cities are predominantly commercial, others are educational centers, governmental centers, or resorts. Moreover, cities that were once expanding and prosperous communities have changed their primary function in the course of time or declined either because of the exhaustion of nearby resources, the development elsewhere of a new industry which made a prior one obsolete, the perfection of transportation facilities, changes in the rate structure, or the rise of a rival city with special advantages. Many communities have become chronically substandard as a consequence of such changes which have deprived them of their economic base.

INDUSTRIAL FACTORS AND TRENDS. While American industry is at present highly concentrated geographically, certain recent shifts in industrial location have occurred which have significantly changed the national urban pattern. In general industry has moved westward with the frontier but this westward movement has been retarded since 1890. Some industries, such as cotton textile, have moved from New England to the South Atlantic States during the post-war period. From 1919 to 1929, for example, the number of cotton textile plants in the four major textile States of New England decreased from 324 to 241, while the number in the South Atlantic textile States increased from 646 to 730. At the same time the average size of the New England plant also decreased, while that of the Southern plant increased. In 1899 over half the wage earners worked in the New England and Middle Atlantic States. By 1933 this had declined to 40 percent, but the intensity of this trend, too, has diminished in the most recent period. In general, there seems to be a tendency for industries to be less tied to the region in which they originally located than at one time was the case. The concentration of industry in given regions is becoming somewhat less marked. While in 1900 three States did over half of the slaughtering and meat-packing in the United States, in 1933 concentration was lessened to a point where it took six of the leading meat-packing States to account for half of the business. The same is true for the glass industry.

Certain types of industry have moved from the centers of the cities to peripheral areas, while industries with large capital investments in huge and complex plants and requiring concentrated pools of labor have shown less tendency to follow. This phenomenon is particularly true of the larger cities. Industries locating or relocating in the suburban and satellite zones of great cities have done so to gain competitive advantages derivable from such factors as lessened transport time and cost, freedom from collective bargaining and urban social control, decreased labor turn-over, and lower land values and taxes. Benefits may accrue to the community from the greater stability, strength, and employing power of the enterprise incident to favorable location, lowered concentration and congestion of transport, improved health standards and public services and stabilized tax revenues. The advantages to the industry, however, are sometimes offset by the disadvantages to the community, and the gains of the peripheral area are sometimes a loss to the central city, especially if they are politically separated, because the central city may continue to render certain public services incident to the industry without receiving proportionate tax revenue.

The greater mobility of goods, persons, and ideas produced by our technological advances has operated, on the whole, to concentrate industry and population into urban areas. Recently this development has been most marked in the West and the South. Within the metropolitan areas themselves the trend has been toward more dense settlements on the margins of the city. Retail trade has begun to disperse with the population into these peripheral areas. But certain types of industry, like clothing, printing, and light manufacturing, as well as commercial offices and large department stores, still favor the center of the city.

A significant trend in American industry is that toward larger corporate units of manufacturing, merchandising, and management. These larger units reflect the swing toward centralization of financial control, the growth of large corporations, and the development of holding companies. This has introduced centralized and absentee control over local industrial activities, and has made industry more detached from the interests of local communities than was true in an earlier period of greater local self-sufficiency and indigenous enterprise. While on the one hand monopoly to some extent limits the mobility of capital and so hinders efficient and desirable relocations, on the other hand centralized control is likely to influence industrial location to some extent in a more rational direction on a national scale by tending toward a more exclusive emphasis of pecuniary factors and the minimization of local pride, traditional attachment, and sentiment.

Among the most significant controlling factors in the establishment in certain locations of industrial enterprises and the communities dependent upon them have been rail facilities and rates. Their supervision by governmental agencies has deterred some rational adjustments of industrial location while furthering others.

An important though short-run factor in plant location has been the existence of diverse wage levels and labor standards in various regions of the Nation and in the more urbanized, as distinguished from the rural, parts of the same region. Federal and State regulation of wages, of hours of labor, and of unfair practices of distribution has tended to promote a more orderly and rational industrial location.

Other underlying factors have been the desire of railroads for tonnage, the desire of realtors for sales, the desire of banks and promotional agencies for new accounts, the cumulative desire of industry for needed services and trade outlets, labor's desire for additional jobs, and the boosting attitudes of the organized communities. In the past, publicity campaigns, special grants and subsidies, including sometimes free sites or free plants, credits, and exemption from or special consideration in respect to taxation, have been employed to attract industries and to lead them to ignore more advantageous locations elsewhere. Such inducements as these have been offered by cities and, especially, small towns without even a guarantee from industry to maintain minimum labor standards, in the attempt to gain advantages by artificial means which they did not possess by nature. Unless communities can be persuaded to pursue sounder principles of industrial planning, large sums will be wasted on the private and community plant in the attempt to expand or strengthen the economic base of the community. This will, in the long run, saddle these communities with debt and an imbalanced and an unstable industrial structure. Community industrial imbalance operates in a vicious circle. The weak industries of the community constantly become weaker and this discourages new industry which might otherwise locate there.

In recent years the use by communities of such incentives to industries as credits, tax exemption and free land has declined, although the depression for a time revived the practice. On the whole it does not appear that such attempts to attract industries have been very successful. Of late more attention has been given to the problem of industrial articulation. There seems to be less of a tendency on the part of both communities and industries to accept surface indications as satisfactory reasons for locations. Only scientifically sound, long-range planning can lead toward a more economical and stable national pattern of industry and prevent and mitigate the evils of substandard, mushroom community structures based upon short-sighted and potentially socially-disastrous perspectives.

TRANSPORTATION. As has already been pointed out, our waterway and railway net has been an important factor in shaping the national urban pattern and, to a lesser degree, the internal urban structure. As the cost of transport has been decreased and facilities have been made available over large areas, greater division of labor and intensified urbanization have been made possible. The points of convergence of a number of railroad and water routes have in general become the sites of the great cities of today. Along the railway and water routes small cities have located at points of transportation breaks, where water route, railways, and roads met. Certain elements in the national environment have significantly influenced the transportation routes and centers and, thereby, the pattern of urbanization. The location of minerals, forests, and agricultural areas, harbors, and other topographical features, combined with such man-made facilities as fords, ferries, portages, bridges, canals, and land routes, have served to direct the form of our railway system. But competition between like and different transport agencies and rivalries between communities had a no less significant influence.

Aside from the physical facilities, the rate structure and transportation practices are significant factors in the location and growth of cities. Some communities and areas owe their growth and present importance in part to the fact that they have enjoyed privileged access to materials and markets because of favorable transportation rates. This has been due sometimes to the initial or potential competition between railroads, and between these and water routes. While certain cities and regions have been favored by the construction of such governmental projects as the Panama Canal, others, like the Middle West, have been adversely affected.

Improvements in transportation technology had a diffusing effect upon urbanization, but the economic influences of rate making gave the established communities, having competitive advantages derived from access to alternative facilities, an initial influence which outweighed the effect of technological improvement. There was thus a cumulatively progressive development starting with locational advantages, such as access to water, physical or institutional breaks in transportation, access to natural resources or markets, which successive developments in transport types and technology accentuated unless they were reversed or impeded by the rate structure or intervention by government.

Although our transportation system and our urban pattern are largely cast, there are dynamic elements in our technology as well as in our social arrangements which render the transport system and the rate structure potential instruments for bringing about a more desirable distribution of population and of cities. Consequently, transportation becomes significant in the social control of economic activity and urbanization.

Certain characteristics of the present transportation technology offer the opportunity to adjust the transportation system to any urban pattern that is considered socially desirable. The increasing use of highways has made transport available over a much wider territory than formerly. The transmission of electric power over large areas through interconnected and coordinated systems offers power advantages in many places where they were not formerly available. The use of the motor truck in conjunction with the railway makes the countryside now less dependent on direct contact with the railway. The efficiency of all forms of transport is increasing by leaps and bounds, while, in general, the costs are being materially and progressively reduced.

Private enterprise has been depended upon to lay out the nation's transportation system. This means that the job has been done piecemeal with an eye always to private and to local interests. Thus facilities have been constructed and rates set so as to encourage and benefit existing communities and the enterprises involved, without adequate regard to questions of economic soundness or social desirability.

2

THE NATURE AND EXTENT OF URBANIZATION
AND POPULATION REDISTRIBUTION

A population within a given territory may redistribute itself through either centripetal or centrifugal movement. *Centripetal movement* is the process by which population and resources are drawn into a center of population concentration—relatively larger numbers and higher density in a given area. *Centrifugal movement* is the process by which population and resources move outward toward the periphery of a center and further develop relations with a hinterland. The major process of centripetal movement is urbanization. *Urbanization* is the process of population concentration in which the ratio of urban people to the total population in a territory increases. From this point of view, an increase in both the size of individual urban concentrations and the number of points of urban concentration may occur without an increase in urbanization of a territory, although these changes usually are accompanied by a rising proportion of the population living in cities. Only when a larger proportion of the inhabitants comes to live in cities is urbanization said to occur.

Five major factors stand out as determinants of city growth and urbanization. While each of these has had its effects upon urban expansion in various periods of history, the period beginning roughly with the middle of the eighteenth century saw them intensified. In a sense, it is rapid changes in these factors which have created what is loosely called "modern society," typified by industrialization and urbanization.

First, there is the effect of the *agricultural revolution*. A city necessarily is composed primarily of persons whose labor is not applied directly to the land. The growth of cities, therefore, is inevitably linked to agricultural productivity. Only with an agricultural system capable of producing a surplus of food is it possible to withdraw labor from the immediate problem of food production and apply it to the many kinds of consumption and capital goods and services characteristic of city life. Thus, the greater the productivity per worker of an agricultural system the greater is the possibility of its supporting large urban populations.

If the transition in the ancient world from digging stick to draft animals and the plough had enormous effects upon the growth of ancient cities, how much greater were the urban consequences of modern technology as applied to farming? In the one hundred fifty years between 1787 and 1937, great shifts in farm and city balances occurred. The produce of nine farms was required to support one city family in 1787, but by 1937 one farm family was feeding seven urban families. Nor has this trend come to an end. The applications of genetics and chemistry to farming are increasingly showing results in regularizing and enlarging agricultural production. New types of machines applicable to a wide variety of crops and adapted to an ever increasing variety of farms are also carrying the agricultural revolution forward. Thus, an increase in the productivity of labor on the farm is not only a precondition of urbanism but a powerful force making it possible for an ever greater proportion of the population to live in cities. At the same time these very developments, by increasing the average size of farms, provide a powerful stream of migrants to the urban centers.

The second major reason for the modern growth of cities and the urbanization of areas is the *technological revolution.* The invention of efficient techniques for converting the energy in fuels, particularly the invention of the steam engine, and the derivative development of mass-production techniques and the factory system made possible the support of masses of people densely settled in small areas and alienated from the land. Thus the modern industrial city and the factory system are closely interrelated. The city requires a means of livelihood for its populace, who in turn can exist apart from the land only so far as a livelihood and an agricultural surplus permit them.

Because of the fact that special conditions exist in particular localities, mass production may be specialized. The power of the factory to support large numbers of people depends upon the availability not only of food but also upon access to the products of a highly varied industrial system. A city which produces large amounts of one product could not support its workers unless the products of other cities could be brought in by the exchange of commodities.

The *commercial revolution* is therefore a third factor in the growth of urbanization. The development of world markets, exchange systems and radically improved means of transportation and communication allowed cities to develop under conditions which otherwise would have prevented their appearance. Cities located in areas which dictate a high degree of specialization are possible as a consequence of trade and transport, and indeed it is no longer necessary nor common for a city to depend heavily upon its own immediate hinterland for

the needed agricultural surplus. In fact, it is much more the case that cities are supported by agricultural products from a far-flung, interrelated trade system which embraces most of the earth. Historically, the impetus to city growth given by the expansion of trade actually preceded the principal effects of industrialization.

The fourth factor in urbanization is *increased efficiency of transportation.* Since cities depend necessarily upon trade, as described above, increases in the efficiency of long-distance transportation (initially the sailing vessel, later the steam railroad and the motor car) have had a powerful stimulating effect upon urban growth. Local transportation, however, must not be ignored. Given the fact that cities contain a highly specialized mass of individuals and functions, they can be integrated effectively only when local transport allows goods and people to move quickly and cheaply from place to place within the city and between the city and its hinterland. Thus, the automobile, the electric car, rapid transit, trucks, buses and elevators all have contributed much to the growth of the huge metropolitan centers of today.

It is obvious that the revolutions in agriculture, commerce, industry and transportation are all aspects of the industrial revolution. A fifth, *the demographic revolution,* is a consequence of these other developments. It does not, however, figure merely as a consequence of the industrial revolution but takes on a certain autonomy as a stimulant of urban growth. The appearance of urban, industrial society brought with it sharp decreases in mortality. Birth rates, however, did not fall so rapidly, and one result was a phenomenal growth of the population in Western society during the nineteenth and early part of the twentieth centuries. These population increments in large measure found their way either to colonial agricultural lands or to the cities. The demographic revolution in this way contributed heavily to needs of the cities for an increasing labor force and consumer markets.

The materials taken from the National Resources Committee monograph on cities, and presented in this section, give a more detailed description of the preconditions for the development of *modern* cities and the urbanization of territories than does the brief description above. Specific elements in the urbanization process also are given a more detailed treatment. It is well to remember that any set of forces which are considered preconditions either for urbanization or a stage of urban development cannot, by definition, be chosen as factors generic to cities; if a particular level of technology is a precondition to cities, then conditions other than urban ones must have produced them.

The process of urbanization in the United States has proceeded at a very rapid rate. A rough comparison of the per cent of the population classified as urban in 1790 as compared with 1950 shows that the United States has changed, in the brief span of 160 years, from a nation with only one-twentieth of the population classified as urban to a nation where almost two-thirds of the inhabitants are classified as urban. Of the nations with 20 million or more inhabitants in 1950, only the United Kingdom with 79.7 per cent of the population classified as urban and the Federal Republic of Germany with 71.1 per cent were more urban.[1] The trend of urbanization in the United States is presented and analyzed in the empirical paper by Bogue. He shows, for example, that in the United States there has been a long-term trend toward concentration of both the total and the urban population in larger places. Bogue also describes gross differences between urban and rural populations in 1950 which neglects both the differences associated with size and type of settlement presented in the

paper by Duncan in the first section and the differences among individual places, some of which are evident in the paper by Reiss on the functional differentiation of cities in Section Seven.

The process of urbanization inevitably involves a multiplication of the points of population concentration in a given territory. These points of population concentration are closely integrated into networks of cities—of local, regional, national and international networks of cities. Cities such as London, New York and Paris are dominant cities in a functionally interrelated international network of cities. They are, for example, major sources of capital for investment and decisions about investment elsewhere. There are a number of ways in which the relationships among cities are described. One of these is Auerbach's rank-size rule, popularized by Zipf, which holds that the product of a community's population size times its rank in size is a constant. Thus, if the largest community has a population of 12,000,000 inhabitants, the tenth ranking community is expected to have 1,200,000 inhabitants and the fiftieth community 240,000 inhabitants. This rule has been shown to hold approximately for the United States city-size distributions of most of the census years, 1790 to 1940, but only the more generalized rank-size rule which allows the rank to have an exponent other than unity holds for the 1950 Census data for size of place.[2] A less precise statement of the rank-size rule is found in the empirical observation that the number of communities of a given size is inversely related to the size of community. Hence, there are nearly 10 times as many places of 2,500 to 5,000 population as there are places of 25,000 to 50,000. The pattern of economic interdependence among cities and other settlements in a region is another aspect of the functional integration of

1. *Demographic Yearbook, 1952,* United Nations, Tables A and B.
2. See Otis Dudley Duncan and Albert J. Reiss, Jr., *Social Characteristics of Urban and Rural Communities: 1950* (New York: John Wiley & Sons, 1956), Chapter 2.

cities. Isard, for example, analyzes the economic structural interrelations of communities in metropolitan regions in terms of economic functions which are categorized as imports (inputs) and exports (outputs).[3] Urban ecologists often have described the functional integration of cities in terms of patterned relationships among types of dominant and subdominant communities. The essay by Vance and Smith in this section describes the pattern of metropolitan dominance and integration for the U.S. South.

The process of urbanization has proceeded at varying rates in different territories and countries of the world, and in different historical periods. The following section describes to some extent the historical growth of cities and of urbanization. Little attention is given to the process of world urbanization, however, and particularly to a description and analysis of the degree to which urbanization has proceeded in given territories. Prior to 1800 there were no highly urbanized countries in the world, since the cities up to that time required large rural populations for their support. The urban revolution, in the sense that a substantially large proportion of a population in a territory came to reside in cities, came with the 19th and 20th centuries. Since 1850 the rate of world urbanization has been very high. The pattern which it has taken in given territories of the world has been a partial function of the relative industrialization of the territory. The relation between urbanization and economic development of a territory, however, is more complex than this statement suggests. Davis and Golden analyze this process in terms of the growth of urbanization in underdeveloped areas of the world. Case

studies of urbanization which show that urbanization is not a simple function of industrialization are found in this essay, as well as in the following case study of urbanization in Latin America by Davis and Casis.

The foregoing discussion has focused largely on a presentation of the centripetal process of population redistribution, particularly as it is represented in the urbanization of territories. There is at the same time the countermovement represented as centrifugal movement. This process is most evident near large metropolitan centers where there is considerable growth at the periphery due to the decentralization of population and activities from the center. Considerable growth at the periphery also occurs, however, because of initial movement into the lower density areas at the periphery. The result has been some dispersion of the population and its activities, since modern transportation and communication has made it possible for large population aggregations to grow without proportionate increases in density. The paper by Hauser in this section describes the relative difference in rate of growth of metropolitan centers as compared with their peripheries. The analysis is set within the framework of decentralization, although the Census data do not permit a separation of movement from the center to the periphery as distinct from the movement which occurs from outside the agglomeration to the periphery. A later paper by Freedman shows there is considerable in-migration from outside the agglomeration to the periphery. The bibliography of this Reader contains a number of references to other studies of centrifugal movement, particularly of industrial decentralization.

---

3. See, for example, Walter Isard, Robert A. Kavesh and Robert E. Kuenne, "The Economic Base and Structure of the Urban-Metropolitan Region," *American Sociological Review*, 18 (June, 1953), 317-321.

URBANISM IN THE UNITED STATES, 1950

Donald J. Bogue

THE UNITED STATES IN WORLD URBANISM. The 1950 Census of Population reported that 64 per cent of the inhabitants of the United States live in urban places. Even though differences in national definitions make exact comparisons difficult, this figure indicates that the United States is now one of the most urbanized nations of the world. Of the larger nations (those with twenty million or more inhabitants), only Great Britain and the Federal Republic of Germany are clearly more urban.[1] Although the United States has only about one-sixteenth of the world's population, it may have as much as one-tenth or more of the world's urban population. Moreover, it is quite probable that at the present time no other nation has an urban population as large as that of the United States. Certainly, no nation has so large an industrial-commercial population.

Much of the 36 per cent of the population classed as rural is also directly tied to urban agglomerations. By 1950 the rural-farm population had declined to 15.5 per cent of the total population (43 per cent of the total rural); a population equaling it could be found in just the four largest urban agglomerations. Moreover, approximately 29 per cent of the employed workers living on rural farms were working in nonagricultural industries in 1950, many being employed in cities. Many workers in cities supplement their income with part-time farming or gardening in the suburbs.[2]

Few of the settlements of rural-nonfarm population are village or crossroad shopping centers for farmers, as was the case a generation ago, Instead, a very large proportion of the rural-nonfarm population is located just outside the urban fringes of cities and along major highways. A part of this population serves the huge flow of traffic between major metropolitan centers. Much of it is suburban: living in the country and commuting to

Reprinted from *The American Journal of Sociology*, Vol. 60 (March, 1955), pp. 471-486, by permission of the author, the *American Journal of Sociology*, and the University of Chicago Press. (Copyright, 1955, by the University of Chicago.)

1. See *United Nations Demographic Yearbook: 1952*, chap. i and Table 6.
2. The 1950 Census of Agriculture reports that, of 5,379,250 farms, 1,029,392 were "residential farms" (those with a total of sales of farm products in 1949 less than $250) and 639,230 were "part-time" farms (those with a value of sales of farm products of $250-$1,199, provided the farm operator reported one hundred or more days of work off the farm in 1949 or the nonfarm income received by him and members of his family was greater than the value of farm products sold). Only 69 per cent of all farms were commercial farms where agriculture was clearly the principal source of livelihood.

work in the city is now a common arrangement for factory and craft workers and no longer uniquely a middle-class and upper-class white-collar trait. Hence, from both an international and a domestic perspective, an urbanism which spreads out to nonagricultural economic institutions centered in and about cities is now one of the outstanding attributes of American life.

The present state of intense urbanism was achieved by rapid city growth during the past one and a half centuries. Although the American colonists and frontiersmen were intent upon developing the natural resources of unsettled areas, they were the offspring of a city-building culture and worked for urban markets within a system of interregional and international trade, improving local production through adopting new machines manufactured elsewhere. At the time of the American Revolution cities were growing at a rapid rate, and this situation has persisted through all but one or two decades. Figure 1 illustrates the rapid urbanization of the population in the last one hundred and sixty years. In 1790, at the time of the first census, 95 per cent of the people lived in rural areas. By the end of the Civil War at least one-fourth was urban. World War I stimulated the urbanization process even further, and by 1920 more than one-half was living in cities. The trend continued with great rapidity between 1920 and 1930 but slackened almost to a standstill during the depression years 1930-40. It enjoyed a renewed upsurge between 1940 and 1950, undoubtedly stimulated by World War II. In broad perspective the urban development of the United States may be viewed as the gradual extension of elements present in the culture from the beginning, hastened by three wars and retarded by depressions, which were, however, only fluctuations in a long-term trend. Meanwhile, the parent-countries, sources of the culture, have followed a parallel development.

RECENT URBAN GROWTH: DEFINITIONS. At the 1940 census only 56.5 per cent of the population had been defined as urban (Table 1). This shifting of 7.5 percentage points (56.5-64.0) from rural to urban within a single decade denotes a very great change. Not all the change resulted from a mass cityward migration, however. About one-third of it is due to a change in the definition of "urban population" employed by the Bureau of the Census, and about two-thirds to further concentration of the population in urban centers. The urban population showed an impressive gain of 22.0 million persons between 1940 and 1950. Of this, 7.5 million is due to urban growth resulting from the change in definitions (Table 2). Thus recent urbanization must be partly explained by the change in census definitions.

The new definition of urban places used in the 1950 census undoubtedly has given rise to some confusion and caused comparisons with the past to be inexact. The old definitions were badly out of focus, but the new definitions divide the population along lines that more nearly coincide with theoretical conceptions.

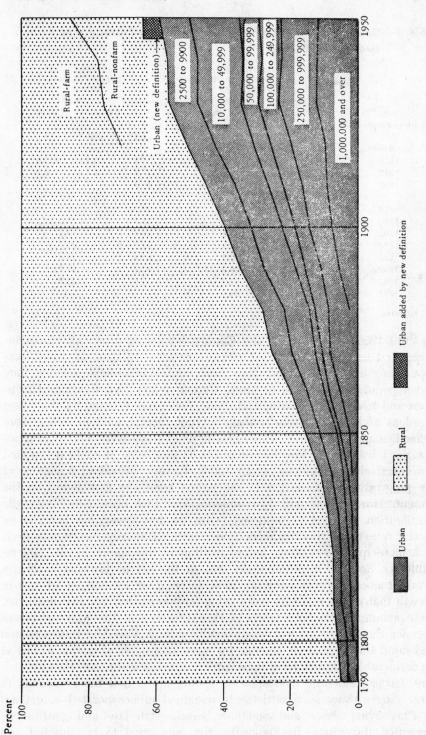

Percent

Rural-farm

Rural-nonfarm

Urban (new definition)

2500 to 9900

10,000 to 49,999

50,000 to 99,999

100,000 to 249,999

250,000 to 999,999

1,000,000 and over

Urban   Urban added by new definition

Rural

FIG. 1—Population of the United States by Size of Place of Habitation, 1790-1950

Table 1—Urban and Rural Composition and Rate of Urban and Rural Growth 1790-1950

| Year | PERCENTAGE OF TOTAL POPULATION CLASSED AS | | | PERCENTAGE CHANGE OVER PRECEDING DECADE | | |
| | URBAN | RURAL | | URBAN | RURAL | |
		Nonfarm	Farm		Nonfarm	Farm
New urban definition:						
1950	64.0	20.7	15.3	22.0*	23.0*	−19.3*
Old urban definition:						
1950	59.0	25.7	15.3	19.5	43.2	−23.6
1940	56.5	20.5	22.9	7.9	14.2	0.2
1930	56.2	19.3	24.6	27.3		
					4.4	
1920	51.2	48.8		29.0	3.2	
1910	45.7	54.3		39.3	9.0	
1900	39.7	60.3		36.4	12.2	
1870	28.2	71.8		42.7	25.7	
1860	19.8	80.2		75.4	28.4	
1840	10.8	89.2		63.7	29.7	
1800	6.1	93.9		59.9	33.8	
1790	5.1	94.9		. . .	. . .	

* Estimated.

Until 1950 the Bureau of the Census defined as urban all places incorporated as municipalities—as cities, boroughs, villages, or towns (except towns in New England, New York, and Wisconsin)—provided they had a population of 2,500 or more. Certain minor civil divisions (townships and towns in New England, New York, and Wisconsin) that were populous and very densely settled, but not incorporated as cities, were defined as urban under special rules; in 1940 there were 141 such areas. A major advantage of this definition was its simplicity. It could be applied retrospectively to previous census totals, thereby providing a picture of the progressive urbanization of the nation from the first census to the present. However, it had two imperfections that eventually forced its modification. First, it presupposed (with the few exceptions handled by special rules) that any agglomeration would voluntarily incorporate itself as a municipality sometime before it attained the minimum of 2,500 inhabitants. Second, it presupposed that in the act of growing each city would succeed in enlarging its area through annexation of all urban growth that might occur by outgrowing its boundaries. For the most part, these assumptions were realistic and satisfactory in the past. In recent decades they became increasingly inadequate. Automobile transportation and rapid transit made it possible for many thousands of people to live at a considerable distance from their work and to commute into the city each day. Large residential developments sprang up around the perimeters of large cities. Many such settlements remained unincorporated—sometimes as a tax-saving device, and sometimes because state laws and constitutions presented difficulties. Resistance by the population to be annexed and legal problems defeated the efforts of the central cities at annexation. As a consequence, the larger cities gradually overflowed their boundaries and became ringed with an urban fringe which had the characteristics of built-up residential areas inside the city. This was in addition to numerous settlements which sprang up about the larger city and incorporated themselves as separate cities. By census definitions, this unincorporated and unannexed urban-like settlement was defined as rural.

Another deficiency in the old urban definition manifested itself as numerous small and unincorporated places located at some distance from other centers grew until they attained the size and characteristics that would permit them to be termed "urban" save for their lack of a municipal charter. (In many cases the growth was very slow and spanned several decades.) Thus, insistence upon municipal incorporation and the use of city boundaries to identify and delimit urban population caused the census to misclassify as rural a large and rapidly growing urban population. Moreover, there was every prospect that this situation would become progressively worse at future censuses.

At least three alternative solutions to the problem of enumerating separately the urban population presented themselves: (a) Minor civil division boundaries (townships or their equivalent) could have been used to delimit, as nearly as possible, the actual limits of urban settlement. A disadvantage of this procedure is that in numerous instances it requires the inclusion of a considerable amount of low-density population (most of it rural-nonfarm) in the urban category. (b) The "special rules" could have

Table 2—Components of Urban Growth, by Sex and Color, 1940-50

Component of Growth	Total	WHITE Both Sexes	Male	Female	NONWHITE Both Sexes	Male	Female
		Number (Millions)					
Total urban increase, 1940-50	22.0	18.8	8.9	9.8	3.3	1.6	1.7
Change in urban definition	7.5	7.1	3.6	3.5	0.5	0.2	0.2
Urban increase, 1940-50, old definition	14.5	11.7	5.4	6.3	2.8	1.4	1.4
Natural increase	8.4	7.5	3.5	4.0	0.9	0.5	0.4
Net migration	3.9	2.2	0.9	1.3	1.7	0.8	0.9
Change in classification	2.1	2.0	1.0	1.0	0.2	0.1	0.1
		Component Composition					
Total	100	100	100	100	100	100	100
Change in definition	34	38	40	36	14	14	14
Natural increase	38	40	39	41	28	29	27
Net migration	18	12	10	13	54	52	55
Reclassification	10	11	11	10	5	5	5
		Color and Sex Composition					
Change in definition	100	94	47	47	6	3	3
Natural increase	100	89	42	47	11	5	5
Net migration	100	56	22	33	44	21	23
Reclassification	100	93	46	47	7	3	4

been modified to include more areas, while retaining the basic definition. This would seem to be only a temporary, not a long-range, solution to the problem. (c) The present actual limits of urban settlement could be determined, their boundaries established without reference to legal or administrative lines, and the boundaries used to define the urban population. This third, most precise, solution was adopted by the Bureau of the Census for the 1950 enumeration.

The details of the new urban definition and how the boundaries were established are reported in the Introduction to all published volumes of the 1950 Census of Population.[3]

In brief, three kinds of areas are defined as urban: (a) all places of 2,500 or more incorporated as municipalities—the basic element of the old definition; (b) the densely settled "urban fringe," including both incorporated and unincorporated areas, around cities of 50,000 or more; and (c) unincorporated places of 2,500 inhabitants or more outside any urban fringe. ("Urban fringes" were defined as continuously built-up areas outside the major city which comprise territory having an average density of about 2,000 persons per square mile.) Elements (b) and (c) in this definition required that the Census geographer establish, in advance of the enumeration, boundaries for urban fringes around cities of 50,000 or more and for unincorporated places outside urban fringes. A city of 50,000, together with its urban fringe, is termed an "urbanized area." A total of 157 of the large urbanized areas was recognized under element (b) of the definition. This element of the new definition added a net increase of 6.2 million persons to the urban category.

Elements (c) of the new definition led to the inclusion of the population of 401 unincorporated places in the urban category. After allowing for population that would have been defined as urban under special rule by the old definition, the net gain for the urban population was 1.3 million persons. Together, elements (b) and (c) led to a net gain of 8.5 per cent for the urban population and a loss of 12.2 per cent for the rural.

If this mode of defining the urban population is continued in the future, the boundaries of the major urban agglomerations must be redefined in advance of each census. Thus, the boundaries will not remain fixed but will change to follow the pattern of actual urban settlement. This definition has the following features which recommend it for social research:

1. It is probably as close an approximation to the truly urban population, as generally conceptualized, as has been achieved by any census and establishes a major precedent for the Bureau of the Census to abandon legal boundaries for delimiting statistical areas where to do so will improve the quality of the data.

2. It recognizes large built-up agglomerations (urbanized areas) as

---

3. See, e.g., Bureau of the Census, *United States Census of Population: 1950*, Vol. I: *Number of Inhabitants, U.S. Summary*, pp. xviii and xxiv.

single urban entities instead of treating the many satellite cities within urbanized areas as separate.

3. It is flexible and can be adapted easily to future needs. Not only does it permit the future adjustment of boundaries of present urbanized areas but it also provides for the recognition of new urbanized areas at each census. If it proves necessary, urbanized areas contiguous to places of less than 50,000 inhabitants may be recognized. Also, if desired, the minimum average density may be either raised or lowered.

4. It makes individual urban clusters much more comparable. In the past, comparisons of cities or the urban-rural composition of states or regions has been complicated by differences in the location of their respective legal boundaries in relation to actual urban settlement as well as by differences in the effect of state laws upon the incorporation of small settlements.

The new definition has the following drawbacks for social research:

1. It is much more difficult than before for organizations other than the Bureau of the Census to collect and tabulate their own statistics by urban and rural areas. The private research worker or survey organization cannot classify data by urban and rural residence without performing the painstaking task of coding street addresses and mapping locations of residences. Informants no longer know whether they live inside or outside the boundaries used to define the urban population and can supply only an address or mapped location which must then be coded from maps and listings of street addresses. This restriction includes the National Office of Vital Statistics, which now finds it virtually impossible and prohibitively expensive to allocate births and deaths by urban and rural residence as now defined.

2. Decennial rates of urban growth can be computed only with difficulty. Much of the increase in urban population at each census actually will consist of people who have resided in the same area throughout the decade but who merely will be shifted from the rural to the urban category. This same situation has existed in the past, but the populations that were reclassified as urban were all the residents of individual incorporated places or minor civil divisions, for which data from previous censuses were available.

3. A great deal of expensive advance preparation is necessary. In the event of a wave of exceptionally stringent economy in government at some future date, the expense of determining urban boundaries in advance of a census might cause the urban definition to be dropped.

In order to bridge the gap between the old and the new definitions, the Bureau of the Census has published a few basic tabulations of data according to both definitions. With these data it is possible to arrive at estimates of the detailed changes which occurred between 1940 and 1950.

Table 1 presents rates of growth according to the old definition and estimated rates using the new definition. (These estimated rates are only

rough approximations and may be in error by as much as 10 per cent.)
Between 1940 and 1950 the urban population, as defined in 1950, grew
by an estimated 22 per cent. This rate was 50 per cent greater than the
average for the nation. The rural-nonfarm population (primarily suburban)
is estimated to have grown at about the same rate. By the old definition
the urban population is reported as growing at a rate only 35 per cent
above the national average and less than one-half as fast as the rural-
nonfarm population. The differences demonstrate the failure of the old
definition to encompass new urban growth; instead, it was attributing the
added growth to rural-nonfarm areas. In retrospect, it appears that the
slow growth of cities between 1930 and 1940, paralleled by a much higher
rate of rural-nonfarm increase, may have been due in part to the definitions then current.

COMPONENTS OF URBAN GROWTH. The 22 million people gained by
urban places between 1940 and 1950 has already been subdivided into a
component of 7.5 million persons attributable to the change in definition
and a component of 14.5 million attributable to growth according to old
definitions. In turn, this latter figure should be broken into three major
components to learn the sources from which cities are now drawing their
growth.

Between 1940 and 1950 the urban population (old definition) increased
in three ways:

a) *Natural increase.* Families residing in cities bore more children than
persons were lost through death.

b) *Net in-migration.* More persons took up residence within cities than
left cities for rural areas.

c) *Reclassification of territory from rural to urban.* At each new census
several incorporated places are found to have attained a population of
2,500 or more, which permits their classification as urban. This procedure,
normal under both the old as well as the new definition, can be a major
source of growth, for the entire population resident in these areas (not
merely the growth during the past decade) is removed from the rural and
added to the urban classification. Between 1940 and 1950 a net total of
559 urban places, averaging 3,750 inhabitants each in 1950, passed from
the rural to the urban category, by old definitions.

By population estimation procedures the urban and rural population
changes between 1940 and 1950 have been subdivided into the above three
components. Because the change in definition makes the task extraordinarily
imprecise, estimates of the components of growth for the 1940-50 decade
were made by two independent methods and the results compared. Table
2 presents what appears to be the best single estimate. Although the figures
should be interpreted with caution, the following conclusions seem warranted:

a) The largest single component of urban growth between 1940 and
1950 was natural increase. Because of an upsurge in fertility, urban popu-

lation produced unusually large annual crops of infants. Of the 22.0 million total increase, 8.4 millions, or 38 per cent of the total increase, is from this source.

b) In-migration, the second source, was comparatively much smaller. It has generally been supposed that cities have grown largely by in-migration from rural areas. During the past decade 3.9 million, or only 18 per cent of the total, came from this source. The rural population has diminished to a point where it can no longer be the major source of supply of urban growth. If cities are to grow in the future, natural increase probably must contribute by far the major share of the increase.

c) The reclassification of places from rural to urban added 2.1 million, or 10 per cent of the total urban increase. Although this is the smallest of the sources of growth, it is more than one-half as important as migration.

d) Of the net in-migration, a very large disproportion was nonwhite. Although one-tenth of the population of cities is nonwhite, over two-fifths (44 per cent) of the net immigration was of nonwhite population. The urbanization of nonwhite population was one of the major changes of the 1940-50 decade.

e) The change in definition and reclassification tended to add white population in disproportion to their share of all urban population.

URBANISM AND SIZE OF PLACE. It might be supposed that there is some optimum or maximum size of city, beyond which growth stops because the place has become highly inefficient and undesirable as a place for living or carrying on economic activities. If such a maximum exists, either cities have not as yet surpassed it, or else exceeding it has not caused sufficient ill effects to prevent growth. In either event many cities in the United States are enormous. The New York urbanized area contained 12.2 million persons in 1950; the Chicago urbanized area contained 4.9 million, and ten other urbanized areas contained a million or more. Twenty-five of the urbanized areas had a 1950 population of 500,000 or more (Table 3). With decreasing size of cities the number of urban places increases. At the lower extreme there were 1,605 urban places containing 2,500-5,000 inhabitants in 1950. Table 3 shows that the 157 urbanized areas contained 46 per cent of the nation's population and 71.8 per cent of its urban population. The 3,253 other urban places contained only 18.1 per cent of the total population and 28.2 per cent of the urban population. Hence, a large proportion not only of the urban population but of all population is concentrated in large urban agglomerations.

Figure 1 traces the rise of the big cities from 1790 to 1950. This illustration fails to show the full extent of the present concentration in large urban places, however, because in it the populations of satellite cities within urbanized areas are classified according to their independent size. It also reports the urban population added by the new urban definition as a separate entity, instead of distributing it among the size classes of cities. This was necessary in order to achieve comparability with the preceding

Table 3—Population of Urbanized Areas and Other Urban Areas, by Size of Place, 1950

Type of Area and Size of Place	Number of Places	Per Cent of Total Population	Per Cent of Urban Population
Total	..	64.0	100.0
Urban, within urbanized areas, total	157*	46.0	71.8
Areas of 1,000,000 or more	12	25.1	39.2
Areas of 500,000 to 1,000,000	13	5.8	9.1
Areas of 250,000 to 500,000	24	5.8	9.0
Areas of 100,000 to 250,000	70	7.2	11.3
Areas of 50,000 to 100,000	38	2.1	3.2
Urban, outside urbanized areas, total	3,253	18.1	28.2
Places of 50,000 or more	21	0.8	1.2
Places of 25,000 to 50,000	172	3.9	6.2
Places of 10,000 to 25,000	547	5.5	8.5
Places of 5,000 to 10,000	908	4.1	6.5
Places of 2,500 to 5,000	1,605	3.7	5.8

* Comprises central city, satellite cities, and unincorporated urban fringe.

censuses. Nevertheless, the figure illustrates, in a general way, the speed with which the population has become concentrated in the larger places.

The characteristics of the urban population tend to vary in several significant ways with changes in the size of the urban place. In other words, the concentration of population into larger agglomerations appears to have an independent effect upon population composition, in addition to the fact of residence. What these effects and conditions are can be learned by examining the population characteristics in terms of the size-of-place continuum.[4]

URBANISM AND METROPOLITANISM. The phenomenon of growth of cities to large size and the fact that large cities acquire unique attributes have given rise to a theory that major cities are focal points in the economic and social organization of modern industrial-commercial nations. From piecemeal evidence it appears that, as a nation becomes highly industrialized and committed to a system of interregional commerce and industry, its economic activities tend to be located with reference to large urban centers, or metropolises, as well as to natural resources and available raw materials. The specific forces and factors that produce a concentration of population and economic activities in metropolitan centers and distribute the remainder in a metropolitan hinterland have not been measured or studied in detail. Among its advantages are, one may say tentatively, low transportation costs, a concentrated market, a joint location for several industries, a large and varied labor supply, a large and varied supply of employment opportunities, and the opportunity for wholesalers and manufacturers to assemble a wide range of items. Also, business management tends to locate sales offices and its home office in large centers to have

4. Otis Dudley Duncan and Albert J. Reiss, Jr., *Social Characteristics of Rural and Urban Communities, 1950* (New York: John Wiley & Sons, 1956).

ready access to other business management, financial institutions, and good transportation and communication facilities. The term "dominance" has been used as a' class name to refer to the combined force of these factors in determining location. New economic units seeking to establish themselves, or old ones seeking to expand their activities, find that these forces are integral parts of the environment over which they have no control and to which they must adjust. Since they emanate from the metropolis and tend to locate activities with respect to the latter, large metropolitan centers are said to be dominant in determining the distribution of population and economic activities. Not an insignificant aspect of the dominant role of the metropolitan centers is the fact that medium-size and small cities, as well as dispersed rural populations, appear to perform their functions with reference to the metropolitan centers, while they themselves exert a more limited and integrative influence upon the territory about them. Thus metropolitan centers are dominant conditioners of the physical environment in the modern industrial-commercial society, while the smaller urban places are subdominant environmental conditioners.

A most familiar aspect of metropolitan dominance is the fact that a large territory outside the metropolis is directly under the influence of the metropolitan center. This territory corresponds approximately to what one would regard as the combined labor market and retail trade area of the metropolis. Since transportation facilities now make it possible to live several miles distant from the place of work, a broad ring outside the urban fringe but adjacent to it is growing rapidly. A high proportion of the population in this ring is rural-nonfarm. Many new factories and other business establishments are locating themselves there. Even the rural-farm population in this zone differs from the farm population elsewhere, for there are numerous residential farms, part-time farms, and specialized farms. After all these aspects are considered, it is evident that the economic and social entity that may be termed "the metropolis and its immediate environs" or "metropolitan area" is much greater in scope than either the central city or even the urbanized area.

In order to provide separate statistics for these areas under direct and daily metropolitan influence, the Bureau of the Census recognized, at the 1950 census, 168 large population clusters that were termed "standard metropolitan areas." They consist of whole counties. In brief, a standard metropolitan area consists of the county containing a central city of 50,000 or more inhabitants plus any adjacent counties that also appear to be metropolitan in character and socially and economically integrated with the central city.[5] The delimitation of standard metropolitan areas was made with the co-operation of several agencies of the federal government. It is based upon a great amount of research, inquiry, and consultation with

---

5. For the full definition, including rules for determining whether adjacent counties are integrated, see U.S. Bureau of the Census, *United States Census of Population: 1950*, Vol. I: *Number of Inhabitants, U.S. Summary*, pp. xxxi-xxxiii.

local authorities. Like the new urban and rural definitions, the use of standard metropolitan areas as statistical areas was an innovation of the 1950 census. However, by combining county statistics from each census since 1900, a recent monograph carries the standard metropolitan area definition back to cover the last half-century of population growth.[6] In order to accomplish this, 16 of the standard metropolitan areas of New England, which had been delimited along town lines by the Bureau of the Census, were redelimited along county lines. In some instances two or more New England standard metropolitan areas fall in the same county. For this reason it was necessary to combine some S.M.A.'s (the common abbreviation) while forming the county equivalent areas. This reduced the total number of S.M.A.'s to 162. The S.M.A. definition was extended to earlier censuses only for "principal S.M.A.'s," those with 100,000 or more total population at a given census. Tables 4 and 5 present data for the S.M.A.'s as thus modified for the half-century, 1900-1950.

Table 4*—Growth Data for Standard Metropolitan Areas, Retrojected to Earlier Censuses, 1900-1950

CENSUS YEAR	NUMBER OF S.M.A.'s	POPU-LATION (millions)	PER CENT OF U.S. POPU-LATION	U.S. Total	RATE OF GROWTH DURING PRECEDING DECADE Standard Metropoli-tan Areas	Nonmetro-politan Areas	PER CENT OF TOTAL U.S. POPULATION GROWTH CLAIMED BY S.M.A.'s DURING PRECEDING DECADE
All S.M.A.'s, 1950	162	85.6	56.8	14.5	21.8	6.0	80.6
Principal S.M.A.'s:							
1950	147	84.3	56.0	14.5	21.8	6.3	79.3
1940	125	67.1	51.1	7.2	8.3	6.2	57.7
1930	115	61.0	49.8	16.1	27.0	7.1	76.2
1920	94	46.1	43.7	14.9	25.2	8.1	67.6
1910	71	34.5	37.6	21.0	32.6	15.0	53.1
1900	52	24.1	31.9	20.7	..	..	..

* Source: Bogue, Population Growth in Standard Metropolitan Areas, 1900-1950 (Washington, D.C., 1953).

In 1950, 56.8 per cent of the population of the United States lived in the 162 S.M.A.'s. These areas covered only 7.1 per cent of the total land area of the nation. Thus, considerably more than one-half of the total pop-lation was concentrated in one-fourteenth of the land area.

In the past half-century there has been a trend toward an increase in the number of S.M.A.'s and toward a rising proportion of the total popu-lation residing in the areas. The record of this trend is contained in Table 4. Had the S.M.A. delimitation been in effect in 1900, there would have been an estimated 52 areas. They would have contained less than one-third of the total population. At each succeeding census from 10 to 23 new

6. Donald J. Bogue, *Population Growth in Standard Metropolitan Areas, 1900-1950, with an Explanatory Analysis of Urbanized Areas* (Washington, D.C.: Housing and Home Finance Agency, 1953).

**Table 5*—Growth Data for Central Cities and Rings of Standard
Metropolitan Areas, Retrojected to Earlier Censuses, 1900-1950**

CENSUS YEAR	NUMBER OF S.M.A.'s	PER CENT OF U.S. POPULATION		RATE OF GROWTH DURING PRECEDING DECADE			PER CENT OF TOTAL U.S. POPULATION GROWTH CLAIMED BY S.M.A.'s DURING PRECEDING DECADE	
		Central Cities	Rings	Metropolitan Areas, Total	Central Cities	Rings	Central Cities	Rings
All S.M.A.'s, 1950	162	32.8	24.0	21.8	13.9	34.7	31.6	49.0
Principal S.M.A.'s:								
1950	147	32.3	23.8	21.8	13.7	34.8	30.7	48.6
1940	125	31.6	19.5	8.3	5.1	13.8	22.8	34.9
1930	115	31.8	18.0	27.0	23.3	34.2	43.3	32.9
1920	94	28.9	14.8	25.2	26.7	22.4	46.8	20.8
1910	71	25.0	12.7	32.6	35.3	27.6	37.4	15.7
1900	52	21.2	10.7	..	..	..	..	..

* Source: Bogue, *Population Growth in Standard Metropolitan Areas, 1900-1950* (Washington, D.C., 1953).

S.M.A.'s would have been added. This, together with the better than average growth rate of S.M.A.'s already defined for earlier censuses, results in a steady rise in the proportion of the total United States population living in metropolitan areas. During every decade except one, the S.M.A.'s as defined for a particular time have grown 50 per cent faster than nonmetropolitan areas and have claimed a disproportionately large share of the total national growth.

The band lying outside the central city but within the S.M.A. is generally termed the "metropolitan ring." During the 1900-1910 and the 1910-20 decades, central cities were growing faster than their rings (Table 5). However, in each decade since 1920, rings have been growing faster than the central cities. Early in the present century, rings had only about one-ninth of the population of the nation; they now have about one-fourth of the national population. Between 1900 and 1910 the rings claimed only about one-sixth of the total national population growth; in 1940-50 they claimed almost one-half. The gap between the growth rate of central cities and the growth rate of rings has become very large; between 1940 and 1950 rings grew almost two and one-half times as fast as central cities. This rapid growth is not confined to the band lying immediately outside the central city (the urban fringe). It is characteristic of a much broader area, much of which has a fairly low population density at the present. (The new urban definition excludes much of the area at the periphery of the city where new growth will occur during succeeding decades.)

To summarize: The larger metropolitan centers are poles to which a very large share of the new population and economic growth are attracted. The sphere of this growth-stimulating influence is quite large. The number of metropolitan centers which exert such an influence is increasing. Meanwhile, except for a few isolated centers that will eventually become metropolitan centers, most of the nonmetropolitan territory grows much more slowly. The progressive urbanization of the population has been, from one point of view, a progressive metropolitanization of the population.

SOCIAL AND ECONOMIC CHARACTERISTICS OF URBAN POPULATION. A discussion of modern urbanism in the United States should include a listing of some of the principal ways in which urban populations differ from the present rural populations. While making such comparisons (using the old definition of urban population), it will be well to check some of our conceptions of the typical urban resident against the facts (Table 6).

Sex Composition. For many years the city has been noted for containing a preponderance of women. By failing to include suburban areas with their family groupings, the old urban definition tended to exaggerate this characteristic. In 1950, cities had a small (1.4 percentage-point) imbalance (51.4 minus 50.0 per cent) toward a deficiency of men. When allowance is made for armed forces overseas, for the tendency of the census to undercount young men in cities, and for the tendency for women to outlive men, the small sex differential reported in 1950 for urban areas loses much of its portentous significance.

Color, Race, and Nativity. About 10 per cent of the urban population is nonwhite. As was indicated earlier, one of the most drastic compositional as well as growth changes that occurred during the 1940-50 decade was an extraordinarily large increase in the nonwhite population (43 per cent, as compared with only 17.2 per cent for the white). This increase was characteristic for both Negroes and other nonwhite races. For many years cities have played the role of "melting pot" and have contained large proportions of the foreign-born. In 1950 one resident in twelve was of foreign

Table 6—Selected Characteristics of the Population, by Urban and Rural Residence, 1950, and Per Cent Change, 1940-1950

Characteristic	PER CENT DISTRIBUTION 1950			ESTIMATED PER CENT CHANGE 1940-50		
	Urban	Rural-Nonfarm	Rural-Farm	Urban	Rural-Nonfarm	Rural-Farm
Total	100.0	100.0	100.0	19.5	43.2	−23.6
Sex, total population:						
Male	48.6	50.9	52.4	18.6	42.6	−24.1
Female	51.4	49.1	47.6	20.4	43.7	−23.1
Color, total population:						
White	89.9	91.3	85.5	17.2	43.4	−22.5
Nonwhite	10.1	8.7	14.5	43.5	40.4	−29.8
Race and nativity, total population:						
Native white	81.1	87.7	83.1	22.6	45.3	−21.8
Foreign-born white	8.8	3.6	2.4	− 7.1	−18.3	−39.5
Negro	9.7	8.0	13.7	43.2	38.0	−29.8
Other races	0.3	0.7	0.8	..	..	..
Marital status, population fourteen years and over:						
Single	22.7	22.3	26.1	−18.7	12.6	−41.1
Married	66.1	68.1	67.2	31.2	48.5	−16.6
Widowed and divorced	11.5	9.6	6.7	29.5	43.9	−28.4

Table 6—Selected Characteristics of the Population, by Urban and Rural Residence, 1950, and Per Cent Change, 1940-1950 (Continued)

Characteristic	PER CENT DISTRIBUTION 1950			ESTIMATED PER CENT CHANGE 1940-50		
	Urban	Rural-Nonfarm	Rural-Farm	Urban	Rural-Nonfarm	Rural-Farm
Age, total population:						
Under 5 years	10.1	12.1	11.4	75.8	87.9	−12.9
5-9 years	7.8	10.0	11.1	33.7	56.8	−18.7
10-14 years	6.3	8.2	10.7	− 5.5	24.3	−26.9
15-19 years	6.4	7.5	9.2	−12.3	13.0	−37.0
20-24 years	8.0	7.6	6.1	5.9	25.8	−43.7
25-29 years	8.7	7.9	5.9	14.5	38.5	−34.5
30-34 years	8.1	7.4	6.0	13.5	40.4	−23.9
35-39 years	7.8	7.0	6.5	17.5	47.9	−13.8
40-44 years	7.1	6.1	6.1	15.9	47.6	−14.6
45-49 years	6.4	5.2	5.6	12.1	36.3	−21.3
50-54 years	5.8	4.6	5.2	19.5	36.5	−21.5
55-59 years	5.0	4.1	4.7	32.2	44.9	−16.4
60-64 years	4.2	3.6	3.9	37.9	48.8	−15.0
65-69 years	3.4	3.3	3.2	42.3	51.9	−14.2
70-74 years	2.3	2.4	2.1	41.5	54.5	−12.3
75 years or older	2.5	2.9	2.3	56.7	67.4	− 6.3
Educational attainment, population twenty-five years and over:						
No school completed	2.3	2.7	3.1	−24.8	20.2	−46.9
Grade school (1-8 years)	39.5	49.3	62.5	− 8.3	28.0	−28.4
High school (1-4 years)	40.2	33.9	26.6	51.5	66.7	9.5
College (1-4 years)	15.2	10.9	6.3	59.0	54.8	6.6
Education not reported	2.7	3.2	1.5	..	..	..
Labor force status, population fourteen years and over (percentage in the labor force):						
White males	79.6	74.7	82.7	11.9	36.5	−23.5
White females	32.2	22.2	14.9	24.9	54.6	11.5
Nonwhite males	76.4	67.4	82.8	31.3	22.7	−34.8
Nonwhite females	42.5	29.0	21.5	25.1	16.5	−37.4
Major industry group, employed labor force						
Agriculture	1.1	9.1	71.0	..	72.7	−25.1
Mining	0.9	4.9	1.3	..	19.5	..
Construction	6.0	8.9	3.1	63.3	89.6	28.7
Manufacturing	29.4	25.6	9.4	31.4	57.1	30.0
Transportation	9.0	7.4	2.1	35.5	54.5	24.9
Trade	21.9	18.0	4.3	33.7	57.3	23.6
Finance	4.4	1.9	0.5	22.8	..	..
Business services	2.7	3.1	0.8	55.1	74.8	..
Personal services	7.2	5.9	1.7	−15.5	6.3	..
Entertainment services	1.2	0.8	0.1	..	..	..
Professional services	9.5	8.4	2.7	44.8	47.8	−12.0
Public administration	5.2	4.0	1.2	74.8	81.4	..
Industry not reported	1.3	1.9	1.8	..	..	..

birth. Between 1940 and 1950 the foreign-born white population declined in all residence groups. It declined least among the urban population, however, for two reasons: First, a high proportion of the older immigrant groups that are dying out at the fastest rates had settled in rural territories.

Second, a high proportion of the immigrants to the United States between 1940 and 1950 settled in urban areas.

Marital Status. Throughout the nation there was a very sharp decline in the proportion of single people in the population and a rise in the proportion of married people. This change occurred primarily through a higher proportion of persons marrying in their late teens and early twenties. Cities lead this very significant change. When allowance is made for differences in total growth rate, the recent tendency toward marriage at younger ages appears considerably greater in urban areas than in rural. In 1950 there were almost one-fifth fewer unmarried persons living in cities than in 1940, in spite of the net cityward migration of young adults. In the city a greater proportion of persons are widowed or divorced than in rural areas.

Age. City populations also have been noted for their youthful age composition. Although the tendency has been to have small proportions of children, by virtue of low birth rates, they have tended to have a larger than average proportion of young adults in comparison with older adults. However, this characteristic has now largely disappeared, and elderly people are comprising an increasing proportion of the total urban population. In 1950, for example, the ratio of persons twenty to forty to persons forty and over in urban and rural areas was as follows: urban .89; rural-nonfarm .93; rural-farm .74. The most youthful population (excluding children) is now the rural-nonfarm population. Although the rural-farm population has the oldest adult age composition, it is only moderately different from the urban. Between 1940 and 1950 the older age groups in the urban population grew at extraordinarily rapid rates, while the population in young adult ages grew at only average rates or below.

The explanation for this aging is evident. The youthful generations of in-migrants of the late nineteenth and early twentieth centuries which created a great urban expansion have remained and are now aged. Meanwhile, the rate of in-migration has slackened sharply, as has been shown. This combination of events can lead only to a rapid advance in the proportion of aged people in the urban population. The process will continue for at least three more decades, barring very high urban fertility that would counteract it. The large streams of migrants that arrived in cities between 1900 and 1930 will be entering the older ages during these decades.

During the depression years between 1930 and 1940, the urban birth rate fell to a very low level. It rose again after 1940 and became very high in the middle and later years of the decade (see below). This trough and crest have left their imprint on the urban age structure. Between 1940 and 1950 there was an actual decline in the number of young people ten to nineteen years of age and an increase of 75 per cent in children under five years of age.

Educational Attainment. The urban population has a considerably higher average educational attainment than the rural population. The proportion of the population twenty-five years of age or older that had not graduated from grade school was only about two-fifths of the urban population, whereas it was about two-thirds of the rural-farm, and more than one-half of the rural-nonfarm. On the other hand, the proportion of inhabitants with college training was about 50 per cent greater among the urban population than among the rural-nonfarm. It was two and one-half times that of the rural-farm population. Between 1940 and 1950 urban growth was highly selective of persons with high-school or college training.

Labor-force Participation. In urban areas women are participants in the labor force to a much greater extent than they are in rural areas. This is especially true of nonwhite women. Between 1940 and 1950 the labor force of urban areas underwent an extraordinary sex-color change. The number of white female participants increased at a rate more than twice that for white males. The number of nonwhite male participants increased at a rate almost three times that for white males. By 1950 the female and the nonwhite segments of the urban labor force were very important and grew rapidly.

Industry. Cities have a unique industrial and commercial composition that distinguishes them from both rural-farm and rural-nonfarm areas. Manufacturing is the largest single type of activity and occupies almost 30 per cent of the breadwinners (it does not differ greatly from the rural-nonfarm population in this respect). Types of manufacturing concentrated in urban areas differ considerably from those in rural areas. The proportions of employed workers engaged in transportation, trade, finance, personal services, entertainment services, professional services, and public administration are relatively greater in urban areas. On the other hand, the fact that all these specialized functions are performed in rural areas to some degree should not be overlooked. The significance of the statistics for rural areas is not clear at this point, however. Since the data are for workers classified by *place of residence* rather than by *place of work,* the data for the rural-nonfarm and the rural-farm population may reflect in part the custom of commuting to work in the central cities from the outer parts of standard metropolitan areas.

Fertility. For more than a century before 1930, the general trend of fertility in the United States had been downward. City populations were considerably less fertile than rural populations. In the mid-1930's urban birth rates had sunk below the replacement level on a long-term basis. The crude birth rates (births per 1,000 population) for the nation began to rise in the late 1930's, and in the 1940's it rose to a peak well above the low point of the 1930's. After some fluctuation, associated with sending armed forces overseas and later demobilization, the birth rate remained high in 1950 (24.1 per thousand). For the year 1954 the rate will be at about its 1950 level, or roughly 30 per cent above its lowest point.

Because cities paced the long-run decline of fertility, it is of extraordinary interest to consider the urban populations during this interruption of the historic trend (Table 7). The urban population experienced the same rise in fertility rates as the nation and appears to have experienced a greater percentage increase in fertility rates than the rural population. This is true for both the white and nonwhite population. But the traditional urban-rural differential has remained. On a ratio basis, the differential is about as large in 1950 as it was in 1940 or 1930, but urban fertility ratios have risen more points between 1930 and 1950 than the rural. This implies that the absolute size of the urban-rural differential has decreased. Urban fertility in 1950 was well above long-run replacement needs. Adverse effects attributable directly to the depression and disruptions created by World War II had largely been equalized by this time. The high rate of fertility for the nation in 1954 indicates that urban fertility also has remained at about its 1950 level. How long this higher-than-expected level of fertility, and especially of urban fertility, will continue cannot be predicted with assurance now. In view of the earlier age at marriage, there is some indication that families are being started earlier and that these families will be completed younger in life. If this is true, urban families of the future may not be so large as it might otherwise appear. A half-dozen or more years will be required before the full implications of the fertility upsurge can be stated. Meanwhile, urban fertility is currently at a much higher level than appeared probable twenty years ago, and there is a good

Table 7—Natality in Urban and Rural Areas, 1930-1950

MEASURE OF NATALITY AND YEAR	UNITED STATES TOTAL	URBAN*			RURAL*		
		Total	White	Nonwhite	Total	White	Nonwhite
Crude birth rate:†							
1950	24.1	22.9	22.0	30.6	25.8	24.5	37.1
1940	19.4	17.1	16.7	20.5	22.5	21.1	32.5
Per cent change, 1940-50	24	34	32	49	15	16	14
Fertility rate:‡							
1950	106.2	95.6	93.2	114.2	123.7	117.1	180.5
1940	79.9	65.1	64.7	69.0	102.8	97.0	143.0
Per cent change, 1940-50	33	47	44	66	20	21	26
Ratio of children to women:§							
1950	587	504	499	541	732	701	1,016
1940	441	334	333	349	618	589	825
1930	517	404	407	369	708	691	813
Per cent change, 1940-50	33	51	50	55	18	19	23
Per cent change, 1930-40	−15	−17	−18	− 5	−13	−15	1
Per cent change, 1930-50	14	25	23	47	3	1	25

* Crude birth rates and fertility rates adjusted for underregistration and misreporting residence, 1940 and 1950.
† Live births per 1,000 population, corrected for underregistration, enumerated as of April 1, for 1940 and 1950.
‡ Live births corrected for underregistration per 1,000 female population aged fifteen to forty-four years, enumerated as of April 1, 1940 and 1950.
§ Ratio of children zero to five years, corrected for underenumeration, to women twenty to forty-four years of age as of census date.

prospect that this situation will persist for some time. However, it should be remembered that urban births, even more than rural births, are subject to planning—both as to ultimate size of family and timing of the arrival of children. In an economic crisis urban fertility may drop precipitously.

QUALIFICATIONS AND IMPLICATIONS. The above quick picture of urbanism in the United States is seriously deficient in one major respect; it neglects distribution. The changes and trends noted for the nation are merely averages of changes and trends in individual urban places. Recent research on this topic has shown that what appears to be a consistent and orderly change at the national or regional level actually is a combination of local changes which frequently run counter to each other and are responsive to forces very different from those considered at the national level. Therefore, the material presented here should be taken as description but not as explanation.

It would be difficult to exaggerate the significance for all social science of certain elements of the broad picture of urbanism presented here. In the United States, the cultural milieu is now predominantly an urbanized and metropolitanized one, and attitude climates are, for the most part, urban climates. Social institutions are, by and large, urban institutions: family life and religious activity are not withering away in the urban milieu but are adapting to it. In a high percentage of cases the socialization and personality-formation process now occurs in an urban setting. People in cities make friends and engage in face-to-face interaction. Unfortunately, much sociological theory and research tends to overlook these facts.

The older research in urban communities is sometimes incomplete if not misleading. Much of the data employed in older studies was unrepresentative in two ways. First, many urban studies have concentrated on the area of lowest incomes and greatest social nonconformity. Second, a high proportion of samples were drawn from immigrants and other newly arrived groups in young and rapidly growing cities. In addition, the rural society was frequently used as a control group. Many accepted sociological assertions about cities in general are based upon social studies which together do not represent all phases of urbanism and which were not arrived at by careful use of modern research techniques.

The urban environment is a setting for a series of social problems, such as crime or delinquency and hostile race relations. To attribute these as inevitable results of urbanism and to specify that disorganization is necessarily the predominant characteristic of urban social process is to commit the same methodological mistake geographers made a generation ago when they attempted to relate climatic conditions to personality types. Within the next century the present built-up urban territory of the nation will probably double or treble in size. Meanwhile, at least one-half of what now exists will be torn down and replaced. Present physical structures will constitute a small portion of the cities of the year 2050. Planning for this building and rebuilding and long-range social work based on scientific research should be able to reduce present inadequacies of the urban environment. Renewed social research upon the urban community, from an objective point of view, using representative samples of data and modern research techniques, should produce much of the knowledge that social engineers will need in order to handle social problems which, in the nature of the case, will be largely urban problems.

METROPOLITAN DOMINANCE AND INTEGRATION

Rupert B. Vance and Sara Smith

Viewed in the national context, southern metropolises are small; they came late upon the scene and they developed on the edge of the great industrial concentration in the Northeast and Middle States. Except for their recent rapid growth, they are unremarkable cities. Human ecologists and students of urbanism in the United States have had little reason to study them. Viewed in the southern context, however, these metropolises are important because the functions which are concentrated in them exert an organizing influence upon the economic and social structure of the communities in their hinterlands. This chapter will be an exploratory attempt to trace the pattern of metropolitan dominance and integration in the South, the myriad nets of intercity relationships which extend from the smallest southern village through the larger cities to the super-metropolises outside the region.

Writers from the time of Aristotle have been aware of the influence of the great city upon its hinterland; but even now so little is known about the dynamics of this influence that metropolitanism must be defined descriptively. It is of course one aspect of the urbanization process. Urbanization in its minimal meaning is the concentration of population and human activities at focal points in space. This concentration proceeds in two ways simultaneously: the multiplying of the points of concentration and the accompanying increase in the size of the individual concentrations. With an increase in both number and size of the city-units, there comes about a territorial division of labor which can be described in much the same way as any division of labor. As differentiation of function develops, communities do not grow in accidental fashion but in terms of the strategic services they develop in relation to each other and to the primary sustenance activity of the area. Functional differentiation here as in other situations creates the necessity for some hierarchy of control; the city which by fortunate location or historical accident becomes the place where the institutions of control center tends to become the largest city—the metropolis—and its sphere of influence, the metropolitan community or region. Whereas urbanization may refer to any aspect of population agglomeration, metropolitanism should be reserved for the organizational component that great cities impose upon the urbanization process. Any

Reprinted from *The Urban South*, edited by Rupert B. Vance and Nicholas J. Demerath, Chapter 6, pp. 114-134, by permission of the authors and the University of North Carolina Press. (Copyright, 1954, The University of North Carolina Press.)

city with a large population is usually referred to as a metropolis, but it may be well to point out that while all metropolises are large cities, not all large cities are metropolises. Population size is a concomitant; function is the keynote.

N. S. B. Gras, the economic historian, has named the economy of the modern world "metropolitan economy" because of the crucial part played by the great cities in organizing and integrating the world's commercial, financial, and communication arrangements.[1] The first of the modern super-agglomerates—the capital markets of the world—developed around the North Sea in London, Berlin, and Paris; the second, for the Americas, grew up along the New York-Chicago axis; and the third developed in the Far East, dominated by Tokyo and Shanghai.[2] World War II has retarded the growth of the first and the third, but the New York-Chicago axis has continued to increase in importance.

As Gras explains, "A metropolitan economy is the organization of producers and consumers mutually dependent for goods and services, wherein their wants are supplied by a system of exchange concentrated in the large city, which is the focus of local trade and the center through which normal economic relations are established and maintained."[3] Implied in this definition are lines of integration tying the central city to other metropolitan centers outside its region. Gras also emphasized the necessity of a sizeable and productive hinterland; there must be a "respectful" distance from other great cities.

The development of the metropolitan center, according to Gras, has four successive and overlapping phases. The first, and probably the basic one, is the *organization of the market*. The second is the *development of industry*, which in the nineteenth century gave such dramatic impetus to population concentration, centering wealth and power in the cities and adding greatly to the primary market function. The third phase, which is closely related to market organization and industrial development, is the *organization of transportation and communication facilities*. The fourth is the *development of financial organization*, the banking and corporate control within the metropolis which is necessary to make the region more independent and without which it will not attain economic maturity. These four developmental stages need not be described as a sequence; they are also a classification of the broad economic functions of the metropolis—distribution, manufacturing, transportation-communication, and finance. If we knew the exact balance and interrelationship of these required for a city to become a true metropolis, we would be closer to a real under-

1. N. S. B. Gras, *An Introduction to Economic History* (New York: Harper and Brothers, 1922).

2. Giles A. Hubert, "A Framework for the Study of Peripheral Economic Areas," *Journal of Farm Economics*, XXVIII (August 1946), 807-808.

3. *Op. cit.*, p. 186.

standing of metropolitanism and would not be limited to a descriptive definition.

The classic study of the metropolitan community as it evolved in the United States is that by the human ecologist, R. D. McKenzie. This study, published twenty years ago, was the first empirical examination of the new "city regionalism" which, as McKenzie said, ". . . differs from the regionalism of former times in that it is the product of contact and division of labor rather than of mere geographic isolation."[4] McKenzie used the bio-social language of ecology to describe the competitive struggle among great cities for dominance and the adjustment process by which those that lost out in the process tended either to become integrated to the dominant metropolis by specialization or to die out, a symbiotic competition for survival similar to that in plant and animal "communities."

McKenzie showed that the particular spatial pattern of the dominant center and its dependent integrated communities in the United States owes much to the organization of modern transportation and communication, which has centralized the control of all types of commodity handling in the larger cities.[5] The axiate spiderweb pattern of city location in most of the nation was laid down in the era of rail transport. Motor transportation, it appears, has not created a new spatial ordering of metropolises but has opened up hinterlands in such a way as to increase interdependence between the central city and its surrounding towns.[6] In a similar way air transport may now be tightening the integration among the dominant centers by providing an improved communication mode—the rapid transit of key personnel.

Location in relation to transportation may give one city initial advantage as a distribution point or industrial site. The larger its population becomes, the larger its local market, and thus the greater its competitive advantage.[7] In the twentieth century it is not so much industrial development that leads to population growth as it is a concentration of what McKenzie calls "center work," highly specialized distributive and control activities.[8] Once this concentration has begun, it becomes in itself an important factor in creating more concentration. As McKenzie says, ". . . once a city becomes established as a regional distributing center, its banking, transportation, and other facilities compel new concerns to select it for their point of operation. This cumulative process is one of the chief factors in explaining the recent rapid growth of many . . . cities."[9]

---

4. R. D. McKenzie, *The Metropolitan Community* (New York: McGraw-Hill, 1933), p. 113.

5. R. D. McKenzie, "Dominance and World Organization," *American Journal of Sociology*, XXXIII (July 1927), 30.

6. McKenzie, *The Metropolitan Community*, pp. 7, 93.

7. R. D. McKenzie, "The Rise of Metropolitan Communities," in *Recent Social Trends in the United States, Report of the President's Research Committee on Social Trends*, I (New York: McGraw-Hill, 1933), 455.

8. McKenzie, *The Metropolitan Community*, pp. 53, 89.

9. *Ibid.*, p. 164.

2.   These statements of Gras and McKenzie have never been challenged;
they have remained in the literature for years as illuminating but untested
hypotheses. In 1949, however, Don J. Bogue took Gras and McKenzie's
theory as the basis for a statistical analysis of the structure of the metropolitan community and established beyond doubt the *fact* of metropolitan
dominance.[10] By an ingenious statistical method he found that cities over
100,000 in population (which he arbitrarily called "metropolises" without
considering their economic function) exert a consistent pattern of influence on the distribution of population and sustenance activities in the area
surrounding them. This influence is direct for a certain distance, roughly
for the retail delivery area or the commuting zone; but most of the influence is indirect and is closely related to the role played by the surrounding
cities and towns in mediating the controls of the central city.

Dominance therefore, according to Bogue, can be understood only if
one relates it to subdominance—successful competition of those hinterland
communities which accept the conditions imposed by the dominant city.[11]
Here is the empirical proof for Gras's dictum that the keynote of the
metropolitan economy is the functional interdependence of city and hinterland and for McKenzie's analogy of the metropolitan region to a symbiotic "community," an organismic whole of differentiated parts. From
Bogue's work it is also possible to learn much about the effects of the size
of the metropolis and of distance from it on the spatial distribution of population and activities related to dominance and subdominance. Unfortunately his statistical size classes lifted the cities from their specific areal
context, making it impossible to apply his findings directly to the metropolitan organization of any one geographical region like the South.

In drawing the lines of metropolitan dominance and integration in the
South, the writers feel that it is better at the present state of knowledge to
be tentative and discursive. Any statistical findings should be overlaid with
evidence about the cities from history, geography, and applied economics.
Certainly the first questions to be answered are *how much* and *what kind*
of metropolitan development can one expect to find at the mid-twentieth
century in the South?

GENESIS OF THE PATTERN. In colonial America, where the most important urban function was to get raw materials into the channels of world
trade, the larger cities were ports. The early struggle for metropolitan dominance was carried on between Boston, Philadelphia, and New York. Boston
led in population until 1750; in 1760 Philadelphia passed Boston, and by
1790 New York had passed Boston. Of the five cities of 8,000 or more population in the Census of 1790, only two—Baltimore and Charleston—were
southern. Baltimore, gateway city to the South, offered some competition

---

10. Don J. Bogue, *The Structure of the Metropolitan Community: A Study of
Dominance and Subdominance* (Ann Arbor: University of Michigan Press, 1949).
11. *Ibid.*, p. 18.

to New York's position at the end of the eighteenth century, but was soon relegated to secondary importance along with Boston and Philadelphia. Logically, Charleston with its fine harbor should have been a national contender against New York, but the collapse of Charleston's plan for a railroad to reach the rich resources of the Mississippi Valley finally forced it out of the running. Interestingly enough, New York's most serious rival in the 1800's was New Orleans, the only town in the United States with comparable inland water connections. In the steamboat period this city flourished even though its imports never equalled New York's. The outcome of the Civil War, however, settled the question. Since then, although New Orleans has often ranked as the nation's second port in tonnage, it has never risen to be a top-level metropolis. Once the east-west railroads had tapped the Mississippi Valley for New York, her ascendancy was assured. New Orleans had not felt the need of railways. Now the difference in the economic positions of New Orleans and Chicago can be gauged by the number of railroads entering each of the cities.

While it is impossible to determine when the pattern of metropolitan dominance was finally laid down in this country, once the New York-Chicago axis was formed, the supremacy of the northern metropolises over the southern was assured. It is doubtful that any of the southern cities could have won pre-eminence after the early nineteenth century, growing as they did under the shadow of the great.

In the ante-bellum plantation South there were four types of urban communities besides the sea ports—river ports, state capitals, county seats, and rural hamlets—all of which were small.[12] The early ocean ports were strictly limited by the size of the sustentation area they could count on with the prevailing mode of inland transportation. This led to the establishment of trading posts at the head of navigation, the fall line of the rivers. The list of these towns carries many familiar names: Richmond, Columbia, Augusta, Macon, Columbus, Montgomery, Selma. When river transport waned, many of these places continued to grow as markets. They were often the cotton collecting places and sometimes the state capitals.

It should not be forgotten that the patterning of urban location in the South took place under the domination of the cotton economy. Whereas financial control centered in several future markets and in points of export like New Orleans, the actual buying, collecting, and storing of cotton was spread among many small communities around railroad stations, cotton gins, and crossroad stores. This resulted in very few large cities and many towns of even size rather than the sharply competitive grading of population found in an industrialized area. In the reorganization of the cotton industry after the Civil War, the same trend can be noted. Thus in

12. *The South in the Building of the Nation.* VI: *Economic History, 1865-1909* (Richmond: The Southern Historical Publication Society, 1909), 607.

South Carolina the number of towns grew from sixteen in 1860 to 493 in 1880; yet only three of the towns in 1880 had as many as 4,000 people.[13]

Because cotton was for so long oriented to world trade, the railroad network may not have had quite as determinate an effect on the actual territorial location of cities in the South as it did in the great interior of this nation, but rail transport has had a great influence on the factors which have caused some cities to grow and others to languish. In the early days, just where the tracks were laid made a difference; later the difference came in the way the freight rate structure was organized. In many cases railroads followed the river transportation routes and merely reinforced the positions of the fall line cities and ports. Sometimes the railroads changed the lines of integration. There was no national policy in railroad building and no national network was envisaged. Cities possessed of capital and local enterprise tried to make rail connections and to capture trade, leaving many gaps that were later remedied by captains of industry who functioned as system builders and consolidators. Thus, in 1860 between the Baltimore and Ohio in the East and the Louisville and Nashville there was a 700-mile vacuum where not a single railroad cut across the Appalachians to tie southern trade with the Middle West. The scheming of all the Atlantic coastline cities from Richmond to Savannah to be the terminus of such an east-west railroad is lost in history.[14] As the main rail lines did develop, they ran north and south along the Piedmont and truncated the hinterlands of the Atlantic coast cities, relegating these ports forever to second place and bringing the life-blood of trade to the market cities of the interior.

The gateways to Europe, the ports, were no longer as important as the rail gateways to the North and Middle States. An example of the bitter rivalry among cities to capture the southern trade was the railroad building feud between Louisville and Cincinnati in the 1870's. Louisville tried to interfere with Cincinnati's efforts to keep her position when the river trade was seized by the railroads by refusing to let her use the Louisville and Nashville and by blocking in the Kentucky legislature Cincinnati's request for a right of way for the railroad she wished to build to Chattanooga. A threat of Congressional action gave Cincinnati her chance in 1872; and when that railroad was completed in 1880, the great Appalachian barrier was finally pierced. Not only did Cincinnati get a good share of the trade from the South, but freight rates to the Middle West were reduced as much as 20 per cent.[15] The location of gateway cities like Cincinnati and Richmond later became even more strategic when the regulations of the Federal Government on freight rates set them within Official Territory, the area of lower rates.

As any region develops its own productivity and economic complexity,

13. E. Merton Coulter, *The South During Reconstruction* (Baton Rouge: Louisiana State University Press, 1947), p. 253.

14. *Ibid.*, p. 236.

15. *Ibid.*, p. 238.

the locus of metropolitan development shifts from the "gateway" cities to those in the interior which the German theorists have called "central place" cities. This began to happen in the South before 1860 in the organization of distribution laid down by the railroads. It is in this trend that we see the beginnings of the phenomenal development of the two great regional metropolises, Atlanta first and later Dallas.

Here is the genesis of Atlanta:

. . . In 1843 it was a railroad station on a hilltop in central Georgia. It was given rail connections with the seacoast in 1845. In 1850 it had a population of 2,372; in 1860, 9,554; in 1870, 21,789. . . . [Located] on the broad inter-stream area of the Piedmont, to the south of the rough mountain and gorge lands of the Southern Appalachians and opposite low-grade gaps across these highlands, it was central to most of the Southeast. Atlanta could have been a few score miles north, south, east or west of its present location and still be the active Atlanta that it is; but the placing of the southern terminus of the first railroad in northern Georgia, the Western and Atlantic, fixed its location and it became a crossroads of railroads in early 1850's when a line was built northwestward from Augusta and another from Atlanta to Montgomery.[16]

A depot for supplies and a seat of manufacturing for the Confederacy, Atlanta rose from its wartime destruction to become a central point in the main currents of traffic and the regional capital for national distributors.

Dallas in the Southwest, as Parkins points out, resembles Atlanta in its location and development. Growing up on broad flat plains in one of the most fertile sections of the Southwest, Dallas reached 10,000 population by 1880 and entered the census classification of cities over 100,000 in 1920. After Atlanta's old cotton lands had reached their maximum production, the lands of Dallas's sustenance area continued in their prime, and the riches of oil from under those soils did far more than cotton to make Dallas a major distribution center.

A city becomes a metropolis, writes Gras, ". . . when most kinds of products of the district concentrate in it for trade as well as transit, i.e., when these products are paid for by wares that radiate from it and when the financial transactions involved in the exchange are provided by it."[17] Thus far in discussing the historical development of the southern metropolises, we have paid attention to trade and transit. Now we must consider what manufacturing can mean to a city. The most dramatic example of the rise of an industrial center to metropolitan status is that of Birmingham. In 1870 it was a cotton field in which two railroads happened to cross, 167 rail miles from the thriving trade center, Atlanta. In 1876 pig iron was first made and in 1879 the Pratt mines of coking coal were opened. It was not until 1888 that Birmingham saw its first ton of steel run through the furnaces. The town then contained about 26,000 people. Today Birmingham

16. Almon E. Parkins, *The South: Its Economic and Geographic Development* (New York: John Wiley and Sons, 1938), p. 461.

17. *Op. cit.*, p. 294.

is the South's one center of heavy industry, has the largest amount of capital invested in manufacturing in the Southeast, and is the region's largest labor employment center. Coal, iron, limestone, cast iron pipe, steel and local manufactures have contributed to the city's position. Because of its manufacturing activities, Birmingham can be its own best market. Without this backlog of local buyers it could not have risen to metropolitan importance so close to Atlanta.

A consideration of the locational pattern of southern industry, however, makes Birmingham's centralization the exception rather than the rule. The well-chronicled recent movement of industry into the South has come about at a time when the combination of hydro-electric power and motor transport has permitted location in the areas around urban centers rather than in them. Bogue proved that if a metropolis can encourage industry within a radius of forty-five miles it has the same effect for metropolitan dominance as location within the central city.[18] McKenzie's insight—that it is not production so much as the "center work" of production that fosters urban growth—is nowhere better proved than in the developmen of Charlotte in an area where industrial plants are scattered over the countryside.

Only within recent years has the South pulled far enough out of its colonial economy to develop much financial organization within the region. Most important in this connection has been the effect of a legislated change—the establishment of the Federal Reserve system in 1914, which provided twelve regional cities with bankers' banks in which reserves against deposits were to be kept. The selection of these centers was on the basis of the "flow of trade" and the urban connections of the small town banks. Whatever mistakes the decision-makers made have been obliterated by the fact that once a city became a regional capital of finance, the flow of trade actually went its way. Federal Reserve cities have had increases in bankers' balances with some repatriation of funds from the New York money market. This has meant lowered interest rates for these communities, a factor which seems of special importance in the higher order distribution (wholesale trade) which is central to metropolitan function. It is also agreed that the system has made for greater elasticity of credit in the movement of regional crops and products and that, as a result, the smaller cities have been tied more closely to the selected financial centers. In the South this has meant a closer tie with Richmond, Atlanta, and Dallas within the region of our study and with St. Louis and Kansas City on its northern edge. The Federal Reserve Branch cities which channel this integration for the South are listed by districts in Table 1.

In all this fragmentary historical evidence of the genesis of the pattern may be found the answers to the question posed earlier: *how much* and *what kind* of metropolitan development may one expect in the South of

18. *Op. cit.*, p. 183.

1950? It is evident that southern metropolises, no matter how rapidly they are now growing, will be smaller than the giants of the New York-Chicago axis because in all specialized functions they are subdominant to these super-metropolises (as in fact is the whole nation). Any change in their general position in the metropolitan hierarchy is unlikely, for it is in the nature of dominance that once it is gained it reinforces itself and sets down a remarkably stable pattern. Meanwhile modifications in the balance of power will continue as the South moves toward economic maturity. The location of industry may modify the kind of constellation these southern cities make when they are considered as a regional unit; but a glance at any map shows that here are no huge industrial satellites crowding the greater cities. Instead there have grown up a number of well-spaced, fairly evenly populated, middle-sized centers which should have considerable autonomy over their surrounding areas, the pattern set down by the market towns of the old agricultural economy.

Table 1—Federal Reserve Banks and Branches for the South

Richmond	Atlanta	Dallas	St. Louis	Kansas City
Charlotte	Birmingham	El Paso	Little Rock	Oklahoma City
	Jacksonville	San Antonio	Louisville	
	Nashville	Houston	Memphis	
	New Orleans			

THE PRESENT-DAY PATTERN. A second important question concerns the individual cities: which of the larger ones may be considered metropolises in 1950 and how do they rank in the dominance they exert? The writers have explored this question with a simple statistical technique which is their own but which is grounded in the suggestions of the theorists and in prior research.

In reviewing the methods used in determining the metropolitan centers of the United States, we find that except for one British geographer, writers have been content to name the Federal Reserve Bank cities and the cities where the Branch Banks are located. Actually this may be as good a rough classification as any simply because financial organization tends to set a capstone on the distributive and control functions crucial to dominance. Gras limited his list of metropolises to eleven of the Federal Reserve cities —the metropolises of the South, therefore, being Richmond, Atlanta, and Dallas. McKenzie, interested in the territorial limits of metropolitan regions, used the circulation areas of great city newspapers as his single index. The basis of his list of metropolises was the Federal Reserve Bank and Branch cities with an occasional Branch city omitted and others added to follow newspaper areas. In the region of our interest, Knoxville was the only addition to the list of Bank and Branch centers (Table 1) and San Antonio was omitted.[19]

19. McKenzie, The Metropolitan Community.

The close relation of these banking centers with wholesale trade has already been pointed out. The market research carried on by the Department of Commerce in the 1920's named as southern wholesale trade centers all the Bank and Branch cities, adding to them only Knoxville and Chattanooga for the Southeast and Fort Worth for the Southwest.[20] The definitive mapping of trade areas done under the NRA in the early 1930's used the Federal Reserve sub-districts, adjusted somewhat to geographical barriers, lines of transport, etc., as wholesale trade areas.[21] This juxtaposition of bankers' banks with specialized distribution seems to point to the heart of metropolitan dominance. In fact, Dorothy Hope Tisdale, in a statistical analysis of the factors involved in urbanization, found the correlation between the higher-order distributive factor (wholesale trade) and the growth of very large cities to be about twice as high as between such growth and the lower-order distribution (retail trade) and production.[22] Bogue found that wholesale sales per capita in the metropolitan centers were seven times those of the hinterland, a degree of concentration far greater than in the other basic sustenance activities he investigated—retail trade, services, and manufacturing.[23]

Dickinson, the British geographer, in his attempt to outline metropolitan regions independent of the Federal Reserve districts, centered his method on the volume of wholesale trade per capita, which he weighted with the volume of manufacturing and two ingenious indices: warehousing space and the number of branch offices listed in Thomas's *Register of Manufacturers*. He came out with a smaller list than McKenzie and with two orders of magnitude. Atlanta and Dallas with Fort Worth were top-level; Birmingham, Jacksonville, Louisville, Memphis, New Orleans, Richmond, and Houston were the secondary metropolises.[24] This has been the most sophisticated attempt to differentiate the true metropolises from the other large cities; but it is twenty years old.

The meager research that has been focused on this problem is perhaps as helpful in pointing out what *not* to do as in providing positive suggestions. There is no question that the most important index to metropolitan status is the concentration of wholesale trade, but it seems that efforts to mark off the areal limits of dominance by either trade or the closely associated newspaper circulation has meant too literal a tie to territory for the different contingencies on space involved in metropolitan influence. In certain specialized functions the whole United States may well be the

20. U.S. Department of Commerce, *Market Data Handbook* (Washington, D.C.: Government Printing Office, 1927).

21. Robert A. Dier, *Natural Areas of Trade in the United States* (Washington: Office of NRA, Division of Review, February 1936).

22. Dorothy Hope Tisdale, Urbanization: A Study of Population Concentration in the United States and its Relation to Social Change (unpublished doctoral dissertation, University of North Carolina, 1942), p. 129.

23. *Op. cit.*, p. 173.

24. Robert E. Dickinson, "Metropolitan Regions of the United States," *Geographical Review*, XXIV (1934), 278-286.

hinterland of one city. On the level of consumer buying, the trade area marked off with pins on a map makes sense, but not for the complexities of economic structure. For this reason no attempt will be made here to outline the area of dominance of each city as has been done heretofore. The assumption is that the extent of influence will be at least crudely reflected in the volume of the activity in the central city. It seems better to use several indices than a single index if for no other reason than the tradition of "safety in numbers." It also seems advisable not to *assume* that the Federal Reserve Bank and Branch cities are the metropolitan centers before investigating their influence. Nor should it be assumed that the largest cities are necessarily the metropolises; here we should use Gras's insight that the size of certain functions and not the size of the population is crucial.

To rank southern cities in their metropolitan function, six indices related to dominance have been selected. The first is *Wholesale Sales* (1948). The second, *Business Services Receipts* (1948), concerns the most specialized type of service which is used by larger concerns, defined in the census as including advertising, consumer credit, adjustment and collection agencies, news syndicates, mailing lists, machine rental and repair, telephone answering, etc. In a sense this measures the degree of specialization, the premise being that the metropolis is the most specialized community of its area and thus the least typical.[25] The third, taken from Dickinson, *Number of Branch Offices*, is an excellent index of the channeling function Gras stressed in his definition. All of the first three factors stress high-level distribution, specialization, and control; and in the construction of the rank-score from the six indices, they are weighted two to one. (The statistical findings of Tisdale and Bogue substantiate this.) The remaining three indices, each with a weight of one, are *Retail Sales* (not a metropolitan specialty but an index of size), *Bank Clearings* (used as an index of business activity which also reveals the presence of Federal Reserve Banks), and *Value Added by Manufacturing* (the most sensitive index of the volume rather than the type of industrial activity). Except perhaps for Bank Clearings of Federal Reserve cities, these last three indices reflect the gross underpinnings a city has for building its market and amassing wealth.

The twenty-nine metropolitan areas of the South which contain central cities of 100,000 and over were chosen as the most likely candidates for metropolitan status. They were ranked according to the six indices. So that their relative positions in each factor would be strictly comparable, z-scores using the standard deviation were constructed for each index; those of the first three indices were weighted by two; the weighted z-scores (actually accurate rank-scores) were converted to make all of them positive numbers, added, and then divided by six to arrive at an average rank-score for *Metropolitan Function*. This score for each of the twenty-nine metropolitan areas can be seen by consulting the first column of Table 2. To point up

---

25. Bogue, *op. cit.*, p. 61.

the difference between size of metropolitan function and population size, a similarly constructed rank-score for size of population is given in the second column. The relation of these two factors for each city is shown in simple graphic form in Figure 1.

Table 2—Cities of Over 100,000 in the South, Ranked by Metropolitan Function

City	Rank Score on Metropolitan Function	Rank Score on Size
SECOND ORDER METROPOLISES		
Atlanta	9.91	6.67
Dallas	9.71	6.38
THIRD ORDER METROPOLISES		
Houston	8.10	7.43
New Orleans	7.36	6.77
Memphis	6.62	5.67
Louisville	6.43	6.18
Birmingham	5.94	6.07
SUBDOMINANTS with METROPOLITAN CHARACTERISTICS		
Richmond	5.34	4.83
Fort Worth	5.24	5.00
Oklahoma City	5.02	4.81
*Miami	4.90	5.71
Charlotte	4.80	4.11
Jacksonville	4.79	4.70
Tulsa	4.60	4.40
Nashville	4.59	4.79
Little Rock	4.54	4.09
*San Antonio	4.48	5.75
*Norfolk-Portsmouth	4.42	5.28
El Paso	4.38	4.12
SUBDOMINANTS		
Tampa-St. Petersburg	4.18	5.26
Chattanooga	4.11	4.38
Knoxville	3.84	4.88
Shreveport	3.62	4.00
Mobile	3.54	4.29
Savannah	3.46	3.87
Corpus Christi	3.30	3.94
Montgomery	3.25	3.79
Baton Rouge	3.25	3.90
Austin	3.19	3.92

* Miami because of its resort function and San Antonio and Norfolk-Portsmouth because of military installations probably rank somewhat higher than their basic metropolitan function would place them. They are essentially Subdominants.

The most certain finding yielded by this method is that Atlanta and Dallas with similar scores on metropolitan function stand head and shoulders above the other cities. There is no doubt about their being the regional capitals. These two cities have been classified as Second Order Metropolises, with the idea that the First Order Metropolis has a nationwide sphere of influence. A glance at Figure 1 will show that the selection of the Third Order Metropolises might be questioned. Houston, New

Orleans, Memphis, and Louisville rank high enough to be considered dominant cities of this class. The question is whether one should include Birmingham and not the Federal Reserve city, Richmond. The evidence of the indices taken singly points to a decline in Richmond's metropolitan function. Only in Bank Clearings and Value Added by Manufacturing does it rank within the first nine cities; its proximity to Baltimore, Philadelphia, and New York means subdominance in many functions. It may be too that the remarkable emergence of Charlotte is infringing on the hinterland of Richmond. Certainly Richmond's metropolitan position must be considered more marginal than it has been in the past.

Class III, which has been named Subdominants with Metropolitan Characteristics, includes a number of smaller cities which have important distributive and control functions over considerable area and which have the balance in specialization associated with metropolitanism: Richmond, Fort Worth, Oklahoma City, Charlotte, Jacksonville, Tulsa, Nashville, Little Rock, and on the geographic fringe, El Paso. Although their scores were fairly high, consideration of their distorted size and specialization should remove Miami, the resort city, and San Antonio and Norfolk-Portsmouth, areas of military installations, to Class IV as Subdominants. It should be noted, however, that Norfolk-Portsmouth is a strong center of wholesale trade and might well qualify for Class III. Class IV is residual as far as metropolitan function is concerned. What is interesting here as well as in Class III is the evenness of the scores. One wonders if there may be very little difference between these urban centers and some of the industrial and distribution centers with populations between 50,000 and 100,000: Roanoke, Winston-Salem, Greensboro, Columbia, Macon—to name a few. In fact, if one looks at the twenty-two cities that have been classified as Subdominants, their independence is striking; not one is a really dependent satellite.

Worthy of note here is the high rank of Fort Worth in metropolitan characteristics. Only thirty-three miles from Dallas, it has managed by organizing the hinterland to the north and west to resemble in dominance a traditional metropolis like Richmond. Dallas and Fort Worth taken together surpass all the cities of the Southeast in their potential. Houston, startling in its rapid development, has taken command as the specialized point of export for the rich oil industry of Texas and Oklahoma. From the day its inland ship channel cut off the growth of Galveston, Houston has offered New Orleans strong competition as a gulf port. Houston has played its important role without blocking the continual development of Dallas and Fort Worth, illustrating again the values of specialization among metropolises. Here an examination of the difference in the import-export trade of New Orleans and Houston would probably explain how they manage to live together.

It seems that we can place some confidence in this method of selecting the metropolitan centers of the region because the seven cities which qualified—Atlanta, Dallas, Houston, New Orleans, Memphis, Louisville,

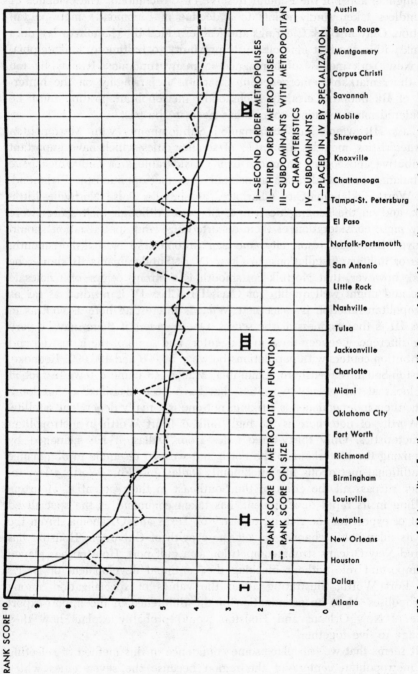

FIG. 1.—Scores of Metropolitan Function Compared with Scores of Size, Metropolitan Areas of the South with Central Cities of over 100,000 in 1950

and Birmingham—are the only ones which have qualified in *every* other attempt to delineate metropolises. The most significant finding, however, is that the pattern of dominance in the South is not nearly as marked as the pattern of strong sub-dominance. Here we may have caught the emerging urban configuration of the twentieth century. Southern cities are growing in the time of hydro-electric power and motor and air transport. The nation is under the shadow of the kind of air attack that may force some modification of the nineteenth-century concentration in the Northeast. The division of labor that is being worked out in the Piedmont of the Carolinas does not involve heavy industry; but it bears watching, as does the little city of Charlotte which already is more of a metropolis than some larger rivals. And of course Charlotte cannot be understood unless one considers its interdependence with Greenville, Winston-Salem, High Point, Greensboro, etc.

In Figure 2, the constellation of cities has been moored to territory so that it is possible to trace the major lines of integration. The great Appalachian barrier set the spatial pattern early in the South's history. Transportation lanes run south to north, toward New York in the east and toward Chicago west of the mountains. The Dallas-Fort Worth metropolitan region is oriented to the Chicago-New York axis through St. Louis and Kansas City. On this map-like diagram, one can also see the vacuum out of which Memphis was able to carve a hinterland. The orientation of the South's great ports—like Houston and New Orleans—to intercoastal traffic is indicated by the broken lines.

THE METROPOLIS AND ITS HINTERLAND. Metropolitan regionlism involves more than the relation of dominance and subdominance among great cities. In the organization of its hinterland, the metropolis extends its sway through subdominant centers to the smallest hamlet and rural homestead within its orbit. In the New South as elsewhere, the metropolis is related to its region in the way it integrates communities of different size, position, and function. Here each center plays a distinct and necessary role and the region itself can be thought of as a constellation of communities.[26]

What processes have been operating here and what changes have occurred in the South within the recent period? As elsewhere, men, activities and products are being drawn into closer relations with central cities and transportation has brought rural life more under the dominance of the metropolis. Warren Wilson once drew the radius of the farm trade center, the basic unit in this hierarchy, as the distance of a day's team haul. The extension of this radius by means of the auto, truck, and hard-surfaced highway created a new pattern of market and service areas. Rural people are tied in with more trading centers and have a wider element of choice and variety; the remaining centers have a broader population base and

26. Radhakamal Mukerjee, *Social Ecology* (New York: Longmans, Green and Company, 1945), p. 87.

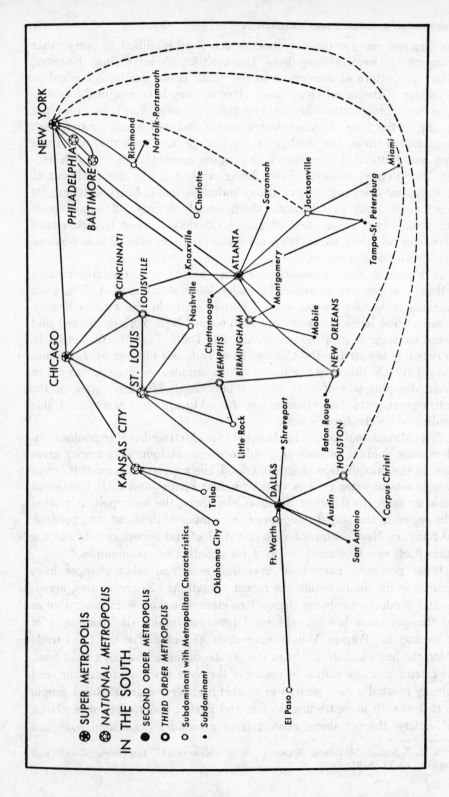

IN THE SOUTH

SUPER METROPOLIS

NATIONAL METROPOLIS

● SECOND ORDER METROPOLIS

◎ THIRD ORDER METROPOLIS

◦ Subdominant with Metropolitan Characteristics

· Subdominant

NEW YORK

PHILADELPHIA

BALTIMORE

Richmond

Norfolk-Portsmouth

Charlotte

Savannah

Jacksonville

Miami

Tampa-St. Petersburg

CINCINNATI

LOUISVILLE

Knoxville

ATLANTA

Montgomery

Nashville

Chattanooga

Mobile

CHICAGO

ST. LOUIS

MEMPHIS

BIRMINGHAM

NEW ORLEANS

Little Rock

Baton Rouge

KANSAS CITY

Shreveport

Tulsa

Oklahoma City

DALLAS

Austin

HOUSTON

Corpus Christi

Ft. Worth

San Antonio

El Paso

FIG. 2—Metropolitan Organization of the South, with Orders of Dominance and Major Lines of Integration

appear more closely related to one another and to dominant metropolitan centers than they did three decades ago.

For the smaller rural centers the problem at times, as H. C. Nixon points out, has seemed to be one of survival. In a Louisiana study T. Lynn Smith found that trade centers less favorably situated in regard to trade and transportation had been smothered out of existence from 1901-1930 while a greater share of activity was organized about the large centers. Division of labor has been taking place among these centers. The tendency for communities of different size and position to compete in supplying every type of service is giving way to a differentiation of function.[27] Many studies indicate that specialized goods and services, those satisfying needs that can be deferred, are concentrated in larger centers. All indications show that the farmers' trading centers are caught in the continuing movement toward urbanization and the dominance of the city.

The South, then, is seen to be following a process already highly advanced throughout the Western world. In recent decades its rate of concentration around metropolitan centers has been exceptionally high. In the past the rural patterns have greatly influenced, if not determined, the cultural and economic life of the region. Today in the South as elsewhere rural and urban ways are merging and folk culture and traditional agricultural modes of life are being influenced in new directions by contacts with the metropolis. Cities are the central source of a new type of uniformity and standardization. To say that the South lags in the process of urbanization, that its subdominant metropolises live in the shadow of the great, that they cannot duplicate the functions of national centers long in existence is not to render an adverse verdict on southern urbanization.

It is reasonable to assume that in the South cities of lesser density and size can satisfy the requirements of metropolitan function. Reaching through the network of communities to the region's farmsteads, they can well meet the tests of economic efficiency and support a mode of life that gives greater accessibility to the open country. This balance of the urban and rural ways of life has often been advocated but rarely achieved.

27. T. Lynn Smith, *Farm Trade Centers in Louisiana, 1901-1931* (Bulletin, Agricultural Experiment Station, Louisiana State University, 1936).

URBANIZATION AND THE DEVELOPMENT
OF PRE-INDUSTRIAL AREAS

Kingsley Davis and Hilda Hertz Golden

The process of urbanization, known to be intimately associated with economic development, deserves close attention if we are to understand the recent and future mechanisms of change in pre-industrial areas. Yet up to the present our comparative knowledge of cities and of urbanization is slight, particularly for underdeveloped areas. Considerable interest was shown in the subject toward the end of the last century—in the works of Levasseur, Meuriot, and Adna Weber—but since then, except for isolated cases such as Pirenne and Mark Jefferson, there has been little work done in the comparative analysis of cities and urbanization.

This does not mean that there has been no interest in cities. On the contrary, the literature on cities and city problems is enormous. But most of this material deals with a particular town or at most with a single province or country. Conspicuously absent are systematic comparative analyses putting together and interpreting data on the cities of different countries and different cultures.

Indeed, the study of cities and of urbanization has been heavily confined to countries of European culture. As a result many of our generalizations about urban phenomena, though treated as if they were universal, are actually limited to Western (and often to American or West European) experience and are wrong when applied to most of the rest of the world. In other words, there is as yet no general science of cities. Without such a general science, one cannot get far in analyzing and documenting the interrelations between urbanization and economic development.

The claim may be made that a comparative science of urban phenomena is impossible because the data are lacking for most of the world. But this view is hardly justified. In the first place, if we always waited for perfect information before attempting to build a comparative social science we would wait forever. In the second place, the data on cities are more numerous, more accurate, and more accessible than most people who have not looked into the matter seem to believe. The fact that the statistical materials are often lacking or inaccurate in a given country or for a given time, is not a signal for defeat. It is rather a challenge to ingenuity to make the best use of what is available and to supplement this with systematic

Reprinted from *Economic Development and Cultural Change*, Vol. III (October, 1954), pp. 6-26, by permission of the authors and the journal.

estimates wherever necessary. In the program of urban studies at Columbia University a modest effort, known as the World Urban Resources Index, is being made to gather and systematize basic data on all large cities. Since material from this project is utilized to some extent in what follows, the Index is described briefly in the Appendix; but the body of the paper draws upon a wider context of comparative work in so far as it bears on the relation of urbanization to economic development in pre-industrial areas.

URBANIZATION VERSUS THE PRESENCE OF CITIES. At the outset a distinction must be made between urbanization and the mere presence of cities. Urbanization as the term is used here refers to a ratio—the urban people divided by the total population. It is therefore as much a function of the rural as of the urban population, the formula being as follows:

$$u = \frac{P_c}{P_t}$$

where "u" is urbanization, "P_c" is city population, and "P_t" is total population.

Obviously the degree of urbanization in a given country or region can vary independently of the absolute number of people living in cities. India has more people in cities than the Netherlands, but it is far less urbanized than the latter. In other words, by transposing in the preceding equation, we find

$$P_c = uP_t$$

Since the two values "u" "P_c" can vary independently, they have to be kept separate in any comparative analysis. Also, the sheer number of cities in a given country may be as much a function of total population as of degree of urbanization. The distribution of urbanization over the globe, in short, is not equivalent to either the distribution of cities or the distribution of urban inhabitants.[1]

---

1. To forestall needless debate, a word should be said about the rural-urban dichotomy. The lack of a standard dividing point between "rural" and "urban" has often been regarded as a serious if not overwhelming handicap to international comparisons of urbanization. Yet such a conclusion is unwarranted. The similarity of definition is greater than the citation of extreme examples usually suggests (see the *Demographic Yearbook* for 1952, pp. 9-12). Also, a detailed study of comparative urbanization would not in any case be satisfied with a simple urban-rural dichotomy, since a continuum is clearly involved. In the past too much emphasis has been placed on the dichotomy. The assumption has been that there are two mutually exclusive but internally homogeneous categories, and that all we need to do is count the number of people falling into each of them. But almost anyone will admit that a man living in a city of several million is, at least demographically, more urban than one living in a town of 10,000.

The better principle is to think in terms of an index of urbanization. One can use as an index the proportion of people in places of 10,000 and over, 20,000 and over, or any other figure one wishes. Actually, since there is a certain regularity about the pyramid of cities by size, the proportion in any major size-class tends to bear a sys-

With respect to urbanization, there can be no doubt that the under-developed areas of the world have less of it than the advanced areas. If we take as underdeveloped, or pre-industrial, all areas with more than 50 per cent of their occupied males engaged in agriculture,[2] we find that only 9 per cent of their combined population lives in cities of 100,000 or over, whereas for the other countries (industrial) the proportion is 27 per cent. Table 1 gives the indices of urbanization for the world's countries and territories classified by degree of agriculturalism. It can be seen that the degree of urbanization increases sharply as industrialism increases.

Table 1—Degree of Urbanization in World's Countries and Territories Classified by Degree of Agriculturalism

Per Cent of Gainfully Occupied Males in Agriculture	Number of Countries	Per Cent of Population in Cities 100,000-plus
0-19	11	32.3
20-29	11	23.6
30-39	7	23.2
40-49	7	21.9
50-59	16	17.7
60-69	17	8.9
70-plus	86	6.3

It follows that those parts of the world still mainly in the peasant-agrarian stage of economic development manifest the least urbanization. A continental breakdown, as given in Table 2, shows that Asia (excluding the USSR) and Africa are the most agrarian and the least urbanized continents.

These results are of course what one would expect, but it is worth having figures to show the precise extent of the association between economic development and urbanization. Another method of showing the relationship is by a correlation coefficient. As of 1950, the (Pearsonian) correlation between degree of industrialization and degree of urbanization, as measured by our indices, was .86, taking the countries and territories of the world as our units.

It is plain, then, that urbanization is unequally distributed in the world. The achievement of high levels of urbanization anywhere in the world had to wait for the industrial revolution. This remarkable transformation had its rise in one part of the world, western Europe, and thence

tematic relation to the proportion in other size-classes. Thus the percentage of a population living in cities above 100,000 has a ratio to the percentage in places above 5,000 which is roughly similar from one country to another. An index of urbanization is therefore quite feasible for comparative purposes.

2. This index of economic development seems to be both convenient and reliable. In the Population Division of the Bureau of Applied Social Research at Columbia University the index has been computed or estimated for all the countries and colonies of the world. These figures are used throughout the present paper in designating countries as "industrial" or "pre-industrial."

spread to other parts as industrialism spread. With the exception of Japan, the centers of urbanization today are the places where industrialization has gone hand in hand with the expansion of European civilization. In many instances, the spread of this kind of civilization has embraced "new" areas of vast extent and sparse native populations, such as North and South America and Australia. The urbanism of Europe was directly transplanted to these new areas, so that they became highly urbanized without acquiring overall dense populations. They were not hampered by the necessity of a slow evolution from densely settled peasant-agrarianism to modern industrialism. Thus we find that some of the most urbanized regions of the world are among the most sparsely settled, whereas some of the least urbanized are among the most densely settled.

Table 2—Per Cent of Population in Cities and in Agriculture in Major World Areas, Ca. 1950

Continent	Per Cent of Economically Active Males Engaged in Agriculture	Per Cent of Population in Cities 100,000-plus
WORLD	60	13
North America	17	29
Oceania	35	41
Europe	38	21
USSR	54	18
South America	62	18
Central America and Caribbean	69	12
Asia	70	8
Africa	78	6

THE SHARE OF CITIES AND PEOPLE IN UNDERDEVELOPED AREAS. The concentration of urbanization in industrial areas should not lead us to believe that most of the cities and most of the city people are found in these areas, as is commonly thought. The truth is that three-fourths of the world's population lives in pre-industrial countries. Although these countries are mainly rural, they are all urbanized to some degree because of the commercial impact of the industrial nations. Consequently, we find that the underdeveloped countries contain as many cities as do the industrial countries, as Table 3 shows. The countries having more than half of their occupied males in agriculture, forestry and fishing (the underdeveloped nations) contain 463 large cities. From the last column of Table 3 it can be seen that the underdeveloped countries have more people (160 million) living in cities of 100,000 or more than do the industrialized nations (155 million).

The same general finding can be shown in another way. If, instead of grouping countries according to their degree of agriculturalism, we group them according to their degree of urbanization, it turns out that the more rural countries have as many large cities and as many dwellers in large cities as the more urbanized ones.

Table 3—Distribution of World's Large Cities and City Population by Degree of Agriculturalism of Countries

Per Cent of Active Males in Agriculture	Number of Countries	Number of Cities	Per Cent of All Cities	Population in Cities (ooo's)	Per Cent of Total City Population
0-29	22	286	31.9	101,438	32.2
30-49	14	148	16.5	53,721	17.1
50-69	33	287	32.0	97,429	30.9
70-plus	86	176	19.6	62,478	19.8
Total	155	897	100.0	315,067	100.0

It becomes clear that the science of cities must concern itself just as much with underdeveloped countries as with advanced countries. Too much of the past study and interpretation of cities has ignored this simple fact. Deductions concerning "the city" have been made principally on the basis of American and European cases, embracing at best less than half of the universe being discussed.

URBANIZATION AND AGRICULTURAL DENSITY. The point has already been made that no relation exists between degree of urbanization and average density of population. Some of the underdeveloped and hence least urbanized countries are among the most densely settled, and some of the most highly developed are among the most sparsely settled; and vice versa. There is, however, a relationship—a negative one—between urbanization and what we call agricultural density (the number of males occupied with agriculture, hunting and forestry per square mile of cultivated land), as exhibited in Table 4. Although this negative relationship seems to affront common sense (for we might think that cities demand more agricultural

Table 4—Agricultural Density According to Degree of Urbanism

Per Cent of Population in Cities 100,000-plus	Agricultural Males per Square Mile of Agricultural Land*
0- 9.9	136
10-19.9	72
20-29.9	67
30-plus	13

* Agricultural males are arbitrarily defined as those gainfully occupied in farming, hunting, fishing, and forestry. Agricultural land is defined as including land under crops, lying fallow, and in orchards. In a few cases the proportion of fishermen or herdsmen is so large as to make the ratio meaningless. In such cases adjustments have been made to approximate the actutal man-land ratio in agriculture. One reason for lumping farmers and fishermen, etc., is tha* the figures are so often grouped that way in census.

products and hence require a dense population in rural areas), the reason for it is apparent upon reflection.[3] As economic development and hence urbanization occur, agriculture tends to become more efficient. Capital equipment, science, and better organization replace manpower. Less labor is required per unit of land to produce the same or even a higher agricul-

---

3. See Kingsley Davis, "Population and the Further Spread of Industrial Society," *Proceedings of the American Philosophical Society*, XCV (Feb. 1951), 10-13.

tural output. The growing cities, in addition to furnishing a market for commercial crops and supplying manufactured goods and services for improving the per-man productivity of agriculture, absorb people from the countryside. As a consequence, the farming population may diminish not only as a proportion of the total population but also in absolute terms (as it has done in the United States and several other industrial countries in recent decades).

The oft-condemned "depopulation" of rural areas is therefore a sign of economic modernization, the growth of cities, a boon to progress. This statement is not only true of densely settled agrarian countries such as those of southeast Asia but also true of sparsely settled ones such as those of central and east Africa. The latter, despite a low overall density, have a high ratio of people to land under cultivation. Their main advantage often lies in the fact that an increase in the land under cultivation is possible on a big scale, so that rural-urban migration does not have to absorb the entire surplus population released by the modernization of agriculture.

THE GROWTH OF URBANIZATION IN UNDERDEVELOPED AREAS. The facts of the current situation—the positive correlation between urbanization and industrialization and the negative association between urbanization and agricultural density—suggest what one might expect to find historically. The present concentration of urbanization (as distinct from cities) in the advanced nations is almost wholly a product of the last 150 years. In 1800 the population in large cities was distributed over the earth in much the same fashion as the general population. With the rise and spread of industrialism in the nineteenth century, the European peoples, as we noted, rapidly and markedly increased their degree of urbanization. The hiatus between the advanced and nonadvanced parts of the world, however, is but a temporary phenomenon—a lag due to the time required for the geographical and crosscultural spread of a radically new type of economic and social organization. As the great transformation has been completed in the most advanced countries, as these countries have achieved a high degree of urbanization, the rate of growth of their cities has begun to slacken. Indeed, this has noticeably happened in the twentieth century in countries such as Britain, Switzerland, the Netherlands, and the United States (see Figures 1 and 2). It is bound to happen, because as the proportion of the population living in cities becomes greater and greater, the chance of maintaining the *rate* of increase in that proportion becomes less and less. Furthermore, we know that the growth of cities has been mainly a result of rural-urban migration, which has contributed at times far more to urban numbers than the natural increase in cities could ever contribute. As the rural proportion declines to a small fraction of the total population, the cities have an ever smaller pool of people to draw on for the maintenance of growth rates.

The charts show the steady decline in the rate of urbanization in the

most advanced countries in recent decades. But at the same time that this
has been happening in industrial areas, the rate of urbanization has been
increasing in most underdeveloped regions, as the charts also show. There
is thus going on today a balancing of accounts, an incipient evening out
of urbanization throughout the world. As a result the next fifty or one
hundred years may find the city population once again distributed roughly
in proportion to the world's total population. If so, it will mark the end
of a gigantic cycle—the urbanization of the world.

The rapidity of urbanization in most of the pre-industrial areas is surprising. Only in such out-of-the-way places as Saudi Arabia, Yemen, and
some African territories has urban expansion failed to make much head-
way, and these countries are few in number and small in total population.
As a group, the underdeveloped countries, with 7 per cent of their people
in 100,000-plus cities and 11 per cent in 20,000-plus cities in 1950, have
moved some distance toward a high degree of urbanization. The general
picture is therefore one of fast urbanization comparable to that experienced at earlier periods in the now industrialized nations. Since the more
recently industrialized countries have tended to urbanize faster once they
started than the older countries did, there is reason to believe that the
future pace of the currently underdeveloped regions may be fast indeed.
Should these regions achieve the rapid rate of urbanization experienced
either by Germany or Japan, they will as a group become highly urbanized (with more than 15 per cent of their population in large cities) within
the next fifty years.

The pace of urbanization in the backward areas shows that they are
anything but static. Sometimes, when one looks at the myriad difficulties
and inefficiencies in the pre-industrial countries, when it appears that immemorial customs still prevail and that there is a vicious circle of poverty
breeding poverty, one is tempted to think that these societies are static.
But the data on trends of city growth and urbanization show them to
possess highly dynamic attributes. Since urbanization is not an isolated
culture trait but is a function of the total economy, its rapid growth indicates that fundamental changes are occurring at a rate sufficient to transform these pre-industrial societies within a few decades.

These generalizations concerning the underdeveloped countries as a
whole seem well worth pondering. They can be documented by statistical
analysis of a comparative kind. At the same time, anyone will recognize
that the pre-industrial countries are not all alike. Some are more urbanized than others. Some differ in demography, economy, and society from
others. It therefore becomes instructive to consider particular countries
which represent types of cases—types that may recur in various underdeveloped countries but are not found everywhere within the pre-industrial category. Accordingly, we have picked out a few countries for
particular analysis.

In this attempt to analyze briefly some particular case, two things

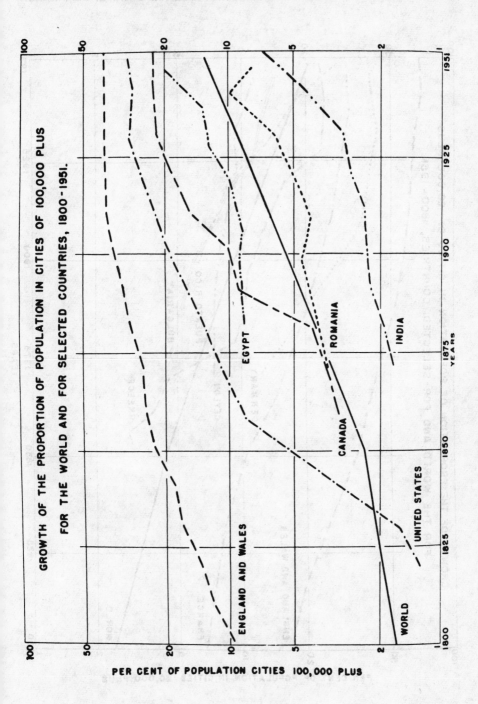

GROWTH OF THE PROPORTION OF POPULATION IN CITIES OF 100,000 PLUS
FOR THE WORLD AND FOR SELECTED COUNTRIES, 1800-1951.

PER CENT OF POPULATION CITIES 100,000 PLUS

FIGURE 1

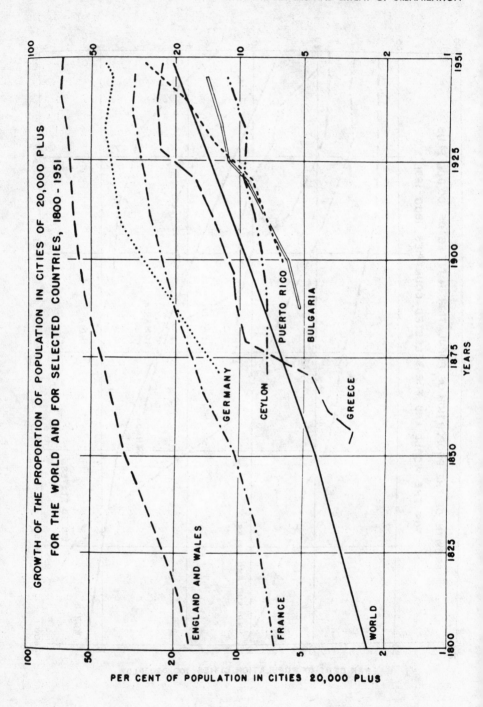

GROWTH OF THE PROPORTION OF POPULATION IN CITIES OF 20,000 PLUS
FOR THE WORLD AND FOR SELECTED COUNTRIES, 1800 - 1951

PER CENT OF POPULATION IN CITIES 20,000 PLUS

FIGURE 2

should be borne in mind. First, as one would expect, our statistics for underdeveloped areas are not as good as those for other areas. They are, however, as good as those we have for industrial nations when they were at a comparable stage of development. As we move back in time the data become poorer, so that long historical series on the underdeveloped countries are quite scarce and our selection of illustrative countries is narrowed. Second, from a scientific point of view little can be learned from a particular case without the benefit of comparative analysis. When a nation is described as a "type" with reference to urbanization it can be so described only in terms of its similarities and contrasts to other countries. Our case analyses are therefore undertaken with comparative statistical analysis in the background, as will become evident.

The particular areas selected for brief presentation below are India, an old agrarian country with a moderate rate of urbanization; Egypt, an over-urbanized and disorganized agrarian country; and central and west Africa, a region of revolutionary new urbanization. The study of these regions in comparative terms raises some fundamental questions about the dynamics of urbanization.

THE CASE OF INDIA.[4] Since pre-industrial countries are not all "underdeveloped" to the same degree, one of the first questions to be asked about any one of them is how its situation compares with that of other countries. India, with respect to our index of industrialization, stands at about the midpoint of the array. Fifty-one per cent of the rest of the world's population lives in countries more industrialized than India and 49 per cent in countries less industrialized. When each country is treated as a unit regardless of population, only 43 per cent of the countries and colonies of the world are more industrialized than India. With 68.9 per cent of her male population dependent on agriculture in 1951, India is definitely in the underdeveloped category, but she is somewhat more advanced than the average country in that category.

But now an interesting question arises. Modernization has different aspects, and if indices can be found which approximately measure these aspects, we can find in what ways a country is more developed and in what ways less developed than its general position would indicate. In other words, in addition to comparing different countries with reference to a particular index, we can compare several indices within the same country. By way of illustration, Table 5 shows that India seems far behind on literacy and considerably behind on per capita income and the reduction of agricultural density. She is best off in terms of occupational structure (our measure of industrialization) and in terms of urbanization. Thus we may say that there is some tendency for urbanization to run ahead of

---

4. This section on India is drawn from Kingsley Davis, "Social and Demographic Aspects of Economic Development in India," to be published soon as part of a symposium sponsored by the Social Science Research Council.

other aspects of development in India, but not noticeably except with respect to educational development.

Without attempting here to explain the particular character of India's situation which these indices point up—which is a significant problem in understanding economic change in pre-industrial countries—let us say that even though urbanization tends to be slightly more advanced than her total economy and society would lead us to estimate, it is still modest in world terms. In 1951, the country had 6.8 per cent of its population in cities of 10,000 or more, as compared to 13.1 per cent for the world as a whole. India manifests less than half the urbanization found in Brazil (13.9 per cent in 100,000-plus cities in 1950) and only one-fourth that found in Chile (26.0 per cent in 1950).

Table 5—India's Relative Position on Selected Indices[1]

	Per Cent of World's Population in Countries Ahead of India	Per Cent of Countries Ahead of India
Non-agricultural employment*	51	43
Agricultural density†	57	69
Urbanization‡	59	51
Literacy§	92	68
Per capita income**	57	73

1. Except for per capita national income, all data were compiled and processed by Division of Population Research, Bureau of Applied Social Research, Columbia University.
    * Percentage of occupied males who are engaged in agriculture, 1947 or near that date.
    † Number of gainfully occupied males in agriculture per square mile or agricultural land (i.e., land under crops or lying fallow). Dates same as (*). A low agricultural density is taken as a sign of efficiency, and hence being ahead of India would mean having a lower agricultural density.
    ‡ Percentage of population living in places of 20,000 or more, 1950.
    § Percentage of population age 10 or over able to read. Dates same as in (*).
    ** Not based on world as a whole, but on 70 countries which include 90 per cent of the world's population. United States, *National and Per Capita Incomes, Seventy Countries—1949.*

The present percentage of India's population living in large cities is about the same as that of the United States in 1855. But urbanization is proceeding somewhat more slowly in India than in the United States at that time, and it went much more slowly in the early periods. From 1820 to 1860 in the United States the average gain per decade in the proportion living in large cities was 63 per cent. In India from 1891 to 1951 it was 22 per cent. In spite of the fact that progress can be faster the more recently it occurs, this is not proving true in India, at least so far as urbanization is concerned. This suggests that there have been dampers on India's development which did not operate in America in its early history. As a result of the unequal rates of development at similar stages of urbanization, India has fallen further behind than it was. Whereas in 1891 India was about 55 years behind the United States in this matter, by 1931 she was over 90 years behind. After 1931, however, India's rate of urbanization increased markedly, almost equalling the United States gain at similar levels. How long she will continue to do so is hard to say, and if she does, it may be a consequence of "overurbanization" such as seems to occur occasionally in other densely-peopled agrarian countries. This possibility is suggested by the apparently static character of India's occupational structure, for the proportion of occupied males in agriculture has shown virtually no sign of change for several decades.

EGYPT: AN OVERURBANIZED COUNTRY.[5] That there is, on a world-wide basis, a high correlation (.86) between urbanization and our index of economic development has already been mentioned. About one-fourth of the variation in urbanization from one country to another, however, cannot be explained by variation in the degree of non-agriculturalism. If the relationship between the two variables is represented in the form of a regression curve, certain countries are found to be off the line to a significant extent. One of these is Egypt, which has far more urbanization than its degree of economic development would lead us to expect. In this sense Egypt is "overurbanized," and since this is a condition found also in certain other underdeveloped areas (notably Greece and Korea, and probably Lebanon), an examination of the case offers some clues to the dynamics of urbanization in underdeveloped areas under certain conditions.

How far out of line Egypt is can be seen from the following figures:

| | Per Cent of Population in Cities | |
	100,000-plus	20,000-plus
Switzerland, 1950	20.6	31.2
Egypt, 1947	19.3	28.5
Sweden, 1945	17.4	29.2
France, 1946	16.6	31.9

By no stretch of the imagination is Egypt as industrialized as the other three countries in the list, yet she is nearly as urbanized as Switzerland and is more urbanized on the 100,000+ level than Sweden or France. Indeed, the urban proportion in the 1947 Egyptian census is so high that some suspicion attaches to the figure,[6] but even if a correction factor is introduced to compensate for overenumeration of the large city population, Egypt is far more urbanized than its industrial position would require. Furthermore, this condition is not of recent origin (i.e., not found in the 1947 census alone) but has characterized the country for at least forty years, as Table 6 shows. The overurbanization is therefore real, and it has increased with time.

5. This section is drawn heavily from Robert Parke, Jr., "Over-urbanization in Egypt," a paper read at the annual meeting of the Eastern Sociological Society, April 3, 1954. Mr. Parke's work on Egypt was developed in the context of the urban research program at Columbia University.

6. Charles Issawi, a well known expert on Egypt, says: "When broken down the census returns show an abnormal increase in Alexandria and even more in Cairo. It is probable that many inhabitants of these cities filled their forms wrongly in the hope of getting extra ration cards." "Population and Wealth in Egypt," *Milbank Memorial Fund Quarterly*, 27 (January 1949), 100. Issawi does not say, however, what he means by "abnormal." He gives no statistical analysis to demonstrate overenumeration.

In looking for an explanation of this situation, one has to take into account the fact that Egypt's cultivated rural area is, to an extraordinary degree, densely settled and impoverished. The density is a product of rapid population growth for a century and a half and the inability of the economy to expand its nonagricultural sector proportionately.[7] The poverty is due to the same factors, plus the familiar pattern of tenancy associated with large landholdings whose absentee owners live in the cities. As the result of the impoverishment of the rural masses and the absence from the countryside of those who utilize the agricultural surplus, a curious thing has happened: nearly everybody who is not actually farming the land has gotten out and gone to the cities. Mr. Parke, on the basis of the 1947 census, has estimated that only 10 per cent of the occupied males living in rural places—i.e., villages and towns of less than 5,000—are engaged in nonagricultural pursuits. For 1950 in Puerto Rico the figure is 23 per cent (except that rural is there defined as places of less than 2,500, which makes the contrast sharper), and in France the figure is estimated at 50 per cent. One cannot avoid feeling that in Egypt the social and eco-

Table 6—Expected and Actual Urbanization in Egypt, 1907-1947*

	Per Cent of Occupied Males in Non-Agricultural Activities	Per Cent of Population in Cities 100,000-plus	
		Expected†	Actual
1907	27	6.6	8.7
1917	30	7.9	9.7
1927	34	9.7	12.2
1937	31	8.4	13.3
1947	38	11.4	19.3‡

* The table was conceived and worked out by Robert Parke, Jr., in the unpublished paper cited in the text.

† The expected figure is derived from the regression equation in which the proportion of non-agricultural male employment is the independent variable and the proportion in large cities is the dependent variable. The compilation of the necessary data and the derivation of the equation are mainly the work of Hilda Hertz.

‡ If a correction is made for overenumeration, the figure comes out to 17.6%.

nomic structure has so deprived the cultivator that he has little or nothing beyond bare subsistence. He cannot command much by way of services or handicraft products, and consequently the people who furnish such goods and services have gone to the cities. In the cities the nonagricultural producer can at least find the people—landowners, government workers, and middle classes—who drain the countryside of its surplus; and it is to them that he looks for support. The city therefore gathers to itself practically everybody who does not actually have to work the land to get a living.

Not only do productive nonagriculturalists come to the cities in Egypt, but also a great many unproductive people. Whereas the cities in indus-

7. *Ibid.*, pp. 98-107. See also Clyde V. Kiser, "The Demographic Position of Egypt" in Milbank Memorial Fund, *Demographic Studies of Selected Areas of Rapid Growth* (New York: 1944).

trial countries normally have a disproportionate share of people in the working ages, the Egyptian cities fail to exhibit this characteristic. They have, to an astonishing degree, the same age-sex structure as the total population. This is particularly strange since normally in an oriental city the sex ratio is heavily distorted in favor of males. Since in Muslim culture women do not usually participate in nonagricultural economic activities, the normal city sex ratio in Egypt, along with an unusually high proportion of children, means that the inactive population in the cities is extremely high. The data indicate, according to Parke, that about 92 per cent of women aged 15 and over in Cairo and Alexandria are economically inactive.

Such facts show that the densely settled and impoverished countryside in Egypt is pushing people into the cities because they have no other alternative. When they get into the cities it is perhaps harder for the government to let them starve, and they run some chance of picking up some crumbs from the wealthy who inhabit only the cities. Issawi has presented evidence showing a sharp decline in the per capita consumption of staple items in Egypt from 1920 to 1937.[8] Much of the migration to the cities seems therefore to be a refugee migration from the countryside where increased population, diminished size of holdings, and absentee landlord exactions have gradually squeezed out families by the thousands.

These facts are sufficient to account for the overurbanization which we found to characterize Egypt. That they do so was found by certain calculations performed by Parke. He first assumed that the nonagriculturalists in Egypt were distributed between the urban and rural sectors in the same ratio as in Puerto Rico. The effect of this assumption was to reduce the population in large cities by 13 per cent. Hence, the concentration of non-agriculturalists and of the inactive population in cities would virtually account for the observed overurbanization in Egypt.

The Egyptian case gains significance by virtue of the fact that some other underdeveloped countries exhibit the same phenomenon. T. O. Wilkinson, working in the comparative urban research program at Columbia University, has shown that in Korea after Japanese occupation in 1910, economic development lagged far behind urbanization.[9] Korean city growth "was more the result of the 'push' from a hard-pressed rural economy than of the 'pull' from expanding opportunities in urban areas." After the departure of the Japanese, this tendency was increased.

During the five-year post-World-War-II period covered in available South Korean census data, urbanization continued at a rapid rate, but even the limited economic base for city growth provided by Japanese activity had disappeared. That 17.2 per cent of South Korea's people in 1949 were in incorporated cities can be accounted for almost wholly by the fact that cities functioned as

8. *Op. cit.*, pp. 106-7.
9. "The Pattern of Korean Urban Growth," *Rural Sociology*, XIX (March 1954), 32-38.

refuges for migrants from the poverty of rural regions and for thousands of repatriates returning to Korea following World War II. An agricultural density approaching 300 per square mile, in addition to the breakdown of rural food-rationing systems, strengthened the tendency for cityward movement. The relief organizations and the employment related to interim military government were almost exclusively in cities.[10]

One's first tendency is to condemn such overurbanization as artificial and perhaps harmful to economic growth. One frequently hears the old plaint that people are being turned off the land and are drifting unhappily to the metropolis, and the temptation is to say that the process should be stopped. The use of the word "overurbanization" may connote such an evaluative interpretation. But the term as used here has only a statistical meaning, with no overtone of evaluation intended. From the standpoint of future economic growth, three considerations stand out. First, over-urbanization surely has its limits. It is possible for city growth to get ahead of general modernization, but not very far ahead for very long. If there is economic stagnation, urban growth itself must ultimately cease. In Egypt we can expect, then, that either the rate of urbanization will fall off sharply or industrialization will gain a new impetus. Second, overurbanization may have some effect in stimulating economic growth. Insofar as the city represents an efficient locale for nonagricultural production (as we believe it does), the accumulation of people in cities represents at least a potential setting for enhanced output. Also, in the process of modernizing agriculture, the more people who can be moved off the land, the better. Third, it is primarily in the cities that the leadership and the mobile following for revolutionary activities are to be found. Overurbanization, as we have analyzed it, is well calculated to provoke the maximum discontent in the population. Faced with idle, impoverished, and rootless urban masses, the government is forced to take drastic action or to allow itself to be displaced by a new revolutionary group. Since economic development is often hindered by outmoded institutional and political arrangements, the role of urbanization in fostering revolutionary activity (whether Communist or not) can be said to be potentially favorable to change.[11] It should be emphasized, however, that we are speaking of potentialities. Whether or not these potentialities are in fact realized depends on other factors in the situation. Urbanization, and particularly overurbanization, is only one of several major variables in industrial change, and so it is wise to avoid the appearance of determinism with reference to its role.

---

10. *Ibid.*, p. 35.

11. It has been shown, for example, that Communist revolutions are largely implemented by the urban intellectual leadership and not by discontented peasants. The urban leadership is needed to mobilize and direct the revolutionary energy which peasant discontent supplies. See Morris Watnick, "The Appeal of Communism to the Peoples of Underdeveloped Areas," *Economic Development and Cultural Change,* I (March 1952), 22-36. This article was apparently reprinted in Bert F. Hoselitz (ed.) *The Progress of Underdeveloped Areas* (Chicago: University of Chicago Press, 1952), pp. 152-72.

Revolutionary New Urbanization in Africa. In cases such as India, Egypt, Korea and Greece, we are confronted with countries that have long experienced the phenomenon of cities and which have old and complex civilizations. In central and west Africa, on the other hand, we find ourselves in a totally different kind of underdeveloped region—one in which primitive tribal life, completely rural in character, has been the dominant mode of existence until very recently. It is still a region of unlettered rurality, its people getting their subsistence mainly by hoe agriculture, by herding, or by hunting and fishing.

Yet into this still heavily primitive region is now being thrust an extremely rapid and patently modern city development. The urbanization that is rapidly taking place is not the urbanization of the late medieval period in Europe, nor the urbanization of the 18th and 19th centuries; it is rather the urbanization of the 20th century. This sudden juxtaposition of 20th-century cities and extremely primitive cultures (virtually stone-age in their organization and technology) gives rise in some respects to a sharper rural-urban contrast than can be found anywhere else in the world. It is the contrast between neolithic cultures on the one hand and industrial culture on the other, not mitigated by intervening centuries of sociocultural evolution but juxtaposed and mixed all at once.

It follows that the flow of migrants from countryside to city in Africa corresponds to a rapid transition telescoping several millennia into a short span. The social disorganization to which it gives rise is probably greater than that ever before experienced by urban populations. The native coming to the city cannot immediately divest himself of his tribal customs and allegiances, his superstitions and taboos; yet these are fantastically inappropriate to a modern urban milieu. Nor can he acquire suddenly the knowledge and habitudes necessary to make city life reasonable and workable. The result is a weird and chaotic mixture which gives to the average African city an unreal, tense, jangling quality.

Yet urbanization is probably going ahead faster in this region than anywhere else in the world. It has to be recalled that great parts of middle Africa were not "discovered" by Europeans until the latter half of the last century, and many parts have been opened to economic penetration only since World War I. As late as 1900, for example, the Katanga area of the Belgian Congo, an area now known to be fabulously rich in mineral deposits, was precariously held by a few isolated military posts which could barely deal with rebellious natives. The site of the present capital of this area, Elisabethville, was not chosen until 1910. By 1912 it already had 8,000 inhabitants; by 1948, over 100,000. Diversifying its industry, stimulating a surrounding modernized agricultural development, Elisabethville today is still growing fast. The growth of other cities has been similarly recent and in many instances even more spectacular. The capital of the Belgian Congo, Leopoldville, had a population of about 34,000 in 1930.

Twenty years later, in 1950, the number of its inhabitants had increased approximately seven times, rising to 211,000. The town was said in 1951 to cover an area equal to a quarter of that of Paris, with sixty miles of streets and roads. In a few more years its population should reach half a million. But the history of Leopoldville is by no means unique. As Table 7 shows, there are several other cities in Negro Africa which have had a comparable rate of growth. Some of them have quadrupled in population since World War II.

Table 7—Population of Some Middle African Cities at Recent Dates*

| | Population (in 000's) | | |
City	1930	1940	1950
Abidjan	22		142
Accra	70		136
Brazzaville		25	83
Dakar		165	209
Elisabethville			101
Kano	89		102
Lagos	126		230
Leopoldville	34		211
Luanda		67	159
Mombasa		57	85
Nairobi		65	119

* Data on these cities are derived from so many different sources that it seems too unwieldy to list them. Few are based on genuine censuses, exceptions being Accra and Lagos. The dates are often a year or two different from those listed in the caption.

The reasons for the rapid growth of cities in this great region are varied. Penetrated by modern economic enterprise only recently, the region has more virtually unexploited primary resources than any other major area of the world. The first notable spurt in the exploitation of these resources came in connection with the demands created by World War I. But the demand during and after World War II was even greater. Both agricultural products (palm oil, cocoa, coffee, pyrethrum, peanuts, cotton, sisal, rubber, hides, timber) and mineral products (tin, copper, gold, diamonds, bauxite, uranium) commanded high prices, so that it was worthwhile to expand their exploitation with modern scientific techniques at the most rapid pace possible. In addition, in connection with World War II, there was apparently a flight of private capital from the politically insecure countries of Europe to the potentially rich colonies of Africa. Not only private but also public capital came. The African colonies had proved to have great strategic value for the free countries of the world, both in war and in the struggle for economic survival. Hence the metropolitan nations were anxious to invest public capital to develop and strengthen them. America was willing to help through Marshall Aid, Mutual Security, Point IV, and private investment. International agencies, such as the World Bank, also lent a hand. As a result of all these funds available for investment in primary resources—resources capable of a rapidly expanding exploitation and fetching good prices on the world market—the economy of Negro Africa moved ahead rapidly. The towns and cities of the region, most of them new, grew with fantastic speed because the invading economic enterprise depended on urban facilities which previously had not existed. The investment of huge capital funds, the organization of business enterprise, the strengthening of governmental control, the mobilization of trained personnel—all were focused in the new urban headquarters. Vast new housing projects for Africans and for Europeans, for public and for private employees, were undertaken; large new administrative office buildings, hotels, stores, storage houses were erected; new utility plants, new light industries, improved harbors, and new amenities were installed. The visitor to these cities, at any time from 1945 and 1954, would see a rate of new construction eclipsing that of American boomtowns in their rosiest periods.

But the rapidity of urban growth today should not lead one to think of the region as highly urbanized. On the contrary, it was so profoundly rural only a short time ago that the recent growth of cities has not yet brought the percentage of urban population to a point of parity with even other underdeveloped areas. The present towns and cities are still urban islands in a sea of rurality.

Furthermore, even though the cities represent mainly an importation by Europeans, their populations are European to only a small extent, being overwhelmingly African. This preponderance of the African means that the cities are composed chiefly of people who only yesterday were living in primitive cultures and who, indeed, are still attached to those cultures. As a result, urbanization achieves in this region an extreme role as a stimulant of social change. The small European populations form the organizing and directing core. Under their stimulus the natives flock from the bush to the city. But they often do not stay. They generally return sooner or later to their tribal home, either for a visit or to stay permanently, being replaced by others while they are away. Thus the effect of the city is diffused outward through the primitive countryside, so that the whole texture of tribal life is being broken down.

What will be the result of this process of rapid and revolutionary urbanization in central and west Africa? On the whole the prospect for complete and early modernization would seem better than in India and Egypt, because the area possesses huge potential resources and a relatively sparse population. The rest of the world, crowded and hungry for industrial raw materials, needs these resources. Thus there is every indication that, barring a world catastrophe, the demand for Africa's primary products will increase and that the region will continue its fast pace of city building. The efficiencies created by wholesale importation of urban and industrial technology will probably provide an adequate economic base for a quick transition to modern conditions. Doubtless, as the tribal peoples recover from the initial shock of quick and massive contact with twentieth-century culture, their natural increase will be great and population will grow for a while. But the urbanization process may be so rapid that, before overwhelmingly dense rural populations are built up, fertility will start declining again and the natural increase will be lowered to manageable proportions. In other words, there is a chance for urbanization to acquire an early predominance as it has done in prosperous new areas such as Australia or Argentina rather than be bogged down in a swamp of densely settled peasant-agriculturalism as in most of Asia.

Our brief analysis of African urbanization has been mainly confined to the middle and western part of the continent where the Europeans are mostly a small directing element, not permanently settled but still attached to their homelands. The case is somewhat different in the Portuguese and Spanish territories where European contact is older, where the cultural differences are less, and where urbanization has not been so recent or so rapid. The case is also different in east Africa where a local northwest European population has made its permanent home and is thus in competition with the native for land and for political advantage. But it still remains true that most of Negro Africa, the world's most rural region, is yielding rapidly to urbanization, and that in spite of (perhaps because of) the disorganization of this twentieth-century intrusion into Neolithic culture, the region stands a chance of shortcircuiting much of the painful evolution that the older partially urbanized civilizations will have to go through before they achieve an urban-industrial society with a commensurate level of living.

CONCLUSION: THE ROLE OF CITIES IN ECONOMIC DEVELOPMENT. Behind much of our reasoning is the assumption that urbanization is not only an excellent index of economic development and social modernization but also itself a stimulus to such change. This assumption should not be taken for granted. It should be examined, and in comparative urban research we have an opportunity to do so. Space does not permit a full treatment of the matter here,[12] but the line of reasoning may be briefly intimated as a fitting conclusion to this paper.

Basically, the city is an efficient mode of human settlement because, with great numbers concentrated in a small area, it minimizes one of the greatest obstacles to human production—what Haig has called "the friction of space." This achievement is not possible without a high degree of urbanization (i.e., not possible in a predominantly agricultural or nonindustrial economy) because by their very nature such activities as hunting and tillage require a large area in relation to number of workers. In nonagricultural production, however, land is not a factor in production but merely a site. Consequently, production can be concentrated in small space; and when this is done in a city, a great variety of goods and services can be

---

12. An attempt to set forth a full theory of the role of cities in economic development will be found in the writers' book, *The Pattern of World Urbanization*, soon to be published.

supplied by numerous specialized producers whose mutual interdependence is facilitated by the possibility of ready and cheap transport and communication within the city. The city thus becomes, in essence, one great factory.

The gain in efficiency thus achieved, though enormous, is not without its limits. The main limitation is that the city is not self-contained. It must export and import to live. It must export either goods or services, or both, to its rural hinterland, and it must usually export to other cities as well. It therefore requires other means of overcoming friction of space than the sheer fact of close settlement within its own boundaries. This is why adequate transportation is indispensable to a high degree of urbanization. Insofar as the technology of rural-urban and of interurban transport and communication is itself an urban product, the city becomes something of a self-generating system, for it is producing the means for ever greater urbanization. The steamboat, railroad, and airplane, by facilitating long-distance transport, made it possible for individual cities to become larger and for a greater proportion of a country's population to live in them. Improved transport made it easier for rural people to migrate to the cities; and the cities, by removing excess rural manpower, by stimulating the demand for agricultural products, and by furnishing capital and new organizational principles and techniques for rural enterprise, contributed to the modernization of agriculture itself.

The efficiency of the city is not limited to the economic sphere. It also makes possible a greater accumulation of capital and personnel for purposes of formal education, public health, science, art, etc. Doubtless much is wasted on excrescences of religious superstition and frivolous fashion and display, but the possibility of specialization in different branches of knowledge, of the accumulation of libraries and the exchange of ideas, exists because of the character of the city.

The requirements of urban living force innovations which those in the countryside, if left to themselves, would never make. The fact of high density in small space gives rise to traffic and sanitary difficulties, to housing problems, to crime conditions, to organized special interests. All of these have to be dealt with in one way or another, and the innovations made sometimes give rise to new patterns of political and social control which can be diffused to the rural population. Furthermore, the competition for space and for special advantage within the urban milieu gives an advantage to individual innovation, to rationalistic calculation, and to individualism—all of which tends to stimulate a faster pace of cultural change than is likely to be seen in a peasant setting.

All told, then, the city makes its own peculiar contribution to the process of economic development. It is no accident that urbanization and industrialization have gone hand in hand. The appearance of rapid urbanization in underdeveloped areas is therefore both a sign of change already under way and an augury of future change. Its stimulating role is possibly more hampered in well-established agrarian civilizations such as those of India and Egypt and least hampered in primitive, but potentially rich, areas such as central and west Africa, but its effect in any case would seem to be substantial.

As yet only a small part of the world has become highly urbanized, but that small part is dominant over the rest and is diffusing its urban pattern widely. As the whole world begins to become highly urbanized, human society can be expected to become more dynamic than in the past. The process of urbanization itself must come to an end when nearly all people live in urban aggregations, but the forms of life and the ecological patterns within these aggregates will doubtless continue to change and the innovating force of urbanism will continue to modify culture and society.

URBANIZATION IN LATIN AMERICA

Kingsley Davis and Ana Casis

An excellent clue to the economic and social development of an area is the growth of cities. For this there are two reasons. First, the city *reflects* the changes in every sphere of social life. Its growth stems from all the factors that change illiterate agriculturalism to literate industrialism; it is correlated with increased industry and commerce, enhanced education, more efficient birth and death control—in short, with the whole process of modernization. Second, the city is a *source* of change in its own right. It is a diffusion center for modern civilization, providing a milieu in which social ferment and innovation can take place. City expansion therefore helps to determine as well as reflect the trend toward more modern conditions.

The present paper, based mainly on analysis of census data, attempts to relate the growth of cities to regional differences and problems in Latin America.[1] "The Growth of Cities," considers the rate of urban as against rural population growth, the development of cities of different size, and the causes and consequences of urban expansion.

Necessarily the treatment cannot be complete, because the data are not available for all areas or for all periods, and when available, are sketchy and unstandardized. It requires a great deal of labor and often a process of estimation to make the statistics comparable from one region to another and from one time to the next.

THE GROWTH OF CITIES. *The Degree of Urban Concentration.* In comparison with more industrialized areas, the Latin American countries do not seem, at first glance, to be highly urban. In the United States in 1940, for example, the percentage of persons living in places of more than 5,000 inhabitants was 52.7, and for Canada 43.0, whereas for most of Latin America it was only 27.1 (Table 1).[2] But when one realizes that the difference in urban concentration is very much smaller than the difference in indus-

Reprinted from *The Milbank Memorial Fund Quarterly*, Vol. 24 (April 1946), pp. 186-207, by permission of the authors and the publisher. (Copyright, 1946, by the Milbank Memorial Fund.)

1. From the Office of Population Research, Princeton University, where the first author is a member of the staff and the second a Milbank fellow. The paper is an outgrowth of a thesis of the same title done by Miss Casis. Though the thesis was for the Master's degree at Syracuse University (1945), the work for it was done in the Office of Population Research under the immediate supervision of Dr. Davis. It was limited to four countries. The present work expands the area covered to as much of Latin America as possible, and is based on further research by both authors.

2. The countries included in Table 1 do not embrace quite all of the Latin American region. They do cover 95.4 per cent of the total area and 94.5 of the total population.

TABLE I—Per Cent of Population in Cities by Size Class [1]

Region and Country	Year	In Cities 5,000 + Per Cent	In Cities 10,000 + Per Cent	In Cities 25,000 + Per Cent	In Cities 100,000 + Per Cent	Index *	Per Cent in the Largest City
Latin America—Total Sample		27.1	23.6	19.0	13.4	20.8	8.2
ABC Area		42.7 [d]	39.6	34.0	25.1	35.4	18.4
Uruguay	e. 1941	55.8	52.0	44.4	32.4	46.2	32.4
Argentina [f]	e. 1943	48.9	46.8	42.7	34.0	43.1	18.5
Chile	c. 1940	44.8	41.1	34.3	23.1	35.8	19.0
Brazil	c. 1940	21.3	18.4	14.6	11.0	16.3	3.8
Paraguay [b]							
Western South America		22.2	18.6	13.0	8.5	15.6	6.1
Ecuador	e. 1944	35.5	29.6	13.2	10.7	22.3	5.2
Venezuela [2]	e. 1936	22.0	17.7	13.0	9.0	15.4	5.8
Peru [2]	c. 1940	18.1	15.4	11.6	7.4	13.1	7.4
Bolivia [f]	e. 1942	16.5	15.3	15.3	8.5	13.9	8.5
Colombia [2]	c. 1938	19.0	15.2	12.1	7.1	13.3	3.7
Middle America, including Mexico		20.0	15.6	12.3	9.6	14.4	8.5
Panama [2]	c. 1940	26.2	24.7	24.7	17.7	23.4	17.7
Mexico [2]	c. 1940	27.5	21.9	16.8	10.2	19.1	7.4
Nicaragua	e. 1941	26.0	20.6	15.6	…	20.7	9.4
El Salvador	e. 1942	20.4	14.7	8.1	5.6	12.2	5.6
Costa Rica [f]	e. 1943	17.4	12.1	10.6	…	13.4	10.6
Guatemala	c. 1940	13.2	8.4	6.0	5.0	8.2	5.0
Honduras	c. 1940	9.5	6.7	4.0	…	6.8	4.0
Caribbean, Major Antilles		26.8	23.6	17.6	11.3	19.8	9.7
Cuba [2]	c. 1943	38.8	35.5	28.8	18.8	30.5	13.8
Puerto Rico [2]	c. 1940	25.8	21.2	15.2	9.0	17.8	9.0
Dominican Republic	e. 1944	15.8	14.1	8.8	6.1	11.2	6.1
Haiti [b]							
Jamaica [b]							
North America		47.8	43.1	36.4	25.9	38.3	6.8
United States [2]	c. 1940	52.7	47.6	40.1	28.8	42.3	5.7
Canada [2]	c. 1941	43.0	38.5	32.7	23.0	34.3	7.8
European Countries [3]							
Great Britain	c. 1931	81.7 [e]	73.6	63.1	45.2	65.9	20.5
Germany	c. 1939	57.4 [e]	51.7	43.5	31.8	46.1	6.3
France	c. 1936	41.7 [e]	37.5	29.8	16.0	31.2	6.8
Sweden	c. 1935	37.1 [e]	33.4	27.0	17.5	28.7	1.0
Greece	c. 1937	33.1 [e]	29.8	23.1	14.8	25.2	7.0
Poland	c. 1931	22.8 [e]	20.5	15.8	10.7	17.4	3.6
Non-European Countries [2]							
India	c. 1931	10.4	8.5	5.8	2.7	6.8	0.3
India	c. 1941	12.3	10.5	8.1 [e]	4.2	8.8	0.5
Australia	c. 1943	[b]	[b]	73.8	45.5	[b]	18.4
Japan	c. 1935	64.5	45.8	36.8	25.3	43.1	8.5
Egypt	e. 1939	[b]	27.0	19.7	13.2	[b]	8.2

* The index of urbanization was computed by adding the percentage in the previous four columns and dividing by four.

[b] Figures not available to the authors.

[c] Percentages based on data from a census are designated by a "c" in front of the date of the census.

[d] All regional percentages are unweighted averages, obtained by adding the percentages of the component countries and dividing by the number of countries.

[e] Percentages based on estimated population figures are designated by an "e" in front of the date of the estimate.

[f] Data on cities incomplete.

[1] Except for those countries otherwise designated, the population figures on which the percentages rest were taken from the *Handbook of Latin American Population Data* (Washington, D. C.: Office of Inter-American Affairs, 1945).

[2] Population figures were taken from census, yearbook, or other government publications.

[3] Figures taken from United States Department of State, Division of Geography and Cartography, *Europe (without U.S.S.R.): Cities of 10,000 Population and Over by Size Categories, circa 1930*, No. 108, April 5, 1944. The percentage for 5,000 + in each case was estimated by us by assuming that the ratio between the percentage in cities 5,000 + and the percentage in cities 10,000 + was the same as the average ratio in the United States and Canada.

trial development,[3] and that, as compared with nearly all other areas the Latin American countries have a very much smaller average density, the percentage of urban dwellers in the countries to the south begins to look fairly high. Indeed, it seems to us that in view of its retarded industrialization, Latin America is urbanized to a surprising degree. In other areas the growth of cities has arisen from large-scale industrial development, but in Latin America it has come more from non-industrial causes.

Table 1 gives for each country the percentage of the population living in cities of various size limits, with an unweighted average for each region. Column 6 of the table provides a rough index of urbanization, obtained by averaging the percentages in the preceding four columns. This index gives greater weight to the larger places and thus expresses the depth, or profundity, of urban concentration.[4] It follows rather closely the percentage of persons in cities of 25,000 or more.

By these figures, the most urbanized countries to the south are Uruguay, Argentina, Chile, Cuba, and Panama, in the order named.[5] The first three, strangely, are more urbanized than France (with 37.5 per cent in cities 10,000-plus); the first four, more urbanized than Sweden (with 33.4 per cent in cities 10,000-plus).

As might be expected, the various regions show sizable differences in the proportion urban. The so-called ABC area of South America has a high degree of urban concentration—an index figure of 35.4 as compared with the North American figure of 38.3.[6] In fact the concentration in the first three countries of the ABC area—Uruguay, Argentina, and Chile—exceeds

---

The areas omitted (mainly Paraguay, British Honduras, the Guianas, and most of the Caribbean islands) are undoubtedly more rural than those included, but since the parts omitted are very small in comparison to the total, the error introduced by this factor cannot be very great. The subregion most poorly covered is the Caribbean, where our sample embraces only 25.2 per cent of the area and 58.0 per cent of the population. Only in the case of this subregion is there a likelihood of serious misrepresentation.

3. "One may conclude that in general the average per capita income in Latin America cannot be much more than $100 per year and is probably less. The national income of all Latin America might then run to about $10 to $15 billion as compared with a current [1944] income of $155 billion in the United States." Harris, Seymour E.: *Economic Problems of Latin America*. New York, McGraw-Hill, 1944, p. 4.

4. It should be borne in mind that the average density in most of these countries is low. Argentina, for example, has only 5 persons per square kilometer, whereas England has 202. A country with as dense a population as England must necessarily have a considerable degree of urbanization, whereas there is nothing in the density of Argentina that would require urbanization.

5. It should be stressed that in a number of cases the urban percentages are approximate only. Since Argentina has not had a census since 1914 and Uruguay has not had one since 1908, the data are deficient both in the numerator and the denominator of the fraction by which the percentages are obtained. In the case of Argentina there have been some special censuses of particular cities and provinces, so that the percentages should be reasonably approximate. Uruguay is more questionable, although observers generally affirm that it is a very urbanized country. The data for Chile, Cuba, and Panama are based on censuses.

6. The regional averages given in Table 1 are obtained by adding the percentages for the countries of the region and dividing by the number of countries. This has the advantage of showing the situation prevailing in the average country of the region, but if the region is viewed as a unit in itself, then the average should be obtained

that of Canada and comes close to that of the United States, although they are far less industrialized than these two countries.

The next most urbanized region is the Caribbean. Doubtless the whole of this sector is not urbanized to the degree indicated by the only three Caribbean countries included in Table 1, but the addition of such places as Jamaica, Haiti, Trinidad, Guadaloupe, Martinique, and Curacao would not bring the region down to the level of either Western South America or Middle America. Cuba stands out in this region with an index of 30.5, which is quite remarkable for a country that is almost purely agricultural. Of course the Caribbean is by far the most densely settled part of the Western hemisphere, with the exception of parts of the United States. In an economy based primarily on the export of raw materials and the importation of manufactured goods by boat, as is the case in Latin America, an island has (in relation to the size of its hinterland) the advantage of maximum exposure to water transport. In the history of Latin America the islands were the first areas to be fully exploited, and their seaport cities grew accordingly. Today the Caribbean islands are the only places already faced with a serious population problem, and they are places where urbanization, in the sense of concentration of people, has gone ahead out of all proportion to the industrial base.

The other two regions—Western South America and Middle America (including Mexico)—have a very similar degree of urbanization. For the most part they are countries with exceedingly mountainous terrain, with large Indian populations, and with inaccessible hinterlands. In view of these characteristics the degree of urbanization, though the lowest in Latin America, is surprisingly large. Ecuador, with nothing but population estimates, is uncertain; the same is true of Bolivia and Nicaragua. Panama, by virtue of its proximity to the Canal Zone, is in a special category. Mexico, the most industrialized country of the two regions, also has the highest degree of urbanization, if only those nations having accurate census information (except Panama) are considered.

The last column in Table 1 gives for each country the percentage of the total population found in the largest city.[7] It is interesting to note that on the average the Latin American countries rank above the United States and Canada in this respect. Also, the ABC area is again outstanding, with the Caribbean, Middle American, and Western South American regions follow-

---

by weighting the percentages according to the population of each country. When this is done, the following averages are obtained for each region.

	Cities 5,000+	Cities 10,000+	Cities 25,000+	Cities 100,000+	Index	Largest City
ABC Area	30.5	27.7	23.5	17.9	24.9	9.2
Western S. America	20.8	17.4	12.7	8.1	14.7	5.9
Middle America	24.3	19.0	14.4	8.4	16.5	7.2
Caribbean	30.7	27.5	21.3	13.8	23.3	11.0

7. This figure is not included in the urbanization index. The largest city does *not* embrace the metropolitan area. In fact, the metropolitan areas have been left out of account in this table entirely. For their treatment see below, especially Table 3.

ing in the order named. Finally, every one of the largest cities in each country is at the same time the political capital of the nation, whereas this is not true of the United States, Canada, India, or Australia. The fact that each country's largest city is invariably the capital and generally holds a sizable percentage of the total population may be an accident, but it is more probably an integral feature of Latin American social structure.

In the entire Latin American region there are twenty cities with more than 200,000 inhabitants, according to figures for 1940 or thereabouts. Of these twenty, the greatest number (13) are to be found in the ABC area, the next largest number (4) in the Western South American area, the next largest number (2) in the Middle American area, and the least number (1) in the Caribbean. (Table 2.)

TABLE II—Twenty Largest Cities in Latin America by Rank, Country, and Region, About 1940 [1]

City and Size Class	Population [a]	Country	Region
1,000,000 +			
Buenos Aires *	2,567,763	Argentina	ABC Area
Rio de Janeiro	1,563,787	Brazil	ABC Area
Mexico City	1,448,422	Mexico	Middle America
Sao Paulo	1,269,319	Brazil	ABC Area
100,000–1,000,000			
Santiago	952,075	Chile	ABC Area
Montevideo *	708,233	Uruguay	ABC Area
Habana [2]	659,883	Cuba	Caribbean
Rosario *	521,210	Argentina	ABC Area
Lima [3]	520,528	Peru	Western S.A.
200,000–500,000			
Avellaneda *	399,021	Argentina	ABC Area
Cordoba *	339,375	Argentina	ABC Area
Recife	327,753	Brazil	ABC Area
Bogota	325,658	Colombia	Western S.A.
La Paz [4]	301,450	Bolivia	Western S.A.
Salvador	293,278	Brazil	ABC Area
Caracas [5]	269,030	Venezuela	Western S.A.
Pôrto Alegre	262,678	Brazil	ABC Area
La Plata *	256,378	Argentina	ABC Area
Guadalajara	229,235	Mexico	Middle America
Valparaiso	209,945	Chile	ABC Area

[a] Except for places marked by an asterisk, the figures came from census reports.
[1] The Office of Inter-American Affairs: *Handbook of Latin American Population Data*, Washington, D. C., January, 1945.
[2] República de Cuba. Dirección General del Censo: *Informe General del Censo de 1943*. Habana, P. Fernández y Cía, S. en C., 1945, p. 843.
[3] República del Perú. Ministerio de Hacienda y Comercio. Dirección Nacional de Estadística: *Censo Nacional de Población y Ocupación, 1940*. Lima, Noviembre, 1944, Vol. 1, p. 36.
[4] H. Alcaidia Municipal de La Paz. Dirección General de Estadística: *Censo Demográfico de la Ciudad de La Paz, 1942*. La Paz 1943, p. 12.
[5] Estados Unidos de Venezuela. Ministerio de Fomento. Dirección General de Estadística: *Anuario Estadístico de Venezuela, 1943*. Caracas, 1938, p. 77.

Nearly all of the twenty largest cities are located either on the coast or on navigable waterways. This fact is not unusual, but the greater part of Latin America is distinguished by very poor communication between city and hinterland. Water-borne transport predominates over rail and highway transport, whereas the reverse is true in most industrialized countries. This fact gives a peculiar orientation to Latin American cities. They tend to face outward toward other countries—even toward other continents—rather than inward toward their own hinterland.

Figure 1 gives, for eight countries with recent and trustworthy census statistics, the percentage of the population living in various size classes of city above 10,000, and in the rest of the country. The major difference between the most urbanized and least urbanized countries lies in the 100,000-plus class. It is in the large cities that urban concentration is having its main effect.

In nearly all cases we have taken the definition of the city's size and area from the censuses or official estimates. The Latin American publications,

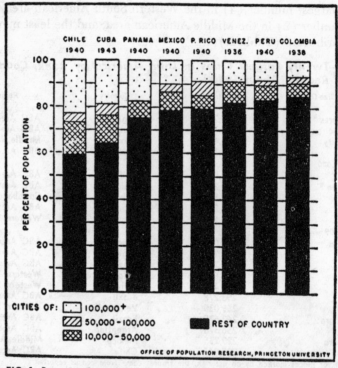

FIG. 1. Per cent of population living in various size classes of city above 10,000, and in rest of country. Selected countries.

however, do not always specify the exact boundary or area of the city. In general it seems that the city is narrowly rather than broadly defined—that is, there is a suburban population around the city that is not included. This means that we have been dealing with cities proper, rather than with metropolitan districts. The question is raised, then, as to what size the metropolitan areas may have.

For Chile the census gives figures for Greater Santiago in 1930. For Puerto Rico, Bartlett and Howell give the municipalities that form the boundary of the San Juan Metropolitan Area.[8] For Caracas and Mexico City the

8. Frederic P. Bartlett and Brandon Howell: *The Population Problem in Puerto Rico*. Government of Puerto Rico: Planning, Urbanizing, and Zoning Board, 1944, p. 47.

Federal District was taken as the metropolitan area. For Cuba the cities immediately around Havana were included in the metropolitan district. For all others (except Panama) a circle with a radius of fifteen miles was drawn around the center of the city, and all the population within this area was included. In most cases, a person acquainted with the locale was consulted before a final decision was reached. All told, seventeen metropolitan districts were worked out. They would seem to be roughly accurate; if anything, they exaggerate rather than minimize the metropolitan population.

TABLE III—Suburban Population as Percentage of Entire Population of Metropolitan Areas, Latin America (Around 1940) and United States (1940) [1]

Size of Metropolitan Area	Number of Metropolitan Areas Included	Percentage of Population in Suburban Part
1,000,000 +		
Latin America	4	12.5
United States	11	35.2
500,000–1,000,000		
Latin America	4	7.7
United States	11	32.5
200,000–500,000		
Latin America	7	23.2
United States	37	26.9
100,000–200,000		
Latin America	2	13.6
United States	37	30.7

[1] The figures for Latin America were derived from censuses and official estimates by procedures described in the text. The countries included, and the number of metropolitan districts dealt with, are Argentina (1), Brazil (2), Chile (2), Colombia (3), Cuba (1), Mexico (3), Panama (1), Peru (1), Puerto Rico (1), Uruguay (1), and Venezuela (1). The figures for the United States were derived from U.S. Bureau of Census, Census of 1940, Vol. 1, *Number of Inhabitants*, pp. 61-65, but only those districts were used which were also metropolitan districts in 1930.

Our hypothesis was that the proportion living in the suburban area would be smaller in Latin America than in more industrialized regions. This turned out to be the case. Table 3 compares the Latin American percentages with those in the United States. Apparently the trend toward suburbanization has not gone so far in the countries to the south, doubtless because of less developed transportation, poorer communication, greater poverty, and the preference of Latin Americans for the central city.

The greatest percentage of the metropolitan population living in the suburbs is found in the following districts:

Puebla (Mexico)	43.6
San Juan (Puerto Rico)	43.3
Medellin (Colombia)	33.6
Havana (Cuba)	21.7
Caracas (Venezuela)	20.3
Mexico City (Mexico)	17.6
Buenos Aires (Argentina)	17.3
Panama City (Panama)	15.3

It should be borne in mind that we have only a sample of such districts, and that the methods of determining their population are crude. Nevertheless, the conclusion seems justified that although urban concentration has gone far in Latin America, the metropolitan tendency has not gone very far. The process of suburbanization should become more prominent in the near future.

The Rate of Urban Growth. When one turns to the history of the urban concentration, one finds that the growth of cities in Latin America has been rapid and that it shows no sign of slowing down. In five countries with available data (Chile, Cuba, Mexico, Panama, and Puerto Rico), the urban population (persons in places of more than 2,500) is growing on an average about twice as fast as the rural population (Table 4). Furthermore, the

TABLE IV—Growth of Population in Rural Areas and in Various Classes of City, Five Countries Combined,[1] 1910–1940

Average Annual Rate of Growth (Per Cent)

Period	Rural	Places 2,500 +	Urban Cities 10,000 +	Cities 100,000 +
1910–1920 [a]	1.24	2.71	3.15	
1920–1930 [b]	0.97	3.03	3.34	
1930–1940 [c]	1.43	2.87	2.93	3.20

[a] In not all cases did the census dates coincide exactly with the periods specified. The first period for Chile was 1907–1920, and for Cuba 1907–1919. In such instances the average annual rate of growth for the period covered by the censuses was assumed to apply to the period mentioned in our table. Also, city boundary changes could not be taken into account.
[b] Cuba, 1919–1931.
[c] Cuba, 1931–1943.
[1] Assembled from census data for the following countries: Chile, Cuba, Mexico, Panama, Puerto Rico. For cities 100,000 + Panama drops out because it had no cities of this size in 1930.

larger the class of city the faster the growth, for the population in places of 10,000 and over is gaining on the 2,500-and-over class, and the population in places 100,000 and over is apparently gaining over all the rest. Figure 2 seems to indicate that the cities between 10,000 and 50,000 are not growing any faster than the general population, but this may be merely a vagary of the particular sample. There can be no doubt that the cities of 50,000 and over are growing at a far more rapid pace than the rest of the population. "Between 1920 and 1940, the population of Brazil increased 36 per cent and the population of the 22 cities for which a 1920 figure is obtainable increased 61 per cent. For the same period, the corresponding per cents for Chile were 34 and 69; for Colombia between 1918 and 1938 they were 49 and 126."[9] The general population of the Latin American countries is growing at an exceedingly fast pace, yet the cities are growing even faster, and the larger cities are growing with phenomenal speed.

In studying the expansion of cities of different size, one should keep in mind two distinct ways of measuring urban growth. One—the class method (used above)—traces the percentage of the population in each class of city from one census to the next, ignoring the shifting of particular cities from

9. Halbert L. Dunn, *et al.*: "Demographic Status of South America," *Annals of the American Academy of Political and Social Science*, 237, January 1945, p. 25.

one class to another. The other—the city method—begins with particular cities and traces their subsequent expansion, ignoring what classes they may later fall into or what cities may later enter the same class. The first measure shows what is actually happening to the population in terms of its distribution by size of city. The second shows what is happening to specific cities as a result of their initial size differences. Since each method supplies an important and complementary kind of information, both are employed in the present study. Having used the first method already, we are now ready to apply the second.

Figure 3 shows for six countries the percentage of the total population

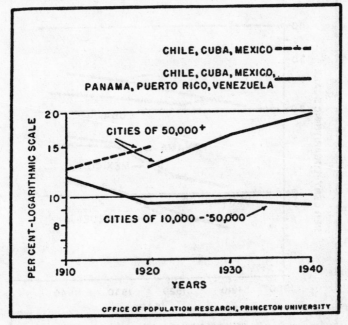

FIG. 2. Per cent of total population living in cities of two size groups. Selected countries.

living, during 1910–1940, in cities that *were* 20,000 or over at the initial date. Without exception these particular cities have grown faster than the general population, but it is worth noting that the rate of increase seems inversely correlated with the initial percentage. Those countries (Chile and Cuba) which had at the beginning the highest per cent living in these cities, showed a slower rate of growth of concentration in these cities throughout the period than did the countries that had a much smaller per cent to start with. This suggests that perhaps the older cities that had the highest proportion of people have not increased their percentage of the country's population as fast as those that did not begin with such a high proportion, but the data are not conclusive.

The Causes of Urban Growth. If the urban concentration in Latin America has already gone beyond that called for by the stage of industrial development, and if it is destined to increase still more in the future, the next question is why such striking urbanization is taking place.

Speaking first in purely demographic terms, we can say that the cause of rapid urban growth is *not* a superior natural increase in cities. In all probability the natural increase of the urban population is less than that of the rural population. Without exception, wherever the data are available, the ratio of children to women in the reproductive ages is lower in the city

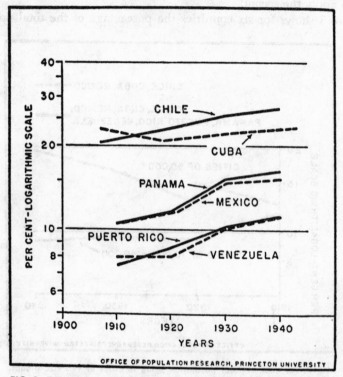

FIG. 3. Per cent of total population, 1910–1940, in cities that were 20,000 and over at beginning of period.

than in the country. Furthermore, when vital statistics are sufficiently reliable for comparisons to be made (as in Argentina, Chile, and Puerto Rico), the urban birth rate is substantially lower than the rural. At the same time, the death rate in the cities is not sufficiently lower than that in the country to balance the inferior fertility; in fact in some cases the urban mortality may be higher.[10]

We must attribute the growth in urban concentration mainly to the other demographic factor—migration. The importance of this factor is shown by the age distribution of the cities. The combined data for six countries (Chile, Colombia, Mexico, Panama, Puerto Rico, and Venezuela) show that

10. The subject of rural-urban vital statistics is discussed in a forthcoming paper.

the cities 10,000 and over had 55 per cent of their population in the ages 15-49, whereas the rest of the population had only 47 per cent in these ages.[11] Statistics on rural-urban migration in Latin American countries are discouragingly scarce, but one or two cases may indicate the general situation. In the Venezuelan capital, Caracas, according to the 1936 census, 47.8 per cent of the population were born outside the City; and in the Federal District 43.2 per cent were born outside the Federal District, a figure which, by 1941, had risen to 50.8. In 1921 the Federal District of Mexico, according to census returns, had 44.1 per cent of its population born outside the District, and in 1930, 50.8 per cent. In 1940 in Peru, the wholly urban province of Callao had 51.4 per cent of its population born outside the province, and the Department of Lima, 67.6 per cent urban, had 35.7 born outside the Department. It is true, too, that the foreign-born population of Latin America is mainly concentrated in the cities. In Panama, for instance, the two cities of Panama and Colon contained in 1940, 72.5 per cent of the total foreign-born population of the country; indeed, more than 23.5 per cent of these cities' inhabitants were foreign-born. In Buenos Aires, according to the census of 1936, the percentage of foreign-born was 36.1, which was much higher than the proportion of foreign-born (estimated at about 20 per cent) in the total country.[12]

But why the migration to the cities? This question raises a paradoxical issue. If, as maintained above, the urbanization has gone beyond its industrial base, compared with other areas, how does it happen that there is considerable rural-urban migration? What is the incentive? The answer seems to lie in Spanish and Portuguese institutions on the one hand coupled with the Latin American environment on the other.

Progress in Latin America did not begin spontaneously or indigenously. Instead, coming as a foreign, ocean-borne intrusion, it began on the coastal borders, where the Europeans first settled and where water transport was available. This might have been a prelude for gradual penetration and settlement of the interior, and so it was in a sense. But the Central and South American land masses were tropical or semi-tropical, mountainous or jungly, excessively wet or dry, and peopled by hostile or at least alien peoples. The conditions offered formidable barriers to settlement, and the Spaniards hardly had hard work in mind. As a consequence, the interior was not developed along the lines of homestead farming, but was given to large landowners (encomenderos) who used native or slave labor and aimed at getting out from forest, field, or mine as quickly as possible a commercial product for foreign shipment. The market lay across the ocean. The city, usually a port, was the necessary nexus, without which the interior would be worthless.

---

11. A part of the difference is probably accounted for by differential fertility, but not all of it.

12. Alejandro E. Bunge: Una Nueva Argentina. Buenos Aires, Guillermo Kraft, 1940, pp. 116, 141.

The interior, inaccessible and undeveloped, had little of culture or convenience to offer. It was remote from the center of civilization (Europe), and from the cities through which European influence filtered. Nobody wanted to stay there any longer than necessary. To live in the city was every man's dream. Persons who owned enough land in the interior lived in the city, where they formed a class of absentee landowners, educating their children abroad, doting on Europe, and in general neglecting the interior from which their wealth came. The existence of this class also drew to the cities a numerous body of retainers giving service to the rich.

As time went by the interior improved very little. Absentee ownership, the use of slave or peon labor, the lack of local industry and local demand all impeded agricultural progress, despite the effort to raise commercial crops. In the absence of mechanization, human labor had to bear the burden of agricultural production.[13] The competition with more mechanized and accessible agriculture in other continents, plus the peon system, drove rural "wages" down to virtual subsistence. To the agricultural worker almost any city wage looked attractive, and he filled the need of the aristocracy in the towns for "unspoiled" menial labor. There was thus a stimulus to cityward migration for both the laboring and landowning classes.

The emphasis upon urban dwelling among the wealthy meant that living conditions in cities were improved greatly, whereas little improvement was made in the country. Sanitation, education, utilities, and amusements were fostered in the city, but not elsewhere. The resulting gulf between city and country, still noticed by travelers and amply documented in rural-urban statistics, served to reinforce the initial preference for the city as a place to live. The idea of a quiet home in the country, far from the urban crowd, was not prominent in the Latin-American mind.

The growth of cities was also fostered by political factors. Despite an expressed preference in the leading republics for federalism and decentralization, the Latin American countries have usually had centralized governments. Since everything, including economic advantage, political patronage, and cultural support revolved about politics, the capitals became the national nerve-centers. It is therefore no accident that in every Latin American country the largest city is also the capital.

In short, the rural-urban migration that has given rise to unusual urbanization has not been due to heavy industrialization, but rather to the peculiar institutions of the Spaniards and Portuguese and the environmental conditions in their part of the new world. Today there is the prospect that industrialization will play a greater role, and that some of the Latin American nations will carry urban concentration still further.

13. There were in 1920, according to the census, some 141,000 plows in all of Brazil. There were six whole states with fewer than 100 plows each, and on the average only 15 per cent of Brazilian farmers possessed this elementary tool. There were 435 agricultural workers per plow. "Recent trips throughout the nation convince me that the same is true today." T. Lynn Smith: *Brazil: People and Institutions.* Baton Rouge, University of Louisiana Press, 1946, pp. 51-53.

The Case of Argentina. The most urbanized of the larger republics, Argentina is experiencing a "de-peopling of the pampas." In 1930 the rural population (persons in places of less than 1,000) was estimated to be 3.58 million; by 1938, 3.32 million. (Figure 4.) In percentage terms, the rural population dropped during this time from 32 to 26 per cent of the total population.[14] Since 1938 the rural population has probably declined still further, both in absolute and in percentage figures.

This rural decline bespeaks a huge rural-urban migration. Between 1930 and 1939, for example, an estimated 260,000 rural dwellers, or 7.3 per cent

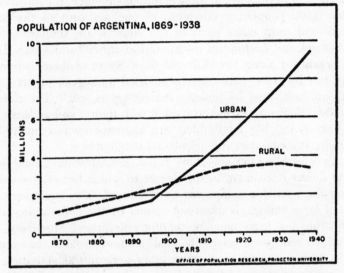

FIG. 4. Growth of rural and urban population in Argentina. (Rural is defined as places having less than 1,000 inhabitants.) Data from Bunge, *op. cit.*, p. 158.

of all such dwellers, migrated to the towns.[15] The rural exodus, plus foreign immigration, explains the phenomenal expansion of the urban population—an expansion that has exceeded the rate of rural growth since 1895.

It is primarily the larger cities that have gained. The census of 1914 showed 24 per cent of the total population living in cities of 100,000-plus, while estimates for 1943 place the figure at 34 per cent. "Between 1914 and 1943 the population of Argentina increased by 74.6 per cent, while the population of the cities that in 1914 had 100,000 or more inhabitants increased by 106 per cent."[16] Greater Buenos Aires contains today close to

14. Bunge: *op. cit.*, pp. 156-158.
15. *Ibid.*, p. 165.
16. Direccion del Censo Escolar de la Nacion: "La distribucion por zonas de la poblacion argentina" (Buenos Aires, 1945, mimeographed), p. 20. All demographic figures for Argentina since 1914 are approximate only, with the exception of those derived from provincial censuses, but it is hard to reconcile our findings with the statement of Preston E. James that "in 1939, approximately two thirds of the population was in cities of more than one hundred thousand." *Latin America.* New York, Odyssey Press, 1942, p. 281.

3.4 million persons, or above one-fourth of the Argentine population. It is, as Preston James points out, the largest city in the Southern Hemisphere and is second only to Paris among the world's Latin cities. Truly, for a predominantly agricultural country, Argentina is extremely urbanized. Its closest parallel is Australia, which is even more urban.

It is the organization of agriculture on the one hand, and the birth of industry on the other, that explains the Argentine phenomenon. Argentina resembles many another Latin American country in the concentration of land ownership.[17] It has been estimated that almost half of Buenos Aires Province, by far the richest and most populous province, is controlled by not more than 3,500 people, or one-tenth of one per cent of the provincial population; and most other parts of the country are similarly controlled. Large *estancias* and *latifundios* dominate the agricultural scene. The holdings are organized along two different lines. Some of them (about 38 per cent) are run by their owners or by salaried managers; others (about 62 per cent) are cultivated by tenants, sharecroppers, etc.[18] The class of persons who own their own farm and work it with their own hands is extremely small. Most of the big landholders are absentee owners—many of them being simply stock-holders in agricultural corporations.

Though resembling her neighbors in the concentration of landownership, Argentina differs from them in the degree to which her estates are mechanized and the need for manpower thus reduced. The equipment, even in the case of large estates, is often not owned by the cultivators; rather it is leased by the day from machine-renting enterprises. Moreover, livestock raising, which requires a relatively small amount of labor, has recently regained its historical dominance over other agricultural activities. The net effect of mechanization and livestock raising has been to reduce the amount of labor needed. Bunge points out that the per capita product of the agricultural population is in Argentina approximately four times what it is in France.[19] Carl C. Taylor has given a graphic account of the labor force of a cattle *estancia*. This *estancia*, covering 50,000 acres, grazing about 32,000 head of livestock, and grossing approximately $300,000 per year, had a permanent working population of 72 persons.[20]

One might think that agricultural mechanization would make rural wages high. But such is not the case in Argentina, because the agricultural proletariat, as against the politically dominant landowning class, has little bargaining power on the *estancia*. It seems generally agreed that rural labor in Argentina is poorly paid and poorly housed, insecure and extremely mobile. If we add that the system of rural credit favors larger holders, and that the tendency toward concentration of ownership is increasing rather than

17. Notable exceptions: Haiti, El Salvador, Costa Rica.
18. Felix J. Weil: *Argentine Riddle*. New York, Latin American Economic Institute and John Day Co., 1944, pp. 94-95, 87-89.
19. *Op. cit.*, pp. 162-163.
20. Carl Taylor: Rural Locality Groups in Argentina. *American Sociological Review*, 9, April 1944, p. 163.

decreasing, it becomes clear why Argentine agriculturalists should desire to leave the land.

At the same time, Argentine industry, concentrated in the cities, has been growing at a fast pace for several decades. It has drawn hard-pressed laborers and tenants from the pampas like a magnet. Thus there have been two forces—agriculture pushing and industry pulling—which have carried huge numbers to the cities.

The cities, in turn, are having a noteworthy effect on the country. Argentina is the first Latin American country to give promise of having a static population. As Figure 5 shows, the birth rate has been steadily de-

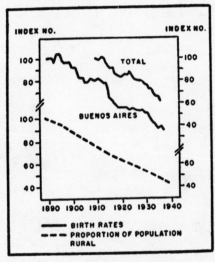

FIG. 5. The trend of fertility in the whole of Argentina and in the capital, and the trend in the population rural (i.e., in places of less than 10,000). Data from Bunge, op. cit., pp. 67, 158; middle line from Bunge's chart, p. 106.

clining as the country has become more urban. On the strength of this trend, Bunge has predicted a maximum population of only 13.7 million for Argentina (without immigration) by 1958, after which he believes it will slowly decline.[21]

The Value of the City. Our discussion may seem to imply that the fast and somewhat anomalous degree of urbanization in Latin America is harmful. Such an opinion is held by some observers, who reason that the cities represent an excessive cost [22] or that they are bringing about an unexpected and premature maturity.[23] One may argue, however, that it is not the cities themselves, but the peculiar conditions underlying their growth, that should be regretted. Though urbanization in the republics may not reflect as much

21. *Op. cit.,* p. 117.
22. Wm. L. Schurz: *Latin America.* New York, Dutton, 1942, pp. 72-73.
23. Bunge, *op. cit.,* Ch. 4.

industrial progress as elsewhere, there can be little doubt that the cities themselves are having a stimulating effect. Their inhabitants are ahead of the rural citizens in nearly every way. As the cities increasingly acquire an industrial base, as they link themselves more closely with the hinterland, as they spread out into suburban zones, their influence in the direction of modernization should increase. If they gradually promote a regime of low birth and death rates and thus halt the region's rapid population growth before it reaches a condition of oppressive density, this too will be a benefit. It is perhaps more, rather than less, urbanization that is desirable.

THE CHANGING POPULATION PATTERN
OF THE MODERN CITY

Philip M. Hauser

The city is a dramatic example of man's ability to fashion the physical and social world in which he lives; and the human products of the city may, in turn, be regarded as exemplifications of the sociologist's description of human nature as "original" plus "acquired" nature. Yet, despite the fact that cities are the works of man and modern man, in many respects, the product of the city, it can hardly be said that our contemporary cities or our contemporary urban human beings have been built according to plan. Nor can it be said that the "urban way of life" was deliberately conceived by man as a preferred means of existence, or as a social heritage for molding the "human nature" of subsequent generations.

Although we know that the city is built by man and that man is to a considerable extent fashioned by the city, there is much that we do not know about the determinants in the structure and process of urban development and growth, and in the socialization of the human being in the urban environment. Horeover, we do know that we are often displeased with many of the physical and cultural aspects of the urban community and with many of its human products.

This somewhat paradoxical introduction is a rather complicated way of calling attention to the fact that modern city, urban culture, and urban peoples are, in many respects, the products of forces which are not controlled by man, which are not yet fully understood, and which have been subjected to research for a relatively short period of time. The social scientist—the sociologist, the human ecologist, the economist, and the political scientist have only in recent years seriously tackled the job of empirically studying the urban community in a comprehensive manner; and the city planner—drawn from diverse professions—has only recently turned to the gigantic task of planning the future direction and character of urban development.

Our cities may be regarded as in transition, in a double sense. Not only are they changing in physical form, in land use, in economic function, in social and political organization and in population type; but they are also in transition in respect to the manner or origin of their change. They are also in transition in the sense that changes are being more and more subjected to control in accordance with a plan.

Published for the first time in this volume.

It would be easy to exaggerate the extent to which the modern city is being influenced by plan. But the rapid out-cropping of city planning boards and commissions, of the city planning curricula in our universities, and of urban research projects bear testimony to the increased attention and energy which are being devoted both to improving our basic knowledge about our cities and using that knowledge to direct the course of their development.

THE PROBLEM AND THE MATERIALS. The following discussion is focused on a very important aspect of urban and metropolitan development—namely, the causes and consequences of metropolitan decentralization. It is my task to discuss the changing population pattern of the modern city.

The distribution of the population as between urban and rural areas, among urban areas and within urban areas, is among the aspects of our culture which is not controlled, which is not the result of a deliberate plan. On the contrary, the distribution of population within the nation, within a region, within an urban community, is a product of many competitive forces of a geographic, economic, social and political character as well as the resultant of the personal choices of individuals and of families. Let us, for a moment, however, set aside the causal factors underlying population distribution and redistribution, and examine the historical and contemporary nature of the urban population pattern.

The rapid growth of the total population of the United States, which increased 34-fold in its first 150 years, is one of the amazing chapters of human history. Even more striking, however, is the growth of the urban population of the United States, which during the same period 1790–1940 increased 372-fold—from 200,000 persons comprising 5% of the total population to a total of over 74,000,000 making up 56.5% of the population of the nation. In 1790, there were only 24 urban places in the United States, only 2, New York and Philadelphia, with a population of 25,000 persons. In 1940, there were 3,464 urban places in the United States, 5 with populations over a million or more, 92 with 100,000 or more.[1]

The data on urban places and urban population do not, by any means, tell the whole story of urban growth. The "urban place"[2] as defined by the Bureau of the Census is necessarily based on aggregations of population in cities as political entities with arbitrary and relatively fixed boundaries. The actual agglomerations of urban population do not conform to the historically fixed political boundaries of our cities. Rather, particularly in our larger cities, the population tends to spill over the city limits into the surrounding area. In an attempt to measure the actual concentrations of population as distinguished from the populations of cities as corporate units, the Bureau of the Census has, since 1910, published data for "metropolitan

---

1. U.S. Dept. of Commerce, Bureau of the Census, *16th Census of the United States, 1940. Population. Vol. I: Number of Inhabitants,* Washington 1942, p. 25.

2. In general, urban place is defined as an incorporated place having 2500 or more inhabitants. For exceptions to this rule, see *ibid.,* p. 10.

districts"[3] in addition to the data for the cities. The 44 metropolitan districts, for which data are available for 1900, contained about ¼th of the total population of the nation (25.5%). By 1940, these districts included well over a third of the total national population (36.8%). The 140 metropolitan districts for which data are available in the 1940 Census, contained almost half of the total population of the nation, 47.8%, in 1940. Although the definitions of a metropolitan district have varied, both for a given census and from census to census, it is possible to use these data to trace the pattern of population distribution within metropolitan areas of the United States since 1900.

The analysis of the metropolitan district data is beset with a number of troublesome problems. In the first place, the number of areas for which metropolitan district data are presented has varied from census to census since 1910. In 1910, the Bureau of the Census published "metropolitan district" data for 25 areas containing 28 central cities with 200,000 inhabitants or more, and data for 19 additional cities of 100,000 to 200,000 inhabitants with their "adjacent territory." In general, the "metropolitan district" data included the central city plus contiguous areas within a 10-mile limit of the city's boundaries, having a population density of 150 or more per square mile. For the city with its "adjacent territory," however, the report included the population of the central city plus the population of all cities, towns, villages, or other political divisions within 10 miles of the city limits of the central city. In 1920, similar definitions were followed, but in that Census there were 29 "metropolitan districts" with 32 central cities of 200,000 or more, and 29 central cities of 100,000 to 200,000 persons with adjacent territory.

In the 1930 Census, the concept of "cities with adjacent territory" was abandoned, and data were published only for "metropolitan districts." The 10-mile limit for the peripheral area of the metropolitan district and the lower limit of 100,000 persons for the central city were dropped, and a metropolitan district report was presented for every city which had 50,000 or more inhabitants in 1920, which together with its peripheral area aggregated 100,000 or more persons. This definition resulted in the publication of metropolitan district data for 96 areas. Finally, in 1940, the concept employed was, in general, the same as that used in 1930. The application of the concept, however, resulted in the publication of metropolitan district data for 140 areas.

Another troublesome problem in attempting to trace the population pattern of the metropolitan area lies in the changing political boundaries of both the central city and its peripheral minor civil divisions from census to census. As a result of new developments and annexations, such boundary changes tend to distort any analysis of relative population growth and the distribution of population within the metropolitan district that is based on

3. Warren S. Thompson, *The Growth of Metropolitan Districts in the United States: 1900–1940*. U.S. Dept. of Commerce, Bureau of the Census, Washington, 1947, pp. 1–3.

differentials between the central city and its surrounding area.

Finally, only limited data are available for analyzing the changing population pattern within the boundaries of the city. The data for wards and other political units within the city, besides varying greatly from census to census as the result of boundary changes, do not permit analysis of a systematic or comparable basis from city to city. The data for census tracts [4] are much better than ward or other political data for this purpose. But census tract data, although available for 60 cities in 1940, were tabulated for only 22 cities in 1930, and the tract boundaries changed too much for the comparative study for five of the latter cities. Moreover, the analysis of census tract data for a large number of cities is an exceedingly burdensome and expensive task.

Fortunately, the larger part of these problems which constituted serious obstacles to the analysis of changes in the population distribution of our metropolitan areas were resolved in a painstaking and comprehensive study by Warren S. Thompson, recently published by the Bureau of the Census.[5] This study not only maximizes the comparability of the data for the various definitions and combinations of metropolitan districts contained in the Census reports, but also contains a careful and exhaustive analysis of differential changes in the population of central cities and their peripheral areas.

DIFFERENTIAL POPULATION GROWTH. Let us examine, first, the changing population pattern of the 44 metropolitan districts, each containing at least 1 central city of 100,000 or more persons in 1910, for which the data are available from the beginning of the century.

It should be observed at the outset that during the past four decades the rate of growth of the country as a whole has been declining rapidly, and that this decline in rate of growth is reflected in the population increases of the metropolitan districts. The percentage increases in the total population of the United States as reported in the Census dropped from 21.0 between 1900 to 1910; to 14.9 between 1910 and 1920; 16.1 between 1920 and 1930; and 7.2 between 1930 and 1940.

For the first 30 years of this period, within the framework of total national growth, these 44 metropolitan districts, however, grew at rates more than twice as great as the remainder of the United States. Only during the depression decade of the 30's did the 44 districts grow less rapidly than the rest of the country. The increases in the population of the 44 metropolitan districts and the remainder of the country for the 4 decades are listed below:

	1930–1940	1920–1930	1910–1920	1900–1910
44 Metropolitan districts	6.9	28.0	25.3	34.6
Remainder of the U.S.	7.4	10.2	10.8	16.4

4. Howard W. Green, *Census Tract Manual*. U.S. Dept. of Commerce, Bureau of the Census, Washington, 1947.

5. Thompson, *op. cit.* The descriptive data which follow are in the main drawn from Thompson's data.

The extent to which the metropolitan districts disproportionately absorbed the total population growth of the country is indicated by comparing the percentage of the total population of the United States resident in these areas with the percentage of the total national increase which they obtained. Thus, although the 44 districts contained about 26% of the total population in the United States in 1900, they absorbed 42% of the increase in national population during the decade 1900–1910. Similarly, although they contained 29% of the population in 1910, they absorbed 48% of the total national increase in the decade 1910–1920; and although they contained 33% of the population in 1920, they absorbed 58% of the national increase in the decade 1920–1930. During the 30's, however, these areas barely managed to get their proportionate share of increase in population. They comprised 37% of the persons in the country but accounted for only 35% of the total national growth.

It is clear that during the first 3 decades of this century, the 44 metropolitan districts under observation absorbed about half of the total national increase in population. In consequence, the concentration of the national population in these areas increased appreciably, from about ¼ of the national total in 1900 to over a third in 1930. During the 30's, however, after this exceedingly rapid period of relative growth, the 44 areas barely held their own as compared with the remainder of the United States.

Although these metropolitan districts, as a whole, showed large population increases there were important differentials in rates of growth within the districts. Throughout the period, for example, the peripheral areas of the districts increased more rapidly in population than did the central cities; and within the peripheral areas, the rural population grew much more rapidly than did the urban.

The disparity between the rates of population growth in the central cities and in the peripheral areas increased from the beginning to the end of the period, as is indicated in the data showing percentage of increase in population, which follow:

	1930–1940	1920–1930	1910–1920	1900–1910
Central cities	4.2	20.5	23.4	33.6
Peripheral areas	13.0	48.7	31.3	38.2

Thus, although the rate of population increase in the peripheral territory was only slightly higher than that of the central cities in the decade 1900–1910, it was almost half again as much in the decade 1910–1920, was almost two and one-half times as great between 1920–1930, and more than three times as great between 1930–1940. The peripheral rural population grew more rapidly than the peripheral urban population throughout the period, but the greatest differences in rates of growth occurred during the last 2 decades. Between 1920 and 1930, the peripheral rural populations increased at a rate almost three-fourths again as much as that of the urban population; while between 1930 and 1940 the rural population increased by a percentage about four times as great as the urban increase. The percentage increases in the population of these areas are shown in the data which follow:

	1930–1940	1920–1930	1910–1920	1900–1910
Peripheral urban	7.3	40.6	30.2	35.9
Peripheral rural	28.1	68.1	34.5	43.1

Part of the more rapid rate of increase in the peripheral rural, than in the peripheral urban, population is to be accounted for by the procedure used by Thompson in the compilation of the data. As indicated above, the population was classified as urban or rural on the basis of the classification of the place at the beginning and not at the end of the decade. If the reverse procedure had been followed, the increase in peripheral urban population would have been somewhat greater than that reported, while the increase for the peripheral rural population would be somewhat less. In either case, however, it would be clear that the rural population of peripheral areas increased more rapidly than did the urban.

The differential pattern of urban-rural population growth in the peripheral areas of the metropolitan districts runs counter, of course, to the differential pattern of urban-rural population growth in the remainder of the country. Throughout the history of the United States the urban population has grown much more rapidly than has the rural population; and with the single exception of the 30's, the urban population of the nation has shown a percentage increase at least twice as great as that for rural areas since 1820. (It was more than nine times as great between 1910 and 1920.) This reversal of the pattern of urban-rural growth within the metropolitan district follows, of course, from the spilling over of population into the unsettled and unoccupied parts of the metropolitan district. Some of these "rural" areas have, in the course of the years, become incorporated and re-defined as "urban." Others have been defined as "urban" for Census purposes, even though they are not incorporated places. Most of these "rural" areas in peripheral parts of the metropolitan districts, however, are not rural in the same sense as in the rest of the nation, and constitute the "urban fringe" or "rural fringe," which is getting increasing attention for statistical and other purposes.[6]

As has been indicated, the data for developing the changing pattern of population distribution within the boundaries of the central city are more limited and the analysis more difficult and costly. The work of McKenzie for the decades 1910 to 1930, for four cities, to which reference is made above, provide sufficient data, however, to permit, at least, a description of the pattern of differential rates of population growth and the changing pattern of population distribution within the entire metropolitan area, including zones within the central city, for the 3 decades from 1910 to 1940.

---

6. Walter Firey, "Ecological Considerations in Planning for Urban-Rural Fringes," *American Sociological Review*, Vol. 11, No. 4, August, 1946, pp. 411-423. Also, Paul H. Landis, *Population Problems: A Cultural Interpretation*, American Book Co., New York, 1943, pp. 346-357.

In these four metropolitan areas, individually, and in the summary form presented below, the pattern of differential population growth for the 30-year period is reasonably consistent. The population of the zones of the cities closest to the center uniformly showed a decline in population for each of the three decades. In the other zones of the cities, population growth was more rapid as distance from the center of the city increased. The peripheral areas of the metropolitan districts, although they grew more rapidly than did the central cities, grew less rapidly than the outer zones of the central cities in the earlier 2 decades; and at about the same rate as the outer zones in the decade, 1930–1940.

The percentage increase in population for the 4 metropolitan areas combined, are shown below:

	1930–1940	1920–1930	1910–1920
4 Metropolitan districts			
(N. Y., Chicago, Cleveland, Pittsburgh)			
Central cities [7]	4.4	20.0	20.6
Inner zones	− 4.2	− 16.8	− 7.2
Middle zone	4.8	18.9	19.5
Outer zone	8.0	51.9	63.0
Periphery [8]	9.0	49.0	34.0

This consolidated table, although to some extent distorted because of variations in the physical size and structure of the cities, provides a good summary of the differential rates of population growth within these metropolitan areas by zones within central cities, as well as for the peripheral areas of the districts.

Of the 16 metropolitan districts for which data are compiled by Thompson for the decade, 1930–1940, 13 have sufficient comparability to permit a similar analysis (Los Angeles, New York, Chicago, Philadelphia, Cleveland, Cincinnati, Boston, Pittsburgh, Buffalo, St. Louis, Indianapolis, Columbus, Ohio and Washington, D. C.). In these 13 areas combined, the pattern of population growth for the decade 1930 to 1940, is identical with that of the 4 districts described above. The inner zone, that nearest the center of the city, showed a decrease in population. The rate of population growth increased for zones within the city with distance from the center; and the rate of population increase in the peripheral area, while greater than that for the districts as a whole, 9.0%, was below that of the outer zones of the central cities, 14.7%. The percentage increases in population between 1930 and 1940 for the 13 metropolitan areas combined are shown below:

	Total	Central City	Inner Zone	Middle Zone	Outer Zone	Periphery
13 Metropolitan areas	7.0	5.2	− 1.3	4.8	14.7	9.0

---

7. For the individual city data, 1910–1939, see R. D. McKenzie, "The Rise of Metropolitan Communities," in *Recent Social Trends in the United States*, President's Research Committee, Vol. I, p. 464.

8. Computed from Thompson, *op. cit.*, Table 3, pp. 33-45.

POPULATION DISTRIBUTION. The net effect of the differentials in population growth within the central cities, and between the central cities and the peripheral areas of metropolitan districts has been to alter significantly the pattern of population distribution within the district. In the 44 metropolitan districts, for example, the central cities in 1900 contained well over three-fourths (77,3%) of the total population of the districts: by 1940, this percentage had declined to slightly over two-thirds or 67.1%. Conversely, the peripheral areas which contained less than one-fourth of the population of the districts in 1900 had approximately one-third of the population by 1940.

The percentage of the total population ot the metropolitan districts resident in peripheral urban areas, increased from 15.5 to 22.6 during the 40 years; while that resident in peripheral rural areas increased from 7.2 to 10.2. The percentage distribution of population within the 44 metropolitan districts for central cities and for peripheral urban and rural areas for each decade follows:

	1940	1930	1920	1910	1900
44 Metropolitan districts [9]	100.0	100.0	100.0	100.0	100.0
Central cities	67.1	68.9	73.4	76.2	77.3
Peripheral areas	32.8	31.0	26.6	23.8	22.7
Urban	22.6	22.5	18.7	17.3	15.5
Rural	10.2	8.5	7.8	6.5	7.2

It is clear that during the 40 years under observation, the differential population growth of areas within metropolitan districts has resulted in marked changes in the distribution of population, as between the central cities and the peripheral areas. In general, in the course of the years, the proportion of the total metropolitan district population resident in peripheral areas has appreciably increased, while that resident in central cities has shown a considerable relative decline.

Many factors, as will be indicated below, are involved in the process of urban decentralization. One factor which is relatively easy to control is worth noting here, namely the rapidity of metropolitan district population growth. Analysis of the relationship between population decentralization and the rate of population increase reveals a positive correlation. That is, the more rapidly an individual metropolitan district grew during the 4 decades studied, the more rapid was its process of population decentralization. This relationship is evident in the data which follow:

Number of Districts	Percentage Increase in Population of Metropolitan Districts, 1900–1940 *	Median Percentage Increase in Proportion of Persons Resident in Peripheral Areas
11	30.0- 83.3	26.2
11	85.2- 137.3	44.6
11	142.4- 162.3	110.7
11	177.8-2260.3	215.0

* The 44 areas were ranked by percentaged increase in population between 1900 and 1940 and grouped into quartiles with the ranges indicated.

A single measure of this association is afforded by the coefficient of corre-

9. *Ibid.*, pp. 33-45.

lation (Pearsonian r) which for these data was .40 (after elimination of 6 extreme cases). This is a relatively high correlation when it is borne in mind that variations in physical size of central cities and peripheral areas, and differences in annexation procedures tend to distort the relationship being measured.

The foregoing analysis of the population shifts between central cities and peripheral areas has been restricted to 44 metropolitan districts because it is only for these areas that data are available for as long as 40 years. It should be observed, however, that for each of the other combinations of metropolitan districts, for which statistics are available for varying periods of time as described above, the pattern of population distribution within the metropolitan district is practically identical with that for the 44 districts for each decade for which comparisons are possible. As an illustration of the correspondence of the data for the various groupings of metropolitan districts, the percentage of the population in the constituent parts of the districts are shown for 1940 for the 44 metropolitan districts and for the group of 140 districts below:

	Total	Central Cities	Peripheral Total	Peripheral Urban	Peripheral Rural
44 Metropolitan districts	100.0	67.1	32.8	22.6	10.2
140 Metropolitan districts	100.0	68.0	32.1	19.8	12.3

Thus, the data for the 44 districts seem to be a good sample for the purposes used to describe the changing population pattern of the 140 metropolitan districts for which Census data are published.

It may also be seen that the differential rates of growth have altered the pattern of population distribution within the city. For the four cities combined, for which data are available from 1910 to 1940, the proportion of the total city population resident in the "inner zone" of the city—that adjoining the central business district—decreased from decade to decade so that the percentage in 1940, 17.8, was less than half that in 1910, 36.3. The "middle zone" showed a remarkable consistency for the four decades, varying in the proportion of total city population from 38.2 to 38.9 percent. The "outer zone," in contrast, consistently increased its proportion of the city population from decade to decade. In 1910 only 24.8 percent of the population of these central cities lived in the outer zone, but by 1940 43.9 percent were located there. The changing pattern of population distribution for those cities is shown:

	1940	1930	1920	1910
4 Cities combined (New York, Chicago, Cleveland, Pittsburgh)	100.0	100.0	100.0	100.0
Inner zone	17.8	19.4	27.9	36.3
Middle zone	38.3	38.2	38.6	38.9
Outer zone	43.9	42.4	33.5	24.8

If the entire metropolitan districts of the 4 cities are considered, the pattern of population distribution, similarly, shows the effect of centrifugal forces. In 1910 well over half of the population of these districts, about 57%, resided in the inner and middle zones of the central cities combined. By 1940, almost two-thirds of the population of the districts, 62%, lived in the outer zone of the central cities and the peripheral areas combined. This remarkable shift in the course of three decades reflects the consistent declines from decade to decade in the proportion of metropolitan district population resident in the inner and middle zones, respectively, of the central cities; and the consistent increase in the proportion of metropolitan district population resident in the outer zones of the central city and in the peripheral areas. The consolidated data for the four metropolitan districts are shown below:

	1940	1930	1920	1910
4 Metropolitan areas combined	100.0	100.0	100.0	100.0
Central cities				
Inner zone	12.0	13.2	20.6	27.5
Middle zone	25.8	26.0	28.4	29.4
Outer zone	29.5	28.9	24.7	18.7
Peripheral areas	32.8	31.8	26.2	24.1

By reason of the relatively small increase in total population of metropolitan areas during the thirties, no significant change in the distribution of population within the 13 metropolitan districts mentioned above is discernible between 1930 and 1940.

REGIONAL DIFFERENTIALS. Although the general pattern described above of differential population growth and its consequent changes in the distribution of population within the district characterizes the metropolitan districts of the nation as a whole, there are important differences in the magnitudes of differential growth and of population decentralization within the district among the major regions of the nation.

In general, the metropolitan districts of the Northeastern states have grown less rapidly and have shown smaller differentials between central city and peripheral area population growth than have the districts of other regions of the nation. In consequence, the 15 metropolitan districts [10] (of the 44 being considered) in the Northeastern states show relatively little shift in the pattern of population distribution within the district during the 40 years under observation. The peripheral areas of the Northeastern metropolitan districts contained 31% of the population of the districts in 1900, and had increased their share of the total to 37% by 1940.

The process of population decentralization was more rapid during these 4 decades in the metropolitan districts in the other regions of the country. Thus, in the South, the peripheral areas which contained about 17% of the total population of metropolitan districts in 1900, increased their share to 23% by 1940; in the North-Central states, they more than doubled their share, increasing from 11% to 26%; while in the West, in which metropolitan districts and urban population in general grew much more rapidly

10. *Ibid.*, p. 47.

during this period than in any other region of the country, the proportion of total metropolitan district population resident in peripheral areas more than trebled, increasing from 11% to 38%. For summary purposes, the percentages of the population of the metropolitan districts resident in peripheral areas are shown by major regions below:

	Total	Northeastern	Northcentral	South	West
1940	32.8	37.8	26.1	22.6	37.8
1900	22.7	30.8	10.9	17.2	11.0

It is evident that the Northeastern metropolitan districts had a relatively high proportion of residents in the peripheral areas at the beginning of the period under observation, from 1900 to 1940; and that they showed relatively little further population decentralization during this period. One factor contributing to an explanation of this regional differential in rate of population decentralization is the relatively slow population growth since 1900 of the Northeastern districts compared with the other districts in the country. This explanation is suggested by the correlation between population growth and decentralization reported above. (This correlation may, in fact, have been considerably higher were it not for the Northeastern metropolitan districts.) The metropolitan centers of the Northeast are older and more stable than the districts of the Northcentral and Western states, while the metropolitan districts of the South, after a long period of relatively slow growth, have shown signs of relatively rapid growth during the past two decades.

DIFFERENTIALS BY SIZE OF DISTRICT. The pattern of population decentralization with metropolitan districts has also shown some variation by size of the district. The proportion of the population resident in peripheral areas is directly related to the size of the district—that is, the larger the population of the district, the larger the proportion of peripheral inhabitants. In 1900 in the 4 districts having 1,000,000 or more inhabitants, ¼ of the population lived outside the central cities. In districts having fewer than 250,000 persons, only 18% lived outside the city limits. The proportion of the population living in the various parts of the districts in 1900 are shown for 4 size groupings of districts below:

	1900 Total	Central Cities	Peripheral Total	Peripheral Urban	Peripheral Rural
Under 250,000	100.0	82	18	5	13
250,000 to 500,000	100.0	79	21	13	8
500,000 to 1,000,000	100.0	76	24	10	14
1,000,000 and over	100.0	75	25	21	4

In 1940, a similar positive association between metropolitan district size and percentage of population in peripheral areas was evident. But the difference in the proportion of the population in peripheral areas between the smaller and larger districts was appreciably increased during the 40 years. The proportion of persons in the peripheral areas of the metropolitan districts with 1,000,000 or more inhabitants increased by nearly half during this period, from 25 to 36%. In districts with populations of from 500,000 to 1,000,000 the proportion in outlying areas increased from 24% to 31%, or by almost ⅓; in districts from 250,000 to 500,000 inhabitants it increased by only 1/10 from 21 to 23%; while in districts with fewer than 250,000 persons it increased by more than a third from 18 to 25%. It is evident that, with the exception of districts from 250,000 to 500,000 persons, the rapidity of the process of decentralization was directly correlated with size of the district—the larger the district the more rapid the population decentralization. A summary of the population distribution within the metropolitan districts for 1940 by size, follows:

	1940 Total	Central Cities	Total	Peripheral Urban	Rural
Under 250,000	100.0	75	25	4	21
250,000 to 500,000	100.0	77	23	8	15
500,000 to 1,000,000	100.0	69	31	20	11
1,000,000 and over	100.0	64	36	27	9

It has already been observed that the proportion of the peripheral population which is resident in urban or rural areas is, to a considerable extent, a function of the incorporation practices of the area and the statistical practices of the Census Bureau. Moreover, the technique employed by Thompson in the compilation of the data tends to over-state the rural at the expense of the urban population (see above). Nevertheless, it is worth noting that there was a definite pattern of direct relationship between percentage of persons in peripheral urban areas and size of district, and of inverse relationship between peripheral rural population and district size. Thus, 27% of the population of the largest districts and only 4% of the population of the smallest districts lived in peripheral urban areas. Conversely, 21% of the inhabitants in the smaller districts and only 9% of the larger districts lived in peripheral rural areas.

THE PROCESS OF DECENTRALIZATION. The modern metropolis, of which the Census Bureau's "Metropolitan District" is necessarily but an approximate and incomplete description, is, in many respects, the unique culture complex of our civilization, embodying, as it does, a great part of the advances in our material culture and many of the distinctive aspects of our nonmaterial culture.

It has already been indicated that the differential rates of population growth among the constituent parts of metropolitan districts, and the changing pattern of population distribution within the district have not followed a man-made plan. On the contrary, they are the resultant of a large number of forces, geographic, economic, social, political, and personal, the interaction of which have produced remarkably consistent and uniform patterns among the diverse metropolitan districts of the country.

The general, and some of the specific, causes of urban concentration and of population decentralization within metropolitan communities have been dealt with in the literature [11] and require only brief mention here. Without question, the invention of the steam engine, the evolution of the factory, the development of the division of labor, the expansion of markets, the emergence of many specialized service functions, great advances in agricultural technology, together with considerations of time and space, were among the key elements which contributed to the centripetal force producing large urban agglomerations of population. Likewise, it is clear that the advent of the automobile and the paved highway; improved and rapid local public transportation; the increasing importance of electricity as a source of power and advances permitting the transmittal of electric power over greater distances; improvement in means of communication—the telephone, the radio, the press; the comparative values of central city and suburban existence; the shortening of the work day and work week; and the decentralization of industry and trade are among the elements contributing to the centrifugal force, manifest in the decentralization of metropolitan populations. Much remains to be learned, however, about the specific ways in which these and other factors operate and about their specific effects.

A useful conceptual framework for approaching the study of the metropolitan community, both in its structural and dynamic aspects, is afforded by the developments in human ecology.[12] It is neither necessary nor appropriate here to eleborate the contribution of human ecology to the understanding of the structure and dynamics of the metropolis. But it would be helpful, briefly, to summarize the highlights in the ecologist's "ideal construct" of the urban community and of a few of the processes underlying urban development and change.

The city as an ideal construct, has been envisaged by Burgess [13] as comprising five major zones, approximating in form a series of concentric circles (the actual geometrical form of the zones is not of major importance for our purposes). These zones consist of the central business district at the center of the city; and successively as one approaches the periphery of the metropolis, of an "area in transition" or "interstitial area"; an area

11. Adna F. Weber, *The Growth of Cities in the Nineteenth Century: A Study in Statistics*, New York, Macmillan Co., 1899. Alfred Weber, *Theory of the Location of Industries*, Chicago, University of Chicago Press, 1929. R. D. McKenzie, *The Metropolitan Community*, McGraw-Hill, New York, 1933. Ernest W. Burgess, "The Growth of the City: An Introduction to a Research Project," in R. E. Park, E. W. Burgess, and R. D. McKenzie, *The City*, University of Chicago Press, Chicago, 1925, pp. 47-62.

12. Park, Burgess and McKenzie, *op. cit*. McKenzie, *op. cit*. E. W. Burgess, *The Urban Community*, University of Chicago Press, Chicago 1926. A. B. Hollinghead, "Human Ecology," in R. E. Park, *An Outline of the Principles of Sociology*, Barnes & Noble, New York, 1939, pp. 65-168. Milla A. Allihan, *Social Ecology: A Critical Analysis*, New York, Columbia University Press, 1939. C. A. Dawson, "The Sources and Methods of Human Ecology," in *The Fields and Methods of Sociology*, L. L. Bernard (ed.), New York, Long and Smith, 1934, Ch. IV. James A. Quinn, "The Development of Human Ecology in Sociology" in Harry Elmer Barnes, Howard Becker, and Frances Bennett Becker (eds.), *Contemporary Social Theory*. D. Appleton-Century Co., New York 1940, pp. 212-244.

13. Park, Burgess and McKenzie, *op. cit.*, pp. 50-58.

of working men's homes; a better class residential area of apartment buildings or single family residence; and finally, the commuters' area—the suburbs.

Land use and population type within these zones is envisaged as the result of a complex process of competition through which the institutions and peoples of the urban community become distributed in space, and the community is structured in a dynamic equilibrium. A major element, and perhaps the major element, in distributing the population within the urban community is the ability to pay for the better, the newer, the most desirable residential facilities.

In general, through "natural" forces, the quality of housing and other residential attractions improve from the center to the periphery of the city, largely because the more modern and more attractive housing facilities are to be found in the newer sections of the city, which are the farthest removed from its center. The population of the area is distributed, therefore, at least initially, by economic class; with the lower economic stratum taking the least desirable facilities, located usually in the interstitial areas; and the higher economic strata, in accordance with their ability to pay, are located in increasingly better residential facilities as the periphery of the area is approached.

The process of urban growth and development is seen as a process of radial expansion from the center with each zone successively invading its adjoining zone towards the periphery of the city, in respect to both land use and population type. With continued successful "invasion," the completed process is denoted as "succession."

Finally, of particular importance for our purpose is a brief description of the interstitial zone, that bordering on the central business district. This is the area characterized by "blight"—the locus of the slums and disproportionate shares of the institutional and personal pathology of the metropolis. Physically, this is the oldest residential area of the city, which is still available for residential use—since the central business district, as it expanded in the growth of the city, absorbed that which may have been older. It becomes an area of decay, partly because of the anticipated expansion of the central business district, which is evidenced by its anomalous relatively high land values and low rents. The land is, in the main, held for speculative purposes frequently under circumstances which do not, on economic grounds, justify further improvement or even reasonable maintenance of the residential housing.

This sketchy and greatly oversimplified vision of ecological structure and process in the city is presented because it helps to clarify and to explain the facts of population decentralization which have been described. It has been noted, for example, that even with a declining rate of metropolitan population growth, there have, nevertheless, during the 40 years observed, been appreciable increases in the population of metropolitan districts with the single exception of the depression 30's. As both a cause and effect of population increase, the expansion of the central business district has forced the emptying of the population of its adjoining area, and invasion, successively, of the other zones towards the periphery of the city. These processes are clearly evident in the data which have been presented on the differential rates of population growth and the changing pattern of population distribution, both within the city and for its adjoining peripheral area. The facts of differential rates of growth and population decentralization tend to confirm the theory of radial expansion; and the theory contributes to a better understanding of the facts.

THE PROSPECT. What is the prospect for the further decentralization of our metropolitan areas? No one can answer this question with certainty and precision, but some considerations can be presented which provide at least a framework for anticipation of the future.

To begin with, it is clear that at least since the turn of the century, the process of population decentralization has been to a considerable extent a function of the rapid growth of population in our metropolitan areas. Further prospect of population growth for the country as a whole and for its various regions may, therefore, shed some light on the prospect of further decentralization.

The abrupt decline in the rate of urban population growth between 1930 and 1940 raised many questions about the future growth of cities in this country. Some of these questions have, in a measure, been answered by the effects of the War on metropolitan growth and development. Data are available, fortunately, which make it possible to assay the impact of the War on urban growth and population decentralization.

Between 1940 and 1943 population estimates released by the Bureau of the Census,[14] based on registration for war-time rationing, indicated that the civilian population of the 137 "metropolitan counties"[15] grew much more rapidly than the remainder of the United States. The metropolitan counties, in fact, increased in civilian population by 2.4 percent, while the balance of the United States, largely because of inductions into the Armed Services as well as out-migration, actually decreased in civilian population by 7.3 percent. The metropolitan areas in the West and the South grew more rapidly under the impact of war-time expansion of production facilities than did those in the North.

The effect of the War in accelerating urban population growth is also evidenced in a sample study of the Bureau of the Census reporting urban and rural population for April 1947.[16] The civilian population in April, 1947,

14. U.S. Dept. of Commerce, Bureau of the Census, "Estimated Civilian Population of the United States, by Counties: November 1, 1943." Series P-44, No. 3, 1944.

15. Metropolitan counties were defined as the county or counties, one-half or more whose population was in the Metropolitan District as defined in the 1940 Census.

16. U.S. Dept. of Commerce, Bureau of the Census, "Urban and Rural Residence, Age, Sex, Color, and Veteran Status of the Civilian Population of the United States: April, 1947," *Current Population Reports: Population Characteristics*, Series P-20, No. 9, Washington, 1948.

numbering over 142,000,000 was 7.9% greater than the total population of the United States in April 1940. The civilian population in urban areas of the United States in 1947, however, was 12.7% greater than the total urban population in 1940. In contrast, the civilian rural population was only 1.7% greater than the rural population of 1940. The relatively large increase in urban population, as the result of war and post-war conditions, resulted primarily from the decline in rural farm population. During this period, the rural farm population declined by 9.6%, whereas the rural non-farm population increased by 14.3%. Thus, under the impact of war, the average annual increase of urban population in the United States between 1940 and 1947 was over twice as great, 1.8%, as that during the decade of the depression 30's, .8%.

Comprehensive data are not available for the analysis of population decentralization since 1940, but such evidence as there is indicates that population decentralization was also accelerated as a result of the conditions generated by the War. A study of 10 "congested production areas" [17] with a total of almost 11,000,000 persons in 1944, excluding military personnel stationed in the area, throws some light on the matter. Between 1940 and 1944 the metropolitan districts in these 10 areas combined increased by 26.4%. The central cities in these areas, however, increased by only 17.3%, while their peripheral areas showed an increase of 42.8%.

Still another piece of evidence on decentralization during the War is afforded by the Special Census of Los Angeles.[18] Between 1940 and 1946 Los Angeles showed a population increase of 20%. Long Beach, which is the largest single peripheral area in the Los Angeles Metropolitan District, however, during the same period showed an increase of 46.8%.

It seems reasonably safe to conclude that the War gave new impetus, not only to the growth of urban population, but also to the further decentralization of population within metropolitan areas.

In considering the prospects of future urban growth and future population decentralization, the trends in the total population growth of the Nation must be considered as an important factor. The declining rate of total population growth will undoubtedly tend to dampen the rate of urban population growth. Projections of urban population growth under varying assumptions strongly point to the possibility that the rate of population increase in our cities will sharply decline by the end of this century. Under the assumption of mixed economic conditions, that is averaging periods of prosperity and depression such as we have experienced in the past, the urban population of the United States would grow more slowly in the coming decades and increase by only 4% between 1990 and 2000. Under

---

17. U.S. Dept. of Commerce, Bureau of the Census, "Total Population of Ten Congested Areas: 1944," *Population*, Series CA-1, No. 11, Washington 1944.

18. U.S. Dept. of Commerce, Bureau of the Census, *Special Census of Los Angeles, California*, Series P-SC, No. 119, April 10, 1946. Also U.S. Dept. of Commerce, Bureau of the Census, *Special Census of Long Beach, California*, Series P-SC, No. 118, April 10, 1946.

conditions of continued economic depression, the urban population would actually decline during the same decade.[19] The projected percentage increase of urban population by decade to 2000, under assumptions of "mixed" economic conditions, is shown below:

	Percentage Increase
1950	10.4
1960	10.8
1970	9.4
1980	7.7
1990	5.5
2000	4.2

We have observed that population decentralization is, in part, a function of rapidity of urban population growth. To the extent that decentralization is dependent upon rapid growth, the declining rate of total population growth and of urban growth will tend to dissipate at least part of the centripetal forces making for population decentralization. It seems reasonably safe to conclude that in the coming decades the population decentralization of metropolitan districts will depend more on factors making for the redistribution within the metropolitan area of the population already resident there, than on the necessity for accommodating or making room for large population increments. On the other hand, the prospect of continued, even though diminished, urban growth points rather definitely to the likelihood, all other factors being equal, of continued decentralization of our urban population for at least the remainder of the century.

The relative importance of rapid population increment as compared with other factors in effecting population decentralization will, for at least a few decades, vary for the different regions of the country. In the North, and especially in the Northeast, rapid population growth may be a relatively unimportant factor in the further decentralization of metropolitan areas. In the South and in the West, on the other hand, rapid population growth may for a longer period continue to be an important element in the decentralization of metropolitan populations.

SOME IMPLICATIONS FOR THE FUTURE. The process of urban growth and of population decentralization within metropolitan areas has, in the main, resulted from the play of "natural forces" of the type briefly described above. With increasing knowledge of the processes involved, and with the dissipation of some of the forces making for decentralization resulting from declining rates of urban growth, the possibilities of, and opportunities for, planning the distribution of populations within metropolitan areas will undoubtedly improve. Considerable knowledge is already at hand, and more can be obtained, to make possible the redistribution of population within metropolitan areas in accordance with a plan, if that should be desired and if planning objectives can be agreed upon.

19. Philip M. Hauser and Hope T. Eldridge, "Projection of Urban Growth and Migration to Cities in the United States." Milbank Memorial Fund, *Postwar Problems of Migration*, New York, 1946, pp. 159-173.

As a result of the "natural process" of urban growth and decentralization, all of our metropolitan districts, for example, are characterized by
large areas of blight which impose a heavy drain on the resources of the
community and produce disproportionately large shares of its physical and
social pathology. An understanding of the processes which produced these
areas of blight constitutes at least the first step in bringing these areas under
control and dealing with the problems which they create.

Similarly, in regard to other areas within the metropolitan district, an
understanding of the natural forces which have been responsible for the
pattern of land use and population type within metropolitan areas constitutes the first step in any attempt to control the development of our metropolitan areas in the interest of their inhabitants, and of the Nation.

Finally, in this atomic age, it is conceivable that it may prove desirable
to hasten decentralization of the population of our metropolitan areas by
reason of considerations of national security. Should the outlook for peace
grow so dim as to make such accelerated decentralization desirable or
necessary, plans for, and actual accomplishment of, the task would undoubtedly benefit from a utilization of the knowledge we have gained about
the "natural" forces and processes involved in urban population growth
and distribution.

3

THE HISTORY OF URBAN SETTLEMENT

Although each city has a history of its own, the history of man can be written in large part as the history of cities and city life. The city introduced a new element into the historical process. Here men created a new mode of living by nonagricultural labor. The origin, growth and dispersion of cities has been traced and described for historical epochs. These historical descriptions usually orient the scholar toward answering such questions as: When, where and under what conditions did this particular city first arise? What is the history of the particular city, and its contribution to the history of a territory or an era? Is there an evolutionary or cyclical development in human history correlated with the rise and development of cities?

The rise and development of cities is difficult to trace with any degree of precision, for a number of reasons. Much of the evidence on cities of antiquity is archeological, and often quite fragmentary. Furthermore, all cities in all historical epochs in all countries have not been studied with equal precision. Much less is known, for example, about the cities of the East than about the cities of antiquity in Western civilization. Some of the oldest known cities are in India and China, although there is a tendency to think of ancient cities solely in terms of cities like Memphis and Thebes on the Nile, or Babylon, Sumer and Ur in the Mesopotamian region. Finally, the absence of extensive written materials on the pre-city and city eras in antiquity means that much of the description of urban life is necessarily gained by inference. Comparisons of these cities with those in later periods, therefore,

are gross, and their description is less precise.

The preconditions for cities in antiquity are those which made it possible for the rise of a sizeable *dependent community*—a community which depends upon a hinterland for at least its food supply. Invention and technology necessary for urban concentration, therefore, existed prior to cities, since the wheel and axle, the plow, metallurgy, the cultivation of crops, and the domestication of animals all appear to be in the nature of preconditions for such concentrated settlement. Once established, of course, cities undoubtedly became the major source of invention and technology, making possible the ever larger population concentrations.

The period in history when cities first arose is difficult to determine. Cities may have existed as early as 6,000 B.C. and certainly existed by 4,000 B.C. These early cities undoubtedly were small and perhaps little different from the residential villages and towns in the society. The apparent reason for their small size was the limited productivity of agriculture and the expense of long-distance transportation. Increased productivity in agriculture, making possible larger concentrations of population, required the later metallurgical innovations in iron, and a technology of agricultural machinery and transportation based on them.

The small cities of antiquity for the most part fell into ruin, and their cultures generally declined as urban civilizations. This was true even of the later cities in Greece and Rome, which depended upon a vast system of trade with, and political domination of, a hinterland. The reasons for their decline are many and complex, including such diverse factors as the conquest of cities by less urbanized peoples and the concomitant failure of cities to evolve systems of defense against them, the failure of cities to develop productive economies of consequence which integrated them more closely with their hinterlands, and the difficulties attendant upon solving certain urban political-economic problems such as taxation.

The Middle ages in western Europe saw the second major development for cities—the development of cities which were functionally specialized in production in a society which came to depend upon this productivity. This means that cities began to specialize in economic activities other than those of trade and transportation. Industry and commerce became the primary functions of many cities in the Middle Ages, and led, as Pirenne has noted, to the rise of the medieval bourgeoisie and the guild system for artisans. The city had become a workshop.

The modern period is characterized less by the existence of large numbers of productive and service cities as such, than by the fact that entire societies have undergone and are undergoing urbanization at an extremely rapid rate, such that a majority of the population in the society lives in cities. There is in these societies a diminution of the differences between the rural and urban inhabitants. Community makes a difference primarily in terms of the size and density of its settlement. Cities in the modern world are either highly specialized or diversified in their economies. Yet, in contrast to the earlier productive cities, modern cities are more likely to produce for their own populations, particularly to provide services for them, than were the earlier production-based cities. In an advanced, urbanized society more than one-half of all the economic activity in the city is solely given to maintaining the physical city, its population, and its institutions.

Cities are an integral part of a larger community. Their number, relative dispersion and functions in a society vary with the complexity of culture and the correlates of cultural change. The functions which cities serve are known to vary somewhat with the nature and complexity of culture, and therefore by historical epoch. There are, for example, predatory, defense, residential, commercial, administrative and specialized or diversified industrial types of cities. From one functional perspective, the development of the city may be seen as moving from a predatory residential community to the modern, dispersed, multifunctional productive community. This change involves a transformation of the city from primarily a place of residence to the city as a workshop. The appearance of the commercial or trading city was an intermediate functional type. Two ancillary functions appear to have characterized some, if not all, cities of historical periods, the city as the repository of certain nonmaterial cultural achievements, e.g., the arts, sciences, and magic and religion, and the city as the administrative center for the government of church and/or state.

The sociologist is not concerned primarily with the historical description of cities *per se*. Rather, sociological interest in historical description of cities, including that of their rise and development, lies in the contribution these descriptions make to analyzing questions such as: What are the functions cities have served in various kinds of societies? What is the contribution of cities to social and cultural change, such as their effect on economic development, the secularization of belief and ritual, and on structural relations such as systems of social stratification? Queries of special interest, for example, are: How were cities in the feudal period related to the structure of feudal society? How did industrial cities alter the structure of feudal societies? What is the effect of urbanization on the ecological organization of a region or territory? How do cities affect the general culture or civilization of a people? Very briefly, the sociological study of the historical dimension of cities permits one not only to make generalizations about how change in cultures and societies is related to the rise and spread of cities and their civilization, and about change in urban phenomena themselves, but it also permits the sociologist to test his hypotheses about cities in a wide variety of historical epochs as well as in different cultures. Examples may aid in seeing how the sociologist uses historical data on cities in these ways. The sociologist may ask a question such as Davis and Golden did in the previous section, *viz.*, how does urbanization contribute to economic development? Historical data for countries which have undergone economic development then may be used to see whether urbanization causes change in the forms and rate of economic production and consumption. Or, historical data could also be employed to examine any observed relationship in a number of historical periods to learn whether there is any variation in the relationship with historical time. The sociologist may also use historical data to answer a series of questions, like Sjoberg does in this section, which relate to the forms of social organization found in cities. The data may show, as Sjoberg maintains, that there are substantial differences between forms of social organization in the pre-industrial as compared with the industrial city. This, in turn, suggests that many phenomena which were thought to be generic to cities probably are generic only to urban industrial places.

The papers in this section, therefore, are not primarily chosen to represent a synoptic view of cities in history, beginning with the first known cities and continuing as a description on to the present day, nor to provide a description of their functions in historical periods. To some extent, of course, the papers fulfill both of these purposes. The papers are primarily chosen, however, to present sociological generalizations about urban phenomena in the perspective of historical change. The paper by Sjoberg on the pre-industrial city hypothesizes, as already noted, that certain structural elements, thought by some students to be universal for all urban centers, are fundamentally different in the pre-industrial city as compared with the industrial urban community. The paper makes historical comparisons of the spatial patterns, forms of economic production, division of labor, social status structure, kinship organization, belief system, and methods of social control in pre-industrial cities, and describes how cities differ in them for the two historical periods. Turner analyzes the effect of industrialization on, among other things, the conditions of urban association. Attention is focused primarily on the industrial city as the initiator and locus of particular forms of culture change, particularly the effect of the industrial city on localism and tradition, behavioral uniformity, individuality, and the right of property.

The rapid growth of cities, and the urbanization of the population which came with the industrial revolution and related technological changes, had a profound effect on the spatial and temporal structure of cities. The result is the metropolitan community, a community form which has become the predominant form in urbanized societies. The metropolitan community is a community of multiple centers and settlements, each more or less specialized in its activities and institutions. McKenzie refers to this phenomenon as a territorial division of labor among multiple centers and settlements. In a sense any dependent community—one which exchanges people, goods, services and ideas with other communities—by definition is involved in a territorial division of labor. The metropolitan community, however, is a dependent community with a large population concentration involved in an intricate network of intercommunity relationships which are made possible only by the modern technology of transportation and communication. The empirical paper by McKenzie in this section documents the rise of the metropolitan community, focusing particularly on the concentration of population in these centers and the effect which the center has on the communities which are related to it—the dominance effect, which is further described and analyzed in sections two and four.

The effects of urbanization on the total population are many. Not only have ever larger numbers of persons been drawn into residence into the larger cities, but the influence of the city has spread to the open-country rural and village communities. The effect probably has been to reduce the differences between urban and rural inhabitants, although the magnitude of this effect is difficult to determine precisely for two reasons. First, the large in-migration of rural inhabitants into cities probably has tended to minimize the effects which cities should theoretically produce without such contact. And, second, certain of the influences on the behavior of rural or urban inhabitants, such as that of technology, derive to some extent from the total cultural setting rather than from cities themselves. For example, the high standard of living in the United States, together with a mass distribution of the rapid means of communication and transportation, has its presumed effects somewhat independent of the level of urbanization in American society, since it has increased and heightened mobility between rural and urban inhabitants. Firey, Loomis and Beegle examine the effect of the highway on the fusion of urban and rural ways of life, advancing the prop-

osition that rural areas, in direct proportion to their time-cost accessibility to urban centers, become culturally urbanized. Since time-cost accessibility is a function of highways, the partial effect of highways on the dissemination of urban values and practices seems evident. The correlative result of this increased accessibility—rural effects on cities—has been given little attention by sociologists, and is not examined in this section.

The previous section in this Reader shows there is a rapid trend toward urbanization in the world since 1800. This trend can be expected to continue and with it the continued fusion of urban and rural ways of life. These associated processes now are taking place at a more rapid rate in countries with a low degree of urbanization. The effect of "complete urbanization" of a country or the world—reaching the maximum of urbanization—on the structure of human society is a matter of conjecture, but complete urbanization must profoundly alter its structure. This is not to say that the fusion of urban and rural must occur exactly as it has in the past. It can, in theory, be quite different, as modern technology and communication make a different spatial pattern possible—as the paper by Vance and Smith in the previous section suggests. As a consequence solely of the fact that the U.S. population probably will double in the next one hundred years, the rural-urban pattern in the United States should be substantially different from the present one. Both greater relative density of settlement and greater dispersion are possible, but the latter seems the more probable pattern.

THE PREINDUSTRIAL CITY

Gideon Sjoberg

In the past few decades social scientists have been conducting field studies in a number of relatively non-Westernized cities. Their recently acquired knowledge of North Africa and various parts of Asia, combined with what was already learned, clearly indicates that these cities are not like typical cities of the United States and other highly industrialized areas but are much more like those of medieval Europe. Such communities are termed herein "preindustrial," for they have arisen without stimulus from that form of production which we associate with the European industrial revolution.

Recently Foster, in a most informative article, took cognizance of the preindustrial city.[1] His primary emphasis was upon the peasantry (which he calls "folk"); but he recognized this to be part of a broader social structure which includes the preindustrial city. He noted certain similarities between the peasantry and the city's lower class. Likewise the present author sought to analyze the total society of which the peasantry and the pre-industrial city are integral parts.[2] For want of a better term this was called "feudal." Like Redfield's folk (or "primitive") society, the feudal order is highly stable and sacred; in contrast, however, it has a complex social organization. It is characterized by highly developed state and educational and/or religious institutions and by a rigid class structure.

Thus far no one has analyzed the preindustrial city *per se*, especially as it differs from the industrial-urban community, although Weber, Tönnies, and a few others perceived differences between the two. Yet such a survey is needed for the understanding of urban development in so-called underdeveloped countries and, for that matter, in parts of Europe. Such is the goal of this paper. The typological analysis should also serve as a guide to future research.

ECOLOGICAL ORGANIZATION. Preindustrial cities depend for their existence upon food and raw materials obtained from without; for this reason they are marketing centers. And they serve as centers for handi-

Reprinted from the *American Journal of Sociology*, Vol. 60 (March, 1955), pp. 438-445, by permission of the author, the *American Journal of Sociology*, and the University of Chicago Press. (Copyright, 1955, by the University of Chicago.)

1. George M. Foster, "What Is Folk Culture?" *American Anthropologist*, LV (1953), 159-73.

2. Gideon Sjoberg, "Folk and 'Feudal' Societies," *American Journal of Sociology*, LVIII (1952), 231-39.

craft manufacturing. In addition, they fulfil important political, religious, and educational functions. Some cities have become specialized; for example, Benares in India and Karbala in Iraq are best known as religious communities, and Peiping in China as a locus for political and educational activities.

The proportion of urbanites, relative to the peasant population is small, in some societies about 10 per cent, even though a few preindustrial cities have attained populations of 100,000 or more. Growth has been by slow accretion. These characteristics are due to the nonindustrial nature of the total social order. The amount of surplus food available to support an urban population has been limited by the unmechanized agriculture, transportation facilities utilizing primarily human or animal power, and inefficient methods of food preservation and storage.

The internal arrangement of the preindustrial city, in the nature of the case, is closely related to the city's economic and social structure.[3] Most streets are mere passageways for people and for animals used in transport. Buildings are low and crowded together. The congested conditions, combined with limited scientific knowledge, have fostered serious sanitation problems.

More significant is the rigid social segregation which typically has led to the formation of "quarters" or "wards." In some cities (e.g., Fez, Morocco, and Aleppo, Syria) these were sealed off from each other by walls, whose gates were locked at night. The quarters reflect the sharp local social divisions. Thus ethnic groups live in special sections. And the occupational groupings, some being at the same time ethnic in character, typically reside apart from one another. Often a special street or sector of the city is occupied almost exclusively by members of a particular trade; cities in such divergent cultures as medieval Europe and modern Afghanistan contain streets with names like "street of the goldsmiths." Lower-class and especially "outcaste" groups live on the city's periphery, at a distance from the primary centers of activity. Social segregation, the limited transportation facilities, the modicum of residential mobility, and the cramped living quarters have encouraged the development of well-defined neighborhoods which are almost primary groups.

Despite rigid segregation the evidence suggests no real specialization of land use such as is functionally necessary in industrial-urban commu-

3. Sociologists have devoted almost no attention to the ecology of preindustrial centers. However, works of other social scientists do provide some valuable preliminary data. See, e.g., Marcel Clerget, *Le Caire: Étude de géographie urbaine et d'histoire économique* (2 vols.; Cairo: E. & R. Schindler, 1934); Robert E. Dickinson, *The West European City* (London: Routledge & Kegan Paul, 1951); Roger Le Tourneau, *Fés: Avant le protectorat* (Casablanca: Société Marocaine de Librairie et d'Édition, 1949); Edward W. Lane, *Cairo Fifty Years Ago* (London: John Murray, 1896); J. Sauvaget, *Alep* (Paris: Librairie Orientaliste Paul Geuthner, 1941); J. Weulersse, "Antioche: Essai de géographie urbaine," *Bulletin d'études orientales*, IV (1934), 27-79; Jean Kennedy, *Here Is India* (New York: Charles Scribner's Sons, 1945); and relevant articles in American geographical journals.

nities. In medieval Europe and in other areas city dwellings often serve as workshops, and religious structures are used as schools or marketing centers.[4]

Finally, the "business district" does not hold the position of dominance that it enjoys in the industrial-urban community. Thus, in the Middle East the principal mosque, or in medieval Europe the cathedral, is usually the focal point of community life. The center of Peiping is the Forbidden City.

ECONOMIC ORGANIZATION. The economy of the preindustrial city diverges sharply from that of the modern industrial center. The prime difference is the absence in the former of industrialism which may be defined as that system of production in which *inanimate* sources of power are used to multiply human effort. Preindustrial cities depend for the production of goods and services upon *animate* (human or animal) sources of energy —applied either directly or indirectly through such mechanical devices as hammers, pulleys, and wheels. The industrial-urban community, on the other hand, employs inanimate generators of power such as electricity and steam which greatly enhance the productive capacity of urbanites. This basically new form of energy production, one which requires for its development and survival a special kind of institutional complex, effects striking changes in the ecological, economic, and social organization of cities in which it has become dominant.

Other facets of the economy of the preindustrial city are associated with its particular system of production. There is little fragmentation or specialization of work. The handicraftsman participates in nearly every phase of the manufacture of an article, often carrying out the work in his own home or in a small shop nearby and, within the limits of certain guild and community regulations, maintaining direct control over conditions of work and methods of production.

In industrial cities, on the other hand, the complex division of labor requires a specialized managerial group, often extra-community in character, whose primary function is to direct and control others. And for the supervision and co-ordination of the activities of workers, a "factory system" has been developed, something typically lacking in preindustrial cities. (Occasionally centralized production is found in preindustrial cities —e.g., where the state organized slaves for large-scale construction projects.) Most commercial activities, also, are conducted in preindustrial cities by individuals without a highly formalized organization; for example, the craftsman has frequently been responsible for the marketing of his own products. With a few exceptions, the preindustrial community cannot support a large group of middlemen.

The various occupations are organized into what have been termed

4. Dickinson, *op. cit.*, p. 27; O. H. K. Spate, *India and Pakistan* (London: Methuen & Co., 1945), p. 183.

"guilds."[5] These strive to encompass all, except the elite, who are gainfully employed in some economic activity. Guilds have existed for merchants and handicraft workers (e.g., goldsmiths and weavers) as well as for servants, entertainers, and even beggars and thieves. Typically the guilds operate only within the local community, and there are no large-scale economic organizations such as those in industrial cities which link their members to their fellows in other communities.

Guild membership and apprenticeship are prerequisites to the practice of almost any occupation, a circumstance obviously leading to monopolization. To a degree these organizations regulate the work of their members and the price of their products and services. And the guilds recruit workers into specific occupations, typically selecting them according to such particularistic criteria as kinship rather than universalistic standards.

The guilds are integrated with still other elements of the city's social structure. They perform certain religious functions; for example, in medieval European, Chinese, and Middle Eastern cities each guild had its "patron saint" and held periodic festivals in his honor. And, by assisting members in time of trouble, the guilds serve as social security agencies.

The economic structure of the preindustrial city functions with little rationality, judged by industrial-urban standards. This is shown in the general nonstandardization of manufacturing methods as well as in the products and is even more evident in marketing. In preindustrial cities throughout the world a fixed price is rare; buyer and seller settle their bargain by haggling. (Of course, there are limits above which customers will not buy and below which merchants will not sell.) Often business is conducted in a leisurely manner, money not being the only desired end.

Furthermore, the sorting of goods according to size, weight, and quality is not common. Typical is the adulteration and spoilage of produce. And weights and measures are not standardized: variations exist not only between one city and the next but also within communities, for often different guilds employ their own systems. Within a single city there may be different kinds of currency, which, with the poorly developed accounting and credit systems, signalize a modicum of rationality in the whole of economic action in preindustrial cities.[6]

---

5. For a discussion of guilds and other facets of the preindustrial city's economy see, e.g., J. S. Burgess, *The Guilds of Peking* (New York: Columbia University Press, 1928); Edward T. Williams, *China, Yesterday and Today* (5th ed.; New York: Thomas Y. Crowell Co., 1932); T'ai-ch'u Liao, "The Apprentices in Chengtu during and after the War," *Yenching Journal of Social Studies*, IV (1948), 90-106; H. A. R. Gibb and Harold Bowen, *Islamic Society and the West* (London: Oxford University Press, 1950), Vol. I, Part I, chap. vi; Le Tourneau, *op. cit.*; Clerget, *op. cit.*; James W. Thompson and Edgar N. Johnson, *An Introduction to Medieval Europe* (New York: W. W. Norton Co., 1937), chap. xx; Sylvia L. Thrupp, "Medieval Guilds Reconsidered," *Journal of Economic History*, II (1942), 164-73.

6. For an extreme example of unstandardized currency cf. Robert Coltman, Jr., *The Chinese* (Philadelphia: F. A. Davis, 1891), p. 52. In some traditional societies (e.g., China) the state has sought to standardize economic action in the city by setting up

SOCIAL ORGANIZATION. The economic system of the preindustrial city, based as it has been upon animate sources of power, articulates with a characteristic class structure and family, religious, educational, and governmental systems.

Of the class structure, the most striking component is a literate elite controlling and depending for its existence upon the mass of the populace, even in the traditional cities of India with their caste system. The elite is composed of individuals holding positions in the governmental, religious, and/or educational institutions of the larger society, although at times groups such as large absentee landlords have belonged to it. At the opposite pole are the masses, comprising such groups as handicraft workers whose goods and services are produced primarily for the elite's benefit.[7] Between the elite and the lower class is a rather sharp schism, but in both groups there are gradations in rank. The members of the elite belong to the "correct" families and enjoy power, property, and certain highly valued personal attributes. Their position, moreover, is legitimized by sacred writings.

Social mobility in this city is minimal; the only real threat to the elite comes from the outside—not from the city's lower classes. And a middle class—so typical of industrial-urban communities, where it can be considered the "dominant" class—is not known in the preindustrial city. The system of production in the larger society provides goods, including food, and services in sufficient amounts to support only a small group of leisured individuals; under these conditions an urban middle class, a semileisured group, cannot arise. Nor are a middle class and extensive social mobility essential to the maintenance of the economic system.

Significant is the role of the marginal or "outcaste" groups (e.g., the Eta of Japan), which are not an integral part of the dominant social system. Typically they rank lower than the urban lower class, performing tasks considered especially degrading, such as burying the dead. Slaves, beggars, and the like are outcastes in most preindustrial cities. Even such groups as professional entertainers and itinerant merchants are often viewed as outcastes, for their rovings expose them to "foreign" ideas from which the dominant social group seeks to isolate itself. Actually many outcaste groups, including some of those mentioned above, are ethnic groups, a fact which further intensifies their isolation. (A few, like the

---

standard systems of currency and/or weights and measures; these efforts, however, generally proved ineffective. Inconsistent policies in taxation, too, hinder the development of a "rational" economy.

7. The status of the true merchant in the preindustrial city, ideally, has been low; in medieval Europe and China many merchants were considered "outcastes." However, in some preindustrial cities a few wealthy merchants have acquired considerable power even though their role has not been highly valued. Even then most of their prestige has come through participation in religious, governmental, or educational activities, which have been highly valued (see, e.g., Ping-ti Ho, "The Salt Merchants of Yang-Chou: A Study of Commercial Capitalism in Eighteenth-Century China," *Harvard Journal of Asiatic Studies*, XVII [1954], 130-68).

Jews in the predominantly Muslim cities of North Africa, have their own small literate religious elite which, however, enjoys no significant political power in the city as a whole.)

An assumption of many urban sociologists is that a small, unstable kinship group, notably the conjugal unit, is a necessary correlate of city life. But this premise does not hold for preindustrial cities.[8] At times sociologists and anthropologists, when generalizing about various traditional societies, have imputed to peasants typically urban kinship patterns. Actually, in these societies the ideal forms of kinship and family life are most closely approximated by members of the urban literate elite, who are best able to fulfil the exacting requirements of the sacred writings. Kinship and the ability to perpetuate one's lineage are accorded marked prestige in preindustrial cities. Children, especially sons, are highly valued, and polygamy or concubinage or adoption help to assure the attainment of large families. The pre-eminence of kinship is apparent even in those preindustrial cities where divorce is permitted. Thus, among the urban Muslims or urban Chinese divorce is not an index of disorganization; here, conjugal ties are loose and distinctly subordinate to the bonds of kinship, and each member of a dissolved conjugal unit typically is absorbed by his kin group. Marriage, a prerequisite to adult status in the preindustrial city, is entered upon at an early age and is arranged between families rather than romantically, by individuals.

The kinship and familial organization displays some rigid patterns of sex and age differentiation whose universality in preindustrial cities has generally been overlooked. A woman, especially of the upper class, ideally performs few significant functions outside the home. She is clearly subordinate to males, especially her father or husband. Recent evidence indicates that this is true even for such a city as Lhasa, Tibet, where women supposedly have had high status.[9] The isolation of women from public life has in some cases been extreme. In nineteenth-century Seoul, Korea, "respectable" women appeared on the streets only during certain hours of the night when men were supposed to stay at home.[10] Those women in

---

8. For materials on the kinship system and age and sex differentiation see, e.g., Le Tourneau, *op. cit.*; Edward W. Lane, *The Manners and Customs of the Modern Egyptians* (3d ed.; New York: E. P. Dutton Co., 1923); C. Snouck Hurgronje, *Mekka in the Latter Part of the Nineteenth Century*, trans. J. H. Monahan (London: Luzac, 1931); Horace Miner, *The Primitive City of Timbuctoo* (Princeton: Princeton University Press, 1953); Alice M. Bacon, *Japanese Girls and Women* (rev. ed.; Boston; Houghton Mifflin Co., 1902); J. S. Burgess, "Community Organization in China," *Far Eastern Survey*, XIV (1945), 371-73; Morton H. Fried, *Fabric of Chinese Society* (New York: Frederick A. Praeger, 1953); Francis L. K. Hsu, *Under the Ancestors' Shadow* (New York: Columbia University Press, 1948); Cornelius Osgood, *The Koreans and Their Culture* (New York: Ronald Press, 1951), chap. viii; Jukichi Inouye, *Home Life in Tokyo* (2d ed.; Tokyo: Tokyo Printing Co., 1911).

9. Tsung-Lien Shen and Shen-Chi Liu, *Tibet and the Tibetans* (Stanford: Stanford University Press, 1953), pp. 143-44.

10. Osgood, *op. cit.*, p. 146.

preindustrial cities who evade some of the stricter requirements are members of certain marginal groups (e.g., entertainers) or of the lower class. The role of the urban lower-class woman typically resembles that of the peasant rather than the urban upper-class woman. Industrialization, by creating demands and opportunities for their employment outside the home, is causing significant changes in the status of women as well as in the whole of the kinship system in urban areas.

A formalized system of age grading is an effective mechanism of social control in preindustrial cities. Among siblings the eldest son is privileged. And children and youth are subordinate to parents and other adults. This, combined with early marriage, inhibits the development of a "youth culture." On the other hand, older persons hold considerable power and prestige, a fact contributing to the slow pace of change.

As noted above, kinship is functionally integrated with social class. It also reinforces and is reinforced by the economic organization: the occupations, through the guilds, select their members primarily on the basis of kinship, and much of the work is carried on in the home or immediate vicinity. Such conditions are not functional to the requirements of a highly industrialized society.

The kinship system in the preindustrial city also articulates with a special kind of religious system, whose formal organization reaches fullest development among members of the literate elite.[11] The city is the seat of the key religious functionaries whose actions set standards for the rest of society. The urban lower class, like the peasantry, does not possess the education or the means to maintain all the exacting norms prescribed by the sacred writings. Yet the religious system influences the city's entire social structure. (Typically, within the preindustrial city one religion is dominant; however, certain minority groups adhere to their own beliefs.) Unlike the situation in industrial cities, religious activity is not separate from other social action but permeates family, economic, governmental, and other activities. Daily life is pervaded with religious significance. Especially important are periodic public festivals and ceremonies like Ramadan in Muslim cities. Even distinctly ethnic outcaste groups can through their own religious festivals maintain solidarity.

Magic, too, is interwoven with economic, familial, and other social activities. Divination is commonly employed for determining the "correct" action on critical occasions; for example, in traditional Japanese and Chinese cities, the selection of marriage partners. And nonscientific

---

11. For information on various aspects of religious behavior see e.g., Le Tourneau, *op. cit.*; Miner, *op. cit.*; Lane, *Manners and Customs*; Hurgronje, *op. cit.*; André Chouraqui, *Les Juifs d'Afrique du Nord* (Paris: Presses Universitaires de France, 1952); Justus Doolittle, *Social Life of the Chinese* (London: Sampson Low, 1868); John K. Shryock, *The Temples of Anking and Their Cults* (Paris: Privately printed, 1931); Derk Bodde (ed.), *Annual Customs and Festivals in Peking* (Peiping: Henri Vetch, 1936); Edwin Benson, *Life in a Medieval City* (New York: Macmillan Co., 1920); Hsu, *op. cit.*

procedures are widely employed to treat illness among all elements of the population of the preindustrial city.

Formal education typically is restricted to the male elite, its purpose being to train individuals for positions in the governmental, educational, or religious hierarchies. The economy of preindustrial cities does not require mass literacy, nor, in fact, does the system of production provide the leisure so necessary for the acquisition of formal education. Considerable time is needed merely to learn the written language, which often is quite different from that spoken. The teacher occupies a position of honor, primarily because of the prestige of all learning and especially of knowledge of the sacred literature, and learning is traditional and characteristically based upon sacred writings.[12] Students are expected to memorize rather than evaluate and initiate, even in institutions of higher learning.

Since preindustrial cities have no agencies of mass communication, they are relatively isolated from one another. Moreover, the masses within a city are isolated from the elite. The former must rely upon verbal communication, which is formalized in special groups such as storytellers or their counterparts. Through verse and song these transmit upper-class tradition to nonliterate individuals.

The formal government of the preindustrial city is the province of the elite and is closely integrated with the educational and religious systems. It performs two principal functions: exacting tribute from the city's masses to support the activities of the elite and maintaining law and order through a "police force" (at times a branch of the army) and a court system. The police force exists primarily for the control of "outsiders," and the courts support custom and the rule of the sacred literature, a code of enacted legislation typically being absent.

In actual practice little reliance is placed upon formal machinery for regulating social life.[13] Much more significant are the informal controls exerted by the kinship, guild, and religious systems, and here, of course, personal standing is decisive. Status distinctions are visibly correlated with personal attributes, chiefly speech, dress, and personal mannerisms which proclaim ethnic group, occupation, age, sex, and social class. In nineteenth-century Seoul, not only did the upper-class mode of dress differ considerably from that of the masses, but speech varied according to social class, the verb forms and pronouns depending upon whether the speaker ranked higher or lower or was the equal of the person being addressed.[14] Obviously, then, escape from one's role is difficult, even in the street

---

12. Le Tourneau, *op. cit.*, Part VI; Lane, *Manners and Customs*, chap. ii; Charles Bell, *The People of Tibet* (Oxford: Clarendon Press, 1928), chap. xix; O. Olufsen, *The Emir of Bokhara and His Country* (London: William Heinemann, 1911), chap. ix; Doolittle, *op. cit.*

13. Carleton Coon, *Caravan: The Story of the Middle East* (New York: Henry Holt & Co., 1951), p. 259; George W. Gilmore, *Korea from Its Capital* (Philadelphia: Presbyterian Board of Publication, 1892), pp. 51-52.

14. Osgood, *op. cit.*, chap. viii; Gilmore, *op. cit.*, chap. iv.

crowds. The individual is ever conscious of his specific rights and duties. All these things conserve the social order in the preindustrial city despite its heterogeneity.

CONCLUSIONS. Throughout this paper there is the assumption that certain structural elements are universal for all urban centers. This study's hypothesis is that their form in the preindustrial city is fundamentally distinct from that in the industrial-urban community. A considerable body of data not only from medieval Europe, which is somewhat atypical,[15] but from a variety of cultures supports this point of view. Emphasis has been upon the static features of preindustrial city life. But even those preindustrial cities which have undergone considerable change approach the ideal type. For one thing, social change is of such a nature that it is not usually perceived by the general populace.

Most cities of the preindustrial type have been located in Europe or Asia. Even though Athens and Rome and the large commercial centers of Europe prior to the industrial revolution displayed certain unique features, they fit the preindustrial type quite well.[16] And many traditional Latin-American cities are quite like it, although deviations exist, for, excluding pre-Columbian cities, these were affected to some degree by the industrial revolution soon after their establishment.

It is postulated that industrialization is a key variable accounting for the distinctions between preindustrial and industrial cities. The type of social structure required to develop and maintain a form of production utilizing inanimate sources of power is quite unlike that in the preindustrial city.[17] At the very least, extensive industrialization requires a rational, centralized, extra-community economic organization in which recruitment is based more upon universalism than on particularism, a class system which stresses achievement rather than ascription, a small and flexible kinship system, a system of mass education which emphasizes universalistic rather than particularistic criteria, and mass communication. Modification in any one of these elements affects the others and induces changes in other systems such as those of religion and social control as well. Industrialization, moreover, not only requires a special kind of social structure within the urban community but provides the means necessary for its establishment.

---

15. Henri Pirenne, in *Medieval Cities* (Princeton: Princeton University Press, 1925), and others have noted that European cities grew up in opposition to and were separate from the greater society. But this thesis has been overstated for medieval Europe. Most preindustrial cities are integral parts of broader social structures.

16. Some of these cities made extensive use of water power, which possibly fostered deviations from the type.

17. For a discussion of the institutional prerequisites of industrialization see, e.g., Bert F. Hoselitz, "Social Structure and Economic Growth," *Economia Internazionale*, VI (1953), 52-77, and Marion J. Levy, "Some Sources of the Vulnerability of the Structures of Relatively Non-industrialized Societies to Those of Highly Industrialized Societies," in Bert F. Hoselitz (ed.), *The Progress of Underdeveloped Areas* (Chicago: University of Chicago Press, 1952), pp. 114 ff.

Anthropologists and sociologists will, in the future, devote increased attention to the study of cities throughout the world. They must therefore recognize that the particular kind of social structure found in cities in the United States is not typical of all societies. Miner's recent study of Timbuctoo,[18] which contains much excellent data, points to the need for recognition of the preindustrial city. His emphasis upon the folk-urban continuum diverted him from an equally significant problem: How does Timbuctoo differ from modern industrial cities in its ecological, economic, and social structure? Society there seems even more sacred and organized than Miner admits.[19] For example, he used divorce as an index of disorganization, but in Muslim society divorce within certain rules is justified by the sacred literature. The studies of Hsu and Fried would have considerably more significance had the authors perceived the generality of their findings. And, once the general structure of the preindustrial city is understood, the specific cultural deviations become more meaningful.

Beals notes the importance of the city as a center of acculturation.[20] But an understanding of this process is impossible without some knowledge of the preindustrial city's social structure. Although industrialization is clearly advancing throughout most of the world, the social structure of preindustrial civilizations is conservative, often resisting the introduction of numerous industrial forms. Certainly many cities of Europe (e.g., in France or Spain) are not so fully industrialized as some presume; a number of preindustrial patterns remain. The persistence of preindustrial elements is also evident in cities of North Africa and many parts of Asia; for example, in India and Japan,[21] even though great social change is currently taking place. And the Latin-American city of Merida, which Redfield studied, had many preindustrial traits.[22] A conscious awareness of the ecological, economic, and social structure of the preindustrial city should do much to further the development of comparative urban community studies.

18. *Op. cit.*

19. This point seems to have been perceived also by Asael T. Hansen in his review of Horace Miner's *The Primitive City of Timbuctoo, American Journal of Sociology,* LIX (1954), 501-2.

20. Ralph L. Beals, "Urbanism, Urbanization and Acculturation," *American Anthropologist,* LIII (1951), 1-10.

21. See, e.g., D. R. Gadgil, *Poona: A Socio-economic Survey* (Poona: Gokhale Institute of Politics and Economics, 1952), Part II; N. V. Sovani, *Social Survey of Kolhapur City* (Poona: Gokhale Institute of Politics and Economics, 1951), Vol. II; Noel P. Gist, "Caste Differentials in South India," *American Sociological Review,* XIX (1954), 126-37; John Campbell Pelzel, "Social Stratification in Japanese Urban Economic Life" (unpublished Ph.D. dissertation, Harvard University, Department of Social Relations, 1950).

22. Robert Redfield, *The Folk Culture of Yucatan* (Chicago: University of Chicago Press, 1941).

THE INDUSTRIAL CITY:
CENTER OF CULTURAL CHANGE

Ralph E. Turner

In 1832 the *Manchester Guardian*, commenting on an exposure of bad living conditions among the factory population, offered as an apology for their existence the following observation: "The manufacturing system as it exists in Great Britain, and the inconceivably immense towns under it, are without previous parallel in the history of the world." This recognition of the industrial city as an unprecedented phenomenon was developed, not as an apology for bad living conditions, but as an explanation of the general changes under way in society, by two English observers of early industrialism, namely, William Cooke Taylor and Robert Vaughan, both of whom, it is worth noting, were historians. Taylor wrote a general history of civilization under the title *The Natural History of Society* (1841), besides many textbooks; and Vaughan, before he became president of the Lancashire Independent College at Manchester, was professor of history at the University of London. In a sense, therefore, it may be said that the view of the industrial city as a center of cultural change belongs peculiarly to historians.

Taylor held that the industrial town was a "new element" in society, which could not develop without deranging old institutions and relationships. It exhibited, he said, "a system of social life constructed on a wholly new principle, a principle yet vague and indefinite but developing itself by its own spontaneous force, and daily producing effects which no human foresight had anticipated." Above all, he was impressed by the formation of the urban masses who, developing new habits of thought without external aid or guidance, would ultimately, like the slow rising and gradual swelling of the ocean, "bear all elements of society aloft upon its bosom." But, although these masses lacked guidance, they were, in his opinion, no worse off than their superiors who, however educated, found little in past human experience of use in understanding the unforeseen innovations of the factory towns. The Greek verse, said Taylor, meant nothing in Manchester, and philosophy knew no circumstances like those which prevailed there.

Vaughan, who pointed out the fact, none too well recognized even

Reprinted from *The Cultural Approach to History*, edited by Caroline F. Ware, pp. 228-242, by permission of the author and the Columbia University Press. (Copyright, 1940 by Columbia University Press.)

today, that rural and urban populations have played different roles in the growth of civilization, argued that in the "unavoidable intercourse" of the new towns there was occurring an education of the people that would stimulate science, advance self-government, improve the arts and literature, and raise the general level of popular life. "Such, indeed, is often the astuteness acquired in the exercise of this greatest of free schools," he said, "that the smith of Sheffield, or the weaver of Manchester, would frequently prove, on any common ground, more than a match for a college graduate." Vaughan saw the new industrial towns as centers of "vast experiments" like those which had occurred in the cities of other lands and ages.

For us who live today in the midst of what is a chaos understood badly if at all, the views of Taylor and Vaughan may provide a point of departure for a consideration of the prevailing confusion. At least, it is clear that, if the English industrial city of the 1840's was a scene of "vast experiments," today, with similar cities having become the dominant type of community in all industrial nations, "vast experiments" have probably been carried further than they had gone in the early nineteenth century. Similarly, if, as Taylor said, the urban masses will ultimately bear all society aloft, it is probable that the tendency of this bearing is more clear today than when he noted it.

An examination of the industrial city as a center of cultural change may indicate something of these "vast experiments," may possibly show the general direction in which the urban masses are tending. It is the purpose of this paper to sketch the outlines of such an examination.

The postulates of the examination are to be found in the concept of culture, as developed in recent social thought, especially by anthropologists and sociologists. According to their views, "a culture" is a socially organized and transmitted structure of behavior and thought. The structure is integrated functionally, that is, its elements provide more of a unity than of a conflict of services to life and have coherence psychologically in terms of a relatively clearly focused outlook on life. The basis of this integration is a process of social interaction, through which individual interests and needs are organized into collective forms or patterns. In the growth of culture, the social process impels individuals to new modes of action and thought—innovations, they are called—and these new modes, in turn, become organized as enduring patterns, through selection in the social process. The evolution of any structure of human behavior and thought, when viewed in historical perspective, is recognizable as the evolution of a cultural tradition which, from time to time as new social conditions arise, assimilates new elements in what may be called a reorientation of the tradition. The newly assimilated elements, it may be believed, seldom outweigh those persisting from the past.

This conception of the evolution of behavior and thought also predicates that, although cultural development goes forward constantly both by the loss of old elements and by the assimilation of innovations, there may be far-reaching disturbances in a cultural tradition which, disorganizing a long-persisting integration, produces finally a new integration. At the base of such new integration, setting its pattern and tendency of growth, is the social process through which individual behavior and thought are originally organized and finally assimilated into transmitted materials. In the words of A. A. Goldenweiser,

> In its constituent elements culture is psychological and, in the last analysis, comes from the individual. But as an integral entity culture is cumulative, historical, extra-individual. It comes to the individual as part of his objective experience, just as do his experiences with nature, and, like these, it is absorbed by him, thus becoming part of his psychic content.[1]

It is from the point of view of these predications that the industrial city can be seen as having special significance for cultural development. Relative to the life that prevailed in the traditional countryside and the old market and port towns, it is not difficult to understand that the industrial city tends to organize a new structure of behavior and thought. The original patterns of this structure, as they emerged in Manchester, England, have been sketched in another essay in this volume;[2] here it is important to emphasize that the industrial city, as a focus of technological, economic, political, intellectual, and esthetic changes, organized cultural influences from many sources in a social process in which the constantly increasing populations participated. Whatever the influences of industrial cities, these influences move in the social interaction that arises in city populations, as individuals carry on their occupations, pursue their interests, and obtain their satisfactions. In terms of the concept of culture, the industrial city is, then, a milieu which everywhere has the same general elements and everywhere supports the development of a structure of behavior and thought from these elements. Because it is a predication of the concept of culture that both behavior and thought, although individually expressed, are socially organized, this milieu may be conceived as bringing about, through time, the transformation of the various organizations of behavior and thought carried in the traditional culture. Thus, for example, the organizations of behavior and thought characterizing the historic sociocultural types—the peasant, the noble, and the priest—are transformed into new structures of behavior and thought, which, however different for workers, technicians, and entrepreneurs, are nevertheless the common base of their lives.

Some of the aspects of this developing structure of behavior and thought may be briefly noted. Its primary elements are evident in the intricate division of labor, which, instead of standardizing and routinizing

---

1. A. A. Goldenweiser, *History, Psychology, and Culture* (New York, 1933), p. 59.
2. See Chap. X in *The Cultural Approach to History*, edited by Caroline F. Ware (New York: Columbia University Press, 1940).

work as commonly supposed, gives it a manifold variety of forms which make the new urban workers not a "uniform mass" but a composite of diversified types. In contrast to the historic peasants, the members of the new industrial working class possess individuality in a great variety of forms. This developing structure of thought and behavior is also evident in new social services, in new amusements, in new intellectual and artistic pursuits, as well as in new technological and economic procedures. Also the new structure of behavior and thought is embodied in new standards of consumption, in new relationships of the sexes and the members of families, in new positions of the several age groups, in new circumstances affecting health, and in new causes of death. For individuals, these aspects are elements of a changing behavior and mentality; for the industrial city milieu, they are attributes fixed upon individuals coming under its influences.

From the point of view of cultural development, it is necessary to conceive of the beginnings of this structure of behavior and thought as appearing in the early industrial cities, of its elements spreading and maturing as industrial cities have grown, and, finally, of these elements becoming integrated through an intellectual outlook upon or a feeling for life shaped in terms of the frame of reference organized in experience as it goes on among the masses who now live in industrial cities. This matter may be stated in another way. If the industrial city, considered as the social milieu of a new structure of behavior and thought, is influencing ever larger parts of national populations, this influence is evident, on the one hand, in the dislocation of old forms of behavior and thought in the several national traditions and, on the other hand, in the appearance and spread of new forms. However, at the moment, because the dislocation of the old forms intensifies the emotional attachments to them, the new ones are not recognized. If at the moment such is the case, the prevailing confusion is understandable in the feeling that, although the old modes of behavior and thought no longer serve life, there is nothing to replace them. In truth, however, the modes of behavior and thought of a *new* culture may be implicit in the industrial city, requiring only recognition and acceptance to become the basis of conscious action. In the words of Robert H. Lowie, the anthropologist, "Culture, it seems, is a matter of exceedingly slow growth until a certain 'threshold' is passed, when it darts forward, gathering momentum at an unexpected rate."[3] The present disturbed situation in western culture, where the industrial city originated and has had its fullest development, may be only the approach to such a "threshold."

Before turning to a consideration of some of the aspects of industrial-city life which may be factors at the "threshold" of a cultural change, it is well to note that no one meant to create the industrial city or, as cur-

---

3. Robert H. Lowie, *Culture and Ethnology* (New York, 1917), p. 78.

rently designated in the United States, the "metropolitan urban area." It arose as entrepreneurs pursued their interest—profits—and engineers served that interest by technological ingenuity. But once created, it became something other than a center of business and machine industry, that is, it became a milieu having the power to organize socially a structure of behavior and thought for those coming under its influence. For this reason the industrial city may ultimately react on business and industry, giving them new forms, in spite of the interests of entrepreneurs. It seems that commonly men do two things when they perform an act, first, what they intend to do and, second, what they do not intend to do. And often the second thing is more important than the first. Certainly this seems to be the case with those persons who, while their intentional activities were chiefly concerned with making money, unknowingly created the industrial city, which, as a social milieu, is now the matrix of cultural change.

An examination of the development of industrial cities shows three classes of factors which may be considered as having significance for further cultural development. Although these factors may not have originated completely in the industrial city, their influence in contemporary life is focused in its milieu, so that they must be considered as elements of a complex of urban psychological influences. These three classes of factors may be designated: (1) the paradox of economic liberalism, (2) conditions having origin in machine technology, and (3) conditions of urban association. Each of these classes of psychological factors ramifies through contemporary society, having many manifestations and exciting many comments. However, only in the industrial city or the metropolitan urban milieu can they be viewed objectively.

By the paradox of economic liberalism, the central predications of which are too widely accepted to require statement here, is meant that entrepreneurial activity has created conditions which not only restrict the freedom of individuals but also reveal that the presumptions that universal competition promotes the automatic realization of a constantly advancing well-being are false. The restrictions on individual freedom of action have objective form in the hierarchies of employment which have appeared as technological developments have brought together ever larger units of capital. For individuals employed in these hierarchies, economic advancement is more a matter of rising from grade to grade than a shift from the status "employee" to the status "entrepreneur." Moreover, in these hierarchies economic power is exercised from the top downward. Through the "right to fire," the qualities of behavior that bring advancement become less and less those summed up in the phrase "individual initiative" and more and more those implied in the word "loyalty." Actually "conformity" rather than "initiative" is the quality desired in an ever-increasing body of individuals who occupy the status of employee. It is also important to note that economic power exerted from the top of these hierarchies upon individuals in the lower levels of employment does interfere upon occasions with the exercise of personal liberties in areas of life quite beyond that of the economic functioning of the hierarchies. The effect of this interference is to impose upon more and more individuals a regimentation in terms of private interests. Indeed, in many ways the current assertion of the doctrines of economic liberalism is merely a defense for economic power that functions as private regimentation.

Probably no more concise statement of the contradiction between the theory of economic liberalism and the fact of the private regimentation which prevails among the populations of industrial cities can be cited than the following words from Walter Lippmann's column, "How Liberty Is Lost":

> To have economic independence a man must be in a position to leave one job and go to another; he must have enough savings of some kind to exist for a considerable time without accepting the first job offered. . . . the industrial worker who has a choice between working in one factory and not working at all, the white collar intellectuals who compete savagely for the relatively few private positions and for posts in the bureaucracy—these are the people who live too precariously to exercise their liberties or to defend them. They have no savings. They have only their labor to sell, and there are very few buyers of their labor. Therefore, they have only the choice of truckling to the powerful or of perishing heroically but miserably.[4]

Who are the great to whom these workers shall truckle? The private employers or the politicians who promise jobs? The economic and political crises which have already swept away some liberal regimes, and which now threaten the remainder, root in this social soil.

In this connection, it is worth observing that, from the cultural point of view, the mere criticism of a social order cannot be the basis of social reconstruction. Indeed, if a program of social reform or amelioration can be successfully based on a critique of a social order, progress away from the conditions giving rise to the paradox of economic liberalism should have been rapid, since the rise of the early industrial cities, for the eloquence of the writers of those times on these conditions has not been surpassed by writers of the present century. But to be able to point out social evils—even, in fact, to understand their origin—is not to become adequate to deal with them. For they cannot be dealt with in terms of themselves or even in terms of the institutions which give rise to them. In other words, the evils cannot be dealt with merely as problems of distress, unemployment, and the like, or as aspects of a social order retaining the essential characteristics described in the doctrines of economic liberalism; they must be dealt with in terms of the potentialities of cultural change, implicit in the industrial city milieu. To know these potentialities involves not the emotional excitement raised by pointing to the evils, but a technique of analysis of the factors in cultural development. And to the development of this technique few social critics have made contributions.

---

4. *New York Herald Tribune*, July 16, 1938.

In turning to a consideration of the two other classes of factors which are elements of the industrial city milieu, namely, conditions having their origin in machine technology and conditions of urban association, it is necessary to point out that the items listed under these headings have been arrived at in a certain way. This way has been an isolation of the repetitive, or recurring elements in industrial urban life, or, in other words, the finding of its continuously pervasive elements. This mode of analysis has been adopted on the ground that a culture, as an integrated and persisting structure of behavior and thought, is constructed psychologically upon a relatively stable order of stimuli, in terms of which patterns of reaction are developed. To such repetitive stimuli the great part of an industrial population react, and the recurring reactions become the determining tendencies of the development of the urban structure of life. Culture, it must be remembered, is both a psychological and a social phenomenon.

This way of analysis is not unfamiliar in American historiography. In fact, the classic essay, "The Significance of the Frontier in American History," by Frederick Jackson Turner, which has received the lip, if not the mind service of a generation of students of American history, embodies it. The fundamental postulate of this essay is that a persisting underlying influence gave distinctive patterns to national life and furthermore created an intellectual outlook which unified the national culture. Certainly the following excerpts can be so understood.

> The existence of an area of free land, its continuous recession, and the advance of American settlement westward explain American development.
>
> Behind institutions, behind constitutional forms and modifications, lie the vital forces that call these organs into life and shape them to meet changing conditions . . . .
>
> The frontier individualism has from the beginning promoted democracy. . . .
>
> The result is that to the frontier the American intellect owes its striking characteristics. That coarseness and strength combined with acuteness and inquisitiveness, that practical inventive turn of mind, quick to find expedients, that masterful grasp of material things, lacking in the artistic but powerful to effect great ends, that restless, nervous energy, that dominant individualism, working for good and for evil, and withal that buoyancy and exuberance which comes with freedom, these are traits of the frontier, or traits called out elsewhere because of the existence of the frontier.[5]

In terms of the concept of culture, the fact of "free land" may be understood as having established patterns which, as the frontier was pushed westward, were worked into the various phases of national life and, as individual experience and behavior were organized in these patterns, came to embody a pervasive psychological reaction which was the source of the subjective tradition of the national culture. In a sense, therefore,

---

5. "The Significance of the Frontier in American History," *The Early Writings of Frederick Jackson Turner*, compiled by E. E. Edwards (Madison, 1938), pp. 185-229, at pp. 186, 220, 227-28.

an analysis of current American developments in cultural terms is not greatly different from the mode of thinking which led Turner to his view of national development.

In every culture the integration of man with physical nature, in terms of technology, is significant in the life of the people who carry the culture. From this integration flows the wealth which supports the social order and certain basic judgments on life that have entered always into social attitudes, religious beliefs, and moral practices. There is no need here to discuss these phenomena, as they have long existed in cultures having an agrarian base. From contemporary technology come, it seems, at least three recognizable conditions that may contribute to the shaping of new cultural forms:

First: The sense of human control. Machine technology is operated by energy produced and controlled by man; in fact, it represents the fullest expression of his rationality. He creates power, orders its flow, governs its movement, and determines its resultant. In this circumstance exists ground for the assumption that what man achieves in one field of action, he may also do in another field. As a result of man's triumph in technology, it may be that he feels more able to command his fate socially. The emergence of the concept "planned economy" roots at least partly in this circumstance.

Second: The utility of objective knowledge. That knowledge is power is appreciated by the simplest mechanic; in terms of a special body of knowledge, every machine operator or machine fixer performs his task. This circumstance boldly insists that it is knowledge which functions to give success in every situation, that myth, tradition, and special interest must give way to knowledge—and the knowledge meant is worldly, factual, and utilitarian. By implication, therefore, machine technology supports the view that social distress exists either because of lack of knowledge or because of the unwillingness to apply what is at hand.

Third: The increasing capacity to produce wealth. With the advent of machinery and applied science in agriculture and industry, man's capacity to produce wealth expanded enormously. For example, between 1920 and 1930 the agricultural population of the United States decreased by 4,000,000 persons, while agricultural production increased by 25 per cent; now agricultural economists estimate that the agricultural population, not counting the backlog of persons who would have migrated to cities if jobs had been available, could be decreased by at least 3,000,000 persons without seriously affecting the agricultural production necessary to maintain national consumption at present standards. It has been estimated that since about 1870 the capacity to produce in manufacturing industries has increased 3 per cent per year. Especially important is the fact that the increase of productivity has gone on steadily during the present depression decade. This fact is relevant to the present situation, which finds industrial production near the 1929 level without the employment of an equal number of workers.

These three conditions having their origin in contemporary technology —the sense of human control, the utility of objective knowledge, and the increasing capacity to produce wealth—point more and more directly to an economy in which human control, exercised with knowledge rather than with self-interest, may utilize the new capacity to produce wealth for the support of a more secure life.

In closing this comment on the new conditions of life that have come with contemporary technology, it should be noted that one does not need to be a philosopher in order to know them, for they run constantly in the experience of all who actually work at the production of real goods. In other words, these conditions are part and parcel of the life of the masses of industrial cities.

The conditions of urban association are certainly no less significant for setting the direction of cultural change than those arising in contemporary technology. In fact, because they have existence in social interaction, they are primary to these influences which, after all, are reactions of men to physical nature and not of men to men. Culture, it may be noted, stands between man and nature, whereas man comes to culture through the social process.

From this point of view four conditions of industrial urban association are significant:

First: The disintegration of localism and tradition. Innumerable social stimuli flow through the contemporary urban population. Newspapers, movies, and radio pour the world into their eyes and ears; from these visual and aural images there is no escape. By the number and impact of these social stimuli, local prejudices and old traditions are disintegrated. By this wearing away, the urban masses are freed to take on views which harmonize with their social environment—the industrial city as a whole, not merely as a place where labor is sold and a profit is made. Indeed, the rise of propaganda, i.e., the organized control of mass opinion, has its origin in this circumstance, for as the masses are released from local and traditional opinions, they become free to move in new directions. Propaganda is organized by special interests in order to determine this direction. In the end, however, the movement of mass mentality will necessarily be in the direction set by the milieu which exists in the going experience of thousands of individuals.

Second: The cult of uniformity. As social stimuli flow continuously through the urban masses by way of machine-made commodities and routinized social services, manners, customs, and tastes are shaped into a wide conformity. This conformity is the necessary base of the organization of a complex social order among a large population; it makes for frictionless movement among large aggregates of individuals, who can, as a result, move together in actions not possible for them when they were embedded in local communities. Conformity serves the need for orderly coöperation in the intricate processes of urban society.

Third: The diversification of individual behavior. In communities antedating industrial cities, refinement, elegance, and taste were, in the main, attributes of small classes; to belong to these classes meant the possession of an explicit moral code, special forms of dress and manner, and particular intellectual affectations. In some respects these class attributes survive now, but among urban masses individual tastes find release from such controls. Thus there appear among urban populations innumerable groups pursuing self-selected interests, and individuals are permitted wide variations from all norms of conduct. The modern urban milieu is fostering a diversification of intellectual, artistic, and amusemental pursuits, unheard of in earlier types of communities. Individual energies are free to find expression in more ways than ever before. The industrial city well exemplifies the sociological principle that as social organization becomes more complex, individuals necessarily have more opportunity for development.

Fourth: The reorientation of the right of property. From the point of view of the concept of culture, the social rather than the economic factor is decisive in historical development. Thus it need cause no surprise that the social milieu of the industrial city is affecting the right of property—indeed, the whole relationship of men and wealth. The prevailing concept of property was derived from societies mainly agrarian in their economic and social organization. It is a concept developed mainly in terms of tangible goods, for it emphasizes possession on the ground that from possessions flow the benefits of ownership. Now it appears that property in this sense has been becoming less and less important in the lives of all urban dwellers. Urban dwellers, even those having great wealth, can own very little of the property upon which their lives continually depend. The rich and the poor alike are dependent upon a continuity of services—water, food, light, heat, protection—which are maintained only through social coöperation. And they demand not ownership of these services, but their continuous functioning, regardless of ownership. Similarly, the owner of tangible property, whatever it may be, can produce little with the property that contributes to real satisfacion. His property probably functions to create any wealth that gives real satisfaction only through a minute division of labor, and such wealth is produced only through the maintenance of this division of labor. Finally, since the individual in the modern urban economy, no matter who he may be, can command few real goods through the possession of real property, he must possess some claim upon wealth which can be executed in diverse ways; for only by such execution can he acquire the diversity of real goods which supports urban modes of living. Thus it appears that in the modern industrial city the ownership of property is far less important to the support of individual life than the maintenance of certain fundamental economic services and the establishment of some kind of claim on currently produced real goods. In fact, the elaboration of the modes of ownership through various kinds of legal claims—securities, trusts, insurance annuities, and social security claims—is an adjustment to this growing social orientation of the right of property.

However confused and clouded this exposition of the factors in the industrial urban milieu has been, it has made these factors far more clear than they are. Actually they exist today as part of the chaos previously noted. They are vaguely felt impulses, uncertain judgments, and befogged visions; they are neither defined nor oriented. However, they run in the experience of urban masses, as life goes on in terms of the labor market, machine technology, and urban association; and, as combined in a day-by-day routine, they form a frame of reference which for these masses, without conscious effort on their part, becomes the point of departure of feeling and thinking. Thus from this frame of reference issues, in the life of the masses, new attitudes toward their problems, new definitions of their interests, and new concepts of what life ought to be like. More important still in the day-by-day routine of behavior, as organized under the influence of this complex of urban forces, are the elements which may be combined in new patterns of behavior that will constitute the culture which is correlative with the modes of thinking and feeling set in this frame of reference. In other words, the frame of reference, as the subjective content of life shaped by the complex of urban forces, and the day-by-day routines of behavior, as the objective content of life shaped by this complex, together form the psychological basis for the integration of thought and behavior in a new culture.

In the concept of culture, it is postulated that at any time there are a limited number of possible modes of thinking and acting; therefore, as far as the contemporary world is concerned, if the old forms of thought and behavior are to be displaced (as, indeed, they are being displaced), the complex of urban forces which shapes this frame of reference and day-by-day routine of behavior of the urban masses fixes the possibilities for the future. It is pertinent to state here that because this frame of reference and this day-by-day routine of behavior are organized through social interaction, they affect, to some degree, the smaller specialized urban groups as well as the urban masses; for this reason contemporary cultural change is not merely an adjustment to the rise of a new social class. It is, in fact, far more fundamental, for it is touching all classes, compelling those which have been dominant to alter the forms of their control if they are to remain dominant. The twentieth century cannot have just any kind of social order; it must have one oriented in terms of the contemporary industrial urban milieu.

If one seeks a general heading under which to sum up the most significant aspect of the cultural change under way in nations whose chief communities are industrial cities or metropolitan urban areas, it would seem to be the phrase "a reëducation of the masses." Before the rise of industrial cities, the overwhelming proportion of population in all lands consisted of peasants—socially isolated, superstitious, tenacious of the land, and illiterate. As industrial cities grew, the peasant element declined and the urban masses formed. It should be recognized that, as the masses shifted to the cities, they brought with them the mentality of peasants; this has been a primary condition in their reëducation which, even today, the contrivers of propaganda know how to use. But, once in the city, the new circumstances of life—the labor market, machine technology, and urban association—began to affect their behavior and thought. It is not contended that the urban masses have been or are now conscious of this process of reëducation; it is only argued that they necessarily act and think under its effects, and that such action and thought are the elements of the cultural change now under way.

THE RISE OF METROPOLITAN COMMUNITIES

R. D. McKenzie

A striking phenomenon of population change in the United States during the past half century has been that which may be described in general terms as a movement from the country to the city. Since 1880 the percentage of population classified as urban has nearly doubled, while that classified as rural has declined proportionately. This statement gives only a very rough idea of what has happened. Urban territory, under the census classification, includes all communities having 2,500 or more inhabitants. Thus Kenilworth, Illinois, with a population of 2,501 in 1930, falls into the same group as Chicago with 3,376,438; and Cooperstown, New York, with 2,909, is "urban" as well as Greater New York with 6,930,446.

More precise results may be obtained by subdividing "urban" communities into nine groups, beginning with those having populations between 2,500 and 5,000 and ending with those having 1,000,000 or more. By dividing our urban population into nine or more fractions according to the sizes of the communities in which it resides it is possible to determine the relative degree of "urbanization" which prevails. But even this method has proved unsatisfactory because it does not give a true picture of the organization of our urban territory. We are coming to think of the city not only as an agglomeration of people but as a way of living, with an influence extending far beyond its own borders. It is the growth of the metropolitan way of living which we now wish to trace rather than merely the increase of metropolitan populations; and it is to the tracing and analyzing of this growth that the present report is largely devoted.

With the increasing ease and rapidity of travel, particularly by motor car, the large city has not only brought under its sway much territory that was formerly rural, but has extended its influence far out into territory that is still classified as rural. Smaller communities within a wide radius of every urban center have lost much of their former isolation, provincialism and independence. Even beyond the commuting area, the city reaches out with its newspapers, radio broadcasts, amusements and shopping facilities. In this process the character of the city itself is somewhat altered. If the suburban and country districts are urbanized the city is in a degree ruralized. Its people more and more go outside the corporate limits to live, to spend their vacations and to find recreation. Thus the city of former days is really being replaced by a new entity, the metropolitan community, with

Reprinted from *Recent Social Trends* by permission of the McGraw-Hill Book Co. (Copyright, 1933, by the Research Committee on Social Trends, Inc.)

a distribution of population shading off from extreme congestion to relative sparseness, yet with some uniformity of character.

Each great city has its sphere of influence. By laying out these spheres on a map of the United States, according to criteria which will be explained in the body of the chapter, it is possible to divide the whole nation into metropolitan regions which economically and sociologically have greater reality than the several states. Three dimensions would be required in order to give a clear picture of this metropolitan organization of the country, for some of our metropolises are regional in character, some are inter-regional and one or two are international in their influence. Neighboring metropolises compete for trade and prestige, and the boundaries between the territories they control may be as fluctuating and as hotly disputed as though each were an independent principality.

At the same time each is likely to be affected in its life by one of the inter-regional metropolises, especially New York or Chicago. Each is increasingly aware of its economic and social unity, yet each tends to imitate the larger centers culturally. Thus the great cities preserve many differences arising from their history, their geographical location, the nature of their population and their sources of livelihood, but they also tend toward cultural uniformity. National advertising, motion pictures, and in recent years the radio play a large part in this latter process. There are also economic influences that cannot be so readily analyzed.

The metropolitan community is not a static thing, though it has some characteristics which are likely to distinguish it for a long time to come. It is a product of development and change and is certain to develop and change in the future. In this chapter an attempt is made to measure, in terms of recent trends, the manner in which our urban population is concentrating itself, the characteristics of the metropolitan region, the nature of the growth process within the region, the part played by regional planning and zoning, and the role of metropolitan governments.

It cannot be too strongly emphasized that the modern metropolitan community is practically a new social and economic entity, comparable in some respects with the city state of ancient and medieval times, but in other respects unprecedented. The metropolitan region is the child of modern facilities for transportation and communication. These facilities, have created the situations and problems of social and economic organization with which the present chapter deals.

I. THE TREND TOWARD METROPOLITANISM. Recent developments in means of communication have so enlarged the scope of local life that the ordinary individual, in the pursuit of his daily activities of work and leisure, is no longer confined to a single village, town or even a city. The modern community usually embraces a number of centers of different size, each more or less specialized in its institutions and its services. In other words it is characterized by a geographical division of labor.

We shall attempt to sketch the rise of this community of multiple centers, to examine some of the important changes taking place in local institutions as a result of specialization and differentiation of function and, finally, to outline a few of the problems associated with this complex pattern of local activities.

Two outstanding factors in the changing character of the local community are: (1) the increase in the aggregate population of the community and the extension of the area within which local activities are carried on in common; (2) the increased mobility of products and people, resulting in a wider range of individual choice, more specialization of local services and a more closely-knit community structure.

Concentration of Population.—Each of the last three censuses has reported an increasing geographical concentration of population. If the total population is divided into one-fourth, one-half and three-fourths, each fraction is found to be contained within an increasingly smaller area, as Table 1 clearly demonstrates.

TABLE I—Population Concentration as Shown by the Smallest Areas[a] Required to Obtain One-quarter, One-half and Three-quarters of the Total Inhabitants of the United States at Each of the Last Three Decennial Enumerations, 1910–1930[b]

		One-quarter of Population		One-half of Population		Three-quarters of Population	
Year	Total Population	Number of Counties	Area (Sq. Mi.)	Number of Counties	Area (Sq. Mi.)	Number of Counties	Area (Sq. Mi.)
1910	91,972,266	39	23,243	312	264,868	1,068	887,829
1920	105,710,620	33	19,270	250	224,944	992	856,820
1930	122,775,046	27	14,431	189	170,517	862	767,403

[a] Table is computed on county units; independent cities are included.
[b] Compiled from U.S. Census reports.

This table understates rather than overstates the actual facts of concentration.[1] Counties are grouped according to rank in population rather than density. This procedure was adopted because the Bureau of the Census did not compute county densities prior to 1920. Occasionally, however, a county with a relatively small population has a high density; consequently, if the table had been based on density, the number of counties listed for each division of the population might be somewhat greater, but the number of square miles of territory would undoubtedly be considerably reduced.

---

1. The converse side of the concentration process, as indicated by Table 1, is reflected in the extent of territory that is declining in population. Out of a total of 2,955 counties whose boundaries remained unchanged during the last decade (the boundaries of 144 counties were changed), 1,220 had less population in 1930 than in 1920. The combined population of these decreasing counties constituted 18 percent of the total population of the country in 1930. This stands in marked contrast to the extent of decreasing area in 1900 when only 368 out of 2,836 counties showed a decrease during the decade and the total population of these decreasing counties was only 7.7 percent of the population of the nation. Nor has the recent declining territory been strictly rural. No less than 102 cities of 10,000 population or more showed declines in population during the last decade as against 57 cities of this class in the decade 1910 to 1920 and 31 in the decade 1900 to 1910.

Population in general is moving toward the areas of high density. In 1920 there were 265 counties [2] with a density of 100 or more per square mile. In 1910 these counties contained 45.1 percent of the total population; in 1920, 48.2 percent; and in 1930, 52.6 percent.

Movement toward Deep Water.—There is a significant but by no means uniform movement of population toward the deep water rim of the country —that is toward the Atlantic and Pacific Oceans, the Gulf of Mexico, and the metropolitan territory adjoining the Great Lakes. Table 2 presents in summary fashion the facts regarding this population increase.

TABLE II—Population Concentration in a Zone Extending Approximately 50 Miles Inland from the Seaboard and the Great Lakes, 1900–1930 [ab]

Census Year	Population Within Zone	Percent of Total U.S. Population in Zone	Increase Within Zone Since Preceding Census	Percent of Total U.S. Increase Within Zone
1900	27,842,288	36.6	5,495,234	42.1
1910	35,633,796	38.7	7,791,508	48.8
1920	43,865,221	41.5	8,231,425	59.9
1930	55,413,567	45.1	11,548,346	67.7

[a] Compiled from U.S. Census reports. The table is computed on county units—a list of which is available from the author on request.
[b] The area of the zone is 435,863 square miles, or 14.65 percent of total land area of the United States. It may be defined as a region approximately fifty miles wide which skirts the salt water rim of the country and the southern shores of Lakes Ontario, Erie and Michigan.

Population moving toward the deep water rim does not, of course, spread itself evenly over this broad strip of territory. It concentrates in the metropolitan centers leaving other sections equally near deep water to decline. The area contains 540 counties and the District of Columbia. Of these counties, 100 actually decreased in population between 1920 and 1930 and 195 others had rates of increase less than the national average. The movement, therefore, is not a mere drift toward open water, but a migration into metropolitan regions which for various reasons are near the water.

Points of Concentration.—Population is moving toward the great cities. Table 3 reflects this movement. The 1930 census lists 93 cities with populations of 100,000 or more. A number of these are so close together, however, that they may be considered as parts of the same metropolitan community. By drawing an arbitrary circle, with a radius of from 20 to 50 miles, around the largest center in such groupings the number of metropolitan regions may be reduced to 63.

As Table 5 shows, about half of the population of the United States at the present time lives within daily access of a city of 100,000 or more. This is approximately the same percentage of the total population as was reported in the 1,208 cities of 8,000 or more in 1930, and only 8 percent less than the total population recorded as urban. The metropolitan region cuts the population in a different way from the urban classification of the census, yet it cuts almost as large a slice.

---

2. Independent cities and the District of Columbia are included.

TABLE III—Total Population in 63 Metropolitan Zones: 1900–1930[ab]

(Cities of 100,000 or more plus adjacent counties; approximately 20 to 50 miles, depending on size of city)

Year	Total Population in United States	Total Population in Metropolitan Zones	Percent Which Population in Zones Formed of Total U.S. Population	Percent Which Net Increase in Zones Formed of Total Increase in U.S. Since Preceding Census
1900	75,994,575	28,044,698	36.9	46.4
1910	91,972,266	37,271,608	40.5	57.7
1920	105,710,620	46,491,835	44.0	67.1
1930	122,775,046	59,118,595	48.2	74.0

[a] Compiled from U.S. Census reports.
[b] Since this table was compiled the Bureau of the Census has published the 1930 report on Metropolitan Districts (U.S. Bureau of the Census, *Fifteenth Census of the United States, 1930, Metropolitan Districts, Population and Area, 1932*), in which 96 districts are outlined, each with a minimum population of 100,000. The 96 districts contained 4.6 percent of the total population of the nation—almost 4 percent less than the percentage found in the districts as outlined in Table 3.

A considerable proportion of the population included in this arbitrary definition of metropolitan territory would naturally be classified as "rural" by the Bureau of the Census. But such rural population is probably more urbanized from an economic and social standpoint than much of the so-called "urban" population living in small centers remote from the larger cities.

TABLE IV—Proportion of Total Population in Different Territorial Classifications, 1900–1930[a]

Territory	1900	1910	1920	1930
Total urban territory	40.0	45.8	51.4	56.2
Cities of 8,000 or more	32.9	38.7	43.8	49.1
Metropolitan zones (Table 3)	36.9	40.5	44.0	48.2

[a] U.S. Census reports.

The Metropolitan Constellation.—Large cities seldom appear isolated. They are almost always surrounded by a cluster of smaller centers, varying in size, which are economically and socially intertwined. There are, to be sure, marked differences in the number of separate political communities that appear around the margins of individual cities. Geography, industry, and the degree of annexation that has occurred seem to be important factors in determining the number of political entities in a territorial grouping of population. But regardless of political boundaries the same general social and economic forces seem to be at work in every metropolitan region.

TABLE V—Incorporated Places of Specified Size in Selected Metropolitan Districts, 1930[a]

Size of Place	New York	Pittsburgh	Chicago	Philadelphia	Boston	Los Angeles	St. Louis	Cincinnati	Detroit	Cleveland	San Francisco
Less than 2,500	112	57	59	43	10	10	27	23	13	24	14
2,500–4,999	49	26	16	25	14	13	4	9	11	5	6
5,000–9,999	49	23	15	14	17	13	8	7	6	4	8
10,000–49,999	48	27	18	7	30	16	7	3	8	5	7
50,000–99,999	8	1	5	1	5	2	1	1	4	2	1
100,000 and over	6	1	2	2	4	2	1	1	1	1	2
Total	272	135	115	92	80	56	48	44	43	41	38

[a] Fifteenth Census of the United States, 1930, Metropolitan Districts.

Table 5 shows the number of incorporated places located within some of the main metropolitan districts as outlined by the Bureau of the Census. But the metropolitan district as delimited by the Census on the basis of density represents only a part of the area that is economically and socially tributary to each of these central cities. Had trading areas been used as the basis of calculation the number of satellites for each of these cities would be greatly increased. The data presented, however, are sufficient to demonstrate the point that smaller cities tend to group themselves around larger ones somewhat as planets group themselves around a sun. They are, so to speak, within its gravitational field. A general analysis of urban statistics without reference to this fact is apt to be misleading. Population increases in the group of small cities are largely in areas exposed to the metropolitan influence. For example, the 78 small urban centers in the state of Illinois, falling in the 2,500 to 4,999 class in 1920, increased in population 32.2 percent in the decade 1920 to 1930; but 93.4 percent of this increase took place in the 25 towns of this size that happened to be suburbs of Chicago or St. Louis. Of the remaining 53 places in this group, located elsewhere in the state, 23 actually decreased in population during the decade. Likewise in Michigan; in 1920 the state contained 32 towns in the 2,500 to 4,999 class, with an aggregate population of 117,178. By 1930 the combined population of these 32 places was 153,538, an increase of 36,360 or 31 percent in the decade. But of the 32 places 4 were suburbs of Detroit, the combined gain of which was 34,009 or 93.5 percent of the gross increase.

The location of places incorporated for the first time during the decade 1920–1930, shows the same trend. The 1930 census records 38 incorporations in Illinois, 26 of which are suburbs of Chicago or St. Louis; the same census lists 33 new incorporations in Michigan, 22 of which are suburbs of Detroit; Ohio is credited with 55 incorporations, 29 of which are suburbs of Cleveland. When the new incorporations suburban to other large cities in these three states are included, practically all the incorporations during the decade are accounted for.

These are random samplings and may not represent conditions everywhere throughout the country. They indicate, however, the tendency toward concentration in certain areas and suggest the importance of taking location into account when interpreting urban statistics.

The Metropolitan Unit.—The essential unity of the central city and surrounding settlement is generally recognized. For the last three decades the Bureau of the Census has published population statistics for the larger cities and their "adjacent territory." No attempt has been made to analyze the relationship existing between the smaller centers and the main city, but from data furnished in the 1930 Census of Distribution it is possible to show certain aspects of commercial interdependence within a metropolitan region. The 37 communities around Chicago, having a population of 10,000 or more, make an excellent illustration. Twenty-one of these cities are located within a zone scarcely ten miles wide lying between the outer limits of the political city and a circle with a 20-mile radius drawn from the Loop, or business center. Six fall within the second concentric zone, lying from 20 to 40 miles distant from the Loop. The remaining ten are located in a third zone, lying from 40 to 80 miles distant from the Loop. An analysis of the average number of persons to a store and the average expenditure for food, wearing apparel and general merchandise in each zone, shows that the central city's influence gradually tapers off. In the first zone stores are relatively few in proportion to population, with an average of 102 persons each. In the second zone this average falls to 69 and in the third to 65. This is a statistical illustration of the common fact of experience, that the nearer one lives to a city's shopping center the more likely one is to shop there.

Other data show that the shopping done in the city by residents of the outlying communities is somewhat specialized. Food makes up 34.1 percent of all retail purchases in the first zone, 26.8 percent in the second zone, 26.4 percent in the third zone. Residents of the first zone spend an average of $26.96 on general merchandise and $25.98 on wearing apparel yearly on their local stores; residents of the second zone, $81.86 and $52.90 respectively; residents of the third zone, $70.93 and $58.38. For other things than food, Zone I depends to a marked extent on the shopping area of the central city, whereas Zones II and III, though obviously not independent of the main shopping center, have gone further in developing local shopping districts.

The same tapering off of the metropolitan influence may be shown by analyses of newspaper circulations, of wholesale selling districts and of the relations of banks with their correspondents. The financial functions of a great city may extend for hundreds of miles, or even be nation wide. More than 60 percent of Chicago's wholesale merchandise buyers come from distances of 200 miles or less, but more than 12 percent come 600 miles or more.[3] Sometimes the metropolitan influence seems to jump an intermediate territory and to be strong at a remote periphery. Thus the banks of Chicago have more than three times as many correspondents among banks between the 1,600-mile radius and the Pacific Coast as they have in the 800-1,200-mile zone.[4] This and other evidence shows that the Pacific Coast cities are more closely integrated with New York and Chicago than are smaller points in intervening zones.

Factors in Metropolitanization.—The tendency of population to concentrate in large metropolitan communities is not wholly due to industrial development. The processes of concentration have been even more rapid during the last decade than formerly, although the total number of industrial wage earners in the country was actually less in 1929 than in 1919.[5]

3. "Merchandise Buyers' Visits to Chicago" listed in the Chicago *Tribune,* January 1 to October 1, 1930, *Bulletin from the Business Survey. No. 293,* December, 1930 (mimeographed sheets for the use of *Tribune* staff).

4. *An Analysis of Bankers' Balances in Chicago,* University of Illinois Bulletin, vol. XXVI, November 19, 1928, Bureau of Business Research, College of Commerce and Business Administration, Bulletin no. 21, pp. 16-17.

5. United States Bureau of the Census, *Census of Manufactures.*

The economic and social advantages of specialization and division of labor seem to apply not only to the production of goods but to most of our institutions and services as well. The larger the population with daily access to a common center of institutions and services, the more specialized and differentiated these tend to become. The individual has a wider range of selection, the institution or service a basis for increased efficiency. The great cities draw to themselves the leaders in business, the professions, the sciences and the arts. Concentration breeds concentration. Functions that require access to numerous or highly selected customers are possible only in cities. As population concentrates spatially a hitherto unparalleled degree of economic and social specialization and diversification becomes feasible. Herein seem to lie the main "attractions" of the city—attractions which evidently outweigh the discomforts and wastes of congestion.

The city dweller may not like crowds. He may, however, find it hard to dispense with the goods and services which crowds make possible. The dispersion of population toward the outer zones of metropolitan regions is obviously an attempt on the part of the city man to have his cake and eat it too.

II. METROPOLITAN REGIONALISM. The larger cities of the country are becoming what might be termed regionally conscious. The mapping of metropolitan regions thus becomes important. Practically every city of more than 50,000 inhabitants has sought to delimit the territory which it considers belongs to it by virtue of proximity and functional relationship. While much of the mapping is still of a rather arbitrary nature—a sort of random staking out of territorial claims for advertising purposes—nevertheless there is a definite trend toward a more careful delineation of regional boundaries for commercial and administrative purposes. In addition to the efforts of the cities themselves to define their primary areas of function, numerous national organizations, including the United States Bureau of Foreign and Domestic Commerce, have sought to divide the country into logical trading areas and sales territories for different types of economic service.

The emergence of regional consciousness seems to be a natural outcome of recent developments in transportation and communication coupled with their effect upon interregional competition. The expansion of the facilities of contact in the form of the motor vehicle, the metropolitan press, the telephone, and even the radio has tended to intensify movement and communication within the local area to an even greater extent than between distant sections. On the other hand the increasing fluidity of commodities and people is exposing cities to new conditions making for growth or decline. Unlike the nation as a whole, which may build tariff walls and set up immigration restrictions to meet foreign competition, the individual city, so far as the domestic economy is concerned, has to meet competition in an open market. In intercity or interregional competition the larger the population group, or in commercial terms the larger the local market, the greater its competitive advantage. It is not surprising, therefore, that cities are devoting increasing attention to questions of transportation rates and routes, which in a sense are to cities what tariffs are to nations. In the recent hearings conducted by the Interstate Commerce Commission with respect to suggested modifications of the freight rate structure in the middle western states—Western Trunk Line Territory—no less than "12,500 pages of testimony were taken and approximately 1,200 exhibits containing more than 12,000 pages were received." [6]

Margins of the Metropolitan Community.—The central city casts its influence over surrounding settlements in the form of traffic zones. This influence goes as far as distance and competition will let it. The boundaries, of course, are seldom definite stable lines which can be graphically shown on a map. They are rather, as has already been shown, tapering zones of influence which vary with changing conditions of transportation and competition.

Two terms have come into common usage to designate areas of community influence: "metropolitan district" and "trade area." The term metropolitan district has come to signify the territory in which the daily economic and social activities of the local population are carried on through a common system of local institutions and services. It is essentially the commutation area of the central city and tends to correspond with the "built-up" area in which public services such as water, light, sanitation and power become common problems.

The second concept, trade area, is used to designate a more extended territory of city influence. The term does not lend itself to precise definition, for different economic functions have different zones of influence. For practical purposes, however, a city's trade area may be defined in the words of John W. Pole, Comptroller of the Currency, as "The surrounding geographical territory economically tributary to a city and for which such city provides the chief market and financial center." [7]

Trends in the Size of the Commutation Area.—For the few cities having railroad commutation service it is possible to gain some conception of the trend in the volume and range of commutation traffic. According to the statistics published by the Interstate Commerce Commission there has been relatively little change in the total commutation traffic on Class I railroads during the nine-year period, 1922–1930, the time interval for which statistics are available. The volume of traffic, measured in terms of revenue passenger miles, increased about 8 percent in this interim and the average length of journey, as indicated by miles per passenger per road, increased from 14.28 to 15.20 miles.

Of course the recent expansion of the metropolitan community is primarily a product of motor transportation. With the exception of a few cities of over a million population there has been a persistent decrease since

6. U.S. Interstate Commerce Commission, *Reports*, vol. 164, no. 17,000, May, 1930, p. 14.

7. *United States Daily*, January 3, 1931.

1920 in the number of revenue passengers carried by street railways and a correspondingly rapid increase in the use of buses and private automobiles. Statistics prepared by the American Electric Railway Association show that in seven cities between 500,000 and 1,000,000 there was a decline of 10.4 percent in the number of revenue passengers carried on street railways from 1920 to 1929, and in 34 cities in the 100,000 to 500,000 class the decline was 27.6 percent. The data are not available for cities under 100,000 but it is reasonable to suppose that the decline in the use of the street railway would be even greater in these small places. According to figures published by the National Association of Motor Bus Operators there were in December, 1930, 222 cities of over 10,000 entirely dependent upon motor transportation.

It is difficult to measure the radius of the motor city. Extensive studies of motor traffic made by the United States Bureau of Public Roads, though not pertaining directly to cities, suggest that the average distance of the local motor trip is relatively short. Various cities have prepared maps showing the flow of motor traffic at different points along arterial highways. Such maps invariably show a rapid tapering off of traffic beyond a ten or fifteen mile radius from the central business district. Certain cities, however, claim a considerable group of daily commuters coming distances ranging between 20 and 40 miles.

The small cities of the nation are tending either to become suburban to nearby larger centers or, if remote from large cities, to assume the role of embryonic metropolises to surrounding villages. The comparatively high rates of population increase in the small cities of the agricultural states in the west north central division suggest the influence of the motor car and paved highway on the extension of their tributary territory. In the seven states [8] comprising this census division there were, in 1920, 55 cities in the 10,000 to 50,000 class. The combined increase of these cities by 1930 was 17.6 percent as against only 6 percent for the region as a whole.

Trends in the Size of the Trade Area.—Important changes are taking place in the marketing territories of most cities. The retail shopping areas of the larger cities, as measured by the daily free delivery service of central stores, have expanded greatly in recent years. It has become common practice for the larger stores throughout the nation to deliver their merchandise regularly within a radius of 30 to 50 miles. City department stores report not only an extension of their delivery systems since 1920 but also an increasing volume of trade from outlying territory. Some stores provide free telephone service to their suburban customers and some rebate fares, depending on distance traveled and volume of purchases. The outward movement of the higher economic elements of the population has been an important factor in the extension of the market areas of department stores. Several stores report a falling off of business within the inner zones; other report that the

8. Minnesota, Iowa, Missouri, North Dakota, South Dakota, Nebraska, Kansas.

volume of the close-in business has been maintained largely as a result of the increase in the hotel and large apartment trade.

Counter to the tendency toward increasing centralization as indicated by department store delivery practice is the rise of the chain store system of retailing, characterized by the centralization of management and warehousing functions in the regional city and the delivery of merchandise to towns and villages located within convenient trucking distance. In either case the city casts its dominance over surrounding settlement and changes the interrelationships of nearby centers.

The enlargement of the marketing territory of the larger cities does not imply that the city's trade area is merely a magnified reproduction of that of the small town. It represents rather the tendency toward greater specialization and division of labor among the different centers located within easy access of a large city. The increasing economic unity of the metropolitan region is chiefly the result of a transformation that is taking place in the field of marketing. The small town is yielding many of its more specialized services to the city, while in turn it is acquiring new services such as the chain store and the motion picture theater. The role of the small center in the retail marketing complex is summarized in *Domestic Commerce* thus:

The Census of Retail Distribution offers, for the first time, a means of accurately determining the position of the small town and the country store as outlets for various types of goods as compared with larger cities. By studying the figures for the state of California, the only complete state released to date, we find 37 percent of the population located outside of the cities of over 10,000 population, but only 32.7 percent of the State's stores and 21.8 percent of total sales.

The extent to which residents of small towns go to the larger cities for apparel, furniture and household goods, and items sold through department or general merchandise stores is evident in that such outlets in the small towns do only 7.7 percent, 11.65 percent and 15.2 percent respectively of the total business done by these types of stores in the state.[9]

The general trend in wholesaling seems to be toward concentration and specialization. The small wholesaling center is surrendering most of its specialized trade to the regional city. The regional city in turn depends upon the larger metropolis for much of its specialized merchandise. The tendency toward hand to mouth buying works in favor of the regional city as against the larger but more distant metropolis especially with reference to staples. On the other hand, the large city, by giving increasing attention to overnight delivery by fast trucks and package rail freight, is succeeding in maintaining its wholesale function over a wide range of territory. In general, however, the tendency for regional cities seems to be toward smaller wholesale territories and more intensive coverage. This doubtless reflects the concentration and regional organization of population. An analysis of reports from 39 wholesale dry goods houses in the Gulf Southwest during the period from 1924 to 1928 showed a decrease in territory

9. June 20, 1931, vol. VII, no. 18, p. 199.

covered in the cases of 28 firms, while 11 reported increases. Of the firms doing over $1,000,000 worth of business a year, six were covering more territory in 1928 than they had covered in 1924 and 12 were covering less.[10]

The Metropolitan Region Comes of Age.—Large cities throughout the nation are gradually maturing in their commercial and industrial structure; in other words, they are "coming of age." As frontier conditions pass there is a tendency for each metropolitan area to become more nearly complete in its economic and institutional structure. In ten out of sixteen cities listed by Glenn E. McLaughlin [11] the number of industries increased between 1921 and 1927. The decline in certain cities, notably San Francisco and Pittsburgh, is in all probability due to the migration of industries into the suburban districts of the region. Diversification is no longer a characteristic of the larger cities alone but is spreading to the outlying regional communities. So far as local conditions permit there is a tendency in each case toward a complete industrial set up. This tendency is, of course, subject to the limitations of accessible raw materials and markets as well as the more subtle ones of commercial and industrial traditions.

Within these limits, however, each large center of population tends to duplicate the occupational structure of similar centers elsewhere. This is particularly noticeable with respect to the manufacturing and mechanical industries. An exception to this rule seems to be the tendency for persons in highly specialized occupations, such as designers, artists, stock brokers, to concentrate in New York City. The New York region, so far as some of these services are concerned, is apparently almost nation wide.

The proportion of the nation's total bank business which it handles is perhaps the best single index of a growing city's maturity. Tables published by *The American Banker* [12] show some striking changes in this respect between 1923 and 1930. An outstanding feature of these tables is that whereas New York City had 48.81 percent of the country's bank deposits in 1923 it had only 32 percent in 1930. Whether the latter figure reflects in part the unusual conditions prevailing in 1930 can only be surmised. It undoubtedly points to an increase in the financial maturity of the outlying regional cities. Chicago, Philadelphia, Boston, Cleveland, Los Angeles, Detroit and Pittsburgh all gained during the period and San Francisco climbed from 5.94 percent to 10.50 percent. Oakland, across the bay from San Francisco, disappeared from the tables between 1923 and 1930, as did Brooklyn and Hoboken, satellites of the New York financial district. Eight cities—Atlanta, Dallas, Oklahoma City, Portland (Oregon), Cincinnati, Seattle, Syracuse and Tulsa—made a showing in 1930, though they were not recorded in 1923.

The economic coming of age of the metropolitan centers of the nation, particularly those on the economic frontiers of the South and West, is

---

10. U.S. Bureau of Foreign and Domestic Commerce, Edward F. Gerish, *Distribution of Dry Goods in the Gulf Southwest,* Domestic Commerce Series, no. 43, 1931, p. 7.

11. Glenn E. McLaughlin, "Industrial Diversification in American Cities," *Quarterly Journal of Economics,* November, 1930, vol. 45, no. 1, p. 137.

12. January 21, 1924 and January 20, 1931.

unquestionably an important factor in intercity competition and in the development of regional consciousness. Cities, like nations, are seeking to develop balanced economies and to protect home industries and regional markets. There are natural limits, obviously, to this sort of development. The major industries of the country are still highly concentrated and, considered from the standpoint of total output, there seems to be but a slight tendency toward industrial decentralization.

But in spite of this concentration of certain industries, the facts indicate that there will continue to be more intensive exploitation of local resources and more effort to build diversified economies on a regional basis. Thus there is the seeming paradox of regional communities growing more alike, yet growing also in independence and self-reliance.

THE FUSION OF URBAN AND RURAL

Walter Firey, Charles P. Loomis, and J. Allan Beegle

THE HIGHWAY AS A FIELD-CENTER NEXUS. Human activities, when viewed in terms of their geographical layout, are of two kinds: "field" activities and "center" activities.[1] The former are directed toward wresting from the land the foods, fibers, ores, and raw materials upon which sustenance depends. The settlements and communities which grow up around these "field" activities, being relatively small and dispersed in character, are generally classed as *rural*. "Center" activities on the other hand, have to do with the processing, distributing, and coordination of field products. Their performance requires great agglomerations of people within rather restricted areas of space. Thus there emerge communities which are commonly called *urban*.

Between the field and the center—between rural and urban—there is an incessant concourse of people and commodities. The channels along which this concourse flows are the roadways of society: the rutted trails, the dirt-and-gravel roads, and the paved highways, all supplemented by the long distance waterways and railroad tracks.

The extent of field-center concourse will, naturally, vary directly with the character of the roadways which connect field with center.[2] Roadways, in other words, are the nexus between rural and urban. Few and poor roadways mean impeded interaction; they involve a sharp distinction between rural and urban. Many and good roadways mean facilitated interaction; they entail a rapprochement between rural and urban. Precisely in this elemental fact lies the clue to the most important processes now under way in rural and urban community formation. Briefly, urban is becoming less urban, rural is becoming less rural.[3] The distinctness of field from center is rapidly being obliterated.

The causative factor in this trend, which is so radically altering the settlement structure and community organization of the American continent, has been the evolution of the roadway system. The highway is the latest type of roadway to have influenced significantly American settlement

Reprinted from *Highways In Our National Life: A Symposium*, edited by Jean Labatut and Wheaton J. Lane, Chapter 13, pp. 154-163, by permission of the authors and the publishers. (Copyright, 1950, by the Princeton University Press).

1. R. D. McKenzie, *The Metropolitan Community* (New York, 1933), 50-65.
2. cf. *loc. cit.*
3. Pitirim A. Sorokin, Carle C. Zimmerman, and Charles J. Galpin, *A Systematic Source Book in Rural Sociology* (Minneapolis, 1932), III, 639.

patterns and community life. Prior to it, in the waterway era and in the railroad era,[4] the city was in very large degree autonomous of its own rural hinterland. One who journeyed from the center of a metropolis outward would always encounter an abrupt, precipitous transition to unspoiled countryside. Socially and culturally the transition was just as abrupt. The city was truly a state of mind; the country was another and very different state of mind.[5] Between them there was an abyss. During the water era New Orleans was literally closer to Memphis than it was to its own rural Louisiana hinterland. Likewise, during the railroad era, Cheyenne was nearer Chicago than it was to nearby rural hamlets which had been stranded by the railroads' passing a few miles away.

But the highway has changed all of this. Because of the peculiar superiority of the automobile as a short-distance, small-load carrier and as a "free agent" whose course and destination need not be confined by waterways or railroad tracks, the advent of highway transportation has meant, for the first time, intimate contact between a city and its hinterland. Rural and urban have truly met. The rapid extension of highways and of automobile ownership has now carried the process so far that "field" and "center" are almost fusing. The consequences of this for settlement patterns, social interaction, and cultural relations cannot be overestimated; they are all-important.

THE INFLUENCE OF THE HIGHWAY UPON RURAL SETTLEMENT PATTERNS. Four main alterations in rural settlement patterns have followed from the proliferation of highways between "center" and "field": (1) the emergence of fringe areas on the outskirts of cities—areas that are half rural and half urban in their characteristics;[6] (2) the appearance of string-along-the-road settlement patterns involving both country-dwelling city people and rural farmers who are interested in accessibility to markets;[7] (3) the development of service areas surrounding towns and cities, generally greater in extent than the "fringe" and differing in certain functional respects as well;[8] (4) the formation of satellite subcenters, out beyond the central service area, each with their miniature fringes, strings-along-the-road, and service areas.[9] All four of these developments may be visualized as aspects of a single process: that of nucleation and subnucleation. Briefly, highways are binding the field areas into organic, functioning unities and subunities which surround and tie in with centers and subcenters. Villages serve as centers for little towns; towns are centers for

---

4. McKenzie, *op. cit.*, 129-143.

5. Howard Woolston, *Metropolis* (New York, 1938), 4.

6. Louis A. Wolfanger, *Your Community and Township Zoning*, Michigan State College, Agricultural Experiment Station, Circular Bulletin 184, (East Lansing, 1945), 12-13.

7. See *ibid.*, fig. 3 and *passim*.

8. See Calvin F. Schmid, *Social Saga of Two Cities* (Minneapolis, 1937), 90.

9. See Noel P. Gist and L. A. Halbert, *Urban Society* (New York, 1946), 2d ed., 171, fig. 9, reprinted from the *Chicago Tribune*.

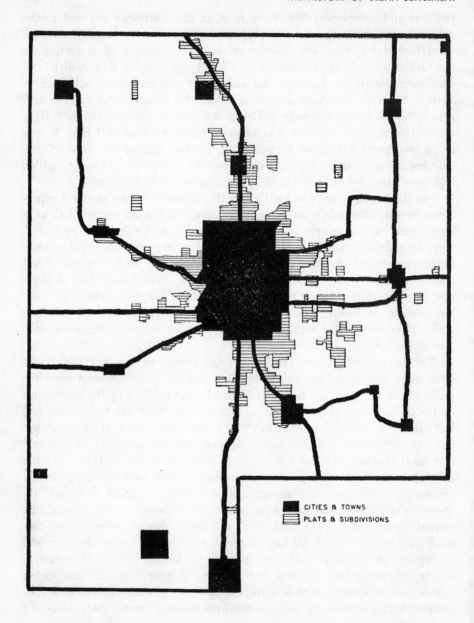

FIG. 1—The Star-like Configuration

The star-like configuration and the string-along-the-road patterns are well shown in the case of Flint, Michigan. The ease of communication afforded by the highways coupled with numerous other factors fosters settlement along the roadways. This leads to the development of the "fringe." In 1940, the incorporated population of Flint numbered 151,543, but the "rural" people who resided in four townships adjacent to Flint numbered 28,641. This number represents the nonvillage rural-nonfarm group, or those persons who live outside of cities or villages and do not farm. This "fringe" population is located for the most part on the highways outside Flint's boundaries, and if added to the incorporated population of Flint would account for 1 out of every 6 persons in the area.

larger fields; and cities function as centers for the largest fields. Each field, with its center, is successively subsumed into the next larger one, in hierarchical fashion.

Thus there emerges a functional pyramid of field-center "organisms," all bound together by a network of highways. The height of the pyramid and the degree of its functional unity is directly contingent upon the number and layout of its sustaining highways. A steep and highly integrated pyramid of field-center areas constitutes a highly "rurbanized" region, to use an accepted sociological neologism. Such a pyramid implies intimate interaction between rural and urban people, a reduction of their differences, a fusion of their interests. In spatial terms it is manifest by relatively dense agglomerations of population surrounding a city, typically assuming a star-like configuration with apices reaching outward along the main highways. Beyond these are subcenters of population, each with their lesser apices reaching out. Thus emerge the fringe and string-along-the-road patterns so typical of the rural areas lying just outside American cities. See Figure 1. In between these centers and subcenters, as well as out beyond them, in the areas more truly rural, are farm families, whose new proximity to the city, made possible by the highway, renders them a little less rural and a little more urban than they had been before. The outer limits of such service areas may be ascertained by minimal traffic counts along outgoing highways, by boundaries of department store deliveries, by the furthermost extent of shopping, or even by the direction which tire tracks take on the dusty roads that run into arterial highways.[10]

The method of delineating trade-center communities is illustrated in Figure 2. The average flow of traffic over a twenty-four-hour period has been recorded by the Michigan State Highway Department for nearly all roads in the state. A record of these counts has been made on the chart for a typical market center and typical small neighborhood, Howell and Hartland. It will be noted that the flow of traffic increases as one moves into each of these centers. At some point on each of the roadways, however, the volume of traffic reaches a minimum and then increases as one moves into another urban center. These points of lowest traffic volume represent the outer boundary of the trade-center community. A line connecting all such minima traffic flow points around a given center may be considered as forming the generalized boundaries of a trading area.

Ordinarily, the frequency of trips to a center is a function of the dis-

___

10. On the techniques of delineating service areas and neighborhoods see: Irwin T. Sanders and Douglas Ensminger, *Alabama Rural Communities: a Study of Chilton County,* Bulletin, Alabama College, Vol. 33, No. 1A, (Montevallo, 1940), 72-80. On the administrative value of these techniques see: Charles P. Loomis and Douglas Ensminger, "Governmental Administration and Informal Local Groups," *Applied Anthropology,* (January-March, 1942), I, 41-59, reprinted in Loomis, *Studies of Rural Social Organization in the United States, Latin America and Germany,* (East Lansing, Michigan, 1945), 151-172. See too: F. Howard Forsyth, "The Use of Road Turnings in Community Research," *Rural Sociology,* (December, 1944), IX, 384-385.

tance. That is, the nearer the center, the more frequently people will visit it, other things being equal. However, if the nearest place is a neighbor-hood center, complete services will not be available. Thus trips to larger centers are essential. The area serviced, or the traffic attraction power of the Hartland neighborhood center and the Howell market center, as shown in Figure 2, is vastly different.[11]

It will be noted from Figure 2 that the contours of the Howell market center are rectangular in form, a characteristic of many communities

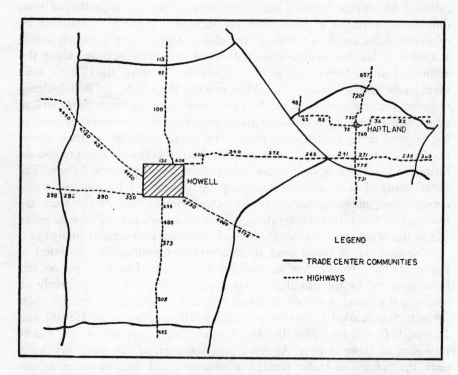

FIG. 2—Trade-Center Communities

The trade-center communities of Howell and Hartland, Michigan, delineated from traffic-flow readings. Note that the community boundaries fall at the minima points on out-going highways. In 1940, Howell's population was 3,748 and that of Hartland township, in which the village is located, only 733. See footnote 11 for other details.

---

11. See J. F. Thaden, *The Lansing Region and Its Tributary Town-Country Communities*, Michigan State College Agricultural Experiment Station Special Bulletin 302, (East Lansing, 1945), 27-30. Thaden's study shows that the Howell community center contains three banks, has a newspaper circulation of 3,892, and has a high school enrollment of 429. In comparison, the Hartland neighborhood center has no bank or newspaper, and has a high school enrollment of only 150. Population estimates for 1940 show that the Howell trade-center area includes 8,670 persons, 57 per cent of whom reside in the tributary area; the Hartland neighborhood contained 509 persons, 61 per cent of whom resided in the tributary area.

throughout the Middle West. In all probability, this form may be attributed to the rectangular or "checkerboard" system of land division which typifies most of the Middle and Far West. In this rectangular system, roads generally run parallel to the longitudinal and latitudinal land division lines. Since diagonal routes to a center rarely exist, the resulting trade-center contours tend to be rectangular. For this reason, it may be necessary to supplement the traffic-flow readings with personal interviews in order to establish certain of the community boundaries. This applies especially to areas comparable to the southwest and northwest corners of the Howell community, Figure 2. Regardless of the pattern that the areas of influence of the emerging centers and subcenters take, the consequence of all these changes has been a "polarizing" of population along the highways, much as iron filings polarize around a magnet. Such polarization is a very tangible thing which is strikingly apparent in the geographical layout of dwellings and outbuildings as seen from the air. It should not be inferred, however, that such population realignments spell the end of small communities—the last harbingers of the rural component in rurbanization. Highways have indeed more fully bound the small community to the large community; they have in many cases led to the demise of some villages and the nascence of other villages. But the small community—the subcenter, as it were—is no less functionally necessary today than it was in the past. Without it the field-center pyramids that have evolved around highway systems would become all apex and no base—monstrously unstable structures that could not function economically or socially.

Conclusive evidence of the continued significance of small communities may be found in areas whose settlement has taken place almost wholly since the advent of the automobile and the highway. Saskatchewan is one such area. There it was found that the number and vitality of small rural communities was fully as great as in areas whose settlement had antedated the highway era.[12] The grounds for this fact lie in the indispensability of the subcenter, with its subfield, as a constituent, functioning "organism" within the more inclusive orbit of the supercenter and its superfield.[13]

THE INFLUENCE OF THE HIGHWAY UPON RURAL SOCIAL INTERACTION. Such realignments of rural settlement patterns as these cannot help but entail corollary changes in rural social interaction. Highways have exerted both an organizing and a disorganizing effect upon rural group life. On the one hand they have broken down the seclusion and provincialism that once characterized rural life. Now more than ever before the farm family can participate in "the larger society" which is borne by metropolitan newspapers, urban recreational facilities, urban libraries and schools, and many other points of contact unknown to the nine-

12. Carle C. Zimmerman, *The Changing Community* (New York, 1938), Ch. 2.
13. See D. G. Marshall, "Hamlets and Villages in the United States: Their Place in the American Way of Life," *American Sociological Review*, (April, 1946), XI, 159-165.

teenth-century country dweller. Organizations and activities once the prerogative of the urbanite are now just as accessible to the ruralite. Aristotle's sly plan to disfranchise the peasantry by stipulating frequent and regular participation in the city assembly as a prerequisite to citizenship—an impossible thing for farmers in an era of donkey-path transportation—would never work in a modern rurbanized society. Farmers now can get to the courthouse about as easily as the townspeople. Such enlarged areas of contact of course mean enhanced political and economic power of farmers—so long a traditionally disadvantaged segment of the American population. Highways, in short, have made the rural population more cosmopolitan.

On the debit side, highways have disrupted the stable, localistic groupings that have been the bedrock of America's rural life. Distinctive neighborhood institutions—the church, the lodge, the country schoolhouse—these have been succumbing before the competition offered by their urban equivalents. Whatever the gain may be, it has certainly been matched by a real social loss. For these old-time localistic institutions, with their typically intimate, face-to-face associations, were potent citizen-building forces. The consolidated school, the federated church, the urban lodge—whatever their advantages, they can never quite replace their rural predecessors. Family life itself is changing. The individualization of activities, long so typical of urban family life, is manifesting itself in rural families as well. In place of family picnics, family reunions, and family churchgoing there is a splitting apart of activities, in which father goes to the lodge meeting, mother attends the church missionary society meeting, daughter goes to the high-school dance, and junior takes in a movie.[14] Traditionalized domestic roles are themselves breaking down under the impact of "equalitarian" family ideals conveyed via the movie, the newspaper, and other concomitants of improved rural-urban transportation.[15]

THE INFLUENCE OF THE HIGHWAY UPON RURAL CULTURE. Such changes, of course, are a reflection of changed values, changed ideals, changed standards—in short, of a changed culture. In this respect the highway has functioned as an artery, bearing outward along its course new values, ideals, and standards. While communication is always a two-way process, by and large most of the diffusion of new cultural patterns has been one-way. Urban patterns are being borne out along the highways into rural areas to a much greater degree than rural patterns are being borne inward toward the cities. Indeed it is possible, by means of maps, to deline-

14. On the remarkable persistence, however, of whole-family activities among rural people, see: W. A. Anderson, "The Family and Individual Social Participation," *American Sociological Review*, (August, 1943), VIII, 420 ff. and (December, 1943), VIII, 721 ff.

15. Ernest W. Burgess and Harvey J. Locke, *The Family* (New York, 1945), 92-110.

ate with remarkable precision the gradients which urban cultural patterns take on in the rural areas contiguous to a city. Data on birth rates, on delinquency, on subscription to daily newspapers, on living levels, and on many other significant items show more or less typical concentric tiers surrounding a central city, each tier revealing successively less urban acculturation as one goes outward from the city.

Research conducted by the Planning and Traffic Division of the Michigan State Highway Department[16] indicates that the flow of traffic is inextricably related to socio-economic factors. In conjunction with such factors, some 1,341 places have been classified. For 416 of the larger centers, the following socio-economic indices were used: (1) the population of the immediate trade area (this includes the population of the center and surrounding area that is dependent upon the center for a majority of its everyday requirements and services); (2) total bank resources; (3) newspaper circulation; and (4) the equalized valuation of a center. Some 1,306 places were classified in accordance with their traffic-attraction characteristics. A determination of the trip frequency by distance relationship for each destination permitted segregation of these places into groups according to their relative traffic-attraction importance. The correlation coefficient between the ratings established by the socio-economic indices and those established by traffic-attraction indices as resulting from a correlation study of 381 places for which both the socio-economic and traffic attraction indices were available is .85.[17]

In respect to ability to attract traffic, centers in Michigan classified as indicated above fall into the following categories: (1) neighborhood centers, or small retail outlets which offer some of the requirements of the immediate surrounding area; (2) minor market centers or those which offer services usually sufficient to meet the general requirements of the center and its trade area; (3) complete market service centers, or those offering services usually sufficient to meet the general requirements (including some recreational and cultural advantages) of the center and its

---

16. For the maps and statistical basis for this discussion of trade-center communities delineated from traffic flow figures, the classification of centers, and the relationships between various indices and the power of centers to attract traffic, we are indebted to officials of the Michigan State Highway Department. Pioneering research is being conducted by the Michigan Highway officials, especially John D. Cruise, Assistant Director of Planning and Traffic, Albert C. Sherman, Highway Planning Engineer, and Earl Fohl, Statistician.

17. Certain of the places used in the correlation study are intense resort and recreational centers. This type of center is extremely difficult to classify using the socio-economic indices. A correlation of the socio-economic ratings and the traffic attraction ratings omitting the resort and recreational centers gave a much higher correlation coefficient. It is known that retail sales is another index of great importance in indicating the traffic attraction power of a center. At the time this study was made, however, complete data were not available, especially for the lesser populated places. Correlation studies relating traffic attraction power of centers and various socio-economic and demographic factors are being made by the Social Research Service of Michigan State College.

trade area; (4) regional centers, or places which offer complete market services sufficient not only to meet the needs of its community and trade area but also to serve as a principal wholesale distributing center; and (5) metropolitan center, or centers which not only offer complete market services sufficient to meet the needs of the trade area but also those which serve as major trade centers in the national economic structure.

Making due allowance for some exceptions and for some degree of variability in the centers, the general principle still seems to hold that rural areas, in direct proportion to their proximity to urban centers, are becoming culturally urbanized. Since proximity is contingent upon time-cost accessibility between country and city, itself a function of highways, the causative agent in this urbanization of rural culture must be evident. It is the highway that has brought city values, ideals, and standards to the country dweller. Notions about life objectives, about loyalties, about modes of living, about consumption tastes, about well-being—all of these are becoming more alike as between country and city. While all this per-force means the loss of quaint, rustic ruralisms, it means, too, the fuller integration of the American people around basic and historic ideals of the nation. More truly than ever before a homogeneous, internally con-sistent, and universally accepted value system, shared alike by urbanite and ruralite, is coming to characterize American society. The role of the highway in effecting this cultural rapprochement between country and city has been decisive.

4

THE SPATIAL AND
TEMPORAL PATTERNS OF CITIES

The modern city is not a large and meaningless agglomeration of people and services. Every urban dweller recognizes, at least implicitly and informally, that there is an ordered spatial pattern in the city's layout and that people and goods follow certain regular and recurrent patterns of movement within it. Human ecology studies, among other things, the spatial and temporal organization of human communities. Looked at another way, space and time are the major dimensions within which the *functional* relationships of the human aggregate are organized.

The spatial and temporal orders of the city are the result of basic processes. There are four basic processes underlying the spatial order of the city: concentration, centralization, segregation, and invasion-succession. Primary aspects of the temporal order are rhythm, tempo and timing.[1] *Concentration* refers to the process whereby a settlement appears and grows. That is, it describes changes in the size of population agglomerations usually involving a change in the density of settlement. When such changes are in the direction of population loss they are usually referred to as "deconcentration." These processes of concentration and deconcentration also are described as aspects of population redistribution, where there is centripetal movement toward a center of activity and centrifugal movement away from

the center or toward the periphery of a settlement.

Cities represent the concentration of population into settlements of relatively high density. Given a relatively large geographic spatial area within which cities could locate, the questions naturally arise, Why are particular geographic locations the place of urban settlement, and Why are particular sites chosen within these locations? These questions also raise the more general ones: How can one account for the distribution of cities in a particular space, and How are cities related to other modes of settlement, i.e., places of varying size and density of settlement? The first papers in this section provide theory and empirical data in partial answer to these questions.

The reasons for the location of a population in a particular settlement which at the same time localizes activities or functions in space, and the reasons for a pattern of distribution among settlements, are not well understood. Scholars from von Thünen to Lösch have devised theoretical models to explain patterns of settlement. The paper by Ullman in this section presents a brief statement of these major theories and gives reasons why they are not altogether satisfactory as theories. A more exhaustive treatment of these theories together with a recent attempt at theoretical formulation is to be found in the writings of August Lösch.[2]

---

1. See Amos Hawley, *Human Ecology* (New York: The Ronald Press), pp. 245 ff.

2. August Lösch, *The Economics of Location*, translated from the Second Revised Edition by William H. Woglom with the assistance of Wolfgang F. Stolper (New Haven: Yale University Press, 1954).

Some of the necessary conditions for the location of cities and the selection of geographic sites are presented in the essay by Harris and Ullman, where the support of cities as suppliers of urban services is discussed. Cities with different kinds of functions are shown to have different patterns of location.

A city is not composed merely of a population agglomeration. Each city is a set of functional interdependences, as each requires a wide variety of productive, distributive and service functions in addition to a residential population. The process by which these functions come together in a relatively permanent location is called *centralization*. The original development of a city requires not only the concentration of a population in non-agricultural pursuits, but the development of areas where functions are centralized. Originally the center of a town or small city may be the only area in which functions are centralized, but other areas in a metropolitan area may show the effect of centralization of functions. These are generally called subcenters. Business, specialized types of manufacturing, wholesaling and recreation are kinds of functions in which subcenters specialize. Decentralization refers to the opposite of this process, or, in other words, to the dispersal of such functions. The paper by Johnson in this section is a detailed description of the ecological center of a metropolitan community—the central business district—and the discrete areas of centralized functions within it. The more specific processes by which this functional differentiation within the center occurs also are discussed.

Metropolitan cities are the centers of a larger ecological community, often called the metropolitan region. The metropolitan city is viewed as a center of dominance over a *hinterland* consisting of satellite cities, subdominant communities, rural towns and villages and open-country residential areas. A metropolitan center is said to be the *center of dominance* when it exercises the predominant influence over other communities in its hinterland, influence being measured on the distribution of the population and sustenance activities in the surrounding area. *Subdominant centers* are communities with lesser influence. The paper by Vance and Smith in Part 3 analyzes patterns of metropolitan dominance and integration in the U.S. urban South. The boundary of the metropolitan region is not necessarily distinct, as it varies for particular functions of the center. The empirical data in the paper by Dickinson show substantial variation in the regional boundary of Salt Lake City when different types of functional areas are considered. The paper also discusses the effect of regional composition on the center of dominance as well as the effect of the dominant on the surrounding hinterland.

The various activities which are integrated both within a metropolitan center and its surrounding community compete for advantageous locations. Their particular location is controlled by what is called the friction of space —the time and cost of transportation which is necessary to overcome distance. In general, activities locate relative to their time-cost advantage in overcoming distance to the community center. The competition for space within the city leads to patterning of these activities in location and subsequent growth of the city. The ordering of the internal spatial structure of the city, the reasons behind such differentiation, as well as the ways these areas are organized into a unity, have occupied an important position in the work of human ecologists. While there is not entire agreement among ecologists as to what the most generalizable pattern is, there is more substantial agreement on the fact that there *is* a pattern, and upon the further question as to what the basic elements of the pattern are. Harris and Ullman present the three major generalizations of arrangement of activities within cities—concentric zones, sectors, and multiple nuclei—to aid in understanding both the internal spatial pattern of cities and the processes which underlie them. The locational pattern of activities in a metropolis is to a great degree a function of the means of transportation available to overcome space. Ogburn shows how the inventions of local transportation have affected the spatial distribution of the residential population of American cities, particularly their effect upon density. The resistances to changing location as a result of these inventions also are discussed.

When people and their institutions come together in a location they do not just "pile up." Rather, they are sifted and sorted by a variety of factors—social and economic—in such a way that concentrations of similar land uses and population types appear. This process is called *segregation*. The overall spatial pattern of the community is a composite of a number of differentiated smaller areas which are the consequence of this process of segregation. Population types are segregated into diverse residential areas. Difference in social status is one such basis of segregation; there are upper, middle and lower social-status areas. family status is another; for example, there are single-person areas and family areas. Race or ethnic background and the degree of acceptance of the folkways and mores are still other ways in which population types are segregated. Ghettos and "Black belts" have been and are common phenomena in American cities. Land use often is an objective index of segregation—the kind and value of property or structure, or the particular function which is localized on the property. Apartment-house districts, rooming-house areas, and "automobile rows" are consequences of segregation. The paper by Beverly Duncan in this section provides some discussion of how different land uses are patterned in an urban area, particularly of their concentric zonation and of the localization of commerce and industry in relation to residence. A detailed ecological analysis of the spatial distance between occupation groups is provided in the paper by the Duncans. Examining the residential distribution of occupation groups in Chicago, they find the most segregated occupation groups are those at the extremes of a socio-economic scale, and that concentration of residence in low-rent areas and centralization of residence both are inversely related to socio-economic status. These findings support the proposition that spatial distances between occupation groups are highly correlated with the social distance between these groups.

The segregation pattern never remains constant, since the process of redistributing a population and its institutions always takes place—particularly when the city grows. Numbers of Negroes, or factory workers, or other population types, increase or decrease as a city grows or changes its functions, and the areas in which they live must change because growth tends to occur in orderly fashion. When the business area at the center of the city expands in response to increasing concentration and centralization, then many areas of the city are forced to respond by changes in their boundaries. This results in the intrusion of a new type of land use or population into an area where formerly it was not functional. Growth in a residential area or a formerly vacant area may also produce such changes in other areas, although their effect usually is more localized. The process of intrusion of a new type of land use or population is called *invasion*. It may involve such widely different phenomena as the entrance of Negroes into a previously white area, the appearance of rooming houses in the midst of single-family dwelling units, or the conversion of a residential area to business or industry. When an invasion has been completed and a new equilibrium is established, the area takes a new position in the pattern of the city. This culmination is called *suc-*

cession. The invasion-succession cycle may occur a number of times for a given area of a city within a particular period of time. A description of internal differentiation within many cities, particularly American cities, and the effect of growth on these spatial patterns is presented in a number of papers in other sections of this Reader, particularly in the papers by Freedman, Heberle, Johnson and Newcomb.

The operation of these ecological processes has the consequence of producing typical areal patterns. The first of these, *natural areas,* are often bounded by such natural barriers as water, abrupt shifts in contour of the land, railroad tracks or heavily traveled streets. Other types of barriers are such social factors as obstacles to communication and consensus. Such areas have an internal coherence based either upon the homogeneity of the population or upon their mutual interdependence for services and social life.

Areas which lie between natural areas in such a way as to render their character ambiguous are called *interstitial areas.* And areas in which land use is undergoing change are called *areas in transition.* The latter term is usually applied to that territory which intervenes between the central downtown commercial land use and the residential regions lying further out. The name also, however, may be given to such changes in land use as territories in which light manufacturing is invading commercial areas, or other similar situations. It is also applied to the rural-urban fringe where residential land use on the periphery of the

growing city is replacing agricultural land use. Such areas are characterized by the problems associated with future but unrealized changes in land values, and thus become sources of considerable concern to cities.

All this taken together indicates the continuous but orderly processes of change leading to the development of basic spatial patterns broadly generalizable from city to city. Time, like space, also is a factor of considerable significance in the organization of the ecological community. The discussion of time and cost in overcoming space suggests how closely the two variables of space and time are related. Space and time are separable, however, for purposes of analysis. There is a kind of metabolism in the movement of people and goods within and between cities so that recurring patterns of movement with time can be observed. The empirical paper by Beverly Duncan presents several patterns of intracity movement and shows how they are related to the spatial structure and functional organization of the city. Her analysis focuses on the most dominant of the daily patterns of movement of an urban population, the movement between workplace and place of residence. Other patterns of recurrent movement have been analyzed, e.g., the movement of persons to other institutions such as schools and churches, or the movement of goods among places of production, storage, and use. The analysis of these temporal processes sheds further light on the ecological organization of the city.

A THEORY OF LOCATION FOR CITIES

Edward Ullman

Periodically in the past century the location and distribution of cities and settlements have been studied. Important contributions have been made by individuals in many disciplines. Partly because of the diversity and un-co-ordinated nature of the attack and partly because of the complexities and variables involved, a systematic theory has been slow to evolve, in contrast to the advances in the field of industrial location.[1]

The first theoretical statement of modern importance was von Thünen's *Der isolierte Staat*, initially published in 1826, wherein he postulated an entirely uniform land surface and showed that under ideal conditions a city would develop in the center of this land area and concentric rings of land use would develop around the central city. In 1841 Kohl investigated the relation between cities and the natural and cultural environment, paying particular attention to the effect of transport routes on the location of urban centers.[2] In 1894 Cooley admirably demonstrated the channelizing influence that transportation routes, particularly rail, would have on the location and development of trade centers.[3] He also called attention to break in transportation as a city-builder just as Ratzel had earlier. In 1927 Haig sought to determine why there was such a large concentration of population and manufacturing in the largest cities.[4] Since concentration occurs where assembly of material is cheapest, all business functions, except extraction and transportation, ideally should be located in cities where transportation is least costly. Exceptions are provided by the processing of perishable goods, as in sugar centrals, and of large weight-losing commodities, as in smelters. Haig's theoretical treatment is of a different type from

Reprinted from *The American Journal of Sociology*, Vol. 46 (May 1941), pp. 853-64, by permission of the author and the publisher. (Copyright, 1941, by *The American Journal of Sociology*.)

1. *Cf.* Tord Palander, *Beiträge zur Standortstheorie* (Uppsala, Sweden, 1935), or E. M. Hoover, Jr., *Location Theory and the Shoe and Leather Industries* (Cambridge, Mass., 1937).

2. J. G. Kohl, *Der Verkehr und die Ansiedlungen der Menschen in ihrer Abhängigkeit von der Gestaldung der Erdoberfläche* (2d ed.; Leipzig, 1850).

3. C. H. Cooley, "The Theory of Transportation," *Publications of the American Economic Association*, IX (May, 1894), 1-148.

4. R. M. Haig, "Toward an Understanding of the Metropolis: Some Speculations Regarding the Economic Basis of Urban Concentration," *Quarterly Journal of Economics*, XL (1926), 179-208.

those just cited but should be included as an excellent example of a "concentration" study.

In 1927 Bobeck [5] showed that German geographers since 1899, following Schlüter and others, had concerned themselves largely with the internal geography of cities, with the pattern of land use and forms within the urban limits, in contrast to the problem of location and support of cities. Such preoccupation with internal urban structure has also characterized the recent work of geographers in America and other countries. Bobeck insisted with reason that such studies, valuable though they were, constituted only half the field of urban geography and that there remained unanswered the fundamental geographical question "What are the causes for the existence, present size, and character of a city?" Since the publication of this article, a number of urban studies in Germany and some in other countries have dealt with such questions as the relations between city and country.[6]

A theoretical framework for study of the distribution of settlements is provided by the work of Walter Christaller.[7] The essence of the theory is that a certain amount of productive land supports an urban center. The center exists because essential services must be performed for the surrounding land. Thus the primary factor explaining Chicago is the productivity of the Middle West; location at the southern end of Lake Michigan is a secondary factor. If there were no Lake Michigan, the urban population of the Middle West would in all probability be just as large as it is now. Ideally, the city should be in the center of a productive area.[8] The similarity of this concept to von Thünen's original proposition is evident.

Apparently many scholars have approached the scheme in their thinking.[9] Bobeck claims he presented the rudiments of such an explanation in 1927. The work of a number of American rural sociologists shows appreciation for some of Christaller's preliminary assumptions, even though done before or without knowledge of Christaller's work and performed with a different end in view. Galpin's epochal study of trade areas in Walworth

5. Hans Bobeck, "Grundfragen der Stadt Geographie," *Geographischer Anzeiger,* XXVIII (1927), 213-24.

6. A section of the International Geographical Congress at Amsterdam in 1938 dealt with "Functional Relations between City and Country." The papers are published in Vol. II of the *Comptes rendus* (Leiden: E. J. Brill, 1938). A recent American study is C. D. Harris, *Salt Lake City: A Regional Capital* (Ph.D. diss., University of Chicago, 1940). Pertinent also is R. E. Dickinson, "The Metropolitan Regions of the United States," *Geographical Review,* XXIV (1934), 278-91.

7. *Die zentralen Orte in Süddeutschland* (Jena, 1935); also a paper (no title) in *Comptes rendus du Congrès internationale de géographie Amsterdam* (1938), II, 123-37.

8. This does not deny the importance of "gateway" centers such as Omaha and Kansas City, cities located between contrasting areas in order to secure exchange benefits. The logical growth of cities at such locations does not destroy the theory to be presented (*cf.* R. D. McKenzie's excellent discussion in *The Metropolitan Community* [New York, 1933], pp. 4 ff.).

9. *Cf.* Petrie's statement about ancient Egypt and Mesopotamia: "It has been noticed before how remarkably similar the distances are between the early nome capitals of the Delta (twenty-one miles on an average) and the early cities of Mesopotamia (averaging twenty miles apart). Some physical cause seems to limit the primitive rule

County, Wisconsin, published in 1915, was the first contribution. Since then important studies bearing on the problem have been made by others.[10] These studies are confined primarily to smaller trade centers but give a wealth of information on distribution of settlements which independently substantiates many of Christaller's basic premises.

As a working hypothesis one assumes that normally the larger the city, the larger its tributary area. Thus there should be cities of varying size ranging from a small hamlet performing a few simple functions, such as providing a limited shopping and market center for a small contiguous area, up to a large city with a large tributary area composed of the service areas of many smaller towns and providing more complex services, such as whole-saling, large-scale banking, specialized retailing, and the like. Services performed purely for a surrounding area are termed "central" functions by Christaller, and the settlements performing them "central" places. An industry using raw materials imported from outside the local region and shipping its products out of the local area would not constitute a central service.

Ideally, each central place would have a circular tributary area, as in von Thünen's proposition, and the city would be in the center. However, if three or more tangent circles are inscribed in an area, unserved spaces will exist; the best theoretical shapes are hexagons, the closest geometrical figures to circles which will completely fill an area (Fig. 1).[11]

Christaller has recognized typical-size settlements, computed their average population, their distance apart, and the size and population of their tributary areas in accordance with his hexagonal theory as Table 1 shows. He also states that the number of central places follows a norm from largest

---

in this way. Is it not the limit of central storage of grain, which is the essential form of early capital? Supplies could be centralised up to ten miles away; beyond that the cost of transport made it better worth while to have a nearer centre" (W. M. Flinders Petrie, *Social Life in Ancient Egypt* [London, 1923; reissued, 1932], pp. 3-4).

10. C. J. Galpin, *Social Anatomy of an Agricultural Community* (University of Wisconsin Agricultural Experiment Station Research Bull. 34 [1915]), and the restudy by J. H. Kolb and R. A. Polson, *Trends in Town-Country Relations* (University of Wisconsin Agricultural Experiment Station Research Bull. 117 [1933]); B. L. Melvin, *Village Service Agencies of New York State, 1925* (Cornell University Agricultural Experiment Station Bull. 493 [1929]), and *Rural Population of New York, 1855–1925* (Cornell University Agricultural Experiment Station Memoir 116 [1928]); Dwight Sanderson, *The Rural Community* (New York, 1932), esp. pp. 488-514, which contains references to many studies by Sanderson and his associates; Carle C. Zimmerman, *Farm Trade Centers in Minnesota, 1905-29* (University of Minnesota Agricultural Experiment Station Bull. 269 [1930]); T. Lynn Smith, *Farm Trade Centers in Louisiana 1905 to 1931* (Louisiana State University Bull. 234 [1933]); Paul H. Landis, *South Dakota Town-Country Trade Relations, 1901–1931* (South Dakota Agricultural Experiment Station Bull. 274 [1932]), and *The Growth and Decline of South Dakota Trade Centers, 1901–1933* (Bull. 279 [1938]), and *Washington Farm Trade Centers, 1900–1935* (State College of Washington Agricultural Experiment Station Bull. 360 [1938]). Other studies are listed in subsequent footnotes.

11. See August Lösch, "The Nature of the Economic Regions," *Southern Economic Journal*, V (1938), 73. Galpin (*op. cit.*) thought in terms of six tributary-area circles around each center. See also Kolb and Polson, *op. cit.*, pp. 30-41.

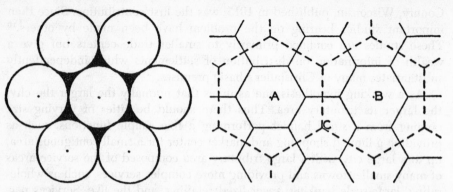

FIG. 1. Theoretical shape of tributary areas. Circles leave unserved spaces, hexagons do not. Small hexagons are service areas for smaller places, large hexagons (dotted lines) represent service areas for next higher rank central places.

to smallest in the following order 1:2:6:18:54, etc.[12]

All these figures are computed on the basis of South Germany, but Christaller claims them to be typical for most of Germany and western Europe. The settlements are classified on the basis of spacing each larger unit in a hexagon of next-order size, so that the distance between similiar centers in the table above increases by the $\sqrt{3}$ over the preceding smaller category (in Fig. 1, e.g., the distance from A to B is $\sqrt{3}$ times the distance from A to C). The initial distance figure of 7 km. between the smallest centers is chosen because 4-5 km., approximately the distance one can walk in one hour, appears to be a normal service-area limit for the smallest centers. Thus, in a hexagonal scheme, these centers are about 7 km. apart. Christaller's maps indicate that such centers are spaced close to this norm in South Germany. In the larger categories the norms for distance apart and size of centers appear to be true averages; but variations from the norm are the rule, although wide discrepancies are not common in the eastern portion of South Germany, which is less highly industrialized than the Rhine-Ruhr areas in the west. The number of central places of each rank varies rather widely from the normal order of expectancy.

	Towns		Tributary Areas	
	Distance		Size	
Central Place	Apart (Km.)	Population	(Sq. Km.)	Population
Market hamlet (Marktort)	7	800	45	2,700
Township center (Amtsort)	12	1,500	135	8,100
County seat (Kreisstadt)	21	3,500	400	24,000
District city (Bezirksstadt)	36	9,000	1,200	75,000
Small state capital (Gaustadt)	62	27,000	3,600	225,000
Provincial head city (Provinzhauptstadt)	108	90,000	10,800	675,000
Regional capital city (Landeshauptstadt)	186	300,000	32,400	2,025,000

TABLE I

12. Barnes and Robinson present some interesting maps showing the average distance apart of farmhouses in the driftless area of the Middle West and in southern Ontario. Farmhouses might well be regarded as the smallest settlement units in a central-place scheme, although they might not be in the same numbered sequence (James A. Barnes and Arthur H. Robinson, "A New Method for the Representation of Dispersed Rural Population," *Geographical Review*, XXX [1940], 134-37).

The theoretical ideal appears to be most nearly approached in poor, thinly settled farm districts—areas which are most nearly self-contained. In some other sections of Germany industrial concentration seems to be a more important explanation, although elements of the central-place type of distribution are present. Christaller points out that Cologne is really the commercial center for the Ruhr industrial district even though it is outside the Ruhr area. Even in mountain areas centrality is a more important factor than topography in fixing the distribution of settlements. Christaller states that one cannot claim that a certain city is where it is because of a certain river—that would be tantamount to saying that if there were no rivers there would be no cities.

Population alone is not a true measure of the central importance of a city; a large mining, industrial, or other specialized-function town might have a small tributary area and exercise few central functions. In addition to population, therefore, Christaller uses an index based on number of telephones in proportion to the average number per thousand inhabitants in South Germany, weighted further by the telephone density of the local subregion. A rich area such as the Palatinate supports more telephones in proportion to population than a poor area in the Bavarian Alps; therefore, the same number of telephones in a Palatinate town would not give it the same central significance as in the Alps. He claims that telephones, since they are used for business, are a reliable index of centrality. Such a thesis would not be valid for most of the United States, where telephones are as common in homes as in commercial and professional quarters.

Some better measures of centrality could be devised, even if only the number of out-of-town telephone calls per town. Better still would be some measure of actual central services performed. It would be tedious and difficult to compute the amount, or percentage, of business in each town drawn from outside the city, but some short cuts might be devised. I_i one knew the average number of customers required to support certain specialized functions in various regions, then the excess of these functions over the normal required for the urban population would be an index of centrality.[13] In several states rural sociologists and others have computed the average number of certain functions for towns of a given size. With one or two exceptions only small towns have been analyzed. Retail trade has received most attention, but professional and other services have also been examined. These studies do not tell us actually what population supports each service, since the services are supported both by town and by surrounding rural population, but they do provide norms of function expectancy which would be just as useful.[14]

---

13. In Iowa, e.g., almost all towns of more than 450 inhabitants have banks, half of the towns of 250-300, and 20 per cent of the towns of 100-150 (according to calculations made by the author from population estimates in *Rand McNally's Commercial Atlas* for 1937).

14. See particularly the thorough study by B. L. Melvin, *Village Service Agencies, New York State 1925;* C. R. Hoffer, *A Study of Town-Country Relationships* (Michigan

A suggestive indicator of centrality is provided by the maps which Dickinson has made for per capita wholesale sales of cities in the United States.[15] On this basis centers are distributed rather evenly in accordance with regional population density. Schlier has computed the centrality of cities in Germany on the basis of census returns for "central" occupations.[16] Refinement of some of our census returns is desirable before this can be done entirely satisfactorily in the United States, but the method is probably the most promising in prospect.

Another measure of centrality would be the number of automobiles entering a town, making sure that suburban movements were not included. Figures could be secured if the state-wide highway planning surveys in forty-six states were extended to gather such statistics.

The central-place scheme may be distorted by local factors, primarily industrial concentration or main transport routes. Christaller notes that transportation is not an areally operating principle, as the supplying of central goods implies, but is a linearly working factor. In many cases central places are strung at short intervals along an important transport route, and their tributary areas do not approximate the ideal circular or hexagonal shape but are elongated at right angles to the main transport line.[17] In some areas the reverse of this normal expectancy is true. In most of Illinois, maps depicting tributary areas show them to be elongated parallel to the main transport routes, not at right angles to them.[18] The combination of nearly uniform land and competitive railways peculiar to the state results in main

---

Agricultural Experiment Station Special Bull. 181 [1928]) (data on number of retail stores and professions per town); H. B. Price and C. R. Hoffer, *Services of Rural Trade Centers in Distribution of Farm Supplies* (Minnesota Agricultural Experiment Station Bull. 249 [1938]); William J. Reilly, *Methods for the Study of Retail Relationships* ("Bureau of Business Research Monographs," No. 4, University of Texas Bull. 2944 [1929]), p. 26; J. H. Kolb, *Service Institutions of Town and Country* (Wisconsin Agricultural Experiment Station Research Bull. 66 [1925]) (town size in relation to support of institutions); Smith, *op. cit.*, pp. 32-40; Paul H. Landis, *South Dakota Town-Country Trade Relations, 1901–1931*, p. 20 (population per business enterprise), and pp. 24-25 (functions per town size); Zimmerman, *op. cit.*, pp. 16 and 51 ff.

For a criticism of population estimates of unincorporated hamlets used in many of these studies see Glenn T. Trewartha, "The Unincorporated Hamlet: An Analysis of Data Sources" (paper presented December 28 at Baton Rouge meetings, Association of American Geographers; forthcoming, probably, in March number of *Rural Sociology*, Vol. VI [1941]).

15. *Op. cit.*, pp. 280-81.

16. Otto Schlier, "Die zentralen Orte des Deutschen Reichs," *Zeitschrift der Gesellschaft für Erdkunde zu Berlin* (1937), pp. 161-70. See also map constructed from Schlier's figures in R. E. Dickinson's valuable article, "The Economic Regions of Germany," *Geographical Review*, XXVIII (1938), 619. For use of census figures in the United States see Harris, *op. cit.*, pp. 3-12.

17. For an illustration of this type of tributary area in the ridge and valley section of east Tennessee see H. V. Miller, "Effects of Reservoir Construction on Local Economic Units," *Economic Geography*, XV (1939), 242-49.

18. See, e.g., *Marketing Atlas of the United States* (New York: International Magazine Co., Inc.) or *A Study of Natural Areas of Trade in the United States* (Washington, D.C.: U.S. National Recovery Administration, 1935).

railways running nearly parallel and close to one another between major centers.

In highly industrialized areas the central-place scheme is generally so distorted by industrial concentration in response to resources and transportation that it may be said to have little significance as an explanation for urban location and distribution, although some features of a central-place scheme may be present, as in the case of Cologne and the Ruhr.

In addition to distortion, the type of scheme prevailing in various regions is susceptible to many influences. Productivity of the soil,[19] type of agriculture and intensity of cultivation, topography, governmental organization, are all obvious modifiers. In the United States, for example, what is the effect on distribution of settlements caused by the sectional layout of the land and the regular size of counties in many states? In parts of Latin America many centers are known as "Sunday towns"; their chief functions appear to be purely social, to act as religious and recreational centers for holidays—hence the name "Sunday town." [20] Here social rather than economic services are the primary support of towns, and we should accordingly expect a system of central places with fewer and smaller centers, because fewer functions are performed and people can travel farther more readily than commodities. These underlying differences do not destroy the value of the theory; rather they provide variations of interest to study for themselves and for purposes of comparison with other regions.

The system of central places is not static or fixed; rather it is subject to change and development with changing conditions.[21] Improvements in transportation have had noticeable effects. The provision of good automobile roads alters buying and marketing practices, appears to make the smallest centers smaller and the larger centers larger, and generally alters trade areas.[22] Since good roads are spread more uniformly over the land

19. *Cf.* the emphasis of Sombart, Adam Smith, and other economists on the necessity of surplus produce of land in order to support cities. Fertile land ordinarily produces more surplus and consequently more urban population, although "the town . . . . may not always derive its whole subsistence from the country in its neighborhood . . . ." (Adam Smith, *The Wealth of Nations* ["Modern Library" edition; New York, 1937] p. 357; Werner Sombart, *Der moderne Kapitalismus* [zweite, neugearbeitete Auflage; Munich and Leipzig, 1916], I, 130-31).

20. For an account of such settlements in Brazil see Pierre Deffontaines, "Rapports fonctionnels entre les agglomérations urbaines et rurales: un example en pays de colonisation, le Brésil," *Comptes rendus du Congrès internationale de géographie Amsterdam* (1938), II, 139-44.

21. The effects of booms, droughts, and other factors on trade-center distribution by decades are brought out in Landis' studies for South Dakota and Washington. Zimmerman and Smith also show the changing character of trade-center distribution (see n. 10 of this paper for references). Melvin calls attention to a "village population shift lag"; in periods of depressed agriculture villages in New York declined in population approximately a decade after the surrounding rural population had decreased (B. L. Melvin, *Rural Population of New York, 1855–1925*, p. 120).

22. Most studies indicate that only the very smallest hamlets (under 250 population) and crossroads stores have declined in size or number. The larger small places have held their own (see Landis for Washington, *op. cit.*, p. 37, and his *South Dakota Town-Country Trade Relations 1901–1931*, pp. 34-36). Zimmerman in 1930 (*op. cit.*, p. 41)

than railways, their provision seems to make the distribution of centers correspond more closely to the normal scheme.[23]

Christaller may be guilty of claiming too great an application of his scheme. His criteria for determining typical-size settlements and their normal number apparently do not fit actual frequency counts of settlements in many almost uniform regions as well as some less rigidly deductive norms.[24]

Bobeck in a later article claims that Christaller's proof is unsatisfactory.[25] He states that two-thirds of the population of Germany and England live in cities and that only one-third of these cities in Germany are real central places. The bulk are primarily industrial towns or villages inhabited solely by farmers. He also declares that exceptions in the rest of the world are common, such as the purely rural districts of the Tonkin Delta of Indo-China, cities based on energetic entrepreneurial activity, as some Italian cities, and world commercial ports such as London, Rotterdam, and Singapore. Many of these objections are valid; one wishes that Christaller had better quantitative data and were less vague in places. Bobeck admits, however, that the central-place theory has value and applies in some areas.

The central-place theory probably provides as valid an interpretation of settlement distribution over the land as the concentric-zone theory does for land use within cities. Neither theory is to be thought of as a rigid framework fitting all location facts at a given moment. Some, expecting too much, would jettison the concentric-zone theory; others, realizing that it is an investigative hypothesis of merit, regard it as a useful tool for comparative analysis.

---

notes that crossroads stores are disappearing and are being replaced by small villages. He states further: "It is evident that claims of substantial correlation between the appearance and growth of the larger trading center and the disappearance of the primary center are more or less unfounded. Although there are minor relationships, the main change has been a division of labor between the two types of centers rather than the complete obliteration of the smaller in favor of the larger" (p. 32).

For further evidences of effect of automobile on small centers see R. V. Mitchell, *Trends in Rural Retailing in Illlinois 1926 to 1938* (University of Illinois Bureau of Business Research Bull., Ser. 59 [1939]), pp. 31 ff., and Sanderson, *op. cit.*, p. 564, as well as other studies cited above.

23. Smith (*op. cit.*, p. 54) states: "There has been a tendency for centers of various sizes to distribute themselves more uniformly with regard to the area, population, and resources of the state. Or the changes seem to be in the direction of a more efficient pattern of rural organization. This redistribution of centers in conjunction with improved methods of communication and transportation has placed each family in frequent contact with several trade centers. . . . ."

In contrast, Melvin (*Rural Population of New York, 1855–1925*, p. 90), writing about New York State before the automobile had had much effect, states: "In 1870 the villages . . . were rather evenly scattered over the entire state where they had been located earlier in response to particular local needs. By 1920, however, the villages had become distributed more along routes of travel and transportation and in the vicinity of cities."

24. This statement is made on the basis of frequency counts by the author for several midwestern states (*cf.* also Schlier, *op. cit.*, pp. 165-69, for Germany).

25. Hans Bobeck, "Über einige functionelle Stadttypen und ihre Beziehungen zum Lande," *Comptes rendus du Congrès internationale de géographie Amsterdam* (1938), II, 88.

Even in the closely articulated national economy of the United States there are strong forces at work to produce a central-place distribution of settlements. It is true that products under our national economy are characteristically shipped from producing areas through local shipping-points directly to consuming centers which are often remote. However, the distribution of goods or imports brought into an area is characteristically carried on through brokerage, wholesale and retail channels in central cities.[26] This graduated division of functions supports a central-place framework of settlements. Many nonindustrial regions of relatively uniform land surface have cities distributed so evenly over the land that some sort of central-place theory appears to be the prime explanation.[27] It should be worth while to study this distribution and compare it with other areas.[28] In New England, on the other hand, where cities are primarily industrial centers based on distant raw materials and extra-regional markets, instead of the land's supporting the city the reverse is more nearly true: the city supports the countryside by providing a market for farm products, and thus infertile rural areas are kept from being even more deserted than they are now.

---

26. Harris, *op. cit.*, p. 87.

27. For a confirmation of this see the column diagram on p. 73 of Lösch (*op. cit.*), which shows the minimum distances between towns in Iowa of three different size classes. The maps of trade-center distribution in the works of Zimmerman, Smith, and Landis (cited earlier) also show an even spacing of centers.

28. The following table gives the average community area for 140 villages in the United States in 1930. In the table notice throughout that (1) the larger the village, the larger its tributary area in each region and (2) the sparser the rural population density, the larger the village tributary area for each size class (contrast mid-Atlantic with Far West, etc.).

	Community Area in Square Miles		
Region	Small Villages (250-1,000 Pop.)	Medium Villages (1,000-1,750 Pop.)	Large Villages (1,750-2,500 Pop.)
Mid-Atlantic	43	46	87
South	77	111	146
Middle West	81	113	148
Far West	. .	365	223

Although 140 is only a sample of the number of villages in the country, the figures are significant because the service areas were carefully and uniformly delimited in the field for all villages (E. deS. Brunner and J. D. Kolb, *Rural Social Trends* [New York, 1933], p. 95; see also E. deS. Brunner, G. S. Hughes, and M. Patten, *American Agricultural Villages* [New York, 1927], chap. ii).

In New York 26 sq. mi. was found to be the average area per village in 1920. Village refers to any settlement under 2,500 population. Nearness to cities, type of agriculture, and routes of travel are cited as the three most important factors influencing density of villages. Since areas near cities are suburbanized in some cases, as around New York City, the village-density in these districts is correspondingly high. Some urban counties with smaller cities (Rochester, Syracuse, and Niagara Falls) have few suburbs, and consequently the villages are farther apart than in many agricultural counties (B. L. Melvin, *Rural Population of New York, 1855–1925*, pp. 88-89; table on p. 89 shows number of square miles per village in each New York county).

In sample areas of New York State the average distance from a village of 250 or under to another of the same size or larger is about 3 miles; for the 250-749 class it is 3-5 miles; for the 750-1,249 class, 5-7 miles (B. L. Melvin, *Village Service Agencies*, New York, 1925, p. 102; in the table on p. 103 the distance averages cited above are

The forces making for concentration at certain places and the inevitable rise of cities at these favored places have been emphasized by geographers and other scholars. The phenomenal growth of industry and world trade in the last hundred years and the concomitant growth of cities justify this emphasis but have perhaps unintentionally caused the intimate connection between a city and its surrounding area partially to be overlooked. Explanation in terms of concentration is most important for industrial districts but does not provide a complete areal theory for distribution of settlements. Furthermore, there is evidence that "of late . . . the rapid growth of the larger cities has reflected their increasing importance as commercial and service centers rather than as industrial centers." [29] Some form of the central-place theory should provide the most realistic key to the distribution of settlements where there is no marked concentration—in agricultural areas where explanation has been most difficult in the past. For all areas the system may well furnish a theoretical norm from which deviations may be measured.[30] It might also be an aid in planning the development of new areas. If the theory is kept in mind by workers in academic and planning fields as more studies are made, its validity may be tested and its structure refined in accordance with regional differences.

---

shown to be very near the modes).

Kolb makes some interesting suggestions as to the distances between centers. He shows that spacing is closer in central Wisconsin than in Kansas, which is more sparsely settled (J. H. Kolb, *Service Relations of Town and Country* [Wisconsin Agricultural Experimental Station Research Bull. 58 (1923)]; see pp. 7-8 for theoretical graphs).

In Iowa, "the dominant factor determining the *size* of convenience-goods areas is distance" (*Second State Iowa Planning Board Report* [Des Moines, April, 1935], p. 198). This report contains fertile suggestions on trade areas for Iowa towns. Valuable detailed reports on retail trade areas for some Iowa counties have also been made by the same agency.

29. U.S. National Resources Committee, *Our Cities—Their Role in the National Economy: Report of the Urbanism Committee* (Washington: Government Printing Office, 1937), p. 37.

30. Some form of the central-place concept might well be used to advantage in interpreting the distribution of outlying business districts in cities (*cf.* Malcolm J. Proudfoot, "The Selection of a Business Site," *Journal of Land and Public Utility Economics*, XIV [1938], esp. 373 ff.).

THE NATURE OF CITIES

Chauncy D. Harris and Edward L. Ullman

Cities are the focal points in the occupation and utilization of the earth by man. Both a product of and an influence on surrounding regions, they develop in definite patterns in response to economic and social needs.

Cities are also paradoxes. Their rapid growth and large size testify to their superiority as a technique for the exploitation of the earth, yet by their very success and consequent large size they often provide a poor local environment for man. The problem is to build the future city in such a manner that the advantages of urban concentration can be preserved for the benefit of man and the disadvantages minimized.

Each city is unique in detail but resembles others in function and pattern. What is learned about one helps in studying another. Location types and internal structure are repeated so often that broad and suggestive generalizations are valid, especially if limited to cities of similar size, function, and regional setting. This paper will be limited to a discussion of two basic aspects of the nature of cities—their support and their internal structure. Such important topics as the rise and extent of urbanism, urban sites, culture of cities, social and economic characteristics of the urban population, and critical problems will receive only passing mention.

THE SUPPORT OF CITIES. As one approaches a city and notices its tall buildings rising above the surrounding land and as one continues into the city and observes the crowds of people hurrying to and fro past stores, theaters, banks, and other establishments, one naturally is struck by the contrast with the rural countryside. What supports this phenomenon? What do the people of the city do for a living?

The support of a city depends on the services it performs not for itself but for a tributary area. Many activities serve merely the population of the city itself. Barbers, dry cleaners, shoe repairers, grocerymen, bakers, and movie operators serve others who are engaged in the principal activity of the city, which may be mining, manufacturing, trade, or some other activity.

The service by which the city earns its livelihood depends on the nature of the economy and of the hinterland. Cities are small or rare in areas either of primitive, self-sufficient economy or of meager resources. As Adam Smith stated, the land must produce a surplus in order to support cities. This does

Reprinted from *The Annals*, Vol. 242 (November 1945), pp. 7-17, by permission of the author and the publisher. (Copyright, 1945, by *The Annals*.)

not mean that all cities must be surrounded by productive land, since strategic location with reference to cheap ocean highways may enable a city to support itself on the specialized surplus of distant lands. Nor does it mean that cities are parasites living off the land. Modern mechanization, transport, and a complex interdependent economy enable much of the economic activity of mankind to be centered in cities. Many of the people engaged even in food production are actually in cities in the manufacture of agricultural machinery.

The support of cities as suppliers of urban services for the earth can be summarized in three categories, each of which presents a factor of urban causation: [1]

1. Cities as central places performing comprehensive services for a surrounding area. Such cities tend to be evenly spaced throughout productive territory. For the moment this may be considered the "norm" subject to variation primarily in response to the ensuing factors.

2. Transport cities performing break-of-bulk and allied services along transport routes, supported by areas which may be remote in distance but close in connection because of the city's strategic location on transport channels. Such cities tend to be arranged in linear patterns along rail lines or at coasts.

3. Specialized-function cities performing one service such as mining, manufacturing, or recreation for large areas, including the general tributary areas of hosts of other cities. Since the principal localizing factor is often a particular resource such as coal, water power, or a beach, such cities may occur singly or in clusters.

Most cities represent a combination of the three factors, the relative importance of each varying from city to city.

Cities as central places. Cities as central places serve as trade and social centers for a tributary area. If the land base is homogeneous these centers are uniformly spaced, as in many parts of the agricultural Middle West. In areas of uneven resource distribution, the distribution of cities is uneven. The centers are of varying sizes, ranging from small hamlets closely spaced with one or two stores serving a local tributary area, through larger villages, towns, and cities more widely spaced with more special services for larger tributary areas, up to the great metropolis such as New York or Chicago offering many specialized services for a large tributary area composed of a whole hierarchy or tributary areas of smaller places. Such a net of tributary areas and centers forms a pattern somewhat like a fish net spread over a beach, the network regular and symmetrical where the sand is smooth, but warped and distorted where the net is caught in rocks.

The central-place type of city or town is widespread throughout the world, particularly in nonindustrial regions. In the United States it is best represented by the numerous retail and wholesale trade centers of the

---

1. For references see Edward Ullman, "A Theory of Location for Cities," *American Journal of Sociology*, Vol. 46, No. 6 (May 1941), pp. 853-64.

agricultural Middle West, Southwest, and West. Such cities have imposing shopping centers or wholesale districts in proportion to their size; the stores are supported by the trade of the surrounding area. This contrasts with many cities of the industrial East, where the centers are so close together that each has little trade support beyond its own population.

Not only trade but social and religious functions may support central places. In some instances these other functions may be the main support of the town. In parts of Latin America, for example, where there is little trade, settlements are scattered at relatively uniform intervals through the land as social and religious centers. In contrast to most cities, their busiest day is Sunday, when the surrounding populace attend church and engage in holiday recreation, thus giving rise to the name "Sunday town."

Most large central cities and towns are also political centers. The county seat is an example. London and Paris are the political as well as trade centers of their countries. In the United States, however, Washington and many state capitals are specialized political centers. In many of these cases the political capital was initially chosen as a centrally located point in the political area and was deliberately separated from the major urban center.

Cities as transport foci and break-of-bulk points. All cities are dependent on transportation in order to utilize the surplus of the land for their support. This dependence on transportation destroys the symmetry of the central-place arrangement, inasmuch as cities develop at foci or breaks of transportation, and transport routes are distributed unevenly over the land because of relief or other limitations. City organizations recognize the importance of efficient transportation, as witness their constant concern with freight-rate regulation and with the construction of new highways, port facilities, airfields, and the like.

Mere focusing of transport routes does not produce a city, but according to Cooley, if break of bulk occurs, the focus becomes a good place to process goods. Where the form of transport changes, as transferring from water to rail, break of bulk is inevitable. Ports originating merely to transship cargo tend to develop auxiliary services such as repackaging, storing, and sorting. An example of simple break-of-bulk and storage ports is Port Arthur-Fort William, the twin port and wheat-storage cities at the head of Lake Superior; surrounded by unproductive land, they have arisen at the break-of-bulk points on the cheapest route from the wheat-producing Prairie Provinces to the markets of the East. Some ports develop as entrepôts, such as Hong Kong and Copenhagen, supported by trans-shipment of goods from small to large boats or vice versa. Servicing points or minor changes in transport tend to encourage growth of cities as establishment of division points for changing locomotives on American railroads.

Transport centers can be centrally located places or can serve as gateways between contrasting regions with contrasting needs. Kansas City, Omaha, and Minneapolis-St. Paul serve as gateways to the West as well as central places for productive agricultural regions, and are important wholesale centers. The ports of New Orleans, Mobile, Savannah, Charleston, Norfolk, and others served as traditional gateways to the Cotton Belt with its specialized production. Likewise, northern border metropolises such as Baltimore, Washington, Cincinnati, and Louisville served as gateways to the South, with St. Louis a gateway to the Southwest. In recent years the South has been developing its own central places, supplanting some of the monopoly once held by the border gateways. Atlanta, Memphis, and Dallas are examples of the new southern central places and transport foci.

Changes in transportation are reflected in the pattern of city distribution. Thus the development of railroads resulted in a railroad alignment of cities which still persists. The rapid growth of automobiles and widespread development of highways in recent decades, however, has changed the trend toward a more even distribution of towns. Studies in such diverse localities as New York and Louisiana have shown a shift of centers away from exclusive alignment along rail routes. Airways may reinforce this trend or stimulate still different patterns of distribution for the future city.

Cities as concentration points for specialized services. A specialized city or cluster of cities performing a specialized function for a large area may develop at a highly localized resource. The resort city of Miami, for example, developed in response to a favorable climate and beach. Scranton, Wilkes-Barre, and dozens of nearby towns are specialized coal-mining centers developed on anthracite coal deposits to serve a large segment of the northeastern United States. Pittsburgh and its suburbs and satellites form a nationally significant iron-and-steel manufacturing cluster favored by good location for the assembly of coal and iron ore and for the sale of steel to industries on the coal fields.

Equally important with physical resources in many cities are the advantages of mass production and ancillary services. Once started, a specialized city acts as a nucleus for similar or related activities, and functions tend to pyramid, whether the city is a seaside resort such as Miami or Atlantic City, or, more important, a manufacturing center such as Pittsburgh or Detroit. Concentration of industry in a city means that there will be a concentration of satellite services and industries—supply houses, machine shops, expert consultants, other industries using local industrial by-products or waste, still other industries making specialized parts for other plants in the city, marketing channels, specialized transport facilities, skilled labor, and a host of other facilities; either directly or indirectly, these benefit industry and cause it to expand in size and numbers in a concentrated place or district. Local personnel with the know-how in a given industry also may decide to start a new plant producing similar or like products in the same city. Furthermore, the advantages of mass production itself often tend to concentrate production in a few large factories and cities. Examples of localization of specific manufacturing industries are clothing in New York City, furniture in Grand Rapids, automobiles in the Detroit area, pottery in Stoke-on-Trent in England, and even such a specialty as tennis rackets in Pawtucket, Rhode Island.

Such concentration continues until opposing forces of high labor costs and congestion balance the concentrating forces. Labor costs may be lower in small towns and in industrially new districts; thus some factories are moving from the great metropolises to small towns; much of the cotton textile industry has moved from the old industrial areas of New England to the newer areas of the Carolinas in the South. The tremendous concentration of population and structures in large cities exacts a high cost in the form of congestion, high land costs, high taxes, and restrictive legislation.

Not all industries tend to concentrate in specialized industrial cities; many types of manufacturing partake more of central-place characteristics. These types are those that are tied to the market because the manufacturing process results in an increase in bulk or perishability. Bakeries, ice cream establishments, ice houses, breweries, soft-drink plants, and various types of assembly plants are examples. Even such industries, however, tend to be more developed in the manufacturing belt because the density of population and hence the market is greater there.

The greatest concentration of industrial cities in America is in the manufacturing belt of northeastern United States and contiguous Canada, north of the Ohio and east of the Mississippi. Some factors in this concentration are: large reserves of fuel and power (particularly coal), raw materials such as iron ore via the Great Lakes, cheap ocean transportation on the eastern seaboard, productive agriculture (particularly in the west), early settlement, later immigration concentrated in its cities, and an early start with consequent development of skilled labor, industrial know-how, transportation facilities, and prestige.

The interdependent nature of most of the industries acts as a powerful force to maintain this area as the primary home of industrial cities in the United States. Before the war, the typical industrial city outside the main manufacturing belt had only a single industry of the raw-material type, such as lumber mills, food canneries, or smelters (Longview, Washington; San Jose, California; Anaconda, Montana). Because of the need for producing huge quantities of ships and airplanes for a two-ocean war, however, many cities along the Gulf and Pacific coasts have grown rapidly during recent years as centers of industry.

Application of the three types of urban support. Although examples can be cited illustrating each of the three types of urban support, most American cities partake in varying proportions of all three types. New York City, for example, as the greatest American port is a break-of-bulk point; as the principal center of wholesaling and retailing it is a central-place type; and as the major American center of manufacturing it is a specialized type. The actual distribution and functional classification of cities in the United States, more complex than the simple sum of the three types has been mapped and described elsewhere in different terms.[2]

2. Chauncy D. Harris, "A Functional Classification of Cities in the United States," *The Geographical Review,* Vol. 33, No. 1 (Jan. 1943), pp. 85-99.

The three basic types therefore should not be considered as a rigid framework excluding all accidental establishment, although even fortuitous development of a city becomes part of the general urban-supporting environment. Nor should the urban setting be regarded as static; cities are constantly changing, and exhibit characteristic lag in adjusting to new conditions.

Ample opportunity exists for use of initiative in strengthening the supporting base of the future city, particularly if account is taken of the basic factors of urban support. Thus a city should examine: (1) its surrounding area to take advantage of changes such as newly discovered resources or crops, (2) its transport in order to adjust properly to new or changed facilities, and (3) its industries in order to benefit from technological advances.

INTERNAL STRUCTURE OF CITIES. Any effective plans for the improvement or rearrangement of the future city must take account of the present pattern of land use within the city, of the factors which have produced this pattern, and of the facilities required by activities localized within particular districts.

Although the internal pattern of each city is unique in its particular combination of details, most American cities have business, industrial, and residential districts. The forces underlying the pattern of land use can be appreciated if attention is focused on three generalizations of arrangement— by concentric zones, sectors, and multiple nuclei.

Concentric zones. According to the concentric-zone theory, the pattern of growth of the city can best be understood in terms of five concentric zones [3] (Fig. 1).

1. *The central business district.*—This is the focus of commercial, social, and civic life, and of transportation. In it is the downtown retail district with its department stores, smart shops, office buildings, clubs, banks, hotels, theaters, museums, and organization headquarters. Encircling the downtown retail district is the wholesale business district.

2. *The zone in transition.*—Encircling the downtown area is a zone of residential deterioration. Business and light manufacturing encroach on residential areas characterized particularly by rooming houses. In this zone are the principal slums with their submerged regions of poverty, degradation, and disease, and their underworlds of vice. In many American cities it has been inhabited largely by colonies of recent immigrants.

3. *The zone of independent working men's homes.*—This is inhabited by industrial workers who have escaped from the zone in transition but who desire to live within easy access of their work. In many American cities second-generation immigrants are important segments of the population in this area.

3. Ernest W. Burgess, "The Growth of the City," in *The City,* ed. by Robert E. Park, Ernest W. Burgess, and Roderick D. McKenzie (Chicago: University of Chicago Press, 1925), pp. 47-62; and Ernest W. Burgess, "Urban Areas," in *Chicago, an Experiment in Social Science Research,* ed. by T. V. Smith and Leonard D. White (Chicago: University of Chicago Press, 1929), pp. 113-38.

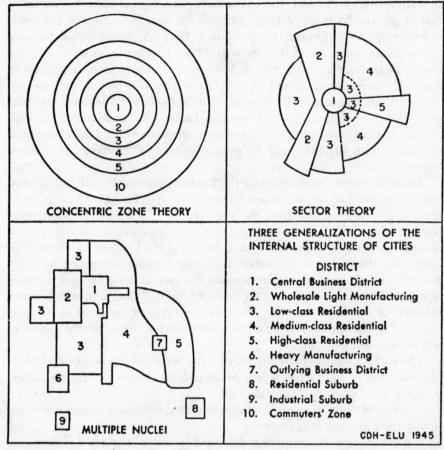

CONCENTRIC ZONE THEORY

SECTOR THEORY

THREE GENERALIZATIONS OF THE
INTERNAL STRUCTURE OF CITIES

DISTRICT
1. Central Business District
2. Wholesale Light Manufacturing
3. Low-class Residential
4. Medium-class Residential
5. High-class Residential
6. Heavy Manufacturing
7. Outlying Business District
8. Residential Suburb
9. Industrial Suburb
10. Commuters' Zone

MULTIPLE NUCLEI

CDH-ELU 1945

FIG. 1. Generalizations of internal structure of cities. The concentric zone theory is a generalization for all cities. The arrangement of the sectors in the sector theory varies from city to city. The diagram for multiple nuclei represents one possible pattern among innumerable variations.

4. *The zone of better residences.*—This is made up of single-family dwellings, of exclusive "restricted districts," and of high-class apartment buildings.

5. *The commuters' zone.*—Often beyond the city limits in suburban areas or in satellite cities, this is a zone of spotty development of high-class residences along lines of rapid travel.

Sectors. The theory of axial development, according to which growth takes place along main transportation routes or along lines of least resistance to form a star-shaped city, is refined by Homer Hoyt in his sector theory, which states that growth along a particular axis of transportation usually consists of similar types of land use [4] (Fig. 1). The entire city is considered

4. Homer Hoyt, "City Growth and Mortgage Risk," *Insured Mortgage Portfolio*, Vol. 1, Nos. 6-10 (Dec. 1936-April 1937), *passim;* and U. S. Federal Housing Administration, *The Structure and Growth of Residential Neighborhoods in American Cities* by Homer Hoyt (Washington: Government Printing Office, 1939), *passim.*

as a circle and the various areas as sectors radiating out from the center of that circle; similar types of land use originate near the center of the circle and migrate outward toward the periphery. Thus a high-rent residential area in the eastern quadrant of the city would tend to migrate outward, keeping always in the eastern quadrant. A low-quality housing area, if located in the southern quadrant, would tend to extend outward to the very margin of the city in that sector. The migration of high-class residential areas outward along established lines of travel is particularly pronounced on high ground, toward open country, to homes of community leaders, along lines of fastest transportation, and to existing nuclei of buildings or trading centers.

Multiple nuclei. In many cities the land-use pattern is built not around a single center but around several discrete nuclei (Fig. 1). In some cities these nuclei have existed from the very origins of the city; in others they have developed as the growth of the city stimulated migration and specialization. An example of the first type is Metropolitan London, in which "The City" and Westminster originated as separate points separated by open country, one as the center of finance and commerce, the other as the center of political life. An example of the second type is Chicago, in which heavy industry, at first localized along the Chicago River in the heart of the city, migrated to the Calumet District, where it acted as a nucleus for extensive new urban development.

The initial nucleus of the city may be the retail district in a central-place city, the port or rail facilities in a break-of-bulk city, or the factory, mine, or beach in a specialized-function city.

The rise of separate nuclei and differentiated districts reflects a combination of the following four factors:

1. Certain activities require specialized facilities. The retail district, for example, is attached to the point of greatest intracity accessibility, the port district to suitable water front, manufacturing districts to large blocks of land and water or rail connection, and so on.

2. Certain like activities group together because they profit from cohesion.[5] The clustering of industrial cities has already been noted above under "Cities as concentration points for specialized services." Retail districts benefit from grouping which increases the concentration of potential customers and makes possible comparison shopping. Financial and office-building districts depend upon facility of communication among offices within the district. The Merchandise Mart of Chicago is an example of wholesale clustering.

3. Certain unlike activities are detrimental to each other. The antagonism between factory development and high-class residential development is well known. The heavy concentrations of pedestrians, automobiles, and streetcars in the retail district are antagonistic both to the railroad facilities and the

---

5. Exceptions are service-type establishments such as some grocery stores, dry cleaners, and gasoline stations.

street loading required in the wholesale district and to the rail facilities and space needed by large industrial districts, and vice versa.

4. Certain activities are unable to afford the high rents of the most desirable sites. This factor works in conjunction with the foregoing. Examples are bulk wholesaling and storage activities requiring much room, or low-class housing unable to afford the luxury of high land with a view.

The number of nuclei which result from historical development and the operation of localization forces varies greatly from city to city. The larger the city, the more numerous and specialized are the nuclei. The following districts, however, have developed around nuclei in most large American cities.

The central business district.—This district is at the focus of intracity transportation facilities by sidewalk, private car, bus, streetcar, subway, and elevated. Because of asymmetrical growth of most large cities, it is generally not now in the areal center of the city but actually near one edge, as in the case of lake-front, riverside, or even inland cities; examples are Chicago, St. Louis, and Salt Lake City. Because established internal transportation lines converge on it, however, it is the point of most convenient access from all parts of the city, and the point of highest land values. The retail district, at the point of maximum accessibility, is attached to the sidewalk; only pedestrian or mass-transportation movement can concentrate the large numbers of customers necessary to support department stores, variety stores, and clothing shops, which are characteristic of the district. In small cities financial institutions and office buildings are intermingled with retail shops, but in large cities the financial district is separate, near but not at the point of greatest intracity facility. Its point of attachment is the elevator, which permits three-dimensional access among offices, whose most important locational factor is accessibility to other offices rather than to the city as a whole. Government buildings also are commonly near but not in the center of the retail district. In most cities a separate "automobile row" has arisen on the edge of the central business district, in cheaper rent areas along one or more major highways; its attachment is to the highway itself.

The wholesale and light-manufacturing district.—This district is conveniently within the city but near the focus of extra city transportation facilities. Wholesale houses, while deriving some support from the city itself, serve principally a tributary region reached by railroad and motor truck. They are, therefore, concentrated along railroad lines, usually adjacent to (but not surrounding) the central business district. Many types of light manufacturing which do not require specialized buildings are attracted by the facilities of this district or similar districts: good rail and road transportation, available loft buildings, and proximity to the markets and labor of the city itself.

The heavy industrial district.—This is near the present or former outer edge of the city. Heavy industries require large tracts of space, often beyond any available in sections already subdivided into blocks and streets. They also require good transportation, either rail or water. With the development

of belt lines and switching yards, sites on the edge of the city may have
better transportation service than those near the center. In Chicago about a
hundred industries are in a belt three miles long, adjacent to the Clearing
freight yards on the southwestern edge of the city. Furthermore, the noise
of boiler works, the odors of stockyards, the waste disposal problems of
smelters and iron and steel mills, the fire hazards of petroleum refineries,
and the space and transportation needs which interrupt streets and accessibility—all these favor the growth of heavy industry away from the main
center of the large city. The Calumet District of Chicago, the New Jersey
marshes near New York City, the Lea marshes near London, and the St.
Denis district of Paris are examples of such districts. The stockyards of
Chicago, in spite of their odors and size, have been engulfed by urban
growth and are now far from the edge of the city. They form a nucleus of
heavy industry within the city but not near the center, which has blighted
the adjacent residential area, the "back-of-the-yards" district.

The residential district.—In general, high-class districts are likely to be on
well-drained, high land and away from nuisances such as noise, odors,
smoke, and railroad lines. Low-class districts are likely to arise near factories
and railroad districts, wherever located in the city. Because of the obsolescence of structures, the older inner margins of residential districts are
fertile fields for invasion by groups unable to pay high rents. Residential
neighborhoods have some measure of cohesiveness. Extreme cases are the
ethnically segregated groups, which cluster together although including
members in many economic groups; Harlem is an example.

Minor nuclei.—These include cultural centers, parks, outlying business
districts, and small industrial centers. A university may form a nucleus for a
quasi-independent community; examples are the University of Chicago, the
University of California, and Harvard University. Parks and recreation areas
occupying former wasteland too rugged or wet for housing may form nuclei
for high-class residential areas; examples are Rock Creek Park in Washington and Hyde Park in London. Outlying business districts may in time
become major centers. Many small institutions and individual light manufacturing plants, such as bakeries, dispersed throughout the city may never
become nuclei of differentiated districts.

Suburb and Satellite.—Suburbs, either residential or industrial, are characteristic of most of the larger American cities.[6] The rise of the automobile
and the improvement of certain suburban commuter rail lines in a few of
the largest cities have stimulated suburbanization. Satellites differ from suburbs in that they are separated from the central city by many miles and in
general have little daily commuting to or from the central city, although
economic activities of the satellite are closely geared to those of the central
city. Thus Gary may be considered a suburb but Elgin and Joliet are satellites of Chicago.

---

6. Chauncy D. Harris, "Suburbs," *American Journal of Sociology*, Vol. 49, No. 1
(July 1943), p. 6.

Appraisal of land-use patterns. Most cities exhibit not only a combination of the three types of urban support, but also aspects of the three generalizations of the land-use pattern. An understanding of both is useful in appraising the future prospects of the whole city and the arrangement of its parts.

As a general picture subject to modification because of topography, transportation, and previous land use, the concentric-zone aspect has merit. It is not a rigid pattern, inasmuch as growth or arrangement often reflects expansion within sectors or development around separate nuclei.

The sector aspect has been applied particularly to the outward movement of residential districts. Both the concentric-zone theory and the sector theory emphasize the general tendency of central residential areas to decline in value as new construction takes place on the outer edges; the sector theory is, however, more discriminating in its analysis of that movement.

Both the concentric zone, as a general pattern, and the sector aspect, as applied primarily to residential patterns, assume (although not explicitly) that there is but a single urban core around which land use is arranged symmetrically in either concentric or radial patterns. In broad theoretical terms such an assumption may be valid, inasmuch as the handicap of distance alone would favor as much concentration as possible in a small central core. Because of the actual physical impossibility of such concentration and the existence of separating factors, however, separate nuclei arise. The specific separating factors are not only high rent in the core, which can be afforded by few activities, but also the natural attachment of certain activities to extra-urban transport, space, or other facilities, and the advantages of the separation of unlike activities and the concentration of like functions.

The constantly changing pattern of land use poses many problems. Near the core, land is kept vacant or retained in antisocial slum structures in anticipation of expansion of higher-rent activities. The hidden costs of slums to the city in poor environment for future citizens and excessive police, fire, and sanitary protection underlie the argument for a subsidy to remove the blight. The transition zone is not everywhere a zone of deterioration with slums, however, as witness the rise of high-class apartment development near the urban core in the Gold Coast of Chicago or Park Avenue in New York City. On the fringe of the city, overambitious subdividing results in unused land to be crossed by urban services such as sewers and transportation. Separate political status of many suburbs results in a lack of civic responsibility for the problems and expenses of the city in which the suburbanites work.

THE FUNCTION OF THE
CENTRAL BUSINESS DISTRICT IN THE
METROPOLITAN COMMUNITY

Earl S. Johnson

The growth of the metropolitan region has raised many new problems in the field of social control. Many of these follow from the nature of the new pattern of land use and population distribution which has developed on the periphery of the central city. Although, on its political side the region is characterized by independence from the central city, social and economic bonds render them highly interdependent. One of the most significant criteria of this unity is that which is furnished by the fact that, in at least its major economic activities, it is organized around a single market. The central business district of the central city is the market place of the metropolitan community.

The method of analysis used here to study the nature of this unity is, primarily, that employed by the human ecologist. In this approach people and institutions are viewed from an external standpoint and largely in their distributive and competitive aspects. The human ecologist is not, however, interested in the graphic and distributive treatment of social data for its own sake. He realizes that in actuality social phenomena are not merely physical things but have their bases in living beings. For purposes of scientific conceptualization, however, he consciously singles out the physical and the external aspects of these essentially social data as the objects of his attention and treats them, as far as possible, as if they operated in isolation.

The central business district of the metropolis is the area in which are located those highly specialized persons and institutions which exert a directing, co-ordinating, and facilitating influence on the market activities of the entire metropolitan region. Its position marks the ecological, though not necessarily the geographical, center of this region. By metropolitan community is meant a spatial and symbiotic pattern, the parts of which are tributary to a city which has reached the stage in which its predominant economic functions have become those of executive management, administration, and financial control. Considered as a spatial and symbiotic pattern, its population is an aggregate of individuals distributed in a determinate order over an area with more or less definite boundaries. If, from the ecological point of view, these units are considered as men rather than

Reprinted from *Third Year Course in the Study of Contemporary Society,* Tenth Edition, 1942, by permission of the author and the publisher. (Copyright, 1942, by the University of Chicago Bookstore.)

as merely physical things, it is as *economic* men, who according to their characteristics, are not social creatures in the sense of admitting any moral claims on one another but whose relations to one another are purely secular and utilitarian—that is, symbiotic.

The fact that the geographical and ecological centers of a community do not necessarily coincide deserves some further elaboration. The geographical center is that point which is equidistant from every point on the periphery of a community. This could, of course, hold only if the periphery described a perfect circle. In any actual urban community, therefore, any point could be only the approximate geographical center, and even if it were this coincidence would be accidental rather than essential in its significance. But obviously even this coincidence could not exist in the case of a port city whose position, with reference to its hinterland, must be off-center. Topographical factors other than bodies of water would likewise render it impossible for the central business district to occupy this approximate position.

But this district does, invariably, occupy the *ecological* center of the metropolitan community. It does so because the ecological center is that position which, owing to the time-cost transportation relations (rather than linear distance relations) which it bears to all parts of the community, permits a complex of economic institutions and persons located there to discharge their functions with a maximum of efficiency. Stated in another way, it is that area in the central city of the metropolitan community where certain market institutions, which are by their very nature dependent upon an extensive market area, are able to maintain themselves despite exceedingly high land values and rents. The boundaries of the metropolitan region are determined by the number and degree of the relations which exist between the central city and its satellite communities. The greater the distance from the central city, the fewer are the functions, though not necessarily less important, for which the satellites depend on it. The ecological pattern of the region may then be conceived of ideally as having a single center, the market place, and varying but concentric peripheries.[1]

The metropolitan community may now be defined in terms of the functional interrelation between the central business district of the central city and the larger metropolitan area. It is *that total area composed of many discrete areas each of which delimits, spatially, a zone over which the central business district exercises a certain degree of dominance.*

It will be noted that this definition makes no mention of the civil divisions into which the community is partitioned. These are omitted here not because they are unimportant but because this analysis is deliberately limited to a consideration of only the economic and spatial aspects of community life. To go beyond this would necessitate treating not only the

1. The classic statement of this is in the conceptual scheme presented by von Thünen in *Der isolierte Staat*. There, interestingly enough, the ecological and the geographical centers are identical. But von Thünen's primary interest was not in geographical position but rather in position measured in terms of transportation costs from concentric zones to a center—or, in other words, in ecological position.

spatial pattern but, as Professor Robert E. Park has expressed it, the "moral order" as well, which would complicate the problem. The object here is to stress the aspects of economic interdependence rather than of political independence. Furthermore, the activities of the market have, historically, been somewhat contemptuous of political boundaries; for, although men have often aimed to achieve for their civil division complete economic independence, this end has more often appeared as a political slogan than as a historical actuality.

The position which the central business district takes within the pattern of the central city can likewise be described with more meaning in ecological than in geographic terms. Ecologically, its boundaries are fixed by the terminal properties of the transportation systems which converge upon it. For the inland city these will be rail and bus terminals; for the port city, both of these and water terminals.[2] These terminals represent breaks in transportation. It is such breaks which have, both historically and causally, been associated with the location of human settlement and the rise of the commercial city and the market. Frederick Ratzel, Adna F. Weber, and Charles H. Cooley have developed this point well. Sir Henry Maine has treated the origin and location of the market in a manner which leads to the same conclusion, for, as he has remarked, the market originated "where the domain of two or three villages converged."[3] This, in principle, holds true for the modern metropolitan market place as well. In the modern city, however, high-speed and long-distance communication facilities permit the convergence upon a central market place of the activities of communities, which communities are, unlike those to which Maine referred, noncontiguous. The location of the market place is, in the modern city, determined not so much by geographical *place* as by technological *process*.

But if transportation facilities fix the margins of the business district, communication facilities fix its center, which is the point of convergence of the telephone and telegraph systems which serve the metropolis. If modern transportation facilities rendered its position less dependent than formerly upon geographic factors, facilities for communication, through their almost complete annihilation of space, have all but completely emancipated it from them. Buyers and sellers may now meet in the market via the telephone, the telegraph, and the radio. This is not to deny that face-to-face relations are still necessary and important, for there appear to be many types of market transactions in which the personal presence of the contracting parties is still indispensable to the consummation of the transaction.

---

2. In the present stage of aviation, landing fields must be located on the periphery of the community; the development of the helicopter may permit the arrival and departure of planes from points within the central business district. The helicopter may also be used more extensively as a kind of "air taxi" between the peripheral landing fields and the business center of the city.

3. *Cf.* Ratzel, *The History of Mankind* (3 vols.); Weber, *The Growth of Cities in the Nineteenth Century;* and Cooley, "A Theory of Transportation," *Sociological Theory and Social Research;* also Maine, *Ancient Law.*

But this distinction between the carrying of persons and goods and the carrying of information in connection with the activities of the market suggest that the central business district has two centers: one defined by the focus of lines of communication, the other by the focus of lines of transportation. With the first center is associated the merchandising of credits; with the second is associated the merchandising of consumers goods and services at retail. Which of these is to be taken as the most significant center depends upon which of the two associated functions—namely, financial control or retail distribution—characterize the economy of the central city. In the sense in which Sombart treats the metropolis in the advanced stage of capitalistic society—namely, as the financial rather than as the industrial or commercial city—the communication center, upon which the financial institutions depend and converge spatially, would constitute *the* center.

Thus, whether it is considered in its local, regional, national, or international setting, the central business district is the focal point of an elaborate transportation and communication structure. Chicago, which is more or less representative of American cities, serves to illustrate this. Except for Lake Michigan on the east, it is, like the city in von Thünen's figure, surrounded by a flat plain. The twenty-odd railroads which converge upon it have pushed their passenger (and less-than-carlot freight) terminals as close as was physically and economically possible into the center of the city. Thus, their inner terminal properties actually define the margins of central business district on three, if not on all four sides. From these passenger terminals more than two hundred thousand persons daily enter the central district; these include suburban commuters, who, from these points of entry, are within walking distance of their places of work. Over these roads, likewise, almost one-half of the population of the United States could, if it cared to, reach Chicago in a journey of overnight or less duration. With respect to the somewhat more strictly local transportation pattern it may be observed, first, that although the street pattern of the city is gridiron in general design, on it are superimposed thirteen diagonal streets, all of which are oriented toward the business center. In addition, this district is the point of convergence of thirty-six surface-car routes, which, through the transfer privilege and by the payment of extra fares, make the district almost hourly accessible to millions of people. The central core of the larger central business district, the "Loop," took its name from the fact that here was established the transfer point for the elevated rapid transit lines which route every train into this area and form an iron ring around it. The bus system of the city is likewise oriented toward this central area, and here also are the terminals of the national passenger-bus lines.

The Chicago central business district is also the area of greatest daily traffic. For a twelve-hour period on a typical business day in 1926, pedestrians excepted, about one and three-fourths million people entered the district, of whom more than 80 per cent came by common carrier. In 1931, during a twenty-four-hour period on a summer week day, over one-half million vehicle trips (by passenger autos and trucks) were exchanged between the central business district and the city and the surrounding metropolitan area. Of these, seventy-two out of every hundred had either an origin or a destination within the district. It is such a network of transportation as this which permits a land area, comprising less than 1 per cent of the total area of the city, to serve as the market place for a regional population of almost five million people.

But the central business district in Chicago, as in every metropolis, is the center of an even more sensitive network, namely, the web of communication lines. From this area originates only slightly less than one-half of the total telegraph traffic of the city. Beneath the pit of its Board of Trade are 2,700 miles of telephone and telegraph wires, while from it wires run directly to scores of offices throughout the building and the city and to 540 cities scattered from coast to coast—in all, over 150,000 miles of wire. In addition to land telegraphic connections, 75,000 miles of nautical cable tie this district to every important market on the face of the earth. To a message sent from this district a cable reply from Europe is only five minutes away.

An analysis of the telephone calls originating in an area almost coterminous with the central business district serves as another significant index to the control functions which the institutions located here perform. This telephone district contains less than six out of every hundred of the total telephone accounts of the city, but from these are made one-fourth of the total number of local calls—slightly less than one-third of the total regional calls and one-seventh of the total long-distance business transacted by the telephone company in Chicago. The ratios which the small number of phones bear to the great volume of the various types of calls originating from them express the degree to which the functions centered in this district depend for their existence upon this form of communication.

The total machinery of transportation and communication devices therefore fixes the central business district at the ecological center of the entire metropolitan community. Furthermore, they bound the district and locate its centers. Associated with the boundaries and with each center are certain market organizations and institutions. Some of the most representative of these deserve mention.

With the transport of goods from these inner terminals, rather than from those farther out which serve the heavier industrial plants, are associated light manufacturing, warehousing, and wholesale distribution. Shipments from these manufacturing concerns are, for the most part, in less-than-carlot quantities. These inner terminals deal generally in this form of freight consignment, hence they and the factories which occupy the zone immediately outside the central business district stand in a symbiotic relation. The warehouse, which is essentially a "bank of merchandise," is also located with reference to these transportation terminals. The railroad carries goods in *space;* the warehouse carries them in *time.* The wholesale establishment is the regional rather than the local store since its customers are middlemen in strategic locations in the region from which they supply the retail demand of the "ultimate consumer." Actually it serves both the regional and the local middlemen as its spatial position near both the freight terminals and the department-store area suggests.

But the metropolitan market is, ideally, the money market rather than the goods and services market. Here are concentrated the bankers' banks, the great insurance companies, the branch of the Federal Reserve System, the investment houses, and the great stock and commodity exchanges. It is at this point that the spatial identity of the central business district with the communication center takes on significance. If it is the center of communication it is, by the same token, also the news center, in both the journalistic and the market sense of what news is. The relation between news and speculation has, historically, been not only close but causal. The rise of the great insurance firm of Lloyd's of London cannot be understood aside from the relation which risk-bearing bears to the availability of reliable news. As Karl Bücher has suggested, it was not accidental that the booth of the independent news bureau on the Venetian Rialto was located between the booths of the changers and the goldsmiths. Furthermore, the fact that the Fuggers were perhaps the greatest bankers and likewise the leading news-gatherers of their day is no less significant in this connection.[4] The central business district as the locus of the market is then the place where both news and credit are created and concentrated and from which both are distributed. Furthermore, it is the area whose risk-taking enterprises depend for their very existence upon the news.

The extreme centralization of men, institutions, and services which rapid communication and transportation have made possible is also expressed in modern industrial organization and control. This is not unrelated to the function of furnishing credit. In the territorial division of labor which has developed in the modern metropolitan community the industrial activities have tended to become reallocated to the satellites, while the financial and executive controls have tended to remain in the central city. Policy-making and executive functions have become concentrated at the focal point of lines of communication. The functional breach between the businessman and the machine, developed so ably by Veblen, here receives its spatial expression, which may in this case, as in others, turn out to be significant for understanding the social processes which underlie and explain it.[5]

This centralization of control and decentralization of fabrication have implications for the distinction between labor and capital and between in-

---

4. For a comprehensive account of the evolution of Lloyd's see Wright and Fayle, *A History of Lloyd's;* also Bücher, *Industrial Evolution,* and Jacob Strieder, *Jacob Fugger the Rich.*

5. See *The Theory of Business Enterprise.*

dustrial and civil politics. Theoretically, in a democratic society policy-making and its execution are divided between the electorate and the executive; in modern industrial organization, in contrast, in the absence of any adequate equivalent to the electorate, both the making and the execution of policy have tended to become the vested rights of the executives, or, as they have come to be properly designated, the "captains of industry." Irrespective of what is held to be true in theory, the organization of the industrial community is, in fact, based on something other than the democratic principle. If, then, the metropolitan community may be considered as an economic or industrial rather than as a civil-political order, the central business district is its capital and its governors the finance capitalists.

The creating and supplying of credit, the primary functions of the metropolitan market, constitute not one but a whole bundle of functions as the foregoing description properly implies. But it, in turn, depends on another bundle of functions. These, among which may be cited accounting, auditing, bookkeeping, insurance, legal counsel, promotion, advertising, and management, have frequently been referred to as the ancillary or secondary functions of the market. Each, whether it be primary or secondary, represents a high degree of specialization, the corollary of which is the need for close integration. The nature of the interrelations dictates, furthermore, that this integration be close both in time and in space. The telephone and the telegraph have effected their temporal integration, but it is chiefly through a special form of housing, and the provision within it of rapid vertical transportation, that their spatial integration has been made possible. The skyscraper, which piles floor upon floor and office cubicle upon office cubicle and connects them by high-speed elevators, has done this. Thus does the division of labor in the metropolitan market place help to explain what is probably the most uniquely urban and at the same time the most uniquely American-urban device—the multistoried office building.[6]

But the need for the spatial integration of many specialists in the central market district is, as has been indicated, but one of a number of the factors with which the appearance of skyscraper is associated. The rise of the great industrial and financial corporations, the separation of executive management and control from the fabrication of the products, the increase in the division of labor in the market place, the complex organization of the marketing machinery, keen competition for the use of the limited land supply at the city's center, the undirected growth and unplanned nature of American cities, the invention of the steel skeleton construction, and the perfection of the electrically operated passenger elevator—all these have converged to make the skyscraper both possible and necessary.

But while the most significant center of the central business district in a metropolitan city is that which fixes the location of the financial and

---

6. The question of the indispensability of the multi-storied structure to the efficiency of the market activities is a real one when it is noted that London, the world's greatest money market, is without a single such building.

office district, the complex of retail establishments constitutes the second most significant center. This is the point on which all local and regional passenger transportation systems, except in some cases of the steam-railroad lines, immediately converge. It is a secondary center not in the sense of its occupying cheaper sites but because in the metropolis retail distribution is secondary in importance to the furnishing of credit. Here, then, is the retail market organized on a grand scale which differs from the provincial market in the extreme specialization of its marketing organization and in its anonymity, which is expressed in the substitution of the "standard price" for the price reached through "higgling." [7]

Some measure of the degree of specialization in the central retail market in Chicago is furnished by the United States Census of Retail Distribution made in 1929. In the downtown shopping district were but 7 per cent of the total number of stores in the city, but these enjoyed a sales volume in excess of one-fourth of the total retail sales made in the entire city. For the department stores the ratio of establishments in this district to the total number in the city was 11.5 per cent, but these did only slightly less than one-half of the total business done in all the department stores in the city. For apparel stores the contrast was even more striking. Only 1.3 per cent of all such stores were located here, but these enjoyed 45 per cent of the total volume of business done in all the city's apparel establishments. [8]

Additional evidence of the specialized character of this retailing-transportation complex is furnished by the medical services in this district. Although these are provided by a professionally trained personnel, they are nevertheless part of the total retailing activity. The Chicago Loop showed an increase of but 17.6 per cent in its total medical personnel in the fifteen-year period between 1914 and 1939. This is not a large increase when compared with other indices of change in this area, such as in daily traffic, retail sales volume, or added office space. This relatively slight increase indicates, as regards *total* medical personnel, that this area was approaching a saturation point. The *selective* or specialized character of the change in medical personnel is, however, highly significant. In the same period the area lost 33.8 per cent of its general practitioners and gained 68.5 per cent in part-time specialists. But for physicians who devoted their full time to the practice of a single specialty, the gain was 118.4 per cent. In other words, the Loop had become less a local and more a regional medical market place, for such an increase in *specialized* medical services could be explained only by reason of the extension of the size of the area from which patients would come with their demand for medical services. [9] The spatial

7. In Chicago the "provincial market," where the price is in part set by "higgling" or bidding, may be found on Maxwell Street just east of Halsted Street.

8. For more recent data see *Geographic Distribution of Retail Trade in Chicago, Illinois* (Bureau of the Census, June, 1939).

9. Increased specialization is equivalent to an increase in the division of labor. Since the time of Adam Smith it has been axiomatic that "the extent of [the division of labor] must always be limited by . . . the extent of the market" (*The Wealth of Nations*).

and temporal integration of these highly specialized medical experts is similar to that in the office section of the market place, effected through the skyscraper. In several instances medical practitioners are housed in buildings designed especially for their occupancy.

The central business district in every metropolitan city has, since its original settlement, been undergoing a process of slow and constant change —a process involving a selection of functions. The basis of this process was indicated earlier, namely, that those enterprises remain whose books, so to speak, still show a profit after the high charges for site rent are subtracted from the gains which accrue by virtue of their location at this strategic communication and transportation center. This is true in large part for the institutions which represent the more cultural or noneconomic aspects of metropolitan life as well as for those which are distinctly economic or profit-seeking in character.

The selective and specialized character of some of these noneconomic institutions may be briefly indicated. The downtown church represents a special form of religious institution. If it was established here when the city was young, the descendants of its original members have perhaps all fled to the residential areas of the central city or to the suburbs. But through its strategic position at the center of transportation and by virtue of its having frequently become self-supporting through its function as landlord, it can still survive without either the financial support or the spiritual co-operation of the descendants of its original members and founders. In the respect that, not infrequently, its drawing-power is due to the dramatic character of its ministerial personnel, a famous pulpit orator or a sort of weekly "headliner type" of speaker, it can continue to carry on even in competition with its more secular neighbors, the legitimate theater and the movie palace, some of whose essential techniques it tends to employ. The Chicago Temple, the Central Church, and the Sunday Evening Club tend to approximate the characteristic forms of the downtown church.

The central business district is, furthermore, the natural habitat of the esoteric cult which, owing to its strange and unconventional beliefs, must recruit its devotees from an area wider than that of any local community. Here too are the theaters, the legitimate, and the gala and gigantic movie and vaudeville houses. Neither could be supported by anything less than a large regional population. Both provide, one might say, a luxury type of retail service in the field of leisure-time pursuits and are therefore to be found not far away from the great retail distributing center and focus of transportation lines. This location is necessary because they must be accessible to not only a large but in many cases a discriminating clientèle.

The great hotels of the district provide a specialized form of housing not primarily for a local but for a regional and national clientèle made up of wholesale buyers and sellers, out-of-town shoppers, tourists, and many others. These institutions also serve an important function as headquarters for the conventions of regional, national, and international business as well as professional and scientific organizations. The modern metropolitan hotel is now an auditorium as well as a dormitory and dining establishment. In this district also are to be found that complement of cultural institutions which can be supported only by the population of a great metropolitan community. These are the opera, the symphony, the public forum, the scientific library, the museum, and the art gallery.

This inventory of central business institutions and functions is of course not complete. Attention must, however, be given to a complex of institutions of which no mention has yet been made—the governmental institutions of the central city. They alone of all the institutions in the district are purely local in the scope of their activity and influence. They symbolize one of the major problems of the metropolitan region, namely, that it constitutes not a *de jure* but a *de facto* community. For this reason it fails frequently to achieve a more complete unity since it lacks a political and administrative machinery of its own. This is not to argue that political controls are necessarily first in importance. It is however, to argue that the socioeconomic order which has evolved in the metropiltan community has proved that it is no longer self-regulatory. There is at present much talk about the relation of the national state to the activities of its traders in the national and international market. Although on a somewhat more complicated level, this relationship represents exactly the problem that exists in the metropolitan community as well. The automobile, rapid transit, the organization of modern industry, and many other technological and social changes have rendered the older set of political implements not only obsolete but also grossly inefficient. Its present socioeconomic organization suggests, furthermore, the anachronism of the old phrase, "the rural-urban antithesis." What exists in its place is well indicated by the more comprehensive concept—the metropolitan community. This provides us with a picture of a co-operating and mutually interdependent set of social and economic processes which, in large part, gives the lie to the old country-city dichotomy and, as suggested above, within which framework the older figure of speech can hardly be imagined.

The central business district has been treated thus far mainly from the ecological point of view. But it is the locus of not only a spatial but also a social order as well, and hence it cannot be thoroughly understood until the dual nature of its organization has been pointed out. To this a brief consideration will be given.

In Chicago, for example, the central business district happens to be an area identical with one of the seventy-five local communities into which the city has been tentatively divided for purposes of social investigation. But the designation of the area as a local community rests only on whatever analysis has been given it as a place of residence, that is, as the home of man rather than his place of work. The study of the local community has, traditionally, included the collection and analysis of such data as the total population, its age and sex composition, nativity, size of family, and similar data. The enumeration of this area in the 1934 municipal census showed that it contained but 3,530 legal residents. Of these, 80 per cent were males; 61 per cent were single; and, most striking of all, among the total population there were but 33 persons under the age of five years. But, in addition to these so-called legal residents, the area contained another population—the one-half million or more daily workers with whom, as such, the census had no concern. It is then only in terms of its 3,530 residents that the area has been designated as a local community. There is, however, little evidence that this population constitutes, in the vicinal and parochial or strictly moral sense of the term, a community. Its hotel and club population is characteristically united, if at all, on the basis of narrow and separate professional or business interests. It possesses little of what Durkheim has called "the patriotism of the parish." Its lodging-house population, which constitutes the bulk of its total number, is largely individualistic, inarticulate, and highly mobile in character. Within it there is little consensus. Likewise, between these two population groups, socially and economically disparate as they are, hotel and club dwellers, on the one hand, and flophouse denizens, on the other, there exists no significant community of interests.

But there is, in this district, another spatial and moral order, namely, the so-called business community. As to its age and sex composition, nativity, marital status, or even its total number but a meager little is known. But this population is the more important for understanding the nature and function of the area as a business district, and this despite the fact that it is, on the average, less than an eight-hour-per-day population. In contrast with the twenty-four-hour population of the area there is within it a marked degree of consensus, some features of which have been indicated above. This is based not upon kinship or geographical propinquity but upon the common professional or business interests generated in the activities of the market place. This consensus is not "all of a piece," but its various segments go to make up a whole which has, undeniably, a common pattern both as to its origin and as to its orientation. This population aggregate is, for the want of a better term, a secular society, but one which, like all secular societies, has its sacred aspects, such as, for instance, the codes and creeds of its business and professional groups. Perhaps its most representative individual is the business executive whose place of business and place of residence are miles apart and frequently under different municipal jurisdictions. His place of residence, on the periphery of the central city or in one of its dormitory suburbs, constitutes his *milicu natal;* the central business district is his *milieu professionel.* In addition he exerts an influence, not infrequently, upon a third *milieu*—the industrial community which responds to his will through the production and wage policies of his corporation. Such a definition of his area of influence, however, takes no account of the national and international range of the industrial and financial policies emanating from this central district.

In an analysis such as has been here presented the institutions of the market place have been made an object of a social, economic, and political theory. This theory should in its turn make for a more comprehensive understanding of the organization of the metropolitan community and, in turn, permit the forging of a set of adequate political tools for its more effective social control.

THE REGIONAL RELATIONS OF THE CITY

Robert E. Dickinson

The city cannot be fully understood by reference only to its arbitrarily defined administrative area. It has to be interpreted as "an organic part of a social group,"[1] and in approaching the analysis of the four main urban functions—dwelling, work, recreation and transport—"it must be remembered that every city forms part of a geographic, economic, social, cultural and political unit, upon which its development depends."[2] The problem of the regional interpretation of the city, of defining and analyzing the functions and limits of the city and the unifying relationships in the surrounding area, is one of disentangling the regional component and examining the multitude of tributary areas served by and serving the city. Each group of functions has its particular extent and characteristics. Many functional areas have no close relation with each other in their geographical extent—which is often difficult to define—or in their causes or characters. But they all have a common denominator in their dependence on the city and, in consequence, in the scientific sense, we may refer to this area that is functionally dependent on the city as the city-region.

The regional interpretation of the functions of the city involves a twofold approach: first, an assessment of the effects of the character of the region—its resources, and economic production—on the character of the activities of the city; and, secondly, an examination of the effects of the city, as a seat of human activity and organization, on the character of the region. There is also involved the question of the limits of the city, and its spheres of influence or tributary areas in its multitude of regional functions. The question of defining the limits of the city as a regional centre, should be subordinated to the main aim of this approach which seeks to evaluate both the city and its region, however vaguely defined, in terms of their mutual relations and in the light of their historical development.

Settlement, route and area are the three facets of the geographical interpretation of urban economy. The commercial output of the area—farming of different types, forestry, industry, or combinations of these—calls into

Reprinted from *City, Region and Regionalism*, Chapter 6, pp. 165 ff., by permission of the author and the publisher. (Copyright, 1947, by the Oxford University Press.)

1. M. Aurousseau, "Recent Contributions to Urban Geography," *Geographical Review*, Vol. XIX, 1934, pp. 444-55.

2. J. L. Sert, *Can Our Cities Survive?*, Harvard U.P., 1943, p. 10.

being centres differing widely both in their interests, their commerce and in the industries arising from the processing of the primary products marketed in them. The quantity of output that passes through commercial channels is the sum total of economic, political, and cultural intercourse.[3] It is, in effect, a measure of the nodality of the urban centre. If all such intercourse is concentrated in one city, all the commerce for the area would pass through the city; and the sum total of this commerce would be the total of its exports and imports. This theoretical state of affairs is never reached because the degree of concentration of circulation in one city in any area depends on the suitability of the area for commerce relative to the location of the city and of its neighbouring cities, to the conditions of historical development, and to the physical build of the land, which may rigidly affect the orientation of routes. Nevertheless, the potency and extent of the sphere of influence of a city are to be measured in theory from the degree of concentration of the circulations of the area around it in the form of freight, passenger and general intercourse.

The city produces goods, and processes and stores imported goods not only for a nation-wide market, but also for the market in its surroundings —whatever it can sell in competition with its neighbours. The city, in addition to its own natural increase (by excess of births over deaths), draws the folk from its surrounding area to enjoy its special amenities—its shops, institutions, markets, art galleries, and theatres. With the great growth of cities in the early nineteenth century, the rural population has been drawn into the towns, with the resultant phenomenon of rural depopulation. The city is a melting-pot and fount of opinion. It disseminates its views on matters relevant to the life and affairs of its citizens and the people of the surrounding towns through the medium of the press. It is a home of learning, culture and political life. The city must be fed, with food for its people and materials for its industry. Before the development of cheap and rapid transport, every city was almost entirely dependent upon its surrounding area for both. Distant supplies of food or materials or immigrants were brought by the only cheap means of transport—water, and it is no accident that in the past, before the railway era, the chief cities in Europe and America were either ports or riverside cities at the heads of river navigation. In the modern era, however, although the movement of foodstuffs and raw materials is world-wide, there is, in fact, a still closer relation between town and country. For all perishable goods must be delivered quickly and daily to the city consumers. Moreover, the economic factor of accessibility to the best market dragoons farm areas to supply large urban markets, so that an even closer tie-up between the great city and its environs results. Again, with the ever-increasing complexity in the social and economic structure of society, in service and organization, the city has acquired a great increase

3. H. Bobek, "Grundfragen der Stadtgeographie," *Geographische Anzeiger*, Vol. XXVIII, 1927, pp. 213-224. This is called *Verkehrspannung* by Bobek.

of functions as a regional centre for the distribution of both consumer goods and producer goods, and as a centre of services—social, economic and administrative. The city makes its impact on the surrounding towns and countryside, especially since the advent of the automobile, by the expansion of urban built-up land—for residence, industry and recreation. It also affects the character and structure of their social and economic life.

The question of the limit of the city when considered as a centre of regional services of collection and distribution may be approached by referring to a theoretical distribution of towns based on the assumption that functions are centred in towns that may be graded according to the importance of these functions. Consequently, a city of the fifth grade in Christaller's scheme, for instance, will combine all the functions of its own and of the four lower grades, and each set of functions in each grade will have its corresponding limits as a series of concentric circles passing through the towns of the next lower grade. This scheme is most nearly approached in extensive and dominantly rural areas with an even distribution of towns and occasional, evenly spaced, large, dominant cities as in eastern England, France, or, indeed, in south Germany. But the following conditions must be added to this distributional pattern—quite apart from irregularities of distribution brought about by topographical and historical conditions, though these, in an evenly settled area, cause relatively small deviations.

First, the modern growth of population has been mainly in urban centres, proportional to the size of the centre. This has meant the snowball growth of existing towns, and in no way interferes with the basic pattern of distribution of service centres.

Secondly, new seats of industrial production, clustered at seats of production of raw materials (or at places of assembly), have given rise to new population clusters, which give rise in turn to central service centres.

Thirdly, the spread of population from the big city results in the spread of the urban area radially and frontally: merging with, often absorbing, pre-existing centres in its closer environs. These outlying centres, though absorbed in the urban mass, usually retain their functions as commercial sub-centres.

Fourthly, the extension of the big city results in the appearance of new settlements, budding off from it, sometimes being independent centres, both legally (if beyond the city boundary) and economically, without any relation to the laws governing the origin and growth of centralized services.

We have already discussed the general structure of the city and its fringes. These, and the outer and more widespread areas influenced by the city, are arranged into three main zones that can be described as the *urban tract*, the *city settlement area* and the *city trade area*.

The *Urban Tract* is used to define the compact and continuous urban built-up area in preference to the term "conurbation." The latter term defines the urban agglomeration that extends beyond administrative boundaries, and was in fact first defined by Geddes as a group of two or more contiguous administrative units that were urbanized. The term has been further elaborated by Fawcett, who describes it as "an area occupied by a continuous series of dwellings, factories, and other buildings, harbour and docks, urban parks and playing fields, etc., which are not separated from each other by rural land; though in many cases in this country such an urban area includes enclaves of rural land which is still in agricultural occupation."[4] This assumes that the conurbation ends with the limit of the compact built-up area, but there is invariably a fringe of rural-urban uses, a fringe that is wide and irregular in this country and still more complicated in other countries. This definition has given rise to much confusion of thought, because with it is associated the idea of several administrative units. An urban agglomeration, no matter what its extent or population, would not be counted, on this definition, as a conurbation if it were one administrative unit.[5] In such cases the administrative boundaries have extended with the growth of the urban area, or the urban area itself has grown by the coalescence of separate units—whether independent towns, villages, or satellites thrown off by a central city and later absorbed in its extension. Moreover, the peripheral rural-urban fringe is so diffuse that there arises the problem of deciding whether to include places that are cut off from the main area but sufficiently near to it to be a part of its economic and social organization. In other words, on the margins the emphasis must change from compactness to function and accessibility.

The limits of an urban tract are to be defined in the first place by mapping the land uses and enclosing those areas that are closely built-up, as suggested by Fawcett. It is of interest to note the minimum density of population for such marginal areas—though it is not suggested that the tract is to be limited on this basis. The Ordnance Survey takes 6,400 per square mile as the limit of "urban"; Jefferson[6] suggested a theoretical limit, many years ago, of 10,000 per square mile for American cities. A recent study of Paris takes 250 persons per square mile as the extreme limit of urban influence against rural areas and 1,250 persons per square mile as the limit of the compact urban tract. A comparative study of German cities shows that in the suburbs (*Vororte*) of the cities fully urban areas have a minimum overall density of 2,500 persons per square mile and that 250 persons per square mile is the outer limit against the rural areas.[7]

The *City Settlement Area* embraces the urban tract and the outer zone or rural-urban fringe. This fringe of settlement and city influence extends as far as communications will allow. A journey-time of one hour is usually

4. C. B. Fawcett, "Distribution of the Urban Population in Britain in 1931," *Geographical Journal*, Vol. LXXIX, 1932, pp. 100-116.

5. This actually is the interpretation given by J. Soulas in his recent study of the French conurbations in the *Annales de Géographie*, Vol. XLVIII, 1939, pp. 466-471.

6. M. Jefferson, "The Anthropogeography of Some Great Cities," *Bulletin of the American Geographical Society*, Vol. XLI, 1909, p. 543.

7. R. Clozier, *La Gare du Nord*, Baillière, Paris, 1940, and M. Reichert, *Die Vororts-bildung der süd- und mitteldeutschen Grossstädte*, Stuttgarter Geog. Studien, Stuttgart, 1936.

considered to be the main limit of daily travel for the city worker, and dormitory settlements lie on the main railway routes outside the greatest cities within a radius of about twenty miles. The map showing isochrones, or lines joining places accessible in the same time to and from a selected centre, is a fundamental basis for planning. This outer area, however, is not merely one of residential and industrial settlement. It supplies the city with milk and vegetables and receives many goods from its wholesale warehouses and its retail shops. It is sufficiently accessible to permit regular visits to the city. It forms a part of the labour market of the city complex and has intimate social and economic associations with the activities of the city. The area has been appropriately called by Chabot the *zone du voisinage*.[8] Its characteristics are summed up by its relatively high densities of population, intermediate between the urban tract and the country, and, more significantly, by its high rate of increase of population.[9]

The City Circulation or Trade Area is the area of wider and more extensive, more occasional circulations to and from the city, these relations being normally more intense and varied as the centre is approached through the fringe and the tract to the core. The great bulk of local circulations, such as are found in the urban tract, are directed to the local towns. The city is the head of affairs, the seat of opportunity, offering in all fields what the local town has not got. Clearly the relations with the big city are occasional and diffuse, and normally (except for through routes) do not appear on the road traffic map until the threads collect on the main roads near to the urban fringe. The city settlement area is, of course, served by a net of routes—rail, bus and tram. The outer limit of this circulation area is vague, and indefinable as a line except very diagrammatically. The ultimate limit of any particular circulation is fixed principally by the accessibility of the city relative to surrounding cities of similar status offering the same service. In fact, the limits will coincide in the peripheral towns, where such goods and services are received for distribution to their local service areas. It is normal for towns of medium size with considerable functional independence to be placed on the border of the sphere of influence of two cities, with close relations with both.

AN AMERICAN EXAMPLE: SALT LAKE CITY.[10] Salt Lake City is "the capital of the State (Utah), the seat of a religious denomination, the Mormons, that has played a dominant role in the regional development of this country and serves as an important basis of regional integration, a nucleus of com-

8. G. Chabot, "La Détermination des Courbes Isochrones en Géographie Urbaine," illustrated by reference to Dijon in *Comptes Rendus Congrès Internationale de Géographie*, Tome II, *Géographie Humaine*, Amsterdam, 1938, pp. 110-113.

9. A particularly interesting study of the *banlieue* of northern Paris will be found in R. Clozier, *La Gare du Nord*, Paris, 1940.

10. *Salt Lake City, A Regional Capital*, by Chauncy Dennison Harris, published by the University of Chicago Press, 1940, Private Edition. We summarize the findings of this work since it illustrates excellently the viewpoint and technique of our approach and the study in itself has a very limited circulation and will therefore not be generally accessible. Maps are reproduced with the kind permission of the author.

mercial and financial enterprises, a focus of transportation, a leading centre in educational activities, and the largest city in a vast section of the United States." In many ways this city of only 150,000 inhabitants both serves and dominates an extensive tributary area that may be called its region.[11] This region is physically diverse, but owes its functional unity to the binding influence of Salt Lake City. It has an area of 185,000 square miles and a population of 790,000 inhabitants (cf. England, 51,000 square miles and 38,000,000 inhabitants). It includes Utah, southern Idaho, eastern Nevada and south-western Wyoming.

Salt Lake City has a well-balanced occupational structure. Its 54,000 gainfully employed persons are occupied as follows (figures for 1930): manufacturing and mechanical industries 25 per cent., trade (wholesale, retail and other) 20 per cent., clerical occupations 15 per cent., transport and communications 11 per cent., domestic and personal service 12 per cent., professional services 11 per cent., public service 3.4 per cent. Harris estimated that a fifth of the total gainfully employed were employed in occupations over and above the needs of the Salt Lake City and its immediate environs—that is, that a fifth of the employed were concerned directly with meeting *regional* as opposed to *local* needs. These "represent merely the elemental occupational base upon which are pyramided many other occupations serving chiefly the inhabitants of the city itself." On this basis Salt Lake City has 62 per cent. of the clerical occupations; 71 per cent. of the wholesale trade; 46 per cent. of the retail trade (which is more evenly distributed with the population in accordance with local needs); 56 per cent. of other trades (bankers, brokers and moneylenders, 61 per cent.; insurance agents, managers and officials, 60 per cent.; commercial travellers, 65 per cent.); 59 per cent. of public service (mainly military service, since the city is a garrison centre); 42 per cent. of professional service [12]; 37 per cent. of transport and communication. Wholesaling is a main regional function, the 407 establishments selling $100,000,000 worth of goods and employing over 4,000 persons in 1935. Two-thirds of the wholesaling of both producers' and consumers' goods of Utah are concentrated in the capital. Manufacturing is not a dominant activity in the occupational structure of Salt Lake City. It produces about a quarter of the value of manufactured products in the State of Utah. But manufactures are none the less important, and figure large in the life and structure of the city.

The Region serving Salt Lake City has a populous core, and scattered oasis and mining settlements in the midst of grazing and desert lands. The boundary of the Region is therefore a wide no-man's land in which there is really no effective competition with other regional capitals. Boundaries are, therefore, more clearly defined in the populous sectors along the main lines

11. The Census metropolitan district had 184,000 and the city 140,000 in 1930.
12. Publishing 66 per cent., baking 60 per cent., clothing 58 per cent., petroleum refining 100 per cent., managers and officials 55 per cent., building (the second largest group) 38 per cent., all other (the largest group) 31 per cent.

of communication. The Region was determined by studying the areas served by a number of important regional functions (Fig. 1). Each of these service areas covers a distinct area that is limited by different factors. Twelve areas were defined and superposed. The service areas for retail trade, wholesale grocery trade, wholesale drug trade, radio broadcasting, and generalized trade were all taken from published sources, and all of them (except the fourth) are the result of careful statistical studies by com-

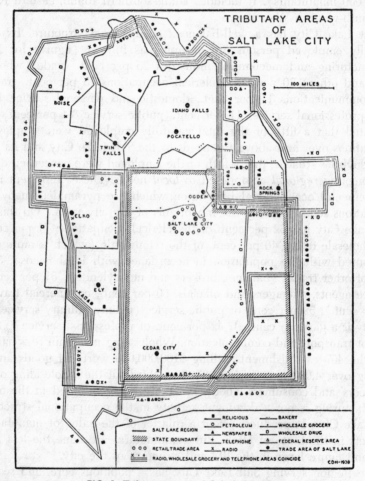

FIG. 1. Tributary areas of Salt Lake City.

petent authorities. Newspaper circulation and the extent of the Mormon religion are also based on statistical study. The former is recognized (if carefully mapped) as a good indicator of potency and extent of metropolitan influence. The latter is a feature peculiar to the State of Utah, which gives to Salt Lake City special claims to leadership over a wide area.[13]

13. Established as the capital of the Mormons in 1847, the settlement of much of

Mormons are still to-day in a majority throughout Utah and in sectors of southern Idaho (except the Twin Falls district), and throughout a wide surrounding area make up to 10 to 20 per cent. of the total population. Interviews provided the author with the extent of telephone, bakery and petroleum distribution areas. From these twelve areas the generalized boundary was drawn. The retail trade area (which is prepared for department stores, clothing, furniture, and jewellery stores rather than for grocery and drug stores) differs from the rest in having a very small service area. The retail trade area is small since it is concerned with a frequent service so that customers will not travel far for it. Local service centres serve, for the same reason, small local areas. The higher quality and higher priced goods have larger areas—both from the point of view of the consumer travelling to the centre or the goods delivered to him. Occasional deliveries (or visits) may cover a long distance, but the area considered is that of regular service. There are other areas of similar restricted extent, such as milk supply and professional service.

Beyond this smaller area comes the wholesale trade area, which again is fixed by the distance factor and its effect on transport costs. Groceries being relatively bulky will not stand the cost of long-distance deliveries from one centre, and smaller towns tend to have their own distributing depots—though the advent of cheap road transport has extended the sphere of delivery from Salt Lake City. Bakery products, being both bulky and perishable, have a range of distribution that is limited by time as well as by transport costs.

Beyond these areas again are the religious, newspaper and generalized trade areas. The religious area represents in part "the distance factor during the early day settlement of Salt Lake City." It is estimated from the area in which the Mormons form over 20 per cent. of the population, though a smaller proportion occurs over a much wider territory. The newspaper circulation limits tend to follow a "time divide" between competing metropolitan centres. These two areas are of the highest significance as cultural and economic agencies. The generalized trade area is the result of a careful synthesis by the United States Bureau of Foreign and Domestic Commerce and closely corresponds with the extent of the Region as finally defined. Five areas extend still farther to the north-west—radio broadcasting, financial, telephone, wholesale drugs, and petroleum service—since these are concerned with services in which the item of transport cost is small and the widest area of distribution is an economy in service.

The Wasatch Oasis, with its combination of agriculture, mining and transport facilities, is the chief support of, and is the section of the region most tied up with, the capital. The irrigation and settlement of this whole area were planned and financed by Salt Lake City and its Mormon com-

the surrounding lands was effected by the religious leadership of the Mormon community, which directed the exploration of irrigable lands, the lay-out of new villages and the settlement of European immigrants.

munity. The very size of the city as a consuming market encourages the specialization and commercialization of farming in the Oasis. The influence of the city in all its regional relations covers the whole of the Oasis, and the business and financial leadership of the city has been influential in the development of its transport facilities. The impact of the city on the types of commercialized farming on the irrigated land is reflected in the importance of dairying, for the Oasis produces half of the milk of the State, and 80 per cent. of the fluid milk consumed in the Oasis is produced in it. There is also a marked specialization on the production of fruit, vegetables and other perishable products.

Salt Lake City, together with Ogden, forms an important nucleus of railways, while the Oasis, in addition to being such a focus, has a closely knit net of electric inter-urban lines. In contradiction to this complicated pattern with its two foci in Ogden and Salt Lake City, the highways are centred on the latter, eight of them radiating in all directions. The business activities of the city and its region are reflected in the trade flows as canalized on rail and road—although it should be noted that such linear routes cannot be used as a means for defining the market area that they serve. Railways dominate this goods traffic. This falls into three categories, through traffic (from California to East or Middle West) making up 54.5 per cent. of the total carload traffic of the region; inter-regional traffic which either originates in or terminates in the Salt Lake City Region, 21 per cent.; and intra-regional traffic, which both originates and terminates in the Region, 24.5 per cent.

The role of Salt Lake City in these traffic movements may be viewed from the standpoint of either the service areas or the mapped streams of traffic flow in which the services are canalized. Ogden is a transfer point between major railway systems, a dispatch centre for certain raw materials such as live stock, and an industrial satellite of Salt Lake City (with railway workshops, meat-packing plants, and flour mills). Salt Lake City handles the trade in diversified wholesale goods, and while Ogden is a through route centre for rail traffic, Salt Lake City is by far the more important terminal for goods and passenger traffic. Inbound shipment of goods far exceeds outbound shipments at Salt Lake City in contrast to Ogden, for it imports valuable and diversified products for distribution (often including processing in the city) by rail and lorry throughout the region. The carloads of goods (in and out) handled by Salt Lake City (1932) amount to a sixth of the total for Utah, and some of these products are handled dominantly by the city for distribution in the region: petroleum at the refinery; miscellaneous products through the hands of distributors; ores and concentrates terminating at refineries in neighbouring satellite towns; imported products such as automobiles, furniture, and machinery (77 per cent. of the trade of Utah); and paper and paper products (83 per cent. of the trade of Utah).

The city plays a much smaller part in exports from the Region, for products from seats of specialized production proceed direct to their re-

gional or national markets. Goods sent to Salt Lake City are mainly consumed in the city itself—milk, building materials, manufactured goods
(sugar and canned goods), coal and coke. It follows that the commodity
movements in which the city exercises its chief regional role are not the
largest in bulk—rather the reverse, for three bulky commodities make up
two-thirds of the freight handled in Salt Lake City: coal, ores and petroleum. The city, like a great national inland port, handles a complex variety
of goods for distribution to its hinterland. Many manufacturing establishments have arisen at railsides to treat these incoming products before their
distribution. The exports of the region, however, proceed from many small
raw material ports, which may be compared to the cotton ports of the
southern states. The total tonnage figures of the Salt Lake City yards, like
those of the great ports, are dominated by a few bulky commodities. It owes
this function not to its location at a physical break of bulk point in the transport system, but to a break in this transport system devised and developed
by man to serve a particular region around it.

COMPARATIVE AMERICAN STUDIES: THE REGIONAL INFLUENCE OF THE
CITY ON RURAL ECONOMY. The city exerts powerful influences on the social
and economic structure of the territory around it. These influences are expressed in the types of rural land use and farm economy, in the nature of
urban land uses, and in the social and economic structure of the villages
and towns affected.

As soon as a city arises it exerts an influence on the uses of the land
around it according to a principle that was clearly expounded by Johann
Heinrich von Thünen in his *Isolierte Staat*—the Isolated State—first published in 1826.[14] The principle was worked out in respect of rural land use
by imagining one large city in the centre of the State in a plain with uniform soil and climate. Types of land use would then be conditioned entirely by the economic factor of distance from the city (by road) as the
market centre. The State, served by the one city, is assumed to be surrounded by a wilderness completely cutting it off from the rest of the world.
The type of crops grown will be determined by the price of the crop in the
city market, a crop, for instance, being grown no farther from the city when
the cost of transport plus cost of production reach the selling price in the
city. Six concentric zones surround von Thünen's city, namely, a small zone
just outside the city producing perishable commodities that cannot stand
long-distance transport, e.g. milk and vegetables; a narrow zone of forest,
wood being used in this pre-industrial era for fuel and building, placed
near to the city owing to its bulk and high cost of transport; third, a zone
of rotation grain cultivation; fourth, a zone of less intensive rotation cultivation with pasture and fallow; fifth, a wide area of widespread three-field
farming, the dominant system in western Europe until the end of the eight-

---

14. J. H. von Thünen, *Der Isolierte Staat in Beziehung auf Landwirtschaft und
Nationalökonomie*, 1826, reprinted, with introduction by Heinrich Waentig, Gustav
Fischer, Jena, 1910.

eenth century; and finally, a zone of cattle-raising and hunting. According to von Thünen's calculations, cereal cultivation would cease at 31.5 miles from the city. It is the competition of land uses through rent that explains these concentric belts of land use in the "Isolated State." The use which can pay the highest rent at a particular place occupies the land.[15] In countries of the present day where road transport is the means of carrying crops to a railhead (rather than to a city), the limit of movement before the advent of the motor lorry was 15 to 25 miles, though the bulk came from a five-mile radius. In Rhodesia the limit is 15 miles. "Roughly the zones are 'farm land' within 25 miles of the railway, 'ranch land' 25 to 50 miles, and land beyond 50 miles is of little practical value to the settler." [16]

This effect of the modern city on the rural land uses and the crops grown in its environs is related to two basic trends: first, the orientation of commercialized farm output towards the city market; secondly, the effect of the spread of the urban area on the values of open land around it. For such land is likely to be used sooner or later for urban uses and will therefore rise in value in anticipation, with the result that farming will be intensive in order to get the maximum returns. Alternatively, if there is immediate likelihood of its being sold for building, it will lie derelict in the hands of the speculative builder, awaiting a purchaser. The location of commercialized horticulture near to cities is due to the high price of land as well as to the proximity of an immediate market. For the same reason the demand of the city market for fresh milk has a marked influence on the spread of dairy farming around cities irrespective of climate and soil. In the United States it has been shown that there is a tendency to the formation of concentric zones around the city market, the sequence being milk production, feeding grains, bread grains and ranching, each fading into the next by a zone of transition from one type of land use to another.[17] The influence of the city market upon the kind of land utilization is thus based on the factor of distance from the market.

The theoretical pattern of land use trends around the great European cities has been summarized by Olof Jonasson.[18]

---

15. R. T. Ely and G. S. Wehrwein, *Land Economics*, New York, 1940, p. 135.
16. *Ibid.*, p. 136, and I. Bowman, *The Pioneer Fringe*, American Geographical Society, 1931, pp. 216-219.
17. Ely and Wehrwein, *op. cit.*, pp. 133-138.
18. *Horticulture.*
    Zone 1. City, plus greenhouses and floriculture.
    Zone 2. Truck products, fruits, potatoes, and tobacco.
Intensive Agriculture with Intensive Dairying.
    Zone 3. Dairy products, beef cattle, sheep for mutton, veal, forage crops, oats, flax.
    Zone 4. General farming—grain, hay, livestock.
Extensive Agriculture.
    Zone 5. Bread cereals and flax for oil.
Extensive Pasture.
    Zone 6. Cattle (beef and range), horses (range), sheep (range), slat, smoked, refrigerated and canned meats, bones, tallow, and hides.

The same principle may be applied to the delivery of goods outwards from a centre. If instead of von Thünen's single city market there are several competitive market centres, then providing these centres serve as equivalent sources of supply and distribution, the price to the consumer becomes the cost price plus the transport charge. Around each centre lines (*isotims*) may be drawn to show the limits to which any commodity can be delivered for the same price and where the lines of neighbouring centres meet is a transition zone in which it is immaterial whence the product comes, or, *vice versa*, in which centres it is marketed. Given the same cost of production, the centre enjoying the more convenient, more efficient, or cheaper, form of transportation will penetrate the market area of the other. This principle is of special importance in respect of retail and wholesale distribution.[19]

THE REGIONAL INFLUENCE OF THE CITY ON SOCIAL AND ECONOMIC CONDITIONS. The impact of urban influences on the country and smaller towns has many and deep-seated effects on their social and economic structure, such influences normally being most intense near the city and decreasing outwards from it. An obvious method, at any rate in theory, for examining the nature of the relations between town and country is to examine various conditions statistically on the basis of small administrative units in the environs of the town. No such studies appear to have been undertaken in Europe, but an attempt has been made in the American researches of Brunner and Kolb in their *Rural Social Trends* Monograph.[20] Eighteen cities were selected with populations ranging from 20,000 to over a half a million. A statistical analysis of concentric zones round each city was made, taking as limits for the area the limits of the wholesale trade area for the city. The county in which the city is situated was taken as a unit, and the counties contiguous to it were called Tier One, counties contiguous to Tier One were called Tier Two, and so on up to Tier Four. The outer boundaries of each tier from the boundary of the city county are approximately 6, 12, 18 and 24 miles respectively.[21] There averaged nineteen counties to each city, covering 10 per cent. of the population of the country. Literally hundreds of indices were taken in these studies, and the characteristics of the tiers or zones in 1930, and the changes in these characteristics since 1910, were determined. The indices include fertility rates, sex ratios, ratio of children, proportion of land in farms, average acreage of improved land per farm, value per acre of farm property, and of farm crops, and value of

Forest Culture.
　　Zone 7. Outermost peripheral areas. Forests.
　　Olof Jonasson, "The Agricultural Regions of Europe," *Economic Geography*, Vol. I, 1925, pp. 284-287.

　　19. Ely and Wehrwein, *op. cit.*, pp. 140-142.
Relationships, 1933, pp. 141-142 and 151-152.

　　20. E. de S. Brunner and J. H. Kolb, *Rural Social Trends*, Chapter V on Rural-Urban
　　21. Wholesale trade areas were taken from the *Market Data Handbook of the United States*, by P. W. Stewart, published by the U.S. Department of Commerce, Domestic Commerce Series, No. 30, 1929.

dairy products. Several significant "gradient relationships" were discovered in the successive concentric zones. The ratio of children under ten years of age to women of reproductive age increased with distance in the first three tiers but declined in the fourth tier. The birth-rate tended to increase with distance of the county from the city. Distance from the city was found to have an important effect on farming. The percentage of farms devoted to dairying tended to increase with distance in the first three tiers and declined rather sharply in the fourth tier. The percentage of truck (market gardening) farms declined in the first three tiers, but showed a slight increase in the fourth. The percentage of poultry farms declined through all four tiers, while the proportion of stock farms increased with distance in all four tiers. The farms tended to increase in size with increased distance from the city. The value per acre of farm land declined consistently with distance and the value per acre of all farm products also declined with distance. The value of dairy products per acre tended to decline in the first three tiers and increase in the fourth tier. These data were then examined for the 1910 to 1930 period and the following conclusions were drawn.

The City County and, to an increasing extent since 1920, Tier One, are likely to be given over to smaller farms for market gardening, fruit growing and intensive dairying. This means more compact communities and relatively high densities of population. It means more frequent contacts of all sorts with the city centre. Demographic trends are akin to those of the city. Tier One and especially Tier Two show an increasing specialization on dairying. Tier Three has many markedly transitional features. Tier Four and beyond, until the influence of another urban centre is reached, form what is described as an outer zone. It has larger farms but fewer cultivated acres per farm. Population densities are lower, communities larger, and there are fewer contacts with the city. City influence in retail sales declines beyond Tier Two, although there is some dependence on the city stores and mail-order houses for clothing, furniture and household effects. But most remarkable are the demographic trends in Tier Four that stand in fundamental contrast to the inner Tiers. There are more children under 10 to women 20 to 45 years of age and there are higher birth-rates. There is a higher proportion of people under 21 years of age, and a higher proportion of males to each 100 females, and this is in turn reflected in the marriage ratios. Children are a distinguishing feature of the farm populations removed from urban influence, and they have been becoming more so, even though the general differences between rural and urban populations in this regard were tending to decrease.[22]

Changes in farming conditions with increased distance from the city were revealed some years ago in a study of Louisville. Within 8 miles of the city market place market garden products and potatoes provided 68 per cent. of the farm income, whereas at a 15-miles radius only 20 per cent.

---

22. Brunner and Kolb, *op. cit.,* Chapter 5, especially pp. 141-142.

was drawn from this source, even though the soil that is especially suitable for market gardening extends more than 20 miles along the river. At 15 miles or more dairying and general farming took the place of the intensive crops. The greater intensity of land use near the city was shown by the smaller farms, greater operating expenses, and higher expenditure on fertilizers. Gross earnings were five times as high per acre 9 miles from the city as 16 miles, and this was reflected in rents paid and land values.[23]

A similar investigation has been made by the Urbanism Committee of the National Resources Committee.[24] It allowed one tier of counties around each county that contained one city with over 100,000 inhabitants, a second tier was added to eight central nuclei with a city with over 500,000 to one million inhabitants (allowing for its greater range and potency of influence), and a third tier for the five central nuclei with a city with over one million inhabitants. On this basis, 89 regions were established around the counties containing the 93 cities of 100,000 inhabitants or over. Data considered were the growth and density of population, industry, income, occupations (grouped as agriculture, industrial non-service occupations, and industrial services),[25] and the percentage of total population ten years old and over gainfully occupied. This investigation showed that an increasing proportion of the total population of the country is concentrating in these regions, and that settlement is, as it were, segregating in wider areas around the central urban districts. The character of these city regions varies from one part of the country to another. In the Atlantic Seaboard, the Great Lakes and California, population is highly urbanized and concentrated and is becoming increasingly so and increasingly industrialized. In the rest of the States, the cities have a more limited range of influence and lead "a more isolated and independent existence." They are primarily commercial distributing points to their agricultural hinterland. It was, moreover, clearly revealed that the city was predominantly engaged in the service trades and professions, as compared with less than a half of the total employed so engaged in the outlying counties, and 25 to 60 per cent. (an average of 40 per cent.) in all the outlying areas. The city is thus clearly revealed as "the centre of managerial, commercial, clerical and professional functions."[26]

---

23. Ely and Wehrwein, *op. cit.*, p. 137, quoting J. H. Arnold and F. Montgomery, *Influence of a City in Farming*, U.S. Dept. of Agriculture, Bulletin 678, 1918.

24. *Population Statistics, 3. Urban Data*, National Resources Committee, October, 1937, pp. 43-45.

25. These included all those engaged in transport, trade, public service, professional service, domestic and private service, and industry not specified.

26. *Population Statistics, 3. Urban Data*, National Resources Committee, 1937, p. 45.

INVENTIONS OF LOCAL TRANSPORTATION AND THE PATTERNS OF CITIES

William F. Ogburn

The air bomber brings the destruction of war to civilians. No longer are the casualties of war confined to combat units. But it is to the cities and not the open country that death is brought by these murderous missiles dropping from the sky. The former cities of Germany laid waste by bombing are a shocking sight as reported by returning visitors.

As one contemplates these ruins, it is easy to observe that if there were no cities there would be no such destruction. If people did not live so close together, the devastation would be less. Why not then spread out our cities and scatter our urban population? Thus modern warfare emphasizes the logical proposal to decentralize our cities.

The atom bomb and the rocket which can travel across the Atlantic Ocean or the Arctic in 15 minutes emphasize the danger to our urban civilian population in another war. One atom bomb of the present type destroys an area of about ten square miles. Twenty such bombs could annihilate the city of Chicago. But the bomb will not remain at its present destructive power. Inventions evolve. Thus the airplane of the Wright Brothers, weighing 750 pounds, has evolved into the Stratocruiser of 135,000 pounds.

This imminent danger to our cities has led to the very sensible proposal to prohibit the manufacture of the atom bomb anywhere in the world. We are in the process of making such an agreement now, which it is hoped will be reached within a period of months. But shall we have security with such an agreement? Ten years after the various nations of the world signed the Pact of Paris not to have recourse to war the world was in flames. The League of Nations was of no avail. So we may be ruined by atom bombs in another war even though our future enemies sign an agreement not to employ this weapon. Furthermore, though the atom bomb was not used our cities could be destroyed by the TNT bombs, which are likely to be more destructive in the next world war, if there is one, than in the last one.

We really ought then, it would seem, to break up our cities over, say, 50,000 inhabitants, 200 of them, into 1000 cities of 50,000 each. The task is so huge and the obstacles, financial, political, economic and social, so great that we shall not do so, despite the fact that not doing so could mean the

Reprinted from *Social Forces*, Vol. 24 (May 1946), pp. 373-379, by permission of the author and the publisher. (Copyright, 1946, by *Social Forces*.)

loss of 40,000,000 civilians in another world war. In considering such a plan of action, however, it is well to note that social action which is in accord with social trends is more likely to succeed than planning in opposition to trends.

Now, the trend in the distribution of cities is one of dispersal. Indeed, a century or two hence the urban population may, by wholly natural processes, be spaced in such a way as to afford protection from bombing. Thus the placement and size of urban communities a century hence may be what we would like to have within the next five or ten years to escape the bombing of the next world war.

In considering these trends, the influence of transportation inventions seems to be the determiner of the distribution of cities. Particularly have the inventions of local transportation been the cause of the patterns of cities taking the shape they have assumed. Students of human ecology have not given adequate recognition to the inventions of local transportation. In the study of social change and of the impact of technology on society a very interesting chapter is the influence of the inventions of local transportation on cities. The singling out of this influence may enable us to speed the natural trends in urban dispersal and to secure a measure of protection from bombing that we would not otherwise obtain so soon.

We have been living in cities only about a century and a half. There were a few cities before then, even in ancient times, but the proportion of the total population living in them must have been very small. Cities, as we know them today, are the creation of the railroad and the factory. They grew up at the junction points of railroads or of railroads and waterways. In them were stores and factories; and, of course, the places of work of those who service the employees of the sellers and manufacturers.

The distribution of residences was determined by the proximity to places of work. In the early cities the only methods of local transportation were based on muscle, except in a few cities like Venice. Donkeys, oxen, and horses were not adequate, hence many workers and shoppers walked. Thus houses were crowded close together. Often the occupants were piled on top of each other in buildings of many stories. The pattern of cities was one of congestion.

The situation was changed with better local transportation. The first electric streetcar was run in 1886. Gradually this faster method replaced the horse-drawn bus and the few horse-drawn rail cars that were found in occasional cities. The streetcar enabled people to live further from their places of work.

However, the effect of the streetcar was not to scatter very much the existing residences of a city. Rather it enabled more people to live in a city, to work in the factories, and to market at the stores. For city populations were growing and needing more or larger stores and factories. Larger establishments were economical and survived. So cities grew in population, and new houses were added to the periphery. Cities continued to be congested, for it was necessary that the stores and factories be near the transportation terminals.

In the course of time, the electric streetcar became faster. It connected towns. The existence of the interurban electric line enabled inhabitants of nearby small towns to work and to shop in the big city. The growth of suburbs was facilitated by local steam lines, too. As more people worked or traded in the city, the residents who serviced them, together with their families, increased the size of cities still further.

Then came the gasoline driven vehicle, the most important invention yet made for local transportation. The private automobile for the individual family was very fast and permitted the owner to live a considerable distance from his place of work and from the market. The automobile bus served the same purpose and was more flexible in its operation than the streetcar. Cities thus took the pattern of a starfish. The urban population strung out along highways and did not fill up the land between the highways, as the radius of the city became longer. They did not string out evenly, though, for people must live around stores, schools, motion picture theatres, etc. So the little clusters of population, to change the simile, were strung out like beads on a string.

This pattern idealizes the structure of the economic city; not necessarily the political city. The political city is a matter of boundary lines drawn by legislative bodies, which are not in recent years identical with economic lines. The political lines lag behind the economic ones.

The outline of this economic urban area is not as compact in design as the shell of a starfish. It is rather as if the prongs of the shell of a starfish were somewhat shattered and broken and the fragments scattered close by. All this area is now customarily called the metropolitan area. The economic city then under the impact of the modern local transportation has become the metropolitan area. The metropolitan area of the automobile age is quite different in shape from the city of the railroad era.

The "economic city" of the automobile age is, *as a whole,* less closely packed with houses than was the city of the railroad era. So it may be argued that the urban population has been becoming more scattered for some time, particularly since the automobile and, perhaps, since the electric streetcar. The density of population is less for the whole economic city. There are more open spaces. Some economic cities have many farms within their borders.

But while the modern economic city as a whole is less densely packed than the city was before the automobile and streetcar, such is not the case with the original area at the center. These earlier cities which depended on muscle for transportation were shaped more like the shell of a clam than the shell of a starfish. The scattering occurs not at the center of the pattern but at some distances out from the center. The center then is no more dispersed than it was before the automobile.

The reason why the original city remains congested is due in part to the slowness of buildings to move. It is easier to break a camp than it is for an owner to move a durable building. Many people have moved from the center out to the suburbs. Their vacant houses have been filled by others. It is a shift of population rather than a depopulation. An owner will sell a building for a loss before he will abandon it and lose all.

To thin out the population as a protection against bombing during wars may then require that the government acquire the land, remove buildings, and prohibit the construction of other buildings thereon. In this case, the cost would be on the taxpayer, rather than a loss occurring to the owner. With land values in cities as high as they are, there has been little thinning out by this type of governmental action; even though such action would lead to wider streets, more parks, more air and sunlight. Action of this type would be governmental, not that of "free enterprise." It would be based on planning and collective direction. Government powers somewhat like those of wartime would be needed. Land values do fall in some parts of a city due to population shifts; but they have not yet fallen very far, not to zero. Though owners do lose, the congestion in buildings remains.

If the process is viewed from the point of view of factories rather than of residences, a variation is noted. Theoretically, if factories move out of a city to a distant location, then an absolute vacancy may be left. For factories are not as easy to sell or to rent as dwellings. If it is good economics for one factory owner to move out where land is cheaper, it will generally be bad economics for another factory to fill the vacancy. Presumably it would be better for the other factory owner to move out to cheaper land too. With the removal of a factory there goes also much of the working population, their families, and those engaged in servicing them.

For a factory to move, though, transportation is needed. While a spur of railroad track may make it possible, small factories or factories making light weight goods can depend much on the auto truck. Trucks and auto-

THE CHANGING PATTERN OF A GREAT CITY, BALTIMORE

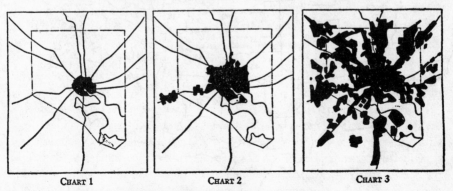

CHART 1   CHART 2   CHART 3

CHART 1. 1850, after the first railroads.
CHART 2. 1900, after the electric streetcar.
CHART 3. 1936, after the automobile.

TRADING AREAS AROUND CITIES

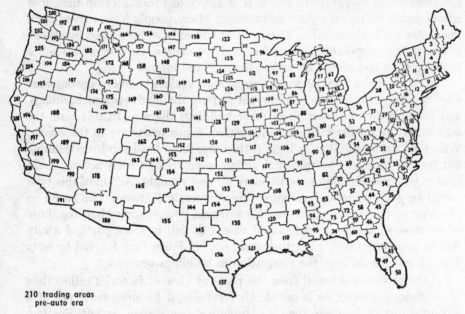

210 trading areas
pre-auto era

MAP 1. In the days of the horse and buggy.

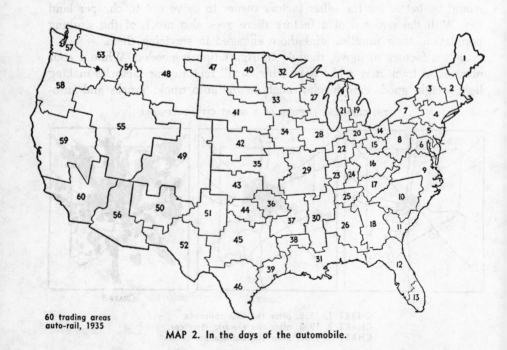

60 trading areas
auto-rail, 1935

MAP 2. In the days of the automobile.

mobiles and buses are forms of local transportation which aid the relocation of factories away from high land values and wages but not too far from a labor supply. The movement of factories from cities then does have possibilities of making a particular area well within a city less densely populated. This process has been taking place on principles of free enterprise without governmental planning and direction.

If the process is viewed from the point of view of stores rather than of factories and residences, it is found also to be different. The success of merchants depends upon shoppers who come to the stores. Hence, subways and elevateds and superhighways are favored by downtown merchants. But many customers do not like to ride crowded subways and elevateds. A surprisingly large number prefer to drive their own automobiles, if the streets are wide enough and if a store has an adequate free parking lot. Hence neighborhood markets, where there is free parking space, are becoming increasingly popular. The downtown market in the center of the city could hold this trade if the streets could be widened and free parking places provided. But the sums of money needed are so large as to be in most cases prohibitive. Hence there are, short of subways, elevateds, and superhighways, tendencies for markets to be dispersed. Still this process does not lead to many vacant lots, which are the desideratum if the problem is that of escaping bombing. But bombing is expected to be directed toward war factories rather than toward stores.

Markets are of various kinds. Food markets can very well be dispersed. But markets for luxury goods such as fine jewelry, fur coats, rare art, etc. need a very large population to support them. As transportation becomes more frequently used these central markets for luxury goods will be made more accessible. Hence the markets in the center of a city are not likely to be diminished very much as the result of any natural process of evolution.

In the future, there will be air transportation. In general, air transportation is, like railroads, for long distances, and hence has the same general effect as railroads. In addition, the larger the city, the more frequent will be the air schedules. Hence air transportation of the type in use today encourages the larger cities to greater growth. The scattering of urban population, as has been shown, is a function of local transportation. To what extent is air transport local? It is hardly worthwhile to travel in a plane for distances less than 50 or 75 miles. But with a helicopter, it may be useful for trips of much shorter distances, provided there are adequate landing places on tops of buildings and in vacant land areas, and provided the helicopter will travel along the ground, also, like an automobile. Then, too, helicopters will be faster than automobiles, perhaps two or three times as fast, and the land distance between two points is about one-sixth longer than the air distance.

The process of dispersal accompanying the private automobile and the autobus will be accentuated by the private helicopter for individual family use and the helicopter bus; but the process will be of the same general

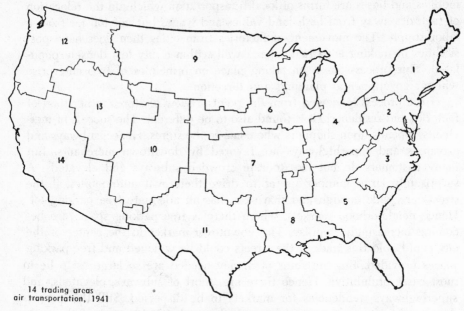

14 trading areas
air transportation, 1941

MAP 3. In the days of aircraft.

nature, as described in previous paragraphs. That is, the prongs of the starfish will be greatly elongated and the number of prongs increased. The extent will depend on the extent of use of the helicopter which in turn rests on price and safety. No use of the helicopter comparable to that of the automobile is expected, though, in the visible future. The price will be high for a long time and the roadable helicopter will not be as good a ground vehicle as the automobile.

Hence not so many persons are likely to come into the city by helicopter as by automobile; but they will come from longer distances. Consequently, the trading area around a city will be much larger in the air age than in the automobile age. The trading center of a city will then probably be increased rather than diminished by aircraft.

The actual thinning out of city populations was found to be dependent on the moving outward of factories. Will the airplane encourage factories to be moved away from the cities? The answer depends on the use of cargo planes. At present, planes in the United States carry profitably only the type of goods that go by railroad express or by mail. Bulky, heavy freight of low unit value is not likely to be transported by air. Hence, the influence of aircraft in moving factories is expected to be slight, as far as we can see.

The natural processes of economics and of technology, then, seem to yield the following picture. Whole areas, larger than the present metropolitan areas, will be urbanized, somewhat as the area in a present economic city limit is urbanized, except that there will be very much more space between the communities. These communities will be of all sizes from small villages to large aggregations around a big trading center. The cities of the railroad age will disappear. The central trading areas and the populations immediately around them are not likely to be thinned out very much, though land values in centers with little vacant space may, of course, be lower. On the other hand the factories will be rather widely scattered, except clusters here and there where integration is highly desirable for production. The wider spacing of factories is most important as a defense against bombing, for they are the most likely targets. Hence the natural process will eventually yield some protection to cities. But these changes are very slow, since buildings are of long life, they cost much money, and we are reluctant to move them or to abandon them.

This process of thinning out cities could be speeded greatly if we would agree to submit to governmental authority and to give up some freedom, as we might do under the threat of war. We are not, however, very likely to break up our large cities quickly under governmental direction to any significant degree, because of the cost, the inconvenience, and the loss of advantages inherent in great cities. To discuss how this might be done is beyond the scope of this article. From the foregoing analysis, however, it can be seen that the first and most important step is to get the factories moved out.

An interesting question is how much would be lost if our city populations were so scattered that no city was over 50,000 inhabitants. We would lose the supermarkets of large cities, the ease of making many contacts quickly, and the cultural advantages dependent upon a large population, such as operas, museums, etc. These advantages could still be had even if large cities were broken up into smaller ones, provided local transportation was cheap, fast, and frequent. Thus, a city of 500,000 occupying an area of 100 square miles, might be broken up into 10 cities of 50,000, placed in an area of 10,000 square miles so that they would be about 50 miles apart with the farthest distance between any two cities not more than 140 miles. Now in a city of 500,000 a citizen can ride anywhere in a streetcar for 10 cents, and the schedules are frequent. If helicopters could furnish sufficiently cheap transportation with frequent schedules, there would be no essential difference between a city of 500,000 on 100 square miles and 10 cities of 50,000 on 10,000 square miles. The breaking up of large cities as a defense against bombing and the spacing of the small cities is thus a function of fast, frequent and, above all, cheap local transportation.

In conclusion, then, there are two observations. One is that the natural process toward dispersal of the urban population could be speeded by governmental planning and direction so as to provide more protection against the very real danger of bombing in the next world war. The second observation is that the placement of city populations, residences, and places of work is singularly a function of local transportation as cities themselves are the creation of long-distance transportation, and that any successful planning and direction of the dispersal of city population must rest on local transportation, which must be fast, frequent, and cheap.

Nothing has been said in this article about values other than safety. But it is obvious that the chance to create new cities presents marvelous opportunities for civilized ways of living. Six- or eight-lane highways would lessen the congestion. Free parking space could be provided by stores, factories, restaurants and even by government. There need to be few highway crossings, thus reducing delay and increasing safety. Accidents on the highways and streets, especially to children, might be greatly reduced. Landing space downtown for helicopters on the ground or on the tops of buildings could be provided. Dwellings would have yards big enough for helicopters to land, for gardens, and perhaps for fruit trees and animals. There need be no smoke, and hence more sunlight with health-giving ultra-violet rays available. New dwellings planned by architects could take advantage of many new inventions, such as a glass wall on the south side for solar heat in winter and radiant heat from steam pipes in the walls.

RESIDENTIAL DISTRIBUTION
AND OCCUPATIONAL STRATIFICATION

Otis Dudley Duncan and Beverly Duncan

The idea behind this paper was forcibly stated—in fact, somewhat overstated—by Robert E. Park: "It is because social relations are so frequently and so inevitably correlated with spatial relations; because physical distances so frequently are, or seem to be, the indexes of social distances, that statistics have any significance whatever for sociology. And this is true, finally, because it is only as social and psychical facts can be reduced to, or correlated with, spatial facts that they can be measured at all."[1]

This study finds a close relationship between spatial and social distances in a metropolitan community. It suggests that a systematic consideration of the spatial aspect of stratification phenomena, though relatively neglected by students of the subject,[2] should be a primary focus of urban stratification studies. Aside from demonstrating the relevance of human ecology to the theory of social organization, the study offers further evidence for the suitability of a particular set of methodological techniques for research in comparative urban ecology.[3] These techniques are adaptable to a wide variety of problems in urban ecological structure, permit economical and objective comparisons among communities, and thus overcome some of the indeterminacy of a strictly cartographic approach. The techniques are here applied to only one metropolitan community, Chicago; however, comparative studies, conducted on an exploratory basis, indicate their ability to produce significant results.

DATA AND METHOD. The sources of data for this study, except as noted

Reprinted from *The American Journal of Sociology*, Vol. 60 (March, 1955), pp. 493-503, by permission of the author and *The American Journal of Sociology*, and the University of Chicago Press. (Copyright 1955 by the University of Chicago).

1. "The Urban Community as a Spatial Pattern and a Moral Order," in *The Urban Community*, ed. Ernest W. Burgess (Chicago: University of Chicago Press, 1926), p. 18.

2. See, however, the discussion of "dwelling area" by W. Lloyd Warner *et al.*, *Social Class in America* (Chicago: Science Research Associates, 1949), pp. 151-54.

3. Otis Dudley Duncan and Beverly Duncan, "A Methodological Analysis of Segregation Indexes," forthcoming in *American Sociological Review*; Donald J. Bogue, *The Structure of the Metropolitan Community* (Ann Arbor: University of Michigan, 1949), p. 72; Richard W. Redick, "A Study of Differential Rates of Population Growth and Patterns of Population Distribution in Central Cities in the United States: 1940-1950" (paper presented at the 1954 annual meeting of the American Sociological Society, Urbana, Illinois).

otherwise, were the published volume of 1950 census tract statistics for Chicago and adjacent areas[4] (coextensive with the Chicago Metropolitan District, as delineated in 1940), and the census-tract summary punch cards for this area obtained from the Bureau of the Census. The ecological analysis pertains to employed males fourteen years old and over, classified into the eight major occupation groups listed in the tables below. The occupation groups disregarded in this analysis (farmers and farm managers, farm laborers, private household workers, and occupation not reported) include only twenty-one thousand of the one and a half million employed males in the Metropolitan District.

A portion of the analysis is carried through with the census tract as the area unit. There are 1,178 census tracts in the Metropolitan District, of which 935 are in the city of Chicago and 243 in the adjacent area. The remainder of the analysis rests on a scheme of zones and sectors, delineated rather arbitrarily. Tracts were assigned to circular zones, concentric to the center of the city at State and Madison Streets, with one-mile intervals up to fourteen miles, two-mile intervals up to twenty-eight miles, and with residual categories of tracts more than twenty-eight miles from the city center and tracts in the adjacent area too large to be classified by zones. The latter category contains only 1.4 per cent of the employed males. Five sectors were established, with boundaries approximately radial lines drawn from the city center. The North Shore sector runs along Lake Michigan through such suburbs as Skokie, Evanston, Lake Forest, and Waukegan; the Northwest sector extends through Park Ridge and Des Plaines to Arlington Heights; the West sector includes the suburbs of Cicero, Oak Park, and Berwyn, running out as far as Wheaton and Naperville; the Southwest sector is approximately bisected by a line running through Blue Island, Harvey, and Chicago Heights to Park Forest; and the South Shore sector runs along Lake Michigan through the Indiana suburbs of East Chicago, Hammond, Gary, and East Gary. Combining the zone and sector schemes yielded a set of 104 zone-sector segments; that is, area units averaging about ten times the size of a census tract, though with considerable variation in area and population.

The spatial "distance" between occupation groups, or more precisely the difference between their areal distributions, is measured by the *index of dissimilarity*.[5] To compute this index, one calculates for each occupation group the percentage of all workers in that group residing in each area unit (tract or zone-sector segment). The index of dissimilarity between two occupation groups is then one-half the sum of the absolute values of the differences between the respective distributions, taken area by area. In the accompanying hypothetical example the index of dissimi-

4. *1950 United States Census of Population,* Bulletin P-D10.

5. For the use of the index of dissimilarity as a "coefficient of geographic association" see National Resources Planning Board, *Industrial Location and National Resources* (Washington, D.C.: Government Printing Office, 1943), p. 118.

larity between occupations A and B is 20 per cent (i.e., 40/2). This may be interpreted as a measure of displacement: 20 per cent of the workers in occupation A would have to move to a different area in order to make their distribution identical with that of occupation B.

Area	A	B	Diff.
1	10%	15%	5%
2	20	15	5
3	40	25	15
4	30	45	15
Total	100%	100%	40%

When the index of dissimilarity is computed between one occupation group and all other occupations combined (i.e., total employed males except those in the given occupation group), it is referred to as an *index of segregation*.[6] An equivalent and more convenient means of computing the segregation index is to compute the index of dissimilarity between the given occupation group and total employed males (i.e., all occupations), "adjusting" the result by dividing by one minus the proportion of the total male employed labor force included in that occupation group.

The indexes of segregation and dissimilarity were computed on both a tract basis and a zone-sector segment basis to determine the effect of the size of the area unit on the results. While the indexes for tracts are uniformly higher than for zone-sector segments, this effect can be disregarded for purposes of determining the relative positions of the occupation groups. The product-moment correlation between the two sets of segregation indexes in Table 2 is .96. The correlation between the two sets of dissimilarity indexes in Table 3 is .98, with the segment-based index (s) related to the tract-based index (t) by the regression equation, $s = .8t - 1.3$. These results indicate that for the kind of problem dealt with here the larger, and hence less homogeneous, unit is as serviceable as the smaller one. This suggests that some of the recent concern about census-tract homogeneity may be misplaced.[7]

The *index of low-rent concentration* is obtained by (1) classifying tracts into intervals according to the median monthly rental of tenant-occupied dwelling units; (2) computing the percentage distribution by rent intervals for each occupation group and for all occupations combined; (3) cumulating the distributions, from low to high rent; (4) calculating the quantity $\Sigma X_{i-1}Y_i - \Sigma X_i Y_{i-1}$, where X_i is the cumulated percentage of the given occupation through the ith rent interval, Y_1 is the cumulated percentage of all occupations combined, and the summation is

---

6. For discussion of the index of dissimilarity as a segregation index see Duncan and Duncan, *op. cit.*, and the literature there cited.

7. Jerome K. Myers, "Note on the Homogeneity of Census Tracts: A Methodological Problem in Urban Ecological Research," *Social Forces*, XXXII (May, 1954), 364-66; Joel Smith, "A Method for the Classification of Areas on the Basis of Demographically Homogeneous Populations," *American Sociological Review*, XIX (April, 1954), 201-7.

over all rent intervals; and, finally, (5) "adjusting" the result (as for the segregation index) to obtain an index equivalent to the one obtained by comparing the given occupation group with all other occupations combined. This index varies between 100 and −100, with positive values indicating a tendency for residences of the given occupation group to be in areas of relatively low rent and with negative values indicating relative concentration in high-rent areas.

The *index of centralization* is computed in the same fashion, except that tracts are ordered by distance from the center of the city, that is, are classified according to the zonal scheme. A negative index of centralization signifies that the given occupation group tends to be "decentralized," or on the average located farther away from the city center than all other occupations, while a positive index is obtained for a relatively "centralized" occupation.[8]

OCCUPATION AND SOCIOECONOMIC STATUS. Selected nonecological indicators of the relative socioeconomic status of the major occupation groups are shown in Table 1. The professional and managerial groups clearly have the highest socioeconomic rank, while operatives, service workers, and laborers are clearly lowest in socioeconomic status. The ranking by socioeconomic level would probably be agreed on by most social scientists. The major occupation groups correspond roughly with the Alba Edwards scheme of "social-economic groups." Edwards does not separate sales workers and clerical workers by "social-economic group," and the group of service workers, except private household, contains individual occupations variously classified by Edwards as skilled, semiskilled, and unskilled, predominantly the latter two.

A ranking in terms of median income results in two reversals in rank. The 1949 median income of male managerial workers in the Chicago Standard Metropolitan Area was about $500 greater than that of professional workers, although both were substantially above that for sales workers. The median income for the craftsmen-foremen group was about $500 higher than that for clerical workers. In fact, the median income for the craftsmen-foremen group was only slightly below that for sales workers, whereas the median income for clerical workers was only slightly above that for operatives.

However, in median school years completed, professional workers clearly rank first, while there is little difference in the medians for the managerial, sales, and clerical groups. The median drops sharply, over 2.5 years, for the craftsmen-foremen group and declines further for each group in the order of the initial listing.

8. The indexes of low-rent concentration and of centralization are formally identical with the index of urbanization proposed in Otis Dudley Duncan, "Urbanization and Retail Specialization," *Social Forces*, XXX (March, 1952), 267-71. The formula given here is a simplification of the one presented there; and the area units and principle of ordering are, of course, different.

In the Chicago Metropolitan District the proportion of nonwhites in an occupation group appears to be closely related to its socioeconomic status. The proportion is very low in the professional, managerial, and sales groups, but it is somewhat higher for clerical workers than for the craftsmen-foremen group. Increasing proportions are observed for operatives, service workers, and laborers, in order.

The suggested ranking is in general conformity with the National Opinion Research Center's data on popular attitudes toward occupations, except that sales occupations appear to rank below clerical and craft occupations in the NORC results.[9] An inadequate sampling of occupational titles within the sales group may account in part for the low prestige rating of sales workers obtained by the NORC. Furthermore, their data do not differentiate prestige ratings by sex. Particularly in a metropolitan area, the male sales worker group is more heavily weighted with such occupations as advertising, insurance, and real estate agents and sales representatives of wholesale and manufacturing concerns than is the case for female sales workers, among whom retail sales clerks are the large majority.

Table 1—Selected Indicators of Socioeconomic Status of the Major Occupation Groups

Major Occupation Group*	Median Income in 1949†	Median School Years Completed‡	Edwards' Socio-economic Group§	Per Cent Non-white**
Professional, technical,and kindred workers	$4,387	16+	1	2.7
Managers, officials, and proprietors, except farm	4,831	12.2	2	2.2
Sales workers	3,698	12.4	3	2.8
Clerical and kindred workers	3,132	12.2	3	7.4
Craftsmen, foremen, and kindred workers	3,648	9.5	4	4.9
Operatives and kindred workers	3,115	8.9	5	12.4
Service workers, except private household	2,635	8.8	5-6	23.0
Laborers, except farm and mine	2,580	8.4	6	27.4

* Does not include farmers and farm managers, private household workers, farm laborers, and occupation not reported.

† For males in the experienced labor force of the Chicago Standard Metropolitan Area, 1950. Source: 1950 U.S. Census of Population, Bulletin P-C13, Table 78.

‡ For employed males twenty-five years old and over, in the North and West, 1950. Source: 1950 U.S. Census of Population, Special Report P-E No. 5B, Table 11.

§ Approximate equivalents. Source: Alba M. Edwards, Comparative Occupation Statistics for the United States, 1870 to 1940 (Washington, D.C.; Government Printing Office, 1943).

** For employed males in the Chicago Metropolitan District, 1950. Based on nonwhites residing in census tracts containing 250 or more nonwhite population in 1950. These tracts include 95.8 per cent of all nonwhite males in the Metropolitan District.

The failure of different bases of ranking to give identical results has been discussed by writers on stratification in terms of "disaffinity of strata" and "status disequilibrium."[10] The reversals in rank between the profes-

9. National Opinion Research Center, "Jobs and Occupations: A Popular Evaluation," Opinion News, IX (September 1, 1947), 3-13.

10. Cf. Pitrim A. Sorokin, Society, Culture, and Personality (New York: Harper & Bros., 1947), pp. 289-94, on disaffinity of strata. On status disequilibrium cf. Émile

sional and managerial groups and the clerical and crafts workers are most frequent. The upshot seems to be that no one ranking can be accepted as sufficient for all purposes. The examination of residential patterns discloses other instances of disequilibrium, which are of interest both in themselves and as clues to the interpretation of those already noted.

RESIDENTIAL PATTERNS. Four aspects of the residential patterning of occupation groups are considered. The first is the degree of residential segregation of each major occupation group with respect to all others, that is, the extent to which an occupation group is separated residentially from the remainder of the employed labor force. The second is the degree of dissimilarity in residential distribution among major occupation groups, that is, the extent to which pairs of occupation groups isolate themselves from one another. The third aspect is the degree of residential concentration of each occupation group in areas characterized by relatively low rents. Finally, the degree of centralization of each major occupation group (i.e., the extent to which an occupation group is concentrated toward the center of the metropolitan community) is examined. In each case the spatial patterning of the residences is considered in relation to socioeconomic level.

A clear relationship of the ranking of major occupation groups by socioeconomic status and by degree of residential segregation is shown in Table 2. Listed in the order given there, the indexes of residential segregation form a U-shaped pattern. The highest values are observed for the professionals and the laborers and the lowest value for the clerical workers. The degree of residential segregation varies only slightly among the professional, managerial, and sales groups; however, it declines markedly for the clerical workers and then increases regularly for each successive group.

This finding suggests that residential segregation is greater for those occupation groups with clearly defined status than for those groups whose status is ambiguous. The latter groups are necessarily subject to crosspressures from the determinants of residential selection; for example, the clerical group has an income equivalent to that of operatives but the educational level of managerial workers.

To check the hypothesis that spatial distances among occupation groups parallel their social distances, the indexes of dissimilarity in residential distribution among major occupation groups are shown in Table 3. As previously indicated, a listing of major occupation groups by socioeconomic level can at best only roughly approximate a social distance scale. Similarly, a measure of dissimilarity in residential distribution can only approximate the spatial distance between groups—the index measures only the dissimilarity of the residential distributions with respect to

Benoit-Smullyan, "Status, Status Types, and Status Interrelations," *American Sociological Review,* IX (April, 1944), 154-61; Harold F. Kaufman, *Defining Prestige in a Rural Community* ("Sociometry Monograph," No. 10 [New York: Beacon House, 1946]).

Table 2—Index of Residential Segregation of Each Major Occupation Group, for Employed Males in the Chicago Metropolitan District, 1950

Major Occupation Group*	By Census	By Zone-Sector Segments
Professional, technical, and kindred workers	30	21
Managers, officials, and proprietors, except farm	29	20
Sales workers	29	20
Clerical and kindred workers	13	9
Craftsmen, foremen, and kindred workers	19	14
Operatives and kindred workers	22	16
Service workers, except private household	24	20
Laborers, except farm and mine	35	29

* Does not include farmers and farm managers, private household workers, farm laborers, and occupation not reported.

a particular set of areas and is insensitive to other important aspects of the spatial pattern such as proximity of areas of concentration.

Nonetheless, the data in Table 3 indicate the essential correspondence of social and spatial distance among occupation groups. If it is assumed that the ordering of major occupation groups corresponds with increasing social distance (e.g., the social distance between professional and sales workers is greater than that between professional and managerial workers), and if it is assumed that the index of residential dissimilarity approx-

Table 3—Indexes of Dissimilarity in Residential Distribution Among Major Occupation Groups, for Employed Males in the Chicago Metropolitan District, 1950 (Above diagonal, by census tracts; below diagonal, by zone-sector segments)

MAJOR OCCUPATION GROUP*

Major Occupation Group*	Prof., Tech., Kindred	Mgrs., Offs., Props.	Sales Wkrs.	Clerical, Kindred	Craftsmen, Foremen	Operatives, Kindred	Service, exc. Priv. Hshld.	Laborers, exc. Farm and Mine
Professional, technical, kindred workers	..	13	15	28	35	44	41	54
Managers, officials, and proprietors, except farm	8	..	13	28	33	41	40	52
Sales workers	11	7	..	27	35	42	38	54
Clerical and kindred workers	20	18	17	..	16	21	24	38
Craftsmen, foremen, kindred workers	26	23	25	12	..	17	35	35
Operatives, kindred workers	31	29	30	16	14	..	26	25
Service workers, except private household	31	31	30	19	25	19	..	28
Laborers, except farm and mine	42	41	42	32	30	21	24	..

* Does not include farmers and farm managers, private household workers, farm laborers, and occupation not reported.

imates the spatial distance between the two groups, the expected pattern would be the following: Starting at any point on the diagonal, the indexes would increase reading up or to the right (down or to the left, in the case of the indexes below the diagonal, based on zone-sector segments). It is clear that the expected pattern, though not perfectly reproduced, essentially describes the observed pattern. The exceptions are few and for the most part can be explained hypothetically; such hypotheses provide clues for additional research.

The least dissimilarity is observed between professional and managerial workers, managerial and sales workers, and professional and sales workers. Furthermore, the dissimilarity of each of these goups with each other occupation group is of approximately the same degree. In fact, three of the inversions of the expected pattern concern the comparison between the managerial group and sales workers; that is, the residential dissimilarity of sales workers with craftsmen-foremen, operatives, and laborers is slightly greater than that of the managerial group, although their difference in terms of socioeconomic level is presumably less.

The residential distribution of clerical workers is more dissimilar to the distribution of sales workers, professional, and managerial workers than to that of the craftsmen or the operatives. Hence, although clerical workers are often grouped with professional, managerial, and sales workers as "white-collar," in terms of residential distribution they are more similar to the craftsmen and operatives than to the other white-collar groups.

The remaining inversions of the expected pattern involve service workers, except private household. One-fifth of these are "janitors and sextons." Presumably a substantial proportion of the janitors live at their place of work in apartment buildings housing workers in the higher status occupation groups.[11] It is hypothesized that this special circumstance accounts for the tendency of service workers to be less dissimilar to the higher status groups than expected on the basis of socioeconomic status.[12] At the same time the color composition of the service group presumably acts in the opposite direction. In so far as residential segregation on basis of color, cutting across occupational lines, exists within the metropolitan community, occupational status is rendered at least partially ineffective as a determinant of residential location. These factors, however, probably do not wholly explain the largest single deviation from the expected pattern, the much larger index of dissimilarity between craftsmen-foremen and service workers than between clerical and service workers.

The first column of Table 4 shows the indexes of low-rent concentration of the occupation groups. Some caution must be exercised in interpreting them, since the tabulation on which they are based did not dis-

---

11. Cf. Ray Gold, "Janitors versus Tenants: A Status-Income Dilemma," *American Journal of Sociology,* LVII (March, 1952), 486-93.

12. This effect has been definitely noted in data, not shown here, for female private household workers, about one-fourth of whom "live in."

tinguish between male and female workers, and the indexes had to be computed for total employed persons rather than males. It is clear, nonetheless, that the degree of low-rent concentration is inversely related to the socioeconomic status of the occupation groups. All four of the white-

Table 4—Indexes of Low-Rent Concentration and of Centralization for Major Occupation Groups, Chicago Metropolitan District, 1950

Major Occupation Group*	Index of Low-Rent Concentration (Total Employed Persons)	INDEX OF CENTRALIZATION (EMPLOYED MALES)					
		Metro-politan District	North Shore	North-west	West	South-west	South Shore
					SECTOR		
Professional, technical, and kindred workers	−32	−14	−15	−20	−29	−20	5
Managers, officials, and proprietors, except farm	−30	−12	−20	−16	−19	−15	1
Sales workers	−25	− 5	−15	−12	−12	− 9	8
Clerical and kindred workers	− 9	5	7	2	1	5	9
Craftsmen, foremen, kindred workers	11	− 8	6	− 6	− 7	− 5	−26
Operatives, kindred workers	29	10	21	16	18	8	− 4
Service workers, except private household	7	21	16	18	20	16	36
Laborers, except farm and mine	32	7	9	21	30	16	− 1

* Does not include farmers and farm managers, private household workers, farm laborers, and occupation not reported.

collar occupation groups have negative indexes, signifying relative concentration in high-rent areas, whereas all four of the blue-collar groups have positive indexes. Again, there is a relatively sharp break between the clerical and the other three white-collar groups. The managerial group has a slightly greater index of low-rent concentration than the professional group, despite the higher income level of the former. It is even more striking that the low-rent concentration of craftsmen-foremen is substantially higher than for clerical workers, again the reverse of the relative positions on income. It can be shown that in 1940 the combined clerical and sales group tended to spend a larger proportion of its income for rent than did the group of craftsmen, foremen, and kindred workers. For example, for tenant families with wage and salary incomes between $2,000 and $3,000 in 1939, and without other income, 63 per cent of the families headed by a clerical or sales worker paid $40 per month or more rent, as compared with only 38 per cent of families whose heads were craftsmen, foremen, or kindred workers.[13]

The index of low-rent concentration for service workers, although positive, is low compared to the other blue-collar groups. This exception

13. Data for the Chicago Metropolitan District, 1940, from Table 11, *Families: Income and Rent, Population and Housing, 16th Census of the United States: 1940.*

to the expected pattern no doubt has the same explanation as advanced above; that is, that a substantial proportion of service workers live in comparatively high status areas in connection with their place of employment.

The indexes of centralization of the occupation groups are given in Table 4, both for the Metropolitan District as a whole and within each of the five sectors. According to the Burgess zonal hypothesis, there is an upward gradient in the socioeconomic status of the population as one proceeds from the center to the periphery of the city. Hence one would expect the degree of residential centralization of an occupation group to be inversely related to its socioeconomic status. The data provide general support for this hypothesis, although there are some significant exceptions. Thus, for the Metropolitan District as a whole, three of the four white-collar indexes are negative (indicating relative decentralization), and three of the four blue-collar indexes are positive (indicating relative centralization). The exceptional cases are again the clerical and craftsmen-foremen groups.

In three of the five sectors (Northwest, West, and Southwest), the hypothesized pattern of centralization indexes is perfectly reproduced, except for the inversion between clerical workers and the craftsmen-foremen group, which appears in all sectors. For the North Shore sector the principal deviation from the pattern is the comparatively low degree of centralization of service workers and laborers. In this sector the managerial group is somewhat more decentralized than the professional group, as is also true in the South Shore sector. The latter sector exhibits a quite marked departure from the expected pattern, in that the only decentralized occupations are those in the blue-collar category. There is a small measure of confirmation for the hypothesized pattern, in that within the white-collar category the least centralized groups are the professional and managerial, and within the blue-collar category the most decentralized is the craftsmen-foremen group. The high index for service workers is doubtless due to the relatively high proportion of nonwhites in this occupation, and the relatively central location of the South Side "Black Belt," a large portion of which falls in the South Shore sector. The decentralization of the other blue-collar groups is attributable to the presence of the Indiana industrial suburbs on the periphery of the South Shore sector. A similar effect of some industrial suburbs at the northern end of the North Shore sector is observable in the low centralization index for laborers in that sector. It is apparent that expectations based on the zonal hypothesis must be qualified by recognizing distortions of the zonal pattern produced by peripheral industrial concentrations. Such concentrations appear only in certain sectors, and, where they are absent, the zonal hypothesis leads to a realistic expectation concerning the pattern of residential centralization by socioeconomic status.

RESIDENTIAL SEPARATION AND DISSIMILARITY OF OCCUPATIONAL ORIGINS. There are good reasons for supposing that residential patterns are related to occupational mobility. For example, ecologists have noted a tendency for advances in socioeconomic status to be accompanied by migration toward the city's periphery. Residential segregation is doubtless one of the barriers to upward mobility, in so far as such mobility is affected by the opportunity to observe and imitate the way of life of higher social strata. Among the findings reported above, at least one may have an explanation that involves mobility. It is surprising that the residential patterns of sales workers do not differ more than they do from those of professional and managerial workers; since the income of sales workers is well below that of either, they rank lower in prestige, and their educational attainment is substantially less than that of professional workers. But there are data which suggest that a sizable proportion of sales workers are moving to a higher occupational level, or aspire to such a move, anticipating it by following the residential pattern of the higher group. The Occupational Mobility Survey found that for males employed in both 1940 and 1950 there was a movement of 23 per cent of the men employed as sales workers in 1940 into the group of managers, proprietors, and officials by 1950. This is the largest single interoccupational movement in the mobility table, except that 23 per cent of laborers moved into the group of operatives and kindred workers.[14]

Another aspect of occupational mobility is illuminated by the data in Table 5, which shows indexes of dissimilarity among the major occupation groups with respect to the distribution of each group by major occupation group of the employed male's father.[15] These indexes, therefore, pertain to differences among the major occupation groups in background, origin, or recruitment. The hypothesis to be tested is that, the greater the dissimilarity between a pair of occupation groups in occupational origins, the greater is their dissimilarity in residential distribution.

The pattern of Table 5 is clearly like that of Table 3. The indexes of dissimilarity with respect to residence, computed on the zone-sector segment basis, correlate .91 with the indexes for occupational origin. The correlation is .94 for the residential indexes based on census tracts, with the regression of the tract-based index (t) on the index of dissimilarity in occupational origin (u) being $t = 1.2u - 1.8$. The hypothesis is thereby definitely substantiated.

---

14. Based on unpublished Table W-56 of the Occupational Mobility Survey, taken in six cities in 1951. For description of the sampling and enumeration procedures see Gladys L. Palmer, *Labor Mobility in Six Cities* (New York: Social Science Research Council, 1954), chap. i and Appendix B.

15. These indexes are based on the aggregated results of sample surveys in six cities in 1951. Although separate data are available for Chicago, these were not used here, because the sample was too small to produce reliable frequencies in most of the cells of the 8 × 9 table from which the dissimilarity indexes were computed. (In the intergeneration mobility table the classification of fathers' occupations included the group "farmers and farm managers" as well as the eight major occupation groups listed in Table 5. This was desirable, since a significant proportion of fathers—though very few of the sons in this urban sample—were farmers.)

In Table 5 all but one of the inversions of the pattern expected on the assumption of an unequivocal ranking of the occupation groups involve the sales and service workers. Sales workers are closer to professional workers with respect to occupational background than are the managerial workers and farther from each of the blue-collar groups. Actually, a more consistent pattern would be produced by ranking sales workers second in place of the managerial group. In this respect the data on occupational origins are more consistent with the ecological data than are the data on socioeconomic status in Table I. In terms of the indexes of dissimilarity in occupational origins, service workers are closer to the first three white-collar groups than are any of the other blue-collar groups. However, in comparisons among the clerical and blue-collar groups, service workers clearly rank next to last, or between operatives and laborers. Again, the factor of occupational origins is more closely related to residential separation than are the indicators of socioeconomic status.

Table 5—Indexes of Dissimilarity in Distribution by Father's Occupation Among Major Occupation Groups, for Employed Males in Six Cities in the United States, 1950*

Major Occupation Group†	MAJOR OCCUPATION GROUP†					
	Mgrs., Offs., Props.	Sales Wkrs.	Clerical, Kindred	Crafts-men, Foremen	Opera-tives, Kindred	Service, Incl. Priv. Hshld.	Laborers, exc. Mine
Professional technical, kindred workers	20	16	27	38	39	34	46
Managers, officials, and proprietors, except farm	..	11	28	31	34	30	42
Sales workers	..	..	26	35	37	35	47
Clerical and kindred workers	..	..	..	18	20	28	39
Craftsmen, foremen, kindred workers	..	..	..	..	14	25	31
Operatives, kindred workers	..	..	..	..	..	22	23
Service workers, including private household	..	..	..	..	..	..	20

* Source: Unpublished data from Occupational Mobility Survey, Table W-9. For description of sampling and enumeration procedures see Gladys L. Palmer, *Labor Mobility in Six Cities* (New York: Social Science Research Council, 1954).

† Does not include farmers and farm managers and occupation not reported. A small number of private household workers are included with service workers, and a small number of farm laborers with laborers, except mine.

The last point deserves emphasis. Not only do the indexes of dissimilarity on an area basis have the same general pattern as those on an occupational origin basis but also the deviations from that pattern occur at the same points and in the same direction. This cannot be said regarding the several indicators of socioeconomic status. If income determined residential separation, managers would outrank professionals, and clerical workers would be virtually identical with operatives in their separation from other groups. If education determined residential separation, there would be substantial differences between the indexes for professional workers and managerial workers. Neither of these hypotheses is borne out by the data, whereas differences in occupational background lead to accurate, specific predictions of the pattern of differences in residential distribution.

The ecological analysis has provided strong support for the proposition that spatial distances between occupation groups are closely related to their social distances, measured either in terms of conventional indicators of socioeconomic status or in terms of differences in occupational origins; that the most segregated occupation groups are those at the extremes of the socioeconomic scale; that concentration of residence in low-rent areas is inversely related to socioeconomic status; and that centralization of residence is likewise inversely related to socioeconomic status. These results are in accord with accepted ecological theory, provide support for it, and demonstrate the relevance of ecological research to the theory of social stratification.

These generalizations, however, are perhaps no more significant to the advancement of knowledge than are the instances in which they do not hold and the additional hypotheses advanced to account for the exceptions. Conventional measures of socioeconomic status do not agree perfectly as to the rank order of the major occupation groups, nor do the several ecological indexes. The prime case in point occurs at the middle of the socioeconomic scale, at the conventional juncture of white-collar and blue-collar occupations. Clerical and kindred workers have substantially more education than craftsmen, foremen, and kindred workers, and the clerical occupations are usually considered of greater prestige than the craft and related occupations. However, craftsmen-foremen have considerably higher incomes on the average, and, among males, their nonwhite proportion is smaller. The pattern of the indexes of dissimilarity in residential distribution clearly places the clerical group closer to the other white-collar groups than the craftsmen-foremen are, and the clerical workers' index of low-rent concentration is less than that of the craftsmen and foremen. But in terms of residential centralization the clerical group tends to fall with the lower blue-collar groups, and the craftsmen-foremen group with the other white-collar groups. In general, it would appear that "social status" or prestige is more important in determining the residential association of clerical with other white-collar groups than is income, although the latter sets up a powerful cross-pressure, as evidenced by the comparatively high rent-income ratio of clerical families. To account fully for the failure of clerical workers to be residentially decentralized like the other white-collar groups, one would have to consider work-residence relationships. Data on work-residence separation for a 1951 Chicago sample show that clerical workers resemble craftsmen, foremen, and kindred workers in the degree of separation much more than they do sales, managerial, or professional workers.[16]

16. Beverly Duncan, "Factors in Work-Residence Separation: Wage and Salary Workers, Chicago, 1951" (paper presented at the annual institute of the Society for Social Research, Chicago, June 5, 1953).

Perhaps the most suggestive finding of the study is that dissimilarity in occupational origins is more closely associated with dissimilarity in residential distribution than is any of the usual indicators of socioeconomic status. This result can only be interpreted speculatively. But one may suppose that preferences and aspirations concerning housing and residential patterns are largely formed by childhood and adolescent experiences in a milieu of which the father's occupation is an important aspect.

The discovery that "status disequilibria" are reflected in inconsistencies in the ordering of occupation groups according to their residential patterns provides a further reason for distinguishing "class" from "social status" elements[17] within the complex conventionally designated as "socioeconomic status." Apparently, attempts to compound these two can at best produce a partially ordered scale; at worst, they may obscure significant differences in life-style, consumption patterns, and social mobility.

There is one important qualification of the results reported. Like census tracts, broad occupation groups are not perfectly homogeneous. The managerial group includes proprietors of peanut stands as well as corporation executives, and night-club singers are classified as professional workers along with surgeons. One would, therefore, expect to find a much sharper differentiation of residential patterns if more detailed occupational classifications were available. In particular, the points at which cross-pressures on residential location develop should be more clearly identified.

Further research should seek other forces producing residential segregation. Ethnic categorizations other than race are doubtless relevant though difficult to study directly for lack of data. In general, the patterns described here would be expected to hold for females, but significant deviations might also occur, in part because the residence of married females is probably determined more by their husbands' occupation than by their own, and in part because the occupations that compose each of the major occupation groups are different for females from those for males (as mentioned above in regard to sales workers). Both race and sex would bear upon residential patterns of private household workers, who are predominantly female and nonwhite. A final class of especially important factors is the effect of the location of workplaces on residence. There is evidence that residences are not distributed randomly with respect to places of work. If location of work is controlled, an even sharper differentiation of residential patterns than that described here may be revealed.

---

17. See "Class, Status, Party," in *From Max Weber: Essays in Sociology,* ed. H. H. Gerth and C. W. Mills (New York: Oxford University Press, 1946).

INTRA-URBAN POPULATION MOVEMENT

Beverly Duncan

The modern city with its complex mosaic of specialized areas can function only if there is a rhythmic flow of people and goods from one part of the city to another. This paper is concerned with the patterns of recurring movement within urban areas.

There are a number of perspectives from which these patterns can be viewed. Patterns of intra-urban movement involve technical problems of transporting people and goods: routing, scheduling, parking, traffic flow, and safety devices are among the relevant considerations.[1] The psychological and physical effects of recurring movement on the individual and effects on the family and other institutions are important areas of study.[2] But here patterns of intra-urban movement are considered in relation to the spatial structure and functional organization of cities.

A comprehensive "explanation" of existing patterns of intra-urban movement requires consideration of the growth of urban concentrations and the technological and organizational innovations which permitted and stimulated their growth. This might be termed a developmental approach to understanding contemporary patterns of intra-urban movement. In this paper, a functional rather than a developmental approach is employed. The spatial structure and functional organization of the differentiated city are, so to speak, taken for granted; then, propositions about intra-urban movement which have been at least partially documented empirically are "explained" in terms of the structure and organization of the city.

PATTERNS OF LAND USE. Different activities are not evenly distributed over an urban area. Rather there is evidence of concentric zonation, i.e., similar or functionally related activities located at the same distance from the center of the city, and localization, i.e., similar or functionally related activities clustered in space, irrespective of distance from the center. A multiplicity of factors produce and reinforce these tendencies toward concentric zonation and localization; only two of the more important factors, the transportation network and land values, will be considered here.

Published for the first time in this volume.

1. See, for example, Robert B. Mitchell and Chester Rapkin, *Urban Traffic: A Function of Land Use* (New York: Columbia University Press, 1954).

2. For a classic study, see Kate K. Liepmann, *The Journey to Work: Its Significance for Industrial and Community Life* (New York: Oxford University Press, 1944).

Because communication and movement among community units are essential to the functioning of an urban area, sites of high accessibility are sought by these units. Generally, the most accessible sites are those at the core of the urban area, for the transportation network, particularly the intra-urban system, tends to converge at the center of the city. Because competition is keenest for accessible sites, their land values or prices are usually higher than those of relatively inaccessible sites. Consequently, land values are at a maximum in the center of the city; they grade downward in all directions, but more slowly along radial transportation lines than in the interstitial areas.

Activities for which the net gain or profit through accessibility is greatest, usually consumption-oriented activities, cluster at the core of the city, driving out production-oriented and residential activities for which centrality is less profitable. Specialized commercial and service facilities whose markets encompass the entire urban area find centrality relatively more profitable than do the less specialized commercial and service facilities whose markets are restricted to local neighborhoods. The former tend to locate in the central area at the focal point of the intra-urban transit system, whereas the latter tend to locate on less valuable sites adjacent to radials of the transportation network. Industry must locate along inter-urban or inter-regional transit routes which provide means of transport for its raw materials and products; in the case of heavy industry, these routes are generally railways or waterways.

Although ready access to workplaces and to commercial and service facilities is desirable, high site costs and proximity to offensive nonresidential uses discourage the location of residence in areas of high accessibility. Where residential use does occur in areas of high accessibility, it must be intensive to compensate for higher site costs—e.g., multi-unit structures crowded on the land rather than single-family dwellings with large lots.

These very general statements are not to be construed as describing with precision the locational patterns of a particular urban area; nor is it denied that cities vary in the degree to which they manifest these general patterns of urban structure. Cogent statements on the theory of location of community units are provided by Hawley[3] and Hoover,[4] whose works have been drawn upon heavily for the preceding discussion.

A concrete example of the tendency toward concentric zonation is illustrated in Figure 1; more detailed data on patterns of land utilization in successive distance zones from the center of the city of Chicago are summarized in Table I. Perhaps the most striking finding is the large proportion of area devoted to transport uses—at the center of the city

3. Amos H. Hawley, *Human Ecology: A Theory of Community Structure* (New York: Ronald Press, 1950).

4. Edgar M. Hoover, *The Location of Economic Activity* (New York: McGraw-Hill, 1948).

nearly half the area comprises streets and alleys, railroads, and waterways, and even at a distance seven to nine miles from the center nearly a
third of the area is devoted to transport uses. This underscores the importance of communication and movement to the functioning of the urban
area.

Residential uses become more prevalent and nonresidential uses more
infrequent in successive distance zones from the city's center. In the central area, over a fourth of the land is in business uses, one-sixth in public
and institutional uses, and only 2 per cent of the land is in residential
use. At a distance seven to nine miles from the center, less than a tenth
of the land is in business uses, a tenth is in public and institutional uses,
and one-third of the land is devoted to residential use. Furthermore, intensity of residential use varies inversely with distance from the city's
center. In successive distance zones, a decreasing proportion of the land
in residential use is devoted to multi-unit structures and an increasing
proportion is devoted to single-family dwellings.

Concentric zonation does not necessarily imply an absence of variation
in land utilization among segments comprising a given zone. Localization
of particular activities occurs within zones, but this is not inconsistent
with the tendency toward concentric zonation.

For example, Table 2 indicates that substantial variation among segments within zones obtains with respect to the proportion of land in
residential use. At a distance one to three miles from the center of Chi-

Table 1—Land Utilization in Successive Concentric Zones from the Center of Chicago: 1939

Type of Land Use	DISTANCE FROM CENTER				
	Within 1 mile	1-3 miles	3-5 miles	5-7 miles	7-9 miles
	Per Cent of Total Area				
All land uses	100.0	100.0	100.0	100.0	100.0
Transport use	48.6	39.8	35.2	34.5	31.8
Streets and alleys	26.5	28.9	26.5	25.8	27.2
Railroads	17.2	9.1	7.7	8.2	4.3
Waterways	4.9	1.8	1.0	0.5	0.3
Business use	27.9	20.9	18.4	13.8	7.2
Industrial	10.4	11.2	11.4	7.8	2.8
Commercial	10.7	4.2	3.1	3.1	2.7
Mixed	4.8	4.8	3.5	2.6	1.5
Temporary	2.0	0.7	0.4	0.3	0.2
Public and institutional use	16.0	9.9	10.5	10.2	10.4
Residential use	2.3	21.3	28.4	32.3	32.7
1-family, detached	0.4	3.6	6.0	10.8	18.3
Other 1, and 2 family	0.4	6.9	10.9	12.2	8.0
3 and 4 family	0.3	5.3	5.3	3.6	2.1
5 families or more	1.2	5.5	6.2	5.7	4.3
Vacant	5.2	8.1	7.5	9.2	17.9

Source: Basic data on land utilization by square mile obtained from *Land Use in Chicago*, Vol. II of the
report of the Chicago Land Use Survey, directed by the Chicago Plan Commission and conducted by the Works
Progress Administration (Chicago: City of Chicago, 1943).

cago, 27 per cent of the land in the North Shore sector is in residential use as compared with 6 per cent of the land in the South Shore sector. But within each sector, there is some tendency for the proportion of land in residential use to increase with distance from the city's center.

Table 2—Percentage of Land in Residential Use, for Selected Zone-Sector Segments in Chicago: 1939

			DIRECTION FROM CENTER			
Distance from Center	All	North Shore	Northwest	West	Southwest	South Shore
All	30.1	32.0	33.9	24.6	28.8	31.5
1-3 miles	21.3	27.4	24.1	21.9	17.8	6.1
3-5 miles	28.4	33.8	34.4	24.3	15.3	36.0
5-7 miles	32.3	36.8	35.1	28.9	28.7	32.1
7-9 miles	32.7	28.0	35.9	20.2	36.6	37.0

Source: Basic data from Land Use in Chicago, Vol. II.

With unpublished data compiled by the Urban Analysis Project of the Chicago Community Inventory, University of Chicago, 1951-53, it is possible to specify the locational patterns of particular types of industrial and commercial use in Chicago.

Manufacturing activities in Chicago are highly localized both with respect to residences and land area. A crude but convenient way to show this localization is to compute for each industry group the proportion of work-places in the five square miles with the greatest concentration of that industry. (The five square miles constitute roughly 2 per cent of the city's land area.) This indicator of concentration registers 20 to 39 per cent for fabricated metals, nonelectrical machinery, chemicals, lumber, and furniture, 40 to 59 per cent for bakeries, confections, beverages, printing, paper, textiles, instruments, primary metals, electrical machinery, and stone, clay, and glass, 60 to 79 per cent for rubber, leather, apparel, transportation equipment, and motor vehicles, and 80 to 99 per cent for meat, tobacco, petroleum products, and blast furnaces.

Only two manufacturing industry groups tend to cluster in the inner zones of Chicago. These industries, apparel and related products and printing and publishing, make intensive use of land. The ratio of workers to occupancy was ten per 1,000 square feet for the apparel industry and seven per 1,000 square feet for the printing industry, as compared with two per 1,000 square feet for all manufacturing industries in Chicago. The nature of the products, the production process, and the market orientation of these industries suggest that centrality is relatively more profitable for the apparel and printing industries than for manufacturing industries in general.

Analysis of the locational patterns of retail outlets in Chicago as of 1935 shows that the most highly centralized and localized of the 31 kind-of-business groups were department stores and specialized clothing stores, and such other specialized types of outlets as restaurants, cigar stores, jewelry stores, second-hand stores, furniture stores, household appliance stores, and florists. On the other hand, grocery stores, meat markets, and filling stations were distributed throughout the city in the same way that residences were distributed. The specialized outlets, concentrated at the core of the urban area, deal in goods which are purchased only occasionally and consumed over an extended period of time; the widely dispersed outlets deal in convenience goods, purchased frequently and consumed quickly.

In the previous discussion of patterns of residential use, it was noted that multi-unit structures predominate in areas of high accessibility, whereas single-family dwellings are more frequent in areas of lesser accessibility. Another indicator of the more intense residential use in areas of high accessibility is monthly rent per acre in residential use. Rent per dwelling unit increases with distance from the city's center, but rent per acre in residential use decreases with distance from the city's center. In general, then, rent per dwelling unit is directly related to distance from the center and inversely related to land value and accessibility; rent per net residential acre is inversely related to distance from the center and directly related to land value and accessibility. The crowding of units on the land in residential use more than compensates for the lower rentals per dwelling unit in the inner zones. For example, in 1940, at distances four to six miles from the center of Chicago, the mean rent per dwelling unit was $31 and the mean rent per net residential acre was over $500; at distances eight to ten miles from the center, the mean rent per dwelling unit was $46 but the mean rent per net residential acre was slightly under $400.

Low rental units tend to concentrate toward the center of the urban area and high rental units to concentrate toward the periphery. There is also evidence that low rental units are concentrated in or toward manufacturing areas irrespective of zonal distance, whereas high rental dwellings are concentrated away from industrial areas. The rent-paying capacity of households is, of course, a function of income, which in turn is related to occupation and education. Consequently, households of lower socio-economic level are concentrated toward the center of the urban area and in or toward manufacturing areas irrespective of zonal distance.

In summary, the commercial-industrial complex of the urban area is substantially localized with respect to residential areas. Commercial and industrial activities are concentrated in areas of high accessibility—virtually monopolizing the core of the urban area and sharing with intensive residential use the sites adjacent to radial transportation lines. Hence, there is a significant daily movement of population between residential areas and the areas in which industrial and commercial activities are carried on.

DISTRIBUTION OF POPULATION. Distributional patterns of residences, or of resident population, are frequently described in terms of variation in population density among areas of the city. Gross population density (persons per unit of gross land area) is very low in the core of the urban area, which is essentially a nonresidential area, rises to a peak in areas adjacent to the core, and then grades downward with increasing distance from the center. The general effect might be described as a volcano with a deep crater.

As an example, in 1950, gross population density in Chicago was 11,400 persons per square mile at the city's center; the density rose to 31,900 at a distance two or three miles from the center, then decreased to 26,500 at distances four to six miles from the center and 12,500 at distances eight to ten miles from the city's center.

Net population density (persons per unit of land in residential use) is, of course, markedly higher than gross population density for areas in which a substantial proportion of the land is devoted to nonresidential uses. But on the basis of analyses for Philadelphia reported by Blumenfeld,[5] it appears that net population density is somewhat lower in the urban core than in the areas immediately adjacent to the center.

The preceding comments apply to the distribution of residences or the residential population. During the daytime, the population in the urban area congregates in the industrial, commercial, and service areas of the city. Daytime population density is highest at the core of the urban area, from which density grades downward rapidly. Within the outlying area, concentrations of population occur at the points where commercial, service, or industrial establishments are clustered.

The influx of population into nonresidential areas during the daytime hours can be readily illustrated. In 1950, only 11,000 employed workers were residing in the central area of Chicago, i.e., within one mile of the center; but not less than 275,000 workplaces were located in the central area. The influx of workers alone produces a net population increase of well over 250,000 during the day. As an isolated example of the daily influx of population to outlying nonresidential areas, consider a half-square-mile area in Chicago, located about four miles southwest of the city's center. In 1950, seventeen persons resided in the area, eight of whom were employed. But 11,200 workplaces in manufacturing industries—10,250 in the meat industry—were located in this area.

The discussion up to this point has been concerned with the distribution in space of the daytime and nighttime, or residential, population, and their patterns of concentration. During the day, people are brought together from their relatively dispersed residences to certain focal points in the urban area where activities essential to the functioning of the city are carried on. Another aspect is the temporal sequence of the concentration and dispersion of daytime population.

The pattern of population accumulation in the central area of Chi-

---

5. Hans Blumenfeld, "On the Concentric-Circle Theory of Urban Growth," *Land Economics*, 25 (May, 1949), pp. 209-12.

cago has been examined by Breese.[6] The peak hour for movement into the central area is 8:30 a.m.; but the maximum accumulation of population at the urban core occurs about 2:00 in the afternoon. Between 7:00 and 9:00 in the morning, the net population gain in the central area (persons entering the area less persons leaving the area) is slightly over 200,000; between 9:00 a.m. and 2:00 p.m., the net gain is slightly over 100,000. Hence, at the peak hour of 2:00 p.m., the population in the central area is some 300,000 greater than at 7:00 in the morning. The rapid net increase between 7:00 and 9:00 is produced by the influx of workers (approximately three-fourths of the workers in the central area begin work between 8:30 and 9:00 a.m.); probably most of the net gain between 9:00 and 2:00 is accounted for by persons entering the central area to use the commercial and service facilities located there. Throughout the remainder of the day, a net loss of population occurs at the urban core. The peak hour for movement from the central area is 5:30 p.m., roughly the end of the working day; and by 6:00 in the afternoon, the population in the central area is only 100,000 greater than at 7:00 in the morning. Although substantial numbers of people enter the central area during the early evening hours, probably attracted by the recreational facilities located there, the absolute size of the central area's population continues to decrease, reaching a low around 4:00 a.m.

It is evident that the distribution of population over the urban area is constantly changing. The "residential" and "daytime" distributions are but two of many distributions which might be observed in the course of a twenty-four-hour period. Further, it seems unlikely that the "residential" distribution could be observed; even during the predawn hours, city residents are absent from their dwellings—for example, maintenance workers, telephone and telegraph operators, employees of the transit system—carrying on activities essential to the functioning of the urban area.

DAILY MOVEMENT OF POPULATION. The vast majority of an urban population is involved in daily movement. An examination of population composition by functional class quickly indicates that this must be the case. Residents of the Chicago urbanized area numbered 4,921,000 in 1950. The 2,143,000 employed workers comprised 44 per cent of the resident population; virtually all workers are involved in daily movement, for workplace and residence are infrequently located in the same structure. The 875,000 persons enrolled in school comprised 18 per cent of the residents; during the academic year, most students travel between place of residence and the educational institution in which they are enrolled. Persons keeping house numbered 1,017,000 and comprised one-fifth of the resident population; each day a substantial proportion of

6. Gerald W. Breese, *The Daytime Population of the Central Business District of Chicago* (Chicago: University of Chicago Press, 1949). See especially Chapter V, "Size of the Daytime Population of the Central Business District," including Tables 18, 26, and 27.

these persons travel between their residences and clusters of commercial and service establishments.

Without doubt, the most important single component of daily population movement is that between residence and workplace. Foley reports that the journey to work accounted for about two-fifths of all daily trips from home for the population in six medium-sized United States cities in the late 1940's.[7] Some propositions about work-residence relationships are discussed below.

In the metropolitan United States in 1954, 18.7 per cent of the workers living in outlying counties traveled to the core county of the metropolitan area for work; 15.7 per cent of the workers residing in the New York metropolitan ring traveled to New York City for work.[8] In 1949, 12.9 per cent of the workers residing in outlying metropolitan counties commuted to the central county of the Chicago metropolitan area for work.[9] Of course, crossing a county line on the journey to work does not necessarily mean travelling a long distance; but there is reason to suspect that a substantial proportion of workers travel rather long distances between residence and workplace. In 1942, 13.0 per cent of the industrial workers in Massachusetts traveled ten miles or more to work;[10] in 1951, 7.6 per cent of the wage and salary workers residing in the City of Chicago traveled ten miles or more to work.[11]

Differences in distance traveled, travel time, or means of transport among component groups of the employed labor force have been observed. Here only differences among socio-economic strata of the labor force and differences between persons working in the central area and other workers are examined.

It appears that distance traveled and means of transport vary with the socio-economic status of the worker, but that average travel time is relatively constant. The length of the journey to work is directly related to the socio-economic status of the worker; the frequency of automobile transportation increases as the socio-economic status of the area in which the worker resides increases, whereas the frequency of walking and public transportation decreases; but, on the average, travel time is about the same for all workers irrespective of the status of the area in which they reside. Relevant data are summarized in Table 3.

By using more rapid and flexible transport means, high-status workers can travel considerably longer distances to work than can low-status work-

7. Donald L. Foley, hectographed tables distributed at annual meeting of Population Association of America, Cincinnati, Ohio, Spring, 1953.

8. U. S. Bureau of the Census, Current Population Reports, Population Characteristics, Series P-20, No. 60, August, 1955.

9. Computed from tabulations of 1949 Chicago Sample Census, Chicago Community Inventory, University of Chicago.

10. J. Douglas Carroll, Jr., "Some Aspects of the Home-Work Relationships of Industrial Workers," Land Economics, 25 (November, 1949), pp. 413-22.

11. Data compiled by the Urban Analysis Project, Chicago Community Inventory, University of Chicago, 1951-53.

Table 3—Selected Data on Means of Transport, Travel Time, and Travel Distance for Wage Earners by Socio-Economic Status

		SOCIO-ECONOMIC STATUS	
Characteristic and Area	All Wage Earners	Highest Status	Lowest Status
Cleveland, 1940*			
Per cent walking to work	10	2	20
Per cent using automobile	47	80	24
Per cent using public transportation	42	18	54
Median travel time (in minutes)	29	32	30
Chicago, 1951†			
Mean linear distance between home and workplace (in miles)	4.7	6.9	4.0

* From J. Douglas Carroll, Jr., Home-Work Relationships of Industrial Employees (Ph.D. dissertation, Harvard University, January, 1950), Table 35, p. 110. Highest status group reside in census tracts with median rental of $45 or more; lowest status group reside in census tracts with median rent of $10-14.

† From Beverly Duncan, "Factors in Work-Residence Separation: Wage and Salary Workers, Chicago, 1951," American Sociological Review (February, 1956). Highest status group are professional workers; lowest status group are laborers.

ers with the same expenditure of travel time. In general, it is neither practicable nor desirable for workers to spend over an hour in reaching their workplace destinations. For persons who must walk to work, the distance between workplace and residence is, then, limited to perhaps three miles; for persons with automobiles, the distance between workplace and residence can be perhaps twenty or even forty miles.

Remuneration, of course, varies directly with socio-economic status; if a fixed proportion of the worker's income is allocated to transportation costs of the work-residence journey, the absolute amount expended by the high-status worker is nearly twice that expended by the low-status worker (median 1949 income was $4,387 for professionals, $4,831 for managerial workers, but only $2,580 for laborers in the Chicago metropolitan area). Consequently, low-status workers are relatively more dependent on inexpensive means of transport than are high-status workers. And the least expensive means of transport are infrequently the most rapid and flexible means.

Rent-paying capacity also varies directly with income. The low-income worker is limited to a rather restricted range of residential rentals; the high-income worker can select from a much wider range of residential rentals. And it has been noted that low rental units tend to be concentrated toward the center of the city and in or toward industrial concentrations in the outlying area, whereas high rental units tend to be concentrated toward the periphery of the city and away from outlying industrial concentrations.

Areas of low rental tend to correspond with areas which permit the worker to travel to his workplace inexpensively. If the worker lives in a low rental area adjacent to the industrial concentration in which his workplace is located, he can walk to work; if he lives in the low rental inner zones of the city, he has ready access to the intra-urban public transit system. Both factors—transport costs and residential rentals—are important determinants of residential location; by residing in areas near the workplace, the worker tends to minimize the combined cost.

The high-status worker, with a larger income, is not under so great a compulsion to minimize transportation and housing costs. Deteriorated housing, congested living conditions, and proximity to offensive nonresidential land uses deter the high-status worker from residing in the low rental areas.

The separation of workplace and residence is greater for persons working in the central area of the city than for other workers; documentary data are summarized in Table 4. Both socio-economic status and work-

Table 4—Average Linear Distance Between Residence and Workplace for Workers in Manufacturing, by Workplace Location and Occupational Level, for Chicago

Occupational Level	WHITES RESIDING IN CITY, 1951*		Employees of Suburban Steel Plant 1950†
	Working in Central Area	Working Elsewhere	
All workers	6.6 mi.	4.0	4.1
White-collar workers	7.3	5.1	5.1
Manual workers	5.7	3.8	4.0

* Beverly Duncan, op. cit.
† Helene M. Conant, The Locational Influence of Place of Work on Place of Residence (M.A. thesis, University of Chicago, 1952), Table 29, p. 118.

place centralization are directly related to the degree of work-residence separation; further, high socio-economic status and workplace centralization operate independently as well as jointly to increase work-residence separation, i.e., the greatest work-residence separation is observed for central area workers engaged in high-status occupations.

But there is little reason to suspect that travel time is greater for persons working in the central area than for persons working in outlying areas. Rapid transit lines and expressways, with their feeders, are oriented toward the urban core; hence, cross-city movement is considerably less rapid than radical movement.

Residences of workers in outlying industrial, commercial, and service establishments are, then, more highly concentrated around the work area than are the residences of central area workers around the urban core. Relevant data are summarized in Table 5. The zonal distribution of the residences of central area workers from the center of the city is similar to the zonal distribution of all residences from the center of the city. The central area workers are highly localized by place of work, but they are residentially dispersed. Some reasons for this pattern of work-residence relationship among central area workers can be tentatively suggested. The nonresidential character of the urban core implies that central area workers cannot reside in proximity to the work area, because of a deficit of available dwellings. The intra-urban transport orientation permits a wider dispersion of the residences of central area workers than of other workers, assuming a fixed travel time. The heterogeneity of the central area working force in terms of socio-economic status suggests that these workers will locate in a wide variety of residential areas, for workers generally reside in areas compatible with their socio-economic status.

Table 5—Zonal Distributions of Resident Population from the City Center and of Selected Groups of Workers from the Workplace for Chicago

| Zonal Distance | Resident Population of City, 1950 | RESIDENTS OF CITY, 1951* | | Employees of Suburban Steel Plant, 1950† |
		Working in Central Area	Working Elsewhere	
All persons	100.0	100.0	100.0	100.0
Within 1 mile	0.7	1.1	18.6	31.7
1-1.9 miles	4.4	3.2	13.1	15.2
2-2.9 miles	8.1	4.6	12.3	5.5
3-3.9 miles	10.5	8.6	11.1	6.2
4-4.9 miles	12.7	11.6	10.1	8.9
5 miles or more	63.6	70.9	34.8	32.5

* From Bevery Duncan, op. cit.
† From Helene M. Conant, op. cit., Table 15, p. 64.

On the other hand, workers in outlying areas tend to concentrate their residences about the work area. One-third of the Chicago residents working outside the central area resided within two miles of the workplace; nearly one-half of the employees of a suburban Chicago steel plant resided within two miles of the workplace. It follows, of course, that in the areas adjacent to their workplace, these off-center workers comprise a disproportionate share of the resident population; and that these workers as a proportion of resident population decrease with distance from their workplace.

This sketches briefly some of the more important propositions about work-residence relationships which have been at least partially documented. Difficulty in procuring data suitable for analyses of work-residence relationships has hampered research workers in their attempts to systematically study the patterns of recurring movement within urban areas. The collection and processing of data on workplace and residence are formidable tasks; but the recent attempt of the Bureau of the Census to secure information on place of work and place of residence, although only on a county basis, is encouraging. Until more adequate data sources are available, knowledge of the patterns and determinants of work-residence relationships will remain fragmentary.

SUMMARY. The land use patterns, patterns of population distribution, and patterns of intra-urban population movement outlined in this paper are by no means universal. But in the absence of systematic, comparative studies, it is virtually impossible to specify their generality or to identify with precision the factors which permit and/or encourage their emergence.

The size and heterogeneity of the urban aggregate, the diversity and scale of economic activities, and the means of transport undoubtedly condition the internal organization of urban areas. The patterns sketched in this paper are descriptive of the contemporary United States city; with some modification, they probably describe the internal organization of contemporary cities in other highly industrialized areas of the world.

The commercial-industrial complex of the city is substantially localized with respect to residential areas. Commercial and industrial activities are concentrated in areas of high accessibility—virtually monopolizing the core of the urban area and sharing with intensive residential use the sites adjacent to radial transportation lines. Less intensive residential uses predominate in the areas of lesser accessibility. As a consequence, there is a significant daily movement of population between residential areas and the areas in which industrial and commercial activities are carried on.

During the day, people are brought together from their relatively dispersed residences to certain focal points in the city where activities essential for its functioning are carried on. Hence, the daytime distribution of population over the urban area differs markedly from the nighttime or residential distribution; in fact, the distribution of population over the urban area is constantly changing through a twenty-four-hour period.

The vast majority of an urban population is involved in daily movement. The most important single component of this movement is that between workplace and residence—accounting for roughly two-fifths of all such movement. The physical separation of residence and workplace varies directly with the socio-economic status of the worker; but, by having access to more rapid and flexible transport means, high-status workers apparently expend no greater time in traveling to work than do low-status workers. The residences of central area workers are more dispersed with respect to the urban core than are the residences of other workers with respect to their work areas. And socio-economic status and workplace centralization operate jointly as well as independently to produce high work-residence separation.

It is true, of course, that large numbers of workers travel long distances on the journey to work; and there is also evidence that, on the average, distance traveled on the journey to work has been increasing.[12] But it is also true that perhaps one-third to one-half of the working force, exclusive of central area workers, reside within two miles of their workplace.

The literature on intra-urban population movements has been increasing; and a number of recent studies have considered the patterns of movement in relation to ecological, socio-economic, or demographic variables.[13] At present, the static aspects of the ecological organization of the

---

12. Beverly Duncan, "Factors in Work-Residence Separation: Wage and Salary Workers, Chicago, 1951," *American Sociological Review*, (February, 1956).

13. As examples, see the following: J. Douglas Carroll, Jr., *op. cit.*; Donald L. Foley, "Urban Daytime Population: A Field for Demographic-Ecological Analysis," *Social*

city have been more fully examined than have the dynamic aspects. But improving data-collection methods and analytical techniques should facilitate more adequate study of the patterns of recurring movement within urban areas.

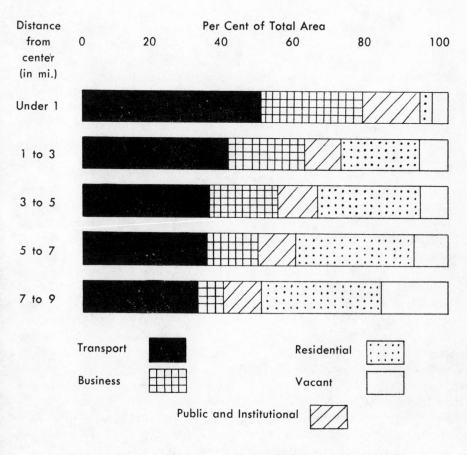

FIG. 1—Major Types of Land Use by Distance from the Center of Chicago: 1939

Forces, 32 (May, 1954), pp. 323-30; Leo F. Schnore, "The Separation of Home and Work: A Problem for Human Ecology," *Social Forces,* 32 (May, 1954).

5

THE DEMOGRAPHIC STRUCTURE
AND VITAL PROCESSES

When the relationship between the functional aspects of a locality and its inhabitants is examined, two broad types of connection emerge. First, the way of life characteristic of a given locality has definite consequences for the nature of its basic demographic processes. Thus, there are different levels of birth rates and death rates, and varied patterns of migration associated with functionally different populations. Second, the consequence of these differential processes is the appearance of typical demographic structures, that is, distinctive combinations of such population characteristics as age, sex, different marital statuses, ethnic or racial backgrounds, etc. These, in turn, by the nature of their differences contribute to the quality of life in the community which they characterize. Thus, demographic processes and structure must be thought of both as independent variables influencing major patterns of community life, and as dependent variables influenced in turn by other aspects of community life.

The division between rural and urban communities is one such broad functional classification. The interdependence between the two extends into the demographic area, and is reflected in complementary patterns of vital rates, migration and population composition. Thus, at present in the United States, fertility is generally lower and mortality is apparently somewhat higher in urban than in rural areas. Migration, however, more than equalizes these differentials re-

sulting in a relative growth of the urban population and a relative decline in the rural population. The effect of a community's structure on its demographic composition also is seen when the demographic composition of communities which vary in size is compared. Duncan shows in Section 1, for example, that the proportion of married women increases from a low point of 61.4 per cent in urbanized areas of 3,000,000 or more inhabitants to a high of 73.7 per cent in rural farm areas when allowance is made for variations in age distribution. Similarly, Duncan finds a gradient pattern in the fertility ratio, defined as the number of children under the age of 5 per 100 married women aged 14 to 44. The rural farm fertility ratio is nearly 50 per cent greater than that of the largest communities. Finally, there likewise is considerable variation in the demographic composition of subcommunities of the larger communities, as the paper by Newcomb in this section demonstrates.

The population in an area may grow, remain stationary, or decline, depending upon the relationship between the births, deaths and net migration of an area. The population increases in size whenever births exceed deaths or in-migration exceeds out-migration, provided that the excess of births over deaths, or of net in-migration, is not exceeded by loss in the other. It declines in size when the reverse conditions prevail—deaths exceed births or out-migration exceeds in-migration provided that the excess of deaths over births or of net out-migration is not exceeded by gain in the other. The population remains stationary in the area when there are enough persons gained from births and/or in-migration to balance losses by deaths and/or out-migration.

In general, it can be stated that rural population growth is typically secured through the excess of births over deaths, while urban growth depends heavily upon migration. The fertility of all segments of the urban population is not equally low, however, nor do all rural groups produce a substantial excess of births. The variation in fertility is particularly striking among urban occupational groups, as the data in the paper by Notestein and Sallume affirm. Whereas cities usually have lower age-specific fertility rates than rural areas, their natural increase tends to be maintained by a favorable age distribution—concentration in the young adult years—produced by rural-urban migration. Rural-urban differences in mortality vary somewhat by cause of death, as illustrated in Wiehl's paper in this section. Though precise data are lacking, it seems probable that rural-urban mortality differentials changed greatly in human history, for the early industrial cities had extremely high morbidity and mortality rates before the advent of modern sanitary facilities and public health measures. There is reason to believe, however, that the city's advantage in having a larger complement of specialized medical personnel and health facilities continues to be offset to some degree by urban environmental factors unfavorable to survival.

Demographic processes and structure substantially influence other organizational elements of cities. The effect of occupational differentials in fertility on the structure and processes of urban societies, for example, are many. A particularly important one is that upward social mobility in the society is facilitated by the generally lower fertility of the upper-status occupational groups in the society. Upward social mobility in cities also is facilitated by the general failure of urban populations to replace themselves, as the research findings by Lipset in the next section make clear.

The structure and process of organizational elements of cities correlatively shape the vital processes which go on in cities. Wiehl, for example, shows in her paper that the death rates from preventable mortality are generally higher in rural than in urban communities. These differences are largely caused by the fact that cities have more effective medical and health programs and practices which reduce the mortality from communicable diseases. The research paper by Keyfitz provides an excellent example of the effect of urban phenomena on the vital process of fertility. It reduces to demonstration the hypothesis that family size patterns are diffused from the city to the hinterland. Family size on French-Canadian farms near cities, when all other accessible variables are controlled, is smaller than on French farms far from cities.

Human populations are heterogeneous aggregates partly owing to their vital processes. They vary according to a large number of characteristics such as age and sex, marital status and family size, race and nativity, labor force, occupation, income and education, religion, etc. The composition of a human population is a description of these differences within the population. Communities are known to vary considerably in demographic composition. A major factor in producing differences in composition is the factor of *natural increase*, or an excess of births over deaths. Natural increase causes demographic differences among communities in two ways: as a result of differences in the rate of natural increase, and by change in the rate of change of size of the population. Two communities differ, as already noted, when there are substantial differences in their birth or death rates, or in both. One, for example, may have relatively more children in the younger age groups relative to the older age groups than the other. This age difference between two communities could even reflect itself in a difference in the ratio of morticians to pediatricians. Two communities also will differ, at least temporarily, when one has a change in the rate of change of size. If the birth rate in one community changes, for example, the two communities will probably show differences in age composition, although initially it would be apparent only in the infant age group.

The demographic composition of two communities likewise differs because of differential effects of the *process of settlement*. The predominant group in the settlement of an area or a community usually is young males. Women and children generally follow the men in the settlement of a community, although seldom in sufficient numbers to establish a normal sex ratio immediately. The data in Chart IV of Newcomb's paper show differences in the age and sex structure of areas of settlement of first, second and third generation immigrants to Chicago. The racial and ethnic composition of cities in the United States evidences considerable variation as the result of the territorial pattern of settlement. Southern cities obviously are more likely to have substantial Negro populations as a consequence of the settlement process than are cities of the West. The ethnic composition of a community as a result of the settlement process may substantially affect the demographic composition of the community in other respects, such as the religious preference of the population.

Migration also exerts a major influence on the composition of a population. The effect of migration is most apparent on the young adult group, since this age group makes up a majority of migrants to almost all cities. Young women predominate over young men in cityward migrations, particularly up to age 30. Freedman presents in this section a description of the migrant as compared with the nonmigrant population of Chicago, showing that in several respects the migrant tends to have the characteristics of the ideal-typical urbanite. It is difficult to separate the effects of natural increase on the demographic composition of the population from the effects of migration by merely observing the difference in the composition of two populations, since they can produce nearly identical effects. Data on the source of the difference therefore is necessary to isolate their separate effects.

Functional specialization of communities similarly produces some differences in the demographic composition of communities. Economic specialization exerts a marked effect on the demographic composition of the total community whenever the specialization accounts for a substantial proportion of the economic base in a community. The very low sex ratio (the number of males per 100 females) in Washington, D. C., for example, is a consequence of its specialization in government, since government work requires a substantial female clerical labor force. By way of contrast, extractive communities, such as mining and lumbering communities, usually have very high sex ratios. The research paper by Reiss in Section 7 provides data on differences in the demographic composition of communities as a consequence of their differences in functional specialization.

The structure of the community has a striking effect on the composition of the labor force, and changes in structure bring changes in labor force composition. Durand describes and analyzes changes in the labor force in the United States. The increase in the ratio of labor force to population, the movement of women into the labor market and of young children out of it, the trend to earlier withdrawal from the labor force, and the decrease in the length of man's working life at the same time that the average age of the labor force is rising, all are presented in the context of a rapidly changing urbanized society.

Emphasis has been placed upon the fact that not all cities are alike in their population composition, their type of selectivity, and the operation of the vital processes. These differences depend upon many factors such as the location and relative size of the community, its relation to a hinterland, its labor force opportunities as determined by the economic base and age of the community, and the institutional structure of the community. Generalizations about rural-urban demographic differentials are somewhat meaningless unless accompanied by some analysis of the variations in patterns—which papers in this and other sections of the Reader try to provide.

Cities not only have a special demographic character, but areas within cities also differ in their demographic composition and the operation of the vital processes, as some of the data in the preceding section manifest. The last two papers in this section present a description of the variation in demographic composition and the operation of vital processes within communities.

Historically, urban communities in the United States have been more heterogeneous from the standpoint of national origins than rural ones. This greater heterogeneity is dependent in part on the fact that migration is a major source of urban growth. Migration to American cities has in the past depended upon both foreign and domestic sources, though the former has been of relatively little importance for the past three decades. The city depends, then, upon a diversity of sources of population and is selective in its recruitment of types of persons. The migrant population not only is different from the nonmigrant population, however, but migrants differ somewhat according to their place of destination in the city. The paper by Freedman in this section presents data for Chicago which attest to differences among migrants according to their place of destination.

There is considerable variation in the demographic composition of areas within the city, including variation in their age and sex composition, the family and work status of inhabitants, and the density of settlement. The age and sex composition of a population often is presented by means of a graphic device known as the population pyramid. The paper by Newcomb portrays area variation in the age and sex distribution of selected areas in Chicago by using the population pyramid.

THE FERTILITY OF SPECIFIC OCCUPATION GROUPS IN AN URBAN POPULATION

Frank W. Notestein and Xarifa Sallume

One phase of the studies on population problems being made by the Milbank Memorial Fund is concerned with a fact of basic importance to any intelligent effort to control the social and biologic character of the people as well as to the planning of future programs of public health. This is the size of the family in different social classes and in urban and rural areas. Since the size of the family depends largely upon the birth rate, this phase of the Fund's inquiries has been concerned primarily with the fertility of women. So far it has shown, probably more accurately than ever before in the United States, that wide differences in fertility in broad social classes have existed for a long time and that the trends of fertility in these classes have been by no means the same.

It has been clearly indicated by our studies that various social factors are involved in these differences, but our knowledge of their causal relationships is much less satisfactory than our description of the differences themselves. It is inherent in the rather nebulous conception of "social class" that the classes, taken as wholes, differ from one another in income, character of employment, interests, standards of living, education, and achievement, and possibly in physical and intellectual capacities. Any or all of these attributes, whether environmental or genetic in origin, may be related directly or indirectly to the fertility of the classes, but by studying the classes as units we observe only the gross resultant of their complex influences and remain entirely ignorant of the part played by any single attribute.

It is the purpose of the present study to examine the data relating to the fertility of urban women whose husbands followed specific occupations, with the hope that such an examination, in addition to indicating the source of the differences in the fertility of the broad social classes, will, because it deals with relatively clear-cut divisions of the social classes, give some indication of the relation which the distinguishing attributes of the groups may have to their fertility. Little more than suggestive results may be expected, but such results may point the way to further investigation of the influence of specific determinative factors.[1]

Reprinted from *The Milbank Memorial Fund Quarterly*, Vol. 10 (April 1932), pp. 120-30, by permission of the authors and the publisher. (Copyright 1932, by the Milbank Memorial Fund.)

1. A number of European investigations of the subject have yielded results roughly

The data employed are those obtained by a special tabulation of samples of the 1910 census returns relating to the total number of children ever born to each married woman, the length of the marriage, and the husband's occupation. Neither the women nor their husbands had been married more than once, and both the husbands and wives were of native-white parentage. The data represent a random sample of this group as found in the thirty-three northern cities with populations of between 100,000 and 500,-000 in 1910.[2]

Since the specific occupations are represented in the sample by a relatively small number of cases, it is desirable to use an index of fertility which will not be disturbed by a few chance early or late marriages. The index employed in previous analyses of the same data, i.e., the number of children ever born to women of specific age groups, has accordingly been replaced by the number of children ever born to women under 50 years of age per 1,000 years of married life.[3] This rate holds the length of "exposure to risk" of childbirth constant, but, in its crude form, it does not insure an equality of exposure. Since the early years of married life are more fertile than the later, a group of women would have a higher ratio of births to married years when thirty than when forty years of age. Therefore, the fertility of occupational groups can be compared only when the age distributions of the wives are not widely dissimilar. This condition is approximated by the standardized rates used in this study. These rates were obtained by computing the number of children ever born per 1,000 years of married life for each of three age groups: under 30, 30 to 39, and 40 to 49, and using an average of these rates weighted by the proportion of women of the total sample found in each age group. The resulting rates are those which would have been characteristic of each occupation had the wives in each occupational group been distributed by age groups in the same manner as those of the entire sample. It should be observed that variation in age at marriage can have little influence on such rates.[4]

These birth rates, the number of cases on which they are based, and

---

similar to those of this study, but the populations considered and the data secured are so different that no direct comparisons have been attempted. Two of the more important of these studies are: *Fertility of Marriage: Census of England and Wales, 1911*, xiii, Part II. J. Sanders, M.D.: *The Declining Birth Rate in Rotterdam* (The Hague: Martinus Nijhoff, 1931).

2. For detailed description of the data and the methods by which they were obtained, see Edgar Sydenstricker, and Frank W. Notestein, "Differential Fertility According to Social Class," *Journal of the American Statistical Association*, March, 1930, xxv, New Series, No. 169, pp. 9-32.

3. In the earlier studies, age 45 was arbitrarily selected as the end of the childbearing period. In this study, the limit has been set at 50 in order to simplify the mechanics of tabulation.

4. It is possible that the adjusted ratio of births to married years reduces the index for early marrying groups somewhat too much. It carries the implicit assumption that the fertility of a given year of married life is independent of that of the preceding years. Doubtless this is not strictly the case. It seems likely that women who married early and had their families well under way might in the succeeding years be less fertile than equally fecund women of the same age whose married life had only begun.

approximations to their standard errors, are presented in the accompanying table for the occupational groups represented in our sample by more than 200 cases.[5] The occupations are shown in order of ascending birth rates within their respective social classes, but the standard errors indicate that in most cases significance cannot be attached to the details of this ranking. The business and skilled-worker classes of the previous studies have been subdivided into proprietors and clerks, and skilled workers and semiskilled workers, respectively. The professional and unskilled-labor classes remain unchanged.

The birth rates for the constituent groups of each social class had such a wide range of variation that there were no clear-cut differences between the classes. When the more extreme cases are disregarded, however, it appears that the majority of the rates fall into three fairly distinct groups, the lowest comprising largely those for the white-collar classes, the middle those for the skilled-worker classes, and the highest those for the unskilled laborers. The similarity of the rates for the professional class and those for the two business classes was in part due, as has been shown in an earlier study, to the fact that our present index is unaffected by the relatively late marriages of professional people.[6] The clerks and semi-skilled workers constituted respectively the low-income groups of the white-collar and skilled-worker classes, but their birth rates were not characteristically higher.

When we come to consider specific occupational groups, it is possible only to speculate as to the reasons for the variation in the birth rates. If groups with similar characteristics have similar birth rates, inferences may be drawn, but such inferences must be in the nature of provisional hypotheses, which can be tested only by more precisely controlled investigations. The reader must also bear in mind the nature of our basic data. They were collected in 1910 and give the total number of children born prior to that date to married women then under 50 years of age. The occupations re-

---

5. The writers are indebted to Professor Lowell J. Reed of Johns Hopkins University, for suggesting the following approximation to the standard error of our rates:

$$\sigma = \frac{\sqrt{(\sigma_1 w_1)^2 + (\sigma_2 w_2)^2 + (\sigma_3 w_3)^2}}{w_1 + w_2 + w_3}$$

where σ_1, σ_2, and σ_3 are the standard errors of the ratios of births to married years for each component age group, and w_1, w_2, and w_3 are the per cent. of women in the whole study who were in each age group. Since the number of births for any one age group was small compared with the number of married years, σ_1, σ_2, and σ_3 were computed by the formula $\sigma = \sqrt{\dfrac{pq}{n}}$ where p equals the number of births per married year, and $q = 1 - p$. The validity of this method of approximating the standard errors of the adjusted rates was tested by drawing twelve random samples of 200 cases each from the 1,944 carpenters' wives, computing the adjusted ratios for each sample, and comparing the standard deviation of their scatter with their standard errors obtained by means of the above formulas. The standard deviation of the rates computed for the samples was 10.5 ± 2.1, and the standard errors of the rates computed by the formulas range from 9.6 to 10.8.

6. Frank W. Notestein, "Social Classes and the Birth Rate," *Survey Graphic*, April, 1931, xix, No. 1, pp. 38 ff.

TABLE I—Children Born to Women Under 50 Years of Age Per 1,000 Years of Married Life, for Specific Occupational Groups of a Native-White Urban Population

Social Class and Occupation	Number of Wives Under 50 Years of Age	Births Per 1,000 Years of Married Life (Adjusted) [1]	Standard Error
Professions			
Dentists	556	124	6
Physicians, surgeons, and osteopaths	1,514	137	4
Accountants and auditors	335	145	7
Architects, artists, sculptors, and teachers of art	373	152	8
College presidents and professors	318	162	10
Engineers (civil, electrical, mechanical, and mining)	1,169	164	4
Authors, editors, and reporters	293	169	9
Lawyers, judges, and justices	1,855	173	4
Teachers, school and athletics	516	175	8
Clergymen	553	175	9
Proprietors			
Hotel, restaurant, cafe, lunch room, and saloon keepers	330	124	7
Druggists and pharmacists	295	125	8
Importers and exporters	336	140	9
Stockbrokers, other brokers, money lenders, promoters, et cetera	472	148	7
Retail dealers (except grocers, druggists, and pharmacists)	1,706	151	4
Insurance agents	550	153	6
Manufacturers	684	157	6
Bankers and bank officials	234	158	15
Grocers	476	158	7
Officials of manufacturing	255	161	9
Managers and superintendents of manufacturing	681	162	6
Real estate agents and officials	1,072	164	6
Conductors (steam railroad)	342	167	7
Builders and building contractors	875	190	9
Clerks and Kindred Workers			
Commercial travelers	1,437	140	4
Salesmen and clerks in stores	2,995	149	2
Bookkeepers and cashiers	1,279	152	4
Agents, canvassers, and collectors	621	157	5
Agents and clerks in railroad employ	423	157	7
Other clerks	2,022	157	3
Shipping clerks	254	171	9
Draftsmen	397	179	8
Skilled Workers			
Barbers and hairdressers	439	133	6
Machinists and loomfixers	1,445	169	4
Foremen and overseers	450	170	6
Engineers (stationary)	550	175	6
Policemen	220	175	9
Electricians	565	176	6
Compositors, linotypers, and typesetters	455	176	6
Locomotive engineers and motormen (steam railroad)	436	176	7
Painters, glaziers, and varnishers (building)	675	185	6
Plumbers, and gas and steam fitters	390	188	7
Carpenters	1,944	193	3
Brick and stone masons	216	202	10
Blacksmiths, forgemen, and hammermen	258	210	9
Moulders, founders, and casters	263	228	8

1. Adjusted by applying the specific rates for women under 30, 30 to 40, and 40 to 50 years of age, to the age distribution of the wives in the entire sample.

TABLE I—Children Born to Women Under 50 Years of Age Per 1,000 Years of Married Life, for Specific Occupational Groups of a Native-White Urban Population—Continued

Social Class and Occupation	Number of Wives Under 50 Years of Age	Births Per 1,000 Years of Married Life (Adjusted) [1]	Standard Error
Semiskilled Workers			
Waiters and bartenders	304	128	7
Brakemen	308	166	7
Switchmen, flagmen, and yardmen	236	175	8
Motormen (street railroad)	480	177	6
Conductors (street railroad)	571	180	5
Semiskilled operatives in metal industries	461	180	6
Semiskilled operatives in other factories and shops	1,488	191	3
Unskilled Laborers			
Deliverymen	497	203	6
Laborers (n.o.s.) [2] in other industries (except building and metal)	254	212	8
Draymen, teamsters, expressmen, and carriage and hack drivers	885	218	5
Laborers (building, general, and not specified)	654	225	5
Laborers in metal working industries	245	228	9

2. Not otherwise specified.

ported for the husbands were those followed at the time of the census. Their characteristics and requirements differed in some cases from those of the same occupations now. Moreover the occupations reported in 1910, especially in the case of the older groups, were not necessarily those followed by the husbands during the most fertile years of married life. Similarly, the families considered were living in the larger cities when enumerated, but we have no way of knowing the length of their residence in those cities. Since the period under consideration was one of heavy migration from country to city, many of the families observed must have moved to the city after at least some of their children were born.

In the professional class the birth rates for dentists and physicians were conspicuously low, and those for lawyers, teachers, and clergymen were high. It is possibly significant that the least fertile occupational groups were also the groups likely to be most familiar with contraceptive techniques. The high birth rates for lawyers and school teachers are particularly striking. In the period under consideration, the education of both groups was substantially less expensive than that of physicians, but not less expensive than that of dentists. School teachers could begin earning at least a regular salary as soon as their training was completed, and lawyers were in a position to supplement their professional fees by a variety of business activities. Probably both the dentists and physicians had greater difficulty in securing a regular income in the early years of their practice. Nevertheless, in view of the similarity of their standards of living, of their positions and obligations in the community, and, presumably, of their social backgrounds, it is somewhat surprising to find physicians and dentists among the least fertile groups considered, and lawyers and school teachers, together with clergymen, among the most fertile occupations of the white-collar classes.

The traditional clergyman's family leads one to expect a high birth rate for the group. It would doubtless have been higher in relation to the other professions and lower in relation to the remaining occupations, if the influence of difference in marriage age had not been eliminated. The relatively high fertility of clergymen is often ascribed to their hesitancy to practice contraception and to their sense of the obligation to "be fruitful." Conceivably a different factor is involved. Many clergymen begin both their professional and married life in the country or small town where large families are relatively common, and only receive a call to the city after their families are well on the way toward completion. It is possible, therefore, that in observing city clergymen, we are observing an unusually large proportion of rural or semirural families which moved to the city too late to be influenced by an urban environment. Much the same thing may have occurred in the case of school teachers. If the migration in these two groups was larger than that in other occupations of the class, their birth rates were not surprisingly high, especially when contrasted with that for lawyers.

The proprietary class had two occupational groups with conspicuously low birth rates. One of these, the druggists, whose birth rate was significantly lower than those for the other retail merchants, like the dentists and physicians of the professional class, probably had more than a lay knowledge of contraception. They also had long and irregular working hours and, doubtless, an interrupted home life. This later characteristic was also common to the other low-birth-rate group of the class, comprising hotel, restaurant, cafe, lunch room, and saloon keepers.

There is no evidence that the higher-income groups of the proprietary class were characteristically either more or less fertile than those with lower incomes. The rates for brokers and bankers, for example, were not significantly different from those for insurance agents and retail dealers (except grocers and druggists), and the rates for manufacturers, officials of manufacturing, and managers of manufacturing were not significantly different from those for grocers and real estate agents. The rate for railroad conductors was the second highest in the class, although it was not significantly different from that of most of the other proprietary occupations. Interestingly enough, it was virtually the same as that for brakemen, from whom conductors are promoted, and was not significantly different from those for locomotive engineers, and flagmen, switchmen, and yardmen in the skilled and semiskilled classes. An even more striking example of the relation of early occupation to fertility is found in the birth rate for builders and building contractors. The rate was significantly higher than that for any group in the proprietary class, and was not significantly different from those of any of the artisan builders for whom data are presented. The explanation is, of course, simple enough. Most of the contractors began as artisans. It appears that neither their "success" nor the factors inherent in it served to affect the fertility of the group.

Two of the clerical groups have almost the same fertility as higher income groups of the proprietary class which had similar working environments and were in the same line of advancement. The birth rate for salesmen and clerks in stores was virtually identical with that for the largest group of retail dealers, and the rate for "other clerks" was not significantly different from rates for bankers, manufacturers, and officials and managers of manufacturing. Commercial travelers appear to have been somewhat less fertile than retail dealers, but this may well reflect the interrupted home life of a conspicuously mobile group. Only two groups of the class, shipping clerks and draftsmen, had relatively high rates. The former was not definitely a white-collar occupation, and the rates for both groups were based on a relatively small number of cases.

Barbers and hairdressers, and the building and heavy metal trades were respectively the least and the most fertile groups of the skilled-worker class. The birth rate for barbers was not significantly different from those for druggists, keepers of hotels, restaurants, et cetera, and commercial travelers; and like these rates, may reflect the influence of long and irregular working hours on the home life of the group. The barber's occupation is definitely skilled, but like other domestic and personal service groups, his working environment is in many respects that of the white-collar classes. The fact that their occupation brings them in daily contact with members of the white-collar classes, whose conspicuous consumption they have a vested interest in maintaining, perhaps influences their own social and economic standards and indirectly their fertility. The rates for artisan builders (and building contractors) are equalled or exceeded only by those for semiskilled operatives in factories and shops; unskilled laborers; blacksmiths, forgemen, and hammermen; and moulders, founders, and casters of metal. It is perhaps suggestive that these groups were without exception engaged in occupations requiring unusual physical exertion.

Waiters and bartenders of the semiskilled class, like barbers, are neither a strictly manual-worker nor white-collar group. Their birth rate further illustrates the characteristically low fertility of persons engaged in domestic and personal service. It was not significantly different either from the rate for barbers or from that of the higher income group, to which they may hope to advance, comprising keepers of hotels, restaurants, et cetera.

The birth rates for the steam and street railroad trainmen were neither significantly different from each other nor from those of a number of other skilled and semiskilled workers. They were somewhat lower than those for the building trades, but were not different from those for machinists. Like the relatively infertile domestic and personal service groups, their home life must have been interfered with by their working hours, but unlike those groups they were not, as a whole, thrown into close personal contact with the white-collar classes.

Only a few occupational groups of the unskilled-laborer class were represented by enough cases to warrant the presentation of birth rates. These few were, without exception, more fertile than the majority of skilled or semiskilled workers. As in the case of the skilled workers, the rates for the building and heavy metal workers were the highest in the class.

This inquiry into the fertility of fairly homogeneous occupational groups of the native-white population of northern cities leads to a number of tentative generalizations, which, though far from conclusive, should point the way to more precisely controlled investigations.

The wide range of variation in the birth rates for the occupational groups of each broad class indicates that factors other than social-economic status affect fertility.

When the more extreme cases are disregarded, however, it appears that, even apart from the influence of differences in marriage age, there was an inverse association between fertility and the social status of the white-collar, skilled-worker, and the unskilled-laborer classes, as usually ranked.

Persons in different income groups but in the same line of occupational advancement had similar birth rates. The validity of this inference will be difficult to test until we have data relating to the entire occupational history of the husband.

There is no evidence that persons of higher economic status had characteristically different birth rates from those of the lower economic status in the same social classes.

The infertility of the three groups which were probably the best informed regarding contraceptive techniques suggests the influence of birth control.

An interrupted home life may have accounted, in part, for the infertility of certain occupational groups. Perhaps it was the principal cause of the low birth rates for commercial travelers, but the similarity of the rates for railroad trainmen and those for certain other skilled workers suggests that some additional factor was involved in the marked infertility of the domestic and personal service groups.

High fertility appears to have been characteristic of persons whose occupations required unusual physical exertion.

A FACTORIAL ARRANGEMENT
OF COMPARISONS OF FAMILY SIZE

Nathan Keyfitz

Whether families are smaller near cities than farther from them has been investigated by a number of writers,[1] and clear-cut differences have generally appeared. There has not, however, been any conclusive finding as to whether the differences can be attributed to the better-known differentials of occupation, income, etc. These latter cannot be simultaneously removed from interarea comparisons, because in general the published census tables on which studies depend are limited in the breakdowns they can show. The present investigation of farm families in the Province of Quebec does not use published census materials but, instead, works with a sample of 1,056 families extracted from original census schedules; there is no difficulty with so small a number in making by hand the cross-tabulation necessary for controlling extraneous variation. The 1941 census of Canada asked the number of children born to each mother, as well as a rather full set of other demographic facts. Within a random sample, tests of statistical significance are available for finding the probability that results are due to sampling error.

MEASURE OF DISTANCE FROM CITIES. Prior to the drawing and hand tabulation of the sample, it was necessary to classify all the counties of Quebec according to distance from a city. There are many ways of allocating areas to the categories of "near cities" and "far from cities." As among the various reasonable methods, we should like to choose one which cannot involve conscious or unconscious reference to the fertility rates of the several counties; we require, that is, an objective criterion in the form of a numerical index.

Such an index plainly should take account of distance (d) of a county from the several cities and also of the sizes (p) of the cities. A combina-

Reprinted from *The American Journal of Sociology*, Vol. 58 (March, 1953), pp. 470-479, by permission of the author and *The American Journal of Sociology*, and the University of Chicago Press. (Copyright, 1953, by the University of Chicago).

1. P. G. Beck, *Recent Trends in the Rural Population of Ohio* (Bull. 533 [Wooster, Ohio: Agricultural Experiment Station, May, 1934]); E. de S. Brunner and J. H. Kolb, *Rural Social Trends* (New York: McGraw-Hill Book Co., 1933), p. 114; P. K. Whelpton, "Geographic and Economic Differentials in Fertility," *Annals of the Academy of Political and Social Science*, CLXXXVIII (November, 1936), 48-50; T. Lynn Smith, *Population Analysis* (New York: McGraw-Hill Book Co., Inc., 1948), p. 230; K. A. Edin and E. P. Hutchinson, *Studies in Differential Fertility in Sweden* (London: P. S. King & Son, 1935).

tion of the form $\Sigma(p^m/d^n)$ adds contributions for the several cities, each contribution being directly proportional to p^m, a (positive) power of the population, and inversely proportional to d^n, a power of the distance. If two cities are close together, one would wish to have the formula for the distance of a county from them give the same result as would be given if they coalesced into a single city of their combined population; this requires that $m = 1$. We might put $n = 1$ also; but, on the intuition that the influence of a city of given distance is more than twice as great as that of a city twice as far away, n was put equal to 2. Cities over 200 miles away from a county are taken as having no effect on it.

The sample was confined to the Province of Quebec. By measurement on a map the distance from the center of each of the cities over 30,000 population in (or near) the province (Montreal, Quebec, Hull-Ottawa, Three Rivers, Sherbrooke) was found for the nearest point of each county; the 1941 census population of the city was divided by the square of the distance of the county from it, and the five such quotients for each county added to make an index of closeness to cities for that county.

CONTRASTS ARRANGED. The investigation was confined to 16 counties, chosen to show maximum contrast in respect to distance from cities. In-

Table 1—Counties Contrasting in Distance from Cities, in Each of Two Income Classes

$195-$290 Average Net Income per Farm Family Worker	$305-$335 Average Net Income per Farm Family Worker	$195-$290 Average Net Income per Farm Family Worker	$305-$335 Average Net Income per Farm Family Worker
Distant from Cities		Near Cities	
Gaspé E.	Chicoutimi	Chambly	Champlain
Gaspé W.	Lac St. Jean E.	Deux Montagnes	Levis
Madeleine Is.	Saguenay	Laprairie	Papineau
Matane		L'Assomption	
Matapedia		Napierville	

come could not be controlled for individual families, since farm income is recorded in the Canadian census on a schedule filed separately from the population schedule, and the two cannot be matched without a great amount of effort; selection of counties was accordingly in income strata. While it was hoped to avoid altogether the matching of areas in this research, yet we can take consolation from the fact that income was the only one of the 15 or so variables that had to be dealt with thus. The two sets of contrasts (strata) that were arranged were (a) one in which the average annual income per farm family worker lay between $195 and $290, and (b) one in which the average was between $300 and $350. Table 1 shows the counties which came into the study.

The choice of these particular counties resulted from the rule that, within the lower-income group, the five lowest and five highest counties on the weighted inverse square measure of distance from cities are drawn;

in the higher-income group are three highest and three lowest. They are in no sense a sample of the Province of Quebec but are rather to be regarded as the complete set of those that show the extreme of contrast within the two income classes; no consideration of a population of counties of which they are samples will enter the subsequent discussion.

Examination of the map of Quebec shows that in the lower-income group the five near counties are all clustered about Montreal, while the five distant ones are along the south shore of the St. Lawrence River and in the gulf. In the higher-income group the three near counties are close to Three Rivers, Quebec city, and Hull, and the distant ones are along the north shore of the St. Lawrence River.

In order to get a sufficient contrast of distance, it was necessary to make the income range rather broad for the low incomes; however, it turned out that the unweighted average of incomes per head in the distant places was $253 and in the near places $252; we may therefore consider that whatever benefit can be secured by the equalizing of the farm incomes of the counties has been secured.

Within the counties an effectively random sample—all those found in one-fifth of the enumeration areas—of all families meeting the qualifications described below was selected. Though the sample was actually every fifth area taken systematically for convenience, there seemed little reason to fear that its departure from randomness would make the usual tests of significance inapplicable.

The conditions of selection of the individual families controlled extraneous factors far more effectively than is possible in published tabulations. The following conditions were imposed: (a) husband and wife both French-speaking and of French origin; (b) husband and wife both of Roman Catholic religion; (c) husband and wife both born on farm and now (1941) living on farm; (d) husband the operator of the farm on which the family lives; and (e) wife between forty-five and seventy-four years of age in 1941, and married at fifteen to twenty-four years of age. Confining the survey to this group excludes widows, French Protestants, and other combinations which, though not numerous, may confuse the results. At the cost of restricting the scope of the investigation, we secure figures whose interpretation will be clear-cut.

Further census information was used to sharpen comparisons without restricting the scope of the survey. The group of families selected were classified according as they showed: (1) net farm income per farm worker in the county low ($195-$290) or high ($300-$350), as mentioned above; (2) 1941 age of wife forty-five to fifty-four years or fifty-five to seventy-four years; (3) age of wife at marriage fifteen to nineteen or twenty to twenty-four; (4) schooling of wife less than seven years or seven or more; thus permitting control of these variables, and the use of the data as well to find the differentials of fertility they represented, if these were significantly revealed in the size of sample used. The families were classified as living in subdistricts which were (5) purely French or mixed, according as they contained fewer than 5 English families or 5 or more, and in counties (6) near or far from cities of 30,000 and over population, as mentioned above.

Because of the vastly simpler calculation needed to extract the information from a table involving only two classes for each variable and also because the problem was conceived essentially as one of finding out whether or not there was an effect due to cities, presence of English, etc., rather than how much effect, two values only of each of the independent variables are recognized.

The design used has been called "factorial" by Professor R. A. Fisher,[2] to whom its theory and early application are due. He points out that it is not a requirement of experimentation that all variables be held constant except the one under investigation; all that is needed is that the effect of the one under investigation be orthogonal to the other effects. This means that each other factor may be included at several levels; the experiment will give, as a by-product, comparisons of these other factors, as well as their interactions. One advantage of this, as against holding other variables constant by confining the experiment to a single set of control conditions, is that the result has wider scope.

EXPERIMENTAL DESIGN IN DEMOGRAPHIC RESEARCH. Though the presentation of data is borrowed from the subject known as experimental design, yet an essential component of the logic of experimental design does not apply. Because residence close to and far from the city can hardly be allocated at random, the theory of probability cannot provide assurance that possible personal variables which might contribute to the differentials have been equally distributed (subject to sampling error only) as among the families close to cities and those far from cities, and hence causation cannot be rigorously inferred. Thus Dr. Yates comments on a survey of fertilizer practice subject to the same difficulty:

We may for instance find that fields receiving fertilizers give higher yields than fields without fertilizers. Yet we cannot attribute the observed differences solely to differences in fertilizers. The farmers using the fertilizers may be farming better land, they may be growing higher-yielding varieties, and they may be carrying out their farming operations with greater skill. . . .

In order to determine with certainty the magnitude in the casual sense of the effect of any given factors experiments must be undertaken. Surveys cannot be regarded as satisfactory substitutes for experiments. Nevertheless they are of value in situations in which experiments are difficult or impossible, though in such cases all conclusions must be tentative.[3]

The logical defect which would apply if the entire population were surveyed applies also to data which have been secured on a sample.

METHOD OF EXTRACTING AND ASSESSING SAMPLE INFORMATION. The first

---

2. R. A. Fisher, *Design of Experiments* (Edinburgh: Oliver & Boyd, 1935).
3. F. Yates, *Sampling Methods for Censuses and Surveys* (London: Charles Griffin & Co., 1948), p. 131.

comparison suggested by the form of the data is between simple average numbers of children. Thus the total number of families living near cities is 496, and the number of children in those families is 4,500, an average of 9.1 children. The corresponding average for the 560 families living far from cities is 10.7 children. The comparison of these averages, however, suffers from the disadvantage that the two groups contain different proportions of well-off and poor, etc.—i.e., they are not orthogonal to the remaining five variables. If such non-orthogonal comparison sufficed, the other variables need not have been tabulated.

A simple way of making the comparison between average sizes in near and distant places in such a way that it is independent of the other variables is to use average numbers of children in the several cells and combine these without weights. There are 32 averages in the various classes in the sample near cities and 32 far from cities (Table 2). The unweighted average of the 32 average numbers of children near cities is 9.5 and of far 10.8, a difference of 1.3 children in favor of far.

This difference of 1.3 children is more suited to answering the main question here and is, in fact, the best answer that can be secured if interactions are large. If interactions are small, as will later be shown to be the case, it is subject to unnecessarily large sampling error, for the cells containing only two or three families have as big a weight as those in which forty families are averaged.

Faced with unequal numbers, we might have rejected observations and, by bringing the cells to equality, made the standard analysis of variance applicable, or else fitted constants by solving a set of simultaneous equations. Luckily, neither the loss of information of the first method nor the great amount of calculation of the second is necessary in the dichotomous case.

The fact is that with only two distances from cities—near and far—under fixed conditions of the other variables, all the information on the effect on fertility of distance from cities is given by the difference between the average number of children in near and far places. Thus for the "block" consisting of women 45-54 years of age in 1941, married at 15-19 years, with 0-6 years of schooling, in French enumeration areas (those in which there are fewer than 5 English families), in low-income counties, the average number of children far from cities is 9.4 and near cities 7.4 (Table 2). The excess for far from cities is 2.0 children, and this is all the information on the subject furnished by the 15 + 5 families of this portion of the sample. If there had been three degrees of distance from cities—say near, middle, and far—it would not have been possible to extract the whole of the information on the effect of distance from each block separately.

A rather considerable number of combinations is involved even in fairly small factorial designs; with two levels of each of n variables, 2^n cells are obtained; in the present instance $n = 6$. A comparison of any two of our 64 cells (Table 2) may be very simply made, but there are not likely to be enough cases for significant results to appear. Thus in the block referred to above in which the average number of children far from cities for 15 families is 9.4 and the average near cities for 5 families is 7.4, we find in the usual way that

$$t = \frac{9.4 - 7.4}{\sqrt{(414.8/[15 + 5 - 2])(1/15 + 1/5)}} = 0.81,$$

414.8 being the pooled sum of squares within the two groups. (Data: far from cities 1, 2, 4, 5, 7, 9, 9, 10, 10, 12, 13, 13, 14, 16, 16 children; near cities 3, 4, 5, 11, 14 children.) An equal or greater difference would arise by chance in almost 1 case out of 2. The information from a number of such "blocks" must be combined to get significant results.

The question, then, is how to weight the 32 differences, such as the 2.0 above, derived from Table 2. The amount of information which is contributed by each difference is exactly that which would be given for an average, in material which varies as our individual families do within

Table 2—Result of Hand Compilation of 1,056 Families from Census Schedules, Showing for Each Cell Average Number of Children Ever Born and Number of Families on Which Average is Based

PRESENT AGE			45-54				55-74	
AGE AT MARRIAGE	15-19		20-24		15-19		20-24	
YEARS OF SCHOOLING	0-6	7+	0-6	7+	0-6	7+	0-6	7+
Average Number of Children								
Low income, French area:								
Far from city	9.4	10.7	10.3	9.8	10.1	14.5	10.4	9.8
Near city	7.4	12.9	8.3	6.7	10.0	11.0	7.6	8.6
Low income, mixed area:								
Far from city	12.9	10.9	8.9	9.8	8.3	12.8	8.4	9.6
Near city	9.7	11.3	9.4	7.1	9.0	9.9	8.6	8.6
High income, French area:								
Far from city	10.9	12.9	10.6	9.8	12.1	12.5	9.0	11.3
Near city	8.3	8.7	7.1	10.3	10.8	13.2	10.9	9.9
High income, mixed area:								
Far from city	12.8	14.3	9.4	11.2	10.6	12.0	9.9	9.0
Near city	10.5	12.2	7.6	8.8	11.0	11.0	8.6	8.4
Number of Families								
Low income, French area:								
Far from city	15	14	35	20	18	6	34	12
Near city	5	8	10	37	9	8	15	22
Low income, mixed area:								
Far from city	14	11	15	21	16	9	16	17
Near city	3	7	14	49	12	8	17	29
High income, French area:								
Far from city	35	29	24	29	31	15	22	27
Near city	6	15	7	28	14	18	14	30
High income, mixed area:								
Far from city	9	10	14	13	14	2	9	4
Near city	15	6	25	12	14	3	26	10

cells, of $n_1 n_2 / (n_1 + n_2)$ cases. For example, the above difference of 2.0 children, which arises from comparisons of 5 and 15 cases, may be thought of as a random variable wtih variance $\sigma^2(1/5 + 1/15)$, where σ^2 is the variance in number of children among individual families; this is the same variance as a mean of

$$\frac{1}{1/5 + 1/15} = \frac{(15)(5)}{15 + 5} = 3.75$$

individual families would be subject to.

In general, if we have averages for numbers of children born in families far from cities, $\overline{X}_{1i}$ (where i ranges over the 32 ways of holding the 5 other variables constant), and corresponding averages for families near cities, $\overline{X}_{2i}$, the unit comparison is $\overline{X}_{1i} - \overline{X}_{2i}$. Being based on n_{1i} and n_{2i} observations, it contains a quantity of information proportional to

$$\frac{n_{1i} n_{2i}}{n_{1i} + n_{2i}} = N_i, \text{ say,}$$

and the efficient combination[4] of all such differences is

$$\frac{\Sigma N_i (\overline{X}_{1i} - \overline{X}_{2i})}{\Sigma N_i}. \tag{1}$$

The error with which this may be compared is easily found. If the within-cell variance is σ^2, then the variance of $\overline{X}_{1i} - \overline{X}2_{2i}$ is

$$\sigma^2 \left(\frac{1}{n_{1i}} + \frac{1}{n_{2i}} \right) = \frac{\sigma^2}{N_i},$$

and the variance of (1) is

$$\frac{\Sigma N_i^2 \sigma^2 / N_i}{(\Sigma N_i)^2},$$

which reduces to

$$\frac{\sigma^2}{\Sigma N_i}. \tag{2}$$

Table 2, along with the fact that the within-cell sum of squares is 18,006, sums up the hand count; it includes all the data needed for the calculation of the six main effects and their errors. For example, the estimated difference between the numbers of children in families far from and near cities is:

$$\frac{3.75(9.4 - 7.4) + 5.09(10.7 - 12.9) + \ldots}{3.75 \quad + \quad 5.90 \quad + \ldots} = \frac{300}{234} = 1.28.$$

Table 3 shows the six main effects calculated in this way. The number of

---

4. This and other theory used in this paper are all implicit in F. Yates, "Analysis of Multiple Classifications with Unequal Numbers in the Different Classes," *Journal of the American Statistical Association*, XXIX (1934), 51.

observations is 1,056, and hence degrees of freedom for error are 1,056 — 64 = 992; the estimated within-cell variance is 18,006/992 = 18.15. From

Table 3—Estimates of Fertility Difference for Six Contrasts, and Their Significance

Contrast	Weighted Average of 32 Differences in Average Children Born = Estimated Number of Children Associated with Contrast (1)	Equivalent Number of Observations = N (2)	Estimated Standard Error of Col. 1 $\sqrt{18.15/N}$ (3)	$t =$ Col. 1/ Col. 3 (4)
Far minus near	1.28	234	0.278	4.6†
French minus mixed enumeration areas	0.15	229	.282	0.5
Law minus high income	−0.90	237	.277	−3.2†
Present age 55-74 minus 45-54	0.38	253	.268	1.4
Age at marriage 15-19 minus 20-24	1.77	231	.280	6.3†
Schooling 0-6 minus 7 and over	−0.72	232	0.280	−2.6*

* Significant at 5 per cent level.
† Significant at 1 per cent level.

(2) we need only divide this by the equivalent number of observations, which is

$$\frac{(5)(15)}{5+15} + \frac{(8)(14)}{8+14} \cdots = 3.75 + 5.09 + \cdots = 234$$

in the case of far minus near; and the result is the variance of the weighted average difference. Table 3 shows three of the effects as highly significant (probability less than 0.01) and one as significant (probability less than 0.05).

The fact that in the sample far places average 1.28 more children than near and that the probability that this difference is due to the particular sample selected is about one in a hundred thousand is the main result of this research. No significant effect attaches to French versus mixed enumeration areas.

The error of 0.278 is applicable only if interactions are negligible. Were this point in doubt, we would have to compare unweighted means, as mentioned above. The unweighted means may be represented as $\Sigma \overline{X}_i/32$ and their variances are easily seen to be

$$\frac{\sigma^2}{32^2} \sum \frac{1}{n_i}, \tag{3}$$

where σ^2 is the variance of family numbers within classes and n_i is the number of families in the ith cell. The variance of a difference is equal to the sum of the variances of the two components, and hence is also represented by (3) if the summation is considered to be taken over all 64 cells. Thus the error of the difference of 1.3 is 0.33, again with 992 degrees of freedom.

Because of the danger that the selection of solid areas or other causes may invalidate the within-class error as calculated here, we are interested in an alternative expression for error. Consider the 32 blocks, each of which gives a difference between the average size of family in near and distant parts and is matched on the other 5 variables. The calculation of the weighted mean difference due to distance has removed 1 degree of freedom; the consistency with which the several blocks resemble their average in respect of excess of children for distant places furnishes 31 degrees of freedom for the error of the weighted mean.

Consider that in each of the 32 pairs of cells there are N_i cases

$$\left(\text{where } N_i = \frac{n_{i1}n_{i2}}{n_{i1} + n_{i2}} \right)$$

and a difference of means equal to $\bar{x}_i$. This is as though we had N_1, $N_2, \ldots, N_{32}$ observations, giving means $\bar{x}_1, \bar{x}_2, \ldots, \bar{x}_{32}$, respectively, of a new variable x which has the same variance as family size, σ^2. We note that t with 31 degrees of freedom for difference due to distance from cities is,[5] as shown in equation (4),

$$\frac{\Sigma N_i \bar{x}_i}{\sqrt{\dfrac{\Sigma N_i(\bar{x}_i)^2 - [(\Sigma N_i \bar{x}_i)^2/\Sigma N_i]}{(k-1)\Sigma N_i}}} \tag{4}$$

$$= \frac{1.28}{\sqrt{\dfrac{3.75(9.4 - 7.4)^2 + 5.10(10.7 - 12.9)^2 + \ldots - 300^2/234}{(31)(234)}}} = 4.4,$$

which is still significant, and for French versus mixed enumeration areas is again 0.5.

An alternative arrangement of the calculation is in the analysis of variance; using the within-class error for distance from cities,

$$F = \frac{385.24}{18.15}$$

5. Based on considerations such as the following: If we knew the true mean μ, then each x_i would furnish an estimate $N_i(x_i - \mu)^2$ of σ^2, the common variance of the hypothetical x_i whose averages $\bar{X}_{i1} - \bar{X}_{i2}$ are given. Each of these estimates is of the same variance, and if they are k in number, then their unweighted average

$$\frac{\Sigma N_i(\bar{x}_i - \mu)^2}{k}$$

estimates σ^2. The variance of

$$\frac{\Sigma N_i \bar{x}_i}{\Sigma N_i} \text{ is } \frac{\sigma^2}{\Sigma N_i},$$

which is estimated by

$$\frac{\Sigma N_i(\bar{x}_i - [\Sigma N_i \bar{x}_i]/\Sigma N_i)^2}{(k-1)(\Sigma N_i)},$$

of which a more convenient form is the denominator of the expression under the radical in (4).

with 1 and 992 d.f.; and using interaction of distance with all combinations of other variables as error

$$F = \frac{385.24}{19.54}.$$

$\sqrt{F} = t$ is 4.6 and 4.4, respectively, as before.

This analysis assumes that interactions are nonexistent; the differences $\overline{X}_1 - \overline{X}_2$ have been weighted by the amount of information contained in each, as is proper only if they are all estimates of the same population difference. If they are estimates of different population differences, i.e., if the interactions do not vanish, there are two consequences: (1) the main effect has a less clear meaning, and (2) weighting must be by some function of the population and not of the sample numbers. A test of the interaction of distance with the 32 combinations of the remaining 5 variables may be made against the within-cell variance. F with 31 and 992 degrees of freedom equals 1.47 at the 5 per cent level; our ratio is

$$\frac{19.54}{18.15} = 1.08;$$

the N_i's are therefore proper weights.

Certain of the results of the hand tabulation appear to contradict other work on differential fertility, and advantage may be taken of the occasion to refer to the possibility that holding relevant variables constant may reverse familiar relationships. Table 3 shows a significant direct relation between fertility and income and between fertility and years of schooling. The relation of fertility to income and schooling was studied by correlation as among whole counties (as has been done independently for the Province of Quebec), and the inverse relation which other students have secured was noted. Income in the present factorial comparison was that of all the farmers in the counties, and not only of the particular French farmers of the study, and this is an objection to the present design. Without assessing this objection we note that it does not apply to years of schooling; it is the women themselves whose education is measured, and not that of their county.

The excess of average children to women with 7 or more years of schooling over those to women with under 7, independent of all other contrasts, is 0.72 child as seen in Table 3. What would the effect due to schooling have appeared to be if we had not been able to make the cross-classifications? This is simply given by the fact that 527 women of 0-6 years of schooling are in the sample, and they reported 5,179 children, an average of 9.83. The corresponding average for women with 7 or more years schooling was 9.99 children. The difference due to schooling hardly appears when other factors are not controlled.

The discrepancies between the usual inverse correlations and the differences here in favor of better-educated and higher-income families seem to be due both to (1) the different extent of control of extraneous variables and (2) the difference between area and individual comparisons.

INTERACTIONS BETWEEN DISTANCE AND OTHER FACTORS. The convenience of the 2^n factorial design for estimating main effects when frequencies in the cells are disproportionate has been noted. It is equally convenient for estimating interactions. For example, considering the four observations in the upper left-hand corner of Table 2, we note that the effect of distance for those with 0-6 years of schooling is $9.4 - 7.4 = 2.0$, and for those with 7 or more years of schooling it is $10.7 - 12.9 = -2.2$. The fact that these differences are dissimilar constitutes the interaction; its amount is estimated by $2.0 - (-2.2) = 4.2$. From the 16 such differences of differences, a weighted average may be calculated, as was done for the main effects. In this case the proper weight for each is the reciprocal of the sum of the reciprocals of the numbers of observations in the four cells, e.g., $1/(1/15 + 1/14 + 1/5 + 1/8) = 2.16$. It turns out that the weighted sum of the 16 interactions is -21.74, and the sum of the weights is 53.37, giving an average of -0.407. The error to which this average is subject is the square root of 18.15 divided by the sum of the weights, i.e., 0.58. No test is required to show that this interaction is not significant.

Table 4

Interaction	Interaction	Estimate of Standard Error of Interaction
With years of schooling	−0.407	0.583
With age at marriage	.009	.588
With present age	+ .958	.571
With income	.156	.581
With French versus mixed areas	0.363	0.585

The five interactions of distance with other factors (or more properly difference of effects, since we have not divided by 2) are given in Table 4. None of these is significant at the 5 per cent level.

PARTITION OF VARIANCE OF FAMILY SIZE. From Table 3 a statement may be made on the partition of variance of family size. We look on each observation as consisting of a sum of terms having independent variation. Thus, in the present case, family size is

$$X_{ijklm} = M + d_i + i + m_k + s_l + e_{ijklm} , \qquad (5)$$

where M is the grand mean, d_i is near or far from cities, i_j is well-off or poor, m_k is young or old at marriage, s_l is more or less schooling, while e is the unexplained variation. To predict the deviation of family size from the grand mean, one-half of the differences of column 1 of Table 3 for the several effects are used. Thus

$$d_1 = 0.64 \text{ for far from city,}$$
$$d_2 = -0.64 \text{ for near city,}$$
$$i_1 = 0.45 \text{ for low income,}$$

$$i_2 \;=\; -\,0.45 \text{ for high income,}$$
$$m_1 \;=\; 0.88 \text{ for married 15-19,}$$
$$m_2 \;=\; -\,0.88 \text{ for married 20-24,}$$
$$s_1 \;=\; 0.36 \text{ for 0-6 years schooling,}$$
$$s_2 \;=\; -\,0.36 \text{ for 7 or more years schooling,}$$
$$e \;=\; \text{a random variable of mean zero and}$$
variance 18.15. The prediction equation
may be written

$$X_{ijklm} - M = \pm 0.64 \pm 0.45 \pm 0.88 \pm 0.36 + e \; ,$$

where choice is made between $\pm$ according to the category of the family whose size is to be predicted.

To find the proportion of total variance which is explained, we square and take expectations. No estimate of the population mean M is required. After making the small allowance for the fact that $d_1 = 0.64$, etc., are subject to sampling error, we find that all four components here account for $1.44/(18.15 + 1.44)$, or 7 per cent of total variance. The factor of special interest to this study, distance from cities, accounts for just under 2 per cent of total variance.

HYPOTHESIS OF DIFFUSION. A word on the sociological interest which has motivated this study of differential fertility is in order here. The initial hypothesis was that diffusion takes place in a geographical dimension as well as in the familiar gradient from high- to low-income classes, better- to less-well-educated persons, etc. Specifically, we suppose that for a new element of culture the point of entry into a society is not only the rich, better-educated, urban population but also that, as among the rural population, those closer to cities are earliest affected. An additional hypothesis was that where elements which have formed part of English-speaking North American life are making their way into French Canada, it might be that those French living nearest to English-speaking people would take up the new elements earlier than their cousins who live far from English-speaking people.

In relation to these hypotheses, family size seems capable of serving as a tracer of culture change in general; it has the advantage of rather complete statistical documentation. We find that family size on French farms near cities, when all other accessible variables have been controlled, is smaller than on French farms far from cities, and we infer that the current of diffusion is from the city outward. On the other hand, no significant difference in family size is shown according to residence close to or away from English-speaking people. We infer that the influence of the English-speaking world upon the French-Canadian farmer is via the French cities.

MORTALITY AND
SOCIO-ENVIRONMENTAL FACTORS

Dorothy G. Wiehl

The association between physical environment and certain diseases was the foundation on which the public health program was built. Through the application of sanitary measures, through control of animal and insect vectors and of food contamination, and through protection of the individual against infectious organisms by immunization, public health brought about tremendous reductions in mortality. Continued progress in the battle to give more and more of the people the opportunity to live out the span of life attained by the healthiest or most fortunate members of society requires persistent study of the conditions which contribute to premature death. Sydenstricker,[1] in HEALTH AND ENVIRONMENT, wrote "failure to survive in the early years of life may be ascribed chiefly to accidents of environment, to conditions of living and to ignorance, . . . in later years of life failure to survive is due chiefly to organic breakdowns." Successful control of environment, improved medical care, and advances in medical science have brought death rates in childhood to a level that is lower than the less optimistic dared to expect a few years ago, and very marked reductions in mortality of young adults. But in late middle life the decrease has been relatively small. Today, therefore, we are concerned with the problem of improving and widening our approach to the prevention or postponement of mortality and especially to the postponement of "organic breakdown." The effect of environmental factors on adult health is not well understood and there is need for more investigation of the possible relationship between early breakdown from the so-called degenerative diseases and such factors as mode of work, level of income and of education with their many related conditions, such as housing, nutrition, social and recreational activities, and concentration of populations.

The ideal method for studying effects of a specific environmental factor on mortality is to compare groups which differ with respect to that factor but are alike in other major respects. This is almost never possible. In fact, only rarely are mortality rates available for population groups that can be

Reprinted from *The Milbank Memorial Fund Quarterly*, Vol. 26 (October 1948), pp. 335-365, by permission of the author and the publisher. (Copyright, 1948, by the Milbank Memorial Fund, 40 Wall St., New York.)

1. Edgar Sydenstricker, *Health and Environment* (New York: McGraw-Hill Book Company, Inc., 1933).

classified according to some one or two well-defined indices of environment. At present, therefore, our evidence concerning the effect of socio-environmental factors on mortality is based largely on deductions from variations in mortality by sex and age and for various causes in populations living in different sections of the country, under various degrees of urbanization, and, for persons living in large cities, variations among different sections of a city. These populations can be described as to some other characteristics such as proportions engaged in different types of occupations, the average income and educational status, but mortality rates specific for such breakdowns are not available. Obviously, such indirect evidence is only suggestive and subject to rather general inferences. Data of this type for the United States have been discussed in two books—one HEALTH AND ENVIRONMENT by Sydenstricker and the other LENGTH OF LIFE by Dublin and Lotka,[2] and in many articles. I shall not attempt to summarize these previous studies but shall limit myself to presenting some of the latest mortality data of this type.

Extensive data on mortality for whites and for nonwhites in the United States are available and the differences in mortality for these groups reflect very largely the results of the lower socio-economic levels of living of the Negroes, although some differences in mortality may possibly be due to racial characteristics. At least the evidence is clear that mortality of the Negroes is susceptible to reduction, and in the period from 1921 to 1940 the average annual per cent of decline in age-adjusted death rates for nonwhites (in 1940, 96 per cent of nonwhites were Negroes) was 1.59 compared with 1.43 for whites.[3] Presumably the same factors are chiefly responsible for the improvement in mortality in both groups. The age-adjusted death rate for nonwhites in 1940 was 16.25 per 1,000, which is 60 per cent higher than the rate of 10.16 for whites. It is not necessary to present evidence that the colored population on the average has a lower economic status than the white population, has poorer housing, less education, and has a generally less favorable standard of living. It is significant that from 1940 to 1945, when Negroes as well as whites had higher incomes than ever before, the mortality decline for Negroes was definitely accelerated. Life tables for 1945[4] and for 1939–1941[5] show that the expectation of life at birth increased 3.8 years for Negro males and 4.1 for Negro females. This increase in five years for males is 80 per cent of that for the previous ten-year period, and for females it is 68 per cent.

---

2. Louis I. Dublin and A. J. Lotka, Length of Life: A Study of the Life Table (New York: Ronald Press Company, 1936).

3. United States Bureau of the Census, Age-Adjusted Death Rates in the United States, 1900-1940. Vital Statistics-Special Reports, June 26, 1945, 23, No. 1, pp. 1-39.

4. United States Public Health Service, Federal Security Agency, United States Abridged Life Tables, 1945. Vital Statistics-Special Reports, April 15, 1947, 23, No. 11, pp. 243-249.

5. United States Bureau of the Census, United States Life Tables, 1939-1941. Vital Statistics-Special Reports, January 11, 1944, 19, No. 4, pp. 31-45.

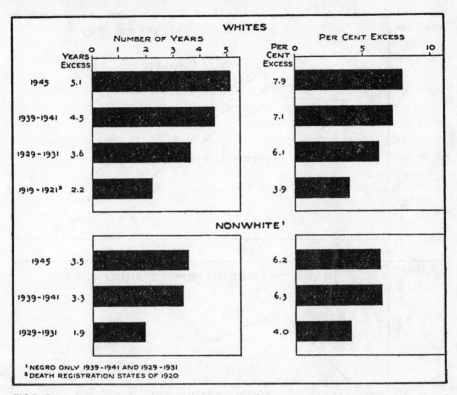

FIG.1. Excess in expectation of life at birth for females as compared with males in the United States. Excess is shown in number of years and per cent for whites and nonwhites.

Differences in mortality trends for sex and age groups, as well as for whites and nonwhites are suggestive of the influence of environmental factors on mortality. The differences between the number of years of life expectancy at birth for males and females over the past twenty-five years are shown in Figure 1. The excess life expectation for white females as compared to males increased from 2.2 years for the period 1919–1921 to 5.1 years in 1945, and this is an increase in the percentage excess from 3.9 to 7.9 per cent. For nonwhites the excess life expectation for females is less than for whites but it too has been increasing.

The greater increase in life expectancy for women than for men is due almost entirely to a more favorable trend in mortality at adult ages. The decrease in life-table mortality at specific ages in the fifteen-year period between 1929–1931 and 1945 is shown in Figure 2 for the white and nonwhite populations. The mortality rates on which this chart is based are the percentages of persons alive at a given age in the life-table population dying before reaching an older specific age. In the upper section of the chart, the percentage decrease in mortality for each of five fifteen-year age periods between birth and age 75 years has been plotted.

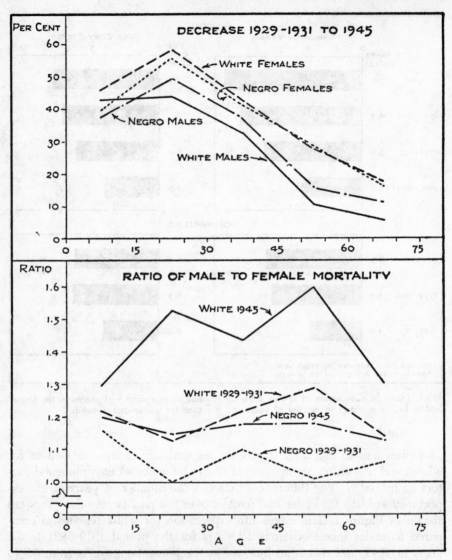

FIG. 2. Per cent decrease in percentage of life-table population dying in five fifteen-year age intervals between birth and age 75 years between 1929–1931 and 1945; and ratios of male to female percentages dying in these age intervals at each period.

Under 15 years of age, the decrease in mortality by sex differs only slightly for both whites and nonwhites. But after age 15 years, the greater percentage decrease in mortality among females is very striking, especially for the white population. Between ages 15 to 30 years, the death rate for white females in 1945 was 59 per cent lower than in 1929–1931 and for white males, the rate declined 44 per cent in the same period; similarly at ages 45 to 60 years, the reduction in mortality was 28 and 10 per cent for females and males, respectively. Thus, the widening difference in expectation of life between males and females is the result of factors operative in adult life, both for Negroes and whites.

It is of interest that in this fifteen-year period the maximum percentage reduction in mortality occurred between ages 15 and 30 years for each sex and color group, although for white males the difference between this age group and the age group under 15 years is negligible. This relatively high reduction in early adult life represents a marked increase in the rate of decline at this age period. For example, comparison of life-table mortality for Death Registration States of 1900 for the ten-year period 1901–1910 with that for the Death Registration States of 1920 for the ten years from 1920–1929 [6] shows that in the twenty-year interval between these life tables, mortality for whites at ages 15 to 30 years decreased 33 and 30 per cent for males and females, respectively, compared with 44 and 58 per cent in the recent period from 1930 to 1945. At ages under 15 years, in the earlier twenty-year interval the decline in mortality was 43 and 46 per cent for males and females and, therefore, much greater than at ages 15 to 30 years during that period, whereas in the recent period, the percentage reduction under 15 years was less than at ages 15 to 30 years. Thus, the factors contributing to an improved mortality have become more effective in preventing deaths of young adults than previously, but white females have benefited much more than white males.

The result of the disproportionate decline in female and male mortality is shown by the ratios of male to female mortality for specific age groups in 1945 and in 1929–1931, which are plotted in the lower half of Figure 2. For every age group the excess male mortality has increased for both whites and nonwhites. For nonwhites, variation in the excess according to age is not large, but for whites the excess male mortality in 1945 was 30 per cent under 15 years of age, rose to 53 per cent at 15-30 years, declined slightly for the next 15 year age group, and increased again to 60 per cent at ages 45 to 60, after which it dropped to 30 per cent. This large excess mortality for adult males as compared with females represents one of our major health problems. Other data relating to it will be discussed later, but it may be said here that the causes are unknown.

URBAN AND RURAL MORTALITY. It has long been known that, in general, urban populations have higher mortality rates than rural populations. Much of the public health program has been directed to the control and elimination of unfavorable conditions in cities, and in the early part of this century urban mortality rates declined sharply. But in the past twenty-five years it has not been possible to follow urban and rural trends in mortality because urban and rural rates were affected by the increasing use of urban hospitals by rural residents. In 1937, the National Office of Vital Statistics began the tabulation of deaths according to place of usual residence of the decedents

6. United States Public Health Service, Federal Security Agency, *United States Abridged Life Tables, 1930-1939 (Preliminary) By Geographic Divisions, Color, and Sex.* Vital Statistics-Special Reports, June 30, 1947, 23, No. 14, pp. 281-295.

and data are now available for somewhat detailed comparisons of mortality in cities and in rural areas. It is of interest to examine the nature of the urban-rural differences in recent mortality of the United States.

For the United States as a whole and for three broad regions, life tables on mortality during 1939 in cities with 100,000 population or more in 1930, in communities having a population of 2,500 to 100,000, and in rural areas have been published by the National Office of Vital Statistics.[7] These life tables and death rates for specific states in 1940 will be used to describe recent urban-rural differences. The movement of the population since the 1940 Census has been so great that more recent urban and rural rates are not very reliable.

In Table 1, expectation of life at birth in the United States for the year 1939 is compared for rural areas and the two urban populations. White females had nearly the same expectation of life at birth in large and small cities; in the country they had an advantage of only a little over one year. For white males also there was little difference by size of city, but at birth rural males had 2.7 years more life expectation than males in small cities and 2.5 years more than those in large cities. These urban-rural differences are much less the differences shown by life tables for the Original Registration States[8] at the beginning of this century (Table 2). In the period 1900–1902, the expectation of life at birth for rural males exceeded that for urban males by 10 years, and for rural females the excess was 7.5 years.

A further point to be noted is that, although the expectation of life has increased greatly for both urban and rural populations, the urban increase has been greater for both males and females.

Trends in sex differences in expectation of life for urban and rural populations are of interest in view of the widening differential already noted. The expectation of life for females exceeds that for males both in urban and rural populations and at all three periods shown in Table 1. For the urban population, females had an average expectation of life four years longer than males had at both earlier periods and the difference increased only slightly (about three-fourths of a year) in 1939. For the rural population, the female expectation of life exceeded that of males by only 1.4 years in 1900–1902, but it has steadily increased and in 1939 the excess was 3.4 years.

Although the population of the Original Registration States is not strictly comparable with that of the total United States, it seems probable that two general conclusions are justified: first, that the urban-rural differential in mortality has been declining due to a more rapid improvement in urban mortality; and second, that the *increase* in the differential between male and female mortality is greater for rural populations than for urban although the absolute difference is greater for urban populations.

7. United States Public Health Service, Federal Security Agency, *United States Abridged Life Tables, 1939, Urban and Rural, By Regions, Color, and Sex*. Vital Statistics-Special Reports, June 30, 1947, 23, No. 15, pp. 299-316.

8. United States Bureau of the Census, *United States Life Tables: 1890, 1901, 1910, 1901-1910*. Washington, 1921.

TABLE I—Average Expectation of Life at Birth for Urban and Rural Populations of the United States

Year and Urban-Rural Class	White		Nonwhite	
	Male	Female	Male	Female
1939—Total United States:				
Cities 100,000 or more	61.6	66.3	51.0	54.6
Other urban	61.4	66.2	46.9	51.1
Rural	64.1	67.5	55.2	57.2
Original Registration States: 1909–1911				
Cities 10,000 or more	47.32	51.39		
Rural	55.06	57.35		
1900–1902				
Cities 8,000 or more	43.97	47.90		
Rural	54.03	55.41		

For nonwhites, the expectation of life at birth for rural males and females exceeded that in both large and small cities by a much greater amount than that found for whites. Under-registration of Negro rural deaths probably is a factor in this large excess but could account for only a part of it. Negroes had a definitely longer expectation of life in large cities than in small cities in contrast to the slight difference for whites.

A higher urban than rural mortality is characteristic of the white populations in nearly all states. Comparison of the age-adjusted urban and rural rates for states (3) in 1940 shows that the urban rate was higher in every state except in Massachusetts where the two rates were equal, and in California and New York where the urban rate was 0.1 per 1,000 less than the rural, and in New Jersey where the urban rate was 0.6 lower. However, the states differ widely as to both urban and rural mortality and the pattern of variation is different.

The geographic variation of urban and of rural mortality for the white population of each state in 1940 is shown in Figure 3. States are grouped into five classes according to the percentage deviation above or below the median rate,[9] as previously described. The urban mortality, shown in the upper half of Figure 3, has a marked geographic pattern. All states in the North which are east of the Mountain region had average or lower rates, except Vermont. Only three states, Wisconsin, Minnesota, and Nebraska, had rates more than 10 per cent below the median rate. All states in the South, except Delaware, the District of Columbia, Florida, and North Carolina, had rates more than 2.5 per cent above the median urban rate, and seven of them had rates more than 10 per cent above the median. In the Mountain and Pacific area, states varied widely as to their urban mortality.

The geographic variation of rural mortality shown in the lower half of Figure 3 follows an east and west division rather than the north and south division of urban mortality. Higher than average rural rates are found in

9. Urban rates are for all places of 2,500 population or more, and the age-adjusted rates are taken from Table 7 of reference 3. Age-adjusted rural rates were computed for each state as described in footnote 2.

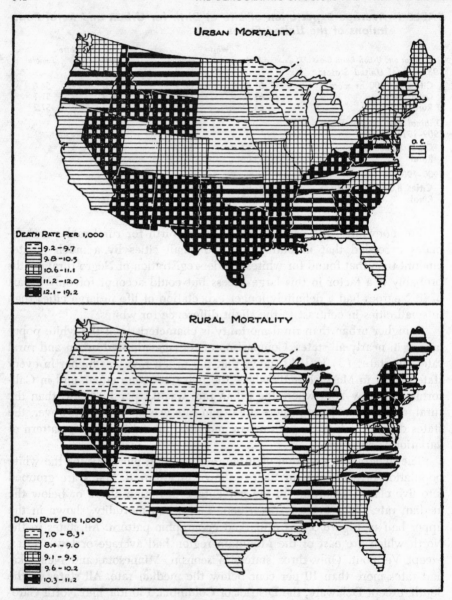

FIG. 3. Geographic variation in age-adjusted death rates in 1940 for the white population of urban and rural areas. Urban includes cities of 2,500 population or more.

most of the states east of the Mississippi River and only four states west of the Mississippi (New Mexico, Utah, Nevada, and California) are in this category. Thus, rural death rates are more consistently high in the industrial states than are the urban death rates. The latter are relatively low in a considerable number of industrial states.

In order to study the possible relation of mortality to some of the characteristics of populations of individual states, correlation coefficients for death rates and a few selected indices were computed. Some of these correlations are sufficiently suggestive of the influence of certain factors on mortality to be helpful in interpreting some of the mortality variations. It must be emphasized that a significant correlation does not demonstrate a causal relation and must be interpreted with great caution.

The rural populations in different states vary tremendously in the percentage that is classified as nonfarm. The range is from 27 per cent in Mississippi to 83 per cent in Connecticut, Rhode Island, and New Jersey. If the rural death rate for the forty-eight states is correlated with the per cent of rural population that was nonfarm, a coefficient of $+ .476$ (P $<.001$) is obtained and it is highly significant. In other words, the greater the proportion of rural population that was nonfarm, the higher the rural death rate. A similar correlation for the nonwhite population in the twenty-eight states in which nonwhites were over 90 per cent Negroes gave a coefficient of $+ .623$ (P $< .001$). In the states west of the Mississippi, where low rural death rates were noted, the rural population is predominantly farm; in the east, especially northeast, the rural population is heavily weighted with nonfarm or small village populations and the mortality was relatively high. Since villages of less than 2,500 population apparently have a less favorable death rate than farm populations, even this degree of concentration of population seems to be unfavorable. However, an additional influence that may affect death rates of rural populations in the highly urban industrial states is the trend toward suburban living. Large numbers of persons live outside city limits and comprise a "fringe population" which finds employment in a nearby city or industrial area and in most respects is similar to the urban populations.

It is well known that the rural populations in various sections of the country differ greatly in their level of living or their socio-economic standards. For farm operators, an index of level of living based on money value of crops and several other items has been published by the Bureau of Agricultural Economics.[10] On the assumption that the prosperity of farm communities closely parallels that of the farmers in the areas, this index of farm living was correlated with the white rural death rate for the thirty states in which the farm population was at least 45 per cent of the total rural population. The coefficient is $- .383$, only moderately high but statistically significant. When the correlation of the proportion of nonfarm families with the death rates in these thirty states is held constant, the coefficient for standard of living and the death rate is raised to $- .625$. Thus we have the suggestion of a second factor associated with the death rates observed for rural populations, namely, the level of living for farm operators. So many conditions of living are associated with income that the specific factors of most importance in this relationship are not easily identified, but

10. Margaret Jarman Hagood, *Farm Operator Family Level of Living Indexes for Counties of the United States, 1940 and 1945*. United States Department of Agriculture, Bureau of Agricultural Economics, Washington, May, 1947, pp. 1-42.

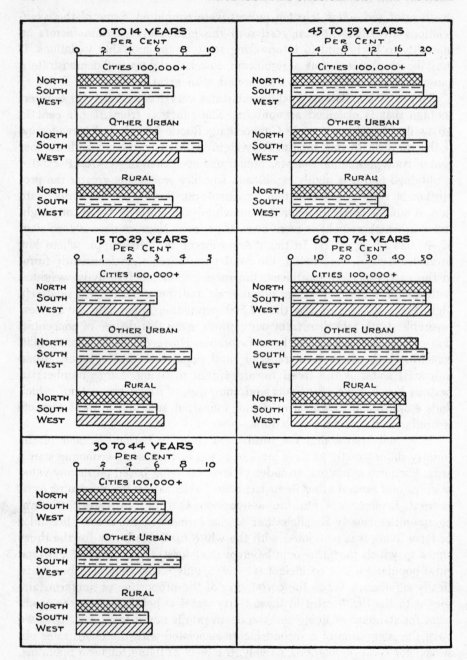

FIG. 4. Percentages of life-table population dying in specific fifteen-year age intervals compared for three regions of the United States for the white population of cities of 100,000 population or more, cities of 2,500 to 100,000 population, and of rural areas, 1939. Per cent dying is average of per cents for males and females.

there are data to show that housing conditions, sanitary conveniences, medical care, and diets are less adequate in rural areas with low economic resources.

The white *urban* death rates (age adjusted) for forty-five states (Arizona, New Mexico, and Nevada excluded) were correlated with the average wage per male white worker who in 1940 received wages taxable for Federal Old Age and Survivors Insurance.[11] The coefficient is − .452 (P < .01) and is statistically significant. This is high enough to suggest a moderate inverse relationship between wage levels and mortality. However, the wage level is highly correlated with the population per physician and per public health nurse in the state and is also associated with the quality of housing and of diet, and with indices of educational and cultural levels. Wages are the means by which the standard of living is modified, and carefully controlled investigations are required for an evaluation of the effect of separate socio-environmental factors on mortality.

MORTALITY BY AGE IN URBAN AND RURAL AREAS. Age-specific mortality by urbanization in the three broad regions of the United States may be analyzed by using life-table mortality for 1939 from the report mentioned above (7). The regions for which urban and rural experience may be compared are: (1) the North which includes the New England states, Middle Atlantic states, East and West North Central states; (2) the South which includes the South Atlantic division, East and West South Central states; and (3) the West, or Mountain and Pacific Coast states. For each region and urban class, the percentages of the life-table population dying within each of five age intervals were computed for each sex and a mortality rate for both sexes obtained by averaging the male and female rates.

Regional Comparison by Urban-Rural Class and Age. The percentages of persons dying within a specified age interval in each of the two urban classes and in rural areas are compared for the three regions in Figure 4. The scale for percentages at each age period has been changed so that an equal distance between length of bars represents roughly equal percentage variation. The regional differences by urban class are not consistent for the various age periods and the three urban-rural classes do not show the same variation. The suggested pattern of variation may be summarized as follows:

1. Mortality is lowest in the North at each of the three fifteen-year age intervals from birth to age 45 years in rural areas, in small cities, and in cities of 100,000 population or more, with the exception that in large cities of the West mortality at ages 0 to 15 years is very slightly lower.

2. In the small cities, mortality is highest in the South at all five age periods and the largest regional differences are shown for this urban class. In large cities the highest mortality under age 30 is also in the South, but from 30 to 75 years mortality in the West is highest.

---

11. Federal Security Agency, Social Security Board, *Social Security Yearbook, 1941.* Washington, June, 1942, p. 131.

3. Rural mortality is highest in the West up to age 45 years, and thereafter the differences are small with minimum rates in the South.

4. The maximum regional variations are found for mortality in childhood and young adult ages.

TABLE II—Age-specific Death Rates [1] Per 1,000 Population in 1940 in Cities of 100,000 Population or Over and in Rural Areas of Selected States [2] in Four Geographic Areas

	Cities 100,000 or More			Rural		
Geographic Area	Under 15 Years	15-44 Years	45-64 Years	Under 15 Years	15-44 Years	45-64 Years
North East	3.20	2.82	17.40	4.03	2.76	13.33
West North Central	2.80	2.17	12.70	2.94	1.95	9.01
South East	3.81	2.94	16.43	4.58	2.82	11.66
Pacific	3.17	2.87	15.44	3.69	2.94	12.61

1. Rates for specific age groups were adjusted by age as follows: "Under 15 years" was adjusted for under 1 year, 1-4 years, and 5-14 years; "15-44 years" and "45-64 years" were adjusted for 10 year age groups. There was no adjustment for sex.
2. For states included see page 353.

Since the North includes the West North Central states which have the lowest urban and rural mortality, the question arises whether the favorable mortality in the North is due to these states. In order to obtain some evidence on this point, Table 2 was prepared. For large cities and for rural communities, it compares the average death rates in 1940 of three age groups in selected states of four geographic areas. The areas and states included are: North East—Pennsylvania, Ohio, and Illinois; West North Central—Iowa, Minnesota, and Nebraska; South East—Alabama, Georgia, Tennessee, and Virginia; Pacific Coast—California, Oregon, and Washington. Rates for these West North Central states are much lower than those in any of the other areas for each age group both in the large cities and rural populations. Among the other three areas, differences in the death rates are less than those shown by the life-table mortality in 1939 for the three regions. However, in the large cities of the South East, mortality under 15 years of age was definitely higher than in the North East or the Pacific area, as was shown by the life-table mortality for the South. The only noteworthy shift in the relative position of geographic areas based on these selected states as compared with the larger regions is for the mortality under 15 years of age in the rural areas of the Pacific states which is lower than in either the North East or South East states, whereas the West region had the highest rate. Thus, although the lower mortality in the North is due to some extent to the low death rates in West North Central states, industrial states in the North East also have a favorable mortality among children and young adults.

Comparison of Urban-Rural Mortality Within Regions. Variation of mortality within regions according to degree of urbanization for specific sex and age groups is shown in Figure 5. Rural mortality for each age group has been taken as 1.00 and the ratio of mortality in each urban class to the rural rate has been plotted in Figure 5.

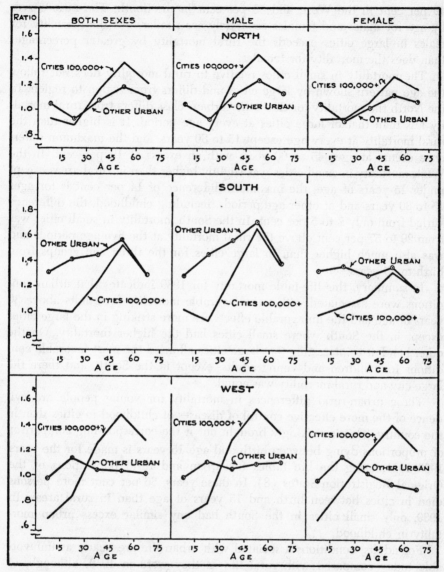

FIG. 5. Ratio of mortality in cities to rural mortality for the white population of three regions of the United States, 1939. Mortality is based on percentages of life-table population dying in fifteen-year age intervals, average of male and female per cent.

The age curve for ratios of mortality in large cities to that in rural areas is quite similar for all three regions. In the North and West, mortality at the two fifteen-year intervals under 30 years is lower than in rural areas, and in the South the rates are about equal. At all older age groups, the mortality is much higher in the large cities than in rural areas. The difference reaches a maximum at ages 45 to 60 years, and at this age period the rate for large cities exceeds the rural rate by 38 per cent in the North,

49 per cent in the West, and 53 per cent in the South. The ratio curves by age for males and females separately are similar, but the mortality for males in large cities exceeds the rural mortality by greater percentages than does the mortality for females.

The mortality in small cities relative to rural mortality does not follow the age pattern shown by large cities and differs from region to region. In the North the mortality for the "other urban" class differs from rural mortality less than that of large cities at every age period. It is higher than the rural mortality at every age except 15 to 30 years, and the maximum difference occurs at ages 45 to 60 years with an excess of 19 per cent. In the West, mortality in small cities was slightly higher than in rural areas except under 15 years of age; the maximum difference of 14 per cent is for ages 15 to 30 years and at other age periods, including childhood, the difference varied from only 2 to 5 per cent. In the South, mortality in small cities was from 29 to 57 per cent above the rural mortality at the five age periods and was also much higher than in large cities for the three age groups from birth to 45 years.

In summary, this life-table mortality for 1939 indicates that urban conditions were associated with an unfavorable mortality for adults above 30 years of age and the unfavorable effects are more striking in the large cities except in the South where small cities had the higher mortality. On the other hand, it is interesting that large cities afforded the most favorable conditions for children and young adults, except in the South, and there the large city and rural mortality was equal.

These urban-rural differences in mortality for young people are evidence of the more effective control of diseases of childhood in cities than in the country. This is strikingly brought out if the corresponding comparison of proportions dying between birth and age 15 years is made for the years 1909–1911, using the life tables for urban and rural populations of the Original Registration States (8). In these years, 36 per cent more persons died in cities between birth and 15 years of age than in rural areas. In 1939, only small cities in the South had any similar excess urban mortality in childhood.

For adults, conditions associated with urban life are nearly as unfavorable today compared with rural life as they were in 1910, although, of course, both urban and rural mortality have declined. For the United States, between age 45 to 60 years, life-table mortality in large cities in 1939 was 43 per cent higher than in rural areas compared with 54 per cent higher urban mortality in 1910. In the South, the urban excess was as high as in 1910. Since adult mortality has become our major health problem, the factors involved in high mortality for urban populations merit intensive study.

Sex Differences for Urban and Rural Mortality. It has been shown that the difference between male and female mortality has been increasing. It is of interest, therefore, to compare the sex ratios for life-table mortality in the three regions according to urbanization. The percentages by which

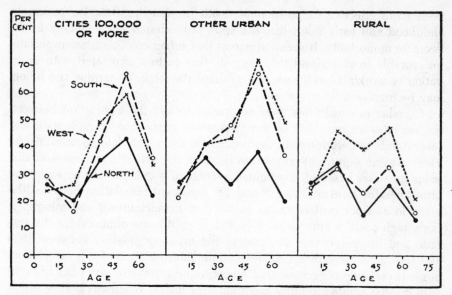

FIG. 6. Percentage excess in percentage of males in the life-table population dying in fifteen-year age intervals over percentage of females dying in the same age intervals for urban and rural populations of the United States in three regions, 1939.

male mortality exceeded female mortality are shown for the five fifteen-year age intervals in Figure 6. Variations in sex differences which seem relevant to this discussion may be briefly described as follows:

1. Under 15 years of age the percentage excess for male mortality varies little among regions or for urban-rural classes, the excess being from 21 to 29 per cent, although there were large differences in mortality by region and urbanization.

2. In both urban classes of all three regions the maximum excess mortality for males was at ages 45 to 60 years, which is the age group at which the greatest difference between urban and rural mortality is found within each region, except for small cities in the West.

3. At ages 60 to 75 years the excess mortality for males drops sharply, and it was less than in childhood except in the urban classes of the South and West.

4. Within each region the excess mortality for adult males in the rural area was less than in either urban class at each age interval except 15 to 30 years.

5. For each urban-rural class the excess mortality for males after age 29 years was least in the North.

In general, the specific regional, urban, and age classes which show a high sex-ratio for mortality are those which had relatively high death rates. In adult life, high mortality is associated with conditions which are more unfavorable to men than to women; or, stated in another way, the complex of factors which have brought about a marked decline in mortality has been more effective in postponing death for females than for males. In childhood and early adult life, the sexes have shared more equally in the decrease in mortality. It seems apparent that urban conditions are especially unfavorable to males and this suggests that factors associated with occupation or working conditions, and perhaps the strain of earning the living, may be involved.

Correlation coefficients were computed to test the association between the sex-ratio for mortality of the total white population of each state and several indices descriptive of the population for which data were available. There was no significant correlation between the sex-ratio and an economic index for states based on a weighted average of wages per worker and rural farm operator level of living;[12] and no significant correlation between the sex-ratio and per cent of males engaged in manufacturing and mining. A fairly high positive correlation (+ .456, P <.01) was obtained for the sex-ratio and the percentage *increase* in the urban population between 1920 and 1940. One can only speculate as to the interpretation of this association, but it is certainly suggestive that recent, rapid growth of cities has brought with it unfavorable mortality experience for males. Whether the new urban workers are those most affected is unknown.

Since urbanization is consistently associated with high sex-ratios for adult mortality, it seems safe to conclude that the steadily rising percentage of the total population that lives in cities is one factor in the increasing excess mortality of males as compared with females. On the other hand, there is evidence that the excess mortality for males has *increased* both in urban and rural areas. In Table 3, the percentage excess in life-table mortality in 1909–1911 for rural and urban males in the Original Death Registration States is compared with similar data for 1939 in the North.[13] For each age interval the excess mortality for males was greater in 1939 than in 1909–1911 both for cities and rural communities. Therefore, the increase in the excess mortality for males in the total population cannot be explained entirely on the basis of the increase in the percentage of population that is urban.

CAUSE OF DEATH. There is time for only a brief reference to specific causes of death but a comparison of death rates for a few causes in different geographic areas affords some significant information on the relative level of control of preventable diseases and on the importance of the degenerative diseases in the task of postponing death among the adult population. For the comparisons of death rates from specific causes, average rates were computed for a few states in four geographic areas, as described on page 322, for each sex in the urban and rural population. Rates were adjusted

12. For each state the average wage per worker (10) and the index of farm level of living (9) was weighted by the per cent of total population in the state which was classified as nonfarm and farm, respectively.

13. This region is more comparable with the Original Registration States than the total United States, but sex-ratios in 1939 were even higher for the United States than for the North region.

TABLE III—Ratio of the Per Cent of White Males in the Life-table Population Dying within a Specified Age Interval to the Per Cent of White Females Dying in the Same Age Interval for Urban and Rural Population in 1909–1911 [1] and in 1939

Age Interval Years	1939—North Region Cities 100,000 or More	Cities 2,500–100,000	1909–1911 [1] Cities 10,000 or More	1939 Rural North	1909–1911 Rural [1]
0-14	1.26	1.27	1.15	1.27	1.17
15-29	1.20	1.34	1.13	1.36	1.03
30-44	1.35	1.15	1.28	1.26	1.04
45-59	1.22	1.26	1.25	1.38	1.09
60-74	1.43	1.13	1.12	1.20	1.07

1. Original Death Registration States.

for differences in the age distribution of the population by the indirect method.[14] The mortality from specific causes is shown in Table 4 and in Figures 7 and 8.

Relatively high rates in the South East area for both urban and rural populations are shown in Table 4 for infant and maternal mortality, typhoid fever, malaria, communicable diseases of childhood, and pellagra. Mortality from these causes is preventable in large part, and this high mortality in the South East is indicative of inadequate health services and low standards of living. In the other three geographic areas, urban mortality from this list of causes was fairly similar, with the exception of pellagra mortality in the Pacific Coast states which was three and a half times that in the North East and West North Central area, although less than one-seventh of the urban death rate in the South East. Rural mortality was more variable than urban mortality from these causes. The North East states had less favorable rural death rates than either the West Central states or the Pacific Coast states for infant and maternal mortality, but for communicable diseases, mortality was similar in the North East and Pacific Coast states and higher than in the rural West North Central states. Only in the West North Central states was the rural death rate from these causes consistently as low or lower than the urban rates.

Mortality from the major causes of death among adults is shown in Figures 7 and 8. In these charts the vertical scale (rate scale) is logarithmic and equal vertical distances between points represent equal percentage differences.

For nearly every cause, or group of causes, the death rate for males is

14. The indirect method used to adjust for age was as follows: (1) the total population by age for each specific subdivision (sex, urban or rural, geographic area) was obtained; (2) the population in each age group for a particular subdivision was multiplied by the age-specific death rate for the United States for the specific cause of death; (3) the products (expected number of deaths for a specific age group) were summed to obtain the number of deaths, all ages, that would be expected if the United States rate applied and this total was divided by the total population for the particular subdivision to obtain the expected death rate; (4) the ratio of the United States rate to the computed expected rate was obtained, and (5) the actual rate for the particular subdivision was multiplied by the ratio to obtain the age-adjusted rate.

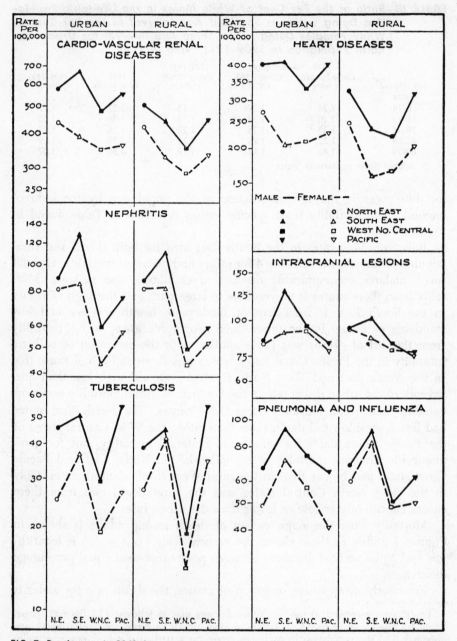

FIG. 7. Death rates in 1940 from several major causes of death for males and females in urban and rural areas of selected states in four geographic areas (see footnote 1, in Table IV). Death rates are adjusted for age by the indirect method. See page 321, footnote 4. Vertical scale is logarithmics.

TABLE IV—Infant and Maternal Mortality and Crude Death Rate Per 100,000 Population from Selected Causes for Urban and Rural Populations of Representative States [1] of Four Geographic Areas, 1940

Cause of Death and Urban-Rural Class	North East	South East	West North Central	Pacific Coast
Infant Deaths—Per 1,000 Live Births				
Urban	37.2	45.4	38.4	35.6
Rural	45.4	52.4	31.2	39.4
Puerperal Deaths—Per 1,000 Live Births				
Urban	3.0	3.5	3.3	2.8
Rural	3.0	4.1	2.4	2.3
Typhoid Fever				
Urban	.48	1.1	.51	.47
Rural	.82	1.5	.25	.80
Scarlet Fever, Whooping Cough, Diphtheria				
Urban	2.0	4.3	2.2	2.2
Rural	3.4	6.5	2.1	3.2
Malaria				
Urban	.09	1.2	0	.08
Rural	.09	2.3	.05	.03
Pellagra				
Urban	.14	3.8	.14	.52
Rural	.20	5.0	.14	.46

1. States included are: North East—Illinois, Ohio, Pennsylvania; South East—Alabama, Georgia, Tennessee, Virginia; West North Central—Iowa, Minnesota, Nebraska; Pacific Coast—California, Oregon, Washington.

higher than that for females, both for urban and rural populations of each geographic area. The differences in the rates by sex are usually greater in urban than in rural areas. Diseases which show the most marked excess mortality for males are the cardiovascular renal diseases, especially heart diseases, tuberculosis, pneumonia and influenza, diseases of the intestines, including appendicitis, hernia, and obstruction. Accidental deaths, especially those due to motor vehicles, show a greater percentage difference in mortality by sex than any of the diseases, both in urban and rural areas, and the actual differences in rates for the two sexes for accidental deaths from motor vehicles and other accidents are exceeded only by the cardiovascular renal diseases.

Higher mortality among females is found for diabetes in urban and rural populations of each of the four geographic areas. Cancer mortality also is somewhat greater for females than males in the rural population of each area, and in the urban population of the North East and South East states but not of the West North Central and Pacific states. The mortality from cirrhosis of the liver and diseases of the gall bladder combined is higher among females in rural sections of each area, except the South East, but is higher for males in urban sections. However, cirrhosis of the liver, separately, causes more deaths among males and gall bladder diseases cause more deaths among females.

Marked geographic differences are shown for most of these causes. Variations of special interest are: (1) the high male urban death rate from

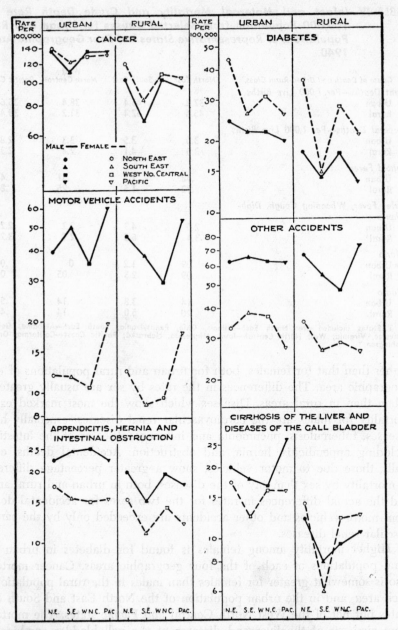

FIG. 8. Death rates in 1940 from several major causes of death for males and females in urban and rural areas of selected states in four geographic areas (see footnote 1, in Table IV). Death rates are adjusted for age by the indirect method. See page 321, footnote 4. Vertical scale is logarithmics.

cardiovascular diseases in the South East states where total urban mortality has been shown to be relatively high; (2) a maximum death rate from influenza and pneumonia among both males and females in urban and rural areas of the South East; (3) the high tuberculosis rate for males and females in the South East states and in the Pacific states, especially among males; and (4) the high accident rate for the Pacific Coast states.

Little is known concerning the effect of social or environmental factors on these causes, except tuberculosis and pneumonia. These two diseases are infectious and a relation to low standards of living, crowding, density of population, and some other conditions has been shown by special studies. The causes of accidents are being intensively studied as a basis for their prevention. Until quite recently the relation of environmental factors to the degenerative diseases has not received much attention. Their epidemiology, in the broadest sense, needs to be studied but the usual published mortality data can afford little more than some clues to be followed up by special investigations.

Some general conclusions that may be drawn from the data presented in the foregoing discussion are as follows:

1. Reductions in mortality have been greatest for children and young adults in large urban centers, where medical and public health services have had the greatest development and are most available.

2. Preventable mortality among children is relatively high in rural communities of most sections of the United States and is high in the smaller cities of the South.

3. In middle life, urban males have a marked excess mortality as compared with females, and the difference has been increasing. Although the excess mortality for rural males is less, it has been increasing also.

4. Geographic and urban-rural variations in adult mortality and in the differences in the sex-ratio for adult mortality suggest the importance of socio-environmental factors.

5. The causes of premature breakdown in middle life, especially for males, need to be studied more intensively.

PAST AND FUTURE LABOR FORCE TRENDS

John Durand

THE RATE OF LABOR FORCE GROWTH. In the past the growth of population in the United States furnished a rapidly increasing supply of labor. The labor force grew from about 22 million workers in 1890 to about 53 million in 1940, according to the estimates "comparable with 1940 census data," or a gain of 140 per cent. In other words, during this half-century the number of workers increased at the rate of about 600,000 annually. Population increase, which amounted to almost 110 per cent during these 50 years, was obviously the main source of the additional labor force.

The era of an expanding labor supply is drawing to a close as the rate of population growth slackens. Because of the decline of the birth rate and the cessation of large-scale immigration, the rate of population increase has been decelerating for many decades. Since the decade of the 1850's, when the population gained about 35 per cent, the percentage increase in successive decades has been declining irregularly, reaching a low of 7 per cent during the decade 1930-40. During the 1930's the increase in absolute numbers, as well as in percentage terms, was smaller than in the preceding decade. According to the latest projections of future population trends, the United States is likely to have a stationary or declining population before the end of the present century.

Slower population growth has resulted in a gradually decelerating rate of increase in the labor force. This tendency can be seen in the following summary of labor force growth during successive periods since 1890:

Census Year	Estimated Labor Force "Comparable with 1940 Census Data"	AVERAGE ANNUAL INCREASE OVER PRECEDING CENSUS YEAR	
		Number	Per Cent of Labor Force in Preceding Census Year
1890 (June)	22,200,000	—	—
1900 (June)	28,400,000	620,000	2.7
1920 (January)	40,700,000	620,000	2.2
1930 (April)	47,600,000	690,000	1.7
1940 (April)	53,300,000	570,000	1.1

The economic import of the slackening rate of labor force growth is most evident when it is viewed in relation to the concomitant reduction in working hours. Statistics on hours of work for the whole labor force

Adapted from *The Labor Force in the United States, 1890-1960,* Chapter 2, pp. 17-46, *passim,* by permission of the author and the Social Science Research Council. (Copyright, 1948, by the Social Science Research Council.)

have been available only since 1940, when they were first obtained in the population census, but it is generally known that hours have been greatly shortened during the last half-century. It is estimated that average full-time weekly hours in manufacturing industries were reduced from 59 in 1899 to 40 in 1939.[1] The reduction for all types of employment combined has probably been less, but still very substantial. Hours were temporarily lengthened during the World War II period but have been greatly shortened since the war ended, as shown by the MRLF estimates.

With shorter hours and slackening labor force growth it is probable that the supply of labor in this country, reckoned in terms of man-hours per year, has increased but little in recent decades, except for the wartime spurt. Henceforth it is quite likely that the trend of labor supply will be downward.

Shrinkage of the quantity of national labor supply of course does not necessarily imply a reduction of potential output of goods and services at full employment. On the contrary, it is probable that increased product per man-hour, due both to an increase in the capacities of the workers themselves and to improvements of technology and capital equipment, will greatly overbalance any reduction in the quantity of labor available. Nevertheless, the trend of labor supply in this country is one factor which tends to put the United States at a disadvantage, by comparison with other countries that have a rapidly growing labor force, in expanding the volume of its potential production and increasing its military power.

TREND OF THE RATIO OF LABOR FORCE TO POPULATION. The trend of the labor force as a percentage of the population is quite different from its trend in absolute numbers. The labor force increased from about 35 per cent of the total population in 1890 to more than 40 per cent in 1940. The sudden jump during the war brought the ratio to 46 per cent in April 1945.

The shift in this ratio during the last half-century does not seem very large, but it was great enough to have considerable economic importance. If average weekly working hours had not changed between 1890 and 1940 and if there had been no gain in productivity, the rise of the labor force ratio would have made possible an increase of one-seventh in the nation's per capita income. The benefit of this change, like the benefit of increasing production per man-hour, has been realized partly in the form of higher income and partly in shorter working hours.

It may be pointed out here that there are two principal explanations of the past increase. First is the decline in the percentage of the population that consists of children too young to be in the labor force. This is a feature of the aging of the population which has occurred mainly as a result of the decline of the birth rate, the improvement of adult mortality rates, and the reduction of immigration. The second major explanation

1. Fabricant, *Employment in Manufacturing, 1899-1939*, Appendix C.

is the increasing proportion of women in gainful occupations. Important offsetting factors have been the increase in the proportion of aged persons in the population, the decline in the proportion of young people in the labor force, and the trend toward earlier retirement of elderly men.

MOVEMENT OF WOMEN INTO THE LABOR MARKET. The increase in the proportion of women in the labor force reflects an important modification of the traditional division of functions between women as homemakers and men as breadwinners. The degree of participation in gainful employment on the part of women from 20 to 64 years of age has increased continuously during the period 1890 to 1940.[2] In the whole female population 20 to 64 years old the proportion of labor force members rose from 17 per cent in 1890 to 29 per cent in 1940.

Even more striking changes are found when the figures for married, widowed, and divorced women are considered separately. In 1890 the estimates show only a negligible proportion of married women in the labor force. Even spinsters were not generally employed in those days. Only about one-half of the single women 25 to 34 years old were in the labor force, and in the higher age groups the proportion was much smaller. Among young widows and divorcees the percentages were about as high as among young single women, or somewhat higher. Many of these women were forced by economic necessity to find what work they could. There was no marital status or age group, however, in which substantially over one half of the women were in the labor force in 1890.

In the half-century that followed, the proportions of married women in the labor force doubled, tripled, or quadrupled in various age groups up to 65 and even showed some increase in the group 65 years old and over. There were also large increases in the percentages for single and widowed or divorced women. By 1940 four-fifths of the single women between the ages of 25 and 35 were in the labor force. Custom has now come to dictate that a young, unmarried woman should earn her living. The proportions of young widows and divorcees in the labor force had also risen quite high by 1940, amounting to about two-thirds of the total at ages between 25 and 45. But responsibilities for the care of children, hindering the employment of many widowed and divorced women, prevented the percentages from rising as high as those for single women.

Under the stimulus of the war labor shortage the percentage of women in the labor force increased between 1940 and 1945 at a rate far above even that of the preceding 50 years. According to the estimates "comparable with the 1940 census," nearly 38 per cent of all women 20 to 64 years old were in the labor force in April 1945, as compared with 29 per cent in 1940.

2. If the 1910 figures (not comparable with those for other census years) are omitted, the data from successive censuses show unbroken upward trends in the percentages of labor force members among each age group of the female population in the age range 20 to 64.

The advantage gained from the employment of more women in the production of economic goods obviously entails some cost. Both the past expansion of the female labor supply and that projected for the future come largely from increased employment of married women. Within the framework of existing customs relating to the care and upbringing of children in this country few women can combine gainful employment and motherhood, at least while their children are too young to take care of themselves. The movement of women into the labor market is therefore a factor tending to reduce the birth rate, though it is easy to overemphasize the importance of this relative to other factors which have contributed to declining fertility. Employment of women also commonly involves some changes in home activities other than child care and thus may tend to alter the character of the family as a social institution. How these changes may affect the welfare of the nation in the long run is a question which merits careful study.

The changing sex ratio of the labor force also gives increasing importance to the problems of women's wages, hours, and conditions of employment, and to their status in labor organizations. When nearly 3 out of every 10 workers are women and nearly 4 out of every 10 women in the productive age groups are workers, as 1960 projections indicate that they are likely to be, working women's problems become major considerations for public policy in regulation of the labor market and for labor union action. It is increasingly important to consider the health and welfare of the feminine segment of the labor force when standards relating to minimum wages, maximum hours, safety precautions, sanitary facilities, etc. are formulated. From the labor unions' point of view, the issues of equal pay, comprehensive organization, maintenance of work standards, etc. become more and more vital as they apply to the female contingent of potential union membership.

CHANGES IN THE AGE OF ENTERING THE LABOR FORCE. The decrease in the proportion of school-age youths in the labor force is also an exceedingly significant trend from the standpoint of social welfare. Between 1890 and 1940 the percentage of boys and girls 14 to 19 years old who were in the labor force decreased by about one fourth. The corresponding figure for boys and girls 10 to 13 years old fell from 7 per cent to virtually nothing.[3]

The average age at which young men entered the labor force in 1940, according to the census figures, was approximately 18 years.[4] The census

---

3. Data on employment status of children 10 to 13 years of age were not obtained in the 1940 census; if they had been obtained, the percentage classified as labor force members would have been very small, as less than 300,000 children of this age reported gainful occupations in the 1930 census. In 1945, however, the percentage of children of this age in the labor force was doubtless much larger. Ducoff and Hagood have estimated that 400,000 children under 14 worked as hired laborers on farms during 1945 (*Employment and Wages of the Hired Farm Working Force in 1945*).

4. This average was calculated from first differences in the percentages of males in

measures of labor force status of youths, however, are somewhat arbitrary and are less reliable than for older groups. The shift from the student category to the labor force is often so gradual that it is hard to say when it has been substantially completed. It may begin with seasonal work during school vacations, or with part-time work after school, and it may continue through various degrees of labor market activity until the individual finally drops school and becomes a full-time member of the year-round labor force. According to the 1940 census definition all the young people who were doing any gainful work or looking for work in the last week of March, a school month, should have been counted as members of the labor force, even though their gainful work may have occupied only a few hours during the week. Actually not all the young people who met this definition were enumerated as labor force members; many of those who were mainly students but were also working part-time at gainful occupations were reported simply as students. Thus the census figures give only a rough and somewhat arbitrarily defined measure of the extent of young people's participation in the labor market.

The fact that young people in 1940 went to work at a later age than they did half a century before is mainly a reflection of a higher standard of education. To be sure, the practice of working at part-time jobs while still in school was probably somewhat less prevalent in 1940 than it was 50 years before,[5] but the main change was a tendency for a larger proportion of young people to finish high school or college before going to work. In 1890 the median number of grades of school completed by boys and girls at the end of their formal education was probably not over 8; in 1940 it was more than 11.[6]

Obviously, later entrance into the labor force means a better-educated and hence a potentially more productive working population. This improvement in the quality of labor resources should be reckoned, along with development of technology and capital equipment, as a major reason for the economic advancement of the nation in the past and an important means of further advancement in the future. The stimulus to cultural and political progress which results from a higher educational level also must not be undervalued.

THE TREND TOWARD EARLIER RETIREMENT. Once a young man has

the labor force at successive single years of age in the range from 14 to 24 years, as shown in 1940 census report B-1, Table 1, adjusted to the level "comparable with the 1940 census." The first differences were weighted according to the age distribution of the stationary male population, as given in the 1939-41 life tables, in order to eliminate the effects of differences in the sizes of successive cohorts of births and to eliminate the effects of irregularities in the reported age distribution.

5. This is probable because of the secular decrease in the percentage of the population living on farms, but the census records do not give any reliable indication of long-term changes in the percentage of young people both in the labor force and attending school.

6. These are the median numbers of school years completed by persons 70 to 74 and 20 to 24 years old in 1940, respectively, as shown in 1940 census report A-4, p. 6.

finished his education and has become a member of the labor force custom demands that he continue in that role, if he is able, until he reaches an age which is socially regarded as appropriate for retirement. Even those few who would be financially able to live without working usually conform to this custom by following some kind of gainful occupation at least until they are 55 or 60 years old. Less than 2 men in 100 between the ages of 25 and 55 were reported in the 1940 census as able to work and not in institutions, but neither employed nor looking for a job. (See Table 1.) In this age group physical disability and institutionalization

Table 1—Functional Distribution of the Male Population 25 Years Old and Over, by Age: April 1940

		PER CENT NOT IN LABOR FORCE	
Age in Years	Per Cent in Labor Force	Unable to Work*	Other
25-34	95.9	2.7	1.5
35-44	95.5	3.5	1.1
45-54	92.8	5.4	1.9
55-59	88.5	8.2	3.3
60-64	79.6	14.2	6.2
65-74	51.6	34.7	13.8
75 and over	18.3	65.6	16.1

* Including inmates of penal and mental institutions and of homes for the aged, infirm, and needy.

are the only important limitations on the proportion of the male population in the labor force. This was true half a century ago as it is today. Between 1890 and 1940 the percentages of men in the labor force at ages between 25 and 55 showed hardly any more variation than might be expected to result from minor differences in the basis of labor force classification in the different censuses. There was some rise in these percentages between 1940 and 1945, doubtless attributable mainly to relaxation of the standards of eligibility, enabling some men to enter the labor force who were previously unable to get jobs on account of physical handicaps. But these men were a relatively unimportant source of additional labor supply.

At ages over 65 the percentage of men in the labor force has followed a downward trend over a long period. The decline in the proportion of men remaining in the labor force at these ages was pronounced and continuous during the whole period from 1890 to 1940.

AGING OF THE LABOR FORCE. In spite of earlier withdrawal from gainful work the average age of the labor force is rising. This anomaly is explained partly by the fact that the average age of the population as a whole is increasing and partly by the reduction in the proportion of youths who enter the labor force before the age of 20.

The close relationship between the age distribution of the population and that of the labor force is illustrated by Chart 1, which shows the functional distribution of men and women in each age group, based on 1940 census data. The relationship is especially close in the case of males because a large majority of men at all age levels from about 18 to 64 years are in the labor force. The age distribution of the female labor force is less closely dependent on the population distribution because of the large group of homemakers making up a changing proportion of the total in each age group. The shift from the homemaker to the labor force group has been proportionally greater among women from about 35 to 55 years of age than among younger women, and this helps to explain why the median age of the female labor force has risen faster than that of the male labor force.

One feature of the aging of the labor force has been a reduction in the number of young workers added annually, in proportion to the size of the whole labor force. This slackening of the labor force replacement

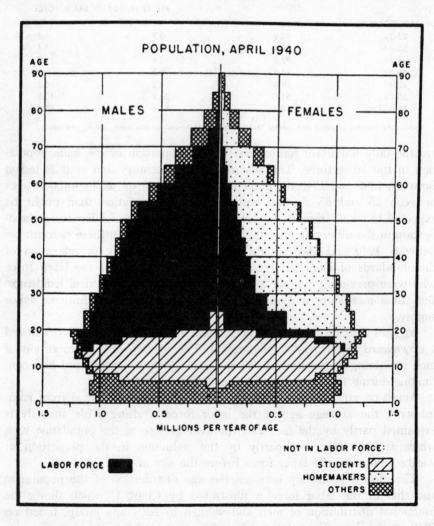

CHART 1—Functional Distribution of the Population, by Sex and Age: 1940

rate results from the fact that the population in the age range from about 15 to 25 years, which provides most of the new recruits to the labor force each year, has constituted a diminishing percentage of the entire adult population.

The number of men and women over 65 in the labor force has remained practically constant in proportion to the total labor force of all ages. Both in 1890 and in 1940 approximately 4 per cent of the labor force consisted of persons over 65, and the projections for 1960 indicate 3.5 per cent. The influence of the aging of the population upon the relative number of workers over 65 is almost exactly balanced by the decrease in the percentage who remain in the labor force after 65 among the men who survive to that age.

The effects of aging can be seen, however, in the projected figures for workers in the ages of the late 50's and early 60's. The age group 55 to 64 years, which made up 7 per cent of the labor force in 1890 and 10 per cent in 1940, will increase to 12.5 per cent of the total in 1960, according to the projections. This group is subject to a comparatively great unemployment risk and will constitute a special problem if a serious threat of unemployment again appears.

How the aging of the labor force may affect productivity is an extremely important question. Present knowledge of differences between the productivity of young and old workers in various occupations is not adequate for an answer. It seems likely that elderly workers suffer a disadvantage on account of waning strength, dexterity, and vigor, and perhaps a greater difficulty in learning new methods. On the other hand, the increased skill which comes with long experience is doubtless an important asset to older workers, and they may also be superior in qualities such as judgment, steadiness, and carefulness. More intensive study of relationships between age and productivity is needed.[7]

THE SHIFTING LOAD OF DEPENDENCY. Trends in the size and characteristics of the population not in the labor force are highly significant in connection with problems of dependency, though persons outside the labor force are not necessarily dependents in every sense. Many of them are financially independent, receiving income from rent, interest, royalties, dividends, pensions, etc. and even those who have no income may contribute as much to the social product in noneconomic terms as the labor force contributes in terms of economic goods. Still, from the standpoint of national economics it is useful to study changes in the relative size of groups who do not take part in the work of producing current income.

It has already been pointed out that the ratio of the labor force to the population has risen substantially during the last half-century—in other words, that the total of all kinds of persons not in the labor force has

7. For an outline of research already done on this subject and of needed studies, see Tibbitts and Pollak, "Employment Problems of Old Persons."

declined in proportion to the number of breadwinners. Certain groups of nonbreadwinners have decreased relatively more than others, and one group, consisting of the aged, retired, and disabled, has vastly increased; so that the composition of the dependency load has been greatly altered.

The 1940 census date is the only one for which detailed information on the composition of the population not in the labor force is available, but estimates have been made for 1890 and projections for 1960.[8] The estimated ratios of various groups not in the labor force to the labor force are shown in Table 2.

Table 2—Persons Not in the Labor Force per 100 Labor Force Members, 1890 and 1940, with Projections for 1960

Functional class	1890 (June)	1940 (April)	1960 (April)
Total not in labor force	182	147	143
Homemakers	66	55	51
Students	52	50	50
Others	64	42	42
Under 14 years old	54	26	22
14-54 years old	5	6	6
55 years old and over	5	11	15

There was a substantial decline in the ratio of homemakers to the labor force between 1890 and 1940. The downward influence exerted on this ratio by the movement of women into the labor force was partly off-set by the changing age composition of the female population, for there was an increase in the proportion of women in the age range which contains the largest proportion of homemakers. Between 1940 and 1960, according to the projections, the net effect of these two influences will be a further decline, from 55 homemakers per 100 labor force members in 1940 to 51 in 1960.

The relative number of students also is affected by influences working in opposite directions, namely, the increase of school attendance and the decrease in the relative size of the school-age population. The net result was practically no change in the number of students per 100 labor force members from 1890 to 1940. The projections indicate that when postwar conditions return to normal, the ratio will resume its prewar level of approximately one student to two labor force members.

During the last half-century the proportion of the "others" not in the labor force considered as a whole has decreased greatly, their ratio to the labor force having dropped from 64 per 100 in 1890 to 42 in 1940. This decrease is attributable entirely to the reduction in the relative number of childen, due chiefly to the declining birth rate. The "others" under 14 years of age, consisting mainly of preschool children, dropped from 54 to 26 per 100 labor force members. From 1940 to 1960 the projections indi-

8. Another set of estimates for 1890 is shown in Hurlin and Givens, "Shifting Occupational Patterns."

cate a slower drop in this ratio because of the abnormally high birth rate at present and during the last few years. The projected ratio falls to 22 in 1960.

Only a small number of persons between the ages of 14 and 55 are included in the "other" group; these are for the most part prematurely disabled persons and inmates of institutions. Their relative number was small both in 1890 and 1940, and the 1960 projections indicate no change. The "others" over 55 years of age, who can be taken as representing principally the dependent aged population, were equally few in 1890 but have increased greatly since then. This group jumped from 5 per 100 labor force members in 1890 to 11 in 1940 and will reach 15 per 100 by 1960, according to the projected figures.

The changing composition of the dependency load which these figures illustrate constitutes one of the great social problems of the century.

THE LENGTH OF MEN'S WORKING LIVES. The significance of labor force trends in relation to old-age security problems is brought out even more clearly by an analysis of the proportion of a man's lifetime which is spent at gainful work. In 1940 conditions of mortality and participation in the labor force at various ages were such that a man at the age of 25 would live on the average of 42.5 years more and would spend 35.4 of these years as a member of the labor force. In other words, he could expect about 7 years of life in retirement, in a state of disability, or in an institution, and these 7 years amounted to about one-sixth of his life expectancy.

The average length of the period of old-age dependency has been increasing gradually during the last half-century. The amount of the increase cannot be determined exactly because only fragmentary data on mortality in the United States toward the end of the last century are available. An indication of the trend is given, however, by a calculation for white males in the Death Registration States of 1900 (10 states and the District of Columbia), for the years 1900 and 1930. This calculation shows an increase in the life expectancy for white men at age 25, amounting to more than 2½ years during the 30-year interval, but no change in the average number of years in the labor force. Thus the average number of years outside the labor force shows a rise from about 4 in 1900 to more than 6½ in 1930.

This trend can be expected to continue as long as reductions in mortality rates continue to improve the chances of surviving to old age while the proportions of the survivors remaining in the labor force after middle age continue to fall. The labor force projections for 1960, together with projections of long-range mortality trends, show a further increase in the average lifetime of men after the age of 25, from 42.5 years in 1940 to 43.9 years in 1960, but still no significant change in the average number of years in the labor force. The expectation of life outside the labor force indicated for 1960 is 8.3 years. In other words, if past trends continue, by 1960 a 25-year-old man will expect nearly 1 year of life in retirement for every 4 years of his remaining working life.

Against this prospect it is not difficult to see the importance of preventing avoidable waste of manpower. To be sure, with increasing productivity and a diminishing burden of child dependency, the future load of old-age dependency may be no harder to bear than the present one. But any lightening of that load which can be achieved without violating the principle of adequate provisions for security of the aged is a clear social gain.

MIGRATION DIFFERENTIALS
IN THE CITY AS A WHOLE

Ronald Freedman

One of the methods of studying the role of the migrant in the life of the city is to study on a city-wide basis the relationships between the migrant status and the social characteristics of the population of Chicago. This is the method customarily employed by students of differential migration. By comparing the non-migrants in the city with the different types of migrants to the city a conception may be developed of the place of each type of migrant in the demographic, social, and economic structure of the city.

In this chapter the relationships between the migrant status and social characteristics of the population of Chicago on a city-wide level will be investigated in detail. The over-all purpose is to discover, as far as possible from census data on a city-wide level, what kind of person the migrant is and how his characteristics are related to his place of origin. In terms of this purpose, several theories will be considered which attempt to relate the characteristics of the migrants to their migrant status.

One theory, suggested for investigation, is that migrants of different types will tend to have in common some social characteristics as well as an attraction to similar areas within the city. Irrespective of type of place of origin, all the migrants have in common the minimum mobility which is associated with migration. If mobility is more closely associated with some social characteristics than with others, migrant groups from different types of places may be expected to have certain common characteristics differentiating them from the non-migrants. The assumption here is that mobility is such an important characteristic that it tends to determine at least some of the other characteristics of mobile persons.

In one respect the theory that all types of migrants have some characteristics in common involves an amendment to Moore's "theory of resembling environments," for Moore indicates that urban migrants from places resembling the city of destination will resemble the non-migrants in that city rather than the migrants from places of widely different cultural levels. The theory advanced here is that, although the cultural level of place of origin (defined in terms of degree of urbanization) determines the variation between migrant groups, all of them will tend to have in common some characteristics which distinguish them as migrants from the non-

Reprinted from *Recent Migration to Chicago,* Chapter 3, pp. 30 ff., by permission of the author and the publisher. (Copyright, 1950, by the University of Chicago Press.)

migrants. The basis for this theory is that even those migrants who came from environments closely resembling that of Chicago must be subject in some measure to the mobility which will affect all migrants, although the migrants from "rural" cultural levels should be affected most profoundly.

The idea that different types of migrants have some social characteristics in common as compared with non-migrants has at least two significant corollaries. In the first place, those migrants for whom the migration process involves the least change (i.e. the least mobility) should tend to resemble the non-migrants most closely. In the second place, those non-migrants who migrate within the city should tend to resemble the migrants more than the other non-migrants.

It is reasonable to assume that the suburban migrants—especially those from the Inner Zone—are the least mobile of the migrant groups. Their movement is within the boundaries of the functional metropolitan community. Presumably, their movement requires a minimum of adjustment to a new institutional structure. On the other hand, the intra-city migrants—those who change residence within the city—may be considered to be the most mobile of the non-migrants. Two points of interest, then, will be the extent to which the characteristics of the Suburban migrants tend to resemble those of the non-migrants and the extent to which the intra-city migrants tend to resemble the inter-city migrants.

The theory that migrant groups of different types may tend to have certain specific similarities as compared to non-migrants does not exclude the possibility of considerable variations among the migrant groups both with respect to the characteristics which distinguish migrants from non-migrants and those which do not. Migrants may be expected to differ from each other in relation to the cultural level of their place of origin. The classifications—"rural farm," "rural nonfarm," and "urban"—have been indicated as representing three different types of environment on a continuum, with the rural-farm environment, on the average, least similar to that of Chicago and the urban environment most similar to that of Chicago. The theory to be investigated here is that the characteristics of the migrants vary in relation to the cultural levels of their place of origin so that the culturally intermediate rural-nonfarm migrants are also intermediate between urban and rural-farm migrants with respect to the proportion of migrants having any given social characteristic. Furthermore, following Moore's "theory of resembling environments" it is hypothecated that the migrants from places whose cultural level is most similar to that of Chicago will have a relatively "high" rank and typically urban characteristics with respect to those characteristics for which "high" and "low" rank have significance. Thus, it is expected that with respect to work status, occupation, and educational attainment the position of the urban migrants will be highest in rank or most favorable and that of the rural-farm migrant lowest in rank or least favorable.

For most of the characteristics to be investigated data are available to determine whether the essential differences between non-migrants and each type of migrant vary with the region of origin of the migrant. Because of the relatively broad regional groupings necessarily employed, regional variations may be expected to be less significant than differences related to the urban-rural classification. Although variations from the general differential pattern associated with each region of origin will be considered in the following sections, special interest will focus on the Southern migrants since their migration probably involves the greatest change in cultural level.

Consideration of the relationship between the characteristics of the migrants and the cultural level of their place of origin should provide a perspective for evaluating that conception of the role of the migrant which has developed out of the interest in the migration to cities from "problem" areas. Novels and Congressional hearings, as well as important research monographs, have centered around the dramatic cityward migration from distressed areas, particularly from rural-farm areas and from Southern regions. The general conception of the "problem" migrants is that they are poorly educated, unaccustomed to the urban environment and a part of a mobile unskilled labor reserve. Here the characteristics of migrants from places of different cultural levels will be compared. On the basis of the "theory of resembling environments" the "problem" migrants should be those from areas whose cultural level least resembles that of Chicago. Insofar as "problem" migrant groups of depressed status are found to exist, the characteristics and numerical importance of such groups may be seen in the perspective of all the different types of migrants who come to a city like Chicago.

FINDINGS ON MIGRANT AGE DIFFERENTIALS. In general, the migration differentials with respect to age have been found to be consistent with those found in previous studies and with the hypotheses suggested for investigation in the introductory section. The principal findings may be summarized as follows:

(1) *In comparison with non-migrants, all types of migrants were concentrated in the late adolescent and early adult years.* This was true irrespective of sex, race, region of origin, or cultural level of place of origin of the migrants. The variations in age distribution as between different types of migrants were in no case great enough to change the central fact that all types of migrants were disproportionately adolescents or young adults.

(2) *The variations in the age distributions of the white migrants were related to variations in rural-urban cultural levels, although the differences in the proportions of migrants from each cultural level in the extreme age groups were not very great.* The rural-urban age differentials were greatest within the age range from 18-54 years. The most significant fact is that the more rural the background of the white migrants, the younger was the average age and the greater was the "excess" in the years of late adolescence and early adulthood. This was true for the migrants from every region

except the Suburban.

(3) *The rural-urban continuum was not found to be related to the age selection of Negro migrants as it was to white migrants. For Negro migrants, the principal contrasts were between the urban migrants on the one hand and the two types of rural migrants on the other hand.* There was no consistent direction of differentiation between rural-farm and rural-non-farm migrants. Among the Negro migrants both rural-farm and rural-non-farm migrants were concentrated in the youngest and oldest age categories in greater numbers than urban migrants. This has been taken as evidence that among Negroes both types of rural migrants tended to migrate in family groups more frequently than urban migrants. The differentials found between Negro rural and urban migrants applied mainly to the migrants from the Southern regions. The rural and urban Negro migrants from areas outside the South were differentiated in a manner more similar to that characterizing white migrants.

(4) *The variations in age distributions related to region of origin were, in most cases, not great enough to affect the essential age differences as between migrant groups or as between migrants and non-migrants.* In terms of this study the most significant fact was the tendency for the age distributions of the Suburban migrants to resemble those of the non-migrants.

Some significant implications are attached to the conclusions summarized in the preceding section. First of all, the "excess" of young adults among every group of migrants indicates that the migrants are potentially a very productive group both from the economic and demographic point of view. The youth of the migrants indicates that large numbers of them are at the beginning of their productive occupational careers and have a full span of working years to contribute to the economy of the city. Relatively few of them are members of those groups above 45 years of age which sometimes encounter difficulty in securing employment in our economy. Among the white migrants the relatively small numbers at either extreme of the age distribution indicates relatively small numbers of persons dependent for economic or other forms of assistance. From the point of view of population growth, the youthfulness of the migrants to the city indicates that they are on the threshold of family life and parenthood and may be expected to contribute more than their proportional share of births to the population. Students of population trends have noted that were it not for the cityward migration of young adults the birth rates of most of our large cities would fall even lower than their present low levels. The fact that all types of migrants are concentrated disproportionately in the fertile young adult years is consistent with this idea.

The disproportionate concentration of white migrants in the young adult years is an indication that they are disproportionately unattached persons or married persons without children. Although satisfactory data on marital and family status for the migrants are not available, this inference is consistent with data on family size, relationship to family head, and living arrangements to be presented later in this chapter.

For Negro migrants, this has been found to be less true. The age distribution of the Negro migrant from the rural South has been interpreted as indicating a family-type migration.

SEX-RATIO DIFFERENTIALS. The sex of the individual is so fundamental in determining his role and status, even in the rational urban environment, that a consideration of the nature of migrant sex-ratio differentials needs no justification. The contemporary social and economic structure of the great American metropolis has a relatively low sex-ratio as one feature of its population base. In 1940, when the sex-ratio for the total non-migrant population of the United States was 100.1, the sex-ratio for the non-migrant population of cities of 100,000 population or greater was 96.0. For Chicago in 1940 the sex-ratio of the non-migrant population was 98.0.[1]

Many students of migration have been concerned with the degree to which various types of cityward migration select females and thereby maintain these relatively low urban sex-ratios. Although these studies have by no means been conclusive, the accumulated weight of the evidence they present indicates that: (1) cityward migration in general is selective of females, (2) the selection of females among cityward migrants is greatest among migrants from nearby places, especially from nearby rural places, (3) the sex-ratio of cityward migrants is lowest in the adolescent and young adult age groups.[2] The applicability of these generalizations to the migration to Chicago will be examined in this section incident to the investigation of whether: (1) all types of migrants differ from non-migrants in having a low sex-ratio, (2) the sex-ratio varies with the rural-urban cultural level of place of origin, (3) the sex-ratio of the Suburban migrants resembles that of the non-migrants.

The sex-ratio for all the migrants to Chicago in 1940 was considerably lower than that of all the non-migrants. The sex-ratio of all the migrants was 89.0 as compared with 98.0 for the non-migrants. The difference between migrant and non-migrant sex-ratios for Chicago was considerably greater than that for all American cities of 100,000 or more in 1940. The Chicago non-migrants had a higher sex-ratio and the Chicago migrants a lower sex-ratio than comparable groups for all cities of 100,000 or more. Migration to Chicago was apparently even more selective of females than migration to metropolitan centers in general.

Each of the major types of migrants of each race had a lower sex-ratio than the Chicago non-migrants. Only the foreign Negro migrants, who were numerically insignificant, had a higher sex-ratio than the non-migrants.

The differences between the migrant and the non-migrant sex-ratios cannot be attributed to age differences. The age-standardized sex-ratios

1. Data on sex-ratios from U.S. Bureau of Census, *Sixteenth Census of the United States, Population, Internal Migration, 1935–1940, Color and Sex of Migrants* (Washington: Government Printing Office, 1943), Table 2.

2. D. S. Thomas, *Research Memorandum On Migration Differentials.* SSRC, Bulletin 43, 1938, pp. 155-69.

were computed by applying the age-specific sex distribution of each migrant group to the non-migrant age distribution. The resulting age-standardized sex-ratios indicate that, even with age eliminated as a variable factor, the sex-ratios of every migrant group (except foreign Negro migrants) are lower than those of the non-migrants. The amount of the differential in sex-ratio is not greatly affected by age standardization in the case of the Negroes, but it is considerably reduced for the whites.

The migrant sex-ratios did not vary consistently in relation to the three rural-urban categories of cultural levels for either whites or Negro migrants. Regional data also indicate that the sex-ratio of the rural migrants is not consistently lower than that of the urban migrants from each region.

The generalization that sex-ratios tend to be lowest for adolescents and young adults is valid for the white migrants to Chicago. For each of the major types of migrants the sex-ratios are lowest both absolutely and relatively in the age groups 18-19 years and 20-24 years. In the age group 18-19 years the sex-ratio is 98 for white non-migrants as compared with 55 for all white migrants and a low of 41 for the white rural-nonfarm migrants. The white migrants have the lowest sex-ratios precisely in those age groups in which they are relatively most numerous.

Among Negroes, also, the sex-ratios tend to be low in the age groups 18-19 years and 20-24 years. Thus, in the age group 18-19 years the Negro non-migrant sex-ratio is 88 as compared with 58 for all Negro migrants and a low of 44 for Negro rural-farm migrants. However, these are not the lowest sex-ratios for the Negro migrants. For all types of Negro migrants the lowest sex-ratios are in the age group 55-64 years (51 for urban, 42 for rural-nonfarm, and 40 for rural-farm). The consistency of this low sex-ratio for the three Negro migrant groups makes it unlikely that it is a chance variation. One possible explanation of the low sex-ratio in this age group is that it reflects the Negro family-type migration and the matriarchal character of the Negro family.

The sex-ratios of the migrants are not lower than those of non-migrants in every age group. Sex-ratios are lower for white non-migrants than any type of white migrant in the age groups from 25-34 years and lower for Negro non-migrants than for any type of Negro migrant in the age groups from 35-54 years.

The low sex-ratios of the white migrants were in large part a function of the distance of their region of origin from Chicago. The low sex-ratio of white rural migrants to Chicago is entirely attributable to migration from regions relatively close to Chicago—the East North Central, West North Central, and Outer Suburban regions. Rural migrants from each of the more distant regions and from the Inner Suburban regions have sex-ratios higher than that for non-migrants. Among urban migrants, also, the lowest sex-ratios were for migrants from the same regions. However, among the urban migrants, only those from the East, the West, and the Deep South had higher sex-ratios than the non-migrants. It is clear that for both urban and rural migrants sex-ratio was a function of the distance of region of origin from Chicago.

Although the sex-ratio of the migrants from the Inner Suburban region is not as low as those of the migrant groups from other regions near Chicago, it does not resemble the sex-ratio of the non-migrants more closely than those of other migrant groups. The tendency for Suburban migrants to resemble the non-migrants is not manifest with respect to sex-ratio.

For Negro migrants the important regional variations in sex-ratio are again with reference to the North-South dichotomy. Sex-ratios were lower for Negro migrants from the three Southern regions than for the Negro migrants from the North and West.

The sex-ratio for white foreign migrants was slightly less than the non-migrant sex-ratio, whether standardized or unstandardized rates are considered. The white foreign migrant sex-ratio was higher than that for any other white migrant group. The sex-ratio for the Negro foreign migrants was very high, but the number of persons in the population from which this ratio was computed was very small.

SUMMARY OF MIGRANT SEX-RATIO DIFFERENTIALS. The findings with respect to the sex-ratio of migrants to Chicago may be summarized as follows:

(1) *Migrants from each rural-urban cultural level, whether white or Negro, had a lower sex-ratio than comparable non-migrants.*

(2) *There were significant regional variations in the sex-ratios. For white migrants the low migrant sex-ratios were mainly attributable to migrants from the regions near Chicago but outside the Inner Suburban Region. For Negroes the low migrant sex-ratios were mainly attributable to Southern Negro migrants.*

(3) *The lowest sex-ratios for white migrants were in the late adolescent and young adult age groups. However, the low migrant sex-ratios cannot be attributed to concentration in these age groups, since each of the major types of migrants had relatively low sex-ratios even when age was held constant.*

(4) *The variations between the migrant sex-ratios were not related consistently to the rural-urban cultural continuum nor did the sex-ratios of the Suburban migrants tend to be similar to those of the non-migrants.* The sex-ratio is apparently not one of the characteristics with reference to which either the cultural level of the place of origin or Suburban residence has the selective effect postulated in the introduction to the chapter.

In general, the investigation of the sex-ratio has shown that the findings of previous studies with reference to sex-ratio migration differentials apply to migration to Chicago but that the more general theories being investigated in this study do not. Age and nearness to Chicago appear to be the significant factors underlying the low sex-ratio of the whole migrant population of Chicago.

SUMMARY OF WORK STATUS DIFFERENTIALS. (1) *The work status of mi-*

grants compared favorably with that of the non-migrants. As compared to non-migrants, most migrant groups were willing to work, as evidenced by the high proportion in the labor force, and they were able to find and hold employment, as evidenced by the low unemployment rates of those migrants in the labor force. While the differences between migrants and non-migrants with respect to proportions in the labor force can be attributed to age differences this is not true for the differences in unemployment rates. The migrants as a whole cannot be characterized as an urban labor reserve. This description properly can be applied only to a limited group of migrants—the Negro rural and urban migrants from the South and the white rural migrants from the South. These "problem" migrants from a "problem" area were distinctive among migrants in having a high unemployment rate.

(2) *For both male and female migrants work status, particularly as denoted by unemployment rates, is associated with the rural-urban cultural level of the place of origin, but the relationship is opposite in direction for males and females.* For males, the more rural the background of the migrants the more unfavorable was the work status as indicated by high unemployment rates. This is consistent with the hypothesis of "resembling environments." For females, the more rural the background of the migrants the more favorable was the work status, as indicated by low unemployment rates. This is apparently inconsistent with the hypothesis of "resembling environments," but some evidence was presented indicating that the high rate of unemployment of the urban female migrants may be a function of higher standards of suitable employment rather than inability to find work. It was not a function of age.

(3) *There is no evidence that the work status of the Suburban migrants deviates from that of other migrants in the direction of the non-migrant work status.*

OCCUPATIONAL DIFFERENTIALS. While the analysis of the work status differentials in the preceding section has indicated that migrants tend to be employed members of the labor force, an analysis of the migrant occupational differentials should give a more precise indication of the migrant's role in the economy by specifying the nature of his employment. Particularly, it should indicate whether the relatively good adjustment of the migrant in the urban labor market in terms of finding employment is a function of his willingness to take poorly paid and poorly esteemed unskilled jobs.

The comparative occupational distribution of the migrants not only indicates their functional position in the economic structure, but also reflects aspects of their social status. For purposes of analyzing the occupational differentials, two broad systems of grouping occupations are to be employed in addition to the analysis of differentials for each occupational grouping for which data are available. In terms of function, the occupations have been grouped into service-production and physical-production occupations. The physical-production occupations are those which are more or less directly concerned with the production and processing of physical goods. On the other hand, the service-production occupations are those which are service or control occupations, involving such functions as management and administration of the productive process, trading, or professional or personal service. The significance of this two-fold functional classification is that the service-production occupations are those generally considered to be typically urban. One significant question concerning the migrant occupation differentials is the extent to which the migrants are concentrated in the typical urban service-production occupations.

A second occupational dichotomy to which reference will be made in this section will be that of "white-collar" as compared to "blue-collar" workers. This division appears to correspond to a rough division of occupations in terms of "high" and "low" status.

In the present section, the concentration of migrants in each occupation as well as in the functional and status occupational groupings will be considered from several points of view. The first question will be whether migrants have distinctive occupational roles in the sense that all migrants or particular groups of migrants are concentrated in specific occupations or in distinctive groupings of occupations as compared with non-migrants. The second question will be the extent to which the theory of "resembling environments" relates to occupations. Jane Moore [3] found that for Stockholm the occupational status of the migrants was "higher" the closer the cultural level of the place of origin was to that of Stockholm. Here the question will be whether the extent of concentration in specific occupations or in service-function or white-collar jobs varies with the categories of the rural-urban cultural continuum. A third question will be the extent to which the occupational status of the migrants varies with their region of origin. With respect to work status, it was found that the only groups unadjusted to the Chicago labor market were those from "problem" regions. Interest will focus on the extent to which similar regional variations affect occupational status.

Compared to non-migrants, male migrants, as a whole, were highly concentrated in the service-production occupations and particularly in those service-production occupations of white-collar status. The male migrants, as a whole, are relatively more numerous than non-migrants in each of the occupations we have designated as service-production occupations and relatively less numerous in each of the physical-production occupations. Sixty-three per cent of all the employed male migrants were in one of the service-production occupations as compared with 48 per cent of the non-migrants. Fifty-two per cent of the migrants were in one of the white-collar occupations as compared with 38 per cent of the male non-migrants. It is clear that the male migrants as a whole were concentrated in the typically urban service-production occupations. Insofar as the white-collar occupa-

---

3. Jane Moore. *Cityward Migration*. U. of Chicago Press, 1938.

tions are those with highest status, they were also concentrated in high status occupations.

The findings with respect to migrant occupational differentials may be summarized as follows:

(1) *In terms of function each major group of migrants, except male rural-farm migrants and female foreign migrants, were concentrated in service-production occupations.* With the exceptions noted, the migrants were drawn into the occupations frequently considered to be distinctively associated with the urban economy. Within the service-production occupations the female migrants were more specifically concentrated in those directly rendering personal or professional services rather than in those involved with control or administration in the productive process. With the exception of the female foreign migrants and the male rural-farm migrants, all types of migrants have a distinctive occupational role as compared to non-migrants in being predominantly in service-production rather than physical-production occupations.

(2) *In terms of status, only the urban male migrants were clearly of higher occupational status than the non-migrants and only the male rural-farm migrants were clearly of lower occupational status than the non-migrants.* The male rural-nonfarm migrants and the four groups of female migrants were concentrated at both extremes of the occupational hierarchy so it is difficult to designate them as of either higher or lower occupational status than non-migrants. The theory of "resembling environments" appears to apply to the migrant occupational differentials.

(3) *Occupational status was directly related to the rural-urban cultural level of the place of origin of both male and female migrants.* The more similar (the more urban) the place of origin to that of Chicago, the higher was the occupational status of the migrants in terms of concentration in white-collar occupations.

(4) *As compared to each other, the groups of migrants from different regions had more significant concentrations of workers in some types of occupations than in others.*

(a) *The migrants from the South and from the regions near Chicago, especially the Suburban region, had significant concentrations of physical-production workers.* Only among migrants from the Inner Suburban region was there a greater proportion of skilled physical-production workers than among the non-migrants. Disproportionate numbers of workers of various skills for Chicago's industries were recruited either from nearby regions or from the disadvantaged South. From the more distant Northern regions the disproportionate concentrations were all in white-collar occupations.

(b) *Migrants from the Suburban regions tended to be concentrated in the occupations in which non-migrants were relatively most numerous.* With reference to occupation this substantiates the theory that Suburban migrants tend to resemble the non-migrants.

EDUCATIONAL DIFFERENTIALS. The relation of educational attainment to migrant status is important as an indication of whether Chicago selected as in-migrants persons who were better prepared for life in terms of formal education than the permanent residents of the city. If our educational system is achieving its stated goals in any substantial part, formal education should constitute at least a rough index of the individual's preparation to make satisfactory adjustments to some of the problems of modern urban life. With specific reference to Chicago, Lang [4] has shown a close relationship between formal educational attainment and other social factors, so that educational differentials may be expected to reflect other social differentials of consequence. There is a general belief that migrants with more than average formal education are an asset to a receiving area. One of the principal arguments for the expenditure of federal funds for education is that certain urban areas are drawing into their own population a disproportionate number of well-educated persons, educated at the expense of other communities—particularly rural communities.

In this section the educational attainment of the migrants is evaluated in terms of data on the years of school completed by persons 25-34 years old. Data for the other age groups are not available. However, there is considerable value in the data for this particular age group alone. It excludes most of the persons who have not completed their formal education. Since the data are limited to a specific age group, age differences will not affect the educational differentials to any substantial amount. This age group includes a substantial number—30 per cent—of the migrants. The educational comparisons made then are between young adults who have presumably completed their formal education.

The educational migration differentials may be summarized as follows:

(1) *The migrants were generally better educated than non-migrants.* Only the male rural-farm migrants and rural Southern migrants, both male and female, had a lower median educational attainment than the non-migrants. Every major migrant group had a considerably higher proportion of college graduates than the non-migrants.

(2) *As between migrant groups, educational attainment varied with the rural-urban cultural continuum so that urban migrants were best educated and rural-farm migrants least well educated.* Insofar as formal education is an index of preparation for the requirements of urban life this is consistent with the theory of "resembling environments."

(3) *Migrants from the Southern regions were the least well educated.* This is consistent with the relatively low work status and occupational status of these migrants.

(4) *Except for Southern migrants, the migrants with the lowest educational attainment were the Suburban migrants, who again tended to resemble the non-migrants.* The migrants from other areas near Chicago also tended to be of relatively lower educational status than migrants from other

---

4. Richard O. Lang, "The Relation of Educational Status to Economic Status in the City of Chicago By Census Tracts, 1934" (Unpublished Ph. D. dissertation, Dept. of Sociology, University of Chicago, 1936).

areas, while the Northern migrants from more distant regions were best educated.

The relatively high educational attainment of the migrants was consistent with their favorable occupational and work status. The only groups of definitely lower educational attainment than the non-migrants were male rural-farm migrants and Southern rural migrants. The migrants in general were of high educational attainment.

FAMILY STATUS DIFFERENTIALS. The comparative family status of the migrants and non-migrants is of great importance, since family relationships are one of the basic determinants of the life pattern of the individual. Persons who live apart from other members of their families are relatively free from the customary restraints and responsibilities of family life. Similarly, persons who live in small families, particularly those who live in two-person families without children or older relatives, are likely to share, in some measure, the relative freedom from customary familial social controls of persons who live alone. The person who is free from customary familial restraints is typically depicted as a mobile individual whose freedom may lead either to the sophistication or to the disorganization typical of different areas of urban life. Since family status is considered to be such a basic factor in creating the distinctive life organization of the urban dweller, it is desirable to describe migrant family status differentials.

The most significant findings with respect to the family status migration differentials have been:

(1) *All types of migrants tended to belong in disproportionate numbers to family units whose size and living arrangements indicated a minimum of family ties.* Among all types of migrants there were disproportionate numbers of persons living alone, in very small family groups, or in extra-familial living arrangements. The role of the migrant in terms of family status was likely to be that of the unattached person with a minimum of immediate family relationships.

(2) *The extent to which migrants were concentrated in extra-familial living arrangements is related to the rural-urban cultural continuum.* The more rural the background of the migrant, the more likely he was to be living in extra-familial living arrangements. It would appear that those groups of migrants who faced the greatest adjustment in the city were most likely to be living apart from family support and control. However, the significance of this relationship is not clear, since the rural migrants in extra-familial living arrangements were the most likely to be living as lodgers in private households rather than in quasi-public households.

(3) *With respect to family size and number of persons living alone the intra-city migrants resembled the inter-city migrants more closely than did the more sedentary non-migrants.*

SUMMARY OF MIGRANT DIFFERENTIALS FOR THE CITY AS A WHOLE. The relationships between migrant status and social characteristics in Chicago in 1940 have been analyzed in this chapter as one indication of the role of the migrant in the life of the city. With respect to some characteristics all types of migrants have been found to be differentiated from non-migrants in the same direction. With respect to other characteristics the nature of migrant-non-migrant differentials has been found to vary with the rural-urban cultural level of the place of origin of the migrants. This relationship with previous cultural level has been found to exist even for those characteristics with regard to which different migrant groups resemble each other more closely than they resemble non-migrants. The evidence has been consistent with the theory that migrants resemble each other in some respects as a result of their common mobility, but also it has been consistent with the theory that the characteristics of the migrants are related to their previous rural-urban cultural background. Although it is possible to describe the migrants as a whole, it is necessary to indicate that different types of migrants frequently differ in fundamental respects.

The migrants as a whole had either equal or higher rank than the non-migrants with respect to those characteristics for which "high" and "low" rank have some meaning in the urban environment. Thus, either male or female migrants as a whole had achieved a higher educational attainment, were more frequently in the labor force and less frequently unemployed, and were less frequently foreign-born or aliens than the non-migrants. Male migrants were of higher occupational status than the non-migrants, while the female migrants were not distinctly either higher or lower than non-migrants in occupational status. Migrant families were generally of higher economic status than non-migrants insofar as rental is an indication of economic status. The stereotype of the "problem" migrants as a group of persons of depressed social and economic status has not been found to fit the migrants as a whole. The migrants as a whole may be described as having had the characteristics associated with a relatively favorable economic and social position in the city.

In addition to the characteristics for which rank evelutions are meaningful, the migrants had other distinctive characteristics as a group. As compared to non-migrants either male or female migrants were predominantly young adults. They were concentrated in typically urban service-production occupations. They were relatively free from primary group controls in that relatively large numbers of them were living alone or in small families and were living under mobile extra-familial types of residential arrangements. The migrants as a whole also had a relatively low sex-ratio.

Some of the characteristics of the migrants as a whole have also been found to characterize each specific type of migrant, as compared to the non-migrants. Thus, each major type of internal migrant has been found to be disproportionately younger, native-born, in the labor force, in service-production occupations, living alone or in small families, and living under extra-familial residential arrangements. Furthermore, for female migrants each type of migrant was better educated and less frequently unemployed than non-migrants and for none of the major female migrant types was occupational status distinctively higher or lower than for the non-migrants. These resemblances between different types of migrants are consistent with the theory that migrants will tend to resemble each other in some respects as a result of their common mobility, irrespective of differences in rural-urban cultural level.

This theory is further strengthened by the fact that the findings have tended to substantiate its two corollaries: (1) the Suburban migrants whose migration presumably involved least mobility tended to resemble non-migrants, (2) the intra-city migrants, presumably the most mobile non-migrants, tended to resemble the inter-city migrants. The postulated tendency for similarity between Suburban migrants and the non-migrants was found to exist in some measure with respect to age, occupation, nativity, education, although the similarity was not consistent for some other characteristics. Apparently there is some tendency for migrants from places functionally a part of the receiving area to resemble the non-migrants in the receiving area. Wherever data have been available, it has been found that intra-city migrants tended to have characteristics deviating from those of other non-migrants in the direction of the characteristics of inter-city migrants.

Although migrants tended to resemble each other in some respects as compared to non-migrants, the characteristics of different types of migrants have been found to vary in relation to the rural-urban cultural level of their place of origin. Where the cultural level of the place of origin of migrants affected the *direction* of the difference in characteristics between the migrants and non-migrants, the urban migrants were generally "higher" and the rural-farm migrants "lower" in rank with respect to specific characteristics than the non-migrants.

Among the three major types of internal migrants only the male rural-farm migrants were found to have characteristics indicative of low social and economic status. Thus with respect to occupational status, employment, educational attainment, and economic status, the male rural-farm migrants were found to be in a less favorable position than non-migrants. The urban migrants were found to be in a better position than the non-migrants in each of these categories, while the rural-nonfarm migrants were either of about equal to or of higher status than the non-migrants. The one major group of migrants (rural-farm) whose social and economic status was clearly lower than that of the non-migrants came from areas culturally most dissimilar to Chicago. The major group of migrants (urban) whose economic and social status was higher than that of the non-migrants came from areas culturally most similar to that of Chicago.

In comparing migrants from different regions with the non-migrants only the migrants from the Southern regions were found to have the relatively low status in specific characteristics noted for the rural-farm migrants. Migrants from the Southern regions, particularly the Deep South and the Border States, tended to be of lower occupational, educational, and work status than migrants from any other region. In large part, this is attributable to the large numbers of Negroes among the migrants from the South. However, even white rural migrants from the South were found to compare unfavorably with Chicago non-migrants in some respects.

Similarly, the foreign migrants to Chicago have not been found to have had the low status characteristics associated with the foreign migrants of the late nineteenth and early twentieth centuries. In many respects the foreign migrants, and especially the males, resembled the internal migrants. The educational attainment and occupational status of the foreign male migrants were higher than that of the non-migrants. The educational attainment and occupational status of female foreign migrants were somewhat lower than that of the non-migrants but the difference was not great enough to designate the foreign migrants as a depressed group.

The role of most migrants as indicated by their social characteristics has not been found to be that encompassed in the stereotype of the "problem" migrants. Only the rural-farm male migrants or migrants from the Southern regions have been found to have the low occupational, educational, or economic status associated with this stereotype. Rural-nonfarm migrants have been found to be of a status equal to or higher than non-migrants in most respects, while the urban migrants have been found to have a status distinctively higher than that of the non-migrants in most respects. Apparently those urban dwellers who moved between cities were likely to be a highly selected group.

One significant aspect of the role of the migrants which emerges from the analysis of the different characteristics is that in many respects the migrants, other than a few small low-status groups, have the characteristics of the ideal-typical urban dweller. The concentration in service-production occupations, high educational status, small families, the extra-familial living arrangements which characterized almost every migrant type are the characteristics frequently associated by sociologists with the ideal-typical urban mode of life. Even male rural-farm migrants, disadvantaged in most respects, share some of these characteristics. There was some resemblance between the ideal-typical mobile urban dweller and the migrant to the city.

GRAPHIC PRESENTATION OF AGE AND
SEX DISTRIBUTION OF POPULATION IN THE CITY

Charles Newcomb

For more than a hundred years literary and descriptive materials have been accumulating which give insight into the structure of the city and the heterogeneous character of the urban population. Notable among the earlier contributions, which influenced government and private organizations, are the writings of Frederick Engels [1] and Charles Booth.[2]

The Census Bureau of the United States, first organized for the Census of 1790, began to publish the composition and characteristics of population for larger cities by political divisions of the city (wards or boroughs) as early as 1900. The use of official units such as wards for tabulating population data has three important limitations: (1) the wards are too large for refined statistical treatment of population [3] since in several cities they include populations as large as those of some large towns; (2) the wards are not planned to include homogeneous population groups, but often cut across racial, cultural, and economic lines for political or other reasons; (3) the ward lines are changed periodically to make an adjustment to population shifts and thus the areas are not comparable from one census period to another.

In order to correct the major faults in the scheme of tabulating population data by wards and boroughs the "census tract" scheme was adopted by the U. S. Census.[3a] This provided for small, constant geographic areas, with tract areas in the more densely populated sections of the city being as small as one quarter square mile, and containing from 2,000 to 5,000 population. For three census periods, 1910, 1920, and 1930, Chicago and several other large cities in the United States have had population data tabulated in as great detail for the small permanent geographic areas as was formerly done for wards. This makes it possible to study the changes

Reprinted from the *Bulletin of the Society for Social Research*, University of Chicago, by permission of the author and the publisher.

1. *Conditions of the Working Class in England* (1838–1844). See pp. 46 ff. for a description of the structure of Manchester and segregation of classes of population.

2. Booth's sixteen-volume work called *Life and Labour In London* gives a wealth of detail about the working class of the period ending 1885.

3. The average population of each of the 50 wards of Chicago at the time of the last redistricting in 1931 was more than 67,500.

3a. This movement was initiated by Dr. Walter D. Laidlaw while acting as Secretary of the Federated Churches of New York City in 1902, but did not come into general use until 1920.

in population in a given area from one period to another without having to resort to estimates as was necessary before. Even more important, it is now possible to speak of death rates, birth rates, marriage rates, delinquency rates, etc., with as much precision when making comparisons of one part of the city with another as it was heretofore when comparing these rates of various cities.

It is not generally known, however, that there are areas within the city, with populations of from two to five thousand persons, which differ more from one another in age and sex distribution than do some types of cities in the United States. It is common to talk about the differences between rural and urban population, but a study of populations in census tracts "Back of the Yards" as contrasted with those of "Hyde Park," or "Hyde Park" with "West Madison Street," reveals even greater differences than can be found between rural and urban people.

Using age and sex distribution as an example of the differences to be found in characteristics of population in different parts of the city, we find that in one census tract just west of the Loop, with a population of over 1,000, more than 90 per cent are male, and of this male population 88 per cent are over the age of 20. On the North Shore, however, there are populations in which 67 per cent are female. In the industrial area on the far south side we find tracts with populations totaling 6,000 or more, in which 50 per cent are under the age of 20. Facts of this sort have not been taken account of heretofore, mainly because the variations of the small segregated groups were obscured in the tabulation of population by wards or boroughs.

Business firms such as newspapers, department stores and public utilities have dealt with population in the city mainly in terms of families, at least, wherever problems of advertising and distribution of commodities were considered. The usual method of procedure is to divide the total population of Chicago by the number of families, giving in 1930 an average size family of 4.01. This average cannot be applied indiscriminately throughout the city, however, since the average size of families varies in a manner comparable to other characteristics of population as has been indicated in the illustration from age and sex distribution. Thus we find in the "Lower North Side" in tract 130 that out of a total of 620 private families 484, or 78.1 per cent, are classified as comprised of only one or two members.[4] Here we find people living alone or as "partners" or "companions." In "Hegewisch," an industrial area, in tract 718 there are 1,389 families, one-half of which contain six or more persons. Nine families in tract 718 reported twelve or more persons. The large families are found for the most part in areas having a high percentage of foreign-born white population. In tract 718, just referred to, 69.8 per cent of the heads of families are foreign-born white.

The selective factors which help to distribute the age and sex elements

_____
4. Census of 1930.

of the urban population have been described for one city in the following terms:

"In the city of Seattle, which has in general a sex composition of 113 males to 100 females, the downtown district, comprising an area inscribed by a radius of a half mile or so, has from 300 to 500 males to every 100 females. But in the outlying districts of the city, except in one or two industrial sections, these ratios are reversed. Females predominate in numbers over males in all the residential neighborhoods and in the suburbs of the city. This same condition is true with regard to the age distribution of the population. The school census shows an absolute decline in the number of children of school age in the central districts of the city although the total population for this area has shown an increase for each decade. It is obvious, then, that the settler type of population, the married couples with children, withdraw from the center of the city while the more mobile and less responsible adults herd together in the hotel and apartment regions near the heart of the community."[5]

The question may be raised whether the tendency which exists in Seattle holds true for other cities and whether there are patterns of distribution of population which are common to all cities. In Chicago we find the situation comparable to that of Seattle and due to the advantage of securing detailed characteristics of population by small areas additional interesting details are revealed.

Let us select for examination certain census tracts along one of Chicago's principal radial streets leading out from the heart of the city and see what changes in population are revealed in the last three census periods. The areas selected for Chart 1 are along Madison Street at the intersections of State, Halsted, Damen, Kedzie, Cicero, Austin, and Oak Park Avenue.[5a] In Figure 1 (of Chart 1) is shown the total population for the last three census periods. Total populations in Figure 1 are plotted on specially prepared paper, called logarithmic scale paper, in order to show rates of change and still retain the actual numerical values. The lowest value on the vertical scale is 800, the next highest is 1,000, the mid-point is 10,000 and the highest is 80,000. We find that the total population has been decreasing in tracts 226 and 232, and that in tract 213 the population is almost at a standstill, the increase in the last decade being only 7.6 per cent. The greatest relative increase for the two decades occurred in tract 149 which is characteristic of the structure and growth of the city. The rising curve for the two decades in this area is indicative of the process of

---

5. R. D. McKenzie, "The Ecological Approach," *The City*, Park and others, p. 78.

5a. All the figures in Chart 1 are designed to read as a map. The left side of each figure is west and the right side is east. Thus each area has been given its true geographic position (according to map usage) and its relative distance from State and Madison Streets. The tract numbers have been substituted for street names at the bottom of each section of Chart 1; thus 298 lies at State and Madison, 226 at Halsted, 232 at Damen, 213 at Kedzie, 149 at Cicero, and 146 at Austin. The numbers appear only at the bottom of Figure 3 and Figure 6, but apply in each case to Figures 1 and 2, and Figures 4 and 5 as well.

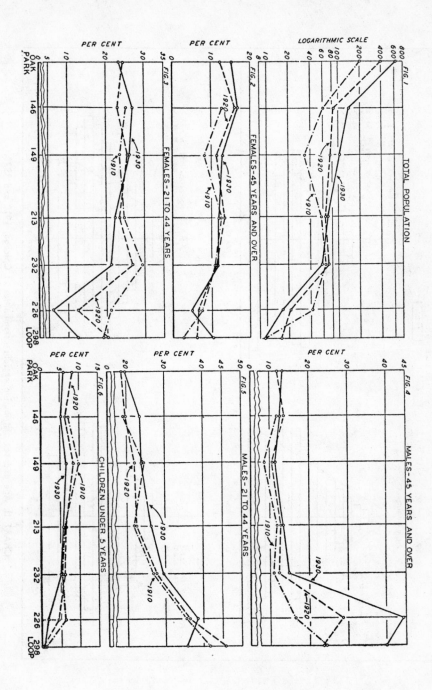

CHART I. Changes in total population and in the proportion of selected age-sex groups for seven census tracts of Chicago, 1910, 1920 and 1930.

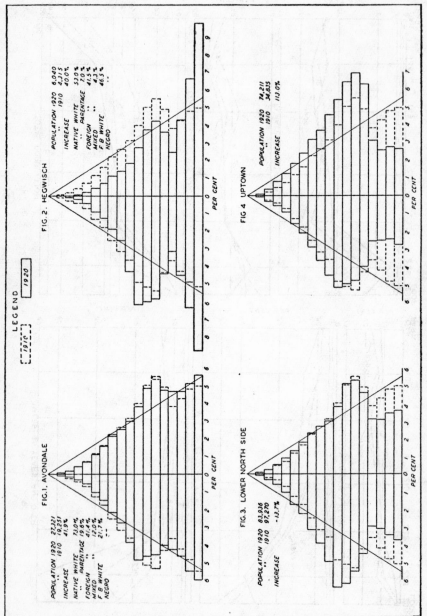

CHART II. Age and sex distribution of four communities of Chicago, 1910 and 1920.

filling in of intervening territory between the city proper and its suburbs, in this case Oak Park. The curves in Figure 1 show a trend of movement of population out from the center of the city, that is, a decrease of population at the center and an increase at the outer edge, which is true for the city as a whole.

We find that for all three periods, 1910, 1920, and 1930, the relative size of the populations in the respective areas remains substantially the same. What we are interested in here is not that populations most distant from the Loop are the largest, but that the changes from one decade to another represent well defined tendencies.

Figures 2, 3, 4, 5, and 6 of Chart 1 show changes in various age and sex groups as proportions of the total population. From these figures we find that the changes for given age groups take place at different rates than the changes of its composite population. Thus the Loop lost 665 persons from 1920 to 1930, but only eight of these individuals were lost in the group of males 45 years of age and over (Figure 4), and even though the number of males in this age group actually declined, their proportion of the total population increased from 23.4 per cent in 1920 to 40.0 per cent in 1930. We find that the proportion of this same age group increased even more for the area just west of this (226), and that beyond that point there is a sharp decline and levelling off so that beyond two and one-half miles from the Loop the range of difference in the proportion of this age group is not more than 4.0 per cent.

The proportion of males 21–44 years of age (Figure 5) does not decline so abruptly as it does for males 45 years and over, but a high proportion of this group extends to six miles beyond the Loop. The proportion of females for this same age group (Figure 3) shows the most marked changes. The proportion of females in tract 232 decreased from 29.1 per cent in 1910 to 21.1 per cent in 1930, but the proportion of females in this age group has increased in all tracts west of this point except Oak Park.

Changes of this sort indicate the order of the movement of population in the city. Thus we find there is not an actual movement of male population toward the center of the city but that the adult males are simply the last to move out and their proportion increases for the most part because the better organized families including women and children move out first.

Given proportions of age and sex groups typify certain areas in the city and, as has been shown, these proportions have a certain order of change. Further, the age and sex distribution also represents, to anyone familiar with the structure of the city, the various occupational and social classes of population. A composite pattern of the proportions of age and sex groups can be made which reveals readily the salient features of the distribution.

This type of diagram, first used in the United States in the Census Atlas of 1874, is called the "Population Pyramid." The population is divided first into male and female, and then each sex group is divided into five-year age groups. The percentage of the total population contained in each age-sex group is computed and a bar representing the given percentage is plotted. The standard form that has come into use is to plot the female age groups as lateral bars according to a suitable scale to the right of a vertical origin line and the male age groups to the left. The youngest age group of the population (under five years) is plotted first, and the next group older in age (from 5 to 9 years) is plotted directly above the first group, and so on in order of age. Since the number in each succeeding age group is diminished by deaths, each succeeding bar must necessarily be shorter, provided of course that the factors of immigration and emigration are excluded. Thus a diagram such as that representing the population of the United States can be used as a norm for comparison with distributions greatly affected by migrations.

In Chart 2 are presented four figures showing selected types of population groupings in which the population changes between two census periods, 1910 and 1920, are compared. Figure 4 (Chart 2) which represents an apartment-hotel area called "Uptown," is an area similar in its social organization to that of tract 146 shown in Chart 1. The increase in the proportion of females 21 to 44 years of age and the decrease in the proportion of children are similar for these two areas, although not so marked for tract 146 as in "Uptown." Figure 4 of Chart 2 should be contrasted with Figure 3 of the same chart. It will be noted that both are decreasing in the proportion of children and increasing in the proportion of adults, but in Figure 3 there is an excess of males while in Figure 4 females are in excess.

Figure 3 of Chart 2 picturing a rooming house district, represents in different graphic form the same type of population as is shown in tract 213 of Chart 1.

Figure 1 of Chart 2 is included to show an area which has increased considerably in population in the decade 1910–1920 but which has attracted substantially the same proportion of age and sex groups as it had in 1910.

A contrasting situation is revealed in Figure 2 of Chart 2, a population found in a manufacturing district, where the increase, as is shown by the long bars representing children under ten, has been mainly due to an increase in births over deaths, and with only slight evidence of an increase due to movement of male population into the area.

So far the emphasis has been placed on the extent and variety of change of population in various parts of the city. The fact of constant change in population in the urban community should be fully realized. It can be shown that there is always some kind of change in population taking place even where the total population is at a standstill. In Chart 3 are shown three census tracts for which no changes in total population are recorded. By comparing the age and sex distribution of 1910 with that of 1920 we find in all tracts, however, an increase in the proportion of children, an increase in the proportion of males 20 to 44, and a decrease in proportion of females. In the case of tract 64 there was a decided shift in the sex ratio of the adult population from an excess of females over males to excess of males over females.

We are led to assume then from the materials so far examined that population in the city is in a constant state of change and adjustment, that the changes so far as age and sex proportions are concerned take place in

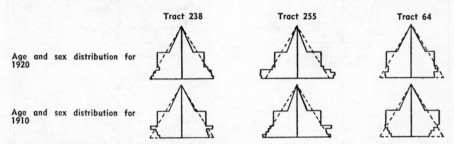

CHART III. Changes in type without change of total population in same tracts, 1910 to 1920

a definite order and that the patterns of age and sex distribution are associated with the basic social and economic character of the area in which they are found.

Treating the population in rather general terms, we find that these assumptions are essentially correct. If we divide the population areas into two classes on the basis of age grouping we find that all areas having a greater proportion of children than the population of the United States (represented in the diagrams by a broken-line triangle) fall into the same general type of area in the city. On the south side of Chicago in 1920 the district embracing the steel mills and factory district had children in excess of the distribution of population of the United States. The industrial area along the north and south branches of the Chicago River also his children in excess of that of the United States. In these areas in which there is a large proportion of children, almost without exception males are in excess over females. This is accounted for by the predominance of immigrant families with large numbers of male boarders and lodgers.

The main area in which adults are preponderant is shaped like the letter "T" with the top extending along the lake shore and the stem projecting out into Oak Park on the west side. A few minor spots also fall into this class, such as the residential settlements in "Morgan Park" and "Beverly Hills" on the southwest side, and in "Logan Square" on the northwest side.

The areas characterized as adult can be sub-classified according to the predominant sex. The Loop and part way out on each branch of the "T" are predominantly male. In the areas where there are many children the economic life of the population is bound up with mechanical and manufacturing trades. Where the adults characterize the area the economic life of the population is related directly or indirectly with the commercial life of the Loop, with the exception of the casual workers who represent a minor part of this population.

CHART IV. Populations of selected census tracts in Chicago—1920, representing types of age and sex distributions in the "City".

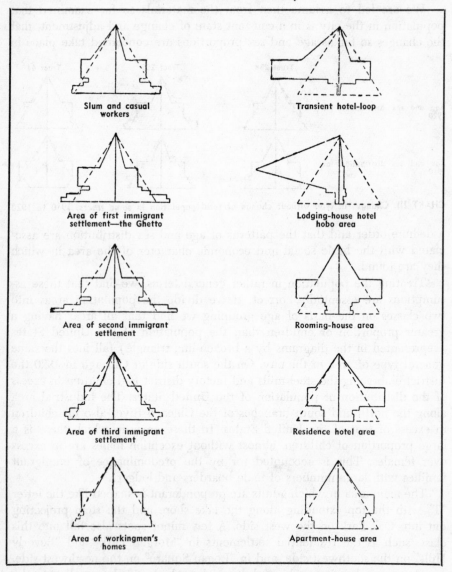

In Chart 4 are shown diagrams which represent types of populations to be found in the city. The left column represents the areas where children are in excess of the proportion of this age group in the population of the United States and following down from the top of the left column of this chart to each succeeding diagram is comparable to starting near the Loop along either branch of the River and following it out toward the city limits.

The slum is an area in which the dwellings are being junked and replaced by wholesale business and light manufacturing. The few remaining families are mixed in with the fringe of casual workers and down-and-outers.

Bordering the slum adjacent to the center of the city is the area of first immigrant settlement. It is an area that is somewhat better organized than the slum and contains immigrants who have brought their cultural institutions with them and maintain them in the new world. The area of second immigrant settlement contains for the most part many of the young native-born whites of foreign and mixed parentage. There are few old people but there are many children. The area of third immigrant settlement represents the attempt of the more assimilated immigrants of the second generation to escape from the old-world culture. It is best typified by the areas that contain a higher proportion of children of school age than the age group under 5. Americans of foreign parentage and their children are therefore moving out of the areas dominated by the old-world culture. The area of working-men's homes, lying as a rule in the general zone of the second immigrant settlement, is often composed of a mixture of the assimilated families of European background and native American stock that has moved into the city. These contain for the most part skilled and semi-skilled workers who have small families, own their own homes, and are the least mobile populations of the city.

The column of diagrams on the right in Chart 4 represents populations where adults are preponderant. This area, already discussed in some detail under Chart 1, contains the transient hotel as in the Loop, together with its business houses which are constantly pushing out and replacing the floating population of the lodging-house and slum area. When the dwellings in this area have been dismantled its population moves on and possesses the rooming-house area which in its turn becomes a hobo lodging-house area. The rooming-house population in its turn moves on and invades the next district, creating a new rooming-house area. The apartment house area draws its population both from the native stock coming into the city and the assimilated elements of the third area of the immigrant settlement and the second generation of the families of the area of working-men's homes. The residence hotel area is isolated from the transient hotel by distance so that it enjoys some of the quiet of the better apartment house district but is also usually isolated from any adjacent rooming-house area by the great difference in rentals. It is an area set aside for endowed widows and families with few children and many servants.

Thus we find that, "Each formation or ecological organization within a community serves as a selective or magnetic force attracting to itself appropriate population elements and repelling incongruous units, thus making for biological and cultural subdivisions of a city's population." [6]

As has been demonstrated in Charts 1 and 2, these populations remain

6. R. D. McKenzie, *op. cit.*, p. 78.

true to type over long periods of time in the city, for although changes are going on continuously the changes follow a regular order of succession.

It is further found that the age and sex distribution of the population disregards entirely the more overt and obvious factors of racial characteristics. The replacement of the Jews in the old Ghetto by the Negroes is a replacement by Negro population that contains essentially the same age and sex elements as the old Jewish population. These are for the most part green, rural Negro families, recruited directly from the plantations in the south. On Chicago's south side, however, we find the large majority of the Negroes are young, unattached males and females from the larger cities in the south who have replaced a white population of essentially the same age and sex characteristics. It is important to note that the Negroes on the south side, especially along the rooming-house section of South Parkway, live much the same kind of lives as the white rooming-house population in the "Uptown" section of Chicago. It is highly probable that the Negroes were the only racial group in Chicago who were socially and economically organized to take possession of Chicago's south side. Thus racial differences disappear when the population formations are reduced to the more abstract form of age and sex distribution. The racial conflicts and antipathies developing out of what is commonly considered invasion of a residence area by another race can be thought of in more abstract terms as the orderly process of city growth or the succession of one population group of lower economic and social status upon the heels of another in the process of assimilation.

6

THE STRATIFICATION STRUCTURE AND PROCESSES

The members of a society identify and interact with one another in terms of symbols or categories. They similarly tend to isolate themselves from contact and interaction in terms of recognized valuations. Members of the society use some of these symbolic categories or valuations to rank one another on an equality-inequality scale, where unequals are more or less superior, or inferior. The extent and kind of inequality and the common basis of valuation varies considerably from culture to culture, and also among communities.

There is no universal basis for social rank valuations. The ranking of persons on a scale of equality-inequality where the members of a group or society share a set of criteria for valuation is called *social stratification*. The scale positions or ranks are generally called *strata*. Every stratum carries with it certain obligations to act, certain rights and privileges conditioning the action, and certain symbolic criteria which characterizes the acts. The obligations to act may include expectations like noblesse oblige, and that one will act in accordance with one's station or family position. The rights and privileges may be such objective conditions as income, leisure and welfare, political power, or such subjective ones as prestige or "psychic income." These conditions generally are represented in symbols of rank such as insignia, styles of life and dress, and group affiliations. Some sociologists distinguish between class and status ranks. *Class position* is defined in terms of the type of chance or power one has in a "market situation" while *status position* is defined in terms of the social prestige or honor

attached to a position. Class and status ranks, in this sense, need not coincide for all persons. A few examples may show how discrepant these ranks can be. A racketeer who amasses a large fortune usually has a higher class than status rank, while a financially impoverished man from an "aristocratic family" usually has a higher status than class rank. Or, a janitor who serves an apartment building often has a higher class position than the tenants, who regard him as being in a status below their own.

There is considerable variation among societies in the relative ease or difficulty with which social rank is changed. A hierarchy of ranks constitutes a *status and/or class structure*. The process by which a person changes rank is called *social mobility*. When a person's position or rank is *ascribed* on the basis of social position at birth alone, the ideal-type system of stratification formed is called a *caste system*. When a person's position is *achieved* solely by individual performance, the ideal-type stratification system formed is said to be "open." There is no known instance where a society empirically fits either of these systems of stratification, for there is some recognition of achievement of social position and some ascribed ranking in every society. Factors which encourage social mobility in a society include: strata differences in the vital processes of fertility and mortality; expansion or contraction of the size of the society by immigration; social and technological changes which affect the distribution of opportunities for movement among the strata; and acceptance of criteria which permit recognition of individual achievement—as, for example, when high valuation is placed on talents such as those which operate in invention or discovery, on abilities such as operate in scholastic or athletic skills, or on personal service to a person of a higher status.

In modern western society, the various sources of strata differentials can be analyzed from two points of view. One of these can be thought of as the stratification system of the local community and the other the stratification system of the larger society of which the local community is a part. Within each of these, a variety of "ranks" contribute to the social position of the individual in the community. Thus, occupational prestige, financial solidity, educational level, family background, or political power, among other factors, may account for high or low rank. The way in which these factors combine in the small community is different from the way they define position in the larger urban settlement or in the more inclusive mass society.

This difference in stratification can be traced to two fundamental differences between the small local community and the urban center. These are the degree to which the division of labor is elaborated and the amount of anonymity present. As the community decreases in size, there is less and less division of labor actually present in the locality. This relative homogeneity in conjunction with the smaller number of people involved and the effect of sheer propinquity, serves to increase the amount and depth of interpersonal knowledge and interaction. This then makes possible the development of a rating system within the community which employs, not only the more "objective criteria," but also the personal reputation of the individual.

As the locality increases in size, the opposite characteristics appear. Increased heterogeneity associated with a more complex division of labor, greater cultural diversity, and increased numbers of persons and distance, all decrease the possibility and, indeed,

the relevance of interpersonal knowledge. The segmented quality of urban interaction therefore emphasizes the importance of the more "objective criteria" for individual identification. There is thus a greater tendency to think of urban stratification in terms of impersonal ranks or institutional niches rather than as a system of rated individuals. In larger cities stratification tends to be analyzed in terms of typical groups of social ranks usually associated with economic, political or other advantages. Thus, for example, a high-school teacher may have a somewhat higher general status in a small city of 5,000 to 10,000 persons than in a large metropolitan community of several million persons.

The first two selections in this section present examples of these two types of analyses. Hollingshead presents a description of a series of cultural characteristics associated with the system of stratification in a small middle western urban community in the United States. Subjective rankings of members of the community were used to determine both the system of ranks in the community, and the rank position each of the families had in its structure. The paper also shows the association between placement in a status ranking of residential areas in the community and placement in the subjective status groups. Mills describes the characteristics of the "middle classes" in small metropolitan cities, using an objective technique for defining the stratification structure and individual placement in it. An objective description of the system of social stratification in a large metropolitan area also is found in the paper by Rogoff.

In modern stratified urban communities, the tendency to change one's social position is more marked than in small-scale societies. Individuals seek to improve their social position by moving to communities where opportunities are prevalent and by changing their occupation for one which provides increased economic power or confers more prestige. Concomitantly, the risk involved in holding one's position is likewise greater and individuals often surrender or lose their position in competition for it. Such changes in social rank are due to a number of factors, as already noted, *viz.*, differences in net reproduction rates, where some strata may fail to reproduce themselves without recruiting persons from other strata; changes in the size and composition of the class or status structures; changes in the relative prestige accorded positions in the status structure; and, by manipulation of specific technical and social skills within an established structure.

A number of the papers in this section describe and analyze the process of social mobility in the society as a consequence of both these changes and the relative openness of the stratification system. The paper by Reiss describes and analyzes broad changes in the composition of the urban labor force of the United States between 1910 and 1950, and suggests some of the effects of these changes on the process of social mobility. It is shown, for example, that changes in the occupational structure during this period resulted in a secular trend toward upward mobility in the occupational structure, when it is assumed there is no equal re-evaluation of the relative occupational ranks during the period. Rogoff's research controls for this secular trend toward upward mobility in the occupational structure, and correlatively, the mobility which is a consequence of it. Her paper describes and analyzes the mobility which takes place solely due to the influence of differently evaluated personal and social characteristics of persons. The effect of the age-grading of occupations on the process of social mobility also is examined. Finally, Rogoff's paper deals with the question whether the occupational system of stratification has tended to become a relatively more open, stationary or closed system, since the turn of the century. Her research paper provides data to show that the channels

to social mobility in contemporary U.S. urban society are about as easily traversed now as they were at the beginning of the century.

Communities appear to vary substantially in their provision of opportunities for social mobility. Both historical and contemporary communities which differ in functional type also differ somewhat in their mobility opportunities. The most obvious examples of the effect of functional specialization in a community on its stratification system are those provided by the description of stratification differences among the agricultural economies, the extractive economies and non-agricultural-extractive economies. Yet there is substantial variation in the system of social stratification within each of these major types of functionally specialized places. The stratification system in agriculturally based communities may be that of feudalism, of a planter aristocracy-laborers, or that of the small entrepreneurial farmer, to name a few of the possible differences. There appears to be even greater possible variation among the functional types of cities. Reference has been made to the joint effect of industrialization and urbanization on the social rank structure of cities. Heberle's paper in this section makes an analytical separation of the two variables, and describes the effect of industrialization on the growth of southern cities and their social structure. Particular attention is given to the consequences of industrialization of cities on the ecological patterning of cities and on their stratification systems.

Investigations of the extent of occupational mobility in the United States have been made in communities which differ considerably in population size. These studies strongly suggest two things: that the small U.S. urban community has less mobility than the larger one, and that communities of different sizes are related to one another in such a way that the larger communities provide mobility opportunities for persons from communities which are smaller in size. They also suggest that there are differences in opportunities for occupational mobility related to the size of the community of origin and destination. The findings of Lipset on occupational mobility and urbanization strongly suggest that a mobility pattern emerges from these movements from small to large communities. The mobility pattern appears to take the form that migrants from the small communities take over the lower occupational positions in the larger ones, while native urbanites move up in the occupational structure. There are no similar findings for the lesser degree of movement from large to small communities. The Lipset paper makes clear some of the effects which size of community can have on a system of stratification. Despite the basic similarity in the system of stratification as one moves from city to city in American and Western culture, there are some observable differences both in the occupational structure and the operation of the mobility process among these communities, particularly when comparisons of structure and process are made for some variable which varies systematically among communities, as, for example, their size.

The stratification system provides barriers to both upward and downward social mobility. There are two major types of such barriers in an occupational structure which affect the kind and degree of occupational mobility. The qualitative differences in kinds of work, including differences in capacities, skill, and training, create one type of barrier to movement. Persons are qualified in this sense to enter work only in jobs where they can use their capacities, skill, and training. There also are artificially maintained barriers to occupational movement beyond the artificial scarcity created by the nature of the work and training for it. These artificial barriers are of two kinds: There are the artificial barriers to entry into the occupation based on such things as ascribed status, criteria for acceptance into training for a job, educational history, personality, and so on. After entry, there are barriers to movement within the occupational category, including the rejection of persons of certain ascribed statuses, organizational criteria for apprenticeships, job ratings, association memberships, and certification. The relative permeability which a barrier has for an individual determines in large part whether he has an opportunity to be mobile, and consequently of his actual mobility behavior. The barriers likewise vary in their permeability for members of different social class and status positions.

Race and ethnic background are important bases for ascribing status in the United States. The ascribed status of the Negro in the United States places rather sharp limitations on the opportunities he has for mobility in the status structure, since racial discrimination operates as an artificially-maintained barrier to mobility. The caste-like structure of Negro and white relations in the United States means that Negroes occupy a dual status, one within the Negro caste, and one in the status structure of the total society. While the ranks which define the American Negro status structure are to a large degree based on valuations within the common mass culture, they also reflect to a degree the valuations of the Negro caste culture. American Negroes move primarily within the status structure created by the barriers to relatively free movement within the mass system of social stratification. The barriers to Negro mobility in the mass system of social stratification are more permeable today than they were even 20 years ago, although there is considerable variation among communities and geographic regions within the United States. Drake and Cayton graphically describe in the last paper in this section the barriers to Negro occupational mobility within the U.S. urban labor market and occupational structure.

SELECTED CHARACTERISTICS OF CLASSES
IN A MIDDLE WESTERN COMMUNITY

August B. Hollingshead

This paper is concerned with a description of a series of cultural characteristics associated with four strata of the social structure in a Middle Western
community of some 10,000 population,[1] which we shall hereafter call "Elmtown."[2] Elmtown is an all white community located near the center of
the corn belt on a rich glaciated plain bisected by a navigable river. Its
highly mechanized agricultural activities are integrated around corn and
hogs, with the production of small grains and soy beans as secondary crops.
Coal mines and three large factories give the community an industrial as
well as an agricultural base.[3] Elmtown is the countyseat of "Home" County,
and the only town in the county with a population above 2,500. All types
of retail and repair businesses, services, and professions common to a prosperous countyseat town of this size are found here. In addition, it has a
locally-owned daily newspaper, hospital, and a central high school.

Elmtown's social structure is composed of five strata[4] whose members
understand with varying degrees of precision how each ranks in the hierarchical order. Assignment to a given stratum or class within the social
structure appears to be dependent upon the possession and expression of a
constellation of culture traits that are evaluated by the members of the
community as appropriate to that particular stratum.

The data used in this paper were collected from two different sources.
On the one hand, the stratification was accomplished by a rating procedure

Reprinted from the *American Sociological Review,* Vol. 12 (August 1947), pp. 385-395,
by permission of the author and the publisher. (Copyright, 1947, by the *American
Sociological Review.*)

1. The town's population was about 6,200 in 1941; rural farm and rural non-farm
population comprised the remainder, 3,800, and was distributed over the 160 square
miles of communal area.
2. Materials discussed here are taken from an extensive study of 735 adolescents
of high school age focused on the relationships between the behavior of the adolescents and the position their families occupy in the social structure of the community.
The field work was completed between June, 1941 and December, 1942.
3. The largest factory normally employed (1939–41) between 450 and 600; the
next sized one 200 to 250; and the smallest 40 to 50 persons.
4. The terminology used here is that developed by Kingsley Davis, "A Concep-
tional Analysis of Stratification," *American Sociological Review,* 7:309-321, Je. 1942.
Also see Kingsley Davis and Wilbert E. Moore, "Some Principles of Stratification,"
American Sociological Review, 10:242-249, Ap. 1945.

developed in the community;[5] on the other, the materials discussed under each class were collected directly from the families concerned, and sources other than the raters by the use of schedules, interviews, and other appropriate field techniques. The scores essential to the stratification of the families of the 735 cases included in the study are presented in Table I.

In the following description of the characteristics associated with each class, a cluster of "typical" traits is emphasized rather than deviant ones. However, the traits are not forced into a procrustean bed for the sake of typology, even though the characterization of cultural patterns associated with each stratum is our general objective. Moreover, our concern is not with the number of classes, but with how fruitful the number used may be in understanding the organization and function of the community as a sociological entity.

TABLE I—Mean Rate(d) Scores of Classes, Number of Raters, and Number of Cases by Class

Class	Scores [2]	Mean Rated Score	A.D.[3]	No. of Raters	Mean No. of Raters	No. of Cases
I [1]	.51–1.50	1.05	.04	21	21.0	4
II	1.51–2.50	1.93	.16	23	14.3	31
III	2.51–3.50	2.91	.25	20	13.4	158
IV	3.51–4.50	4.17	.37	26	12.1	312
V	4.51–5.50	4.71	.21	22	10.5	230

1. The data on families in Class I are combined with Class II hereafter in the tabular materials.
2. Persons assigned to each class by each rater were given a weighted score. The weights used were Class I, 1; Class II, 2; Class III, 3; Class IV, 4; Class V, 5. The interval is the theoretical range of scores except for Classes I and V where the functional intervals were only one-half of the theoretical range; that is, 1.50 to 1.0 and 5.00 to 4.51.
3. Average deviation was calculated from the mean.

CHARACTERISTICS OF FOUR STRATA.[6] Almost exactly one-half of the families in Class II have achieved their positions through their own efforts (the remainder have inherited them), but a further rise is virtually impossible as their origins are too well known and not enough time has elapsed between the start of their ascent and the present to accord them recognition within Class I. Psychologically, Class II persons are aware of the prestige differential between themselves and Class I. Nevertheless, they attempt to identify themselves with it in every possible way and exaggerate the social distance between themselves and Class III.

----

5. 31 Raters placed the families of the 735 adolescents in the social structure. The technique followed differs from the rating devices used by a number of sociologists in the past decade in that it was based on the use of a standardized Control List of 20 families. See: Wilson Gee, "A Qualitative Study of Rural Depopulation in a Single Township: 1900–1930," *American Journal of Sociology*, 33:210-221, Se. 1933; Carl Frederick Reuss, "A Qualitative Study of Depopulation in a Remote Rural District: 1900–1930," *Rural Sociology*, 2:66-75, Mar. 1937; George A. Lundberg, "The Measurement of Socio-economic Status," *American Sociological Review*, 5:29-39, Fe. 1940; Edgar A. Schuler, "Social and Economic Status in a Louisiana Hills Community," *Rural Sociology*, 5:69-87, Mar. 1940; Harold F. Kaufman, *Prestige Classes in a New York Rural Community*, Memoir 260, Cornell University Agricultural Experiment Station, Ithaca, New York, 1944, 3-46; Harold F. Kaufman, "Members of a Rural Community as Judges of Prestige Rank," *Sociometry*, IX, 71-85, Fe. 1946. Detailed procedures used are described in a forthcoming monograph.
6. Class I is omitted here since only four families came from this stratum.

TABLE II—Ecological Area and Class for Families Residing in Elmtown

Ecological Area [1]	Class			
	I + II	III	IV	V
"The 400"	15	26 } [3]	3 }	0 }
"Old Residential"	13	57	26	0
"The East End"		2	12	4
"Down by the Mill"		6	46	21
"The Mill Addition"		7	54	21
"Down by the Canal"		7	58	75
"North of the Tracks"		3 }	21 }	22 }
"Below the Canal"		0	5	48
Total	28 [2]	108	225	191

$\chi^2 = 283.6807,$ $P < .01$
$C = .59$ $\bar{C} = .73$ [4]

1. Ecological areas are arranged in order of prestige value.
2. Cases in Class I and II are not included in the chi square analysis or the coefficient of contingency.
3. These cells were combined in the chi square analysis.
4. C = Coefficient of Contingency. $\bar{C}$ = coefficient of contingency corrected for broad grouping by formula given in Thomas C. McCormick, *Elementary Social Statistics*, McGraw-Hill, New York, 1941, p. 207.

Income is earned largely by the male head who actively follows a profession, operates a family-owned business, industry, or farm, or is engaged as a salaried executive in an enterprise owned by Class I families. (See Table III) Family income may be supplemented by income from a farm or two, securities, perhaps some rental houses.[7] Most, but seldom all, family income is spent on daily living. Security rather than wealth appears to be the economic goal. They were successful enough in the depression years to avoid all types of direct public assistance. All families had commercial and savings accounts in the local banks. In a crisis bank credit is available and used when necessary. Another important point is that lawyers are used extensively in normal business activities rather than in a crisis only.

TABLE III—Occupational Group of Father by Class

Occupational Group	I + II [1]	III	IV	V	Total
Professionals and proprietors	21	41 }	23 }	8 }	100 [2]
Farm owners	9	26	2		
Clerical	3	18 }	8 }		44
Sales	2	10	6	2 }	
Skilled craftsmen		37 }	54 }	31 }	185
Semi-skilled machine operators		2	44	17	
Farm tenants		20	54	9	83
Services		3 }	25 }	16 }	288
Unskilled		1	96	147	
Total		158	312	230	700

$\chi^2 = 293.0819$ $P < .01$
$C = .55$ $\bar{C} = .68$

1. Classes I and II are not included in the chi square analysis.
2. Cells combined in chi square analysis.

Class II focuses its attention upon the aggressive manipulation of economic and political processes; consequently, its members are hyperactive in the power wielding associations, such as Chamber of Commerce, Rotary,

7. Annual family incomes ranged between $3,000 and $10,000, with the mode at $4,500 and the mean at $4,650. These are 1941 figures.

Masons, country club, and the major political parties. The women are as active as the men within their own sphere. A considerable proportion of the working day of many men and women is donated to community affairs without the donors receiving or expecting any direct, tangible compensation for their efforts other than the pleasure derived from the manipulation of human relationships in a controversial situation. As the outwardly prominent prestige bearers of community leadership, they are generally respected by the bulk of the population who look to them for community betterment. Few people realize these overt community leaders may be controlled, and often are, from behind the scenes by Class I persons.

All of these families paid personal property taxes, 90 per cent owned real estate, and 80 per cent owned the home they lived in. The town dwellers lived in the two highest ranking residential areas (Table II), with 54 per cent in the "400" and 46 per cent in the "Old Residential" area. The homes, while not as large as those of Class I, are interspersed in the same areas. They are well kept, and furnished nicely. An automobile is a necessity and custom decrees it shall be a new one, preferably large, but not necessarily so; and in excellent repair.

Class II wives are homemakers and the family's social secretary.[8] Their homes are well-managed and run with the help of one general servant or with hourly services of a cleaning woman. Although their homes are a source of pride, an ambitious wife must not allow her home interests to out-weigh her community activities. Their community activities generally are arranged to take place in the afternoons; only occasionally is the wife expected to be out in the evening, since this is the time the husband will be free from his occupational restrictions. However, demands on the husband's evenings are so numerous, he is home only a few nights a week. Thus, the home tends to be a service station and a place of relaxation on week-ends.

Approximately four out of five families come from pioneer American stock. The remainder trace their origins directly to Norwegian, German, and Irish elements who have lived in the area for three generations; no ethnic groups are represented.

Marriage occurs in the middle twenties between persons of approximately the same educational and economic backgrounds. Since Class II is upwardly mobile, marriages with Class I persons are preferred by IIs but not by Is. Marriages between equals are approved, those between a II and a III are not, but they are tolerated when they occur. Few marriages occur below this level. Marriage is for life, not until divorce breaks it. Children are expected and, in most cases, desired and planned; thus, families are small in size.[9] The mother is confined in a hospital in a distant city and cared for by a specialist; the local hospital is seldom used. Parents strive to rear their children properly and to give them advantages they may not

---

8. Only 1 wife out of 31 was gainfully employed.

9. The mean was 2.3 per family; the range from one to four.

have had themselves. The children expect their parents to assist them in reaching and consolidating a desirable future. The boys are headed for business or a profession. The girls are steered toward a desirable marriage after an education has been secured.

Church affiliation and active participation in religious affairs are emphasized. Class II is relied upon by the ministers for lay leadership in church activities. Religious goals are achieved through church work, such as dinners, welfare drives, Sunday School, missionary societies, and young people's affairs, instead of through large pecuniary pledges as is the rule in Class I.

The adults of Class II are the most highly educated persons in the community (Table V). Education is viewed as a requisite to success in business, and indispensable in the professions. The college educated males are concentrated in the large professions, only a few are in business. The non-college men are all in business enterprises of one kind or another. Those who achieved success without a college education admit the lack of it, often in an indirect way; and indicate, none too subtly, they believe they could have gone much farther if they had been better educated. Both college and non-college parents emphasize to their children the need for a college education.

Class II families do not have the time or the money to travel extensively, but they usually make a few trips each year to a neighboring city to shop, to attend the theater or an inter-collegiate football game. Their vacations are spent in automobile trips to various parts of the country or in a rented cabin at one of the northern lakes. The younger children go to summer camp for a few weeks, but the older boys work in the fields or in the town's stores. The adults make only limited use of public recreational facilities, such as parks and playgrounds, as they have access to the country club.[10] Almost every Saturday night, there are get-togethers in the homes where the numerous cliques of husbands and wives drink, eat, play cards, talk freely, and relax from the strains of daily life.

Class III adults have strong feelings about their position in the social structure. Above them they see the Is, who they realize are much higher in prestige because of their wealth, lineage, and way of life. Likewise, they know the IIs occupy a position superior to their own, but a position that rests on different bases: dignified occupations, more income, higher education, and leadership in the prestige-giving activities—traits they too possess, but not in such generous amounts. The cavalier treatment they receive from IIs in community activities and the fact that IIs identify themselves psychologically with Class I, and many times act as its agents in community enterprises builds resentment among IIIs toward the IIs rather than the Is. IIIs look down upon IVs as "the common man," but they do not condemn or scorn them as many IIIs trace their immediate background to this stratum. Proportionately, there probably has been more upward mobility

10. Eighty-five per cent belonged.

in this stratum than any other in Elmtown. Mills found evidences of the same thing in Central City.[11]

Income is derived from profits, fees, and salaries earned by both the father and the mother.[12] The men largely own and operate small retail businesses, own medium sized farms, operate as large tenants,[13] or pursue the lesser professions. Many are highly skilled craftsmen, a considerable number are foremen. Others are clerks in the mill offices, the banks, and other businesses. One-sixth of the wives were gainfully employed outside the home largely as small professionals, some operated small businesses, such as corner groceries, tobacco, and dress shops.

All families maintained commercial accounts and three out of four had savings accounts. Bank credit was available to those who had savings accounts, insurance policies, and owned real property. One-fifth however, did not have bank credit and resorted to the local small loans broker to tide them over a crisis. Class III families invest their small savings in real estate, insurance, or speculative enterprises, only to lose much of it to financial sharpers. Lawyers are not consulted as guides to business activities before action is taken, but afterwards when difficulty arises.

IIIs strive to live in the better residential areas and, in large part, they succeed (Table II). Sixty-one per cent of the homes are owned.[14] Class III families have sufficient income for the conveniences and comforts of life, possibly part-time help, money for a two weeks' vacation each year, popular magazine subscriptions, automobiles, and other externals of a successful standard of living that may be typified as comfort without luxury. Home furnishings tend to be uniform in quality, similar in price, and standardized as to the kind of articles in a room, one might almost say the way they are arranged.

Descendants of the ethnic groups that settled in Elmtown a half century and more ago are represented disproportionately in this stratum.[15] Since ethnic background is connected directly with religious affiliations in most families, the Catholic and Lutheran churches claim large blocks of Class III people. The distribution of religious affiliation in the several classes is shown in Table IV.

Church activities, such as guilds, study groups, missionary societies, and welfare organizations are kept alive, in large measure, by Class III women.

---

11. C. Wright Mills, "The Middle Classes in Middle-Sized Cities," *American Sociological Review*, 11:520-529, O. 1946.

12. Family income ranged from $2,000 to $4,000 in 1941 with the mode at $2,800-$2,899, and a mean of $2,867.

13. A medium sized farm owner usually operates his own farm. In size it ranges from 150 to 300 acres. A large tenant is one who operates 300 or more acres.

14. Home ownership is almost universal among the small business and professionals, but only 43 per cent of the farm families were owners, and one-third of the foremen, salesmen, and service workers owned their homes.

15. 30 per cent were of Norwegian descent, 20 per cent Irish, and 10 per cent German. No "Poles," however, had achieved a Class III station. The remaining 40 per cent traced their descent to American stock.

TABLE IV—Religious Affiliation by Class

Religious Affiliation	I + II	III	Class IV	V	Total
Federated [1]	20	26	16	1	63
Methodist	5	31	45	12	93
Lutheran	3	45	80	32	160
Catholic	3	35	57	48	143
Baptist; others [2]	3	12	72	71	158
No affiliation	1	9	42	66	118
Total	35	158	312	230	735

$$\chi^2 = 244.4319 \qquad P < .01$$
$$C = .50 \qquad \bar{C} = .58$$

1. Created by the official merger of the Presbyterian and Congregational groups and the unofficial affiliation of local Episcopalians.
2. Free Methodist, Pentacostal, Church of God, Christ Scientist, Pilgrim Holiness.

Church attendance and church work are major functions in their lives. While the women are twice as likely to be avid church workers as men, there is a significantly higher average attendance at church services among both men and women than in any other class.[16] Regular church attendance appears to confer a kind of moral respectability peculiar to Class III. These people along with the IIs run the activities of the socially desirable churches —Federated, Methodist, Lutheran, Catholic, and Baptist.

Marriage occurs a year younger than in Class II and the women give birth to their first child 18 months earlier in life than Class II. Class III women also have more children than Class II women; [17] practically all babies are delivered in the local hospital. Strict sexual fidelity is required of the wives, but the husbands are known, on occasion, "to play around with other women." The wives do not "run around with other men" to any appreciable extent, and they bitterly condemn a woman who does. Class III is not as well educated as the higher classes; moreover, there is a distinct difference in the amount of education received by the men and women. (See Table V).

It has often been observed that Americans are joiners; this is particularly true in Class III where membership in many associations, implemented by active participation, confers high prestige within the class; to be elected to an office, or to be on a committee adds a few additional cubits. The most coveted memberships are the country club and Rotary for most of their members come from Classes I and II.[18] Although IIIs could not "make the grade" to these relatively exclusive organizations in appreciable numbers, a few did, thus preserving the traditional belief that "one can go anywhere if he only has the stuff in him."

16. Each minister rated the church activity of each family. These ratings were analyzed by chi square for significance of difference and association. For father's church activity with a 20 cell table and 18 degrees of freedom $X^2 = 239$; the coefficient of contingency for the raw scores was .49; when corrected for broad groupings it was .55. The contingency table for the mother's activity had 20 cells and 18 degrees of freedom, $X^2 = 350$; the coefficient of contingency, uncorrected was .57, corrected, .66.

17. The mean size of Class III families was 3.6; standard deviation 1.9.

18. 15 per cent of the country club's membership and 10 per cent of Rotary came from Class III families. However, 84 per cent of the Lion's Club membership was

TABLE V—Educational Level Attained by Each Parent by Class

Education Completed	I + II	III	Class IV	V	Total
			A. Fathers		
College [1]	17 $\}$[2]	11 $\}$	4 $\}$	0 $\}$	87
High school	11 $\}$	26 $\}$	17 $\}$	1 $\}$	
9–11 grades	2	26	32	6	66
8th grade	5 $\}$	74 $\}$	158 $\}$	67 $\}$	582
5–7 grades	.. $\}$	13 $\}$	61 $\}$	80 $\}$	
Less than 5th grade	.. $\}$	8 $\}$	40 $\}$	76 $\}$	
Total	35	158	312	230	735

$\chi^2 = 244.2504$ P < .01   C = .50 $\bar{C} = .64$

Education Completed	I + II	III	Class IV	V	Total
			B. Mothers		
College [1]	18 $\}$	63 $\}$	10 $\}$	.. $\}$	166
High school	10[2] $\}$	33 $\}$	28 $\}$	4 $\}$	
9–11 grades	5	55	39	2	101
8th grade	2 $\}$	5 $\}$	174 $\}$	70 $\}$	468
5–7 grades	.. $\}$	1 $\}$	42 $\}$	99 $\}$	
Less than 5th grade	.. $\}$	1 $\}$	19 $\}$	55 $\}$	
Total	35	158	312	230	735

$\chi^2 = 444.6439$ P < .01   C = .62 $\bar{C} = .84$

1. Includes all formal training beyond high school, such as college, university, professional, and vocational courses. It ranged from 6 months to 8 years in length.
2. Figures combined for chi square analysis.

Although political activity is more widespread than in any other stratum, and from two-thirds to three-fourths of the several county offices are staffed by persons either elected or appointed from this class, these facts do not lead to the conclusion that Class III is politically powerful. On the contrary, it looks to Classes I and II for leadership. Many politically active IIIs resent their subordinate positions in the political system in view of the work they do, but their control is limited by all policy-making offices being in the hands of the higher classes.

Class III advertises its activities in the "Society" column of the local paper. When Mrs. John P. Doe gives a party or chairs an activity, she is expected to "write a piece" for the paper which tells when and where the party occurred, who was there, the kind of entertainment offered, the refreshments served, and a detailed description of the decorations. If she does not, her friends are likely to inquire why she did not have a "piece in the paper." Afternoon affairs are advertised in this manner and, in most cases, mixed Saturday evening parties attended by cliques. Trips out of town for almost any reason are mentioned in the paper. IIIs might be said to be seekers after respectable personal publicity of any kind—to have one's name in the paper adds to one's prestige. Class I persons, on the other hand, avoid personal publicity; IIs do not seek it—as a rule, they try to keep from being mentioned too frequently in the local press.

Class IV persons are aware of the inferior position they occupy in the prestige hierarchy, and they resent the attitudes most persons in the higher classes exhibit toward them. They discriminate sharply between "people

drawn from the III fathers. The picture was similar for the exclusive women's organizations.

like us" and the "socially ambitious" IIIs who they believe "put on airs" they do not rightfully deserve. Conversely, they are convinced Vs are inferior to themselves because they live in hovels and shacks, are dirty, immoral, and do not "try to get ahead." Consequently, a self-respecting IV avoids contact with Vs whenever possible. On the whole, Class IV people consider themselves to be "the backbone of the community." The higher ranking classes do not expect community leadership from Class IV, but they do expect them to work, produce, pay taxes, vote right, pay their bills, and buy the things they need locally while the higher classes provide the direction and reap the profits from their efforts.

Class IV members are employees who work for wages day after day on the farms, in the mines, the mills, and the shops of Elmtown.[19] Although class folkways indicated the family should be supported by the father, 30 per cent of the mothers were gainfully employed outside the home either as supplementary or chief breadwinner in occupations that carry little prestige and low hourly or weekly wages.[20] Their income was large enough to provide the necessities of life, a few comforts, but few, if any, luxuries. Family income was spent as it was earned; little was left over for "a rainy day." Family possessions were limited to a few clothes, household goods, and a car. However, 25 per cent did not own an automobile, and only 35 per cent either owned or were buying a home.[21] Thirty-five per cent had small commercial bank accounts and 17 per cent had savings accounts. The commercial bank accounts were limited largely to the farmers, little business men, and the craft and skilled workers. Laborers and service workers had commercial accounts in but 11 per cent of the cases. Bank credit was available to approximately two families out of five. The local small loans broker acted as the credit agency for families who did not have bank credit.

Although many families were on relief during the worst years of the depression in the 1930's, specific data were not available in the county and it was not considered advisable to ask the families directly about their relief experiences. The Supervisor of the poor, between January 1937 through December 1941, gave township relief to 8 per cent of the families for periods varying from one month to three years. None of these cases involved "total relief." On the contrary, the relief given acted as a subsidy to a family in dire need that could not get help elsewhere. No family in the higher classes found it necessary to "go on relief."

All ethnic elements are found in Class IV. In Elmtown proper their homes are found in all residential areas, as Table II shows, but they are largely

---

19. The chances were 12.5 to 1 against a Class IV father owning a business. When he did, it was a very small one, as defined by Dun and Bradstreet's *Registry* for Elmtown, May, 1941. A very small business is therein defined as one with a value between $500 to $2,000.

20. Annual family incomes ranged from $800 to $2,700, with the mode at $1,500 to $1,599 and a mean of $1,541.

21. The point should be made here that these families were in the prime of life; the mean age of the father was 45.5 years and the mother 42.1 years. These families had all been established 15 years or more.

excluded from the best residential area by economic factors, and they avoid the area "Below the Canal" as being beyond the pale of respectability.

The family pattern is sharply different from that found in the higher classes. Marriage between class equals is the rule, although a small minority marry one class up or down. Males marry in their very early twenties and females in the late teens. Children normally are born from 9 to 18 months after marriage,[22] and more are born per family than in Class III.[23] Also, the family is broken by divorce, desertion, or death twice as often as in III.

The mother does her own housework with the aid of the children even though she may be gainfully employed part or full-time. There is no help except in an emergency, such as childbirth or illness; even then, it is dispensed with as soon as possible. The wife and mother's role in the community is encompassed by domestic duties. She is judged by the way she keeps her house, dresses her children, and manages the family budget. The community does not expect these women to join the Women's Club or other social organizations and they are discriminated against if they have ambitions along this line. The men are judged by how well they provide and by their moral actions, not by their business or organizational contacts.

Formal educational experience is limited almost exclusively to elementary and high schools. The Class IV adult might be characterized as literate, but not educated. (See Table V).

Many families claimed they had neither time nor money to support the churches, and one-third indicated hostility toward religion for one reason or another. Fourteen per cent had no affiliation with a local church, and out of those who did, two-thirds of the fathers and one-half of the mothers did not attend church services. These people claimed to be church members, but by the practical test of whether they actually participated in church activities, they were not.[24] This class may be as devout as the higher classes, but its members do not work on church boards, committees, and societies. When they do, especially in the high prestige churches, they are most likely to be found in menial positions. For instance, the chances are about 20 to 1 that an active Class IV woman in the Methodist Church, let us say, will be found in the kitchen at a church dinner rather than on the planning committee for the affair.

Leisure is limited for both men and women to the hours outside the daily, weekly, and yearly work routines. Approximately, three leisure hours out of four are spent at home listening to the radio, looking over the local paper, "working around the place," "fixing things up," and, for the men

---

22. 55 per cent of Class IV mothers gave birth to their first child before they were 20 years of age, whereas only 19 per cent of the Class III mothers were in this category.

23. The mean number was 4.3 per family; range 1-10, standard deviation 2.2.

24. Twenty-four per cent of fathers and 19 per cent of the mothers were completely unknown to the ministers of the churches with which they claimed they were affiliated.

especially, cleaning and repairing the car. There is very little reading of magazines, books, or newspapers. Outside the home, recreation occurs in public or semi-public places. The most popular spot, visited by the average family once a week, is the motion picture theater. Visiting friends and relatives is also a very popular pastime. People meet informally on the street and stop to visit when the weather permits; if it does not, they congregate in the grocery, ten cent, and hardware stores. On a warm Saturday evening, Main Street swarms with people from the two lower classes who visit along the sidewalks and curbs. The family does not travel for travel's sake, as is often the case in the higher classes. An extended trip may be made for a definite purpose, such as visiting a relative, but these trips are not viewed as pleasures in themselves, but a means to renew family ties.

Intimate association in cliques is limited almost exclusively to intraclass relationships as IIIs avoid clique ties with IVs, and IVs, in turn, avoid Vs. Clique activities are highly informal and consist of visiting back and forth between couples in the evening, Sundays, and holidays rather than planned parties and dinners with drinks, games, and polite conversation as their central focus. Clique relations are more definitely on an age and sex basis, and more leisure time is spent by adults with their own sex in various clique activities than in the higher classes.

Periodically, attention is focused very briefly on some person who has committed a crime. This occurs more frequently in Class IV than in III, for 13.8 per cent of the fathers had been convicted in local courts of offenses between 1934 and 1941, but only 4.4 per cent of the Class III fathers. None of the mothers in either class had been accused or convicted of an offense.

Class V occupies the lowest stations in the social structure. Its members are looked upon by the higher ranking classes as the "scum of the city." It is believed nothing beyond charity can be done for them, and only a minimum is justified since they show little or no inclination to help themselves. Class V persons realize they are "on the bottom" and they know they are discriminated against by the higher classes, but most of them do not have enough insight to realize why. Class V persons give the impression of being resigned to life in a community that despises them for their disregard of morals, lack of "success" goals, and dire poverty.

Family support comes from many sources. The father is the chief breadwinner in some three families out of five, but their earnings are meager.[25] Fifty-five per cent of the mothers were gainfully employed outside the home part or full-time as waitresses, dishwashers, cooks, washwomen, janitresses, cleaning women, and general unskilled domestic workers. Income from

---

25. Ninety-two per cent were unskilled and semi-skilled laborers or machine operators; none was a farm owner, eight were farm tenants, two were salesmen; and eight operated very small businesses, such as hauling coal from local mines, ash and trash hauling, repair and sales of old cars.

wages provides the families with just enough to obtain the meagerest necessities of life, supplemented by private charity and public relief.[26] Between 1937 and 1941, the private earnings of 52.6 per cent were supplemented by township relief at least one-fourth of each year.[27] Bank accounts and credit are non-existent and even the small loans broker has learned, as he said, "through experience to be careful with that class. Before I loan one of them a cent, I investigate carefully and make sure they own what they put up for security."

All population elements (American, German, Norwegian, Irish, and "Polish") are represented, but three families out of five (58 per cent) traced their ancestry to old American stock that came to Elmtown before the Civil War. In spite of popular belief, "the Irish element" has contributed less than 9 per cent to the ranks of Class V. The "Poles" are found here twice as frequently as would be expected by chance as measured by chi square; the Germans and Norwegians only one-third as frequently as we could expect if chance factors alone were operating.[28] Many families have lived in Elmtown as long as the "leading families." In their long history, they have achieved notorious histories. The unsavory reputation of an ancestor is remembered and often used as an explanation for present delinquency.[29]

Class V families are excluded from the two leading residential areas (Table II). They are found in the others, with large concentrations "north of the tracks" and "below the canal." Ethnic background acts as a selective factor within these areas. "Below the Canal" and "The Mill Addition" are populated almost exclusively by old American stock. "Down by the Mill" is "Irish heaven," whereas "North of the Tracks" is divided into "Norwegian" and "Polish" areas.

The family residence, a box-like structure of two or three rooms, is rented in four cases out of five (81 per cent). The few that are owned have either been inherited or built along the canal and in the tannery flats by their present owners. Although it is popularly believed these people buy cars rather than homes, only 57 per cent owned an automobile.[30]

The family pattern differs sharply from that found in the other classes. Marriages are limited almost exclusively to class equals. For instance, in 61

26. Annual family income ranged from a low near $500 to a high of about $1,500. The modal income fell in the $800 to $899 bracket, with the mean at $842.

27. This figure does not take into consideration federal subsidies, such as W.P.A. and N.Y.A. that prevailed in that period. Neither does it include private charity in its many forms.

28. A chi square of 43.9513 was found with 9 degrees of freedom between ethnic antecedents and class. This is significant at the .01 level.

29. The doctrine of "blood" used to explain the rise to eminence of Class I is used in the same way to justify the derogation of Class V. Such remarks as the following were made about these notorious families or some member of them, "blood will out," "you can't expect anything else from such people," "his great-grandfather was hung for killing a neighbor in cold blood!"

30. Eighty per cent were more than seven years old and only 5 per cent were under two years of age.

out of 65 marriages where the class positions of the families were traced both partners were Class V (93.7 per cent); the other four involved the marriage of Class V with Class IV persons. Marriage takes place in the middle teens for the girls, and the very early twenties for the boys. In the present adult generation, 78 per cent of the mothers reported they had given birth to their first child before they were 20 years of age. Another trait that marks the family complex is the number of children produced by these women.[31] There is little prenatal or postnatal care of either mother or child. The child is delivered generally at home, usually by a local doctor, the county nurse, or midwife, but in the late 1930's, some expectant mothers entered the local hospital. Hospital deliveries, however, are very new to Class V and not widely diffused.

Death, desertion, separation, or divorce has broken more than half the families (56 per cent). The burden of child care, as well as support, falls on the mother more often than on the father when the family is broken. The husband-wife relationship is more or less an unstable one even though the marriage may be sanctioned either by law or conventional understandings between the partners. Disagreements leading to quarrels and vicious fights followed by desertion on the part of either the man or the woman are not unusual. There are few compulsive factors, such as neighborhood solidarity, religious teachings, or ethical considerations operating to maintain a stable marital relationship.

Formal educational experience is limited almost exclusively to the elementary school. (See Table V). It is easy to calculate that a generation ago the odds against a V boy finishing high school were 230 to 1; for the girls they were 57 to 1. It may seem surprising, but they have not improved.[32]

Religious ties are either very tenuous or non-existent. Only 71.3 per cent of the families claimed any religious connections, and many of these were "in spirit" rather than in fact. More than 9 families out of 10 have no functional connections with any church.

Class V persons are isolated from organized community activities. A few men claimed membership in veterans' organizations, but they neither paid their dues nor attended meetings. Those who worked in the mill belonged to the union, the others did not belong to unions as the other shops were open; besides most of the men followed lines of work the unions had not organized.

Time has little value in the daily routine beyond the demands of the job. Since they do not participate in organized community affairs, hours off the job and during the periods of unemployment or lay-off are spent the way the person chooses without too much interference from neighbors.

31. The mean was 6.6 per mother, with a range from 1 to 13 and a standard deviation of 3.1.

32. In 1941–1942, there were 6 freshmen and 2 sophomore boys, and 18 girls, 6 were juniors, and 3 were seniors, from Class V in the Elmtown High School. Two of the three senior girls graduated in June, 1942.

Their extensive leisure is spent in loafing around the neighborhood, in the downtown district, along the river, and at home. Intimate associations are limited in large measure within the class. Social life consists of informal visits between neighbors, gossip, petty gambling, visits to the cheaper theaters, "going to town," drinking in the home or public taverns, with now and again a fist fight. Since the family is organized loosely, the members usually go their own way in search of amusement or pleasure. The cliques are severely age and sex graded. Men associate with men and women with women, except in their ubiquitous sex activities.

The police, sheriff, prosecuting attorney and judge know these families from frequent contact through the years, whereas the ministers and school officials may be only slightly acquainted with them. Between 1934 and 1941, 8 per cent of the mothers and 46 per cent of the fathers had been convicted once or more in the local courts. Public drinking, disorderly conduct, family neglect, and sex offenses were the most frequent charges. Some were chronic offenders who were hauled into court a few weeks after they had either worked out a fine or served their previous sentence; others were single offenders. The group as a whole average 4.1 convictions each. The misdeeds of these people are publicized on the front page of the local paper and by word of mouth to such an extent that many people expect nothing better from them.

On the basis of the data presented, certain tentative conclusions appear to be warranted. First, each of the five strata, as delimited by the procedures used, has a distinct subculture. Second, identification with a given class or stratum is dependent upon the possession of a constellation of appropriate traits. Third, the members of each class participate in community activities in significantly different ways from the members of other classes.

THE MIDDLE CLASSES IN MIDDLE-SIZED CITIES

C. Wright Mills

The problems which the middle classes pose for the social scientist are typically metropolitan in character and nation-wide in scope. White-collar workers in particular, are thought of in connection with big cities, and most recent discussions of the middle classes as a whole focus either upon the nation or upon the metropolis. The sociology and politics of these strata in middle-sized [1] cities may nevertheless be worthy of study.

Such cities are convenient units for empirical analyses; they offer a point of contrast for information and theory dealing with nations or with big cities, and despite the fact that many large problems may be more sharply posed in national and metropolitan areas, some of the issues of politics and social structure take on fresh meaning and reality when translated into the concrete terms of smaller and more readily understood units.

If one keeps in mind the "place" of the middle-sized city in the nation and in relation to various city-size groups, it is a convenient point of anchorage for more extensive analysis of stratification, politics, and ideology. The position of the U. S. middle classes cannot be fully determined without attention to those living among the 15 million people who in 1940 resided in the 320 middle-sized cities.

STRATIFICATION AND POLITICAL MENTALITY. A city's population may be stratified (a) objectively in terms of such bases as property or occupation or the amount of income received from either or both sources. Information about these bases may be confined to the present, or may include (b) the

Reprinted from the *American Sociological Review*, Vol. 11 (October 1946) pp. 520-529, by permission of the author and the publisher. (Copyright, 1946, by the American Sociological Society).

1. Middle-sized cities include those between 25,000 and 100,000 population. Middle classes include the smaller business and the white-collar people. The small business stratum includes retail, service, wholesale, and industrial proprietors employing less than 100 workers. (In the present data from Central City, the small business men employ far fewer, on the average 2 to 4). The white-collar strata include families in the salaried professions and minor managerial positions, clerks and stenographers and bookkeepers, salesmen in and out of stores, and foremen in industry.

Materials used in this paper were gathered, in connection with studies having quite other purposes, for the Office of Reports, Smaller War Plants Corporation (6 cities extensively covered), and the Bureau of Applied Social Research, Columbia University (one city intensively covered). This is publication number A-70 of the latter institution. My colleague, Miss Helen Schneider, has been most helpful in her criticism of this manuscript.

extractions, intermarriages, and job histories of members of given strata. Such "depth stratification" adds a time dimension to the contemporary objective bases of stratification. Subjectively, strata may be constructed according to who does the rating: (c) each individual may be asked to assign himself a position, (d) the interviewer may "intuitively" rate each individual, or (e) each individual may be asked to stratify the population and then to give his image of the people on each level.[2]

Properly designed studies in stratification will use both objective and subjective criteria: indeed, one of the key problems of stratification theory is to account for such discrepancies as may thus appear.

The general problem of stratification and political mentality has to do with the extent to which the members of an objectively defined strata are homogenous in their political alertness, outlook and allegiances, and with the degree to which their political mentalities and actions are in line with the interests demanded by the juxtaposition of their objective position and their accepted values.

Irrational discrepancies between the objectively defined bases of a stratum, the subjectively held policies of its members and their commonly accepted values do not necessarily point to problems of method. They may indicate the "false consciousness" of the stratum we are examining.[3] Lack of structural unity and of political direction are symptoms of the many problems covered by this term that have as yet only been touched by modern empirical research.

Political mentalities may or may not be closely in line with objectively defined strata, but a lack of correspondence is a problem to be explained— in terms of the homogeneity of the situation of the stratum, the social relations between its members, the reach and content of the mass media and of the informal networks of communication that lie along each stratum, etc.

In examining the stratification and politics of the white collar and small business strata in middle-sized cities, we are concerned with whether or not each of them is a homogeneous stratum, with the degree and the content of political consciousness that they display, and with whether they reveal any independence of policy, or are politically dependent upon the initiative and ideologies of other strata.

The objective stratification of the U. S. middle-sized city has fallen into a rather standardized pattern. It will naturally vary from one city to another in accordance with the degree and type of industrialization and the extent to which one or two very large firms dominate the city's labor mar-

2. In the present paper, we are not concerned with the intuitive ratings of interviewers, and space will not permit us to utilize fully the quantitative data available.

3. "False consciousness," the lack of awareness of and identification with one's objective interests, may be statistically defined as the deviant cases, that is, those which run counter to the main correlations in a table: for example, the rich who vote Socialist, the poor who vote Republican. "Objective interests" refer to those *allegiances and actions* which would have to be followed if the *accepted values* and desires of the people *involved in given strata situations* are to be realized.

ket. But the over-all pattern is now fairly set:

When the occupations of a cross section of married men in Central City [4] are coded in 24 groups and ranked according to average family income, five strata are crystallized out: between each of them there is a "natural" break in average income whereas the average income of the occupations making up each income stratum are relatively homogeneous. These strata, with their average weekly income (August, 1945), are as follows:

(1) Big Business and Executives $137.00
(2) Small Business and Free Professionals 102.00
(3) Higher White-collar [5] 83.00
(4) Lower White-collar [6] 72.00
(5) Wage Workers [7] 59.00

These strata fall objectively into the "old" (1 and 2) and the "new" middle classes (3 and 4). Both these classes, however, are definitely split by income, and this split, as we shall see, is also true of other variables.

There is one point on which both objective and subjective methods of strata construction give similar results: Of all the strata in the middle-sized city, the small businessmen and the white-collar workers occupy the most ambiguous and least clearly defined social position: (a) The images which observers on other objective levels of the city ascribe to these occupational groups seem to vary the most widely and to be the least precise; (b) Correspondingly, in terms of a great many attributes and opinions, the white-collar people and, to a lesser degree, the smaller businessmen are the least homogeneous strata. Both in the subjective images held of various strata and in their objective attributes, the city is polarized; the small businessmen and the white-collar workers make up the vaguer and "somewhere in-between" strata.

I. THE SMALL BUSINESS STRATUM. *Its Social Composition and Prestige.* When we ask people in the several objectively defined strata to discuss the position and rank of the small businessman, a fundamental difference occurs between the ranking given him by upper-class and that given him by lower-class observers.[8]

To the lower-class observer, little businessmen are very often the most

4. A mid-western city of 60,000 population selected as "the most typical" on the basis of 36 statistical indicators gathered on all mid-western cities of 50-80,000 population. On the over-all index for all cities of 100, Central City was 99.

5. Salaried professional and semi-professional, salesmen, government officials, minor managerial employees; income range: $80.00 to $87.00.

6. Government protection and service, clerks, stenographers and bookkeepers, foremen; income range: $71.00 to $76.00.

7. Due to wartime "up-grading" there are in this sample very few "manual laborers"; these make about $14.00 less than the skilled and semi-skilled average.

8. These remarks are based on 45 open-ended interviews in Central City, a baby sample within the parent sample; and some 60 random interviews in 6 other middle-sized cities.

apparent element among "the higher-ups" and no distinctions are readily made between them and the "business" or "upper-class" in general. Upper-class observers, on the other hand, place the little businessmen—especially the retailers—much lower in the scale than they place the larger business-men—especially the industrialists. Both the size and the type of business influences their judgment.

In fact, two general images are held of small businessmen by upper-class people. They correspond to two elements of the upper class: (a) The so-cially new, larger, industrial entrepreneurs rank small business rather low because of the *local* nature of these little businessmen's activities. Such upper-class people gauge prestige to a great extent by the scope of a busi-ness and the social and business "connections" with members of nationally known firms. These criteria are opposite to the status-by-old-family-resi-dence frequently used by the second upper-class element: (b) The old family rentier ranks the smaller businessmen low because of his feeling about their background and education, "the way he lives." And, as we shall see, the smaller businessmen cannot often qualify with these standards.

Both upper-class elements tend to stress a Jewish element among the smaller business stratum (although there are very few Jewish families among the smaller businessmen in Central City) and both more or less agree with the blend of "ethical" and "economic" sentiment expressed by an old-family banker: "The independent ones are local operators; they do a nice business, but not nationally. Business ethics are higher, more broad-minded, more stable among industrialists, as over against retailers. We all know that."

But wage-worker families do not know all that. They ascribe power and prestige to the small businessman without really seeing the position he holds within the upper strata. "Shopkeepers," says a lower-class woman, "they go in the higher brackets. Because they are on the higher level. They don't humble themselves to the poor."

(a) The social composition and (b) the actual power position of the small business stratum help us to understand these ambiguous images.

(a) Since they earn about the same average income as the free pro-fessionals, the small businessmen are in the Number Two income bracket of the city. But they are not at all similar to the other high income groups in occupational, intermarriage and job histories. In these respects, the free professionals are similar to the big business owners and executives, whereas the smaller businessmen crystallize out as a distinct stratum different from any other in the population.[9]

Almost three-fourths of the small businessmen are derived from the upper half of the occupational-income hierarchy. Yet this relative lack of

9. The figures on small business men which are given below are quite small: in an area sample of 882 homes we caught 37 small business men. No per cents from such a small base are given unless they are significant according to critical ratios. Nevertheless, the results should be taken with a grain of salt, and caution exercised in any further use made of them: in reality, we are here dealing with qualitative materials.

mobility is not the only, nor necessarily the most relevant point at hand: when we compare small business with other occupations of similar income level, we notice that they contain the greatest proportion of ascending individuals now in the higher income brackets: 18% of those who are urban-derived had wage-worker fathers and 9% had low-income white-collar fathers. Thus 27% come from the lower groups. The free professional and big businessmen, on the other hand, do not include any individuals who derive from wage-worker or low income white-collar.

Slightly more than half of these small businessmen have married girls whose fathers were in the upper-half of the income-occupation ranks. About 40% of them married daughters of wage workers; the remaining married into the lower income white-collar stratum. This 40% cross with wage workers is well over three times greater than for any other of the occupational groups in the higher income brackets.

The job histories of these little businessmen reval the same basic pattern. Only one out of five of them were in a job as high as small business at the time of their marriage (their average age is now around 48) whereas almost half of them were working for wages at that time. Well over half (57%) did wage work for their first full-time job.

In contrast, all the free professionals were professionals by the time they married, and three-fourths of the salaried professionals—who make on the average $13.00 a month less than the small businessmen—were in their present jobs when married. At the bottom of the society we find the same type of rigidity: 9 out of 10 of all grades of labor were wage workers at their time of marriage.

There is rigidity at the bottom and at the top—except among small businessmen who, relative to comparable income groups, have done a great deal of moving up the line.

Almost twice as high a proportion of the big business and free professional men have graduated from high school as is the case for small businessmen, despite the fact that the small businessmen are slightly younger. Moreover, the wives of small businessmen rank fourth in education, just above laborer's wives, in our five-fold occupation-income strata; over half of their wives never finished high school, as compared with only one-fourth of the wives of men in comparable income groups.

The small businessmen are of the generally upper ranks only in income; in terms of occupational origin, intermarriage, job history, and education, more of them than of any other occupational group of such high income are "lower class." A good proportion of them have rather close biographical connections with the wage worker strata. These findings help us explain the difference between the images held of them by members of the upper and of the lower strata. The upper class judges more on status and "background"; the lower more by income and the appearances to which it readily leads.

(b) The ambiguous prestige of small business people has to do with power as well as with "background"; the small businessmen, especially in cities dominated by a few large industrial firms, are quite often "fronts" for the larger business powers. They are, civically, out in front busily accomplishing all sorts of minor projects and taking a lot of praise and blame from the rank and file citizenry. Among those in the lower classes who, for one reason or another, are "anti-business," the small business front is often the target of aggression and blame; but for the lower-class individual who is "pro-business" or "neutral," the small businessmen get top esteem because "they are doing a lot for this city."

The prestige often imputed to small business by lower-class members is based largely on ascribed power, but neither this prestige nor this ascribed power is always claimed, and certainly it is not often cashed in among the upper classes by small businessmen. The upper-class businessman knows the actual power setup; if he and his clique are using small businessmen for some project, he may shower public prestige on them, but he does not "accept" them and he allows them only such "power" as he can retain in his control.

Organizational Power of Small Business. The centers of organizational life for the top are the Chamber of Commerce and the service clubs, and for the bottom, the several trade unions. There are vast differences in their scope, energy and alertness to chances to play the larger civic role. The Chamber of Commerce is more compact and disciplined in its supporting strata and more widely influential in its infiltration and attempted manipulations of other voluntary associations. It is, in many towns, a common denominator of other voluntary organizations. Its hands, either openly *via* "committees," or covertly *via* "contacts," are in all "community" affairs of any political consequence. But the trade unions do not typically reach out beyond themselves, except when their leaders are included in projects sponsored by the Chamber of Commerce.

If both CIO and AFL unions operate in a city, the Chamber of Commerce can very often play them off against one another; usually the old AFL men are quite flattered by being included in Chamber of Commerce committees which thus build them up before the citizenry as representing "labor" in this town. The younger CIO men are confronted with the choice of following this older route of compromised inclusion or of playing the lone wolf, in which case they rest their civic chances entirely upon their strictly union success.

The organization of the Small Business Front is quite often in the hands of the Chamber of Commerce; and many of the hidden wires behind the scene are manipulated by the local bank setup, which is usually able to keep The Front in line whenever this is considered necessary by large industrial firms. The political and economic composition of a well-run Chamber of Commerce enables the organization to borrow the prestige and power of the top strata; its committee includes the "leaders" of practically every voluntary association, including labor unions; within its organizations and through its contacts, it is able virtually to monopolize the organizing and publicity talent of the city. It can thus identify its program with the unifying myth of "the community interest."

This well-known constellation of power underpins the ambiguity of prestige enjoyed by small businessmen, and provides the content of their ideology and political efforts.

Ideologies of Small Business. The ideology of small businessmen rests upon their identification with business as such. They are well organized, but "their" organizations are pretty well under the thumb of larger businesses and the banks. The power of big business is exercised by means of threats "to leave town," by simply refraining from participation in various organizations, by control of credit sources, and by the setting up and using of small businessmen as fronts. The small businessmen, nevertheless, cling to the identity: "business is business." They do not typically see, nor try to act upon, such differences as may exist between the interests of big and little business. The benefits derived from "good relations" with the higher-ups of the local business world, and the prestige striving, oriented towards the big men, tend to strengthen this identification, which is organized and promoted by their associations.

One of the best contemporary sources of information on small business ideology is provided by the field hearings of the SWPC.[10] These are "gripe sessions" usually held in local hotels in the presence of a congressman or his delegate. A rough content analysis of these discussions, occurring during the late war, reveals that the bull's-eyes of the small businessman's aggression are labor and government. The attitude toward "labor" magnifies its power: "We know that labor, at the present time, has the upper hand. They tell us what to do." And the resentment is quite personalized: "Think of the tremendous wages being paid to laboring men . . . all out of proportion to what they should be paid . . . a number of them have spoken to me, saying they are ashamed to be taking the wages." And another one says: "I had a young man cash a check at the store on Monday evening for $95.00 . . . Another case . . . made a total of $200.00 for 30 days . . . We would not class him as half as good as our clerks in our store . . . Naturally to hire men today to do this common labor we are going to have to compete with (war factories)." "A man has to run short-handed or do the work himself."

Toward government, the attitude is resentment at its regulations and at the same time many pleas for economic aid and political comfort. The only noticeable talk against big business is in such governmental statements, by staff members of Senate committees, as: the definition of a small businessman is one who "hasn't got an office or a representative in Washington." The independent little businessman believes: "We are victims of circumstances. My only hope is in Senator Murray, who, I feel sure, will do all in his power to keep the little businessman who, he knows, has been the foun-

10. See, e.g., *Hearings,* Senate Small Business Committee, S. Res. 298 (76th Congress) Part 6.

dation of the country [etc.] . . . We all know no business can survive selling
. . . at a loss, which is my case today, on the new cost of green coffee."

"Small business . . . what is it?" asks the manager of a small business
trade association. "It is American Business . . . it is the reason we have an
American Way." Such phrases as "the little businessman who has built up,
by sweat, tears and smiles, a business . . ." underline the importance placed
by this stratum on its own virtue. The ideology of and for small business
thus carries self-idealization to the point of making it the content of nationalism.

The attitude towards "government" is blended with a self-estimate of
virtue: the criterion of man is success on Main Street: "Another thing that
I resent very much is the fact that most of these organizations are headed
by men who are not able to make a success in private life and have squeezed
into WPA [sic] and gotten over us and are telling us what to do, and it is to
me very resentful. And all these men here know of people who head these
organizations, who were not able to make a living on Main Street before."

This ideology apparently rests to some extent upon a sense of insecurity.
For example, in Central City, the wives of low income businessmen worry
about "how the postwar situation will affect you and your family" more
than any other strata, although they are followed closely by the lower
white-collar people. Sixty per cent of the low income business people worry
a great deal, as against 45% of those of higher income. The small business
families are apparently aware that they make up the margins of free private
enterprise. And—in view of their ascent—perhaps they remember that everything that goes up can come down.

It is also of interest to notice that the wives of smaller businessmen are
not nearly so sure as one might expect that "any young man with thrift,
ability and ambition has the opportunity to rise in the world, own his own
home, and earn $5,000 a year." In Central City [11] only 40% of them believe
it, as against 68% of the higher income business people. They are still, however, a good deal more optimistic than the low income white-collar people
(26%) who are the most pessimistic stratum in the city. About 37% of the
wage workers' wives, regardless of income, are optimistic of the climb.

II. The White Collar Strata. *Social Composition and Images of
White-Collar People*. The lower classes sometimes use the term, "white-
collar," to refer to everybody above themselves. Their attitude varies from
the power-class criterion: they are "pencil pushers" who "sit around and
don't work and figure out ways of keeping wages cheap," to the social-
pragmatic criterion: "The clerks are very essential. They are the ones who
keep the ball rolling for the other guy. We would be lost if we didn't have
the clerks." This latter attitude may be slightly more frequent among those
workers whose children have become clerks.

---

11. We first asked this ascent question in general; then we followed it up with:
"Could he do it in (Central City)?" The optimism of all strata dropped greatly when
the question was brought closer home to them.

The upper classes, on the other hand, never acknowledge the white-collar people as of the top and sometimes place them with laborers. An old upper-class man, for instance, says: "Next after retailers, I would put the policemen, firemen, the average factory worker and the white-collar clerks." Interviewer: "You would put the white-collar people in with the workers?" "Well, I think so. I've lived in this town all my life and come to the bank every day but Sunday, and I can't name five clerks downtown I know."

The white-collar people are split down the middle by income, extraction, intermarriage, job history, and education. Of the men in the higher of the two white-collar income classes, 61% are derived from the upper-half of the extraction-income hierarchy, as compared with 49% of the lower white-collar men who are from the upper half by extraction.[12]

The *urban* origins of the several occupations of the higher white-collar stratum are homogeneous as regards extraction; but the lower white-collar stratum of urban origin contains occupations of quite different extraction which cancel out into a misleading average: The clerks are closer in origin to the higher white-collar as a whole, about 50% being from the upper half, whereas the foreman are quite like labor,[13] only 25% being from the upper half.

In intermarriage, job mobility and education similar situations exist: members of the higher white-collar bracket are homogeneous in intermarriage: about half of them have married women whose fathers were in the upper half of the hierarchy. The lower white-collar stratum is split: the women whom clerks marry are similar in background to the wives of the upper white-collar. Foremen, on the other hand, show a tendency to marry more along the lines that the labor strata follow; yet they marry small businessmen's daughters in about the same proportion (27%) as clerks, minor managerials and salaried professionals, thus forging another link between small businessmen and the laboring class.

The salesmen and the salaried professionals have not experienced much job mobility: 6 out of 10 of them were in higher white-collar at the time of their marriage. In the lower white-collar, again foremen stand out as exceptions: 67% of them were wage workers at their time of marriage and 75% worked for wages in their first full-time job.

Whereas the formal education of the clerks is similar to that of higher white-collar (only 5 to 11% of high white-collar and clerks never going beyond grade school), 40% of the foremen have never gone beyond grade school; this places them educationally only a little above skilled workers.

The lower white-collar is thus not a homogeneous stratum by extraction, intermarriage or job history: some of the occupations in it are socio-

12. There are 117 families in our higher white-collar group, and 92 in the lower. In the general origin table, farm owners are put with upper half, farm tenants and laborers with the lower half.

13. The cases of government protection and service were too few to permit a reliable calculation.

logically affiliated with labor and some with the occupations we have
ranked by income as higher white-collar.

The white-collar people are, as we have seen, split by income. But the
images held of them as a whole seem to be drawn from the occupations
belonging to the lower half of the white-collar income level. The upper
white-collar people, especially the salesmen, tend to merge with the sponge
term, "business," and are thought of as "businessmen" by many members
of the upper class. Most upper-class people derive their images of the
white-collar people largely from stereotypes of "the clerk."

The ambiguous rank of the small businessman is explained by his social
origin and by the "power" which is ascribed to him by the lower but denied
to him by the upper. The ambiguous position of the white-collar worker,
on the other hand, rests less upon *complications* in, and pressures on his
power position than upon his absence of power. They have no leaders active in civic efforts; they are not, as a stratum, represented in the councils;
they have no autonomous organizations through which to strive for such
political and civic ends as they may envision; they are seldom, if ever, in
the publicity spotlight as a group. No articulate leaders in these cities appeal directly and mainly to white-collar people or draw their strength from
white-collar support.

The few organizations in which white-collar employees predominate—
the Business and Professional Women's Clubs, the Junior Chamber of Commerce, and the YWCA—are so tied in with business groups as such, that
they have little or no autonomy. Socially, the lower white-collar is largely
on "the Elk level" and the higher white-collar usually is in the No. 2 or 3
social clubs; in both these situations they form part of a "middle-class
mingling" pattern. They are "led," if at all, by salesmen and other such
"contact people" who are themselves identified with "business."

The organized power of the middle-sized city does not include any
autonomous white-collar unit. Which way the unorganized white-collar people will swing politically and which of the two civic fronts they will support seems to depend almost entirely upon the strength and prestige of
autonomous labor organizations within the city.

White-Collar Ideologies. The ideology of the white-collar people rises
rather directly out of their occupations and the requirements for them. They
are not a well defined group in any other readily apparent sense. This
ideology is not overtly political, yet by political default, it is generally "conservative" and by virtue of the aspects of occupation which it stresses, it
sets up "social" distinctions between white-collar and labor and makes the
most of them.

Those white-collar people in middle-sized cities, for example, who "contact the public" exhibit the psychology of people working a small and
personally known market from within small and moderate-sized firms. In
this respect, they are the typological opposites of salesgirls in metropolitan
department stores who work a mass public of strangers. Fifty-three small

merchants and salespeople in Central City,[14] almost unanimously knew personally the people they served and were very "happy" about their work. Their attitude towards this work is seldom material. It rests upon a communalization between buyer and seller: 63% spontaneously mentioned enjoyment at contacting their public, which is twice as high as for any other single reason for liking their work.

This general ideology has four discernible contents: (a) the idea that they are *learning about human nature,* which is mentioned by about one-fourth of them; (b) the feeling that they *borrow prestige* from their customers; sometimes the prestige source includes the merchandise itself or the store, but its center is normally the customer; (c) the opposite of prestige borrowing: the feeling of *power in manipulating the customer's appearance and home;* this is more apparent, of course, among cosmetic and clothing sellers; (d) the idea of *rendering service:* about one-fourth speak explicitly in terms of an ideology of service, which is interwoven in various ways with the other contents.

These key elements in the occupational ideology of salespeople in medium-sized cities, (1) rest upon the facts of a small and personally known market; (2) in emphasizing just this contact aspect of their work, the white-collar people seize upon precisely an occupational experience which wage workers do not and cannot have; they make a fetish of "contacts"; and (3) the ideology, as a whole and in its parts, is either neutral or pro-business in orientation.

Similar ideological analysis of other occupations making up our two white-collar strata reveal similar tendencies. Nothing in the direct occupational experience of the white-collar people in middle-sized cities propels them towards an autonomous organization for political or civic power purposes. The social springs for such movements, should they occur, will be elsewhere.

The direct appeal to higher wages, through collective action, which the trade unions hold out, is in tension with these occupational ideologies.

"I can't understand why they don't organize," says a business agent for an old-line union. "They got a high school education or more. Looks to me like they'd be the ones to organize, not the man in the ditch with fourth grade education. But it seems to work out just the other way . . . The solution is to come down to earth and realize that the prestige of this would-be manager and assistant manager is camouflage for cheap wages. The glory of the idea of the name takes the place of wages . . . that's all I can figure out." [15]

---

14. Twelve were small business operators; two-thirds are women; about one-half of the total have finished high school. The implicit contrast with metropolitan salesgirls is anchored on quotational materials gathered over several years by Mr. James Gale, "Types of Macy Salesgirls," seminar paper, University of Maryland, Graduate School.

15. There are of course other reasons, besides status claims and occupational ideologies for the difficulties of unionizing white-collar workers; see C. Wright Mills, "The White Collar Unions: A Statistical Portrait and an Outline of Their Social Psychology" (forthcoming).

Such a contrast between status and class interest, which is rather typically known by alert trade union men, leads us to expect that only if labor gets civic power and prestige will the white-collar people in these cities string along. So long as their occupational ideology and status claims remain as they are, they will not make a "class fight," although they will try to share in the results, if those who make it for them win out.

White-Collar Politics. In the general polarization of the middle-sized city's stratification, the top and the bottom are becoming more rigid: 73% of the upper half of the income-occupation scale is descended from the upper half. There is also a rather distinct polarization in organization life, in ideological loyalty, and in political tendency.

There are no available symbols which are in any way distinctly of the white-collar strata. Contrary to many expectations, these middle groups show no signs of developing a policy of their own. Neither in income nor mentality are they unified. The high white-collar are 40% more Republican than their lower white-collar colleagues.

They do not feel any sharp crisis specific to their stratum. They drift into acceptance of and integration with a business-run society punctuated by "labor troubles." In these cities, it may be pretentious to speak of "political tendencies" among white-collar workers. And such problems as the relations of party, trade union, and class cannot even be posed: The white-collar people are not a homogeneous class; they are not in trade unions; neither major party caters specifically to them, and there is no thought of their forming an independent party.

Insofar as political and civic strength rests upon organized economic power, the white-collar workers can only derive such strength from "business" or from "labor." Within the whole structure of power, they are dependent variables. They have no self-starting motor moving them to form organizations with which to increase their power in the civic constellation. Estimates of their political tendencies in the middle-sized cities, therefore, must rest upon larger predictions of the manner and outcome of the civic struggles of business and labor.

Only when "labor" has rather obviously "won out" in a city, if then, will the lower white-collar people go in for unions. If the leaders of labor are included in compromise committees, stemming from Chamber of Commerce circles, then such white-collar groups as exist will be even more so.

Lenin's remark that the political consciousness of a stratum cannot be aroused within "the sphere of relations between workers and employers" holds doubly true for white-collar employees in these cities. Their occupational ideology is politically passive. They are not engaged in any economic struggle, except in the most scattered and fragmentary way. It is, therefore, not odd that they lack even a rudimentary awareness of their economic and political interests. Insofar as they are at all politically available, they form the rear guard either of "business" or of "labor"; but in either case, they are very much rear guard.

Theories of the rise to power of white-collar people are generally inferred from the facts of their numerical growth and their indispensability in the bureaucratic and distributive operations of mass society. But only if one assumes a pure and automatic democracy of numbers does the mere growth of a stratum mean increased power for it. And only if one assumes a magic leap from occupational function to political power does technical indispensability mean power for a stratum.

When one translates such larger questions into the terms of the middle-sized American city, one sees very clearly that the steps from growth and function to increased politicial power include, at a minimum, political awareness and political organization. The white-collar workers in these cities do not have either to any appreciable extent.

CHANGE IN THE OCCUPATIONAL STRUCTURE
OF THE UNITED STATES, 1910 TO 1950

Albert J. Reiss, Jr.

The United States has changed from a primarily agricultural nation to a highly industrialized one in the past 130 years. The nature of this change is easily seen from the fact that only 12 per cent of all employed persons were in agricultural occupations in 1950 as compared with almost three-fourths in 1820. This predominant shift in industrial composition brought with it marked changes in the occupational composition of the working force. There were striking changes in the composition and complexity of the division of labor. Some of these changes are presented below, and a few reasons for them are suggested.

An advanced urban economy such as that found in the United States has an extensive division of labor. The degree of occupational differentiation in an urban economy is not easily conveyed. The second edition of the *Dictionary of Occupational Titles of the United States,* for example, contains 22,028 job descriptions and a total of 40,023 defined occupational titles.[1] These descriptions include a diversity of occupational titles such as collator operator, ear cutter, fish-liver sorter, mutuel option cashier, pedodontist, red-lead burner, third-cure man, tree warden, and zig-zag machine operator, in addition to the more easily recognized titles such as architect, carpenter and patrolman. Each of these jobs performs a particular function for the society. Such functions can be grouped, however, into classes of similar occupations and they, in turn, into an occupational structure. The number and kind of occupational classes obtained depend upon the criteria employed for a functional differentiation among occupations.

The sociologist is primarily interested in occupational position as a symbol of prestige in a status structure. Various criteria are said to be involved in prestige status rankings of occupations, such as the income derived from the occupation, the amount of education or training required to enter the occupation, and the nature of the work itself. Broad occupational classifications like white-collar and manual work, or head and hand work, are indicative of such classifications. Frequently the occupational structure is defined as a socio-economic status structure where the groups represent strata with different ways of life. The United States Bureau of

---

1. United States Employment Service, *Dictionary of Occupational Titles of the United States* (Washington: USGPO, 1949).

the Census has developed one such operational classification for urban occupations, which generally consists of six major nonfarm occupational groups.[2] More detailed classifications and scales of occupations are used in the research literature. The Census hierarchy is presented in Table 1 with information on the occupational composition of the farm and non-farm categories of occupations for decennial periods from 1910 to 1950. The data are only roughly comparable from decade to decade, as both the procedures of classification and the basis of classification have changed somewhat.

The data in Table 1 show the changes in occupational composition that have obtained in the work force of the United States during a forty-year period. These changes are presented and discussed below. Table 1 also presents an *index of net redistribution* in occupations for the adja-

Table 1—Per cent Distribution of Employed Workers, by Occupational Groups and by Decennial Periods, 1910-1950

Occupational Group	1950*	1940*	1930†	1920†	1910†
Total	100.00	100.0	100.0	100.0	100.0
Nonfarm	87.9	82.5	78.7	74.6	67.6
Professional and Semiprofessional	7.2	6.9	6.0	4.9	4.3
Proprietors, Managers and Officials	10.4	7.8	7.5	6.7	6.4
Clerical and Sales	19.0	17.2	16.3	13.7	10.3
Skilled Workers and Foremen	12.9	12.8	12.9	13.4	11.3
Semiskilled Workers	20.9	17.9	16.3	16.0	14.3
Unskilled Workers	17.5	19.9	19.7	19.9	21.0
Farm	12.1	17.5	21.3	25.4	32.4
Operators and Managers	7.0	10.4	12.3	15.3	16.1
Laborers	5.1	7.1	9.0	10.1	16.3
Index of net redistribution‡		7.8	3.9	4.8	8.1

SOURCE: U. S. Bureau of the Census.
* Data are for labor force; all experienced workers 14 years of age and over. The groups are not directly comparable to those for preceding years owing to differences in the population for which data are compiled, and in classification into occupational groups.
† Data are for gainful workers, 10 years of age and over.
‡ Computed as the index of dissimilarity between the occupational distributions for any two decades. The index is one-half the sum of the absolute values of the differences between the occupational differences for any two decades, taken occupation by occupation.

cent pairs of decades: 1910-1920, 1920-1930, 1930-40, and 1940-1950. The index may be interpreted as a measure of displacement. It specifies the per cent of the workers in the more recent decade who would have to move to another occupation in order to make its occupational distribution identical with that of the previous decade. Data from other sources are used to present a somewhat more detailed statement of changes over the forty-year period.

(1). THE PREDOMINANCE OF URBAN OCCUPATIONS. The change from a primarily agricultural nation to a highly urbanized one in the last 130

---

2. Sixteenth Census of the United States, *Population: Comparative Occupation Statistics For the United States, 1870 to 1940* (U.S. Bureau of the Census, 1943), pp. 179-80.

years already has been noted. During the past forty years this trend appears as a continued decrease of both farm operators and managers and of farm laborers. The lower-paid farm laborers, on the average, have decreased by over two-thirds during this period while there were somewhat fewer than one-half as many farm operators and managers in 1950 as in 1910. The mechanization of agriculture, of course, is largely responsible for the sharp decrease in the farm work force, since the amount of agricultural product has grown at a rate far greater than that of the general population to create an agricultural surplus for present levels of living.

Not all of the persons employed in nonfarm occupations in 1950 lived in urban areas, however. Of the 49,053,900 employed nonfarm persons in the labor force in 1950, only 77.1 per cent were classified as living in urban areas, while 18.1 per cent were classified as rural nonfarm and 4.8 per cent as rural farm persons. Correlatively, of the 6,700,860 labor force employed in farm occupations in 1950, 83.8 per cent lived in rural farm dwellings, 11.5 per cent in rural nonfarm dwellings and 4.7 per cent in urban areas.[3] Thus, while the occupation of a person is largely related to his place of residence; it is not necessarily determined by it. Some persons, in fact, both operate a farm and work in a nonfarm occupation. The 1950 Census of Agriculture found that 38.4 per cent of the 2,069,152 farm operators had some work off their farm in 1949. The proportion of these persons with off-farm employment has been increasing, since only 30.3 per cent of farm operators reported off-farm employment in 1930.[4] Farm operators who work off the farm can work in other farm occupations, of course. The 1940 Census of Agriculture found that three out of every four farm operators with off-farm employment in 1939 were employed in nonfarm occupations, however.[5]

There also is considerable evidence that the nature of farm operation and employment itself has been steadily changing to a more urban pattern of industrial operation. The size of the average farm has been increasing, the total number of farms is decreasing and the rate of mechanization of labor is increasing. The proportion of farm laborers, in fact, has decreased at a somewhat greater rate than that of farm operators and managers over the past forty years. Many farms today are operated as large-scale business enterprises.[6]

(2). THE PROFESSIONALIZATION OF JOBS. The professional and semi-professional occupations for the most part have shown substantial increases during the past forty years. The old established professionals such as doctors, lawyers and clergymen have had relatively smaller increases than the newer ones of scientists, engineers, professional entertainers and

3. These percentages are based on data in Table 1, *United States Census of Population: 1950*, "Occupational Characteristics," Volume IV, Part 1, Chapter B.

4. *United States Census of Agriculture: 1950*, Volume II, Chapter II, p. 74.

5. *16th Census of the United States: Agriculture, 1940*, Volume 3, Chapter 5, p. 325.

6. See Walter Goldschmidt, *As You Sow* (Glencoe, Ill.: The Free Press, 1947).

technicians. Compulsory education laws together with the increased demand for higher education as a prerequisite to many jobs undoubtedly have contributed to the expansion of some old professions, such as the teaching profession. The semiprofessions, comprised to a great extent of technicians, testers, and analysts, have shown phenomenal growth since 1900. The growing application of science—in the medical arts, industry and the professions generally—has substantially increased the proportion of semiprofessional technicians. The development of modern medicine alone has contributed well over 100 different kinds of technicians who assist professional medical personnel.

There are a large number of occupations which increasingly seek and are granted professional status. The administrators and staff persons of institutions in the health, education and welfare field and a growing number of entertainment and recreation personnel in the mass communication industries of radio and television are examples of such would-be and quasi-professionals which have shown substantial increase. In brief, the practice of science and the mass arts has led to considerable professional expansion in the past forty years. It is quite likely they will continue to show substantial growth, given American value emphasis on science, the medical arts, and mass education and entertainment.

(3). THE BUREAUCRATIZATION OF THE ADMINISTRATION AND OPERATION OF INSTITUTIONS. The past forty years have seen a substantial increase in the number of white-collar workers who are responsible for the management and operation of both governmental and private institutions, and in the size of the employing establishment. This has meant a growth of the "office" and the personnel associated with it. Government officials and administrators, private managers and their assistants, clerical workers and business machine operators all contribute to the relatively efficient operation of a network of relations associated with the *large* corporation, institution or agency. Even the small business, institution or agency, however, increasingly accepts bureaucratic routines and operations which in turn lead to the employment of a variety of managerial, clerical and other technical specialists.

The clerical and sales worker group, in fact, has shown the greatest relative increase of any occupation group in the past seventy years. It grew from 2.9 per cent of the total workers in 1870[7] to almost one-fifth of all workers in 1950. Technology, of course, has made possible an increasing number of clerical specialists which has in turn made possible a vast number of business records and controls. Technology, likewise, has made possible improved communication and its use in large-scale organization. Telegraph and telephone operators, for instance, have shown sizeable increase since 1900. Increasingly, of course, women have come to comprise a large segment of the employed in the clerical and sales occupations, partly because technology has made their entry more favorable.

---

7. Bureau of Labor Statistics, *Monthly Labor Review*, 39 (March, 1934), p. 504.

(4). THE CHANGING CONCEPT OF SKILL. Table 1 shows that the skilled worker and foreman occupations have remained fairly stable in growth over the past forty years, while the semiskilled worker occupations have shown substantial increase and the unskilled laborer jobs an actual decrease. These patterns usually are attributed to several related factors: the development of mass-production methods of manufacture; the changing technology of work processes so that machines perform complex operations formerly done only by skilled artisans; an increased demand for installers, service and repairmen for the newer transportation, communication and household appliance industries; and, the changing methods of packaging, labeling, canning and preserving, and storaging activities in all industries.

Industrial occupations vary considerably in the degree to which they require that the worker perform skilled manual operations in a job or technical process. At one extreme are the skilled artisans where variation in skills usually leads to considerable product variation, while at the other extreme is a machine operator on a mass-production line who simply determines whether the machine continues to perform its uniform mechanical operation. One produces the entire artifact; the other performs only a minuscule operation in an elaborate production process. Most occupational tasks lie between these extremes.

The growth of the semiskilled occupations during the past forty years has largely at the expense of the unskilled rather than the skilled laboring jobs. Mechanization of labor in construction, the handling of goods, the extraction of raw materials and similar operations has made machine-operator jobs of formerly unskilled ones. There is, for instance, much less need for the unskilled laundress today because she is largely replaced by a host of operatives such as bleachers, ironers, dyers and pressers. Despite this upgrading of unskilled to semiskilled jobs, there has been considerable shifting of formerly skilled jobs to semiskilled ones and of semiskilled and unskilled jobs to skilled ones. The unskilled ditch-digger or excavator, for instance, now often is replaced by a skilled diesel-scoop operator, a dragline operator, or a trenching-machine operator, while the skilled weaver is more likely to be replaced by a semiskilled textile weaver or spinner. At the same time, both new skilled and semiskilled jobs have arisen, particularly in mass-production processes. Thus, for example, highly skilled installers, repairmen and maintenance men are required for many factory machines operated by semiskilled operators.

The relative stability of the skilled worker class with the accompanying increase in the semiskilled and decrease in the unskilled laboring classes of work does not mean that modern industry is less dependent upon skilled labor for efficient operation.[8] Rather, skill has a somewhat different meaning when applied to the semiskilled occupations. The high

---

8. See Harry Ober, "The Worker and His Job," *Monthly Labor Review,* 71 (July, 1950), pp. 14-15. This section is indebted to Ober's discussion of skill changes.

degree of precision and skill required in many processes today is either divided among a large number of workers such that it is relatively limited for a particular job for a particular employer, or the skill is transferred to a machine where the worker skill lies only in its operation. In many cases, the worker gains his experience in a semiskilled occupation in a relatively short period of on-the-job training with a particular employer. Much of this "skill" is not transferred to another employer unless the plant operations and product are very similar. The semiskilled worker is geared to a particular machine or process in a particular plant making a specified product, or to a specific task such as operating a means of transportation.

The significance of this change in relative skill required of the labor force since the turn of the century, then, lies in the diffusion of some skill to a larger segment of the labor force. Technology has reduced the need for as large a proportion of the unskilled worker and the highly skilled artisan while increasing the need for workers in the semiskilled occupations. The result is a revaluation of skills which has led to less emphasis on training and experience as criteria for entry into jobs which are part of a complex technological system. Since technology should continue to make inroads on worker skill, the semiskilled group may well become the largest single occupational group in the U. S. labor force.

(5). THE SECULAR TREND TOWARD UPWARD MOBILITY IN THE OCCUPATIONAL STRUCTURE. The expanding occupational groups in the occupational structure of the United States during the past forty years are largely those with relatively higher status. If we call the first three nonfarm occupation groups in Table 1 the white-collar occupations, we note that white-collars have increased from 21 per cent of all gainful workers in 1910 to 36.6 per cent of all employed workers in the labor force in 1950. The other nonfarm occupations showed a relatively smaller rate of increase, from only 46.6 per cent of all gainful workers in 1910 to 51.3 of all employed in the labor force in 1950. A great deal of the loss of agricultural employed in fact has been taken up in the expansion of the white-collar rather than the manual nonfarm occupations. Assuming next that the nonfarm occupational groups in Table 1 represent a status rank order or hierarchy of occupations, the other major status upgrading in the occupational structure since 1910 has been the decrease in the low-status unskilled laborers and an increase in the higher-status semiskilled workers. Assuming further that the major occupational groups have maintained the same rank order from 1910 to 1950, many persons have been able to move to higher-status occupations in the occupational hierarchy simply because of this secular trend for the higher-status occupations to expand.

The predominant shift in the occupational structure over the past forty years has been upward—to the semiskilled manual jobs and to all major white-collar occupational groups. The loss occurred primarily for the farm occupations and the nonfarm manual laborers. A second type of shift can also be discerned in the occupational structure—a shift toward the occupational center of gravity.[9] Considering only the nonfarm occupational structure in Table 1, it can be seen that the greatest expansion of the structure occurred at the lower white-collar level—the clerical and sales group—and the semiskilled level. The lowest-status occupational group of unskilled laborers showed an actual decrease while the upper-status ones had smaller increases. Viewed in terms of actual numbers, and considering a mass skill group of white-collar clerical and sales group and the manual skilled and semiskilled groups to be at the "center of occupational gravity," the proportion of workers at the "center" increased from 35.9 per cent of all gainful workers in 1910 to 52.8 per cent of all employed in the labor force in 1950, or a majority of all employed persons in 1950.

(6). THE ABSENCE OF A DECLINE IN THE RATE OF OCCUPATIONAL MOBILITY. There is considerable interest in the question of whether the opportunities for movement in the occupational structure of the United States have been declining in recent decades. The data in Table 1 give a negative answer to this question. The fact that there is no downward trend in the index of net redistribution negates the idea that the rate of social mobility is slowing down. The 1940-1950 index, in fact, is twice that of the 1930-1940 index, and roughly comparable to that of the 1910-1920 decade. At the same time the data for the index of net redistribution show that there is considerable variation in these opportunities over time.

SUMMARY. The data on changes in the occupational structure from 1910 to 1950 broadly show a substantial increase in the proportion of workers in the clerical and kindred worker and the semiskilled occupations and a sharp decline in the farm occupations. Fairly substantial increase occurred too for the highest-status professional, proprietary, managerial and official occupations while there was a small decrease for the lowest-status unskilled worker occupations, which includes private household and servant occupations. Employment in skilled occupations was fairly stable for the period.

The changing industrial composition of the United States economy, of course, is a factor in this changing occupational composition. The growth of the mass transportation and communication facilities and the increase in public employment are two major examples of such changes in industrial composition. The rise of such industries can have a marked effect on the prestige of particular occupations. Generally, it is thought that the declining occupations lose prestige while the growing occupations and those in the newer industries gain in prestige. The development of automotive transportation and the application of motor power to agricultural machines have had profound effects on our occupational composition since 1910. The automobile, for example, led to a decline in demand for work-

---

9. The term and a discussion of the trend from 1870 to 1930 can be found in Elbridge Sibley, "Some Demographic Clues to Stratification," *American Sociological Review,* 7 (June, 1942), p. 323.

ers in such occupations as coachmen, harness makers, wagon makers, teamsters and livery stable proprietors during this period. Increasing utilization of automotive transport on the other hand led to a demand for workers in such a diversity of occupations as automobile designers and engineers, construction workers, automobile repair mechanics, gasoline station proprietors and attendants, automobile sales proprietors and sales agents, truck, bus, and taxi drivers, traffic engineers and officers, and licensing agents—to mention only a few of the occupations in addition to those directly involved in the manufacture of automobile parts and automobile assembly.

Science and technology, through discovery and engineering application, doubtlessly will continue to exert a profound influence on the specific occupational group composition of the occupational structure over the next decades. The direction of the changes in major occupation group composition should not materially differ from those outlined above, however, since the character of the change is generally orderly and predictable. One of course cannot have as much of a decrease, because the farm group has substantially decreased in size. For the same reason, the rate of urbanization cannot long continue as rapidly as it has in the past.

RECENT TRENDS IN
URBAN OCCUPATIONAL MOBILITY

Natalie Rogoff

The following report presents the results of a study of social mobility in an urban American community of the twentieth century. The procedure used in this research was to collect information concerning the occupations of male applicants for marriage licenses and the occupations of their fathers, for residents of the city of Indianapolis and the surrounding suburban and rural fringe which make up Marion County, Indiana. These data were collected for two time periods: a seven-year period preceding the first World War (1905–1912), and a three-and-one-half-year period preceding the second World War (1938–1941).[1]

The first question which this study raises, then, concerns the degree to which social mobility has increased or decreased in the recent history of American society. This question has provoked considerable speculation, but little concrete research. It has been supposed that one of the consequences of the depression of the nineteen thirties was a fixing or hardening of the social structure, so that the channels of entrance to the differing layers of the hierarchy were either closed or greatly narrowed. The findings given below will show that probably no such categorical description is adequate, but rather that the degree and direction of the changes which have occurred vary with such factors as the age of the men being considered and the particular occupational or social position to which they have gone.

In addition to these inter-generational trends in social mobility, the influence of a number of personal or social characteristics on mobility were also studied. Because of limitations of space, only one of these factors will be discussed here—age. Consideration of mobility in relation to age is important, since a good deal of occupational movement takes place not only from one generation to the next, but also from one time point to others during the career of an individual. Therefore, in measuring the mobility of a son relative to the starting point represented by his father's position, it is desirable to know for what point in the career of the son his occupational status is reported. By controlling the son's age, as is done here, we can determine the age at which mobility becomes most evident for sons

This article is based on Natalie Rogoff, *Recent Trends in Occupational Mobility* (Glencoe, Ill.: The Free Press, 1953).

1. For an evaluation of the procedures used in the collection of the data, see Chapter 3 of the book.

originating in each of the social classes. Age is also relevant in considering the movement into occupations whose requirements include, for example, physical strength versus long experience.

Before presenting the results of this study, a parenthesis must be opened concerning certain definitional and technical problems.

A number of important questions concerning modern communities and societies are implied in the study of social mobility. On the one hand, this term refers to the variation in the social origins of the members of a given social stratum. This aspect of mobility helps us to understand, for example, the quality of leadership furnished by the elite, or the aspirations or behavior of the middle or lower classes. If, for instance, the members of the upper class of one generation are exclusively the sons of the upper class of the previous generation, we expect a wholly different kind of community of social life from that which obtains when there is complete turnover in the membership.

On the other hand, social mobility also refers to the way in which the opportunities available to a given generation of men are distributed among them, according to their various social characteristics. This is, in effect, the opposite side of the coin to the aspect discussed above, and it is at least of equal importance. The difference between the two hinges on whether we begin with the members, say, of the upper class or the working class of today, and ask the question: in what social classes did the men now in these positions originate; or whether we begin with the men who were born into each of the social milieux and trace the different social destinations at which they have arrived.

Implicit in the phenomenon of social mobility is the element of change over time. Any measurement of mobility must therefore involve a comparison of two or more points in time. As is done in the study to be described, it is usual to compare the social positions of sons and their fathers. However, it must be realized that two types of social change are included in these comparisons, and for the sake both of precision and theoretical usefulness, these two types ought to be dealt with separately.

First is the type of social and technological change which is seen in the secular trends in the occupational structure. From one generation to the next in any large American city, the proportion of semi-skilled, clerical, and professional workers has tended to increase, while all other occupational groups have either declined or remained constant in numerical importance. This is obviously an important source of inter-generational occupational mobility, since men are constantly recruited from the declining occupations into the expanding ones, either at the onset or during the course of their careers.

However, we can imagine an occupational structure which is unvarying from one decade to the next, but in which mobility nevertheless takes place. In this case, mobility would be due solely to the influence of the differently evaluated personal and social characteristics, such as talent, ambition, or family background, which the individuals in the labor force possess. The *proportion* of highly rewarded and poorly rewarded positions would remain the same, but the men whose fathers occupied a given position need not themselves remain there.

It is clear that both types of mobility are simultaneously operating in contemporary American society. In most previous research on this subject, the measurement techniques used have not been such as to distinguish between the two.[2] In contrast, the present study uses a measure of mobility which is geared to answer the following question: *Has more or less occupational mobility taken place than can be accounted for by the concurrent changes in the occupational structure?*[3]

This technique will be explained as the data are introduced. Let us consider first the problem of how much change in the over-all amount of mobility occurred between the periods centering around 1910 and 1940, as indicated by the two Indianapolis samples of about ten thousand men each.

The last two lines in Tables 1 and 2 represent the percentage and the actual distribution of all the white male residents of Indianapolis who applied for marriage licenses during the specified time periods.[4] These total distributions will serve as a standard against which the mobility of men stemming from each occupational origin will be compared. For example, 3.8 percent of all just-married Indianapolis residents were engaged in professional work about the year 1910. Reading down the first column of percentages in Table 1 shows that the proportion of men in the professions ranges from 21 per cent of the men who were sons of professionals, to less than 1 per cent of the sons of unskilled workers and personal service workers (janitors, cooks, elevator operators). If we compute the ratio of each of these proportions to the total proportion of 3.8, these ratios will indicate the "surplus" or "deficit" of mobility into professional work by men coming from each of the various occupational origins. For the example given, these ratios range from a high of 5.5, or a more than five-fold surplus, for men who are sons of professionals themselves, to a low of 0.2, a deficit of four-fifths, for sons of unskilled and service workers. Note that a ratio of one, as is approximately the case for sons of semi-professionals and farmers, indicates that men stemming from such origins are just proportionately represented in the given occupational group. These ratios provide a clear

---

2. The two outstanding exceptions in the previous research literature are Federico Chessa, *La Trasmissione Ereditaria delle Professioni* (Torino: Fratelli Bocca, Editori, 1912), and F. W. Taussig and C. S. Joslyn, *American Business Leaders: A Study in Social Origins* (New York: The Macmillan Co., 1932).

3. This technique was developed by Herbert Goldhamer, to whom the author was research assistant in 1947–1948. It was first presented in a paper read before the Society for Social Research in Chicago, May 1948.

4. A sample of about one thousand Negroes was also gathered for the later time period, but not the earlier, due to the small size of the non-white population in Indianapolis before the first World War. These Negro cases are not included here. For a separate analysis of them, see Chapter 5 of the book.

TABLE I—Occupational Mobility, Indianapolis, 1910: Proportion of Sons in Each Occupation According to Their Fathers' Occupation

Father's Occupation	Professional	Semi-professional	Proprietors, Managers, Officials	Clerks and Salesmen	Skilled	Semi-skilled	Unskilled	Protective Service	Personal Service	Farming	All Fathers	Number of Fathers
	%	%	%	%	%	%	%	%	%	%	%	
Professional	27.0	3.7	12.2	24.1	21.8	10.9	3.2	0.5	2.1	0.5	100.0	377
Semi-professional	4.1	27.0	9.5	21.6	13.1	13.5	5.4	2.7	2.7		100.0	74
Proprietors, managers, officials	7.3	2.8	21.1	27.5	20.2	10.5	5.0	1.0	3.8	1.0	100.2	1,253
Clerks and salesmen	5.6	2.9	7.4	43.7	22.0	10.6	3.6	0.5	2.4	1.2	99.9	659
Skilled	1.9	1.6	4.1	15.2	48.7	16.9	7.0	0.8	3.2	0.7	100.1	2,720
Semi-skilled	2.4	1.5	3.6	13.7	31.8	31.6	10.3	0.7	3.3	1.0	99.9	940
Unskilled	0.8	0.7	2.8	10.9	26.8	19.0	34.2	0.9	3.3	0.6	100.0	1,256
Protective service	1.3	0.6	10.6	21.3	32.5	19.4	8.8	2.5	3.1		100.1	160
Personal service	0.8	3.1	3.9	17.8	26.4	20.9	11.6	0.8	14.7		100.2	129
Farming	3.4	1.2	6.1	14.6	27.8	16.7	14.0	1.3	4.3	10.7	100.1	2,685
Sons of all fathers	3.8	1.9	7.1	18.2	32.0	17.1	12.0	1.0	3.7	3.4	100.2	.....
Number of sons	389	190	731	1,869	3,280	1,753	1,225	98	374	344	10,253	10,253

TABLE II—Occupational Mobility, Indianapolis, 1940: Proportion of Sons in Each Occupation According to Their Fathers' Occupation

Father's Occupation	Professional	Semi-professional	Proprietors, Managers, Officials	Clerks and Salesmen	Skilled	Semi-skilled	Unskilled	Protective Service	Personal Service	Farming	All Fathers	Number of Fathers
	%	%	%	%	%	%	%	%	%	%	%	
Professional	28.3	6.3	7.6	27.9	15.4	9.5	2.5	0.8	1.5	0.2	100.0	474
Semi-professional	15.8	19.3	3.5	17.5	23.7	12.3	2.6	1.8	3.5		100.0	114
Proprietors, managers, officials	7.7	3.4	17.6	30.6	14.3	19.8	2.5	1.6	2.1	0.5	100.1	1,203
Clerks and salesmen	7.7	5.2	7.6	42.2	15.1	16.4	2.4	1.3	1.9	0.2	100.0	1,092
Skilled	3.3	2.9	4.3	19.1	32.3	26.9	5.6	2.1	3.0	0.6	100.1	2,729
Semi-skilled	2.5	2.1	4.1	17.3	18.4	43.2	5.3	2.2	4.3	0.6	100.1	1,520
Unskilled	2.4	1.5	2.8	13.1	15.4	30.0	28.6	2.4	3.6	0.3	100.1	720
Protective service	2.5	0.8	6.6	22.8	17.0	31.5	8.7	8.3	1.2	0.4	99.8	241
Personal service	4.9	4.3	5.5	17.1	22.6	29.9	3.7	1.8	10.4		100.2	164
Farming	3.8	1.6	5.9	15.2	23.1	28.7	8.9	3.6	5.1	4.2	100.1	1,635
Sons of all fathers	5.5	3.1	6.6	22.1	21.9	27.1	6.9	2.3	3.4	1.1	100.0	
Number of sons	548	307	656	2,188	2,163	2,678	684	229	334	105	9,892	9,892

measure of the first aspect of mobility mentioned above: the extent of variation in the social origins of the members of a given stratum.[5]

It should be pointed out that this measure of mobility is in no way
influenced by changes in the occupational structure from one generation
to the next. For example, Table 2 shows that the proportion of professional
workers in the sample had increased almost one-and-one-half times to 5.5
per cent by 1940. Consequently, we cannot directly compare the percentage
distributions of the first column in each of the two tables, in order to ascertain whether or not there have been changes in the social origins of the
members of the liberal professions. But by computing a separate set of
ratios for each sample, the increase in the total proportion is automatically controlled. We can then compare these two sets of ratios, and determine whether professional, as well as other types of work have become
more or less accessible to men coming from the different ranks in the social
structure.

To what extent, then, did the amount of mobility into various occupations change between the two periods centering around 1910 and 1940?
Based on the mobility ratios described above, Table 3 summarizes this
information in the form of averages. Each figure represents an average of
the ratios for the corresponding column in Table 1 or 2, and hence, the
average rate of mobility into each type of occupation. In these averages,
the diagonal cells have been omitted, since they represent occupational
stability, rather than mobility.

TABLE III—Average Mobility Into Each Occupation, 1910 and 1940

Occupation	Average, 1910	Mobility, 1940
Professional	0.81	1.01
Semi-professional	1.09	1.01
Proprietors, managers, officials	0.94	0.80
Clerical and sales	1.02	0.91
Skilled manual	0.77	0.84
Semi-skilled	0.90	0.84
Unskilled	0.64	0.68
Protective service	1.06	0.84
Other service	0.86	0.86
Farming	0.17	0.29
All occupations	0.82	0.81

For each of the samples taken as a whole, the average amount of mobility is expressed by a ratio of about four-fifths. This signifies that about
eighty percent as much occupational mobility occurred, in each of the time
periods, as would have occurred if all the men had been proportionally distributed in the occupational hierarchy, according to their social origins.
That there was no change between 1910 and 1940 belies the notion that the
social structure has grown more rigid in recent years. But for a more differ-

5. The similarity of this technique to orthodox contingency analysis should be apparent. The modification introduced is the computation of individual ratios of actual to
expected values, rather than a sum of the differences between actual and expected
values.

entiated answer to this question, let us consider also the mobility rates into each of the separate occupational groups.

Table 3 shows that, although the over-all mobility rate did not vary between the earlier and later years, there was some change in mobility among the separate occupations. The most striking of these was in the professions, where the average mobility increased about twenty-five percent over the thirty year period. It should perhaps be recalled that these figures in no way reflect changes over time in the availability of positions in the given occupation; nor, in ranking the various occupations with respect to mobility rates during a single time period, do such rates vary with the increasing or decreasing importance of the occupation since the fathers' time. They show, rather, whether more or less men than "expected" (as this term is used in contingency analysis) moved into a given occupation. In this sense, then, the professions were more accessible in 1940 to men coming from all other strata of society than they had been in 1910. On the other hand, semi-professional, business, and clerical work all slightly decreased in accessibility. There was small, and inconsistent change among the manual occupations, skilled and unskilled work increasing slightly, semi-skilled decreasing slightly.

In spite of these inconsistent changes, the relative positions of the various occupations, with regard to their accessibility, varied little between 1910 and 1940. At both times, somewhat more mobility took place into those occupations representing "head" work, than into those representing "hand" work. The differences in these average mobility rates are not, however, of a large order; this suggests that the effect of such opposing factors as occupational rewards—prestige, income, etc.—and qualifications—academic training, manual skills or strength—have been to some extent cancelled out in the computation of means. This is verified by an examination of the separate cells in Tables 1 and 2, which show wide variation in the amount of mobility into a given occupation, depending on the social origins of the men involved. In order to summarize this dispersion, the coefficients of variation from each mean mobility rate have been computed, and are given below in Table 4. These coefficients, which express the standard deviation as a percentage of the corresponding mean, measure what might be termed the level of "indifference" with which the members of a given

TABLE IV—Coefficients of Variation from Average In-Mobility Rates by Occupation, 1910 and 1940

Occupation	Coefficient of Variation	
	1910	1940
Professional	69.1%	75.2%
Semi-professional	53.2	55.4
Proprietors, etc.	50.0	31.3
Clerical and sales	27.5	27.5
Skilled	23.4	19.0
Semi-skilled	25.6	34.5
Unskilled	46.9	52.9
Protective service	62.3	36.9
Personal service	19.8	43.0
Farming	16.5	72.4
All occupations	57.3	53.1

occupation were recruited from various social origins. Thus, a low coefficient of variation indicates that all men, no matter what origins they came from, experienced about the same degree of ease or difficulty in, or about the same degree of attraction for, entering the occupation. A high coefficient of variation reveals that there has been a selective recruitment of the members of an occupation, most of them coming from one or a few social origins and a disproportionately small number from the rest of the social hierarchy.

On the whole, the occupations which are either highest or lowest in the rewards which they offer show the highest amounts of dispersion from their mean mobility rates. Thus, professional and semi-professional work and, in 1910, independent commerce as well, were highly selective in nature; more than other occupations, they recruited their personnel disproportionately from some ranks to the exclusion of others. The same is true of unskilled manual labor, farming, and to a lesser extent, the service jobs. But the occupations in the middle of the hierarchy—clerical work, skilled and semi-skilled work—were not far from the indifference point in their recruitment; mobility into these ranks was almost evenly distributed throughout the population, irrespective of social origins.

It should be pointed out that, once again, little change is shown with respect to this measure of mobility from the earlier to the later time period. The over-all coefficient of variation from average mobility is almost identical in 1910 and 1940; with the exception of commercial work and the two small groups of service workers, the same is true of each of the occupational groups taken separately. Mobility, then, was as evenly distributed in the occupational structure of 1940 as it had been in 1910.

To give a still more differentiated measure of trends in mobility between the two time periods studied, rates are presented below for the amount of movement which took place among three large blocs of occupations, considered both as points of origin and destination. This is, in effect, a collapsed form of the detailed presentation of mobility from each occupation to every other occupation. It permits measurement of the variation in mobility into a given occupation, in relation to the *particular* social origins of the men involved. It also permits an analysis of the amount of mobility *out of* various occupations, a parameter not as yet considered.

TABLE V—Average Inter-Occupational Mobility, 1910 and 1940

Occupational Origin	"Head" Work	"Hand" Work	Farming
1910:			
"Head" work	1.47	0.72	0.20
"Hand" work	0.69	0.91	0.14
Farming	0.80	1.10	...
1940:			
"Head" work	1.39	0.59	0.21
"Hand" work	0.71	0.92	0.35
Farming	0.70	1.29	...

For purposes of convenience, all of the "head" work occupations—professional, semi-professional, commercial and clerical—have been grouped together; all of the "hand" work occupations—skilled, semi-skilled, and unskilled manual work, and the service occupations—have been grouped; and farming is considered separately. Average mobility rates into and out of each of these three large blocs are presented in Table 5. Once again, rates concerning occupational stability, those which measure the propensity of sons to follow in their fathers' occupations, have been omitted here.

The "isolation" of the head work occupations from all others is clearly shown here. Men stemming from white collar, business, or professional origins moved with great frequency within this bloc of occupations. Both in 1910 and in 1940, this type of mobility was much more commonly achieved than any other.

In both time periods, sons of manual or service workers, and farmers' sons, entered the more prestigeful non-manual jobs only half as frequently as sons of non-manual workers. It is this considerable difference which accounts for the high coefficients of variation described above. The highly selective recruitment manifested in the non-manual occupations is clearly to the disadvantage of men stemming from a background of manual or rural work, and to the advantage of men coming from closely related white collar, business, or professional origins.

There was almost perfect reciprocity between the manual and the non-manual occupations in their "interchange" of personnel. Both in the earlier and the later time periods, the rate of mobility into non-manual work by the sons of manual workers was about the same as the rate of mobility from a non-manual origin to a manual occupational destination. Making allowances for the looseness of such a definition, we may say that downward mobility and upward mobility were about equally common, with respect to these two large groups. In both directions, and at both times, about two-thirds as much mobility took place as would have under conditions of perfect interchange between the two large occupational groups.

Mobility from one manual or service occupation to another was at a relatively low level. Although these occupations are closely related to one another, and often are carried on at the same place of work, the sons of men who were engaged in one manual occupation moved less often to another in the same bloc than would have occurred if they had been distributed simply at random in the occupational structure. Stemming from a family whose breadwinner was a manual worker does not mean that one will, with great likelihood, enter another manual occupation.

The men who are most likely to enter manual occupations are the sons of farmers; and the move from country to city is made more often by way of the factory or the independent craft than the office or the shop.

No consideration has yet been given to the rates of occupational inheritance, or immobility. In all the above discussion, these data have been eliminated, since they refer to a different, although not independent, phenomenon. The propensity of sons to enter the same occupation as their fathers is shown below for each of the several classes in the occupational structure.

One of the most recurrent findings in previous research on occupational mobility is that sons are more likely to enter their father's occupation than to enter any other single occupation. This is upheld, without exception, by the data in this study. It is also true, that, of the men who go into a given type of work, those who are most heavily represented are the sons of men who were themselves engaged in that occupation. Stability is always greater than average mobility into or out of an occupation. However, there are variations in these measures from one occupation to another.

In both time periods, inheritance was lowest in the clerical, skilled, and semi-skilled classes. The degree of inheritance in an occupational class can probably be accounted for by (a) the extent to which the sons consider the fathers' occupation to be rewarding and (b) the extent to which characteristics associated with the sons' origins, such as education, ambition, etc., inhibit or induce mobility out of his origins. It is likely that in the case of the clerical and semi-skilled occupations, these two factors are relatively weak, and inheritance can therefore be expected to be relatively small.

TABLE VI—Occupational Inheritance in Each Occupation, 1910 and 1940

	Occupational Inheritance	
Occupation	1910	1940
Professional	5.53	5.10
Semi-professional	14.61	6.23
Proprietors, etc.	2.96	2.66
Clerical and sales	2.40	1.91
Skilled	1.52	1.47
Semi-skilled	1.85	1.60
Unskilled	2.87	4.14
Protective service	2.60	3.58
Personal service	4.04	3.07
Farming	3.17	3.92
All occupations	4.16	3.36

However, the degree of inheritance in skilled work cannot be explained by these factors. In both time periods, there was less inheritance of skilled work than of any other type of occupation. The concept of Berufsehre, or occupational pride, was developed specifically in connection with the skilled trades. It was expected that this pride in occupations which offer the rewards of security, high income, and prestige, would operate to produce a high degree of occupational inheritance. The familiar notion of sons following their fathers in occupational choice is probably more commonly associated with skilled work than with any other occupation. Yet the table above shows that sons of skilled workers were least likely, in a relative sense, to enter the same kind of work as their fathers.

Professional and semi-professional occupations are characterized by high rates of inheritance, both in 1910 and in 1940. Almost as high was the immobility of sons of unskilled and service workers, especially in 1940. It seems likely that the first two occupations attract their "own" sons because of the rewards in income and prestige that they offer. On the other hand, the immobility of sons of unskilled and service workers is probably due to their restricted economic and educational opportunities, or to restricted ambition; the sons "remain" in their fathers' occupations because they cannot leave.

SUMMARY. The following chart summarizes the results presented above with respect to most of the aspects of occupational mobility dealt with. This summary is in the form of a series of mobility patterns characterizing various occupations. Only those occupations are discussed for which the data seem sufficiently reliable and consistent to warrant classification.

CHART 1

Occupation	Average Mobility into the Occupation	Dispersion from the Average	Occupational Inheritance
Professional and semi-professional	Average to High	High	High
Clerical	High	Low	Low
Skilled and semi-skilled	Average	Low	Low
Unskilled	Low	Average	Average to High

These four sets of occupations represent the top and the bottom of the "head" work and the "hand" work hierarchies, respectively. As such, each presents its own pattern of occupational mobility. The highly rewarding professions have a high power of attraction both for their "own" sons and for sons originating in other occupations; but the entrance qualifications cannot be met with equal ease by men coming from all ranks of the social hierarchy. Clerical and sales work serve as the point of first entry into the non-manual occupations; they are easily and equally accessible to men from all social origins, since they do not impose barriers of long and costly preparation. But they do not "hold" their own sons, who use their fathers' white collar position primarily as a point of departure for advancement into business or professional work.

The skilled and semi-skilled manual occupations seem to be at what might be termed the fulcrum of the occupational hierarchy. The flow of movement into them corresponds to the average for the occupational structure as a whole, suggesting that the rewards are about equal to the barriers to mobility into these manual positions. (It should be understood that what are termed here as barriers to mobility may be self-imposed; e.g., the businessman or professional's son who would not consider working in a factory.) Skilled and semiskilled work are also relatively indifferent to the social origins of the men who enter them. Contrary to expectations, skilled work is the most unstable of all occupations, as defined by the rate of occupational inheritance. Reference to Tables 1 and 2 will show that almost fifty percent of the population analyzed here, both in 1910 and in 1940, had entered skilled or semi-skilled work; it cannot be assumed, therefore, that mobility into them was "sluggish," in absolute terms; rather, such movement was only at moderate frequency and was evenly distributed among men coming from all social origins.

Although the requirements for entering unskilled manual work are minimal, the rewards which such occupations offer are lower still, or even negative. Consequently, mobility into them is low. Furthermore, the men who do enter such work are less evenly distributed, with respect to their social origins, than is so for the men who enter skilled, semi-skilled, or clerical work. In this sense, unskilled work resembles the occupations at the top of the social hierarchy.

The return to the leading question in this research, the mobility patterns just described for a number of occupations are quite consistent in the two time periods. The most important change, already mentioned, is the increase in mobility into professional work from 1910 to 1940. Perhaps also worthy of mention is the decrease of mobility into commercial and managerial positions, accompanied by a decrease in the dispersion from this rate. Movement into business positions took place at a lower rate, on the average, but the men who made such a move were more proportionately distributed in their social origins than they had been in 1910. On the whole, however, there data support the statement that no great change has taken place in recent times in the extent to which men may move from the occupational origins represented by their fathers' positions. The channels to social mobility afforded by the contemporary occupational structure are about as easily traversed now as they were at the beginning of the century.

OCCUPATIONAL MOBILITY IN RELATION TO AGE. One of the characteristics of the contemporary occupational structure is that occupational affiliation tends to be age-graded. This can be attributed to a number of factors. First, the requirements for entrance into some occupations are directly or indirectly associated with age. For example, the specialized education required by the professions, the accumulation of capital necessary for becoming a proprietor, and the experience required of managers, all tend to preclude the entrance of very young men into these occupations. On the other hand, unskilled clerical and laboring jobs, requiring physical strength and alertness, are more likely to be filled by younger than older men. Secondly, changes in the occupational structure bring about the development and expansion of new occupations, and the decrease, either in absolute or relative importance, of outmoded occupations. It is to be expected that workers for new occupations will be recruited mainly among younger men, while the men in declining occupations will be older.

Still a third aspect of mobility in relation to age is our concern with the changes that have occurred from the earlier to the later of the two time periods. It has already been shown that little variation in mobility occurred for the population as a whole. However, we can raise the further question as to whether mobility may not have been deferred until a later age as a result of the depression of the nineteen thirties; or whether some other type of change took place in the age-grading of mobility.

In principle, the same measuring technique described above has been used in analyzing the influence of age on mobility. However, one modification has been introduced. After separating the men in each time period into three age groups—those under twenty-four, those twenty-four to thirty, and those over thirty—the mobility of each group was measured against the distribution of all three groups combined. In this way, each age group is compared with a standard distribution, in order that the influence of age may operate.

In 1910, a man's chances of experiencing occupational mobility in-

TABLE VII—Average Mobility Rates, by Age, 1910 and 1940

	Average Mobility	
Age	1910	1940
Under 24	0.69	0.77
24-30	0.85	0.85
Over 30	1.01	0.83

creased constantly with age. The older he was, the more likely he was to be in an occupation different from that of his father. But in 1940, there was almost no variation at all in mobility according to the men's age. Younger men found mobility harder to achieve in 1910 than in 1940; for men over thirty, mobility was more probable in 1910 than in 1940. Recall, however, that these rates refer to mobility in both the favorable and unfavorable sense.

Although the details cannot be given here, the amount of mobility into each of the various occupations, by each of the age groups, is consistent with the general averages shown above. In 1910, it was more than three times as likely that men over thirty would enter professional or commercial work as would men under twenty-four. With two exceptions, older men achieved more mobility than younger men into all other occupations as well, although the probabilities are not as disparate. The two exceptions are clerical and unskilled work, which younger men were about one-and-one-half times more likely to enter than their older contemporaries. These exceptions are consistent with expectations, however, since these are precisely the occupations which require the least qualifications in either training or experience.

In 1940, business and professional work were still predominantly older men's occupations, and unskilled work still primarily young men's work. But in all other types of work, no consistent relation of age to mobility is revealed in the 1940 data. Some occupations show a maximum in the age group twenty-four to thirty, others a minimum in this age group, still others almost no variation at all with age. Before attempting any interpretation of these findings (and any such interpretation must necessarily be ex post facto), let us present even more differentiated information than that already given. The mobility rates just discussed include both upward and downward movement, and movement between occupations that are distantly and closely related; those given below indicate both the origins and the destinations of men of various ages who achieved occupational mobility in each of the time periods studied. As in the earlier section, the "head" work and "hand" work occupations have been grouped together to facilitate presentation.

For the men whose fathers were engaged in a business, professional, or clerical occupation, and who themselves moved into another occupation in the same bloc, mobility increased with age both in 1910 and in 1940. But the increase with age in this type of "near" move was more marked in the earlier years than in the later.

TABLE VIII—Average Inter-Occupational Mobility, by Age, 1910 and 1940

| | Occupational Destination | | | | | |
| | "Head" Work | | "Hand" Work | | Farming | |
Occupational Origin	1910	1940	1910	1940	1910	1940
"Head" Work:						
Under 24	1.09	1.16	0.59	0.72	0.23	0.22
24-30	1.50	1.50	0.77	0.55	0.11	0.10
Over 30	2.00	1.76	0.98	0.43	0.43	0.36
"Hand" Work:						
Under 24	0.57	0.45	0.86	0.95	0.13	0.27
24-30	0.84	0.84	0.84	0.95	0.09	0.41
Over 30	0.70	0.78	1.05	0.85	0.23	0.42
Farming						
Under 24	0.56	0.47	0.96	1.56	...	...
24-30	0.77	0.71	1.11	1.25	...	...
Over 30	0.98	0.72	1.20	1.16	...	...

About the same may be said for mobility from an origin in one manual or service occupation to a destination in another such type of work. In 1910, older men were more likely to make this move than younger; in 1940, there was almost no difference from one age group to another, and the slight variation was in favor of the younger men. In general, then, "near" mobility was less influenced by age in 1940 than it had been in 1910.

A much more significant difference between the two time periods is revealed in the rates of downward mobility—from a non-manual origin to a manual or service occupational destination. In 1910, these rates increased regularly with age; the older a man was, the more likely he was to move down in the occupational scale. In 1940, exactly the reverse is true. Downward mobility decreases regularly with age, and at no age is it as high as the maximum achieved by the men over thirty in 1910.

Upward mobility, or movement from a manual to a white collar or professional occupation, was quite similar in the two time periods. In both cases, it reached a maximum for the men in the age group twenty-four to thirty. And for sons of farmers, mobility into a non-manual job increased regularly with age both in 1910 and in 1940, although the maximum was higher in the earlier than in the later years.

In 1910, the likelihood of farmers' sons moving into a manual or service occupation increased regularly with age. But in 1940, the older a farmers' son was, the less likely he was to have moved into manual work. This latter trend is consistent with the findings already mentioned with respect to manual work: from all classes of origin, mobility into these occupations decreased with age in 1940.

Summary. What are the principal changes that have taken place, then, in the influence of age on social mobility? In the earlier of the two time periods studied in this research, mobility varied consistently and directly with age. The older a man was, the more likely he was to have moved from his occupational origin; this was so, almost without exception, irrespective of the direction or the distance moved. The chief exceptions involve the occupations at the bottom of the manual and the non-manual hierarchies: unskilled labor and clerical work. In these pursuits, mobility was at a maximum among the younger men and decreased regularly with age.

Thirty years later, the relation of age to mobility was more complex. For those men who moved into manual or service work, no matter what their occupational origins, (and hence, no matter whether they moved up or down) mobility decreased with age. This can perhaps be partly accounted for by the industrial expansion over the years in the city of Indianapolis, which provided a large number of semi-skilled factory jobs attractive primarily to younger men.

On the other hand, with only one slight exception, upward mobility and "near" mobility into white collar, commercial, or professional work increased regularly with age in the 1940 period. The variation with age for this type of mobility is not as great as it had been in the earlier period, but the direction of this variation is the same.

Thus, in 1940, the relation of age to mobility depended upon the occupation into which the men moved; in 1910, this relation had been consistent and positive no matter what the men's occupational destination. The result of this may be seen by comparing the relative position of young men and older men with respect to upward and downward mobility (movement from "hand" work to "head" work and vice versa). In 1910, young men were equally likely to move down as to move up, while men over thirty were *more* likely to move down than up. In 1940, young men were in the less favorable position—more liable to have moved down the occupational scale than up—but men over thirty achieved almost twice as much upward as downward mobility. In this sense, then, changes over time with respect to occupational mobility have worked to the detriment of the youngest members of the active population, and to the advantage of those already well into their careers.

SOCIAL CONSEQUENCES OF THE
INDUSTRIALIZATION OF SOUTHERN CITIES

Rudolf Heberle

The subject to be discussed in this paper is the effect of the growth of manufacturing industries upon cities and towns in the South or, more precisely, upon urban society. Although we have a wealth of good studies of urbanization and of industrialization in this region, very little actual research seems to have been done on our particular subject.

I. INDUSTRIALIZATION VERSUS URBANIZATION. Industrialization and urbanization should not be considered as identical processes, as we might be tempted to do because of the decisive influence which modern industry has had upon the development of cities in the last century and a half. But cities have been in existence before industrialization began, and not all cities are highly industrialized. This certainly holds for many cities in the South. Furthermore, much of the industrial development has been a consequence rather than a cause of city growth.

II. ORIGIN AND DEVELOPMENT OF SOUTHERN CITIES. 1. With few exceptions, southern cities did not originate as industrial communities. This is particularly true of the larger cities, with Birmingham as the most notable exception. The South being a rural region with a colonial type of agriculture, most of its older cities developed as ports, railway and commercial centers, or as local trading and marketing towns [1] and as temporary residences of wealthy planter families. The oldest industries in the South, those engaged in processing the products of the farm and the forest, were largely located in rural communities and small towns. The cities had to depend almost entirely on commerce and trade. Purely commercial cities, however, seldom attain very large size. Those old cities of the South whose commercial function faded away through changes in the transportation system were doomed to stagnation unless they offered also factors of attraction for manufacturing industries. Like some of the old cities of Europe that ceased

---

Reprinted from *Social Forces*, Vol. 27 (October 1948), pp. 29-37, by permission of the author and the publisher. (Copyright, 1948, by *Social Forces*.)

1. Walter J. Matherly, "The Emergence of the Metropolitan Community in the South," *Social Forces*, 14 (March, 1936), p. 323. "The cities of the Old South were exclusively commercial; they were centers of surrounding agricultural territories; they were largely the product of agrarianism. But with the rise of industrialism, new types of cities appeared. Since the turn of the century the industrial cities emerged. . . . The growth of trade has likewise contributed, more greatly than any other factor to the rise of metropolitan centers in the South. . . ." See also Francis Butler Simkins, *The South, Old and New* (New York: Knopf, 1947), pp. 68-69.

to grow when trade routes changed, many of the older cities in the South stagnated when the transatlantic and inland trade shifted to northern cities; and just as some of the old commercial towns of Europe experienced another spell of growth when, for some reason or other, manufacturing industries began to locate in them, thus New Orleans, Mobile, and other southern cities experienced an economic rejuvenation when manufacturing industries began to develop, while Savannah, Georgia (population, 1940–118,000), and Charleston, South Carolina (population 1940–99,000), illustrate the other type.[2]

Contrary to the most important European commercial cities which were also old centers of handicraft, producing many commodities for long distance trade, the older southern cities lacked such a broad basis of industrial production. Until late in the nineteenth century they were places of export and import trade, exporting mainly products of primary industries and importing the products of European handicraft and manufactures. Apparently, the wealth of planters and merchants did not support a broad layer of local artisans and craftsmen. This fact has been of great significance for the social changes that took place when industrialization began.

2. We shall now turn to our second question: The role of industrialization in the development of southern cities. By industrialization we mean the development and growth of "secondary" industries: the extraction of coal, oil, natural gas, and other minerals, the construction industry and, most important of all, the manufacturing and mechanical industries. The role of an industry in urbanization depends in the first line on the factors that determine its location. Some of these industries are *consumer-oriented*,[3] like bakeries, printing shops, gas, power plants, and to some extent the construction industry. Their location tends to correspond to the distribution of population; they are to be found in all larger communities and in fairly fixed ratios to the population of the community and its trade area. In the case of these industries it is hardly meaningful to speak of a contribution to urbanization or an "effect" upon urban society. They develop as urban society develops and they are part and parcel of it. A great deal of the earlier growth of secondary industries in the South has been in this class and a great deal of recent development also belongs to it.[4]

Other industries are either *raw-material oriented*, like steel mills and sugar refineries, or *labor oriented* like most of the southern textile industry. Among these two groups are the truly city-building industries, those that

<hr/>

2. See Simkins, *op. cit.*, p. 375.

3. The terminology with regard to location of industries is that of Alfred Weber's, on whose theory this section is based. See Alfred Weber, "Industrielle Standortslehre," in *Grundriss der Sozialökonomik,* VI (Tübingen, 1923).

4. It should be noted, however, that with the increasing dependence of the rural population upon urban industry and commercial services, the development of these consumer-oriented industries tends to be increasingly influenced by the demands of rural customers in the metropolitan region of the city. Bakeries, for instance, sell increasing proportions of their production in rural territory. But a large-scale bakery is not likely to be established except in a city of considerable size.

draw people into cities and whose growth tends to speed up the growth of an urban population. Consequently, our analysis should be primarily concerned with them.

Now it so happens that in the South a large proportion of the important secondary industries are raw-material oriented. This is not merely due to the presence of resources, but also a consequence of the well-known freight rate structure. Whether these industries will be located in cities or in rural areas, whether they tend to develop large industrially diverse urban communities or tend to create only small or medium-sized industrially specialized towns, depends on the nature of their main raw materials and the location of resources, together with the industry's dependence upon cheap transportation facilities and other factors.[5]

One of the oldest industries in the South and one of the most important industries in regard to employment is the lumber industry. It is definitely raw-material oriented. The rapid exhaustion of timber resources made it a temporary industry in many localities. The sawmills were rarely located in large cities, but rather spread and scattered over the country side. Consequently, this industry created a large number of small mono-industrial communities, but contributed little directly to the growth of larger cities. However, in many cases it laid the foundation for a larger community, as some of the sawmill towns developed beyond the mono-industrial stage and became cities of more diversified industrial structure. In some cases this was due to the establishment of additional wood-using industries. The furniture industry, the production of paper and cardboard containers, and the rayon industry belong in this group. The wood-using industries are, as a rule, more concentrated locally than the lumber industry. Consequently, the workers in these industries tend to be living in cities, while the sawmill workers tend to be living largely in rural areas and small towns. A striking example of city development due to the sequence of sawmills and paper mills is the town of Bogalousa in Louisiana, an urban community of very recent origin. Another example is Monroe in north Louisiana.

5. Harriet L. Herring, *Southern Industry and Regional Development* (Chapel Hill: University of North Carolina Press, 1940), p. 72 shows the share of the South in 55 industries in 1937. Among the twenty industry groups of whose total wage earners the Southeast had 25 percent or more, only about ten may be considered as definitely city-building industries. Of the entire list the same proportion is probably in this class. See also Rupert B. Vance, *All These People* (Chapel Hill: University of North Carolina Press, 1945), p. 276.

In Louisiana we found that of all workers in manufacturing industries in 1940, 57.6 percent were living in urban communities, 33.7 percent were rural-nonfarm, and 8.7 percent rural farm. In the lumber industry, however, only 29 percent of the workers were living in urban communities, whereas in the paper industry 51.5 percent were classified as urban residents. In the crude petroleum and gas production, only 41.0 percent were living in urban communities, 49.6 were classified as rural-nonfarm residents, and 9.4 percent lived on rural farms, while in the group petroleum products and chemical industries, 51.0 percent were urban, 42.8 percent rural nonfarm, and 6.2 percent rural farm. Although these data need considerable refinement, they do give an idea of the differences in urbanizing effect between various industry groups. See Rudolf Heberle, *The Labor Force in Louisiana* (Baton Rouge: L.S.U. Press, 1948).

In other cases the continued growth of lumber towns was due to the agglomeration of new industries oriented towards different raw materials at the locations of the lumber industry. This happened in several cities of the deep South and coastal Southwest with the coming of the petroleum industry. Refineries and chemical plants using the products and by-products of oil refineries—as well as natural gas—were in several cases established in old lumber industry towns.

Reasons for this "agglomeration" of two entirely different industries were probably the dependence of both upon water transportation,[6] the location of their respective raw materials in the same general areas, and the advantage, for the more recent industries, of finding already a local nucleus of industrial labor. Baton Rouge or even better Lake Charles and the area of Beaumont-Port Arthur in the southeastern corner of Texas are good examples of this sequence.

However, the job-creating capacity of the petroleum and basic chemical industries is low[7] and the direct effect of these industries upon urban growth is not very strong. On the other hand, these are high wage industries which exert a considerable stimulus upon the development of trade and services, and they also attract a variety of auxiliary industries. Among the raw-material oriented branches of the food industry, which are very important with regard to employment in the deep South, none can be considered as city-building industries if taken by themselves. The canning and drying of seafood and of fruits and vegetables are typically rural industries, scattered over many small towns and villages. Cane sugar refineries, too, tend to be located in rural communities.

The greatest city-building industry, the iron and steel industry, is so far almost entirely concentrated in the Birmingham metropolitan area. Here, of course, was an ideal location for this industry because iron, coal, and limestone—the three basic materials in steel production—occur in this same locality. Birmingham, which incidentally was founded in the same year of 1871, when the German steel magnate, Friedrich Krupp, had already reaped great profits from his armament factory in Essen, is an outstanding example of the urbanizing force of the iron and steel industry. It is probably the most outstanding example in the South of purely industrial origin of a *large* city. However, Birmingham has for a long time been lagging behind the chief northern centers of iron and steel production as far as diversification is concerned. This has been explained by the relatively restricted size of the

6. Oil refineries are not necessarily located near the origin of petroleum, which can be transported economically over long distances by pipeline or water transportation. The Baton Rouge refinery receives petroleum in both ways, from oil fields in the region and from Venezuela. Coastal lumber mills also receive part of their raw material (valuable tropical timber) from overseas. The shipment of bulky products like saw timber and gasoline by waterway is of course also advantageous.

7. See Herring, *op. cit.* Some recent expansions at the Esso Standard Oil Co. refinery at Baton Rouge indicate a range of investment per job created from about 10,000 to about 90,000 dollars per job (*State Times,* Baton Rouge, April 13, 1948, p. 1).

southern market for steel products.[8]

Another and most striking example of industrial origin of a city is Oak Ridge, Tennessee, child of World War II and product of the most recent industry in the region. While its population in 1946 was estimated at 48,000, it may grow into a considerably larger center, provided that other industries will locate at the same place.

If we turn now to the *labor-oriented* industries in the South, we have to consider in the first line the South's most notorious problem child: the cotton textile industry. One of the main city builders in nineteenth century Europe and in New England, this industry had its main period of growth in the South at a time when electrification in connection with a relatively ample labor supply in rural areas made concentration in large cities unnecessary and decentralization in small urban communities possible. Thus, the growth of the textile industry in the Piedmont, while certainly contributing to urbanization, did not result in the development of an American Manchester or Chemnitz. With few exceptions, the southern textile communities are small.[9] However, in some cases textile mills have been located in cities where an already established but more or less exclusively men-employing industry left a sufficient supply of female labor unutilized. The agglomeration of the hosiery industry at a furniture manufacturing center like High Point, North Carolina, illustrates this case. The fuller utilization of the labor force will, of course, result in larger aggregate payrolls and thereby stimulate the growth of trade and services.

The concentration of the cigarette and tobacco industry in two larger North Carolina urban areas, Winston-Salem and Durham, is most likely the result of a combination of labor- and raw-material orientation, and without the additional factor of an extraordinary concentration of capital, this industry as such would scarcely have created any important urban centers.[10]

So much for the urbanizing effect of southern industries. A more refined and comprehensive analysis would have to take into consideration the importance of secondary factors of location, such as water transportation, water supply, and the availability of electric power and natural gas.

The indirect effects of industrialization upon city development were

8. Andreas Predoehl, "Die oertliche Verteilung der amerikanischen Eisen-und Stahl-industrie," *Weltwirtschaftliches Archiv,* 27 (Jena, 1928), pp. 240, 246, 270, 276, 289. Also: Temporary National Economic Committee, Investigation of Concentration of Economic Power. Monograph No. 42. *The Basing Point Problem* (Washington, D.C., 1941), pp. 17, 18 and *passim.*

9. According to R. B. Vance, *op. cit.,* p. 307, Table 84 (Percent of Manufacturing Establishments by Size of City and Type of Manufacture, North Carolina Catawba Valley, 1938), the furniture and chemical industries were more concentrated in larger cities than the textile industry. Among the latter, plants making wearing apparel, silk, rayon, and dyeing and finishing plants were more concentrated in cities of 10,000 or over than plants making cotton yarns and cotton fabrics. Only 35 percent of all establishments in the area were in cities of 25,000 and over (65.1 percent in cities 10,000 or over).

10. Simkins, *op. cit.,* p. 377 "Concentration of the [tobacco] industry into fewer cities in larger factories . . . [was] part of the Duke strategy."

demonstrated in a highly dramatic fashion during the Second World War when increases in manufacturing employment in cities like New Orleans were accompanied by very strong increases in employment in trade, transportation, and services.[11]

Before we proceed to discuss the consequences of industrialization for urban society, let us briefly consider the pattern of geographic distribution of cities in the South as it results from the factors determining the location of raw-material-oriented and labor-oriented industries.[12]

We saw that the South has relatively few large cities which owe their existence to the agglomeration of raw material oriented industries, like the big manufacturing cities of the North. In the labor oriented industries, two contradictory tendencies can be observed in a society where labor is free to move: the workers tend to concentrate at the large labor markets, where employment opportunities are most numerous and diverse, while employers, unless the nature of their enterprise ties them also definitely to the large labor markets, tend to move away from the big cities in order to evade high land prices and high wage levels. This latter tendency has been strong in the South. One recalls the typical advertising of entrepreneurs who want to establish a plant in a small community with an ample supply of labor and without competing enterprises, in order to attain a virtual monopoly over the local labor market. This tendency has been favored on the workers' part by lack of knowledge of employment opportunities in distant large cities and probably in many cases by the desire to be able to fall back on farming in old age or depression,[13] all of which factors have contributed to hold labor in small cities and in the surrounding country. The result has been a wide dispersion of manufacturing industries in many but relatively small cities and a relative sparsity of large cities.

Distances between large cities are much greater than in the older manufacturing regions of the North, and there are in the South no very large clusters of smaller cities. While we find in some highly industrialized subregions, like the Piedmont, strings of cities lined up along the highways, there are no large compactly urbanized areas; even in the more densely industrialized parts of North Carolina, which have been studied by Howard W. Odum, Rupert B. Vance, Harriet L. Herring and their associates, there appears to be evolving a new constellation pattern of urban communities,

11. Rudolf Heberle, "Survey of the War-time Labor Force of Louisiana" (U.S. Employment Service, Louisiana, 1945), p. 22 f. and *passim*. In New Orleans these increases were concentrated in the central business district rather than in the "neighborhood" shopping centers; in other words, they occurred in establishments serving the war-industry workers (and soldiers).

12. The important work of the late August Lösch, *Die räumliche Ordnung der Wirtschaft* [2.ed. Jena 1944] came to my attention too late to find consideration in this article. If translated it should prove to be of great value in all studies dealing with the location of cities and industries.

13. Therel R. Black, Part-Time Farming among Industrial Workers in East Baton Rouge Parish (M.A. Thesis in Sociology, L.S.U., 1941) finds that this was one of the most frequent reasons given for acquisition of a farm by petroleum refinery workers.

consisting of small central cities with still smaller satellite communities and considerable dispersion of workers in the open country.[14] Similar patterns can be observed along the Gulf Coast from Pensacola to Galveston and Houston.

However, in order to see this pattern in its true significance, one ought to realize that the war-time industrial boom did not result in much further decentralization of industry in the region; on the contrary, most of the gains in population and increases in industrial employment were concentrated in already established centers of manufacturing.[15] Oak Ridge is an exception rather than a typical case.

These statements concerning the pattern of city location are, of course, more or less hypothetical. To analyse the economic factors which have contributed to the development of the present geographic distribution of cities in the South would be very interesting. One would probably find: (1) a system of major export- and import-trade cities, (2) a much more numerous system of smaller local trading centers, and (3) a system of industrial cities, partly new, partly evolved out of cities of type (1) or (2).

III. THE EFFECTS ON URBAN SOCIETY. 1. The most obvious, most easily observable effects of industrialization are changes in the social ecology or human geography of the cities. These changes have been far from uniform.

In the older cities of the South, where industrialization began in the age of the steam engine and the street car, the pattern of ecology and the process of its evolution has been quite similar to that of American cities in general. This led authors like E. W. Parks to the conclusion that *all* southern cities would become more like the northern and eastern cities.[16] But in the majority of cities, especially the smaller ones, where industrialization occurred mainly in the age of electrification and the automobile, the ecological pattern seems to deviate from the older one. The more recent the industry, the greater seems to be the deviation.

In many cases the industrial plants were from the beginning located far outside the city, where unobstructed sites were available at low cost. If there had not yet been developed any large working class areas, the workers tended to live near the plants, even where the employer did not, as in the case of textile mill villages, provide dwellings for the employees. This tendency towards peripheral location of factories and plants is particularly pro-

---

14. Rupert B. Vance, *op. cit.*, chaps. 19 and 20, especially pp. 306, 317.

15. Rudolf Heberle, "The Impact of the War on Population Redistribution in the South," *Papers of the Institute of Research and Training in the Social Sciences*, Vanderbilt University, Number Seven (Nashville, Tennessee, Vanderbilt University Press, 1945), pp. 24 to 30.

16. The statement by E. W. Parks that "Every possible forecast implies that the continued growth of the city, with the concomitant advance of industrialism, will tend to standardize our cities and make them completely like all other American cities," appears exaggerated in the light of more recent developments. See: E. W. Parks, "Towns and Cities," in W. T. Couch (ed.), *Culture in the South* (Chapel Hill: University of North Carolina Press, 1933), p. 518. I owe this quotation to Ira de A. Reid's stimulating paper "Methodological Notes for Studying the Southern City," *Social Forces*, 19 (December, 1940), pp. 228-35.

nounced in the case of the more recent basic industries, which, like the petroleum refineries and chemical plants, require ample space and cannot be located in densely populated areas, for reasons of health and security. The location of the major industrial plants at Baton Rouge and the development of adjoining suburban areas inhabited by the employees is an outstanding example. The same pattern exists in an even more extreme form in Lake Charles, Louisiana, where the plants which were established during the second world war are located far out in the country, and where entirely separate workers' communities have sprung up at considerable distance from the old town. A more or less typical "ribbon" development along the main highways leading out of town is a characteristic element in this pattern.

This scattered growth may agree with the prevailing inclinations or preferences and particularly with the likings of workers of rural origin; it may make their accommodation to urban life easier; and it has definite military advantages as it reduces the vulnerability of a city from air attacks. But it certainly increases the overhead cost of road maintenance, sewerage, and utilities if it results in a population density below the minimum at which, according to the experience of city planners, those services cannot be provided at reasonable rates.[17]

The general extent of suburban expansion can be inferred from the high rate of population increase in the outlying parts of metropolitan districts [18] and also from the high rates of increase of "rural nonfarm" population in counties containing large urban centers, an increase which is largely concentrated in suburban areas.

Another significant development can be observed with regard to the location of wealthy people's homes. It seems to be characteristic for the older, smaller, cities in the South that the homes of the socially prominent families were to be found just outside the central—and only—business district. A few streets with not too pretentious homes under magnificent old trees in luxuriant gardens usually made up the areas of highest social status. As the city grew and as wealth increased, the "old" families tended to move towards the periphery—following the general fashion of our age. The more industrialized the area, the better are most likely the roads and the greater the inducement to move into the cooler countryside. The old homes are then converted into rooming houses and "tourist homes." This in itself is nothing peculiar to the South. However, it so happens that in the kind of

---

17. Bartholomew and Associates, "The 25-Year City-Parish Plan for Metropolitan Baton Rouge, Louisiana, Preliminary Reports," chap. 3, Population (1945), p. 13 f. See also Th. R. Ford, Maplewood: A Planned Community in the Industrial South (M.A. Thesis in Sociology, L.S.U., 1948).

18. During the period 1930 to 1940 the population growth in southern metropolitan districts conformed to the national pattern: higher rates of growth in outside areas than in the central city. The rates were very high in some cases. There seems to exist a fair correlation between rates of population increase of the total metropolitan district and rates of growth in outside areas. See: U.S. Bureau of the Census, Release P-3, No. 26.

city under consideration, the poorer people usually lived at the edge of the town. This was particularly the case with Negroes. It happens, therefore, quite frequently that white people infiltrate into suburban areas occupied by Negroes, buying their property or cancelling their leases. This process, which has been observed by Woofter and others, has been studied in Baton Rouge by my former colleague, Edgar A. Schuler; here the same process of displacement of Negroes by whites has also occurred in the more desirable parts of the old town.[19] As a result, the Negroes now tend to congregate in poorly drained and otherwise disadvantageous areas.[20] The close ecological symbiosis of whites and Negroes which seems to have been characteristic at least of the older cities in the coastal plantation zone,[21] gives way to spatial segregation. Neighborly contacts become rare, and estrangement between the two races tends to increase. At the same time, industrialization is likely to reduce the frequency of interracial contacts through domestic and other personal service (because larger proportions of Negroes find other employment, and because the proportion of whites not wealthy enough to keep servants increases), while on the other hand, contacts in the industrial plants tend to be more formalized and restricted. The same tendency is, of course, observable in the relations between various social strata of the white population: greater isolation and exclusivity of "upper class" residential areas on the one hand, and the growth of exclusively working class areas on the other hand tend to widen the social distance between the top and the bottom of the social pyramid. At the same time, the concentration of large masses of factory workers, their living together in relatively crowded and less desirable urban areas is likely to contribute to the strengthening of their class consciousness.

2. Thus, the effects of industrialization in the South upon the social stratification of urban society are in principle the same as everywhere. The main differences in the South are due to the late beginning of industrialization and to the presence of the Negroes. In the old cities, the former social pyramid tends to be broadened at the base and perhaps to become more pointed at the top. The old "independent middle class" consisting of cotton merchants, bankers, small manufacturers and other small businessmen as well as lawyers and other professional people is gradually being superseded by a smaller but economically more powerful group composed of larger

19. See: Reid, *op. cit.*, quoting Woofter. Schuler's study is not published. See also: Bartholomew and Associates, *op. cit.*, chap. 3, *passim*. The same phenomenon has been observed in Jackson, Mississippi, by Dorothy Melvin (unpublished paper in urban sociology).

20. A similar change in racial ecology was observed in New Orleans by Harlan W. Gilmore, "The Old New Orleans and the New" *American Sociological Review*, 9 (Aug. 1944), pp. 385-394. Here the Negroes, formerly in close symbiosis with the whites, moved into the low-lying areas as these were drained and public transit system developed. Industrialization invariably leads to the growth of racially segregated suburban working-class areas.

21. Concerning differences in Negro concentration in southern cities, see: Reid, *op. cit.*, p. 232.

manufacturers and of the executives of big corporations. It is essentially the same process which has been described by Lynd in *Middletown in Transition* and by C. Wright Mills in *Small Business and Civic Welfare*.[22] Whether these changes in the local élite are always detrimental to the civic spirit in the community, as Mills thinks, remains to be seen. From personal observation it would seem to me that the executives and higher professional personnel of big corporations are sometimes more far-sighted and progressive in civic affairs, such as public health work or city planning, than the old local ruling class. It is undeniable, however, that the latter tends to lose in power and prestige.

At the same time, there occur changes in the stratification of the middle and lower classes of white people. On the one hand, industrialization opens a greater variety of job opportunities to these people, especially to the women, who formerly were very limited in their employment opportunities because the large traditional field of domestic service was closed to them in the South. Thus a broad layer of clerical, technical and supervisory personnel develops, mostly recruited from the "lower middle class" of white people.

On the other hand, there is now developing a permanent, more or less hereditary class of white factory workers. The older southern cities did not have a large class of white manual workers. The Negroes did most of the menial work, and the relatively few white craftsmen and artisans were not widely separated in status from the middle classes. Now, with the increase in white wage earners employed in capitalistic manufacturing enterprises, there develops a new class of city-born and industry-bred factory workers, whose socio-economic position tends to be passed on from one generation to the other. This process is even more evident in the textile mill towns. While the large proportion of the older workers in these communities is still farm born, the great majority of the younger generation are now natives of industrial communities.[23] Like the mill workers who are set apart ecologically and in status as a separate class, the masses of white factory workers in the cities are becoming more separated by widening social distances, emphasized by ecological segregation, as indicated before, from the middle and upper strata. The craftsman in the smaller cities came into frequent personal and business contacts with the socially more prominent people in the community; the factory worker of today tends to live in a separate world. This change has occurred in all American and European cities under the impact of industrialization. In the South, however, it is taking place at a late hour when the industrially more advanced sections of the country have already found new patterns and new institutions in employer-employee relationships. The diffusion of these new patterns into

22. *Small Business and Civic Welfare*, Report of the Smaller War Plants Corporation to the Special Committee to Study Problems of American Small Business, United States Senate (Washington, 1946).

23. R. B. Vance, *op. cit.*, pp. 285-287.

a region where until now the white upper strata have adhered to a paternalistic pattern of labor relations is bound to result in frictions and conflicts of a somewhat different sociological quality than those familiar to us from other regions where these changes began earlier and extended over a longer period of time. Here lies an important field for empirical research.

Further complications arise from the transformation of an increasing proportion of the Negro population from an agricultural and domestic labor group into an industrial working class. The modern industrial system requires a maximum of interchangeability of workers, particularly in the semi-skilled jobs. Any factors that impede the free movement of workers from job to job will interfere with the rational allocation of the labor force and therefore appear objectionable to the emtrepreneurs. Everywhere in the world industrialization has tended to break down barriers of nationality, caste and status in industrial employment. This at least has been the long run trend. In the short run it may be advantageous for the employer to exploit status differentials among the workers in order to strengthen his bargaining power and his authority. Contrary to the long run trend the recruitment of supervisory personnel from those classes of white people who have traditionally looked upon the Negro primarily as a potential competitor rather than as a servant or employee also operates. These are the people who now have most of the direct personal relations with the Negro industrial worker. They have none of the elements of an aristocratic code of social conduct which was the basis of the relations between master and slave, or landlord and tenant, where they were at their best. Consequently, the old paternalistic pattern cannot endure. What will follow in its place depends on a variety of factors which cannot be discussed in this paper.[24]

In many of the smaller industrial cities and towns of the South, employers have been able to establish and maintain an unusual degree of control over the entire social existence of "their" workers. The devices used—such as the unincorporated company town or mill village—and the conditions which made such policies possible are too well known to need further elaboration. But it is quite inconceivable and would be contrary to all experience in older industrialized sections of the country that such practices should continue in the long run. Some are, in fact, already disappearing. The main reason for our forecast is, of course, the increasing significance of the labor vote in southern urban areas. We indicated before how the growth of a city is usually accompanied by an increasing diversification of industries. This is bound to result in greater economic independence of workers from employers and to reduce the control of employers over the workers' vote.

---

24. While the caste or status system becomes more and more annoying to the employer, and while labor's objective interest lies in the abolition of discriminations, non-economic motivations may prevail and prevent the evolution of a new harmony in race relations.

In summary we may say that manufacturing in the South began chiefly in rural locations and in smaller urban communities; the older larger cities owe their growth primarily to commerce and transportation and only in the second line to manufacturing industries. Very few major cities of the South were from the beginning primarily manufacturing cities.

The relatively late beginning of industrialization has significant consequences for the ecological development of southern cities as well as for the changes in social stratification. The impact of technically most advanced recently developed branches of manufacturing upon ecology and the rather immediate transition from traditionalistic patterns of labor and race relations to more contractual forms represent some of the significant aspects of the social consequences of industrialization for urban society in the South.

SOCIAL MOBILITY AND URBANIZATION*

Seymour Martin Lipset

Discussion of the factors which have helped preserve the "open" character of the American class system has traditionally pointed to the role of the immigrant as the base of the class ladder upon which the native-born climbed. Until the end of mass immigration in the 1920's, millions of immigrants entered the economic structure in unskilled and semiskilled occupations. The children of the previous generation of immigrants were, presumably, able to secure the next highest level of jobs which opened up in an expanding economy. The end of mass immigration is, therefore, now cited as a major reason for predicting the emergence of rigid class stratification in the United States. In this paper, evidence will be presented which suggests that certain internal structural trends—specifically those associated with increased urbanization and internal migration—operate to continue to make possible a pattern of social mobility similar to that posited as resulting from high rates of immigration.

Heavy internal migration is a continuing aspect of American society, occurring in depression, in wartime, and in prosperity. What is the effect of the movement of tens of millions of Americans on their socio-economic position, on that of their children, and on the structure of communities? Such questions would best be answered by a systematic research project designed to analyze the relationship between migration and social mobility. As a preliminary contribution to such research, the data collected in the Oakland mobility study have been subjected to a secondary analysis to learn what hypotheses are suggested by examining the relationship between geographical and occupational social mobility.[1]

Reprinted from *Rural Sociology*, Vol. 20 (September-December, 1955), pp. 220-228, by permission of the author and *Rural Sociology*. (Copyright, 1955, by the *Rural Sociology Society*).

* This article is one of a series based on the Oakland labor-mobility survey, conducted by the Institute of Industrial Relations, University of California, Berkeley, during 1949-50. In this survey, 935 principal wage earners were interviewed, chosen as a random sample from Oakland, California households after eliminating the highest and lowest socio-economic areas in the city. A standardized questionnaire was used, covering the subject's family background, education, area shifts, job history since leaving school, and other factors considered to be important in an analysis of labor mobility in this community.

1. Since the Oakland mobility study was not designed for the purpose, this paper, like all secondary analyses, cannot pretend to offer a rounded presentation. Nevertheless, it may serve as another example of the way in which sociologists may profitably re-analyze some of the vast amounts of empirical data collected in the past two decades.

EXTENT OF MOBILITY, The geographically mobile character of the members of the sample can be seen from the following data. Only 24 per cent were born in the San Francisco Bay Area, with an additional 8 per cent born in other parts of California. A large majority of the respondents, 61 per cent, began their working careers outside the San Francisco Bay Area. Once having reached adulthood, as defined by entrance into the labor market, the sample's members continue to reveal a pattern of migration. More than three-quarters of them have worked in two or more communities; as many as a third have held jobs in five or more areas.

In an attempt to analyze the effect of migration on current position in the occupational structure, the respondents were classified according to the size of the community in which they spent their teens (community of orientation).[2] While there is a certain amount of unreliability in such information, the data revealed significant differences between the size of the community in which the respondent spent his most important pre-employment years and his later job career. For example, a comparison of the total work careers of men coming from communities of different sizes indicates that the smaller the community of orientation of present (1949) Oakland residents, the more likely they are to have spent a considerable proportion of their work careers in manual occupations. (See Table 1.)

EFFECT OF ORIGINAL COMMUNITY BACKGROUND. The data clearly point to the role which original community background plays for residents of large cities. Those coming from a rural background are most likely to have been manual workers for most of their careers. Those from towns and small cities reveal a similar job history. The typical member of the sample coming from a village under 2,500 in population spent an average of 41 per cent of his work career in nonmanual occupations, as compared with 53 per cent for one who spent his teens in a metropolitan center.[3] The data indicate two principal "breaking points" in the influence of community of orientation on job careers: (1) There is a sharp break between those from farms and all others; and (2) among those from villages, towns, and cities, the largest differences are between communities under and over 250,000 in population.

While Table 1 treats the entire work history of the respondents, regardless of where the jobs were located, Table 2 presents the relationship

---

2. The community of orientation was obtained by asking the respondents: "Where did you live most of the time between the ages of 13 and 19? Did you live inside the city limits? Did you live on a farm?" Each community was then classified according to the population size reported by the census.

3. The analysis revealed that size of community of orientation, rather than migration background *per se*, was most crucial in affecting subsequent career patterns. That is, there is little difference between natives of metropolitan San Francisco and natives of other large urban centers. If anything, migrants from other metropolitan areas were even more successful than native Bay Area residents. The difference, however, seems in large part related to the fact that the natives in the sample were somewhat younger than the migrants, and consequently were not as close to the peak of their careers as migrants.

Table 1—Relation of Community of Orientation to Average Proportion of Career Spent in Each Type of Job*

			TYPE OF COMMUNITY OF ORIENTATION			
	RURAL			URBAN, BY POPULATION SIZE		
	Farm (N = 131)	Nonfarm (N = 87)	2,500- 24,999 (N = 71)	25,000- 249,999 (N = 75)	250,000 749,999 (N = 42)	750,000 and over (N = 250)
			Average Per Cent of Career			
Nonmanual	27	41	45	46	52	53
Manual	57	52	52	49	44	43
Farm	11	2	1	2	1	1

* Includes only respondents aged 31 and over. The average proportion of career spent in a specified type of job applies to the group of respondents in the size-of-community category. Each respondent's career was individually analyzed, and the proportion of career time spent in each type of job was calculated. These individual percentages were averaged to obtain the group averages presented in the above table. Because of the biases involved in averaging unweighted percentages, the proportions cannot be summed nor do the implicit sums account for the total career.

between community of orientation and present job. If we examine this table. a clear pattern emerges—the larger the community of orientation, the higher the status of the job held in San Francisco. Sixty-seven per cent of the business executives and upper white-collar workers grew up in large cities (250,000 or over in population) as compared with 60 per cent of the lower white-collar workers, 51 per cent of the sales personnel, 44 per cent of the skilled, 40 per cent of the semiskilled, and 21 per cent of the unskilled. These data suggest that migration from rural areas and smaller communities to metropolitan centers is playing the same role in ordering people in the occupational structure that immigration once played.

The deviations from the above trend lie mainly in two groups, the self-employed and the professionals. Other data in this study suggest that the deviation of the self-employed is related to the unique position that

Table 2—Relationship Between Community of Orientation and Present Job

		TYPE OF COMMUNITY OF ORIENTATION			
		Farm	Rural- nonfarm, and Urban, Under 250,000	Urban, Over 250,000	All Types
		Percentage Distribution of Respondents			
All types	(N = 898)	19	33	48	100
Nonmanual	(N = 510)	14	31	55	100
Professional	(N = 68)	12	48	40	100
Self-employed	(N = 114)	21	30	49	100
Upper white-collar*	(N = 105)	8	25	67	100
Lower white-collar	(N = 159)	12	28	60	100
Sales	(N = 64)	16	33	51	100
Manual	(N = 388)	25	36	39	100
Skilled	(N = 195)	24	32	44	100
Semiskilled	(N = 136)	23	37	40	100
Unskilled	(N = 57)	35	44	21	100

* Includes business executives and other high-status white-collar jobs.

self-employment plays in our society.[4] The self-employed have the most heterogeneous occupational career of any group in the sample. Many of them have had unskilled and semiskilled jobs previous to entering business for themselves. Of all the nonmanual occupations, this group contains the largest number of former manual and farm workers. The data also indicate that self-employment is the principal means of upward mobility for manual workers and the less educated, while the better-educated nonmanual workers tend to move up the occupational ladder within the

Table 3—Relationship Between Occupations of Fathers and Sons, by Type of Community Orientation

	FATHER'S OCCUPATION*				
Son's Present Job	Professional, Self-employed, and Business Executives	White-collar and Sales	Manual— Skilled	Manual— Semiskilled and Unskilled	Farm
	Percentage Distribution of Respondents				
COMMUNITY OF ORIENTATION—FARM, RURAL-NONFARM, AND URBAN UNDER 250,000					
Manual	31	37	65	54	61
Nonmanual	69	63	35	46	39
All	100	100	100	100	100
	(N = 115)	(N = 30)	(N = 97)	(N = 55)	(N = 147)
COMMUNITY OF ORIENTATION—URBAN, 250,000 AND OVER					
Manual	28	21	43	50	52
Nonmanual	72	79	57	50	48
All	100	100	100	100	100
	(N = 106)	(N = 52)	(N = 106)	(N = 70)	(N = 33)

* These categories differ from those for present job (Table 2). The data on father's occupation did not permit distinguishing between upper and lower white-collar jobs but did make it possible to separate business executives, who have been grouped here with professionals and the self-employed.

bureaucracy of large-scale organizations. Owning a business, therefore, is the pattern of upward mobility of the lower-class migrants. If they do not enter self-employment, they tend to remain in lower-status manual jobs.

The professionals, on the other hand, present a different problem. Most professionals have spent their entire working career in this category. It is probable that many natives of small communities who become professionals leave their home town to go to the larger cities, where greater opportunity exists in their field. Thus, we find that size of community of orientation is related to occupational position within the ranks of industry and large-scale organization. The smaller the community of school-age training, the more obstacles the individual is likely to encounter in his attempt to be upward-mobile within bureaucratic structures.

The hypothesis *that the larger the community of orientation of individuals living in metropolitan areas, the more successfully mobile they will be* may be tested directly by examining the difference between the occupations of the respondents and those of their fathers as an indicator of generational mobility, and the variations between the first jobs of the

---

4. See Seymour M. Lipset and Reinhard Bendix, "Social Mobility and Occupational Career Patterns, II, Social Mobility," *American Journal of Sociology* (Mar., 1952), pp. 497-499.

sample members and their present positions as a measure of intragenerational mobility, holding size of community of orientation constant in both cases. Tables 3 and 4 present the results of this analysis.

Table 4—Relationship Between First Job and Present Job, by Type of Community of Orientation*

	FIRST JOB		
Present Job	Nonmanual	Manual	Farm
	Percentage Distribution of Respondents		
COMMUNITY OF ORIENTATION—FARM			
Nonmanual	60	29	40
Manual	40	71	60
All	100	100	100
	(N = 20)	(N = 62)	(N = 48)
COMMUNITY OF ORIENTATION—RURAL-NONFARM, AND URBAN UNDER 250,000			
Nonmanual	73	31	44
Manual	27	69	56
All	100	100	100
	(N = 94)	(N = 120)	(N = 9)
COMMUNITY OF ORIENTATION—URBAN, 250,000 AND OVER			
Nonmanual	88	42	..
Manual	12	58	..
All	100	100	..
	(N = 129)	(N = 158)	

* Includes only respondents aged 31 and over, in order to eliminate those men who have not been in the labor force for a considerable length of time.

It is clear from the above tables that the larger the community in which one is brought up, the greater the likelihood that a man will be successfully upward-mobile, or conversely, the lower the possibility that he will fall in occupational status.[5] There are many factors which underlie these relationships; some are discussed below. One important element, however, is the fact that educational opportunities are greater in larger cities and the potential rewards for educational attainment are more visible to those who live in larger cities while attending school. Natives of large cities are generally better educated than those living in smaller communities, and the data indicate that the same differentials in educational backgrounds exist among residents of Oakland, when they are compared according to community of orientation (Table 5).

While the lower educational attainments of those residents of Oakland who grew up in smaller communities explain in large part why native metropolitan urbanites are more likely to attain nonmanual positions, it is interesting to note that, even when amount of education is held constant, more of the metropolitan residents hold nonmanual positions (Table 6). Similar findings have been reported in European studies of social mo-

---

5. While the differences in some of the internal comparisons are slight and the number of cases in some of the cells is small, the fact that in each of the ten possible comparisons the difference is in the direction indicated by the hypothesis suggests that the results have some validity.

Table 5—Relationship between Community of
Orientation and Education

TYPE OF COMMUNITY OF ORIENTATION

Years of schooling completed	Farm (N = 167)	Rural-nonfarm, and urban under 250,000 (N = 305)	Urban, 250,000 and over (N = 434)
	Per cent	Per cent	Per cent
0-11	65	53	42
12	23	22	35
13+	12	25	23

bility. A recent Swedish study indicates clearly that the manual working class of Stockholm is primarily recruited from smaller urban communities and rural areas, while the majority of the sons of manual workers who grow up in the metropolis move up to the middle class.[6] An early German study of the relationship between migration and social mobility also reported comparable results.[7]

INTERPRETATION. The cycle in which immigrants or migrants into large cities take over the lower-status positions while native urbanites move up in the occupation structure has been one of the more important processes underlying social mobility ever since cities began to expand rapidly. It is this cycle which gives to cities their character of great mobility and ever present change. Of those persons born and raised in cities, some are socially mobile and some, of course, are not. But they all tend to stay in the city (although they frequently move from one urban center to another). On the other hand, rural and small-town dwellers, if they move out of their parental status, are most likely to do so in a large city—while their more stable neighbors remain in their place of origin.[8] Thus, more

Table 6—Relationship Between Community of Orientation and
Occupation, with Education Held Constant

TYPE OF COMMUNITY OF ORIENTATION

	Rural-Farm			Rural-Nonfarm and Urban under 250,000			Urban, 250,000 and over		
	Years of Schooling Completed			Years of Schooling Completed			Years of Schooling Completed		
	0-11	12	13+	0-11	12	13+	0-11	12	13+
	(N = 157)	(N = 55)	(N = 34)	(N = 108)	(N = 51)	(N = 57)	(N = 185)	(N = 151)	(N = 97)
	Percentage distribution of respondents								
Nonmanual	36	49	79	36	63	79	50	72	82
Manual	64	51	21	64	37	21	50	28	18
All	100	100	100	100	100	100	100	100	100

6. See Gunnar Boalt, "Social Mobility in Stockholm" in *Transactions of the Second World Congress of Sociology*, Vol. II (London: International Sociological Association, 1954).

7. See Otto Ammon, *Die Gessellschaftsordnung und ihre natürlichen Grundlagen* (Jena: Verlag von Gustav Fischer, 1895), p. 145.

8. It may, indeed, be suggested that the more ambitious small-town and city lower-class youth leave their home community for "greener pastures" in large cities. This hypothesis was in part validated by Scudder and Anderson, who compared the patterns of social mobility of "migrant" sons and those who remained at home with those of their

mobility takes place in the city than in the country or in small communities. But this conclusion still leaves unexplained the factors which facilitate the social mobility of native urbanites. While little research has been done which bears directly on this problem, it is possible to suggest a number of processes which seem significant:

1. Greater social mobility in large urban centers as compared with smaller communities is inherent in the simple fact that metropolitan areas are characterized by a greater degree of specialization and a more complex division of labor than smaller communities. The economies that flow from specialization of function are able to take effect primarily in metropolitan centers. Consequently, increased size of community is related to the existence of a greater variety of positions. This means that there is a greater likelihood, on a chance or random basis alone, that people in large cities will move occupationally than will small-community dwellers.

2. Since the beginnings of the great urbanization and industrialization trends in the nineteenth century, cities have experienced considerable population and economic growth. They have far *more* than matched the expansion in total inhabitants and total economic activities of the countries in which they are found.[9] This pattern of urban growth necessarily means that there are more new (and higher level) positions to be filled in metropolitan centers than in smaller and demographically more stable communities.

3. In spite of their rate of rapid growth, large cities have a lower birth rate than smaller communities and rural areas. Except for a brief period after World War II, cities over 100,000 in size in the United States have not been reproducing their population. Thus, migration to metropolitan areas not only accounts for the expansion of urban population, but also fills in the gap created by low birth rates. And within urban society, the wealthier and higher-status socio-economic strata have the lowest reproduction rates. Consequently, variations in fertility rates help account for the maximization of social mobility in the city.[10]

The processes cited above clearly indicate why metropolitan areas have a higher rate of social mobility than smaller communities. They do not, however, suggest why men raised in large cities are more likely to be upward-mobile than migrants from smaller communities and rural areas. A few hypotheses may be suggested.

---

fathers in a small Kentucky community. They found that "sons who migrate out of small or moderate-size communities are more likely to rise above their parents' occupational status than sons who remain in the home town." [Richard Scudder and C. Arnold Anderson, "Migration and Vertical Occupational Mobility," *American Sociological Review*, XIX (1954), pp. 329-334.]

9. Between 1870 and 1950, the proportion of the population living in cities over 100,000 jumped from 11 to 30 per cent in the U.S., from 5 to 27 per cent in Germany, from 26 to 38 per cent in Great Britain, and from 9 to 17 per cent (1946) in France.

10. See Pitirim Sorokin, *Social Mobility* (New York: Harper & Bros., 1927), pp. 346-360; and E. Sibley, "Some Demographic Clues to Stratification," *American Sociological Review*, VII (1942), pp. 324 f.

As was indicated earlier, lower-class individuals growing up in a large city are more likely to secure high education than their brethren in smaller communities. Almost every major city in the Western world has one or more universities, and natives of such communities can attend college or university while living at home. In addition, the simple fact of living in a community which has a college or university within it should mean that a school youth will be more aware of the possibilities and advantages of attending an institution of higher learning than will one who grows up some distance from a college. Metropolitan youth also benefit from the fact that the teaching staffs in their high schools are usually better paid and trained than those in smaller communities, and consequently are more likely to give their students more incentive to attend college.

Related to the greater propensity of urban youth to obtain higher education is the fact that they are more likely to be acquainted with the occupational possibilities which exist in such communities than will those who are raised in the occupationally less-heterogeneous smaller community. In re-analyzing the occupational choices of school youth in a number of Geman and Austrian cities, Lazarsfeld reported that "local variations in occupational choice are parallel to differences in the economic structure."[11] Thus, the larger the proportion of jobs in a given occupation in a city, the greater the number of fourteen-year-old school youth who desired to go into that occupation. Lazarsfeld interpreted this finding as follows:

> . . . the nature of occupational choice is not determined primarily as an individual decision, but rather is a result of external influences. For the occupational impressions offered by daily life are proportional to the actual occupational distribution. The greater the number of metal workers, the more frequently will young people hear about it, and the greater will they be stimulated to choose it.[12]

Lower aspirational levels derived from their immediate class and community environment probably result in lower-class small-town or rural youth being less likely to try to obtain the education or skills which will permit them to be successfully upward-mobile. Thus, lower goals, plus the objectively greater difficulty in securing such training, result in lower-class youth not raised in a metropolitan center entering the labor market with greater handicaps than their big-city class-cousins. And in the labor market of the metropolitan centers, we find that working-class youth who are native urbanites are, in fact, more successful than migrants with similar class backgrounds.

The fact that urban origins are conducive to upward social mobility may help account for a phenomenon that has long puzzled students in this field: the success of the Jews in moving out of lower-class occupations. As compared with any other *visible* social group, the Jews are the

---

11. Paul F. Lazarsfeld, *Jugend und Beruf* (Jena: C. Fischer, 1931), p. 13.
12. *Loc. cit.*

urbanites *par excellence*. The mobility patterns of the Jews, therefore, may in some part be a consequence of the fact that they are urban dwellers. Other natives of metropolitan areas are also successful in moving up, but this is observed as individual rather than group mobility.

CONCLUSIONS. This article has focused primarily on the ways in which the relative size of the community of orientation affects the training, opportunity, perceptions of the occupational structure, and occupational aspirations of individuals, and thus increases or decreases men's chances for an advantaged position in the occupational structure. It should be recognized, however, that variation in the size of community of orientation is only a special case of the variables which structure the horizons and opportunities of individuals. The sociological and psychological mechanisms involved are little different from the restrictions set by socioeconomic origins, education, or ethnic background. When documenting the effect of each variable on a given behavior pattern, the sociologist is calling attention to the way in which an individual's potential behavior is limited or responsive to factors derivative from his location in the social structure. For example, Herbert H. Hyman pointed out that lower-status individuals are less likely to appreciate the value of higher education, or to recommend high-status jobs as occupation objectives to youth.[13] The members of the lower strata not only are disadvantaged in terms of economic resources, but, like the residents of small communities, they take their cues about opportunity or education from their immediately visible social environment.[14] Given the fact that most people in that environment do not have high-status jobs or good educations, many of them are not even aware that these goals are attainable. Thus, a self-perpetuating cycle exists for men in less-privileged environments. The fact remains, however, that many men do break this cycle; and it is the further task of research in this and other areas of behavior to locate the sources of such "deviant" behavior.

---

13. See Herbert H. Hyman, "The Value Systems of Different Classes," in Reinhard Bendix and Seymour Martin Lipset (eds.), *Class, Status and Power* (Glencoe, Ill.: The Free Press, 1953), pp. 426-442.

14. The question may be raised as to how these findings may be reconciled with those of Scudder and Anderson, who, as was previously noted, found that individuals who migrated from small communities were more mobile than those who remained. It is obvious that this study is not in conflict with that of Scudder and Anderson. The latter report more mobility by small-town out-migrants than natives, while the present study indicates greater mobility by large-city natives than by migrants from small towns. If these two studies are typical of patterns in the whole country, then they suggest the following relationship between social mobility and community of orientation: Those who grow up in small communities and remain in them are least mobile, those who leave these communities are more mobile than the stay-at-homes, while those who are socialized in metropolitan areas have the most opportunity for mobility. This pattern indicates why students of the status structure of small towns and cities report the existence of a relatively static structure. Unwittingly, they select for research the communities which are least representative of mobility trends in American society.

THE JOB CEILING

St. Clair Drake and Horace Cayton

NEGRO WORKERS ON DEPRESSION EVE. To understand the intense feeling within Black Metropolis about job discrimination, it is important to visualize the economic position of Negroes in Chicago on the eve of the Depression, at the end of a ten-year wave of "prosperity." It is obvious from a careful study of the figures that Negroes were doing a disproportionately large amount of the city's servant work, a disproportionately small amount of the "clean work," and a little above their "proportionate share" of the "manual labor." The term "proportionate share" as used throughout this chapter is simply a device for comparing the occupational status of Negroes and whites by assuming: (1) that Negroes and whites have the same conception of what constitutes a "good job"; (2) that Negroes, if permitted, would compete for these good jobs; (3) that there are no inherited mental differences between the races; (4) that if competition were absolutely unfettered by racial discrimination, Negroes, being approximately 8 per cent of the workers in 1930, would tend to approximate 8 per cent of *each* occupational group.[1]

Reprinted from *Black Metropolis*, Chapter 9, "The Job Ceiling," pp. 219-232, by permission of the publisher. (Copyright, 1945, by Harcourt, Brace and Company.)

1. This method of analysis is, of course, open to the criticism that it does not take into account the time factor—that the fifteen years beween 1915 and 1930 may not have constituted a sufficiently long period of time for such a distribution to take place. At the rate of speed with which industry was expanding during the Twenties, and with the amount of turnover in personnel which seems to have been involved in the crucial fields of skilled labor and white-collar employment, it seems reasonable to assume that the differentials between the actual proportions and the theoretical "proportionate share" would not have been so great if barriers had not been placed against the use of Negroes.

The concept of the "proportionate share" has more than theoretical interest, however. During the Depression several Federal agencies reserved a certain quota of jobs for Negroes based on their numbers in the population. Thus, on a job in area where Negro carpenters were 3 per cent of all carpenters in 1930, this percentage of Negroes was hired. In the autumn of 1944, the Communist Party raised the issue sharply within a number of unions as to whether seniority provisions should not be waived during postwar cut-backs in order to let Negro workers retain the same proportion of jobs in the plant which they had gained during the War period. This tendency to think in terms of "quotas" and "proportions" of Negro workers is admittedly an unsatisfactory approach to the problem of integrating Negroes into the economic life of the country, but some people feel that it is the only method of making sure that Negroes will secure broadened economic opportunity.

The *"Clean Work":* Professional, proprietary, managerial, and clerical work was almost a white monopoly on the eve of the Depression. Negro representation in Chicago's large white-collar class was very small. Those few Negroes who did "clean work" were almost entirely confined to the Black Ghetto and were dependent upon the wage-earning masses for a livelihood, or upon the ability of white people to pay for their services as entertainers. (See Table 1.)

TABLE I *—The Ten "Clean" Occupations in Which Negroes Were Most Heavily Represented: 1930

Negro Men			Negro Women		
Occupation	Number of Men	Share of Work (Per Cent)	Occupation	Number of Women	Share of Work (Per Cent)
Mail carriers	630	16	Restaurateurs	235	19
Clergymen	390	15	Physicians' attendants	55	12
Undertakers	120	12	Actresses	145	10
Musicians	525	10	Messenger girls	30	6
Actors	215	9	Musicians	205	7
Messengers and office boys	385	6	Religious workers	45	6
Taxicab owners	110	8	Social workers	50	5
Government officials	40	5	Designers	25	5
Physicians	265	5	Physicians	17	4
Dentists	130	5	Photographers	10	4
			Decorators	20	4

* The number of people in each occupational group in Tables 1 and 2 is given in round numbers, and is based on data from Tables 110, 111, 112 in Estelle Hill Scott, *Occupational Changes Among Negroes in Chicago* (mimeographed), Works Projects Administration, 1939.

Servant Work: Over twenty-five out of every hundred employed Negro men and fifty-six out of every hundred Negro women were doing some kind of servant work on the eve of the Depression. This was at least four times their "proportionate share," for Negroes did over a third of all the servant work performed by women, and a fourth of that done by men. *While only twelve out of every hundred white women were in service occupations, over half of the colored women did such work.* The Negro woman's share of the various types of service work is indicated in Table 2.

TABLE II—Service Occupations with Highest Proportion of Negro Women: 1930

Occupation	Number of Negro Women	Share of Work (Per Cent)
Laundry work done in homes	1,600	55.9
Elevator service	200	42.7
General domestic and personal service	20,000	42.5
Charwomen and cleaners	450	20.4
Janitors	180	9.6
Waitresses	1,100	9.5

Negro men had a virtual monopoly of some types of service jobs—jobs that depended upon an affluent white population, traveling, spending freely, and passing out tips (Table 3).

TABLE III—Servant Occupations with Highest Proportion of Negro Men: 1930

Occupation	Number of Negro Men	Share of Work (Per Cent)
Railroad porters	3,600	94.9
Other types of portering	2,100	82.5
Domestic and personal service	3,500	82.2
Waiting table on trains, in hotels, etc.	3,000	31.4
General service	5,000	26.6
Janitors	4,000	19.1
Elevator men	5,000	10.6

Manual Labor: Negroes were not overrepresented among the people who did the city's manual labor, but if we go behind the bare figure of nine per cent we find that they were doing a disproportionately large share of the poorly paid and less desirable work. They were concentrated in the unskilled labor categories which suffered heaviest from unemployment. Over half of all the Negro men who earned their living by manual labor were employed in the jobs listed in Table 4.

TABLE IV—Manual Labor Jobs with Highest Proportion of Negro Men: 1930

Occupation	Negro's Share of Work (Per Cent)	Number of Negroes	Desirable Aspects of Job	Undesirable Aspects of Job
Garage labor	58.5	1,860	Easy to get, not monotonous	Low pay, exposure, very dirty
Coal yard labor	40.5	1,525	Easy to get	Low pay, exposure, very dirty
Stockyard labor	34.2	1,640	Relatively good pay	Very heavy and dirty
Labor in stores	31.8	3,360	Relatively clean	Low pay
Packing and slaughter labor	28.7	1,960	....	Very dirty
Laundry operatives	26.3	1,470	Easy to get	Low pay, extreme heat and dampness
General labor	25.0	7,500	Easy to get	Low pay, insecurity, exposure
Steel mill labor	15.0	4,000	Relatively good pay	Heavy work, often very hot and hazardous
Railroad labor	14.0	1,815	Easy to get	Low pay, exposure
Building labor	13.3	2,850	Fairly well paid	Insecurity and intense competition of foreign-born
Road and street labor	13.0	567	Easy to get	Low pay and intense competition of foreign-born

Total number of Negro men employed   28,547

About 100,000 women were doing manual labor when the Depression began. Of these about 15,000 were colored women—twice their proportionate share. Some three out of four of the Negro women doing manual labor were employed in the occupations listed in Table 5. All of these were marginal occupations, and the dress industry in which Negro semi-skilled women were concentrated was one of the industries hardest hit by the Depression.

THE JOB CEILING. The Depression began fifteen years after the Great Migration and at the halfway mark between the two World Wars. Despite

TABLE V—Manual Labor Jobs with Highest Proportion of Negro Women: 1930

Occupation	Negro's Share of Work (Per Cent)	Number of Negroes
Laundry operatives	55.4	5,000
Railroad labor	44.3	140
Labor in steel	20.2	80
Clothing factory operatives	20.0	3,000
Slaughter and packing operatives	21.5	300
Labor in packing	17.0	130
Semi-skilled in boarding houses	16.2	1,000
General labor	11.5	360

Total number Negro women employed   10,010

fifteen years of urbanization during a period of industrial expansion, Negroes had not attained a proportionate share of the skilled and clerical jobs or of the professional and business occupations. They were clinging precariously to the margins of the economy. As former sharecroppers and underpaid southern city workers, they had "bettered their condition"; but they had not made the type of rapid progress which white European immigrants had made in an equal period between 1895 and 1910. This was due primarily to the fact that they had not been allowed to compete freely, *as individuals,* for any types of jobs to which they aspired and for which they

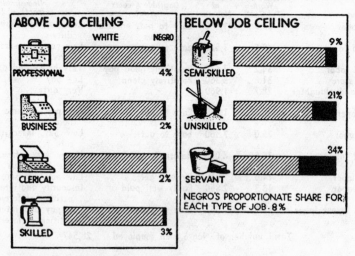

FIG. 1. Negro's share in selected work groups. (Prepared from tables in Scott, "Occupational Changes Among Negroes in Chicago: 1890–1930." Data for 1930.)

were qualified. The result of these limitations was the crystallization of a "JOB CEILING."

The nature of this ceiling in terms of the "proportionate share" is indicated in Figure 1. All other things being equal, Negroes might have been expected by 1930 to approximate eight per cent of each occupational category.

The Job Ceiling also has its reflection in the internal structure of the white and the colored communities. These differences are depicted in Figures 3 and 4. Out of these differences in occupational distribution arise many of the peculiarities of social life within Black Metropolis. Over half

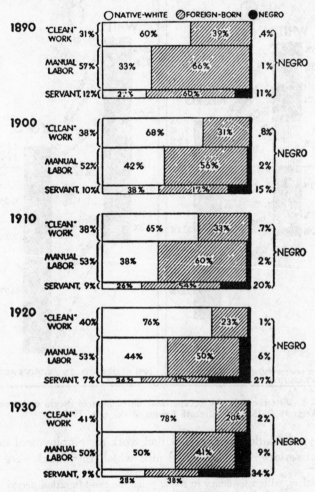

FIG. 2. Trends in job distribution: 1890–1930. (From tables in Scott, "Occupational Changes Among Negroes in Chicago: 1890–1930.")

of the white workers were doing skilled labor or "clean work." Over two-thirds of the Negroes were doing semi-skilled, unskilled, or servant work.

EVOLUTION OF THE JOB CEILING. Between the first World's Fair and the Great Migration, Negroes constituted only a minute proportion of the city's workers. (See Figure 2.) As late as 1910 only three out of every hundred workers in Chicago were colored and at no time during this period did these few thousand Negroes offer any significant competition to the foreign-born who did the city's industrial work. Although they occasionally complained of discrimination in the building trades, Negroes, on the whole,

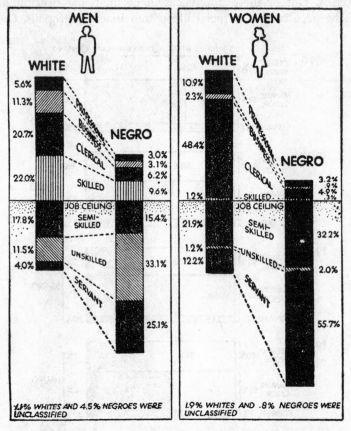

FIG. 3. Differences in the occupational distribution of Negro and white workers: 1930. (Source: Fifteenth Census of the U.S., 1930.)

tended to bypass skilled and semi-skilled work for employment in domestic and personal service.[2] The unskilled jobs which they held were largely in

2. Old Settlers, with a tendency to romanticize the pre-Migration period, consistently minimize the extent of the Job Ceiling prior to 1914. That it was a reality, however, is evident from an examination of the few careful studies that are available for that period. The Juvenile Protective Association sponsored an investigation in 1913 which was released in the form of a pamphlet, *The Colored People of Chicago*, by Louise De Koven Bowen. There are references to "the tendency of the employers who use colored persons at all in their business to assign them to the most menial labor." It was asserted that "the colored laborer is continually driven to lower kinds of occupation which are gradually being discarded by the white man." The larger corporations were accused of refusing to employ Negroes. It was stated that while most labor unions did not refuse to accept Negro members, some consistently denied work opportunities to Negroes after they had accepted their initiation fees and dues. These charges were thoroughly documented and the conclusion was drawn that Negroes were gradually being "crowded into undesirable and underpaid occupations." (Bowen, *op. cit.*, pp. 1-10.)

stores and transportation. A very small business and professional class existed, and a few Negroes held responsible political posts. But neither in the "clean work" nor in the industrial sphere had Negroes yet raised an insistent claim for a "proportionate share" of the jobs.

The First World War brought over 50,000 southern Negro workers into the city within eight years. Most of them went into unskilled labor and

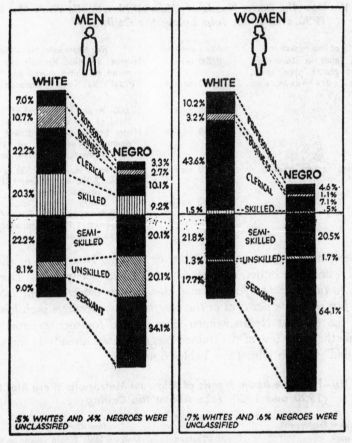

FIG. 4. Differences in the occupational distribution of Negro and white workers: 1940. (Source: Sixteenth Census of the U.S., 1940.)

domestic service, but at least 10,000 took semi-skilled jobs. There were also sizable gains in the clerical field. When the war was over, however, there was a wholesale displacement of Negro workers from both industry and clerical work and a sharp increase in the proportion of Negroes doing domestic and personal service. They held what they could and took what they could get. But Negro women in the garment factories had won a permanent place as semi-skilled industrial workers, and Negro men had become an integral part of the steel and packing industry as unskilled and semi-skilled laborers.

The ten years between the First World War and the Depression witnessed a tremendous expansion of Chicago's industries. The city's share of America's total industrial production rose to fifteen per cent, and this expansion required nearly 328,000 new workers. During this ten-year period, 64,000 additional Negro workers filtered in from the South. Two-thirds of the women and a fourth of the men became servants. Over a half of all the

TABLE VI—How the Boom Needs of Midwest Metropolis Were Met Between 1920 and 1930: Jobs Below the Ceiling

Type of Employment	Number of Workers Absorbed	How Negro Labor Was Utilized
Unskilled labor in stockyards, packing plants, steel mills, stores, warehouses, and wharves	10,000 men	Negroes supplied virtually the whole demand as whites moved up.
	2,670 women	Virtually no Negro women used.
Servants	28,000 men	10,000 Negro men supplied about one-third of the demand for men.
	14,000 women	Negro women supplied almost all of the demand. Two-thirds of the Negro women migrants became servants.
Semi-skilled factory workers	36,000 men	8,000 Negro men used: 500 in the stockyards; 2,000 in garages; 1,100 in laundries; others general.
	11,000 women	8,000 Negro women used, supplying three-fourths of the demand: 5,000 to laundries; 1,100 to garment factories; others general.

men went into either unskilled labor or service. Nearly all of the Negro women went into either servant or semi-skilled occupations. *During this period, forty per cent of the new white women workers went into "clean work," but only five per cent of the Negro women secured such jobs.* While few of the migrant Negro women were trained for such occupations it is probable that very few of the trained Negro women already in the city were "upgraded" to such jobs. (See Tables 6 and 7.)

TABLE VII—How the Boom Needs of Midwest Metropolis Were Met Between 1920 and 1930: Jobs Above the Ceiling

Type of Employment	Number of Workers Absorbed	How Negro Labor Was Utilized
Clerical work	35,800 men	Only 2,500 Negro men used, largely within Black Metropolis. A proportionate increase, but not enough to "catch up." At least 7,000 jobs were needed to give Negro men 8.0 per cent of clerical jobs.
	42,000 women	Only 300 Negro women secured such jobs. Ten times as many jobs—at least 3,000—would have been necessary to give Negroes their 8.0 per cent of the new workers.
Skilled labor	19,400 men	4,000 Negro men secured jobs in the building trades, but few in industry.
	2,700 women	Less than a hundred Negro women.
Professional, proprietary, and managerial	53,000 men	3,000 Negroes.
	16,000 women	1,800 Negroes.

In fact, Negroes who were already in the city, as well as the newcomers, found it impossible to secure a "proportionate share" of the good jobs even when they were qualified for them. They were not permitted to "advance on the job" or to secure apprenticeship opportunities. Instead, white male

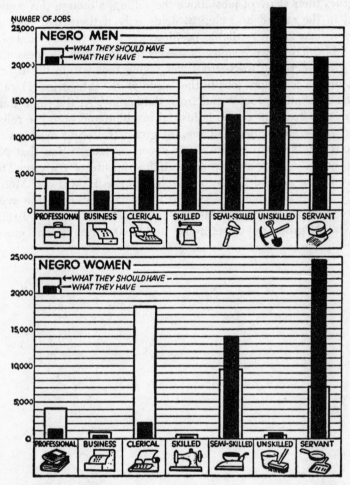

FIG. 5. Negro's "proportionate share" of jobs. (From tables in Scott, "Occupational Changes Among Negroes in Chicago: 1890–1930." Data for 1930.)

workers moved up, and white women either moved up or left industry to become housewives. Those Negroes who had entered industry during the Great Migration tended to advance to the level of semi-skilled workers, but no farther. The 64,000 new Negro workers found their place as servants and unskilled workers. (Tables 6 and 7.)

Had competition been entirely free, with advancement upon individual merit; had Negroes been integrated and promoted in accordance with principles of seniority and at the same rate as white workers, the difference between the jobs the Negroes secured between 1920 and 1930, and the approximate number of jobs they might have been expected to get is illustrated in Figure 5.

A continuously expanding economy might conceivably have operated to give Negroes their share of jobs above the ceiling, although this could have happened in the skilled and clerical fields only if there had been such a phenomenal increase in available positions as to create an actual shortage of white labor. There were signs, however, that a Negro business and pro fessional group catering to Negroes was taking root within the Black Belt, thus providing a few more jobs in the "clean work" categories. The Depression halted the entire process and froze the ceiling. At the same time, Negroes were squeezed out of the industrial machine and onto the relief rolls at a rapid rate—semi-skilled and servant groups suffering most severely.

But it is significant that there was never any suggestion that Negroes should be entirely eliminated from the industrial life of the city. This was due partly to the general temper of public opinion in Midwest Metropolis, and partly to the fact that by 1934 the WPA had stabilized the system so that everybody could at least eat and get some clothing. By 1940, there were 20,000 Negroes on direct relief and 40,000 on various emergency projects.[3]

---

3. The Illinois Emergency Relief Commission reported in 1939 that 44.9 per cent of all "general relief" cases were Negro—a term embracing families without a wage-earner and all "problem" families.

INSTITUTIONS AND
ORGANIZATIONAL STRUCTURES AND PROCESSES

The city as a social system can be perceived as a set of social institutions and special modes of social organization. If urbanism is a characteristic way of life, it should be exhibited in institutions, for institutions are, after all, normatively crystallized ways of acting. Institutions are not to be confused with organized behavior, however. An *institution* is a set of norms governing a specific form of socially organized activity or behavior in group situations. The *group* is an organized aggregate of persons in interaction. A social group, for instance, may behave with respect to a large number of institutions, while a single institution may govern behavior in a large number of social groups. The institution of property, for example, governs behavior in a large number of groups in the society—families, corporations, parishes and governments, to name only a few. It is obvious, of course, that each of these groups practices a large number of institutions. Thus, families in American society practice the institutions of romantic love, monogamous marriage, private property, and so on; and they are primarily organized as nuclear families with multilineal kinship, neolocal residence, and so on.

There are various organized ways in which human beings behave—in social systems, field structures, collectivities and social groups—and there are many techniques for organizing behavior, as for example, love, monetary exchange, conflict, etc. It appears that city-dwellers may utilize some forms of social organization and specific techniques

for mobilizing behavior more often than persons in smaller and, perhaps, more isolated societies. Some say, for example, that crowd behavior is more readily mobilized in cities than in open-country areas, that behavior is more rational and calculative in cities and that kinship becomes a less effective institution. But the evidence for these assertions is far from clear. The essays in this section are largely empirical descriptions of institutions and organization which seem typically to emerge in highly industrialized cities of Western societies with a high rate of urbanization. Their generic urban character is in no way adequately demonstrated.

The city is a place where new institutions often are formed and where deviant institutions exist precariously. This is particularly true for cities in a society undergoing rapid urbanization, as the rate of change in these societies is very great. The high geographic and social mobility of the population, recruitment from diverse social and cultural groups and the character of secular change in the city, constantly threaten urban institutions. The traditional institutions of the U.S. agrarian society, e.g., its sacred religious belief systems, magic, the sanctity of marriage, the extended family, and sexual fidelity, are subject to considerable modification in U.S. cities. These changes in turn have a strong impact on the structure of groups and their activities or functions. The first essays in this section deal with changes in institutions in an urbanized society and their impact on the structure and process of urban based groups.

The changing institutions of marriage and divorce, kinship, private property, level of living and the valuation of children—to mention only a few—all have had their profound effects on the structure of families in cities. The paper by Burgess characterizes some of the major changes in family structure and processes in the United States as a result of changes in these institutions, and of secular trends in the society. His thesis is that the American family can be viewed as in transition from an older rural structural form to a democratic companionship type of family relationship adapted to an urban environment. Frazier's discussion of the impact of urbanization on Negro family life shows how the four major types of Negro family groups which arose in a rural setting are changed by transposition to an urban environment. The emerging forms of family organization in the city are described, as are changes in institutions practiced by Negro families. The data from Kinsey's research report on sexual behavior of men in rural and urban areas describe similarities and differences in sex practices in the two types of environment. The differences in certain institutionalized practices and their availability in the two environments are analyzed. Prostitution, for instance, is considered more of an urban-based set of institutions and practices.

Students of urban life have emphasized that there is a general trend toward secularization of human behavior. Nowhere is this more apparent perhaps than in the institutions of religion and in the organized church and sect. The major changes in religious institutions and their organization, as one moves from the small isolated society to the large urbanized ones, can generally be characterized as follows: (1) a decrease in anthropomorphism; (2) a decline in the belief that supernatural forces are directly involved in natural processes and local events; (3) an increase in the diversity of religious beliefs, practices and organizations, particularly in the spread of sects; (4) the maintenance of religious practices or rituals apart from their belief content or the specific norms of religions. The paper by Chapin in this section deals primarily with the ways in which the traditional organizational practices of Protestant churches have adapted to the urban environment. Particular attention is given to a description of the contrasting types of churches which emerge in cities.

The rapid urbanization attendant upon the industrialization of Western societies markedly changed the relationship of work to play. Technology and its organization changed the productivity of an individual worker both by the use of machines and the organization of work in the factory and mass production, and by the formation of large collectivities of owners-managers and workers. The substantial changes in the work-leisure relationship can perhaps easily be conveyed by the simple statistic that the industrial work week declined from an average of 64 hours in 1860 to an average of 40 hours by 1950. Recent projections place the 1960 figure close to 37 hours, which would mean that the work week would be reduced by roughly three-fifths within a century of rapid industrialization and urbanization. The technology of automation makes even greater reductions within a shorter period of time likely.

The effect of this changing work-leisure relationship, then, is to create ever larger amounts of leisure time for the average city-dweller. This basic change has brought with it a whole series of changes both in the institutions of work and leisure, and in their organization. There are a number of distinctive characteristics of leisure in modern urbanized societies. They include the organization of leisure on a large scale, both as a business enterprise and as a service of governments, and an increase in the passivity of participants on the one hand and the mass organization of participants on the other. Steiner's analysis of recreation in the United States describes and analyzes some of these leisure trends.

The rapid changes in behavior attendant upon urbanization and industrialization bring with them problems of political organization. One of the consequences of these changes is a disjuncture between the ecological community and the politically organized one, resulting in such phenomena as a discontinuity between the metropolitan community and the politically organized city, the overrepresentation of less urbanized constituencies in political groups and systems, and the development of new modes of organizing the interdependencies of politically separate aggregates, as in the formation of port authorities. The essay by Hauser describes these and other consequences of urbanization on political institutions and organizations.

When enough people feel that a function is vital to them, a new set of institutions usually arises. Many of these are characteristically found in cities, as they arise to meet the needs of people who must deal with one another in rational and impersonal situations. The complex division of labor and the productive and marketing institutions together provide the city's economic integration. These give rise to a host of such characteristically urban milieu result in numerous and izations as the factory, the exchange, and the newspaper. The problems which confront persons living in an urban milieu result in numerous and varied institutions and organizational arrangements to resolve crises. The settlement house, the mission, the home for aged, and the hospital are examples of these crises-solving institutions. Some organizational structures in cities are particularly adapted to the migrant, the intinerant and the single person. Certain of these, such as the hotel, the roominghouse, the nightclub, and the restaurant support the impersonality and anonymity readily generated in large-scale contexts. Others, such as the mission and the precinct organization, personalize relationships to manipulate their impersonality. Even the housing arrangements of the city's inhabitants

reflect the effect of urban variables. There are, for instance, the apartment buildings which mirror such facts as the land values, urban densities, and family size. There also are the roominghouses which reflect the marital status and family size, as well as economic status and mobility; and there are the Skid Rows, which are, above all, the abodes of older, downwardly mobile, economically dependent males, many with unresolved personal crises.

All these instances serve as examples of how cities affect to some degree the character of established institutions and organizations, and perhaps of how they generate some which are peculiar to cities. However, it is likely that the character of the institutions and organizations in cities is as much affected by the dominant cultural valuations, the level of urbanization and industrialization of the society, and the societal modes of organization, as it is affected by specific urban variables themselves. Many institutions thought to be characteristic of American cities today, reflect Western capitalistic, religious and democratic political values. They also manifest the effects of a high rate of urbanization, of the changing nature of industrial organization and of large-scale modes of organization. But these conditions also are changing ones. The growing urbanization of the world and the technology of automation, to mention but two trends in organization, will exert still further changes on institutions and their organization in cities. The paper by Hoselitz in this section makes some comparisons of the differential effects of industrialization and urbanization on the social structure of cities in western and nonwestern countries during periods of economic growth.

The principal form of economic organization in rural open-country or village communities has been *primary* industry, that is, the agricultural and pastoral pursuits. To some extent the extractive industries are primary industries, and for the most part they are based in very small settlements, unless the extractive industry is linked with manufacturing. The major basis for the rapid urbanization of countries in modern times has been through the growth of secondary manufacturing industries as the principal basis of production. The pre-industrial cities, by way of contrast, owed their growth primarily to the *quaternary industries* of transport, commerce, communication, finance and administration. The *tertiary industries* of domestic and quasi-domestic services and the *quinary industries* of medical care, education, research and recreation (including the arts) contributed to some urban growth in all historical periods. They have come, however, to form an important part of the industrial structure of all modern metropolitan cities.[1] While all relatively large cities have some employment in all but the primary industries, cities vary considerably in the degree to which an industry is part of the economic base or export function of the community. This industry specialization, in turn, has consequences for the demographic and socioeconomic structure of communities. The paper by Reiss in this section describes different kinds of functional specialization of cities and shows how these differences are related to demographic, economic, and socio-economic differences among cities.

In the urban world, control through the mores tends to weaken, and group organizational techniques often are insufficient to bring conformity. External control through a series of formal institutions such as law, and organizations such as the courts and police, then become more essential. Such control is applicable to only a minimum of conduct, however. This means that urbanites generally must permit a wider range of behavior than rural dwellers, since minimum rather than optimum conduct is achieved by such manipulation. This fact often gives to city life an appearance of lawlessness. It means too that the line between the "legitimate" and the "illegitimate" is faint since what is often proscribed by law is facilitated by customs of local groups. Whyte's essay on the social structure of racketeering shows how certain "illegitimate" institutions are rationalized by the social structure of the slum community. The folkways, if not the mores, of the slum dweller in U. S. cities support the institutions which give rise to organized gambling. Whyte also analyzes the modification of the behavior of the law enforcement officers under direct contact with the local informal modes of control in the rackets and among their participants.

The struggle to keep life organized probably is at its height in the modern city. People in cities do not fit easily into an ordered pattern of social relationship surrounding their interests. Social groups, often tangential to one another, are some times in conflict. The population of the city may take on the characteristics of a mass, since individual interests often remain essentially unorganized. Despite these barriers to interaction, urbanites frequently get together when they are motivated by common interests, articulated as they are through associations and voluntary organizations growing up around these common though segmental interests. Goldhamer analyzes these associations from the perspective of their function in urban industrialized societies.

Communities vary considerably in their social integration, i. e., the degree to which there is a coordination of individual and group behavior according to the normative expectations of the collectivity. Sociologists have observed that the major focal points of urban integration are their functional organization on the one hand and the articulation of interests through associations and voluntary organization on the other. While the interests of urban individuals often are dominated by extra-local community orientations, the neigh-

1. These distinctions among types of industry are an extension of Colin Clark's industry groups by Nelson N. Foote and Paul K. Hatt. See their "Social Mobility and Economic Advancement," *American Economic Review*, 43 (May, 1953), 364-378.

borhood and local community remain as focal points of social integration. Organizations such as schools, stores, and taverns, and media such as newspapers may, under certain circumstances, orient and integrate urbanites into local groupings. On this point, Foley presents data on the use of local facilities by metropolitan inhabitants and shows the equilibrium between local and metropolitan patterns of behavior. The study of local community newspapers by Janowitz shows the role of this medium in the integration of urbanites around local activities, sentiments and symbols. An essay by McKay in the next section shows how the neighborhood furnishes the setting in which the urban child is educated either for conventional or delinquent behavior.

Some sociologists have observed that cities have less social integration than rural societies, but this assertion remains essentially without proof. Part of the reason for the failure to develop tests of the hypothesis is the fact that it is so very difficult to measure a complex group attribute such as its integration. Angell reports on his indexes of moral integration of cities in this section, and tries to account for observed differences in their variation on these indexes.

THE FAMILY IN A CHANGING SOCIETY

Ernest W. Burgess

The title of this symposium "The American Family" may seem a misnomer. In this country the patterns of family life are so numerous and varied that it appears more appropriate to speak of American families rather than of any homogeneous entity, as implied by the term "*the* American family."

Never before in human history has any society been composed of so many divergent types of families. Families differ by sections of the country, by communities within the city, by ethnic and religious groups, by economic and social classes, and by vocations. They are different according to the family life-cycle and by number and role of family members. They vary by the locus of authority within the family and by widely different styles of life. There are the families of the Hopi Indian (primitive maternal), of the old Amish of Pennsylvania (patriarchal), of the Ozark mountaineers (kinship control), of the Italian immigrant (semipatriarchal), the rooming-house (emancipated), the lower middle class (patricentric), the apartment house (equalitarian), and the suburban (matricentric).

With due recognition of all the diversity in American families, it is still possible and desirable to posit the concept of *the* American family. In a sense it is an ideal construction in that it attempts to concentrate attention upon what is distinctive of families in the United States in comparison with those of other countries. These differential characteristics are largely in terms of process rather than of structure and represent relative, rather than absolute, differences from families in other cultures. Chief among these distinctive trends are the following:

1. *Modifiability and adaptability* in response to conditions of rapid social change

2. *Urbanization,* not merely in the sense that the proportion of families living in cities is increasing but that rural, as well as urban, families are adopting the urban way of life

3. *Secularization,* with the declining control of religion and with the increasing role of material comforts, labor-saving devices, and other mechanical contrivances like the automobile, the radio, and television

Reprinted from the *American Journal of Sociology,* Vol. 54 (September 1948), pp. 118-125, by permission of the author and the publisher. (Copyright, 1948, by the *American Journal of Sociology*).

4. *Instability,* as evidenced by the continuing increase in divorce, reaching in 1945 the proportion of one for every three marriages

5. *Specialization,* on the functions of the giving and receiving of affection, bearing and rearing of children, and personality development, which followed the loss of extrinsic functions, such as economic production, education, religious training, and protection

6. The *trend to companionship,* with emphasis upon consensus, common interests, democratic relations, and personal happiness of family members

These distinctive trends in the American family will not be elaborated. Certain of them, however, will receive additional comment at appropriate places in this paper.

With all the variations in American families, it is apparent that they are all in greater or less degree in a process of change toward an emerging type of family that is perhaps most aptly described as the "companionship" form. This term emphasizes the point that the essential bonds in the family are now found more and more in the interpersonal relationship of its members, as compared with those of law, custom, public opinion, and duty in the older institutional forms of the family.

The point is not that companionship, affection, and happiness are absent from the institutional family. They exist there in greater or less degree, but they are not its primary aims. The central objectives of the institutional family are children, status, and the fulfilment of its social and economic function in society.

The distinctive characteristics of the American family, as of the family in any society, are a resultant of (1) survivals from earlier forms of the family, developing under prior or different economic and social conditions; (2) the existing social and economic situation; and (3) the prevailing and evolving ideology of the society.

1. SURVIVALS. The American family has had a rich and varied historical heritage, with strands going back to all European countries and to the religious ideologies of the Catholic, Jewish, and Protestant faiths. What is distinctive in the American family, however, has resulted from its role, first, in the early rural situation of the pioneer period, and, second, in the modern urban environment.

The growth of democracy in the family proceeded in interaction with the development of democracy in society. Pioneer conditions promoted the emancipation both of women and of youth from subordination to the family and to the community. Arrangements for marriage passed from the supervision of parents into the control of young people.

The rural family of the United States before World War I, however, had progressed toward, but had not achieved, democratic relations among its members. Control was centered in the father and husband as the head of the farm economy, with strict discipline and with familistic objectives still tending to be dominant over its members. Children were appraised in terms of their value for farm activities, and land tenure and farm operations were closely interrelated with family organization and objectives.

2. THE EVOLVING URBAN ENVIRONMENT. The modern city, growing up around the factory and serving as a trade center for a wide area, provided the necessary conditions for the development of the distinctive characteristics of the American family. It still further promoted the equality of family members and their democratic interrelationships, initiated and fostered to a certain degree by the rural pioneer environment. In the urban community the family lost the extrinsic functions which it had possessed from time immemorial and which continued, although in steadily diminishing degrees, in the rural family. The urban family ceased to be, to any appreciable extent, a unity of economic production. This change made possible a relaxation of authority and regimentation by the family head. Then, too, the actual or potential employment of wife and children outside the home signified their economic independence and created a new basis for family relations. In the city the members of the family tended to engage in recreational activities separately, in their appropriate sex and age groups. Each generation witnessed a decline of parental control over children.

This increased freedom and individualization of family members and their release from the strict supervision of the rural neighborhood was naturally reflected in the instability of the family. The divorce rate has averaged a 3 per cent increase each year since the Civil War.

Urbanization involves much more than the concentration and growth of population. It includes commercialization of activities, particularly recreational; specialization of vocations and interests; the development of new devices of communication: telephone, telegraph, motion picture, radio, the daily newspaper, and magazines of mass circulation. All these still further promote the urbanization and secularization of families residing not only in cities but even in remote rural settlements.

3. THE IDEOLOGY OF AMERICAN SOCIETY. Democracy, freedom, and opportunity for self-expression are central concepts in the American ideology. The frontier situation favored their expression in the social, economic, and political life of the people. As they found articulation in the American creed, they reinforced existing tendencies toward democracy and companionship within the family.

Urban life in its economic aspects provided less opportunity than did the rural environment for the exemplification of the American ideology. For example, the development of big business and enormous industries decreased the opportunities for the husband and father to run his own business. But the city greatly increased the economic freedom and independence of the wife and children by providing employment outside the home. The social conditions of the modern city led to the emancipation of family members from the institutional controls of the rural family. The urban family tended to become an affectional and cultural group, united by the interpersonal relations of its members.

The paradox between the unity and the diversity of the American family can be understood in large part by the conception of the family in process. This means, first of all, that it is in transition from earlier and existing divergent forms to an emergent generic type and, second, that it is in experimentation and is developing a variety of patterns corresponding to the subcultures in American society.

THE FAMILY IN TRANSITION. Much of what is termed the "instability" of the American family arises from the shift to the democratic companionship type from the old-time rural family of this country and the transplanted old-world family forms of immigrant groups.

Many of the current problems within the family are to be explained by the resulting conflicting conceptions in expectations and roles of husbands and wives and of parents and children. The husband may expect his wife to be a devoted household slave like his mother, while she aspires to a career or to social or civic activities outside the home. Immigrant parents attempt to enforce old-world standards of behavior upon their children, who are determined to be American in appearance, behavior, and ideas.

THE FAMILY IN EXPERIMENTATION. The changes taking place in the family have constituted a vast experiment in democracy. Hundreds of thousands of husbands and wives, parents and children, have participated in it. Couples have refused to follow the pattern of the marriages of their parents and are engaged in working out new designs of family living more or less of their own devising. This behavior has been fully in accord with the ideals and practices of democracy and has exemplified the American ideology of individual initiative and opportunity for self-expression.

This experiment in family formation, while apparently proceeding by individual couples, has been essentially collectivistic rather than pluralistic behavior. Each couple has naturally cherished the illusion that it was acting on its own. To be sure, individual initiative and risk-taking were involved.[1] Many individual ventures have ended in disaster. But actually it has been a collective experiment in the sense that the couples were acting under the stimulus of current criticisms of family life and were attempting to realize in their marriage the new conceptions of family living disseminated by the current literature, presented by the marriages of friends, or developed in discussion by groups of young people.

In the past, stability has been the great value exemplified by the family and expected of it by society. This was true because the family was the basic institution in a static society. American society, however, is not static but dynamic. The virtue of its institutions do not inhere in their rigid stability but in their adaptability to a rapid tempo of social change.

The findings of two recent studies underscore the significance of adaptability for the American family. Angell began his study of the family in the depression with the hypothesis that its degree of integration would deter-

---

1. See Floyd Dell, *Love in Greenwich Village* (New York: Doubleday, Doran & Co., 1926).

mine its success or failure in adjustment to this crisis.[2] He found, however, that he needed to introduce the concept of adaptability to explain why certain families, highly integrated and stable before the depression, failed, and why some moderately integrated families succeeded, in adjusting to the crisis. A restudy of these cases indicated that adaptability was more significant than integration in enabling families to adjust to the depression.

Another study[3] arrived at a similar conclusion. In predicting success and failure in marriage, data were secured from couples during the engagement period. Certain couples with low prediction scores were later found to be well adjusted in their marriage. The explanation seemed to lie in the adaptability of one or both members of the couple, which enabled them to meet and solve successfully difficult problems as they developed in the marriage.

Adaptability as a personal characteristic has three components. One is psychogenic and represents the degree of flexibility in the emotional reaction of a person to a shift from an accustomed to a different situation. The second component is the tendency of the person as culturally or educationally determined to act in an appropriate way when entering a new situation. The third component of adaptability is the possession of knowledge and skills which make for successful adjustments to a new condition.

Successful marriage in modern society with its divergent personalities, diversity of cultural backgrounds, and changing conditions depends more and more upon the adaptability of husbands and wives and parents and children. The crucial matter, then, becomes the question of the adaptability of the family as a group, which may be something different from the adaptability of its members.

The growing adaptability of the companionship family makes for its stability in the long run. But it is a stability of a different kind from that of family organization in the past, which was in large part due to the external social pressures of public opinion, the mores, and law. The stability of the companionship family arises from the strength of the interpersonal relations of its members, as manifested in affection, rapport, common interests and objectives.

Flexibility of personality is not sufficient to insure adaptability of the family to a changing society. Its members should also be culturally and educationally oriented to the necessity for making adjustments. For example, the prospects of successful marriage would be greatly improved if husbands on entering wedded life were as predisposed in attitudes as are wives to be adjustable in the marital relation. Finally, adaptability in marriage and family living demands knowledge and skills on the part of family members. These are no longer transmitted adequately by tradition in the

2. Robert C. Angell, *The Family Encounters the Depression* (New York: Charles Scribner's Sons, 1936).

3. See E. W. Burgess and Paul Wallin, "Engagement and Marriage," chapter on "Adaptability" (unpublished manuscript).

family. They can be acquired, of course, the hard way by experience. They can best be obtained through education and counseling based upon the findings of social science research.

The instability of the American family as evidenced by its rising divorce rate is, in general, incidental to the trial-and-error method by which divorced persons ultimately find happiness in a successful remarriage.[4] But trial and error is a wasteful procedure. It involves tragic losses both to husbands and wives and to their children. So far as possible, it should be replaced by a more rational and less risk-taking planning.

The solution, however, does not lie fundamentally in legislation. Laws, within limits, may be helpful as in the insuring of economic and social security, the improvement of housing and nutrition, in the exemptions from income taxes for wives and children, and in family allowances for children.

The state and federal governments have taken steps to undergird the economic basis of the family and are likely to be called upon for further aid. But assistance to young people entering marriage and to the family in attaining its cultural objectives is coming from other institutions and agencies.

The school and the church have for some time shown a growing interest in assuming responsibility for education for marriage and family life. This is most marked in colleges and universities, a large majority of which, upon demand of the student body, now offer one or more courses in the family, family relations, marriage and the family, and preparation for marriage. High schools are experimenting with different types of courses in human relations and in family relations or with the introduction of family-life education material in existing courses. Churches, through Sunday school classes, young peoples' societies, young married couples' clubs, and Sunday evening forums, have promoted programs in family-life education. Community programs have been organized under the auspices of the Y.M.C.A., the Y.W.C.A., settlements, social centers, associations for family living, parent-child study associations, and other agencies.

Marriage and family counseling are developing under both older and newer auspices. The public still turns to the minister, the physician, and the lawyer for assistance upon spiritual, physical, and legal aspects of marriage. Theological, medical, and law schools are beginning to realize their responsibilities for training their students for this activity. The family social case workers, particularly those with psychiatric training, are at present the persons best trained professionally for marriage and family counseling. The identification in the public mind of family-service societies with relief-giving has largely limited this service to dependent families, although in some cities special provision has been made to extend marriage and family counseling on a fee basis to middle-class clientele.

Beginning with the Institute of Family Relations in Los Angeles, estab-

---

4. Harvey J. Locke, "Predicting Marital Adjustment by Comparing a Divorced and a Happily Married Group," *American Sociological Review*, XII (1947), 187-91.

lished in 1930, and the Marriage Council of Philadelphia two years later, marriage-counseling centers under independent auspices are now functioning in an increasing number of our largest cities, in some smaller communities, and in a growing number of colleges and universities.

The growing disposition of young people is, as we have seen, to make their own plans for marriage and family living. They are, at the same time, interested in the resources available in education, in counseling, and in the findings of research in the psychological and social sciences. Leaders in the family-life educational and counseling movement are also looking to research to provide the knowledge which they may use in giving more efficient service.

This paper attempts only to state the role of research in relation to the solution of the problems of the family in our modern society. Its role is to provide the knowledge which an increasing number of young people are desirous of using in planning marriage and parenthood.

The outstanding evidence of this attitude and expectation is the reliance upon science of upper- and middle-class parents in the rearing of children. Their diet is determined upon the advice of a pediatrician, and their rearing is guided by the latest book on child psychology. This is a wide and significant departure from the older policy of bringing up the child according to methods carried down by tradition in the family.

A second illustration is the growing interest of young people in the factors making for the wise selection of a mate and for success or failure in marriage as derived from psychological and sociological studies.

A third significant fact is the widespread public interest in A. C. Kinsey's book, *Sexual Behavior in the Human Male,* containing the first report of sex behavior of 5,300 male Americans, based upon a very complete schedule and a carefully organized interview.

These are but three of the indications of the receptivity of intelligent young people to the findings of the psychological and social sciences and of their willingness to utilize them in planning for marriage and parenthood. In short, these activities are being taken out of the realm of the mores and are being transferred to the domain of science.

The findings of research do not, in and of themselves, provide the data for a design for marriage and family life. It is, however, the function of social science research to collect and to analyze the fund of experience of young people in their various experiments in achieving happiness in marriage and family life. Therefore, these findings of research should be made available to them through books, magazines, and newspapers; through motion pictures and radio; and through marriage counseling and programs of family-life education.

In conclusion, the main points of this paper may be briefly summarized. The American family, both in its apparent variety and in its essential unity, needs to be viewed in the perspective of social change. It is in transition from older rural institutional forms to a democratic companionship type of family relations adapted to an urban environment. This great change in the mores is a vast social experiment, participated in by hundreds of thousands of families under the collective stimulation of the American ideology of democracy, freedom, and self-expression. This experimental situation places the emphasis upon the adaptability rather than upon the rigid stability of the family. This experiment provides an unusual opportunity for the study of the family in transition. Moreover, participants in the experiment are demonstrating an increasing interest in utilizing research findings in designing their own patterns for marriage and family life.

THE IMPACT OF URBAN CIVILIZATION
UPON NEGRO FAMILY LIFE

E. Franklin Frazier

INTRODUCTION. The urbanization of the Negro population during the present century has effected the most momentous change in the life of the Negro since his emancipation. During the first three decades of the century, nearly two and a half million Negroes moved from the rural South into the urban areas of the North and the South.[1] Public attention has been directed to the northward movements because they were dramatized by the mass migrations to northern industrial centers during the World War; whereas, the million or more Negroes who drifted into southern cities attracted little or no attention.[2] However, the shift from country to city in both the North and the South has been accompanied by profound changes in the Negro's behavior and general outlook on life. Because of the fundamental role of the family in social organization, the study of the Negro family offers the most fruitful approach to an understanding of these important changes in the social and cultural life of the Negro.

I. Although the great majority of Negroes who have migrated to urban areas have been simple peasant folk, the economic and cultural differences among the migrants as a whole have determined largely the kinds of accommodation which they have made to their new environment. Therefore, on the basis of a large body of documentary material we shall undertake first to describe four fairly distinct types of traditional patterns of family life found among the Negroes who make up communities in American cities.[3] There is first the maternal family pattern which is found in its purest and most primitive form in the rural South. By a maternal pattern of family organization we mean a family that is based primarily upon the affectional ties and common interests existing between the offspring and the mother who is the head of the family. As one would expect, many of

Reprinted from the *American Sociological Review*, Vol. 2 (October, 1937), pp. 609-618, by permission of the author and the *American Sociological Review*. (Copyright, 1937, by the American Sociological Society.)

1. Frank A. Ross, "Urbanization of the Negro," *Pub. Amer. Sociol. Soc.*, 26, 118.
2. *Ibid.*, p. 21. For literature on the movement of the Negro to northern cities one should consult Louise V. Kennedy. *The Negro Peasant Turns Cityward*, New York, 1930. This study lists books, articles, and editorials by 159 authors and organizations.
3. A detailed discussion of these four types may be found in the author's "Traditions and Patterns of Negro Family Life in the United States," in *Race and Culture Contacts*, edited by E. B. Reuter, New York, 1934, pp. 191-207.

these families owe their origin to illegitimacy, often involving several men. In such cases the man's or father's function generally ceases after impregnation; and if he continues to show interest in the woman and the offspring his contacts are casual and his contributions to the household are of the nature of gifts. But he has no authority in the family and the children may not even be aware of his relationship to them. This type of family pattern has existed since the days of slavery when the mother was the dominant and most stable element in the Negro family. Even after emancipation, which resulted in a general loosening of social bonds, the Negro mother continued in her accustomed role unless perchance the father acquired some interest in his family. The high rate of illegitimacy among southern Negroes represents family mores and folkways that have their roots in a natural maternal family organization that flourished during slavery.

The second type of family pattern shows many of the characteristics of the traditional family pattern of the American whites. In fact, the histories of the families of this type provide the source materials for studying the genesis of the traditional family type. It is possible to trace in the histories of some Negro families the actual process whereby the father's interest in the family became consolidated with the common interests of the various members of the family group of which he was the recognized head. In some cases traditions in these families go back to the time when the family was still in slavery. Where conditions were favorable to stable family life, the father's interest in his family was often bound up with his status among the slaves, as well as his trusted position in relation to the whites. The moralization of his behavior was further facilitated by incorporation into the household and church of his master or the Negro's own church. Under such circumstances the transition from serfdom to freedom did not result in a breakdown of family relations. In fact, when the father began working as a free man his authority was undisputed in his family. It has been upon such families that the development of the race as a whole in respect to character and culture has depended.

The third type of family pattern is sharply differentiated in regard to social heritage from the great mass of the Negro population. These families originated in the communities of free Negroes, usually of white and Negro and sometimes Indian ancestry, that existed in various parts of the country during pre-Civil War times. Many of these families not only achieved stability but also assumed an institutional character. The founders of these families in some cases inherited wealth from their white ancestors and generally showed the advantages of educational opportunities and white contacts. The families were as a rule patriarchal in organization with the female members playing roles similar to those of the slave-holding class in the ante-bellum South. Pride in white ancestry exercised considerable influence on their conception of themselves and their role in relation to the Negroes of unmixed blood and of slave origin. Many of the old established families in the North sprang from this group, families which were often forced to migrate before as well as after the Civil War in order to maintain their self-respect and secure advantages for their children.

We come finally to the fourth class of families who have been relatively isolated from the main currents of Negro life. These families originated in isolated communities of persons of Negro, white and Indian ancestry, and branches and remnants of these families may still be found in these communities, which are located in Alabama, North Carolina, Ohio, New Jersey, and New York. They are not a homogeneous group but are classified together because they show certain common characteristics. Usually they regard themselves as a distinct race from the Negroes and show in their behavior the clannishness of an isolated group. Their family organization is sternly patriarchal and is usually closely tied up with the religious organization of the community. Negro families that have their roots in such communities generally show in their behavior the influence of their peculiar cultural heritage.

II. Before considering the significance of these various patterns of family life in the accommodations which the Negro family has made to the urban environment, let us turn our attention to the sex behavior and familial life of the thousands of solitary men and women who have found their way into the towns and cities of the North and South. It is necessary to distinguish this group from the great body of black migrants, because their attitudes towards sex and family life have resulted from their mobility and emancipation from the most elementary forms of social control. Such a group of men and women have formed a part of the Negro population since the confusion and disorder following the Civil War. Although after emancipation the great mass of the Negro population settled down under a modified form of the plantation system, a fairly large number of Negro men and to a less extent Negro women continued to wander about in search of work and new experience. The size and character of this migratory element has been continually affected by the condition of southern agriculture and industry. On the other hand, when mass migrations were set in motion by demands of northern industries during and following the World War, many unattached men and women were among the migrants.

When the present economic crisis disrupted the economic life of the rural South, as well as that of industrial areas, the number of these unattached migrants was greatly augmented. A study by the Works Progress Administration showed that for the country as a whole, unattached Negro transients constituted 7 to 12 per cent of the total during the nine-month period, August 1934 through April 1935.[4] In Chicago, during the first six months of 1934, 1,712 of the 10,962 unattached persons registered with the Cook County Bureau for Transients were Negro men and women. In the Harlem area of New York City, during the period from December 1931 to January 1936, there were 7,560 unattached Negro men registered with

4. *The Transient Unemployed.* Research Monograph III, Washington, 1935, p. 33.

the Emergency Relief Bureau.[5] However, these figures include only those unattached Negro men and women who have sought relief; they leave out of account the thousands of roving men and homeless women who support themselves by both lawful and unlawful means.

Although we can not describe in detail the various types of sexual unions which these migratory men and women form in the course of their wanderings from city to city, we may safely draw some conclusions concerning the general character of their sex behavior and mating. In a sense, one may say that the "Blues," those distinctive creations of the black troubadours in our industrial civilization, epitomize the sex and family behavior of this class. In these songs the homeless, wandering, intermittent black workers sing of their disappointments and disillusionment in the city. An oft-repeated cause of this disillusionment is the uncertainty and instability of romantic love, if one might apply the term to the emotions of these migratory men and women. Yet, in a very real sense, one might say that in these songs one can discover the origin of romantic sentiments among the great masses of the Negro population. These songs record the spontaneous responses of strange men and women to each other in an unfamiliar environment. More important still, they reveal an awakening imagination that furnishes a sharp contrast to the unromantic matings of Negroes in the isolated peasant communities of the rural South.

It is not our purpose to give the impression that the "Blues" furnish historical data on the sex and familial behavior of this migratory group. Through life history documents we have been able to distill from these songs their true significance. We find that in many cases these men begin their migratory careers by going first to nearby sawmills or turpentine camps, in order to supplement the landlord's allowances to their families. In fact, if one goes to one of the "quarters" near a sawmill in the South, one may find these foot-loose men and women living out the stories of their loves and disappointments which have become fixed in the "Blues." On the whole, their sexual unions and matings are characterized by impulsive behavior. However, just as their natural impulses urge them to all forms of anti-social behavior, spontaneous sympathy and tender emotions create the temporary unions which these men and women often form. In this connection one should not overlook the fact that a recurring theme of these songs is the longing for the intimate association of kinfolk, or wife and children, who have been left behind. Although the temporary unions which these men and women form are often characterized by fighting and quarreling, they supply a need which these wanderers feel for warm and intimate human association.

If the sawmill closes or the man feels the "itch" to travel, or some "Black Ulysses" from the outside world lures him by stories of a more exciting existence or a tale of fabulous wages in a nearby city, he takes to the road. In some cases, the girl may follow to the next city; but in the

---

5. From the records of the Unattached and Transient Division.

end she loses her temporary lover. During the course of their wanderings, these men may pick up lonely Negro women in domestic service who gratify their sexual longings and provide them with temporary lodging and food. While these men are acquiring sophistication in the ways of the city, they are becoming thoroughly individuated men. By the time they reach Chicago, Detroit, or New York, they have learned how to survive without labor. Some of them have acquired the art of exploiting women for their support. Girls who have run away from their homes in the South and sought adventure in these large cities often become, in spite of their callousness and boasted toughness, the tools of these men. However, these same women sometimes during their sentimental reflections disclose a hidden longing for the security and affection of their families, or betray an abiding attachment to an illegitimate child that they have left with a parent or relative during their wanderings.

III. From this migratory group of men and women, we turn now to the great mass of the Negro migrants who have come to the city in family groups or in remnants of family groups. This movement was at its peak during the World War when not only whole families but entire communities picked up their meagre possessions and joined the flight from the semi-feudal conditions of the South to the modern industrial centers of the North. One can get some notion of the volume of the tide of black humanity that overwhelmed the comparatively small Negro communities in northern cities by considering the increases in the Negro population of the four principal cities to which these migrants were attracted. Between 1910 and 1920, the Negro population of Detroit increased 611.3 per cent; that of Chicago 148.2 per cent; that of the Borough of Manhattan in New York City 80.3 per cent; and that of Philadelphia 58.9 per cent. The immediate effect of the inundation of Negro communities in northern cities was conflict with the white population in contiguous areas. However, the subsequent expansion of the Negro communities proceeded in accordance with the natural growth of these cities.

What especially interests us in regard to the expansion of these Negro communities is that, through selection, various elements of the population have become segregated, thus causing the spatial organization of these communities to reflect their economic and cultural organization. In the case of Chicago, it was possible to divide the Negro community into seven zones of about a mile in length indicating its southward expansion along and parallel to one of the arterial highways radiating from the center of the city.[6] The selection which had taken place during the expansion of the Negro population was indicated by the decline in the percentage of southern-born Negroes and illiteracy, the decrease in the proportion of persons engaged in unskilled labor and domestic service and the percentage of

---

6. See the author's *The Negro Family in Chicago*, Chicago, 1932, chap. 6, for detailed information on the character of these zones as well as the method used in defining them.

women employed, and a corresponding increase in the percentage of mulattoes in the population and of persons in professional and public service in the successive zones. A similar selection was found in the Harlem Negro community in New York City. However, whereas the Chicago Negro community in its expansion has cut across the concentric zones of the larger community and shows the impress of the larger community, the Harlem Negro community has expanded radially from the area where Negroes first settled and has assumed the same pattern of zones as a self-contained city.[7]

When the Negro family is studied in relation to the economic and cultural organization of these communities, we are able to obtain a rough measure, at least, of the Negro's success in the struggle to support himself or family and attain a normal family life. Therefore, let us consider first the question of family dependency. From the records of the United Charities it appears that under normal conditions between 8 and 9 per cent of the families in the poorer areas of Chicago are dependent upon charity. However, the rate of family dependency showed a progressive decline in the successive zones marking the expansion of the community. In the seventh zone only one per cent of the families were dependent.[8] Although we do not possess considerable data for Harlem, we know that prior to the crash in 1929 between 25 and 30 per cent of the "under care" families handled by the Charity Organization Society in an area in New York City including a part of Harlem were Negro cases. The present economic crisis has tended to emphasize the precarious economic situation of a large percentage of Negro families in our cities. According to the 1933 report of the Federal Emergency Relief Administration, as high as 85 per cent of the Negro families in some cities were receiving relief. The percentage of Negro families receiving relief was highest in such highly industrialized areas as Toledo, Akron, and Pittsburgh, where large numbers of Negroes are employed in unskilled labor; the percentage in Chicago and New York was around 46 per cent and 30 per cent respectively.

In the case of the Harlem community, we are able to study the incidence of relief in relation to the spatial organization of the Negro area. During the first week of September, 1935, there were 24,292 Negro families on Home Relief, this being 43.2 per cent of the 56,137 Negro families in this area. However, the incidence of relief varied considerably in the zones marking the outward expansion of the community from its center. The percentage of families receiving relief declined rapidly from 70.9 per cent in the central zone to 28.4 per cent in the outermost zone. This is of special interest because, although in some areas of the peripheral zone were found some of the poorest Negro families in the entire community, the incidence in these areas did not vary greatly from the average for the zone as a whole. The only explanation that occurs to us is that the family groups that

---

7. See the author's article, "Negro Harlem: An Ecological Study," *Amer. Jour. Sociol.*, July 1937.

8. See *The Negro Family in Chicago*, pp. 150 ff.

tended to be segregated in the peripheral zones were better able to meet collectively the economic crisis than the single, unattached, separated and widowed men and women who tended to congregate in the center of the community. This selection was shown in the marital status of the population in the various zones. The percentage of single men declined in the successive zones outward from 42.6 to 31.1 per cent and that of single women from 30.9 to 23.5 per cent. On the other hand, the proportion of men and women married increased from about 50 per cent each to 64 per cent for the men and to 60 per cent for the women.[9] A similar tendency was discovered in the case of the Negro community in Chicago.[10]

The selection and segregation of the population with reference to marital status coincides with other processes of organization and disorganization of Negro family life in the city. In Chicago, home ownership was closely correlated with family stability, whereas, in Harlem, with its apartments and multiple dwellings, it was not significant. Similarly, the relationship between family organization and disorganization and the spatial organization of the Negro community was more evident in Chicago with its relatively simple pattern than in Harlem with its more complex pattern. For example, the desertion and non-support rates declined regularly from 2.5 per cent of the total families in the poorer-zone near the Chicago loop to less than one half of one per cent in the outermost zone. Although a similar tendency in regard to desertions was discernible in the Harlem Negro community, the various zones did not show the same degree of cultural homogeneity as the Chicago zones. Thus, in Chicago the delinquency rate declined from 42.8 per cent in the zone of considerable family and community disorganization near the center of the city to 1.4 per cent in the outermost zone of stable family life and home ownership. However, in Harlem, no such decline in the successive zones of population expansion was discernible in regard to juvenile delinquency. It would require a more intimate study of the character and culture of the various zones in order to determine the relationship between community factors and juvenile delinquency. Nevertheless, it is apparent that as a result of competition, various elements of the Negro population in both cities are selected and segregated in a way which enables the student to get some measure of the processes of organization and disorganization.

This is seen most clearly in regard to the question of the survival of the Negro in the city. The low fertility of Negro women in cities has been shown in a number of studies. According to Thompson and Whelpton, Negroes in large cities, including Chicago and New York, "were not maintaining their numbers on a permanent basis in either 1920 or 1928."[11] Lately, Clyde Kiser has found that the fertility of Negro women in a health

---

9. See "Negro Harlem: An Ecological Study," loc. cit.
10. See The Negro Family in Chicago, chap. 7.
11. Warren S. Thompson and P. K. Whelpton, Population Trends in the United States, New York, 1933, p. 280.

area in New York was lower than that of white women of similar and higher occupational status in several urban communities.[12] However, if we study the fertility of Negro women in relation to the organization of the Negro community, some important facts are revealed. For example, in Chicago in 1920, the highest ratio of children under five to women of child-bearing age, i.e., 15 to 44, was found in the two peripheral zones, or the areas of stable family life and home ownership. The ratio was higher in these zones than in the zones where the poorer migrant families settled and almost twice as high as the ratio in the bright light area with its cabarets, saloons, and houses of prostitution.[13]

Harlem offers even more striking evidence of the influence of selective factors on the survival of the Negro in the city. In 1920, the ratio of children under 5 to 1,000 women 20 to 44 years of age increased in the successive zones outward from the center of the community from 109 in the first to 274 in the fifth, with a slight variation in the fourth. However, in 1930, the ratio of children increased regularly from 115 in the first to 462 in the outermost zone. This latter figure is about the same as the ratio in towns with from 2,500 to 10,000 population. Differential survival rates were revealed also in the ratio of deaths to births in 1930 in the various zones. In the central zone, the population was dying out, there being 112 deaths to each 100 births. However, the ratio of deaths to births declined in the successive zones until it reached less than 50 to 100 in the areas near the periphery of the community. Looking at the situation from the standpoint of births alone, we find that in 1930 there was one child born to each 25 women, 20 to 44 years of age, in the central zone. From this zone outward, the number of women of child-bearing age per child born declined regularly until it reached eight in the outermost zone. Thus the survival of the Negro in the city seems to be influenced by the same selective factors which determine the spatial organization and social structure of the Negro community.

Let us return now to the four traditional patterns of family life described above and consider them in relation to the selective process at work in these communities. The first or maternal type of family offers little resistance to the disintegrating forces in the urban environment. Because of their poverty, these families are forced to seek homes in the poorer sections of the Negro community. Moreover, since these families are supported solely by the mother who is generally employed in domestic service or at unskilled labor, they easily slip into the ranks of those dependent upon charity. The children suffer not only from the lack of parental control but are subjected to the vicious environment of disorganized areas. Consequently, many of the boys become members of delinquent gangs, while

---

12. Clyde V. Kiser, "Fertility of Harlem Negroes," *The Milbank Memorial Fund Quarterly*, 13, July, 1935, 273-285.
13. See *The Negro Family in Chicago*, pp. 136-144.

the girls are guilty of sex delinquency, which often leads to unmarried motherhood.

In these same areas may be found the poorer families of the paternal type. In these families, as well as those of the maternal type, a large percentage of the mothers are forced to be wage earners. Whether they maintain their paternal organization depends upon a number of factors, including the vitality of family traditions, the security and regularity of employment of the father, the development of common interests, and the degree to which these families are integrated into the institutions of the Negro community. But, it often happens that the father's interest in his family rests upon some immediate interest, or is based upon mere sympathy and habit. Under such circumstances, if the father loses his job or if he develops new interests in the urban environment that are antagonistic to the common interests of his family, he may easily join the ranks of the large number of Negro deserters. In this connection, it should be pointed out that the families inhabiting these blighted areas are free from the censure of public opinion, as well as other types of communal control. On the other hand, those families that succeed in maintaining a community of interest or develop new ambitions for their children generally move, if their economic resources permit, towards the periphery of the Negro community. Their movement at first may be just beyond the area of extreme deterioration and poverty.

It may take another generation for these families to reach the periphery of the Negro community where one finds the families of the third type—those having a background of several generations of stable family life and firmly rooted traditions. It was old mulatto families of the third type who sometimes fled before the onrush of the uncouth Negroes from the South to areas beyond the borders of the Negro community. But as a rule they sought the periphery of the Negro community as is shown in the case of the seventh zone in Chicago, where half of the inhabitants were mulattoes.[14] Then, too, sometimes these old established families have isolated themselves and have regarded with mixed feelings of contempt and envy the rise of the ambitious elements in the lower and, on the whole, darker elements in the Negro population. But, just as in the rigorous competitive life of the northern city, the poor and illiterate Negroes with no other resources but their folk culture are ground down by disease, vice, and poverty, those possessing intelligence and skill and a fund of family traditions find a chance to rise beyond the caste restrictions of the South. Thus, there has come into existence in these cities a fairly large middle-class element comprised of the more ambitious elements of the second type of families and representatives of the third type with a few descendants of the fourth type of families. Their pattern of family life approaches that of the white middle class. It is the emergence of this class which accounts largely for those orderly and stable areas on the periphery of the Negro

14. See *The Negro Family in Chicago*, pp. 101-105.

communities in our cities. In between such areas and the areas of extreme deterioration where family disorganization is highest, there are areas of a mixed character in which the more stable and better-paid industrial workers find homes.

In view of the process described here, it is not surprising that in the area occupied by the middle-class families, there may be on the average more children, as for example in Chicago, than in the areas of extreme poverty and family disorganization. In the case of the Harlem community which resembles in its spatial organization a self-contained city, relatively large family groups of working class as well as middle class status tend to become segregated on the periphery, though they occupy different areas. In the center of the Harlem community, which is essentially a non-family area, one may find the emancipated from all classes and elements.

IV. Our discussion points to a number of conclusions which may be stated briefly as follows. First, it seems inevitable that, as long as the bankrupt and semifeudal agricultural system in the South continues to throw off men and women who lose the restraints imposed by a simple folk culture, there will be a class of roving Negroes who will live a lawless sex and quasi-family life. Secondly, the great mass of migrants who, as a rule, manage to preserve remnants of their family organization must face in the competitive life of the city a severe struggle for survival and, at the same time, be subjected to the disintegrating forces in the urban environment. The fate and fortunes of these families will depend upon both their economic and their cultural resources. Many of the poorer families that are held together solely by the affectional ties between mother and children, will be ground down by poverty and the children will be scattered and are likely to become delinquent. Those families in which the father's interest rests upon no firmer basis than some passing attachment, or mere sympathy and habit, may suffer a similar fate. But, if such families succeed in becoming integrated into the institutional life of the community and have sufficient income to avoid dependence upon charity, they may achieve a fair degree of stabilization. On the other hand, the economically better situated families, in which the father's interest is suported by tradition and tied up with the common interests of the family, may resist the disintegrating effects of the city and some of the children will enter the middle class. The traditions of these families will become merged with the traditions of mulatto families, many of free origin, who once formed an upper social class. The economic and cultural organization of the Negro community which emerges as the result of competition indicates the selective influence of the urban environment on these various family heritages.

RURAL-URBAN BACKGROUND
AND SEXUAL OUTLET

Alfred C. Kinsey, Wardell B. Pomeroy, and Clyde E. Martin

The city boy's failure to understand what life can mean to a boy who is raised on a farm, and the farm boy's idea that there is something glamorous about the way in which the city boy lives, apply to every avenue of human activity, including the sexual. This popular interest in knowing how another group lives is projected into the sociologist's invariable search for basic differences between the mores of city groups and the mores of farm groups; and this accounts for the fact that the few data which have been available on the sexual life of the rural male have commanded widespread attention.

Persons have been considered rural if they lived on an operating farm for an appreciable portion of the years between 12 and 18. This is the late pre-adolescent and adolescent period which is so important in the shaping of sexual patterns. Persons have been rated as urban if they never had more than incidental residence in rural areas, or if their rural residence occurred only after the age of 18, which is the age by which most of the patterns of sexual behavior are already laid down.

FREQUENCIES OF TOTAL OUTLET. For the population as a whole, it has been shown that frequencies of sexual outlet depend upon the age of the individual, the age at which he became adolescent, his educational background and occupational class, and his religious background. This is equally true of the rural portion of the population and of the urban portion of the population, and no comparison of the frequencies of total sexual outlet or of the sexual outlet from the several sorts of sexual activity can mean much unless there is a preliminary breakdown on most of these other factors.

An examination of Figure 1 will show that the differences between the total outlet of the rural males and the total outlet of the urban males are never very great. In general, the differences would not be particularly significant if they did not all lie in the same direction, which is almost without exception in the direction of a lower frequency of total sexual outlet for the rural males. The differences are most marked in the lower educational level, where the rural males may not have more than three-

Adapted from *Sexual Behavior in the Human Male,* Chapter 12, pp. 449-464, *passim,* by permission of the authors and the publisher. (Copyright, 1948, by the W. B. Saunders Company.)

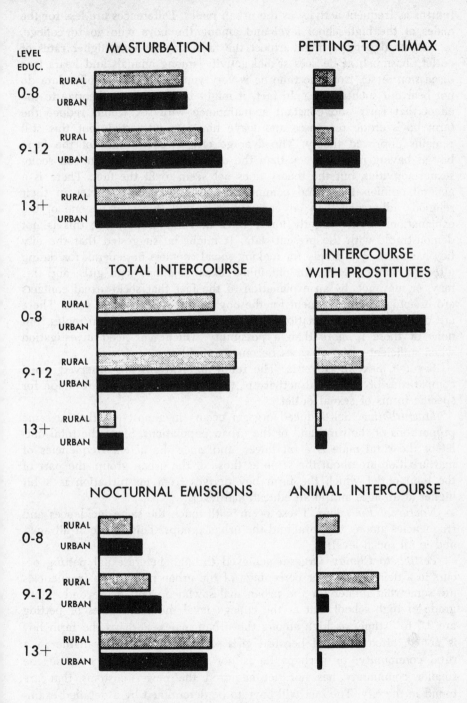

FIG. 1—Comparisons of Sexual Activity in Rural and Urban Groups.
Comparing mean frequency data for the age period 16-20, for three educational
levels. Black bars for urban population, shaded bars for rural groups.

fourths as frequent activity as the urban males. Differences are less for the males of the high-school level and among the boys who go to college.

City-bred persons might expect the farm boy to have higher rates of outlet, inasmuch as he sees sexual activity among animals and hears free discussion of sex from the time he is very young; but the specific data do not bear out such an idea. In fact, it might be possible to theorize to the effect that early and constant acquaintance with sex would reduce the farm boy's erotic responses and leave him less interested; but this still remains unproved theory. The average city dweller thinks of the farm boy as having more privacy than the city boy has for carrying on socio-sexual activities, but the theory does not seem to fit the fact. There is a general opinion that rural communities are in general stricter in their religious adherence than city communities, and this may be one of the explanations of the slightly lower rates of rural groups, but this is not demonstrable with the present data. It might be suggested that the city boy has more opportunity for making social contacts in general, for dating girls and, consequently, for obtaining sexual relations with girls; and this may, or may not, be an explanation of the fact that socio-sexual contacts are in actuality less frequent for the boy who is raised on the farm. There are other possible explanations of the lower rates of the rural males, but none of these is more than a possibility which will need investigation when sufficient series of cases become available.

SPECIFIC SEXUAL OUTLETS. The following patterns are observed when comparisons of the sexual activity of rural and urban males are made for specific forms of sexual outlet.

Masturbation. Self-induced orgasm occurs in almost exactly the same proportions of the rural and of the urban populations. Since the total outlet of the rural male is a bit lower, and since the actual frequencies of masturbation are about the same as those of the urban group, the part of the total outlet which the farm boy derives from masturbation is a bit higher at all ages and in all educational levels.

Nocturnal Emissions. These occur with much the same incidences and frequencies among the rural and the urban groups. This is true at all ages, and in all social levels.

Petting to Climax. Orgasm achieved through heterosexual petting occurs in a definitely higher percentage of the urban males. The frequencies are somewhat higher for the urban males who do not go beyond eighth grade or high school, but at the college level the frequencies of petting are 2.5 to 3 times as high among the urban males. Perhaps the farm boy is not so often involved because girls simply are not so available in a rural community; or perhaps he is not so often involved because the smaller community has not yet acquired the newer customs that are found in the city. The fact will have to be determined by a detailed examination of more histories.

Premarital Intercourse. The differences between rural and urban groups are greater in regard to premarital intercourse than they are for any of the preceding activities. In most age groups and at all educational levels, more of the city boys are involved and fewer of the farm boys. At the grade school level, 91 per cent of the city boys may be involved between the ages of 21 and 25, but only 80 per cent of the farm boys. At the college level in the same age period, 55 per cent of the city boys have some premarital intercourse and about 47 per cent of the farm boys. The differences in frequencies of premarital intercourse between rural and urban groups are of about the same order.

Intercourse with Prostitutes. Premarital relations with prostitutes are even more distinctively an activity of the city group. While it is commonly believed that farm boys are particularly interested in securing intercourse with prostitutes when they go into the city, the record indicates that fewer of them ever arrive at such experience. The frequency with which they have relations with prostitutes is definitely lower than the frequency with which city boys have such relations.

Marital Intercourse. In marital relations, the rural male again has a slightly lower rate of outlet than the city male. The differences are not great but are consistent in several groups, as far as our limited data apply.

Homosexual Outlet. Orgasm effected by contacts with other males is, on the whole, less frequent among the farm boys who have contributed histories to this study, more frequent among the urban males. The two groups are most distinct at the grade school and high school levels. The differences in incidence are very minor at the college level.

There is a widespread theory among psychologists and psychiatrists that the homosexual is a product of an effete and over-organized urban civilization. The failure to make heterosexual adjustments is supposed to be consequent on the complexities of life in our modern cities; or it is a product of a neuroticism which the high speed of living in the city imposes upon an increasing number of individuals. The specific data on the particular rural and urban groups do seem to suggest that there is something in city life which encourages the development of the homosexual. But the distinctive thing about homosexuality in the city is the development of a more or less organized group activity which is unknown in any rural area.

Large cities have taverns, night clubs, restaurants, and baths which may become frequented almost exclusively by persons interested in meeting homosexual friends, or interested in finding opportunities for discussions with others who do not object to the known homosexuality of their companions. In this city group, the development of an elaborate argot gives a sense of belonging which may defend a minority group against the rest of society; but it also intensifies a feeling which the group has that it stands apart from the rest of the population. Moreover, it is this city group which exhibits all the affectations, the mannerisms, the dress, and the other displays which the rest of the population take to be distinctive of all homosexual persons, even though it is only a small fraction of the males with homosexual histories who ever display such characteristics. None of these city-bred homosexual institutions is known in rural areas, and this may well account for a somewhat lower rate of the homosexual among farm boys.

On the other hand, the highest frequencies of the homosexual which we have ever secured anywhere have been in particular rural communities in some of the more remote sections of the country. The boy on the isolated farm has few companions except his brothers, the boys on an adjacent farm or two, visiting male cousins, and the somewhat older farm hand. His mother may see to it that he does not spend much time with his sisters, and the moral codes of the rural community may impose considerable limitations upon the association of boys and girls under other circumstances. Moreover, farm activities call for masculine capacities, and associations with girls are rated sissy by most of the boys in such a community. All of these things are conducive to a considerable amount of homosexuality among the teen-age males in the most isolated of the rural areas. There is much less of it in the smaller farm country of the Eastern United States.

Animal Contacts. Sexual relations with animals of other species are, of necessity, most often found in rural areas. Ultimately about 17 per cent of the farm boys have complete sexual relations with other animals, and perhaps as many more have relations which are not carried through to climax.

In summary, it may be emphasized again that there are few material differences between the histories of farm boys and the histories of boys raised in the city, or between adult males living in the two places. In general there are slightly lower frequencies of total sexual activity in the rural population, and lower frequencies in most of the particular sources of outlet. Nocturnal emissions occur with nearly identical incidences and frequencies in rural and in urban groups. The rural population is most distinct in having fewer socio-sexual contacts (meaning premarital heterosexual petting, premarital and extramarital intercourse, and homosexual relations), and in its much higher frequencies of animal intercourse. But the city boy's interest in animal contacts as soon as they are available makes it clear that it is simply a question of opportunity which differentiates the rural and urban groups on this latter point.

THE PROTESTANT CHURCH
IN AN URBAN ENVIRONMENT

F. Stuart Chapin

Animal and plant organisms are found to be adapted to their environments in structure and function. Similarly we find that social institutions have patterns that are related to the field of culture in which they live and grow and have their being. The Protestant church is a religious institution whose pattern of organization and rate of growth have been found to be closely correlated with certain measured characteristics of the urban environment in which it exists.

In the scientific study of such a complex entity as the Protestant church, we must decide upon some objective—that is, measurable and verifiable—criteria of growth. Church membership, Sunday school enrollment and total expenditure were the criteria selected by the Institute of Social and Religious Research as objective measures of growth in their study of 1950 churches in 16 large American cities.[1] Figure 1 shows a comparison for three of the cities.

In general, the percentage of churches growing in membership in each of the 16 sectors [2] corresponds roughly to the population growth. Sunday schools increased somewhat more rapidly. The variation among the percentages reflects the age of the city as well as population growth. In the category of total expenditures there is distinctly less variation among the churches.

Unless we have an equally significant measure of environment, the analysis by the three criteria of growth—membership, Sunday school enrollment, and total expenditure—becomes useless. After ten years of study and experimentation, the Institute adopted eight measures of the urban environment as significant in the wider social sense. These are: (1) population growth or loss; (2) increase or decrease in the elements likely to affiliate with a white Protestant church; (3) change in characteristic economic status of residents; (4) change in desirability of residence; (5) increase or decrease in the unstable elements of population; (6) increase or decrease

Reprinted from *Contempo. ary American Institutions,* Chapter 11, pp. 177 ff., by permission of the author and the publisher. (Copyright, 1935, by Harper and Brothers, Publishers.)

1. Ross W. Sanderson, *The Strategy of City Church Planning,* Harper & Brothers, 1932.

2. *Ibid.,* chap. ii.

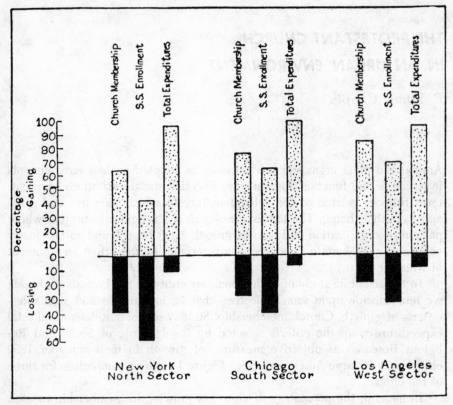

FIG. 1. Percentage of churches gaining or losing on each of three indices of church progress, in sectors of three typical cities. (Taken from Chart V, R. W. Sanderson, *op. cit.*, p. 78.)

in dependency; (7) increase in juvenile delinquency; and (8) improvement or deterioration in health.[3]

When rankings of each church on all three of the criteria of growth (membership, Sunday school enrollment and total expenditure) are taken in a combined index of growth, the grades of growth—A, B, C, D, and E— are defined as follows:

A—highest fifth, 55 per cent to 127 per cent increase, 1920–1930.
B—above average, 25 per cent to 54 per cent increase.
C—average fifth, 8 per cent to 24 per cent increase.
D—below average, 24 per cent decrease to 7 per cent increase.
E—lowest fifth, 41 per cent to 25 per cent decrease.

With these combined indices [4] of growth available, it is interesting to observe the relation between growth and social environment. There seems

3. *Ibid.*, pp. 40-42, 62.
4. *Ibid.*, pp. 79-80.

to be a very close relation between church progress and social conditions, since the churches with A and B rankings are more numerous in the better territory (area of best and above-average social tendency), and churches of D and E rankings are more numerous in poorer territory (area of below-average or worst social tendency).

Thus far we have examined only the larger and more general relations between the church and its urban environment as these relations are revealed in the distribution of churches in different zones of the social environment, and in the incidence of churches with different rates of growth in these different zones. It now becomes important to examine more closely the relationship between church membership and the area in which the church is located. Table 1, covering 813 churches, shows the church mem-

TABLE I—Membership Living Within a Mile of All Churches and of Variant Churches, by Type of Parish and of Territory [5]

Type of Parish	All Churches Number	All Churches Per Cent	Churches in Better Territory All Number	Churches in Better Territory All Per Cent	Churches in Better Territory Sub-modal Number	Churches in Better Territory Sub-modal Per Cent	Churches in Poorer Territory All Number	Churches in Poorer Territory All Per Cent	Churches in Poorer Territory Super-modal Number	Churches in Poorer Territory Super-modal Per Cent
Scattered										
Less than 50% of membership within a mile of the church	287	35.3	61	15.9	5	11.1	226	52.6	43	46.7
Medium										
50-59%	103	12.7	50	13.1	8	17.8	53	12.3	10	10.9
60-69%	79	9.6	32	8.4	2	4.4	47	10.9	11	12.0
Compact										
70-79%	94	11.6	58	15.1	10	22.2	36	8.4	11	12.0
80-89%	73	9.0	48	12.5	7	15.6	25	5.8	5	5.4
Very Compact										
90-99%	143	17.6	105	27.4	10	22.2	38	8.8	10	10.9
100%	34	4.2	29	7.6	3	6.7	5	1.2	2	2.1
Total	813	100.0	383	100.0	45	100.0	430	100.0	92	100.0

bership residing within a one-mile circle. When less than 50 per cent of the members live within a mile of the church, the parish is regarded as scattered. A medium parish is one in which from 50 to 69 per cent of the members live within this distance. It will be noted that this table also shows the churches classified by better territory and by poorer territory. Thus it is possible to see how churches with a scattered parish tend to be found in the poorer territory and churches with compact parishes tend to be found in the better territory.

Although this is the general trend, it is interesting to inquire what sort of churches tend to succeed in poorer territory. Are there exceptions to the trend? To answer this question, the Institute made a special study of churches whose rankings differed most widely from the characteristic rank-

5. Ross W. Sanderson, *op. cit.*, p. 210.

ings in each type of territory. Such churches were called variants.[6] Thus there were below-average or sub-modal churches in better territory, and above-average or super-modal churches in poorer territory. Further study of Table 1 shows that these variant churches show a definite trend. The sub-modal or relatively unsuccessful churches in the better territory tend to have more compact parishes than all churches in the same territory. The super-modal or successful churches in the poorer territory tend to have more compact parishes than all churches in the same territory. Why should compactness be associated with failure in better territory and, at the same time, with success in poorer territory? The answer to this question requires still more intensive analysis.

Table 2 lists the frequency of the chief factors found in the variant churches. It is evident that psychological factors, such as adaptability, group

TABLE II—Frequency of Chief Factors of Variance in Sub-modal and Super-modal Churches [7]

Factors of Variance	Frequency Among 82 Sub-modal Churches	
	Number of Churches	Per Cent of Churches
Border territory or "pocket"	3	4
Revision of rolls	5	6
Poor location or equipment, or both	8	10
Meager program	11	13
Recently moved to new neighborhood	13	16
Inadequate size	17	21
Lack of lay leadership	18	22
Inadequate paid leadership	24	29
Lack of financial resources	24	29
Competition	27	33
Lack of group solidarity	31	38
Lack of adaptability	42	51
	Frequency Among 134 Super-modal Churches	
Border territory	2	1
Absolute increase too small to be significant	12	9
No competition	33	25
Exceptional lay leadership	56	42
Prestige	58	43
Exceptional financial resources	58	43
Program varied or intense	61	46
Excellent location, new equipment, or both	97	72
Exceptional paid leadership	99	74
Exceptional group solidarity	107	80
Adaptability	118	88

solidarity, leadership and a varied program, play an important part in the life of the super-modal churches, and that the lack of these favorable psychological qualities bulks large in the patterns of the sub-modal and unsuccessful churches.

It is a commonplace of sociological research that any given situation is

6. *Ibid.*, p. 104.
7. *Ibid.*, p. 111.

likely to be the product of many factors in functional relationships rather than the result of single causes. Investigation shows that at least twelve factors are involved in the careers of these institutional units. The questions arise, Do these factors operate together and in combination? Is there any connection between the number of these factors present and the degree of success of the church? Table 3 is a partial answer to these questions. Here

TABLE III—Distribution of Variant Churches According to Number of Chief Factors of Variance [8]

82 Sub-modal Churches		134 Super-modal Churches
19	One factor	5
24	Two factors	7
17	Three factors	14
12	Four factors	20
5	Five factors	25
3	Six factors	23
2	Seven factors	29
0	Eight factors	5
0	Nine factors	6

Average number of factors per sub-modal church, 2.7; per super-modal church, 5.2. Most frequent number of factors among sub-modal churches, 2; among super-modal churches, 7.

we find that sub-modal and super-modal churches show strikingly different distributions. The modal number of factors for the unsuccessful churches (sub-modal churches) is two, whereas the number of concurrent factors for the successful churches (super-modal churches) is five. Obviously the successful churches in the poorer territory are more complex institutions. Their success is due to the way they have adapted to many different conditions. In short, they are successful because their pattern is flexible and capable of adjustment to a complex environment.

If complexity of influences in the urban environment of the church forces intricate adjustments and adaptations of the institutional pattern as the condition of success,[9] then the rôle of leadership, energetic, varied, resourceful and specialized, should be related to the larger evidences of institutional prosperity. Table 4 presents an analysis of the presence of different types of specialized staff in 994 churches. It is evident that the unsuccessful churches in the better environment (sub-modal churches) show smaller percentages of staff in 11 of the 13 categories of specialized leadership. As compared with this situation, the successful churches in the poorer environment show a larger percentage of staff in 9 of the 13 categories of leadership than the average church in the better territory. Here seems to be some objective proof [10] of a positive relation between the presence of

---

8. *Ibid.*, p. 112.

9. It should be remembered that the criteria of success are church membership, Sunday school enrollment and total expenditures. These are tangible attributes of each church as an institution. Back of these attributes lie such psychological factors as loyalty, cooperativeness, self-denial and devotion. Although these factors are not measured at this stage of our analysis, they underlie it.

10. Objective, because separate types of leadership are present in a certain number of cases and hence subject to counting and verification.

TABLE IV—Staff Service Employed by All Churches and by Variant Churches, by Type of Territory [11]

	Better Territory		Poorer Territory		Total
	454	54	540	112	994
	Churches	Sub-modal	Churches	Super-modal	Churches
Staff Position	(Per Cent)	(Per Cent)	(Per Cent)	(Per Cent)	(Per Cent)
Minister	97.4	85.2	92.5	86.6	94.6
Assistant minister	6.2	.0	12.6	8.0	9.7
Pastor's assistant	7.3	5.6	8.1	13.4	7.8
R. E. director	9.3	3.7	9.8	9.8	9.6
Young people's worker	3.5	1.9	4.8	1.8	4.2
Athletic or recreational director	3.3	.0	4.1	2.7	3.7
Church secretary	20.9	16.7	34.3	17.9	28.2
Finance secretary	5.7	3.7	8.1	7.1	7.0
Visitor	3.3	1.9	11.1	7.1	7.5
Deaconess	2.6	3.7	5.9	6.2	4.4
Part-time boys' or girls' worker	1.3	3.7	3.3	2.7	2.4
Part-time assistant minister	.7	1.9	1.9	.0	1.3
Miscellaneous	13.7	7.4	29.6	23.2	22.2

specialized leadership and success in rising above a poor institutional environment, and between lack of specialized leadership and submergence below the average in a good institutional environment. The table also seems to show that variety of specialized leadership (types of staff position) is characteristic of a larger proportion of churches in a poor environment than of churches in a better environment, and that, in general, the staff of churches in the poorer territories is superior in specialization to the staff of the average church among the 994 studied.

If we turn to the larger area of the country, we discover from the tabulated information of Table 5, that the more complex church institutions,

TABLE V—Frequency of Certain Subsidiary Church Organizations in Rural Churches and in Churches in Small Cities [12]

	Per Cent Frequency, Rural Churches			Small City Churches
Organization	Open Country	Village	Town	
Some subsidiary organizations besides Sunday school	52	79	93	100
Women's organization	42	70	87	100
More than one women's organization	17	21	44	90
Mixed sex organizations (usually Young People's)	25	47	67	66
More than one mixed sex organization	5	14	37	0
Men's organization	2	5 [a]	10	55
Boys' organization	1	6 [a]	15 [a]	11
Girls' organization	3	8 [a]	20	33

[a] Less than 1 per cent have more than one.

judged by the constituent organizations, exist in the more complex environments of cities, whereas in the open country are found simple organizations. This is true also of small city churches. Douglass [13] has worked out a method

---

11. Ross W. Sanderson, *op. cit.*, p. 210.
12. H. Paul Douglass, *1000 City Churches*, Harper & Brothers, 1926, p. 81.
13. *Ibid.*, pp. 54, 67.

of graphic analysis to show the relation between the type of church and the type of its constituent group organization. This is shown in Figure 2.

The method identifies, by objective devices, six types of church with some subtypes, in accordance with the program of the church and the number of its constituent groups. The types are: the unadapted church, the slightly adapted, the internally adapted, the socially adapted, the adven-

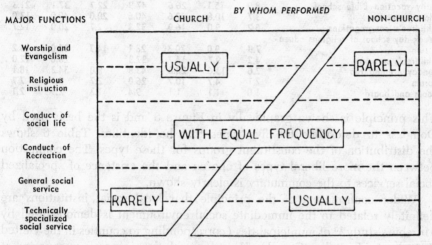

FIG. 2. Division of functions between churches and non-churches. (Taken from Chart I, H. P. Douglass, *op. cit.*, p. 50.)

turous, and the conservative (widely variant). This plan of classification rests upon a careful count of the number and type of constituent groups within each church. If we select examples of the major church functions and consider how frequently they occur in churches in comparison to non-church institutions, we may represent the frequency as in Figure 2. Worship, evangelism, and religious instruction are usually found in the church, but rarely in non-church institutions. Such functions as those that relate to the conduct of social life and of recreation are found with equal frequency in the contrasted social institutions. But the functions of general social service and technically specialized social service, which are rarely carried on by churches, are usually carried on by non-church institutions. If, now, we classify the different types of constituent groups and services of churches, we discover the ones that are usual and the ones that rarely occur. Douglass did this in a more elaborate manner than that shown in Table 6, and discovered the existence of 33 different kinds of activities. The most specialized occurred in less than 10 per cent of the churches; the most conventional religious activities were found in over 80 per cent of the churches. Thus the church may increase the *size* of its program by having many subgroups and activities of the limited religious sort, or it may increase the *range* of its program by spreading the activities it does support over the list so that its program includes some of the more novel features.

TABLE VI—Percentage of Churches Reporting Certain Specified Activities, in Each Type of Church [14]

Activities	Un-adapted	Slightly Adapted	Inter-nally Adapted	Types Socially Adapted	Widely Adven-turous	Variant Con-servative	Total
Cooperation with social agencies	26.7	43.4	61.6	84.4	41.3	77.1	49.2
Church office open daily	16.8	34.1	64.4	72.9	18.7	65.7	40.8
Organized athletics	13.1	27.2	52.0	69.8	20.0	54.3	34.5
Church open daily for devotion	8.4	14.7	26.0	41.7	10.7	25.7	18.8
Daily vacation Bible school	8.9	15.1	26.6	47.9	22.7	37.1	21.3
Motion pictures	3.7	10.8	22.6	40.6	20.0	40.0	17.0
Children's congregations	5.2	9.0	16.9	32.3	2.7	20.0	12.7
Week-day school of religious education	7.9	9.0	20.3	28.1	14.7	20.0	14.2
Children's sermons	4.2	9.7	14.7	32.3	. . .	28.6	12.0
Sunday evening tea	2.6	13.6	28.8	43.8	8.0	34.3	18.1
Forum	2.1	4.7	10.7	26.0	2.7	3.6	7.7
Room and board	1.0	1.1	1.1	9.4	1.3	2.9	2.1

This principle is shown graphically in Figure 3 and is the basis used by Douglass to determine the five types that he identifies. Table 6 shows the distribution of the constituent groups for these types. The connection between the more liberal types of church and the existence of specialized social services to the community is clearly shown.

Wider confirmation of the principle that local social institutions are definitely related to the immediate social environment is demonstrated by Murchie's study [15] of municipalities (corresponding to counties in the United States) of Manitoba, Canada. He measured the economic prosperity of municipalities by developing an index of economic productivity. Table 7

TABLE VII—The Relation of Local Institutions to Fundamental Economic Conditions [a]

Productivity Index Average = 100	Municipality with Special School Grants	Religious Services, No Resident Clergy	Medical Services, No Resident Physicians	Neither Medical Nor Religious Services Locally
Over 50	2	1	3	. .
41 to 50	2	3	3	2
31 to 40	5	4	5	3
0 to 30	12	13	15	13
Total	21	21	26	18

[a] Shows how with decline of economic conditions (productivity index) the ability to support locally such social institutions as schools, churches and medical services, diminishes.

shows how the ability of a locality to provide local support for its social institutions, schools, churches and medical services, varies with the economic condition of the locality; for when the economic index fell below 31, a considerable number of municipalities had to secure support for local institutions from the province of Manitoba or from the nation.

A picture of these contrasting types of churches, more graphic than that presented in statistical tables, may be obtained by considering brief case descriptions. We therefore reproduce descriptions of an unadapted church, a sub-modal church, and a slightly adapted church.

14. H. Paul Douglass, op. cit., p. 229.
15. R. W. Murchie, Unused Lands of Manitoba, 1927, p. 205.

THE UNADAPTED CHURCH. This diminutive Swedish Baptist Church has thirty-one members. There are only two smaller churches in the Northeastern city of 130,000 people in which it is located. It has no morning service. Its range of organizations and activities consists merely of an evening and a mid-week service, a Sunday school of twenty-eight members, a small young people's society and a ladies' aid organization to which the men of the

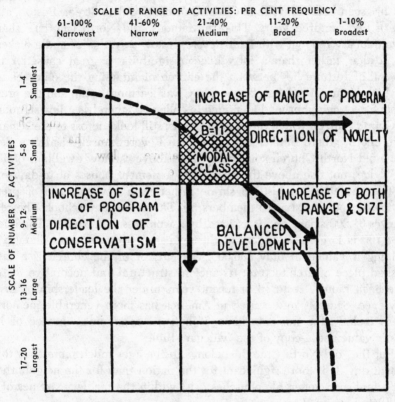

FIG. 3. Possible directions of development toward complexity of program. (Taken from Chart VI, H. P. Douglass, op. cit., p. 67.)

church are attached as honorary members. Twenty-five people constitute its average congregation and its weekly total of service-hours is 126. The Sunday school is made up exclusively of children, and has no adolescent classes. The pastor is neither theologically trained nor ordained. The place of worship is a room twenty-eight by thirty-seven feet in dimensions, built as a one-story addition against the small residence in which the pastor lives. Under these circumstances it is natural that the salary and average expenditures of the church are far below normal, while the total value of its property is but $6,000.

For ten years a mission of the Swedish Baptist Church in a neighboring city, this little group was recognized as a full church organization in 1905.

But throughout the last two decades it has had losses relatively larger than those of any other church in the city that still survives. Like other little churches, the only terms on which it can live at all, even with so limited a program, is by demanding a very high number of hours per week from its members. In this respect its record is sixteen and three-tenths hours per member—more than 50 per cent above the city average.[16]

THE SUB-MODAL CHURCH. No better example could be found of a church that has seen better days than Christ Church on Salem Street, Boston, at the end of two hundred years. This, the famous "old North Church," sharing Revolutionary renown with Paul Revere, is now a symbolic candle flickering on an altar rather than a lofty beacon signifying a great cause. A total reversal of fortune lies between the church maintaining the élite academy in which Henry Ward Beecher as a boy was learning Latin, and the present Salem Street neighborhood identified in college doggerel as a Jewish quarter.

Copp's Hill, on which the church stands, still looks across to the "Charlestown Shore" where Bunker Hill rises. Paul Revere himself has left a sketch of the old North Church spire rising high above the low dwellings of 1723; but it does not rise above the many-story tenement houses of to-day.

The church is an historic shrine rather than a vital place of present service. It counts sixty-two members but has no Sunday school. The rector receives $1,200 salary and is assisted by a woman social worker. The budget of $8,700 is largely expended on the upkeep of the property. Though this building is valued at only $56,000, the interior of the church is a distinguished piece of architecture. Its ancient structural and decorative features have been piously restored in recent years under the leadership of Bishop Lawrence. Scarcely any church in America has more venerable memorials. These include the ancient chime of bells, a communion service of high artistic value and a copy of the "vinegar" Bible.

But the "old North Church" belongs to the ages much more than to the present day. It is more significant for the nation than for the neighborhood. Not a few such venerable churches exist within the feebler extremes of the unadapted group.[17]

THE SLIGHTLY ADAPTED CHURCH. Urban conservatism rather than rural finds an example in a church of solid Teutonic virtues, though largely Americanized, located in a metropolitan city. Its relatively large and well-balanced Sunday school is a mark of the American rather than German traditions, and shows that the younger generation is ready to move on. For thirty-six years it has occupied the center of the middle-class residential district a little apart from the brewery industrial section, where the old-world flavor of the original German quarter is left behind and the tree-lined streets are fronted by houses showing the substantial and ugly American city architecture of a generation ago.

The present membership is just over 600. The pastor, a fully educated

---

16. H. Paul Douglass, *op. cit.*, p. 144.
17. *Ibid.*, p. 145.

man with twenty years' experience, has been seven and one-half years in his present position and seceives a salary of $1,650. The total budget of the church is $5,460 for current expenses—less than $10 per member—and nearly $1,200 for missions. With a well-equipped, though old-fashioned, building of ten rooms, seating 525 in the auditorium, and with thriving subsidiary organizations within a narrow range, the church is, nevertheless, unadapted from the standpoint of the average American city organization. It has no boys', girls' or young people's organizations. This reflects the pull-back of conservative tradition. In spite of its size and resources it stands a little to the rear of average American church progress.[18]

We may conclude from this study of the church as a social institution that its pattern of structure as well as its vitality is related to certain factors in its environment. Thus we have presented a picture of a social institution as an entity against the field of culture upon which it occurs.

---

18. *Ibid.*, p. 146.

MODERN RECREATION:
BACKGROUNDS AND PRESENT TRENDS

Jesse F. Steiner

THE LIMITED RECREATIONAL WORLD OF THE PAST. The unprecedented expansion of leisure during recent years is rapidly creating a new world with possibilities for the enjoyment of life that would have been deemed impracticable a generation ago. For long centuries the prodigal expenditure of time and strength in the struggle for a livelihood forced leisure into the background except for the favored few who were in a position to profit by the toil of the masses. Now, within the short period of a lifetime, the rapidly improving means of production have not merely banished all fears of inability to supply our needs, but have made it possible to shorten the hours of labor for many thousands of workingmen and give them more time for recreation than they are required to spend in their regular employment.

It is only within recent years that the public has taken any active interest in dealing with the problems of leisure. In these days when recreation is looked upon as a necessary part of life, it is difficult to realize that only a generation ago leisure-time activities were much less emphasized and in many cases were even frowned upon as a waste of time and energy. Ordinarily it was only on special holidays that our forefathers would turn aside from their daily pursuits to enjoy such outdoor games as were then available and many felt apologetic in this unaccustomed role. Even children were not permitted to give full vent to their irrepressible urge to play and had to content themselves with simple games that required a minimum of equipment. Recreational grounds provided at government expense were rarely found, and the so-called worldly amusements were only for the bolder spirits who were not deterred by the religious taboos of their day.

From the point of view of the present generation, the recreational opportunities of the past century were decidedly limited. The urban parks of today with their crowded beaches and swimming pools and athletic fields stand in striking contrast to the scenic but little-used parks of an earlier period. The automobile, which opened up a new world of pleasure,

Adapted from *Recreation and Morale: Teaching American Youth How to Plan and Use Leisure Time*, National Council for the Social Studies and National Association of Secondary-School Principals, by permission of the publisher. (Copyright, 1942, by the National Association of Secondary-School Principals, and the National Council for the Social Studies.)

travel, came into general use little more than two decades ago. The preceding generation knew nothing of the allurements of the motion picture. The popular use of the radio as a means of entertainment dates back no farther than the 1920's. The modern business or professional man who permits nothing to interfere with his round of golf and frequently enjoys a weekend motor trip to a distant place of interest belongs to a new recreational era without precedent in our earlier history.

It is well to remind ourselves that the present recreational pattern that has attained such wide vogue developed very slowly and for a long time was very limited in scope. Not only was it unfashionable for the past generation of adults to participate actively in athletic sports, but the lack of facilities made it impossible for them to do so. Even as late as 1900 participation in outdoor games was largely limited to members of athletic teams and to the wealthier classes who could afford to belong to private athletic or country clubs. It was in fact not until America's entrance into the World War in 1917 with the new emphasis upon wholesome outdoor games that recreation for adults gained wide popular support.

THE ROLE OF URBANIZATION. The rising tide of leisure-time activities during the past few decades marks the beginning of a new period in which the traditions of rural America finally gave way to the advance of an urbanized, industrial world. The new emphasis upon recreation first arose in cities and gained acceleration as urbanization advanced. As long as Americans were occupied chiefly with land settlement and the exploitation of natural resources, there was neither opportunity nor great necessity for an elaborate system of leisure-time pursuits. But with the growth of industry, cities began to expand and the whole tempo of American life changed. Large numbers of people hitherto accustomed to outdoor life were forced to work in factories and live in congested urban districts. As machinery improved, routine tasks became the common lot of workmen, thus adding greatly to the monotony of labor. With their work speeded up by the machine and their hours of labor measured by the time clock, there was little opportunity to mingle pleasure with toil as had been possible under more simple conditions of employment. The traditional amusements of a rural people became pitifully inadequate and unsatisfying for factory workers and businessmen.

One of the reactions to this advancing urbanization was a vigorous and successful demand for shorter hours of labor. The growth of machine industry has been accompanied by an expansion of leisure which would have been regarded as impossible at the beginning of the industrial revolution. It has been within this enlarged urban world of leisure that modern recreation has developed. Released from long hours of monotonous labor, workers in many different lines of employment have eagerly turned to recreational activities as an important part of their daily routine.

RISING STANDARDS OF LIVING. Closely associated with expanding leisure in urban communities has been the increasing capacity of a large proportion of the American public to make purchases beyond the mere necessities of life. While the general upward trend in money wages in this country during the past forty years has been in a considerable measure offset by higher prices of commodities, there can be no doubt of the wide prevalence of a higher standard of living than at the opening of the present century. One automobile for approximately every five persons in the population and a radio in almost every American home are facts indicative of a new scale of living unique in the history of our nation. It has been this financial surplus remaining after essential needs are met that has brought recreational activities within the reach of so many people. Increased purchasing power gave momentum to the recreation movement and made possible its recent expansion along so many lines. It could have developed in such an extensive manner only in a period when there was capacity on the part of the majority of the people to meet a rising tide of expenditures.

CHANGING ATTITUDES TOWARD RECREATION. This building of an urbanized, industrial world in which leisure-time activities found a congenial soil for development has been accompanied by a changing outlook on life with greater emphasis upon the values of play and recreation. The earlier prejudices against recreation gradually disappeared and were replaced by an almost equally intolerant belief in its value and necessity. In the eager rush to secure more time for recreational activities, Sunday blue laws were swept aside and the entire weekend has, for large numbers of people, been entirely turned over to the pursuit of pleasure. The growing interest in adult recreation has brought a new and powerful force into the struggle for shorter hours of labor. The opening of the doors of recreation to the mass of the people strengthens their determination to attain a standard of living that will include ample provision for the enjoyment of leisure. Municipalities have found it profitable to build up public recreational facilities and give them wide publicity in their efforts to attract new industries and increase their population. Breaking almost entirely with past traditions, the church and the school have expanded their activities to include recreational programs. Many industrial plants have adopted the policy of making some provision for the leisure-time activities of their employees. The exclusive country clubs of a generation ago have been supplemented by the organization of innumerable recreational associations designed to meet the needs of all classes of people.

RECENT TRENDS IN AMERICAN RECREATION. This extraordinary turning of the whole range of our institutional life toward the satisfaction of leisure-time needs is a revolutionary change of great significance. Never before has there been such a concentration of money and effort in building up the field of recreation. So elaborate are the provisions for the enjoyment of leisure that the more simple amusements and diversions of the past make no longer a wide appeal. The modern city-dweller lives and works under high tension and demands a great variety of thrilling pleasures.

Moreover, he does not now regard recreation as something to be reserved for an occasional holiday or even merely as a weekend activity. Each day must provide for hours of leisure a recreational program adjusted to the seasons as well as to the changing weather. No modern recreational program is complete unless it is varied enough to meet the needs of people of all ages with their widely varying interests and capacities. The unique characteristic of modern American recreation is the multiplicity of games, amusements, hobbies, and diversions widely available to all classes of people and utilized to an extent never dreamed possible in earlier years.

Any effort to sum up modern trends in American recreation must lay emphasis upon its universality, its wide diversity of activities, and the tendency toward frequent rather than occasional participation in its enjoyment. Other aspects of almost equal importance are the wide vogue of amusements that provide thrills and excitement, the desire to be on the move and to seek diversion through travel to distant places, the extraordinary interest in the outcome of competitive sports, both professional and amateur, the growing popularity of forms of recreation that can be jointly participated in by both men and women, the willingness to spend a considerable proportion of the family income for recreation, and the widespread use of the device of organization for the promotion of leisure-time interests.

THE VARIED NATURE OF RECREATIONAL PROBLEMS. Whatever may be our judgment concerning the desirability of these present trends in American recreation, it is clearly apparent that they have brought in their train a host of challenging problems to which serious attention must be given. These problems ramify in many directions and assume varied forms as they invade different areas of our community life. The family, the state, the school, the church, and the industrial and business world have been compelled to abandon traditional policies and procedures that have been outmoded by the changing recreational habits and attitudes of the people. No part of our institutional framework has escaped the impact of the modern recreation movement.

The widespread scope of the recreational problem stands out most clearly, however, when we think of it as an insistent demand on the part of vast numbers of people for more abundant and satisfying recreational facilities and leisure in which to enjoy them. Recreation has become so securely entrenched in the habits and folkways of the people that it is a dominating force affecting the whole range of their activities. Adults as well as our youth have become impatient with the failure of leisure-time facilities to keep pace with the expansion of leisure and mounting recreational desires. The problem that looms large before them is how can the world of recreation meet the needs of the vast mass of our people. It is this phase of the recreational problem that comes closest home to the general public and gives it a significance it never possessed during the earlier years of our history.

EXPANSION AND DISTRIBUTION OF LEISURE. Without the spectacular expansion of leisure during recent years, the present emphasis upon widespread recreational opportunities and facilities could not have been possible. This boon of greater leisure for our toiling millions made its most rapid advance during the preceding decade and represents one of the great achievements of modern civilization. The widespread acceptance of the forty-hour week has multiplied free time enormously.

A slight computation makes clear the amount of free time at the disposal of the worker employed on a forty-hour-week schedule. Allowing twelve hours a day for sleep, eating, travel to and from work, and so forth, the spare time remaining for the cultivation of his own interests is more than five hours a day for six days a week with Sunday thrown in as an additional full day of leisure. Or if his forty hours of work are completed within five days, he has remaining two full days of leisure besides four hours of free time on each of his working days. Computed in a similar way, the worker who formerly was compelled to work twelve hours a day had no free time except on Sunday, and the one working ten hours had only two hours of free time each working day.

This new leisure is by no means an entirely new development for it has been coming in cumulative fashion during the past 100 years. In the early part of the nineteenth century when even children were working in English mills sixteen and eighteen hours a day and when a twelve-hour day was regarded as a goal difficult of universal attainment, leisure for the mass of the working people was nothing more than an illusive dream. But with the advance of the machine age hours of labor began to be shortened. The twelve-hour day became less common, and finally in 1923 it was routed from the steel industry, its last great stronghold. Strikes for a shorter workday characterized the closing quarter of the last century, and progress was made gradually toward the goal of an eight-hour day. The forty-hour week, to which so much publicity was given during the financial depression of the 1930's, was by no means a new attainment, but its sudden application to so many lines of work and the remarkable manner in which it was accepted as a method of overcoming unemployment caught the imagination of the American people and gave new impetus and status to this long and dramatic struggle for a larger amount of leisure.

This new leisure has without doubt come to stay. The shorter workday and the shorter workweek must be reckoned with as permanent facts. The busy bee that toils early and late so that it may not come to want is no longer an appropriate symbol for our modern industrial world. We have entered upon a period when we do not point with pride to achievements made possible by unremitting toil. Our emphasis upon the beneficence of labor now includes also provision for adequate leisure. The old idea that "the devil finds work for idle hands to do" expresses a suspicion of leisure out of touch with our new thought and practice. The American ideal is to do our work expeditiously so that plenty of time may remain for the cultivation of leisure-time interests.

This struggle to reduce the hours of work has brought forcibly to our attention the great inequalities in the distribution of leisure. Many thousands of farm laborers, domestic servants, and unorganized workers in various occupations and places have as yet made little advance toward the goal of a shorter workday. Much still remains to be accomplished before the trend toward reduction of the hours of employment has successfully invaded all the fields of labor. When this problem of unequal distribution of leisure is examined more closely, it is found to be too complicated to be solved merely by limiting the length of the workday or the work week. Not all have regular employment, and vast numbers are not forced to work by the clock. The farmer's work is largely seasonal, followed by periods of comparative idleness. The casual and seasonal labor of hundreds of thousands employed in agriculture, business, and industry is characterized by extreme irregularity. The free time of housewives varies widely depending upon labor-saving devices, number and age of children, and standards set up by the family for housekeeping activities. Small shopkeepers and professional people operating independently have their hours of work determined largely by the demands made upon them in their competitive struggle for a living. School children spend no more than half their waking hours in school and home work, and during week ends and vacations the vast majority under the legal working age have almost unlimited free time at their disposal.

These examples are sufficient to show the impracticability of setting up the forty- or the thirty-hour week as a pattern to be followed in reducing the inequalities in the distribution of leisure. In a complex civilization not all can have free time at week ends or during early evenings when leisure seems so highly desirable. Some kinds of employment must continue throughout the night hours, and the seasonal nature of certain jobs cannot be entirely eliminated. For large numbers of people leisure can be made available only during inconvenient hours or in large blocks of time interspersed with long periods of intensive labor. The nature and amount of leisure vary with the different occupations and types of employment and should be taken into consideration when choice of a vocation is made. No doubt the desirability of various lines of work is being measured more and more not merely by the financial rewards, but by the extent to which they make possible regular hours of leisure.

COMMERCIALIZATION OF SPORTS AND GAMES. The modern expansion of recreational facilities owes a great deal of its rapid advance to business enterprise. Commercial interests were quick to take advantage of the rising tide of recreation and exploit for financial profit the growing leisure of the people. This provision of recreation on a commercial basis is as legitimate and inevitable as is the supply of food and other articles needed in daily living. So widespread has been this movement toward the commercialization of leisure that it is now a dominant force in the recreational world. At the present time commercial interests are in control of many different forms of sports and amusements, and their position is becoming more securely entrenched by greater efficiency in business organization. The total amount of recreation that is made available on this commercial basis is enormous and provides for a very considerable share of the leisure time of a large portion of our population.

The widespread interest of the public in games and sports has made this type of recreation a very lucrative one for those engaged in exploiting it for financial gain. Baseball, for example, has been so thoroughly commercialized that it is operated as a big business with its leading players on a professional basis devoting their whole time to the game during the playing season. College football, on the other hand, is played by men who maintain their amateur standing, but the huge investments in grandstands and stadiums, the publicity designed to attract large crowds, the high prices charged for admission, the efforts made to recruit secondary-school graduates known to be good players, and the large profits in many instances at the end of the playing season, make it clearly evident that the game is dominated by the commercial spirit even though not promoted by commercial interests. This tendency toward commercialization has brought upon this popular sport a storm of criticism on the part of those who feel that college youth should not be exploited for the financial gain of the institution they represent. Already some of the colleges and universities have taken steps toward a reorganization of their athletic programs with less emphasis upon intercollegiate football. Students are urging the adoption of a policy that will give them wider opportunities for participation in games of their choice. Perhaps the increasing difficulties in arousing popular interest in football games where championships are not at stake indicate a decline in the overemphasis of this college sport. Apparently professional football, which has rapidly advanced in public favor, may eventually supplant the college game because of the superior skill of the players. In the future, public interest may shift from the college to the professional game—as has been the case with college baseball, which continues to be a popular sport among college students without being exploited as a public spectacle.

This exploitation of a sport for financial gain can be seen most clearly in the field of professional boxing or prize fighting which draws huge crowds and stands first in its ability to produce large gate receipts. At ten boxing matches held during the decade 1921-30, the amount paid for admission tickets averaged more than a million dollars at each contest. The receipts at the famous Dempsey-Tunney fight for the heavyweight championship at Chicago in 1927 totalled $2,650,000. During recent years these extravagant expenditures have not been duplicated, but professional championship bouts are still sufficiently popular to make this sport profitable for those engaged in its promotion. Its fascination for many people consists in the fact that it is a bodily combat sport with serious risks of physical injury. Some of the most popular boxers have been sluggers capable of giving and taking a large amount of punishment. It is this aspect of boxing that makes possible the high prices of admission to championship fights, but it prevents the sport from winning complete public approval.

Among the indoor games that have been exploited by commercial interests, pool, billiards, and bowling have long occupied a position of importance. These games make their appeal to participants rather than to spectators and are well adapted to wide use, since they do not require great physical strength and can be played enjoyably by persons of moderate skill. Unfortunately, the unsavory reputation of many commercial pool halls caused by their close association with gambling interests has retarded their growth and limited their patronage. The present trend seems to be away from the small, ill-kept places in second-rate business sections to large well-equipped halls better located and designed to appeal to a higher type of clientele. The bowling alleys have been especially successful in breaking away from many of their undesirable associations and now enjoy a much higher status. Nevertheless, in spite of improved conditions in many instances, these commercial amusement centers are frequently headquarters for racetrack and baseball pools and attract among their patrons many who are chiefly interested in their betting and gaming devices.

Wrestling, ice hockey, basketball, tennis, and golf are other sports which have produced professional players whose skill has been utilized in public contests and exhibitions for the making of money. The commercialization of sport can be further seen in the opportunities presented to popular amateur athletes and winners of championships to capitalize their fame by starring in moving pictures, appearing in vaudeville skits, giving endorsements of commodities, or engaging in professional exhibitions of their skill. The financial rewards that may be secured by athletes during the height of their fame are greater than ever before and are made possible by wide publicity in the sports pages of newspapers, which make their names household words throughout the nation. After the amateur sportsman of the present day has won his cups and medals, it is taken for granted that he will sacrifice his amateur status for financial gain. Not all respond to this lure of gold, but the public looks with toleration, if not with full approval, upon this growing tendency to commercialize fame and skill in the field of sports.

SPECTATORISM VERSUS ACTIVE FORMS OF RECREATION. The extraordinary public interest in commercialized sports and amusement during recent years has led to a rather widespread belief that Americans prefer to be amused by others rather than to participate actively in sports and games. There can be no doubt that opportunities to enjoy passive amusements have recently become more numerous and attractive. Moving pictures provide a form of entertainment that is far more popular than dramatic plays of a generation ago. Athletic contests and games may be no more interesting than formerly, but great advance has been made in providing comfortable and commodious seating facilities for spectators. Those who do not wish to venture forth from their own homes can through the radio or television follow the progress of important games and enjoy a wide variety of entertainment. Under these circumstances it is inevitable that passive amusements should form a very considerable part of our leisure-time activities.

While huger crowds assemble to witness sports and amusements than was customary a decade or two ago, this growth of spectatorism has been a part of the expansion of cities and has been paralleled by advances made in many other lines. The building of large stadiums, and the expansion of other facilities for passive amusements have been accompanied by increased acreage of public parks, and by a rapidly growing number of athletic fields, golf courses, tennis courts, swimming pools, and bathing beaches constructed for the use of large numbers of people. The crowds that fill the baseball and football stadiums are apparently matched, although in a less spectacular way, by the hundreds of thousands of golf and tennis enthusiasts and by the multitudes that throng the municipal bathing beaches.

As a matter of fact, in the development of American athletic sports, the two roles of participant and observer have been combined in a very effective manner. The profits from college football have in many instances been utilized in building up a comprehensive system of intramural athletics. Attendance at professional games has stimulated interest in outdoor sports and aided in developing a public opinion that has insisted upon municipal appropriations for playing fields for the people. Grandstands and stadiums for spectators represent the most economical use of space for the enjoyment of sports and make possible wholesome entertainment for the many thousands who for various reasons cannot actively participate in sports and games.

In spite of the fact that many people spend much of their leisure in watching others play, it is noteworthy that it is becoming difficult to get public support of games where championships are not at stake or where widely known and popular players do not participate. The major-league ball parks are crowded to full capacity during the world series, but the teams that fall behind during the playing season do not attract many spectators. The curve of football attendance at universities rises and falls each year depending upon the quality of the team and its chance of winning a championship. A certain number of people may attend games simply because of their interest in watching a contest, but the large crowds are found only at important games to which wide publicity has been given by the newspaper press. The most striking fact about athletic sports today is not the cheering crowds on the sidelines but the large numbers of players, both young and old, the men and women, who are eager to improve their own game in competition with their fellows.

The widespread tendency of people to play more or less passive roles in their leisure-time pursuits is a part of the growing emphasis upon what may be called mass recreation. When leisure becomes more widely available, as has been the case in recent years, more attention must be given to forms of diversion that are inexpensive to the individuals as well as economical in the use of space. Bathing beaches and public parks where crowds can congregate—grandstands, field houses, and auditoriums which facilitate picture and the radio and television that enable millions to spend leisure hours enjoyably at minimum expense—fulfill to a remarkable degree the essential conditions for giving recreation greater universality. In view of the great need for interesting diversions on a wide scale at a low per capita cost, more efforts should be made to canvass the possibility of developing new types of mass recreation that would be both satisfying and inexpensive. It is especially important to know, as we make further plans for public recreation, whether there should be greater emphasis upon grandstands, auditoriums, and similar facilities designed to bring together people *en masse* during their leisure hours. Perhaps this aspect of the public recreation movement has been neglected because of our interest in developing wider participation in competitive sports and games for those full of youth and vigor.

COMMERCIAL EXPLOITATION OF NIGHT LIFE. The leisure time most available for the vast mass of the people comes at the close of the normal working day and extends for many far into the night. It is during this period of relaxation in the evening hours that the streets in urban amusement centers are filled with people seeking amusements and diversions of their choice. For the most part they must look to commercial enterprises for the entertainment they seek, a large share of which is of high quality and is provided without excessive cost. Theaters, moving-picture houses, dance halls, cafes, night clubs, road houses, and playlands abound in urban centers and their adjacent hinterlands and provide popular diversions patronized by immense numbers of people. Cities take great pride in their amusement streets or white ways with their bright lights and attractive establishments for the enjoyment of evening leisure. This provision of entertainment on a profit basis has developed into one of our most important industries employing large numbers of people and representing investments of more than two billion dollars. Through this utilization of competitive business methods a large world of amusement has been built up with types of activities and prices adapted to the requirements of people in widely different walks of life.

However desirable or necessary this invasion of business into the world of leisure, the desire to increase financial profits frequently leads to the promotion and establishment of demoralizing forms of popular entertainment. The exploitation of leisure has proved to be a profitable financial venture for those business interests that play upon human weakness and promote habits that tend to degrade rather than to build up. Liquor, gambling, and vice have long been favorite money-making devices found not only in the underworld but closely associated with socially approved forms of entertainment patronized by the general public.

Prior to the World War of 1914-18, the purveyors of liquors were among the most successful exploiters of the surplus time and money of the rank and file of our working people. The saloon was popularly known as the workingmen's club, and behind its swinging doors and glazed windows were found stimulation for jaded nerves, social intercourse with congenial friends, and forgetfulness of the toil necessary in the struggle for existence. But the evils of this way of spending leisure overbalanced its contribution as a needed social center, and it was legally abolished in 1918 as a festering sore in American urban life. It is not without significance that the repeal of the Eighteenth Amendment in 1933 which ended the Federal experiment with prohibition coincided with the remarkable expansion of leisure during the financial depression. Immediately beer parlors, cabarets, night clubs, road houses, and similar types of liquor dispensing places were established in large numbers and strong efforts were made through advertising and entertainment features to build up patronage and make institutions of these kinds popular places for the spending of leisure. The large amount of liquor consumed in recent years and the mounting Federal tax receipts from cabarets and night clubs furnish some evidence of the growing popularity of forms of amusement associated with the sale and drinking of liquor. Under conditions as they exist today, this expansion of the cafe type of entertainment constitutes an even more serious problem than it did during pre-Volstead days. The larger role of semi-automatic and high-speed machinery that requires skillful handling, the streets congested with automobiles with their constant menace to human life, and the growing amount of leisure to be spent either constructively or destructively are among the new conditions that make extremely dangerous a close alliance between liquor and entertainment as a means of financial gain. The old cafe type of spending leisure drinking with a party of friends will doubtless remain in popular favor as one of our many forms of recreation. Public interest, however, demands that this way of spending leisure should not through the efforts of commercial interests become a dominant feature of the modern recreaional world.

SOME POLITICAL INFLUENCES
OF URBANIZATION

Philip M. Hauser

The Constitution of the United States which established the framework of our Federal government and, in the main, the constitutions of the individual states, which created our forms of local government were drawn in a pre-industrial rural setting. The political thought which dominated the minds of early Americans in the critical period during which the Federal government, and many of the State and local governments were established, was a complex compact of many strains reflecting the transition of the political order from a feudal-autocratic to a liberal-democratic state. The technological, economic and social changes introduced by the industrial revolution and urbanization of America have posed problems of political organization and policy which our founding fathers could not possibly have foreseen. It is small wonder then that our inherited political institutions and thought have been greatly altered and that they are still in process of accommodation to the rapidly changing urbanized scene.

A good starting point for our examination of some of the political influences of urbanism is the government of the city itself.

GOVERNMENT IN THE METROPOLITAN AREA. Our city governments are creatures of the State. They owe their corporate existence to charters granted by the State which frequently contain more or less arbitrary delineations of their legal boundaries. Thus, the American city as a legal entity is more or less rigidly defined by constitutional or legislative provision.

But the American city as an economic, population and social phenomenon has not been rigidly defined. Our expanding economy and rapid urban development have had little regard for the political boundaries of the city. In fact, a study of United States Census volumes restricted to a consideration of the population and other characteristics of the city as a political unit obscures rather than reveals the nature of our contemporary urban agglomerations.[1] The American city as an economic and social reality has long since spilled over its political boundaries and has assumed quite altered patterns of organization within them. The story of this development

---

Portion of an essay originally presented to the Conference on Evaluation of Social Institutions in America at the Princeton University Bicentennial, October, 1946.

1. That the U.S. Bureau of the Census is aware of this is evidenced by its ever expanding publications of data for metropolitan areas.

is the story of the growth of the metropolitan area. The metropolitan area [2] is more nearly the unit of urbanism than is the city for it more nearly includes the entire group of economic and social structures and processes and population aggregations which make up our urban communities.

The failure, to date, of our inherited local political structures to adapt themselves to the changed urban economic and social environment is strikingly portrayed by two startling anomalies. The first is the complete lack of coincidence between the jurisdictional boundaries of local governments and the real boundaries of the urban community as represented by the metropolitan area. The second is the maze of overlapping and duplicating governmental units within our cities as well as in our metropolitan areas.

It is to these anachronisms that one can trace many of the major problems besetting local government and the aura of confusion which surrounds the many well intentioned efforts to cope with these problems. The almost complete inability of our inherited forms of local government to cope with the problems of contemporary urban life are at once brought to mind by merely pointing to the revenue and expenditure muddles both within local governmental units and in the relation of local to other levels of government; and to the many specific problems in respect to housing, transportation, utilities, traffic congestion, slums and blighted areas, sanitation and public health, and planning and zoning. Nor are the evidences of political disorganization represented by the corrupt political machine, graft, favoritism, the "big fix" and election frauds unrelated to this basic "lag" in the accommodation of our local political institutions to the changed urban environment.

LEVELS OF GOVERNMENT. The creation and development of the Federal, State and local levels of government in the United States may be regarded as a natural outgrowth of the pre-industrial, rural structure of our nation. In a country comprising relatively homogeneous self-sufficient, rural units, it was plausible and feasible to delineate arbitrary boundaries as jurisdictional units of government both within and between the historic levels of government framed in our Federal and State constitutions.

The complex, interdependent and urban character of contemporary life imposes many strains on this governmental heritage. The metropolitan dis-

---

2. The Bureau of the Census and other federal agencies have attempted to delineate this more realistic urban agglomeration. For the 1940 and some prior censuses, the "metropolitan district" was defined by the Bureau of the Census for cities with 50,000 or more inhabitants as consisting of the central city plus all continguous minor civil districts having a population density of at least 50 per square mile. For the 1950 census, the Bureau of the Census has adopted the new "standard metropolitan areas" prepared by an interdepartmental committee of the federal government under the leadership of the Division of Statistical Standards of the Bureau of the Budget in the Executive Office of the President. These areas consist of groupings of counties containing one or more central cities having a population of 50,000 or more inhabitants. For the 1950 census, the Bureau of the Census has also devised a new urban geographic concept, the "urbanized area." This area is, in general, defined as the built-up area contiguous to, as well as including the central city.

trict has disregarded State as well as city limits. The problems of the river valley, often augmented by urban complications, transcend city and state boundaries. The clash of "urban" and "rural," "upstate" and "downstate" and sectional interests cut across our traditional governmental jurisdictions. The new requirements and problems of urban existence which have necessitated the expansion of government functions have posed new problems of division of labor and cooperation among the agencies in our different levels of government.

New agencies and procedures of intergovernmental cooperation, designed to deal with the new problems with which our inherited governmental structures could not cope, have emerged; such as those represented by the New York Port Authority, the Tennessee Valley Authority; the Federal grant-in-aid, the United States Employment Service (in varying forms), the Federal Security Agency, the various cooperative agricultural programs, and the State and City Planning Commission. In the main, however, the problems of intergovernmental cooperation are yet to be resolved and the course of future developments in intergovernmental level cooperation will, in large measure, reflect the attempts of the Federal, State and local governments to come to grips with the new and real problems of urbanization.

THE ROLE OF GOVERNMENT. Much of our current political controversy hinges around divergence in concepts of the proper role of government. To this divergence in concepts the rapid urbanization of America has made a major contribution.

At the risk of extreme oversimplification, it may be said that foremost in the concept of the role of government in our political heritage is emphasis on the tenet that "that government is best which governs least." This doctrine coupled with the liberal tradition in economic thinking that each man acting in his own interest automatically acts in the interest of the larger whole constitutes, fundamentally, the inherited framework of principles central to the bitter contemporary debate over the function of our Federal government.

It is a tribute to the forces of social change that despite the dominance of these principles in our political philosophy the record shows that the functions of American government, on all levels, have tremendously expanded and multiplied in the course of our history; and that the expansion has been continuous without regard to the complexion of the political party in power.

The major explanation for the rapidly expanding functions of our governments is to be found in the complex of technological, economic and social changes which constitute "urbanization." The new physical and economic structure produced by the industrial and urban revolutions, the increasing interdependence of the various elements of our economic and social order, the breakdown of traditional social controls, the inability of our inherited social institutions to cope with the new situations and new problems of urban life led inexorably to the manifold expansion of government functions and powers—a process by no means yet complete.

A few concrete examples may serve to clarify this point. Certainly there is some relationship between the inability of the family to meet the educational requirements of our contemporary urban civilization and the expanded participation of government in formal education. Similarly, there is more than a casual connection between the inability of the family as an inherited social institution to cope with the security problems posed by urban health hazards, industrial accidents, and unemployment; and the development of public health services, workmen's compensation laws and unemployment insurance benefits.

The creation of the Interstate Commerce Commission, the Federal Trade Commission, the Federal Security Agency, the Securities and Exchange Commission, the Council of Economic Advisers, and the Atomic Energy Control Commission, to confine ourselves to selected agencies in the Federal government, are but a few examples of expanded functions of government necessitated by the voids and gaps created by differential rates of growth and development of our economic, social and political orders. Additional examples could be multiplied almost indefinitely, ranging from the government interventionism represented by the installation of traffic signals and parking meters to the development of the T.V.A. and the growing pressure for a strong United Nations.

The influence of urbanization is by no means restricted to political philosophy of domestic import. Urbanization as both a cause and effect of increasing international economic and social interdependence is exerting pressures on other aspects of our political heritage. Our traditional concepts of "nationalism" and "sovereignty," for example, no more than the negative concept of the role of government have been subjected to strain. The historic offer to abrogate at least a part of our national sovereignty contained in the recent so-called Baruch proposals in respect to international control of atomic energy is at least one indication of how far modern urban civilization has undermined our inherited concept of sovereignty; and the new forms of international organization emerging from current efforts to weld the United Nations, afford striking examples of the deterioration of our traditional concept of nationalism. If developments in nuclear physics permit the continuation of our urban civilization, it may confidently be expected that our historical conceptions of nationalism and sovereignty will be forced to retreat even further, no matter how brilliant and forceful may be the rear guard delaying action.

All of the agencies which emerged with new responsibilities and new functions in our local, State and Federal and now international levels of government, may be regarded as social inventions, originating in the needs created by the frictions and problems engendered in a changing social order. It is a significant indication of the present stage of our development that such social inventions are by no means received with the same acclaim and reward afforded to the physical and mechanical inventions; despite the fact that it is the effects of the latter that frequently create the economic, social or political dislocation which the social inventions are designed to meet.

PUBLIC ADMINISTRATION. It is evident that urbanization has greatly altered the character and the problems of public administration particularly as they affect the executive and the legislative branches of government. The increased complexity and technical character of urban problems, coupled with the expanded functions of government have placed a premium in public administration, on the one hand, on the specialist and technician in government; and, on the other hand, on the coordinator and integrator to bring cohesion and unity into a complex and far-flung government structure.

Many phases of public administration in the urban setting call for highly professionalized skills—and, in fact, the record clearly shows that great advances have been made in the acquisition by government agencies, on all levels, of competent professional personnel. Yet the boundary between the technical province of the specialist, and the policy province of the legislator or executive is by no means clearly drawn and recognized. The result is seen in the widespread confusion and distrust that exists among officials in the executive branch of government, between the legislative and executive branches of government and often between these branches and the judiciary on the Federal, State and local levels. It is seen also in the lack of adequate mechanisms within the executive branches of government to assure coordination and integration of policy and program; and often in the absence of sufficient specialized skills within legislative bodies or on their staffs to comprehend, let alone intelligently deal with, some of the problems with which they are confronted.

These difficulties are another example of the lag in the adjustment of our inherited political institutions to the new conditions of urban existence. That there is increasing awareness of this lag is, among other things, evidenced by such recent actions of the Congress as in the "streamlining" of its organization and procedures, and in providing for the Council of Economic Advisers; and in the efforts of the President to reorganize the Federal establishment.

REPRESENTATIVE GOVERNMENT. Urbanization has also had, and is still exerting, an influence on the nature of "representative" government. The representative form of government for which provision was made in the Constitution of the United States represented a departure from the democracy of the Greek city-state, but was certainly "democratic" in its rural setting in the sense that delegates of the people in the Congress could be expected to represent the relatively homogeneous population of their districts (that is, the enfranchised part of their districts). The heterogeneous character, even more than the size, of the Congressional district or the State in contemporary life, poses the question of just how a member of the Congress "represents" his constituents.

On the one hand, despite the broadened base of the electorate, improved and widened public education, and almost instantaneous forms of public communication, the typical voter often has little knowledge of the personal attitudes, opinions and principles of the official for whom he votes; and frequently not much knowledge of the principles of the political party, particularly as they affect his interests, with which his candidate is affiliated. On the other hand, the elected public official from any of our urban areas is faced with the almost impossible task of determining just what are the interests of his own heterogeneous constituency as well as of the city, of the State and of the nation as a whole.

It may be argued, and often is, that better government can be achieved if our representatives think in terms of the interests of the population as a whole rather than special sectional or regional interests; and that the judgment of the official is often better than the judgment of the electorate. However this may be, it is clear that the complexity and heterogeneity of urban existence have introduced new variables into the theory of "representative" government.

In the absence of clearly defined mandates by the people or explicit formulation of principles by the candidate and official, policy and specific legislation in our political process has become more and more the resultant of the forces set in motion by the lobby and insistent pressures of special interest groups. These forces do not necessarily result in "bad" policy or in "bad" legislation but neither do they necessarily result in policy or legislation accurately reflecting the "will of the people."

Recent developments in the measurement of public opinion made possible by advances in the science and art of sampling, psychometrics and sociometrics afford some clue to means by which the "will of the people" can more directly be reflected in the political process. Certainly the results of some of the public opinion polls suggest that our legislatures defy as well as follow the wishes of the electorate.

When one considers, on the one hand, the heterogeneous character of urban life, its diversity and conflict of interests and its dynamic and rapid tempo; and, on the other hand, the electoral process and the relative insensitivity of our form of government to public opinion (as contrasted with the Parliamentary form of government), it is clear that urbanism poses new questions of "representative" government that have not yet been squarely met.

It is partly in recognition of these problems that our political leaders, political scientists and others have been paying increasing attention to problems of public opinion and its measurement, to problems of political psychology, and to the study of the political party.

THE POLITICAL PARTY. The complexity and heterogeneity of urban life also affect political parties as an element in our form of representative government. The two party system which many regard as a necessary adjunct of our form of government also shows many evidences of strain emanating from the problems of urbanization.

It does not take a profound student to detect a greater range of interests and principles and a wider diversity of political philosophies within than between each of the contemporary major political parties. It is easy to see the historic differences that led to the founding of our great parties; and to distinguish between the historical differences in the political philosophy of the solid Democratic South, and rockbound Republican New England. But the new maze of local, regional, national and international issues introduced in no small measure by the complexities and problems of urban civilization has obscured the historic differences between our parties.

It is a wise voter who knows just what he is espousing when he votes in national elections for a Republican party which embraces Taft and Vandenberg on the one hand; and Morse and LaFollette on the other; or a Democratic party which contains Bilbo and Rankin and also Wallace and Pepper.[3] To be sure, many voters if they make their choice on the basis of rational rather than traditional or emotional considerations, may do so in terms of difference of degree in liberalism or conservatism or differences in degree of other attributes of the respective parties; rather than on the basis of clear-cut differences of policy on general or specific issues. In the main, however, it is clear that there is considerable confusion and no clear-cut party differences as such, in many of the major issues that enter the political process.

A number of factors, some of which derive from the urban setting, account for this state of affairs. For one thing, our major political parties have in the nature of their historical development encompassed both urban and rural populations. The conflict of interests between farm and city populations has in recent years been both ameliorated and augmented. They have been softened by the increasing awareness on the part of both urban and rural populations of their mutual interdependence; but they have, also, been sharpened by the strengthened organization of the farmer and the increased organization of the urban worker. These organized groups often pressing for their own special interests have exerted pressures on both of the political parties and forced similar concessions from both.

The city has had still another important effect on the political party. Just as other forms of tradition tend to be modified or to break down in the urban environment, so also does the tradition of political party affiliation. In the urban environment there is an ever increasing proportion of persons who select rather than inherit their party affiliation. The "independent" voter has demonstrated that he holds the balance of power in national elections; and it is in seeking the support of the urban independent voter, therefore, that another force is set in motion which tends to obscure the differences in party principles and in party platform planks.

Certainly the attempts of both parties to capture the "farm vote," the "vote of organized labor" and the urban "independent vote" account in some measure for the increasing pressure placed on parties for drawing platforms

---

3. Editor's note: This was written in 1946.

designed to reconcile the interests of conflicting groups and for the increased difficulty of distinguishing between the parties. It may be that the function of reconciling conflicting special interests is one of the important contributions of the political party to our form of government, but in practice it has often resulted in platforms that have evaded rather than dealt squarely with difficult issues. In such a situation the citizen, in voting, frequently has no knowledge of just what principles and policies he is supporting; and the elected officer in the performance of his duties has no more knowledge of the policy preferences of his constituents.

The multi-party system prevalent in parts of Europe may in part be ascribed to the expression of the diversity of interests produced by modern life. To that extent it may provide a better vehicle for "representative" government. Yet the apparent difficulties of the multi-party system, especially if transplanted to the American scene and the American form of government, would probably afford no solution to these problems.

Here again is ample evidence of the frictions produced by a rapidly changing social order. It remains for the future to produce the right kind of lubricant to reduce the evident heat and the wear and tear that this political friction has injected into the contemporary scene.

POLITICAL ISSUES. The pervasive and insistent character of the problems of urbanization are also evident in an examination of some of our major contemporary political issues.

Even before the "New Deal" of Franklin D. Roosevelt, problems originating in the urban community came to the fore as major national political issues. The battle for the "income tax," and the Federal Reserve System, the enfranchisement of women, workmen's compensation laws, and antitrust legislation are but a few examples that can in large measure be interpreted as issues having their origin in the changing urban order. More recently, the "New Deal" itself, as well as many of the specific innovations it introduced into the political arena, affords additional testimony of the extent to which the city has contributed to our political battlefront.

The election of President Roosevelt in 1933 and in his three additional successful campaigns can be attributed largely to the dissatisfaction of the people of this nation with the failure of his predecessors to deal with perhaps the major problem of American urban civilization—economic depression. Although the farmer is also adversely affected by depression, he, by reason of his tie to the soil, can usually manage to survive it on a low subsistence level of existence. The major brunt of depression is undoubtedly borne by the urban population—by the large masses of under-employed and unemployed, the small businessman and other urban residents with limited savings.

The proliferation of alphabetical agencies in the early days of the "New Deal" was largely designed to deal with urban problems of depression. Much of the permanent legislation resulting from this period, such as that relating to Social Security, labor organizations, the stock market, the banks, and housing, were aimed directly at the unsolved problems of urbanism. The embittered debate over "full employment," resulting in the enactment of "The Employment Act of 1946," still reflects the force of this major political issue which will undoubtedly remain with us as long as the fluctuations of the business cycle.

A major part of President Truman's legislative program which was rejected by the 79th Congress was addressed to urban problems—for example, the extension of Social Security, public health insurance, an expanded housing program and minimum wage laws. It can confidently be predicted that these and similar issues are in American politics to stay; and that the changed pattern of urban existence will continue to be fertile soil for the production of new political issues.

SUMMARY AND CONCLUSION. The United States in the course of a single century has developed from a small, homogeneous and predominantly rural society into a large, heterogeneous, industrialized and urbanized nation. The rapid industrialization and urbanization which we have experienced, in a basic sense, may be described as a major technological and economic revolution. They have introduced major changes in the material and structural elements of our economic and social organization which have produced great strains and stresses on other elements in our social heritage— in our institutions and mores, our systems of conduct and thought.

The material elements of culture seem, in general, to be much more subject to change than do the non-material elements. Thus the technological aspects of culture change more rapidly than do our social and political institutions and our mores. This differential rate of social change among the elements of our social heritage result in cultural frictions, lags, and anachronisms. Certainly the differential rates of change between the material and non-material aspects of culture is particularly characteristic of our own culture in which a great premium is placed on physical invention and innovation, with no counterpart in the realm of non-material or social invention.

The selected political influences of urbanization discussed above may be readily comprehended within this framework. The non-material elements of our contemporary economic, social and political order may be described as being in various stages of accommodation to the new technology and economic structure produced by the industrial revolution. The major influence of urbanization on our social and political institutions and ideologies has been, in brief, to make them, in varying degrees, obsolescent.

The problems of urbanization—personal, social and political—are but symptoms of the frictions produced by the differential rates of change in our social heritage. But reorganization can never be achieved without a certain amount of disorganization. There are always among us nostalgic souls who feel that the price of adjustment to a changing world is not "worth the candle" and who long for a return to the "good old times." Certainly this position can be defended, but it is on the face of it romantic and unrealistic. We can be comforted, if we need comfort, by the many obvious advantages and advances which the industrial revolution and the city have brought with them, including an ever rising standard of living and an unprecedented opportunity for personal expression and creation.

The adjustments necessary to achieve an integrated and consistent social heritage can conceivably be attained in time through "natural" processes—through the forces which produce the "strain toward consistency" in our culture. This process of social evolution is perhaps something paralleling the biological "struggle for existence" and the "survival of the fittest" in respect to culture traits and culture complexes.

Unlike the rest of the animal kingdom, however, man has it within his power to speed up the social evolutionary process—to accelerate the adjustment of social and political institutions and ideologies to the new requirements forced by technological and structural change. Indeed, one of the most important influences of urbanization lies in the emancipation of the person from the rigidities and restraints imposed upon him by tradition —in the new opportunity—in large measure forced upon him by the nature of urban existence—to be a rational animal and to intervene in the processes of social change so as to exert some control over its tempo and its direction.

That we have, in some measure, availed ourselves of this opportunity is clear. For example, the "natural" processes through which the American city has grown, which have been described in some detail by the ecologist and sociologist, are being subject to the increasing interference and interventionism of city planning and city zoning. The new functions of governments on the local, State and Federal levels include increasing provision for planning for the future as well as for dealing with the immediate frictions, voids and lags of social change. The National Resources Planning Board did not fare so well, but there can be but little doubt that its functions will be assumed by other branches of the government, and in time even become respectable.

It is one of the paradoxes of modern life that increased freedom in the urban environment often is attained only through increased restraints—that is through the increased interventionism of private or governmental agencies into the social and political process. Intelligent social planning, obnoxious as this concept may be to many of us in the light of some of our inherited ideologies, is a device for effecting integration, coordination, cohesion and order within the urban setting or in the largely urbanized nation. It is a social invention necessitated, on the one hand, by the new problems created by the city, and, on the other, by the rapid deterioration in the urban environment of some of the elements of our rural social heritage.

It is a happy combination of circumstances that the same urban environment which is breaking down our inherited system of social and political organization and our traditional patterns of conduct and thought is also producing the means whereby we can weld a new order better adapted to our changed technology and economic structure. An increasing awareness of this happy combination of circumstances would undoubtedly accelerate the process of cultural adjustment which still confronts us.

THE CITY, THE FACTORY,
AND ECONOMIC GROWTH

Bert F. Hoselitz

In a generally accepted view, the economic development of underdeveloped countries is contingent upon the introduction of industry. Industrialization, in turn, is associated with urban growth, and the relationship of these two processes is usually assumed to be so close that some writers speak of industrialization and urbanization as two facets of one and the same process. The evidence for the need for industrialization and urbanization is found in the historical experience of the economically more advanced countries and in general considerations on the economic situation of the farm populations in many underdeveloped countries.

The advanced countries contain the most heavily industrialized and at the same time most densely urbanized regions of the world, and to the extent to which industrial cities have grown up in underdeveloped countries, they have been patterned after British, German, and American models.

The improvement in the economic position of subsistence farmers who make up two-thirds or more of the people in many underdeveloped countries is dependent upon industrialization. There are scarcely any underdeveloped countries in which there is not a large surplus of unemployed agricultural labor. This surplus farm labor represents a tremendous waste of human resources, and the obvious remedy is the transfer of these "redundant" persons into industry. But their removal from the farms may not always be sufficient and may have to be implemented by removal from the villages to urban areas.

We may conclude, therefore, that industrialization and urbanization are effective means for economic advancement. But this process is not one of unmixed blessings. The social consequences of the growth of industrial urban centers in underdeveloped countries are well summarized by Motwani, when he describes the cities of South Asia as "huge mausoleums of coal, smoke, iron and steel, of dirt and squalor, of overcrowding, of cooly-lines, and human warehouses. Long hours, low wages, bad housing, woman and child labor, infant mortality, accidents, high rents, poor sanitation, prostitution, gambling, racing, dope dealing, dance halls, cabarets and night clubs were features of all the cities. The noise corroded

Reprinted from the *American Economic Review*, Vol. 45 (May, 1955), pp. 166-184, by permission of the author and the *American Economic Review*. (Copyright 1955 by the American Economic Association.)

the nerves of the city dwellers, while absence of neighborhood restricted their social contacts and made them strangers to each other."[1]

Much of this is true. But many of Motwani's charges are not the consequences of the growth of cities but rather of general conditions of economic backwardness and poverty. His reproach against urbanization and industrialization is too undifferentiated to be fully effective. Infant mortality is much higher in the rural areas of underdeveloped countries than in their cities; the standards of housing are also, on the whole, rather better in cities; and many of the rural laborers work long hours and receive pitifully low incomes for their toil. Normally the small subsistence farmer works harder and gets less than the factory worker or the workers on plantations, mines, and railways.

But although industrialization and urbanization go usually hand in hand, there is no necessary connection between the two processes. Industries can be and have been established in rural districts, and cities have grown up without large industrial plants. The introduction of new technology may sometimes change existing social relations very little and sometimes subvert them completely. The social relations created by modern factory organization, implying new hierarchial relations in the work situation, discipline, the dependence of the worker upon a money wage, the uncertainties and insecurities connected with the proletarian style of life, are not peculiar to urban industry. These same conditions hold in plantations and mines which are typically located in rural surroundings, on railways and other means of transportation and communication which stretch far out into the countryside. The almost automatic association of industrialization with the introduction of the factory system as it was practiced in the mid-nineteenth century made us forget that the advantages and disadvantages of technological change in underdeveloped countries may be attributed to different factors and that the relative contribution of each of these factors in the overall process of economic development and technological change must be more clearly determined in order to provide guiding principles for developmental planning. For if certain "undesirable" outcomes can be associated with one factor alone, it may be possible to plan in such a way as to eliminate or at least mitigate the incidence of the undesirable outcome.

In order to isolate the impact of industrialization from that of urbanization, we will examine each of these processes separately. In the subsequent discussion the contrasts and differences will appear sharper than they are in reality. By describing situations which approximate idealtypes, some of the variables are placed in greater prominence than if an attempt is made to present a fully realistic description with all shades and qualifications. I do not maintain that the sharp contrasts which will appear in the discussion are necessarily present in all the developments

---

1. Kewal Motwani, "The Impact of Modern Technology on the Social Structure of South Asia," *International Social Science Bulletin*, Winter, 1951, p. 787.

described. They are emphasized here because by this method attention is drawn to the most important tendencies accompanying industrialization and urbanization in a developing economy.

Let us begin with the analysis of "industrial" cities. Firstly, they are new, not merely in the sense that most of them are the product of urban growth of the last 150 years, but rather that many industrial cities arose in places where earlier there had been no places of settlement at all or only small villages or hamlets. Manchester, which has been called the "first industrial city," was described by Daniel Defoe in 1727, as a "mere village." (Daniel Defoe, *A Plan of the English Commerce* [reprint ed.; Oxford, 1928], page 64.) Also other heavily industrialized areas of Great Britain—the Glasgow region, the Newcastle region, the Rhondda Valley, and parts of the Black country—were wasteland or farmland with few and unimportant settlements up to the middle of the eighteenth century. Extensive evidence for the rural character of the Ruhr Valley at the beginning of the nineteenth century was collected by Pierre Bernaerts. He cites accounts of the time which state that the Westphalian region in the 1830's presented "the character of an agricultural country with a few market towns which also had some handicraft trades. No contemporary document envisages by any means the extraordinary upheaval which, in the course of one generation, was to bring forth in this territory the most extensive industrial region of the European continent. . . . Essen is described as an agreeable small town . . . in which in summer the cows were taken to the communal grazing grounds. . . . Oberhausen, Gelsenkirchen and Ruhrort were tiny dots on the map." (Pierre Benaerts, *Les origines de la grande industrie allemande* [Paris, 1933], pages 101-102.) It is superfluous to point out that the great industrial metropolitan centers in the United States, Canada, and Australia grew in places where not even villages had been before the first settlers decided to build their cities in these spots.

The newness of the industrial city—the absence of a long urban tradition with guilds and market privileges and other vested interests—was doubtless an important factor in their rapid rise. Although urban growth in England was rapid everywhere during the nineteenth century, the new cities grew faster and ultimately reached larger size than the older cities. Manchester outstripped Birmingham and Leeds, the cotton towns of Lancashire overtook the woolen towns of Yorkshire, the coal towns and the iron towns of the north and west overtook the commercial and small-industry centers of southern and eastern England.[2] But although the new cities did not have deep historical roots, they grew up in a cultural environment in which there existed a long urban tradition. They adopted

---

2. On the differential growth of British cities in the nineteenth century, see the forthcoming article by Eric Lampard, "The History of Cities in Economically Advanced Areas, *Economic Development and Cultural Change* (January, 1955), pp. 111-112.

and modified the old institutions, but there was never any question that each of these rapidly growing entities formed a "corporation," a whole of some sort, that the inhabitants of the city were the members of one and the same community, and that they had rights and privileges in the community and duties towards it. Classical liberalism at its height saw some experiments in municipal "socialism" in such fields as sanitary provisions, street lighting, gas and water works, and other services. Municipalities entered the field of education and culture: they built libraries and schools and recreation grounds and parks. In spite of the intense ego-orientation stimulated by classical liberalism in the economic sphere, the older collectivity-oriented values prevailed even in Cobden's Manchester. In spite of slums and low housing and sanitary standards in many parts of the industrial cities, the whole city formed a community. It was not merely altruism or beneficent self-interest which made some municipal reformers agitate for slum clearance and municipal improvement. An important role was played by the sentiment of community; i.e., the conception that any blemish in the city's landscape was a matter of concern for all its citizens.

This sentiment of community became concretized in at least two institutions and types of attitude which persisted throughout the Western world. One was the tradition of self-government—of the city's taking care of its own present and evolving needs. This found expression in at least some political consciousness and activity of most of the city's inhabitants. The vigorous development of municipal self-government and public services in all Western cities is largely an outflow of this tradition, although it developed different forms in different localities. Secondly, there persisted, even if in a changing and transformed way, the attachment of the city's population to the urban way of life. This became manifest on the one hand in the clearer distinction between city and country and the city-dwellers' self-consciousness of the differences in their attitudes and objectives from those of the countryside. On the other hand, it showed itself in the development of functionally specific areas in the city itself. The concentric arrangement of modern industrial cities, with their central business districts and their changing belts of industrial and residential areas, the location and function of district shopping centers, the pattern of intracity communications, and many other features of a similar kind, show the interdependence of all parts of a city upon one another and are proof of the overall unity of the urban community in spite of its internal wide diversity.

A second common characteristic of the industrial cities in the advanced countries is that their growth was by and large associated with the demand for labor and that people moved to the cities because employment opportunities existed there. This process was made possible by the often rapid growth of industrial investment in the city. Let us again take the example of Manchester, which exhibits this pattern clearly. In 1780 only one factory, that of Richard Arkwright, could be found within the perimeter of Manchester; in 1790 the first Bolton and Watt steam engine was installed in a cotton mill; and by 1820 there were sixty-six cotton, six silk, and six woolen spinning mills in Manchester. By that time factory spinning became unprofitable unless combined with weaving. As a consequence, the manufacturing capitalists were obliged to install the improved power loom and to integrate the spinning, weaving, and finishing processes in one single establishment, each of which employed between three hundred and a thousand workers. By 1845 there were more than a hundred integrated factories in Manchester and Salford. But in addition to this growth of the cotton industry, subsidiary industries were progressing. Machine makers, forges, tin plating establishments, leather workers, braziers, harness makers, as well as railways, canals, breweries, and chemical industries, were clustering around the cotton mills of Manchester and Salford. This expanding concentration of industry called forth a secularly ever increasing demand for labor.[3] As a city grew in population and as subsidiary production developed around each city's main specialized industrial branches, external economies for these main industries increased. Anyone newly establishing a cotton mill in Manchester could count not only on the presence of a skilled and disciplined labor force, but he had suppliers of raw materials, wholesalers to whom he could easily sell his output, sources of credit, repair shops for his machinery, and many other subsidiary services near at hand. This in turn encouraged the further expansion of the industrial base of the city and called for further increase in employment opportunities and a growing demand for labor.

A third characteristic of the industrial city in economically advanced countries is the role it plays in the process of cultural change. Robert Redfield and Milton B. Singer distinguished two phases of cultural change which are mediated primarily by urban centers ("The Cultural Role of Cities," *Economic Development and Cultural Change*, October, 1953, page 59). One is the phase of "orthogenetic" and the other of "heterogenetic" cultural transformation. By orthogenetic cultural transformation Redfield and Singer mean the development of a great tradition, such as took place in the cities of ancient Egypt, China, Mayan Yucatan, and the Christian centers of the European middle ages. Heterogenetic cultural transformation, on the other hand, is a process in which acculturation—the absorption of new culture elements from the outside—takes place and in which predominantly rationalistic tendencies prevail. It is obvious that the growth of the industrial city is a process of heterogenetic cultural transformation. However, the industrial cities were not the spearheads in this process but latecomers. The phase of heterogenetic transformation of Occidental cities began with the end of the middle ages, and the "spirit

---

3. Leon S. Marshall, "The Emergence of the First Industrial City: Manchester, 1780-1850," in Caroline F. Ware, *The Cultural Approach to History* (New York, 1940), pp. 140-143.

of capitalism" and of rationality were well developed and fully accepted into the pattern of Western social values when the rise of the industrial city began. In other words, the growth of industrial cities took place in a cultural climate favorable to the further development of the technical order in which the modern industrial city could flourish. The industrial city, in turn, soon became one of the chief centers of social change and played an important role in strengthening the new technical order based on rational allocation of resources, competitive markets, and the pursuit of self-interest in economic action.

The development in the value system of the modern world, of which the industrial city is one of the most characteristic symbols, has sometimes been expressed by stressing the presence of universalist, achievement-oriented norms, as against the predominance of particularistic, ascription-oriented norms in less developed societies.[4] This transition in value structures is accompanied by stresses and strains which tend to produce features of social disorganization in various degree. The impact of the modern industrial city, as a latecomer in this transformation process, made itself felt at a time when the basic alteration in social values had already been achieved and its main role has been to reinforce an already existing system of social values rather than to participate in the creation of new ones. Although the industrial cities of the Western countries have witnessed episodes of severe social disorganization, they have been able to overcome these disruptive tendencies better because they were not places of cultural innovation but rather of cultural consolidation.

Before examining to what extent the origins of industrial cities in the underdeveloped countries differ from those of Western industrial cities, we must take a look at one group of Western cities which have performed chiefly functions other than specialization in given branches of industrial production or the supply of specified services. These cities are usually referred to as "central cities."[5] The most characteristic central cities are the capitals of some European countries; for example, Paris or London. They are not only political and cultural centers of their respective countries but also perform some of the central economic functions in the national economies. The money markets, often the transactions with foreign countries, the main wholesale and retail houses, and several important industrial and manufacturing branches are concentrated in these cities.

4. The original definition of these variables was given by Talcott Parsons, *The Social System* (Glencoe, 1951), pp. 58 ff. They were applied to the analysis of economic growth in general by Bert F. Hoselitz, "Social Structure and Economic Growth," *Economia Internazionale*, August, 1953, pp. 52-72. The same conceptual scheme was applied to the analysis of the modern industrial city by William L. Kolb, "The Social Structure and Function of Cities," *Economic Development and Cultural Change* (October, 1954), pp. 30-46.

5. Edward L. Ullman, "A Theory of Location for Cities," in Paul K. Hatt and Albert J. Reiss (ed.), *Reader in Urban Sociology* (Glencoe, 1951), pp. 123-132.

The history and role of central cities differ markedly from the industrial cities. Central cities—even central cities of only provincial importance —are on the whole older than industrial cities. They developed out of towns which already had some political importance in medieval times, and many of them have tended to perform "central city functions" for a considerable period of their history. Economic growth has been more halting in them, traditions have lingered longer, and their influence has often been on the conservative side. Although some capitals grew as rapidly as some industrial cities, many provincial central cities developed much more slowly.[6] They resisted industrialization more effectively than the newer cities, and the influx of migrants into these central cities was motivated not always by search for employment or economic betterment but by expectations of political promotion, or simply the desire to be on the scene where important new events were taking place. The general transformation in the value system has affected the central cities as well as the industrial cities. But in the former the raw edges were somewhat smoothed, extremes were, on the whole, avoided, and the impact of the new economic ethic was less drastic. It is probably no accident that the economic ethic extolling universalist, achievement-oriented norms is referred to as "Manchesterism" and that American sociologists have chosen Chicago as the model when they wished to describe the specific flavor of the sprawling, big, American industrial metropolis.

If we now compare industrial and central cities in the underdeveloped countries with their counterparts in the advanced countries, we find several rather startling differences. Above all, there are hardly any genuine industrial cities in underdeveloped countries. Though the absolute number of cities with population 100,000 and above is as large in "preindustrial" countries as it is in industrial countries, the very fact that in the former set of countries more than half the males are occupied in agriculture, fishing, or forestry explains the scarcity of genuine industrial cities in these countries.[7] Though such cities as Kanpur or Ahmedabad in India, Maracaibo or Monterrey in Latin America, and Dharan in the Middle East may be regarded as genuine industrial cities, the majority of the cities of underdeveloped countries perform numerous central city functions and industry plays often only a relatively subordinate role. Thus, if Motwani designates the cities in underdeveloped countries as "mauso-

6. On the different ranks of central cities see especially Walter Christaller, *Die zentralen Orte in Sueddeutschland* (Jena, 1935), and Ullman's discussion of Christaller's schema, *op. cit.*, pp. 126-127.

7. Kingsley Davis and Hilda Hertz Golden have shown in the article, "Urbanization and the Development of Pre-Industrial Areas," *Economic Development and Cultural Change* (October, 1953), p. 9, that of the world's 897 cities with populations of more than 100,000 persons, 463 are located in countries with more than half the occupied males in agriculture and 434 in other countries. The total population of the first group of cities is roughly 160 million; that of the second group, only approximately 155 million.

leums of coal smoke, iron and steel," he can speak only of very few such cities, and even there of relatively limited quarters only. The appropriate counterpart for comparisons with cities in underdeveloped countries is, therefore, not the industrial cities, but the central cities of the advanced countries. But the central cities have shown themselves more stable and more resistant to the introduction of new values. They have also resisted to some extent the introduction of industry. They have had fewer upheavals, there was less disorganization, and there was maintained a higher degree and more profound sense of collectivity-orientation than in the industrial cities of the advanced countries. It is the contrast between places like Toulouse, Munich, Edinburgh, or Albany—cities with important central city functions and a fair degree of industrialization—and centers such as Dakar, Djakarta, or Mexico which comes under scrutiny.

If we trace the actual origins of the cities in underdeveloped countries, we find that many of them, like the bulk of the industrial cities of Europe and North America, are new. They were founded by foreign traders or invaders; in the colonial and excolonial countries, by representatives of the colonizing power. Some of the cities in underdeveloped countries are planted upon the native cities which existed previous to contact with the West. These last cities—places like Mandalay or Benares, Mecca or Fez— have been most refractory against change and the introduction of industry. They often played an important role in the orthogenetic transformation of the urban culture of the underdeveloped country; they were "sacred" cities in which important traditions of the cultural past of these countries were preserved. They have resisted the introduction of new values and new methods; the Westerners found it often easier to leave these cities as oases of "backwardness and superstition" and to construct their own cities elsewhere. This experience has occurred also in tropical Africa. The relatively large settlements of indigenous peoples which existed before the full penetration of parts of West Africa by Europeans appeared to be ideal sites for the establishment of commercial and industrial activities by the colonizing powers. Often these settlements (as for example some of the larger towns of the Yoruba in Nigeria) were situated on favorable spots on rivers or in sheltered bays. There was a large population nearby which offered a potential ample labor supply and housing of a sort already existed in the native town. Hence these towns appeared, on the surface, as the most promising places for economic development. But it was soon found that the very existence of a previous settlement, with all the customs and beliefs which had developed in it and around it, proved a very unsuitable place for rapid change. There were serious rigidities, even revolts. The generalization that a city is, in general, the readiest place for innovation proved fallacious with respect to these towns. The most rapidly growing and most "Westernized" settlements in Africa were not the places with a long urban history, but the recent creations of the Europeans.[8] Thus many cities—even in countries with old cultures—are new and, in addition, creations of outsiders. Balandier says of West and Central Africa (an area with considerable urban traditions) that the only city "which has risen to the scale of a great European town" is Ibadan in Yorubaland, Nigeria (op. cit., pages 3-4). All the other cities were founded and built by whites, although they are inhabited predominantly by Negroes.

It is, therefore, not surprising that in African cities a sense of community, as we know it in Western cities, is absent. This does not mean that Africans are not collectivity-oriented. On the contrary, they are more deeply tied to the group to which they feel they belong than Westerners. But the group to which the African is loyal is not the city in which he lives, but his family, his kin, his tribe, his village. African cities are, therefore, collections of many separate compounds. This characteristic is confirmed by the all-too-few social surveys which have been made in Africa. For example, Mrs. Sofer writes that the African population of Jinja is heterogeneous and variable (op. cit., page 1), and Balandier prefers to speak of "les Brazzavilles noires," indicating that the various African quarters of Brazzaville are as many separate towns (op. cit., passim). This lack of unity in urban agglomerations is found also in other underdeveloped countries. Redfield describes Mérida of 75 years ago and shows that by that time the various barrios formed virtually self-contained independent villages. Though some integration has taken place since that time, many particularistic features still prevail. Pierre George discusses the bidonvilles of the cities of French North Africa, and finds there also a high degree of particularism. Finally, and most importantly, the lack of internal cohesion and unity has been found to be characteristic of the cities of India, Burma, Thailand, and Indonesia. In fact, in some Indian cities it appears to be so pronounced that some students believe this trend towards particularism to be a lasting feature of Indian urban development.[9]

One of the great contrasts between the cities of the underdeveloped countries and those of the West is therefore the absence of a "city-consciousness" in Asia and Africa and perhaps also in Latin America. This implies, at the same time, that the distance between urban and rural

8. On urbanization in Africa, see the Working Papers submitted at the Conference of Social Scientists on the Social Impact of Industrialization and Urban Conditions in Africa, held from September 29 to October 7, 1954, at Abidjan, Ivory Coast, under the auspices of UNESCO. Cf. especially the papers by Rhona Sofer, "Adaptation Problems for the African Population in a Society of Early Industrialization at Jinja, Uganda," and by Georges Balandier, "Urbanism in West and Central Africa: Suggested Trends of Research" (mimeographed).

9. See Robert Redfield, The Folk Culture of Yucatan (Chicago, 1941), pp. 25-28; Pierre George, "Bidonvilles, a Form of Urban Development in Underdeveloped Countries" (lecture presented at the International Conference on Underdeveloped Areas at Milan, October 10-15, 1954); McKim Marriott, "Some Comments on William L. Kolb's 'The Structure and Function of Cities,' in the Light of India's Urbanization," Economic Development and Cultural Change (October, 1954), pp. 51-52.

styles of life is less pronounced than in Europe; that the loyalties of the urban dwellers are frequently to groups whose center of gravity is outside the city; that the sojourn in the city is regarded often as only temporary; that migrants to the city from one village or province not only tend to settle in clusters of their own, but that even when they have become permanent city dwellers they maintain some ties with the region they came from; and that each district of the city forms a community of its own, often rigorously separated from the others. These differences were pointed out almost twenty-five years ago by Max Weber. He examined the pecularities of Chinese, Indian, and Arabic cities and concluded that "only the West has known an urban community [*Stadtgemeinde*] in the true sense of the word as a mass phenomenon." (*Wirtschaft und Gesellschaft* [3rd ed.; Tübingen, 1947], Vol. II, pages 523-528, especially 523).

The consequences of this fact are of considerable gravity. Most of the European migrants to the cities in the eighteenth and nineteenth centuries came from the countryside, just as the migrants to cities in underdeveloped countries today. But whereas the European, once he had reached the city and lived there for a short time was able to cut himself loose from his old home because he found a new home with new loyalties in the city, the Asian or African does not experience such a transfer of loyalty. He continues to "belong" to the place whence he came and he never feels fully and exclusively at home in the city. The migrant to the city in underdeveloped countries lives in a strange and foreign place as long as he remains in the city, and this alone increases the psychological stress he experiences. It means, also, that he seeks as associates only persons who come from the same kinship group, village, or province as he himself. In this way almost all interpersonal relations into which he enters are strongly influenced by the pattern of group formation peculiar to his native culture. He works with men who have the same ethnic and often even the same local origin. He lives in a social structure in which authority and responsibility are distributed according to patterns characteristic of his native culture rather than that of the city and its economic needs. His relationships with his fellow-workers, his supervisors on the job, his trade-union—if he is a member of one—are expressions of the culture and social structure of his native environment and not of the city or even of the European model after which they were patterned. It is therefore not surprising that we find among the noncommunist union leaders in South Asian countries two groups, one of which "consists of leaders whose authority is local and based on native traditions" and the other of which, though inspired by Western models, tends to "resort to autocratic measures, making it hardly distinguishable from traditional forms of leadership, except perhaps in its professed ultimate objectives." (George E. Lichtblau, "The Politics of Trade Union Leadership in Southern Asia," *World Politics*, October, 1954, pages 92 and 98.)

The urban environment in underdeveloped countries has therefore the effect of increasing greatly the anxieties and uncertainties of the recent migrant, to make him look for security in familiar surroundings, and to seek out associations in which familiar patterns of social structure, authority, and responsibility prevail. This creates a sentiment of strong ambivalence towards the city, even on the part of those who have come to the city because they were attracted by its glamor and of those who have no place else to go, for whatever reason they came. It further explains why the pushes in order to impel people to migrate to the cities must be so strong, and why, in spite of apparently appalling conditions in some of the overcrowded rural areas of India, Java, and other parts of the underdeveloped countries, people continue to remain in their villages.

And yet we find cityward migrations in underdeveloped countries which are larger than is warranted by the newly created economic opportunities in the cities. Here is another difference between the cities of underdeveloped countries and those of the advanced countries. The rapid growth of the industrial cities of Western countries occurred simultaneously with the rapid growth of industrial investment, and hence the movement to the cities was in large part a response to the opening up of new employment opportunities there. To be sure, many migrants had only very dim expectations as to what they would find in the city, but wave after wave of migrants found even fairly optimistic expectations confirmed. Sometimes they had to suffer hardships and deprivation for a period; sometimes they flourished as soon as they arrived. But during the entire growth process of the cities in advanced countries, the expectations of the migrants to find employment and improve their economic position were confirmed in the long run.

The pattern of cityward migration in the underdeveloped countries is different. Some migrants are attracted by the glamor of the city and some by expectations of economic improvement. But most persons who come to the city are pushed out from where they have lived before by events beyond their control. In some cases it may be the rigors of famine and other material hardships which drive people out, in other instances it may be civil war and banditry, but in most cases the forces which succeed in pushing people into the cities are persistent and strong.[10]

The most rapid growth of cities in underdeveloped countries took place in the last few years. Accurate figures are not available for all countries,

---

10. See Wilbert E. Moore, *Industrialization and Labor* (Ithaca, 1951), especially pp. 48-70 and 94-96. On cityward migrations due to famine, see Owen Lattimore, "The Mainsprings of Asiatic Migration" in Isaiah Bowman (ed.), *Limits of Land Settlement* (New York, 1937), p. 133, and Walter H. Mallory, "The Northward Migration of the Chinese," *Foreign Affairs*, October, 1928, pp. 80-81 (migration of Chinese to Manchuria out of famine-stricken areas in Shantung and Hopei). The main instances of cityward migration as a consequence of civil war and banditry occurred in recent years in Indonesia, Burma, Malaya, and the Philippines.

but we have fairly good estimates for the growth of cities in some countries. Some very interesting estimates of urban growth in Indonesia have been published by W. L. Utermark. He presents a table in which he lists fourteen of the largest Indonesian cities, dividing them into two groups. One group is composed of cities which grew primarily because of cityward migration from their immediate hinterland, apparently motivated largely by economic opportunities in the city. The other group is made up of cities which grew primarily because people from all over the country hoped to find in the city shelter from insecurity, political advancement, or other opportunities associated with the rapid social and political change of the times. The first group embraces seven cities which in 1930 had a combined population of 536 million and in 1950-51 of 977 million. The second group also embraces seven cities which were inhabited by 1,386 million people in 1930 and by 4,329 million in 1950-51. The rate of growth in the first group was 82 per cent and in the second 212 per cent.[11] This shows that not only are the largest cities growing faster than the smaller ones, but also that cityward movement was motivated considerably more by noneconomic reasons than by economic ones.

It is not difficult to assess the consequences of this form of development. In the first place, it adds to the insecurity and stress which the migrant to the city experiences. Not only is he torn from his accustomed environment, but he finds that his very existence is put in question in the city. He literally lives from hand to mouth; he is available for any job to be had (including hiring himself out for political demonstrations or rioting);[12] he becomes demoralized and an easy prey for radical agitators of all hues; he lives in unspeakably rotten slums, much worse than those of Manchester in early Victorian times, and scarcely equaled by the *bidonvilles* of North Africa and Spain. A large proportion of the poor people in many underdeveloped towns are not an "industrial reserve army," but a demoralized, unhealthy, pitiful *lumpenproletariat*. Even if a sudden spurt of industrial investment were to take place in these cities, it would be difficult to transform these people into disciplined, effective factory workers.

Another aspect of this recent in-migration is the very high sex ratio in many cities of underdeveloped countries. This phenomenon is not unknown in advanced countries. Among the immigrants from Europe to the New World, men were in the majority, and if we omit persons under eighteen years of age, the proportion of male immigrants increases. Most of these immigrants went to cities, and hence one may say that here was

---

11. W. L. Utermark, "Aspect économique de l'attraction exercée par les centres urbains et industriels en Indonésie," in *L'attraction exercée par les centres urbains dans les pays en voie d'industrialisation* (Brussels: Institut International des Civilizations Différentes, 1952), pp. 226-234, especially p. 232.

12. I am told by an American official, resident in Iran, that participation in political rioting—one day for and the next against Mossadegh—was one of the more attractive forms of making a livelihood for a portion of Tehran's *lumpenproletariat*.

a predominantly male cityward migration. In the underdeveloped countries, also, men predominate so strongly among the migrants that the sex ratios in cities are extremely uneven. For example, in four of the eight largest Indian cities the preponderance of males is very strong. In Calcutta there are 602, in Bombay 569, in Ahmedabad 764, and in Kanpur 699 women per 1,000 men. Similarly, in Africa the male urban population is much larger than the female. In the Belgian Congo, for example, there are 696 women per 1,000 men.[13] In many of the mining camps of the Copper Belt in Rhodesia or the Rand in the South African Union the imbalance is even stronger.

The consequences of these facts are not difficult to assess. The great preponderance of males means that stable families are rarer in cities than in the country. The men who come to the city are single or leave their wives behind. In the former case they may regard their stay in the city as temporary, since they often come in the hope to make enough money to go back and get married. In the latter case they do not break their close tie with their native village; they are not city dwellers but temporary residents. This situation adds to the instability of the city population in underdeveloped countries. It also adds to the stress experienced by the new immigrants and is one of the chief causes of the prostitution, gambling, racing, dope dealing, and other forms of social disorganization and crime which Motwani notes with so much displeasure.

All these factors conspire to make the large cities in underdeveloped countries highly unsuitable places for the development of new forms of social cohesion and solidarity. Although whatever change in the culture and social values occurred in Asia and Africa did primarily take root in the cities and then emanated from them, the changes that have actually been achieved have been slow and halting, often impeded by the lack of unity, instability, and heterogeneity of the city population. If progress towards universalistic, achievement-oriented social values has been difficult in the cities of Asia and Africa, it is not due to the stubbornness of the people or their "superstitious" adherence to old ways of life, but rather to the very unfavorable conditions under which they have been brought to the city and under which they continue to exist.

It is in the light of this contrasting impact which cities have exercised in advanced countries and now exercise in underdeveloped countries that we have to appraise the industrialization of less advanced countries. The analysis of this aspect of economic development can be short because there already exists a considerable literature on this subject.[14] In principle, we

---

13. The figures for India are for 1951. Cf. India, Census Commission, *Census of India, 1951* (Delhi, 1953), Vol. I, p. 56. The figures for the Belgian Congo are for 1949. Cf. A. J. Moeller de Laddersous, "Attraction exercée par les centres urbains et industriels dans le Congo Belge" (Institut International des Civilizations Différentes), *op. cit.,* p. 192.

14. In addition to Wilbert E. Moore's book, mentioned earlier (in note 10) there

may distinguish three types of impact exercised on a nonindustrial labor force by the introduction of mechanized industry. The first is the need for adjustment to the new environment, and it is particularly in this area that the new urban agglomerations are important factors in the formation of an industrial labor force in underdeveloped countries. The second impact is that of a new technology: the replacement of handicraft work by machine work, the acquisition of new skills, and the co-ordination of the tempo and rhythm of work with the machine rather than the freer and less rigorously structured pace of the artisan. The third impact is the imposition of new social relations appropriate to modern forms of industrial organization: new hierarchies, new social groups, new patterns of authority develop which are strange and often contrary to those to which the new recruits of industry are accustomed. The workers find themselves in situations which in terms of their old culture either have no analogue or which are flatly opposed to the old culture. The high-caste Indian, working side by side in a factory with a low-caste Indian; the mixture, in a factory, of different racial or ethnic groups who previously held strictly aloof from one another; the congregation of people who previously had known co-operation only on the basis of kinship ties, in a labor union or a sectional work crew in a factory—all are cases in point.

As concerns the impact of the urban environment, little needs to be added to what has been said before. The city in an underdeveloped country is an inhospitable environment for many actual or potential laborers. Reference is made not so much to slum conditions and bad housing, although these have detrimental effects on the morale of an industrial labor force. Nevertheless, in many underdeveloped countries actual health, sanitary, and housing standards are no worse, and often better, than in the rural areas whence the workers come. To be sure, conditions are often worse than they were in nineteenth-century Europe, but compared with what the cityward migrant in many underdeveloped countries left behind, his standard of real welfare suffers hardly any diminution. The inhospitality of the urban environment expresses itself rather by the serious psychological strains it exerts on the worker. Employment is uncertain and wages too low to permit savings for a rainy day. Families are torn asunder; the comforting security of a known and accustomed environment is lost. The number of face-to-face relationships with persons whom one does not know is increased; the loneliness of the individual becomes, in some cases, almost absolute. These conditions impair morale, discipline, and steadfast devotion to a given task. It is not the noise or the soot in the city which corrodes the nerves of the worker, as Motwani has it, but rather

is a considerable literature on this topic sponsored by UNESCO, ILO, and various national governments. A good bibliography is contained in Wilbert E. Moore, op. cit., pp. 365-398. Other writings are listed in Current Sociology: International Bibliography of Sociology, Vol. I and ff.; and Daniel Craemer, Bibliography on Income and Wealth, Vol. II (Cambridge, 1953), especially under the headings "Estimates of Labour Force by Geographic Areas" and "International Comparisons of Labour Force Estimates."

the "absence of neighborhood"—the anonymity and impersonality of life in a big city. These factors go far to explain the high absentee rate, the high rate of turnover, and the low standard of performance of many industrial workers in underdeveloped countries.

The impact of the new technology pales in importance beside this impact of the urban environment. New skills can be learned and have been learned with surprising speed by many peoples. It has been pointed out again and again by anthropologists that the technical manipulations involved in handling complex machines have been learned with relative facility by peoples in underdeveloped countries who had no previous knowledge of these machines and whose general standards of literacy and education left much to be desired. No less an authority than the late Ralph Linton wrote: "I would back certain Polynesian and Swahili mechanics of my experience against nine-tenths of American garagemen for ingenuity and mechanical know-how."[15] The retarding factor is not the incapacity or lack of interest on the part of workers in underdeveloped countries to acquire the requisite skills, but rather the inadequate provision for training, the great shortage of educational facilities, and the impediments, in many instances, to advancement which deprive workers of incentives to improve their performance. The "demonstration effect" described by Ragnar Nurkse with reference to changes in consumption patterns of the peoples in underdeveloped countries exercises an influence here also. (*Problems of Capital Formation in Underdeveloped Countries* [New York, 1953], pages 64-65.) Imitation of Western methods and the use of Western machines are recognized as means to increased output and ultimately better living standards. What is absent is not the willingness or human ability to use these machines and methods, but the social institutions which permit their use to these ends.

This leads us to the knottiest and most difficult problem in the industrialization process in underdeveloped countries: the impact of the new forms of social structure and the requirements of new types of social behavior appropriate to large-scale production in the factory. The restructuring of social relations occurs as a result of the mobilization of the labor force implying the imposition of canons of employment prevailing in the industrial communities of Europe and America. It is hardly necessary to point to the striking differences between the economy in the West and that of most other societies. In the West it is based upon individual effort, whereas most of the other peoples are communally oriented. Hence in the West the worker acts as an individual. In the economies of most underdeveloped societies, on the other hand, the individual acts usually as a member of a group based on kinship or residence or both. His responsibilities are considered not merely those he individually undertakes, but also those of the

---

15. "Cultural and Personality Factors Affecting Economic Growth," in Bert F. Hoselitz (ed.), *The Progress of Underdeveloped Areas* (Chicago, 1952), p. 78. Linton presents an exhaustive discussion of this point, giving other examples on pp. 77-79.

other members of the group to which he pertains. Similarly any compensation he may get for his effort is regarded by him not merely as a reward to be employed for his individual purposes, but as something to be shared with the other members of the collectivity of which he forms a part. In many societies there are still recognized traditional arrangements for the control of money income which secure to the older members of the community the major handling of what money income is secured. Laborers must share their income with chiefs, parents, fathers-in-law, or other relatives and persons of respect.[16] In addition to this, the ranking of persons in terms of traditional status relations may differ considerably from that established in a factory work situation. Older men or chiefs or other persons with high traditional status may be subordinate in the factory to younger men, and this subordination may express itself not merely in a lower wage but in actual positions of inferiority in the factory hierarchy or a work crew. The disruptive effects not only on traditional social structures but also on the psychological security of the persons involved are obvious if a man with high traditional status must obey orders of someone who in the traditional ranking is far below him simply because the new distribution and valuation of skills makes this new relation mandatory.

I do not wish to suggest that these changes should be prevented in order to maintain an old cultural tradition or even to preserve certain traditional social structures from disruption or disorganization. I am merely pointing to those changes which, in the light of productive efficiency, may be necessary in the new work situation, in order to explain why the new social relations established in the factory are often contradictory to the traditional and accepted views of a man of himself and his relation to his fellow-men. It is also important to state that, other things being equal, the farther removed the factory is from the locus in which traditional social relations exist, the easier will it be accepted and the fewer psychological or cultural impediments will stand in its way. A factory located in a village in which the old culture is still strong and vigorous is likely to create more conflict than one located in a far-away city. The more homogeneous, moreover, the labor force in a given factory, the more likely will be its resistance against changes in the accustomed patterns of authority and responsibility. (An instance of this is reported by John Useem, "South Sea Island Strike" in Edward H. Spicer [ed.], *Human Problems and Technological Change* [New York, 1952], page 149-164.)

We are now in a position to draw together the various strands of this analysis. The impact of the modern factory is exerted along technological and social-structural lines. The former create relatively few difficulties, but

---

16. A number of such instances are reported by Raymond Firth, "Money, Work, and Social Change in Indo-Pacific Economic Systems," *International Social Science Bulletin*, 1954, pp. 406-407.

the latter may be a cause of serious maladjustments and resistances reflected in the overall low productivity of the labor force. These impediments to effective control over the labor force result from the contradictions—which are not necessarily present, but do in actual fact occur often—between the traditional structure of the social status system and the new social relations created by the work situation in the factory. The city, on the other hand, has a definite tendency to break down the old cultural traditions and to weaken the influence of traditional status considerations and interpretations of the worker's place in the social hierarchy. Though residence in a city may create anxieties and stress often bordering on *anomie,* this very same process may produce the result of creating in the co-operation with other workers in the factory an environment in which the new social relations established there may come to be regarded rather as a positive integrating than a disorganizing factor. A recent migrant who feels lonely in the city may welcome the relative security resulting from his being placed in close daily contact with individuals whom he gets to know and with some of whom he may become friendly. To be sure, one should not exaggerate the loneliness experienced by many recent migrants to the cities of underdeveloped countries. They usually find some person to whom they are related by kinship ties or ties of previous residence. And if this fails, they get in contact with persons who speak the same dialect and come from the same general portion of the country as they themselves. This enables them to maintain at least a semblance of group relations along traditional patterns. But the closer these group relations are to the traditional pattern and the more intimate the cohesion of this traditional collectivity, the greater will be the difference between the interpersonal relationships in this group and the pattern of social relations in the factory.

This, then, is the price paid by peasants who come to the city where they are forced to become industrial workers. The transformation of a predominantly rural society, based on the relatively complete self-sufficiency of a village or a group of villages, into an urban society, based on the interdependence of various portions of a country, is necessarily associated with features of social disorganization. On the sociopolitical level they appear in the form of increased crime rates, imbalanced sex ratios, political extremism, and various other kinds of social maladjustment which usually demand some centrally implemented policy in order to be remedied. On the level of the individuals most concerned, i.e., the nascent industrial workers, this process manifests itself in the increase of stress either due to the new urban environment or the new social relations prevailing in large-scale factory production. In many cases these two sources of stress pull in opposite directions. If the migrant to the city finds an already established community there in which accustomed intergroup relations prevail, the impact of the new social relations in the factory tends to produce the stress. If he does not find a group in the city resembling those of his home, the loneliness and anxiety which he experiences are the chief causes of stress, and the entry into a new system of social relations in the factory, in a work crew, or a trade union may be a factor mitigating this stress.

The persons who in the last few years have swelled the cities of underdeveloped countries do, in a sense, play the role of pioneers. The gap in culture, form of economic activity, and patterns of social relationships which they had to bridge will become narrower for those who follow. But the magnitude of the task and its ultimate importance for the welfare of the total population of underdeveloped countries appear to make these sacrifices justified. It is the toll which a rural peasant society has to pay to become urbanized and industrialized.

FUNCTIONAL SPECIALIZATION OF CITIES

Albert J. Reiss, Jr.

The principal economic activity of open-country communities ordinarily is either agriculture or an extractive industry. These communities, of course, may perform other economic functions for the population, such as providing for trade and other services. The pattern of economic activity in modern urban communities is more varied, however. Some places specialize in one or more forms of economic activity, while others have a more or less diversified set of industries. All relatively large cities nevertheless have some employment in each major non-agricultural industry group: construction; manufacturing; transportation; telecommunication; utilities and sanitary services; wholesale and retail trade; finance, insurance and real estate; business and repair services; personal services; entertainment and recreation services, professional and related services; and public administration. The relative importance of these industries in the economic structure varies from city to city. This variation reflects functional differentiation.

The purpose of this paper is twofold: (1) to describe different kinds of functional specialization for cities, and (2) to determine demographic, economic and socio-economic differences among cities with different kinds of function specialization.

CRITERIA OF FUNCTIONAL SPECIALIZATION. There are a number of functional classifications of cities representing a variety of approaches to the problem of classification.[1] The theory followed in this paper bases functional specialization on the export of goods and services which brings in income to the community. Urban land economists refer to this export activity as the "economic base" of a community.[2]

A community may be thought of as having two major kinds of economic activity. There are those activities which satisfy *local demand*. These constitute the *maintenance activity* of a community. They include

Published for the first time in this volume.

1. See in particular, Chauncy D. Harris, "A Functional Classification of Cities in the United States," *Geographical Review*, 33 (January, 1943), 86-99; Grace M. Kneedler, "Functional Types of Cities," *Public Management*, 27 (July, 1945), 197-203; Victor Jones, "Economic Classification of Cities and Metropolitan Areas," *The Municipal Yearbook*, 1953, pp. 49-57; John Fraser Hart, "Functions and Occupational Structures of Cities of the American South," *Annals of the Association of American Geographers*, XLV (September, 1955), 269-286.

2. See, for example, Richard B. Andrews, "Mechanics of The Urban Economic Base: The Problem of Terminology," *Land Economics* 29 (August, 1953), 263-268.

the activities required to maintain the physical city, such as construction, utilities, sanitary services and transportation; the services, including trade, necessary to maintain the level of living of the population; and manufacturing for local use or consumption. The *export activity* of the community, by contrast, depends on *extra-local demand* for goods, services or capital which are exported to and consumed by persons in other communities. Export and maintenance activities, then, make up the total economic activity of a community. The percentage of local employment in maintenance activities generally is greater than that in export activities. Hoyt, for example, estimated that about 68 per cent of the employed persons in the New York metropolitan region in 1940 were engaged in producing for, or servicing, residents of the region.[3]

Most cities export a number of goods and services, and in this sense have a more or less diversified economic base. The contrast between "diversified" and "specialized" cities, therefore, is only a matter of the number of specialized activities or the degree of functional specialization. In this paper, an urban or metropolitan community is said to be diversified if its export activity is about the same as that of the "average" community, while it is a functionally specialized one when the export activity is greater than that of the average community. Unfortunately, data are not available to measure or estimate directly the kind and volume of export activity for each S.M.A. and urban place with 10,000 or more population in 1950. Functional specialization, therefore, is measured indirectly. It is assumed that a high proportion of employed persons or a high per capita output in a given industry, relative to other comparable communities, represents an export of the products or services of that industry. A place is classified as specialized when it meets this criterion. For example, when a community has a much larger proportion of its labor force employed in manufacturing than the average of a comparable group of communities, it is presumed to export manufactured goods, and therefore to be specialized in manufacturing.

Two other factors affect the criteria of functional specialization: the size and metropolitan status of a place. Communities which differ in size and location in a region "divide" the goods and services to be exported. The study, therefore, does not apply a uniform criterion of specialization to all places. Rather, the criteria are varied for the eight groups of places included: four metropolitan status groups, consisting of standard metropolitan areas, central cities, suburbs and independent cities; and two size classes within each group.

TYPES OF FUNCTONAL SPECIALIZATION. The type and number of economic activities in which a city can specialize depends upon the degree of specificity given the definition of the activities. The following economic activities were selected for this study: manufacturing; wholesale and retail

3. The New York Regional Plan Association, Inc. *The Economic Status of the New York Metropolitan Region in 1944* (New York: 1944), Table 4, p. 6.

trade; public administration; higher education; transportation; military; entertainment and recreation; finance, insurance and real estate; and medical and other health services. There follows a brief statement of the criteria for determining operationally whether a city may be said to specialize in the activity.[4]

Manufacturing: A place is said to be specialized if it falls in the upper quintile on the distribution of places by the percentage of all employed persons in manufacturing. The quintile limits range from 39 per cent for large independent cities to 50 per cent for suburbs.

Higher Education: A place is defined as specialized if it falls in the upper quintile on the distribution of the percentage of all persons in the age interval, 20 to 24, enrolled in school. The upper quintile is about 19 to 20 per cent, depending upon size and metropolitan status.

Public Administration: A place is said to be specialized if it falls in the upper decile on the distribution of places by the percentage of employed males in public administration. The upper decile ranges from 7 to 10 per cent, depending upon size and metropolitan status.

Transportation: A place is designated as specialized if it falls in the upper decile on the distribution of places by the percentage of all employed persons in transportation .The upper decile ranges from 8 to 12 per cent depending upon size and metropolitan status.

Military: A community is designated as a "military center," given evidence that there is a sizeable military establishment located in or near it. Central cities and S. M. A.'s with more than 100,000 inhabitants are classified as military centers if they contained 2,000 or more members of the Armed Forces in 1950. All other S. M. A.'s and all urban places of 50,000 to 100,000 population are required to have at least 500 military persons, and all urban places with less than 50,000 population are required to have 200 or more military persons residing within their boundaries to be classified as military centers. These statistics almost necessarily understate the size of the military establishment, since only a fraction of the military personnel are ennumerated as residents of the community.

Entertainment and Recreation: A place is defined as specialized if it falls in the upper decile on the distribution of places by the percentage of employed males in entertainment and recreation. The upper decile is roughly 2 per cent for all but the S. M. A.'s, where it is 1.5 per cent.

Finance, Insurance and Real Estate: A place is designated as specialized if it falls in the upper decile on the distribution of places by the percentage of employed persons in finance, insurance and real estate. The upper decile is defined by from 4 to 9 per cent, depending upon size and metropolitan status.

Medical and Other Health Services: A place is said to be specialized if it falls in the upper decile on the distribution of places by the percentage of all employed persons in medical and other health services. The upper decile is defined by from 5 to 8 per cent, depending upon size and metropolitan status.

Trade: Each of the eight groups of places is subdivided into high and low income catagories to control the correlation between income and trade. Then each urban place and S. M. A. is classified by its quartile position on both wholesale and retail trade. This yields 16 classes: four wholesale times four retail quartiles. By combining certain of these, five categories are obtained.

---

4. A more detailed statement of the operational procedures and their limitations is to be found in Otis Dudley Duncan and Albert J. Reiss, Jr., *Social Characteristics of Rural and Urban Communities: 1950* (New York: John Wiley & Sons, 1956), Chapter 16.

These are identified as: *Wholesale Trade Center*, a high per capita value of sales in wholesale trade but a low per capita value of retail sales; *Retail Trade Center*, a high per capita value of retail sales with a low per capita value of sales in wholesale; *Trade Center*, a high per capita value of sales in both wholesale trade and retail trade; *Maintenance Trade Center*, the per capita value of wholesale trade and retail sales is about average for that of all cities, and it is therefore roughly considered to be a level of trade necessary to maintain the local population; *Non-Trade Center*, a low per capita value of sales in both wholesale and retail trade. It can be seen that every S. M. A. and urban place will be classified in one of the five trade center classifications. Only those classified as Wholesale Trade, Retail Trade, or Trade Centers are considered to export trade, however.

RELATIONSHIP AMONG TYPES OF FUNCTIONAL SPECIALIZATION. Many communities show more than one form of specialization, given the operational definitions employed in this research. The occurrence of several types of specialization in a community is referred to as "linkage" among these types. Table 1 presents information on the extent of linkage among manufacturing, retail trade, and the minor types of functional specialization.

There is some variation in the percentage of places with a type of functional specialization among the S.M.A. and urban place groups, but the variation is quite small. Roughly 85 per cent of the places in each group are functionally specialized. The absence of specialization in a place is not due to any artifact of definition, since the categories are inclusive enough to permit every urban place to be specialized and, in addition, at least two-fifths of the places in each group to have two forms of functional specialization. Each metropolitan status-size of place group has approximately the following proportions of specialized places: manufacturing centers, 20 per cent; higher education, 20 per cent; trade centers, 30 per cent; wholesale trade centers, 11 per cent; retail trade centers, 9 per cent;[5] public administration centers, 10 per cent; transportation centers, 10 per cent; entertainment-recreation centers, 10 per cent; finance, insurance and real estate centers, 10 per cent; medical and other health service centers, 10 per cent. To the total represented by these ten types of specialization, a percentage of military centers, varying in proportion by metropolitan status and size of place, must be added. The third line from the bottom in Table 1 gives the per cent of places which are expected to have a double specialization, given the fact that by definition the number of specializations is greater than the number of places in any metropolitan status-size of place group and the assumption that each place has at least one specialization. About one-seventh of the places in each group have no functional specialization, so that the expected percentage of places with a double specialization is even greater. In point of fact, about 10 per cent of the places in each group have three types

5. The percentages reported for trade centers, wholesale trade centers and retail trade centers are the percentages for all urban places. The percentages vary somewhat for metropolitan status-size groups, since the proportion in each type of trading center is a function of the correlation between wholesale and retail trade in that group.

of functional specializations, and at least an additional 2 per cent have four types, so that the number of places with a double specialization is less than the number expected. The difference between these expected and actual values in the last line of Table 1 varies from —2.9 per cent for small suburbs to —41.5 per cent for large S.M.A.'s. In general, small places are somewhat less likely to have multiple forms of specialization than are large places.

The results from Table 1 clearly show that although most S.M.A.'s and urban places are functionally specialized, the majority of them develop only a minimum of functional specialization, i.e., either a single specialization (50.6 per cent of all urban places) or a double specialization (34.3 per cent of all urban places), give a fairly definite number of types of functional specialization by definition. Only a relatively small percentage of specialized places (less than one-fifth in every metropolitan status-size group) have more than a single or a double specialization.

The extent of linkage among the types of specialization is related to the nature of the specialization. It is related, for example, to the percentage employed in the industry of specialization. Table 1 shows that no more than 9 per cent of any group of places has manufacturing linked with trade, a minor form of functional specialization, or both. Manufacturing is more likely to be linked with trade, however, than with a minor form of functional specialization. That manufacturing is more likely to be linked with trade is surprising, as manufacturing and trade are the two largest single industry group employers in the United States. Both trade and the minor forms of specialization nevertheless are more likely to occur with one another than with manufacturing. The linking of trade with a minor form of functional specialization occurs with relatively greater frequency than the linking of two or more minor forms of specialization. This suggests that perhaps certain, if not all, minor forms of specialization are more likely to occur with trade than with one another. Detailed examination of the data shows that specialization in entertainment and recreation and in finance, insurance and real estate is more likely to occur with retail trade than with other minor forms, that transportation and wholesale trade are quite frequently linked in an urban place, and that specialization in higher education is linked with specialization in both wholesale and retail trade.

About 22 per cent of all urban places in 1950 were specialized in two or more functions. The majority of these involved a double specialization, as only about one-fourth of these places had three or four types of functional specialization. Examination of the kinds of linkage among the minor forms of specialization shows the following patterns predominating. Higher education is most likely to be linked with entertainment and recreation, and the converse is true. Places where this linkage occurs include the central cities of Los Angeles, Calif. and Salt Lake City, Utah, and the independent cities of Santa Barbara, Calif. and Saratoga Springs, N. Y. Higher

Table 1—Percentage Distribution of Places by Type of Functional Specialization and Degree of Linkage Among Types of Specialization, by Metropolitan Status and Size: 1950.

Functional Specialization and Degree of Linkage	S.M.A.'s		All Urban Places	CENTRAL CITIES		SUBURBS		INDEPENDENT CITIES	
	50,000 to 250,000	250,000 or More		Under 100,000	100,000 or More	10,000 to 25,000	25,000 or More	10,000 to 25,000	25,000 to 50,000
Total places	91	77	1262	98	95	276	134	502	157
Per cent	100.0	100.0	100.0	100.0	100.0	100.0	100.0	100.0	100.0
Manufacturing specialization	19.8	20.8	19.6	20.6	18.9	19.9	20.1	19.3	19.7
Manufacturing, only	12.1	13.0	13.7	13.3	9.5	12.3	11.2	15.3	15.9
Manufacturing & Trade	4.4	3.9	4.0	5.1	8.4	4.7	8.2	2.2	1.3
Mfg. & Minor Specialization	3.3	3.9	1.8	1.1	1.0	2.9	0.7	1.8	1.9
Mfg., Trade & Minor Specializations	0.0	0.0	0.1	1.1	0.0	0.0	0.0	0.0	0.6
Trade specialization*	39.5	45.4	36.7	42.6	45.3	29.0	36.6	37.5	38.2
Trade, only	12.1	14.3	13.3	16.2	11.6	12.7	12.7	12.7	15.9
Trade & 1 minor specialization	14.3	13.0	13.8	14.3	20.0	10.9	10.4	15.6	11.4
Trade & 2 minor specializations	8.8	7.8	7.4	8.1	8.4	5.1	10.4	6.8	9.6
Trade & 3 minor specializations	4.3	10.3	2.2	4.0	5.3	0.3	3.1	2.4	1.3
Minor forms of specialization only†	25.3	20.8	27.5	21.5	23.2	32.7	27.6	26.7	28.1
Single specialization	13.2	13.0	15.4	9.2	10.5	15.6	16.4	17.1	15.9
Double specialization	11.0	5.2	9.5	9.2	9.5	12.7	9.0	8.4	8.3
Triple specialization	1.1	2.6	2.2	3.1	3.2	3.3	2.2	1.0	3.2
Quadruple specialization	0.0	0.0	0.4	0.0	0.0	1.1	0.0	0.2	0.7
No specialization	15.4	13.0	16.2	15.3	12.6	18.4	15.7	16.5	14.0
Total number of specializations	138	129	1777	148	159	370	198	678	224
Number of specializations minus number of places	47	52	515	50	64	94	64	176	67
Expected per cent of places with a double specialization‡	51.8	67.5	40.8	51.0	67.3	34.1	47.7	35.1	42.7
Actual per cent of places with a double specialization	33.0	26.0	19.1	29.5	38.9	31.2	28.3	28.0	22.9
Actual minus expected per cent	-18.8	-41.5	-21.7	-21.5	-28.4	-2.9	-19.4	-7.1	-19.8

* Places specialized in trade are: Wholesale Trade Centers; Retail Trade Centers; and Trade Centers, specializing in both wholesale and retail trade.
† Minor forms of specialization are: Education; Transportation; Public Administration; Military; Entertainment and Recreation; Finance, Insurance and Real Estate; and Medical and Other Health Services.
‡ Assuming no linkage among the types of specialization.

Table 2—Summary of Comparisons Among Five Types of Wholesale-Retail Trade Centers for All Standard Metropolitan Areas and Urban Places of 10,000 Population or More by 1949 Income Level

NUMBER OF COMPARISONS IN WHICH THE FIRST NAMED TYPE OF SPECIALIZED PLACE HAS A HIGHER FIGURE THAN THE SECOND NAMED TYPE OF SPECIALIZED PLACE*

Characteristic	Ww-Rr	Ww-Tc	Ww-MT	Ww-NT	Rr-Tc	Rr-MT	Rr-NT	TC-MT	TC-NT	MT-NT
Per cent of population 21 years old and over	0	1	3	6	12	15	15	14	14	9
Sex ratio	10	12	8	6	11	5	3	3	1	3
Persons per household	10	16	13	10	7	5	1	5	1	1
Per cent living in same house, 1949 and 1950	12	10	9	6	7	8	3	4	4	3
Per cent in labor force										
Male	12	7	9	9	3	4	6	8	8	9
Female	8	2	7	10	4	10	12	14	16	12
Per cent employed in manufacturing	10	12	6	4	8	3	0	3	2	4
Per cent government workers	4	7	8	5	11	10	10	8	8	10
Per cent employed in transportation	16	11	12	14	1	4	5	9	11	9
Per cent employed males in—										
Public administration	6	8	7	9	10	9	10	9	10	11
Hotels and lodging places	3	1	3	7	8	9	11	12	14	11
Entertainment and recreation	5	3	5	10	9	8	13	12	13	13
Per cent of males employed as white collars	3	2	6	10	9	12	16	15	13	13
Per cent of males employed as—										
Professional, technical & kindred workers	1	2	4	6	12	11	13	10	11	10
Managers, officials, and proprietors, except farm	4	4	8	11	5	12	16	15	12	12
Clerical and kindred workers	12	10	10	13	5	2	7	12	12	12
Sales workers	4	2	7	11	7	9	15	14	14	13
Craftsmen, foremen and kindred workers	7	10	6	6	10	5	5	1	4	6
Operatives and kindred workers	14	16	9	3	5	1	0	1	3	3
Private household and service workers	5	5	7	12	7	12	13	14	13	11
Laborers, except farm and mining	11	11	9	9	5	4	4	9	6	6
Per cent of females employed as—										
Sales, clerical and kindred workers	8	4	7	10	4	5	10	10	11	13
Operatives and kindred workers	11	12	9	3	7	4	2	1	3	5
Private household and service workers	7	6	6	10	10	11	12	9	15	14
Median school years completed	2	2	5	5	11	13	11	11	11	9
Per cent enrolled in school, persons 20 to 24 years old	5	4	3	9	10	11	13	10	12	11
Per cent of dwelling units owner-occupied	4	8	5	4	9	10	8	5	3	6

* Sixteen comparisons are involved; two income groups by two size groups, each, of S.M.A.'s, central cities, suburbs and independent cities.

education also is fairly closely linked with both finance, insurance and real estate and medical and other health services, although the latter two types of specialization are seldom linked. Examples of places where all three of these specialties are linked include the Boston, Mass., S.M.A., the central city of Columbia, S. C., and the suburb of Evanston, Ill. Specialization in public administration is more often linked with military specialization than with any other type, and vice versa. The central cities of Washington, D.C. and Montgomery, Ala. illustrate this pattern. Transportation is infrequently linked with other minor forms of specialization.

CORRELATES OF FUNCTONAL SPECIALIZATION. Structural characteristics of a community are intimately related to the functions its population performs. To the degree that all cities share common maintenance functions and a characteristic division of labor, their structure will be very similar. A city that is highly specialized, however, is apt to have a distinctive social structure. For example, manufacturing centers employ large numbers of semiskilled operatives. Hence, manufacturing cities like Detroit, Mich. have a high ratio of manual to white-collar workers. The question arises, however, *whether most functionally specialized places of a given kind differ significantly in their demographic, economic, and socio-economic characteristics from communities which lack this particular functional specialization.* This question is considered for each of the functional types defined above.

TRADE SPECIALIZATION. Trade, historically, was one of the major forces producing urbanization. The typical preindustrial city was a trade center. Today, despite extensive industrialization, many American communities continue to specialize in trade because they are the source of goods and the center of exchange for a rural hinterland. In the urban United States as a whole, wholesale and retail trade employ a larger proportion (21.9 per cent) of the urban working force than any other major industry group except manufacturing (29.4 per cent).[6] A community may specialize in wholesale trade, in retail trade, or in both. The average U. S. urban community has a smaller volume of wholesale than of retail trade, since wholesale trade is concentrated in fewer places. Retail trade, of course, also provides relatively more urban employment (17.6 per cent) than does wholesale trade (4.3 per cent). The effect of wholesale specialization on an urban place, therefore, may be less pronounced than that of retail specialization.

Table 2 summarizes comparisons of the demographic, economic, and socio-economic characteristics of the five classes of trade community considered in this paper. Comparisons among the types of trade centers and of each type with those lacking specialization in trade shows that the degree of retail trade specialization affects a number of the differences among communities. The major contrast occurs between communities which specialize in retail trade, either as Retail Trade (Rr) or Trade

---

6. Table 55, *U.S. Census of Population: 1950*, Vol. II, Part I, p. 102.

Centers (TC), and those which do not, i.e., Wholesale Trade (Ww), Maintenance Trade Centers (MT) and Non-Trade Centers (NT). This contrast reflects the fact that employees in retail trade are on the average four times as numerous as in wholesale trade.

The impact of specialization in retail trade on community morphology may be summarized as follows: (1) Rr and TC have somewhat older populations and smaller households, on the average, than do Ww, MT or NT places. (2) Rr and TC places have somewhat greater labor force participation rates for women, but not for men, than do Ww, MT, or NT places. This is not surprising in view of the heavy employment of females in retail trade. (3) Rr and TC places have higher proportions of males in hotels and lodging places and in entertainment and recreation than do Ww, MT or NT places. These findings can be explained in part by the frequent occurrence of entertainment and recreation in conjunction with retail eating and drinking places and undoubtedly with other retail places as well. A disproportionate number of the entertainment and recreation centers, as compared with all places, in fact, are Rr and TC places. (4) Rr and TC places have a higher socio-economic status level, as indicated by occupational composition and educational attainment, than do Ww, MT and NT places. These differences are probably explained by the fact that both wholesale and retail trade are substantial employers of white-collar workers, particularly of male managers, officials and proprietors, and of sales workers. In 1950, only two major industry groups had a larger proportion of male white-collar workers than did the combined wholesale and retail trade industries with 61.8 per cent. They were finance, insurance, and real estate with 81.9 per cent, and professional and related services with 71.3 per cent.[7] The fact that Ww centers do not show the expected predominance of white-collar workers seems due to other factors, primarily the fact that industries with a quite low proportion of white-collar workers tend to locate with wholesale trade. (5) Rr and TC places have relatively high proportions of male private household and service workers; this seems to be related to the occupational composition of retail trade. The proportion of male service workers is greater in retail trade (11.3 per cent) than in wholesale trade (1.2 per cent).[8] (6) Rr and TC places have a somewhat higher percentage enrolled in college than do Ww, MT and NT places. A number of factors undoubtedly account for this difference. Among them is the fact that specialization in higher education more often is linked with specialization as a Trade Center than one would expect given the percentage of Trade Centers among all places.

The share of wholesale trade in total employment in an urban place is relatively small. Despite this fact, specialization in wholesale trade

---

7. The foregoing statements are based on data in Table 134, *U.S. Census of Population: 1950,* Vol. II, Part II, pp. 290-91.

8. *Ibid.,* p. 291.

has a discernible effect on the social morphology of communities. (1) It increases the proportion of males in the labor force above that produced by retail specialization. This effect may be due to the circumstance that the ratio of employed men to employed women is much greater in wholesale than in retail trade. (2) Transportation accounts for more of the total employment in Ww and TC than in Rr, MT or NT places. There seems, in fact, to be a fairly clear rank order of types of trade centers by percentage employed in transportation: Ww centers have the highest proportion employed in transportation, followed by TC, MT, NT and Rr places, in that order. Wholesale trade, of course, requires more transport facilities and access to a large geographical network of transportation than does retail trade. (3) The percentage of employed male clerical and kindred workers is greater in Ww than in Rr communities. The fact that a larger proportion of the male workers in wholesale than in retail trade are clerical workers may explain this difference.

The relative absence of trade specialization also conditions the social morphology of urban communities. (1) NT centers have higher proportions of persons living in the same house in 1949 and 1950 than do centers with trade specialization. MT centers have higher proportions than do Rr or TC, but not Ww places. These findings are consistent with the opinion that trading communities should have more in-migration than places with little trade activity. The several exceptions to the finding mean that other factors are involved, however. (2) NT and MT places have a greater percentage of persons employed in manufacturing than do Rr, Ww or TC communities, except for Ww and TC suburbs. As manufacturing and retail trade are the largest industry groups in terms of employment, the fact that the two forms of specialization seldom occur together is not unexpected. Detailed examination of the data shows that wholesale trade is more likely to locate with manufacturing than is retail trade, a fact which human ecologists often have noted. (3) NT, MT and Ww places have higher proportions of male operative and kindred workers than do Rr and TC places, while the proportion of females so employed is generally highest in NT and MT places. This relatively high proportion of operatives and kindred workers in places with a relative absence of trade as compared with those specialized in trade probably can be attributed to the higher percentages employed in manufacturing in the former, although some minor types of functional specialization also are associated with a relative absence of trade.

Manufacturing Specialization. Manufacturing exerts a powerful influence on the morphology of a community which specializes in it. This influence is partly due to the fact that specialization in manufacturing, except in suburbs, decreases employment in other industries. The data in Table 3 disclose, in fact, that the percentages employed in transportation, public administration, hotels and lodging places, and entertainment and recreation, and the per capita wholesale and retail sales, are lower in manufacturing centers than in all places of comparable size and metropolitan status. Specialization in manufacturing furthermore, shows very little linkage with the minor forms of specialization, or with trade. Only two per cent of all urban places combine specialization in manufacturing with a minor form of specialization.

Manufacturing specialization exerts a substantial influence on the labor force of a community in that the proportion of males in the labor force is considerably higher in manufacturing communities than in all places. The demographic composition of manufacturing centers, however, generally differs little from that of other specialized places, except that the populations of manufacturing places are residentially more stable and the average household is larger.

The data in Table 3 show that manufacturing specialization exercises its greatest influence on the socio-economic level of the community. Specialization in manufacturing produces substantially *smaller* proportions of all white-collar workers and of manual service workers and laborers than are found in all places. There are substantially larger proportions only of craftsmen, foreman and kindred workers, and of operative and kindred workers, who, of course, comprise a sizeable proportion of all manufacturing workers. The effect of manufacturing specialization, then, is to truncate the occupational distribution for all places by employing disproportionate numbers of workers at the top of the working class and fewer at the top and the bottom of the rank order of all occupations. *Both* the highest and lowest paid occupational categories consequently have fewer workers in manufacturing centers than in all comparable places. This results in a higher median income level for manufacturing places than for all places of comparable size and metropolitan status, except for suburbs.

College Communities. The community specializing in higher education typically exports a service, education, by importing students into the community as temporary residents. The college or professional school student purchases a rather large number of goods such as food, clothing and housing, and services such as entertainment, recreation, and personal services. The selective nature of these purchases appears to have important consequences for the social morphology of college communities. Only a very small proportion of the employed persons in communities specializing in higher education are employed by educational institutions. Unless a place is very small, therefore, actual employment in higher education has relatively less effect on the social morphology of the community than do the purchases made by the student population.

College communities, when compared with places of comparable size and metropolitan status in Table 3, have an above-average socio-economic status level. Their economic base is favorable to employment in white-collar occupations. A higher percentage of men and women in college communities than in all comparable places are employed in all specific white-collar occupations, except that of male clerical and kindred workers, and the median level of school completed is higher. Correlatively, places specialized in higher education have a lower percentage of men and women in all manual occupations, other than private household and service workers. The relatively high socio-economic level of a college community cannot be traced solely to the fact that it specializes in an industry with

Table 3—Summary of Comparisons With All Standard Metropolitan Areas and Urban Places of 10,000 Population or More, for Manufacturing Centers and Each of the Minor Types of Functional Specialization

	NUMBER OF COMPARISONS IN WHICH SPECIALIZED PLACES HAVE A HIGHER FIGURE THAN ALL PLACES*							
	Mfg.	Ed.	PA	Tr.	My.	ER	F,I,RE	MHS
Per cent of population 21 years old and over	5	5	2	1	3	7	8	5
Sex ratio	7	4	6	4	7	4	2	1
Per cent nonwhite	2§	2	8	5	6	7	1	4
Per cent living in same house, 1949 and 1950	8	0	0	2‡	1	1	0	2
Per cent married males, 14 years old and over	5	0	4	6	3	6	5	2
Persons per household	8	1	3	5	3	0	1	2
Per cent in labor force								
Male	8	0	4	6	6	3	1	0
Female	5	4	5	2§	3	4	6	5
Per cent employed in manufacturing	8	0	0	0	0	0	0	0
Per capita wholesale trade	1	0	1	6	5	3	6	3
Per capita retail trade	1	6	1	1	3	8	7	4
Per cent government workers	0	7	8	6	8	6	6§	8
Per cent employed in transportation	0	0	4	8	3	1	4	4
Per cent employed males in—								
Public administration	0	6	8	6	8	6	6	6
Hotels and lodging places	0	5	7	3	6	8	8	6
Entertainment and recreation	0	8	2	1	7	8	6	2
Per cent of males employed as white collars	0	8	7	3	5	8	8	8
Per cent of males employed as—								
Professional, technical and kindred workers	0	8	7	0	5	7	8	8
Managers, officials and proprietors	0	8	4	6	5	8	8	6
Clerical and kindred workers	1	3	8	6	4	1	6	3
Sales workers	0	8	4	0	6	8	8	6
Craftsmen, foremen and kindred workers	8	2†	5	6	5	2	1	0
Operatives and kindred workers	8	0	0	2§	0	0	0	0
Private household and service workers	0	6	7	4	8	7	7	8
Laborers, except farm and mining	2§	0	7	8	6	4	2	3
Per cent of females employed as—								
Sales, clerical and kindred workers	0	8	8	6	6	1	8	3
Operatives and kindred workers	8	0	0	2§	1	0	0	0
Private household and service workers	0	7	8	7	6	7	6	8
Median school years completed	0	8	6	2	5	8	8	4
Per cent enrolled in school, persons 20 to 24 years	1	8	4	1	2	5	8	7
Median income, families and unrelated individuals	6	3	2	1	1	2§	7	3
Per cent of dwelling units owner-occupied	5	6	2	4	0	3	6	2

* Eight comparisons are involved; two size groups each of S.M.A.'s, central cities, suburbs, and independent cities. The symbols refer to the following types of specialized places: Manufacturing (Mfg.); Education (Ed.); Public Administration (PA); Transportation (Tr); Entertainment and Recreaiton (ER); Military (My); Finance, Insurance and Real Estate (F,I,RE); Medical and other Health Services (MHS).

† S.M.A.'s only.

‡ Independent cities only.

§ Suburbs only.

a relatively large proportion of white-collar workers. The higher socio-economic level also can be attributed to the fact that college communities attract other industries employing white-collar workers, as is shown by the relatively higher levels of employment in government, public administration, and entertainment and recreation than in all comparable places.

As to demographic composition, the male population in college communities is less likely to participate in the labor force than is the male population generally. This, of course, is expected since a majority of college students are not in the labor force. The proportion of men 14 years old and over who are married is somewhat lower in college communities than in all comparable places, although this finding is not consistent with the findings for the sex ratio. The population of college communities is somewhat more residentially mobile than that of all comparable places. This does not appear to be primarily due to the college population itself, suggesting that the mobility is due to other causes.

Public Administration Centers. Governments employ rather substantial numbers of persons in American communities, since a large number of community functions now are carried on by government. Public administration includes only those government activities, however, which are uniquely governmental functions, such as legislative and judicial activities and most of the executive agency activities of Federal, State and local governments. Government provision of educational and medical services, for example, is not classified as public administration, while government employment in the administration of the law—police, courts, penal and treatment institutions—for example, is considered public administration. Most municipal administrative activity functions solely to meet the needs of the local population. By contrast, Federal, State and county agencies function largely for the population beyond the confines of the place in which the agency is located. These centers are said to export administrative services, or to specialize in public administration. They often are referred to by particular names such as "county seat," "state capitol," or by the name of some government institution which is localized in the community, such as a penal institution or a military installation.

The demographic composition of public administration centers is similar to that of all places (Table 3). The stability of residence is somewhat below that of all places, however. This seems due in part to the fact that centers of public administration induce residential mobility through personnel transfer policies, patronage systems of employment, bureau changes, and so on. There also are somewhat greater sex ratios and percentages of nonwhite persons in public administration centers.

Employment opportunities in centers of public administration are similar to those in the average place of comparable size and metropolitan status. Specialization in public administration markedly affects the industry composition of a place, however. Centers of public administration are below the average place with respect to employment in manufacturing, wholesale and retail trade, entertainment and recreation, and finance, insurance, and real estate. By contrast, specialization in public administration increases employment in hotels and lodging places and is often linked with military specialization.

Public administration centers have a substantial excess of white-collar workers as compared with the average place, mainly accounted for by clerical and kindred workers and male professional, technical, and kindred workers. The percentage of female sales, clerical, and kindred workers in public administration centers is greater than that in any of the other minor types of specialized places except those specialized in finance, insurance and real estate. The occupational composition of public administration undoubtedly accounts for the relative importance of clerical and professional workers. Public administration centers show an overall deficiency of manual workers as compared with all comparable places. Table 3 discloses that there are slight excesses in some lower-status manual occupations—male laborers, and male and female private household and service workers. The average educational level of the population in public administration centers is consistent with the occupational composition, but the income level of the population is not. The excess of the lower-income clericals among white-collar workers and of laborers and private household and service workers among the manual workers may account for the relatively low median income level of public administration centers.

Transportation Centers. Cities of any substantial size require some employment in transportation to facilitate the local movement of goods and services. There are urban places which specialize in transportation, nevertheless, in that they either are the place of residence or of employment for workers who are connected with the movement of people and goods to and from a hinterland or other centers by motor, rail, air, or water transport. Transportation usually becomes a specialized function in a city that is a collection point for distribution to other places, or when the city is located at the point where people and goods are shifted from one means of transportation to another, e.g., from rail to motor transport.[9] There also are some places which become specialized in servicing transportation at a convenient point. The railroad town of Altoona, Pa. is such a servicing point at the foot of the Alleghenies, although dieselization of railroads has somewhat reduced this function.

There is very little to distinguish the demographic composition of centers of transportation from that of all places of comparable size and metropolitan status (Table 3). Opportunities for male, but not female, employment seem to be increased by specialization in transportation. This is not surprising, as transport employs relatively few women. The labor force participation rate of women in transportation centers, in fact, is gen-

---

9. See James A. Quinn, *Human Ecology* (New York: Prentice Hall, Inc., 1950), pp. 173-176 for a discussion of the "median location" and "break-in-transportation" theories of urban location.

erally below that of all comparable places or that in the other minor types of functionally specialized places.

Transportation fails to induce above average employment in any major industry group, other than wholesale trade. There is relatively little employment in manufacturing, retail trade or the minor types of specialized places, except public administration, in transportation centers in comparison with all other places.

Transportation centers have a relatively low socio-economic status level compared with the average place. Income and educational levels are somewhat below those of all places, and the transportation center has relatively small excess of manual workers. (See Table 3). The substantially lower median income in transportation centers cannot be attributed directly to specialization in transportation, however, since transportation provides a higher average income than most industry groups, including manufacturing. The occupational composition of transportation, however, would indicate lower levels of educational attainment. The deficiency of male white-collar workers in centers of transportation is largely due to a deficiency of professional, technical, and kindred workers, which counterbalances a slight excess of male managers, officials and proprietors, and of clerical and kindred workers. Transportation centers clearly reflect the fact that transport requires a relatively large unskilled work force, for there are substantially greater proportions of male laborers in these places than in all places. Transportation centers do not favor the employment of male operative and kindred workers, if suburbs are excluded, but they do have somewhat higher proportions of male craftsmen, foremen and kindred workers. Specialization in transportation can exercise little direct effect on the employment of women in specific occupations, for relatively few women work in transportation. The relatively higher proportions of employed women in sales, clerical and kindred jobs or in private household and service work in transportation centers must therefore be due to other selective factors.

Military Centers. Historically, military centers usually were true "fortress towns." The early frontier in the United States had a number of such places. The typical military center in the United States today, however, is an S.M.A. or urban place which serves as a host community to a military establishment located either within its boundaries or in a nearby open-country area. The geographical location of these military bases was determined by federal executive and legislative authority. It is less likely, therefore, that an ecologically competitive relationship determined their location than is true for other kinds of specialized places such as transportation centers. The size and number of military bases varies with national policy. The military centers in the comparisons which follow probably include only the relatively "permanent" military establishments prior to the Korean hostilities.

A military base has a double effect on the host community. It provides for some civilian employment at the military base, and it creates a demand for goods and services which the host community may be said to export to the establishment and its personnel. The comparisons below do not permit one to discriminate between these effects.

A military establishment appears to have two major effects on the demographic structure of the host community. Table 3 discloses that the sex ratio is somewhat higher, reflecting the presence of relatively larger numbers of males, and that the population is less stable residentially, reflecting the high residential mobility of military personnel and their families. The relatively low rate of home ownership in host communities also reflects the high residential mobility.

Military specialization stimulates the demand for extra-family services, since the majority of military personnel at a base are either unmarried or without their families. The effect of this demand on industrial employment can be seen in that military centers have somewhat larger proportions of males employed in entertainment and recreation and in hotels and lodging places than does the average place. Military specialization also appears to provide increased opportunity for civilian work with a government employer; host communities have substantially greater proportions of employed persons in government, and of employed males in public administration.

The socio-economic level of military centers probably is somewhat above that of all places of comparable size and metropolitan status when occupational composition and level of educational attainment in Table 3 are taken as indicators of socio-economic level. The occupational composition of military communities is primarily influenced by the relative absence of employment in manufacturing and trade as compared with the average place, and relatively more employment in the industries which cater to a transient population.

Entertainment and Recreation Centers. A community specializes in leisure by meeting extra-local demand for such services. A number of factors give rise to this extra-local demand. Local conditions may create an extra-local demand for their leisure facilities. This demand may be created by such diverse conditions as the legalization of gambling, the development of a religious shrine, or natural scenic endowment. Or, the demand may come from a nonlocal population or a transient sub-community which make demands on the larger or host community for special forms of leisure, such as the demand by populations with unbalanced sex ratios found at military installations, mining, or lumbering camps. Three major types of leisure centers are produced by these differences in demand —those based primarily on (a) recreation and natural endowment, generally called resorts; (b) commercial forms of amusement or entertainment, often characterized in terms of a particular commercial form, such as the commercial and legalized gambling for which Las Vegas is known or racing at Hialeah; (c) aesthetic institutions devoted to the arts and sciences, e.g., museums, art galleries, botanical and zoological gardens, musical festivals, and opera. Generally speaking, the United States has relatively fewer places which "export" the advantages of their aesthetic institutions, and large numbers of resort and commercial recreation centers. These several types of centers are treated as a single unit of entertainment and recreation centers in the comparisons below. Separate comparison would undoubtedly show, however, that the effects of the three types are not always the same.

The demographic composition of entertainment and recreation centers as a whole is substantially different from that of all places or any other type of specialized place. These specialized places have, as Table 3 shows, comparatively older populations, small households and a high incidence of residential mobility—characteristics expected of resort and retirement centers, if not of all types of entertainment and recreation centers.

The pattern of economic activity and the occupational structure of entertainment and recreation centers are conditioned somewhat by a complex of industries closely related to specialization in entertainment and recreation, as well as by the specialization itself. The centers show high per capita retail expenditures and fairly sizeable male employment in hotels and lodging places. The occupational structure shows a relative excess of male white-collar workers, largely accounted for by the excess of male managers, officials and proprietors, and male sales workers. Specialization in the commercial forms of entertainment and recreation, together with the auxiliary stimulation of the hotel business and of retail trade, probably accounts for this finding. The same complex of industries probably accounts too for the slight excess of both male and female service workers. The median level of educational attainment in entertainment and recreation centers is consistent with the excess of white-collar workers.

Finance, Insurance and Real Estate Centers. A community specializes in finance, insurance, or real estate when it exports these goods and services to a hinterland, region or territory. The institutional facilities which export these goods or services include Federal Reserve and private banking facilities, investment companies, security and commodity brokerage, insurance firms, insurance sales offices, and real estate sales offices. Cities which are specialized in finance, insurance and real estate may export one or more of these goods or services. Hartford, Conn. and Bloomington, Ill., for example, are recognized as cities providing sizeable employment in insurance, as the home offices of some very large insurance companies are located there. A few very large S.M.A.'s and central cities are highly specialized in all of the major forms of finance, insurance and real estate. Boston, Mass., New York City, N.Y., and San Francisco, Calif. are examples.

An examination of the demographic structure of finance, insurance and real estate centers summarized in Table 3 reveals that these centers have a substantial excess of older persons, a lower sex ratio, and a more mobile population than the average place. The need for a sizeable female clerical work force in finance, insurance and real estate firms undoubtedly affects both the sex ratio and the average residential mobility in these specialized places. Of the employed persons in finance, insurance and real estate in 1950, 41.7 per cent were women;[10] 72.5 per cent of these employed women were clerical and kindred workers.[11] The sex composition of finance, insurance and real estate probably accounts, too, for the fact that the labor force participation of women but not of men is slightly greater than that of the average comparable place.

Like all places specialized in a minor type of economic function, places specialized in finance, insurance and real estate have comparatively low manufacturing employment. Generally, employment in other minor forms of specialization is greater than that of the average place, except for transportation. The per capita expenditures for both wholesale and retail trade are also generally higher.

The striking feature of places specialized in finance, insurance and real estate, however, is their occupational composition. Among all minor types of functionally specialized places, finance, insurance and real estate centers have the highest percentage of white-collar workers in suburban and independent city comparisons. At least two-fifths of the workers in each size group of S.M.A.'s and type of urban place are white-collar workers, as are almost three-fourths of those in small suburbs. This white-collar excess is made up of substantial excesses in all major white-collar occupation groups, except that of male clerical workers. There are substantially fewer male and female manual workers, except for private household and service workers. The socio-economic level of finance, insurance and real estate centers is well above that of the average place, too, as measured by the educational attainment of the adult population. It is, in fact, generally as great as that of places specialized in higher education. Except for small central cities, the median income level of residents in finance, insurance and real estate centers is above that of all comparable places. The differences are relatively small, however, except for suburbs.

Medical and Other Health Service Centers. Every city maintains some medical, dental and other health services for its local population. There is a tendency, nevertheless, for such services to concentrate in a few centers. This is so for a number of reasons. First, State and Federal governments locate large, specialized medical-health facilities in centers to serve primarily extra-local populations. Examples of such centers are Kankakee, Ill., where a state mental hospital is the basis of specialization; Chippewa Falls, Wis., where it is a state hospital for mentally deficient persons; and Coatesville, Pa., where it is a Federal Veterans Administration hospital. The development of a medical center for the diagnosis and treatment of diverse forms of illness is a second basis for specialization. Such centers

10. Based on data in Table 55, *U.S. Census of Population: 1950*, Vol. II, Part I, *op. cit.*, p. 102.

11. Based on data in Table 2, *U.S. Census of Population: 1950*, Vol. IV, p. 61.

generally serve both local and extra-local populations. The most famous of these specialized centers in the United States is Rochester, Minn., where the privately developed Mayo Clinics serve a national patient clientele.

Specialization in medical and health services may affect the demographic structure of the community substantially. The effect is not uniformly the same, however, since it is a function of the kind of specialization, often, in fact, of the kind of medical institution or patient population. A medical custodial institution such as a mental hospital will have disproportionate numbers of older persons, while one for the mentally deficient will tend to have disproportionate numbers of younger ones; veterans' hospitals usually have a high sex ratio, while other hospitals have a more balanced one. Despite this lack of uniformity in effect, small differences were observed in the demographic composition of medical and other health centers and the average place of comparable size and metropolitan status. The sex ratio and the per cent of males 14 years old and over who are married are somewhat less than that of the average place, the average size of household is smaller, and the population is somewhat less stable residentially. These latter measures suggest a greater transiency rate in the population.

Places specialized in medical and other health services are somewhat more favorable to the employment of women than is the average comparable place, while the reverse is true for men. This is not surprising, since of the major industry groups treated in this study, only educational services and medical and other health services, each with 63.9 per cent of all employed persons who are women, employ more women than men.[12] Government is a substantial employer of persons in places specialized in medical and other health services. Only public administration and military centers of the specialized types of places considered in this study have higher ratios of government workers to all workers. Government is a substantial employer in places specialized in medical and other health services since the larger medical-health institutions usually are government supported—mental hospitals, hospitals for tuberculars, the mentally deficient, the physically handicapped, veterans hospitals, charity patient hospitals, and state or municipally supported research hospitals.

Specialization in medical and other health services should affect the occupational composition for employed women more than that for men, since men comprise a relatively small proportion of all employed in these services. Among men, however, the proportion of professional, technical and kindred workers and of service workers should be higher than that of the average place, as four-fifths of all employed men in medical and other health services are professional, technical and kindred workers (55.4 per cent) and service workers (25.1 per cent). This is the case in

12. Based on data in Table 55, *U.S. Census of Population: 1950*, Vol. II, Part I, *op. cit.*, p. 102.

Table 3, as only these two major occupation groups appear in consistently higher proportions for employed males than in the average comparable place. The same occupational expectations exist for women in places specialized in medical and other health services, as 50.4 per cent of the employed women in medical and other health services are professional, technical and kindred workers and 26.6 per cent are service workers.[13]

CONCLUSIONS. This paper examines some of the demographic, economic and socio-economic consequences which particular forms of economic specialization have on the social morphology of human communities. The largest impact of economic specialization generally is on the socio-economic status structure of the community. Several points are worth noting, since they are significant for theories of social stratification. (1) Specialization in manufacturing decreases the proportion of workers in both the highest and lowest paid occupational categories in our society and leads to substantial excesses in the middle occupational categories of craftsmen, foremen and kindred workers and operative and kindred workers; hence, there is a fairly high median income for the average family in the community, but fewer extremes in income. The population in manufacturing communities tends, in most ways, to be less consumption oriented than the population in the average community. There is a smaller per capita expenditure for both wholesale and retail trade, relatively fewer employed in hotels and lodging places, entertainment and recreation, medical and other health services, relatively fewer younger persons locally enrolled in institutions of higher learning, and a lower average level of educational attainment than in the average place. (2) The specialized community providing the sharpest contrast to the manufacturing community is the center of finance, insurance, or real estate. The community specialized in finance, insurance and real estate has substantial excess of all types of white-collar workers, but most particularly the male managerial, proprietary, and official and s worker white-collar occupation groups. Manual workers are relatively absent, except for the male and female private household and service workers associated with higher socio-economic levels. The extremes of education, income and occupation are more apparent in these communities, particularly since both the lower-status clerical white-collar workers and higher-status craft and operative manual workers are relatively absent. The average person who resides in these communities, however, has a relatively higher educational and income level and is more likely to own his own home than is the average urban person in the United States. Residents of places specialized in finance, insurance and real estate are more consumption oriented than is the average urban resident. (3) Communities specialized in higher education or in retail trade are reasonably similar to those specialized in finance, insurance and real estate, and therefore form a similar, though less marked, contrast to manu-

---

13. The percentages for men and women are based on data in Table 2, *U.S. Census of Population: 1950*, Vol. IV, Part I, p. 68 and p. 71.

facturing centers. (4) Centers of public administration show substantial excess of workers in the bureaucratic clerical occupations, and induce a relatively low consumption orientation.

In summary, almost every aspect of a community's structure is related to its basic functions. Reliable differences among the functionally specialized types of communities are found with respect to age and sex structure, mobility rates, labor force participation, educational attainment, industrial and occupational composition, income and home ownership. This does not imply that every functional type of community has a distinctive pattern for each of these characteristics, but that at least one functionally specialized type of place deviates considerably from the average for all places on each characteristic examined. The conclusion, therefore, seems warranted that type of functional specialization is a principal determinant of structural differences among communities.

THE SOCIAL STRUCTURE OF RACKETEERING

William F. Whyte

History of the Rackets. The liquor traffic of prohibition provided many of the prominent racketeers of today with their business experience and financial resources. In the early years of prohibition there were a large number of small liquor dealers in active competition. Prices fluctuated, and spheres of operation were not clearly defined. Competition often led to violence.

As time went on, some of the more skilful, energetic and daring of the dealers gained in financial status and power, so that they were able to push a number of the smaller independents out of business and extend their control over others. This combination movement continued steadily and, in Eastern City, reached its height shortly before repeal under the leadership of a man who became known as "the Boss."

The depression fell heavily upon the liquor industry. With improvements in production and distribution, a constantly increasing supply was becoming available just when the demand fell off. Many of the bootleggers became insolvent and defaulted on their debts to the producers. This provided the Boss with his opportunity. He organized a combination of about ten of the leading wholesalers (gang leaders) for the purpose of controlling all the imports of Canadian liquor into this section of the country. The Boss signed an agreement to pay the debts incurred by the delinquent bootleggers and in return was granted exclusive control over all the liquor produced by the distilleries for the American trade in the section where the combination was operating. The monopolists also operated their own stills. Toward the end of 1932 the combine held complete control over the distribution of liquor in the Eastern City region.

Then the Boss was murdered. His killing, accomplished by some relatively unimportant gangsters, seems to have grown out of a dispute unconnected with the monopoly; but, even with the Boss alive, it would have been difficult to maintain unified control over illegal activities in such an unsettled time as that which came with repeal in 1933. The members of the combine were unable to agree upon a successor. Instead, they divided the field that the Boss had controlled.

Reprinted from *Street Corner Society*, Chapter IV, pp. 111 ff., by permission of the author and the publisher. (Copyright, 1943, by the University of Chicago Press.)

The lessons in working together that had been learned by the combine members were to have a strong influence upon the subsequent organization of illegal activities in the vicinity of Cornerville. As the end of prohibition approached, the racketeers needed to find an alternative field into which to expand their activities. The policy racket seemed to provide this opportunity. Since bets of a dime, a nickel, and even a cent were taken, the racket appealed particularly to the poor man. At the height of prohibition profits, few of the top racketeers had paid attention to the exploitation of the numbers, but now many were beginning to see that small change would be worth collecting if it came in fast enough.

ORGANIZATION OF THE POLICY RACKET. Doc once commented:

I'm batted out. I'm so batted out that I didn't have a nickel to put on the number today. When a Cornerville fellow doesn't have the money to put on a number, then you know he's really batted out. Put that in your book.

Women as well as men play the numbers. When a mother sends her small child to the corner store for a bottle of milk, she tells her to put the change on a number. The racketeers themselves play the numbers. Tony Cataldo once told me:

I play a dollar every day on a three-number play and a quarter on four numbers. If the four numbers come out, I get a thousand dollars. Then, once a month, I put twenty dollars on a number. I figure if that comes out, I'll really have some money.

When the horse races which determine the day's number have been run, people lean out of the windows of their houses to look for the agent who can tell them what it is. The corner boys gather around and ask one another, "What's the number?"

If the Cornerville man does not obtain the information from his friends, he can get it in the newspapers. Every evening a local tabloid appears on the streets with a "Pay-off Edition," which contains not only the results of the races but also a convenient table, like the one in the following example. The morning papers also print this table on their sports pages.

$$
\begin{array}{ll}
\text{1-2-7 races} \dots\dots\dots\dots\dots\dots & \$145.20 \\
\text{1-2-3-5-7 races} \dots\dots\dots\dots\dots & \$209.80 \\
\text{[All] 7 races} \dots\dots\dots\dots\dots\dots & \$323.60
\end{array}
$$

The table is made up from the prices paid on two-dollar bets on winning, second-, and third-place horses in the designated races at a particular track. The digits in the table have no meaning except to the person interested in the number pool. The number is discovered by reading the first digit to the left of the decimal point, from the top down, on the table. In this case, it would be 5-9-3. The winning "four-number play" is determined in the same way, with the addition of the second digit to the left of the decimal in the bottom figure. While all important racketeers have interests in certain legal and illegal business activities besides the numbers, I shall concentrate upon describing the policy-racket organization, for that seems to provide a framework for the other activities and to give in most complete detail the relations among the men involved at various levels in the structure.

Cornerville men who seek to explain the policy racket always begin by saying, "It's run just like a business." The analogy serves to point out certain distinctive features of the racket. It runs from day to day in smoothly organized routines. Violence is held to a minimum, and other controls, including financial pressure, are used to regulate it. The syndicate in control of the numbers makes agreements to regulate competition among its members and to eliminate competition from outsiders. The leading figures in the rackets maintain efficient organizations with good discipline over their subordinates. They have fixed arrangements which enable them to deal smoothly with their legal problems.

At the bottom level of the racket organization are the agents who take the bets. Some have regular rounds of customers to be solicited, others are storekeepers or employees who "write numbers" for customers who come into the store. The agent writes the bets on a pad, gives a carbon slip to the customer, and turns the other over to his employer with his day's collections. He may accept bets of any amount from one cent up. The customer who "hits" receives odds of 600 to 1 on a three-number play, 4,000 to 1 on a four-number play, 80 to 1 on two digits, and 8 to 1 on one digit.

The agent is paid a percentage of the amount by which his total collections exceed the amount of the winnings to be paid to his customers. His share may run anywhere from 10 to 40 per cent, depending upon the amount of his daily collections and also upon his relations with his employer. In addition, whenever one of his customers makes a hit on a three-number play (the most popular type of play), the agent receives from the company (through his employer) 10 per cent of the amount of the customer's winnings.

Some of the larger agents have smaller agents working for them. If an agent's collections are large enough ($50 or more a day), he can turn in his numbers directly to "the office" and become a "50 per cent man."

All numbers collected by the agent are turned in to his 50 per cent man (except in the case of the small agent working for the larger agent, when the collections pass through an intermediate step before they reach the 50 per cent man). If both employer and employee are working in the same district, the agent personally turns in his collections, but if the 50 per cent man has a number of agents operating far away from his office, he sends out a collector (or "pickup man") to bring in the numbers written by these agents. The collector is paid a small salary. Some 50 per cent men write numbers themselves and have only a few agents working for them. Others have scores of men under them and never write a number.

The 50 per cent man turns over all his collections to "the office" or "the company," as it is variously known. The company backs the numbers. After all the collections are in and the number has "come out," the company office force calculates the amount of winnings to be paid on the numbers turned in by each 50 per cent man. This sum is turned over to the 50 per cent man, who passes it to his agents, and the agents pay off their customers.

Like legitimate businesses, the numbers companies meet their obligations to the customers. I have never heard of a Cornerville man who hit the number in recent years and was not paid in full. Customers have been paid even when agents have proved untrustworthy. As one agent told me:

Once a certain fellow hit for $4,000. The agent went up to the office and got the money to pay off with. Then he skipped town. When this fellow didn't get paid, he went to see T. S. T. S. says, "Wait awhile, maybe he'll be around later." After a couple of days this fellow goes up to T. S. again, and he's crying about that $4,000. So now T. S. knows the agent really skipped town, and he pays out the $4,000 himself. If they ever find that man that skipped town, his life won't be worth a nickel.

In maintaining their own positions, it is clearly in the interests of the companies to co-operate with one another—and they do. Perhaps the most common form of such co-operation is known as "edging off." When the agents turn in their number-pool slips, they write on the outside of the envelopes on what numbers they have bets totaling a dollar or more. The bookkeepers can then tell at a glance whether some numbers have been played so heavily that the company could not afford to pay the possible winnings. Then, as Tony Cataldo explained,

the big companies get together. I'll give you five dollars on 6–4–3. You might ask me if I can take five on 4–1–1, and I'd say, "I can't afford it; I already have too much on that number." That way, we have a chance to trade around before the number comes out.

This manner of spreading the risks is an important factor in the stability of the business.

One of the most important functions of the heads of the companies is the establishment and maintenance of close relations with politicians and high police officials. It is particularly important for them to have "connections" in the district attorney's office, and in this respect they have at times been very fortunate. The chief of police is obviously a key man for the operation of their business, and in the past they have had connections with at least one man who filled that office. Even if no such connection is available, the business may thrive on the basis of connections with the police captains, who are in charge of their districts. If the numbers business is flourishing in any district, it is safe to assume that the captain is "getting paid off." Political connections are important for the influence that may be brought to bear through them upon all the agencies of law enforcement. The chief of police is a political appointee. If he cannot be "reached" directly, pressure may be brought upon the man who appointed him.

A connection does not always mean bribery in the strict financial sense of the word. For example, there is one prominent law-enforcement official who does not take any money from the racketeers but who likes to bet on the horses himself. Crusades against gambling do not appeal to him. The racketeers have always given this man their political support and have been able to secure a number of favors from him.

Horse-race betting is controlled by the same organization which operates the policy racket. While the largest horse rooms are operated by the heads of the syndicate, some of the 50 per cent men have their own betting establishments. They turn in all bets to the company and receive 50 per cent of the profits. Protection is organized according to the policy-racket system.

RELATIONS WITH THE POLICE. It is the function of the 50 per cent men to provide police protection for their agents. As a 25 per cent man explained to me:

The cops are paid off. They call it the "union wage." The patrolman gets five dollars a month for every store on his beat that sells numbers. The plain-clothes men get the same, but they can go anywhere in Cornerville. They divide up the territory between themselves. They get on different pay rolls, and they divide up the graft, but even so a plain-clothes man can make more than a patrolman. The sergeant gets ten dollars [on every store]. The men in the cruising car get two-fifty each—some men sell themselves cheap. Of course, they got a lot of territory to cover.

The lieutenants and the captain in the local station are said to receive correspondingly larger payments, but these are handled above the level of the 50 per cent man by "the office." According to local accounts, the captain does not receive his money directly. It is placed in the hands of a patrolman or sergeant whom he trusts. Then, in case of some slip, the captain is protected as long as his subordinate does not testify against him, and, if the subordinate is accused of taking graft, the captain does all in his power to clear him of the charge.

The policeman's graft is not limited to money payments, as the 25 per cent man explained.

There's plenty of extras. Every Christmas and Easter my boss makes up a big bundle of groceries from his store for all the cops he pays off, and I deliver it for him to their houses. And then the cop never pays for nothing. They'll go in to my boss and ask for groceries and walk right out without even offering the money. That's the bad thing about having a grocery store. A man that don't have no business like that is better off in some ways. If a cop does pay, he gets a discount that you and I couldn't get. I give the cops cigarettes for ten cents. I lose two cents a pack on that. The cops get all their groceries free on market days—and other times. Some of them do it pretty raw. You come down some Saturday, and I'll show you one cop. He parks his car—it's a big Packard—on King Street, and then he loads up. And I mean he really loads up. He fills the back of that car from the floor to the roof. One family couldn't eat all that stuff. He must take care of all his relatives on that.

Not all this goods is provided by people in the racket. There are all sorts of city ordinances that can be invoked against the pushcart peddler and the small shopkeeper, if the policeman cares to take such action. Ordinances passed to meet conditions in other parts of the city can be used as weapons to force the Cornerville man to "take care óf" the police. If a man were thoroughly conversant with his legal rights, he might find that he could safely refuse to give the officers anything, but few know the law well enough to take the risk. There are many small businessmen who feel secure in their legal positions but nevertheless provide the officers with free goods. They explain that it is always advantageous to have a friend on the force and that there might come a time when he could do them a favor. Graft is given as a matter of course by men connected with the racket, but even outside the racket it is not always provided reluctantly.

It is not necessary to have connections with all the members of the police department. One officer in a district who is intent upon cleaning up the racket can cause considerable trouble, but in such cases the racketeers bring pressure upon politicians and police superiors to have him transferred to another section. One sometimes hears remarks such as this:

John Doe was one cop that caused a lot of trouble when he was down here, but they had him shifted. Now he's out patrolling the cemetery in ——, and don't he wish he could get back in Cornerville. It's lonely out by the cemetery. Nothing ever happens out there.

There are other weapons with which police superiors can discipline their subordinates. The captain may assign the officer to extra duty without financial compensation. It is understood in the department that there are two sorts of extra duty. When there is a parade, convention, band concert, or something of that nature which obviously requires a larger number of officers than are ordinarily in the area at one time, the officers detailed do not consider it punishment. At other times assignments to extra duty are recognized by the captain and his subordinates to be disciplinary measures. This is entirely unofficial. If the captain announces that the extra duty is a punishment, the subordinate has a right to appeal the decision to a trial board of the department. Naturally, most such penalty assignments are simply made "for the good of the service," and the captain is required to give no other explanation.

Some officers hate night work; others prefer it. Some dislike traffic duty; others like it. The captain who is familiar with the tastes of his men can penalize his subordinates by assigning them to jobs that they do not like. This, again, is not officially recognized as discipline, but it is so understood by the men concerned and thus serves its purpose.

The offering or withholding of promotions can be used as a reward or penalty. For several years recently, the police chief could promote to fill vacancies any officers who had passed the civil service examinations for the positions. Such discretionary powers were in his hands that there was a widespread belief that the jobs could be bought by anyone who passed and had the right political connections. The political requirements were a strong incentive to aspirants to refrain from bothering racketeers who had influential political friends. Now the chief is restricted to the top three men on the list when he has a vacancy to fill, to the top four when he has two vacancies, etc., but still it is commonly believed that a policeman's career is aided by his connections.

The threat of transfer is particularly effective with those officers who become attached to the district in which they are assigned, and this is true of many of the Cornerville officers. One agent said to me:

You know, Bill, I've known cops that have cried when they got transferred out of Cornerville. They all want to stay here. There's plenty of graft, and then they don't have to work around here. There's one cop comes into my store as soon as I open up in the morning, and he stays there until I go away at noon. He sits in the back and reads the morning paper, and we play cards. He goes out when he has to punch the box, but outside of that he's in taking it easy all the time. In some other sections you couldn't get away with that. I know one Cornerville cop that used to be in ——. Out there he wouldn't be in a store five minutes before somebody would call up the station-house, and they would have to send for him and tell him to keep out of there. A cop in a district like that really has to pound the pavement. He can't sit around all day like he does here. Down here there is so much numbers and horses going on that the less the people see of the cops the better they like it. Then, in other districts, the people have got telephones in their houses, they call up the station-house right from there to complain about a cop. Down here, how many people have telephones in their houses? Not one out of twenty families—less than that. And how many people are going to walk out and put a nickel in a pay phone to call the station-house? Besides, the people down here don't complain. The people that have made good, most of them have moved out. The people that are left—they just don't care. They let it ride.

Cornerville people look upon the local officers as parasites and feel that the dregs of the department have been foisted upon them. It is not exceptional to hear of an officer drunk or asleep while on duty. While this does not engender respect, it is convenient for the racketeers, who find the local force easier to deal with than officers of other sections.

There are prevalent in society two general conceptions of the duties of the police officer. Middle-class people feel that he should enforce the law without fear or favor. Cornerville people and many of the officers themselves believe that the policeman should have the confidence of the people in his area so that he can settle many difficulties in a personal manner without making arrests. These two conceptions are in a large measure contradictory. The policeman who takes a strictly legalistic view of his duties cuts himself off from the personal relations necessary to enable him to serve as a mediator of disputes in his area. The policeman who develops close ties with local people is unable to act against them with the vigor prescribed by the law.

Local people do not know what to make of a 100 per cent copper like Sergeant Clancy. His unorthodox behavior impels some to consider him crazy and others to admire him. One racketeer said to me: "You know,

Bill, I respect a man like that even though he hurts my business. If all cops were like him, we could have law and order in every city in the country."

However, this respect does not lead to friendship. In spite of the prevailing hostile attitude toward the police, all the other officers can count at least a few friends in the district. But not Clancy. Since he does not conform to the prevailing pattern of behavior, he has become socially isolated from his colleagues and from the people of Cornerville. At the same time, because he does his duty according to the *legal* requirements of his position, Sergeant Clancy forces the other officers to simulate conformity with his behavior.

It is not only the officers who are in the pay of racketeers who stress the importance of using discretion in enforcing the law. A police captain who was well known for his incorruptibility once said to me:

We don't judge the efficiency of an officer by the number of arrests he makes. There are so many arrestable offenses committed even by the law-abiding citizen that if the officer made all the arrests that he could, he would be a very, very busy man. If a man makes too many arrests, he isn't doing his job right. Of course, if he doesn't make any arrests at all, we know something is wrong. We rate the efficiency of the man as a variable considering the character of his route and how quiet he keeps it. If a man has a difficult section and he keeps it quiet so that there isn't much violence, places aren't being robbed, and the women aren't being bothered, then we know he is doing a good job.

I commented that, according to such a rating, an officer could be doing a good job while numbers were being sold all over his beat as long as the business was carried on in an orderly fashion.

That's right. There are so many millions of people in this country, and about half of them play the number pool. We all know it's going on. Why, one of those three men at the desk outside my office can play a number for you any time. He just calls up the office. The number pool isn't considered such a serious thing. The only bad thing is that it's run by men who don't want to work. As long as it is kept quiet, the cop can't complain. We might say, "For God's sake, don't write them under my nose. Go in the back street." The police have to see that it doesn't become too open. Of course, if an officer accepts money to let them do business, that's a very serious thing.

The captain's remarks are representative of the police attitude toward gambling. Many policemen have grown up in the same environment as the racketeers, where gambling is taken for granted. Some like to gamble themselves. At one time numbers were written in police headquarters, and, I am told, an officer handled the business. Gambling involves personal relations quite different from those to be found in other illegal activities. As long as the gambler feels that he is being fairly and honestly treated, he does not think of complaining to the police when he loses money. He participates of his own volition. But when a man is held up or has his home or store broken into, he complains to the police. Holdup men and burglars do not develop the routine day-to-day relations with the police that characterize the racket organization; their more spectacular breaches of the law receive more publicity and necessitate more energetic police action.

Observation of the situation in Cornerville indicates that the primary function of the police department is not the enforcement of the law but the regulation of illegal activities. The policeman is subject to sharply conflicting social pressures. On one side are the "good people" of Eastern City, who have written their moral judgments into the law and demand through their newspapers that the law be enforced. On the other side are the people of Cornerville, who have different standards and have built up an organization whose perpetuation depends upon freedom to violate the law. Socially, the local officer has more in common with Cornerville people than with those who demand law enforcement, and the financial incentives offered by the racketeers have an influence which is of obvious importance.

Law enforcement has a direct effect upon Cornerville people, whereas it only indirectly affects the "good people" of the city. Under these circumstances the smoothest course for the officer is to conform to the social organization with which he is in direct contact and at the same time to try to give the impression to the outside world that he is enforcing the law. He must play an elaborate role of make-believe, and, in so doing, he serves as a buffer between divergent social organizations with their conflicting standards of conduct.

In times of crisis it becomes difficult for the policeman to play his dual role. An outbreak of violence arouses the "good people" to make demands for law enforcement which must be carried out to a certain extent, even when they disturb police-racketeer relations. Therefore, it is in the interest of the department to help maintain a peaceful racket organization. Since competition in illegal activities leads to violence, it is also in the interest of the department to co-operate with the racket organization in eliminating competition. By regulating the racket and keeping the peace, the officer can satisfy the demands for law enforcement with a number of token arrests and be free to make his adjustment to the local situation.

Periodic crises in law enforcement require a high degree of flexibility on the part of the police department. In order to play the dual role, the organization must be able to move in opposite directions according to the requirements of the situation. The 100 per cent copper helps to maintain the necessary flexibility. When a racket scandal breaks, he is let loose upon the case. His reputation for incorruptibility is accepted by the public as a sign that the police are in earnest. When the furore dies down, he is shifted into the background. A man so prominent as Captain O'Leary cannot be too obviously penalized or shelved, but, if he is kept within certain bounds, his actions serve to strengthen the police organization. If there were no untouchables on the force, police-racketeer relations known as corruption would develop to such an extent that, when finally a crisis arose to bring this condition to public notice, the department would lack the men necessary to bring about an apparent reversal of policy. The resulting scandal might assume such proportions as to threaten the prevailing system of police organization with destruction. Then, presumably, a period of confusion would follow while a new (or similar) social system was developing. The untouchable officer therefore helps to keep the police organization in a state of equilibrium between the pressures which are exerted upon it from both sides.

These generalizations do not mean that the police department and the racket organization enter into a great conspiracy and agree upon a common policy. The relations between them are established not in the mass but between individuals of both groups, and the actions on both sides become a matter of habit and custom just as they do between other people and other groups. While a study reveals certain consistent patterns in the actions of men, it is not correct to assume that anyone planned them to be such as they are.

THE RACKETEER IN HIS SOCIAL SETTING. The strength of the racketeer rests primarily upon his control of gambling activities. In our middle-class society gambling is a disreputable activity. In Italy, as in many European countries, gambling is taken for granted, and the state promotes its own lotteries. Protestants tend to identify law and morality and therefore to consider illegal acts as immoral. The Catholic church makes no such identification. Gambling is a temporal matter. The state has the right to forbid it, but the legal prohibition does not make it immoral. According to the church, gambling is immoral only when the gambler cheats, uses money which is not his own, or deprives his dependents of what is needed for their maintenance. Recognizing that it often involves such deprivation and that it tends to be associated with immoral activities, the church looks with suspicion upon gambling; but that is quite different from an outright moral ban.

The common Cornerville attitude toward gambling was expressed to me in this way by a corner boy:

Suppose I'm a rich man, and I like to follow the horses. When they're running in Crighton, I can go out there and bet my money. When they're in Florida in the winter, I can go down there and play them. That's all legal. That's all right. But suppose I'm a poor man. In the summer I go out to Crighton. In the winter I can't afford to go to Florida, but I still want to play them. I don't lose interest just because they're in Florida. Is it immoral for me to bet them in a horse room? Why should it be immoral for me if it ain't for the rich man?

Cornerville people have quite a different attitude toward robbery and murder. They draw a sharp line between respectable and nonrespectable illegal activities. Gambling is respectable.

Gambling plays an important role in the lives of Cornerville people. Whatever game the corner boys play, they nearly always bet on the outcome. When there is nothing at stake, the game is not considered a real contest. This does not mean that the financial element is all-important. I have frequently heard men say that the honor of winning was much more important than the money at stake. The corner boys consider playing for money the real test of skill, and, unless a man performs well when money is at stake, he is not considered a good competitor. This helps to fix the positions of individuals and groups in relation to one another.

In individual and team competitions the corner boys organize their own gambling. If they wish to play the horse or dog races or the numbers, they cannot handle the situation in the same informal way. It is here that the racketeer comes in. He organizes gambling as a business.

The corner boy knows very well that, in playing the number pool or betting on the horses, he will lose on the average. For him the financial incentive is not the only one. He enjoys studying the horse-racing lore and matching his skill at selecting winners against that of his friends. There is no skill involved in playing the numbers, yet people develop attachments to their "steady numbers," and they enjoy discussing their experiences with the numbers.

A corner boy who saved his nickels and dimes would have more money in the long run than if he bet them on the numbers, but he could not pursue this course without disagreeable social consequences. The corner boy who has money is expected to help his friends. The free spender is popular and respected. Saving, therefore, is not a real alternative to gambling on the numbers. The small change would be dissipated in one way or another, whereas the large amounts occasionally won have real meaning for the corner boy. The sixty dollars that comes from a ten-cent three-number hit is used to pay off debts, to buy an outfit of clothes, to treat his friends, to give some money to his parents, and to gamble again.

The racketeer conducts activities which lend themselves particularly to the extension of his social influence. In retail trade, price and quality of goods have some influence upon sales, but the odds paid on winning numbers and horses are exactly the same throughout Cornerville. Personal ties and personal trust are, then, the only factors which influence the customers to place their bets with one agent instead of another. The corner boy wants to give his business to a friend, and close ties are established between the agent and his customers. Those on a higher level in the organization have risen to their positions through forming the same sort of relations of friendship and trust with the Cornerville people. These relations continue to exist, though in somewhat modified form. T. S., for example, cannot have close relations with all those who do business with his organization, but he spends much of his time in Cornerville, and, when he is there, he hangs on a certain corner, or in a certain barbershop, and has his "coffee-and" in a certain restaurant like any of the corner boys. Although he lives outside the district, he has not cut himself off socially from the corner boys as have most successful business and professional men.

Organized gambling activities tend to place a number of the corner boys in a position of dependence upon the racketeers. It is part of the code of the man who makes a profession of gambling that he gives back some of his winnings to the losers who are "cleaned out." I know one crap-game holder who used to take home all his days' earnings to his mother. He came to be regarded as "a cheap no-good" fellow, and, had his associates in promoting the game not abided by the code in quite a liberal manner, he would have lost his customers.

In Cornerville the racketeers are known as free spenders and liberal patrons of local enterprises. They spend money in local stores. They patronize the activities of the corner boys with purchases of blocks of tickets to dances and with other contributions.

One young man in a legitimate business said of T. S. and his associates:

These gangsters are the finest fellows you want to meet. They'll do a lot for you, Bill. You go up to them and say, "I haven't eaten for four days, and I haven't got a place to sleep," and they'll give you something. Now you go up to a businessman, one of the respected members of the community, and ask him. He throws you right out of the office.

This pattern of action is substantially the same for all racketeers. While the generosity of outlaws is a theme as old as time, it is important to understand it in this case not as a peculiar personality trait but as an important aspect of the racketeer's adjustment to his society.

Generosity creates obligations which are recognized by its recipients. Beyond the group of "parasites" who are completely dependent upon his support, there are a large number of corner boys who are at some time or other beholden to the racketeer for money lent to them or spent upon them.

The racketeer's power is seen in clearer perspective when he is compared with some of his possible competitors for influence. Legitimate business and professional men are usually considered the leading members of the community. There are a number of prosperous business and professional men who grew up in the district and still have their stores or offices in Cornerville, but most of them have made their homes in less congested and more socially desirable sections. They spend many of their working hours in Cornerville, but they have little time and usually little inclination to "hang with the boys." Even those few who have continued to live in Cornerville tend to be limited socially by the nature of their activities. A storekeeper must remain in his store and wait for the customers to come to him. He must rely upon the steady trade of his circle of friends and acquaintances, and yet he cannot afford to become too intimate with the corner boys. In fact, sometimes one hears it said that a man failed in business because he had too many friends—because too much of the business of these friends was on a credit basis. If a man is too closely tied to the corner boys, he will have difficulty in refusing them credit, whereas if he avoids becoming involved with them he may still have their business if his products are good, his prices reasonable, and his location central to their activities. However, in the latter case, he will not have the influence of the man who is "one of the boys."

Many stores are dependent upon the numbers business, and the storekeepers thus become a part of the racket organization. Numbers are sold in all kinds of stores, but they are most commonly found in small variety stores, barbershops, lunchrooms, and poolrooms. It is significant that these are places which are used as hangouts by the corner boys. The boys are friendly with the owner of the store, and the owner depends for much of his income upon his numbers business. In such circumstances the influence of the racketeer needs no further explanation.

While the Cornerville rackets are organized around gambling, local racketeers have a number of other interests. Some still deal in bootleg liquor, underselling the legal product by evading the government tax. However, this business is insignificant compared with the prohibition traffic, and there are many racketeers who have nothing to do with it. At times certain men in the organization have furnished strike-breakers to industry, but this work has been sporadic. At present there are no houses of prostitution in Cornerville. The dope traffic is little in evidence in the district, though some local men have been arrested and sentenced on dope charges. There may be a tie-up between the racket syndicate and these businesses. "The Boss" who organized the liquor monopoly also controlled the Eastern City dope traffic. However, there is no evidence that any Cornerville racketeers up to and including the 50 per cent men have business interests in prostitution or dope.

There are in Cornerville some small gangs indulging in holdups and burglaries. While some prominent racketeers began their careers in this line, they have discontinued such activities since becoming established in the more secure and respectable field of gambling. Some agents occasionally participate in holdups, but this is discouraged by those prominent in the organization. It is bad business for the racketeers to have their subordinates get in trouble with the police any more than is necessary in the operation of the rackets. The holdup men usually operate independently with a few associates. Some of them are friendly with racketeers and seek their help when in trouble with the law. While the racketeers look down upon holdup men, there are informal relations existing between them.

If they exist at all, protection rackets preying upon legitimate Eastern City businesses have certainly not been organized to the extent found in other cities. Some years ago in Cornerville the racketeers forced all the bakeries to pay them protection, but the racket was short lived. On another occasion in a near-by city, racketeers attempted to set up control of the poultry market, but the murder of a well-known local businessman and member of the American Legion upset their plans at the outset.

In all their activities, legal or illegal, the racketeers perform the important function of providing employment for a large number of men. Most of the employees have no background of experience and skill to prepare them for jobs in private industry. Furthermore, it is widely believed in Cornerville, and not without considerable evidence, that a Cornerville Italian is discriminated against when he applies for a job. The corner boys do not fit into the socially approved economic organization, and in the depression the rackets provided them with jobs difficult to find by other means.

The racketeers also provide investment capital for new enterprises. One story will serve as an example. Tom Leonardi was a young Cornerville man who worked for a large corporation. Tom learned the business well and saw opportunities for profits if he started out for himself. Without any capital to back him, he began selling the product among his friends. He built up a small trade, but he needed capital to expand his operations. City investment bankers would hardly be interested in backing an unknown young Italian who was entering into competition with firmly intrenched corporations. Tom approached several Italian racketeers, and they agreed to invest. With their capital, he was able to buy the plant and equipment necessary for the expansion of his business. At the same time his board of directors pushed sales with enthusiasm—which sometimes led to coercion. Today the business is firmly established, and certain "tough" sales methods of earlier years are less in evidence. The company produces a product of excellent quality and seems likely to enjoy a long and prosperous existence. The evidence indicates that Tom Leonardi had superior business ability, and yet, had it not been for the support of his racketeer friends, he would still be struggling to get ahead. This is not an isolated example. The support of racket capital has helped a number of able men to rise to positions otherwise unattainable.

Racket capital in Eastern City has been invested in a large number of legitimate enterprises. It is most in evidence in the production and sale of liquor, in finance companies, in night clubs and restaurants, in race tracks, and in sports promotion.

From the racketeer's standpoint there are several advantages to having legitimate business interests. Profitable investments are welcomed for obvious reasons. Even unprofitable interests serve as convenient "fronts" for the illegal activities.

The promotion of prize fights is an uncertain and frequently unprofitable business. I understand that the racketeer most prominent in this line cleared a profit of less than a hundred dollars on the operations of a recent year. Nevertheless, he and his associates considered it well worth the trouble.

They pass out the tickets to certain police officers and businessmen. Suppose they send ten tickets to a certain officer every time there is a fight. He uses them and passes them out among his friends. Sometime if they need a favor from him, he is supposed to do it for them. That's why it's good business. . . . And then they pass out tickets to all their numbers writers—to show their appreciation.

It appears that one of the chief incentives for entering legitimate business is the hope of becoming "respectable," as the following story indicates. Joe the Wolf started out as a bodyguard for a prominent gang leader. He had frequent clashes with the law. Once, when a gangster was shot, Joe the Wolf was caught running away from the scene of the crime. He was tried for murder and acquitted. For some time after that Joe was picked up by the police whenever a gang murder had been committed. He complained that he was being hounded. His activities were changing. He made money in the numbers and acquired some legitimate business interests. He played up the respectable side of his career and discouraged the use of his nickname. He refused to allow his daughter to go out with racketeers. She married a man of a respectable family who was engaged in a legitimate business. The elaborate wedding reception attracted a large gathering, including many local businessmen and prominent politicians. Newspaper accounts of the affair described the bride's father as a "well-known sportsman." Although Joseph Lupo is still known to the corner boys as Joe the Wolf, he has traveled far toward respectability since his early days.

The rackets function in Cornerville as legitimate business functions elsewhere. The racketeer patterns his activity after the businessman and even strives to gain respectability so that he may become accepted by society at large as he is accepted in Cornerville.

VOLUNTARY ASSOCIATIONS
IN THE UNITED STATES

Herbert Goldhamer

Despite a tendency toward individualism, Americans have long been known as a "nation of joiners." Over a hundred years ago a Frenchman, Alexis de Tocqueville, observed that "in no country in the world has the principle of association been more successfully used, or applied to a greater multitude of objects than in America. . . . Wherever, at the head of some new undertaking, you see the government in France, or a man of rank in England, in the United States you will be sure to find an association." Toward the end of the nineteenth century an equally eminent observer, Lord Bryce, noted that "associations are created, extended and worked in the United States more quickly and effectively than in any other country." And in our own day, speaking of the twenties, the historian Charles Beard has written: "The tendency of Americans to unite with their fellows for varied purposes . . . now became a general mania. . . . Any citizen who refused to affiliate with one or more associations became an object of curiosity."

The fact is, of course, that we are never in any exclusive sense members of a society at large. Rather, we are members of a variety of social groups within the society. What we have seen in the United States (and in modern Western civilization in general) is an extension of this principle.

In earlier and simpler societies the individual usually belonged only to three groups: his community, his church, and his family. Most of the activities or work of the society was carried on by these groups or by the individual himself. Today, however, the activities of our society are carried on by a great variety of groups. We are, perhaps, most aware of this in the field of economic activity. In an earlier period most of the economic activity was carried on either by the family or by individual workers and businessmen, whereas now the major portion of the American national income is produced by organized groups called "corporations." Many of our economic activities could not be undertaken or the advantages of large-scale production secured by the single individual operating by himself. It is for this reason that the modern world has seen the phenomenal growth of the stock company—a type of organized group whose members pool their

Reprinted from *Third Year Course in the Study of Contemporary Society*, Vol. 1, Tenth Edition, September 1942, by permission of the author and the publisher. Copyright, 1942, by the University of Chicago Bookstore.

resources in order to undertake what the individual could not do by himself. In 1857 an American judge went as far as to say that the Illinois legislature had created more corporations in its last session than existed in the whole world at the beginning of the nineteenth century. And in 1929 we find that over 90 per cent of the income produced by manufacturing was produced by corporations.

Most persons are aware of the very great part played by corporations in our national economy. But probably fewer people realize how much of our noneconomic activity is carried on by the thousands of clubs and associations that exist in the United States. A great part of our recreational, educational, philanthropic, political, protective, and social activities are now carried on not by the family or by the single individual but by participation in a great variety of organized groups such as fraternal societies, civic associations, social clubs, businessmen's organizations, trade-unions, athletic clubs, scientific societies, and many other types of organizations. One might perhaps say that the club and association have tended to become in the noneconomic life of our society what the corporation is to its economic life.

We may be sure that the organized group or association could not be so widespread in its application and so adaptable as an instrument for achieving the most diverse aims without being deeply rooted in the conditions and nature of American life. Nor is it very difficult to see what those factors are in American society that have led to the organization of so many associations.

People organize themselves into groups only if they are in some way different from other persons in the society, only if they have special interests that serve to bring them together and mark them off from others. Consequently we find in the United States that the more differentiated the members of a community are, the more associations they tend to have. In the early American rural community most persons were very much alike; they had very largely similar occupational and economic interests, similar leisure time interests, similar racial, nationality, and religious backgrounds. They had, therefore, very little incentive to organize themselves into separate groups. But in the typical American urban community of today the situation is quite otherwise. There is, for instance, a very great variety of occupations, and consequently a very great diversity, often divergence, of occupational, economic, and political interests. If an individual is a manufacturer of mop and broom handles, he will find a trade association devoted to the interests of that industry; if he is a trainer of thoroughbred horses, a society exists for him; if he is an opera singer, he may join a trade-union that protects the interests of his craft. Similarly, we find that in the American community of today there are a very great number of specialized recreational interests. Bridge players, chess players, tennis players, stamp collectors, garden enthusiasts, amateur astronomers—these and hundreds of other groups organize themselves into associations for the pursuit of their common interests. Even a common enthusiasm for the same movie actor or actress has proved sufficient to draw people together into "fan clubs." Only an extraordinarily individuated person would be unable in any large American city to find an organized group whose members are devoted to his own leisure-time interests.

But the organization of associations in the American city does not merely proceed along the lines of the specialized interests referred to above. Age, sex, racial, nationality, and religious differences cut across these lines and provide still further incentives for group organization. For these differences tend to make persons socially exclusive and also to provide them with different interests. People are frequently forced to, or else prefer to, associate with persons of the same race, nationality, religion, or social standing. And consequently one finds that even in relatively small towns there may be not one athletic club but several, each club drawing its members from a different income, religious, or racial segment of the population.

But there is another reason why the city, as compared with the small community, tends to breed organizations. Even where there are many specialized interests in the small community, the persons who have these common interests usually know one another and can meet without being brought together through the machinery of a formal organization. The checker player knows that he has only to go down to the general store to find his fellow-players. But, in the city, persons having common interests could not come together or easily find one another in order to pursue together the activity in which they are interested without some degree of formalization of their relationship. The city person may not even know that his next-door neighbor has interests similar to his own. And so we find that, in the city, associations serve to advertise to persons that here other individuals may be found who are interested in the same things in which they are.

Since the specialization of interests leads to a specialization of associational activities, the members of associations tend to associate with one another or pursue common activities only in respect to relatively narrow segments of their total life-activities. This contrasts strongly with the type of total participation or association characteristic of such groups as the small community and the family. When the individual's social relationships increasingly occur within the framework of specialized associations there tend to follow as consequences both a diminution of the affective or emotional content of the social relationships and a diminution of social control over the individual by the groups in which he participates. It is characteristic of many contemporary urban associations, especially those that are not primarily "social" or convivial in nature, that they are more concerned with controlling the behavior of nonmembers than they are with controlling the behavior of their own members. The latter type of control tends, furthermore, to be confined only to the spheres of behavior which are regarded as instrumental to the association's attaining its specified goals. While the associations to which an individual belongs may exercise a rather limited control over him, it is important to realize that there are many other groups to which he does not belong that are actively interested in controlling his behavior. One might summarize this point by saying that the individual in contemporary society (as contrasted with earlier and simpler societies) tends to be controlled less by his "ingroups" and more by his "outgroups." Another aspect of this situation is that whereas in the past total participation in an inclusive group gave direction to an individual and prescribed his choices, segmental participation, such as is widespread today, gives to the individual a multiplicity of possible choices, some of which are mutually contradictory. The individual is thus forced to decide for himself which of these choices is most congenial to him to a considerably greater degree than in the past, increasing both his freedom and his responsibility.

Most of us today are very conscious of the terms "pressure groups" and "pressure politics." The very important part that is played by pressure politics in American government provides us with an additional explanation of why organized groups have been so important throughout the greater part of American history. Democracy in the sense of an active, immediate, and direct participation of the people in the details of the governmental process has long ceased to exist. The conditions which enabled the New England town-hall meeting to function have receded into a distant past; it is no longer possible for citizens of even a relatively small town to meet for the discussion of common problems. In its place has come government by representatives of the people. Democracy under such conditions is dependent upon the degree to which the people are still in a position to make important political judgments and to direct their elected representatives in accordance with their wishes. In a sense an election provides an opportunity for a canvas of opinion. Few elections, however, are waged in terms of specific issues. Hence citizens require a method of securing organized expression on issues as they arise. Such expressions, of course, do not represent merely the statement of a position in regard to an issue but also a demand, backed by whatever means of pressure are available to the organization, that the issue be settled in accordance with its desires. Now it is precisely this function of expressing and enforcing the wishes of its members that has characterized the activities of many American organizations. In this way these organizations appear to revive once more, in varying degrees, the participation of citizens in the governmental process. This would certainly seem to be a very definite gain. Yet it is not difficult to see that this process has at the same time created grave problems. For the groups which attempt to influence governmental policy are in too many cases merely devoted to furthering their own special interests. This fact is hardly likely to surprise anyone. What is significant, however, is not that particular groups favor measures of special benefit to themselves but that all sections of the population are not equally organized for the expression of their opinion and that many organized groups, because of greater financial resources or other strategic advantages, are able to acquire an influence in public affairs disproportionate to their numbers. In a democracy it would certainly seem desirable that governmental authorities, whether municipal, state, or federal, should be responsive to public opinion, and that public opinion, failing frequent referendums, may very well be expressed through organizations of citizens. It becomes all the more important, therefore, that there should be more equal opportunities for people to organize for the study of problems that concern them and more equal opportunities for the expression of a genuinely public opinion. It has, in part, been because of a greater awareness of this necessity that the number of organizations has increased so rapidly in the past years and that so many of these new organizations have been concerned with public issues.

Desirable as the multiplication of such voluntary associations may be, their development is often a matter of great concern to those who control the apparatus of government. Most groups seek, at least to some extent, to attach the loyalties of their individual members to themselves and to direct the behavior of the individual in all or some of his activities. Consequently groups, and especially organized associations, are likely to be regarded— and may, in fact, be—rivals of the "great association," the state, for control over the members of the society. Loyalty toward a special group need not, of course, necessarily be incompatible with loyalty toward the state or, more specifically, incompatible with the individual's conformity to the laws and directives promulgated by those who conrol the governmental apparatus. But, in fact, this situation occurs with considerable frequency. It is most clearly illustrated in the case of many sectarian religious movements that have attempted to direct the total life-activities of their adherents along lines conformable with certain religious convictions. Since such sectarian movements usually oppose any show of loyalty toward "nonbelievers" and since their injunctions are almost always in conflict with at least some of the decrees of the state authorities, they tend to create a "state within a state"—a situation which is likely to be intolerable to state officials jealous of any rivals to their power and fearful of the consequences of any successful opposition to their decrees. The formula "Render unto Caesar that which is Caesar's and unto God that which is God's" is an attempt at compromise intended to smooth over the conflicts inherent in the situation just described.

Sectarian groups frequently desire only "to be left alone" and to be able to construct for themselves a type of communal life consistent with their convictions. This separatism from the general life of the society sometimes renders them relatively tractable and innocuous from the standpoint of the state authorities. Of more direct threat to the state power are those associations that do not withdraw their members from the life of the society but which seek instead to influence or attain control over its decisions. Associations with political and economic aims are especially likely to be regarded as objects of suspicion, although in general any association that may be able to control the behavior of its members to the extent of offering opposition to state decrees or rendering its members more impervious to "official" ideologies is a potential threat to the state authorities.

Because of actual or potential conflict between the "great association" and the lesser associations the latter have had in most countries to carry on a continuous struggle for freedom of association. This struggle, especially in recent times, has been necessary only for certain restricted categories of associations such as trade-unions, radical political parties, cooperatives, and business corporations. The restrictions on association and governmental control over associational activities are, then, largely confined to those groups whose interests tend to be opposed to the interests of the power-holders in the society. The power-holders in the society themselves make use of associations to consolidate their position and to attain their ends. They are not interested, therefore, in restricting the action of all associations, but only those which threaten their position. Associations become, then, for the power-holders an auxiliary form of control. In the totalitarian countries power has become so concentrated in the hands of the state authorities—that is, power has tended so largely to become purely political power—that the attack on associations has been much more widespread. Since it is relatively unnecessary to maintain fictions of democratic control in the totalitarian countries, the remaining important associations which are tolerated in such countries are those which are more or less openly under the direct control of the state authorities.

The emergence of organized groups that held property precipitated both for this and for other reasons serious legal problems. Law defines the obligations and rights of persons, but it became progressively impossible to deal legally with organized groups as so many separate individuals. In order to deal with associations, especially in their capacity as holders of property, the Roman jurists developed the notion of associations as *personae fictae*—that is, fictitious persons. Associations achieved thereby legal recognition from the state. Early in the fourteenth century English jurists, faced with a similar problem, made the legal recognition of organized groups dependent upon the receipt of a royal charter or franchise. It became customary, therefore, to look upon associations as a creation and hence a "creature of the state." Incorporation of organized groups for the attainment of full legal status is still today subject to rules promulgated by the state authorities. Only in a purely juridical sense, however, would it be possible to say today that the associations in the United States are "creatures of the state." And perhaps at no previous period in the history of the United States have the problems of policy involved in defining the relations between associations and the state been so acute as at the present time.

THE IMAGERY OF THE URBAN COMMUNITY PRESS

Morris Janowitz

Within the city limits of Chicago, in 1950, 82 community newspapers were being published with a total weekly circulation of almost 1,000,000. With the exception of New York City, similar patterns could be found in every metropolitan center in the United States of over one million residents, for it is at this population level that the urban community press begins to develop.[2]

The urban community press is defined as any weekly (or more frequent) English language publication addressed to the residents of a specific locality or area of the metropolitan district. Their mode of production and distribution may vary considerably as well as their financial base. Nevertheless the urban community press—city and suburban—can be considered as a homogeneous class insofar as it is directed to a geographically and ecologically delimited audience within the metropolitan district.

Coordination and the maintenance of consensus within the urban community has been closely associated with the development of interrelated systems of mass media, of which the community press is a part. The mass media have contributed to the growth of the urban centers by providing the channels of mass information and symbolism required for the integration and social solidarity of vast aggregates of population. In turn, urbanism has promoted the development of the mass media by providing geographically a concentrated audience and a concentrated market for their support.

In particular, since 1920, the growth of urbanism in the United States has been accompanied by a growth of the urban community press. Just as the development of urbanism allowed for and stimulated the organization of various local and specialized institutions in the community, so the growth of the mass media was accompanied by the development of specialized and local channels of communications. The growth of the community press, although subject itself to tendencies of consolidation and large-scale organ-

1. Excerpted and adapted from *The Community Press in an Urban Setting* (Glencoe, Illinois, The Free Press).

2. It appears that a tremendous daytime population concentration, a transportation system which de-emphasizes satellite business districts, a high population concentration, shifts in land utilization which alter local residential communities wth great rapidity, and the persistence of the foreign-language press have prevented the development of an urban community press on Manhattan Island.

ization, stands in opposition to the development of these tendencies more generally in modern society and in the mass media.

As a specialized system of communication the community newspaper stands in contrast to most mass media in that it is not designed to reach the widest possible audience and/or to promote the most general identifications. In terms of its function, the community newspaper is a ready sociological index to community organization and community orientations. As such, it is one of the many institutions and agencies which participate in the process of integrating the individual into the urban social structure by assisting him to maintain the complex balance between local and non-local practices and orientations.

Analysis of its historical growth, ecology, ownership, control, content and audience response to content are all involved in understanding the community press' function and implications, with audience response being of crucial importance. Audience response itself involves numerous dimensions: *exposure*—the amount of content to which the individual attends; *involvement*—degree of importance the individual attaches to the content in meeting his needs and interests; *interest pattern*—portions of the communication to which the individual attends; *penetration*—the conscious recall or remembrance of content to which the individual has exposed himself; and *imagery*—verbalized responses to the ongoing flow of communication which reflect less reactions to specific content and more basic attitude to its overall format, style and character.

Six hundred interviews with men and women respondents of three Chicago communities in which separate community newspapers were published supplied data on the extent of readership. The three communities represented a lower class community (designated as Atwater), an upper-lower and lower-middle class community (Bethel Park) and a lower-middle and middle-middle class community (Carleton Manor).

The amount of readership encountered according to an elaborated set of criteria measuring both exposure and involvement is presented in Table No. I, which indicates the extensive readership of the community press in the face of strong competition from the other mass media.

The data presented here deal only with certain aspects of reader imagery, although the correlates and dimensions of exposure, involvement, interest pattern and penetration are all required to describe audience response and impact. The analysis of reader imagery, in particular, is of importance in indicating the manner in which the urban community press operates as a counter-force against the individuating influences in the metropolitan community. The material presented emerges not only from direct questions but, more relevantly, from associative comments throughout the interviews.

Four themes in general encompass the main elements of the image of the community press held by its *readers:*

1. The community press is generally perceived as an auxiliary not as a

competing news source with the daily press (and tends to be viewed favorably for its preoccupation with the details of the local community which are unreported in the daily press);

2. The community press is not generally perceived as a medium which is "commercialized";

3. The community press is not generally perceived as political or partisan but rather as an agent of community welfare and progress;

4. The community press is generally perceived as an extension of the reader's personal and social contacts because of its emphasis on news about voluntary associations and local social and personal news. As such it constitutes a device for democratizing prestige. For the majority, this functions as an extension and reenforcement of social contacts which have real existence in the local community. Only for a minority does involvement with the news and personalities of the community press operate as substitute gratifications because of the individual's lack or paucity of social contacts in the local community. This proposition as it applies to the urban community press stands in contradistinction to the current view of the mass media which contends that significant portions of the mass media substitute for real social contact.

TABLE I—Readership of Three Community Newspapers

	Community Residents %
Fans	11.0
Regular	40.0
Partial	33.0
Non-readers	16.0
	100.0
Total cases	(600)

1. *The community newspaper is generally perceived as an auxiliary not a competing news source with the daily press (and tends to be viewed favorably for its preoccupation with the details of the local community which are unreported in the daily press).* When readers were asked whether the community newspaper devoted too little or too much news to the local community, the response was an acceptance by the majority (72.5%) of the present balance which overwhelmingly emphasizes local news and local orientations. (A quantitative content analysis of a three-month sample of the community press in Chicago revealed that in 1949, 75.4% of the space dealt with local community affairs, 9.3% with sectors of the city, 14.8% with city-wide affairs, while the rest was concerned with state, national, international or was not classifiable.) [3] However, where the present balance was questioned, it was almost all in the direction of demanding more local news (15.5%). Among the readers—fans, partial and glancers—all displayed inter-

3. Local was defined as taking place within the territory of one of the seventy-five local communities of Chicago in which the paper was published. Cf. Louis Wirth and Eleanor Bernert, *Local Community Fact Book of Chicago,* Chicago, 1949.

est in the local news content while only a scattered few felt that too much attention was paid to local affairs. For the community editor, the decision has to be made continually as to how many events shall be selected from outside the limits of the community for publication in his paper. Interview data with editors indicates that rather universally, his horizons are broader than his readers' who emphasize the purely local aspects of the community press.

Opinion became highly articulate among the readers about the distinct purpose a community newspaper serves.

"My goodness, the daily can't take the place of the paper in the community. There are two different functions; the community paper is the only way to keep up with the local area." (36 year-old taxi driver, resident of Carleton Manor).

An occasional enthusiast even stated:

"You can learn all about your neighborhood. It is more important than the daily paper." (42 year-old housewife of Atwater.)

This image of community newspapers as a source of information missing in the daily press, expressed in varying forms, was almost universal for even the non-readers subscribed to it.

This image, together with the mass of examples volunteered by respondents on specific overt responses to content, support the proposition that the community newspaper assists adjustment to the institutions and facilities of urban life through the factual information it supplies. However, local news also has a purely symbolic effect. The phrase "keeps us informed" and its often encountered variants not only refer to information but has many overtones. The printed word has authority and still quite a bit of magic. Local news incorporates a strong feeling of local pride and personal respect which print enhances. Printing news in the local community paper—for all but those completely disenchanted—identifies and glorifies the persons and institutions reported. If the individual has any knowledge of these persons and institutions close at hand or any sense of identification with them, he in turn feels a sense of solidarity and cohesion well beyond merely being informed.

Moreover, community news is local news of events and people which the individual is in a better position to verify personally, directly or indirectly, than non-local news. The potentiality for verification is there, and this potentiality is a real factor in conditioning the reader's attitude and relation to the editor. In effect, many readers seem to attribute a higher degree of veracity and trust to community newspaper content than to daily newspaper content. The actual and potential confirmation of specific items casts a halo effect over the entire contents:

"There's more news in our neighborhood paper than in the big ones. And most is the truth too, not like the big papers—they print what they want." (27 year-old housewife of Atwater, with two children.)

"I think the *Advocate* is more important than the daily paper. Dailies are filled with lies and scandal." (53 year-old transit engineer, resident of Carleton Manor.)

Community newspaper readers do in effect make use of their closer ties in that errors in the community newspaper seldom go by unchallenged. Publishers are always complaining about the volume of complaints covering even apparently the most trivial errors.

2. *The community press is not generally perceived as a medium which is "commercialized."* Commercialism in the case of the community newspaper would mean an image that the paper is merely published for profit, that it contains too many ads, and that it is guilty of a tone of high pressure tactics, sharp practices and unbridled pursuit of business incentives. To the contrary, the advertising in the community newspaper generally is regarded with real interest and considered as a genuine aid to daily living.

The community newspaper is frequently considered by daily newspaper publishers, the heads of advertising agencies and sophisticated critics of contemporary culture to be "all advertisements." The conclusions of the content analysis indicate that this is a case of distorted perception. Percentage-wise, the difference between the amount of advertising in the daily and the community newspapers is trivial; in fact specific issues of the daily press contain a higher proportion of advertising.

In contrast to such an appraisal, is the image held by those who actually read the community press. In the readership study with six hundred households, less than ten percent of all respondents—readers and non-readers combined—claimed that there were too many advertisements in their local community newspapers. While the bulk felt that the amount of advertisements was all right, there was a minority (6.5%) who claimed that the newspaper had too few ads. Among the non-readers, reasons given for indifference or hostility to the community press hardly emphasized the amount of advertising.

More positive indication of the lack of a "commercialized" image comes from the high interest among both men and women in display advertisements as an aid to shopping (51.5%) and in the classified advertisements as an aid to the respondent's own commercial transactions (37.6%).

Readers' beliefs as to why community newspapers are published supply a further clue to imagery. Questions were put to the readers: did they believe the papers were published to develop community spirit, make profit, or better community facilities. Only half said that their community newspaper was published to make profit. Getting better community facilities scored equally high while developing community spirit received more affirmative replies. The lack of a conception of the community newspaper as a "commercialized" vehicle seems reasonable in view of the positive attitude towards its content in general and to advertisements as well. But attributing such altruistic motives to community newspaper publishers is difficult to understand. The powerful dailies which appear more prosperous may help to condition such an image. The low emphasis on controversy and scandal which arises from the reluctance of the community newspaper publisher to take a purely impersonal view of his content and "do anything for money" is apparently recognized by his readers and blocks the commercial image. But the readers surely are engaged in some self deception. They must have a powerful desire not to want to view all media of communication as commercialized and therefore untrustworthy. The community press does display some of the characteristics of non-economic incentives and practices; but this imagery is elaborated by the readers themselves.

3. *The community newspaper is not generally perceived as political or partisan but rather as an agent of community welfare and progress.* None of the three papers could be considered politically neutral. The quantitative content analysis revealed a low news coverage of politics and almost complete absence of editorializing. In a non-election period only about one percent of the content dealt explicitly with political party activities and five percent with public affairs material related to politics. However, many of the categories of content supply a vehicle of reporting the activities of local politicians and of offering "news" support to favored candidates in an apparently unpolitical tone. Thus in Atwater, the editor of the *Atwater News* supports the old line Democratic machine which, at the time of the study, had temporarily lost control of the central ward in the community to Polish Republican forces, but which was returned to office in the last elections. In Bethel Park, the publisher's independent stands confuse the issues, but he supports the Fair Deal and their local Democratic candidates. The *Northeast Advocate* in Carleton Manor, over the issue of civil rights and public housing has shifted from traditional Democratic to publicizing Republican candidates.

A small minority of politically alert readers were aware of the political forces at work and the subtle but influential support the papers give to favored candidates. In answer to the question "what does (the name of the paper) stand for in politics?" only 15.4% replied either Republican or Democratic. The overwhelming bulk of the respondents gave answers which clearly indicated that they did not perceive of the paper in political terms ("it is impartial") or that they were disinterested in its politics.

Low political sensitivity led to the frequent expression of the incompatibility of politics and the community newspaper.

"They stand for progress in the community rather than for anything political." (42 year-old dry cleaner, resident of Carleton Manor.)

"They aren't political, they're a community paper." (22 year-old married laborer, resident of Atwater.)

In fact, politics stand as a threat to the appeal of the paper.

"You feel more intimate with local papers because big papers take sides in politics." (31 year-old resident of Carleton Manor.)

Such an underlying attitude toward the community newspaper was succinctly summarized by the comments of one reader.

"Well, it don't take stands for anything but whatever is in the interest of the community." (36 year-old pharmacist, resident of Carleton Manor.)

The extent of this attitude can be inferred from the fact that despite the lack of an explicit political imagery, over fifty percent of the sample believed that one of the consequences of their community newspaper was to get better community facilities.

By contrast, among the politically alert, there was some tendency to express strong likes or dislikes for the political slant of the paper:

"That fellow . . . writes sensible editorials. I swear by them . . . In fact, I take them to the shop and pin them up for the fellows to see." (46 year-old machinist, resident of Bethel Park.)

"That's a grade school paper. I never look in there for news. I wish they would cease publishing it. It is vicious, always panning something . . ." (36 year-old housewife, resident of Carleton Manor.)

4. *The community newspaper is perceived generally as an extension of the reader's personal and social contacts because of its emphasis on news about local voluntary associations and local social and personal news. As such it constitutes a device for democratizing prestige.*

Thomas and Znaniecki in their analysis of the development of social cohesion among the peasants of Poland saw much of the contents of the Polish press operating in such a fashion:

"Now the psychological mechanism through which satisfaction of the social instinct is obtained in the wider community also consists in a large measure in supplementing actually experienced response and recognition by imagined response and recognition. The individual who sees his name or his contribution in print imagines the attitude of the readers and this has on him an effect attitudes would have." [4]

The significance of Thomas and Znaniecki's proposition rests on the key phrase *supplementing actually experienced response and recognition by imagined response and recognition.* For them, actuality of social contact was requisite and conditioned the use of the press as an extension of primary group relations as the basis of larger social cohesion. They did not examine the implication of mass media impact where primary group contacts did not exist. Under such conditions the content would be more likely to serve the individual as a substitute for actual contacts and therefore operate as a substitute gratification.

Therefore, in analyzing the image of the community press connected with social and personal news, a basic distinction was made. For one group, such content might serve as an extension and reinforcement of social contacts which have real existence. For another group, such content would serve as a substitute gratification for the absence of social contacts. The

---

4. W. I. Thomas and Florian Znaniecki, *The Polish Peasant,* Vol. 4, p. 264-265.

number for whom such community press content serves as a substitute, it seemed would be small as compared with the first group. The community press here loses in the competitive struggle with the mass media, for it is not melodramatic enough to serve the function of supplying phantasy and substitute gratifications effectively. (The likelihood that the same persons may get different gratification from different media must also be taken into account.)

Relevant systematic evidence was difficult to gather for it involved investigating underlying motivations which are not readily apparent within the scope of the interview design employed. Nevertheless, much confirming evidence can be marshalled. First, however, it should be noted that although the reading of social and personal news was extensive, for a significant group there was no reading involvement at all. (Readership ranged from 51.5 percent in Carleton Manor, to 61.0 percent in Atwater.) Readership by women exceeded readership by men, and women who read such content were more prone to volunteer their positive attitudes. Readership of social and personal news was associated with length of residence in the community. Even more relevant, such readership was associated with the extent of neighborhood contacts—more contact was linked to higher readership—indicating again that real participation conditioned interest in the social and personal news. Yet the question of distinguishing more precisely those whose readership was motivated by pseudo-involvement and substitute gratification required fuller analysis.

Pseudo-involvement or substitute gratification could best be identified in the instances where the respondent himself voluntarily attested to that fact in describing his reactions and interests in social and personal news. There was a group who claimed that they read the social and personal news and were strongly interested. Yet these stated that they were unfamiliar or unacquainted with the people reported, thereby indicating pseudo-involvement.

"It's very neighborly even if you don't know the people; you know the streets and you can just about figure out which house they live in."

"I always look for names, maybe you do not know them, but you know they're neighbors."

"The socials are fine—I enjoy reading them even if I don't know the people."

By contrast are the comments highlighting the extension of real involvement:

"We are interested in the neighborhood—that's what it gives you . . . names of people we know. It always has something interesting in the ward, something the city paper hasn't got, you know, it gives the local news about stores and people. You know, about churches and activities in your ward. We're going to put in a notice of the birthday of our little daughter . . ."

"I think the *Northeast Advocate* is a very nice paper, so many people you see in it that you know."

"The *Bethel Park Bulletin* is just as good as the Times paper. You don't read about the President's daughter or some prince. That gets tiresome. I like to read about the people I know."

In all, fourteen cases were found that clearly revealed themselves as being in the "substitute gratification" category in that they were interested in social and personal news without having acquaintance with those mentioned. The statements of 33 additional respondents were of such a character as to raise strong presumption of substitute gratification. Direct questioning would have put the respondent on the defensive and produced distortion, yet all the respondents who read the community press had equal opportunity during the probing to express themselves in this regard. Thus, it should hardly be assumed that all who had such attitudes revealed themselves, although it is quite likely that they did.

In any case, these "substitute gratification" cases are extremely revealing. They were distributed through the three communities, and their length of residence was roughly the same as the total sample. Nor were they characterized as falling into any particular social status group. Yet, all but two had no or few contacts with their neighbors, seldom visited in the neighborhood, and in general claimed that their friends were located outside the community. The number of children in their households is also interesting in the light of the fact that community newspaper readership was markedly concentrated in unbroken families with two or three children, as compared with incomplete families or households of single individuals. The families in which "substitute gratification" was found had either no children, or in a few cases, very large families—four children and over. Thus marked deviations from primary group and community orientations led to the use of these social and personal items in the community press as a substitute gratification. It was impossible to investigate to what extent the community newspaper reader fans—who are markedly integrated into the local community—still found substitute gratification in the other mass media, in particular those who boasted loudest of all the people they know in the columns of the community press (26 cases).

An additional observation can be made on this imagery. Readership of social and personal news involves "equals." The individuals publicized are men and women quite similar to the reader. Associative remarks revealed not only an interest in the names of neighbors but also a preoccupation with the democratic aspects of prestige. Community social news is written with a bland flair not designed to create special distinction and was perceived in these terms. Easy accessibility to the columns of the paper was frequently mentioned as concrete proof of this point.

"Anyone who wants an item or picture in can get it by sending it in—no special group is a social elite." (56 year-old Carleton Manor contractor).

Almost ten percent of all respondents voluntarily mentioned some recent personal or family publicity in the community newspaper. This number who actually made use of the community newspaper facilities is difficult to describe as either large or small. But actual numbers are no more important than an image or ideology which is based on the widespread recognition of the potentialities for prestige which are available for each individual.

Democratization of prestige encompasses not only news and announcements of the various stages of the life cycle, but ultimately death. In addition to high interest in obituaries, the following attitude was repeatedly offered voluntarily:

"We don't get our names in the big papers even when we die; but the local paper prints everybody's death notice who wants it." (28 year-old Bethel Park pressman.)

"You can get news to be published in the *Atwater News* about deaths without having to pay for it and that's a good thing." (42 year-old Atwater housewife.)

The community press, long recognized by certain types of commercial advertisers, politicians and community leaders as a relevant media of communication, has been neglected by students of urbanism. The findings of the over-all study from which the data presented here has been excerpted, attest to the high impact of the urban community press in certain areas. However, it appears that such impact cannot be traced merely to extensive exposure to its contents, if exposure is defined as the amount of content to which the reader gives his attention. The imagery of the community newspaper in the mind of its readers which is built on and in turn contributes to local social solidarity is a significant underlying element in accounting for its impact.

THE USE OF LOCAL FACILITIES IN A METROPOLIS

Donald L. Foley

The rise of metropolitan centers has undoubtedly been accompanied by significant changes in social pattern. Few urban studies have directly investigated the place of neighborhood or local community life within the larger metropolis. It is not yet known, for example, to what extent individual metropolitan residents carry out their various out-of-the-home activities locally, as in a rural village or in a small community, or, conversely, to what extent they carry out these activities on the metropolitan scale.

Previous research has demonstrated a decline in the primary-group type of urban neighborhood.[1] Such concepts as "communality" and "personal neighborhood," for example, have been suggested as more accurately descriptive of current urban life.[2] The implication is that an individualistic type of social bond, such as that of the voluntary association, has extensively displaced traditional neighborhood ties. The dearth of neighborhood or local-community sentiments and association patterns has been included as an integral feature of the "urban society" when conceived as an ideal type.[3] In certain of these previous studies it has been inferred that, paralleling the decline of the urban neighborhood as a social entity, urban residents were becoming less locally self-sufficient in their use of facilities,[4] coming rather to depend upon facilities located throughout the city.

Reprinted from *The American Journal of Sociology*, Vol. 56 (November 1950), pp. 238-246, by permission of the author and the publisher. (Copyright, 1950, by *The American Journal of Sociology*.)

1. Roderick D. McKenzie, *The Neighborhood: A Study of Local Life in the City of Columbus, Ohio* (Chicago: University of Chicago Press, 1923); M. Wesley Roper, "The City and the Primary Group" (unpublished Ph.D. dissertation, Department of Sociology, University of Chicago, 1935); Bessie A. McClenahan, *The Changing Urban Neighborhood* (Los Angeles: University of Southern California, 1929).

2. McClenahan, *op. cit.*, and "The Communality: The Urban Substitute for the Traditional Community," *Sociology and Social Research*, XXX (March-April, 1946), 264-74. Frank L. Sweetser, Jr., "A New Emphasis for Neighborhood Research," *American Sociological Review*, VII (August, 1942), 525-33.

3. *Cf.* Louis Wirth, "Urbanism as a Way of Life," *American Journal of Sociology*, XLIV (July, 1938), 1-24.

4. "Use of facilities" and "facility use" are used synonymously as generic terms meaning the functional dependence by residents on such organized, specifically located meeting places or service centers as stores, places of employment, schools, churches, doctors' offices, and movie theaters. Whereas the "primary-group type of neighborhood" involves informal social relations of "neighboring," the "use of facilities" is conceived of as being more formal and as involving specific, organized "facilities."

This article reports a study made in 1947 of facility use by residents of a district in northwest St. Louis.[5] Questions were asked to discover the relative extent of the residents' use of local facilities in contrast to their use of nonlocal facilities; what proportion of their facility use could be classified as local; what proportion as nonlocal or metropolitan; with what factors local- or nonlocal-facility use was associated; which facility uses were the most local; which the least local; what types of residents tended to be locally oriented in their use of facilities; which nonlocally.

To answer these questions required an examination of day-to-day, away-from-the-home activities of the urban dweller. Has he lost touch with local activities? Or does there still remain a vestige of the local community, in the sense of a service center at least, within the larger metropolitan area? It was the writer's hypothesis (using the term in a general or guiding sense) that metropolitan residents make relatively little use of local facilities.[6]

That the approach in this research is ecological is admitted; and, if this study were to be considered in isolation, it might be appraised as peripheral to sociology. But the study of as complex a phenomenon as metropolitan social life presents an unusual challenge to the researcher to utilize an assortment of complementary research techniques. The present study, then, is most logical if its findings are treated as but one segment of a more comprehensive framework of urban analysis.[7]

A five-square-mile residential district in northwest St. Louis was selected for the study. The district is located between 4.5 and 6.5 miles from downtown St. Louis and is just within the political limits of the central city. The characteristics of the district and its residents are generally intermediate between those of the more central portions of the city and of the suburbs beyond; it could probably be termed middle class, shading toward lower middle class. That the population of the area is generally representative of St. Louis is shown in Table 1.

5. More completely reported as the writer's "Urban Neighborhood Facilities: A Study of a Residential District in Northwest St. Louis" (unpublished Ph.D. dissertation, Department of Sociology-Anthropology, Washington University, 1948), esp. chap. iii.

6. Literally to test this hypothesis was difficult, for the hypothesis assumed that one could determine with some finality just where the line was to be drawn between "local" and "nonlocal" facilities and what in a metropolitan setting would constitute "relatively little use" of local facilities. Lacking previous definitions, an attempt to force a strict test of the hypothesis would have involved a certain arbitrariness, unwarranted at this stage of the research, in selection of appropriate criteria. Consequently the findings are offered in such form as to be relevant to the hypothesis, without definitely upholding or rejecting it. The findings as they are reported are, then, largely descriptive, with certain tentative classifications suggested upon which further research could draw.

7. An exploratory attempt to use this general approach in studying social organizational and social psychological aspects is being undertaken in the sociology department of the University of Rochester. Under way is an attempt to translate the idea of a "local-community" to "metropolitan" continuum into workable terms. Pilot research in Rochester has included such aspects as neighborliness and sense of local identification as well as use of facilities. The goals of such an undertaking include the possibility of stating where, along this continuum, various activities and/or attitudes of urban residents seem to belong.

In a number of ways this district is more homogeneous than is St. Louis as a whole. For example, the range of 1940 average-block rentals for the district is from $15.00 to $83.00; for the city as a whole (not known for the county) it was from $1.00 to $293.00. In one important respect, intentionally a part of the research design, the district differs from the larger St. Louis community: it contains practically no Negroes—although Negroes constituted 11 per cent of the total population of St. Louis City and County in 1940—and was selected because such complications as segregation were thereby avoided. The leading foreign-born nationality represented in the district is Russian, presumably Jewish, on the whole, while the nationality in the city is German. The southern portion of the district is generally the older and the more densely developed (35 persons per gross acre) and is better served by commercial facilities. The largest single outlying shopping center in metropolitan St. Louis—Wellston, with nearly four hundred retail

TABLE I—Selected Characteristics for the Residential District Studied and for St. Louis City and County

Characteristics (from the 1940 Census Unless Otherwise Stated)	District Studied	City of St. Louis and St. Louis County *
Percentage of population under 14 years of age	19.8	18.7
Percentage of population 65 years of age and over	6.6	7.3
Percentage of population foreign-born	11.6	6.7
Percentage of population 25 years and over with 6 years or less schooling	18.8	21.4
Percentage of employed population 14 years old and over classified as "operatives and kindred workers" or as "laborers"	29.0	28.1
Average monthly dwelling-unit rental	$27.53	$29.24
Percentage of dwelling units owner-occupied	37.4	34.4
Ratio of dwelling units to residentail structures	1.5	1.7
Ratio of population per passenger automobile †	5.6	5.2
Total population	71,899	1,090,278

* These two units represent roughly the Missouri portion of the St. Louis metropolitan district as defined in 1940. The Illinois segment of the district (with about 268,000 population) was not included, because certain needed statistics were not available.
† Estimated as of 1946 by the writer.

stores—lies at the southwest corner of this southern segment, and other commercial centers and clusters are also readily accessible. The northern portion of the district, with its single-family-home type of development, is somewhat suburban in character, with a lower density (20 persons per gross acre). Many of its residents are a considerable distance from any shopping center.

Schools, churches, movie theaters, and other facilities are generally available. There is probably more than typical opportunity for employment, particularly in the industrial area within the district. Not available in the district, although accessible in varying degrees, are public high schools; large parks (of which St. Louis has several); and facilities, other than movie theaters, providing professional entertainment such as major-league baseball or the outdoor municipal opera.

To obtain a representative sample of the estimated 20,000 families living in the district, an areal sampling technique was used and an optimum sample size of about 400 families was set. A panel of addresses was selected by drawing every nth dwelling unit from the most recent Polk city directory, using only street addresses falling within the district. After 12 addresses were dropped as nonresidential and 36 addresses were substituted (from certain predesignated extras) for a similar number of nonresponses, the final sample numbered 401 families. At lease one member of each family was interviewed on the use made by the various family members of selected facilities. Each address was revisited, if necessary, as many as five or six times, in an effort to locate some family member. Straight refusals to answer were given in 10 families; illness, summer vacationing, and odd working hours accounted for the remaining cases where substitution was necessary.

Each respondent was asked to tell where every family member (over five years of age) went for the following: (1) employment, (2) food, (3) clothing, (4) furniture or household equipment, (5) school, (6) church, (7) medical care, (8) outdoor recreation, (9) miscellaneous indoor activities. Each member's use of a specific facility was treated as a "report." (For example, the use of two different food stores by a housewife was treated as two reports; the use of a church by all four members of a family was treated as four reports.) On this basis, there was an average of sixteen reports per family—6,216 reports in all. Each report included background information about the family member involved, location of home, type and location of the facility, type of transportation used, and the distance from home to facility. The interviewing was carried out from June to August, 1947, and reflects summertime uses of the facilities.

The major variable was the airline distance from home to facility, and this served as the primary index of local use.[8] The frequency distribution of this major variable provided a primary answer in itself. In addition, the distribution of facility's uses as falling within, adjacent to, or away from the district was examined. Also analyzed were the relations between the major variable—distance—and the following: (1) type of facility use, (2) type of transportation, and (3) certain other variables pertaining to family or personal background.

One could undoubtedly interpret the findings in a number of ways. One could point to very considerable evidence that the residents made relatively great use of facilities located well outside the district and often several miles from the users' homes, thus indirectly supporting the writer's hypothesis. Or, one could find strong supporting evidence that the use of facilities located near home and within the immediate district was surprisingly extensive considering the fact that the district is in a metropolis. A third interpretation—and one that tends to take both of the former ones into

---

8. This use of distance as an index excluded trip time and cost and did not measure either frequency or intensity of facility use. Methodological research considered beyond the scope of this particular study was called for. In the writer's pilot study of 50 families he used travel time as an index and ascertained the frequency of each facility's use. The final decision simply to use distance was based on these considerations: Distance provides a clear-cut, reliable measure along a single continuum; it reduces the time and complexity of interviewing and analysis operations; and for the purposes of this study (for the question of transportation economics was not being raised) it provides a generally valid measure of local versus nonlocal facility use.

account—is that large-city living involves an intricate balance between the relative use of local and nonlocal facilities. The writer was impressed by the different "levels" of facility use that were observed and the wide distribution of facility uses among the levels.

The study revealed that 47 per cent of the reported facility uses were within 1 mile of the user's home, 20 per cent were between 1 and 3 miles from home, and 33 per cent were at least 3 miles away. About 30 per cent were within 0.5 mile; 10 per cent were at least 6 miles away. The median distance from home was 1.2 miles, while the arithmetic mean was estimated as about 2.4 miles. (See Table 2.) It is thus apparent that a little over half of all the reports involved the use of facilities located in or near the residential district.

The transportation, as facility-use reports showed, was: walking from home, 36 per cent; public transit from home, 31 per cent; and automobile

TABLE II

Location of Facility Use		Percentage Distribution of Reports Analyzed
Within or adjacent to district		53
Within the district	41	
Adjacent to the district *	12	
Away from district		47
In central business district †	14	
Other "away" location	33	
Total of all facility uses		100

* Included as "adjacent" were facilities that were within about a quarter-mile of the district. For the commercial facilities, the bulk of those classed as adjacent were located in four outlying shopping centers—Wellston, Pine Lawn, Jennings, and Easton and Kingshighway (including a Sears, Roebuck store)—on the periphery of the district.

† The 84-block area bounded by Franklin Avenue, Third Street, Market Street and Twelfth Boulevard.

from home, 30 per cent.[9] (Three per cent were classed in a miscellaneous category including "from other than home," such as shopping from place of work.)

Thus between one-third and one-half of the reported facility uses could be classified as "local." Table 3 gives alternative pertinent measures and

TABLE III

Facilities	Per Cent
Within ½ mile from home	30
To which walked from home	36
Within the district	41
Within 1 mile from home	47
Within or adjacent to the district	53

corresponding percentages, 100 per cent in each case equaling the total of all the facility-use reports. There could be two possible interpretations here of "nonlocal": (1) Local and nonlocal might be dichotomous, nonlocal

9. Of the families sampled, 48 per cent had no automobile; 37 per cent had an automobile, but, because it was used as transportation to and from work, it was not available during the day; 15 per cent had an automobile available for family use during the day, although not necessarily driven then.

including all those facilities not classed as local. In such a case, obviously, between two-thirds and one-half of the reports of facility uses were non-local. (2) Local and nonlocal might be conceived of as extreme positions on the continuum with a middle or intermediate classification as well. Non-local would include only facilities 3 miles or more (3 miles representing a little over halfway downtown), in which case one-third of the facility-use reports would be included.

It is to be expected that children in attending school will go a shorter distance than will adults in shopping for items that are mainly carried in downtown department stories. How various types of facility uses were arrayed according to their average distance from the user's home is shown in Table 4. Whether the particular distance involved choice as between local and nonlocal facilities or whether the distance reflected merely a particular situation as to local or nonlocal availability is indicated in the

TABLE IV—Selected Facility Uses Ranked According to Localization

Facility Uses *	Availability of Facility †	No. of Reports Analyzed	Mileage from User's Home to Facility Median	Standard Error
Food shopping, at small stores	A	351	0.23	.06
Attendance at Orthodox Jewish synagogues	L	67	0.23	.04
Elementary-school attendance	L	148	0.35	.05
Children's use of playgrounds	L	58	0.49	.06
Catholic church attendance	L	395	0.50	.03
Food shopping, at large stores	A	222	0.55	.09
Movie attendance, at small theaters	A	1,081 ‡	0.57	.05
Protestant church attendance	A	342	0.66	.09
Clothing, household-equipment, or furniture shopping at small stores §	A	241	0.82	.18
Bowling	A	60	1.39	.23
Attendance at Reformed Jewish temples	N-L	27	1.55	.21
Playing organized ball	A	24	2.01	.70
High-school attendance	A	51	2.02	.26
Visiting doctors' offices	A	556	2.17	.09
Part-time employment	A	21	2.40	.75
Municipal-opera attendance	N-L	93	2.56	.12
Going to ball games (mostly major league)	N-L	164	2.70	.08
Meetings of fraternal or military organizations	MN-L	51	2.74	.49
College or trade-school attendance	N-L	24	2.86	.66
Meetings of business or professional organizations	MN-L	16	3.53	.64
Full-time employment	MN-L	427	3.87	.14
Outdoor swimming	N-L	86	3.93	.31
Meetings of labor organizations	MN-L	40	3.96	.35
Movie attendance, at large theaters	N-L	204 ‡	4.42	.10
Playing golf	N-L	25	5.12	.79
Clothing, household-equipment, or furniture shopping at large stores §	MN-L	633	5.39	.07
Going on picnics and outings	N-L	241	6.81	.28
Hunting and fishing	N-L	44	‖	..
Total	.....	5,999 ⧣	1.21	.04

* Since interviewing was done in the summer, facility uses and amounts of participation are valid for summer.

† A, available both locally and nonlocally; L, available (either physically or for administrative or practical reasons) only locally; MN-L, available mainly only nonlocally; N-L, available only nonlocally.

‡ In most cases involves reports on two different theaters per person; hence the large number of reports.

§ Reports were secured only on purchases of clothing of $5.00 or more and of furniture or household equipment of $10.00 or more.

‖ Indeterminate from data, but over 7 miles.

⧣ Grand total of 6,216 reports less 217 for which distance was indeterminate.

second column. (A in the column indicates more choice on the part of the user as between a local and a nonlocal facility than does L, MN-L, or N-L [see table footnotes].)

An over-all summary of the distribution of facility-use groupings as within or away from the residential district studied is provided in Table 5. The groupings are arranged so as to rank the percentage located away from the district. Rather different types of facilities, such as elementary and secondary schools and colleges, small local stores, and large downtown department stores, are in some instances here grouped intentionally in order to summarize major functions.

From the data presented in Table 5 it is evident that the four general types of facilities that are used preponderantly within or adjacent to the residential district studied are food stores, churches, schools, and movie

TABLE V—Location of Facility Uses in Relation to Study District

Major Groupings of Facility Uses *	No. of Reports Analyzed	Percentage Distribution by Location			
		Within District	Adjacent to District †	Away from District	Total
Food shopping	573	69.3	26.5	4.2	100.0
Church attendance	831	77.1	5.2	17.7	100.0
School attendance	223	68.2	9.0	22.8	100.0
Movie attendance	1,285 ‡	58.4	15.6	26.0	100.0
Miscellaneous indoor activities (association meetings, sports, etc.)	380	35.5	9.7	54.8	100.0
Visiting doctors' offices	563	29.7	8.5	61.8	100.0
Clothing, household-equipment, or furniture shopping §	874	5.1	19.7	75.2	100.0
Employment	434	17.5	5.3	77.2	100.0
Miscellaneous outdoor activities (sports, outings, etc.)	795	10.1	0.4	89.5	100.0
Total	5,958	41.0	11.7	47.3	100.0

* Since interviewing was done in the summer, facility uses and amounts of participation are valid for summer.

† Included as "adjacent" were facilities that were within about a quarter-mile of the district. For the commercial facilities, the bulk of those classed as adjacent were located in four outlying shopping centers—Wellston, Pine Lawn, Jennings, and Easton and Kingshighway (including a Sears, Roebuck store)—on the periphery of the district.

‡ In most cases involves reports on two different theaters per person; hence the large number of reports.

§ Reports were secured only on purchases of clothing of $5.00 or more and of furniture or household equipment of $10.00 or more.

theaters. A more detailed breakdown of these major groupings shows certain exceptions. For example, while the attendance at Orthodox Jewish synagogues is 100 per cent within the district, that at Reformed Jewish services is completely away from the district, because there is no local Reformed temple. While movie attendance is heavily concentrated within the area, there is also considerable attendance at the large theaters in or near the central business district. Elementary-school attendance is 98 per cent within or adjacent to the district, and high-school attendance is 49 per cent; attendance at college or trade school is only 8 per cent.

The summertime participation in outdoor activities is completely non-local except for the children's use of playground facilities. Practically 100 per cent out of the district are major-league ball games, the municipal opera, the zoo or large parks, outdoor swimming, golf, hunting and fishing, and picnics and outings. Attendance at union meetings and at business and professional meetings is about 90 per cent out of the district. Employment is preponderantly nonlocal, although there are firms that hire large numbers of employees within or adjacent to the district.

Further general findings are as follows:

1. The distance from home to facility varies directly with the mode of transportation employed, as is shown in Table 6. The shorter median distance for automobile use was interpreted as being due partly to the many

TABLE VI

User's Transportation	Median Mileage, Home to Facility
Walking from home	0.35
Automobile from home	2.70
Public transit from home	3.50

short trips which one would take with an automobile but which one might not care or be able to take by public transit and partly to the extensive use of good public transportation for the five- or six-mile trip downtown.

2. Family nonownership of automobiles is associated with a proportionately greater use of local facilities (Table 7). This held true in spite of

TABLE VII

Family Ownership of Automobile	Median Mileage, Home to Facility
Ownership	1.68
Nonownership	0.82

the fact that the automobile trips per se were of shorter median distance than were trips by public conveyance.

3. Young persons, especially those under twelve years of age, and persons over sixty-five make relatively the most extensive use of local facilities. Young adults, aged eighteen to thirty-four, make the least (see Table 8).

TABLE VIII

User's Age in Years	Median Mileage, Home to Facility
5-12	0.70
13-17	0.99
18-24	2.29
25-34	2.28
35-49	1.51
50-64	1.18
65 and over	0.68

4. Table 9 shows that the less the user's formal education, the more use he makes of local facilities. In this statement of relationship, however, age and other factors were not held constant.

TABLE IX

Education of Users 18 Years of Age and Over	Median Mileage, Home to Facility
3 Years' high school or more	2.05
2 Years' high school or less	1.23

5. Females use local facilities more than males do (Table 10). In contrast to that of the adult male, the adult-female average is kept closer to home by nonemployment, by the need to do extensive shopping, and by considerable participation in local leisure activities.

TABLE X

User's Sex	Median Mileage, Home to Facility
Male	1.77
Female	1.15

6. On the surface there appears to be a direct relation between lower economic status and greater use of local facilities, but when automobile-ownership is held constant, the economic status factor loses most of its significant association with the major variable.

7. Residential density appears to be of greater significance than home-ownership in its association with local-facility use. Thus, within the district the older and more densely built-up section, with greater relative tenancy, shows somewhat more extensive use of local facilities than does the sparser, single-family section where homeownership rates are high.

CONCLUSIONS. For the student of urban social organization this study should demonstrate the variety of "levels" at which facilities in a metropolis are used.

A number of facilities are extensively used at the local level. Food and certain other types of shopping, children's attendance at elementary schools and use of play facilities, attendance at certain churches, and patronage of certain small movie theaters take place to a great degree within a neighborhood or local-community sphere. It would be unrealistic to neglect this important local phase of urban social life either as a basis for understanding the present organization or for future planning. Inasmuch as this important condition of city life exists, it appears that the thoroughgoing, ideal-type urban pattern falls short of applicability *in toto*. Our large cities, for all their urbanity, seem to contain an impressive degree of local community life within their metropolitan limits.

But urban life involves more than this local level; many lines of functional interdependency extend out from any designated residential district. In spite of the fact that the area studied was approximately a half-hour or more from St. Louis' central business district, the dependence by residents on that business district was striking—especially for employment, for shopping, and for miscellaneous services. With adequate transportation urban residents will and do go far out of their local districts to make use of many types of facilities. It is apparent that most residents accept the longer trip as a counterpart of the specialization that is so intrinsically a part of metropolitan growth. Thus, trips to the large department stores downtown, to the large theaters, and to doctors' offices in established medical-office buildings are widely and casually reported.

The study—although not specifically carried out with this in mind—suggests striking differences in uses of facilities, even within the same family, and indicates the divisive influences and interests not atypical, it would seem, of the urban family. This phase of the picture deserves further study. One possible classification of facility-use patterns or complexes at a family level might distinguish (1) employment and related facility uses, (2) keeping house and related facility uses, (3) children's use of facilities, and (4) various adult leisure uses of facilities.

The relations between urban-facility-use patterns and users' attitudes were only briefly explored in the present study. Further research is needed so that the association between the level of facility use and the degree to which a resident may or may not be characterized as holding metropolitan (or urban) attitudes can be stated with some degree of certainty. To date there is little research literature on any special operational definition of "metropolitan" (or "urban") attitudes. Is there one continuum along which attitudes may be measured as more, or less, urban? Or are there many continua involved? This, in turn, raises the whole question of the rural-urban dichotomy: Are there degrees of what we call "urban," and are there shades that can be termed "metropolitan"?

THE MORAL INTEGRATION OF AMERICAN CITIES

Robert C. Angell

THE FACT OF MORAL INTEGRATION AND ITS MEASUREMENT. A term like "moral integration" is a scientific concept. It points to something believed to be important in understanding and in generalizing what happens in social groups. Since one cannot see or hear or touch this something, there arises the very proper question: How do we know it exists? This problem is not peculiar to the social sciences. The atom is not present to the senses either, but physicists have a very definite concept of its character and structure. We accept the existence of the atom because a great many things are thereby explicable which otherwise would be inexplicable. Its nature is inferred from the manner in which events that can be sensibly perceived occur. In order that we can think about this unsensed object, communicate ideas concerning it, put it into generalizations as one of their terms, and develop tests of its reality, we give it the label "atom." The meaning of the term evolves, but at any given time the concept is a clustering of inferred characteristics that fit both practical experience and accepted theory.

With respect to moral integration there is a tremendous amount of common-sense experience that testifies to the reality behind the concept, but this field of experience has been little probed by research. In view of the widespread appreciation that team "spirit" is important to success in athletics, it is surprising that more social scientists have not followed the path blazed by the great French sociologist, Émile Durkheim. In his *Suicide* and *The Elementary Forms of Religious Life* he demonstrated the importance of moral integration, first, to the individual and, second, to society. In this country good work has been done by Elton Mayo and his followers at the Harvard Business School[1] and by the late Kurt Lewin and his students, a group of whom now constitute the Research Center for Group Dynamics at the University of Michigan.[2] Both of these research

Adapted from "The Social Integration of American Cities of More than 100,000 Population," *American Sociological Review,* Vol. 12 (June, 1947), pp. 335 ff., and *The Moral Integration of American Cities,* Chapters 2 and 3, Chicago, Illinois: The University of Chicago Press, 1951, by permission of the author and the publishers. (Copyright by the American Sociological Society, 1947, and the University of Chicago, 1951.)

1. Elton Mayo, *The Human Problems of an Industrial Civilization* (New York, 1933), and *The Social Problems of an Industrial Civilization* (Boston, 1945); F. J. Roethlisberger and W. J. Dickson, *Management and the Worker* (Boston, 1934); Fritz Jules Roethlisberger, *Management and Morale* (Cambridge, 1941).

2. Kurt Lewin, *Authority and Frustration* (Iowa City, 1940), *Resolving Social Conflicts* (New York, 1948), and *Field Theory and Social Psychology* (New York,

teams have been interested primarily in small groups, like the factory department or the nursery school. They have made contributions of great theoretical importance to our knowledge of how such groups function.

Although it is true that small groups are the seedbeds of character, the most challenging problems of moral integration today seem to lie in very large groups. It is these that have been fostered by modern means of transportation and communication, and it is in these that social cohesion breaks down most frequently. To investigate the grounds of moral integration in these large, loose aggregates is therefore essential. The present study is designed to make a contribution in this direction.

It hardly seems necessary to point out the importance of research on moral integration at the present time. At the level of the community, the nation, and the world, we are faced with grave problems resulting from the lack of a firm moral order to which people are loyal and in terms of which conflicting parties may be reconciled. Research upon the integration of cities is therefore important not only in its own right, but also because an understanding of the phenomenon of integration at the local level may suggest hypotheses respecting the national and international levels. Granted that there are important emergent properties at those higher levels, it seems probable that the phenomenon of moral integration has some elements in common wherever it occurs.

In planning this piece of research two objectives stood out: (1) to obtain the best possible index of integration for cities; and (2) to isolate the most important causal factors. In reaching these objectives, deductions from sociological theory and clues from the previous empirical research have both been influential. In the first place, it was assumed on the basis of a former study that the crime index, taken negatively, was the best single index of integration, and that other indexes should be tested against it. One that appeared promising was a welfare effort index, since such an index had been used with success in the previous study. Exactly the same index could not be used, however, since it was developed from a U. S. Children's Bureau study of only twenty-nine cities. Secondly, sociological theory, as well as many empirical studies including my first one, suggested that mobility of the population and racial and cultural differences within it should be negatively related to integration. Since my previous study had shown size in cities of more than 100,000 not to be significantly related to crime, and since this was confirmed by the correlation of size with crime in this one ($r = -.06$ for "independent" cities of more than 100,000), size was dropped as a causal factor. The plan was to determine the influence of mobility and population composition and then search for other factors.

The total number of 92 cities of more than 100,000 in 1940 was con-

1949); Ronald Lippitt, *Training for Community Relations* (New York, 1949); Leon Festinger, Stanley Schachter, and Kurt Back, *Social Pressures in Informal Groups* (New York, 1950).

siderably reduced for this study by the availability of data with respect to the characteristics mentioned. In- and out-migration figures between 1935 and 1940, which were determined upon as the basis of a mobility index, did not exist for Charlotte and Sacramento. The obviously inaccurate reporting of crime in New Orleans, when it was compared with cities of like situation, led to its elimination. Later, when it was decided to use the data supplied by Community Chests and Councils for a welfare effort index, six other cities dropped out for lack of information on this point— Chicago, Fort Wayne, Knoxville, Philadelphia, San Antonio, Washington. And, after computation of the welfare effort index, Salt Lake City was dropped because it was apparent that the welfare role of the Mormon Church rendered the efforts through the Community Chest an inadequate measure for that city. But the most important reason for elimination was something quite different. I decided at the start that, since this was a study of moral integration, the cities should be independent in the sense that they should not be satellites of larger cities and that they should not have "twins" or very large satellites in their own metropolitan districts. The requirement laid down was that three-fifths of the population of the metropolitan district must be within the city and that not more than half of the remainder of the population within the district should be in a satellite city. This eliminated thirty-eight cities,[3] and to them New York was added because of its complex relationship to surrounding communities. This left a total of forty-three cities.

The crime index, which was to be basic in the integration index, was computed in almost the same way as in the previous study. It was made up from the murder and non-negligent homicide, robbery, and burglary rates,[4] weighted in accordance with the square roots of their frequencies in cities of more than 100,000. Thus one murder equalled 7.97 burglaries and one robbery equalled 2.49 burglaries. The sums for each city were divided by the population fifteen years of age and over. The data were for 1938, 1939 and 1940.

Experimentation with other data in order to find indexes that could be combined with the crime index to form the integration index proved disappointing. In two cases preliminary work with the data showed them unacceptable. It is a plausible theory that communities in which a higher percentage of newspapers are delivered to homes are better integrated than those in which street sales are more common, but this proved to be a poor "hunch," probably because of differing costs of distribution in the various cities. It might also seem that amounts spent by municipalities on sanitation, health and hospitals, and recreation, divided by retail sales

---

3. Albany, Boston, Cambridge, Camden, Canton, Cincinnati, Duluth, Elizabeth, Fall River, Gary, Hartford, Jersey City, Kansas (Kan.), Kansas City (Mo.), Long Beach, Los Angeles, Lowell, Minneapolis, Newark, New Bedford, New Haven, Norfolk, Oakland, Omaha, Paterson, Pittsburgh, Providence, St. Louis, St. Paul, San Francisco, Scranton, Somerville, Springfield, Tampa, Utica, Wilmington, Yonkers, Youngstown.
4. As given in *Uniform Crime Reports* of the Federal Bureau of Investigation.

would be a good index, but cities known to be well integrated, like Milwaukee, did not show up well. This was perhaps because cities already well integrated may not need to spend money heavily for these purposes. In two other cases work was carried through to definite results. The proportion of husbands or wives not living with their spouses seemed a likely indicator of low social integration, but this figure correlated with crime only + .32. On a theory of anomie the ratio of receipts from commercial amusements to retail sales appeared to be a similar indicator, but it correlated with crime only + .06.

Because none of these other indexes had worked out well, it was decided to rely upon only one index additional to crime, a welfare effort index. Community Chests and Councils, Inc. kindly supplied their information for 1940 on cities of more than 100,000. Their cards show the population covered, the quota assigned, the amount raised, and the number of persons making pledges. The following formula was constructed to give a welfare effort index:

$$\frac{\text{Amount Raised}}{\text{Quota}} + \frac{\text{Pledgers}}{\text{No. of Families in Area}} + \frac{\text{Amount Raised}}{.003 \times \text{Retail Sales}^5}$$

Each one of these ratios fluctuates around unity, so that the index fluctuates around 3.0. It will be seen that each of the three ratios measures one aspect of welfare effort—degree of achievement of goal, proportion of families giving, and economic sacrifice involved. This index correlated with crime — .43.

In Table 1 the Crime Index and the Welfare Effort Index for the forty-three cities have been so adjusted that they have the same mean and the same range of scores. The crime series has been reversed so that high scores indicate little crime. Although the relationship appears fairly close between the two series, there is the same tendency as before for some cities to be markedly inconsistent. Of the seven cities in the previous study that were inconsistent, only five appear in this one—Grand Rapids, Wichita, Richmond, Indianapolis, and Louisville. All show the same trends as before—Grand Rapids and Wichita to make a better crime score than welfare effort score, and the other three the reverse. This time, however, the inconsistencies of Grand Rapids and Indianapolis are not great, and that of Wichita only moderately large. Richmond and Louisville again show great inconsistency. Milwaukee, Baltimore, and Buffalo, cities that were labeled consistent before, now appear to be inconsistent. In the case of the first two, the trends now noted are merely an exaggeration of those that appeared before, but in the case of Buffalo there is a great change in the Welfare Effort Index. For this city it would be a mistake to rely upon either score, since we have no way of knowing which one to trust. Three cities not studied before—San Diego, Tacoma, and Chattanooga—appear to be inconsistent. Among the cities in this study, then, those that

---

5. The factor .003 was used to bring this ratio to unity in the mean case.

seem to be somewhat "passive" are Milwaukee, Buffalo, Wichita, San Diego, Baltimore, and Tacoma. They have better routine than intentional moral integration. The converse list is made up of Richmond, Chattanooga, and Louisville. They are the "quickened" ones. These terms should not be misinterpreted. All three of the quickened cities make a poorer

Table 1—Measures of Moral Integration, Forty-three Cities of More than 100,000

City	Adjusted Crime Index	Adjusted Welfare Effort Index	Integration Index
Rochester	17.3	22.4	19.0
Syracuse	17.1	16.9	17.0
Worcester	14.8	19.6	16.4
Erie	15.0	18.6	16.2
Milwaukee	18.4	10.5	15.8
Bridgeport	15.6	14.8	15.3
Buffalo	17.8	9.9	15.2
Dayton	13.4	16.1	14.3
Reading	14.2	14.2	14.2
Des Moines	14.5	13.4	14.1
Cleveland	12.3	17.4	14.0
Denver	14.8	12.0	13.9
Peoria	14.4	12.5	13.8
Wichita	15.6	9.7	13.6
Trenton	12.6	13.7	13.0
Grand Rapids	14.5	9.3	12.8
Toledo	11.5	15.0	12.7
San Diego	15.5	6.5	12.5
Baltimore	14.2	7.6	12.0
South Bend	12.7	9.9	11.8
Akron	12.0	9.8	11.3
Detroit	12.4	8.6	11.1
Tacoma	13.3	6.1	10.9
Richmond (Va.)	7.4	16.4	10.4
Houston	9.4	12.0	10.3
Fort Worth	10.4	9.8	10.2
Flint	11.7	6.0	9.8
Oklahoma City	9.8	9.6	9.7
Spokane	9.7	9.4	9.6
Chattanooga	7.2	13.4	9.3
Seattle	8.9	9.2	9.0
Indianapolis	7.5	11.4	8.8
Nashville	8.2	9.5	8.6
Birmingham	7.9	8.7	8.2
Columbus	6.2	11.7	8.0
Dallas	9.4	5.2	8.0
Louisville	4.1	15.0	7.7
Portland (Ore.)	6.7	8.1	7.2
Jacksonville	6.2	5.5	6.0
Memphis	3.8	8.7	5.4
Tulsa	3.7	8.5	5.3
Miami	5.8	3.6	5.1
Atlanta	2.5	7.6	4.2

over-all showing than do the passive cities. The point is merely that the former are evidently striving hard to overcome their low status, while the latter are to some extent resting on their laurels.

The third column in Table 1 gives a Moral Integration Index that was obtained by combining the Crime Index and the Welfare Effort Index. In the process of combination, however, the two constituent series were not weighted equally. By a rather elaborate calculation it was decided that the Crime Index was more reliable than the Welfare Effort Index, and the crime scores were therefore given twice the weight of the welfare effort scores in the inclusive index of moral integration.

It is felt that the array of moral integration scores gives a quite accurate picture of the relative standing of these large cities. The differences from top to bottom are very great. Rochester and Syracuse have a much stronger moral order than Miami and Atlanta. To say this is not to praise or to blame, since Miami and Atlanta are undoubtedly subject to much greater stresses than are Rochester and Syracuse. But the difference is a fact, and a very important one. To the matter of causes we now turn.

THE SIGNIFICANCE OF POPULATION FACTORS. It is one thing to demonstrate that cities are different with respect to moral integration; it is quite another to determine what the causal factors are. In the first place, there are so many influences working in one of our large cities that the task might appear a hopeless one. Cities differ in size, in age, in the backgrounds of their populations, in their religious makeup, in the stability of residence of their inhabitants, in their standards of living, in the proportions of the labor force in different occupations, in the kinds of organizations developed locally, in the quality of community leaders—to name only a few of the more obvious factors. Second, there is the problem of whether a particular feature, even if shown to be related to moral integration, is cause or effect of that integration. For instance, it can be argued that the organizations possessed by a city are influenced by the degree of solidarity of the community as well as being a cause of that solidarity. In meeting both of these difficulties one obtains much help from existing theory. This enables the research worker to select from the host of variables that present themselves for possible study those which are most likely to give significant results. Theory also helps one to assess the probability that a factor that varies with moral integration is cause or effect.

One of the best-established generalizations of the sociologist is that social problems tend to multiply, not only absolutely but relatively, with increase in community size. It is evidently more difficult to maintain a satisfactory social order over a large number of people than over a small number. This principle agrees with everyday observation. Indeed, the longing for "the good old days" is largely a nostalgia for the simple, small community where the pattern of life was well ordered. Although in towns and villages there may be unfriendly gossip about neighbors and even occasional overt violence, there are rarely organized centers of corruption.

Tocqueville painted a glowing picture of such American communities about 1835 in his *Democracy in America*. Probably his account is unduly laudatory, but it does underline the solid virtues of the small town.

Table 2*—Offenses Known to the Police (Rates per 100,000 population)

Size of Cities	Murder and Non-negligent Manslaughter		Robbery		Burglary	
	1947	1940	1947	1940	1947	1940
More than 250,000	7.11	6.1	85.7	74.7	450.6	397.3
250,000-100,000	7.71	6.5	68.9	50.8	508.3	418.4
100,000-50,000	6.30	5.7	43.0	37.8	392.3	364.8
50,000-25,000	4.14	3.4	32.3	32.2	343.8	313.5
25,000-10,000	4.30	3.9	27.1	23.3	295.1	253.7
Less than 10,000	4.33	4.1	24.8	22.2	248.2	234.1

* Source: Uniform crime reports of the Federal Bureau of Investigation.

In view of the testimony both of science and of common observation, it is a distinct surprise to find that, once a population of 100,000 is passed, size is not negatively related to moral integration. If we take crime as a measure, we can see from Table 2 that there is a fairly steady loss of integration with increasing city size below 100,000. But above that figure crime trends are irregular. One explanation for this leveling-off of crime rates would be that all the evils of the largest cities are already present in the 100,000-250,000 group. Another possibility is that the cities above 250,000 are on the average older than those in the next group and that greater maturity is a positive influence which is just about offsetting the negative influence of larger size.

Since the Crime Index is the principal constituent of the Integration Index in the second study, size of the city was dropped as a causal factor as soon as it was discovered that the correlation of crime with size was only — .06 for the forty-three cities—a random relationship.

Although Thorndike had found income to be significant for the goodness of a community, experimentation with his data in my first study had not convinced me of its significance for moral integration. In the second study I used the per capita retail sales of each community as a measure of its level of income and found that the correlation with moral integration was zero. Hence a second hypothetical cause was proved worthless for our purposes and banished from the study.

The conclusion that the economic factor is unimportant for moral integration may well surprise the layman. He is so likely to think that all the good things of life are dependent upon the possession of money that it may be a shock to learn that this is not so. However, the cultural anthropologist will not be surprised. His contact with primitive peoples has made him aware that social solidarity is a result of quite other forces. As a matter of fact, it has been argued by sociological historians that the higher standard of living that has come with increasing division of labor has actually served to lessen social cohesion by expanding the opportunities for individualistic consumption of economic goods and services.

Both the layman and the sociologist would expect that, the more the population of an American city is a mixture of races and nationalities, the greater the difficulties of moral integration. In the first study I obtained srtiking confirmation of this generalization from the analysis of Thorndike's data on the fourteen "consistent" cities. Table 3 shows the ratio of native-born whites to nonwhites for the well-integrated, moderately inte-

Table 3—Ratio of Native-born Whites to Nonwhites in Fourteen "Consistent" Cities, Grouped According to Levels of Moral Integration

Well integrated:		Moderately integrated:		Poorly integrated:	
Milwaukee	49.7	Hartford	16.8	Houston	2.6
Syracuse	82.2	Bridgeport	29.1	Columbus (Ohio)	7.3
Springfield (Mass.)	34.6	Canton	28.1	Dallas	4.7
Providence	31.4	Dayton	10.1	Birmingham	1.6
		Kansas City (Mo.)	7.9	Atlanta	1.9
Mean	49.5	Mean	18.4	Mean	3.6

grated, and poorly integrated cities. This ratio was used as an index because it was felt that the foreign-born whites constitute a middle category the members of which deserve to be in neither the numerator nor the denominator. The striking thing about this series is that there is no overlapping of scores among the three groups of cities. Since the ratio of native-born whites to non-whites in a city can hardly be attributed to that city's moral integration, the inference is strong that heterogeneity of population is a negative factor causally related to moral integration.

In my second study I followed up this clue. I constructed a new index of heterogeneity as follows:

$$\text{Heterogeneity} = \frac{\text{Foreign-born whites} + 2\,(\text{Nonwhites})}{.01\,(\text{Total population of city})}$$

It was assumed on the basis of American sociological findings that it is twice as difficult to integrate a member of another race into a community chiefly made up of native-born whites as it is to integrate a foreign-born white into that community. Later work with these data indicate that it is actually three times as difficult to do so.

The heterogeneity scores are given in the second column of Table 4. They tend to rise as integration falls, in accordance with our hypothesis. The correlation coefficient between the two series is $-.59$. This is a fairly significant relationship. Since the real meaning of such a coefficient is more accurately expressed by its square, this one signifies that 35 per cent of the variation in moral integration can be laid to differences among the cities in their heterogeneity. This does not prove that different races and nationality groups in a population always affect moral integration unfavorably. Where there is racial tolerance, as in Brazil, or where the government has made strong efforts to overcome the prejudices of nationalities toward one another, as in Russia, heterogeneity may not be a handicap to moral integration.

There is a great deal of support in sociological studies for the proposition that the movement of population makes for disorder. Solidarity can be more easily maintained in a stable group than in one with a high turnover of members. We should therefore expect that the shift of residents into or out of a community would lessen moral integration. This hypothesis can be tested by the data for in- and out-migration between 1935 and 1940 gathered by the United States Census in 1940. For all cities of more than 100,000 the number of persons living in each city who lived elsewhere in 1935 and the number of persons living elsewhere in 1940 who lived in each city in 1935 were tabulated. By adding the percentage of in-migrants to the percentage of out-migrants we obtain a rough measure of the total movement during the five years. This we call the Mobility Index. The mobility scores for our forty-three cities are given in the third column of Table 4.

Casual inspection shows that there is a tendency for the mobility scores to increase as the integration scores fall. As expressed in a correlation coefficient, this relation is − .49. This signifies that about one-quarter of the variation in integration among the cities is attributable to the differing degrees of mobility of their populations.

When the two factors of heterogeneity and mobility are correlated with each other, the coefficient is found to be − .06. This may seem odd when it is recalled that both series tend to rise as integration falls. However, careful inspection of Table 4 will reveal that the southern cities, where heterogeneity scores are high, have rather low mobility scores, while the northern cities have high mobility scores and fairly low heterogeneity scores. Because these two factors are independent of each other, their multiple correlation with integration is − .79. Translated into layman's language, this means that 63 per cent of the variance in integration among the forty-three cities is accounted for by these two factors.

This result is very gratifying, since it is not often in social research that so much of the variation of an abstract characteristic like moral integration can be attributed to so few factors. The important question still remains, however: To what is the remainder of the variation in integration due? Five other possibilities had occurred to me by the time I had finished working with heterogeneity and mobility. These factors were: the rate of growth of the city, the proportion of absentee-owned to locally-owned businesses, the proportions of the population adhering to various religious denominations, the proportion of married women working, and the pattern of social classes in the community.

Although I realized that the rate of growth of a city would probably be associated with the mobility index already computed because the in-migrants between 1935 and 1940 would be important to both, I thought it worth while to determine whether the rate over a longer period might not be independently significant. The hypothesis was simply that integration is easier the more slowly newcomers are added to the aggregate. The percentage growth between 1920 and 1940 was taken as the index. This was found to correlate — .43 with integration, but, when it was added to mobility and heterogeneity, the multiple correlation with integration was

Table 4—Moral Integration and Causal Factors, Forty-three Cities of More than 100,000

City	Integration Index	Heterogeneity Index	Mobility Index
Rochester	19.0	20.6	15.0
Syracuse	17.0	15.6	20.2
Worcester	16.4	22.1	13.6
Erie	16.2	14.0	14.8
Milwaukee	15.8	17.4	17.6
Bridgeport	15.3	27.9	17.5
Buffalo	15.2	22.3	14.7
Dayton	14.3	23.7	23.8
Reading	14.2	10.6	19.4
Des Moines	14.1	12.7	31.9
Cleveland	14.0	39.7	18.6
Denver	13.9	13.0	34.5
Peoria	13.8	10.7	35.1
Wichita	13.6	11.9	42.7
Trenton	13.0	32.5	15.8
Grand Rapids	12.8	15.7	24.2
Toledo	12.7	19.2	21.6
San Diego	12.5	15.9	49.8
Baltimore	12.0	45.8	12.1
South Bend	11.8	17.9	27.4
Akron	11.3	20.4	22.1
Detroit	11.1	38.3	19.5
Tacoma	10.9	17.8	31.2
Richmond	10.4	65.3	24.9
Houston	10.3	49.0	36.1
Fort Worth	10.2	30.5	36.8
Flint	9.8	19.3	32.2
Oklahoma City	9.7	20.7	47.2
Spokane	9.6	12.3	38.9
Chattanooga	9.3	57.7	27.2
Seattle	9.0	23.9	34.2
Indianapolis	8.8	29.2	23.1
Nashville	8.6	57.4	25.4
Birmingham	8.2	83.1	25.9
Columbus	8.0	27.4	25.0
Dallas	8.0	36.8	37.8
Louisville	7.7	31.5	19.4
Portland (Ore.)	7.2	16.4	35.8
Jacksonville	6.0	73.7	27.7
Memphis	5.4	84.5	26.7
Tulsa	5.3	23.8	44.9
Miami	5.1	50.2	41.8
Atlanta	4.2	70.6	32.6

not improved over the — .79 previously obtained. This can be attributed to the fact that the rate of growth was positively related both to mobility (+ .53) and to heterogeneity (+ .27), so that its influence is expressed through those two variables.

The hypothesis that absentee ownership of industry might have something to do with integration was derived from the *Report of the Smaller War Plants Corporation to the Special Committee To Study Problems of American Small Business* (79th Cong., 2d Sess.; Senate Doc. No. 1350). It was there suggested that cities in which small businesses predominate will have more civic enterprise than cities in which large businesses predominate because of a greater number of "independent" businessmen in the former who are not oriented to the head offices elsewhere of giant corporations. The index suggested was the ratio of proprietors, firm members, and officials of corporations to the total nonwage-working employees as indicated by the 1939 Census of Manufactures. In absentee-owned plants this index would be low, since the local executives would be counted as nonwage-working employees, not as officials of the corporation. The correlation of the ratio with my Integration Index, however, proved to be negative, rather than positive and to be substantial: — .46. And the correlation remained the same even when a correction was made to include all businesses as well as manufactures. This surprising result is probably a consequence of the greater frequency of small businesses in mobile and heterogeneous communities rather than of any direct causal influence of large businesses on integration. At any rate, it is clear that the scale of enterprise is not closely related to moral integration, as the congressional committee supposed.

Sociological theory and popular belief agree in assigning positive importance to religious values in the moral integration of the community. The last Census of Religious Bodies, taken in 1936, was used to investigate this matter. I tried out two hypotheses. One was that the larger the proportion of church members in the community, the better the integration. Another was that the larger the ratio of Catholics to all church members, the better the integration—on the theory seemingly proved by Durkheim in the case of suicide that Protestants are more individualistic in their outlook. Neither of these hypotheses was substantiated by the facts, and I therefore abandoned church membership as a factor in moral integration. Thorndike reached similarly negative conclusions. He states: "On the whole, unless the better communities under-report their church membership or the worse communities over-report theirs, we must suspect that churches are clubs of estimable people and maintainers of traditional rites and ceremonies rather than powerful forces for human betterment."[6]

This result will surprise many readers, who are perhaps aware of the role that religion plays in their own lives. One possible explanation is that the statistics are for church membership, not for degree of participation.

6. *Your City,* p. 99.

If figures for the latter were obtainable, they might well show a significant relation to a city's moral integration.

Another clue from my first study that seemed worth following up was the possibility that the proportion of married women gainfully employed was causally significant for the moral integration of the city. In Table 5 are shown the figures given in Thorndike's study for the three groups among the fourteen "consistent" cities. Although there is considerable overlapping of scores among these groups, there is enough of a trend to suggest the hypothesis that the working of married women is detrimental to the moral integration of a community. However, caution is necessary here. The proportions may be effect of moral integration as well as cause. Where there is not much sense of civic responsibility, mothers may pay less attention to the upbringing of their children. Despite this, I felt that the matter should be explored with reference to the forty-three cities of my second study. It turned out that there was a negative correlation between this factor and integration of $-.54$ but that the positive correlations of this factor with heterogeneity and mobility were so great—$+.67$ and $+.21$, respectively—that the addition of this factor to the other two did not raise the multiple correlation of $-.79$ already established between

Table 5—Married Women Gainfully Employed per 1,000 Population,
Corrected for Sex Ratio, for Fourteen "Consistent" Cities
Grouped According to Levels of Moral Integration

Well integrated:		Moderately integrated:		Poorly integrated:	
Milwaukee	25.1	Hartford	33.0	Houston	50.7
Syracuse	30.2	Bridgeport	28.9	Columbus (Ohio)	40.1
Springfield (Mass.)	28.1	Canton	21.4	Dallas	52.8
Providence	22.9	Dayton	36.5	Birmingham	39.6
		Kansas City (Mo.)	45.4	Atlanta	56.4
Mean	26.6	Mean	33.0	Mean	49.9

those two and moral integration. Undoubtedly the chief reason for the close correspondence of the series on the employment of married women with that on heterogeneity is the fact that Negro wives are employed proportionately much more often than white wives. The effect of wives working, therefore, is already taken into account through our other two causal factors.

A hypothesis that to a sociologist obviously merits testing is that cities that have a larger middle class to mediate between the extremes in social status will have higher moral integration than those that have fewer in the middle class. It would appear almost axiomatic that, the smaller the mediating group, the greater the likelihood of severe friction between the upper and lower groups.

I first tried to test this hypothesis with census figures on occupations. In the attempt to get at the relative size of the mediating group in each city, I used both the percentage of clerical workers and, later, the combined percentage of clerical workers and skilled manual workers. Although small proprietors certainly deserve to be in the middle class too, as well as many professionals, there is no way to separate them satisfactorily. The two series that I did compare with the integration scores showed no tendency whatever to validate the hypothesis. Cities that were well integrated seemed just as likely to have small as large middle groups.

This result seemed so inconsistent with accepted sociological doctrine that I tried again, this time using figures on rentals rather than occupations. The index for each city was what is known as a coefficient of variation. This gives a measure of the relative degree of dispersion in rentals for each city. Thus a city that had unusually large proportions of its population at the extremes of wealth and poverty would have a high score, while a city in which a disproportionate share of the families were near the rental average would have a low one. The correlation with moral integration proved to be very high: $-.65$. This was the best simple correlation yet obtained, and I therefore hoped that the addition of this factor to heterogeneity and mobility would raise the multiple correlation above the $-.79$ previously recorded. However, this hope was in a large measure disappointed. The relations of rental spread to heterogeneity and mobility (respectively, $+.71$ and $+.28$) were such that the multiple correlation of the three factors with moral integration turned out to be only $-.80$, a negligible improvement over the former figure. What this means is that income spread, though an important causal factor in moral integration, is already represented pretty completely in heterogeneity and mobility. On the scientific principle of parsimony, it is better to regard the latter two as the principal causes, since no combination of three causes accounts for significantly more of the variance in moral integration than do these two alone, and no other combination of two causes accounts for as much.

Table 6—Population Factors and Moral Integration

VARIABLE	WITH INTEGRATION		WITH MOBILITY		WITH HETEROGENEITY	
	r	σ_r	r	σ_r	r	σ_r
Mobility	$-.49$	.12	..	..	..	..
Heterogeneity	$-.59$	.10	$-.06$	.15	..	..
Rate of growth	$-.43$	.12	$+.53$	.11	$+.27$	.14
Percentage of married women working	$-.54$	.11	$+.21$	.15	$+.67$	.08
Rental spread	$-.65$	.09	$+.28$	.14	$+.71$	.08
Mobility and heterogeneity	$-.79$	.06	..	..	..	..
Mobility, heterogeneity, and percentage of married women working	$-.79$	.06	..	..	..	..
Mobility, heterogeneity, and rental spread	$-.80$	.05	..	..	..	..

Of the nine variables that had been tested for their causal relation to moral integration in cities of more than 100,000, four had proved to have no significance—size, income level, church membership, and percentage of small businessmen among all businessmen. Five had shown definite relationship to moral integration—heterogeneity, mobility, rate of city growth, percentage of married women working, and rental spread. The correlations of these with moral integration and with one another, together with the standard deviations of the several correlation coefficients, are shown in Table 6. Of the five, heterogeneity and mobility appear to be the key factors in the sense that the influence of the others is almost completely included in the influence of these two.

8

THE URBAN DWELLER:
PERSONALITY AND SOCIAL PARTICIPATION

Some of the characteristics of urban social structure and the manner in which they function for subgroups in society have been presented. Several further questions can now be raised. What kinds of human beings live in the city? How does urban living affect the social self or personality of urbanites? What is the character of interpersonal relationships among them?

An early essay in this Reader by Louis Wirth provides an ideal-typical description of interpersonal relationships among urban inhabitants. A major factor conditioning these relationships is the large size of the community and the density of settlement. A series of interrelated factors undoubtedly are jointly linked with these —such as the level of urbanization in the society and the complexity of the technological system—since they affect such factors as the size and density of settlement, the complexity of the division of labor, the scale of the social organization, and the increased mobility of the urban population in search of livelihood and status in the society.

A number of hypotheses about the quality of interaction among urban as compared with rural inhabitants, and of the consequences of these differences for personality integration, often are made on the basis of the ideal-typical description of interpersonal relationships in cities as compared with rural areas. They include the following hypotheses: (1) Within a given period of time, urban dwellers will have *a greater average number of interpersonal contacts* than rural ones; (2) Urban individuals are *more likely to inter-act with others as occupants of specific social roles,* as human contacts in cities are segmentalized as role contacts, while rural dwellers are more likely to interact as full personalities; (3) *Primary social contacts comprise a smaller proportion of the total interpersonal contacts* of city than of country people; (4) Urban individuals have *greater anonymity in social contacts,* permitting extensive interaction among persons who have little, if any, knowledge of the life history of the other, while rural individuals interact primarily in terms of a known life history; (5) Urbanites interact outside the primary group by *utilizing one another almost exclusively as means to ends—* the utilitarian quality of interpersonal relations; (6) The *interpersonal contacts of city persons tend to be spatially more diffuse* than those of rural dwellers; (7) The basis of social integration is more likely to reside in *segmental contacts around common interests* in cities than it is in rural areas; (8) City dwellers are more likely to be *detached from organized aggregates* than are rural ones, because of the greater spatial and social mobility in cities; (9) The interaction system of urbanites as compared with rural folk is more likely to encompass seemingly contradictory behaviors—*urbanites in interaction are more likely to accentuate the unique qualities of actors and their roles, while standardizing the interactions;* (10) Urbanites are *more likely to tolerate social differences and to develop a relativistic perspective,* given their greater exposure to a diversity of groups, ideas and persons, than are rural dwellers.

The data available to test these hypotheses are meager and the tests far from rigorous. Despite the plausibility of these hypotheses, their validity as propositions is open to question.

The personality structure of city dwellers is thought to be developed and changed by the nature of interpersonal relations in the city. Persons in cities find it difficult to maintain an integrated personality, it is said, as the quality of interpersonal relationships in many urban situations fails to insure consistency in behavior, the stability of reference points, and the personal integrity of the individual. Simmel's essay in this section emphasizes that the exposure to constant shifts in external and internal situations renders participation difficult on an affective basis. The result is a calculus of expediency and sophistication where the rationale of efficiency takes the place of feelings in personal relationships. The degree to which the empirical behavior of persons in cities is consistent with these ideal-typical descriptions of the behavior of urbanites is not altogether clear. Other papers in this section represent empirical attempts to study the personality integration and patterns of social participation of urban dwellers. They permit only a limited evaluation of the adequacy of these descriptions.

The high degree of concentration in urban centers presumably has its subjective effects. The close physical contact of urbanites, the marked contrasts in ways of life, the destruction of traditional models of behavior with increasing freedom for the individual, and the segmental character of contacts all appear to affect the *level* of personality integration of the city dweller. The selection from Plant suggests that the effects of living under conditions of close physical proximity are to heighten personal insecurity, to destroy the illusions which make for personal integration, and to substitute personal satisfaction for mutual satisfaction. Urban living is seen as tending toward the privatization of activity—the divorcement of the person from a sense of mutual participation in the society, resulting in increased withdrawal into the self.

Social control in cities proceeds in large degree through formal mechanisms. Law is a major institution of formal control in cities, and it is organized through enforcement agencies. Laws generally express a minimum rather than a maximum of conduct. A great deal of normative variation therefore is permitted in conduct, since the formal mechanisms generally operate only when behavior fails to conform to the minimum conduct standard. The individual is thus given a great deal of freedom to deviate from convention, if not from law. This apparent toleration of deviation from convention seems to lead, in fact, to a selective migration to cities, at least to very large ones, of persons who reject prescribed conformity to social norms in their community, or who because of their actual normative and behavioral deviation are social outcasts or isolates in their community of origin. The metropolitan city, itself, at the same time has a sizeable number of native inhabitants whose behavioral deviation from the social norms leads to rejection by the more conventional groups in the urban society. Formal mechanisms of social control in cities operate to sanction the behavior of these deviates; particularly when they persist in their behavior in the more conventional urban residential areas. It is characteristic of metropolitan cities that they provide an organized way of life for these types of normative deviants. Cities actually develop residential and quasi-productive communities for persons who deviate rather markedly from the prevailing norms. These areas tend to be characterized by a distinct subculture, the normative content of it changing with changes in the content of the dominant culture. Caroline Ware provides a description of one such subculture and its "Village" in New York City. The types of Villagers or residents also are described, largely in terms of a continuum of normative deviation or rejection.

There are a number of studies which try to compare the personality of rural and urban inhabitants in order to determine whether there are substantial qualitative differences in their personalities and in personal integration. The evidence from these studies is not altogether consistent. Some show substantial differences between rural and urban inhabitants (usually U.S. high-school children), while others do not. There are many measurement problems which render such comparisons difficult. A formidable problem in comparison is to control the fact that the differences between rural and urban dwellers appear to diminsh in highly industrialized-urbanized societies. Parenthetically, let it be said that this means that factors other than the size of the community must produce the original differences. One of the more careful investigations of personality differences between rural and urban children is that by Mangus presented in this section. Comparing the personality adjustment of a sample of rural and urban children, Mangus concludes there is evidence that farm children tend to be more self-reliant, have a greater sense of self-esteem and belonging, and greater freedom from withdrawing tendencies.

Ideal-typical descriptions of city dwellers generally present urbanites as less conservative in their behavior than their rural counterparts. Evidence supporting observations about this attitude difference for the most part are based on comparisons of the voting records of rural and urban legislators, and of the urban locus of so-called radical movements and their spread. Contrary evidence perhaps is quite frequently ignored in these observations. Recently the public opinion polls made it possible to learn whether there are substantial differences in the verbalizations of rural and urban inhabitants on opinion issues. The papers by Haer and Beers in this section report such opinion comparisons. Haer concludes that

the hypothesis that conservatism is positively associated with rurality, as designated on a continuum of places of residence which vary in size, is not tenable for residents of the State of Washington. The review of national sample poll data by Beers concludes that rural dwellers seem more conservative than urban ones primarily on issues which are of direct personal and group concern to farmers. Furthermore, unanimity of opinion among farmers or urban dwellers is not found for any issue. Rather, there is considerable overlap in the separate distributions of opinion for farmers and urban status groups.

The normative beliefs, attitudes and opinions of urban persons vary considerably within American cities. There is evidence, in fact, that this variation is at least as great as the contrast between large and small communities. The paper by Sykes in this section reports an investigation of the social location of knowledge of the community among its inhabitants. A high level of community knowledge in the community he studied was found to be associated with active membership and participation in the community, while a low level of community knowledge was related to orientation away from the community of residence.

Students of urban life have observed that there appears to be more organization of special interests and attitudes on a specialized group basis in cities than in rural areas. This is particularly true for those organizations where membership is achieved on a voluntary basis, as already noted in Section Seven. There is some difficulty in determining the degree to which observed differences in the extensity of organizations and participation in them is a true community difference. The values of the culture in which the city is located and the level of urbanization in the society—to mention but two factors—undoubtedly affect the extensity of, and participation in, organizations. Current research on the organization of the city in terms of a large number and variety of groups focuses more on the study of differential participation in these groups, than on a study of group structure and process. These studies generally emphasize that there are sizeable differences in organizational patterns of participation among persons in different strata and positions in the society. The paper by Axelrod in this section provides data on differential social participation in formal and informal groups for a sample of the Detroit, Michigan, population. The evidence suggests that formal group membership seems less extensive and the participation less intensive than the polar ideal type of urban participation leads one to hypothesize. Substantial variation in membership and participation in organizations occurs for variables which are indicators of social status. The paper by Zimmer compares the social participation of migrants with nonmigrant natives of a small city. There is evidence that both the size of the community of migrant origin and the length of time a migrant resides in the community affect the level of social participation. This single case study of a community suggests, however, that the native urban pattern of participation in a community of this size is generally adopted by migrants within a period of five years of migration to the community.

THE METROPOLIS AND MENTAL LIFE

Georg Simmel

The deepest problems of modern life derive from the claim of the individual to preserve the autonomy and individuality of his existence in the face of overwhelming social forces, of historical heritage, of external culture, and of the technique of life. The fight with nature which primitive man has to wage for his *bodily* existence attains in this modern form its latest transformation. The eighteenth century called upon man to free himself of all the historical bonds in the state and in religion, in morals and in economics. Man's nature, originally good and common to all, should develop unhampered. In addition to more liberty, the nineteenth century demanded the functional specialization of man and his work; this specialization makes one individual incomparable to another, and each of them indispensable to the highest possible extent. However, this specialization makes each man the more directly dependent upon the supplementary activities of all others. Nietzsche sees the full development of the individual conditioned by the most ruthless struggle of individuals; socialism believes in the suppression of all competition for the same reason. Be that as it may, in all these positions the same basic motive is at work: the person resists to being leveled down and worn out by a social-technological mechanism. An inquiry into the inner meaning of specifically modern life and its products, into the soul of the cultural body, so to speak, must seek to solve the equation which structures like the metropolis set up between the individual and the super-individual contents of life. Such an inquiry must answer the question of how the personality accommodates itself in the adjustments to external forces. This will be my task today.

The psychological basis of the metropolitan type of individuality consists in the *intensification of nervous stimulation* which results from the swift and uninterrupted change of outer and inner stimuli. Man is a differentiating creature. His mind is stimulated by the difference between a momentary impression and the one which preceded it. Lasting impressions, impressions which differ only slightly from one another, impressions which take a regular and habitual course and show regular and habitual contrasts —all these use up, so to speak, less consciousness than does the rapid crowd-

---

ing of changing images, the sharp discontinuity in the grasp of a single glance, and the unexpectedness of onrushing impressions. These are the psychological conditions which the metropolis creates. With each crossing of the street, with the tempo and multiplicity of economic, occupational and social life, the city sets up a deep contrast with small town and rural life with reference to the sensory foundations of psychic life. The metropolis exacts from man as a discriminating creature a different amount of consciousness than does rural life. Here the rhythm of life and sensory mental imagery flows more slowly, more habitually, and more evenly. Precisely in this connection the sophisticated character of metropolitan psychic life becomes understandable—as over against small town life which rests more upon deeply felt and emotional relationships. These latter are rooted in the more unconscious layers of the psyche and grow most readily in the steady rhythm of uninterrupted habituations. The intellect, however, has its locus in the transparent, conscious, higher layers of the psyche; it is the most adaptable of our inner forces. In order to accommodate to change and to the contrast of phenomena, the intellect does not require any shocks and inner upheavals; it is only through such upheavals that the more conservative mind could accommodate to the metropolitan rhythm of events. Thus the metropolitan type of man—which, of course, exists in a thousand individual variants—develops an organ protecting him against the threatening currents and discrepancies of his external environment which would uproot him. He reacts with his head instead of his heart. In this an increased awareness assumes the psychic prerogative. Metropolitan life, thus, underlies a heightened awareness and a predominance of intelligence in metropolitan man. The reaction to metropolitan phenomena is shifted to that organ which is least sensitive and quite remote from the depth of the personality. Intellectuality is thus seen to preserve subjective life against the overwhelming power of metropolitan life, and intellectuality branches out in many directions and is integrated with numerous discrete phenomena.

The metropolis has always been the seat of the money economy. Here the multiplicity and concentration of economic exchange gives an importance to the means of exchange which the scantiness of rural commerce would not have allowed. Money economy and the dominance of the intellect are intrinsically connected. They share a matter-of-fact attitude in dealing with men and with things; and, in this attitude, a formal justice is often coupled with an inconsiderate hardness. The intellectually sophisticated person is indifferent to all genuine individuality, because relationships and reactions result from it which cannot be exhausted with logical operations. In the same manner, the individuality of phenomena is not commensurate with the pecuniary principle. Money is concerned only with what is common to all: it asks for the exchange value, it reduces all quality and individuality to the question: How much? All intimate emotional relations between persons are founded in their individuality, whereas in rational relations man is reckoned with like a number, like an element which is in itself indifferent. Only the objective measurable achievement is of interest. Thus metropolitan man reckons with his merchants and customers, his domestic servants and often even with persons with whom he is obliged to have social intercourse. These features of intellectuality contrast with the nature of the small circle in which the inevitable knowledge of individuality as inevitably produces a warmer tone of behavior, a behavior which is beyond a mere objective balancing of service and return. In the sphere of the economic psychology of the small group it is of importance that under primitive conditions production serves the customer who orders the good, so that the producer and the consumer are acquainted. The modern metropolis, however, is supplied almost entirely by production for the market, that is, for entirely unknown purchasers who never personally enter the producer's actual field of vision. Through this anonymity the interests of each party acquire an unmerciful matter-of-factness; and the intellectually calculating economic egoisms of both parties need not fear any deflection because of the imponderables of personal relationships. The money economy dominates the metropolis; it has displaced the last survivals of domestic production and the direct barter of goods; it minimizes, from day to day, the amount of work ordered by customers. The matter-of-fact attitude is obviously so intimately interrelated with the money economy, which is dominant in the metropolis, that nobody can say whether the intellectualistic mentality first promoted the money economy or whether the latter determined the former. The metropolitan way of life is certainly the most fertile soil for this reciprocity, a point which I shall document merely by citing the dictum of the most eminent English constitutional historian: throughout the whole course of English history, London has never acted as England's heart but often as England's intellect and always as her moneybag!

In certain seemingly insignificant traits, which lie upon the surface of life, the same psychic currents characteristically unite. Modern mind has become more and more calculating. The calculative exactness of practical life which the money economy has brought about corresponds to the ideal of natural science: to transform the world into an arithmetic problem, to fix every part of the world by mathematical formulas. Only money economy has filled the days of so many people with weighing, calculating, with numerical determinations, with a reduction of qualitative values to quantitative ones. Through the calculative nature of money a new precision, a certainty in the definition of identities and differences, an unambiguousness in agreements and arrangements has been brought about in the relations of life-elements—just as externally this precision has been effected by the universal diffusion of pocket watches. However, the conditions of metropolitan life are at once cause and effect of this trait. The relationships and affairs of the typical metropolitan usually are so varied and complex that without the strictest punctuality in promises and services the whole structure would break down into an inextricable chaos. Above all, this necessity is brought about by the aggregation of so many people with such differentiated interests, who must integrate their relations and activities into a highly complex organism. If all clocks and watches in Berlin would suddenly go wrong in different ways, even if only by one hour, all economic life and communication of the city would be disrupted for a long time. In addition an apparently mere external factor, long distances, would make all waiting and broken appointments result in an ill-afforded waste of time. Thus, the technique of metropolitan life is unimaginable without the most punctual integration of all activities and mutual relations into a stable and impersonal time schedule. Here again the general conclusions of this entire task of reflection become obvious, namely, that from each point on the surface of existence—however closely attached to the surface alone—one may drop a sounding into the depth of the psyche so that all the most banal externalities of life finally are connected with the ultimate decisions concerning the meaning and style of life. Punctuality, calculability, exactness are forced upon life by the complexity and extension of metropolitan existence and are not only most intimately connected with its money economy and intellectualistic character. These traits must also color the contents of life and favor the exclusion of those irrational, instinctive, sovereign traits and impulses which aim at determining the mode of life from within, instead of receiving the general and precisely schematized form of life from without. Even though sovereign types of personality, characterized by irrational impulses, are by no means impossible in the city, they are, nevertheless, opposed to typical city life. The passionate hatred of men like Ruskin and Nietzsche for the metropolis is understandable in these terms. Their natures discovered the value of life alone in the unschematized existence which cannot be defined with precision for all alike. From the same source of this hatred of the metropolis surged their hatred of money economy and of the intellectualism of modern existence.

The same factors which have thus coalesced into the exactness and minute precision of the form of life have coalesced into a structure of the highest impersonality; on the other hand, they have promoted a highly personal subjectivity. There is perhaps no psychic phenomenon which has been so unconditionally reserved to the metropolis as has the blasé attitude. The blasé attitude results first from the rapidly changing and closely compressed contrasting stimulations of the nerves. From this, the enhancement of metropolitan intellectuality, also, seems originally to stem. Therefore, stupid people who are not intellectually alive in the first place usually are not exactly blasé. A life in boundless pursuit of pleasure makes one blasé because it agitates the nerves to their strongest reactivity for such a long time that they finally cease to react at all. In the same way, through the rapidity and contradictoriness of their changes, more harmless impressions force such violent responses, tearing the nerves so brutally hither and thither that their last reserves of strength are spent; and if one remains in the same milieu they have no time to gather new strength. An incapacity thus emerges to react to new sensations with the appropriate energy. This constitutes that blasé attitude which, in fact, every metropolitan child shows when compared with children of quieter and less changeable milieus.

This physiological source of the metropolitan blasé attitude is joined by another source which flows from the money economy. The essence of the blasé attitude consists in the blunting of discrimination. This does not mean that the objects are not perceived, as is the case with the half-wit, but rather that the meaning and differing values of things, and thereby the things themselves, are experienced as insubstantial. They appear to the blasé person in an evenly flat and gray tone; no one object deserves preference over any other. This mood is the faithful subjective reflection of the completely internalized money economy. By being the equivalent to all the manifold things in one and the same way, money becomes the most frightful leveler. For money expresses all qualitative differences of things in terms of "how much?" Money, with all its colorlessness and indifference, becomes the common denominator of all values; irreparably it hollows out the core of things, their individuality, their specific value, and their incomparability. All things float with equal specific gravity in the constantly moving stream of money. All things lie on the same level and differ from one another only in the size of the area which they cover. In the individual case this coloration, or rather discoloration, of things through their money equivalence may be unnoticeably minute. However, through the relations of the rich to the objects to be had for money, perhaps even through the total character which the mentality of the contemporary public everywhere imparts to these objects, the exclusively pecuniary evaluation of objects has become quite considerable. The large cities, the main seats of the money exchange, bring the purchasability of things to the fore much more impressively than do smaller localities. That is why cities are also the genuine locale of the blasé attitude. In the blasé attitude the concentration of men and things stimulates the nervous system of the individual to its highest achievement so that it attains its peak. Through the mere quantitative intensification of the same conditioning factors this achievement is transformed into its opposite and appears in the peculiar adjustment of the blasé attitude. In this phenomenon the nerves find in the refusal to react to their stimulation the last possibility of accommodating to the contents and forms of metropolitan life. The self-preservation of certain personalities is bought at the price of devaluating the whole objective world, a devaluation which in the end unavoidably drags one's own personality down into a feeling of the same worthlessness.

Whereas the subject of this form of existence has to come to terms with it entirely for himself, his self-preservation in the face of the large city demands from him a no less negative behavior of a social nature. This mental attitude of metropolitans toward one another we may designate, from a formal point of view, as reserve. If so many inner reactions were responses to the continuous external contacts with innumerable people as are those in the small town, where one knows almost everybody one meets and where one has a positive relation to almost everyone, one would be completely atomized internally and come to an unimaginable psychic state. Partly this psychological fact, partly the right to distrust which men have in the face of the touch-and-go elements of metropolitan life, necessitates our reserve. As a result of this reserve we frequently do not even know by sight those who have been our neighbors for years. And it is this reserve which in the eyes of the small-town people makes us appear to be cold and heartless. Indeed, if I do not deceive myself, the inner aspect of this outer reserve is not only indifference but, more often than we are aware, it is a slight aversion, a mutual strangeness and repulsion, which will break into hatred and fight at the moment of a closer contact, however caused. The whole inner organization of such an extensive communicative life rests upon an extremely varied hierarchy of sympathies, indifferences, and aversions of the briefest as well as of the most permanent nature. The sphere of indifference in this hierarchy is not as large as might appear on the surface. Our psychic activity still responds to almost every impression of somebody else with a somewhat distinct feeling. The unconscious, fluid and changing character of this impression seems to result in a state of indifference. Actually this indifference would be just as unnatural as the diffusion of indiscriminate mutual suggestion would be unbearable. From both these typical dangers of the metropolis, indifference and indiscriminate suggestibility, antipathy protects us. A latent antipathy and the preparatory stage of practical antagonism effect the distances and aversions without which this mode of life could not at all be led. The extent and the mixture of this style of life, the rhythm of its emergence and disappearance, the forms in which it is satisfied—all these, with the unifying motives in the narrower sense, form the inseparable whole of the metropolitan style of life. What appears in the metropolitan style of life directly as dissociation is in reality only one of its elemental forms of socialization.

This reserve with its overtone of hidden aversion appears in turn as the form or the cloak of a more general mental phenomenon of the metropolis: it grants to the individual a kind and an amount of personal freedom which has no analogy whatsoever under other conditions. The metropolis goes back to one of the large developmental tendencies of social life as such, to one of the few tendencies for which an approximately universal formula can be discovered. The earliest phase of social formations found in historical as well as in contemporary social structures is this: a relatively small circle firmly closed against neighboring, strange, or in some way antagonistic circles. However, this circle is closely coherent and allows its individual members only a narrow field for the development of unique qualities and free, self-responsible movements. Political and kinship groups, parties and religious associations begin in this way. The self-preservation of very young associations requires the establishment of strict boundaries and a centripetal unity. Therefore they cannot allow the individual freedom and unique inner and outer development. From this stage social development proceeds at once in two different, yet corresponding, directions. To the extent to which the group grows—numerically, spatially, in significance and in content of life—to the same degree the group's direct, inner unity loosens, and the rigidity of the original demarcation against others is softened through mutual relations and connections. At the same time, the individual gains freedom of movement, far beyond the first jealous delimitation. The individual also gains a specific individuality to which the division of labor in the enlarged group gives both occasion and necessity. The state and Christianity, guilds and political parties, and innumerable other groups have developed according to this formula, however much, of course, the special conditions and forces of the respective groups have modified the general scheme. This scheme seems to me distinctly recognizable also in the evolution of individuality within urban life. The small-town life in Antiquity and in the Middle Ages set barriers against movement and relations of the individual toward the outside, and it set up barriers against individual independence and differentiation within the individual self. These barriers were such that under them modern man could not have breathed. Even today a metropolitan man who is placed in a small town feels a restriction similar, at least, in kind. The smaller the circle which forms our milieu is, and the more restricted those relations to others are which dissolve the boundaries of the individual, the more anxiously the circle guards the achievements, the conduct of life, and the outlook of the individual, and the more readily a quantitative and qualitative specialization would break up the framework of the whole little circle.

The ancient *polis* in this respect seems to have had the very character of a small town. The constant threat to its existence at the hands of enemies from near and afar effected strict coherence in political and military respects, a supervision of the citizen by the citizen, a jealousy of the whole against the individual whose particular life was suppressed to such a degree that he could compensate only by acting as a despot in his own household. The tremendous agitation and excitement, the unique colorfulness of Athenian life, can perhaps be understood in terms of the fact that a people of incomparably individualized personalities struggled against the constant inner and outer pressure of a de-individualizing small town. This produced a tense atmosphere in which the weaker individuals were suppressed and those of stronger natures were incited to prove themselves in the most passionate manner. This is precisely why it was that there blossomed in Athens what must be called, without defining it exactly, "the general human character" in the intellectual development of our species. For we maintain factual as well as historical validity for the following connection: the most extensive and the most general contents and forms of life are most intimately connected with the most individual ones. They have a preparatory stage in common, that is, they find their enemy in narrow formations and groupings the maintenance of which places both of them into a state of defense against expanse and generality lying without and the freely moving individuality within. Just as in the feudal age, the "free" man was the one who stood under the law of the land, that is, under the law of the largest social orbit, and the unfree man was the one who derived his right merely from the narrow circle of a feudal association and was excluded from the larger social orbit—so today metropolitan man is "free" in a spiritualized and refined sense, in contrast to the pettiness and prejudices which hem in the small-town man. For the reciprocal reserve and indifference and the intellectual life conditions of large circles are never felt more strongly by the individual in their impact upon his independence than in the thickest crowd of the big city. This is because the bodily proximity and narrowness of space make the mental distance only the more visible. It is obviously only the obverse of this freedom if, under certain circumstances, one nowhere feels as lonely and lost as in the metropolitan crowd. For here as elsewhere it is by no means necessary that the freedom of man be reflected in his emotional life as comfort.

It is not only the immediate size of the area and the number of persons which, because of the universal historical correlation between the enlargement of the circle and the personal inner and outer freedom, has made the metropolis the locale of freedom. It is rather in transcending this visible expanse that any given city becomes the seat of cosmopolitanism. The horizon of the city expands in a manner comparable to the way in which wealth develops; a certain amount of property increases in a quasi-automatical way in ever more rapid progression. As soon as a certain limit has been passed, the economic, personal, and intellectual relations of the citizenry, the sphere of intellectual predominance of the city over its hinterland, grow as in geometrical progression. Every gain in dynamic extension becomes a step, not for an equal, but for a new and larger extension. From every thread spinning out of the city, ever new threads grow as if by themselves, just as within the city the unearned increment of ground rent, through the mere increase in communication, brings the owner automatically increasing profits. At this point, the quantitative aspect of life is transformed directly into qualitative traits of character. The sphere of life of the small town is, in the main, self-contained and autarchic. For it is the decisive nature of the metropolis that its inner life overflows by waves into a far-flung national or international area. Weimar is not an example to the contrary, since its significance was hinged upon individual personalities and died with them; whereas the metropolis is indeed characterized by its essential independence even from the most eminent individual personalities. This is the counterpart to the independence, and it is the price the individual pays for the independence, which he enjoys in the metropolis. The most significant characteristic of the metropolis is this functional extension beyond its physical boundaries. And this efficacy reacts in turn and gives weight, importance, and responsibility to metropolitan life. Man does not end with the limits of his body or the area comprising his immediate activity. Rather is the range of the person constituted by the sum of effects emanating from him temporally and spatially. In the same way, a city consists of its total effects which extend beyond its immediate confines. Only this range is the city's actual extent in which its existence is expressed. This fact makes it obvious that individual freedom, the logical and historical complement of such extension, is not to be understood only in the negative sense of mere freedom of mobility and elimination of prejudices and petty philistinism. The essential point is that the particularity and incomparability, which ultimately every human being possesses, be somehow expressed in the working-out of a way of life. That we follow the laws of our own nature—and this after all is freedom—becomes obvious and convincing to ourselves and to others only if the expressions of this nature differ from the expressions of others. Only our unmistakability proves that our way of life has not been superimposed by others.

Cities are, first of all, seats of the highest economic division of labor. They produce thereby such extreme phenomena as in Paris the remunerative occupation of the *quatorzième*. They are persons who identify themselves by signs on their residences and who are ready at the dinner hour in correct attire, so that they can be quickly called upon if a dinner party should consist of thirteen persons. In the measure of its expansion, the city offers more and more the decisive conditions of the division of labor. It offers a circle which through its size can absorb a highly diverse variety of services. At the same time, the concentration of individuals and their struggle for customers compel the individual to specialize in a function from which he cannot be readily displaced by another. It is decisive that city life has transformed the struggle with nature for livelihood into an interhuman struggle for gain, which here is not granted by nature but by other men. For specialization does not flow only from the competition for gain but also from the underlying fact that the seller must always seek to call forth new and differentiated needs of the lured customer. In order to find a source of income which is not yet exhausted, and to find a function which cannot readily be displaced, it is necessary to specialize in one's services. This process promotes differentiation, refinement, and the enrichment of the public's needs, which obviously must lead to growing personal differences within this public.

All this forms the transition to the individualization of mental and psychic traits which the city occasions in proportion to its size. There is a whole series of obvious causes underlying this process. First, one must meet the difficulty of asserting his own personality within the dimensions of metropolitan life. Where the quantitative increase in importance and the expense of energy reach their limits, one seizes upon qualitative differentiation in order somehow to attract the attention of the social circle by playing upon its sensitivity for differences. Finally, man is tempted to adopt the most tendentious peculiarities, that is, the specifically metropolitan extravagances of mannerism, caprice, and preciousness. Now, the meaning of these extravagances does not at all lie in the contents of such behavior, but rather in its form of "being different," of standing out in a striking manner and thereby attracting attention. For many character types, ultimately the only means of saving for themselves some modicum of self-esteem and the sense of filling a position is indirect, through the awareness of others. In the same sense a seemingly insignificant factor is operating, the cumulative effects of which are, however, still noticeable. I refer to the brevity and scarcity of the inter-human contacts granted to the metropolitan man, as compared with social intercourse in the small town. The temptation to appear "to the point," to appear concentrated and strikingly characteristic, lies much closer to the individual in brief metropolitan contacts than in an atmosphere in which frequent and prolonged association assures the personality of an unambiguous image of himself in the eyes of the other.

The most profound reason, however, why the metropolis conduces to the urge for the most individual personal existence—no matter whether justified and successful—appears to me to be the following: the development of modern culture is characterized by the preponderance of what one may call the "objective spirit" over the "subjective spirit." This is to say, in language as well as in law, in the technique of production as well as in art, in science as well as in the objects of the domestic environment, there is embodied a sum of spirit. The individual in his intellectual development follows the growth of this spirit very imperfectly and at an ever increasing distance. If, for instance, we view the immense culture which for the last hundred years has been embodied in things and in knowledge, in institutions and in comforts, and if we compare all this with the cultural progress of the individual during the same period—at least in high status groups—a frightful disproportion in growth between the two becomes evident. Indeed, at some points we notice a retrogression in the culture of the individual with reference to spirituality, delicacy, and idealism. This discrepancy results essentially from the growing division of labor. For the division of labor demands from the individual an ever more one-sided accomplishment, and the greatest advance in a one-sided pursuit only too frequently means dearth to the personality of the individual. In any case, he can cope less and less with the overgrowth of objective culture. The individual is reduced to a negligible quantity, perhaps less in his consciousness than in his practice and in the totality of his obscure emotional states that are derived from this practice. The individual has become a mere cog in an enormous organization of things and powers which tear from his hands all progress, spirituality, and value in order to transform them from their subjective form into the form of a purely objective life. It needs merely to be pointed out that the metropolis is the genuine arena of this culture which outgrows all personal life. Here in buildings and educational institutions, in the wonders and comforts of space-conquering technology, in the formations of community life, and in the visible institutions of the state, is offered such an overwhelming fullness of crystallized and impersonalized spirit that the personality, so to speak, cannot maintain itself under its impact. On the one hand, life is made infinitely easy for the personality in that stimulations, interests, uses of time and consciousness are offered to it from all sides. They carry the person as if in a stream, and one needs hardly to swim for oneself. On the other hand, however, life is composed more and more of these impersonal contents and offerings which tend to displace the genuine personal colorations and incomparabilities. This results in the individual's summoning the utmost in uniqueness and particularization, in order to preserve his most personal core. He has to exaggerate this personal element in order to remain audible even to himself. The atrophy of individual culture through the hypertrophy of objective culture is one reason for the bitter hatred which the preachers of the most extreme individualism, above all Nietzsche, harbor against the metropolis. But it is, indeed, also a reason why these preachers are so passionately loved in the metropolis and why they appear to the metropolitan man as the prophets and saviors of his most unsatisfied yearnings.

If one asks for the historical position of these two forms of individualism which are nourished by the quantitative relation of the metropolis, namely, individual independence and the elaboration of individuality itself, then the metropolis assumes an entirely new rank order in the world history of the spirit. The eighteenth century found the individual in oppressive bonds which had become meaningless—bonds of a political, agrarian, guild, and religious character. They were restraints which, so to speak, forced upon man an unnatural form and outmoded, unjust inequalities. In this situation the cry for liberty and equality arose, the belief in the individual's full freedom of movement in all social and intellectual relationships. Freedom would at once permit the noble substance common to all to come to the fore, a substance which nature had deposited in every man and which society and history had only deformed. Besides this eighteenth-century ideal of liberalism, in the nineteenth century, through Goethe and Romanticism, on the one hand, and through the economic division of labor, on the other hand, another ideal arose: individuals liberated from historical bonds now wished to distinguish themselves from one another. The carrier of man's values is no longer the "general human being" in every individual, but rather man's qualitative uniqueness and irreplaceability. The external and internal history of our time takes its course within the struggle and in the changing entanglements of these two ways of defining the individual's role in the whole of society. It is the function of the metropolis to provide the arena for this struggle and its reconciliation. For the metropolis presents the peculiar conditions which are revealed to us as the opportunities and the stimuli for the development of both these ways of allocating roles to men. Therewith these conditions gain a unique place, pregnant with inestimable meanings for the development of psychic existence. The metropolis reveals itself as one of those great historical formations in which opposing streams which enclose life unfold, as well as join one another with equal right. However, in this process the currents of life, whether their individual phenomena touch us sympathetically or antipathetically, entirely transcend the sphere for which the judge's attitude is appropriate. Since such forces of life have grown into the roots and into the crown of the whole of the historical life in which we, in our fleeting existence, as a cell, belong only as a part, it is not our task either to accuse or to pardon, but only to understand.[1]

---

1. The content of this lecture by its very nature does not derive from a citable literature. Argument and elaboration of its major cultural-historical ideas are contained in my *Philosophie des Geldes* [The Philosophy of Money; München und Leipzig: Duncker und Humblot, 1900].

THE PERSONALITY AND AN URBAN AREA

James S. Plant

Within the area served by the Essex County Juvenile Clinic is a close-packed triangle bounded by three railroads and containing a high percentage of foreign-born and second-generation individuals, ranging from skilled artisans down to unskilled laborers. The families are large and there is much crowding. The lines between various racial groups are not clearly marked off though there is somewhat of a tendency to cluster.

Here we shall list what we have seen of the cross-currents between the pattern of living conditions found in such an area and the personality. We have chosen this sort of illustration because social institutions, such as the Family, grow and change in themselves through the growth and change of their members. On the other hand, areas within a city are changed rather by forces outside of the personality—industrial spread or new means of transportation—the inhabitants usually moving to other areas when the distinction between what they wish to be and what the area makes them becomes too great. In the case of the Family, we were able to speak realistically of integrated and purposeful changes, as we could in dealing with the Church, Industry, or the School. It is hard for people to move into or out of the Family or the School; people stay in them and change them. It is relatively easy to move into or out of a geographical area; the sociological factors within the area seem to the individual to be distinctly more static.

However, the fundamental issues are the same. Study of the casual breakdown shows us that the personality can be understood only if the cultural pattern in which it has grown, and from which it has taken its coloring, is understood; that it can be molded, "cured" if you please, only in the light of these cultural factors and perhaps only by altering them. Nor is this alteration merely to "better the surroundings of the individual" but also to better the individual. Social work of any sort is only forging its own fetters so long as it accepts the ancient dichotomy of personality and culture. The recent trend towards building a personal security, towards mending attitudes, towards a preoccupation with individual mechanisms is important; but it may be a comfortable escape from reality unless one keeps in mind that the personality is in the cultural pattern; to phantasy that

Reprinted from *Personality and the Cultural Pattern*, Chapter 8, by permission of Mrs. James S. Plant and the publisher. (Copyright, 1937, by the Commonwealth Fund.)

one may be changed without altering the other ranks with much of the magnificent but futile daydreaming of our various patients.

While we shall fail to see in this example the working through of a problem because the individual moves away from the area instead of enduring the growing tensions between what he wishes to be and what the pattern would make of him, we feel that our data from other areas indicate the probability that here too we are dealing with the individual's adjustment to problems rather than his adjustment of problems.

There are certain limitations in the materials. We have selected an area of the City of Newark in which children come to us almost entirely through the Juvenile Court (the schools of this city operate their own clinic). This may skew our material somewhat to the side of those less able to adjust to the pattern about them. However, scattered material from other crowded areas which provide contact with children not referred by the courts seems to indicate that this factor of selection does not materially distort the fundamental issues.

We chose this in preference to other possible samples as perhaps throwing some light upon a prevalent theory of the economic causes of maladjustment. Whether this be expressed in the social worker's finality in declaring the home a "bad one" (intending thus to characterize its poverty and crowding), or in statements from judges or officers of the law who assure the public that poverty is a large factor in crime, the implication is that certain economic conditions are the source of our social ills. It is simple to show that only poor people appear in our criminal courts, that the incidence of school retardation is much higher in the crowded areas, that mortality statistics and disease show here a most unfavorable comparison with those of advantaged areas—in short, that every form of social ill is increased in those areas of marked poverty.

If poverty were the cause of delinquency instead of the cause of being haled into court, if crowding rather than carelessness were the source of disease, if wealth meant the absence of problems instead of ability to care for them without recourse to formal social agencies—a better day would be but around the corner. Actually poverty and crowding seem to develop attitudes which in turn play into the hands of economic disadvantage—and any theory as to the economic sources of social ills must consider what these disadvantages mean to the personality and what meaning the proposed changes will have in terms of personality values and attitudes. It is the people themselves who are caught in the dragnet of sickness and death and no mere reallocation of the goods of the world—no resharing without consideration of what it will mean to those whom it affects—will accomplish anything more than show. The two (the person and the pattern) interact and (as we may have reiterated too frequently) those who would merely alter attitudes show the same blindness and the same parochial satisfaction as those who would merely alter dollars or houses.

POVERTY AND THE INDIVIDUAL. *"Hardening."* The first phenomenon that we have observed is what might be termed the hardening or brutalizing effect of constant financial menace. The psychological and physiological factors in "hardening" are difficult to assay though the process has definite reality and seriously affects much of our work with the dependent and delinquent. Every experience has a certain emotional value, a certain affect content. As an experience is repeated its emotional value or affect content is lessened so far as the individual is concerned. Possibly the mechanism is one of a more rapid and facile "draining off" of the disturbances and tensions set up by the event. Thus the criminal can with ease recall his first break with established law—though that break was really a minor one in relation to many later offenses. This is possibly because the visceral disturbances occurring at the time of the first break, through their very newness and strangeness, had not set those patterned modes of arrangement and draining off which would be developed by repeated experience. Thus the hardening process would be not a decreased emotional reaction but a sort of ordering of reactions into something like habitual patterns which obviate those disturbing reverberations appearing in the first "casual" act. This may be measured in many ways—one of the more dramatic being that given us by a nineteen-year-old "beginner." In holding up a store he realized that his trembling voice would betray his emotional excitement and therefore, in self-defense, he wrote out his demands in advance. After his sixth successful effort he was able to use his voice calmly.

Similarly, occasional poverty affects individuals in a very different way from persistent threats to shelter and food. Occasional and relatively short periods of financial stress are met as a disturbing challenge, are not lacking in thrill. One "didn't think he could do it" or "didn't know he had it in him"—so he expresses something of the pleasure of a challenge met or of a sharp crisis escaped. Where the problem is met every day and perhaps to an even more serious extent, a new quality of response sets in. We believe that this is not a mechanism of resignation, but the development of patterns of response (or draining off) that prevent each experience of want (it matters little how drastic!) from resulting in the emotional reverberations which accompanied the first such experience. This hardening or brutalizing process has certain practical implications.

There are many situations which the children of the area we are discussing seem to be able to meet with relatively little emotional disturbance—situations which would seriously disturb children of advantaged areas. (An example appears in their reactions to bullies and to losing out in competition and games even though they have a strongly competitive spirit.) It is as though the process of hardening could be used to advantage in meeting problems other than poverty. The social worker meets the relative equanimity of the child with "Well, he *ought* to be disturbed about it." A somewhat wide-flung belief that the children of the poor are lacking in the finer sensibilities is perhaps correct only in the sense that out of self-protection accustomed or habituated pathways of emotional reaction to crises are formed. The disturbance that the poor little rich child shows over what his hard-boiled cousin takes so nonchalantly is not then so much a matter of degree of feeling as that the former has not learned what to *do* with his feelings. Thus these two individuals in the presence of a crisis which is absolutely new to each frequently show the same reaction. A boy of sixteen who since seven had roamed the country with his father, experiencing the direst poverty, was entirely "taken off his guard" by the plight of a small youngster who had lost her parents. Joe knew and accepted every form of social evil but it was weeks before he could forget that experience, during which he had shown the tenderest regard for the child's feelings.

Corollary to this is the question as to the reaction a child who has long been hungry and cold has to a sunset or a painting in which there are nicely blended touches of color. Such different answers come from those who see much of these children (and our own findings are so various) that the answer must be a highly individualized one. The whole problem needs illumination and is of great educational value.

Finally one looks for a moment at this "hardened" person when a change of fortune occurs. If the essential element in continued and insistent poverty is the attitudes which it arouses, then some evidence of this should occur with the release of this pressure of stress and difficulty. And this is what actually happens. The individual now surrounds himself with gaudy symbols of a new day. The world knowingly shakes its head, confirmed in its assurance that here is "poor taste." If one "pinches himself to be sure that he is awake," he is simply stimulating a reaction which will not in empty fashion drain off along habituated and patterned pathways.

Feeling of insecurity. Continued poverty of an insistent sort seems to produce a vague and generalized picture of insecurity. The repeated, particularized reactions of hunger and cold may develop an habituation that means that each day's lack does not arouse those reverberations that appear in any serious emotional crisis, but an underlying pervasive sense of insecurity nevertheless develops.

The development of security is to a great extent a family affair—some sense of belongingness that the psycho-motor tensions of the parents transmit to the child. The resulting satisfaction is so basic a sentiment that it is only the most serious or prolonged series of threats that disturb it. The child who has not achieved this sense of security, the child who has not ever had a feeling that he has an unassailable place because of who he is regardless of what he is or what he does, shows a rather typical picture of anxiety and panic. However, this same picture appears in children who have suffered continued and serious blows at their sense of adequacy. It has been this that has led us to accept provisionally the conclusion that it is possible to produce a destruction of the feeling of security where the blows at adequacy are of sufficient strength and frequency. We recently saw a ten-year-old boy who unmistakably in his school and family history gives the picture of earlier security. For three years he has been living at places to which he is ashamed to take his companions, he has had clothes which practically preclude his going to school, and he has been without money to meet the small needs of boys of his age. He now gives the typical picture of not wishing to undertake the difficult task and of meeting every situation in rather panicky fear.

Children in families that have long had marginal or even lower status do show the picture of insecurity. It is without question affected by other security-giving mechanisms so that in well-knit family groups the picture does not appear as soon as in others, if at all. The data are not entirely clear, in the sense that one can never be sure whether long-continued financial reverses of themselves bring about the insecurity or whether they simply accentuate a condition previously existent in such mild degree as not to be recognizable in the sort of retrospective analyses which clinic procedure often has to use.

In either case it must be apparent that the poverty itself is vitalized and made important only as it touches upon and is given meaning by the personality. In this new setting of its meaning to the individual it undergoes enough transformation so that the mere removal of poverty and need does not solve the problem.

Feeling of inferiority. Perhaps the outstanding problem from the point of view of conduct disorders is that of the feeling of inferiority arising from the specific things which the less advantaged child lacks and desires. The matter is of course a relative one. One's feeling of insecurity comes from a long-continued, real fear of cold and hunger; the hardening effects of poverty are the hardening effects of real need; but the feeling of inferiority is one that is in relation to other persons. The inferiority reactions of children appear in many situations considerably removed from the brink of actual need. When children of the poor steal, it is usually to obtain those things which they themselves actually want—those things which give them that satisfaction of possession which they dream that children of other strata have. On the other hand, children equally deprived but in contact with more advantaged children come to us involved in stealing those objects which more directly compare with what the others have or those things with which they may buy favor. In areas of Essex County where patterns of the sort that we are discussing are contiguous to those of greater advantage, so that the children from the two groups are thrown together in school, we often deal with the latter phenomenon. Thus one finds the stealing of money which is used to buy candy which is used to buy social favor. (Our best examples of this last have been a handful of the children of the janitors who live in the apartment houses occupied by the well-to-do. These children did not steal what looked good to them but what looked good to the children of the tenants.) The group described here represent only a fraction of those to whom stealing *means* something else than merely the possession of a prized object.

One meets the distinction in the effectiveness of treatment. It is very difficult to provide any satisfactory therapy for the insecure child—the various attempts at answering his needs by giving him preference in the schoolroom or athletic team are tawdry and bedraggled answers to his deep distress. However, answers to the feeling of inferiority are relatively simple and easy. Teacher and social worker have long recognized this in handling a wide range of conduct disorders through giving to such children a feeling of success through any one of a host of resourceful ways. This type of treatment does not relieve the situation where it has progressed to the point of meaning insecurity to the child.

Because the narcissism of adolescence so much emphasizes whatever may be the child's problems, the feelings of inferiority from poverty are more acutely seen then than at other times. The problem of clothing families under the Emergency Relief program, for instance, has had its peculiar difficulties with the adolescent children. Where the adults and younger children were pressed enough by need to go for clothes thus provided, the more acutely sensitive adolescents have rebelled against this sort of regimentation. Similarly in another less-advantaged area of the county we have found that the teachers of the primary schools (up through sixth grade) knew much of the struggle of poverty-stricken families whereas in the junior and senior high schools in these same areas the teachers had no such data though their children came from the same families. "Well, we know they are having an awful time but they never say anything to us about it." "We can never get them to admit they are having any troubles at home." This is affected undoubtedly by the fact that high school teachers know their pupils less well than do grade teachers. However, in clinic or elsewhere the typical reaction to inferiority, the able and relatively sure-footed ability to cover over the matter that really disturbs the child, is much more frequently seen in the adolescent members of needy families than in their younger siblings.

STREET PLAY AND THE INDIVIDUAL. *The meaning of play.* The play life of the children of the area under consideration is very largely confined to street play and we have, again, been making an effort over these years to determine what street play means to the personality.

Play life—at least for children—is very largely emotional in its connotations. Even such intelligence as is required is of a highly contentional sort, demanding more of shrewdness or "cuteness" than that sort which is measured by the formal intelligence tests. This is amply supported by frequent lack of correlation between "intelligence" (in the sense used by the psychometrists) and success in ordinary street play. The school teacher marvels —and is often irritated—over children's preferences in their play life and games for those who far from shine in the classroom. (This has been perhaps the most persistent and jarring challenge that she has met to her faith in the relationship of what she teaches to the real problems of life.)

Those parts of the nervous system which are involved—and their order of appearance—in an "emotional reaction" are still the subject of dispute.

Yet somewhere in the emotional experience the body enters, as is not the case in purely intellectual operations. Thus when one is ashamed he is ashamed in his face. When one fears, the roots of the hair and the whole gastro-intestinal tract are involved. When one is happy or gay there is a certain feeling of the lightness of the whole body. And depression equally seems to load the entire body with a weight of lead. In other words, the completion of an emotional reaction involves expression through the visceral or sympathetic system. (One has to use the word "completion" here due to the present uncertainty of the exact relationship in time and stimulus between the visceral and the cerebro-spinal elements of the nervous system.) We take it that the ability of the higher animals, who are quite as well equipped in this visceral system as are we to express—and apparently to experience—emotions, is some support of this. Certainly the dog, the anthropoids, and to some extent the horse, seem quite as competent to enjoy, to hate, to show loyalty or jealousy, as we are.

Accepting this, accepting the concept of the maturation of the visceral system, accepting the hypothesis that the cultural pattern coerces and molds these visceral expressions in quite an autocratic (though, obviously, less direct) a manner as it imposes its wishes upon the intellectual life, a vast field of training and education opens before us. The early activities of the parents play their part—just as they sincerely affect the child's approach to the field of symbolic thinking—but the major "education" of the visceral system at least through childhood probably occurs through the play life. In play, more than in any other adjustment, the conditions surrounding emotional expression can be varied to meet the child's needs. The cultural pattern of any civilization delays and thwarts emotional expression and through this sets up appetite for expression—which appetite it seeks to train to be satisfied with reactions acceptable to the pattern. Anger which is aroused in early experiences in football is thus restrained (at least in its expression) and the individual is taught to satisfy the appetite aroused in this way by controlled acts of playing valor. The football coach will even deliberately attempt to anger his players that they may execute a better game. We earlier questioned the value of thwarting the emotions from the point of view of the individual's mental health but of course any other practice would lead to so sudden and complete a disintegration of our entire pattern that individual as well as social destruction would occur. Love, hatred, jealousy, joy, and sorrow receive the same treatment. And while there are many tools at the hand of society, it is, for the child, in the field of play that the outstanding mode of this control and substitution presents itself. (The ramifying implications of this fundamental task seem so clear that one marvels that the school has let itself be so completely monopolized by the intellectual field—only recently entering the field of play and still insisting upon the "coldness" of knowledge. Why has a cultural pattern so definitely committed to the policy of indoctrination through the schools neglected this richest of all fields?) These considerations lead us to the field of play with much more than relaxation at stake, interested in something besides taking the child out from under the mother's feet. The implications of such an approach are dealt with elsewhere and only this need be said here: that a program of "exercises" and drills (the ordinary school program of physical education) is entirely inadequate to the needs and promise of the whole field of the education and training of the emotions or expression of the emotions, and that the mere provision of a place to play is equally lacking in vision. A program of molding the entire individual to the efficiency of the cultural pattern is at best questionable business—but it is a program to which our civilization is committed and in its present blindness to the importance of play it is doing itself poor justice.

Effect of street play on mental health. From this point of view the street play of children becomes of increasing interest and importance. One asks what its characteristics mean to the development of the emotions. In this inquiry one is forced to take the indirect approach of seeing the problem in the light of the bodily expressions involved.

Street play is artificially confining in two ways. Few games requiring extensive running are possible. "Cops and robbers" and similar games are played within confined limits and the exciting phantasy content is of more importance to the child than is the physical activity of capture or escape. Such games as baseball maintain their ideational content at the same time that they are materially limited in physical expression. Children of the streets in their first days at camp show an unbelievable bursting forth of physical and vocal expression. To what extent the limitation in actual physical activity and in the type of game that can be played is actually, day by day, affecting the child, we do not know. From what we see there seems to be set up a mechanism of protection—a way of draining off the dammed-up tensions—that at least allows the child for each day of city living to be free of the feeling of the lack of healthy outlet. Thus we are quite unaware of what this all means to the child until we take him into a rural situation where his sudden uncontrollable exuberance gives us a picture of the previous confinement.

Street play lacks continuity. Of course, a great deal of the unsupervised play life of children lacks continuity. (One of the disasters dependent upon adult supervision of children's play comes in our effort to lengthen the span of attention beyond what is normal for the age involved. "They never stick at anything" is the disgusted formula which the adult brings to the clinic.) However, in street play there are other factors of disruption which rather brusquely break into the picture. The first is the needs of other groups. In crowded areas the opportunity of a group to play out its own game without interference from another group which wishes more space, or merely shows the normal desire to be in the midst of anything that is "going on," is relatively limited. There is, of course, also the breaking in of street traffic. Not only do these factors break the continuity of the game itself but they imply fear and defense as constant concomitants of the play process.

Street play involves a heterogeneity of collaborators which is of questionable hazard. What does it mean that the wealth of available players brings into any game a wide variety of ages and abilities? In talking with children of the street about their playmates one is amazed at the wide range of age (this excludes the "pal" or inner circle of special friends where there is rather marked homogeneity of age or ability). However, one's disturbance over this is unquestionably affected by the tradition of age distinction which the school stratification of children has built in us all. Perhaps the heterogeneity in maturity of emotional life and in span of attention which the play of the street provides is salutary relief from the regimentation of school grading. We are also, perhaps, unduly affected by our experience with youngsters who play habitually with older children and show a tense, uneasy restlessness which seems to be the result of the child's having forever to "reach up" to an integration and length of span of attention which is beyond his ability. In other words, we are at present without adequate data as to the effect of the age variation of play groups—and our natural distrust is perhaps dependent entirely on considerations which are not pertinent here.

We are not implying a disparagement of street play in comparison to what is available to children of more advantaged families. We find the latter frequently quite without adequate physical outlets in play—the fact that a family owns a lawn unfortunately does not guarantee that the children are allowed to romp upon it. Here, as elsewhere, we have simply used a certain area to illustrate an approach to the problem that asks what a certain social situation means to the development of the child—means in terms of certain rather well-defined needs in growth.

In the area which we are discussing some playgrounds have been developed. These alter in certain ways the matters discussed above. Crowding and confinement still exist, though not so markedly. There is a distinct difference in the factor of disturbance—the children are free from fear of automobiles and the crushing of their game by rival groups. To what extent adult supervision is going to control and regiment the child's activities rather than make way for their free expression remains for time to tell. For those interested in conduct disorders perhaps the most interesting question is whether the children who most need the playground will go there. In company with many similar ventures the playground is still viewed with suspicion by the type of child who fears the loss of freedom that is threatened when adults enter his life.

CROWDING AND THE INDIVIDUAL. The area under discussion has a large number of industrial plants interspersed in a general housing pattern of low rentals, large families, and few rooms for each. In the working out of the problems of life what does this pattern mean to the individuals living within it?

Lack of self-sufficiency. Crowding seems very definitely to affect the self-sufficiency of children—their ability to be alone. This is a matter entirely different from that of the close-drawn walls about the ego which are built when others threaten. Here we are dealing with a certain uncomfortable ill-at-ease-ness when there are not many others about. The search is for games, for work, where many others are close by. Also we have found difficulty in placing girls of this area in house-servant positions, a difficulty made up of many elements apparently, one of which at least is revealed by the girls' statement that "the work is too lonely." Every social engineer has had the experience of the loneliness of these children of crowded areas when placed in the country. It is as though they felt incomplete—without the necessary supports to the personality. It seems that persistent and constant crowding from early life destroys the sense of individuality—which without doubt is fostered by opportunities for privacy. (McDougall in discussing this same phenomenon uses the term "incomplete personality." [1]

These children seek in all their activities situations in which there are others—the movies, the factory. Their panic over country placement is not due merely to the strangeness of the surroundings, as many do not show this when placed in equally new situations where there are plenty of people about—in other cities or in other parts of the same city. (Country children brought to the city similarly complain of "loneliness"—but this is a different matter. Here the child feels that he is no factor in all that goes on about him—that persons do not nod a "good morning"—that his place of importance in the community is lost.) Our work in suburban and rural districts has convinced us that periods of being alone, of playing alone, of having the privacy of one's own room, are important fostering agents in a feeling of individuality, of self-sufficiency.

The other side of the picture is that there is a certain sensing of the needs of others, a certain understanding of others that comes from always living with them, not provided otherwise. Those who have periods of privacy, of being alone, have the opportunity to arrange their clothes before they appear in public. One often hears the complaint that the ward leader, the "typical politician," represents the crowded, less advantaged area, but at the same time the admission that he has a certain understanding of people that seems to come only from close contact with people in all their moods.

(The United States is rapidly being urbanized and, if we see the effects of crowding correctly, its results should appear in our cultural pattern. Is our growing reputation as a nation of joiners in any sense dependent upon this same factor? Here seems again to be this feeling of incompleteness if there are not many around.)

Destruction of illusions. Crowding serves to destroy the illusions which children build about other people. The word "illusion" is perhaps unwisely chosen. These images we build of others are of the material of our dreams

1. William McDougall, *Character and the Conduct of Life,* New York, Putnam's, 1927.

and goals. They are of great dynamic power—leading us to the best we can attain. Indeed the hero we thus invest is little more than the dramatizer, the personalization of what is perhaps otherwise too intangible a goal. We nevertheless use "illusion" here because its opposite has such a fixed and real meaning. When we speak of "disillusionment" we recognize the breaking of that which has been of tremendous worth.

There seems to be a certain optimum amount of contact for the construction of illusions. This differs for different individuals. At times chance meeting serves for the building of a complete hero picture. This phenomenon is not common, and depends entirely upon the extent to which some presenting symbol has been previously associated with an acceptable ideal image ("I *always* like people with that sort of hand"). Most of the children we see build much more definitely upon persons whom they know better—with whom they have carried through a number of conversations or projects. We have become quite certain that there is a point of contact beyond which these illusions stand the hazard of complete destruction. In this mechanism the child puts into the individual what he would like to be there rather than accepting what actually is there. This means that with rare exceptions the process of disillusionment must come with better acquaintance and more frequent contact.

Crowding, as we have said, destroys these illusions. People are seen when not on dress parade, they are seen often—they must be seen as they are rather than as they would wish to be or as one would wish to see them. For instance, the boys of this area do not want to follow in their father's footsteps. Of course, these families represent the least advantaged groups so that the children would naturally look to some other lines of work than those which seem so patently to have brought this lowly result. We have felt however that there is, too, the factor that the child knows his father too well. One idealizes out of dream material—the clatter and push of crowded living conditions too easily wake him up.

Does crowding prevent the formation of these illusions or break them down soon after they are formed? Our present feeling (without adequate data) is that the latter is the case. The discovery that these children continue the construction of these illusions (though now about new persons) would, in part, constitute such data. Would individuals show an insistent urge to form these idealized goals, if they had never done so at least in embryo form? One may add, for what it is worth, the observation that the descriptions of persons which these children give carry that certain sort of crispness that comes from something broken ("Everybody is a gyp," "There isn't a one I'd really trust"). Admittedly our data for this area only cover the delinquent group, which perhaps considerably skews the findings. The child describes his lack of goal images in the people about him with a certain attitude of rebuff. It is not alone that these children of crowded families are much more realistic about other people than are the children of well-to-do families. They are realistic on the negative or discouraging side—

that they know that you cannot trust people, that people are fundamentally selfish and looking for the attainment only of their own ends. They are much more on the defensive as to other people.

If crowding actually prevented the formation of ideal images then we should find hero worship absent in these groups. But if, as we believe, crowding merely served to break the images which are formed, then in some form or other hero worship should be found quite as much as at other levels of social stratification. The latter is what we find in our group. The older children have their highly idealized heroes and follow their lead as best they can. But these heroes are now peculiarly depersonalized. Thus, if one talks about some baseball hero he finds that nothing is known of the person. The hero is one of power and numbers. A home run is not a crisis met by a person but "his forty-first." Is this just the short-cut symbol for the more personal image? We think not—we have not been successful in getting back of batting averages and home-run accomplishments to the personality involved. This same "emptying" of the personality makes their description of the movies amusing. These children use the true names of the actors in describing their activities on the screen—again "protecting themselves" from the true personality of the movie hero or heroine. ("Clark Gable almost lost his life saving her.") Watching the face of the child through this gives ample evidence that the star is separated entirely from his or her own personality. If one now turns the child to the actual life of her favorite actress there is either a quick "Oh, I don't know anything about that" or a projection from a film that again leaves the star without much that she could really call her own.

Such observations led us to the following formulation: that the crowding of individuals does not prevent the development of image goals or hero worship; that the crowding of individuals repeatedly disillusions children, breaks the images that are formed; that what is left open to the child is an interesting form of depersonalized hero in which the name of an individual stands for such abstractions as numbers, high averages, power, or victory; that, in other words, the child learns that he cannot "afford" to worship a person *as such*.

This realism, this clearness of vision as to people, works peculiarly in another way, so that children seem to see more clearly what is "good" in people just as they see what is, for them, "bad." How else can one understand the ability of children to see the love that lies behind the harsh hand and voice? For often love is there—often it is precisely this force that impels the harshness. (One is tempted to amusement at a naïveté that fails to see that it is the errors only of those for whom we care that stir our deepest feelings. How often must we strive for calmness, plan for objectivity, scheme for a certain coldness in the feeding of the child—all to gain victory over a dish of spinach! How often the child senses in the parent's disturbance the tie of belongingness it craves! Well can we afford to be cold and objective about those things which do not touch us and about those for whom we do not care! We have had some rather rude jolts from children in families where statistics as to tempests ran high—only to find ties of loyalty and love that seemed incomprehensible. "Sure the old man beat me up—lots of times—but it was because he loved me. He wouldn't a done it if he didn't care a lot.") The child of the crowded home senses motives—sees what really lies behind conduct—and if this breaks his brittle idols it often too gives him strength and the sense of belongingness in the face of what seems to the objective outsider to be unreasonable and cruel treatment.

(We earlier essayed a parenthesis as to cultural drifts and here we raise another general question. In the light of growing urban concentration, and the disruption of the drive to the idealization of others which it seems to imply, we have been interested in the recent development of "realism" in our biographical literature. People turn out to be only real people after all—national heroes of just the same ordinary clay as the rest of us. This form of biography would be no more "realistic" than the earlier romantic types if we continued to live as far away from others as we earlier did. The important factor in our illusions about others is their intense realism and power. Their disappearance from our lives is not so much a matter of their weakness and lack of substantiality as it is of our having destroyed them through the way in which we live.)

Sexual maladjustment. Crowding also prevents the building of illusions about sex. (Again we impute a realism and dynamic power to "illusions" that is scarcely connoted in the word itself.) This demands that something be said of the meaning of sexual adjustments.

In any of the biological sciences it is difficult to set up a true dichotomy. If one sets up a dichotomy in the field of what sexual expression means to people, it is done only for the sake of clearer exposition; one accepts the premise that each of the two elements runs into the other, with indistinct borders between them. On this basis sexual expression can be said to play two quite distinct roles which are in large measure separable though both have a part in most sexual acts.

Sexual phenomena, on the one hand, serve the individual in high degree as the source of direct pleasurable experiences. It is uncertain at how early an age this appears though certainly, from birth, the genital region is provided with a greater concentration of sensory nerves than practically any other part of the body. The individual comes into the world already equipped to receive through this region satisfying responses which are not of a sexual nature as the adult knows it but rather of something merely more marked and striking than are other body reactions. However, the sexual connotations (in an adult sense) of these reactions rapidly grow, being aided by the biological process of the specialization of sensation and by the social process which hastens to give meaning to all life experiences. Thus occasionally one finds children up to ten years old, let us say, who turn to stimulation of the genital region as a means of attaining a direct satisfying physical response (in distinction to those who use these activities for their social value—a group discussed in a moment). From ten years on the opportunity for this direct satisfaction develops and is worked out largely in the problem of masturbation. We have seen both girls and boys who, we are convinced, have no phantasy life during masturbation beyond the contemplation of the pleasure of the act itself. Here one finds the establishment of various sorts of so-called perverted sexual acts because the individual is primarily interested in any procedure which will develop actual physical expression of the sexual hunger. Such an individual very soon loses all compunctions (as to following what Society is pleased to call "normal" heterosexual procedures) and is quite ready to find expression in the homosexual or heterosexual, in the normal or perverted field, whatever gratification can be found.

Sexual phenomena on the other hand serve a high symbolic or language-value purpose for the individual. Just how early this begins is again unknown although perhaps some of the rudimentary patterns are set down in late infancy when the child discovers that masturbation has a high social value in the temper tantrums his act causes in the nearby adults. Soon children learn that certain words serve the same purpose of attracting attention. By six the boy learns that there are sexual acts which connote that one is grown up, and children of both sexes at this time, or before, use sexual information as valuable coin—buying respect and admiration from other children through particular bits of information. Most masturbation (at least this is true of our group) carries a high degree of heterosexual phantasy. By far the larger fraction of the "perversions" which we see at this period (sodomy and the like) are rich in heterosexual phantasy, are undertaken as a means of showing that one is "grown up" and spontaneously disappear just as soon as social sanctions allow of true ("normal") heterosexual experiences. The sexual phenomena through this whole adolescent period run rampant as the symbols of having grown up. One sees something of this as one listens to the tale of many a boy or girl who defies social condemnation in an effort to show through these fabrications that full growth has by now been attained. Similarly one talks with many of these children who actually dread definite heterosexual experience but who try to drive themselves to it because it is their best established symbol of maturity. The boy who has attempted but failed to consummate the heterosexual act never comes to us with a story of physical thwarting or unpleasantness, but with the shame that he is not yet grown up. So for the adolescent one could multiply by hundreds the examples of the use of the sexual life to attain in one's own eyes and the eyes of others, age, maturity, social prestige victory in sibling rivalry, and the like.

Interwoven with the above and developing rapidly in adolescence is the use of the sexual life as a means of expressing relationships which are beyond the power of words. It is at this level that the sexual aspects of the marital relationships work themselves out. The intimacy ties involved in marriage are idiomatic for the individual; the partners labor to develop a feeling that here exists a relationship that could exist between no two others. The sexual act is of the highest importance here—entered upon only by "agreement" of both partners and turned to by them as a means of expressing some sort of idiomatic tie that seems to defy any other form of expression. So-called "perversions" (as Havelock Ellis long ago pointed out so well) [2] have frequently now a particular value as they represent to the partners symbols of "what other people wouldn't do."

Physical gratification of course plays a part in practically all the sexual phenomena. Equally, the symbolic values of the sexual life appear to some degree in most of its manifestations. The matter is one, then, of the relative degree to which each is present. We have dealt with boys and men who in fear and actual physical discomfort attempt to carry through various forms of sexual expression as symbolizing maturity. (This is apparently more common in girls and women—many of whom go through the entire sexual life with nothing beyond the experience of the sexual activities as the "proper thing to do" or what is "expected of one in marriage.") Of the existence of the various onanistic, homosexual, and heterosexual acts as no other than means of physical gratification, we are decidedly more certain.

What now are the "illusions" about sex? We think that they are the realistic, dynamic images that are set up in a vague way about this use of sex as a symbol of relationship. And what now does crowding do to these illusions, which ordinarily begin to appear at seven, eight, or nine years of age? If our observations are correct then an individual can understand the use to which those who love each other put the sexual life only when he or she has had that experience. It is precisely the idiom of the relationship which defies teaching it to others. Yet our clinic records of crowded families quite abound in instances of children surreptitiously or more openly viewing those sexual activities to which they can give no other connotation than that of physical gratification. In other words, the "illusions" about sex are not formed because the child views the whole gamut of sex activities for those years during which he can give them practically no other connotation than that of direct physical gratification.

What meaning do such views give to "sexual perversion"? Evidently the important matter is whether or not the act leads towards a better heterosexual adjustment. Sexual acts carried out upon individuals of the same sex or of a masturbatory nature where the phantasy is entirely heterosexual and where the deterrence to heterosexual approach is social tabu, can hardly be called perversions—indeed, these individuals turn to "correct" heterosexual outlets as soon as the social sanctions allow. Similarly the most eminently "proper" relations of the marital state may be carried through with so overwhelming a drive on the part of one of the partners for physical gratification and so complete a disregard for the language values of the

2. In various places; particularly see Havelock Ellis, *Studies in the Psychology of Sex*, Philadelphia, F. A. Davis, 1927. Volume VI, pages 523, 531 (footnote), 544, and 554.

sexual act in the expression of the affectional ties, as to constitute definitely a perversion. In other words, a perversion in sexual expression has nothing at all to do with the form of the act but only with its purpose (which, of course, has been already recognized by a number of writers).

Does crowding prevent the development of illusions about sex or does it break them down after they have been formed? We get the impression from our clinic children that these illusions are never formed. In talking with us they do not manifest the elements of disappointment—the sharpness as of something broken—that appears in the discussion of broken idols. It has been this in part that has built our theory that the symbolic language values of sexual phenomena appear later in childhood and are prevented from appearing where the child has first seen so much of what is to him meaningless ("meaningless" beyond their prevision of physical satisfaction) physical expression.

We are aware that a large and voluble group of psychoanalytic persuasion have felt that it has been precisely the illusions about sex that have led to most of our difficulties. They would have us realize that hiding from children the strength and undaunted drive of the sexual urge has been really what has led to neuroses and conflicts when the child actually meets the overpowering character of his or her own sexual hunger. This may be a correct view of the situation. If it is, then the various interesting (not to say exotic) mechanisms which this school has uncovered should be quite lacking in crowded families where children from tender years are accustomed to see a rather florid display of the sexual urge. Up to the present time certain quite impelling urges have almost entirely prevented the psychoanalysts from investigations among the poor. Our experience is that among the poor these difficulties are at least as frequent as among their more advantaged cousins. We are still persuaded that any arrangement which brings to the child an important and insistent urge at a time when he is utterly unable to understand its perspective in the total life situation of the adults involved must color the child's whole future attitude.

We are also aware of the arresting nature of the facts supplied by the divorce courts. In the Los Angeles courts, for instance, it is reported that "the primary cause of discord was . . . mostly based on complaints of sexual maladjustments."[3] Data such as these have strengthened the present fervid group who seek to cure the ills of family life through sexual education. We would be willing to accept the validity of these findings. We have ourselves every indication that a difficulty in the affectional ties first shows itself in sexual expression. How can people talk if they have nothing to say? The most subtle rift in the affectional ties is quite obviously magnified and dramatized in the sexual act which is no less than a highly complicated mutual act of expression. The analogy from the field of speech seems fair.

---

3. J. E. Wallace Wallin, *Personality Maladjustments and Mental Hygiene*, New York, McGraw-Hill, 1935.

Because speech difficulties such as stammering are so very dramatic and noticeable, generations have been busily engaged in attempting to cure these through various exercises directed to the speech trouble itself. If those interested in speech trouble now see that their point of attack is the fundamental emotional adjustment of the individual, may we not hope that in time there will be similar recognition that the sexual act is a mode of expressing certain deeper relationships?

There is an interesting type of document developing with some rapidity at this time—the volumes devoted to the technique of the sexual act. These Emily Posts of the sexual field have convinced themselves that one can make people happily married by telling them what happily married people do. Nor would one too quickly turn from this approach—writers are aided by a larger vocabulary, artists by better colors, carpenters by a wider range of tools. But first there must be something to be expressed.

Similar considerations threaten any movement which is directed at merely a symptom of a relationship. The pleasure factors in the sexual relations—in distinction to the language factors—are indeed persistent. However, propaganda which stresses solely these pleasure factors and their enhancement through freedom from fear of consequences runs the danger of emphasizing what we would consider the least constructive and most rapidly disintegrating factor of the marital relationship. It would be difficult not to support the dissemination of sane and correct information concerning a matter which is very widely practiced at the present time—namely, birth control—so long as there continued through the whole procedure the proper primary emphasis of the part that the sexual life plays in the preservation and enrichment of the love relationship.

What does all this mean in the matter of sexual education for children and young adults? There is nothing to be gained in a program that keeps the nature of the physical acts of sex in the realm of mystery and tabu. It is equally fatuous to feel that we are covering the sexual education of youngsters by describing in detail the overt sexual phenomena. If children are to be given an insight into a vocabulary they must recognize that it is a vocabulary. The child eight or nine years old cannot understand why "people do such things." They have for him value only as objective phenomena. Admittedly, this is the only value which they have for many adults. This is not, however, the point here. Perhaps with children we can never go beyond the matter of teaching them that sex is "all right," that their questions about it are not tabu, that their interest is not evil. In other words, the important aspect of sexual education for young children is not the so-called "facts" which are taught them but the attitude with which these are taught. We have become rather certain that many parents have done more harm in blushing and blundering their way through a detailed and exact account of affairs than have others who have dispensed such old favorites as the magnanimity of the stork in a way that has made the child feel that it was all right to have asked the question.

But, frankly, we have felt that up to the present we could not answer the question of sexual education of the adolescent. The physical manifestations of the sexual life are not only highly individual but they attain, for any pair of persons who are what one calls "happily married," validity precisely on the basis of their individuality—or at least on the basis of their supposed individuality. Perhaps it is only this setting forth of principles that could ever be given to adolescents. The high degree of individuality in the sexual relationship of itself seems to defy further "teaching."

(Again we return to our parenthetical statements. If population-concentration grows and if it indeed skews the interest of the child towards the physical-gratification side of sexual phenomena, is there any general cultural trend which might be thought of as developing from this? In this light we have been interested in the development in our literature, as well as in psychiatric theory itself, of a marked increase in preoccupation with the sexual acts themselves rather than with them as an expression of the affectional ties.)

Mental strain: Negativism and irritability. A fourth effect of crowding we have called—for lack of a better term—"mental strain." It is that which arises from always having to "hold on to oneself." We have discussed the walls that are built about the ego to preserve its sanctity from prying eyes. That these are walls of fear seems certain—nor can watchful guardianship over them be relaxed as long as many others are about. So one meets many adults—and some children—who "want to get away from everybody" they know, who feel the need of some surcease from this eternal vigilance. The results, when these periods of freedom are lacking, are either those of a somewhat forbidding negativism or of irritable outbursts of temper which belong definitely to the phenomena of fatigue. We see much of the latter either alone or associated with the former. The fatigue phenomenon seems to come from failure ever to be free from the task of guarding the status-preserving walls.

Or the matter may be expressed in another way—amounting, we guess, to the same thing. Earlier we pictured our children's inability to integrate the ego into a whole unit. Perhaps the walls of protection for the integrated ego are, in crowded families, never really completely formed. Perhaps this "mental strain," the fatigue phenomenon which we see, arises from the never-ending effort to integrate the ego under conditions which do not allow of this integration.

However this may be, one sees a constantly recurring picture of "touchy" reactions and irritability as the personality is pressed. Often one sees it covered, for protection, by an assumed nonchalance or braggadocio. When we realize that for many of these individuals from one year's end to the other, there is never a time that they are alone, we begin to get some picture of what this tension must be. Even the nights conspire to the same end; three to five children sleeping in the same bed means that even during the periods of relaxation and for the deeper levels of the unconscious there must always be this awareness of the imminence of others and the compromises and surrenders which this entails.

The reader recognizes that it is not alone the phenomenon of crowding that leads to this picture of mental strain. Nor, unfortunately, are touchy, irritable reactions confined to those of these less advantaged groups.

Lack of objectivity. Finally, among these individuals of crowded areas and crowded families there is what one describes as the phenomenon of being so much in the world that there is no chance to look at it. We have already discussed objectivity and attempted to show its basic importance to the developing personality. We believe that the degree of one's objectivity is largely if not entirely an inherent matter. However, even for individuals with a high degree of this objectivity this characteristic is in abeyance where the hurly-burly of life forever presses upon them. This is not a difficult matter to measure, our conclusions being based upon the relative ability of children from different areas to describe themselves and the situations in which they have been as onlookers rather than as participants.

VILLAGERS

Caroline F. Ware

The Village acted as a magnet which drew to it a wide variety of people with one quality in common, their repudiation of the social standards of the communities in which they had been reared. Here gathered in these years a whole range of individuals who had abandoned their home pattern in protest against its hollowness or its dominance, and had set out to make for themselves individually civilized lives according to their own conceptions. They had found the traditional Anglo-Protestant values inapplicable and the money drive offensive. In the Village, some sought to discover other positive values upon which to reconstruct a social system in America; many carried on those activities, especially artistic, which had little or no place in a civilization dominated either by the remains of the Calvinist ethic or by the purely acquisitive impulse; an increasing proportion simply sought escape, and brought with them little except negative values, throwing over more or less completely whatever smacked of 'Puritanism' or 'Babbittry'; the more serious sought some compromise which would enable them to avoid the features which they did not like, but to retain those which they consciously or unconsciously cherished.

The Village was not the only place where those who repudiated their traditions took refuge. Although it was the most notorious of such places, its counterpart could be found in Chicago, San Francisco, and other large cities, and elsewhere in New York. Its notoriety did not make it unique, but only made it an advantageous point from which to observe the disintegration of old American culture in the post-War years in an acute, and, therefore, clearly visible form.

The Villager population, in 1930 and the years preceding it, included at one end of the scale those who cherished old American values, but found them so lost or submerged in the bourgeois world that they took refuge from the pressures of that world and sought the opportunity to re-create the old values in their own lives. At the other extreme were those who threw over altogether both the American and the bourgeois patterns and sought complete freedom, defiance, or escape in flight to Greenwich Village. In between these two elements was the great mass of Village residents whose

Reprinted from *Greenwich Village*, Chapter VIII, pp. 235 ff., by permission of the publisher. (Copyright, 1935, by Houghton Mifflin Co.)

repudiation of their background was only partial and who consequently presented various conflict situations where that which they had retained interfered with that which they had cast aside. The first of these groups was the one which discovered the Village in its early, unsung days. The second gave it its reputation. The third made up by 1930 the largest element in its Villager population. Though these groups were not completely separated from each other, and lines between them were not hard and clear, they presented essentially distinct forms of adaptation and associated in groups which roughly followed these lines. All, however, shared certain basic common qualities which distinguished them both from their neighbors in that other social world and from their home communities—namely, a disregard for money values and for prestige based on either income or conspicuous expenditure, an awareness of some sort of cultural values, and tolerance of unconventional conduct even when their own habits were more constrained.

Unconventionality, especially in the matter of sex, was taken for granted, and attitudes ranged from tolerance of experimentation to approval rather than from condemnation to tolerance. The sober superintendents of 'respectable' apartment houses made no bones about enumerating 'girls and their fellers' among the occupants of their houses when trying to rent an apartment to a middle-aged lady. Villagers of conventional tastes were distinctly on the defensive in explaining to the interviewer that 'all the people in Greenwich Village aren't the kind that you expect to find. There are plenty of ordinary respectable people like us.' No one felt called upon to be on the defensive about the opposite type of conduct.

All types of Villagers were intensely individualistic in both their social relations and their point of view. Their social contacts were confined to more or less purposeful relations with those who had common interests. Independent of virtually all institutions and scorning the joining habit, taking full advantage of both the selectiveness and the anonymity which the city offered, they avoided the usual casual contacts with family, neighbors, or members of the same economic or social class and the relations growing out of institutional connections. Instead, they maintained individual ties with friends scattered all over the city. If they had professional or artistic interests, these were apt to furnish a basis for their social life. The pursuit of an avocation or common tastes in recreation brought others together.

It was possible to block out the main types of adaptation and repudiation and to describe the groups which fell within those types. The members of the groups did not remain constant, but the types endured, represented by some old and some new individuals from year to year. Succeeding groups with their different sorts of reactions in turn imparted their reputation to the Village as its dominant element, at least in the eyes of the outside world. In 1930, all these groups were still present, the earlier represented either by remnants of the personnel which had constituted the original groups or by newcomers of the same type as those who had left. The same range of types found in 1930, moreover, had been present in the years before, differing only in their relative numerical strength and in some of the specific attitudes which characterized them.

As the backflow to the Village increased, however, the relative prominence of different types changed. The first group of Villagers had been made up of individuals of exceptional independence, who had faced social problems with earnestness and had sought positive solutions. When the community had come to contain a large proportion of persons of ordinary caliber whose position reflected the social situations from which they had come more than the personal quality of the individuals, the negative desire to escape took the place of any positive quest, and social earnestness gave way to a drifting attitude. At the same time, the actual expression of repudiation became more extreme as the conduct which had constituted social defiance at one time became commonplace a few years later. The disappearance of smoking as an issue, the spread of drinking, and the passing on from free love to homosexuality were only the more obvious of the manifestations which were successively adopted to mark the outposts of revolt.

Art, sex, and a disdain for the pursuit of wealth were the key points by which it was possible to test the nature and the degree of departure from the old American tradition.

Interest in money-making for its own sake and in the world of business was rare among all types of Villagers. Though those who refused to compromise with the materialistic world even to the point of earning a living were a small minority, even a sample of distinctly conservative Villager men showed sixteen per cent never looking at the financial section of the newspaper, in contrast to a corresponding group of townspeople in similar occupations where only two per cent failed to follow the financial news.[1]

Neither in the old American culture pattern nor in that dominated by bourgeois values had either artist or writer an integral place. Although it was the part of cultivation to know the works of classical writers, it was not in the genteel tradion to be an artist or a writer by profession, particularly either a struggling or an experimental one who was not a success on the money-making front and who did not accept the dictates of respectable taste. Except for the circumstances which produced the Concord group in the years before the Civil War, artist and writer had found the American environment thoroughly uncongenial and, in the absence of social status or a critical audience, they had either been driven, like Henry James, to seek expatriation or to retire into themselves like Emily Dickinson. Those who made much of art were, by the mere fact of this emphasis, registering a repudiation of traditional attitudes. In addition, the Village artists departed conspicuously from those forms of art expression which were acceptable

---

1. L. M. Moshier, A Comparison of the Reading Interests of a Selected Group of Adults in New York City, and Similar Group in a Town in New York State. MS. Thesis, Columbia University, 1931.

to the American community. The attack on the genteel tradition, led by the genuine artists, became a secondary symbol of the scorn in which the staid world was held, and those whose art registered their social attitude rather than their talent felt compelled to violate all the established rules of versification, punctuation, or composition.

Art, moreover, served a purpose which no other form of repudiation filled in that it offered positive as well as negative values, not simply the discarding of an empty or unacceptable social pattern, but a way of life in itself. And upon this fact rested its relation to the many groups in the Village, none of whom possessed any coherent alternative to the social pattern which they more or less vigorously despised. It was to art as a way of life that all turned, either as a means of satisfying themselves or of giving themselves status in a society in which art was the one recognized form of divergence. Hence, practically all groups in one way or another, even though they had no artistic capacities themselves, attempted to justify themselves to themselves and to society in some artistic or literary terms or longed to be able to do so.

In throwing over traditional attitudes toward sex, the Villagers were, again, attacking simultaneously Puritanism and bourgeois morality. Their attitudes toward sex were the product of a combination of trends—the attack on Puritanism which gave the *American Mercury* its vogue, the growing equality between men and women of which the success of the suffrage movement was only one manifestation, and the 'arrival' of Freud and psychoanalysis to bring sex into the center of the stage. They ranged from those engaged in a serious and genuine effort to discover a basis for a freer relationship to those for whom sex was merely a symbol and who turned to promiscuity or homosexuality to express the completeness of their defiance. The former struggled against the odds of economic and personal insecurity and the strain of city living to find a basis for personal independence. The latter used Freud to rationalize as all-important what was much nearer sheer lust than the experience with whose ramifications the psychologist dealt. In between were many who were honest in their desire to cast off the shackles of Puritanism, who might or might not lean on Freud for support, and who used the equality of the sexes as a useful concept to justify the new conduct of girls. Characteristically the latter found themselves in a conflict situation, for they had often not changed their attitudes as completely as they thought, and in spite of lip service to freedom and equality, they retained many of their bourgeois values.

In contrast to the Babbitt-ridden communities from which they had escaped, virtually every group in the Village at any time was definitely art-conscious. The professional, conventional people looked upon the genuine arts with respect and discrimination, entertained a hearty contempt for the pseudos, and were quite likely to pursue some form of artistic expression themselves as an avocation. The bohemians and those whose repudiation was complete, claimed efforts toward creative expression as their *raison d'être,* quite regardless of the success of those efforts, while those who had partially discarded their traditions were more than likely to yearn toward the arts, perhaps maintaining some form of expression as an avocation, and in some cases, hoping to abandon their bread-and-butter jobs in favor of an artist's life if they should ever become sufficiently proficient to do so. The social adjustments of the artist, in their turn, varied through the whole range of Village groups, with some concentration at the more experimental end of the scale.

The group which first sought social readjustment in the Village and which numbered some of the serious artists and writers among its members was genuine in its effort to discover new values and far from wishing to abandon all parts of the code of behavior in which it had grown up. Rather, its members sought to carry forward what they regarded as vital in the American tradition and to maintain, in the face of disrupting influences, the cultural values which they had inherited. What they repudiated primarily was the money drive, the 'Babbittry,' the purely acquisitive values which had come to dominate the American scene.

This group, which remained well represented in the area in 1930, was made up chiefly of professional people, social workers, and teachers, drawn largely from cultivated families of old American stock who had occupied comfortable middle-class or professional positions in widely scattered communities. Single women, living alone or in groups of two or three, predominated over either families or single men. Some had made their first acquaintance with the neighborhood by way of residence at the local settlement house; others had been among the first occupants of remodeled stables. They had come to the Village in search of a place where they could live inexpensively, conveniently, and with taste. These people had always considered themselves the 'real' Villagers, regarding the Village very much as theirs and resenting equally its reputation for bohemianism and the building of expensive, respectable apartments.

The elements in the American tradition which the members of this group cherished included a taste for the way of life and the standards of conduct which went with its simpler, less industrialized, more rural stage. City life was rarely congenial to them. Many maintained camps or cottages in the country to which they escaped over the week-ends. Others joined the Appalachian Mountain Club and spent Sundays on long tramps. They relished the charm of old, brick houses and greatly preferred their made-over interiors with high-ceilinged rooms and fireplaces to better-equipped apartments in buildings served by liveried doormen. They preferred the Village to other parts of the city because its buildings were low, its streets 'quaintly' violated the checkerboard principle, and the green of Washington Square lent a sense of space. Some liked to praise the Village for its Old World or colonial atmosphere. With slight variation on account of income level, they exerted every effort to make their apartments into homes rather than dormitories, with antique furniture, etchings, perhaps some old European brass, and many books. The tea-rooms which they patronized were in the same decorous taste as their homes, with a fire burning on the hearth and excellent and inexpensive food tastily served on well-worn wooden tables set with peasant pottery or English ware.

Their leisure was quietly spent in 'cultural' pursuits, in reading, conversation, or in trips to the country. They rarely played cards; they attended the theater frequently, but condemned the movies as cheap. Few by 1930 had come to the point of recognizing in the movies a contemporary art form in which varying quality was to be critically distinguished. If they had a radio, they listened to the Philharmonic concerts and perhaps to political speeches, but not many of this group felt it necessary to own a radio. Their reading included the classics and the more serious of modern works. Their magazine reading was confined to the quality journals. They prided themselves on taste, simple living, and wholesomeness. They considered it their duty to vote and frequently supported the Socialist candidate, especially after the Socialist Party acquired a new respectability under the lead of Norman Thomas.

With all the conventionality of their own behavior, however, members of this group were intensely individualistic and conscientiously tolerant of the conduct of others. Eminently sincere themselves, they respected sincerity even where it led to forms of behavior which they found unpalatable. On most questions of conduct they were unwilling to be dogmatic, taking the position that the individual was in a position to judge what was right and wrong for himself. Though they had mostly dropped away from the Church, they had retained the assumptions of individual conduct guided by individual conscience which was fundamental to the Protestant faiths. Again in the best tradition of the old American community, they possessed a strong social consciousness and sense of social responsibility which frequently expressed itself in interest in reform. Many who worked for social betterment or educational advance were pioneers in fields of technique, yet the concepts of the society which they sought to rebuild were essentially those which retained the values of early American life. Though the genteel tradition no longer dominated their literary horizon, it continued to tinge their taste.

The distinction of this group lay in the fact that the social values which it sought to preserve had come to rest on taste rather than on social pressure. Enforcement by community pressure of forms of behavior which they regarded as the mere empty shell rather than the essential spirit of American institutions, they repudiated as readily as the money drive. They had as little sympathy for Mrs. Grundy's social pressure as for the race to keep up with the Joneses. But they confidently hoped that the good judgment and taste of individuals would lead them into lines which would include a preference for antique furniture and Anglo-Saxon decency.

Some had gone over to the 'psychological' camp of those who accepted a complete breakdown of social patterns and sought to build on the basis of the individual as a psychological entity. For those who taught in the progressive schools or shared the views of the more advanced social workers, this emphasis on the psychological individual was easily grafted onto their traditional acceptance of the individual as an independent moral entity. But the tastes and points of view which they hoped the individuals would freely develop, and the cultural values which they, perhaps unconsciously, supported, were largely those which had come down from the past rather than those imaginatively conceived for the future.

Closely resembling this old professional group in background, attitudes, and manner of living, but unrelated to it through social contact, was a body of young professional and business people who had come in in increasing numbers to be close to their work in the near-by laboratories, the adjacent university, or the downtown area. Economic reasons primarily had brought them into the city and convenience and the availability of suitable apartments had led them into the local community. These were drawn largely from the same old American background as the older professional group, and, like them, had little or no desire to throw overboard entirely the values of their home communities. They ate at the same kind of well-appointed tea rooms and took their entertainment, in so far as limited finances permitted, in much the same ways, with theaters, reading, and parties. Perhaps they were a shade more inclined toward 'Babbittry,' a bit less cultivated, and a little more likely to patronize a speakeasy, go to the movies, or read the *Saturday Evening Post*. Because they had reached maturity during the post-War years, they were less universally possessed of a social consciousness. Their interest in the neighborhood and their conception of the Village as an interrelated community were non-existent. On the whole, however, they were not in revolt, and would have liked to mould their lives fairly close to the pattern in which they had grown up.

These younger people, though similar in taste and point of view to the older professional group, rarely had any contact with the latter, for in the community no means of making such contacts were open to them. Even among themselves there was little social organization or opportunity for contact. Apart from an occasional encounter with someone in the same house, most of their connections were made through work, and their friends were scattered through the city. A real need of providing an organized means for making social contacts was revealed by the response of this group to the organization of a young people's society by one of the Protestant churches. In view of the fact that the Church had been more consistently dropped than any other institution among all the Villager groups, the readiness to join church activities was an indication of how little of its background this particular group had cast off.

Some members of this group—how representative of the whole body it was difficult to ascertain—felt their position a difficult and anomalous one. They desired to live according to the standards of their homes and to found homes of their own which would carry on those same standards. But their income was low and there was slight possibility, in the community in which they found themselves, of securing either the physical surroundings which they deemed necessary for the maintenance of inherited standards or the social position which they felt they should achieve.

Although some of them mingled with people who came to the Village because of its unconventional reputation and patronized the speakeasies and entertained at Village parties, the majority were only a little less disgusted with the Village's reputation and what passed as Village life than the older, conventional group. In their own communities they might lean in the direction of the Babbitts. Here in the city, the absence of social pressures had freed them from the necessity of conforming to the Babbitt mould, but it had not given them the opportunity to carry with them the rest of their social inheritance which they desired to retain. They had brought the values and ambitions of an economically freer society, where their fathers had been able to count on rising to positions of independence and prominence, into a situation in which they found themselves parts of closely organized, gigantic economic units with little chance at independence or much more than a meager economic competence. In their own way, too, this group yearned for the traditional values for which they saw little opportunity in their own future. Their attempt at a solution was likely to be a move to the suburbs, with the accompanying discomfort of commuting, as soon as they started to raise children.

At the extreme opposite end of the scale from those professional groups who sought to perpetuate in taste their cherished social values were the out-and-out bohemians whose repudiation of the values and the controls of organized society was complete. These discarded money values to the point of making little or no provision for self-support and tossed all trace of moral earnestness and other aspects of old American culture into the scrapheap as well. The influence of this group was out of all proportion to its actual numbers. It had come in originally, as 'bohemias' are prone to do,[2] in the trail of the Village's early artist colony, and had then become a distinct group in itself. In spite of the reputation which the bohemians' publicly led lives gave to the Village, not more than a small group at any one time would truly have answered to this description—would really have fallen within the category of those who deliberately disregarded the standards and the drives which governed the ordinary world, either on grounds of philosophy, preoccupation with art, or laziness.

Certain houses, owned by a landlord whose reputation for befriending bohemians was known from coast to coast, housed most of these, although some were scattered in the garrets of unremodeled houses. In these apartments, no one was put out for failure to pay the rent, but was simply moved to smaller quarters or put in with another occupant. The landlord even went so far as to help out his tenants with money or food when they were badly off, or lent them typewriters. He recognized that many were shiftless and

2. A. Parry, *Garrets and Pretenders,* New York, 1933, *passim.*

took advantage of him, that others lived from drink to drink, while others were really struggling and devoting themselves to artistic or literary pursuits. This group drifted in and out, but some members stayed on for years. The type and its habits remained constant from the earliest days of the Village until 1930, though the proportion whose artistic pretensions were real appeared to have dropped, and the homosexual types became somewhat more prominent.

The influence of the genuine bohemians extended beyond the confines of the houses where they lived and the eating-places where they met, for their reputation lured many young people who were not really bohemian in their philosophy and temperament, but eager to 'see life' by living in what they considered the bohemian manner. In the course of the decade, more and more of the Village population came to consist of young single people holding ordinary jobs, coming from ordinary backgrounds. Some of these had come with the deliberate intent of following the bohemian path. Many had come to live in the Village simply because it was convenient or offered the right type of apartment, but even these found themselves exposed to the contagion of bohemianism. Other people who did not live in the Village, but resided with their families in other parts of the metropolitan area, were also drawn there for social life. The hangouts which went in most heavily for 'bohemian atmosphere' were centers for people from Brooklyn or the Bronx.

The pseudo-bohemians developed two closely related social institutions, the hangout and the studio party. Since their daytime occupations were the minimum compromise with economic necessity, their night activities were the focus of their life. Formal societies constituted to them part of the pattern which they repudiated. At the same time their insecurity and the directions of their escape produced a gregariousness of habit which led them to gather nightly in some studio apartment or public meeting place. To capitalize this gregariousness, a succession of gathering places were opened, some serving sandwiches and furnishing informal entertainment, others, more imposing in name but not in practice, calling themselves studio salons or clubs. They offered unlimited opportunities for contacts to those who sought to join this type of group.

For this group sex in its most irresponsible form was a means of escape either from the type of life in which they had grown up or from some inadequacy in themselves. In the absence of clinical data, it was not possible to determine how many of the group were running away from personality problems and family situations and how many from the emptiness of inherited social codes. Neither was it possible to determine the extent to which repudiation was a mere episode or a permanent attitude. A little fragmentary and inconclusive evidence suggested that, for a substantial number, this type of escape was more than a temporary phase. For those who lived elsewhere in the city and simply came down for their entertainment, it may well have had little permanent importance. But for those who came from a distance to live in the Village, a more serious break may well have been involved. The testimony of the doctor whose office was located most conveniently to the center of such activity bore vigorous witness to the number of girls whose health was permanently impaired. For individuals who for any long period of time remained part of this group, the possibility of returning to the home communities, once they had so thoroughly repudiated the values of these communities, was certainly reduced. The older persons who had become long-time habitués testified by their persons to this potentiality. On the other hand, the proprietor of one of the less extreme of the hangouts reported many former patrons who had settled down to bourgeois lives.

Of all the groups in the Village, this one had the widest influence on the rest of the country, for it helped to popularize the 'wild party' from one end of the land to the other; it was the purely negative set of values which this group developed that set its stamp upon America during these years. 'It's well to remember that the Village isn't unique,' observed one of the interviewers who was working on this study. 'If that necking party I went to in Brooklyn last night had been in the Village, I'd have taken it for "typical"—but there it was, as wild as you please, and right in the most substantial part of respectable Brooklyn.'

Between the professional group which, while repudiating bourgeois values, definitely retained its appreciation of old American culture and those who repudiated that culture altogether, were various groups, mostly but not all made up of younger people, who attempted to make some combination between what they wished to retain and what they sought to discard. They ranged all the way from completely unsophisticated youngsters who knew enough to 'hate their jobs, of course,' and wanted to 'see life,' but could feel satisfactorily devilish as soon as a little gin began to flow and noise to mount, to those who attempted, seriously and thoughtfully, to solve the problems of their personal lives with as much emancipation as possible from the pressure of social standards.

These groups were all less scornful of the money drive than both the more conservative and the more bohemian, for they were apt to feel the force of economic pressure more acutely. Most looked to art as the positive alternative to those standards of their home communities with which they had little sympathy. All were preoccupied to some degree with the problem of sex, giving lip service, at least, to the principle of sex equality, ready to use 'Puritan' as a term of reproach, and equipped with at least a second-hand version of Freud.

The conduct of these groups varied widely, but it involved conflicts and inconsistencies arising out of the effort to hold some attitudes and to break through others. The types of conflict situations in which they found themselves reflected the problems of adjustment faced by many, here and elsewhere, during these years of social breakup.

Characteristic of a growing proportion of Village residents was a group of girls with fair to good stenographic or secretarial positions and men in moderately paid office jobs with large corporations, banks, or brokers. Their reason for residence in the Village was principally convenience and the type of apartment available, but often also a slight desire for freedom and adventure. Some considered it a distinct advantage to be able to give a Greenwich Village address to new acquaintances, while others found it a great nuisance. Members of this group found themselves often in an *impasse* because they had retained too much of the traditional conception of the relation between men and women to take advantage of the changed positions into which they had put themselves. The girls were self-supporting and independent, and, though not preoccupied with sex, were not inhibited from such experiences as might occasionally 'grow out of an evening.' Yet they counted on balancing their budgets by being taken out by men two or three times a week. The men would admit, if pressed, that if a married woman wanted to work she should, but, for their own part, they felt that they must not marry until they could support their wives. The girls who wished to marry and were prepared to go on supporting themselves were prevented by the attitude and the low earnings of the men. These young people represented a group which valiantly kept its head above water, but saw little chance of achieving either the status or the security which it wished to combine with its city freedom.

Somewhat more experimental than these, but at the same time not free from conventional attitudes which got in their way, were groups of young people who thought they had repudiated certain standards, but found that they had not fully done so and could not be comfortable when not living up to them. Typical of this sort of conflict was a couple who despised bourgeois standards, to whom the worst of all crimes was to be boring, and whose conscious ideal was to live vividly and intensely with cultivation, ardor, and creative expression. But though the man scorned his prosaic job, he was too much bound by the convention of what a man should do not to care whether he made a masculine success or not. The girl, though she had been attracted by his sensitiveness and artistic leanings, found herself resenting his lack of success and nagging him into an added sense of inferiority. In less than a year their marriage had broken down.

In most groups, pressure toward sex experimentation was strong. There was difference of opinion as to the most desirable sorts and quantity of sex experience, but there was general intolerance of any who were disinclined toward experimentation, and a virgin was the object of expressed contempt. Although their vocabulary on the subject contrasted radically with that of the Italian young men of the neighborhood, the conduct of many Villagers differed much less. They differed from their local neighbors chiefly in expecting the girl to be the one taking the necessary precautions, in assuming that they would not become infected, while the Italians took venereal disease as a matter of course, and in having enough medical friends to make it easier for them to see that the necessary abortion was performed in case their contraceptive measures had been ineffective.

In those groups where the women tried to achieve a genuinely emancipated status, difficulty often arose out of the fact that the men gave only
lip service to the principle of equality and took advantage of the girls' seri-
ousness to exploit them. The changed attitudes toward sex were much more
of a wrench for the girls than for the men, for the latter could fit the facts
of freedom and experimentation in sex relations into the tradition of the
double standard which they might have officially abandoned, but which
remained an essential part of their attitude. The girls, on the other hand,
had the whole weight of their tradition against them, and could not go in
for 'experimentation' as lightly as could the men. The result was that when
the girls talked about sex equality they really meant it, while the men often
did not. The very girls whom men persuaded to sleep with them by a
learned discourse later became objects of their contempt, and their conversation when no women were present would have done credit to any
similar bourgeois group.

The status of the 'emancipated' woman, whose living as well as her
thinking was unconventional, but who remained serious and self-respecting
and had not taken to sex and gin as an avenue of escape, was thus very
insecure. Uncertain of respect, whatever her choice, she had to battle her
lonely way without the assurance of social support. Upon her fell the whole
brunt of an uncertain position in a shifting culture, for she embodied in
herself much of the break with tradition. Upon her vitality and the capacity
to effect an individual solution rested much of the success or failure of her
adaptation. Where her economic position was also precarious, the strain was
acute. Without sufficient vigor and toughness and enough economic security to keep afloat, she was in danger of drifting into a state of instability
from which little but good luck could extricate her.

For those who could not accept the social pattern into which they had
been born, the constructive alternative to escape into art or drink was social
reorganization. The pre-War Village had been a center for radical thought
—not, to be sure, the fighting Marxism of the East Side ghetto, but nevertheless, the literary proletarianism of the *Masses,* the vigor of the suffrage
drive, and the challenge of I. W. W., anarchists, and socialists. In the decade
of the twenties, few had the heart or the faith to predicate their conduct
and their thought on the assumption of a new social order. The negative-
ness of all the forms of protest except the artistic, and the pursuit of art for
its own sake rather than its use as a social tool, reflected the eclipse of the
revolutionary spirit.

In the defection of some members, the failure to enlist new blood, and
above all in the psychological reaction to the War, lay at least a partial
explanation of the Village's loss of vigor as a radical center. The first break
in the ranks had been made by the War itself when some of the better-
known Village socialists went patriot in 1917. But vigor enough remained
to organize the Civic Club as one of the few places in the city where free

discussion could be carried on in spite of the Espionage Act. It was the close of the War rather than the War itself which took the wind out of the radical sails, as post-War disillusionment replaced the faith and zeal which had propelled both radical and patriot in the crisis years. The 'tired radical' of these post-War years was as familiar a figure as the 'younger generation' which kicked over the traces in scorn at the failure of their elders.

In communities where a body of conservative people had retained their pre-War attitudes, there might be something to fall back upon, but in the Village, where those pre-War codes had already been repudiated, there was no heart left in the drive for any form of social action. In the field of literary and artistic expression and of social freedom, much of the fight had been won. There was no zest in battling for free verse and free love as social issues when these bade fair to become commonplace. The social radicals who had survived the wartime defection found the radical ranks split and their parlor radicalism reduced to an amateurish pastime by the realities of the Russian Revolution. They faced the choice of placing themselves under discipline as active party members—a bitter pill for any Village individualist to swallow!—of contributing to various of the national organizations which were striking at specific social evils, or of taking the side lines as observers. A few chose the first course, many responded to appeals for funds by various organizations, but most chose the third line.

As a radical center, the Village ceased to function, in spite of the feeble survival of the Civic Club and the presence of radically minded individuals, including members and officers of liberal, socialist, anarchist, and communist organizations, and in spite of the fact that a local Tammany judge's epithet for women with low heels was 'socialist' and the priest was quick to dub any Village activity he could not identify as 'communist.' A considerable measure of social and political radicalism was taken for granted in most Village circles, but, as one of the old radicals who, in 1930, still had the confidence to try to 'start something,' said, 'It does not seem as if it was possible to get people together to do anything nowadays. They used to be all for action, but now they cannot be made to care.' Even in thought, very few were prepared to push their way through to any revolutionary philosophy.

Thus the Villagers, virtually without social institutions, scornful of bourgeois values, seeking escape through sex, rationalizing their conduct with the aid of Freud and of art, and in despair of social reconstruction, developed an individualism as irresponsible and as extreme as that of the local Italians who were out for themselves. Through their actions, they made the Village a symbol of defiance to whatever the established social order might be. It mattered little that most who lived in the Village did not share in the extremer forms of its reputation or that the rest of the country adopted many of the habits which had been unique in the Village at an earlier time. Greenwich Village remained always the place where one could go farther than in other communities, and as such it acted as a social leaven for the rest of the country. Its manners and attitudes, its art forms and its gin parties, became familiar from coast to coast. Herein lay its entirely uncalculable social influence, an influence which grew as it drew less exceptional and adventurous residents than it had in its early days.

But in its own social life the Village offered no solution to the cultural problems which drove people to the area. Escape it offered but not solution. It accelerated the breaking of old forms, but it contributed no new ones to take their place. In the face of cultural disintegration, it either fostered escape or erected the individual as a psychological entity into an end in himself.

PERSONALITY ADJUSTMENT
OF RURAL AND URBAN CHILDREN

A. R. Magnus

This paper presents some results of a study of personality adjustment of school children in Miami County, Ohio. The basic data were collected during the spring of 1946 as part of the Miami County Health and Human Development Project. The main sponsors of this project were the Ohio State Department of Public Welfare, Division of Mental Hygiene, the Ohio State University, Ohio Agricultural Experiment Station, and the local County Mental Hygiene Association.[1]

The original data for this paper consisted of test results and ratings for 1,229 third and sixth grade children living on farms, in villages and in urban homes. Of these subjects 371 lived on farms, 573 lived in rural-nonfarm homes, and 285 lived in a city of about 17,000 inhabitants.

THE PROBLEM. Does living on a farm and growing up in a farm home prove a help or a hindrance to the achievement of desirable personality adjustment as compared to living in a village or in a city? This is the general problem of concern here.

Personality is considered a social product. It is made up of various systems of habits and attitudes built up in the individual on the basis of his native endowments but as resultants of his life experiences. The term "adjustment" refers to the extent to which the person's systems of attitudes, feelings, and actions, which make up his personality, function harmoniously together. In other words, the extent to which a person functions efficiently in a world of other persons. Good personality adjustment is considered synonymous with good mental and social health.

The question as to whether rural homes and rural communities provide a relatively favorable environment for healthy personal and social development of children was magnified by results of Selective Service rejection rates during the recent war period. Throughout the history of the Selective Service personality disorders and character defects constituted the leading causes for rejection. Special studies indicated that these personality difficulties were even more prevalent among farm men than among those in

---

1. See A. R. Mangus and John R. Seeley, "Mental Health Needs in a Rural and Semi-Rural Area." Mimeo. Bull. No. 195. Ohio State Univ., 1947.

Reprinted from the *American Sociological Review*, Vol. 13 (October 1948), pp. 566-575, by permission of the author and the publisher. (Copyright, 1948, by the *American Sociological Review*.)

nonfarm occupations. Various explanations have been offered to account for these differentials in farm-nonfarm rejection rates. One assumption was that rejection rates for personality disorders were higher among farm men because, as compared with cities, farm homes and farm communities provide a relatively unfavorable setting for healthy personality adjustment in children and youth, and that the effects show up in adult life. To test this assumption is the major purpose of this report.

It may be taken for granted that in any area *some* farm children will achieve better personality adjustment than will *some* city, or small town boys and girls. Also that some farm children will lag behind some city children in their personal and social growth and development. The problem here is to discover whether farm children as a group are as well adjusted as are comparable groups of rural-nonfarm and of city children. How does a representative group of farm boys as a group compare socially and emotionally with representative groups of boys living in village and in city homes? How do groups of farm and nonfarm girls compare with respect to their personality adjustment?

CRITERIA OF ADJUSTMENT. In the present study of personality adjustment of school children, three instruments were used in recording data. These included:

1. A standardized personality test.

2. A device by which each classroom teacher ranked her students according to her best judgment of their mental health.

3. A "Guess Who" test by which students in each classroom recorded their own observations of deviant attitudes, and roles in other members of their class.

The Elementary Series of the California Test of Personality [2] was the standardized test employed. This test contains 144 items of "self" and "social" adjustment. The authors of this test obtained a high degree of statistical reliability by using standard methods of determination. They tried to assure its validity by careful selection of items, and by disguising them to prevent the subject's ready detection of their purpose and his likelihood of presenting a self-profile better than the original.

In obtaining the teacher's judgment of her students each instructor was requested to arrange the members of her class in rank order. This she did on the basis of her best judgment of each child as a "normal, wholesome, happy, well-adjusted person."

It is well known that children are acutely sensitive to deviant attitudes and behavior in other children. The "Guess Who" device was used to record children's judgments of one another. This device was constructed in the form of a game. It contained 42 significant descriptions of normal and deviant personality characteristics. For example, one item was "This person has an awful temper. Can you guess who?" Each child was asked to write

2. Published by the California Test Bureau, 5916 Hollywood Blvd., Los Angeles, California.

in for each item the name of the person who fitted the description, or write in "nobody." [3]

METHODS OF ANALYZING STANDARDIZED PERSONALITY TEST RESULTS. The California Test of Personality, Elementary Series, was administered to children in the third and sixth grades of the schools in Miami County in the spring of 1946. This standardized test was designed to reveal characteristic tendencies on the part of each child to respond to a variety of situations of major importance in his life. Its major purpose is to provide measures of the extent to which the child is adjusting to the problems and conditions which confront him, in other words, the extent to which he is developing a normal, happy, and socially effective personality.

This test is divided into two major sections so that it yields scores pertaining to personal, or "self-adjustment" and scores pertaining to "social adjustment." Within each of these general sections are six subtests. These scores are designed to provide estimates of the child's self-reliance, his feeling of personal worth, his feeling of belonging, his sense of personal freedom, his tendencies to withdraw from social contacts, and of his nervous or neurotic symptoms. These all relate to the concept of personal adjustment. The six sub-tests of the social adjustments provide scores pertaining to the child's attitudes toward social standards, his social skills, his freedom from anti-social attitudes, and his family, school, and community relationships.

The basic data used here consisted of the scores achieved on these various tests by the 1,229 children included in this report. The scores for self-adjustment and for social adjustment had a possible range from 0 to 72. The actual range was from 18 to 72. The possible range of scores for each sub-test was 0 to 12. The actual range of scores varied among the several tests.

The methods of analysis and comparison followed the usual statistical procedures applied to data of this kind. The scores for each test were arranged in frequency distributions. Separate distributions were made for farm, village (rural nonfarm), and city children. Also, separate classifications were made for boys and girls. The usual methods of summarization, comparison, and analysis were applied to these frequency tables.

RESULTS OF ANALYSIS OF STANDARDIZED PERSONALITY TEST RESULTS. As a result of statistical analyses it appears conclusive that in Miami County in the spring of 1946, farm children as a group had achieved a somewhat higher level of personal and social adjustment than urban children living in the small city included in the study. This assumes, of course, that the California Test of Personality provided a valid measure of these group differences.

While Miami County farm children differ favorably from city children

---

3. See "A Study of the Mental Health Problems in Three Representative Elementary Schools," *Ohio State University Studies*, Bureau of Educational Research Monograph No. 25, 1942, Chapter VIII, pp. 130-161.

in that county in personality adjustment no significant differences either in self-adjustment or in social adjustment were found between rural farm and rural nonfarm boys and girls. (The results are shown in detail in Table 1.)

TABLE I—Comparison of Mean Adjustment Scores for Third and Sixth Grade Children in the Public Schools of Miami County, Ohio, 1946

A. Means and Standard Deviations

Residence	Number of Children	Self-adjustment		Social Adjustment	
		Mean Score	Standard Deviation	Mean Score	Standard Deviation
Farm	371	48.68	10.20	56.25	9.00
Village [a]	573	47.95	10.40	56.58	9.65
City	285	45.52	10.60	54.08	10.35

B. Group Differences

Groups Compared	Self-adjustment			Social Adjustment		
	Difference in Mean Scores	Standard Error of Difference	Critical Ratio	Difference in Mean Scores	Standard Error of Difference	Critical Ratio
Farm—city	3.25	.824	4.0	2.17	.770	2.8
Farm—village	.73	.683	1.1	— .33	.611	0.5
Village—city	2.53	.762	3.3	2.50	.732	3.4

a Includes some children living in open country nonfarm homes.

The mean self-adjustment score for the 371 farm children in this study was 48.68. This mean was 3.25 points higher than that for the city children at the same grade levels in school. This difference favoring farm children was 4 times greater than its standard error. Its probability of chance occurrence is only about 1 in 1,000. In other words, it represents a statistically significant difference in mean scores for the two groups of boys and girls.

Similarly farm children as a group differed favorably from city children with respect to social adjustment. The difference of 2.17 in mean social adjustment scores between the two groups was not quite as great as the difference in self-adjustment but was nevertheless a significant difference as indicated by a critical ratio of 2.8 (Table 1).

Village and open country nonfarm children also differ favorably from the city children in this study, both in self-adjustment and in social adjustment. On the other hand, such differences as appeared between the farm and rural nonfarm groups proved to be small and of no statistical significance, the critical ratios being in each case considerably less than 2.

RESIDENCE COMPARISONS BY SEX. In the Miami County study it was found that boys and girls generally differ considerably with respect to personality adjustment, the difference favoring girls. The question may also be raised to how farm boys compare with village and city boys, and how farm girls rate in relation to nonfarm girls. This question was made a subject for investigation for the samples included in this study. The findings may be briefly summarized.

It was found that both farm and village boys differ favorably from city boys but did not differ significantly from each other. The statistically significant differences in mean scores favored the rural boys both with respect to self-adjustment and with respect to social adjustment (Table 2).

TABLE II—Comparison of Mean Adjustment Scores for Third and Sixth Grade Children by Residence and Sex

A. Means and Standard Deviations

Sex and Test	Mean Score City	Rural Nonfarm	Farm	Standard Deviation City	Rural Nonfarm	Farm
Boys (number)	158	272	190	....	....	....
Self-adjustment	44.33	47.47	46.91	10.35	10.95	10.45
Social adjustment	51.17	54.07	54.15	11.40	10.75	9.80
Girls (number)	127	301	181	....	....	....
Self-adjustment	47.90	50.23	50.61	10.60	10.25	9.60
Social adjustment	57.94	59.68	58.49	8.85	7.70	7.55

B. Group Differences

Sex and Test	Farm—City Diff.	S.E.	C.R.	Farm—Nonfarm Diff.	S.E.	C.R.	Nonfarm—City Diff.	S.E.	C.R.
Boys									
Self-adjustment	2.58	1.118	2.3	— .56	1.010	0.6	3.14	1.058	3.0
Social adjustment	2.98	1.153	2.6	.08	.964	0.1	2.90	1.118	2.6
Girls									
Self-adjustment	2.71	1.095	2.5	.38	.933	0.4	2.33	1.049	2.2
Social adjustment	.55	.892	0.6	— 1.19	.720	1.7	1.74	.844	2.1

Farm girls differed favorably from city girls with respect to self-adjustment but not with respect to social adjustment. Village girls on the other hand showed superior adjustment both personally and socially as compared to those living in the city. As in the case of the boys, farm and village (or rural nonfarm) girls did not differ significantly from each other (Table 2).

RESIDENCE COMPARISONS ON SUBTESTS. On what particular components of personal and of social adjustment are farm and village children favored when compared to those in the city? Are rural boys and girls more self-reliant? Do they have a greater sense of security, of self-confidence, of personal freedom? Are they better adjusted to home, school, and community?

Answers to these questions were sought by analyzing the scores of the various subtests of the California Test of Personality in the same way as were the scores for total adjustment (Table 3).

It was found that farm children differed favorably and significantly from city children in every component of self-adjustment save one. This one related to a sense of personal freedom. Even in this quality, however, farm children were on a par with their city cousins. The average farm child was also superior to city boys and girls in three of the 6 components of social adjustment.

The findings pertaining to the several phases of self-adjustment may be briefly summarized.

Self-reliance. The farm group was significantly more self-reliant than was the one city group included in this study. This would indicate that the

TABLE III—Comparison of Mean Adjustment Scores for Third and Sixth Grade Children in the Public Schools of Miami County, Ohio, by Residence, 1946

A. Means and Standard Deviations

Test	Mean Score			Standard Deviation		
		Rural			Rural	
	City	Nonfarm	Farm	City	Nonfarm	Farm
Self-adjustment						
Self-reliance	7.18	7.58	7.49	2.02	1.76	1.81
Sense of personal worth	7.38	7.92	8.51	2.36	2.46	2.36
Sense of personal freedom	8.50	8.85	8.41	2.41	2.24	2.61
Sense of belonging	9.14	9.85	10.04	2.32	2.18	1.93
Withdrawing tendencies	6.60	6.85	7.15	3.17	3.10	3.11
Nervous symptoms	6.62	6.90	7.08	2.93	3.01	2.77
Social Adjustment						
Social standards	10.04	10.12	10.01	1.76	1.64	1.66
Social skills	8.10	8.96	8.80	2.24	1.91	1.80
Anti-social tendencies	9.16	9.33	9.25	2.47	2.25	2.27
Family relations	9.20	9.53	9.45	2.57	2.65	2.49
School relations	7.74	8.45	8.56	2.87	2.74	2.57
Community relations	9.84	10.19	10.18	2.30	1.76	1.58
Number of children	285	573	371	. . .	. . .	. . .

B. Group Differences

Test	Farm—City			Farm—Rural Nonfarm			Rural Nonfarm—City		
	Diff.	S.E.	C.R.	Diff.	S.E.	C.R.	Diff.	S.E.	C.R.
Self-adjustment									
Self-reliance	.31	.155	2.0	— .09	.123	0.7	.40	.138	2.9
Personal worth	1.13	.187	6.0	.59	.162	3.6	.54	.176	3.1
Personal freedom	— .09	.195	0.5	— .44	.165	2.7	.35	.171	2.0
Sense of belonging	.90	.171	5.3	.19	.135	1.4	.71	.165	4.3
Withdrawing tendencies	.55	.247	2.2	.30	.208	1.4	.25	.228	1.1
Nervous symptoms	.46	.226	2.0	.18	.192	0.9	.28	.215	1.3
Social Adjustment									
Social standards	— .03	.135	0.2	— .11	.110	1.0	.08	.127	0.6
Social skills	.70	.165	4.2	— .16	.123	1.3	.86	.155	5.5
Anti-social tendencies	.09	.187	0.5	— .08	.152	0.5	.17	.173	1.0
Family relations	.25	.200	1.3	— .08	.171	0.5	.33	.187	1.8
School relations	.82	.217	3.8	.11	.176	0.6	.71	.205	3.5
Community relations	.34	.162	2.1	— .01	.110	0.1	.35	.155	2.3

country children, more than the urban, had learned to do things independently of others, and to depend upon themselves and to direct their own activities to a favorable degree. Village children likewise were on the average more self-reliant than those in the urban sample.

Sense of personal worth. Farm boys and girls were especially favored in their possession of a sense of personal worth. It is well known that one of the basic foundations for mental health, or adequate personality development, is a reasonable degree of confidence in oneself and in those about one. This study showed that farmers' sons and daughters were blessed with this quality to a greater degree than either city or village children in Miami County. Their average score in this trait was 8.51 as compared to scores of only 7.38 for the city group and 7.92 for the village group. The differences among these means were all significant of real differences in the groups compared (Table 3).

Sense of belonging. Another basic foundation for mental health, it is widely agreed, is the child's sense of personal security, or his sense of belonging in his relations with other persons and groups that exert determining influences in his development. In this quality rural children both farm and nonfarm differed favorably from the city group.

Withdrawing tendencies. Normal personality adjustment is characterized by reasonable freedom from withdrawing tendencies. Such tendencies when present are seen in the child who is sensitive, timid, and lonely, and who tends to daydream and to concern himself with fantasy as a substitute for successes in real life. In the test of this quality farm children again excelled when compared with the city sample.

Nervous symptoms. Emotional conflicts frequently give rise to such symptoms as loss of appetite, frequent eye strain, inability to sleep, or a tendency to be chronically tired. This study showed that farm children were freer from such symptoms than were urban children.

Personal freedom. It is believed that a reasonable sense of personal freedom is conducive to good personality adjustment. A person enjoys such a sense of freedom when he is permitted to have a reasonable part in the determination of his activities and setting the rules which will determine his life. Farm children did not excel in this component of self-adjustment. This result is not surprising since other studies indicate that the farm family is generally less democratic than the typical urban family. The farm children did not differ significantly from urban children, but they differed unfavorably from village boys and girls in this trait (Table 3).

With respect to the components of social adjustment farm children did not fare quite so well. In no component, however, did they compare unfavorably either with city or village children.

Social skills. The achievement of good mental health, or good personality adjustment, depends to a considerable degree upon the development of skills in getting along with other people. Since farm children are thought of as being rather isolated from many social contacts it was surprising to find that they showed decided superiority over urban children in being socially skillful or socially effective, as measured by test results. Village boys and girls, including those living in open country nonfarm homes, also showed superiority over the urban group in this component. As in most other respects the farm and village groups did not differ significantly from each other.

School relation. Rural children, both farm and nonfarm, were on the average better adjusted to the school situation than were those in the city. Those pupils living on farms had an average adjustment score nearly one point higher than urban pupils on the 12-point scale designed to measure adjustment to school. The difference was statistically significant as indicated by the fact it was 3.8 times greater than its standard error (Table 3).

Farm and village students did not differ significantly with respect to their school adjustment.

Community relations. Farm and village children as groups were making relatively good adjustments to community situations as indicated by the test results. The indications were that the average rural child was mingling more happily with his neighbors, taking more pride in his neighborhood; more tolerant of strangers and more respectful of laws and regulations than was the average city child of elementary school age in the survey county.

Family relations. The young person who exhibits desirable family relations generally feels that he is loved, wanted, and well-treated at home. He lives easily and comfortably with other members of his family. He is usually subjected to parental control that is neither too strict nor too lenient.

It is interesting that no one of the three groups of children—city, farm, and village—excelled over another in this respect. The average score on the family relations test was highest for village children and lowest for those in the city. The differences were too small, however, to be considered statistically significant.

Social standards. Another component of social adjustment is an understanding of what is regarded as being right and wrong in one's group and an appreciation of the necessity of subordinating one's own desires to the demands of the group. In this component as in the case of family relations no significant group differences appeared among the three residence groups of children in this study.

Freedom from anti-social tendencies. The anti-social boy or girl is generally thought of as one who tries to satisfy his own wants in ways that are damaging or unfair to others. Anti-social behavior is seen in such acts as bullying other children, frequent quarreling, property destruction and other socially unacceptable tendencies. Normal personality adjustment is characterized by a reasonable degree of freedom from these tendencies. This study showed that farm, village, and city children were about on a par with respect to this component of social adjustment. The mean scores for these groups did not show any significant differences among the three residence groups (Table 3).

COMPARISON OF RURAL CHILDREN WITH A STANDARD GROUP. Results presented up to this point indicate that there are factors involved in rural living that are favorable to personality adjustment in children as compared to children of comparable age in an adjacent city of small size. The question remains as to whether the mean adjustment scores found for the groups of children in this study are as high or higher than would normally be expected for children of elementary school age.

It so happens that the California Test of Personality was standardized by its authors on a group of more than 1,000 children in grades four to eight inclusive. This standard group consisted of boys and girls in a dozen different schools in and around Los Angeles, California. A table of percentile norms [4] based on the test data for this metropolitan group is available for use as a standard of comparison for other groups.

When the rural farm and rural nonfarm children in the present study were combined, their average score on the self-adjustment scale was found to be 48.2. This average score corresponds to the 40th percentile in the published table of norms. This may be taken to indicate that the average rural child in Miami County exceeded 40 per cent of the children on whom the test was standardized but fell short of 60 per cent of the standard group. This would indicate that the rural students in the present study compare somewhat unfavorably in self-adjustment with the highly urban group on which the norms are based.

The average social adjustment score for the rural children in the present study was 56.5. This corresponds to the 45th percentile of the standard group. This would indicate a slight disadvantage for the rural children since it would be expected that their average score would correspond to the 50th percentile in the table of norms.

Further comparisons involving the various components of self and social adjustment show some interesting results. The rural children as a group showed superiority over the standard group in only two components. In self-reliance the average rural pupil had a score which corresponded to the 63rd percentile of the standard group. In a sense of personal worth the average rural child also had a score which exceeded the 50th percentile of the Los Angeles group.

Compared with the standard group the rural children in this study made the poorest showing in freedom from nervous symptoms, in their sense of personal freedom, in their school relations, and in their family relations (Table 4).

TEACHERS' RANKING OF FARM AND NONFARM CHILDREN. It will be recalled as a part of this study of personality adjustment of rural and city children teachers were asked to rank the members of their respective classes. In response each teacher ranked the members of her class into 7 groups on the basis of her considered judgment of the normality of their personal and social development.

Did the teachers tend to rank farm or nonfarm children higher as normal, healthy, wholesome persons? Unfortunately this question could be answered only for those teachers in the county and village school systems, and comparisons could be made only as between rural farm and rural nonfarm children. This was due to the fact that while both rural farm and rural nonfarm students were found in the classes of the county and village schools, only city children attended the city schools.

Interestingly enough teachers tended to rate farm children above rural nonfarm children as normal, healthy, wholesome persons. Students living in farm homes made up 39.5 per cent of all rural students, but they made

---

4. *Manual of Direction*. California Test of Personality. Elementary Series. P. 16.

TABLE IV—Percentile Value of Self and Social Adjustment Scores for Average Third and Sixth Grade Rural Children, 1946

Test	Mean Score	Percentile Value[a]
Self-adjustment	48.2	40
Self-reliance	7.5	63
Sense of personal worth	8.2	53
Sense of personal freedom	8.7	27
Sense of belonging	9.9	39
Freedom from withdrawing tendencies	7.1	41
Freedom from nervous symptoms	7.0	20
Social Adjustment	56.5	45
Social standards	10.1	37
Social skills	8.9	44
Freedom from anti-social tendencies	9.3	35
Family relations	9.5	33
School relations	8.5	28
Community relations	10.2	39

[a] Expected value approximately 50. Percentile values derived from published table of percentile norms.

up 47.2 percent of those that teachers ranked highest. On the other hand the farm children who constituted 39.5 per cent of all rural students comprised only 32.6 per cent of those ranking lowest in the teacher's estimation (Table 5).

TABLE V—Teachers' Ranking of Third and Sixth Grade Students by Residence and Sex, 1946

		Number					Per Cent		
Rank	Total	City	Rural Nonfarm	Farm		Total	City	Rural Nonfarm	Farm
				Both Sexes					
Total	1225	285	569	371		100.0	100.0	100.0	100.0
1	107	18	47	42		8.7	6.3	8.3	11.3
2	134	33	58	43		10.9	11.6	10.2	11.6
3	146	38	70	38		12.9	13.3	12.3	10.2
4	493	131	214	148		40.3	46.0	37.6	39.9
5	139	33	65	41		11.3	11.6	11.4	11.1
6	104	16	57	31		8.5	5.6	10.0	8.4
7	102	16	58	28		8.3	5.6	10.2	7.5
				Boys					
Total	618	158	270	190		100.0	100.0	100.0	100.0
1	36	6	12	17		5.7	3.8	4.4	8.9
2	56	12	26	18		9.1	7.6	9.6	9.5
3	64	20	29	15		10.4	12.7	10.7	7.9
4	237	70	89	78		38.2	44.3	33.0	41.1
5	82	20	73	25		13.3	12.7	13.7	13.2
6	74	16	39	19		12.0	10.1	14.8	10.0
7	70	14	38	18		11.3	8.9	14.1	9.5
				Girls					
Total	607	127	299	181		100.0	100.0	100.0	100.0
1	72	12	35	25		11.9	9.4	11.7	13.8
2	78	21	32	25		12.9	16.5	10.7	13.8
3	82	18	41	23		13.5	14.2	13.7	12.7
4	256	61	125	70		42.1	48.0	41.8	38.7
5	57	13	28	16		9.4	10.2	9.4	8.8
6	30		18	12		4.0	...	6.0	6.6
7	32	2	20	10		5.3	1.6	7.6	5.5

COMPANIONS' JUDGMENT OF FARM CHILDREN. Farm children also received fewer adverse judgments from companions than did nonfarm children. In the third grade 15.1 per cent of all farm children received negative scores on a "Guess Who" test, as compared to 18.7 per cent of the city group and nearly 20 per cent of the rural nonfarm group. At the sixth grade level 16.9 per cent of the farm boys and girls and 17.2 per cent of the village group received unfavorable "Guess Who" test scores as compared to nearly 28 per cent of the city children (Table 6).

TABLE VI—*Third and Sixth Grade Children in the Public Schools of Miami County Who Received Negative Scores on Guess Who Test, 1946, by Residence and Sex*

| | | Third Grade | | | Sixth Grade | |
| | Total | With Guess Who Scores | | Total | With Guess Who Scores | |
Residence and Sex	Number	Number	Per Cent	Number	Number	Per Cent
Total	654	118	18.0	575	112	19.5
City	155	29	18.7	130	36	27.7
Boys	81	24	29.6	77	23	29.9
Girls	74	5	6.8	53	13	24.5
Rural nonfarm	294	58	19.7	279	48	17.2
Boys	144	36	25.0	128	29	22.7
Girls	150	22	14.7	151	19	12.6
Rural farm	205	31	15.1	166	28	16.9
Boys	109	25	22.9	81	19	23.5
Girls	96	6	6.3	85	9	10.6

COMPOSITE ADJUSTMENT SCORES. Personality test scores were combined with teachers' rankings, and companions' ratings to get a composite personality adjustment index for each child in the present study. On the basis of this index about 1 child in every 8 was classified as having superior personality adjustment. A somewhat larger proportion of rural than of urban children were in this class.

On the same basis about 1 child in every 5 was classed as poorly adjusted, and showing evidences of poor mental health. The proportions of these poorly adjusted children were about the same for the different residence groups.

At the time of the present survey the average level of personality adjustment was significantly higher among farm children than among those living in city homes in the one city included in the study. Between rural farm children and those from rural nonfarm homes very few significant differences were found. Both groups differed favorably from the city boys and girls in the study.

Farm children differed favorably from city children in a number of ways. They were more self-reliant, they had a greater sense of personal worth, a greater sense of belonging, greater freedom from withdrawing tendencies and nervous symptoms. Also they showed evidence of greater social skills and rated superior in school and community relations. They failed to show any superiority in their sense of personal freedom and in their adjustments in the family. Neither did they show superior adjustment in social standards or in freedom from anti-social tendencies.

While the farm children in this study differed favorably in most respects from the city children they tended to compare somewhat unfavorably with a standard group in California studied by the authors of the personality test administered in Miami County. These farm children did, however, rise above the standard group in self-reliance and in self-confidence.

Teachers tended to rank farm children above nonfarm children as "normal, healthy, wholesome persons."

Farm children also received relatively fewer adverse judgments from companions than did nonfarm children.

The proportion of children of superior personality adjustment was found to be highest among farm and village children and lowest among city children. The category of superior personality adjustment established by the study included about 13 per cent of the rural children and around 11 per cent of the city group.

The proportion of children classified as very poorly adjusted was not significantly different among farm, village and city children. About 1 in each 5 or 6 was in this category.

Finally no claim is made for the generality of these results. They are reported with certain validity only for the time and places designated for the present study.

A follow-up study indicates that since 1946, when the original study was made, the average level of personality adjustment has risen among the city children but has not improved much among the rural children.

CONSERVATISM-RADICALISM AND
THE RURAL-URBAN CONTINUUM

John L. Haer

THE PROBLEM. One of the most persistent contentions found in the literature of rural sociology concerns the importance of "conservatism" as a
personality trait characterizing rural people as contrasted with urban
people. Indeed, the image of the "conservative farmer" seems to have the
status of a venerable stereotype in some of the literature. The purpose of
this paper is to determine to what extent this image is an accurate description of the farm and urban populations in at least one part of the country,
and to determine whether this personality trait is found differentially
according to the degree of rurality exhibited by a group of individuals.
In this latter connection, the concept of a rural-urban continuum rather
than the more conventional dichotomous classification will be employed.

In recent years an increasing number of writers have declared that
research and theory in rural sociology would be facilitated by the substitution of the concept of a rural-urban continuum for the conventional
rural-urban dichotomy. Loomis and Beegle[1] have shown how the continuum
concept may be utilized to make more precise the meaning of the attributes
usually subsumed under the rubrics "rural" and "urban." In a recent
article, Spaulding not only suggested the usefulness of this concept, but
asserted that "In the light of the fusion of characteristics which has taken
place, we recognize that the dichotomous concept of 'rural-urban' is not
at this 'day and age' a verifiable description of the empirical situation."[2]
These and other suggestions lead to the conclusion that the searcher for
"differences" in the personality patterns of rural and urban people might
well test the hypothesis that such differences are found to occur in relative
degrees in a range extending between rural and urban polarities, rather
than in an all-or-none, qualitative sense.

Many kinds of evidence have been proposed to support the idea that
conservatism and rurality are intimately associated. Foremost among the
sources of evidence are what may be termed common-sense observations

Reprinted from *Rural Sociology*, Vol. 17 (December, 1952), pp. 343-347, by permission of the author and *Rural Sociology*. (Copyright, 1952, by the Rural Sociological
Society.)

1. C. P. Loomis and J. A. Beegle, *Rural Social Systems* (New York: Prentice-Hall,
Inc., 1950).
2. I. A. Spaulding, "Serendipity and the Rural-Urban Continuum," *Rural Sociology*,
XVI (March, 1951), p. 33.

of the incidence of this trait. As a result of certain conditions in his way of life, the farmer is said to develop a frame of mind characterized by introversion, provincialism, fatalism, conservatism, and numerous other traits peculiar to the rural setting.[3] Another type of evidence, treated more often in works written for popular consumption, are the citations of "isolationist" tendencies in various farm organizations. Although, in dealing with this point, Carl C. Taylor has concluded that such groups "did not promote or oppose any measure which could in any way reflect farmers' attitudes toward international issues,"[4] his analysis does not point to the existence of tendencies which might in any sense be considered radical. Two other sources of evidence are sometimes put forth to substantiate the claim of rural conservatism—the results of opinion and attitude studies, and election returns. The former, in the writer's opinion, provide information which is at best inconclusive;[5] the latter, election returns, seem to indicate that farmers have indeed voiced provincial interests, and have seldom sided with forces (e.g., organized labor) whose ultimate aims may be considered radical.[6]

Although few rigorous studies have supported the idea of rural conservatism, the wealth of common-sense observations to that effect and the findings stemming from indirect approaches to the problem lead one to believe that there is sufficient reason for the testing of such a hypothesis. Relating the notion of rural conservatism to that of the rural-urban continuum, this paper investigates the hypothesis that, in the state of Washington, conservatism as a personality characteristic is positively associated with the degree to which people exhibit a rural way of life.

METHODOLOGY. The procedure undertaken for the testing of this hypothesis involved first deciding upon an appropriate index to represent the rural-urban continuum in the state. Then, the degree of conservatism-radicalism evidenced by the people in each of the classes of the continuum was ascertained in order to determine the extent to which each of the classes as a whole was conservative. Once the latter was accomplished it became possible, within the framework of this research, to answer the question whether conservatism is positively associated with rurality on a rural-urban continuum.

The rural-urban continuum used was the range in the *size of the place of residence* of a sample of 441 adults in the state of Washington. These adults were selected by means of stratified area sampling in October, 1950.[7] The following classification of size of place of residence was em-

3. P. H. Landis, *Rural Life in Process* (New York: McGraw-Hill Book Company, Inc., 1948), pp. 127-128.

4. C. C. Taylor, "Attitudes of American Farmers—International and Provincial," *American Sociological Review*, IX (Dec., 1944), p. 662.

5. Cf., *Fortune*, March and April, 1943.

6. S. A. Rice, "Farmers and Workers in American Politics," *Studies in History, Economics, and Public Law*, XIII (New York: Columbia University, 1924): L. H. Bean, *Ballot Behavior* (Washington, D. C.: American Council on Public Affairs, 1940).

7. *Sample Design Number 4*, Washington Public Opinion Laboratory, 1950, Pull-

ployed: places of 100,000 and over; 25,000 to 100,000; 10,000 to 25,000; 2,500 to 10,000; under 2,500, in metropolitan areas; under 2,500, incorporated areas; under 2,500, unincorporated areas. It is assumed that this classification is a good indicator of density of population in the various parts of the states, and as such is an adequate (and common) index of the degree to which areas do or do not possess rural and urban characteristics. The classification is designated as a continuum in that it permits the ranking of individuals in a number of positions on a single dimension extending between urban and rural extremes.

To secure a measure of the degree to which each of the persons in the sample was characterized by conservatism, the responses of these individuals to a battery of questions from a conservatism-radicalism scale were obtained.[8] These questions, and the proportion of persons in the sample endorsing conservative or radical answers, are listed below. In each case the conservative answer is denoted with a (C), and the radical answer as (R).

1. Do you agree or disagree that America is truly a land of opportunity and people get pretty much what's coming to them here?
   (C) Agree 93.6%
   (R) Disagree 6.4%
2. As you know, during this last war, many private businesses and industries were taken over by the government. Do you think wages and salaries would be fairer, jobs more steady, and that we would have fewer people out of work if the government took over and ran our mines, factories, and industries in the future; or do you think things would be better under private ownership?
   (C) Better under private owners 80.0%
   (R) Better under government 12.2%
   Don't know 7.8%
3. Which of these statements do you agree most with?
   The most important job for the government is to make it certain that there are good opportunities for each person to get ahead on his own.
   (C) Agree 68.4%
   Other response 1.4%
   The most important job for the government is to guarantee every person a decent and steady job and standard of living.
   (R) Agree 30.2%
4. Would you agree that everybody would be happier, more secure, and more prosperous if the working people were given more power and influence in government; or would you say we would all be better off if the working people had no more power than they have now?
   (C) No more power 44.3%
   (R) More power 44.1%
   Don't know 11.6%
5. Do you think working people are usually fairly and squarely treated by their employers, or that employers sometimes take advantage of them?
   (C) Fair treatment 43.2%

man, Washington. This type of sample is regarded as representing all segments of the population of the state over twenty-one years of age.

8. R. Centers, *The Psychology of Social Classes* (Princeton, New Jersey: Princeton University Press, 1949), pp. 39-46.

(R)   Employers take advantage 46.8%
       Don't know 10.0%
6. In strikes and disputes between working people and employers, do you
   usually side with workers or the employers?
   (C)   Employers 16.1%
   (R)   Workers 48.2%
          Don't know 35.7%

The responses of the sample to these questions were then scaled according to the technique developed by Louis Guttman.[9] Scalogram analysis
resulted in a quasi-scale having a coefficient of reproducibility of .88. The
scale contained nine scale types which enabled a ranking of the individuals
in the sample according to the pattern of their responses. This ranking
provided a basis for designating the degree to which individuals manifested a conservative or radical attitude. Since the radical answers were
given positive scores, the higher an individual's score the greater the
degree to which he indicated a radical response to the questions. Thus,
persons in scale rank 8 endorsed radical answers on all the questions, and
hence are designated the most radical people in the sample; persons in
scale rank 7 endorsed all radical answer categories except that in question
1; persons in scale rank 6 endorsed all radical answers except those in
questions 1 and 2; and so on, until in scale rank 0 there remain those persons who endorsed none of the radical responses.

For practical purposes, the existence of a quasi-scale in this area
indicates that the battery of conservatism-radicalism questions are measuring a single dominant variable (conservatism-radicalism) and a number
of small random factors. The usefulness of this quasi-scale for determining
whether conservatism is related to the rural-urban continuum is denoted
by the fact that such an ordering of respondents in terms of scale positions
"is perfectly efficient for relating any outside variable to the area."[10]

After determining the conservatism-radicalism scores for the individuals in the sample, the degree to which each of the classes in the rural-
urban continuum evinced this trait was determined by computing the
mean of the scores of the individuals in each of the categories. These means
are used to represent the degree of conservatism for each class, and their
use affords a method for deciding the issue raised in the initial hypothesis.
Table 1 shows the classes in the rural-urban continuum, and their mean
conservatism-radicalism scores.

CONCLUSIONS AND SUMMARY. On the basis of the evidence presented
here, the hypothesis that in the state of Washington conservatism is positively associated with rurality, as designated on a rural-urban continuum,
is not tenable. According to the hypothesis, one would expect that metro-

---

9. S. A. Stouffer, *et al.*, *Measurement and Prediction* (Princeton, New Jersey:
Princeton University Press, 1950), chap. 3. Scalogram analysis of these data was per-
formed by Herman M. Case, Department of Rural Sociology, the State College of
Washington.

10. *Ibid.*, p. 160.

politan areas having populations of 100,000 and over would exhibit the highest mean score. Instead, it is observed that the mean score of this class ranks below that for unincorporated towns, villages, and open countryside. The table indicates that this is not the only instance in which the hypothesis is not borne out—in fact, nowhere in the ranking of mean scores is there evidence of an ordering which would suggest even partial substantiation of the hypothesis.

Table 1—Conservatism-Radicalism Scale Scores, by Population of Place of Residence

Population of Place of Residence	Mean Scale Scores*
10,000 and over	3.37
25,000 to 100,000	3.85
10,000 to 25,000	3.52
2,500 to 10,000	3.76
Under 2,500 (unincorporated places in metropolitan areas)	3.33
Under 2,500 (incorporated)	3.06
Under 2,500 (unincorporated)	3.39

* An analysis of variance test revealed that the differences between these means were significant beyond the .01 level.

Not only must the notion of a rural-urban continuum in regard to this question be discarded, but also the table indicates that even the conventional rural-urban dichotomy would not adequately explain the findings. The fact that the mean score for the most highly urban group is found below that for unincorporated rural areas would make any such interpretation suspect; and one can see from this table that, had the areas been dichotomized into rural and urban *before* the comparisons, the resulting conclusion concerning rural-urban "differences" would have had an extremely tenuous foundation.

The unexpected findings of this study do not, it seems, accord with any systematic rationale which might explain the lack of order or direction in rural-urban conservatism. Furthermore, it appears that no overall statement can be made concerning the association between conservatism-radicalism and the rural-urban continuum in the state of Washington. Although it is not implied that these findings may be expected to hold for all areas in the nation, this conclusion does caution against the making of high-order generalizations not supported by research findings.

It should be pointed out that these results accord with the findings of some studies in this state, but are contrary to others. Rural-urban continua with reference to certain traits have been found in some instances,[11] while in other studies the differences between rural and urban segments

11. P. H. Landis, *The Territorial and Occupational Mobility of Washington Youth*, Wash. Agr. Exp. Sta. Bull. No. 449 (July, 1944). See also "Personality Differences of Girls from Farm, Town, and City," *Rural Sociology*, XIV (March, 1949).

of the population seem almost nil.[12] It has been suggested that the lack of rural-urban differences may be explained, in part at least, by such factors as high mechanization of agriculture, a predominance of consolidated schools in rural areas, and a rural standard of living that facilitates the introduction of urban devices.[13] Thus, it might be expected that persons living in states typified by these conditions (e.g., in Washington or California) will in many instances exhibit a way of life that can not be grasped conceptually with either the dichotomous or continuum classification.

12. P. H. Landis, *Two Generations of Rural and Urban Women Appraise Marital Happiness*, Wash. Agr. Exp. Sta. Bull. No. 524 (March, 1951).

13. *Ibid.*, pp. 17-18.

RURAL-URBAN DIFFERENCES: SOME EVIDENCE
FROM PUBLIC OPINION POLLS

Howard W. Beers

RURAL SOCIOLOGY AND SOCIOLOGICAL RURALITY. The conventional socio-logical description of rural-urban differences is frequently said to have lost its empirical reference in American society. Now and then one hears or reads that rural life is chiefly memory and hardly any more a fact. The argument runs that America now is urban; and one implication, which many critics are too polite to make explicit, is that rural sociologists are already vestigial specialists who may now or soon be released to other occupations. In recognition of these points and in keeping with current preoccupations of rural sociologists, this paper reports a preliminary and partial checkup of rurality in the United States.

The problem is to see what positions rural life has come to occupy in American society, and especially whether in certain aspects rural life cor-responds any more or less now than formerly with the ideal-type of rural society. An introductory pause over data on population and technology is followed by a cautious exploration of newly available materials from public opinion polls. Opinions reflect values; so the discussion of the problem moves from demography over into sociology and social psy-chology.

Since 1910, the whole demographic position of rural life in American society has changed. The reversal of dominance in population numbers appeared first with the census of 1920. By 1950—partly because of new definitions—our population was nearly two-thirds (64 per cent) urban.

In the forty years after 1910—while rural sociology sought maturity as a discipline and as a field of service—agriculture in the United States experienced a technological revolution, and the number of farmers de-clined by eight million. The number of farms declined by 15 per cent, and the average size of farm increased from 138 to 215 acres.[1] Between 1940 and 1947 alone, there was a net loss to the farm population of three mil-lion by out-migration. In 1950, only 16 per cent of the people of the United States were rural farm, and this is the population segment to observe in a test of rural-urban differences, for farmers are the prototype of rural.

Reprinted from *Rural Sociology*, Vol. 18 (March, 1953), pp. 1-11, by permission of the author and *Rural Sociology*. (Copyright, 1953, by the Rural Sociological Society.)

1. Arthur F. Raper, *A Graphic Presentation of Rural Trends* (Washington, D. C.: Extension Service and Bureau of Agricultural Economics, USDA, May 2, 1952).

But farmers recently were informed in a pamphlet from the Department of Agriculture that "the number of people in the U. S. A. is increasing at an average rate of more than 6,000 persons a day. . . . There will be 38 million more people at the table by 1975." To feed this fifth person at every table we must, the pamphlet says, increase our total agricultural production by one-fourth over 1950.[2]

To meet this responsibility there will be still fewer farmers. They will, of course, have more and better machines, better crop and livestock varieties, more effective procedures for conserving soil, more and better fertilizers and pest controls—a more productive technology. In efficiency, from 1910 to 1950, farm output per man-hour more than doubled. As to machinery, we need only remember that automobiles, trucks, tractors, cornpickers, combines, and milking machines came from virtual nonexistence in 1910 to wide prevalence in 1950, when for example, there were over 3.5 million tractors!

On the level-of-living side, radio wasn't dreamed of by farmers in 1910; forty years later, 9 out of 10 farm operators had radio sets. Electricity on farms jumped from less than 5 per cent to more than 78 per cent in prevalence. The installation of running water in farm homes has been slower; the number of homes with this convenience went from 10 per cent in 1910 to 40 per cent in 1950. A summary of the farm level-of-living changes is seen in the Hagood index, which moved from 79 in 1940 to 122 in 1950.[3]

In addition to the reduced farm population and the improved agricultural technology, there have been the various notorious advances in urbanization. Especially there are the ecological, social, and cultural penetrations of the country by the city at what has been called the "fringe." There has been extensive occupational diversification within the farm population, even within the farm labor force. The 1950 census is yielding many tabulations that confirm these trends, and the practical problem of how to define *farm* population and *rural* population is increasingly vexing.

It is clear, then, that farmers have dwindled in number and proportion, but have gained spectacularly in technical knowledge, in tools of production, and in the physical "amenities" of living—and, although evidence will not be introduced here, they have retained considerable political power. They now face a greatly expanded task of production for an enlarged society. The demographic and agricultural statistics point to changes that have narrowed many of the ranges of difference between the rural and urban sectors of American society. Taeuber has made a specific statement on this and related points:

Whether the measures of level of living are taken in terms of housing and household conveniences, or in increased health as measured by infant mortality

2. *The Fifth Plate* (Washington, D. C.: Production & Marketing Administration, USDA, Dec., 1951), p. 191.

3. Arthur F. Raper, *op. cit.*

or expectation of life, there appears to be a lessening of the differences between the most favored and the least favored groups. Differences have been lessened as between farm and nonfarm, between rural and urban, South and North, Negro and white.[4]

Against this background of conspicuous demographic and technological development, what can be seen of corresponding social changes? Attention in this discussion will be focused on one central feature of social change—that which comprises values.

POLLS OF OPINION AS EVIDENCE.[5] The Cantril compendium of national polls taken in the United States between the middle 1930's and middle 1940's,[6] together with quarterly summaries of polls through 1950,[7] make available a new variety of evidence on the place of rural life in American society.

Norms, values, and attitudes lie behind expressions of opinion on the economic activities of government, labor issues, international relations, various public issues, and questions of personal belief and satisfaction. Selected topics in each of these fields have engaged pollers in recent years; and a preliminary foray into the multitude of responses, tabulated by categories of residence and occupation, is here summarized. The procedure suggests a simple way of using opinion polls, and yields some data which may help to delimit problems of defining rural and urban society and culture.

Over three hundred polls (on subjects other than national elections) in fifteen years can be identified as having relevant topics and as having been tabulated by some criterion of rurality. For this study, a selection of polls was made on the basis of (a) time: prewar and wartime polls were excluded; only the first five postwar years, 1946-1950, were included; (b) topic: polls asking for prediction of future events and those surveying current customs and practices were excluded; only polls of opinion or attitude were included; (c) use of occupational categories: division by rural-urban residence was excluded; only those with a category based on "farmer" status or farm residence were included.

The tabular arrangements here presented are simplified from table forms prepared in earlier stages of the analysis. The first tables presented more data, but were too bulky and space-consuming for printing as part of a journal article. The condensed tables use only one statistic. To simplify description at the risk of literary criticism, this statistic is here called the *pro-percentage*. It is the percentage of a sample that responded with

4. Conrad Taeuber, "Current Population Trends" (paper presented before the National Industrial Conference Board, New York City, Jan. 24, 1952).

5. Acknowledgment is made to colleagues at the University of Kentucky, especially to C. Arnold Anderson for suggesting the use of poll data and to A. Lee Coleman for his suggestions on tabular organization.

6. Hadley Cantril (ed.), *Public Opinion: 1935-1946* (Princeton, N.J.: Princeton University Press, 1951).

7. *Public Opinion Quarterly*, X-XIV (1946-1950).

"yes," or approval. This is probably adequate for the current illustrative analysis, but it would also be useful to examine intergroup differences by *con-percentages* and by the percentages of "no-opinion" answers—considering, in fact, the "yes-no-other" distribution rather than just one position on the distribution.

Hence, the present analysis is in small scale, and hardly more than suggestive. Further exploitation of the available data is indicated. Some of the possibilities which should be of interest to workers in rural-urban research are the following: analysis of polls related to elections; comparisons (in the few cases possible) of United States polls with those for other countries; comparisons among the three time-periods—prewar, war, and postwar; interregional comparisons, where possible; analysis on the basis of rural-urban residence as well as on the occupational breakdowns; inclusion of polls that survey practices and conditions, or deal with predictions.

The pollsters choose their subjects of inquiry on other bases than the research interests of sociologists, and one may well be perplexed in a desire to group the topics by satisfactory classifications. The classifications adopted here were developed by the simple process of clustering the polls into seemingly related groupings, and assigning a descriptive name to each grouping. The polls mentioned touch on enough aspects of the sociologically orthodox conceptions of rurality, however, to provide support of some and challenge to other elements in the traditional ideas of what is rural.

ECONOMIC ROLE OF GOVERNMENT: A REVIEW OF POLLS. Those polls which elicited opinions on certain economic actions of government do not cover a random or representative sample of such governmental functions. However, at least seven of the postwar polls, for which the tabulators have separated farmers from other categories, do deal with selected aspects of this field and may profitably be explored for evidence of rural-urban or inter-occupational differences (Table 1).

Only governmental price guarantees for farm crops drew favor from a larger percentage of farmers than of the general public, or of any other subgroup. Here the interest of farmers in the prices of what they sell apparently overcame what appears in most of the polls as an opposite reaction. On each of the six other poll topics the farmer pro-percentage was less than that for the general public, and on five topics it was less than that for any other subgroup, making farmers the most reluctant of any of the groups to favor the extension of economic action by the government.[8] True, "government appropriations for slum clearance and housing" was the only one of the seven proposals that as many as half of the general public favored. Approval of each other item was granted by only

---

8. Cf., John L. Haer, "Conservatism and the Rural-Urban Continuum," *Rural Sociology*, XVII, No. 4 (Dec., 1952), pp. 343-347 (published since this paper was prepared).

a minority. The farmer minority on each topic in these postwar polls, however, is considerably lower than the general-public minority.

This array of the subsamples by pro-percentages puts farmers and laborers at opposite ends of the range on five issues, with city dwellers and farmers at opposite ends on a sixth topic. If no farmers and all laborers had approved these governmental excursions into economic activity, the current existence of the orthodox ideal-type rural society would have some confirmation. But on each issue the general public was divided, as was every subsample, including farmers. The question of intersample differences such as rural-urban or farmer-labor suggests the usual classroom discussions of overlapping curves.[9] Most of the farmers and most of the general public or any of the subsamples on any issue are under overlapping distribution curves, where they hold common territory in Cartesian space. With reference to a given origin of coördinates, however, the distribution curves for farmers on most of these economic-role-of-government issues were farther removed along the line of abscissas from the distribution curve for some classification of laborers than from the distribution curve for any other segment of the public. To shorten and oversimplify this observation, we may say that farmer distributions of opinions on the economic role of government were more like the distributions of executives, proprietors, businessmen, and white-collar samples than like the distributions of samples of laborers. The temptation is to oversimplify by one degree more, and say that farmers think like business-

Table 1—Comparison of Farmers with Total Sample and Most Extreme Subsamples, by Percentage Approving Specified Economic Action by Government (Postwar National Polls, 1946-1950)

Topic	Farmers	Total	EXTREME GROUPS	
			Least Approval	Most Approval
	Pro-percentages		Pro-percentages	
Keeping price guarantees on farm crops	62	39	33 (City dwellers)	62 (Farmers)
Government appropriations for slum clearance, housing	56	69	56 (Farmers)	79 (Union members)
Government guarantee of standard of living for all	36	43	28 (Professionals & businessmen)	57 (Union members)
Retention of price ceilings on meat, etc.	34	42	34 (Farmers)	47 (Manual workers)
Rationing and price ceilings on some products	31	48	31 (Farmers)	53 (Manual workers)
Government ownership of railroads	18	26	18 (Farmers)	32 (Union members)
More government regulation of business	14	21	14 (Farm owners)	32 (Factory workers)

9. This is more readily apparent from the percentage distributions of "yes-no-other" responses, but may also be inferred from these tables of pro-percentages.

men and not like laborers when it comes to the economic functions of government. This might make interesting conversation, but it is not an accurate statement of the findings.

One begins to suspect here that certain distributions of subsamples within the farmer or rural category, as within urban categories, may be more in contrast to each other than are the overall rural and urban distributions. A suspicion must be confessed at this point, also, that the representation of farmers in national polls may not be adequate at all strata of rural society. Unfortunately, the tabulations presently available do not permit more than cursory exploration of such hypotheses.

LABOR ISSUES: A REVIEW OF POLLS. A number of polls in recent years have sought the public's pulse on labor issues. Farmer groups have been singled out in ten accessible postwar tabulations on labor topics so-stated that an opinion of approval may be classified as "pro-labor" (Table 2). Incidentally, the separation of these polls from those dealing with the economic functions of government is somewhat artificial, because most of them relate directly to some question of governmental policy with regard to labor.

The pattern of farmer opinion on these labor issues is very much like the pattern on topics dealing with economic actions of government. On each of the ten topics, views favorable to labor were offered by smaller percentages of farmers than of the general public. Inspection of the corresponding no-opinion percentages and con-percentages (not presented in Table 2) confirms an inference from study of the pro-percentages that the distributions of farmer groups were like the distributions of professional, white-collar, business, and executive groups, but unlike the distributions of labor groups. There is one suggestion of a contradiction in the inference that many farmers, normally hesitant to have government enlarge its powers, approved using the power of government to restrain labor (Table 2), as they approved also the use of the power of government to support farm prices (Table 1).

On nine of the ten polls, farmers are at the lowest extreme and laborers at the highest extreme, when the subsamples are arrayed by the percentages of pro-labor response. Even the labor pro-percentages, however, are under 50 on six of the ten topics, representing minority rather than majority approval.

A bare majority of the farmers approved raising minimum wages; nearly half of them acknowledged the general right of labor to strike; four in ten approved of labor unions "in general." On no other issue did as many as a fourth of the farmers register the pro-labor position. Even on the most unpopular propositions—that unions be permitted to contribute to political campaign funds, and that unemployment benefits be paid to strikers—one farmer in ten gave the pro-labor reaction.

Again the analyst faces a temptation to simplify description by elliptical sequences of words. It would be easy to say that farmers feel more strongly than do workers that unions should be regulated by the government, because only 17 per cent of them, compared with 36 per cent of the manual workers, want the Taft-Hartley Law repealed. Actually, all that we are shown is that relatively (percentage-wise) fewer farmers than workers want the restrictions of a law removed. Even so, nearly one farmer in six favors its repeal. It is not accurate to say that "farmers are for regulation" and "laborers are not for regulation." And in this case the fact that majorities of manual workers, the general public, and farmers were on the same side of the issue is more significant than the percentage-point differences. The worker public—the farmer public—the general public, to that extent, are one public; and the farmer class is more in than out, more like than unlike the general public.

INTERNATIONAL ISSUES: A REVIEW OF POLLS. Farmers are generally thought to be provincial and ethnocentric. A comparison of their stands on international matters should provide a good test of the rural-urban difference hypotheses. On the international issues for which poll tabulations are available, the distributions of farmers by shadings of opinion were, in general, not unlike the distributions for the public at large (Table 3). Neither farmers nor the general public seemed clearly isolationist or internationalist—the pro-percentages for the two were very close

Table 2—Comparison of Farmers with Total Sample and Most Extreme Subsamples, by Percentage Expressing Pro-Labor Opinion on Ten Specified Issues (Postwar National Polls, 1946-1950)

Topic	Farmers	Total	EXTREME GROUPS	
			Least Approval	Most Approval
	Pro-percentages		Pro-percentages	
Raising minimum wage from 40c to 65c	51	68	51 (Farmers)	81 (Manual workers)
Right to strike, in general	47	62	47 (Farmers)	67 (Professionals & businessmen)
General approval of unions	41	*	41 (Farmers)	67 (Manual workers)
In refereeing disputes, would favor labor	24	26	18 (Executives)	39 (Workers)
Right to strike in public services	22	30	22 (Farmers)	33 (Manual workers)
Higher union wages	19	38	19 (Farmers)	59 (Union members)
Repeal Taft-Hartley Law	17	30	17 (Farmers)	36 (Manual workers)
Prefer union shop over other types	11	18	11 (Farmers)	33 (Union members)
Union contributions to campaign funds	10	17	10 (Farmers)	26 (Union members)
Paying unemployment benefits to strikers	10	21	10 (Farmers)	38 (Union members)

* Not available.

(within three percentage points of each other) on 6 of the 11 topics in the field of international relations.

Farmers appeared at the lowest extreme, or were the subgroup with the smallest pro-percentage, on 6 of the 11 topics; but, in contrast to their

Table 3—Comparison of Farmers with Total Sample and Most Extreme Subsamples, by Percentage Favoring Selected Propositions Concerning International Relations, Particularly United States-Russian Relations (Postwar National Polls, 1946-1950)

| Topic | Farmers | Total | EXTREME GROUPS | |
| | | | Least Approval | Most Approval |
	Pro-percentages		Pro-percentages	
International Affairs in General:				
To declare war, Congress should have national vote of approval	71	71	66 (Small-town dwellers)	72 (City dwellers)
U.S. should join World Congress to solve problems between countries	56	62	56 (Farmers)	67 (Large-city dwellers)
U.S. should send enough food to Europe for health, even if we have less at home	33	43	33 (Farmers; factory workers)	60 (Professionals & businessmen)
Send food to Europe only if paid for	19	14	7 (Professionals & executives)	19 (Factory workers; farmers)
Relations Between the U.S.A. and Russia:				
Russia is building up merely for self-protection	29	29	26 (Manual workers)	36 (Professionals & businessmen)
U.S. should not go ahead with treaties without Russia	19	25	19 (Farmers)	31 (White-collar workers)
Russian government sincerely desires peace	13	16	13 (Farmers)	18 (White-collar workers; professionals & businessmen)
U.S. should give Berlin to the Russians	11	11	8 (Professionals & businessmen)	12 (Manual workers)
U.S. should pull out of U.N. if Russia continues to block	11	13	11 (Farmers)	16 (Manual workers)
Business firms should continue selling to Russians	9	15	9 (Farmers)	21 (Professionals & businessmen)
U.S. is too tough on Russia	5	6	4 (Manual workers)	9 (Professionals & businessmen)

alignment on economic-action and labor issues, farmers here are set off against labor as the opposite extreme only once, and are more typically in opposition to the business and professional or the white-collar sub-grouping. Labor, "small-towners," and farmers held all but 2 of the 11 "low score" positions, yielding the position of smallest pro-percentage on only those two items to professional and business groups.

The subgroupings were less widely separated in the degree of approval they gave these issues than they were on economic-action and labor issues, although alignments varied more. Even so, it is apparent that the percentage of farmers expressing approval exceeded that of the general public on only 1 of the 11 polls. Many of the postwar polls on international questions have concerned Russian-United States relationships specifically. On the six topics mentioning phases of our relations with Russia, the pro-Russian view was expressed by small minorities of the general public, but by even smaller minorities of farmers and workers.

It can be concluded that farmers were no more or no less international-minded than the public at large, labor groups, or business and professional groups. Rural-urban or inter-occupational differences on these issues were clearly less pronounced than on the domestic issues of government economic roles and labor policy. Perhaps during and after the tensions of war the traditionalism of farmers had been pressed into accord with the views of the urbanites.

SELECTED PUBLIC QUESTIONS: A REVIEW OF POLLS. Polls dealing with a variety of topics are here grouped under "selected public questions," for want of a better classification (Table 4). On each of the eight issues, farmers were at either one extreme or the other in relation to other subgroups. They had the largest percentage favoring prohibition, wanting membership in the Communist party to be forbidden, and preferring standard to daylight-saving time. They had the smallest percentage for including farmers under Social Security, for a national health act, for universal military training, and for Negro-white equality in rights to jobs. There are moral overtones of Puritanism, individualism, loyalty, and related values in these reactions—as well as strength of vested interest in oleomargarine taxes (protecting the butter market) and just plain traditionalism as in the repudiation of daylight-saving time.

Here, as in issues dealing with international matters, there is no consistent opposition of the farmer and labor subgroups as extremes. Farmers are set off against workers on only two items; they are opposite white-collar groups on four items and dwellers in the largest cities on two items. The divergence of the farmer from other groups was sharpest on the prohibition and daylight-saving questions. The old matrix of rurality is evident, but it is not fully determinant of the opinions expressed. Whether there is a farmer-labor or rural-urban difference depends upon the issue.

EDUCATION, EMPLOYMENT, "LOT IN LIFE": A REVIEW OF POLLS. Other polls have dealt with questions of more personal reference than those considered under the previous headings: the desirability of education for one's children; one's preference for type of work, one's satisfaction with conditions of living, or "lot in life" (Table 5).

The proportion of farmers wanting sons to go to college, although a majority (53 per cent), is lower than that of any other group—and quite in contrast to the white-collar pro-percentage. The presence of education as a white-collar value in American life is conspicuous; but who can say college education is not also a rural value if half the farmers are for it? The difference between the pro-percentages for sons and daughters is only five percentage points (53-48), and is less significant than the fact that nearly half of the farmers would send their daughters to college ("other things being equal"). Among the subgroups here studied, the approval of college education as a value seems less developed in worker than in farmer or white-collar occupational grades.

Table 4—Comparison of Farmers with Total Sample and Most Extreme Subsamples, by Percentage Approving Specified Statements on Public Questions (Postwar National Polls, 1946-1950)

			EXTREME GROUPS	
Topic	Farmers	Total	Least Approval	Most Approval
	Pro-percentages		Pro-percentages	
Social Legislation:				
Would vote for national prohibition	53	35	27 (Residents in largest cities)	53 (Farmers)
Including farmers in social security programs	49	57	49 (Farmers)	59 (Manual workers)
Preference for national health act over Blue Cross plan	26	33	26 (Farmers)	39 (Manual workers)
Universal Military Training:				
Universal military training for one year	69	74	69 (Farmers)	81 (White-collar workers)
Control of Communism:				
Membership in Communist party should be forbidden	69	62	56 (Professionals & businessmen)	69 (Farmers)
Special Taxes:				
Removal of taxes on oleomargarine	39	69	39 (Farmers)	78 (Professionals & businessmen)
Race Relations:				
Negroes and whites should have same chance to get any job	40	47	40 (Farmers)	65 (Professionals)
Daylight-Saving Time:				
Prefer standard over daylight-saving time	71	42	24 (Residents in largest cities)	71 (Farmers)

Large majorities preferred security of work to high wages, and farmers were with the general public on this item (81 per cent). A characteristic reaction also is the preference of the farmer—like that of professional and business people—for self-employment. This is a high-priority value for manual workers, too (61 per cent). The value of self-employment must have outlived the possibility of its fulfillment in a society of mass production and group business. As a value, however, it is apparently no more rural nor urban than it is "American."

Table 5—Comparison of Farmers with Total Sample and Most Extreme Subsamples, by Percentage Approving Specified Statements on Education, Types of Employment, and "Lot in Life" (Postwar National Polls, 1946-1950)

Topic	Farmers	Total	EXTREME GROUPS	
			Least Approval	Most Approval
	Pro-percentages		Pro-percentages	
Importance of Education:				
Would want a son to go to college	53	62	53 (Farmers)	77 (White-collar workers)
Would want a daughter to go to college	48	50	38 (Wage earners)	74 (Professionals & executives)
Young men need college training to get along well	47	54	35 (Nonfarm labor)	74 (Professionals)
Preferred Types of Employment:				
Prefer secure job to high-paying job	81	81	76 (Professionals & businessmen)	84 (Manual workers)
Prefer own business to working for others	80	68	61 (Manual workers)	81 (Professionals & businessmen)
Rather work for private firm than government	39	41	33 (Professionals & businessmen)	49 (Manual workers)
Satisfaction with "Lot in Life":				
Satisfied with "lot in life"	84	*	71 (Manual workers)	88 (Professionals & businessmen)
Satisfied with present housing	84	66	50 (Residents in largest cities)	84 (Farmers)
Farmer is better off than city dweller	83	73	66 (Residents in largest cities)	83 (Farmers)
Farmer is happier than man in city	73	65	55 (Residents in largest cities)	73 (Farmers)
If beginning again, would enter same work	70	55	46 (Manual workers)	70 (Farmers; professionals & businessmen)

* Not available.

In satisfaction with "lot in life," expressed variously in five polls here reviewed, farmers were ahead of the general public. On four of the five items they were in the most-approval position, and apparently were closer to business and professional groups than to any other subgroups in general satisfaction with "lot in life" and with work. The public generally, and especially the residents of large cities, were less satisfied with housing and less certain that farmers are better off or happier than city people.

Satisfaction is probably an accompaniment of conservatism, and here seems more characteristic of farmers than others, but clearly evident for a majority of each subgroup. Such rural-urban differences as exist are only in degree.

CONCLUSIONS FROM THE REVIEW OF POLLS. The review here presented does not complete the analysis of farmer opinion as an expression of rural values and, thus, as an index to the character of rural society. Certain details of tabulation are as yet unattended to. The grouping of polls into prewar, war, and postwar time-blocks will permit more thoroughgoing analysis. Another possible grouping would be by issues on which farmer-labor or rural-urban contrasts are sharpest or agreement most pronounced. No doubt conclusions would thus be revealed.

The effort thus far, however, raises important research questions. If farmer opinions could be sorted by type-of-farming areas and cultural regions, what further diversities might we find? If they could be sorted on more issues by income and land-tenure status, what varieties would be revealed? If the statistical adequacy of farmer samples were more carefully tested for representativeness of types of farming and of social strata, what qualifications in interpretation might we have to state. If international comparisons were made, what universalities might be isolated? What would be the result of special studies of the no-opinion, no-information, undecided responses?

The review of polls also yields some tentative conclusions, appropriate to offer at this point. When table forms were first being set up and captions chosen for the table columns to be used in this study, the plan was to speak of the general public, the farmer public, and the publics most extremely like and unlike farmers. When the distributions within each category were noted, however, this application of the concept "public" was abandoned. The "public" that approved giving Berlin to the Russians includes 11 per cent of the farmers, 8 per cent of the business and professional people, and 12 per cent of the manual workers; but neither the pro-public nor con-public includes all the farmers, or all the business and professional workers, or all the laborers.

On most issues of national interest, the majorities of farmers express opinions consistent with and supported by the values and attitudes associated with orthodox (classical) sociological concepts of the nature of rural society and culture. On no issue of national interest do all farmers alone present a solid front of opinion either *pro* or *contra*. On all issues, there are divisions of pro and con, and intervening distributions—among farmers themselves, and among the members of any other group. Unanimity is not found on any topic.

Strains of conservatism have influenced farmer pro-percentages and con-percentages most conspicuously in areas of personal and social concern, and least conspicuously in areas of international relations. It might have been expected that our "rural heritage," to borrow Williams'[10] phrase, would lead farmers to differ from the general public as much in opinions on international matters as on other issues. Apparently the character of world events in recent years has affected farmers as much as any others in American society, and farmers have been pressed by the urgency of the times to lean away from their former provincialism—at least far enough to bring them into general conformance with the views of Americans at large.

Most reactions on public questions, labor issues, and economic functions of government betray also the operation of underlying rural values; but many of these issues deal with situations beyond the range of everyday contact, beyond the scope of intimate participation. They are not so close to the individual as are matters moral, social, and personal.

---

10. James Mickel Williams, *Our Rural Heritage* (New York: Alfred A. Knopf, 1925), pp. xvii-246.

THE DIFFERENTIAL DISTRIBUTION
OF COMMUNITY KNOWLEDGE

Gresham M. Sykes

Although many studies have been made of normative standards, moral beliefs, opinions, and similar social phenomena in terms of their differential distribution in various social groups, there have been few empirical inquiries into the distribution of knowledge and its relationship to such phenomena.[1]

Our understanding of the forms of social action cannot be complete unless we have some idea of the knowledge with which the individual and the group operate. Such knowledge forms, as it were, the basis for the actor's orientation. It makes known alternative goals, available means, and what is normatively prescribed or proscribed. The "rationalistic bias" is, of course, dangerous;[2] but the individual and the group must be provided with some knowledge, whether it is erroneous or not, which gives expectations of probable consequences, and the nature of past and present conditions, as they are believed to exist.

This study represents one such investigation, but is limited in its concern with only one type of knowledge, knowledge of the community, and emphasizes only one aspect—the social location of such knowledge. It is plain that a thorough study of community knowledge would have to include not only such social location, in terms of status, occupational role, ethnic group, position in the power structure, and so forth, but also its historical origins and social functions.

Aside from its scientific interest, such an inquiry may be significant in relation to the value system of a democratic society; there is an obvious need for more information as to who is the "informed voter," the "political participant," and the "civic-minded" individual.

The city of Plainfield, New Jersey, with an estimated population of

Reprinted from *Social Forces*, Vol. 29 (May, 1951), pp. 376-382, by permission of the author and *Social Forces*. (Copyright, 1951, by the Williams and Wilkins Co.)

1. The knowledge of which we are speaking might better be termed the level of information; it is not a systematic body of thought, but rather the "isolated fragments of information available to the masses of the people." Robert K. Merton, *Social Theory and Social Structure*, p. 201. But the term is convenient, and will be used in this paper for that type of thought which refers to objectively verifiable "facts," as the word is understood in common usage.

2. See, for example, Wilbert E. Moore and Melvin M. Tumin, "Some Social Functions of Ignorance," *American Sociological Review*, 14 (December, 1949), pp. 787-788.

41,000 in 1949, was chosen for the location of the study because the writer was familiar with the city, the necessary cooperation could easily be secured, the city was convenient in terms of a time-budget, and Plainfield is a city within the metropolitan region of New York. As such it could be expected to show two primary orientations: the local community itself, and the metropolis as a surrogate of the Great Society.

In the summer of 1949 a questionnaire was constructed and administered to a small random sample of white male principal wage-earners in the city of Plainfield.[3] The questionnaire was composed of three parts: a test of knowledge of the community; a set of questions concerning attributes such as income, occupation, and length of residence; and a group of questions dealing with political participation. Scores representing levels of knowledge of the community were obtained on the basis of the test which consisted of forty questions. These questions were divided into three groups relating to the areas of government, education, and welfare. For those questions requiring a numerical answer, such as the tax rate, a certain amount of leeway was provided—in most cases, approximately 12 per cent either above or below the actual figure. A score of one was given for each correct answer or item of information. Thus the highest possible total score was 40; and, in the three areas of government, education, and welfare, 12, 15, and 13. (For the distribution of the sample by total scores, see Figure 1.)

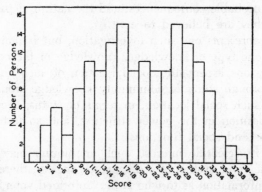

FIG. 1—Distribution of 165 White, Male, Main Wage Earners in Plainfield, New Jersey, by Total Score.

3. A sample of 213 individuals was selected by taking the first name on the top of every fourth page of the Plainfield City Directory. All women and students, when so listed, were eliminated and the next name on the page selected. Negroes were eliminated by inspection at home calls, and all addresses at which there were no principal wage-earners for reasons of retirement, death, and so on, were also discarded. This method is open to criticism in that it does not conform to strict sampling theory, although no known bias has been introduced. The sample also possesses some upward socio-economic tendency in so far as there is undoubtedly a selective factor as to who is listed in the directory. Of the 213 addresses selected, there were 165 completed interviews, 7 refusals, 6 on vacation, 4 not reached, 3 sick, and 21 who failed to fulfill the criteria of membership in the universe.

There are of course no absolutes in tests of this kind, and therefore the interpretation of the scores is difficult. It was decided that the most fruitful method would be to dichotomize the scores at some point which could be taken as dividing "knowledgeable" individuals from "non-knowledgeable." This procedure is essentially the same as that used by Seba Eldridge in his study of public intelligence.[4] The mean score of the group in each area was taken as the point of division. In all areas the median score was close to the mean, so that in each case approximately half the group could be termed knowledgeable (Table 1).

Table 1—Summary of All Scores

Score	Mean	Median	Standard Deviation of the Mean
Total score	19.7	19.4	8.8
Government score	7.5	8.0	2.5
Education score	6.7	6.6	3.9
Welfare score	5.4	5.2	3.1

Knowing and not knowing as used here are thus quite relative, and this character of the scores should be kept in mind in any interpretation of the results. Hereafter, scores higher than the mean of the group will be referred to as high scores; scores below the mean will be termed low scores. Knowledgeable and non-knowledgeable will be used interchangeably with these two terms.[5]

The attributes about which questions were asked were: socio-economic status, length of residence, children in school, geographical mobility, location of work, home ownership, and participation in political affairs. The method of statistical analysis used was the test for significant differences between percentages of individuals termed knowledgeable, at the .05 level of probability. The relevant empirical data may be summarized as follows:

1. *Income.* As income levels rise, the proportion of knowledgeable individuals increases. When the sample is dichotomized into those earning $5,000 or more per year and those earning less, the former group shows a significantly higher percentage of knowledgeable individuals. However, it is those earning $2,000 or less per year who are primarily responsible for the relatively smaller percentage of knowledgeable persons in the less than $5,000 per year group.

2. *Occupation.* Occupational classifications were made on the basis of the U. S. Census groupings.[6] In general, as occupational status falls, the

4. Seba Eldridge, "Public Intelligence," *Bulletin of the University of Kansas,* Humanistic Studies, V, No. 1, June, 1935.

5. Since the scores in the three areas consistently follow the pattern of the total scores, only the latter will be dealt with in this paper, as an aid in simplicity of presentation.

6. *Alphabetical Index of Occupations,* 1937, U. S. Department of Commerce,

proportion of high scores become smaller. When the occupational statuses are grouped, the two highest categories (professional, proprietors, managers, and officials) show a significantly higher proportion of high scores than do semiskilled workers and lesser-ranked occupations.

3. *Education.* The sample shows a consistent increase in the percentage of knowledgeable individuals with an increase in the educational level, until the group "completed college" is reached, at which point the proportion decreases slightly. When grouped by those having completed high school or less, and those having "some college or more," the higher educational level group shows a significantly higher proportion of high scores.[7]

The findings suggest that (1) a certain amount of education is essential for the acquisition of community knowledge, but that this level is soon reached (approximately some high school); (2) educational level is importantly associated with the level of community knowledge within the context of lower economic status, but not within the context of relatively high economic status; and (3) there is a tendency for the highest educational levels—completed college and beyond—to have a lower level of community knowledge than the educational level immediately below.

4. *Length of residence.* There is evident a more or less consistent increase in the proportion of high scores as the length of residence increases. When grouped by those who have lived in the community more and less than ten years, there is a significantly greater proportion of knowledgeable persons in the group of longer residence.

5. *Home ownership.* Home owners show a significantly higher percentage of knowledgeable individuals than does the group which rents its home. Since to own one's home requires a relatively large financial outlay and presumably a stability of occupation and way of life, we may suspect that these individuals are of a somewhat higher economic status and tend toward a longer period of residence than do individuals who rent their homes; an examination of the sample data indicates that this in fact is the case.

6. *Geographical mobility.* An index of mobility was constructed in terms of the number of changes in residence since 1940. The findings indicate an inverse relationship between knowledge and mobility. However, when length of residence is held constant, a reversal of this occurs, when *only* those who have lived in the community for more than ten years are

---

Bureau of the Census. The supposition here is that the ranking from professional to servant classes indicates a roughly descending order in the socio-economic scale, in so far as occupation is relevant to such stratification.

7. As is to be expected, educational level and income are related. Of those who are in the "some college or more" category, 70 per cent receive $5,000 or more per year; but of those who are at the "completed high school or less" level, only 22 per cent do so. When income level is held constant, the amount of education would seem to make little difference among those who receive $5,000 or more per year—high educational level and high scores are associated primarily in the lower income group.

considered. Within the context of long residence, relatively numerous changes of residence would seem to be associated with a comparatively high level of community knowledge; for those who have lived in the community less than ten years, the opposite relationship holds true. Since those who have lived in the community more than ten years have made all their moves within the community since 1940; and since mobile persons who have lived in the community less than ten years have made one or more moves either outside the community or to the community, it suggests that mobility *within* the community is associated with a high level of community knowledge.

7. *Reading the local newspaper.* The group that regularly reads the local newspaper contains a higher percentage of knowledgeable persons than does the group which does not. "Regularly," however, was not defined in the questionnaire, and thus was susceptible to the varying interpretations of the respondents; furthermore, no attempt was made to ascertain what was read in the paper, or the order of reading.[8]

8. *Location of work.* When the sample is grouped on the basis of the location of work (inside or outside of the community), there would seem to be little difference in knowledge between the two groups. However, of those who work in the community, 28 per cent receive $5,000 or more per year, whereas of those who work outside the community, 53 per cent do so. In regard to occupational status, 38 per cent of those who work in Plainfield are in the two highest categories, but 55 per cent of those who work outside the community are professionals, proprietors, managers, and officials. In so far as high income and high occupational status are associated with a greater proportion of high scores, this would tend to obscure the relation of place of work and community knowledge. When income levels are held constant, for example, location of work in the community is associated with a higher percentage of high scores in all areas.

9. *Children in school.* When the sample is grouped on the basis of those having children in school in the community, and those having no children in school, the former group has a higher proportion of knowledgeable individuals.

10. *Political participation.* This was taken as referring to registration for voting, voting in primary elections, voting in general elections, attending public meetings, and belonging to a political organization. Each of

---

8. Among those who do not read the paper must be included the foreign born who have not learned English, the illiterate, and the like, who on this basis alone might be expected to have a low level of community knowledge. On the other hand, there are those who in all probability read newspapers other than the local one. When we compare the nonreading group with those who read, we find that 83 per cent of the former are in the two highest occupational categories, whereas only 43 per cent of the reading group is so ranked. In regard to income, 83 per cent of those who do not read the local paper receive high incomes ($5,000 or more per year), and only 40 per cent of the readers do so. The nonreading group is largely of an upper socioeconomic status, in this limited sense, as compared with the group that reads.

these attributes is associated with a significantly higher percentage of high scores than is the non-possession of these attributes.

The possession of the attributes discussed in section III may be considered as marking certain statuses; the individual having those attributes plays his role in a set of patterned relationships. As previously noted, the attributes or statuses may be divided into those having to do with socio-economic status, those concerning community relationships, and those involving political participation.

Of those statuses having the community as a significant element in their definition, long residence, ownership of home, location of work in the community, children in school in the community, and geographical immobility will be termed *local*. When combined in one individual they will be said to constitute a local position or station. Short residence, renting of home, no children in school, working outside of the community, and geographical mobility will be termed *nonlocal* statuses; and, when combined, make up a nonlocal position.

This terminology is derived from Merton's local and cosmopolitan types, formulated in reference to individuals exercising influence in a community.[9] The statuses making up these types of influentials are strikingly similar to the statuses found to be associated with differing levels of community knowledge. The terms have been modified in this paper (cosmopolitan to nonlocal) in order to distinguish two types of individuals oriented away from the total local community; those oriented toward the Great Society, and those oriented toward some sub-unit of the community, such as the neighborhood or clique.

The phenomenon of knowledge of the community, when regarded as a process of learning, may be roughly divided into four elements: *exposure, selection, interpretation,* and *retention.* These elements can be discussed in two ways: one, as a formal sequence of events, leading to the demonstration of knowledge, i.e., answering a questionnaire, "rational"

---

9. Robert K. Merton, "Patterns of Influence," *Communications Research 1948-1949,* Paul F. Lazarsfeld and Frank N. Stanton (eds.). Merton's description of locals and cosmopolitans in the town of "Rovere" is particularly germane: "The chief criteria for distinguishing the two is found in their orientation toward Rovere. The localite largely confines his interests to his community. Rovere is essentially his world. Devoting little thought or energy to the Great Society, he is preoccupied with local problems, to the virtual exclusion of the national and international scene. He is, strictly speaking, parochial.

"Contrariwise with the cosmopolitan type. He has some interest in Rovere and must of course maintain a minimum of relations with the community since he, too, exerts influence there. But he is also oriented significantly to the world outside Rovere, and regards himself as an integral part of that world. He resides in Rovere, but lives in the Great Society. If the local type is parochial, the cosmopolitan is ecumenical." pp. 189-190.

The author from whose article the above has been quoted has previously noted the similarity of the concept to the distinction made in the writings of Simmel, Cooley, Weber, Durkheim, and others, with somewhat different terminologies. The terms local and cosmopolitan are adopted from Carle C. Zimmerman who uses them as translations of Tönnies' *Gemeinschaft* and *Gesellschaft.*

action, etc.; and two, as interconnected causative factors.[10] They will be discussed here in the latter sense.

1. *Exposure.* Local statuses have a common element by definition; they all involve comparatively closer and stronger ties with the community than do nonlocal statuses. These ties provide channels through which knowledge about the community can flow. The individual filling a local position has had time to form extended friendships of long standing. As a home owner, he must conform to certain regulations of the community, and he is aware of the services, or the lack of them, provided by the community for property owners. Through his children he comes into contact with the school system. Working in the community, he has face to face relationships, both of a contractual and particularistic nature, with many of the individuals living in the community. Much of this is lacking for the non-local. What relationships he does have will tend to be in a limited range of brief duration. In short, it is to be expected that the local's exposure to knowledge of the community is of longer duration, of greater frequency, more varied, and of greater intensity than that of the nonlocal.

2. *Selection.* It is when we come to selection—the differential extraction of certain portions of the presented material—that we must consider the matter of orientation. Selection is here considered not only as the attention given to portions of factual material to which an individual has been exposed, but also, and less passively, as a determining factor in deciding what knowledge an individual will expose himself to. It is suggested that the complex of goals underlying the local position helps to determine the nature of this selection, and the complex is such that a knowledge of the community (1) is obtained as a by-product in striving for these goals; and (2) provides an efficient means, in some cases, for reaching these goals. The goals of the nonlocal, on the other hand, would seldom involve the community.[11]

3. *Interpretation.* In the matter of interpretation, the local position would seem to provide a framework of knowledge in which new material could be weighed and evaluated, a framework more or less lacking for the nonlocal. In this sense, the local position provides a check for the

---

10. The following citations exemplify discussions of these factors at the psychological level: F. C. Bartlett, *Remembering*; Muzafer Sherif, *The Psychology of Social Norms*; J. S. Bruner and C. C. Goodman, "Value and Need as Organizing Factors in Perception," *The Journal of Abnormal and Social Psychology*, XLII (1947), 33-44; Jerome M. Levine and Gardner Murphy, "The Learning and Forgetting of Controversial Material," *The Journal of Abnormal and Social Psychology*, XXXVII (1943), 507-517; John A. McGeoch, *The Psychology of Human Learning*; A. L. Edwards, "The Retention of Affective Experiences," *Psychological Review*, 49 (1942); Frederick Williams, "Information as a Determinant of Opinion," in Hadley Cantril, *Gauging Public Opinion*.

11. For a relevant discussion, in a slightly different frame of reference, see James E. Murray, chairman of the Special Committee to Study Problems of American Small Business, *Small Business and Civic Welfare*, U.S. Gov. Printing Office, Document No. 135, 79th Congress, 2nd session, pp. 22-23.

accuracy of new knowledge, assuming a certain amount of community knowledge is already associated with the position. Thus a nonlocal may brand as false a statement which is in fact true.[12]

The usefulness of this typology of locals and nonlocals in distinguishing between knowledgeables and non-knowledgeables is borne out when individuals possessing all local and nonlocal attributes are compared. The group of locals in the sample contains a much greater proportion of high scores than does the non-local group (Table 2).

A more refined use of this typology is made possible if its relationship to socio-economic and participation status is considered. The findings suggest that high or comparatively high socio-economic status is associated with a high level of community knowledge. However, such status would seem to operate in this manner only in conjunction with the local position which has already set the pattern for the acquisition of knowledge. This would give a fourfold modification of the heuristic typology: high socio-economic status locals; high social economic status nonlocals; low socio-economic status locals; and low socio-economic status nonlocals. It is here suggested that the first group has the highest level of community knowledge; they occupy statuses such that they are oriented toward the community. And their high socio-economic status facilitates the acquisition of knowledge by its association with leisure, positions of responsibility, possibilities for extended personal interaction. Not to be overlooked here, perhaps, is the tradition of "leaders of the community" which may be more or less operative.

The second group—high socio-economic status nonlocals—would tend to be oriented toward the Great Society. In a professional or managerial position outside the community, the majority of their daily personal relationships will not take place within the context of community life. This group would tend to come third in regard to knowledgeability.

The third group—low socio-economic status locals—forms the majority of locals, but they would tend to be second in regard to knowledgeability. Their area of exposure and selection is probably somewhat more restricted than that of the first group. One would expect to find among them the rank and file of local political organizations, welfare groups, and so on. They would form the majority of participants. This opens the possibility that such locals substitute community goals for more individualistic goals of material success. On the other hand, participation in community affairs may be used as a means for personal advancement.

The fourth group—low socio-economic status nonlocals—would be the

---

12. In regard to retention, it has been assumed for the purposes of this paper that if an individual has been exposed to certain factual material, if he has selected from it certain portions, and if he has interpreted these portions correctly, he will be able to supply such portions on demand. Such an assumption would of course have to be examined more closely in a more complete investigation. The effects of age, education, intelligence, facilities for reference, and so on, probably would all be relevant.

least knowledgeable. It is in all probability an extremely heterogeneous group and would include among its members such persons as the young unmarried highly mobile individual, the older immigrant who confines

Table 2—Distribution of All Scores, by Locals and Nonlocals

Position	Number in Group	Number with High Scores (Total)	Number with High Scores (Government)	Number with High Scores (Education)	Number with High Scores (Welfare)
Locals	14	12	11	12	9
Nonlocals	13	2	3	1	3

his attention to his ethnic neighborhood, and the unskilled worker from the nearby industrial plants.

When this more precise heuristic typology is applied to the empirical data, it would seem that our hypotheses are essentially correct. Taking occupational level as the best single index of socio-economic position, and forming six types of "locals" ranging from nonlocals (I) to locals (VI), by number of local statuses possessed,[13] it is clear that the four extreme types follow the pattern suggested (Table 3). Furthermore, it can be seen that (1) high occupational levels have higher scores than low occu-

Table 3—Mean Total Score of Community Knowledge, by Occupational Level and Number of Local Statuses

Type	Number in Group	MEAN SCORE* Proprietors, Managers, and Officials	Clerks, Skilled Workers, and Below
I (nonlocal)	13	15.0	11.5
II	18	18.1	12.1
III	33	19.8	16.1
IV	50	24.1	19.2
V	37	25.8	18.9
VI (local)	14	25.8	23.9

* Underlined mean scores are those of the original fourfold typology: high socio-economic status locals, low socio-economic status locals, high socio-economic status nonlocals, and low socio-economic status nonlocals.

pational levels, *within a given type;* and (2) as the number of local statuses possessed becomes greater, the level of knowledge is higher.

Again the number of individuals in each type is too small to allow statistical tests of significance, but the consistency of the pattern displayed is highly suggestive.

In regard to participation statuses, it is to be expected that participation in community affairs provides some exposure to knowledge about the community. These statuses, however, are probably more important as an index of existing orientation, since such a relatively small proportion

13. Types I to VI have from none to five local statuses. Whether there is an underlying continuum of "localism" is difficult to establish, although the data suggest the possibility of scale types in terms of Guttman's scalogram analysis. This problem is now being investigated.

of individuals are participants as here defined. Thus we find the majority of participants occupying the local position, but not the majority of locals being participants. Why some locals become participants, however, is somewhat outside the scope of the present analysis.

In spite of the small size of the sample, the rather gross determination of attributes, and the tentative nature of the test of community knowledge, it is felt that this study has made possible a more precise formulation of the social location of community knowledge and some of the factors involved.

A high level of community knowledge would seem to be associated with a cluster of statuses which have as their common element orientation toward the community. "Local" individuals possessing such statuses are, in a certain sense, truly members of the community. They live there, they work there, their goals and interests are intertwined with those of the community itself. Such individuals apparently are tied to the community by a multitude of bonds; and it is this cohesion which provides both the means of obtaining knowledge and the motivation to do so.

It is important to recognize, however, that this relationship is in all probability somewhat circularly self-reinforcing. Not only does orientation to the community produce knowledge, but knowledge may be an important factor in producing such orientation.

Those persons who are relatively well-to-do, who have reached the college level of education, and who have jobs that are fairly high on the occupational ladder, also tend to know a good deal about their town. But this association of high socio-economic status and community knowledge is by no means a simple one. Such a position would seem to be helpful in gaining knowledge about the community mainly when the basic orientation toward the community is already present. If this orientation is lacking, the "upper class" individual is more than likely to have little interest in his town and to have a low level of community knowledge. And of those persons having high socio-economic staus, there would seem to be more who are oriented away from the town than toward it. In other words, many of the persons of whom knowledge of the town is normally expected, who are looked to for leadership in civic affairs, are precisely those persons who are not likely to assume such a role.

This raises a still further problem concerning the association of high socio-economic status and knowledge. Community knowledge may accrue to high social status because of certain advantages which are more or less independent of the relative ranking of such status in the community. On the other hand, knowledge of the community may be associated with a certain income, occupational and educational level because of the position of individuals filling such statuses in relation to the specific community power structure, prestige system, or political hierarchy.

If, as the data suggest, the person oriented away from the community has a low level of knowledge about the community, we are confronted with a problem in regard to our democratic value system. The ideal is the informed citizen, actively participating in the life of the community in which he lives. And yet if long residence, home ownership, and location of work in the community, coupled with high socio-economic status, are related to a high level of community knowledge, it would seem that there are serious obstacles in the way of obtaining such an ideal. The evidence indicates that this is a set of attributes possessed by only a relatively small proportion of the members of the community.

URBAN STRUCTURE AND SOCIAL PARTICIPATION

Morris Axelrod

Two views which have been stressed in the sociological literature have to do with the relation of urbanization to group membership. The more traditional view emphasizes the impersonality of relationships in the urban community, the wide importance of formal and secondary group association, and the decline of the kinship group. The "Chicago School" of sociology was founded on the study of the unique characteristics of the city.[1]

The newer view, while admitting this, gives informal group contacts a more important place.[2] The traditional view sees the family and the extended kin group as playing a much circumscribed role, while the second emphasizes more the changed role of the family.

The resolution of these different emphases is a critical and fundamental problem, necessary to the better understanding of community organization in particular, and social organization in general. This study did not attempt a definitive resolution of these problems but attempted rather to provide some answers to several questions bearing on the more general problem. These questions are:

1. What is the extent of participation in formal groups in the large urban community—that is, how many people participate in formal groups?
2. What is the extent to which various economic and social segments of the community are characterized by distinctive or different patterns of group participation?
3. What is the extent of participation in informal groups in the large urban community?
4. To what extent are kinship relationships important in different economic and social segments of the community?
5. In what way and to what extent is participation in formal groups related to participation in certain types of informal groups, other than the immediate family?

Reprinted from the *American Sociological Review*, Vol. 21 (February, 1956), pp. 14-18, by permission of the author and the *American Sociological Review*. (Copyright, 1956, by the American Sociological Society.)

1. For the classic expression of this view, see Louis Wirth, "Urbanism as a Way of Life," *American Journal of Sociology*, 44 (July, 1938), pp. 1-24. See also the monographic literature on Chicago published in the 1930's.

2. Some recent works which reflect this point of view include: W. F. Whyte, *Street Corner Society: The Social Structure of an Italian Slum*, Chicago: University of Chicago Press, 1943; Floyd Dotson, "Patterns of Voluntary Association Among Urban Working Families," *American Sociological Review*, 16 (October, 1951), pp. 687-93; Donald L. Foley, *Neighbors or Urbanites*, Rochester, New York: Department of Sociology, The University of Rochester; Morris Janowitz, *The Community Press in an Urban Setting*, Glencoe, Illinois: The Free Press, 1952.

This paper is a report of the data obtained in one metropolitan community which bear on these questions. The data were collected by the Detroit Area Study. Interviews were obtained from a cross-section sample representative of the Detroit Area population. The sample size was 749 and was a probability sample selected by the method known as "area sampling." The generalizability of the data to this particular community is limited by the fact that the institutional population, which includes rooming houses of ten or more, dormitories, hospitals, prisons, etc., were not included in the sample. It is estimated that these comprise less than 5 per cent of the total population.

FORMAL GROUP ASSOCIATION.[3] Nearly two-thirds (63 per cent) of the population are members of formal groups. Thus it is seen that membership in formal groups is widespread in this urban community, but far from inclusive of the whole adult population. The number of memberships is shown in Table 1. One-half of all the members belong to only one group, and three-quarters to one or two groups. Although membership is widespread, comparatively few people belong to more than one group.

Table 1—Number of Formal Group Memberships

Number of Groups	Per Cent of Population	Per Cent of Members
None	37	
One	31	50
Two	16	26
Three	8	13
Four	4	6
Five	2	3
Six or more	2	2
Total	100	100
Number of cases	749	471

Participation in formal groups may also vary in intensity. Table 2 shows how the population is distributed from nominal and inactive membership to a high degree of involvement. Among members about one-quarter had not attended any meetings during the three months preceding the study, one-third had attended rarely, and one-quarter had attended frequently. The remaining one-fifth of the members can be considered as very active in that they not only attend frequently, but hold office, are committee members, or are active in other ways.

---

3. In general, the sense in which "formal organization" is used corresponds to that of "voluntary association" in the following quotation: "The term 'voluntary association' is used in this report to denote those groups which are private (as distinguished from public or governmental bodies) and entrance into which rests on the choice of the individual (as distinguished from involuntary formations such as family, church, and nation into which the individual is born). The term 'voluntary association' is also restricted in this report to nonprofit voluntary associations (as distinguished from profit making corporations, partnerships, etc.). More specifically, then, this section deals with such groups as fraternal orders, civic and reform societies, cooperatives, trade unions, trade associations, youth associations, and recreation and leasure-time groups." [*Our Cities, Their Role in the National Economy* (June, 1937), Report of the Urbanism Committee to the National Resources Committee, Washington, D. C.: U.S. Government Printing Office, 1937, p. 24.]

The extent of participation in formal groups was found to vary for different subgroups in the population. The greatest difference occurred between groups varying in amount of education, family head's occupation and in family income. These, of course, are all highly interrelated as measures of socio-economic status apart from their independent effects.

Table 3a demonstrates that extent of involvement varies with income: higher income is associated with a greater probability of membership and higher activity. Less than one-half of those whose family income is under $3000 have formal group membership, while twice this proportion among those whose family earnings exceed $7000 are group members.

The effect of education is shown in Table 3b. Education is quite strikingly related to the extent of formal group participation. More than three-quarters of all persons with some college experience have formal group membership, while only half of those with grade school experience have formal group membership.

The relationship between formal group participation and occupation of the head of the family is shown in Table 3c. This table suggests that where the head is engaged in a white-collar occupation, the family member is somewhat more likely to belong to a formal group.

Social status as inferred from income, occupation, and education may be viewed as an index to a persons' power position in the social structure. We expect the high status person to join with others, who are in a similar position, in such organizations as will safeguard his position. In addition, high status represents a convergence of many kinds of interests arising in part from higher education, more and more varied contacts, and inter-

Table 2—Extent of Formal Group Participation

Formal Group Participation	Per Cent of Population	Per Cent of Members
Non-members		
No association	20	
Church only	17	
Total	37	
Members		
Never attends*	15	24
Attends rarely†	22	34
Attends frequently‡	14	23
Very active§	12	19
Total	63	100
Grand Total	100	100
Number of cases	749	471

* Includes members who had attended no meetings in the three month period preceding the interview.
† Includes members who reported attending one or two meetings in the three month period preceding the interview.
‡ Includes members who reported attending at least three meetings in the three month period preceding the interview.
§ Includes members who reported attending at least three meetings in the three month period preceding the interview and were additionally active in one of the following ways: holding office, having committee membership, participating outside of regular meetings on at least two occasions during the three month period.

action arising from demands of the occupational role. The factory worker at the conclusion of his day's work may dismiss his work from his mind. The professional or the executive finds the dividing line between his work and his other activities a tenuous one.

Table 3—Extent of Formal Group Participation for Selected Characteristics

	Per Cent Who Are Members	Per Cent Who Are Very Active	Number of Cases
a. Family Income			
Under $3000	42	8	106
$3000-3999	66	9	164
$4000-4999	67	14	138
$5000-5999	62	12	102
$6000-6999	65	12	77
$7000 and over	81	21	116
b. Education			
0-6 years	52	2	92
7-8	60	9	158
9-12 years	63	14	402
some college	78	19	95
c. Occupation of Family Head			
Service worker or laborer	50	19	36
Operative	40	8	107
Craftsmen, foremen, etc.	40	11	93
Clerical, sales, etc.	62	21	37
Professional, managers, and proprietors	61	11	70

Apart from these specifics which contribute and are related to status, status once achieved becomes a value which must be maintained. Exclusive clubs, rather than inclusive clubs, are instruments for maintaining this status. Higher status roles carry the obligation of participation in various kinds of community activity. Community Chest activities are almost obligatory on the part of the junior executive. Some memberships such as the country club are the conspicuous trappings of status. In this connection, Svend Riemer has observed, "The social assets of belonging to the right country club, the right church, and the right service club, and participating in charities are ignored only at the cost of economic loss."[4]

It was found that a large proportion of the whole population are members of formal organizations, although not many are active. It is not surprising this should be true for a large complex population such as we are concerned with here. The secondary groups link together the various roles necessary to maintain the routine activities of the community in meeting its daily needs. As noted earlier, in the view of traditional sociology, this was considered the main way in which a large urban community is integrated.

INFORMAL GROUP ASSOCIATION. A principal function of informal association seems to be that of creating cohesive and common values in the population. Apart from the functional integration of specialized roles into

4. *The Modern City*, New York: Prentice-Hall, Inc., 1952, p. 208.

working relationships through the specification of proper role behaviors associated with the various socio-economic roles, there are universal norms in the society which must regulate behavior. These have to do with the relations among all people and not some circumscribed segment. There are rules, standards, norms, and behaviors which all members of a given society share and that have to do with "common decency," and etiquette. An important source of such norms is the intimate informal group, such as the family and the peer group. To the extent that these assumptions are true, the question of the extent of participation in informal groups in this community is an important one.

Table 4 reports the frequency with which the general population associates with each type of informal group. More people get together

Table 4—Frequency of Association with Several Types of Informal Groups, in Percentage

Frequency of Association	Relatives	Friends	Neighbors	Co-Workers
At least once a week	49	28	29	12
A few times a month	13	19	9	8
About once a month	12	18	9	14
Less often	22	31	50	62
Not ascertained	4	4	3	4
Total	100	100	100	100
Number of cases	749	749	749	749

frequently with their relatives outside of the immediate family than they do with friends, neighbors, and co-workers. About one-half of the population report that they see these relatives at least once a week. Nearly three-quarters see relatives about once a month or more often. This is in sharp contrast to the stereotype which pictures the city dweller as devoid of kinship associations.

Although many of the functional prerequisites which previously bound members of the extended kinship group into a unity may no longer exist, the family apparently continues as a most important form of informal association. Urban man apparently does get together with his relatives more frequently than on ceremonial occasions such as christenings, marriages, and wakes.

Of the remaining types of informal association, more people report getting together with friends (other than friends among their neighbors or work associates). Nearly two-thirds of all people see their friends at least once a month, and nearly one-half get together with their neighbors at least once a month. About one-third associate with co-workers at least once a month.

Perhaps a better picture of the total amount of such informal participation is afforded by the composite of the frequency of each of these contacts as shown in Table 5. Nearly two-thirds of the whole population get together with such groups more than once a week. About one-sixth have such informal association once a week, and nearly all of the remaining one-sixth of the population do have some informal association, if not so frequent.

This very dense network of informal relationships must have an important effect in determining attitudes, in organizing actions, and supporting and sustaining norms.

Table 5—Total Frequency of Informal Group Participation

Total Association with Relatives, Friends, Neighbors and Co-Workers	Per Cent of Population
At least twice a week	30
Every 4 or 5 days	35
Once a week	16
Less often	18
Never	1
Total	100
Number of cases	749

As we have just seen, from the point of view of frequency of contact, relatives constitute the most important informal group. The rank order of the comparative importance of the types of informal groups is (1) relatives, (2) friends, (3) neighbors, (4) co-workers.

Not only does this pattern of relatives, friends, neighbors and co-workers, in that order, hold for the general population, but it is also true for almost every important segment of the population we have studied. Whether people are young or old, teachers or laborers, high or low in social status, they are more likely, with only a few exceptions, to get together frequently with their relatives outside of the immediate family than with any other type of informal group. Some examples of this are shown in Table 6.

The extended family may have lost its function as an economic producing unit in the city, but relatives continue to be an important source of companionship and mutual support, to judge from the frequency with which people in this urban population see their relatives.

It seems clear that the school of urban sociologists which has emphasized the decline of the kinship relationship has exaggerated a trend to an extreme which is inconsistent with the facts obtained here.

This consistency in pattern of association with relatives, friends, neighbors, and co-workers does not hold for the small group with exceptionally high status, high income, or some college education. Within each of the highest categories, friends tend to replace relatives as the group seen frequently by most persons. Even among these exceptional groups, however, from one-half to three-quarters get together with their relatives frequently.

One may speculate that education and sophistication give the higher status individual resources for integration which are more frequently provided by the family in the general population.

No substantiation of the view that formal association substitutes for informal association was found in this study. On the contrary, there is

Table 6—Types of Informal Groups with Which People Have Frequent Association by Selected Characteristics, in Percentages*

	Relatives	Friends	Neighbors	Co-Workers	No. of Cases
a. Social Status†					
1 (low)	60	34	37	18	104
2	64	50	48	19	108
3	62	47	37	20	97
4	74	55	28	22	111
5	65	54	37	23	87
6 (high)	58	62	41	28	106
b. Family Income					
Under $3000	52	37	37	12	106
$3000-3999	68	50	39	19	164
$4000-4999	67	48	40	22	138
$5000-5999	74	43	35	25	102
$6000-6999	64	44	29	23	77
$7000 and over	54	57	44	28	116
c. Education					
0-6 years	53	24	26	8	92
7-8 years	59	42	40	13	158
9-12 years	69	61	39	25	402
some college	50	61	37	25	95

* "Frequent association" is defined as getting together with the specified type of informal group at least a few times a month.

† The measure of "social status" used was an index constructed by Gerhard E. Lenski and Werner Landecker. Its components are education, income, occupation, and ethnic background of the head of the family. These components were weighted equally, and each individual's score was based on the percentile rank in the population of each of his component characteristics. Thus the status score is an average of the percentile ranks for each person.

some suggestion, in Table 7, that they vary directly. Although there are no sharp differences, the relationship is in a positive direction.

SUMMARY AND CONCLUSION.[5] Several of the findings which emerged from the study of one urban community:

1. A majority of the population had formal group membership. However, membership was neither markedly intensive nor extensive for most organizational members, and at least one-third of the population had no such membership.

2. Formal group membership and participation were not randomly distributed throughout the population, but were related to what are considered to be some basic and fundamental differentiating characteristics in our society.

3. In the population studied informal group association was well-nigh universal with only a small segment entirely devoid of such association.

4. Relatives emerged as the most important type of informal group association.

5. Formal and informal group participation were found to vary positively together.

Formally organized associations have unquestionably an important

5. The extent to which these findings are applicable to other metropolitan communities is limited by the fact that only one community has been studied at one point in time. The characteristics of Detroit—a large population, a history of fairly rapid population growth, a high degree of industrialization and heterogeneous population—are almost ideal-typical of the modern urban community. These data provide a benchmark from which we can observe other communities as well as this one over time.

role in the urban community. The ultimate logic of urban life might conceivably still be towards a universal and intensive membership in such groups. However, in the present scene their *direct* influence does not touch a large part of the population. The less than massive character of participation in formal organizations suggests that insofar as such organizations exercise any pervasive influence in the urban community, it may be through the links between its minority of active members and the underlying network of informal association in the community at large.

Table 7—Extent of Formal Group Association by Extent of Informal Group Association, in Percentages

| | NUMBER OF INFORMAL CONTACTS IN TWO MONTH PERIOD | | | |
	0-4	5-12	13-19	20 and Over
Non-members	56	41	32	32
Members	44	59	68	68
Total	100	100	100	100
Number of cases	71	229	225	224

PARTICIPATION OF MIGRANTS
IN URBAN STRUCTURES

Basil G. Zimmer

Historically cities have been dependent upon migration for growth or even maintenance of size. Important as migration is to the city, very little is known concerning the behavior of migrants in these centers. It has long been known that cities are made up of migrants, but just what this means to the city is as yet relatively unexplored. Most of the work in the area of migration to date has been concerned with the volume and direction of movement, reasons for movement, and the demographic characteristics of the persons engaged in the movement. From these kinds of data the significance of migration to the receiving communities has been inferred.

There is a great deal of conjectural literature concerning the social implications of migration, but the empirical studies attempting to measure some of the implications, as far as specific types of behavior are concerned, are limited. Generally, those available have been concerned with very select groups.[1]

The only type of behavior which has received systematic analysis in relation to migration status is occupational role both before and after migration. Perhaps the reason for this is that migration studies have been, for the most part, limited to census materials.

Significant as these studies have been, it appears to the writer that a fruitful area for research, in order better to understand both the city and the consequences of migration, is to measure selected types of behavior in the urban community of destination in relation to migrant status. This is the problem of the present study. Specifically, we will test whether migrants to an urban center, considered as a group, ever become participants in the activities of the community to the same extent as the non-migrant natives, and if so, how long a period of time is required. Further, we will test whether specific types of migrants enter the formal activities of the community more rapidly than other types of migrants. It is expected that migrants coming from an environment culturally similar to the present

Reprinted from the *American Sociological Review*, Vol. 20, (April, 1955), pp. 218-224, by permission of the author and the *American Sociological Review*. (Copyright, 1955, by the American Sociological Society.)

1. Louis Killian, "Southern White Laborers in Chicago's West Side" (unpublished Ph.D. dissertation, University of Chicago, 1949). Grace G. Leybourne, "Urban Adjustment of Migrants from the Southern Appalachian Plateaus," *Social Forces*, XVI (December, 1937), pp. 238-246.

community will participate more rapidly than persons coming from dissimilar environments.[2]

We will test the following hypotheses:

Hypothesis I. Migrants differ from the natives in level of participation but they become more similar to the natives in their behavior the longer they live in the community.[3]

Hypothesis II. Urban migrants tend to enter the activities of the community more rapidly than farm migrants.[4]

The data on which this investigation is based were gathered by the personal interview survey method during the spring and early summer of 1951. The interviews were obtained from the occupants of a random sample of dwelling units in a midwestern community with a population of nearly 20,000. The data presented here are limited to married males. Thus, marital status and sex are automatically controlled.

Three different types of activity in the community are studied: membership in formal organizations,[5] officership in organizations, and registration to vote. The analysis of participation[6] in each type of behavior is a separate test of the general hypotheses. If the hypotheses are valid they should be supported for each type of behavior studied.

Prior researchers have investigated these types of behavior but most studies have emphasized that participation varies by demographic characteristics such as age, sex, education, and occupation.[7] The importance of these variables is already known; the present study will employ these as controls. Thus, the significance of migrant status itself can be demonstrated.

MEMBERSHIP IN FORMAL ORGANIZATIONS. Membership in formal organizations tends to increase directly with length of time in the community within age, occupational and educational categories, as is shown in Table 1. Migrants, as a group, within each control category, have a lower participation rate than the natives, but the rate among the migrants becomes more similar to the natives the longer the former reside in the community.

---

2. This is based on the notion that even though migration itself may limit behavior, previous training to live in an urban setting will facilitate participation in the urban community, whereas, the lack of such training or experience will retard participation.

3. Natives include those who have lived in the community since birth, and those who entered the community before attaining ten years of age and have lived in the community continuously since that time.

4. Migrants are classified according to type of community of birth.

5. Formal organizations refer generally to those groups which are ordinarily thought of as clubs and societies by the people in the community. However, church organizations, such as missionary societies, usher clubs, choir, and the like, have not been included. Although not reported here these latter have been analyzed separately.

6. Participation means only that persons belong to any organization, holds or has held an officership position, or is registered to vote. It does not measure intensity of activity.

7. Mirra Komarovsky, "The Voluntary Associations of Urban Dwellers," *American Sociological Review,* II (December, 1946), pp. 468-98. Herbert Goldhamer, "Some Factors Affecting Participation in Voluntary Associations" (unpublished Ph.D. Dissertation, University of Chicago, 1943). William C. Mather, "Income and Social Participation," *American Sociological Review,* VI (June, 1941), pp. 380-84.

Within each subgroup the lowest participation rate is found among migrants in the community less than two years, whereas, migrants who have been in the community twenty years or more have the highest participation. Among the white-collar workers and the college-trained, migrants who have been in the community over twenty years have a participation rate higher than the natives. In all other subgroups, the natives have the highest membership rate.

Table 1—Per Cent Belonging to Formal Organizations Within Age, Occupational, and Educational Categories, by Length of Time in Community

Length of Time in Community (Years)	AGE Under 40 Yrs.	AGE 40 Yrs. Plus	OCCUPATION WC	OCCUPATION MW	EDUCATION GS	EDUCATION HS	EDUCATION Col
Less than 2	25*	22	33	16	5	10	47
2-5	37	36	53	22	15	37	54
6-10	45	31	46	35	18	42	58
11-19	50	40	67	30	29	49	60
20 and over	..†	51	73	37	35	47	92
Natives	56	54	63	48	33‡	50	74
Total	41	42	56	32	24	41	61

* The complement of this percentage would be the percentage of those who do not belong.
† Less than 10 cases.
‡ Less than 20 cases.

Within age groups we note that, among the younger persons, migrants approximate the level of participation of the natives after ten years of residence, whereas in the older age group this does not occur until migrants have been in the community for twenty years or more. Apparently younger persons are less affected by migration than older persons.[8]

Among white-collar workers the difference between migrants and natives in membership also tends to disappear after ten years of residence. At this point white-collar migrants seem to participate at about the same rate as the natives, or even at higher rates. However, among the manual workers, migrants never do attain the level of participation of the natives at the same occupational level. It may be that there is a standardized urban culture shared by white-collar workers which soon transcends the limiting influence of migration. This is to say that, in preparing for or in the pursuit of white collar work, persons learn at the same time an urban way of life, which is carried with them in their migration. The urban culture makes for a more rapid adjustment in the new community. Such a culture is not found among manual workers. Thus it takes the manual worker longer to become similar to the native in participation. In each length of time in the community category white-collar workers have a much higher membership rate than manual workers. The importance of

8. From these data differences by age are not evident. However, a more detailed breakdown by age shows the middle age groups to have the highest participation, whereas the rate is lower for the younger and older migrants. A similar pattern was observed in a preliminary report issued by the Detroit Area Study.

occupational status is strikingly evident when we note that white-collar workers in the community from two to five years, have a higher membership rate than native manual workers.

Within each educational group participation increases consistently with length of time in the community; however, marked differences by education are found. The lowest membership rate, only 5 per cent, is found among grade school persons with less than two years of residence in the community. At the college level nearly half are members. The importance of education is also strikingly evident by the fact that college migrants who have lived in the community less than two years have a membership rate which is much higher than the natives in the grade-school group and is nearly equal to the natives at the high-school level.

At each educational level it takes at least ten years or more before migrants approximate the natives of equal education in level of participation. Generally, after ten years of residence, migrants become quite similar to the natives, however it seems that, at the lower levels of education, migrants become similar to the natives of equal education sooner than at the college level. It may be that college persons join more exclusive groups which are more difficult to enter. Such groups are likely to offer more restrictions to migrants than other types of formal organizations.

At any rate Hypothesis I is supported by the data. The length of time required to become active in the community varies according to the personal characteristics possessed by the migrants. High status facilitates participation. However, regardless of status, it takes migrants ten years or more to become integrated in this aspect of the organized structure of the community.

The rate of entering formal organizations varies by migrant type as demonstrated in Table 2. However, for each migrant type, membership increases with length of time in the community. Farm migrants have the slowest entrance rate, but contrary to expectations urban migrants do not enter more rapidly than rural nonfarm migrants. Nevertheless, they do exceed them in memberships after the first two years. Persons from rural nonfarm areas tend to enter the organizations sooner than those from urban areas, but after a time in the present community the urban born have a higher membership rate than is found among the rural nonfarm

Table 2—Per Cent Belonging to Formal Organizations, by Length of Time in Community, by Migrant Type

| Length of Time in Community (Years) | TYPE OF MIGRANT | | | | | |
| | FARM | | RURAL NONFARM | | URBAN | |
	Per Cent	Number	Per Cent	Number	Per Cent	Number
Less than 2	14	(29)	41	(17)	26	(39)
2-5	29	(56)	38	(29)	43	(60)
6-10	29	(56)	39	(23)	47	(62)
11-19	39	(49)	53	(17)	41	(44)
20 and over	48	(54)	52	(25)	57	(35)
Total	33	(244)	44	(111)	43	(240)

migrants. Thus, eventually urban migrants attain the highest participation rate.

The high participation on the part of rural nonfarm migrants as a group was not expected according to our cultural similarity hypothesis. It may be that the rural nonfarm category does not properly "fit" on a rural-urban continuum since it is a recognizable ambiguous category. For this reason the emphasis of our discussion is centered on the differences between urban and farm migrants. These two categories do clearly represent distinctly different types of communities.

A second possible explanation for this finding is that, insofar as rural nonfarm areas are small villages, it may be that formal organizations play a more important role in such communities than in larger urban areas. These organizations may be quite accessible to all members of the community in that sharp status differences on which to select members may be lacking or at least quite limited. Thus, living in rural nonfarm areas may expose persons to formal organizations even more so than living in the city. It is suggested that the diversity of such groups may be rather limited in small villages as compared to urban centers, but the actual level of participation may be more frequent in the former. Thus, rural nonfarm migrants may have learned to participate in such groups more so than other types of migrant. It may be that their participation rate decreases proportionately because of migration, but they continue to have a higher level of participation than other types of migrant. Perhaps an analysis of membership before and after their migration would show that their high participation rate in the present community is due to the fact that they have transferred their memberships to local chapters of national organizations to which they had previously belonged. One of the important functions of national organizations may be to cushion the limiting effects of migration.

Although membership increases steadily for the farm migrants by length of time in the community, these never do reach the level of participation of the natives. Also, we note that no matter how long farm migrants have been in the community, they have a lower participation rate than do other types of migrant who have lived in the community the same length of time.

For memberships in formal organizations, Hypothesis II is also supported by these data. Farm migrants enter this activity less rapidly than rural nonfarm or urban migrants. Here also, as within subgroups, we find that, regardless of type, it takes at least ten years or more for migrants to become similar to the natives in level of participation. Farm migrants, however, never do attain the level of participation of the natives.[9] We will now turn to a different type of behavior in order to test further the same hypotheses.

---

9. When migrants are classified according to last place of residence the participation rate of farm migrants is lower than is found according to the place of birth criterion.

OFFICERSHIP. The extent to which migrants may obtain officership positions is dependent upon their rate of membership in the organizations of the community. For this reason our discussion on officership is limited only to those persons who belong to an organization in the community and are thus exposed to officership positions.[10] Officership refers to any specially recognized position in the group.

The participation rate in the officership class increases directly by length of time in the community within each control category. These data are presented in Table 3. As in formal organizations, those who have been

Table 3—Per Cent in Officership Class Within Age, Occupational, and Educational Categories, by Length of Time in Community

| Length of Time in Community (Years) | AGE | | OCCUPATION | | EDUCATION | | |
	Under 40 Yrs.	40 Yrs. Plus	WC	MW	GS	HS	Col
Less than 2	23	8†	33	10	8†	..‡	45
2-5	23	26	37	13	9	29	31
6-10	37	31	53	27	16	36	58
11-19	37	35	47	30	31	33	50
20 and over	..*	37	58	24	19	36	64
Natives	31	56	49	33	17†	42	48
Total	30	34	46	24	18	32	48

* Less than 10 cases.
† Less than 20 cases.
‡ None in the officership group.

in the community less than two years have the lowest proportion in the officership group, whereas those who have lived in the community twenty years and over have the highest percentage. Even though there tends to be a steady increase in the proportion who are in the officership group by length of time in the community, within age groupings, the main difference among the younger persons is found between those who have lived in the community five years or less and those who have lived in the community for more than five years. However, among the older people the migrants never do reach the natives in the proportion who are in the officership class. Thus, for this category, the effects of migration are never overcome. Differences in the officership rate are also found by age. Older persons, as a group, have a higher proportion in the officership class than do younger persons.

When we control for occupation it is only during the first five years that migrants are distinct by their low participation. Migrant white-collar workers, after living in the community more than five years, have a higher percentage in the officership class than the natives of equal status. However, among the manual workers, as among the older people, migrants never do reach the natives in level of participation, but the differences are

10. All persons without an affiliation have been dropped from the sample for this discussion. Included here are members of formal organizations, church organizations, and of the union. Therefore, the differences reported are not due to differential membership by length of time in the community.

not marked after the first five years. Thus, among manual workers, it seems that during the second five years in the community the officership rate is more than double the rate for the first five years. Thereafter, even though the proportion in the officership class increases, the differences are slight. Marked differences by occupation are found. High-status migrants enter officership positions more rapidly than low-status workers. For example, white-collar migrants, in the community less than two years, have an officership rate equal to the natives in the manual worker group. White-collar workers, as a group, have an officership rate double that of the manual workers.

Similarly, within each educational level, migrants approximate the natives in the proportion who are in the officership class after five years of residence. Again we find that after long residence migrants are likely to have a higher participation rate than the natives. In other words, the limiting influences of migration are lost. Marked differences are found by education. The college trained migrants enter officership positions much more rapidly than migrants at the lower levels of education. Again we observe that the possession of high status characteristics facilitates adjustment. For this type of behavior also Hypothesis I is supported by the data.

Within each migrant type (Table 4) the proportion in the officership class also tends to increase with length of time in the community. Farm migrants, however, take longer to enter the officership roles than do the other types of migrant. Farm migrants have a particularly low participa-

Table 4—Per Cent in Officership Class, by Length of Time in Community, by Migrant Type

| Length of Time in Community (Years) | TYPE OF MIGRANT | | | | | |
| | FARM | | RURAL NONFARM | | URBAN | |
	Per Cent	Number	Per Cent	Number	Per Cent	Number
Less than 2	12	(17)	28	(14)	20	(20)
2-5	18	(40)	30	(20)	32	(41)
6-10	20	(41)	29	(17)	44	(52)
11-19	25	(40)	31	(13)	43	(35)
20 and over	42	(38)	32	(22)	35	(29)
Total	24	(176)	30	(86)	37	(177)

tion rate during the early years in the community. Among the farm migrants we note a steady increase in the proportion in the officership group by length of time in the community, whereas the proportion of the other migrants in the officership class increases only during the first five years in the community, then begins to level off and remains relatively constant. Apparently rural nonfarm and urban migrants attain their normal participation rate in about five years, whereas, farm migrants are continually adjusting.

Thus, Hypothesis II is again found to be supported by the data in that urban migrants tend to make a more rapid adjustment than other migrants. The effects of migration appear to be temporary, for migrants soon approximate the native population in level of participation and in many instances the migrants are even more active than the nonmigrant natives. A third test of the hypotheses is presented below in terms of registration to vote.

REGISTRATION TO VOTE. Insofar as registration to vote is a measure of the level of participation in the political affairs in the community, the data presented here do not indicate that migration cuts a person off from participation. On the contrary, after living in the community for a certain length of time, migrants become as active, and in some cases even more active, than the native population in terms of the proportion who are registered. It is evident from the data in table 5, that only those who have

Table 5—Per Cent Registered to Vote Within Age, Occupational, and Educational Categories by Length of Time in Community

| Length of Time in Community (Years) | AGE | | OCCUPATION | | EDUCATION | | |
	Under 40 Yrs.	40 Yrs. Plus	WC	MW	GS	HS	Col
Less than 2	18	44	24	25	20	28	25
2-5	63	77	74	63	51	77	70
6-10	82	97	87	89	89	88	94
11-19	92	93	..†	89	90	91	..†
20 and over	..*	94	98	91	93	95	96
Natives	84	89	89	83	86‡	84	93
Total	66	88	79	77	75	81	76

* Less than 10 cases.
† All registered.
‡ Less than 20 cases.

been in the community less than five years have a lower proportion registered to vote than do the natives.[11] Thus, migration has the effect of decreasing participation in the political life of the community, but this is only temporary. Registration to vote varies also by age. Older persons are more likely to be registered than younger persons.

Within each occupational and educational category a similar pattern is found. After five or more years in the community the migrants become very similar to the natives of equal status and even exceed the natives in the proportion who are registered voters. No consistent difference in the proportion registered is found by occupational or educational status.

Thus, in terms of this type of behavior also, Hypothesis I is supported by the data. After a period of adjustment, migrants as a group, tend to become quite similar to the natives.

The rate of entering the formal political activities of the community varies by type of migrant. Our data[12] show that it takes the farm and the rural nonfarm migrants ten years or more in the community before they equal or exceed the natives in proportion registered, whereas, the urban migrants exceed the natives after they have lived in the community for

11. The same pattern of difference is found when those who have not yet established legal residence are dropped from the sample.

12. Due to space limitations these data are not presented here, but are available upon request to the writer.

only five years or more. After ten years in the community the migrant types can no longer be clearly distinguished from each other in the proportion registered, and in most cases migrants have a higher proportion registered than do the natives. Here again, Hypothesis II is supported by our data.

SUMMARY. These data have shown that: (1) migrants differ from the natives in level of participation, but they become more similar to the natives in their behavior the longer they live in the community, and (2) urban migrants tend to enter the activities of the community more rapidly than farm migrants.

On the basis of a case study of a single community, it seems that migration does limit participation in community activities, but the initial limiting influences of migration are only temporary for these types of behavior, at least in that, with time, migrants either equal or exceed the natives in level of participation. When migrants first enter the new community they are much less active in the formal structure than are the natives, but with time their participation rate increases. The adjustment takes at least five years, however, and in some types of behavior migrants possessing low-status characteristics never do attain the same level of participation as the natives. The possession of high-status personal characteristics facilitates the adjustment.

Farm migrants have the slowest rate of entering. They seem to be particularly limited during the first five years or so in the community. However, the longer they live in the community, the higher their rate of participation. All migrant types eventually become similar to the natives in their behavior.

9

THE CITY AS AN ARTIFACT

A full understanding of the city requires a knowledge of how the concerted efforts of men make and remake cities. The city is a product of processes of growth and change. Some of these processes involve deliberate human endeavor to alter the structure and processes of cities.

No one has been able to assess accurately the degree to which urban structure and organization is the unintended or unanticipated result of growth and change processes as compared with the extent to which it is contrived by deliberate social acts. Social scientists frequently assume that natural social processes produce urban structure and organization to the degree that they show similarities in structure and organization which cannot be traced to *deliberate group activity toward the specific goal of planned change*. This statement does not justify a conclusion, however, that systematic relationships between certain processes and certain elements of urban structure or organization have been scientifically demonstrated. The scientific investigation of urban phenomena is too imprecise and our knowledge of relationships too incomplete to warrant this conclusion.

The organized activity of persons directed toward the isolation of socially acceptable group goals and the setting up of means for implementing these goals is called *planning*. Planning, in this sense, may occur with or without the sanctions of the governing bodies of a collectivity. The planned direction of urban growth and change is not a recent phenomenon, although the social movement to undertake city planning in a specialized administrative structure of municipal governments is of fairly recent origin.

Planning can be thought of as a process of social change. The process of social planning involves a number of stages where decisions are made or actions are taken. These stages now are briefly described. Planning involves, first, a choice among ends to select the specific goals which the group desires to implement. It requires, therefore, the isolation and description of values which can direct the group activity. The choice among values is not a task, in and of itself, for the social scientist, as science is not a sufficient basis for making value decisions in planning. The social scientist, though, can assist planners by scientifically ascertaining facts such as the values which groups hold, the intensity with which they hold them, their basis of value choice, and so on. The second planning step is to establish a priority among the desired goals. These decisions likewise are not the task of the social scientist, although they can aid planners by answering questions such as, What are the priorities which publics place on goals? What consequences can be expected to follow from particular goal priority systems? and What is the relationship of the priorities to the means of implementation?

The selection of means to implement goals and an assessment of their effectiveness in achieving the goals is the third major planning task. Here the sociologist makes a potentially large contribution to planning by providing scientific knowledge of the relationship of particular means to the implementation of given ends. This knowledge must be of a predictive order, since the planning process involves taking action on the basis of choices for which there are predicted consequences. The fourth stage in the planning process is the organization of action to insure that the plan is implemented. Urban planning agencies seldom have either the authority or the organizational mechanisms to carry out the planning actions. They may plan and co-ordinate these actions, however. Sociologists aid the planner in this phase by providing factual knowledge on such questions as the selection of techniques of manipulating groups toward the chosen ends, the power structure of the community, and the assessment of group conflicts and their resolution. All processes are dynamic. As the actions of the community are taken, both with and without reference to plans, the planning process requires an assessment of the results of planned action. The sociologist may aid the planner in this fifth step of assessment by isolating the unanticipated consequences of planning activities, investigating the reasons for planning successes and failures, and by analyzing the planning process itself. The final step in the planning process is more or less a recapitulation of previous ones. There is a revision of group goals, new selection of means, and so on, as the result of the assessment of progress toward planned group goals.

The planning process also can be viewed as a set of value decisions, the prediction of consequences from planning actions, and the carrying out of these actions. At least three levels of value decisions are involved in the planning process: the decisions as to what kind of urban community is wanted; decisions as to whether this kind of community is possible, given the kind of resources available; and decisions as to how best to go about getting this kind of community. An effective planning program must be based on valid relationships from which predictions can be made. The factual sociological information includes knowledge of the structure and problems of the urbanized society, the directions in which social forces are tending, the relationship of means to ends and of how planning acts may be realized in the community. The limitations of sociological knowledge at the present time render difficult the prediction of consequences of planning acts. The studies sociologists make for individual cities often prove useful to the planning organizations in those cities, however, and there is a growing body of basic knowledge of cities from which valid predictions can be made, particularly in urban ecology. Perhaps a major failure of city planning has been the failure of planning agencies actually to achieve the implementation of their plans. No plan would seem complete without a set of organizational plans for achieving the planning ends. To make plans effectively to reach the planning ends is to make possible, too, a more realistic assessment of the successes and failures of the plan.

Planning often is the consequence of situations or conditions which the inhabitants or publics of urban centers define as problems requiring amelioration. Such problems as those outlined in the report of the National Resources Committee, presented in this section, delimit the planning area. Urban planning can be for a neighborhood, a local community, the municipal city, a metropolitan region, or an urbanized nation. But the extent of the planning area varies with the particular problem. Thus, planning a health control program usually requires a different planning area from that of a housing program. A major concern of the planner, then, is to delimit his planning scope in terms of the types of problems he wishes to plan for.

Planning requires, among other things, that the limits within which the corporate activity may and does take place is known. It requires, therefore, an isolation of the major trends in urban society, the discovery of how these trends may be effectively altered, and of how to plan in accord with them. In the previous sections and in the selection from the National Resources

Committee report on problems confronting city dwellers, these trends are pointed up.

The primary concern in this section is with the question as to how the sociologist of city life may make significant contributions to effective planning. A number of studies which show the contributions of sociologists to effective planning programs therefore are presented.

One such planning problem is the examination of the empirical relationship between the goal selected and a choice among means. Planners, for example, have been concerned with a general question of determining the optimum size of cities, given certain planning goals they may seek, such as a healthy population and a low crime and delinquency rate. Duncan's research paper makes an important contribution to understanding this problem of optimum city size by investigating the empirical relationship between variation in city size and variation in the situation which is positively or negatively valued. The empirical relationships warrant the inference that it probably is meaningless for planners to seek a unique optimum city size. This is so for two reasons: (1) optimum size varies considerably among the value criteria of planners and, (2) there is no known way to objectively weight or balance them to yield an unequivocal figure for *the* optimum population of a city. Duncan's paper shows, at the same time, that while the achievement of a planned size should make certain goals possible, it should also necessitate the sacrifice of others.

The kinds of problems for which cities must plan and the planned goals they wish to implement generally require a planning area of considerable size—at least the equivalent of what is called the standard metropolitan area or the primary metropolitan area. The implementation of planning goals generally requires, too, the authority and procedures of governmental bodies in addition to support and action from private organizations. Most municipalities with 25,000 or more inhabitants in the United States in fact have planning bodies as part of the administrative structure of the city government There frequently is a discontinuity between these two areas so that the authority of a single government and the means it has to implement the decisions of the planning body is not coterminous with the effective or natural planning area. Special problems in planning often arise as a result of this discontinuity. The functional integration of an urban area has profound effects on the services which the government of an urban area provides for its inhabitants. Many of the services for the population of a metropolitan area are provided by the government of the central city. The situation therefore arises that a large number of users of the service are neither involved in decisions about the service nor in financial support of it through municipal government. Hawley's paper in this Section shows how the development and clarification of planning policy and objectives on this question may be influenced by the research findings of sociologists. The empirical data in his paper show that the municipal costs of central cities in the United States vary directly with the sizes of their satellite populations. Several examples of how this finding can be applied in the development of planning policy and objectives are given. One implication of the specific findings on cost, for instance, is that a single taxing and administrative agency would apparently make for a more equitable distribution of costs and a more adequate complement of services for the entire metropolitan area. Discussions of the wisdom of policies of annexation to the central city should profit from Hawley's finding that area size as such has an almost negligible association with government costs while population and housing densities show a more substantial relationship with costs.

A major controversy among city planners in recent years surrounds the problem of whether and how to plan neighborhood unit organization in metropolitan cities. Some planners argue for a planned city comprised of neighborhood units which integrate inhabitants into a local life. Others challenge this conception of the urban residential area and tend to argue for less localistic residential units. The controversy, of course, rests in part on the positive or negative valuations which are attached to particular residential conditions called neighborhood. It can be analyzed to a degree, however, in terms of more factual descriptions of neighborhood structure both within and among communities which vary in size, and by relating types of neighborhood structure to other aspects of community structure, as, for instance, segregation patterns. Dewey's first paper in this section tries to show how sociologists may contribute to a clarification of the neighborhood unit controversy. His paper also provides a critical discussion of needed sociological research on the zone of transition in growing cities.

The paper by McKay shows how the neighborhood furnishes the setting in which the child is socialized either for conventional or for delinquent behavior. By critical analysis, McKay shows that recreation is not a means of preventing delinquency in cities and develops the idea that delinquency prevention programs must be developed on a neighborhood basis, involving action programs by the residents of a neighborhood. The Institute for Juvenile Research in Chicago, Illinois actually has developed such neighborhood action programs under the general program of the Chicago Area Projects.

The growth of the city since the development of modern means of transportation has led to a discontinuous expansion of population into the unincorporated areas surrounding the built-up city. This expansion of the population into suburban areas and fringe settlements occasions problems for the metropolitan area planner. The paper by Firey in this section shows how a successful land use planning program for the rural-urban fringe must be designed in terms of its essential nature—that it is a marginal land use area in which the only order and stability that can ever exist must come from the imposition of a comprehensive planned development. The delineation of the major ecological characteristics of the fringe area provides a more consistent and rational basis for the development of these areas. Dewey's second paper shows how planners may utilize scientific procedures to learn more about the goals people have in choosing a residential location at the fringe of a city. The investigation of reasons persons gave for movement to the peripheral areas of Milwaukee County, Wisconsin, and their attitudes toward their present residence and area are reported. If the reasons given by these peripheral inhabitants hold for other urban fringe residents, the results of the investigation suggest that where one of the planning goals is to retard movement from the central city to the periphery, the movement can be decreased somewhat by replanning the deteriorating areas of the city to meet the goals of people who move to the fringes.

THE PROBLEMS OF URBAN AMERICA

National Resources Committee

In the wake of the process of urbanization, a series of maladjustments have bobbed up which militate against the attainment of a satisfactory urban life. The difficulties now confronting the urban community not only prevent the city from making the maximum contribution to our national economy, but in some instances they actually menace urban existence.

POVERTY AND INEQUALITY. Poverty stalks the city streets in good times and bad. In spite of the increasing standard of living of the city worker, there still exists a large number of individuals and families who are without the essentials necessary to sustain life on even a minimum standard.

While poverty is not exclusively an urban phenomenon, since privation is widespread among the farm population and especially the tenant farmers and share croppers, the city is, nevertheless, the home of the most drastic inequalities in wealth and income. In contrast to their rich fellow citizens, the poor are poorer in the city than they are elsewhere.

It is not merely the existence of large numbers of poor and underprivileged families, nor the philosophic implications of economic inequality, which constitutes a basic problem of urban life. An interdependent, mass production economy rests upon mass purchasing power. Widespread poverty, therefore, threatens the stability and even the survival of such an economy and the society based upon it. Extreme concentration of wealth, on the other hand, leads to personal and corporate oversaving and overexpansion, and is regarded as an important factor in the periodic dislocation of our national economy. The Nation must look to the abolition of poverty and to the reduction of glaring inequalities in wealth and income, because in that direction lie the beginnings of the essential reforms of our economic system and the improvement of urban life.

INSECURITY AND UNEMPLOYMENT. Poverty and inequality in the city, though relieved by economic opportunities of various kinds in good times, are accentuated by the insecurities and uncertainties which in some measure characterize the problem of the breadwinner at all times, particularly in times of depression. The causes of our economic cycles may be Nation-wide or even international, but it is the city, as the nerve center of the country's

Reprinted from *Our Cities: Their Role in the National Economy,* published by the National Resources Committee, Washington, D.C., United States Government Printing Office, 1937, pp. 55-70.

commerce and industry, that is most immediately affected. The stock market crashes, the banking house calls in its loans, the factory cuts production and wages, business offices slash their overhead, the city workers lose their jobs, interest payments on home and farm are defaulted, the banks fail, purchases are curtailed, the retailer's business slumps, orders cease, the factory stops production, and the vicious circle is complete. The depression hits hard and suddenly in the city, which is precisely the spot where lives the mass of people, both factory and white collared workers, who are dependent on their jobs and possess little beyond their ability to work. They have few or no reserves to fall back on in case of unemployment. In fact, they do not have even a meager food supply which, on the farm at least, helps to sustain life.

VULNERABILITY OF CITY LIFE. The tenuousness of the urban economy, which expresses itself particularly in the rapid and cumulative effects of depressions, is actually a characteristic that is basic to urban life generally. On the technological side, for example, it is apparent that the city is a delicate mechanism which can be thrown out of gear and demoralized at a number of vulnerable points.

How hazardous a place the city can be is indicated by events in time of epidemic, storm, accident, conflagration, war, internal strife, sabotage, strike, or flood. Death and disaster wrought by the recent floods in the Ohio and Mississippi Valleys and the suspension of vital municipal services in the cities, large and small, illustrate in a dramatic way what happens when the mechanism of public services is disrupted. Even in normal times, the breakdown of an electric power station or a transmission line may paralyze the city. A subway accident leaves hundreds of thousands stranded. The bursting of an important water main leaves a whole section of the city without water and exposes it to the hazards of conflagration. The fact that these and other difficulties do not arise more often is a tribute to the smooth functioning of our technology, but when they do happen the effects are swift and serious.

Recognizing this vulnerability of the city and foreseeing the havoc that may be and actually is being wrought by military attacks on cities, European authorities are making provisions for the required emergency facilities and administrative machinery, and are equipping and preparing the cities and their inhabitants for such eventualities. Bomb-proof cellars, gas masks, mock air raids, warning sirens, rescue squads, and the even more fundamental steps drastically of replanning the cities, illustrate the frantic efforts to lessen the extreme vulnerability of the city in case of war.

DEPENDENCY. Insecurity of the urban worker, his lack of reserve resources, and the impersonality and mobility of urban life combine to make the problems of dependency more acute and more widespread in the cities than in rural areas. A much greater proportion of the urban population was forced on the relief rolls during the depression than was the case in rural areas. One-fifth of all the employable persons on relief in 1935 were located in the 10 largest cities and consisted mainly of unskilled workmen. The need for the amelioration and prevention of distress brought forth in the cities organized agencies supported by private funds, but, as is well known, these found themselves unable to cope with the task during the recent depression when dependency assumed extraordinary proportions. Experience of the past few years has also shown that urban local government and State governments were financially unable and otherwise unprepared to take over the task from the hard-pressed private relief agencies and to meet the tremendously increased problem of dependence. It remained for the Federal Government to come to the rescue of the States and urban communities in meeting the problems of dependency and relief.

Municipal welfare activities are lacking in uniformity because of the varying distribution of functions among county and city authorities. Together with the counties and States, the cities have assumed greater responsibilities during the recent depression, and welfare organization in general is in a state of transition from an emergency to a permanent basis.

The important problems in caring for dependency include those of finance, the inability of the less wealthy communities and regions to bear the cost of local needs, the constitutional or statutory limitations on taxation, regional organization through city and county collaboration, interstate cooperation in the planning of legislation and administration, adequate standards of administration and professional personnel, and closer Federal-city cooperation.

RACIAL HETEROGENEITY. Racially and from the standpoint of national origin the urban population of America is more heterogeneous than in cities of other countries. Foreign-born parents and their children constituted in 1890, 1910, and 1930, 73.0 percent, 74.3 percent, and 63.7 percent, respectively, of the populations of cities of over 1,000,000. The proportion of foreign stock was smaller in the smaller cities. The proportion of Negroes is increasing rapidly in cities of over 250,000, though it is declining in the smaller cities and in the rural districts. Heterogeneity of origin also results in heterogeneity of language and customs, and accounts for the disunity of American urban culture and for some of the conflicts and difficulties in regulating and stabilizing behavior.

With the curtailment of immigration such distinctions may become less marked. But in any case, we are very far from a uniform national type even if this should appear to be desirable.

FAMILY AND COMMUNITY DISORGANIZATION. Racial heterogeneity contributes in some measure to family misunderstanding and disruption, particularly between the Americanized child attracted by the variegated outlets of urban existence and parents with an unassimilated outlook and culture. Forces are at work which make divorce and family desertion more prevalent in the city than on the farm. Anonymity of human relations in the city further contributes to the weakening of family and community ties. In the face of these disintegrating forces there is urgent need and great opportunity for finding a new anchorage for the urban dweller who now lives in a social void. This is a task for the church, the voluntary association, and other community institutions.

EDUCATION. Although educational facilities are widely developed in American cities, the problems of making a living preclude a large proportion of the urban population from taking advantage of them. Children and minors have opportunity for free education even when they have passed the compulsory school age, but they are often barred from such opportunity because they must too frequently supplement the family income by going to work.

Classes for adults have also been made available, but mass adult education has until recently not made much progress. Designed primarily to serve immigrants, public-school facilities for adults have only lately begun to catch up with the apparent demand for a more mature program of adult education. Public facilities for adult education, except for the emergency educational program, are still limited primarily to the night schools. The proper use of the public forum and of the radio for adult education and mass enlightenment in America promises to become one of the outstanding problems in this field.

DANGERS TO PUBLIC HEALTH. The provision of adequate public-health services is a significant problem of urban life. While urban morbidity and mortality rates in such fields as infants' diseases and tuberculosis compare favorably with the rural rates, in blighted areas and among low-income groups in the city the rates are higher than they would be with adequate, modern, public-health services.

The difficulties of urban public-health regulation are not merely financial, but they involve such irrational and incongruous factors as group selfishness and prudishness. Only under a fearless program recently launched with Federal aid have we deigned to admit the vast prevalence of syphilis and to attack it on a national scale with direct cooperation between the Public Health Service and the cities. It should be possible to restrict within much narrower bounds the common cold so easily transmitted in an urban environment, and its associated diseases of influenza and pneumonia.

DIRT, SMOKE, AND WASTE. Inimical also to the public health are the polluting effects of industrial waste and urban waste in general. In spite of valiant efforts to enforce smoke abatement ordinances, the belching chimneys of factories, office buildings, and apartment houses fill the air with smoke injurious to the respiratory organs, and are inducing neo-modern man to take refuge in air-conditioned buildings. Soot and grime settle on buildings, dirt blackens the streets, and dust seeps into the homes. Garbage, considering the size of the task, is generally well disposed of, but it sometimes piles up in alleys and in outlying dumps, with extremely noxious if not unhealthful consequences. One or a few misplaced industries emitting obnoxious odors at times pollute the air of large sections of the city. Worse still, communities and industries often dump their wastes untreated into the source of the water supply where regulation and legal powers are not adequate to prevent this, or where conflicting State, county, and city boundaries encourage it, with the result that drinking water must be so highly treated with purifying agents as to be nearly unpalatable. The usefulness of many bodies of water is destroyed for much needed recreational purposes as a result of pollution.

NOISE AND STRAIN. The large city and especially its central business district is so characteristically a place of noise that a sudden wave of silence frequently proves to be oppressive to the urbanite for he is accustomed to distracting sounds of all kinds. Screeching brakes, screaming trolley cars, rumbling trucks, rasping auto horns, barking street vendors, shouting newsboys, scolding traffic whistles, rumbling elevated trains, rapping pneumatic hammers, open cut-outs, and now advertising sound trucks and aircraft with radio amplifiers, when added together, constitute a general din for which it would be difficult to find a precedent in the history of cities.

With the development of techniques for measuring the intensity of city noise, and with the experiments now conducted through municipal regulation and informal antinoise campaigns, as in New York City, urban noise and the consequent nerve-racking strain of urban life promise to be recognized in the near future by the American city as problems calling for a serious attack.

INSANITY AND SUICIDE. There is some evidence of a higher rate of institutional commitments from urban than from rural communities of people suffering from mental diseases. In 1932, admissions to hospitals for mental diseases were 78.8 per 100,000 population for the urban population and 41.1 for the rural. The rates for feeble-mindedness and epilepsy are also higher in urban areas, although some States have higher rates in rural areas. In interpreting these facts, the question occurs at once whether the contrast is not distorted by the greater tendency in urban areas to institutionalize individuals who in the country would continue to live at home. In addition there is the related problem of personal disorganization leading to suicide which is closely related to the degree of urbanization. In any case the tensions of urban existence give rise to serious problems of mental hygiene.

DELINQUENCY AND CRIME. The outstanding characteristics of urban delinquency and crime are the emphasis on crimes against property rather than persons, the greater tendency toward organized and commercialized crime and the wide opportunities for juvenile delinquency. There is no evidence, however, that, as compared with rural areas, the city has looser morals, particularly in matters of sex crimes, like rape. Rackets, and the extortion of tribute from legitimate business are restricted mainly to some large cities, but commercialized crime of the type characterizing the prohibition era had its origin not only in the conditions of urban life but also in an unenforceable code of behavior dictated by the nation at large and especially by the rural areas. The remedying of the failure to provide outlets for juvenile energy and the combating of delinquency are among the primary problems the city will have to face and solve in the future.

INADEQUATE RECREATIONAL FACILITIES. The most obvious problem in urban recreation arises out of a lack of sufficient space for play and recreation in some cities and, still more, out of the poor distribution and the consequent ineffectiveness of existing recreational areas in many more cities. This difficulty is due mainly to the failure of municipal authorities to realize the need for recreational facilities until after the cities were built up. As a result, the establishment of adequate parks and playgrounds in the congested sections of cities is made prohibitive by the high cost of land in such districts.

Another emerging problem is that of providing the type of cultural services suitable to a city population which is growing "older" and which is coming to have more leisure time at its disposal. Music, art, light opera, movies, and the theater have not played a large part in the public recreation programs of the past, but with some notable precedents going back to the pre-war period and with the stimulus of the Federal arts, music and theater projects, these forms of recreation may become more widely incorporated into the recreational programs of American cities.

The 200 million dollar annual public expenditure for recreation is made largely by municipalities, which accounted for roughly three-fourths of the total public recreational expenditures during the year 1930. State and Federal park facilities and expenditures, in spite of their conspicuous growth in recent years, thus still lag far behind the municipal or urban figures. This does not mean, however, that cities can continue their programs without outside aid. The depression especially had a curtailing effect. Recently the deficiencies have been reduced in many cities by Federal and State work relief expenditures which, according to estimates held to be reliable, have advanced recreation facilities in some cases 5 or 10 years ahead of expected normal development.

Whether or not this type of Federal aid is to continue, particularly for cities which lack adequate facilities or minimum recreation opportunities, it is apparent that the Nation as a whole has a large stake in urban recreation, not only because it will have to adjust this function to the changes in the industrial economy and leisure-time utilization, but because recreation has wide social implications as well. The problem is not only one of providing more adequate facilities for physical recreation, but of putting forth greater national, State, and community effort to offer adequate opportunities for cultural self-development, artistic self-expression and group participation.

CONGESTION. The problem of urban congestion arises from the fact that as the city spreads out at its periphery it almost invariably also rises at the center. The skyscraper is a visible symbol of this congestion. As it fills and empties, the streets and traffic facilities, which were designed for smaller cities and lower buildings, are no longer able to carry the load without friction and delays. The extensive remodeling of these facilities to bring them again in scale with the new and greatly more intensive use of private property is inordinately expensive in most cases. For it is precisely at the center, where the region-wide functions of the city are concentrated, where the daily ebb and flow of the human tides converge and where the acquisition of every foot of additional space involves high land costs and building damages, that this remodeling is most needed and space is at a premium.

While the elimination of congestion would involve enormous costs, the aggregate cost of permitting this congestion in our cities to continue represents an imposing waste. Traffic delays where speed and promptness are at a premium, overcrowding of sites and buildings, dark and badly ventilated dwellings and offices, overtaxing of public facilities and services, deficiency in public open space combined with a surplus of unused private open space, undue concentration of land values, and unfair apportionment of the local tax burden—these and other detriments to urban well-being are present in varying degrees in practically every American city. These conditions generally accompany the type of urban growth which is characterized by uninterrupted accretion at the periphery and increasingly more intensive building development, concentration, and congestion in the center, seldom relieved for long, but rather aided and abetted by subways, traffic lights, one-way streets, and the staggering of office hours.

One of the most serious consequences of traffic congestion at the center of urban areas and of the high-speed radial traffic to their outskirts is the increasing rate of street-traffic accidents and the appalling number of fatalities. These constitute a hazard in present-day city life comparable in some respects with the plagues of old.

DISPERSION. Just as extreme concentration is wasteful, so is extreme dispersion. The suburbanite aims to escape at least some of the disadvantages of living in the densely built city but by coming to the central city to earn his living, he creates new problems of overcentralization. The advantages of residential dispersion are coupled with the disadvantages of atomized administrative areas which tend to break up urban regions into suburban bailiwicks and dormitories independent of the central city.

The real difficulty with the dispersive tendencies of suburbanization and other centrifugal movements lies in the lack of planning and the consequent waste in public facilities, services, and the use of urban land and space. Urban expansion being left largely to the whim of the subdivider, discontinuous, sporadic, suburban settlements or ribbon developments along the highways, with large undeveloped interstices between them, greatly increase the cost and difficulties of providing the essential public facilities and services. On his part the subdivider has so thoroughly pursued his job—in many cases at the expense of either the land owner, the gullible home seeker, or the community—that even now enough land is subdivided in the outskirts of many of our larger cities to exceed any prospective need of these communities for building sites for a great many years to come.

EXPLOITATION OF URBAN LAND. Gambling in land values has contributed to alternate booms and depressions, raising false hopes, encouraging over-ambitious structures, wiping out private investors, and, all in all, has been one of the major tragedies of American urban life. Inflated valuations have contributed to vertical expansion and over-intensive land utilization, with the result that the private use of land has far outgrown public facilities and services, including water, sewerage, health, police and fire protection, street and transit facilities, and has created all sorts of congestion.

The dispersive developments of recent years have left blighted vacuums in the interiors of our cities and have themselves been vitiated by land prices at a level too high to permit a desirable standard of urban development. Boom subdividing has resulted in paper streets with impossible grades and unintelligent gridiron patterns, as well as unnecessary or premature and poorly planed subdivisions.

The plight of our cities is commonly ascribed to the unbridled exploitation of land by private owners. But in fairness, the blame cannot be fixed so simply and definitely. Indeed, candid analysis must place the major responsibility on our lack of urban land policies and on the consequent failure of our public authorities to afford to private owners and developers adequate opportunities for sound and profitable land uses. It is the guidance and protection rather than the restriction of land users that need major emphasis in the formulation of land policies for desirable urban development. For every landowner who wishes to exploit his property to the detriment of his neighborhood or community, there are hundreds who desire to be safeguarded against such antisocial uses. But where community protection is lacking, it is quite natural for the average property owner to try to secure, in self-protection and at the expense of his neighbors, advantages which they might otherwise secure at his expense.

The basic problem then is not private exploitation alone but also our failure to realize that the tenure and use of urban land are matters of urgent public concern; that a larger measure of protection for socially beneficial private uses and of public ownership of land would be in the public interest; that orderly and speedy reform is essential to the present well-being and future progress of our cities; and that few of these reforms can be worked out on an exclusively local scale but require new principles and policies in urban land economics, country-wide in effect and expressed through State, local, and, perhaps, even through national legislation.

SLUMS AND BLIGHTED AREAS. The slum is the most glaring symptom of urban disintegration. Much more than the rural slum and the village hovel, the urban slum is a contagious blight on a large scale. It is by no means limited to derelict, residential areas, but often consists of decaying business and industrial sections. Neither is the location of the slum limited to the older, central parts of the city. Actual or potential suburban slums are probably developing faster than the older, centrally located slums are being eradicated.

The areas of blight and decay drag down neighboring values, reduce rentals, restrict tax paying ability, and curtail those community services which could be used to supplement the waning facilities of the neighborhood. In this sense, the slum is a drain on the resources of the community and is inimical to the welfare of the entire city.

As to residential buildings of the cities, a substantial proportion of these are substandard in respect to structure, open space, overcrowding, sanitary conditions, and conveniences. Of approximately 1,500,000 residential buildings in 64 cities, between one-sixth and one-fifth were found to be substandard on the basis of the Real Property Inventory made in 1934 by the Department of Commerce and the Civil Works Administration.

Numerous local studies indicate that inadequate housing conditions are causally connected with high infant mortality rates, high tuberculosis rates, high incidence of delinquency and crime. Likewise, there is a close coincidence between poor housing conditions and social disorganization; similarly, between fire hazards and poor housing. The cost per capita of providing fire, police, and other services for the population in the areas of poor housing is usually much higher than for other sections, while the tax revenues from these areas are disproportionately low. The community thus subsidizes areas of poor housing, when it might employ such resources constructively for good housing.

HOUSING DIFFICULTIES. Even the more desirable homes of the urban community present problems. In the first place, there is an inadequacy of acceptable housing facilities. Urban home ownership, though it had been rising in the decade 1920–30, was still as low as 46.8 percent in 1930. In fact the larger and the more industrialized a city, the greater the tenancy. Principally, however, the problem lies in the fact that family incomes are inadequate or the cost of satisfactory housing is too high and that, consequently, too large a proportion of the family budget is spent for rentals. To aggravate the problem, families with low incomes generally must spend a larger proportion of their income for rent than those of the higher income groups.

National policy has recognized, through the establishment of such Federal agencies as the Home Owners' Loan Corporation, the Federal Housing Administration, the Housing Division of the Public Works Administration, and the Resettlement Administration, that Government lending for and the construction of housing is a public responsibility, not only as a means of economic recovery but for the sake of improving housing facilities.

But even with the adoption of this national policy, problems still persist. The States, even with the enactment of limited dividend and housing authority laws, are not moving fast enough to give general and nation-wide encouragement to housing. State and local authorities are but slowly appreciating the necessity for vigorous action and for a definite acceptance of public responsibility and leadership. The problems of slum eradication are still being confused with those of low-rent housing. Areas which should not again be used for housing, because they are functionally unfit and undesirable for this purpose and are not in proper relation to the desirable development of the whole community, are being enthusiastically rebuilt, often on such a limited scale that shortly they may be subjected to and are likely to be the victims of the same forces of deterioration which dragged down the old development before them. Similarly, loans are being made on homes which by no means meet minimum requirements of neighborhood, space, construction, and sanitation, and will contribute to future deterioration and blight. A national housing policy to be fully effective must not only be tied in with the national economy and financial structure, but it must be an integral part of a comprehensive long-range plan for the development and redevelopment of the community, in order to prevent patchwork projects and to insure against the instability of new developments, new dislocations in the community structure and, in general, the very unsoundness and deterioration which caused the conditions that the new policy and program are intended to remedy.

DISLOCATION OF INDUSTRY. One of the principal urban problems is the articulation of the industries of the community into a structure which will secure the maximum employment of the available labor supply, the minimizing of seasonal and cyclical fluctuations in the total employed pay roll of the community, the optimum use of the advantages of location from the standpoint of raw materials and markets, and a balance between the cost of community services to industry and the income derived by the community from industry.

Lacking an appreciation of the need for a selective program of industrial development, communities have attracted and subsidized enterprises without adequate attention to their effects upon the total industrial structure. Too frequently, the test has been not the qualitative test of the effect upon the various parts of the community's industrial mechanism, but the quantitative test of increasing the total amount of industrial activity at the time the new enterprise is established. A poorly balanced local industrial structure throws the entire industrial front out of joint by causing migration of labor, unemployment, lower wages, curtailed purchasing power, less trading business, lower living standards, high cost of relief, high taxes, tax delinquency, untenanted property, stagnation of building enterprises, obsolescence of community plant and depreciation of industrial equipment.

On a national scale, too, the industrial pattern has developed from a background of factors which either have never been or are no longer sound. The location of an industry in one region or another, in one city or another, was too frequently decided on the basis of the internal economy of that particular industry with no reference to the possible ill effects upon other and related industries or upon the community. It was, on too many occasions, influenced by a transportation system and a rate structure which favorably beckoned the enterprise to locate at a particular place at the expense of the entire productive balance of an industry of nation-wide importance. Stranded industrial population groups are not local phenomena. In origin and consequence they are nation-wide.

URBAN PLANNING AND ZONING. Although city planning and zoning as practiced during the past 20 years has, by and large, been beneficial, it has fallen short of expectations and potentialities. It has been, and still is, handicapped by a combination of obstacles, the removal of which is held to be fundamental to really effective and successful urban planning and zoning.

To begin with, city planning bodies lack sufficient legal powers to guide effectively the physical, social, and economic structure of the community through the instrumentality of a comprehensive plan broadly construed. They are subject to uninformed official and public opinion which does not fully appreciate the great importance of community planning. They often encounter jealousy and even opposition on the part of administrative departments. They suffer from insufficient appropriations and a scarcity of competent technical planning personnel. They are themselves sometimes at fault, because they lack sincere interest and vigor in performing their task of which they often have but a limited understanding or a narrow view.

Even where legal powers and planning practices are most advanced, local planning agencies seldom have even advisory authority over *all* public works projects within the area under their jurisdiction, but are limited to projects of their own local government. Nor do they have such authority over the facilities of transportation, transit, and utility agencies, except when the proposed changes directly affect a public facility or public property. Their powers over the layout of real estate subdivisions are inadequate to be fully effective and they are without authority to regulate the quantity of such subdivision developments. In general, local planning agencies need stronger and wider authority in order to exercise jurisdiction over all matters relating to community development, and, where a county or regional planning agency does not exist, not only within the municipal boundaries, but over the entire area now urbanized or likely to become so and as much of the region beyond as bears relation to the proper development of the urban community itself.

Another weakness in local planning has been the absence of more general plans for larger areas—the region, the State and the Nation—which might have furnished a framework and much needed over-all controls for local effort.

In fact, the entire scope and conception of local urban planning needs broadening. While the influence of the physical environment upon the economic and social structure of the community is everywhere in evidence, planning agencies and planners have been slow to recognize and give proper emphasis to the social and economic objectives and aspects of planning and zoning. Studies of the economic base of the community, its soundness, deficiencies, and its prospects, and the need for a selective program of industrial development, have been almost completely overlooked. The pressing problem of housing has not received the attention from planning agencies that it deserves.

Local planning should be given or must gain for itself a place in the structure of government where it will be closer to the local legislative body, the chief executive and the administrative departments. A possible way to achieve this might be the transforming of the independent planning commission or board into a planning department as one of the staff agencies of the local government, with or without an advisory committee of citizens. However, thorough understanding and acceptance of planning by the local legislative body, the chief executive and, most of all, by the citizenry in general, would appear to be a prerequisite for such a change.

LAG IN PUBLIC IMPROVEMENTS. Urban communities have shown a widespread need for the stimulation of public works and facilities. The difficulties of urban public improvement programs arise first from the historic practice of cities to dispose of their land holdings for a pittance only to be compelled in many cases to buy them back later for their own use at exorbitant prices. The problem of financing public improvements has been only partially relieved by Federal grants and loans recently made available for worthy or self-liquidating public works. The planning of public works has also been neglected both locally as part of the city plan, and nationally, as part of a broad program for increasing employment directly and for stimulating industrial activity during slump periods.

An additional difficulty has been the existence of a number of overlapping and coordinate governmental authorities in the urban region. Each of these authorities may have a veto power over essential improvements, such as roads, sewers, and sewage disposal plants, and may be unprepared to proceed when all the others are able and willing to do so. Moreover, the obvious advantages of combining the office buildings of all governmental authorities in the community into a "governmental center," have been achieved in but a very few instances because of the lack of unified control over public works projects. City and county, school board and special district, State and Federal Governments almost invariably pursue their land purchasing, construction, or rental policies irrespective of the needs of the others, regardless of the increased bargaining strength of a joint program and apparently unaware of the symbolic and practical values of a single, planned community center for all governmental buildings.

However, the most important and fundamental reason for the lag in public works is the difficulty of finding the funds to pay for them. Municipal governments are hard pressed to raise funds for even the most essential public improvements, because the tax on real property is practically the only source of general revenues for local government, or because of rigid tax limitations, or the taxpayers' reluctance to vote for bond issues. A further handicap in the financing of public works is the lack of legal powers to use more up-to-date methods, such as special district assessments, excess condemnation, and land-value increment taxes, in order to finance improvements more nearly from the increased values which they create.

INADEQUATE GOVERNMENTAL POWERS. In contrast to the rapidly increasing responsibilities and services of urban governments, their legal powers are relatively stationary. Legally, the city is the creature of the State, and in practice the city must contend with all sorts of meddlesome State statutory details or conversely with statutory gaps which prove judicially fatal when the city embarks upon new programs. All ranges of urban activity, from petty questions of administrative procedure to general questions of urban policy, are determined by State law. Between 1896 and 1936 the number of Supreme Court cases, State and Federal, involving the exercise of municipal powers, has increased fourfold, and one-third of these cases have been decided against the city. Even constitutional home rule over municipal affairs, though it has been adopted in 18 States, has become a waning movement, and where it has been adopted, courts have, on the whole, tended to construe the grant of municipal powers more narrowly than was expected.

DUPLICATION OF GOVERNMENTAL LEVELS. A problem which underlies the difficulties of regulating urban affairs in the United States is the duplication of governmental levels—local, State, and national. Whenever a program of municipal reform and reconstruction is initiated, either locally or on a national scale, this dilemma has to be faced: our constitutional system forces the cities to work largely through the States which, either singly or collectively, have been unable to deal adequately with urban problems.

Where, for example, the State's power has been practically exclusive in matters of distinct urban significance, such as the criminal law and judicial procedure, the Nation has witnessed one of the most hesitant and barren fields of governmental endeavor, and the cities have been forced to experiment with police and judicial reforms without the encouragement of advanced State laws. On the other hand, in fields where cities do possess the power and have developed an adequate program of regulation, the States have engaged in a subtle process of invading municipal activities. A study of a dozen major regulatory State acts in one State, for example, shows that the usual practice has been for the city to initiate a regulation, to develop technical standards for its enforcement, and to install an inspection service, and then for the State to step in, enact some of the standards set up by the city and take over the licensing powers and the licensing fees without, however, enforcing adequate standards or inspections itself.

GOVERNMENTAL DISORGANIZATION OF METROPOLITAN REGIONS. As has already been pointed out, the process of urbanization has brought larger aggregates of population and wider areas within the orbit of a central dominant city. In continuing to treat the city as a municipal corporation, however, we have obviously allowed the realities of today to be obscured by the artificial and often arbitrary administrative boundaries which are a heritage of the past. Taking only the largest urban areas, i. e. the 96 metropolitan districts containing 55 millions of people or 45 percent of our total population, it is found that the urban governmental system of these districts consists of a bewildering maze of overlapping authorities and of a growing number of suburban and satellite cities.

The municipality of governments in the metropolitan areas is best indicated by the fact that, besides a very large number of overlapping authorities, in 1930 there were 272 separate incorporated places in the New York-Northeastern New Jersey metropolitan district, 135 in the Pittsburgh district, 115 in the Chicago area, 92 in the Philadelphia district, and 56 in the Los Angeles district. Together with their over-layers of counties, townships, school districts, sanitary districts, sewer districts, library districts, health districts, park districts, forest preserve districts, street lighting districts, utility districts, water districts, and even mosquito-abatement districts—each of them a separate body politic and corporate—these communities present an odd picture of independent bailiwicks performing related or even identical governmental functions with some degree of cooperation, but with a great degree of competition for municipal revenues, for administrative prestige and for legal powers. Frequently, these districts are too small in area or have insufficient tax resources to support essential public services. All this governmental duplication, confusion and localism are in sharp contrast to the obvious disregard of the network of urban boundary lines by epidemics which complicate urban health work, by criminals who are not stopped by city limits, and by the city and suburban users of highways and transportation facilities who seldom know or care about the maze of political boundaries in metropolitan districts.

The whole problem is aggravated by the customary legal difficulties in applying the earlier, and now unusual, solutions of annexation, consolidation, and federation of metropolitan authorities and suburbs, and in utilizing the more frequent and current devices of special metropolitan authorities, intermunicipal and extra-territorial contractual and functional relations, and interstate and Federal arrangements.

On the latter point in particular, the difficulty is not merely in the lack of urban imagination or in the restraints of State law, but again it lies in the fact that the legal pattern of the nation consists of sovereign States and subordinate cities, while the concrete facts of our urban and administrative life defy State lines and State control. Twenty-two metropolitan districts containing 26,000,000 people, more than one-half of our metropolitan inhabitants and over one-fifth of our total population, straddle State lines. Since many of our cities are located along navigable rivers and since such rivers also generally serve as boundaries between States, it is to be expected that as some of these cities grow they will increasingly transcend the political units of which they are a part. For rivers, while they divide areas politically, generally unite them economically. But these populous urban regions and their administrative problems receive scant recognition in the existing machinery of our States and our National Government.

In their daily or periodic contacts the inhabitants of the metropolitan region, irrespective of municipal, township, county, State, or even national lines, are bound together into a community through industry, public utilities, social and cultural institutions, an interdependent system of transportation and communication, the newspaper, radio, telephone, and postal service, if not through a sense of social solidarity and common interests arising out of common problems. The greatest obstacle to the full emergence of a metropolitan community is the great number of conflicting and overlapping political and administrative units into which the area is divided. It is to be expected that as cities grow, an increasing proportion of their population will be found outside of their official boundaries. In fact, in the highly urbanized areas of the North Atlantic seaboard, even the different metropolitan regions shade almost imperceptibly into one another, constituting a vast aggregation or a super-metropolis. Under such circumstances, the daily interrelations of the population are so far flung spatially and so intimate socially and economically that the official place of residence of the person scarcely defines the locus of his actual interest. In these areas with their concentration of population, commerce, and industry, their convergence of lines of transportation and communication, where mobility is high and spatial separation great, government, since it is not unified, is heavily taxed in dealing with the problems and functions that in smaller communities are not present, or are easily solved. In view of the relative inflexibility of political and administrative areas, the necessity of cooperation among and integration of the separate units of government has led to the development of *ad hoc* governments and to the increasing demand for greater freedom to deal adequately with the task of planning the physical structure and the functional coordination of the government constituting the region.

Unless, therefore, the boundaries of the political city can be stretched to include its suburban and satellite industrial and residential colonies, the economic and social base, upon which rests the welfare of both those who remain in the city and those who seek a partial escape from it, will eventually disintegrate. For no community in a democratic society can long remain a sound functioning organism, if those among its members who gain the greatest benefits from it, escape from most of the obligations communal life imposes, and if those who obtain the least returns in the way of the necessities and amenities of life are left to bear the brunt of civic responsibility and taxation. If an orderly development and a higher level of life for the people of the imposing supercities are to be attained, some measures calculated to endow them with the capacity to act collectively as a political unit are indispensable.

DISUNITY OF THE CITY. Fundamentally, the United States is suffering from a lack of balance between the urban economy and the entire national economy, between the city and the country, and between the various aspects of urban life itself.

One of our basic urban problems consists of the widespread neglect of cities as a major segment of national existence, the consequent derision of urban politics and depreciation of urban administration as a career, and the cumulative disregard of the city hall as a principal center of American urban life. Indicative of this neglect is the fact, although the United States has been a predominantly urban nation for more than two decades, this report of the National Resources Committee is the first inquiry on a national, official, and comprehensive scale into the problems of the American urban community.

The disfranchisement or underrepresentation of the city in the political and administrative councils of the Nation also contributes to the disunity of the city and its inability to deal effectively with its problems. In the United States we have little hesitancy in relating rural distress to the need for a national agricultural policy. The same connection, however, is not made between urban distress and the need for a unified urban policy. Perhaps the reason for this may be found in the fact that the country has a uniform economic base in agriculture, the farm and the farmer, while the city cannot be characterized by any such common symbol, institution, or group. Agriculture is identified with the farm and the rural community, but when we speak of manufacturing, of commerce, of banking, of professional or service enterprises, these are not synonymous with the city and do not exhaust the major interests of the urban community. This may make the urban problem more difficult than the rural, but it is no justification, it seems, for applying national directives and policies to rural life while hesitating to in the case of urban life.

Even the contrast between the common economic base of the country and the mixed economic interests of the city as an explanation for the nonexistence of a national urban policy is being whittled away by time and experience. Farm tenancy and share-cropping, which is the lot at present of one-half of our rural inhabitants, is setting up a dependent economic class which, unless steps are taken to avert it, may soon resemble the economic disfranchisement which the city artisan suffered when the factory succeeded the household unit of production and when the machine supplanted the hand tool.

Yet, in contrast to the problem of urban enterprise and the city, the problem of agriculture and rural life is treated by our national policy-making bodies as a unified economic problem. If the city possesses any economic unity, our political economy apparently has not been ready to permit its expression to this extent.

OPTIMUM SIZE OF CITIES

Otis Dudley Duncan

What is the best size for a city?—The question can only be answered intelligently (if, indeed, there is an answer) by assuming a general viewpoint from which criteria of good, better, and best can be derived; working out an explicit set of such criteria; and examining the empirical validity of the criteria.

This procedure will be illustrated here by (1) assuming the viewpoint of the theorist of city planning interested in setting general standards for the planning of cities; (2) abstracting from the literature of city planning theory a list of specific criteria which have been offered therein for determining optimum city-size; and (3) examining each of the criteria on the list from the standpoint of observable relationships between city-size and the empirical variables involved in the criteria. The logical justification for this approach rests on the truism that any criterion of optimum population involves, implicitly or explicitly, two elements: first, the normative element, which places a positive or negative valuation on a particular situation; and second, a factual element which has the force of a statement of empirical relationships between variation in city-size and variation in the situation in question.

Suppose a criterion of optimum city-size is that a city's size should be that which is most favorable to the health of its population. This criterion takes health as a positive value, and ill health a negative one. Beyond this, it implicitly posits some significant correlation between city-size and health; for if there were no such correlation, there would obviously be no "most favorable" size, i.e., no optimum.

The establishing by scientific inquiry of a dependable relationship like that implied by a given criterion may be termed a process of empirical *validation* of the criterion. Normative issues are not involved here:—the value once assumed, validation of a criterion of optimum city-size is a purely empirical procedure, which, to be sure, may be carried out more or less adequately, depending on quality of data, soundness of method, and the like.

Clearly, examining optimum city-size from the viewpoint of the city planning theorist provides only one illustration of the proposed procedure for validating the concept of optimum city-size. It is, however, not a trivial illustration. There is good reason to suppose that the list of criteria fur-

nished by the planning literature includes many criteria which would also
be forthcoming under alternative viewpoints. There is the further point
that planning standards based on the notion of optimum city-size have historically played an important role in the development of the theory and
practice of planning. Some writers on city planning—notably those influenced by Ebenezer Howard [1]—have gone so far as to insist that realistic
planning presumes some initial consensus as to the desirable size of the
urban units planned for; [2] while others have urged that control of city-size
is among the most important means of achieving the ends of city planning.[3]
Though these may be extreme positions, they are influential ones, as is in-
stanced by the planning efforts got under way in Britain after World War
II.[4] Both enthusiasts for and opponents of such positions would do well to
subject to searching scrutiny the underlying concept of optimum city-size.
Thought and discussion on this question have been jolted by the recent bold
proposals for meeting the threat of atomic war by dispersing the urban
population. The idea that cities should be small enough to have a low probability of atomic destruction is, of course, a criterion of optimum size, and
the discussion of this idea has raised anew the question of size considerations in city planning.[5]

General population theory discusses optimum population in terms of an
economic criterion applicable, abstractly, to a closed economy.[6] This formulation has little application to the present problem, since cities are intrinsically "open" economies. Though some writers have sought to justify
city optima on economic grounds, the economist himself has by and large
remained neutral on the question of optimum city-size.[7] The general trend
of discussion is in line with Firey's view that in this area explicit recognition
should be given to a variety of interests, all having just claims as criteria
of optimum population, and not all mediated in any obvious manner by
purely economic factors.[8] The criteria considered in this paper are those
which appear in discussions of optimum city-size in the literature of city

1. Howard's *Garden Cities of To-Morrow* first appeared at the turn of the century;
it was reissued in 1946 (London: Faber and Faber, Ltd.).

2. F. J. Osborn, *Transport, Town Development and Territorial Planning of Industry*, No. 20, The New Fabian Research Bureau (London: Victor Gollancz, Ltd., 1934),
p. 20.

3. Lewis Mumford, *The Culture of Cities* (New York: Harcourt Brace, 1938),
p. 488.

4. Ministry of Town and Country Planning, New Towns Committee, *Final Report*,
Cmd. 6876 (London: H. M. Stationery Office, 1946).

5. William F. Ogburn, "Sociology and the Atom," *American Journal of Sociology*,
LI (January, 1946), 267-275; Tracy B. Augur, "The Dispersal of Cities as a Defense
Measure," *Bulletin of the Atomic Scientists*, IV (May, 1948), 131-134.

6. Manuel Gottlieb, "The Theory of Optimum Population for a Closed Economy,"
Journal of Political Economy, LIII (December, 1945), 289-318.

7. Paul Samuelson, "The Business Cycle and Urban Redevelopment," *The Problem
of the Cities and Towns*, ed. Guy Greer (Report of the Conference on Urbanism,
Harvard University, March 5-6, 1942).

8. Walter Firey, "The Optimum Rural-Urban Population Balance," *Rural Sociology*,
XII (June, 1947), 116-127.

planning and allied disciplines.[9] The classification of these criteria is the writer's and has merit only for reasons of its convenience. It will be obvious that, at least in the aggregate, planners have been hopeful of attaining far-reaching transformations and ameliorations of the urban way of life through control of city-size. The realism of such hopes is closely bound up with the validity of the concept of optimum city-size.

While the data on which this paper is based are to be summarized rather sketchily, most of them are from published sources; and in any case, there is elsewhere available to the specialist a complete and critical exposition of detailed empirical and methodological problems.[10]

EMPIRICAL OBSERVATIONS. 1. *Physical Plan of the City.*—The theorist of optimum city-size frequently demands that cities be small enough to enable ready access to the country-side and a reasonably moderate journey to work. The desirable area of a city is in question here, along with the bearing of area on transportation problems. According to a relationship between population size and area demonstrated for our cities as of 1940,[11] the average city of 10,000 will have a radius of one mile; the city of 100,000 a radius of 2.3 miles; and the city of a half-million 4.1 miles, on the idealized assumption of circular areas. For the average resident, accessibility to the various functional areas of the city varies inversely with its radius. With increasing city-size walking or cycling to work and play rapidly becomes out of the question, and automotive and mass transportation become indispensable. A 1942 survey showed that the average resident of cities over a half-million lived 4.8 miles from work, and required 24 minutes to get to his job. In these cities three-fifths traveled to work by mass transportation media, and three-tenths by auto. In the cities of 5,000–25,000 the median distance to work was but 0.8 of a mile, the journey to work requiring 9 minutes. Fewer than half utilized automotive and mass transportation. Respondents in large cities expressed somewhat more dissatisfaction than those in small cities over parking facilities and the distance their children had to travel to high

---

9. The following are representative: National Council of Social Service, *The Size and Social Structure of a Town* (London: George Allen & Unwin, Ltd., 1943); William F. Ogburn, *op. cit.*; F. J. Osborn, *op. cit.*; *Report of the Royal Commission on the Distribution of the Industrial Population*, Cmd. 6153 (London: H. M. Stationery Office, 1940); Thomas Sharp, *Town Planning*, rev. ed. (Harmondsworth, Middlesex: Penguin Books, 1945); Raymond Unwin, "The Town and the Best Size for Good Social Life," *Town Theory and Practice*, ed. C. B. Purdon (London: Benn Brothers, Ltd., 1921).

10. Otis Dudley Duncan, "An Examination of the Problem of Optimum City-Size," microfilm (Chicago: University of Chicago Libraries, 1949). See also the following compilations of data on differential characteristics of cities by size: Fenton Keyes, "The Correlation of Social Phenomena with Community Size," Ph.D. dissertation, Department of Sociology, Yale University, 1942; *The Municipal Year Book* (Chicago: The International City Managers' Association, annual); William F. Ogburn, *Social Characteristics of Cities* (Chicago: The International City Managers' Association, 1937); U.S. Bureau of the Census, *Cities Supplement, Statistical Abstract of the United States* (Washington: Government Printing Office, 1944).

11. John Q. Stewart, "Suggested Principles of 'Social Physics,'" *Science*, CVI (August 29, 1947), 179-180.

schools.[12] Some form of local mass transportation is apparently required in cities over 15,000, since virtually all cities of this size have buses or street cars.[13] The automobile is a much less effective mode of transit in the large city: A fragmentary survey in 1942 indicated that in cities of 25,000-100,000 about four-fifths of vehicular passengers arriving in the central business district travelled by auto, as against only two-fifths in cities over a half-million; the remainder in each case arrived by some means of mass transportation.[14] Families in cities over 100,000 spend more than four times as much for non-automotive transportation as families in smaller cities.[15]

Although the statistical data are not adequate for a thorough cost analysis of transportation, the unequivocal indication is that the advantages of time, expenditure, and convenience all lie with the moderate sized or small city.

2. *Health.*—One of the most frequently mentioned criteria of optimum city-size concerns the environmental and institutional aspects of the city-dweller's health. It can readily be shown that the ratio of physicians to population increases with increasing city-size, at least up to the million mark, with even more marked differences between large and small cities in the ratios of medical specialists to population than holds for general practitioners. Of the eleven numerically most important types of medical specialists, eight are regularly found only in cities over 50,000 population (as indicated by a ratio of one such physician per city).[16] Ninety-five per cent of the cities over 10,000 have general hospitals, as compared to three-fourths the cities of 5,000-10,000 and two-fifths the cities of 2,500-5,000; and the model size of these hospitals varies directly with city-size.[17] Nine-tenths of the births to residents of cities over 10,000 now occur in hospitals, as compared to three-fourths in the case of cities below 10,000; and over half the large city deaths occur in hospital beds as compared to one-third in the smaller centers.[18] Health services and facilities are, therefore, clearly more accessible to large city residents than to small.

The actual health status of the populations of different sized cities is perhaps most reliably, though indirectly, shown by mortality statistics. In-

12. Melville C. Branch, Jr., *Urban Planning and Public Opinion* (Princeton: Princeton University Bureau of Urban Research, 1942).

13. "Suburbs' Growth Expands Use of Cars," *Automobile Facts*, III (March, 1944), 1, 3.

14. Kendrick Lee, "Local Transportation," *Editorial Research Reports*, I, No. 18 (May 15, 1942), 311-325.

15. National Resources Planning Board, *Family Expenditures in the United States, Statistical Tables and Appendices* (Washington: Government Printing Office, 1941), Tables 1, 196, 198, 200, and 202.

16. R. G. Leland, *Distribution of Physicians in the United States* (Chicago: Bureau of Medical Economics, American Medical Association, rev. ed., 1936).

17. Commission on Hospital Care, *Hospital Care in the United States* (New York: The Commonwealth Fund, 1947), Table 14.

18. U.S. Bureau of the Census, *Vital Statistics—Special Reports*, vol. 22, no. 1, 1945; and vol. 10, no. 51, 1941.

fant mortality varies inversely with city-size, and in recent years the smallest cities have had rates two-fifths larger than cities over the million mark. The association with city-size is uniform, and the differentials by city-size have increased, rather than diminished, with the nation-wide improvements in infant mortality rates of the past three decades.[19] Likewise, the larger cities experience an advantage with regard to maternal mortality, though here the differences are smaller—perhaps of the order of ten per cent—and have diminished considerably in recent years.[20] For combined sexes in the total white population, the life expectancy at practically all ages was higher in 1940 for residents of cities of 10,000-100,000 than for residents of cities larger or smaller than this. The superior longevity in this city-size group is a function of age, increasing to age 35 and being most marked in the age range 35–65. However, at best these cities experience only a three per cent superiority over larger cities, and a much narrower margin over smaller cities.[21] Further, there are important variations by population subgroups. In the West and the North, life expectancies of both races are higher in the smaller cities, but the reverse is true in the South. In general, the advantage of the smaller cities increases with advancing age, amounting to as much as 5 to 15 per cent at the old ages in the North and West.[22] Among the important causes of death, large cities have the highest death rates from cancer, heart disease, tuberculosis, diabetes, stomach ulcers (white population), and suicide. Small cities have higher rates for pneumonia and influenza, appendicitis, intracranial lesions, nephritis, and hernia and intestinal obstruction.[23] Recalling the higher infant and maternal mortality of the small cities, and the fact that their life expectancies are relatively greater at advanced than at early ages, there is, therefore, some indication that the principal health advantages of the large cities are in regard to the immediate accessibility of superior services for the treatment of acute diseases and childbirth; whereas the populations of these large urban centers are more vulnerable to the long-term, accumulative environmental hazards eventuating in chronic and psychosomatic disorders. This picture is, of course, much different nowadays from that of a few decades ago before the control of epidemic infectious diseases. Recent advances in public health have presumably benefited the large cities more than the small. It is impossible to make a categorical generalization about the relative advantages of large and small cities with regard to health; but the probability is that the magnitudes of the historical differences in the health of populations in cities of different sizes are diminishing, on the whole.

19. U.S. Bureau of the Census, *Vital Statistics of the United States* (Washington: Government Printing Office, annual).

20. *Ibid.*

21. Life tables computed from data in U.S. Bureau of the Census, *Vital Statistics Rates in the United States, 1900–1940* (Washington: Government Printing Office, 1943).

22. U.S. Bureau of the Census, *Vital Statistics—Special Reports*, vol. 23, no. 15, 1947, Table IV.

23. U.S. Bureau of the Census, *Vital Statistics—Special Reports*, vol. 23, no. 1, 1945.

City-Size:	100,000 and Over	25,000– 100,000	10,000– 25,000	2,500– 10,000
Per cent of cities with psychiatric clinics, 1947	83	25	4	1
Per cent of births occurring in hospitals, 1943	92	88	84	74
Infant deaths per 1,000 births, 1948	29	31	33	36
Life expectancy, 1940:				
—At birth (sexes combined)	64.3	64.0		62.5
—At age 45 (sexes combined)	26.0	26.7		26.6
Age-adjusted death rates per 100,000 population, 1940:				
—From heart and circulatory diseases	354	309		295
—From pneumonia and influenza	64	67		77

3. *Public Safety.*—It is sometimes stated that small cities are safer places in which to live than large cities. This assertion may be checked against the statistics of crime, auto accident deaths, and fire losses.

Most of the 24 offense categories used in *Uniform Crime Reports* show a tendency for crime rates, as measured by crimes known to police, or by persons charged, to increase with city-size. The relationship is not always of a simple character, but in general cities over 50,000 have higher rates than cities under 50,000, though the very largest cities by no means have the highest rates in all or most of these categories.[24] Lacking data to measure directly the cost of crime, it may be observed that per capita expenditures for city police forces increase directly with city-size, differences among city-size groups being of the order of three or four to one, comparing cities over a half million to cities below 10,000.[25] A similar comparison for per capita size of police force gives a ratio of roughly two to one.[26] These ratios of differential effort and expenditure are greater than the ratios of differential incidence in most categories of crime. Therefore, it may be generalized that the large city not only experiences a greater relative amount of crime, but also pays proportionately more heavily for it.

Statistics of automobile accident death rates are none too reliably compiled, and consequently exhibit certain illogical irregularities over the years. In general, occurrence rates based on population are lower for cities between 10,000 and 50,000 than for larger cities, for the recent years for which data are relatively complete. Occurrence rates based on numbers of registered vehicles give a somewhat clearer picture. Again cities of 10,000-50,000 have the lower rates, with the rates increasing regularly with city-size in the statistics of recent years. Although it is not entirely clear in what size group of cities there is the greatest personal risk of dying in an auto accident, it is obvious that the larger the city, the more lethal an instru-

24. Federal Bureau of Investigation, *Uniform Crime Reports* (Washington: Government Printing Office, semiannual).

25. U.S. Bureau of the Census, *City Finances: 1942,* Vol. III; and *Finances of Cities Having Populations Less Than 25,000: 1942* (Washington: Government Printing Office, 1944).

26. *Uniform Crime Reports, op. cit.*

ment the automobile becomes. And it seems fairly clear that the cities below 50,000 enjoy the greatest safety from auto accidents, by perhaps ten
per cent as measured by population based rates, and by a much larger
margin in relation to the number of automobiles owned by residents.[27]

City-Size Group	Average Annual Auto Accident Deaths per 100,000 Vehicles, 1942–46	Per Capita Police Expenditure, 1942	Average Annual Criminal Offense Rate per 100,000 Population, 1940–1947		
			Murder	Robbery	Rape
1,000,000 +	68	$6.71	5	73	
500,000 —	54	5.80	}8	}74	}14
250,000 —	50	3.80			
100,000 —	46	3.57	7	56	11
50,000 —	40	3.37	6	40	9
25,000 —	35	2.89	4	29	7
10,000 —	35	2.34	4	23	8
5,000 —	..	2.06	}4	}22	}8
2,500 —	..	1.64			

In regard to fire hazards, the results vary according to the statistical
measure chosen. Per capita fire loss, in dollars, shows little systematic association with city-size, except for the possibility that within a given city-size
group, there is greater variation in the scale of losses by individual cities
among the smaller cities. This would indicate a greater vulnerability of
the small city to losses from an occasional large fire.[28] Fire loss expressed
as a percentage of total real property value is larger in the cities of 30,000-
50,000 than in the cities over 1,000,000, the differences being greater when
measured by the size group mean than when measured by the size group
median—again indicating a skewing toward extreme values among smaller
cities.[29] The annual number of fires per capita is related inversely to city-size,
with fires being relatively one-third more frequent in cities 25,000–50,000 than
in cities 500,000 and over.[30] On the other hand, the loss per building fire is
more than fifty per cent greater in the larger of these two city-size groups.[31]
There are only slight differences by city-size in regard to per capita size of
fire departments, but the cities over a half-million spend 15 per cent more
for them in relation to their population, than do the cities of 10,000-25,000.[32]
While there is no unequivocal measure of fire hazard and of fire-fighting
efficiency, the suggestion is that among all sizes of city larger than 25,000
the differences in fire losses are rather due to inherent fire hazards than
to differences in the mobilization of resources for fire protection. While the
choice among the above quoted indices is somewhat subjective, perhaps
a fair case could be made for the greater safety of the small or medium
sized city, on the average.

27. National Safety Council, *Accident Facts,* Annual editions of 1933–1947.
28. *The Municipal Year Book, op. cit.,* editions of 1940 and 1945.
29. Mabel L. Walker, *Municipal Expenditures* (Baltimore: The Johns Hopkins
Press, 1930), Table II.
30. *The Municipal Year Book, op. cit.,* annual editions of 1941–1945.
31. *Ibid.*
32. *The Municipal Year Book, 1945, op. cit.*

In most persons' minds, no doubt, the preeminent question about a city's public safety nowadays is its potential destruction by the Bomb in a future war. Fortunately, there are no statistics on the relative vulnerability of cities of different sizes to A-bombs; we have to rely on statements of authorities and certain *a priori* considerations. The question is not, of course, one of the destructive power of the Bomb in a direct hit, but rather of the probability of a city's suffering such a hit. It has been argued that the small city is safer, first because it is a smaller target, more difficult to locate and hit directly; second, because it is likely to be a less attractive target; and third, because the potential enemy's A-bomb supply may be limited, thus diminishing the probability of an A-bomb attack on any given small city. From considerations such as these, the National Security Resources Board urges that "further urban concentrations of more than 50,000 people . . . be avoided." [33]

4. *Municipal Efficiency.*—It is a plausible hypothesis that the efficiency with which municipal services can be rendered should increase with increasing city-size to a point of diminishing returns, with an optimum size somewhere between the extremes. However, it is virtually impossible to get data to test this hypothesis. The existing data on municipal expenditures show, in general, a direct relationship between city-size and per capita costs in most of the 14 categories of expenditure: The larger cities spend more for highways, sanitation, public welfare, correction, schools, etc., than small.[34] However, these data reflect the separately varying factors of unit costs, amount, and quality of services. Hence they show little about municipal efficiency. From previously cited data, it may be seen that despite their greater expenditures, the large cities apparently enjoy no better situation than small with regard to crime and traffic control, fire protection, or health. This would argue that either these services are rendered less efficiently in large cities, or—what is more probable—that the initial problems of large cities are intrinsically more difficult. On the other hand, as will appear later, the higher levels of expenditure for schools, libraries, and recreation apparently reflect greater amounts and/or qualities of these services. Whether the increment of service is commensurate with the increment of cost cannot be accurately judged.

In only one area of municipal service can some tentative optimum population be established—the provision of residential electric service. Unit costs decline with increasing city-size up to the million mark, with cities between a half and one million getting electricity the cheapest.[35] Except for this one observation—which can by no means be immediately generalized—

33. *National Security Factors in Industrial Location*, NSRB Doc. 66 (Washington: National Security Resources Board, rev., July 22, 1948), p. 4.

34. *City Finances: 1942, op. cit.; Finances of Cities Having Populations Less Than 25,000: 1942, op. cit.*

35. *Cities Supplement, Statistical Abstract of the United States, op. cit.*, Table 4.

optimum city-size from the standpoint of municipal efficiency is still *terra incognita*.

5. *Education and Communications.*—A variety of measures of city school systems may be cited. Larger cities have longer school years—one week longer in cities over 100,000 as compared to those below 10,000. But the difference is smaller in regard to average per pupil school days attended. The average annual salary of teachers increases markedly with city size, quite overshadowing any cost-of-living differentials. Likewise, per pupil expenditures of large city schools exceed those of small city schools, and a greater proportion of the total school budget goes directly into costs of instruction. Large cities are much more frequently able to provide such special services as summer schools and night schools. On the other hand, the pupil/teacher ratio is greater in large cities, though the difference between large and small cities is only of the order of ten per cent.[36]

Facilities for advanced education are considerably limited by city-size. If we somewhat arbitrarily estimate the "population base" for a facility as that city-size at which 50 per cent of cities have the facility, the population base for a college or university is around 100,000, about the same for a junior college, and about 25,000 for a business college.[37] Accredited professional schools in such fields as business, engineering, law, medicine, and social work require larger population bases, of the order of 500,000.[38]

Despite the demonstrably superior educational facilities of large cities, their populations are at but slightly higher levels of educational status than those of small cities. As between cities of 250,000 and over and those below 25,000 superiorities of 0.2-0.3 in median school years completed are typical for ages below 18, but the slight observed differences amongst the adult populations are not all in this same direction.[39]

With regard to agencies of public enlightenment other than schools, estimates of population bases have been made as just indicated. For an art museum the population base is 100,000, with a somewhat higher figure for science and historical museums. The population base for a public library

36. U.S. Office of Education, "Statistics of City School Systems 1937–1938," *Biennial Survey of Education in the United States*, Bull. No. 2, 1940 (Washington: Government Printing Office, 1940), Ch. III; and "Statistics of City School Systems 1939–1940 and 1941–1942," *Biennial Surveys of Education in the United States 1938–1940 and 1940–1942* (Washington: Government Printing Office, 1944), Vol. II, Ch. VII.

37. Clarence Stephen Marsh, ed., *American Universities and Colleges* (Washington: American Council on Education, 4th ed., 1940); *Directory of Private Business Schools in the United States* (Washington: War Emergency Council of Private Business Schools, 1943); *Directory of Junior Colleges, 1941* (Washington: American Association of Junior Colleges, 1941).

38. U.S. Office of Education, *Education Directory 1941, Part III, Colleges and Universities*, Bulletin 1941, No. 1 (Washington: Government Printing Office, 1941).

39. U.S. Bureau of the Census, *Sixteenth Census of the United States: 1940. Population. Education, Educational Attainment of Children by Rental Value of Home* (Washington: Government Printing Office, 1945), Table III; and *Educational Attainment by Economic Characteristics and Marital Status* (Washington: Government Printing Office, 1947), Table 17.

is 2,500, for a daily newspaper 5,000, for a radio station 10,000, for an FM station 50,000, and for television 500,000. Current trends suggest a raising of the required population base in the future for newspapers, and a lowering for libraries, FM, and television.[40]

| | | | Per Cent of Cities with— | | |
City-Size Group	School Expenditures Per Pupil, 1937–38	Median School Years Completed, Native White Males, 18–44, 1940	College or University, 1940	Art Museum, 1938	AM Radio Station, 1946
250,000 +	} $120	11.0	100	86	100
100,000 —		⎫	56	53	89
50,000 —	99*	⎬ 11.2†	43	25	72
10,000 —	85*	⎭	19	4	39
2,500 —	75	11.1†	6	1	5

* The dividing line between these two groups is 30,000, rather than 50,000.
† The dividing line between these two groups is 25,000, rather than 10,000.

A more detailed analysis of libraries shows that they generally meet desirable minimum professional standards only in cities as large as 50,000-75,000.[41] Although libraries in large cities have larger book stocks and spend more money per capita, their service to the population is less as measured by per capita book circulation. For a sample of 103 cities in 1943 there was a negative correlation of —.64 between city-size and per capita circulation. Holding constant percent of population registered as borrowers, book stock in volumes per capita, branch libraries per capita, and per capita expenditures, the correlation remained at —.51.[42] Another writer has demonstrated a negative correlation between city-size and per capita museum attendance.[43] Apparently for those facilities which do not operate by mass distribution, the superior facilities of the large city are purchased at the price of diminished community participation.

6. *Public Recreation.*—An accepted professional standard for park acreage is one acre per 100 population. This standard is attained by one-fifth the cities between 50,000 and 250,000, by practically no city above that size, and by somewhat lesser percentages of the smaller cities. Parks in large cities have a much wider variety of recreation facilities, special use areas and buildings, and spend larger per capita amounts for operation and maintenance. On the other hand, the accessibility of parks, as indicated by the number of parks per capita is much greater in the small cities. In those

40. Laurence Vail Coleman, *The Museum in America* (Washington: The American Association of Museums, 1939), Vol. III; *The American Library Directory, 1939* (New York: R. R. Bowker Co., 1939); *Directory, Newspapers and Periodicals, 1946* (Philadelphia: N. W. Ayer & Son, 1946); "Directory of Broadcasting Stations of the United States," *Broadcasting, 1946 Yearbook Number,* pp. 71-190; Jack Alicoate, ed., *The 1947 Radio Annual* (New York: Radio Daily, 1947).

41. Lowell Martin, "The Optimum Size of the Public Library Unit," *Library Extension: Problems and Solutions,* ed. Carleton B. Joeckel (Chicago: University of Chicago Press, 1945), pp. 32-46.

42. Original data taken from "Public Library Statistics," *Bulletin, American Library Association,* XXXVIII (April, 1944), 154-167.

43. Paul Marshall Rea, *The Museum and the Community* (Lancaster: The Science Press, 1932).

cities reporting parks there are four for every 10,000 persons in the city of 25,000-50,000 as compared to 1 in the city over 1,000,000.[44] The optimum population for parks, on any equilibrium of these four variables, is clearly in the middle size range of cities.

The population base for zoos (estimated as before) is 100,000; [45] approximately the same figure holds for symphony orchestras.[46] Resident grand opera is found in only three or four of the country's largest cities, and the population base for opera of any sort is apparently above a quarter million.[47] On the other hand, motion picture theaters are found in every city, and even cities as small as 10,000-25,000 have variety and choice of cinematic offerings, with an average of three movies each.[48]

City-Size Group	At Least One Park Acre Per 100 Population 1940	Park Expenditure of at Least $1.00 Per Capita, 1940	Zoo, 1940	Symphony Orchestra, 1946
		Per Cent of Cities with—		
1,000,000 +	0	80	100	100
500,000 —	0	100	100	89
250,000 —	9	58	76	78
100,000 —	20	42	57	55
50,000 —	21	42	32	18
25,000 —	17	27	15	5
10,000 —	15	14	8	0
5,000 —	14	13	2	0
2,500 —	12	7	1	0

7. *Retail Facilities.*—The oft mentioned values of the large city as a shopping center cannot be denied. However, in many standard lines of merchandise this advantage is slight, the real superiority of the large city being in style and specialty trade. It is worth observing that in no more than three of the 65 kinds of retail outlet listed by the census is a population base of over 50,000 apparently required.[49] Another study suggests that for some lines of specialty goods, stores in the largest cities apparently have no more "drawing power" for non-resident trade than those in cities of 100,000.[50] The optimum city population for adequate retail outlets, even for specialized trade, may therefore be no higher than 50,000 to 100,000.

8. *Churches and associations.*—Criteria of optimum city-size involving

44. National Recreation Association, *Municipal and County Parks in the United States, 1940* (New York: National Recreation Association, 1942).

45. *Ibid.*

46. "Symphony Orchestras in the United States and Canada," *The International Musician*, XLIV (June, 1946), 7-8.

47. *Pierre Key's Music Year Book, 1938* (New York: Pierre Key, 1938).

48. *Motion Picture Theatres in the United States: A Statistical Summary, 1948* (New York: Motion Picture Association of America, Inc., 1948).

49. Population base estimated as city-size where number of stores per city is 1.0, by graphic interpolation; U.S. Bureau of the Census, *Sixteenth Census of the United States: 1940. Census of Business: 1939. Retail Trade Analysis by City-Size Groups* (Washington: Government Printing Office, 1942), Table 12C.

50. John Adams Pfanner, Jr., *A Statistical Study of the Drawing Power of Cities for Retail Trade* (Studies in Business Administration, The Journal of Business of The University of Chicago, Vol. X, No. 3, April, 1940).

the organized group life are ordinarily not precisely stated. Rather there is usually some general reference to the desirability of a certain degree of variety and diversity of groups, preferably without too much loss of community consensus and cohesion. The following data will doubtless seem somewhat tangential to this formulation.

There are only 20 religious denominations in the United States (1936) which have as many as 1,000 urban local churches. These cover three-fourths of all local churches and nine-tenths of all memberships in urban areas. Perhaps 20 could therefore be regarded as a generous estimate of the minimum desirable number of denominations. From census data on number of denominations per city, it is estimated that 30,000 is the population base for this degree of denominational variety.[51]

There are no comparative statistics on the variety of voluntary associations present in cities of different sizes, and only fragmentary data on certain national organizations. From these, the estimated population bases for certain kinds of organization are as follows: Rotary Club, 5,000; Elks lodge, 10,000; Lions Club, 15,000; Boy Scout Council, 25,000; YMCA, 25,000; YWCA, 25,000.[52] The population base for any two or more of these would be somewhat higher, but in all probability most organizations of these types are well represented in cities no larger than 25,000-50,000.

9. *Family life.*—Advocates of small cities and decentralization often stress the greater strength of the family institution in small cities. Statistical support for this position may be found in the data on marriage and fertility. Of the native white population 18-64, only three-fifths are married in cities over a quarter million as against over two-thirds in cities 2,500-25,000.[53]

In 1940 no city-size group in the urban white population had a fertility level up to the permanent replacement quota. The cities of 2,500-10,000 were reproducing at 15 per cent below replacement, whereas cities over 1,000,000 were 35 per cent below.[54] In previous census periods the persistent inverse association of city-size and effective fertility has also been marked.

Another important aspect of family living—housing—has been minutely described by the 1940 census. The principal differentials by city-size are as follows: Home ownership is more frequent in small cities; rentals increase with increasing city-size; and owner-occupied units are less frequently mortgaged in small cities. Thus both ownership and rental are easier propositions in the smaller centers. Dwelling units in large cities are better equipped

---

51. U.S. Bureau of the Census, *Religious Bodies: 1936, Vol. I. Summary and Detailed Tables* (Washington: Government Printing Office, 1941), Table 13.

52. Official Directory 1935–1936 (Chicago: Rotary International, 1935); Keyes, *op. cit.*, p. 162.

53. U.S. Bureau of the Census, *Educational Attainment by Economic Characteristics and Marital Status, op. cit.*, Table 37.

54. Warren S. Thompson, *The Growth of Metropolitan Districts in the United States: 1900–1940* (Washington: Government Printing Office, 1947); and special computations from 1940 Census data.

with regard to private bath, running water, central heating, flush toilet, mechanical refrigeration, and gas or electric cooking. They are also in better repair, being somewhat newer on the average. In small cities a majority of dwelling units are in single family structures, whereas the reverse is true of large cities. However, there is somewhat more room overcrowding in small cities, as measured by the standard of more than one and one-half persons per room.[55] In sum, not all the advantages in regard to good housing lie with any one size group of cities.

Housing Characteristics, 1940	Cities of—			
	250,000 and Over	50,000– 250,000	10,000– 50,000	2,500– 10,000
Home ownership	29%	38%	45%	49%
Average rent, tenant units	$32	$25	$23	$18
Single family units	33%	51%	61%	71%
Room overcrowding	5%	6%	6%	7%
Units needing major repairs	8%	11%	14%	17%
Units without running water	3%	6%	8%	15%

10. *Miscellaneous Psychological and Social Characteristics of Urban Life.*—There remains a residual category of attributes, desirable and undesirable, which are sometimes mentioned as criteria of optimum city-size. Such epithets as provincialism, friendliness, community participation, standardization, anonymity, strain, spontaneity, and the like are perhaps applied with more heat than light in the absence of precise specification and reliable measurement of such urban traits.

One writer claims to find evidence of greater "social contentment" in cities below 25,000 in the fact that survey respondents there voice fewer complaints on certain questions about neighborhood and community characteristics.[56] Another attempt to get at some of the more intangible traits of cities through an analysis of student community reports[57] must be deemed methodologically unsound.

There is but one trait of this miscellany for which some approximate measurements can be made. This is the status of the city as a center of innovation and cultural diffusion. Rose's data indicate a positive correlation between city-size and cultural innovation.[58] Bowers has shown that amateur radio followed a diffusion cycle from large to small cities.[59] Data assembled for the present study indicate that commercial broadcasting, FM, and television follow a similar pattern. Another kind of measurement is the per capita incidence of persons in certain eminence groups. Inventors, artists,

55. *Housing—Special Reports,* Series H-44, Nos. 1-7 (Washington: U.S. Bureau of the Census, 1944–1945).

56. Branch, *op. cit.,* p. 31.

57. Walter T. Watson, "Is Community Size an Index of Urbanization?" *The Southwestern Social Science Quarterly,* XVII (September, 1936), 150-160.

58. Edward Rose, "Innovations in American Culture," *Social Forces,* XXVI (March, 1948), 255-272.

59. Raymond V. Bowers, "The Direction of Intra-Societal Diffusion," *American Sociological Review,* II (December, 1937), 826-836.

and persons in *Who's Who* are present in greater numbers, relative to population, in large cities than in small.[60]

DISCUSSION. The above summary of a considerable mass of data leads to the following comments: The optimum size of cities is quite different from the standpoint of certain criteria from what it is on the basis of others. It is found that even an apparently unitary criterion—e.g. health—may give conflicting indications of the optimum. There is no immediately obvious way in which these various optima may be objectively equilibrated, compromised, weighted, or balanced to yield an unequivocal figure for *the* optimum population for a city. Any numerical choice of a figure for the optimum population is involved in subjective value preferences and impressionistic weighting systems. Most theorists proposing a size or size range as the optimum adopt this procedure, or the alternative one of confining attention to a few of the many criteria of optimum city-size that have been proposed in the literature. Thus if the preeminent interest is in the planning of cities for safety in atomic war, some population, say 25,000 or 50,000, will be taken as a maximum desirable city-size. Some other interests will be compatible with this choice, e.g. those of physical plan, health, and public safety. Attention to the remaining criteria which indicate larger sizes is then shifted to a consideration of the sacrifices involved in limiting city-size. Data such as those cited in this paper furnish the starting point for such a consideration, assuming the relationship between city-size and urban characteristics to be those of the present time. The degree to which city and national planning could mitigate these sacrifices is a question which is still open, scientifically speaking, though there is no dearth of assertion on the subject.

The problem of optimum city-size originates in the realm of values and, ideally, eventuates in action. Only the middle term of the translation of values into action is open to scientific procedures, for the choice of values and the decision to act are intrinsically beyond the scope of science. Nevertheless, both valuation and action should profit from an occasional summing up of the evidence and its implications. This paper has reported an initial effort of that kind.

---

60. Sample of inventors from U.S. Patent Office, *Index of Patents, 1940* (Washington: Government Printing Office, 1941); sample of artists from *Who's Who In American Art, Vol. III, 1940–1941* (Washington: The American Federation of Arts, 1940); R. D. McKenzie, *The Metropolitan Community* (New York: McGraw-Hill Book Co., Inc., 1933), Table 48.

METROPOLITAN POPULATION AND MUNICIPAL GOVERNMENT EXPENDITURES IN CENTRAL CITIES

Amos H. Hawley

The importance of the population occupying the land surrounding and adjacent to urban centers for the maintenance of facilities and services within such places has been indicated in many ways. Delimitations of zones of influence, tributary areas, trade areas, etc., have been made by Galpin, McKenzie, and many others.[1] These studies, using both direct and indirect measures, have dealt with all sizes of places and always with the same general result, namely, they consistently show that the effective population is considerably greater than what is contained within incorporated boundaries. This conclusion is also supported by studies of the spatial distribution of urban functions, such as those by Bogue, Isard, and Whitney.[2] Empirical findings of this sort have found practical expression in the Census Bureau's concept of the metropolitan district.

The purpose of this paper is to test another hypothesis regarding the interdependence of populations lying within and without urban centers. This involves the use of municipal government expenditures. A first assumption is that city services, which are bought with municipal government expenditures, are developed to meet the total need generated by activity carried on within the city. Secondly, it is assumed that some of that activity, and hence some of the need for city services, arises from the population residing outside the city boundaries. The outlying population uses the city streets and public buildings; it multiplies police problems, thus affecting the costs of that service; it creates additional fire risks which must be included in the allocation of funds for fire protection; its congregation in and traffic through the city is a factor in the budget of the health department.[3] No doubt the impact of the outlying population

---

A condensed version of this paper originally appeared in the *Journal of Social Issues*, Vol. 7, (Nos. 1 and 2, 1951), pp. 100-108. Reprinted with the permission of the *Journal of Social Issues*.

1. C. J. Galpin, *The Social Anatomy of an Agricultural Village*, Agri. Experiment Stat. of the University of Wisconsin, Research Bulletin 34 (Madison, Wis., May, 1915); R. D. McKenzie, *The Metropolitan Community* (New York, 1933).

2. Don J. Bogue, *The Structures of the Metropolitan Community: A Study of Dominance and Subdominance* (Ann Arbor, 1949); Walter Isard and Vincent Whitney, "Metropolitan Site Selection," *Social Forces*, 27 (March 1949), 263-69. See also R. R. Dickinson, *City, Region and Regionalism* (London, 1947).

3. See Edward Blythin, "The Dangers of Metropolitan Decentralization," *National Municipal Review*, XXXI (Sept. 1942), 442-44.

is felt in the costs of many of the lesser services provided by municipal government. That influence also probably operates indirectly through the costs of services to factories and retail establishments which derive portions of their labor forces and clienteles from outside the city. It is for reasons such as these that some cities have felt justified in assessing a payroll tax, sometimes referred to as a "privilege" tax, on all who live or work within their boundaries.

Given the assumptions that (1) municipal government costs are developed to meet the total need for services generated within the city, and (2) some of that need arises from the population living outside the city's boundaries, then the annual expenditures of city governments should vary with the sizes of populations occupying adjoining areas. Likewise, the larger the proportion of the total population living outside the central city, the heavier should be the tax burden on the population living within the city. The investigation reported in the following paragraphs is designed to demonstrate these hypotheses, particularly the former. More than that, however, it analyzes the interrelations among selected demographic and related variables that may be expected to have some bearing on the costs of city government.

The data employed pertain to seventy-six cities of 100,000 or more population and their metropolitan districts.[4] Excluded from consideration as central cities are those with 100,000 or more population but which occupy a metropolitan district containing a larger city.[5] The fifteen cities excluded on this basis are regarded as satellite cities and they are added to the totals for the remainders of their respective districts. New York City, with its metropolitan district, is also omitted because of its exceptional size.

All characteristics of the seventy-six units are for the year 1940, except the variable of growth rate which is computed for 1930-1940. Municipal government expenditures are reduced to amounts per capita of the population living within the corporation limits of the central city.[6] The remaining variables are described on the stub of Table 1.

---

4. Akron, Albany, Atlanta, Baltimore, Birmingham, Boston, Bridgeport, Buffalo, Canton, Charlotte, Chattanooga, Chicago, Cincinnati, Cleveland, Columbus, Dallas, Dayton, Denver, Des Moines, Detroit, Duluth, Erie, Flint, Fort Wayne, Fort Worth, Grand Rapids, Hartford, Houston, Indianapolis, Jacksonville, Kansas City (Mo.), Knoxville, Los Angeles, Louisville, Lowell, Memphis, Miami, Milwaukee, Minneapolis, Nashville, New Haven, New Orleans, Norfolk, Oklahoma City, Omaha, Peoria, Philadelphia, Pittsburgh, Portland, Providence, Reading, Richmond (Va.), Rochester, Sacramento, St. Louis, Salt Lake City, San Antonio, San Diego, San Francisco, Scranton, Seattle, South Bend, Springfield, Spokane, Syracuse, Takoma, Tampa, Toledo, Trenton, Tulsa, Utica, Washington (D.C.), Wichita, Wilmington, Worcester, Youngstown.

5. These cities are: Cambridge, Camden, Elizabeth, Fall River, Gary, Jersey City, Kansas City (Kan.), Long Beach, Newark, New Bedford, Oakland, Paterson, St. Paul, Somerville, Yonkers.

6. Data derived from *Statistical Abstract of the United States, 1942* (Washington, D. C., 1943), 264-267.

The procedure used is correlation analysis. While the relationship between all costs of city government per capita and city population (r = .398) is slightly curvilinear (p = .513), the position adopted in this study is that the curvilinearity may be due to lack of control of related variables. Hence it is assumed, though not tested, that multiple correlation will correct the curvilinearity.

FINDINGS. In Table 1 are presented the zero order coefficients for all government expenditures, operating expenditures, and capital improvement expenditures[7] with eight variables of central cities and ten variables of remainders of districts. A number of interesting observations may be made from these data. Perhaps the most singular finding is that per capita costs of government (computed on the population residing within the city) are more closely related to population living outside the city (r = .554) than with the population occupying the city (r = .398). The disparity is even greater where per capita operating costs alone are considered (r = .398 and r = .560 respectively). Thus, on the basis of this gross comparison, the first hypothesis of the study appears to be true. The correlation coefficients for government expenditures with the per cent of the

Table 1—Zero Order Correlation Coefficients* of Municipal Government Expenditures with Selected Charactristics of 76 Metropolitan Districts, 1940

Metropolitan District Division and Other Characteristics		MUNICIPAL GOVERNMENT EXPENDITURES PER CAPITA		
		All Expenditures (y_1)	Operating Expenditures (y_2)	Capital Improvement Expenditures (y_3)
Central city				
Population size	(x_1)	.398	.398	.156
Population per square mile	(x_2)	.526	.509	.286
Population growth rate, 1930-1940	(x_3)	−.171	−.215	.028
Labor force, number in	(x_4)	.394	.393	.159
White-collar occupations, no. in	(x_5)	.403	.403	.161
Houses, number of	(x_6)	.403	.422	.163
Houses, per square mile	(x_7)	.546	.536	.273
Area, square miles	(x_8)	.241	.241	.083
Remainder of district				
Population size	(x_a)	.554	.560	.200
Population per square mile	(x_b)	.501	.531	.093
Population growth, 1930-1940	(x_c)	−.197	−.229	.027
Labor force, number in	(x_d)	.321	.325	.107
White-collar occupations, no. in	(x_e)	.417	.430	.106
% of population incorporated	(x_f)	.559	.567	.195
% of total district population	(x_g)	.560	.577	.169
Houses, number of	(x_h)	.535	.546	.177
Houses, per square mile	(x_i)	.545	.595	.052
Area, square miles	(x_j)	.364	.352	.165

* Coefficients of .325 and higher are reliable at the 1% level. Coefficients of .250 or higher are reliable at the 5% level.

7. Including interest charges.

total district population living outside of the central city indicate that the corollary hypothesis is also correct (all costs: r = .560, and operating costs: r = .577). That is, government costs are somewhat more closely associated with the proportion of the total population living outside of central cities than with the size of the outlying population as such.

Before pressing further with the major concern of the study, it is well to note certain other relationships shown in Table 1. Of interest is the fact that capital improvement costs are only slightly associated with the independent variables under study. In all probability this reflects the inadequacy of a single year for a study of capital improvement expenditures.

The dependence of government costs on population characteristics is most pronounced in respect to operating costs. The data in Table 1 suggest that this observation applies most markedly to the remainder of the district. Operating costs, in other words, are much more sensitive to variation in population characteristics than are capital improvement costs.

Government expenditures are more closely associated with density of population within the city (r = .526) than with the size of city population. But this is not true of density (r = .501) as compared to population size in the remainder of the district. While the difference between the coefficients for size and density of population outside the city is small, it is in the expected direction. City government costs are affected mainly by the number of people who reside in or who come into the city; only in a few instances are city services extended beyond the limits and thus are subject to the influence of congested settlement.

The association with growth rates is slight and inverse. Central cities and remainders of districts show no appreciable difference in this respect. This finding is in accord with the conclusions of others regarding the lag in the development of government services as population changes.

The correlation of government expenditures with labor force size is unimpressive, both where the central city and the remainder of the district are involved. Higher correlation coefficients obtain between the numbers of people employed in white-collar occupations and municipal government expenditures, though the difference is not significant.

Housing density, i.e., the number of houses per square mile, is more consistently related to government costs than is either the number of houses or the number of square miles. In the remainder of districts the influence of housing density is much greater than is that of either of the variables it combines.

Having noted that municipal government expenditures in central cities of metropolitan districts are more closely related to population size in satellite areas than to population size within the cities themselves, the question we ask is to what extent is the association between expenditures and population influenced by, or dependent on, variations in other characteristics. It is possible, for example, that certain demographic characteristics are distributed in such a manner as to obscure the relationship between government costs and population. A preliminary step toward uncovering a truer relationship may be made by successively adding the effect of each of the several independent variables by multiple correlation shown on the stub of Table 1. The results of this operation are in Table 2.

Table 2—First Order Multiple Correlation Coefficients. Population Size in Central Cities, Paired Successively with Each of Seventeen Independent Variables, and Municipal Government Expenditures in 76 Metropolitan Districts, 1940

Independent Variable Paired With Size of Population in Central City		MUNICIPAL GOVERNMENT EXPENDITURES PER CAPITA		
		All Expenditures Y_1	Operating Expenditures Y_2	Capital Improvement Expenditures Y_3
Central city				
Population per square mile	(x_{12})	.551	.538	.286
Population growth rate	(x_{13})	.401	.445	.160
Labor force, number in	(x_{14})	.417	.535	.170
White-collar workers, number in	(x_{15})	.444	.403	.161
Houses, number of	(x_{16})	.434	.437	.166
Houses per square mile	(x_{17})	.569	.561	.274
Area, square miles	(x_{18})	.398	.400	.158
Remainder of district				
Population size	(x_{1a})	.553	.560	.202
Population per square mile	(x_{1b})	.531	.554	.157
Population growth rate	(x_{1c})	.431	.442	.162
Labor force, number in	(x_{1d})	.442	.444	.166
White-collar workers, number in	(x_{1e})	.574	.585	.188
% of population incorporated	(x_{1f})	.559	.567	.198
% of total district population	(x_{1g})	.560	.579	.177
Houses, number of	(x_{1h})	.537	.547	.184
Houses, per square mile	(x_{1i})	.567	.610	.158
Area, square miles	(x_{1j})	.433	.428	.182

As may be surmised from data presented earlier, the density of population within central cities exerts an important influence on the association of all expenditures and population size. The measure of relationship changes from $r_{y1.x_1} = .398$ to $R_{y1.x_{12}} = .551$, when the effect of density is added. Of the characteristics found within central cities, population density is surpassed in influence only by housing density — $R_{y1.x_{17}} = .569$. No other central city variable deflects the relationship in question to any important degree. The addition of the influence of area exerts no effect on the relationship obtained in the zero order correlation. Growth rate is almost equally unimportant. The size of the labor force, the number of white-collar workers, and the number of houses produce slightly higher, but still unimportant, improvements in the measure of association.

Variations in nearly all characteristics of the satellite areas exert greater influence on the relationship than do the corresponding variables within central cities. The principal exception occurs in connection with housing density, which exerts substantially the same effect from the satellite areas as from the central cities. It is noteworthy that the association of all government expenditures with size of central city population is affected equally by the size of satellite population and by the density of central city population. No doubt these two variables are interdependent. The most impressive result gained from adding variables in the satellite area, however, is that involving the size of the white-collar occupational population ($R_{y1} \cdot x_{1e} = .574$). Thus, it appears that the number of white-collar workers in the outlying areas constitutes a much more important influence than does the number of such workers within the central cities ($R_{y1} \cdot x_{15} = .444$). The former seems to be considerably more important too than the size of the labor force in satellite areas ($R_{y1} \cdot x_{1d} = .442$).

Very similar patterns of association appear when operating costs are substituted for all costs as the dependent variable. The one slight exception occurs in connection with the size of the labor force within central cities ($R_{y2} \cdot x_{14} = .535$). Housing density in the satellite area affects the relationship of size of central city population and operating costs very significantly ($R_{y2} \cdot x_{11} = .610$).

In the association with capital improvement costs the patterns for paired variables within the central city are the same as those observed for all costs. Differences appear, however, in the measure of relationship involving satellite area variables. Density of satellite population, for example, has no added independent effect on the relation of central city population and capital improvement costs ($R_{y3} \cdot x_{1b} = .157$). And the independent effect of per cent of total district population is not great ($R_{y3} \cdot x_{1g} = .177$). Again, housing density in the satellite area adds nothing to the relationship ($R_{y3} \cdot x_{1i} = .158$). In short, once more it is evident that capital improvement costs are responsive to different characteristics than are operating costs.

A question which now arises is: To what extent do the eighteen independent variables explain all of the variation in government costs in central cities? An answer may be found by accumulating the effects of the independent variables in multiple R's. The results of such a calculation are shown in Table 3. The last coefficient in each column expresses the combined effect of all variables for each type of government cost. Thus the association of all government costs with the eighteen independent variables taken together ($R_{y1} \cdot x_{12345678abcdefghij}$) is .755. In other words, the total effect of the several characteristics accounts for approximately 57 per cent of the variation in all municipal expenditures in central cities. The percentage of determination rises slightly to 59 for operating costs and capital improvement costs, the R values for these dependent variables being .768 and .733, respectively.[8]

About 40 per cent of the variation in municipal government costs remains unexplained. It is quite likely that so large a residue reflects on the adequacy of the metropolitan district definitions employed in the 1940

8. The differences between the $r_y x_1$ values and their respective $R_y \cdot x_{12345678abcdefghij}$ values are significant at the .001 level.

Census. With a different definition, the same eighteen independent variables may have accounted for a much larger proportion of the variation. It is probable, too, that other independent variables are closely associated with government costs in central cities. Per capita income, for example, may have considerable importance in this respect. A high-income population is able and perhaps willing to support a larger municipal budget than is a low-income population. Furthermore, the high-income population living outside the central city may use the city's facilities more intensively than the low-income population. Still another factor of possible significance is the nature of the local economy. While that is partly involved in some of the demographic characteristics already used, its influence probably is not entirely contained in such characteristics. For instance, a concentration of heavy industry in the satellite area may cause a large flow of truck traffic over the central city's streets, thus raising the costs of street maintenance and traffic control above what would be necessary in the absence of an industrial concentration. The ramifications of composition of the local economy are numerous and merit much more investigation than they have received to date.

Returning to the data at hand, it is apparent that many of the independent variables are of negligible consequence in accounting for the variations in municipal government costs. That is particularly true of growth rate, size of the labor force, number of houses, and area, both within and without the central city. It applies to a lesser extent to several other factors. Nor is this surprising, for the influences of many of these factors are contained in and are, therefore, adequately represented by other factors. The size of the labor force, for example, is so closely associated with population size ($r_{lf} = .999$) that little or nothing is gained by using both.

No doubt closely comparable results could be obtained by using fewer than eighteen independent variables. By inspection it appears that seven factors are so closely associated with central city government expenditures and sufficiently unrelated to one another that they may explain most of the variation in the dependent variables. These are: Population density and housing density within the central city; and population size, number of white-collar workers, proportion of the satellite population incorporated, proportion of the total district population in the satellite area, and housing density in the satellite area. The multiple correlation coefficients based on these factors are:

$$R_{y1.x27aefgi} = .670$$
$$R_{y2.x27aefgi} = .680$$
$$R_{y3.x27aefgi} = .392$$

For total costs and for operating costs the seven independent variables produce R values which, when the numbers of variables involved are considered, do not differ significantly from those obtained when the eighteen factors are used. The percentages of variation explained thereby, however, are 44.9 and 46.2 respectively. But the seven selected variables used with capital costs produce a rather small R value; the .392 indicates that together they account for less than 16 per cent of the variation in expenditures for capital outlay. In fact, to obtain an R value which differs insignificantly from that secured with the eighteen independent variables (i.e., $R = .773$) requires the combined influence of at least sixteen of the eighteen.[9]

CONCLUSION. The initial hypothesis of this paper—that the municipal government costs of metropolitan centers vary with the sizes of their satellite populations—is clearly confirmed. In fact, the association with satellite

Table 3—Multiple Correlation Coefficients for Eighteen Independent Variables with Per Capita Government Costs in Central Cities of 76 Metropolitan Districts, 1940

		MULTIPLE CORRELATION COEFFICIENTS			PER CENT OF ASSOCIATION EXPLAINED		
Independent Variables Accumulated		All Costs Y_1	Operating Costs Y_2	Capital Costs Y_3	All Costs Y_1	Operating Costs Y_2	Capital Costs Y_3
Central city							
Population size	(x_1)	.398	.398	.156	15.8	15.8	2.4
and population per square mile	(x_{12})	.551	.537	.286	30.4	28.9	8.2
and population growth rate	(x_{123})	.554	.549	.302	30.7	30.1	9.1
and labor force	(x_{1234})	.558	.556	.305	31.2	30.9	9.3
and white collar workers	(x_{12345})	.622	.631	.312	38.6	39.8	9.8
and number of houses	(x_{123456})	.624	.633	.314	38.9	40.0	9.8
and house density	$(x_{1234567})$	.630	.641	.314	39.8	41.1	9.8
and area	$(x_{12345678})$	.647	.655	.333	41.9	42.9	11.1
Remainder of district							
and population size	$(x_{12345678a})$	.664	.676	.334	44.0	45.7	11.2
and population density	$(x_{12345678ab})$	.669	.685	.362	44.8	47.0	13.1
and population growth	$(x_{12345678abc})$	.670	.686	.364	44.9	47.1	13.3
and labor force	$(x_{12345678abcd})$	.675	.689	.383	45.6	47.4	14.7
and white collar workers	$(x_{12345678abcde})$	.709	.722	.383	50.2	52.1	14.7
and per cent incorporated	$(x_{12345678abcdef})$	.745	.726	.392	55.4	52.8	15.4
and per cent of total pop.	$(x_{12345678abcdefg})$	.749	.749	.419	56.0	56.1	17.6
and number of houses	$(x_{12345678abcdefgh})$	.751	.749	.519	56.5	56.1	26.9
and house density	$(x_{12345678abcdefghi})$	.751	.767	.682	56.5	58.9	46.5
and area	$(x_{12345768abcdefghij})$	.755	.768	.773	57.0	59.0	59.7

---

9. Trials of various combinations of fifteen variables failed to produce an R value which differed by an insignificant amount from the value obtained with the eighteen independent variables.

population is closer than with size of population in the cities concerned. That is true, moreover, of virtually every population variable employed as well as of such nondemographic factors as number of houses and housing density. The difference in degree of association as between central city and satellite area variables is most pronounced when operating costs alone are used. The hypothesis is not so consistently supported, however, when capital improvement costs is used as the dependent variable.

Analysis of the combined effect of numbers of variables on all costs and operating costs reveals that the most important factors of the eighteen studied are population density and housing density within central cities and, in the satellite area, size of population, number of white-collar workers, per cent of the population incorporated, per cent of total district population, and housing density. But at least sixteen of the factors are needed to explain variations in capital costs.

It may be of interest, particularly to those involved in debates over the wisdom of annexation, to note that area as such has an almost negligible association with government costs, though it does exercise some independent influence as may be seen in its effect in the multiple correlation coefficients. On the other hand, both population density and housing density show a well-marked relationship with government expenditures over and above that which may be attributed to size of population and number of houses. Does this mean that a decline in the intensity of land occupance may be accomplished without a corresponding increase in government costs? Clearly there is a problem for further investigation here.

Although in the zero order correlations (Table 1) the association of numbers of white-collar workers with central city government costs is not very close, nevertheless that variable exerts a highly significant (.001 level) independent influence. The inference suggested by this finding is that white-collar workers utilize the central city's facilities more intensively than do other classes of workers. Whether this may reflect differences in expectations of urban government, or simply differences in ability to pay the incidental costs of transportation and use is not known.

The relation of per cent of satellite area population incorporated to central city government costs also poses an interesting problem. It may mean, perhaps, that incorporation in the vicinity of a large city is less costly than if it takes place elsewhere, that, in other words, incorporation in the satellite area may depend partly on the existence of the central city's service facilities. It is just as possible, of course, that the equipment of the central city may serve as a model and a stimulus to incorporation in the surrounding area.

The findings reported here appear to have significance for municipal administrators and for planners, if not in the solution of day-to-day problems, then at least in the development of objectives and general policy. They indicate that the size of the metropolitan population not included in the corporation limits of the metropolitan center represents a cost factor to the residents of the center.[10] The latter are carrying the financial burden of an elaborate and costly service installation, i.e., the central city, which is used daily by a noncontributing population that in some instances is more than twice the size of the contributing population. Thus from the standpoint of fiscal policy alone a strong case for the establishment of a single metropolitan-wide government may be made. A single taxing and administrative agency would doubtless make for a more equitable distribution of costs and a more adequate complement of services for the entire metropolitan area.

A second implication of these findings—one which is becoming generally appreciated—is that the appropriate territorial unit for planning purposes is the metropolitan area rather than the municipal area. A smaller unit fails to encompass many of the factors that directly influence the events which the planner seeks to control. In this instance, changes in population size, shifts in population composition, the rate of incorporation, and the trend in housing construction in the satellite area present the planning agency in the central city with many problems, which sooner or later are apt to be reflected in a rising cost of government. In the absence of a government which embraces the entire metropolitan area, the planner's chief recourse would seem to be an alertness to developments in the satellite zone as one of the important variables affecting the success or failure of his efforts.

Whether the metropolitan area constitutes a community in any sentimental or sociologically abstruse sense may be uncertain. But that it is a community in the sense of functional interdependence and the mutual sensitivity of parts can scarcely be doubted. The former may well be a derivative from the latter. It is not unique to find men slow in perfecting their adaptations to altered circumstances. After well over a century of experience, men are just beginning to learn how to live in industrially contrived cities. That they should require more time than has yet passed to accommodate their actions and their perspectives to the more extensive and more ramified metropolitan community should surprise no one.

---

10. On the assumption of a linear relationship, every increase of one person in the central city population is accompanied by an increase of $1.30 in government costs, whereas each increase of one person in the satellite area is accompanied by an increment of $2.77 in the cost of government in the central city.

THE NEIGHBORHOOD, URBAN ECOLOGY, AND CITY PLANNERS

Richard Dewey

The modern period of city planning, which dates roughly from the World's Fair of 1893, has been dominated from its inception by architects, landscape architects, and engineers. Their domination has spread from the private consulting firms to the established planning commissions and departments on federal, state, and local levels. For years the problems faced and dealt with in the planning field were problems with which these specialists were equipped to deal, and the buildings, fountains, civic centers, lagoons, monuments, and even the highways were treated in isolation from the thinking and research of the social scientists. The latter were pursuing the problems of urbanism in their own way, and for the most part with neither knowledge of, nor concern for the efforts of those technicians in the drivers' seats of the planning firms, commissions, or departments. What has resulted from this nearly complete divorce of actual city planning on the one hand from the studies of the city by sociologists and other social scientists on the other hand is clearly visible. Any sociologist, social psychologist, economist, or political scientist who takes the time to examine the master plans which line library shelves, and the current versions which will find their way to those shelves, is soon convinced of the inadequacy of these plans from the social science viewpoint. However, the divorce has not only accrued to the disadvantage of the planner, but has lulled the urban sociologist, among other social scientists, into an uncritical complacency. Inasmuch as he has not been called upon to test his observations, nor to measure the adequacy of his concepts in the day-by-day application of the planners who are shaping the growth and changes of urban communities, his concern with historical developments and with the grosser outlines of theory has apparently met the needs of those enrolling in his courses. Few if any of the students taking courses in urban sociology are called upon to apply their newly gained information in actual attempts to understand or control urban behavior.

However, there is increasing evidence that this situation is changing, and that the long-term estrangement of social scientist and city planner is coming to a close. Upon the initiative of the engineers, landscape archi-

Reprinted from the *American Sociological Review*, 15 (August, 1950), pp. 502-507, by permission of the author and the *American Sociological Review*. (Copyright, 1950, by the *American Sociological Society*.)

tects, and architects who do the actual planning, research positions calling for training in the social sciences have become integral parts of planning staff organizations of most large cities.[1] The felt need for information
and viewpoints which are not provided in the training of engineer or
architect has been expressed formally by the American Institute of Planners
in a report by their committee on "The Content of Professional Curricula
in Planning," a committee made up of "firing line" planners, and not of
academicians.[2] That report stresses the need for knowledge of economics,
sociology, and political science equally as much as it does the need for
technical knowledge of materials and/or for skill in design.

It is the purpose of this paper to urge the urban sociologist to overcome
certain of the shortcomings which are the result of the separation of his
efforts from those of the city planners. As a means to that end, two of the
several weak spots of the urban sociologists are briefly discussed. In both
instances the errors are of omission rather than of commission; the one
concerning ecological theory directly, the second only indirectly.

The first instance concerns the sociologists' treatment of those urban
areas denoted by the ecological terms "transition" or "conversion" zone.
Whatever may have been written and said by the critics of the concentric
circle analysis of city patterns and growth (which was initiated by Park
and developed by Burgess), and we all know that the criticism has been
considerable, none has denied that the terms "transition zone" or "conversion zone" denote valid structure and processes which are associated
with rapidly growing American cities.[3] These areas of mixed land uses
immediately adjacent to central and auxiliary business and industrial districts characterize all such urban areas. Nor would planners deny, once
they discover what is meant by the "transition zone," that herein lies a
major problem area, if not *the* problem, of today's metropolis. Yet the
plans for the problem's solution as recommended by the planners usually
entail either some form of superhighway which would permit the employees
of the central business district to ignore the problems of slum, blight, and
confused land use by speeding past them en route to job or suburban
residence, or else the construction of low-cost subsidized housing on high-
cost land. These plans evidence a basic lack of understanding of the nature
of the so-called "transition" zone, and this is one point at which the social

---

1. It is true that there are instances where social scientists have sought entrance to
planning activities and have been denied, but this is not the rule.
2. "Content of Professional Curricula in Planning," *Journal of American Institute
of Planners,* XIV (Winter, 1948), 4-19.
3. Cf. R. E. Park & E. W. Burgess, *The City,* Chicago: University of Chicago Press,
1925; Maurice R. Davie, "The Pattern of Urban Growth," in *Studies in the Science of
Society,* ed. by G. P. Murdock, New Haven: Yale University Press, 1937, pp. 133-161;
Walter Firey, *Land Use in Central Boston,* Cambridge: Harvard University Press, 1947;
Homer Hoyt, *The Structure and Growth of Residential Neighborhoods in American
Cities,* Washington, D.C.: Federal Housing Administration, 1939; James A. Quinn,
"The Development of Human Ecology in Sociology," in Barnes, Becker, and Becker,
Contemporary Sociological Theory, New York: D. Appleton-Century Co., Inc., 1940.

scientists, urban sociologist and land economist particularly, have failed in their obligation to the planners. One looks in vain through current literature for an adequate discussion of the nature of this area. Even the continued use of the terms "transition" and "conversion" zones evidence the outdated nature of the ecological concepts. These dynamic concepts of urban patterns and growth were derived from observation of rapidly growing cities, and are no longer applicable to central cities which are growing very slowly or not at all. The less flattering term of "stagnation" zone better describes the actual present-day scene. The problem of slum and blight in the past was frequently one of a moving target: the ecological processes of invasion and succession kept the situation fluid, creating problems of mixed land use on the periphery of the transition zone where business and industry pressed into residential areas, but solving problems on the inner side of the zone where the transition or conversion from residential to nonresidential use had become complete. That period of rapid growth of the city is gone, in all probability permanently, and the planner will find the concepts of invasion and succession of waning importance. As Stuart Queen has said, the problems now facing the planner of cities lie primarily in those areas where the conversion process stopped short of completion. Because these ecological processes are slowing down, even stopping or reverting in certain instances, the slum of today will not be the business district of tomorrow, nor can the planner meet his obligation through zoning regulations and control of expanding growth. The problem has become one of urban *re*-development, not one of controlled growth. The addition of this information, supplemented by that provided by needed research in the area, would not be difficult from the point of view of the sociologist or economist, yet would add greatly to the planner's ability to cope with his problems. Failure to provide the planner with such basic information accounts in no small part, it would seem, for the apparent willingness of many planners to accept as inevitable the present ecological patterns of large urban communities. The social scientist has some obligation to point out to the planners that the land use pattern of the erstwhile transition zone is the heritage of miscalculations of speculators as to the rate of future urban growth, the extreme overcrowding of low-income residents as a *temporary expedient* in the speculation process, and of unfortunate tax policies which encouraged deterioration of the area. This much can be done immediately, despite the tremendous need for research as to the best use to be made of the extensive slum and blighted areas.

The second point selected to illustrate the costs of estrangement of planner and sociologist concerns the "neighborhood unit" principle. This principle was given its clearest formulation and greatest impetus by the late Clarence Perry in connection with his work for the New York regional plan. The neighborhood unit, as defined by Perry, is a residential area which

. . . should provide housing for that population for which one elementary school is ordinarily required, its actual area depending upon its population density . . .

should be bounded on all sides by arterial streets, sufficiently wide to facilitate its bypassing, instead of penetration, by through traffic . . . [should include] a system of small parks and recreational spaces. . . . Sites for the school and other institutions having service spheres coinciding with the limits of the unit should be suitably grouped about a central point. . . . One or more shopping districts . . . should be laid out in the circumference of the unit . . . [and] the unit should be provided with a special street system . . . being designed to facilitate circulation within the unit and to discourage its use by through traffic.[4]

Until very recently this principle rode unchallenged at the vanguard of planning concepts, sharing the spotlight with the over-emphasized express or limited-access highways. Although the remarks which follow are directed primarily toward the small group of extremists among planners who have exceeded Perry himself in their enthusiasm for the plan (Perry readily admitted that the principle was applicable only to certain parts of the city, being limited by both physical and social factors, see *ibid.*, pp. 52, 61), Mr. Perry did leave room for the inference that the principle still embodied for him much of the small village flavor. Witness his statement that

Thus the square itself will be invested with a meaning, a symbolism, more significant than the mere sum of its parts. It will be a visible sign of unity. . . . The square itself will be an appropriate location for a flagpole, a memorial monument, a bandstand, or an ornamental fountain. *In the common life of the neighborhood* it will function as the place of local celebrations. Here, on Independence Day, the Flag will be raised, the Declaration of Independence will be recited, and the citizenry urged to patriotic deeds by eloquent orators.[5]

It is to this aspect of Perry's writings, but more particularly to his less critical followers, that we now turn attention. Reginald Isaacs, planning director of Michael Reese Hospital in Chicago, caused no small amount of consternation among planners with his recent analytical attack upon the neighborhood-unit principle as a guide for urban planning. His main points of criticism, that the very social and physical nature of the metropolitan regions makes the creation of the small-town type of neighborhood an improbability, and that where the development of such neighborhoods has been attempted, the efforts were often motivated by the desire to segregate socio-economic groups, are not without verifying data.[6]

Isaacs makes a good, some persons think an overemphatic, case against certain aspects of the principle, but perhaps his most telling attack was against the misuse of it. In response to the criticism, Frederick Adams, head of the department of regional and city planning at Massachusetts Institute of Technology, accused the sociologist of having presented a

4. *Housing for the Machine Age*, p. 51.
5. *Ibid.*, p. 65. Italics not in the original.
6. "Are Urban Neighborhoods Possible?" *Journal of Housing*, July, 1948, pp. 177-180; "The 'Neighborhood Unit' Is An Instrument for Segregation," *loc. cit.*, August-1948, pp. 215-219. The essence of these arguments also published in "The Neighborhood Theory," *Journal of the American Institute of Planners*, XIV (Spring, 1948), 15-23. See also Max S. Wherly's answer to Isaacs' position, "Comment on the Neighborhood Theory," *loc. cit.*, XIV (Fall, 1948), 32-34.

principle to the planners, and then criticizing them for accepting it as valid. Professor Adams credits us with activity which is not ours, because the sociologists have been most conspicuous by their absence in both the development of the principle and in the ensuing controversy. In James Dahir's recent comprehensive annotated bibliography, containing well over 100 titles dealing directly and indirectly with the neighborhood-unit principle, only six titles are the works of sociologists.[7] Surely it is within the province of sociology that the neighborhood concept falls, yet the treatment of it there has left much to be desired. Nor can we plead that the lack of research justifies our neglect, because there is much that we can contribute even today. It can be pointed out that much of the difficulty associated with the attempt to use the concept in planning lies in the planner's interpretation of it as a unitary concept, whereas it is a dual concept as they employ it.[8] It embodies a service area concept designed to reduce the need for undue expenditure of time and energy, and for this part of the principle there are research findings which will permit the planners to proceed with the assurance that their reports will result in satisfaction for the residents of the service area.[9]

The other embodiment of the neighborhood principle is a nostalgia for the rural way of life with its closely compacted primary groups. The misconceptions of many planners as to the nature of the neighborhood as a

---

7. *The Neighborhood Unit Plan—Its Spread and Acceptance,* New York: Russell Sage Foundation, 1947; Cf. "The Neighborhood Concept in Theory and Application," in *Land Economics,* XXV, Feb., 1949 (Supplement: "Symposium on Frontiers of Housing Research") articles by Svend Riemer, Reginald Isaacs, Robert B. Mitchell, and Gerald Breese; Judith Tannenbaum, "The Neighborhood—A Psycho-Sociological Analysis," *Land Economics,* November, 1948; Walter Gropius, "Organic Neighborhood Planning," *Housing and Town and Country Planning,* United Nations Bulletin, 2, April, 1949, pp. 2-8; *Planning the Neighborhood,* American Public Health Association, published by Public Administration Service, Chicago; Catherine Bauer, "Good Neighborhoods," *The Annals of the American Academy of Political and Social Science,* November, 1945.

8. One sociologist has broken the concept down into even more parts, viz., the primary neighborhood, the concentric service neighborhood, the relational personal neighborhood, the areal neighborhood, and the residential area. Frank L. Sweetser, Jr., *Neighborhood Acquaintance and Association—a study of personal neighborhoods,* New York: Columbia University Press, 1941, p. 91. Professor Sweetser's study concerns itself with the "relational personal neighborhood," which he describes as being "socially definite, although it is areally indeterminate."

9. *Better Housing for the Family,* published by the Woman's Club of New York City, 1948; Theodore Caplow, "Home Ownership and Location Preferences in a Minneapolis Sample," *American Sociological Review,* 13 (December, 1948); *Present Housing of Former Project Tenants,* New York City Housing Authority, May, 1943; *Survey of Tenant Opinion in Charter Oak Terrace,* Hartford Housing Authority, 1942; *Urban Planning and Public Opinion,* Bureau of Urban Research, Princeton, N. J., September, 1942; *Why do Tenants Move?,* Citizens Housing Council of New York, 1940; *The Milwaukee Survey,* Urban Redevelopment Study, Chicago, 1949; Richard Dewey, "Peripheral Expansion in Milwaukee County," *American Journal of Sociology,* LIV (September, 1948). Further evidence of the practicality of the service area aspect of Perry's principle is found in the many residential areas already built which embody service units in keeping with the original principles. The best illustrations are Greenbelt, Greenhills, and Greendale.

primary group will thwart any real success of shaping social relationships by means of physical design. Among the questions to be raised by the sociologist for the benefit of the planner are the following:

The first question relates to the nature of the rural setting in which the neighborhood seemed to function best. Might it not be the homogeneity of income classes, nationality, racial, and religious composition that made random neighboring possible? Have the planners taken into account the marked heterogeneity of the city and considered the probability of the attempts to recreate rural patterns of social relationships in an urban setting floundering upon the stark realism of habitual prejudices? Can the sociologist disagree with Isaacs' assertion that application of the neighborhood principle will either result in segregation on a scale hitherto unknown or will fail completely? He makes his point well when he asks how the neighborhood unit principle can be applied to a population which is approximately equally divided between parochial and public school attendants. What sociologist would claim that sheer juxtaposition of peoples with irreconcilable convictions is sufficient for the resolution of these differences?

A second query we might raise is whether or not the rural community with its prototype of the neighborhood was ever the social paradise it is often assumed to have been. Isn't it more than likely that the advocates of the neighborhood principle look upon the small-town social patterns from the vantage point of the leader or outstanding citizen of the community? This fact is illustrated by Oliver Goldsmith in his famous *Deserted Village*, a source often quoted in support of the small-town ideal. One seldom-remembered paragraph reveals that Goldsmith's principal concern with the passing of "Sweet Auburn, Fairest Village of the Plain" is his frustration at not being able to return to his former haunts and to show his worldly wisdom before the local yokels who never left the village.[10] Had he written as much and as well about the reasons why he left the village in the first place, we might have a more balanced picture of "Sweet Auburn." Might it not be of service to the planner to emphasize the simple truth that whereas high social visibility plus high status adds up to genuinely satisfactory way of life, high visibility added to mediocre or low social status results in a social situation that falls far short of satisfaction.

---

10. "In all my wand'rings round this world of care,
In all my griefs—and God has given my share—
I still had hopes my latest hours to crown,
Amidst these humble bowers to lay me down;
To husband out life's taper at the close,
And keep the flame from wasting by repose.
I still had hopes, for pride attends us still,
Around my fire an evening group to draw,
And tell of all I felt and all I saw;
And, as a hare, whom hounds and horns pursue,
Pants to the place from whence at first she flew,
I still had hopes, my long vexations passed,
Here to return—and die at home at last."

A third point requiring emphasis concerns the nature of the small town's primary groups. It is often overlooked that there are two types of primary groups operating in the rural setting. In the first, group membership is voluntary and is made up of friends and associates of one's own choosing. The second group is made up of those whose attention is unsolicited and often unwelcome, but the small-town resident cannot escape membership in this primary group. The former type of primary group is essential to man's welfare regardless of his residence, but the latter type is neither essential nor desirable, and is frequently the reason for persons migrating from rural areas. The sociologist and social psychologist can aid planners by pointing out that a large primary group is *not* essential to the development of an adequate personality. However, this misconception is integral to the thinking of those who would plan our cities in terms of neighborhoods. As one English writer has said, "Many worthy people do not want formal social organizations. They are happy among their family and their friends." He adds that ". . . when exiles think of their home town they are as likely to recall the pub, the snack bar or Sunday evenings in the park as they are to think of the church, the school or the community centre."[11]

A fourth point is found in the fact that the ideal-type neighborhood was congruent with the economic community wherein the populace spent all of their time. This fact, plus the slower modes of transportation and communication, enforced the close-knit community neighborhood. The resulting social pattern was born of necessity, not desire. Does not the fact that the breadwinner, and often other members of the urban family, must go outside of the proposed neighborhood for work, school, and special services destroy one of the prerequisites for the creation and maintenance of urban neighborhoods? The primary group activities, such as bowling teams and bridge groups, which are centered around place of work rather than residence, reduce the necessity of neighboring in the rural sense. It certainly is true that the planners who are ". . . trying to revive community life based upon place are moving against the tide of people's wishes. With modern communication there is no need for people to focus their interests on a particular locality."[12] In fact, it may be inviting a form of parochialism to do so. Svend Riemer cautions us that "cultural stagantion may well be expected where the individual is challenged to escape from participation in city-wide and nation-wide problems into the parochial haven of neighborhood affairs."[13]

Further evidence of the improbability of any successful re-creation of the rural neighborhood in metropolitan communities is found in the attempts to do this by copying certain activities which were carried on in the

11. "Can Communities Be Planned?," *Planning*, (London), Vol. XV, No. 296, March 28, 1949.
12. *Ibid.*
13. *Loc. cit.*, p. 71.

rural setting. In certain housing projects in large cities attempts have been made to foster handicrafts in the neighborhood centers, thinking thereby to recapture the neighborhood pattern of social activity. Actually, the result is an intensification of the division and specialization of labor which characterizes urbanism generally.[14] Even though such activities as quilting, weaving, and hooking rugs are engaged in, they are the activities of the specialist, whereas in the original rural setting every one in the community engaged in them. This affords one more example of the essential difference between the rural community of yesterday and the urban one of today.

In closing these remarks about the nature of the neighborhood-unit principle, it may be desirable again to make explicit the point that the target of such remarks is the extremist who has gone even farther than Clarence Perry ever did in espousing attempts to re-create the rural neighborhood within the metropolitan community. Such planners constitute a minority, albeit a vociferous one, among planners generally. Nor is this action on their part mystifying when one knows of the ugly, haphazard, and costly physical structure of modern metropolitan centers and of the genuine loneliness that characterizes much of the urban social life. The criticisms given here are more of the misapplication of the principle rather than of the principle as Perry outlined it in his *Housing for the Machine Age*. If the principle proves to be of prime importance in making our cities more livable, if it be the means of bringing more democratic control to the city as Cooley warned must be done, it will not be because of the uncritical application of it by ardent advocates, but because of its cautious application in accord with the best available knowledge of man's behavior in an urban environment.

Although it is probably true that urbanism is as neglected by adequate research as any other field of sociology, the sociologist and other social scientists can do much to bring greater realism into the present and future efforts of those whose responsibility it is to plan and redevelop our urban centers. But in order that this contribution may be made, the social scientists must learn what the planners are doing and what concepts are shaping their efforts. The plea made by this paper is that the social scientist in general, and the urban sociologist in particular, make certain amendments and additions before the planners come to us and find us wanting.

---

14. This point was suggested by Prof. J. E. Hulett, Jr., University of Illinois.

ECOLOGICAL CONSIDERATIONS IN PLANNING FOR RURBAN FRINGES

Walter Firey

From the standpoint of ecological theory the rurban fringe may be viewed as a marginal area. In this respect, it is comparable to the blighted zone which generally lies between a city's business district and the surrounding residential districts, as well as to the many inaccessible rural areas whose isolation makes them indifferently suited to farming as against forestry or grazing. Common to all three of these land use phenomena is the fact of marginality between alternative types of utilization. This marginality derives, not so much from any intrinsic qualities of the land as such, but rather from what is known as "position" or "situs" as distinct from "location."[1] In other words, the rurban fringe is a marginal land use area, not because of its geographical location, its soil type, or its topography, but rather because of its particular degree of accessibility (relative to that of other land uses) to some central transportation point. The same is true of the other two marginal land use types.

This fundamental identity between seemingly unrelated land uses suggests the possibility of a single inclusive theory of slums in which the rurban fringe, the ghetto, the rooming house area, and the rural creek-bottom or forest-farm slum all appear as varieties of a single land use phenomenon. The hypothesis to be advanced rests upon the substitution principle of marginal utility economics,[2] but goes somewhat farther than a strictly economic analysis. The theory is diagrammatically represented on the following page.

Accessibility may be defined in terms of the savings in time and cost attendant upon location near major points of population confluence. Social utility refers to the degree of *optimal functioning* of the community viewed as a going system of spatially contingent processes. As such it is to be sharply distinguished from the concept of "economic rent." Economic

Reprinted from the *American Sociological Review*, Vol. 11 (August, 1946), pp. 411-21, by permission of the author and the *American Sociological Review*. (Copyright, 1946, by the American Sociological Society.)

1. On "position" see R. D. McKenzie, "Spatial Distance," *Sociology and Social Research*, 13: 536-544, July-August, 1929, p. 536; on "situs" see H. B. Dorau and A. G. Hinman, *Urban Land Economics*. New York: 1928, pp. 167-169.

2. Applied to land use the principle might be stated thus: That one use which can so combine land with other productive agents as to achieve the greatest returns with the least cost will be the one to which the land will eventually devolve. For a generalized application of the substitution principle to land use see Andreas Predöhl, "The Theory of Location in its Relation to General Economics," *Journal of Political Economy*, 36: 271-390, June, 1928.

rent is a measure of the utility of disparate competing entrepreneurs. Social utility, on the other hand, refers to the utility of the community *sui generis*. Thus it includes not only a community's economic requirements in the way of adequate tax base, reasonable fire insurance rates, etc., but also a community's functional requirements in the way of civic participation, health and sanitation, and other strictly sociological factors. Between rent and social utility there is an undoubted correlation, but only within a limited range of values of the two variables. Beyond that range the relationship becomes inverse.[3] Thus up to a certain point the progressive sub-

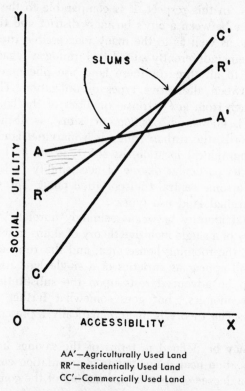

AA'—Agriculturally Used Land
RR'—Residentially Used Land
CC'—Commercially Used Land

FIG. 1—Amount of Social Utility Yielded by Specified Land Uses at Varying Degrees of Accessibility to a Population Center.

dividing of vacant lands around a city will entail both increased economic rent and increased social utility. But beyond that point a continuation of the subdividing process, while further increasing the land's economic rent, will entail diminished social utility to the community. This will manifest itself in higher fire insurance rates, new health and santation problems arising out of inadequate water and sewerage facilities, a decreased tax

3. For demonstration of this see: A. C. Pigou, *The Economics of Welfare*. Second Edition, London: 1924, Part II, ch. 8; Vilfredo Pareto, *The Mind and Society*. New York: 1935, section 2115-2139.

base attendant upon population outflow, and diminished civic participation on the part of suburban dwellers.

Thus formulated, the theory constitutes an analytical definition of a functional relationship between two variables. One of these, accessibility, has been taken as the independent variable and the other, social utility, has been taken as the dependent variable. With equal right one might of course posit some other variable as the independent one and define another functional relationship. Slums are certainly the product of many "causes"; the task of scientific analysis is to ferret out and analytically define the variables of which they are a function. In this paper we shall try to establish the pragmatic value of selecting accessibility as an independent variable in understanding the characteristics of rurban slums.

As the diagram shows, land that is close to a population center and is used agriculturally will yield more social utility than land which is remote from a population center and is used agriculturally. If all a city's food could be raised on the most accessible land, food would cost less, truck traffic would be smaller, farmers could more fully participate in community organizations, and a better correspondence might be achieved between the territorial extent of municipal taxation and the territorial area within which people benefit from municipal services. And yet, there are other spatially contingent requirements besides food. Residence is one of them. Space must be allocated for homes and in that way become removed from agricultural productivity. Here again, accessible land which is put to residential use yields more social utility than inaccessible land which is put to residential use. Indeed, the social utility which attends the residential use of land diminishes very rapidly with decreasing accessibility.[4] This is because the outer limits of the area within which daily commuting is possible are much more circumscribed than are the limits for hauling agricultural produce. Ultimately the matter reduces to one of differential transportation costs and the unequal importance of the time factor. For this reason the utility slope RR′ rises much more steeply than the slope AA′. Below the point at which the two intersect, land yields more social utility when used agriculturally than when used residentially, and for that reason it generally becomes farmland. But beyond the intersection point, land yields more social utility when used for residential purposes than when used for farming. Hence farms are seldom found amidst residential neighborhoods. Similarly the slope CC′ indicates that below a certain point land put to commercial use will yield practically no social utility at all, so inaccessible is the area from the flow of shoppers. But beyond the intersection of RR′ with CC′ land used commercially yields so much more utility over alternative uses that it becomes almost wholly put to business.

---

4. This of course assumes as a constant the very important symbolic qualities that may attach to residential land use and which yield just as real a social utility as does the quality of accessibility. In other words it fictionalizes actual land use to the extent of supposing this symbolic utility to be uniform throughout all residential districts.

It is the points at which the utility slopes intersect that are of greatest interest in the present study. For at these points land becomes indifferently suited to either of two alternative uses. There is no inexorable economic necessity for its being used in either way. As a result land uses interpenetrate. At the RR'-CC' intersection, businesses and residences exist side by side; at the AA'-RR' intersection, farms and residences intermingle. Each depreciates the value of the land for the other use. People of means do not want to live near stores, so house rents drop and dwellings deteriorate. Farmers cannot stand the taxes which must be levied if essential sewage and water facilities are to be provided for rurban residences, so they give up and their land reverts to the county. In this process slums have their origin.

In the present paper we shall limit our attention to the AA'-RR' intersection. At this intersection there exists what has come to be called the "rurban fringe," an area occupied by tar paper shacks and stately estates, large commercial farms and one-acre part-time farms, golf courses and cemeteries, airports and obnoxious industries. Our analysis of this phenomenon will have a twofold object: (1) to summarize some research findings concerning land use in the rurban fringes of Detroit and Flint, Michigan; (2) to indicate through these findings the usefulness of our theory in parsimoniously ordering research data into a coherent body of statements that will be of practical value to land use planners.

Following out the logic of our theory, we find in the rurban fringe three land use characteristics which are common to all marginal areas, and two additional characteristics unique to the rurban fringe but nonetheless resulting from its marginality. They are, respectively, as follows: (1) a capriciousness and diseconomy in private developmental plans; (2) variability and instability in the spatial patterns of land use; (3) a tendency for residences to gravitate to the lowest use in terms of class status; (4) an irrelevance of settlement patterns to soil capability; (5) the removal of the land from agricultural productivity. Let us consider each of these in order.

(1) Being marginal between alternative land uses, the rurban fringe represents a "dead center" between conflicting ecological forces. Some of these forces incline the land toward agricultural use, others incline it toward residential use. But neither clearly prevails over the other. There is no economic necessitousness that would dictate one or the other use. As a result there exist, side by side, blocks of subdivided lots lined with sidewalks and dwellings, numerous vestigial commercial farms standing off the side roads and to the rear of platted frontages, trailer camps and squatter towns, great expanses of land grown up to weeds, well-tended country estates owned by corporations and city businessmen—all spottily distributed in clusters and in string-along-the-road patterns.

The diseconomies which result from this are numerous. Not only is land removed from agricultural productivity, but all too frequently it fails to be put to any residential use either. This is because the subdividing process has usually surpassed the rate of population growth. In the Detroit metropolitan area, between 1900 and 1930, population increased 479 per cent; in the same period platted acreage increased 1,105 per cent.[5] Thus at a time when there were 224,092 vacant lots within municipal Detroit— enough to serve another one million persons—there were enough newly platted lots outside of Detroit to accommodate an additional two million persons.[6] It is not surprising that a survey made by the Michigan Planning Commission revealed the average utilization of lots in four townships near Detroit to be only 4.3 per cent. Those lots which were occupied were spottily distributed, thus giving rise to excessive expenditures for police and fire protection, school maintenance, and street and utilities upkeep.[7] Moreover, a high proportion of the vacant lots eventually became tax delinquent. Indeed, in the four townships studied by the Commission fully 61.2 per cent of all subdivided lots were advertised in the 1938 tax sale for delinquency. Of these, 98.3 per cent were vacant.[8] Since vacant and tax delinquent lands yield little or nò revenue to governmental units, the burden of necessary expenditures must fall upon the remaining taxpayers. Naturally this only worsens things. Farmers find agriculture unprofitable and quit. People having large homes and estates seek less expensive places where assessments will be lower. In time only shop workers and transients remain; their assessments are generally low because of the small valuation of their dwellings, so that they can well afford to remain.

The city of Flint presents a similar picture. Within the city there were, at the outbreak of the war, 40,000 vacant subdivided lots, most of which are distributed around the fringe of the city (Figure 2). Moreover, since the city limits of Flint at a number of points fall within rural areas, there are extensive tracts of first-class agricultural land that lie within the city. Being in the city they are, of course, subject to municipal tax rates. As a result farming on such land has become unprofitable and much of it has reverted to the state for tax delinquency. The fringes of Flint are lined with such lands, standing idle and devoted to no productive use whatsoever. Even outside the city, land that has once been subdivided and equipped with water, sewerage, and other utilities acquires a valuation that far exceeds its agricultural earning capacity. If such land cannot sell for residential purposes neither can it easily revert to agricultural productivity. So it remains idle—an unproductive burden to the community.[9]

Unregulated wildcat subdividing is, of course, responsible for this. Real

---

5. Michigan Planning Commission, *A Study of Subdivision Development in the Detroit Metropolitan Area*. Lansing: 1939, p. 10, table 2.

6. *Ibid.*, p. 11.

7. *Ibid.*, pp. 2-4. The four townships were Dearborn, Nankin, Redford and Taylor.

8. Computed from *ibid.*, p. 27, table 10; p. 31, table 15. There were 560,788 subdivided lots, of which 364,894 were tax delinquent.

9. *Report of Genesee County Land Use Planning Committee* (ms). Genesee County Agricultural Agent's Office, Flint, 1940, p. 25.

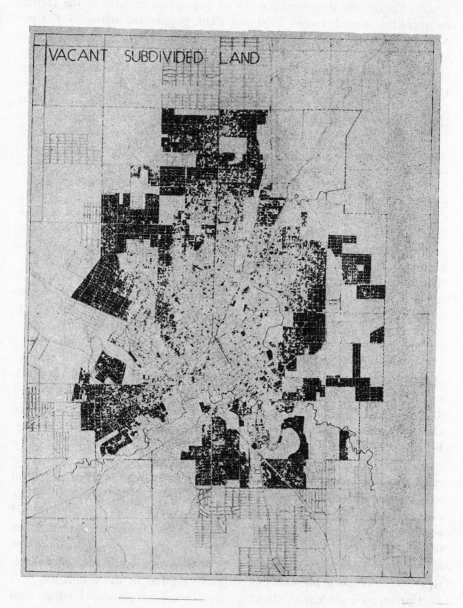

FIG. 2—Vacant Subdivided Land, Flint, Michigan.
Reproduced from: map in C. W. A. Housing Survey of Flint, Mich. (unpublished)

estate developers, farmers, township officials—all have contributed to the dividing of excessive and unplanned subdividing of fringe lands. The uses to which these subdividers have designed their plats are often wholly capricious and devoid of any respect for established land use principles. It is quite common for much more land to be allocated for business purposes than can ever be so used. In the four townships near Detroit that were referred to above, an average of 25.4 per cent of platted lots had been planned for business occupancy. Only 1.7 per cent of these lots have actually been occupied by business.[10] That this is more than a temporary lag or "waiting period" intervening between the time of subdividing and the time of occupancy[11] is suggested by the fact that in one of the townships, Redford, the utilization of platted business lots thirteen years after the original subdividing was only 0.3 per cent; utilization of residential lots was 6.9 per cent.[12]

Quite clearly, projected land uses in the fringe area have had little correspondence with feasible or needed land uses. Whim and caprice have had considerable scope, for the simple reason that no one use has been able to yield unmistakably greater utility than the alternative use. The rurban fringe is just so far out from the central points of population confluence that its superiority for residential as against agricultural utilization is unclear. Enough speculators are willing to gamble on its residential superiority, however, to plat it out for such use. Only in a marginal area, having an equipotency between competing uses, could such wildcatting operate. In an area clearly superior for residential use or in an area clearly superior for agricultural use no such speculative development could appear, for the reason that there would not be any scope for chance to operate, upon which the speculator is so dependent. Thus it becomes clear that the capriciousness and diseconomy so typical of the rurban fringe is predicated upon the marginal nature of the area, upon its indifferent suitability to two alternative land uses.

(2) From this it follows that the spatial patterns of land use in the rurban fringe are quite variable and unstable. Side by side there may be trailer camps, cemeteries, golf courses, country estates, junk yards, wayside stands and taverns, country clubs, part-time acreages, general farms and obnoxious industries. To the east of Flint one finds, in segmental arrangement along a main highway, extensive tracts of vacant land, an oil depot and gas works, a preferred residential suburb protected by high deed restrictions, and a shop workers' residential suburb built up with small, inexpensive homes. To the rear of the highway frontages are substantial commercial farms. South of Flint, on another main highway, are two

---

10. *A Study of Subdivision Development in the Detroit Metropolitan Area, op. cit.,* p. 24, and computations from p. 19, table 6.

11. Cf. Ernest M. Fisher and Raymond M. Smith, *Land Subdividing and the Rate of Utilization.* Michigan Business Studies, vol. 4, no. 5, 1932, p. 3 and *passim.*

12. *A Study of Subdivision Development in the Detroit Metropolitan Area, op. cit.,* p. 16.

compact subdivisions platted out in 50' x 100' lots and closely built up with small shop workers' homes. Across the highway is a large trailer camp. Surrounding both are large farms and unoccupied subdivided lands. Such a conglomeration of land uses could only exist where the utility curves of alternative land use types intersected and thus defined a dead-center of ecological forces. In such marginal areas no one land use type yields clearly greater utility than another and hence none is able to preempt the land for itself. As a result both alternative uses coexist, as well as a number of other uses which by their very nature seek out non-homogeneous areas that cannot offer resistance to their incursions (obnoxious industries, junk yards, taverns, etc.).

One manifestation of the variability in fringe land use patterns is the juxtaposition of subdivisions having incompatible deed restrictions. In one subdivision to the west of Flint, lots were sold with restrictions that stipulated a minimum residential building cost of $3,000. An adjoining subdivision had a minimum restriction of $600. In the course of time the blighting influence of the second subdivision led to the construction of cheap shacks throughout the vicinity, thereby vitiating the force of the first subdivision's restrictions. In this way subdivisions with lower deed restrictions have literally strangled subdivisions with higher restrictions.

Another example of this may be seen in Figure 3, which shows race occupancy and building cost restrictions in subdivisions in Garden City and Inkster, lying to the west of Detroit.[13] As the map shows, the distribution of subdivisions having varying types of deed restrictions is utterly chaotic. Highly restricted subdivisions are scattered among subdivisions having no restrictions whatsoever. Even the restricted areas vary considerably in the minimum building costs specified. They range all the way from $1,000 to $7,000, as the figures in each subdivision on the map indicate. In one community not shown on the map, a subdivision with minimum residential building cost restrictions of $15,000 became lined on two sides with unrestricted subdivisions. One of these subdivisions had, in 1939, an average building assessment of $538, with about 30 per cent occupancy. The other had an average building assessment of less than $400 and about 82 per cent occupancy.[14] Both are built up with inexpensive and even shacky houses. As a result the highly restricted area stood vacant for twelve years. In 1939 its restrictions were finally lowered from $15,000 to $4,000 and $3,000.[15]

All of this lends to the rurban fringe a highly unstable character. Repeated changes in land use are typical.[16] In parts of the Flint fringe one

13. Reproduced from *ibid.*, p. 21, map 4.

14. *Ibid.*, pp. 20-23.

15. *Ibid.*, p. 23, n.

16. William R. Gordon and Gilbert S. Meldrum, *Land, People and Farming in a Rurban Zone.* Bulletin 285, Rhode Island Agricultural Experiment Station and Bureau of Agricultural Economics, United States Department of Agriculture, cooperating, 1942, p. 44.

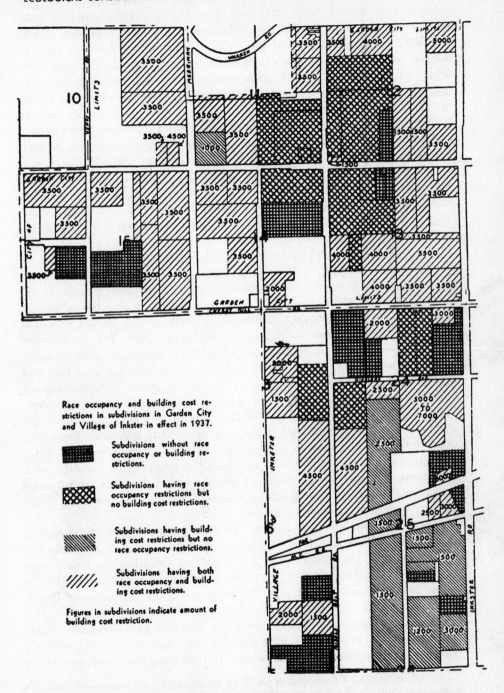

FIG. 3—Race Occupancy and Building Cost Restrictions in a Fringe Area Near Detroit, Michigan.

Reproduced from: Michigan Planning Commission, *A Study of Subdivision Development in the Detroit Metropolitan Area.* Lansing, 1939, map 4.

actually finds platted tracts that have reverted to agricultural use, naturally at great loss to the original subdividers. Farmers who had platted out highway frontages during the 1926 boom are now back to farming among the sidewalks they built. Families who had invested several thousand dollars in attractive suburban estates, in a subdivision protected by high deed restrictions, have seen the value of their property depreciated by the appearance of shacks in an adjoining subdivision which had no such restrictions. Commercial farmers, burdened with taxes, operate on a slender margin and frequently give up. Shop workers, interested in part-time farming near the city, commonly buy acreages that are utterly unsuited to cultivation. Typically they buy on easy down payments but on terms they will never be able to meet. Eventually many of them give up, forfeiting both land and payments, and the land is sold to another buyer, only to repeat the cycle all over again.[17] Such instability is the inevitable concomitant of marginality in land use.

(3) Another concomitant is a tendency for residences to gravitate to the lowest use in terms of class status. Cheaper residential land uses seem generally to drive out the higher ones or inhibit their development. In the four suburban Detroit townships surveyed intensively by the Michigan Planning Commission, approximately 25 per cent of the platted area had residential building cost restrictions of $5,000 or more. Yet, as of 1938, only 1.5 per cent of all residences had actually cost that much. Ninety-one per cent had cost under $3,000 and more than forty per cent had cost under $1,000.[18] People of means simply will not build in neighborhoods which are likely to be invaded by shacks. If any portion of a neighborhood is platted out with no restrictions, or with low ones, the higher restrictions of an adjoining area become in effect null and void. Moreover, deed restrictions are only as good as the residents of an area make them. If transgressions are overlooked, and building proceeds in violation of a restriction, all rights of enforcement become forfeit. For this reason deed restrictions are never sure guarantees against the encroachment of blight upon a preferred residential district.

There are fundamental reasons for this precariousness of desirable residential land use in the rurban fringe. Being marginal as it is between alternative uses, the fringe lacks any clear-cut valuation for either residence or agriculture. Hence whatever fashionable residential utility a fringe neighborhood may acquire depends, not upon the objective dwelling requirements of a city's upper class population, but solely upon the neighborhood's symbolic quality, upon the desirable or fashionable "reputation" which it happens to gain through the vagaries of a subdivider's plans. So long as this symbolic quality lasts the neighborhood can retain

17. Of 84 families interviewed in the Flint fringe during the summer of 1945, 25 were either undecided as to future residential plans or were definitely intending to leave when circumstances permitted.

18. *A Study of Subdivision Development in the Detroit Metropolitan Area, op. cit.,* p. 25.

its higher-class families. But, again through the vagaries of subdividers' plans, there is nothing to prevent the platting out of adjoining areas into unrestricted subdivisions for working-class occupancy. Such plats, with their symbolic connotations of lower class status, seem nearly always to have a blighting effect upon other subdivisions whose symbolic quality denotes higher class status.

The dynamics of ecological symbolism are as yet insufficiently known to warrant anything more than an *a priori* explanation of why this must be. Whatever the explanation, it obviously must be on a sociological rather than an economic level. In the first place, the high- or low-class connotations of a fringe subdivision rest wholly upon the circumstance that a subdivider has, by arbitrary fiat, decided to lay out a plat with or without certain restrictions.[19] In effect this foreordains the economic level, and thereby the class status, of the families which will occupy that plat. No economic analysis in terms of the substitution principle is adequate to explain this phenomenon. Secondly, the invasion of preferred residential areas by cheaper dwellings actually represents a smaller capitalization on the land's earning capacities than would expensive upper-class dwellings. Thus the process becomes, in some respects at least, a diseconomic one.

The most plausible explanation of the competitive superiority of cheaper residential land uses would seem to lie in the analysis which Durkheim has made of symbolism. As Durkheim indicates, symbols denoting radically divergent values ("sacred" versus "profane") must be spatially distinct and separate lest their values become confounded.[20] This is all the more necessary because of the "contagious" character of symbolism, by which the meanings attaching to a symbol tend to proliferate and fix onto other objects associated with the symbol. Apply this to land use. The symbolism of residential areas falls on a single scale of prestige valuation, ranging from "low" to "high." A district platted out with high deed restrictions will attract families of corresponding class status and will thus come to symbolize that class status to the community at large. Similarly a district platted out with no restrictions will attract families of lower class status and will acquire a corresponding reputation or symbolic quality. If the two districts happen to adjoin one another, their respective symbolic qualities will tend to diffuse. This means a devaluation, in terms of prestige, of the upper-class area, and a heightened valuation of the lower-class area. The former thus loses the very quality (and the only one) to which it owes its hold upon upper-class families. The latter gains somewhat, but not enough to lift it out of the lower-class category owing to the actual class affiliations of its residents. Presently

19. Such arbitrariness could only operate in an area defined by the intersection of the utility curves of alternative land use types.

20. Emile Durkheim, *The Elementary Forms of the Religious Life*. London, 1915, pp. 40, 219-220, 308.

upper-class families begin to sell their homes, property values decline, restrictions lose their force, and blight sets in. In this way residential land use in the rurban fringe tends "immanently" to gravitate toward lower-class occupancy, thereby creating slums.

(4 and 5) The three foregoing characteristics of rurban land use are in some degree common to all marginal areas, the commercial-residential fringe as well as the farm-forest fringe.[21] There are two additional characteristics, unique to the rurban fringe, which may be briefly noted before turning to a consideration of the planning implications of our analysis. First of all, settlement patterns in the rurban fringe bear little relation to soil capability. This follows from the fact that accessibility rather than agricultural suitability is the main criterion by which fringe dwellers choose a location. And yet, some very real problems result from this disregard for soil capability. Most fringe residents engage in some gardening or part-time farming. Yet often the land is unsuited to this, thereby burdening families with unnecessary labor and often preventing altogether any agricultural use of the land. For many families this may represent the difference between self-support and public assistance.

Secondly, the rurban fringe involves a removal of land from agricultural production. In spite of the prevalence of part-time gardening in the fringe, the agricultural productivity of the land falls sharply with the platting out of subdivisions. Not only do buildings, roads, and service utilities require space, but more than that, the land becomes so cut up and so irregularly occupied, with vacant tracts being interrupted in spotty designs by dwellings, that extensive commercial farming becomes impossible. Thus arises the frequent paradox of first-class agricultural land standing idle, grown to weeds, too small in size to be farmed because of the surrounding residential lots, yet unmarketable because of the surfeit of lots relative to housing demand.

These are facts with which rational planning for the rurban fringe must comply. Yet, as this paper has attempted to show, all these land use characteristics are logically implied in the very nature of the fringe as a marginal area. A successful land use planning program for any rurban fringe must take its cue from the basic, essential nature of the fringe as a dead center area in which the only order and stability that can ever exist will be that imposed by a comprehensive and inclusive plan. It is, of course, impossible to outline any detailed, step by step planning program that would be applicable to all rurban fringe areas. But there are a few general principles of rurban planning which seem to logically follow from the nature of the fringe as a point of intersection of the utility curves of

---

21. Supporting evidence for this statement obviously lies beyond the space limitations of this paper. On its plausibility with regard to the commercial-residential fringe see Harvey Warren Zorbaugh, *The Gold Coast and the Slum*. Chicago, 1929, ch. 1-2; with regard to the farm-forest fringe see Carter Goodrich *et al.*, *Migration and Economic Opportunity*. Philadelphia, 1936, pp. 165-175, 193-201.

alternative land use types. These principles correspond to the five rurban land use characteristics discussed above.

(1) To begin with, if caprice can play so great a part in private developmental plans for the rurban fringe, it is no less true that rational planning can do so too. The very "failing" of the fringe may be its redemption. This is because the scope for planning increases in direct ratio with the non-necessitousness or indeterminateness of land use. Since the fringe is a marginal area it presents a minimum of necessitous land uses and should therefore be highly amenable to rational planning. If this opportunity is to materialize, however, it is necessary that determinateness be created by will where it did not exist of itself. If consistency and rationality are to replace caprice and diseconomy, some effective and territorially extensive planning authority has to be set up. Such a planning authority must be so constituted as to encompass all the municipal, township and county jurisdictions that fall within a given fringe area. It must, moreover, be invested with the policy-forming and judicial authority necessary for it to create and maintain a sustained, consistent, yet flexible land use program. Whatever program is drawn up by such an authority can have a considerable degree of randomness without running into serious economic difficulties, owing to the marginal nature of the fringe. There are less likely to be the serious strains and conflicts of interest such as arise in urban zoning systems. Unlike the latter, where sites have more of an intrinsic appropriateness to certain uses and not to others (thus leading to difficulties when zoning plans fail to recognize this), fringe lands do not have such a right-or-wrong, this-and-no-other quality as to the uses they may be put to. The opportunities for planning become all the greater.

(2 and 3) There are, of course, certain limits to the randomness with which a rurban planning program may be drawn up. We have seen that the variability and instability of land use patterns in the fringe conduces to blight. We have seen, too, that preferred residential subdivisions have little or no competitive strength against low-rent residential subdivisions that may be platted out on adjoining territory. Hence the first prerequisite to any rational plan must be the regulation of platting activities. This regulation must be directed, first, toward synchronizing the rate of subdividing with the rate of population growth and, second, toward zoning off large areas to homogeneous land uses and giving them an assured immunity against encroachments from other land uses. Such regulation of platting activities of course presupposes the state authorization of township or county zoning, the required recording of plats, and the legal specification of minimum plat improvements (sewerage, water, power, etc.) prior to the sale of lots. Along with such authority must go the granting of discretionary powers which would permit the varying of zoning regulations when circumstances might require; for the very marginality of the fringe is bound to occasion unexpected shifts in ecological pressures, such as the sudden demand for "victory gardens" during the war or for sub-

sistence gardens during periods of protracted unemployment. With powers like these an impartial and well-informed planning authority could check the blight which comes from variable and unstable land use patterns and the competitive weakness of better residential land use.

(4 and 5) The same powers would enable a planning authority to forbid the platting out of land that is unsuited to gardening. This is essential if the interests of part-time farmers are to be protected and unnecessary dependency and tax delinquency be avoided. Rural land should be zoned, first, according to soil capability classes, and second, with regard to maintaining as much fringe land in cultivation as possible. The lower soil capability classes, while not suited to farming, are certainly no more suited to gardening. Hence they should not be platted out in small acreages; if platted at all they should be designed strictly for residences and small yards. Land that is open to platting should be zoned to form compact, contiguous tracts rather than the spotty, randomly distributed clusters which typically prevail. This is necessary if there is not to be the waste of potential farm land which follows from unguided subdividing. Agriculture cannot be economically pursued when land is cut up into the small, detached fragments that now dominate most rurban fringe areas. Through zoning fairly large, contiguous areas into like uses, the loss of potential farm land in metropolitan districts can be minimized.

Implied in each of the foregoing suggestions is the idea that a fringe planning program will be guided by a continuing social and economic survey of metropolitan trends. For the contours and even the location of a rurban fringe can change significantly within a very few years. Hence accurate factual knowledge of building activities, employment trends, directions of population growth, the living levels of migrants, and agricultural marketing trends is indispensable to the success of any planning program. In the compilation and interpretation of these research findings one may look to systematic land use theory for direction. For only through theory, whether it be explicit or implicit, can one assess the relative importance of particular trends and recognize their bearing upon a planning program.

PERIPHERAL EXPANSION IN MILWAUKEE COUNTY

Richard Dewey

The expansion of population into the unincorporated areas surrounding the central city and its incorporated suburbs presents metropolitan-area planners with numerous problems. The present analysis of this trend in one of the Middle West's large cities was undertaken with the hope that some light could be cast upon the future direction of peripheral expansion in order that the needs for highways, parks, airport facilities, restrictive zoning, etc., might be anticipated more accurately.[1] In only a limited sense was this hope realized, but the study yielded information which is of both interest and value to planners in urban areas. In some respects the principal merit of the research lies in its confirmation of hunches which planners have cherished for years.

The bulk of the information yielded by the study was secured from approximately twelve thousand questionnaires which were circulated through the rural school system. By inclusion in the schedule of a question in which the county school superintendent was interested, the use of this medium of research was greatly facilitated. Approximately one-third (3,970) of the questionnaires were filled out sufficiently to permit their use.[2] In addition to the questionnaires, use was made of aerial photographs; county land-use maps; city, village, and township directories; county plat books; actual on-the-spot observations of the areas in question; and personal inter-

Reprinted from *The American Journal of Sociology*, Vol. 53 (May 1948), pp. 417-422, by permission of the author and the publisher. (Copyright, 1948, by *The American Journal of Sociology*.

1. The research was carried on in 1945 while the writer was planning analyst for the Milwaukee County Regional Planning Department.

2. The representativeness of the sample was checked by calculating the percentage of each minor political unit's population represented by the sample and by checking the occupational distribution of the persons filling out and returning the schedule against the occupational distribution in each civil unit according to the census. Both checks gave evidence of the sample's being representative of the total population. The writer interviewed some seventy persons living in unincorporated areas before making up a preliminary schedule which was tested on some two hundred persons. After further interviewing, the final questionnaire was drafted and circulated. There was little opportunity to test the reliability of the schedule, but, in the limited areas where interview, preliminary questionnaire, and final form were used, the answers on the final form were generally the same as they had been on the previous ones. There is no guaranty, of course, that the final questionnaires were filled out by the same persons who filled out the original ones.

views. The manner in which some of these sources of information were employed will be revealed in this paper. Because it is a marked condensation of the original study, a few of these sources were not drawn upon for the paper.

Although Milwaukee County is by far the largest in population of all Wisconsin counties, it is the second smallest in area, being only twenty-four miles in length from north to south and something less than ten miles in width, on the average, from Lake Michigan on the east to its western boundary. At the point of greatest population density it is but eight miles wide. Aside from the presence of Lake Michigan there is little in the topography which would direct the population flow as it moved into the peripheral districts. The land is flat to slightly rolling, punctuated by several rivers and creeks which converge and enter Lake Michigan near the heart of the city. With one exception the rivers are unimportant in determining the distribution of population in the outlying areas. The lake shore has been a significant force in the location of residential areas but not uniformly so, much of the south shore having been monopolized by industry.

Both as to class and status groups, Milwaukee is divided sharply on a north-side-south-side basis. One gains in prestige by moving to the north side, and to particular areas of the north side. The latter's high status is but little depressed by the presence within its borders of the city's worst slums, which fact permits of the juxtaposition of "Gold Coast" and slum as in Chicago and other American cities. The suburbs to the south and southwest—South Milwaukee, Cudahy, West Milwaukee, and West Allis—are industrial towns peopled for the most part by laboring groups. The suburbs to the north and west—Wauwatosa, Shorewood, Whitefish Bay, Fox Point, and River Hills—are residential suburbs peopled by the upper economic classes. Greendale, the demonstration housing project owned by the United States government, lies to the south and west of Milwaukee, separated from the built-up areas by several miles of open countryside. Milwaukee's remarkable likeness to the Chicago area is undoubtedly explainable in large part on the basis of the comparable geographical factors, viz., the confluence of rivers in the heart of the city and the presence of Lake Michigan on the east.

Ecologically, it is interesting to note the way in which the city of Milwaukee illustrates both the Burgess concentric-circle pattern and the Hoyt sector scheme. The concentration of upper-class residential districts along the north shore of Lake Michigan, extending from the central part of the city northward to the county border, and the similar patterning of the industrial sectors which extend along the lake shore to the south and along the river valley in the central part of the city illustrate the Hoyt thesis. However, in the areas which are not influenced by these geographical features, the Burgess concentric-circle pattern is clearly in evidence. The northwest quadrant of the city particularly exhibits land-use patterns which approach the ideal sequence of zones according to Burgess as closely as it is possible to conceive of any city evidencing an ideal ecological patterning of natural areas.[3]

In the questionnaire mentioned above, persons were asked: "Where did you live before moving to your present address?" Analysis of the returns showed that 60 per cent came from the city of Milwaukee, 20 per cent from the six largest suburbs, 12 per cent from other rural areas of Milwaukee County, and 8 per cent from outside the county. The movement of population into the rural-urban fringe is thus shown to be a movement of urban people. It is known that many, probably the majority, of those migrants from rural areas of the county or from outside the county were urban in origin. Available data permitted further analysis of only the city of Milwaukee. The areas in the center of the city supplied the smallest percentage, while those on the periphery of the city gave the greatest percentage. Thus the movement in its immediate aspects is not a decentralization movement but is a continuation of the time-honored centrifugal expansion which has been, and still is, characteristic of American cities. In Table 1, the four quartiles of census tracts are characterized as to monthly rentals, percentage of home owners, and single-family dwellings. The peripheral expansion is clearly not a movement of slum dwellers desiring to escape substandard blighted areas.

TABLE I—Comparison with the City Average of Emigration Areas within the City by Quartiles

(Quartiles Ranked in Order of Least to Most Emigration)

Quartiles	Average Rent	Single Family Dwellings (%)	Home Ownership (%)
1	$27.22	44.50	24.60
2	31.50	48.10	29.80
3	34.77	50.20	32.60
4	39.27	58.90	39.60
City average	33.26	29.08	32.20

To check and amplify the data secured from the schedules, a simple, if laborious, technique was employed. This entailed the taking of a 5 per cent random sample of the names in the most recent directories of the unincorporated townships, the smaller cities, and the villages in the county, noting street addresses in each case. The second step was the seeking of these names in the 1930, 1934, and 1937 directories of the city of Milwaukee, West Allis, Wauwatosa, South Milwaukee, and Cudahy. To insure selection

---

3. Cf. R. E. Park and E. W. Burgess, *The City* (Chicago: University of Chicago Press, 1925), and Homer Hoyt, *The Structure and Growth of Residential Neighborhoods in American Cities* (Washington, D.C.: Federal Housing Administration, 1939). See also Walter Firey, *Land Use in Central Boston* (Cambridge: Harvard University Press, 1947), for an extended, if somewhat labored, discussion of ecological patterns in urban areas. It seems to the present writer that Firey errs when he implies that Burgess, Hoyt, and other writers in the field of urban ecology are not aware of the influence of non-economic values on land-use patterns in cities.

of identical names, only those cases were used in which both husband and wife were listed. The trend of population movement revealed by this technique paralleled that reported by the questionnaires. It also indicated that persons who moved orginally from the central part of the city reached the periphery via a series of short moves and not by a single move. The data from these two sources were combined and incorporated in a map of the county. It was clearly demonstrated that, in general, the migration into rural areas came from no specific area of the city, nor was it directed into any specific rural area. The rural areas in each of the townships surrounding the incorporated areas drew the bulk of their migration from the nearest urban areas, again emphasizing the general centrifugal nature of the migration.

The only exception to this general trend was the clear-cut directional movement of the upper-class migration. This movement was to the upper east side of Milwaukee proper, thence to Shorewood, Whitefish Bay, Fox Point, and River Hills. One climbs the social ladder by following this route, as is evidenced by the fact that the persons whose names are listed in the *Social Register* live almost exclusively in the areas named. Fox Point and River Hills have the greatest proportions of population listed in the *Social Register*. It is interesting to note that Wauwatosa, a suburb which in some ways is aesthetically and economically superior to much of Shorewood, does not have the social prestige of the latter. Several residents of Wauwatosa referred to Shorewood as a "social climber's" town. Interviews revealed the desire of persons in Shorewood to move to Whitefish Bay, and a certain portion of the residents of Whitefish Bay dream of the time when they can afford to move to Fox Point.[4] In the latter two areas, housewives have been frowned upon for doing their own shopping for groceries. There is a strong awareness of the high-status value of residence in the northshore suburbs. The writer observed this when teaching in a college (Lawrence College, Appleton) which drew many students from the Milwaukee area. Students from the industrial suburbs did not object to being classified as coming from Milwaukee, while those from the higher-status suburbs voiced definite protest to the effect that they were *not* from Milwaukee but from Wauwatosa, Shorewood, etc. This status awareness accounts in no small degree for the resistance to any suggestions of consolidation of suburbs and central city. In an advisory referendum on the consolidation of services and governments held in 1934, of the total vote from the industrial suburbs, 58 per cent was registered in favor of consolidation. This contrasts with only 33 per cent of the population in the residential suburbs voting for consolidation; and, if the north-shore suburbs—those with the higher social status—are taken as a unit, only 25 per cent voted for

---

4. These interviews were with upper-middle-class persons and not with the upper economic classes whose homes line the lake shore. In general there is a tendency for values to decline in direct relationship to the distance from the lake shore. This trend is interrupted, to be sure, by shopping districts but holds true generally.

consolidation.[5] Although there are other reasons which motivated the voters on the consolidation issue, the strong in-group attitude of the residential suburbs surely is the strongest of these motives.

In Figure 1 are shown the reasons given for moving from the urban to the unincorporated areas of Milwaukee County. The reasons are not, of course, mutually exclusive; surely the second, third, and fourth reasons are components of the most important reason given for moving, namely, "better for children." Although "lower taxes" and "cheaper land" were reported as important reasons motivating the moving to rural land, these advantages are at best illusory, as is admitted readily by most residents of the rural-urban fringe. It is a conservative estimate that, if one uses private modes of transportation, it costs twenty-five dollars per year for every mile that he moves away from his place of employment, recreation, shopping

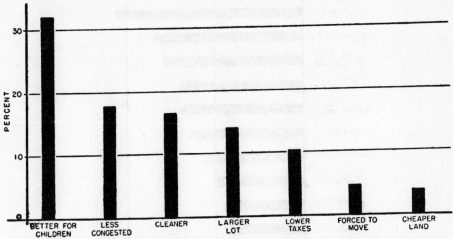

FIG. 1. Reasons for moving into unincorporated areas of Milwaukee County.

center, school, and church. This, plus the additional cost of providing his own utilities, quickly erases any financial gain secured through cheaper land or lower taxes. Illustrative of the general disillusionment is this excerpt from a newspaper published by and for residents of several subdivisions in the rural-urban fringe: "The dream of low taxation in our community, which was prevalent when people moved in five years ago, has faded away and is today replaced by exorbitant sums which have incensed many residents. . . . Total cost $145. Compare this with $78, four years ago." [6] The strong demand for the urban conveniences accounts for the increase in taxes.

When answers were sought to the question of why persons moved to a particular place in the rural-urban fringe, once they had decided to leave

5. Paula Lynagh, *Metropolitan Milwaukee* (Citizens' Bureau of Milwaukee, 1936).
6. *Tri-Town News*, February 7, 1946 (published in Hales Corners, Milwaukee County, Wis.).

the city, the reasons shown graphically in Figure 2 were given. These reasons were largely self-explanatory. It was of interest to note, during interviews with dwellers in the rural-urban fringe, the emphasis placed upon the aesthetic appeal of the house and subdivision. Purchases often resulted from Sunday and holiday rides into the rural areas: a Chicagoan, returning from a hunting trip in northern Wisconsin, was so attracted by the appearance of one of these subdivisions that he returned the following week, purchased a lot, built a house and moved in, retiring from his professional work in Chicago.

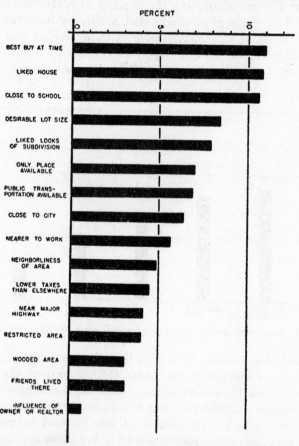

FIG. 2. Reasons for moving to particular site in preference to other sites in unincorporated areas of Milwaukee County.

Once the people have moved into the open area on the periphery of the urban areas, the question of what they think of their home and neighbors arises. Their general attitude is indicated by the fact that approximately 65 per cent preferred to remain in their present position, some 30 per cent expressed a preference for some other areas in the rural-urban fringe, and only approximately 5 per cent reported a desire to return to built-up urban areas. It is significant, too, that nearly 80 per cent found in the subdivision more of a neighborly and community spirit than in the city, and many of the others found the subdivision at least equal to the city areas in this respect. In one instance a woman reported that primary-group relations of some twenty years' standing had been replaced by the congeniality which was found in the subdivision. Particularly in the smaller subdivisions there appeared to exist a genuine neighborhood primary group which had not been known in the urban areas. It is of interest to note, too, that this intimate acquaintance seemed not to limit social mobility; nor did it appear to impose inhibitions upon the residents. The fact that the population was urban with regard to social values may account for this situation. To what degree an urban way of life with its heterogeneity of values and insistence upon living one's life according to one's own code can be maintained in the face of loss of social anonymity which the urban world affords is an interesting question. In at least one instance a family sold their home and returned to the city because they felt that the "neighborliness" was merely curiosity which bred gossip, but, for the present at least, this is an exception.

One of the results of the study which corroborated city planners' beliefs is the clear-cut preference for large lots. The average width of lot preferred was approximately seventy-five feet. Figure 3 indicates in detail the attitude of rural-urban-fringe residents toward the width of lot they now occupy. The preference for the larger lots is evident, and, even in the instances in which the smaller lots appear to be satisfactory, it was discovered that many of these were persons who either had just moved from the city where lots were even smaller or did not have buildings on the lots adjacent to theirs. There is limited evidence to suggest that the longer the person remains in rural areas, the less satisfied he is with lots of forty- and fifty-foot widths. It should be noted, however, that few were interested in acreage which would permit any part-time farming. Supporting the expressed preference for the larger lots is the fact that approximately 81 per cent of all lots fifty-nine feet or less in width still remain vacant, while approximately 60 per cent of the lots of sixty feet or more in width are vacant. This difference is all the more significant when one takes into consideration the fact that the larger lots are newer lots and therefore have not been on the market for nearly so long as the smaller ones. Only some 14 per cent of the lots subdivided prior to 1930 were sixty feet or more in width, whereas 43 per cent of the more recently divided lots were of this size.

Certain services and utilities are essential to the way of life which urban Americans have come to know, even in suburban America. Inquiry concerning the distance which persons deemed desirable to certain places of business, recreation, etc., yielded the following information: the average rural-urban-fringe dweller wants to have food market, grade school, and drug store reasonably close to home, which in most instances means within walking distance. Beauty parlor, gas station, high school, church, parks, and movies are close enough if they lie within a radius of a mile and a half.

If taverns and airports are five miles or more away, that appears to be satisfactory, and astronomical distances were frequently given with regard to taverns. Places of employment, according to the study, need not be close. The nature of the place of employment has some bearing, of course, on this attitude. In the higher-income groups the distances to all these services were

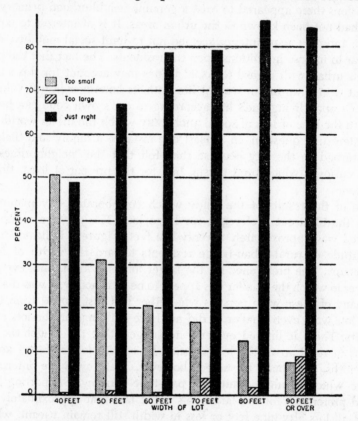

FIG. 3. Attitude toward width of lot now occupied.

deemed to be less important than in the lower-income groups, the most significant difference being found with regard to food markets.[7]

When asked to evaluate a list of utilities and services, a majority checked as essential the following: public transportation, sewer, garbage collection, ash collection, gas connection, and street lights. Even such services as public water supply, sidewalks, and to-the-door mail service were held to be either

7. These expressed desires give evidence of the realism of the planning based upon the neighborhood principle which has been espoused by several planners, the most explicit of whom has been the late Clarence Perry. The neighborhood units described in his *Housing for the Machine Age* (New York: Russell Sage Foundation, 1939) are illustrations of the sort of planning which would permit the residents to secure the satisfaction of their needs. This should not be interpreted as meaning that all persons would find this neighborhood type of life desirable. There is still need for a planned area of apartments in the central part of cities.

essential or desirable. The list is given here in order of preference, and it should be noted that electricity and telephone are not included. Few, if any, felt that these were not essential. With regard to the list of utilities services, the economic-class differential observed with regard to the foregoing set of services (food market, school, etc.) was not in evidence. There appeared to be as strong a demand for public transportation in the upper-middle class as among the middle-class groups. This was true even in homes in which there were several cars, but wherein the wife did not drive or did not want to use private cars for transporting children to school. Of interest, also, is the attitude of the upper classes toward sidewalks and street lights, which attitude seems to have been motivated by the desire to maintain a stereotyped rural-manor appearance in the subdivision. Emulation of wealthier persons in certain of the élite-studded areas of the country explains a part of this disdain for sidewalks. One price which the residents of such subdivisions pay for this dubious advantage is the sacrifice of an important part of the children's playground. Macadam and blacktop road surfaces rule out roller skates, and the use of the streets for baby buggies and tricycles is hazardous. The precarious task of driving through such subdivisions when the neighborhood youngsters are out in full force is well known to anyone who frequents such areas.

The implications of this study for the planners whose task it is to plan for the rural-urban fringe are, it would seem, clear. The dweller in this area is seeking a cleaner, less congested community in which he can live an urban way of life.[8] Only in a very limited sense is it a manifestation of return to a rural life; if rural social characteristics arise, they will be incidental phenomena. On the basis of the expressed desires of the rural-urban-fringe dwellers in Milwaukee County, objectively verified, it was possible to construct an ideal type of rural-fringe community. If the people's desires are to be met, the planners should bend their efforts to encourage, by every means known to them, the building of subdivisions of no smaller than three hundred homes. Persons living in neighborhoods smaller than this will of necessity be deprived of some of the desired services and utilities. The federally owned demonstration project of Greendale is the community which most closely approximates the ideal.

Greendale has a population of about two thousand, provides a service center which includes grocery store, drug store, small service shops, a tavern, and a theater. Public facilities include a fire department and excellent school facilities through the eighth-grade level. Churches are planned, and at present church services are held in the school building. Thus Greendale is not a community in the meaning of the term as used by the soci-

8. By urbanism is meant a way of life characterized by (1) marked division and specialization of labor, (2) heterogeneity of social values, (3) relative anonymity regarding individual behavior, (4) formal laws, and (5) symbols of class and status independent of intimate acquaintance.

ologist, because most residents must find employment elsewhere, and also such services as high school, department store, and professional services are not provided. Nevertheless, the enthusiasm of the residents for Greendale justifies the selecting of it as the closest approach to the ideal rural-urban-fringe community.

The movement into the rural-urban fringe is not a desire to escape anything that is inherent in urbanism as a way of life. Rather it is a desire to retain this way of life and yet to avoid some of the incidental disadvantages which are, it is hoped, only temporary characteristics of most built-up urban areas. If this study is representative of general trends and attitudes, realistic and imaginative replanning of the blighted and near-blighted areas of the cities should be expected to check the peripheral expansion to some significant degree. Too much of present-day urban planning is focused upon transportation lines which are designed to facilitate escape from the city into peripheral districts. This approach, it would appear, is motivated by a desire to circumvent, rather than to solve, the leading problems of contemporary city life. The near-cessation of city growth which can be expected in the not too distant future will give the planners an opportunity to catch their breath and to plan not for an expanding city area but for a rationally oriented, stable one.

THE NEIGHBORHOOD AND CHILD CONDUCT

Henry D. McKay

The introduction of cause-and-effect explanations into the field of children's behavior has thus far brought about only a partial metamorphosis in thinking habits. It has long been recognized that the child's attitudes, habits, and mode of life are natural products of his experience, and that not much is gained by blaming him for being a problem. What has happened, however, is that the blame has been transferred. During the past decade or more, the practice of blaming the parents for the misconduct of their children has been very prevalent. Now, in turn, there are some signs that this practice is being challenged, and that some other object of blame is being sought.

This discussion is not an attempt to replace the parents with another scapegoat. The neighborhood is not to be blamed for the misbehavior of youth. Just as first blaming the individual and later the parents proved to be futile, so it would be futile to place the blame elsewhere, because blame is not a concept of science and understanding. Instead, an effort will be made to describe the roles of the neighborhood and leisure-time activity in the whole education and socialization process. Particular emphasis will be given to the process through which the child becomes a delinquent, and its counterpart, the process through which he is remade into a conventional citizen. For emphasis, in this discussion the neighborhood and leisure-time activities will be considered separately, although it is recognized that they are inseparable parts of the same situation.

THE AREA OF PARTICIPATION. The term "neighborhood" is used here as a general concept to describe the world of the child exclusive of his family on the one hand, and of the radio, newspapers, and other symbols of the larger community on the other. It is essentially the area known to him through participation—it is the area in which he works and plays.

The activities of the child in the neighborhood tend to be organized around basic institutions and groupings such as the church, the school, the playgrounds, and perhaps the movie theater. In addition it may include participation in teams, clubs, or other groups organized on the basis of in-

Reprinted from *The Annals of the American Academy of Political and Social Science*, Vol. 261 (January, 1949), pp. 32-41, by permission of the author and the publisher. (Copyright, 1949, by *The Annals of the American Academy of Political and Social Science*.)

terests, talents, or accomplishment. Collectively these groups may represent the most meaningful part of the child's social world. The neighborhood of the child includes also institutions and activities in which he does not participate but with which he is familiar. Thus local lodges, taverns, clubs, and adult sport organizations are part of his world in a very real sense. In many but not all neighborhoods, other institutions and activities, such as picnics, carnivals, fights, weddings, funerals, and celebrations in which persons of all ages participate, are integral parts of the social life.

In short, everything that happens on a group-wise basis constitutes part of the setting for the neighborhood stage on which the drama of socialization and education is played.

The importance of the neighborhood in the conduct of the child is seen most clearly in an examination of the educational process. Formal education outside of the home takes place in the school where the child spends approximately one-sixth of his waking hours. But education in the broad sense goes on continuously, either in the home or in the neighborhood, during the remaining five-sixths of his waking hours. It is with this informal, continuous, educative process that we are primarily concerned here.

The basic task of the school is instruction, but it is involved directly in conduct problems also. If the school is well integrated in the neighborhood life, if the values of the teachers coincide with the values of the parents, and if there are no status or communication barriers between teachers and pupils, the effect of the school in the area of moral instruction may be very great. But if there is a cleavage between the school and the neighborhood, and if teachers exhibit attitudes of superiority or intolerance, the influence of the school upon individuals or on the moral tone of the neighborhood is greatly reduced.

Even when the school is effective, a large part of the child's moral education is acquired outside its walls; and when it is ineffective, the role of the informal and noninstitutional aspects of neighborhood life in the educational program is proportionately greater. In this situation the child takes over whatever the neighborhood has to offer—its traditional leisure-time activities, its standards of sportsmanship, its characteristic way of expressing anger, pleasure, or hostility, its philosophy of life, its moral codes, and its language. These come not only from the institutions in which the child participates directly, but also from his vicarious participation in all the activities which the neighborhood encourages or tolerates.

It is not possible to evaluate precisely the relative importance, in the education of the child, of the influence of the neighborhood on the one hand, and the influence of movies, radio, printed matter, and other contacts with the world outside of the neighborhood on the other. Each is part of his world and each must have some influence. But it is felt that the personal contact and participation in the neighborhood groups make neighborhood education more dynamic and significant than the education which is acquired more indirectly from the outside.

As a result of the relatively large amount of time spent at the movies, listening to serials or murder mysteries on the radio, or reading comic books, the modern child can imitate a machine gun, shoot or be shot with appropriate histrionics, anticipate the plots of murder mysteries, or play the role of superman. But there is reason to believe that these are just forms of play, without much meaning or significance in the formation of conduct patterns. Basic attitudes and values, it is felt, are not effectively transmitted through these more impersonal media of communication.

IMPORTANCE OF THE PLAY GROUP. On the other hand, it is known that attitudes and values are transmitted effectively through the personal relationships of the play group. Impersonal communication must depend upon abstract symbols, but direct personal communication is augmented by the immediate sensory impressions of four of the five senses. Moreover, the communication of the personal groups has emotional overtones which arise out of identification with the group, and the communication of meanings is facilitated by the successive responses of each person to each of the other participating persons. And it is just because this communication is so effective that the group is so important in the educational process.

The play group, in addition, is able to enforce conformity. Its sanction is more openly sought, and its disapprobation more carefully avoided, than is that of other groups. The family may decide how the child shall dress, but the verdict on whether the form of dress is satisfactory depends upon play-group reaction. The accepted standards in speech, clothing, manners, relationships with the other sex, and entertainment, all are decided by this same group. If these decisions do not coincide with those of the home, the church, and the school, the resulting conflict often reveals that the sanction of the play group is more important to the child than is the sanction of any other group or institution. When this is true, the conventional neighborhood institutions may find that they are relatively ineffective in their efforts to regulate conduct.

NEIGHBORHOOD TYPES AND DELINQUENCY RATES. Since the child reflects the influences of the neighborhood, it follows that if there are differences in the adequacy of neighborhoods, these differences should be reflected in variations in rates of law violations. Or, stated conversely, variations in rates of law violations should indicate discernible differences among neighborhoods or areas. The data on the number of juvenile offenders are so variable that valid comparisons cannot be made between rates for rural and urban areas or among cities, but within the same judicial area or city, defensible comparisons can be and have been made.

Rates of official delinquents based on several different kinds of indexes vary widely among areas in Chicago and other large American cities.[1] Every city has its sections where the rates of delinquents are high and its sections where the rates are low, with the areas of intermediate rates spread

---

1. See Clifford R. Shaw and Henry D. McKay, *Juvenile Delinquency and Urban Areas*, Chicago: University of Chicago Press, 1942.

out over the wide range between these two extremes. Rates of school truants, young adult and adult offenders, and female offenders, all are distributed about the same as rates of delinquents. Likewise, studies of rates for widely separated periods of time indicate that areas of high rates tend to remain areas of high rates, and vice versa.

Studies of areas within the city reveal also that the distribution of other community problems resembles the distribution of delinquents. The areas of high rates of delinquents also are the areas of highest rates of morbidity, infant mortality, mortality, dependency, and physical deterioration. And the areas of highest rates in one city have external characteristics in common with areas of high rates in other cities. There is little question that rates of delinquents vary with types of neighborhood situations.

The only other possibility would be the association of high rates of delinquents with particular nativity, nationality, or racial groups. Studies in Chicago have revealed, however, that the variations in rates among areas within nativity, nationality, or racial groups are as great as the variations in total rates. Moreover, in the same types of areas the different groups have approximately the same rates. This point is further reinforced by the fact that in Chicago different nationality and nativity groups have succeeded one another in the areas of high rates of delinquents without any appreciable change in the relative magnitude of the rates. Thus it appears that nativity or nationality does not explain the difference in rates among areas, and that the social life of the neighborhood should be examined in somewhat greater detail.

CONFLICTING VALUES. Areas of high rates of delinquents are areas of conflicting values—areas in which alternative educational processes are in operation. Part of the social life with which the child comes in contact is conventional and part of it is nonconventional. The result is that he may be educated in either or in both of these lines of activity. This is described by Sutherland as differential participation in conventional and non-conventional group activities.

An adequate explanation for the lack of consensus in the areas of high rates of delinquents is not easily found. The problem is: Under what conditions do alternative value systems come into existence in an area, and why are they not driven out by groups representing the dominant conventional values? It is suggested here that these alternative values arise most frequently in the struggle for position or status where the institutional organization is inadequate. If the institutional arrangements were completely adequate, the competition and conflicts through which persons and groups establish their status would be regularized. But in the absence of such adequacy, alternative devices for making a living and for getting ahead develop and are tolerated. A few of the conditions which seem to be favorable for such developments will be discussed briefly.

The alternative devices for the acceleration of the process of upward mobility outside of the traditional institutional arrangements have been developed most openly in the areas of low economic status in large cities. But many elements common to other types of situations are involved in the process. Among them are the traditions of a fluid status structure in which the possession of material goods is the symbol of power and prestige; free competition for the acquisition of goods; the weakening of traditional controls through the organization of society on an impersonal basis; and the presence of obstacles to the acquisition of the technical skills or education which are so important in the status struggle. Implicit also in our literature, radio programs, and advertising is the assumption that all persons have access to the luxury pattern of life, and that if the person does not have access he is being deprived of what he justly deserves. It is when these elements are coupled with the institutional weakness of inner city areas that the competitive process is most likely to take on new forms. And where it does take alternative illegal forms, the child is exposed to illegal modes of behavior.

LEISURE-TIME PROBLEM. Another element which complicates the education of the child in the neighborhood of high rates of delinquents is the problem of leisure time. In the Old World or in rural America the leisure-time problem for children was not serious because the child was part of the economy. He did his share of the family work and by so doing earned his share of the family income. But in the city he is not part of the income-earning group, and as a result he is free from income-procuring activity a large proportion of the time.

Since the problem did not exist before arrival in the city, no institutional forms were brought by the groups in the inner city areas to meet these particular needs. Likewise, the city has not developed adequate institutions for this purpose, since the large city in America is itself comparatively new. The result has been that children, especially boys, do not have any meaningful or acceptable way of employing their leisure time. And in gaining leisure time they have lost the devices through which, historically, they have established themselves in the neighborhood. Children now have freedom, but they are not important in the economy. As the late Professor Reuter has pointed out, the lack of any real function leaves the urban adolescents in a position of tolerated parasitism.[2]

INDIGENOUS INSTITUTIONS. In this situation where the traditional institutional arrangements do not control the status struggle or provide for the needs of young people, new native or indigenous institutions come into existence. Some of these institutions are conventional and some are either criminal or quasi criminal. Examples of the former are ethnic group organizations and social-athletic clubs. The ethnic group organizations are concerned both with welfare problems in the narrower sense and with efforts to improve the position of the group in the total society. Social-athletic clubs, it would seem, are perfect illustrations of natural institutions which

2. E. B. Reuter, "The Sociology of Adolescence," *American Journal of Sociology,* Vol. 43 (Nov. 1937), pp. 414-27.

have arisen to meet the social and recreational needs of young men in the inner areas of large cities.

Examples of nonconventional institutions are organized crime (often designated as the syndicate) and delinquent boys gangs. The power and prestige of the former guarantees that the boys in the area of operation will have access, in their education, to knowledge of this mode of getting on in the world. The presence of the delinquent gang means in addition that some boys will have an opportunity to participate in illegal activities. Delinquent gangs, as differentiated from play groups, encompass only some of the boys in a neighborhood; none of the boys can escape the influence of the presence of adult organized crime.

The other type of institution which comes into existence in the areas where the institutional arrangements are inadequate are the superimposed or nonindigenous welfare institutions such as boys clubs or social settlements. These can be distinguished from local institutions by the fact that they are developed, controlled, operated, and financed largely from outside the neighborhood. It is quite clear that the addition of these institutions on the side of conventionality has not materially reduced the operation of illegal or quasi-legal devices for making a living, nor has it resulted in the child's being insulated or protected from these influences. Gangs prosper in the very shadow of these institutions, and rates of delinquents continue to be high in spite of efforts to reduce them.

When examined from the point of view of the education of the child in the neighborhood, however, these nonindigenous institutions could hardly be expected to bring about important changes. Their number is small in the total number of neighborhood institutions, and participation in their activities represents only a segment of the child's total participation in the life of the neighborhood. Moreover, these institutions have the disadvantage of being "foreign" to the area where they are located, with all that is implied by that term. Although this does not prevent children from engaging in the activities of these institutions, it does reduce their value for the purpose of moral instruction.

RECREATION AND DELINQUENCY COMPARED. As forms of activity, recreation and delinquency have many qualities in common. In its early stages, delinquency is clearly a form of play. It is easy to see that running away from home, stealing pies from a pie wagon, or driving a stolen car may satisfy some of the basic needs or desires that are satisfied conventionally by baseball, pleasure riding, or going on a camping trip. In fact, it is easy to see that for those involved in them, many forms of delinquency, although costly to the community, may satisfy more of the immediate needs and wishes of children than are satisfied by more conventional forms of recreation. And this competition between the two types of activity is further complicated if the delinquency becomes financially profitable.

Both delinquency and recreation are essentially group activities. Each can be participated in alone, but in the more prevalent and meaningful forms, two or more persons usually are involved. Each type of activity has a tradition. Children's groups are the recipients and bearers of tradition governing rules, regulations, and mode of play of a great variety of games and means of entertainment, ranging from the rhymes which are sung while skipping rope to the techniques for playing third base. Similarly, in those neighborhoods where there are delinquent groups, the members are the recipients and bearers of a tradition on such subjects as how to break into a car, shoplift from a store, or avoid a policeman. The latter groups may be the recipients, also, of the conventional traditions.

In spite of these similarities, from the point of view of the larger community, these two forms of group activity are widely different. One is destructive, the other is constructive; one is dangerous, the other is desirable; one is law violation, the other is recreation. Even random play-group activity, which in its beginnings is inherently neither delinquent nor recreational, becomes one or the other in terms of whether or not the culmination of the activity is acceptable to the community. Thus a visit to an old house may be defined as an adventure; but if there is destruction it may be defined as law violation. In this connection it should be noted that the likelihood that random behavior will become destructive or malicious probably varies with the extent to which the neighborhood has provided for the needs of children along conventional lines.

Not only are recreation and delinquency both group activities, but in areas of high rates of delinquents the groups resemble each other in terms of physical characteristics, mental abilities, economic status, and family situations. Both delinquent and play groups have in their membership large boys and small boys, smart boys and dull boys, boys from broken homes and boys from integrated homes, and boys from families economically deprived and boys from families economically self-sufficient. In fact, with reference to these and similar characteristics, both kinds of groups are cross sections of the membership of the neighborhoods from which they are drawn.

The importance of this point is that there is no inherent reason why one group engages in delinquent activity and the other in recreation. The delinquent boys might just as well be limiting their activities to conventional games, and vice versa. The important variable is to be found, not in the boys, but in the variations in the educational process in the neighborhood. Of course after habits of delinquency have been established, it may not be easy to substitute less exhilarating conventional activities. It is not easy to satisfy a champagne taste with Coca-Cola.

ORGANIZED RECREATION NOT A PREVENTIVE. If the rate of delinquency in an area is high, often it is assumed that there is a dearth of organized recreation, and that if more organized recreation were introduced, the rate of delinquents would show a reduction. Probably neither one of these propositions is completely valid. They are true to the extent that a child engaging in organized recreation cannot at the same time be involved in delinquency. They are false to the extent that it is assumed that participation in organized recreation makes it unlikely that the child will engage in delinquency.

Organized recreation and delinquency are not mutually exclusive activities. In the summary of the findings of a study of recreation and delinquency in Chicago the following proposition is set forth: "In all of the areas studied, of those children who took part in recreation activities, delinquent boys spent more time in such activities than did nondelinquent boys." [3] These findings based on five areas in Chicago may or may not hold true for all of Chicago or for other cities, but they do establish, at least, that participation in one of these types of activity does not preclude participation in the other.

Another reason why recreation programs will not, by themselves, prevent delinquency is that participation in organized recreation represents such a small proportion of the total life experience of the child. In the study just mentioned, it was pointed out that during any one three-month season, between one-third and one-half of the recreation participants took part in supervised programs for less than ten hours, that a smaller proportion of boys over fourteen years took part in such activities, and that twice as much time was spent by boys in the movies as in supervised recreational activities. Thus it is clear that even for those who do participate, organized recreation consumes but a small part of their total leisure time.

The fact that organized recreation does not eliminate delinquency has little to do with its value. It is suggested here that it is a mistake to attempt to justify recreation in terms of delinquency or any other such activity. Actually, recreation needs no such justification. A chance to engage in leisure-time activities through which energies and creative urges are satisfied and which are not harmful to the neighborhood should be the heritage of every child, regardless of where he lives. Moreover, play has a defensible role in the socialization process. To suggest, however, that a boy will not be delinquent because he plays ball is no more valid than to say that he will not play ball because he is delinquent. He may do either, neither, or both.

BASIS OF PREVENTION PROGRAMS. Implicit or explicit in every program for the prevention of delinquency is some conception of the nature of the problems. Thus, if delinquency were assumed to be caused by mosquitoes, the prevention program would be mosquito abatement; or if the cause were assumed to be inadequate diets, the treatment program would be diet improvement. By the same logic, if it is assumed that the delinquent is a neighborhood product, a program of prevention must be related to the life of the neighborhood.

Prevention means that something is kept from happening which might otherwise have happened. As applied to delinquency in the community,

<hr />

3. Ethel Shanas, "Recreation and Delinquency," Chicago Recreation Commission, 1942.

this means that the probability of education for delinquency must be reduced or eliminated, and that the probability of education for conventional behavior must be increased. In some neighborhoods, where the rates of delinquents are low, education for accepted behavior need only be maintained; but in other areas, where rates of delinquents are high, some characteristics of the neighborhood must actually be changed.

Real achievement in this direction involves several kinds of endeavors. The first is the recognition of the need for the satisfaction of human needs and desires within the framework of conventional life. If the institutions and organizations are not available for this purpose, prevention may require their development. Another necessary step is the elimination of conflicting elements in the neighborhood. If delinquency is to be prevented, alternatives to conventional behavior cannot be tolerated. As was indicated earlier, organized crime, delinquent gangs, fences, and other illegal or quasi-legal activities are indications that the child is being subjected to alternative systems of values. It is evident that the influence of these alternatives must be reduced if delinquency is to be prevented.

Another kind of conflict which makes for appearance in court, if not for actual delinquency, is the conflict between the court and the local community in the way behavior is defined. If children are taken to court for engaging in practices which are tolerated or considered to be acceptable in the local neighborhood, they are the victims of such conflicts. Shoeshining, junking, and picking up coal along the railroad are examples of the types of behavior which the neighborhood may endorse, but which the police and the court, representing the attitudes of the wider community, may define as illegal. Attempts to remove or reconcile such variations of definitions are in themselves attempts at prevention.

STIGMA OF DELINQUENCY. An entirely different kind of preventive program can be directed at a reduction in the number of children defined as problems or as delinquents either by neighborhood action or by experience in legal agencies. Technically a child is a delinquent only when so defined by a court, but he may come to conceive of himself as a delinquent either through official action or by being pointed out as a delinquent in the neighborhood. This neighborhood definition, which may result in ostracism or exclusion from participation, has far-reaching consequences. Surely if it interferes with participation, it interferes with the normal socialization process and also may drive children who are rejected or ostracized into groups which furnish their own sanction and approval for retaliatory acts against the neighborhood.

Similarly, when children are arrested for relatively minor offenses, the treatment accorded them in the police station, the detention home, or the court may provide the basis for their coming to conceive of themselves as offenders or as delinquents. From this point of view it may be seen that neighborhood reaction or the action of neighborhood or community officials may be part of the process through which the minor offender is made into a delinquent. Thus efforts to prevent misbehavior may be the efforts through which it is created.

Prevention of delinquency, so conceived, would involve such action or restraint from action in the neighborhood as would keep children from being defined as problems or delinquents. Keeping good little boys from playing with Johnny, the bad boy, may be justified from the point of view of righteous citizens, but it is also part of the process through which Johnny is cast permanently in the role of a bad boy. Similarly, calling the police and sending boys to the station because they have been playing ball in the streets may be the beginning of the process through which they may become real offenders.

TREATMENT. Effective treatment means that the offender who has been devalued, ostracized, or incarcerated, must be helped to establish himself in a satisfactory role in the conventional community. This proposition has few exceptions; for if the offender is not re-established in conventional activity, it is probable that once more he will re-establish himself in the world of the delinquent. The alternative is that temporarily he may belong to some groups in both the delinquent and the conventional world without being fully incorporated into either. Such a person is a potential candidate for either conventionality or delinquency, and, as such, is a good subject for treatment.

This fact brings to the foreground the dilemma of treatment. It is: How can the society which casts out the offender because he has violated its laws be induced to accept him again for the purpose of treatment? "Casting out" the offender, either actually or symbolically, has been accepted practice throughout the written history of man. At the present time with juveniles our "casting out" usually takes the form of a sentence to a training school, followed by a period during which the offender is designated either as a delinquent or as a criminal and treated with suspicion and hostility both by the ordinary citizen and by our representatives of the law and order. Yet as a logical proposition this offender must be reincorporated into conventional groups before it can be said that he has been successfully treated. Therein lies the problem.

Treatment, like prevention, must be formulated with reference to a theory of causation. If it is assumed that delinquency and crime are products of education in situations where there are alternative systems of values and ways of getting ahead in the world, then treatment involves getting the person to be treated to accept the values and mode of life of the conventional group. This must be accomplished either in opposition to the conflicting values or through their elimination.

Treatment programs not involving major changes in the community include attempts to introduce nondelinquent types of activity into the delinquent groups and attempts to induce the offenders being treated into conventional groups. The process is facilitated through the use of persons of prestige in the world of the offender, and it is encouraged by sympathetic understanding and the avoidance of evidence of moral indignation or recrimination. Only when the person has been incorporated into conventional groups long enough to have experienced a re-education in terms of conventional values can the treatment be said to have been complete. Such a program applies, of course, to children who are physically and mentally normal.

Finally, neighborhood treatment, like prevention, is more likely to succeed if the opportunities for participation in delinquent activities are reduced and the opportunities for satisfactory participation in conventional activities are increased. This cannot be accomplished by enacting harsher laws or selecting a new chief of police. It might come, however, from neighborhood action. If illegal activities meet with organized neighborhood opposition they may be driven out or closed. Likewise, organized activity on the part of adults may strengthen the conventional aspects of neighborhood life both through participation in constructive neighborhood activities and through the stimulation of such goals. To the extent that these activities create consensus and uniform values, they are changing the community and increasing the probability that the offender will be re-educated in terms of conventional conduct.

RECAPITULATION. The neighborhood furnishes the setting in which the child is educated either for conventional or for delinquent behavior. If the values of the neighborhood are consistent, this consistency is likely to be reflected in conventional behavior. If, however, conventional institutions are not completely adequate, and illegal institutions and activities develop and persist in the neighborhood, the conflict of values is likely to be reflected in high rates of violation of the conduct norms. Such neighborhoods are found in the inner areas of large cities.

Both recreation and delinquency are group activities, and although one is legal and the other illegal, both satisfy many of the same basic needs in the child. Recreation is not a cure for delinquency, although it can be defended in its own right as a socializing agency. Delinquency prevention involves the elimination of conflicting values from the neighborhood and the protection of the child from definition as a delinquent. Successful treatment of delinquents necessitates the reincorporation of the offender into conventional groups. Such a program clearly requires some type of neighborhood action.

The following abbreviations for journals and periodicals are used in the bibliography.

AER	American Economic Review
AJES	American Journal of Economics and Sociology
AJS	American Journal of Sociology
ASR	American Sociological Review
BJS	British Journal of Sociology
EDCC	Economic Development and Cultural Change
GR	Geographic Review
JASA	Journal of the American Statistical Association
JPE	Journal of Political Economy
JSI	Journal of Social Issues
JSP	Journal of Social Psychology
LE	Land Economics
MMFQ	Milbank Memorial Fund Quarterly
POQ	Public Opinion Quarterly
PS	Population Studies
RES	Review of Economics and Statistics
RS	Rural Sociology
SF	Social Forces
SSR	Sociology and Social Research

I. Theory and Method

A. Theory: General Community.

Bates, Marston. *The Nature of Natural History*. New York: Charles Scribner's Sons, 1950.

Bernard, Jessie. *American Community Behavior*. New York: The Dryden Press, 1949.

Blackwell, Gordon W. "A Theoretical Framework for Sociological Research in Community Organization," *SF*, 33 (October, 1954), 57-64.

Firey, Walter. "Review of Current Research in Demography and Human Ecology," *ASR*, 17 (April, 1952), 212-215.

Galpin, C. J. "The Social Anatomy of an Agricultural Community," *Agricultural Experiment Station Research Bulletin*, 34, Madison, Wisconsin, 1915.

Green, James W. and Mayo, Selz C. "A Framework for Research in the Actions of Community Groups," *SF*, 31 (May, 1953), 320-327.

Hawley, Amos. *Human Ecology: A Theory of Community Structure*. New York: The Ronald Press Company, 1950.

Hill, Mozell C., and Whiting, Albert N. "Some Theoretical and Methodological Problems in Community Studies," *SF*, 29 (December, 1950), 117-124.

Hollingshead, A. B. "A Re-examination of Ecological Theory," *SSR*, 31 (January-February, 1948), 194-204.

———. "Community Research: Development and Present Conditions," *ASR*, 13 (April, 1948), 136-155.

Murdock, George P. "Feasibility and Implementation of Comparative Community Research," *ASR*, 15 (December, 1950), 713-720.

Quinn, James A. *Human Ecology.* New York: Prentice-Hall, Inc., 1950.

Park, Robert E. *Human Communities.* Glencoe: The Free Press, 1952.

Redfield, Robert. "The Folk Society and Culture," *AJS*, 45 (March, 1940), 731-42.

————. "The Folk Society," *AJS*, 52 (January, 1947), 292-308.

————. *The Little Community: Viewpoints for the Study of a Human Whole.* Chicago: University of Chicago Press, 1955.

————. "The Natural History of the Folk Society," *SF*, 31 (March, 1953), 224-228.

Tönnies, Frederick. *Fundamental Concepts of Sociology.* Translated by C. P. Loomis. New York: American Book Co., 1940, pp. 70-73, 265-67, and 271-72.

Wirth, Louis. "Human Ecology," *AJS*, 51 (May, 1945), 483-88.

B. Theory: Urban Community.

Bogue, Donald J. (ed.). *Needed Urban and Metropolitan Research.* Scripps Foundation Studies in Population Distribution, No. 7. Miami, Ohio: Scripps Foundation, 1953.

Burgess, E. W. (ed.). *The Urban Community.* Chicago: University of Chicago Press, 1926.

Dickinson, Robert L. *City, Region and Regionalism.* New York: Oxford University Press, 1947.

Fisher, Robert M. (ed.). *The Metropolis in Modern Life.* New York: Doubleday & Co., 1955.

Gillen, Paul Bates. *The Distribution of Occupations as a City Yardstick.* New York: The King's Crown Press, 1951.

McClenahan, Bessie A. "The Communality: The Urban Substitute for the Traditional Community," *SSR*, 30 (March-April, 1946), 264-274.

Miner, Horace. "The Folk-Urban Continuum," *ASR*, 17 (October, 1952), 529-37.

National Resources Committee. *Our Cities: Their Role in the National Economy.* Washington, D.C.: U.S. Government Printing Office, 1937.

Park, Robert E. and Burgess, E. W. (ed.). *The City.* Chicago: University of Chicago Press, 1925.

Park, Robert E. "The City: Suggestions for the Investigation of Human Behavior in the Urban Environment," *The City.* Edited by R. E. Park and E. W. Burgess. Chicago: University of Chicago Press, 1925, pp. 1-46.

Peterman, Theodor (ed.). *Die Grosstadt.* Dresden, 1903.

Reiss, Jr., Albert J. "An Analysis of Urban Phenomena," *The Metropolis in Modern Life.* Edited by Robert M. Fisher. New York: Doubleday & Co., 1955, Chapter 3.

Schmid, Calvin F. "Generalizations Concerning the Ecology of the American City," *ASR*, 15 (April, 1950), 264-281.

Sjoberg, Gideon. "Urban Community Theory and Research: A Partial Eavluation," *AJES*, 14 (January, 1955), 199-206.

Sorokin, P. A. and Zimmerman, C. C. *Principles of Rural-Urban Sociology.* New York: Henry Holt and Co., 1929.

Spaulding, Irving A. "Serendipity and the Rural-Urban Continuum," *RS*, 16 (March, 1951), 29-36.

Truesdell, Leon E. "The Development of the Urban-Rural Classification in the United States: 1874 to 1949," *Current Population Reports.* U.S. Bureau of the Census, Series P-23, No. 1.

Weber, Max. "Die Stadt," *Wirtschaft and Gesellschaft.* Tubingen, 1925. pp, 514-601.

Wirth, Louis. "Urban Communities," *AJS*, 47 (May, 1942), 829-840.

————. "Urbanism as a Way of Life," *AJS*, 44 (July, 1938), 1-24.

"World Urbanism," *AJS*, 60 (March, 1955), 427-492.

C. Method and Techniques of Community Study.

Arensberg, Conrad M. "The Community Study-Method," AJS, 60 (September, 1954), 109-124.

Baur, Edward J. "Statistical Indexes of the Social Aspects of Communities," SF, 33 (October, 1954), 64-75.

Bell, Wendell. "A Probability Model for the Measurement of Ecological Segregation," SF, 32 (May, 1954), 357-364.

Bogue, Donald J., and Harris, Dorothy L. Comparative Population and Urban Research via Multiple Regression and Covariance Analyses. Oxford, Ohio: Scripps Foundation, Miami University, 1954.

Duncan, Otis Dudley and Beverly. "A Methodological Analysis of Segregation Indexes," ASR, 20 (April, 1955), 210-217.

Fessler, Donald R. "The Development of a Scale for Measuring Community Solidarity," RS, 17 (June, 1952), 144-152.

Form, William H., et al. "The Compatibility of Alternative Approaches to the Delimitation of Urban Sub-Areas," ASR, 19 (August, 1954), 434-440.

Goodman, Leo. "On Urbanization Indices," SF, 31 (May, 1953), 360-362.

Green, Norman E. "Scale Analysis of Urban Structures: A Study of Birmingham, Alabama," ASR, 21 (February, 1956), 8-13.

Hauser, Philip M., Duncan, Otis Dudley, and Duncan, Beverly Davis. Methods of Urban Analysis: A Summary Report. Lackland Air Force Base, San Antonio, Texas: Air Force Personnel & Training Research Center; AFPTRC-TN-56-1, January, 1956.

Hawley, Amos. "The Approach of Human Ecology to Urban Areal Research," Scientific Monthly, LXXIII (July, 1951), 48-49.

Hornseth, Richard A. "A Note on 'The Measurement of Ecological Segregation' by Julius Jahn, Calvin F. Schmid, and Clarence Schrag," ASR, 12 (October, 1947), 603-604.

Jahn, Julius A. "The Measurement of Ecological Segregation," ASR, 15 (February, 1950), 100-104.

Jahn, Julius, Schmid, Calvin F., and Schrag, Clarence. "The Measurement of Ecological Segregation," ASR, 12 (June, 1947), 293-304.

Jonassen, Christen T. "A Re-evaluation and Critique of the Logic and Some Methods of Shaw and McKay," ASR, 14 (October, 1949), 608-618.

Kimball, Solon T. "Some Methodological Problems of the Community Self-Survey," SF, 31 (December, 1952), 160-164.

Myers, Jerome K. "Note on the Homogeneity of Census Tracts: A Methodological Problem in Urban Ecological Research," SF, 32 (May, 1954), 364-366.

Reiss, Albert J., Jr. "Some Logical and Methodological Problems in Community Research," SF, 33 (October, 1954), 51-57.

Robinson, W. S. "Ecological Correlations and the Behavior of Individuals," ASR, 15 (June, 1950), 351-356.

Smith, Joel. "A Method for the Classification of Areas on the Basis of Demographically Homogeneous Populations," ASR, 19 (April, 1954), 201-207.

Strodtbeck, Fred L. "Equal Opportunity Intervals: A Contribution to the Method of Intervening Opportunity Analysis," ASR, 14 (August, 1949), 490-497.

Williams, Josephine J. "Another Commentary on the So-Called Segregation Indices," ASR, 13 (June, 1948), 208-304.

II. The City in History

Bridenbaugh, Carl. Cities in the Wilderness: The First Century of Urban Life in America, 1625-1742. New York: The Ronald Press, 1938.

Childe, V. Gordon. Man Makes Himself. London: Watts and Company, 1937.

——. *What Happened in History*. Harmondsworth: Penguin Books, 1942.

Clerget, Pierre. "Urbanism: A Historic, Geographic and Economic Study," *Annual Report of the Board of Regents of the Smithsonian Institution*. Washington: USGPO, 1913.

Davis, Kingsley. "The Origin and Growth of Urbanization in the World," *AJS*, 60 (March, 1955), 429-437.

Diamond, William. "On the Dangers of an Urban Interpretation of History," *Historiography and Urbanization*. Edited by Eric F. Goldman. Baltimore: John Hopkins Press, 1941, Chapter IV.

Dickinson, Robert E. "The Development and Distribution of the Medieval German Town," *Geography*, (March and June, 1942).

——. *The West European City*. London: Oxford University Press, 1951.

Dopsch, Alfons. *The Economic and Social Foundations of European Civilization*. London: Kegan Paul, Trench, Trubner & Co., Ltd., 1937.

Fleure, H. J. "The Historic City in Western and Central Europe," *Bulletin of the John Rylands Library*, 20 (July-August, 1936), 312-331.

Fustel de Coulanges, Numa Denis. *The Ancient City*. Boston: Lee and Shepard Company, 1889.

Geddes, Patrick. *Cities in Evolution*. London: Williams and Norgate, 1915.

Gras, N. S. B. *Introduction to Economic History*. New York: Harper and Brothers, 1922.

——. "The Rise of the Metropolitan Community," *The Urban Community*. Edited by E. W. Burgess. Chicago: University of Chicago Press, 1925.

Homans, George C. *English Villagers of the Thirteenth Century*. Cambridge: Harvard University Press, 1941.

Lampard, Eric E. "The History of Cities in the Economically Advanced Areas," *EDCC*, III (January, 1955), 81-136.

McKenzie, R. D. "The Rise of Metropolitan Communities," *Recent Social Trends*. New York: The McGraw-Hill Book Co., 1933, pp. 443-96.

Maine, H. S. *Village Communities in the East and West*. London (7th ed.), 1913.

Miner, Horace. *The Primitive City of Timbuctoo*. (American Philosophical Society, Memoir No. 32). Princeton: Princeton University Press, 1953.

Mumford, Lewis. *The Culture of Cities*. New York: Harcourt, Brace and Company, 1938.

Munro, W. B. "The City," *Encyclopedia of Social Sciences*.

Nussbaum, F. L. *A History of the Economic Institutions of Modern Europe*, 1940.

Park, Robert E. "The City and Civilization," *Second Year Course in the Study of Contemporary Society*. University of Chicago Bookstore, Sixth Edition, September, 1947, pp. 204-220.

Piganiol, A. "The City State," *Encyclopedia of the Social Sciences*.

Piggott, Stuart. "The Role of the City in Ancient Civilizations," *The Metropolis in Modern Life*. Edited by Robert M. Fisher. New York: Doubleday & Co., 1955, Chapter 1.

Pirenne, Henri. *Medieval Cities: Their Origins and the Revival of Trade*. Princeton: Princeton University Press, 1945.

Rostovtzeff, Michael I. "Cities in the Ancient World," *Urban Land Economics*. The Institute of Land Economics, Ann Arbor, Edwards Bros., Publishers, 1922.

Schlesinger, Arthur M. "The City in American History," *Mississippi Valley Historical Review*, 27 (June, 1940), 43-67.

——. *The Rise of the City 1878-1898*. New York: The Macmillan Company, 1933.

——. *Paths to the Present*. New York: The Macmillan Co., 1949.

Sombart, Werner. *Der Moderne Kapitalismus*. Munich and Leipzig: Dunckes and Humblat, 1928.

Sorokin, P. A., Zimmerman, C. C., and Galpin, C. J. *Systematic Source Book in Rural Sociology*, Minneapolis: University of Minnesota Press, 1930, Vol. I.

Spengler, O. *The Decline of the West*. New York: A. A. Knopf, 1926-28, 2 vols.

Wirth, Louis. "The Urban Society and Civilization," *AJS*, 45 (March, 1940), 743-755.

III. Population Redistribution

A. Urbanization and Urban Growth.

Allen, G. R. "The 'Courbe des Populations': A Further Analysis," *Bulletin of the Oxford University Institute of Statistics*, 16 (May-June, 1954), 179-189.

Blumenfeld, Hans. "On the Growth of Metropolitan Areas," *SF*, 28 (October, 1949), 59-64.

Bogue, Donald J. *Population Growth in Standard Metropolitan Areas, 1900-1950: With an Explanatory Analysis of Urbanized Areas.* Washington, D.C.: Housing and Home Finance Agency, 1953.

———. "Urbanism in the United States, 1950," *AJS* 60 (March, 1955), 471-486.

Clark, Colin. "Urban Population Densities," *Journal of the Royal Statistical Society*, 114 (No. 4, 1951), 490-496.

Cole, William E. "Urban Development in the Tennessee Valley," *SF*, 26 (October, 1947), 67-75.

Cooper, Eunice, "Urbanization in Malaya," *PS*, 5 (November, 1951), 117-131.

Davis, Kingsley. "The Origin and Growth of Urbanization in the World," *AJS*, 60 (March, 1955), 429-437.

———. "The World Demographic Transition," *The Annals*, 237, pp. 1-7.

Davis, Kingsley and Casis, Ana. "Urbanization in Latin America," *MMFQ*, 24 (April and July, 1946) Part I, pp. 186-207; Part II, pp. 292-314.

Davis, Kingsley, and Hertz Golden, Hilda. "Urbanization and the Development of Pre-Industrial Areas," *EDCC*, III (October, 1954), 6-26.

———. "The World Distribution of Urbanization," *Bulletin of the International Statistical Institute*, XXXIII, Part IV.

Ginsberg, Norton S. "The Great City in Southeast Asia," *AJS*, 60 (March, 1955), 455-462.

Gross, Edward. "The Role of Density as a Factor in Metropolitan Growth in the United States of America," *PS*, 8 (November, 1954), 113-120.

Harris, Chauncey D. "The Cities of the Soviet Union," *GR*, 35 (January, 1945), 107-121.

Hauser, Philip M. and Eldridge, Hope T. "Projection of Urban Growth and Migration to Cities in the United States," *MMFQ*, 25 (July, 1947), 293-307.

Hawley, Amos and Bogue, Donald J. "Recent Shifts in Population: The Drift Toward the Metropolitan District: 1930-40," *RES*, 24 (August, 1942), 143-148.

Jaffe, Abram J. "Population Trends and City Growth," *The Annals*, 242 (November, 1945), 18-24.

Jefferson, Mark. "Distribution of the World's City Folks," *GR*, 21 (1931), 446-65.

Keyes, Fenton. "Urbanism and Population Distribution in China," *AJS*, 56 (May, 1951), 519-527.

Lee, Rose Hum. *The City: Urbanism and Urbanization in Major World Regions*. Philadelphia: J. B. Lippincott Co., 1955.

Leonard, Olen. "La Paz, Bolivia: Its Population and Growth," *ASR*, 13 (August, 1948), 448-54.

McKenzie, R. D. "The Rise of Metropolitan Communities," *Recent Social Trends*. New York: McGraw-Hill Book Company, 1933.

McLaughton, Glenn E. *Growth of American Manufacturing Areas*. Pittsburgh, 1938.

Singer, H. W. "The 'Courbe des Populations': A Parallel to Pareto's Law," *Economic Journal*, 46 (June, 1936), 254-263.

Thompson, Warren S. *The Growth of Metropolitan Districts in the United States: 1900-1940*. Washington: Government Printing Office, 1947.

Tisdale, Hope. "The Process of Urbanization," *SF*, 20 (March, 1942), 311-316.

Weber, Adna Ferrin. *The Growth of Cities in the Nineteenth Century: A Study in Statistics*. Columbia U. Studies in History, Economics and Public Law, New York, 1899.

Wilkinson, Thomas O., "The Pattern of Korean Urban Growth," *RS*, 19 (March, 1954), 32-38.

B. Population Redistribution in Metropolitan Complexes.

Armstrong, Robert H. and Hoyt, Homer. *Decentralization in New York City*. Chicago: The Urban Land Institute, 1941.

Blizzard, Samuel W. "Research on the Rural-Urban Fringe," *SSR*, 38 (January-February, 1954), 143-149.

Blizzard, Samuel W. and Anderson, William F. *Problems in Rural-Urban Fringe Research: Conceptualization and Delineation*. Pennsylvania Agricultural Experiment Station, Progress Report No. 89, November, 1953.

Bogue, Donald J. *Metropolitan Decentralization: A Study of Differential Growth*. Scripps Foundation Studies in Population Distribution, No. 2. Oxford, Ohio, August, 1950.

Gist, Noel P. "Developing Patterns of Urban Decentralization," *SF*, 30 (March, 1952), 257-267.

———. "The New Urban Fringe, *SSR*, 36 (May-June, 1952), 297-302.

Harris, C. D. "Suburbs," *AJS*, 49 (July, 1943), 1-13.

Martin, Walter T. *The Rural-Urban Fringe: A Study of Adjustment to Residence Location*. Eugene: The University of Oregon Press, 1953.

Mumford, Lewis. *City Development: Studies in Disintegration and Renewal*. New York: Harcourt, Brace, and Company, 1945.

Redick, Richard W. "Population Growth and Distribution in Central Cities, 1940-1950," *ASR*, 21 (February, 1956), 38-43.

Reeder, Leo G. "The Central Area of Chicago: A Re-examination of the Process of Decentralization," *LE*, 28 (November, 1952), 369-73.

Reeder, Leo G. "Industrial Deconcentration as a Factor in Rural-Urban Fringe Development," *LE*, 31 (August, 1955), 275-80.

Reiss, Jr., Albert J. "Research Problems in Metropolitan Population Redistribution," *ASR*, 21 (October, 1956), 571-77.

Riemer, Svend. "Escape into Decentralization," *LE*, 24 (February, 1948).

U.S. Federal Housing Administration. *The Structure and Growth of Residential Neighborhoods in American Cities*. Washington: USGPO, 1932.

Whitney, Vincent Heath. "Rural-Urban People," *AJS*, 54 (July, 1948), 48-54.

IV. Urban Ecological Organization

A. Location.

Cooley, Charles H. "Theory of Transportation," *Sociological Theory and Social Research*. New York: Henry Holt and Company, 1930.

Dennison, S. R. *The Location of Industry and the Depressed Areas*. 1939.

Gilmore, Harlan W. *Transportation and the Growth of Cities*. Glencoe, Ill.: The Free Press, 1953.

Hoover, Edgar M., Jr. *Location Theory and the Shoe and Leather Industries.* Cambridge: Harvard University Press, 1937.

———. *The Location of Economic Activity.* New York: McGraw-Hill, 1948.

Hoult, Thomas Ford. "Research Note on the Hypothesis of Median Location," *AJS,* 59 (May, 1954), 536-538.

Isard, Walter and Whitney, Vincent. "Metropolitan Site Selection," *SF,* 27 (March, 1949), 263-269.

Lösch, August. "The Nature of Economic Regions," *Southern Economic Journal,* 5 (July, 1938), 71-79.

———. *The Economics of Location.* Translated from the Second Revised Edition by William H. Woglom, with the assistance of Wolfgang F. Stolper. New Haven: Yale University Press, 1954.

National Resources Committee. *Industrial Location and National Resources.* Washington, D.C.: USGPO, 1937.

Ratcliff, Richard U. "Efficiency and the Location of Urban Activities," *The Metropolis in Modern Life.* Edited by Robert M. Fisher. New York: Doubleday & Co., 1955.

Von Thünen, J. H. *Der Isolierte Staat, in Beziehung auf Landwirtschaft und Nationalökonomie,* Rostock, 2nd edition, 1942.

Ullman, Edward A. "A Theory of Location for Cities," *AJS,* 46 (1941), 853-64.

Van Cleef, Eugene. *Trade Centers and Trade Routes.* New York: Appleton-Century Company, 1937.

Weber, Alfred. *Theory of Location of Industries.* Chicago: University of Chicago Press, 1929.

B. Urban Functional Organization and Integration.

Alexander, John W. "The Basic-Nonbasic Concept of Urban Economic Functions," *Economic Geography,* 30 (July, 1954), 246-261.

Andrews, Richard B. "Mechanics of the Urban Economic Base," *LE,* 29 and 30 (1953-1954), series of seven articles, variously subtitled.

Batten, Thelma F. *Flint and Michigan: A Study in Interdependence.* Ann Arbor: Social Science Research Project, University of Michigan, 1955.

Clark, Colin. "The Economic Functions of a City In Relation to Its Size," *Econometrica,* 13 (April, 1954), 97-113.

Conway, Freda. "The Industrial Structure of Towns," *Manchester School of Economic and Social Studies,* 21 (May, 1953), 154-164.

Cuzzort, Raymond P. *Suburbanization of Service Industries within Standard Metropolitan Areas.* Scripps Foundation Studies in Population Distribution, No. 10, Oxford, Ohio, 1955.

Duncan, Otis Dudley. "Urbanization and Retail Specialization," *SF,* 30 (March, 1952), 267-271.

Duncan, Otis Dudley and Reiss, Jr., Albert J. *Social Characteristics of Rural and Urban Communities, 1950.* New York: John Wiley & Sons, 1956, Part IV.

Harris, C. D. "A Functional Classification of Cities in the United States," *GR,* 33 (1943), 86-99.

Hart, John Fraser. "Functions and Occupational Structures of Cities of the American South," *Annals of the Association of American Geographers,* 45 (September, 1955), 269-286.

Isard, Walter, Kavesh, Robert A. and Kuenne, Robert E. "The Economic Base and Structure of the Urban-Metropolitan Region," *ASR,* 18 (June, 1953), 317-321.

Kitagawa, Evelyn M. and Bogue, Donald J. *Suburbanization of Manufacturing Activity within Standard Metropolitan Areas.* Scripps Foundation Studies in Population Distribution, Number 9. Oxford, Ohio, 1955.

Kneedler, Grace. "Functional Types of Cities," *Public Management,* 27 (July, 1945), 197-203.

Mattila, John M. and Thompson, Wilbur R. "The Measurement of the Economic Base of the Metropolitan Area," *LE,* 31 (August, 1955), 215-228.

Sargant, Florence P. "Economic Efficiency in the Metropolis," *The Metropolis in Modern Life.* Edited by Robert M. Fisher. New York: Doubleday & Co., 1955, Chapter 6.

Schnore, Leo F. "The Functions of Metropolitan Suburbs," *AJS,* 61 (March, 1956), 453-458.

Smith, Jr., George C. "Lorenz Curve Analysis of Industrial Decentralization," *JASA,* 42 (December, 1947), 591-596.

C. Urban Spatial Organization and Processes.

Bogue, Donald J. *The Structure of the Metropolitan Community: A Study of Dominance and Subdominance.* Ann Arbor: The University of Michigan Press, 1949.

Blumenfeld, Hans. "On the Concentric-Circle Theory of Urban Growth," *LE,* 25 (May, 1949), 209-212.

Carroll, J. Douglas, Jr. "The Relation of Homes to Work Places and the Spatial Pattern of Cities," *SF,* 30 (March, 1952), 271-282.

Clark, Colin. "Urban Population Densities," *Journal of The Royal Statistical Society: Series A,* 114 (Part IV, 1951), 490-496.

Duncan, Beverly. "Factors in Work-Residence Separation: Wage and Salary Workers, Chicago, 1951," *ASR,* 21 (February, 1956), 48-56.

Ikle, Fred Charles. "The Effect of War Destruction Upon the Ecology of Cities," *SF,* 29 (May, 1951), 383-391.

Gist, Noel P. "Ecological Decentralization and Rural-Urban Relationships," *RS,* 17 (December, 1952), 328-335.

———. "Developing Patterns of Urban Decentralization," *SF,* 30 (March, 1952), 257-67.

Isard, Walter, Kavesh, R. A. and Kuenne, R. E. "The Economic Base and Structure of the Urban Metropolitan Region," *ASR,* 13 (June, 1953), 317-321.

Kinneman, John A. "Newspaper Circulation from Small Metropolitan Centers," *ASR,* 11 (April, 1946), 150-155.

Ogburn, W. F. "Inventions of Local Transportation and the Patterns of Cities," *SF,* 25 (May, 1946), 313-19.

Park, R. E. "Urbanization as Measured by Newspaper Circulation," *AJS,* 35 (July, 1929), 60-65.

Stolper, Wolfgang. "Spatial Order and the Economic Growth of Cities," *EDCC,* 3 (January, 1955), 137-146.

D. Intra-Urban Spatial Organization.

Andrews, Richard B. "Elements in the Urban Fringe Pattern," *Journal of Land and Public Utility Economics,* 13 (May, 1942), 169-183.

Bartholomew, Harland. *Land Uses in American Cities.* Cambridge: Harvard University Press, 1955.

Bell, Wendell. "Economic, Family, and Ethnic Status: An Empirical Test," *ASR,* 20 (February, 1955), 45-52.

———. "The Social Areas of the San Francisco Bay Region," *ASR,* 18 (February, 1953), 39-47.

Blizzard, Samuel W. "Research on the Rural-Urban Fringe: A Case Study," *SSR,* 38 (January-February, 1954), 143-149.

Bloom, Leonard and Shevky, Eshref. "The Differentiation of an Ethnic Group," *ASR,* 14 (August, 1949), 476-481.

Bourland, D. David. "The Distribution of Professions within Cities in the United States," *American Journal of Psychology*, 63 (April, 1950), 244-249.

Bowers, R. V. "Ecological Patterning of Rochester," *ASR*, 4 (April, 1939).

Caplow, Theodore. "The Social Ecology of Guatemala City," *SF*, 28 (December, 1949), 113-133.

———. "Urban Structure in France," *ASR*, 17 (October, 1952), 544-549.

Duncan, Otis Dudley. "Urbanization and Retail Specialization," *SF*, 30 (March, 1952), 267-271.

Duncan, Otis Dudley and Beverly. "Residential Distribution and Occupational Stratification," *AJS*, 60 (March, 1955), 493-503.

Dunham, H. Warren. "Current Status of Ecological Research in Mental Disorder," *SF*, 25 (March, 1947), 321-326.

Federal Housing Administration. *The Structure and Growth of Residential Neighborhoods in American Cities*. Washington, D.C.: United States Government Printing Office, 1939.

Firey, Walter. *Land Use in Central Boston*. Cambridge: Harvard University Press, 1947.

Freedman, Ronald. "Distribution of Migrant Population in Chicago," *ASR*, 13 (June, 1948), 304-309.

Gilmore, Harlan W. "The Old New Orleans and the New: A Case for Ecology," *ASR*, 9 (August, 1944), 385-394.

Harris, Chauncey D. and Ullman, Edward S. "The Nature of Cities," *The Annals*, 242 (November, 1945), 7-17.

Hatt, Paul K. "The Concept of Natural Area," *ASR*, 11 (August, 1946), 423-427.

Hawley, Amos H. "Land Value Patterns in Okayama, Japan, 1940 and 1952," *AJS*, 60 (March, 1955), 487-492.

Hayner, Norman S. "Criminogenic Zones in Mexico City," *ASR*, 11 (August, 1946), 428-438.

Holt, A. E. "Ecological Approach to the Church," *AJS*, 32 (1927-28), 72-79.

Hoyt, Homer. *One Hundred Years of Land Values in Chicago*. Chicago: University of Chicago Press, 1933.

Hurd, Richard M. *Principles of City Land Values*. New York: The Record and Guide, 1903.

James, John. "A Critique of Firey's Land Use in Central Boston," *AJS*, 54 (November, 1948), 228-234.

Kish, Leslie. "Differentiation in Metropolitan Areas," *ASR*, 19 (August, 1954), 388-398.

Lee, Rose Hum. "The Decline of Chinatowns in the United States," *AJS*, 54 (March, 1949), 422-432.

Sainsbury, Peter. *Suicide in London: An Ecological Study*. London: Chapman and Hall, Ltd. for the Institute of Psychiatry, 1956.

Schmid, Calvin F. "Generalizations Concerning the Ecology of the American City," *ASR*, 15 (April, 1950), 264-281.

———. *Social Saga of Two Cities*. Minneapolis: Council of Social Agencies, 1937.

Shaw, Clifford and McKay, H. D. *Juvenile Delinquency and Urban Areas*. Chicago: University of Chicago Press, 1942.

Shevky, Eshref and Bell, Wendell. *Social Area Analysis*. (Stanford Sociological Series, Number 1) Stanford: Stanford University Press, 1955.

Shevky, Eshref and Williams, Marilyn. *The Social Areas of Los Angeles, Analysis and Typology*. Los Angeles: University of California Press, 1949.

Swanson, G. E. "The Disturbances of Children in Urban Areas," *ASR*, 14 (October, 1949), 676-678.

U.S. *Census of Population: 1950*. "Census Tract Statistics," Vol. III.

E. Intra-Urban Spatial Organization and Processes.

Blumenfeld, Hans. "On the Concentric-Circle Theory of Urban Growth," *LE*, 25 (May, 1949), 209-212.

Brussat, William K. "Incidental Findings on Urban Invasion," *ASR*, 16 (1951), 94-96.

Cressey, Paul F. "Population Succession in Chicago, 1898-1930," *AJS*, 44 (July, 1938.

Davie, Maurice. "The Pattern of Urban Growth," *Studies in the Science of Society*. Edited by G. P. Murdock. New Haven: Yale University Press, 1937.

Dotson, Floyd, and Ota, Lillian. "Ecological Trends in the City of Guadalajara, Mexico," *SF*, 32 (May, 1954), 367-74.

Firey, Walter. "Sentiment and Symbolism as Ecological Variables." *ASR*, 10 (1950), 140-48.

Ford, Richard G. "Population Succession in Chicago," *AJS*, 56 (September, 1950), 156-160.

Form, William H. "The Place of Social Structure in the Determination of Land Use: Some Implications for a Theory of Urban Ecology," *SF*, 32 (May, 1954), 317-23.

Jonassen, Christen T. "Cultural Variables in the Ecology of an Ethnic Group," *ASR*, 14 (February, 1949), 32-41.

Jones, Clifton R. "Invasion and Racial Attitudes: A Study of Housing in a Border City," *SF*, 27 (March, 1949), 285-90.

Myers, Jerome K. "Assimilation in the Political Community," *SSR*, 35 (January-February, 1951), 175-82.

Park, Robert E. "The Urban Community as a Spatial Pattern and a Moral Order," *The Urban Community*. Edited by E. W. Burgess. Chicago: University of Chicago Press, 1926.

Scaff, Alvin H. "Cultural Factors in Ecological Change on Mindanao in the Philippines," *SF*, 27 (December, 1948), 119-123.

Schietinger, E. F. "Racial Succession and Value of Small Residential Properties," *ASR*, 16 (December, 1951), 832-35.

Sellew, Gladys, and Nuesse, C. J. "Recent Changes in Washington Alley Slums," *SF*, 27 (October, 1948), 61-67.

F. Inter-Urban Spatial Organization and Processes.

Anderson, Theodore R. "Intermetropolitan Migration: A Comparison of the Hypotheses of Zipf and Stouffer," *ASR*, 20 (June, 1956), 287-291.

Bogue, Donald J. *The Structure of the Metropolitan Community: A Study of Dominance and Subdominance*. Ann Arbor: University of Michigan Press, 1949.

Brush, J. E. "The Urban Hierarchy in Europe," *GR*, 43 (1953), 414-16.

Dickinson, Robert E. *City, Region and Regionalism*. London: Oxford University Press, 1947.

———. "The Metropolitan Regions of the United States," *GR*, 24 (April, 1934), 278-91.

———. *The Regions of Germany*. New York: Oxford University Press, 1945.

Friedmann, John R. P. "The Spatial Structure of Economic Development in the Tennessee Valley," Department of Geography, University of Chicago, Research Paper No. 39 (March, 1955; planographed).

Haig, Robert M. and McCrea, Roswell C. "The Assignment of Activities to Areas in Urban Regions," *Major Economic Factors in Metropolitan Growth and Arrangement*. New York, Regional Plan of New York and Its Environs, pp. 31-43.

Hoover, Edgar M., Jr. "The Concept of a System of Cities," *EDCC*, 3 (January, 1955), 196-98.

Isard, Walter. "Interregional and Regional Input-Output Analysis: A Model of a Space Economy," *RES*, 33 (November, 1951), 318-28.

———. "Regional Commodity Balances and Interregional Commodity Flows," *AER*, 43 (May, 1953), 167-80.

Isard, Walter and Kavesh, Robert. "Economic Structural Interrelations of Metropolitan Regions," *AJS*, 60 (September, 1954), 152-62.

Isard, Walter and Kuenne, R. "The Impact of Steel Upon the Greater New York-Philadelphia Urban-Industrial Region," *RES*, 35 (November, 1953), 289-301.

Jefferson, Mark. "The Law of the Primate City," *GR* (April, 1939).

Lösch, August. "The Nature of Economic Regions," *The Southern Economic Journal*, 5 (July, 1938), 71-78.

———. *The Economics of Location*. (Translated from the 2nd Revised Edition by William H. Woglom with the assistance of Wolfgang F. Stolper.) New Haven: Yale University Press, 1954.

Stouffer, S. A. "Intervening Opportunities: A Theory Relating Mobility to Distances," *ASR*, 5 (December, 1940), 845-67.

Vance, Rupert B., and Smith, Sarah. "Metropolitan Dominance and Integration," *Virginia Quarterly Review*, 31 (Spring, 1955).

———. "Metropolitan Dominance and Integration," *The Urban South*. Edited by Rupert B. Vance and Nicholas J. Demerath. Chapel Hill: The University of North Carolina Press, 1954.

Vining, Rutledge. "A Description of Certain Spatial Aspects of an Economic System," *EDCC*, III (January, 1955), 147-95.

Von Thünen, J. H. *Der Isolierte Staat, in Beziehung auf Landwirtschaft und Nationalökonomie*. Rostock, 1942.

G. Temporal Organization and Processes.

Batten, Thelma F. *Flint and Michigan: A Study in Interdependence*. Ann Arbor: Social Science Research Project, University of Michigan, 1955.

Breese, Gerald. *The Daytime Population of the Central Business District of Chicago*. Chicago: University of Chicago Press, 1949.

Caplow, Theodore. "Incidence and Direction of Residential Mobility in a Minneapolis Sample," *SF*, 27 (May, 1949), 413-17.

Carroll, J. Douglas, Jr. "The Relation of Homes to Work Places and the Spatial Pattern of Cities," *SF*, 30 (March, 1952), 271-82.

Foley, Donald L. "Urban Daytime Population: A Field for Demographic-Ecological Analysis," *SF*, 32 (May, 1954), 323-30.

———. "The Daily Movement of Population into Central Business Districts," *ASR*, 17 (October, 1952), 538-44.

Henry, Andrew F. "Residential Turnover and Family Composition of Home Owners in Four Subdivisions in Natick, Massachusetts," *SF*, 31 (May, 1953), 355-60.

Landis, Paul H. "Rural-Urban Migration and the Marriage Rate—An Hypothesis," *ASR*, 11 (April, 1946), 155-158.

Lambert, Richard D. "Method of Measuring Intra-Urban Population Movements," *SF*, 27 (March, 1949), 269-71.

Liepmann, Kate. *The Journey to Work*. London: Kegan, Paul, Trench, Trubner and Company, 1944.

Reeder, Leo G. "Social Differentials in Mode of Travel, Time and Cost in the Journey to Work," *ASR*, 21 (February, 1956), 56-63.

Rossi, Peter. *Why Families Move: A Study in the Social Psychology of Urban Residential Mobility.* Glencoe, Illinois: The Free Press, 1955.

Schnore, Leo F. "The Separation of Home and Work: A Problem for Human Ecology," *SF,* 32 (May, 1954), 336-43.

Sullenger, T. Earl. "The Social Significance of Mobility: An Omaha Study," *AJS,* 55 (May, 1950), 559-64.

V. The Demographic Structure and Processes

A. Population Composition.

Duncan, Otis Dudley and Reiss, Jr., Albert J. *Social Characteristics of Urban and Rural Communities, 1950.* New York: John Wiley and Sons, 1956.

Durand, John D. *The Labor Force in the United States 1890-1960.* New York: The Social Science Research Council, 1949.

Durand, John D. "Married Women in the Labor Force," *AJS,* 52 (November, 1946), 217-23.

Monthly Labor Review. "Occupational Changes Since 1850 as Shown by Census Reports," 37 (November, 1933), 1017-1027.

Newcomb, Charles. "Graphic Presentation of Age and Sex Distribution in the City," *Bulletin of the Society for Social Research* (1938), 79-85.

Ogburn, William F. *Social Characteristics of Cities.* International City Managers Assoc., 1937.

Schmid, Calvin. *Social Saga of Two Cities.* Minneapolis: Council of Social Agencies, 1937.

Schnore, Leo F. and Varley, David W. "Some Concomitants of Metropolitan Size," *ASR,* 20 (August, 1955), 408-14.

Thompson, Lorin A. "Urbanization, Occupational Shift and Economic Progress," *The Urban South.* Edited by Rupert B. Vance and Nicholas J. Demerath. Chapel Hill: The University of North Carolina Press, 1954.

B. Vital Processes.

Benyon, Erdman Doane. "The Southern White Laborer Migrates to Michigan," *ASR,* 3 (June, 1938), 333-43.

Buckatzsch, E. J. "The Influence of Social Conditions on Mortality Rates," *PS,* 1 (December, 1947), 229-48.

Dinkel, Robert M. "Peopling the City: Fertility," *The Urban South.* Edited by Rupert B. Vance and Nicholas J. Demerath. Chapel Hill: University of North Carolina Press, 1955, Chapter 5.

Freedman, Ronald. *Recent Migration to Chicago.* Chicago: University of Chicago Press, 1951.

———. "Health Differentials for Rural-Urban Migration," *ASR,* 12 (October, 1947), 536-541.

Hamilton, C. Horace. "Population Pressure and Other Factors Affecting Net Rural-Urban Migration," *SF,* 30 (December, 1951), 209-214.

Hauser, Philip M. and Eldridge, Hope T. "Projection of Urban Growth and Migration to Cities in the United States," *MMFQ,* 25 (July, 1947), 293-307.

Hawley, Amos and Freedman, Ronald. "Migration and Occupational Mobility in the Depression," *AJS,* 55 (September, 1949), 171-77.

Heberle, Rudolf. "The Causes of Rural-Urban Migration," *AJS,* 43 (May, 1938), 932-50.

Innes, John W. *Class Fertility Rates in England and Wales, 1874 to 1934.* Princeton: Princeton University Press, 1938.

Isbel, Eleanor Collins. "Internal Migration in Sweden and Intervening Opportunities," *ASR,* 9 (December, 1944), 627-639.

Jaffee, A. J. "Urbanization and Fertility," *AJS*, 48 (July, 1942), 48-60.

Keyfitz, Nathan. "A Factorial Arrangement of Comparisons of Family Size," *AJS*, 58 (March, 1953), 470-80.

————. "Differential Fertility in Ontario: An Application of Factorial Design to a Demographic Problem," *PS*, 6 (November, 1952), 123-134.

Kiser, Clyde V. *Group Differences in Urban Fertility*. Baltimore: Williams and Wilkins Co., 1942.

————. *Sea Island to City*. New York: Columbia University Press, 1932.

Moore, Jane. *Cityward Migration*. Chicago: University of Chicago Press, 1938.

National Resources Committee. "The Social Effects of Migration," *The Problems of a Changing Population*. Washington: USGPO, 1938, pp. 108-111.

Notestein, Frank W. and Sallume, Xarfia. "The Fertility of Specific Occupational Groups in an Urban Population," *MMFQ*, 10 (April, 1932), 120-30.

Ogburn, W. F. "Size of Community as a Factor in Migration," *SSR*, 28 (March-April, 1944), 255-61.

Palmer, Gladys L. *Labor Mobility in Six Cities*. New York: Social Science Research Council, 1954.

Price, Daniel O. "Nonwhite Migrants to and from Selected Cities," *AJS*, 54 (November, 1948), 196-201.

Reiss, Jr., Albert J. and Kitagawa, Evelyn M. "Demographic Characteristics and Job Mobility of Migrants in Six Cities," *SF*, 32 (October, 1953), 70-75.

Schmitt, Robert C. "Migration and City Population Estimates," *SSR*, 37 (May-June, 1953), 327-328.

Thomas, Dorothy S., *et. al. Research Memorandum on Migration Differentials*. New York: Social Science Research Council, Bulletin 43, 1938.

Valien, Preston. "Internal Migration and Racial Composition of the Southern Population," *ASR*, 13 (June, 1948), 294-98.

Vance, Rupert B. *Research Memorandum on Population Redistribution Within the United States*. New York: Social Science Research Council, Bulletin 42, 1938.

Wattenberg, William W. "Attitude Toward Community Size as Evidenced by Migratory Behavior, 1935-1940," *SF*, 26 (May, 1948), 437-442.

Wiehl, Dorothy G. "Mortality and Socio-Economic Factors," *MMFQ*, 26 (October, 1948), 344-65.

Wolfbein, S. L. and Jaffe, A. J. "Demographic Factors in Labor Force Growth," *ASR*, 11 (August, 1948), 392-96.

Yankauer, Alfred, Jr. "The Relationship of Fetal and Infant Mortality to Residential Segregation," *ASR*, 15 (October, 1950), 644-648.

Zimmer, Basil G. "Participation of Migrants in Urban Structures," *ASR*, 20 (April, 1955), 218-24.

Zipf, George K. "The $\frac{P_1 \, P_2}{D}$ Hypothesis: On the Intercity Movement of Persons," *ASR*, 11 (December, 1946), 677-686.

VI. The Stratification Structure and Processes

A. The Nature and Effects of the Stratification System.

Anderson, C. Arnold. "Social Class Differentials in the Schooling of Youth Within the Region and Community Size Groups of the U.S.," *SF*, 25 (May, 1947), 434-40.

Bendix, Reinhard and Lipset, Seymour Martin. *Class, Status and Power: A Reader in Social Stratification*. Glencoe, Illinois: The Free Press, 1953.

Duncan, Otis Dudley and Beverly. "Residential Distribution and Occupational Stratification," *AJS*, 60 (March, 1955), 493-503.

Durkheim, Emile. *The Division of Labor in Society*. Translated by George Simpson. Glencoe: The Free Press, 1947.

Edwards, Alba M. *A Socio-Economic Grouping of the Gainful Workers of the United States*. Washington, D.C.: United States Government Printing Office, 1938.

Goldstein, Harold. "The Changing Occupational Structure," *Monthly Labor Review*, 65 (December, 1947), 654-59.

Gross, Neal. "Social Class Identification in the Urban Community," *ASR*, 18 (August, 1953), 398-404.

Hatt, Paul K. "Occupation and Social Stratification," *AJS*, 55 (May, 1950), 533-43.

Kaufman, Harold. "An Approach to the Study of Urban Stratification," *ASR*, 17 (August, 1952) 430-37.

Knupfer, Genevieve. "Portrait of the Underdog," *POQ*, 11 (Spring, 1947), 103-14.

Kornhauser, Arthur W. "Analyses of Class Structure of American Society: Psychological Bases of Class Divisions," *Industrial Conflict*. Edited by George W. Hartmann and Theodore Newcomb. New York: The Gordon Co., 1939, 250-57.

Lenski, Gerhard E. "American Social Classes: Statistical Strata or Social Groups," *AJS*, 58 (September, 1952), 139-144.

Mills, C. Wright. "The Middle Classes in Middle-Sized Cities," *ASR*, 11 (October, 1946), 520-28.

North, Cecil C. and Hatt, Paul K. "Jobs and Occupations: A Popular Evaluation," *Opinion News*, September 1, 1947, 3-13.

Pfautz, Harold. "The Current Literature on Social Stratification: Critique and Bibliography," *AJS*, 58 (January, 1953), 391-419.

Sibley, Elbridge. "Some Demographic Clues to Stratification," *ASR*, 7 (June, 1942), 322-30.

Spier, Hans. "Social Stratification in the Urban Community," *ASR*, 1 (April, 1936), 193-202.

B. Patterns of Stratification in Communities.

Davis, A., Gardner, B. and Gardner, M. *Deep South*. Chicago: University of Chicago Press, 1941.

Dollard, John. *Caste and Class in a Southern Town*. New Haven: Yale University Press, 1937.

Gross, Neal. "Urban Class Identification in the Urban Community," *ASR*, 18 (August, 1953), 398-404.

Hatt, Paul K. "Stratification in the Mass Society," *ASR*, 15 (April, 1950), 216-22.

Hawthorne, Harry B. and Audrey E. "Stratification in a Latin American Community," *SF*, 27 (October, 1948), 19-29.

Hollingshead, August B. *Elmtown's Youth*. New York: John Wiley & Sons, 1949.

———. "Class and Kinship in a Middle Western Community," *ASR*, 14 (August, 1949), 469-77.

———. "Selected Characteristics of Classes in a Middle Western Community," *ASR*, 12 (August, 1947), 385-95.

Hill, Mozell C. and McCall, Bevode C. "Social Stratification in a Georgia Town," *ASR*, 15 (December, 1950), 721-30.

Kaufman, Harold F. "Social Class in the Urban South," *The Urban South*. Edited by Rupert B. Vance and Nicholas J. Demerath. Chapel Hill: The University of North Carolina Press, 1954.

King, Charles E. "The Process of Social Stratification Among an Urban Southern Minority Population," *SF*, 31 (May, 1953), 352-55.

King, C. Wendell. "Social Cleavage in a New England Community," *SF*, 24 (March, 1946), 322-27.

Mills, C. Wright. "The Middle Classes in Middle-Sized Cities," *ASR*, 11 (October, 1946), 520-29.

Spier, Hans. "Social Stratification in the Urban Community," *ASR*, 1 (April, 1936), 193-202.

Warner, Lloyd, *et al. Democracy in Jonesville.* New York: Harper and Bros., 1947.

Warner, Lloyd and Lunt, Paul S. *The Social Life of a Modern Community.* New Haven: Yale University Press, 1941.

C. Selected Types in Stratification Systems.

Bell, H. M. *Youth Tell Their Story.* Washington, D. C.: American Council on Education, 1938.

Davis, Allison. "The Motivation of the Underprivileged Worker," *Industry and Society.* Edited by William F. Whyte. New York: McGraw-Hill Book Co., 1946.

Drake, St. Clair and Cayton, Horace. *Black Metropolis.* New York: Harcourt, Brace and Co., 1945.

Frazier, E. Franklin. "Occupational Classes Among Negroes in Cities," *AJS*, 35 (May, 1929), 718-38.

Hughes, E. C. "Dilemmas and Contradictions of Status," *AJS*, 50 (1944), 353-57

Ober, Harry, "The Worker and His Job," *Monthly Labor Review,* 71 (July, 1950), 13-22.

Sutherland, E. H. and Locke, H. *Twenty Thousand Homeless Men,* Philadelphia: J. B. Lippincott, 1936.

Thomas, W. I. and Znaniecki, F. *The Polish Peasant in Europe and America.* New York: Alfred A. Knopf, 1927, 2 Vols.

Ware, Caroline. *Greenwich Village.* New York: Houghton Mifflin Co., 1935.

Warner, W. Lloyd and Srole, Leo. *The Social System of American Ethnic Groups.* New Haven: Yale University Press, 1945.

Warner, W. Lloyd and Low, J. J. *The Social System of the Modern Factory.* New Haven: Yale University Press, 1945.

Wirth, Louis. *The Ghetto.* Chicago: University of Chicago Press, 1929.

Young, Pauline. *Pilgrims of Russian Town.* Chicago: University of Chicago Press, 1932.

Zorbaugh, Harvey. *The Gold Coast and the Slum.* Chicago: University of Chicago Press, 1929.

D. Social Mobility

Bendix, Reinhard and Lipset, Seymour Martin. *Class, Status and Power: A Reader in Social Stratification.* Glencoe, Illinois: The Free Press, 1953.

Centers, Richard B. "Occupational Mobility of Urban Occupational Strata," *ASR*, 13 (April, 1948), 197-204.

Davidson, P. E. and Anderson, H. D. *Occupational Mobility in an American Community.* Stanford University Press, 1937.

Foote, Nelson N. and Hatt, Paul K. "Social Mobility and Economic Advancement," *AER*, XLIII (May, 1953), 364-378.

Freedman, Ronald and Hawley, Amos. "Migration and Occupational Mobility in the Depression, 1930-1935," *AJS*, 54 (September, 1945), 171-77.

Glass, D. V. (ed). *Social Mobility in Britain.* Glencoe: The Free Press, 1954.

Lipset, Seymour Martin. "Social Mobility and Urbanization," *RS*, 20 (September-December, 1955), 220-28.

Lipset, Seymour and Bendix, Reinhard. "Social Mobility and Occupational Career Patterns," *AJS*, 57 (January and March, 1952), 366-374 and 494-504.

Rogoff, Natalie. *Recent Trends in Occupational Mobility*. Glencoe: The Free Press, 1953.

Scudder, Richard and Anderson, C. Arnold. "Migration and Vertical Occupational Mobility," *ASR*, 19 (June, 1954), 329-334.

Sibley, Elbridge. "Some Demographic Clues to Stratification," *ASR*, 7 (June, 1942), 322-330.

Sorokin, P. A. *Social Mobility*. New York: Harper and Brothers, 1927.

VII. Urban Social Institutions and Organization

A. Institutions and Their Urban Modes of Organization.

Booth, Charles. *Life and Labor of the People in London*. New York: The Macmillan Co., 1902, 9 vols.

Broden, Charles S. "The Sects," *The Annals*, 256 (March, 1948).

Bultena, Louis. "Church Membership and Church Attendance in Madison, Wisconsin," *ASR*, 14 (June, 1949).

Bushee, Frederick A. "Small Organizations in a Small City," *AJS*, 51 (November, 1945), 217-26.

Chapin, F. Stuart. "The Protestant Church in an Urban Environment," Chapter XI of *Contemporary American Institutions*. New York: Harper and Bros., 1935.

Chicago Recreation Commission, *Chicago Recreation Survey, 1937-39;* Vol. I, *Public Recreation;* Vol. II, *Commercial Recreation;* Vol. III, *Private Recreation;* Vol. IV, *Summary*.

Clark, S. D. *Church and Sect in Canada*. Toronto: University of Toronto Press, 1948.

Cohen, Lillian. "Los Angeles Rooming-House Kaleidoscope," *ASR*, 16 (1951), 316-26.

Cressey, Paul G. *The Taxi-Dance Hall*. Chicago: University of Chicago Press, 1932.

Denney, Reuel, and Riesman, David. "Leisure in Urbanized America," *Reader in Urban Sociology*. Edited by Paul K. Hatt and Albert J. Reiss, Jr. Glencoe: The Free Press, 1951.

Detroit Area Study. *Social Profile of Detroit*. Ann Arbor: University of Michigan Press, 1952, 1953 and 1954.

Douglas, H. P. *The Church in the Changing City*. New York: George H. Doran Company, 1937.

———. "Some Protestant Churches in Urban America," *Information Service*, 29 (January 21, 1950), 1-8.

Drake, St. Clair. *Churches and Voluntary Associations in the Chicago Negro Community*. District 3, W.P.A., Chicago, December, 1940.

Drake, St. Clair and Cayton, Horace. *Black Metropolis*. New York: Harcourt, Brace and Company, 1945.

Fichter, Joseph H. "Conceptualizations of the Urban Parish," *SF*, 31 (October, 1952), 43-46.

———. *Dynamics of a City Church: Southern Parish*. Chicago: University of Chicago Press, 1951.

Frazier, E. Franklin. "The Impact of Urban Civilization Upon Negro Family Life," *ASR*, 2 (October, 1937), 609-18.

———. *The Negro Family in Chicago*. Chicago: University of Chicago Press, 1932.

Geiger, Kurt. "Deprivation and Solidarity in the Soviet Urban Family," *ASR*, 20 (February, 1955), 57-68.

Harlan, William H. "Community Adaptation to the Presence of Aged Persons: St. Petersburg, Florida," *AJS*, 59 (January, 1954), 332-39.

Heberle, Rudolf. "Social Consequences of the Industrialization of Southern Cities," *SF*, 27 (October, 1948), 29-37.

Hughes, E. C. "The Ecological Aspects of Institutions," *ASR*, 1 (April, 1936), 180-92.

Hughes,, Helen McGill. *News and the Human Interest Story*. Chicago: University of Chicago Press, 1940.

Jaco, E. Gartly and Belknap, Ivan. "Is A New Family Form Emerging in the Urban Fringe?" *ASR*, 18 (1953), 551-57.

Jones, Alfred. *Life Liberty and Property*. New York: J. B. Lippincott, 1941.

Killian, Lewis M. "The Adjustment of Southern White Migrants to Northern Urban Norms," *SF*, 32 (October, 1954), 66-69.

Kincheloe, Samuel C. "The Behavior Sequence of a Dying Church," *Journal of Religious Education*, 24 (November, 1929), 329-45.

———. *The American City and Its Church*. Missionary Educational Movement, 1938.

———. "Major Reactions of City Churches," *Religious Education*, 23 (November, 1928), 868-74.

Kobrin, Solomon. "The Conflict of Values of Delinquency Areas," *ASR*, 16 (October, 1951), 653-61.

Komarovsky, Mirra. "The Voluntary Associations of Urban Dwellers," *ASR*, 11 (December, 1946), 686-97.

Koos, Earl Lomon. *Families in Trouble*. New York: Kings Crown Press, 1946.

Lee, Frank F. "The Race Relations Pattern by Areas of Behavior in a Small New England Town," *ASR*, 19 (April, 1954), 138-143.

Leevy, J. Roy. "Leisure Time of the American Housewife," *SSR*, 35 (November-December, 1950), 97-105.

Lillywhite, John D. "Rural-Urban Differentials in Divorce," *RS*, 17 (December, 1952), 348-55.

Lundberg, George A. *Leisure: A Suburban Study*. New York: Columbia University Press, 1934.

Lynd, Robert and Helen. *Middletown*. New York: Harcourt, Brace and Co., 1929.

McDougal, Myres S. "The Impact of the Metropolis Upon Land Law," *The Metropolis in Modern Life*. Edited by Robert M. Fisher. New York: Doubleday & Co., 1955, Chapter 10.

Masuoka, Jitsuichi. "Urbanization and the Family in Japan," *SSR*, 32 (September-October, 1947).

Mayhew, Henry. *London Labor and the London Poor*. London: Griffin, Bohn and Co., 1862.

Merton, Robert K. *Mass Persuasion*. New York: Harper & Bros., 1947.

Merton, Robert K. "Social Structure and Anomie: Revisions and Extensions," *The Family: Its Functions and Destiny*. Edited by Ruth Anshen. New York: Harper and Bros., 1949, Chapter XII.

Minnis, Mhyra S. "Cleavage in Women's Organizations: A Reflection of the Social Structure of a City," *ASR*, 18 (February, 1953), 47-53.

Minton, Arthur. "Marlovian 42 Street: Folkways of the Megalopolis," *SF*, 24 (May, 1946), 393-397.

Moses, Earl R. "Differentials in Crime Rates Between Negroes and Whites, Based on Comparisons of Four Socio-Economically Equated Areas," *ASR*, 12 (August, 1947), 411-20.

Murphy, Raymond E. and Vance, J. E. Jr. "A Comparative Study of Nine Central Business Districts," *EG*, 30 (1954), 301-36.

Ogburn, William F. "The Changing Family," *Pub. American Sociological Society.*

Porterfield, Austin L. "Suicide and Crime in the Social Structure of an Urban Setting," *ASR*, 17 (June, 1952), 341-48.

Porterfield, Austin L. and Talbert, Robert H. "A Decade of Differentials and Trends in Serious Crimes in 86 American Cities by Southern and Non-Southern Pairs," *SF*, 31 (October, 1952), 60-67.

Parsons, Talcott and Fox, Renee. "Illness, Therapy and the Modern American Family," *JSI*, 8 (No. 4, 1952), 31-44.

Pope, Liston. "Religion and The Class Structure," *The Annals*, 356 (March, 1948), 84-91.

Reckless, W. C. *Vice in Chicago.* Chicago: University of Chicago Press, 1933.

Reed, Ruth. *The Illegitimate Family in New York City.* New York: Columbia University Press, 1934.

Reeve, Harold L. "Recent Developments in the Law of Property," *The Metropolis in Modern Life.* Edited by Robert M. Fisher. New York: Doubleday & Co., 1955, Chapter 9.

Rose, Arnold. "Interest in the Living Arrangements of the Urban Unattached," *AJS*, 53 (May, 1948), 483-95.

———. "Voluntary Associations in France," *Theory and Method in the Social Sciences.* Minneapolis: University of Minnesota Press, 1954.

Steiner, Jesse. *Recreation and Morale.* National Council for the Social Studies, and National Association of Secondary School Principals, 1942.

Thomas, W. I. and Znaniecki, Florian. *The Polish Peasant in Europe and America.* Boston: The Gorham Press, 1920.

Veblen, Thorsten. *The Instinct of Workmanship and the State of the Industrial Arts.* New York, 1914.

Ware, Caroline. *Greenwich Village.* New York: Houghton, Mifflin Company, 1935.

Warner, Lloyd and Low, J. O. *The Social System of the Modern Factory.* New Haven: Yale University Press, 1947.

Webber, Irving L. "The Organized Social Life of the Retired in Two Florida Communities," *AJS*, 59 (January, 1954), 340-46.

West, James. *Plainville, U.S.A.* New York: Columbia University Press, 1945.

Williams, Robin, and Ryan, Margaret. *Schools in Transition.* Chapel Hill University of North Carolina Press, 1954.

B. Local Community Institutions and Organization.

Bell, Wendell, and Force, Maryanne T. "Urban Neighborhood Types and Participation in Formal Associations," *ASR*, 21 (February, 1956), 25-34.

Caplow, Theodore, and Forman, Robert. "Neighborhood Interaction in a Homogeneous Community," *ASR*, 15 (June, 1950), 357-66.

Clarke, Alfred C. "Residential Propinquity as a Factor in Mate Selection," *ASR*, 17 (February, 1952), 17-22.

Cohen, Lillian. "Los Angeles Rooming-House Kaleidoscope," *ASR*, 16 (June, 1951), 316-26.

Dewey, Richard. "The Neighborhood, Urban Ecology, and City Planners," *ASR*, 15 (August, 1950), 502-08.

Ellsworth, John S. "The Relationship of Population Density to Residential Propinquity as a Factor in Mate Selection," *ASR*, 13 (August, 1948), 444-47.

Fava, Sylvia Fleis. "Suburbanism as a Way of Life," *ASR*, 21 (February, 1956), 34-38.

Foley, Donald. *Neighbors or Urbanites? The Study of a Rochester Residential District.* Rochester, New York: University of Rochester, 1952.

Foley, Donald. "The Use of Local Facilities in a Metropolis," *AJS*, 56 (November, 1950), 238-47.

Greer, Scott. "Urbanism Reconsidered: A Comparative Study of Local Areas in a Metropolis," *ASR*, 21 (February, 1956), 19-25.

Janowitz, Morris. *The Community Press in an Urban Setting*. Glencoe: The Free Press, 1952.

Keller, Marvin R. "Residential Propinquity of White Mates at Marriage in Relation to Age and Occupation of Males, Columbus, Ohio, 1938 and 1946," *ASR*, 13 (October, 1948), 613-16.

McClenahan, Bessie. *The Changing Urban Neighborhood*. Los Angeles: University of Southern California, 1929.

Marches, Joseph R. and Turbeville, Gus. "The Effect of Residential Propinquity on Marriage Selection," *AJS*, 58 (May, 1953), 592-95.

Wallin, Paul. "A Guttman Scale for Measuring Women's Neighborliness," *AJS*, 59 (November, 1953), 243-46.

Wirth, Louis. *The Ghetto*. Chicago: The University of Chicago Press, 1928.

C. Urban Social Organization and Integration.

Anderson, C. Arnold. "Community Chest Campaigns as an Index of Community Integration," *SF*, 33 (October, 1954), 76-81.

Angell, Robert C. *The Moral Integration of American Cities*. Chicago: University of Chicago Press, 1951.

Cuber, John F. "City and Country Services Utilized by Farm Families," *SSR*, 23 (November-December, 1938), 157-61.

Dotson, Floyd. "Patterns of Voluntary Association Among Urban Working-Class Families," *ASR*, 16 (1951), 687-93.

Firey, Walter, Loomis, Charles P. and Beegle, Allan. "The Fusion of Urban and Rural," *Highways in Our National Life*. Edited by Jean Labatut and Wheaton J. Lane. Princeton: Princeton University Press, 1950.

Gist, Noel P. "Ecological Decentralization and Rural-Urban Relationships," *RS*, 17 (December, 1952), 328-35.

Hatt, Paul K. "Stratification in the Mass Society," *ASR*, 15 (April, 1950), 216-23.

Hawley, Amos H. "An Ecological Study of Urban Service Institutions," *ASR*, 6 (October, 1941), 629-39.

Hayes, Wayland J. "Revolution Community-Style," *SF*, 28 (October, 1949), 1-6.

———. *The Small Community Looks Ahead*. New York: Harcourt, Brace & Co., 1947.

Hunter, Floyd. *Community Power Structure: A Study of Decision Makers*. Chapel Hill: University of North Carolina Press, 1953.

Jonassen, C. T. *The Shopping Center Versus Downtown*. Columbus, Ohio: Bureau of Better Business Research, Ohio State University, 1955.

Kolb, William L. "The Social Structure and Functions of Cities," *EDCC*, 3 (October, 1954), 30-46.

Reitzes, Dietrich. "The Role of Organizational Structures," *JSI*, 9 (No. 1, 1953), 37-44.

Remmers, H. H. and Kerr, W. A. "Home Environment in American Cities," *AJS* 51 (November, 1945), 233-37.

Schettler, Edward. "Relation of City-Size to Economic Services," *ASR*, 8 (February, 1943), 60-62.

Sjoberg, Gideon. "The Pre-Industrial City," *AJS*, 60 (March, 1955), 438-45.

Thorndike, E. L. and Woodyard, Ella. "Individual Differences in American Cities," *AJS*, 43 (1937), 191-224.

Wirth, Louis. "Consensus and Mass Communication," *ASR*, 13 (February, 1948), 1-15.

D. Cities and Social Change.

Baltzell, E. Digby. "Urbanization and Governmental Administration in Lower Bucks County," *Social Problems*, 2 (July, 1954), 38-46.

Basom, William. "Urbanization Among the Yoruba," *AJS*, 60 (March, 1955), 446-53.

Carr, Lowell Julliard and Stermer, James E. *Willow Run: A Study of Industrialization and Cultural Inadequacy*. New York: Harper & Bros., 1952.

Comhaire, J. "Some Aspects of Urbanization in the Belgian Congo," *AJS*, 61 (July, 1956), 8-13.

Crane, Robert I. "Urbanism in India," *AJS*, 60 (March, 1955), 463-70.

Havighurst, Robert J. and Morgan, H. Gerthan. *The Social History of a War-Boom Community*. New York: Longmans, Green & Co., 1951.

Heberle, Rudolf and Betrand, Alvin. "Social Consequences of the Industrialization of Southern Cities," *SF*, 27 (October, 1948), 29-37.

Hoselitz, Bert F. "The City, The Factory, and Economic Growth," *AER*, XLV (May, 1955), 166-84.

———. "Generative and Parasitical Cities," *EDCC*, 3 (April, 1955), 278-94.

———. "The Role of Cities in the Economic Growth of Underdeveloped Countries," *JPE*, 41 (June, 1953), 195-208.

Hughes, E. C. *French Canada in Transition*. Chicago: University of Chicago Press, 1943.

Hughes, R. H. "Hong Kong: An Urban Study," *Geographic Journal*, 117 (March, 1951), 1-23.

LeTourneau, Richard. "Social Change in the Muslim Cities of North Africa," *AJS*, 60 (May, 1955), 527-35.

Lynd, Robert M. and Helen. *Middletown in Transition*. New York: Harcourt, Brace & Co., 1937.

McCall, Daniel F. "Dynamics of Urbanization in Africa," *The Annals*, 298 (March, 1955), 151-60.

Marsh, Charles F. (ed.) *The Hampton Roads Communities in World War II*. Chapel Hill: University of North Carolina Press, 1951.

The Role of Cities in Economic Development and Cultural Change: Proceedings of a Conference Held at the University of Chicago, May 24-26, 1954. *EDCC*, III (October, 1954).

Ruttan, Vernon W. "The Impact of Urban-Indusrtial Development on Agriculture in the Tennessee Valley and the Southeast," *Journal of Farm Economics*, 37 (February, 1955), 38-56.

Sjoberg, Gideon. "The Pre-Industrial City," *AJS*, 60 (March, 1955), 438-445.

Turner, Ralph E. "The Industrial City: Center of Cultural Change," *The Cultural Interpretation of History*. Edited by Caroline F. Ware. New York: Columbia University Press, 1940, 228-242.

University of Pennsylvania, The Institute for Urban Studies. *Accelerated Urban Growth in a Metropolitan Fringe Area: A Study of Urbanization, Suburbanization and the Impact of the U. S. Steel Plant in Lower Bucks County, Pennsylvania. Vol. I. Summary Report. Vol. II. Project Report*. Philadelphia: The Institute for Urban Studies, University of Pennsylvania, 1954.

Vance, Rupert B. and Demerath, Nicholas J. (eds.) *The Urban South*. Chapel Hill: University of North Carolina Press, 1955.

E. Social Control in Cities.

Agger, Robert E. "Power Attributions in the Local Community: Theoretical and Research Considerations," *SF*, 34 (May, 1956), 322-31.

Burgess, E. W., Lohman, Joseph and Shaw, Clifford R. "The Chicago Area Project," *Yearbook of the National Probation and Parole Association*. New York, 1937, 8-28.

Cantril, Hadley, *The Invasion from Mars*. Princeton: Princeton University Press, 1940.

Clark, Robert E. "Size of Parole Community as Related to Parole Outcome," *AJS*, 57 (July, 1951), 43-47.

Fanelli, A. Alexander. "A Typology of Community Leadership Based on Influence and Interaction within the Leader Subsystem," *SF*, 34 (May, 1956), 332-38.

Gosnell, H. F. *The Negro Politician in Chicago*. Chicago: University of Chicago Press, 1935.

———. "How Negroes Vote in Chicago," *National Municipal Review*, 22 (May, 1933), 238-43.

———. "The Chicago Black Belt as a Political Battleground," *AJS*, 29 (November, 1933), 329-41.

———. *Machine Politics: Chicago Model*. Chicago: University of Chicago Press, 1937.

Gremley, William. "Social Control in Cicero," *BJS*, 3 (December, 1952).

Hunter, Floyd. *Community Power Structure*. Chapel Hill: University of North Carolina Press, 1953.

Jones, Victor. *Metropolitan Government*. Chicago: University of Chicago Press.

Killian, Lewis M. "The Significance of Multiple-Group Membership in Disaster," *AJS*, 57 (January, 1952), 309-14.

Kurtzman, D. H. *Methods of Controlling Votes in Philadelphia*. Philadelphia, 1935.

Landesco, John. "Organized Crime in Chicago," *The Illinois Crime Survey*. Chicago: Illinois Association for Criminal Justice, 1929, Part III.

Lohman, Joseph. "The Social Situations in Which Tensions Arise," *The Police and Minority Groups*. Chicago Park District, 1947, pp. 59-74.

McKay, Henry D. "The Neighborhood and Child Conduct," *The Annals*, 261 (January, 1949), 32-41.

Mannheim, Karl. *Man and Society in an Age of Reconstruction*. New York: Harcourt, Brace & Co., 1948.

Merriam, Charles. *A More Intimate View of Urban Politics*. New York: The Macmillan Co., 1929.

———. *et. al. The Government of Metropolitan Chicago*. Chicago: University of Chicago Press, 1933.

Merriam, C. E. and Parratt, S. D. and Lepawsky, Albert. *The Government of the Metropolitan Region of Chicago*. Chicago: University of Chicago Press, 1933.

National Resources Planning Board. *Urban Government*. Washington, D.C.: USGPO, 1939.

Peterson, Virgil. *Gambling: Should It Be Legalized?* Springfield: Charles C. Thomas, 1951.

Park, Robert E. *The Immigrant Press and Its Control*. New York: Harper & Bros., 1922.

———. *Society: Collective Behavior, News and Opinion, Sociology and Modern Society*. Glencoe, Illinois: The Free Press, 1955.

Reckless, Walter C. *Vice in Chicago*. Chicago: University of Chicago Press, 1933.

Report of the Smaller War Plants Corporation to the Special Committee to Study Problems of American Small Business. *Small Business and Civic Welfare*. Senate Document 135, 79th Congress, 2nd Session. Washington: USGPO, 1946.

Warner, W. L., *et al. Democracy in Jonesville*. New York: Harper & Bros., 1949.

Warren, Roland L. "Toward A. Typology of Extra-Community Controls Limiting Local Community Autonomy," *SF*, 34 (May, 1956), 338-41.

Whyte, William Foote. *Street Corner Society*. Chicago: University of Chicago Press, 1942.

VIII. Personality and Social Participation of Urban Dwellers

A. Personality Effects of Urbanness.

Anderson, Nels. *The Hobo*. Chicago: University of Chicago Press, 1923.

Burgess, E. W. "Educative Effects of Urban Environment," *Education and Environment*. Chicago: University of Chicago Press, 1942.

Cavan, Ruth S. *Suicide*. Chicago: University of Chicago Press, 1928, Part II.

Emmett, W. G. "The Intelligence of Urban and Rural Children," *PS*, (March, 1954), 207-221.

Faris, R. E. L. and Dunham, H. Warren. *Mental Disorders in Urban Areas*. Chicago: University of Chicago Press, 1939.

Goldschmidt, H. "Social Aspects of Aging and Senility," *Journal of Mental Sciences*, 92 (1946), 182-94.

Hayner, Norman. "Hotel Life and Personality," *Personality and The Social Group*. Chicago: University of Chicago Press, 1932.

———. *Hotel Life*. Chapel Hill: University of North Carolina Press, 1936.

Hughes, E. C. "Personality and the Division of Labor," *AJS*, 33 (March, 1928), 754-68.

Mangus, A. R. "Personality Adjustment of Rural and Urban Children," *ASR*, 13 (October, 1948), 566-75.

Merton, Robert. "Bureaucratic Structure and Personality," *SF*, 18 (May, 1940), 560-68.

———. "Social Structure and Anomie," *ASR*, 3 (1938).

Meyer, Julie. "The Stranger and the City," *AJS*, 56 (March, 1951), 476-83.

Oeser, Oscar A. (ed.) *Social Structure and Personality*. London: Routledge and Kegan Paul, 1954.

Park, R. E. "The Concept of Social Distance," *SSR*, 8 (May-June, 1924), 339-44.

———."Human Migration and the Marginal Man," *AJS*, 33 (May, 1928), 881-93.

Park, Robert E. and Miller, Herbert A. *Old World Traits Transplanted*. New York: Harper & Bros., 1921.

Patterson, Cecil H. "The Relationship of Bernreuter Scores to Parent Behavior, Child Behavior, Urban-Rural Residence, and Other Background Factors in 100 Normal Adult Parents," *JSP*, 24 (August, 1946), 3-49.

Pear, T. H. "Psychological Aspects of English Social Stratification," *Bulletin of the John Rylands Library*, 26 (May-June, 1942).

Plant, James S. *Personality and the Culture Pattern*. New York: The Commonwealth Fund, 1937, Chapters 5, 6 and 8.

Riemer, Svend. "Villagers in Metropolis," *BJS*, 2 (March, 1951), 31-43.

Riesman, David, *et al. The Lonely Crowd: A Study of the Changing American Character*. New Haven: Yale University Press, 1950.

———. *Faces in the Crowd: Individual Studies in Character and Politics*. New Haven: Yale University Press, 1952.

Scheutz, A. "The Stranger: An Essay in Social Psychology," *AJS*, 49 (1943).

Seeman, Melvin. "An Evaluation of Current Approaches to Personality Differences in Folk and Urban Societies," *SF*, 25 (December, 1946), 160-65.

Sewell, William H. and Amend, Eleanor E. "The Influence of Size of Home Community on Attitudes and Personality Traits," *ASR*, 8 (April, 1943), 180-84.

Shils, Edward A. "Human Nature in Industrial Societies," London, BBC. Third Channel Broadcast, 1948.

Simmel, Georg. "The Stranger," *The Sociology of Georg Simmel*. Translated by Kurt Wolff. Glencoe, Illinois: The Free Press, 1950.

———. *Die Grosstadt und das Geistesleben*. Translated by E. A. Shils in *Third Year Reading Course in Contemporary Society*. Chicago: University of Chicago Bookstore, September, 1942.

Stonequist, E. "The Problems of the Marginal Man," *AJS*, 41 (1935).

Sutherland, E. H. and Locke, H. J. *Twenty Thousand Homeless Men*. New York: J. B. Lippincott and Co., 1932.

Thomas, W. I. "The Problem of Personality in the Urban Environment," *Pub. of Am. Soc. Society*, 20 (1926), 31-40.

———. *The Unadjusted Girl*. Boston: Little Brown and Company, 1923.

Zorbaugh, Harvey. "The Dweller in Furnished Rooms as an Urban Type," *Pub. of Am. Soc. Society*, 32 (May, 1933), 83-89, Part I.

———. *The Gold Coast and the Slum*. Chicago: University of Chicago Press, 1929.

B. Attitudes of Urbanites.

Beers, Howard W. "Rural-Urban Differences: Some Evidence from Public Opinion Polls, *RS*, 18 (1953), 1-11.

Grieffer, J. "Attitudes to the Stranger," *ASR*, 10 (1945).

Haer, John L. "Conservatism-Radicalism and the Rural-Urban Continuum," *RS*, 17 (December, 1952), 343-47.

Hellpach, Willy. *Mensch and Volk der Grosstadt*. Stuttgart: Ferdinand Enke, 1952.

Jonassen, C. T. *Downtown Versus Suburban Shopping: Measurement of Consumer Practices and Attitudes in Columbus, Ohio*. The Ohio State University Bureau of Business Research, 1953.

Kornhauser, Arthur. *Detroit as the People See It: A Survey of Attitudes in an Industrial City*. Detroit: Wayne University Press, 1952.

Masuoka, Jitsuichi. "The City and Racial Adjustment," *SF*, 27 (October, 1948), 37-41.

Rose, Arnold M., Atelsek, Frank J. and McDonald, Lawrence R. "Neighborhood Reactions to Isolated Negro Residents: An Alternative to Invasion and Succession," *ASR*, 18 (October, 1953), 497-507.

Stone, Gregory P. "City Shoppers and Urban Identification: Observation on the Social Psychology of City Life," *AJS*, 60 (July, 1954), 36-45.

Sykes, Gresham M. "The Differential Distribution of Community Knowledge," *SF*, 29 (May, 1951), 376-82.

Turner, Ralph H. "Migration to a Medium-Sized American City: Attitudes, Motives, and Personal Characteristics Revealed by Open-End Interview Methodology," *JSP*, 30 (November, 1949), 229-49.

Watson, Jeanne, Breed, Warren and Posman, Harry. "A Study in Urban Conversation: Sample of 1,001 Remarks Overheard in Manhattan," *JSP*, 28 (1948) 121-33.

C. Social Participation and the Quality of Social Interaction in Cities.

Bell, Wendell and Force, Maryanne T. "Urban Neighborhood Types and Participation in Formal Associations," *ASR*, 21 (February, 1956), 25-34.

Caplow, Theodore and Forman, Robert. "Neighborhood Interaction in a Homogeneous Community," *ASR*, 15 (June, 1950), 357-66.

Dotson, Floyd. "A Note on Participation in Voluntary Associations in a Mexican City," *ASR*, 18 (August, 1953), 380-86.

———. "Voluntary Associations Among Urban Working-Class Families," *ASR*, 16 (October, 1951), 687-93.

Fanelli, A. Alexander. "Extensiveness of Communication Contacts and Perceptions of the Community," *ASR*, 21 (August, 1956), 439-45.

Foley, Donald L. *Neighbors or Urbanites? The Study of a Rochester Residential District*. Department of Sociology: University of Rochester, 1952.

Komarovsky, Mirra. "The Voluntary Associations of Urban Dwellers," *ASR*, 11 (December, 1946), 686-98.

Martin, Walter T. "A Consideration of Differences in the Extent and Location of the Formal Associational Activities of the Rural-Urban Fringe Residents," *ASR*, 17 (December, 1952), 687-94.

———. *The Rural-Urban Fringe: A Study of Adjustment to Residence Location*. Eugene: The University of Oregon Press, 1953.

———. "The Structuring of Social Relationships Engendered by Suburban Residence," *ASR*, (August, 1956), 446-53.

Reissman, Leonard. "Class, Leisure and Social Participation," *ASR*, 19 (February, 1954), 76-84.

Roper, M. Wesley. *The City and the Primary Group*. Chicago: University of Chicago Libraries, 1935.

Rose, Arnold M. "Interest in the Living Arrangements of the Urban Unattached," *AJS*, 53 (May, 1948), 483-94.

Scaff, Alvin H. "The Effect of Commuting on Participation in Community Organizations," *ASR*, 17 (April, 1952), 215-20.

Shuval, Judith T. "Class and Ethnic Correlates of Casual Neighboring," *ASR*, 21 (August, 1956), 453-58.

Smith, Joel, Form, William H. and Stone, Gregory P. "Local Intimacy in a Middle-Sized City," *AJS*, 60 (November, 1954), 276-84.

Sorokin, P. A. and Berger, Monroe Q. *Time Budgets of Human Behavior*. Cambridge: Harvard University Press, 1939.

Sweetser, Frank. *Neighborhood Acquaintance and Association: A Study of Personal Neighborhoods*. New York, 1941.

Tannenbaum, Judith. "The Neighborhood: A Socio-Psychological Analysis," *LE*, 24 (November, 1948), 358-69.

Tomars, Adolph S. "Rural Survivals in American Life," *RS*, 8 (December, 1943), 378-86.

Ware, Caroline. *Greenwich Village*. New York: Houghton Mifflin Company, 1935!

Zimmer, Basil. "Farm Background and Urban Participation," *AJS*, 61 (March, 1956), 470-75.

IX. The City As An Artifact

A. The Planning Process for Urban Communities.

Breese, Gerald and Whiteman, Dorothy E. (eds.) *An Approach to Urban Planning*. Princeton: Princeton University Press, 1953.

Buttenheim, Harold S. "Land Policies and Land Uses Which Affect Rational Urban Development," *Urban Planning and Land Policies*. National Resources Committee, Washington, D. C.: USGPO, 1937. Pp. 217-24.

Churchill, Henry S. *The City Is the People*. New York: Reynal and Hitchcock, 1945.

Colean, Miles L. *Renewing Our Cities*. New York: Twentieth Century Fund, 1953.

Federal Housing Administration. *A Handbook for Urban Redevelopment for Certain Cities in the United States; Suggesting Certain Powers and Procedures, and Integrated Long-Term Program for Dealing with Slums and Blighted Urban Areas*. Washington, D. C.: USGPO, November, 1941.

Goodman, Percival and Paul. "The Conditions of Planning," *Communities: Means of Livelihood and Ways of Life.* Chicago: University of Chicago Press, 1947.

Greer, Guy (ed.). *The Problems of the Cities and Towns: Reprint of the Conference on Urbanism.* Cambridge: Harvard University Press, 1942.

Haig, R. M. *Regional Survey of New York and Environs.* New York: N.Y.C. Plan Commission, Vol. I.

McDougall, Myres S. "Municipal Land Policy and Control," *The Annals,* 242 (November, 1945), 88-95.

Mitchell, Robert (ed.). "Building the Future City," *The Annals,* 242 (November, 1945).

Mumford, Lewis. *City Development.* New York: Harcourt, Brace and Co., 1945.

National Resources Committee. *Urban Planning and Land Policies.* Vol. II, Part II, "Urban Living Conditions," by Louis Wirth and Edward A. Shils. Washington, D. C.: USGPO, 1939.

———. *Federal Aids to Local Planning.* Washington, D. C.: USGPO, 1938.

National Resources Planning Board. *Better Cities.* Washington, D. C.: USGPO, 1942.

———. *The Problems of a Changing Population.* Washington, D. C.: USGPO, 1936.

———. Regional Factors in National Planning and Development. Washington, D.C.: USGPO, December, 1935.

———. *Transportation and National Policy.* Washington, D. C.: USGPO, May, 1942.

———. *The Role of the Housebuilding Industry.* Washington, D. C.: USGPO, 1942.

Public Administration Service. *Action for Cities.* Chicago: Public Administration Clearing House, 1943.

Segoe, Ladislas. *Local Planning Administration.* Chicago: Institute for Training in Municipal Administration, 1941.

Walker, Robert A. *The Planning Function in Urban Government.* Chicago: University of Chicago Press, 1941.

Weimer, A. M. and Hoyt, Homer. *Principles of Urban Real Estate.* New York, 1939.

Wirth, Louis. *Community Life and Social Policy.* Chicago: University of Chicago Press, 1956.

———. *Community Planning for Peacetime Living.* Stanford University Press, 1946, Chapters 1, 2, 3, 4, 7, 8, and 24.

———. "Sociological Factors in Urban Design," *1948 Convention Seminars,* The American Institute of Architects, 43-49.

Woodbury, Coleman (ed.). *The Future of Cities and Urban Redevolpment.* Chicago: University of Chicago Press, 1953.

———. *Urban Redevelopment: Problems and Practices.* Chicago: University of Chicago Press, 1953.

B. Planning Urban Communities and Their Services.

Bauer, Catherine. *Modern Housing.* New York: Houghton Mifflin Co., 1934.

Buell, Bardley, and associates. *Community Planning for Human Services.* New York: Columbia University Press, 1952.

Carnovsky, Leon and Martin, L. A. (eds.). *The Library in the Community.* Chicago: University of Chicago Press, 1944.

Ford, James. *Slums and Housing.* Cambridge: Harvard University Press, 1936, 2 vols.

Isaacs, Reginald A. "Educational, Cultural and Recreational Services," *The Annals,* 242 (November, 1945), 129-38.

National Resources Committee. *Our Cities: Their Role in the National Economy.* Washington, D. C.: USGPO, 1937.

Orlans, Harold. *Stevenage: A Sociological Study of a New Town.* London: Routledge, and Kegan Paul, 1952.

Walker, Mabel L. *Urban Blight and Slums*. Cambridge: Harvard University Press, 1938. (Harvard University Planning Series, Vol. IV.)

Wood, Edith E. *Slums and Blighted Areas in the United States*. Federal Housing Administration: Washington: USGPO, 1936.

C. Selected Sociological Contributions to the Urban Planning Process.

Burgess, E. W., *et al.* "The Chicago Area Project," *Yearbook of National Probation Association*, 1937. Pp. 8-28.

Burgess, E. W. "The New Community and Its Future," *The Annals*, 149 (May, 1930), 157-64.

Dean, John P. "The Myths of Housing Reform," *ASR*, 14 (April, 1949), 281-88.

Dewey, Richard A. "Peripheral Expansion in Milwaukee County," *AJS*, 54 (September, 1948), 118-25.

–––. "The Neighborhood, Urban Ecology, and City Planners," *ASR*, 15 (August, 1950), 502-07.

Duncan, Otis Dudley. "Optimum Size of Cities," *Reader in Urban Sociology*. Edited by Paul K. Hatt and Albert J. Reiss, Jr. Glencoe: The Free Press, 1951.

Ericksen, E. Gordon. "The Superhighway and City Planning," *SF*, 28 (May, 1950), 429-34.

Firey, Walter. "Ecological Considerations in Planning for Rurban Fringes," *ASR*, 11 (August, 1946), 411-23.

–––. "The Optimum Rural-Urban Population Balance," *RS*, 12 (June, 1947), 116-27

Hauser, Philip M. "How Declining Urban Growth Affects City Activities," *Public Management*, 22 (December, 1940), 355-58.

Hawley, Amos. "Metropolitan Population and Municipal Government Expenditures in Central Cities," *JSI*, 7 (Nos. 1 and 2, 1951), 100-08.

Housing Authority of the City of Newark. *A Study of the Social Effects of Public Housing in Newark, N. J.* Newark, November, 1944.

Kuper, Leo. "Social Science Research and the Planning of Urban Neighborhoods," *SF*, 29 (March, 1951), 237-43.

Phillips, H. S. "Municipal Efficiency and Town Size," *Journal of the Town Planning Institute*, (May-June, 1942).

Riemer, Svend. "Hidden Dimensions of Neighborhood Planning," *LE*, 26 (May, 1950), 197-201.

Schmitt, R. C. "Demography and City Planning," *SF*, 30 (March, 1952), 300-04.